NINTH EDITION

MEN'S LIVES

Michael S. Kimmel
State University of New—Stony Brook

Michael A. Messner
University of Southern California

PEARSON

Boston   Columbus   Indianapolis   New York   San Francisco   Upper Saddle River
Amsterdam   Cape Town   Dubai   London   Madrid   Milan   Munich   Paris   Montréal   Toronto
Delhi   Mexico City   São Paulo   Sydney   Hong Kong   Seoul   Singapore   Taipei   Tokyo

For Gary Barker, Byron Hurt, Jackson Katz,
Michael Kaufman, and Rob Okun, whose work for
gender equality also enhances men's lives.

Editor in Chief: *Dickson Musslewhite*
Publisher: *Karen Hanson*
Associate Editor: *Mayda Bosco*
Executive Marketing Manager: *Kelly May*
Marketing Associate: *Diana Griffen*
Marketing Assistant: *Janeli Bitor*
Production Manager: *Fran Russello*
Editorial Production and Composition Service: *ShreeMohanambal Inbakumar / PreMediaGlobal*
Cover Administrator: *Jayne Conte*
Cover Designer: *Karen Noferi*
Cover Image Credit: *Blend Images / Alamy*
Printer/Binder: *Courier Companies, Inc.*

Credits and acknowledgments borrowed from other sources and reproduced, with permission, in this textbook appear on appropriate page within text.

Library of Congress Cataloging-in-Publication Data
Men's lives/[compiled by] Michael S. Kimmel, Michael A. Messner. —9th ed.
  p. cm.
  ISBN-13: 978-0-205-09641-1
  ISBN-10: 0-205-09641-7
  1. Men—United States—Attitudes. 2. Masculinity—United States. 3. Men—Sexual behavior—United States. I. Kimmel, Michael S. II. Messner, Michael A.
  HQ1090.3.M465 2013
  305.310973—dc23

2012000942

2 3 4 5 6 7 8 9 10 V092 16 15 14

www.pearsonhighered.com

ISBN-10: 0-205-09641-7
ISBN-13: 978-0-205-09641-1

CONTENTS

PREFACE

For nearly three decades, we have been teaching courses on the male experience, or "men's lives." Our courses have reflected both our own education and recent research by feminist scholars and profeminist men in U.S. society. (By pro-feminist men, we mean active supporters of women's efforts against male violence and claims for equal opportunity, political participation, sexual autonomy, family reform, and equal education.) Gender, scholars have demonstrated, is a central feature of social life—one of the chief organizing principles around which our lives revolve. Gender shapes our identities and the institutions in which we find ourselves. In the university, women's studies programs and courses about women in traditional disciplines have explored the meaning of gender in women's lives. But what does it mean to be a man in contemporary U.S. society?

This anthology is organized around specific themes that define masculinity and the issues men confront over the course of their lives. In addition, a social-constructionist perspective has been included that examines how men actively construct masculinity within a social and historical context. Related to this construction and integrated in our examination are the variations that exist among men in relation to class, race, and sexuality.

We begin Part One with issues and questions that unravel the "masculine mystique" and reveal various dimensions of men's position in society and their relationships with women and with other men. Parts Two through Ten examine the different issues that emerge for men at different times of their lives and the ways in which their lives change over time. We touch on central moments related to boyhood, adolescence, sports, occupations, marriage, and fatherhood, and we explore men's emotional and sexual relationships with women and with other men. We also inlude a section on Violence and Masculinities. We have done so because violence remains the single behavior, attitude, or trait for which there are overwhelming, significant, and seemingly intractable gender differences. It affects so many other arenas of our lives that we have decided that we need to highlight this important feature of men's lives. The final part, "Men, Movements, and the Future," explores some of the ways in which men are changing and some possible directions in which they might continue to change.

Although a major component of the traditional, normative definition of masculinity is independence, we are pleased to acknowledge those colleagues and friends whose criticism and support have been a constant help throughout our work on this project. Karen Hanson and Jeff Lasser, our editors at Allyn and Bacon, inherited this project and have embraced it as their own, facilitating our work at every turn. Chris Cardone and Bruce Nichols, our original editors, were supportive from the start and helped get the project going. Many other scholars who work on issues of masculinity, such as Bob Blauner, Robert Brannon, Harry Brod, Rocco Capraro, Raewyn Connell, James Harrison, Jeff Hearn, Joe Pleck, Tony Rotundo, Don Sabo, and Peter Stein, have contributed to a supportive intellectual community in which to work.

Colleagues at the State University of New York at Stony Brook and the University of Southern California have been supportive of this project. We are especially grateful to Diane Barthel-Bouchier, John Gagnon, Barry Glassner, Norman Goodman, Carol Jacklin, and Barrie Thorne. A fellowship from the Lilly Foundation supported Kimmel's work on pedagogical issues of teaching about men and masculinity.

This book is the product of the profeminist men's movement as well—a loose network of men who support a feminist critique of traditional masculinity and women's struggles to enlarge the scope of their personal autonomy and public power. These men are engaged in a variety of efforts to transform masculinity in ways that allow men to live fuller, richer, and healthier lives. The editors of

Changing Men (with whom we worked as Book Review Editor and Sports Editor), the late Mike Biernbaum and Rick Cote, labored for more than a decade to provide a forum for antisexist men. We acknowledge their efforts with gratitude and respect.

Our families, friends, and colleagues have provided a rare atmosphere that combines intellectual challenge and emotional support. We thank the reviewers of this edition of the book. We want especially to acknowledge our fathers and mothers for providing such important models—not of being women or men, but of being adults capable of career competence, emotional warmth, and nurturance (these are not masculine or feminine traits).

Finally, we thank Amy Aronson and Pierette Hondagneu-Sotelo, who have chosen to share our lives, and our sons, who didn't have much of a choice about it. Together they fill our lives with so much joy.

M.S.K.
M.A.M.

ANCILLARY MATERIALS

The ancillary materials that accompany this textbook have been carefully created to enhance the topics being discussed.

FOR THE INSTRUCTOR:

Instructor's Manual and Test Bank (ISBN 0205096468). This carefully prepared manual includes the following elements for each Article: Summary, Learning Objectives, Key Words, Weblinks, and test questions in Multiple Choice, Essay, and Discussion format. The Instructor's Manual and Test Bank is available to adopters at www.pearsonhighered.com.

MyTest (ISBN 020509645X). This computerized software allows instructors to create their own personalized exams, to edit any or all of the existing test questions and to add new questions. Other special features of this program include random generation of test questions, creation of alternate versions of the same test, scrambling question sequence, and test preview before printing. The MyTest is available to adopters at www.pearsonhighered.com.

PPTs (ISBN 0205096476). The Lecture PowerPoint slides are uniquely designed to present concepts in a clear and succinct manner. They are available to adopters at www.pearsonhighered.com.

For the Student

www.mysearchlab.com

SAVE TIME. IMPROVE RESULTS.

MySearchLab is a dynamic website that delivers proven results in helping individual students succeed. Its wealth of resources provides engaging experiences that personalize, stimulate, and measure learning for each student. Many accessible tools will encourage students to read their text, improve writing skills, and help them improve their grade in their course.

FEATURES OF MYSEARCHLAB
Writing

- Step by step tutorials present complete overviews of the research and writing process.

Research and citing sources

- Instructors and students receive access to the EBSCO ContentSelect database, census data from Social Explorer, Associated Press news feeds, and the Pearson bookshelf. Pearson SourceCheck helps students and instructors monitor originality and avoid plagiarism.

Etext and more

- **Pearson eText**—An e-book version of Men's Lives, 9th Edition, is included in MySearchLab. Just like the printed text, students can highlight and add their own notes as they read their interactive text online.
- **Chapter quizzes and flashcards**—Chapter and key term reviews are available for each chapter online and offer immediate feedback.
- **Primary Source Documents**—A collection of documents, organized by chapter, are available on MySearchLab. The documents include head notes and critical thinking questions.
- **Gradebook**—Automated grading of quizzes helps both instructors and students monitor their results throughout the course.

INTRODUCTION

This is a book about men. But unlike other books about men, which line countless library shelves, this is a book about men *as men*. It is a book in which men's experiences are not taken for granted as we explore the "real" and significant accomplishments of men, but a book in which those experiences are treated as significant and important in themselves.

MEN AS "GENDERED BEINGS"

But what does it mean to examine men "as men"? Most courses in a college curriculum are about men, aren't they? But these courses routinely deal with men only in their public roles, so we come to know and understand men as scientists, politicians, military figures, writers, and philosophers. Rarely, if ever, are men understood through the prism of gender.

But listen to some male voices from some of these "ungendered" courses. Take, for example, composer Charles Ives, debunking "sissy" types of music; he said he used traditional tough guy themes and concerns in his drive to build new sounds and structures out of the popular musical idiom (cf. Wilkinson 1986: 103). Or architect Louis Sullivan, describing his ambition to create "masculine forms": strong, solid, commanding respect. Or novelist Ernest Hemingway, retaliating against literary enemies by portraying them as impotent or homosexual.

Consider also political figures, such as Cardinal Richelieu, the seventeenth-century French First Minister to Louis XIII, who insisted that it was "necessary to have masculine virtue and do everything by reason" (cited in Elliott 1984: 20). Closer to home, recall President Lyndon Baines Johnson's dismissal of a political adversary: "Oh him. He has to squat to piss!" Or President Johnson's boast that during the Tet Offensive in the Vietnam War, he "didn't just screw Ho Chi Minh. I cut his pecker off!"

Democrats have no monopoly on unexamined gender coloring their political rhetoric. Indeed, recent political campaigns have revolved, in part,

around gender issues, as each candidate attempted to demonstrate that he was not a "wimp" but was a "real man." (Of course, female politicians face the double task of convincing the electorate that they are not the "weak-willed wimps" that their gender implies in the public mind while at the same time demonstrating that they are "real women.")

These are just a few examples of what we might call gendered speech, language that uses gender terms to make its case. And these are just a few of the thousands of examples one could find in every academic discipline of how men's lives are organized around gender issues and how gender remains one of the organizing principles of social life. We come to know ourselves and our world through the prism of gender—only we act as if we didn't know it.

Fortunately, in recent years, the pioneering work of feminist scholars, both in traditional disciplines and in women's studies, and of feminist women in the political arena has made us aware of the centrality of gender in our lives. In the social sciences, gender has now taken its place alongside class and race as one of the three central mechanisms by which power and resources are distributed in our society and the three central themes out of which we fashion the meanings of our lives.

We certainly understand how this works for women. Through women's studies courses and also in courses about women in traditional disciplines, students have explored the complexity of women's lives, the hidden history of exemplary women, and the daily experiences of women in the routines of their lives. For women, we know how gender works as one of the formative elements out of which social life is organized.

THE INVISIBILITY OF GENDER: A SOCIOLOGICAL EXPLANATION

Too often, though, we treat men as if they had no gender, as if only their public personae were of interest to us as students and scholars, as if their interior experience of gender was of no significance. This became evident when one of us was in a graduate seminar on feminist theory several years ago. A discussion between a white woman and a black woman revolved around the question of whether their similarities as women were greater than their racial differences as black and white. The white woman asserted that the fact that they were both women bonded them, in spite of their racial differences. The black woman disagreed.

"When you wake up in the morning and look in the mirror, what do you see?" she asked.

"I see a woman," replied the white woman.

"That's precisely the issue," replied the black woman. "I see a black woman. For me, race is visible every day, because it is how I am not privileged in this culture. Race is invisible to you, which is why our alliance will always seem somewhat false to me."

Witnessing this exchange, Michael Kimmel was startled. When he looked in the mirror in the morning, he saw, as he put it, "a human being: universally generalizable. The generic person." What had been concealed—that he possessed both race and gender—had become strikingly visible. As a white man, he was able not to think about the ways in which gender and race had affected his experiences.

There is a sociological explanation for this blind spot in our thinking: the mechanisms that afford us privilege are very often invisible to us. What makes us marginal (unempowered, oppressed) are the mechanisms that we understand, because those are the ones that are most painful in daily life. Thus, white people rarely think of themselves as "raced" people, and rarely think of race as a central element in their experience. But people of color are marginalized by race, and so the centrality of race both is painfully obvious and needs study urgently. Similarly, middle-class people do not acknowledge the importance of social class as an organizing principle of social life, largely because for them class is an invisible force that makes everyone look pretty much the same. Working-class people, on the other hand, are often painfully aware of the centrality of class in their lives. (Interestingly, upper-class people are often more aware of class dynamics than are middle-class people. In part, this may be the result of the emphasis on status within the upper class, as lineage, breeding, and family honor take center stage. In part, it may also be the result of a peculiar marginalization of the upper class in our society, as in the overwhelming number of television shows and movies that are ostensibly about just plain [i.e., middle-class] folks.)

In this same way, men often think of themselves as genderless, as if gender did not matter in the daily experiences of our lives. Certainly, we can see the biological sex of individuals, but we rarely understand the ways in which *gender*—that complex of social meanings that is attached to biological sex—is enacted in our daily lives. For example, we treat male scientists as if their being men had nothing to do with the organization of their experiments, the logic of scientific inquiry, or the questions posed by science itself. We treat male political figures as if masculinity were not even remotely in their consciousness as they do battle in the political arena.

This book takes a position directly opposed to such genderlessness for men. We believe that men are also "gendered" and that this gendering process, the transformation of biological males into socially interacting men, is a central experience for men. That we are unaware of it only helps to perpetuate the inequalities based on gender in our society.

In this book, we examine the various ways in which men are gendered. We have gathered together some of the most interesting, engaging, and convincing materials from the past decade that have been written about men. We believe that *Men's Lives* will allow readers to explore the meanings of masculinity in contemporary U.S. culture in a new way.

EARLIER EFFORTS TO STUDY MEN

Certainly researchers have been examining masculinity for a long time. Historically, there have been three general models that have governed social scientific research on men and masculinity. *Biological models* have focused on the ways in which innate biological differences between males and females program different social behaviors. *Anthropological models* have examined masculinity cross-culturally, stressing the variations in the behaviors and attributes associated with being a man. And, until recently, *sociological models* have stressed how socialization of boys and girls includes accommodation to a "sex role" specific to one's biological sex. Although each of these perspectives helps us to understand the meaning of masculinity and femininity, each is also limited in its ability to explain fully how gender operates in any culture.

Relying on differences in reproductive biology, some scholars have argued that the physiological organization of males and females makes inevitable the differences we observe in psychological temperament and social behaviors. One perspective holds that differences in endocrine functioning are the cause of gender difference, that testosterone predisposes males toward aggression, competition, and violence, whereas estrogen predisposes females toward passivity, tenderness, and exaggerated emotionality. Others insist that these observed behavioral differences derive from the differences between the size or number of sperm and eggs. Since a male can produce 100 million sperm with each ejaculation, whereas a female can produce fewer than 200 eggs capable of producing healthy offspring over the course of her life, these authors suggest that men's "investment" in their offspring is significantly less than women's investment. Other authors arrive at the same conclusion by suggesting that the different size of egg and sperm, and the fact that the egg is the source of the food supply, impels temperamental differences. Reproductive "success" to males means the insemination of as many females as possible; to females, reproductive success means carefully choosing one male to mate with and insisting that he remain present to care for and support their offspring. Still other authors argue that male and female behavior is governed by different halves of the brain, males are ruled by the left hemisphere, which controls rationality and abstract thought, whereas females are governed by the right hemisphere, which controls emotional affect and creativity. (For examples of these works,

see Trivers 1972; Goldberg 1975; Wilson 1976; and Goldberg, 1986.)

Observed normative temperamental differences between women and men that are assumed to be of biological origin are easily translated into political prescriptions. In this ideological sleight of hand, what is *normative* (i.e., what is prescribed) is translated into what is *normal,* and the mechanisms of this transformation are the assumed biological imperative. George Gilder, for example, assembles the putative biological differences between women and men into a call for a return to traditional gender roles. Gilder believes that male sexuality is, by nature, wild and lusty, "insistent" and "incessant," careening out of control and threatening anarchic disorder, unless it can be controlled and constrained. This is the task of women. When women refuse to apply the brakes to male sexuality—by asserting their own or by choosing to pursue a life outside the domestic sphere—they abandon their "natural" function for illusory social gains. Sex education, abortion, and birth control are all condemned as facilitating women's escape from biological necessity. Similarly, he argues against women's employment, since the "unemployed man can contribute little to the community and will often disrupt it, but the woman may even do more good without a job than with one" (Gilder 1986: 86).

The biological argument has been challenged by many scholars on several grounds. The implied causation between two observed sets of differences (biological differences and different behaviors) is misleading, since there is no logical reason to assume that one caused the other, or that the line of causation moves only from the biological to the social. The selection of biological evidence is partial, and generalizations from "lower" animal species to human beings are always suspect. One sociologist asks, if these differences are "natural," why must their enforcement be coercive, and why must males and females be forced to assume the rules that they are naturally supposed to play (see Epstein 1986: 8)? And one primatologist argues that the evidence adduced to support the current status quo might also lead to precisely the opposite conclusions, that biological differences would impel female promiscuity and male fragility (see Hrdy 1981). Biological differences between males and females would appear to set some parameters for differences in social behavior, but would not dictate the temperaments of men and women in any one culture. These psychological and social differences would appear to be the result far more of the ways in which cultures interpret, shape, and modify these biological inheritances. We may be born males or females, but we become men and women in a cultural context.

Anthropologists have entered the debate at this point, but with different positions. For example, some anthropologists have suggested that the universality of gender differences comes from specific cultural adaptations to the environment, whereas others describe the cultural variations of gender roles, seeking to demonstrate the fluidity of gender and the primacy of cultural organization. Lionel Tiger and Robin Fox argue that the sexual division of labor is universal because of the different nature of bonding for males and females. "Nature," they argue, "intended mother and child to be together" because she is the source of emotional security and food; thus, cultures have prescribed various behaviors for women that emphasize nurturance and emotional connection (Tiger and Fox 1984: 304). The bond between men is forged through the necessity of "competitive cooperation" in hunting; men must cooperate with members of their own tribe in the hunt and yet compete for scarce resources with men in other tribes. Such bonds predispose men toward the organization of the modern corporation or governmental bureaucracy.

Such anthropological arguments omit as much as they include, and many scholars have pointed out problems with the model. Why didn't intelligence become sex linked, as this model (and the biological model) would imply? Such positions also reveal a marked conservatism: The differences between women and men are the differences that nature or cultural evolution intended and are therefore not to be tampered with.

Perhaps the best-known challenge to this anthropological argument is the work of Margaret Mead. Mead insisted that the variations among cultures in their prescriptions of gender roles required the conclusion that culture was the more decisive cause of these differences. In her classic study, *Sex and Temperament in Three Primitive Societies* (1935), Mead observed such wide variability among gender role prescriptions—and such marked differences from our own—that any universality implied by biological or anthropological models had to be rejected. And although the empirical accuracy of Mead's work has been challenged in its specific arguments, the general theoretical arguments remain convincing.

Psychological theories have also contributed to the discussion of gender roles, as psychologists have specified the developmental sequences for both males and females. Earlier theorists observed psychological distancing from the mother as the precondition for independence and autonomy or suggested a sequence that placed the capacity for abstract reason as the developmental stage beyond relational reasoning. Because it is normative for males to exhibit independence and the capacity for abstract reason, it was argued that males are more successful at negotiating these psychological passages and implied that women somehow lagged behind men on the ladder of developmental success. (Such arguments may be found in the work of Freud, Erikson, and Kohlberg.)

But these models, too, have been challenged, most recently by sociologist Nancy Chodorow (1978), who argued that women's ability to connect contains a more fundamentally human trait than the male's need to distance, and by psychologist Carol Gilligan (1982), who claimed that women's predisposition toward relational reasoning may contain a more humane strategy of thought than recourse to abstract principles. Regardless of our assessment of these arguments, Chodorow and Gilligan rightly point out that the highly ideological assumptions that make masculinity the normative standard against which the psychological development of *both* males and females was measured would inevitably make femininity problematic and less fully developed. Moreover, Chodorow explicitly insists that these "essential" differences between women and men are socially constructed and therefore subject to change.

Finally, sociologists have attempted to synthesize these three perspectives into a systematic explanation of "sex roles." These are the collection of attitudes, attributes, and behaviors that is seen as appropriate for males and appropriate for females. Thus, masculinity is associated with technical mastery, aggression, competitiveness, and cognitive abstraction, whereas femininity is associated with emotional nurturance, connectedness, and passivity. Sex role theory informed a wide variety of prescriptive literature (self-help books) that instructed parents on what to do if they wanted their child to grow up as a healthy boy or girl.

The strongest challenge to all these perspectives, as we have seen, has come from feminist scholars, who have specified the ways in which the assumptions about maturity, development, and health all made masculinity the norm against which both genders were measured. In all the social sciences, these feminist scholars have stripped these early studies of their academic facades to reveal the unexamined ideological assumptions contained within them. By the early 1970s, women's studies programs began to articulate a new paradigm for the study of gender, one that assumed nothing about men or women beforehand and that made no assumptions about which gender was more highly developed. And by the mid-1970s, the first group of texts about men appeared that had been inspired by these pioneering efforts by feminist scholars.

THINKING ABOUT MEN:
THE FIRST GENERATION

In the mid-1970s, the first group of works on men and masculinity appeared that was directly influenced by these feminist critiques of the traditional explanations for gender differences. Some books underscored the costs to men of traditional gender role prescriptions, exploring how some aspects of men's lives and experiences are constrained and underdeveloped by the relentless pressure to exhibit other

behaviors associated with masculinity. Books such as Marc Feigen-Fasteau's *The Male Machine* (1974) and Warren Farrell's *The Liberated Man* (1975) discussed the costs to men's health—both physical and psychological—and to the quality of relationships with women, other men, and their children of the traditional male sex role.

Several anthologies explored the meanings of masculinity in the United States by adopting a feminist-inspired prism through which to view men and masculinity. For example, Deborah David and Robert Brannon's *The Forty-Nine Percent Majority* (1976) and Joseph Pleck and Jack Sawyer's *Men and Masculinity* (1974) presented panoramic views of men's lives from within a framework that accepted the feminist critique of traditional gender arrangements. Elizabeth Pleck and Joseph Pleck's *The American Man* (1980) suggested a historical evolution of contemporary themes. These works explored both the costs and the privileges of being a man in modern U.S. society.

Perhaps the single most important book to criticize the normative organization of the male sex role was Joseph Pleck's *The Myth of Masculinity* (1981). Pleck carefully deconstructed the constituent elements of the male sex role and reviewed the empirical literature for each component part. After demonstrating that the empirical literature did not support these normative features, Pleck argued that the male sex role model was incapable of describing men's experiences. In its place, he posited a male "sex role strain" model that specified the contemporary sex role as problematic, historically specific, and also an unattainable ideal.

Building on Pleck's work, a critique of the sex role model began to emerge. Sex roles had been cast as the static containers of behaviors and attitudes, and biological males and females were required to fit themselves into these containers, regardless of how ill-fitting these clusters of behaviors and attitudes felt. Such a model was ahistorical and suggested a false cultural universalism, and was therefore ill equipped to help us understand the ways in which sex roles change, and the ways in which individuals modify those roles through the enactments of gender expectations. Most telling, however, was the way in which the sex role model ignored the ways in which definitions of masculinity and femininity were based on, and reproduced, relationships of power. Not only do men as a group exert power over women as a group, but the definitions of masculinity and femininity reproduce those power relations. Power dynamics are an essential element in both the definition and the enactments of gender.

This first generation of research on masculinity was extremely valuable, particularly since it challenged the unexamined ideology that made masculinity the gender norm against which both men and women were measured. The old models of sex roles had reproduced the domination of men over women by insisting on the dominance of masculine traits over feminine traits. These new studies argued against both the definitions of either sex and the social institutions in which those differences were embedded. Shapers of the new model looked at "gender relations" and understood how the definition of either masculinity or femininity was relational, that is, how the definition of one gender depended, in part, on the understanding of the definition of the other.

In the early 1980s, the research on women again surged ahead of the research on men and masculinity. This time, however, the focus was not on the ways in which sex roles reproduce the power relations in society, but rather on the ways in which femininity is experienced differently by women in various social groups. Gradually, the notion of a single femininity—which was based on the white middle-class Victorian notion of female passivity, langorous beauty, and emotional responsiveness—was replaced by an examination of the ways in which women differ in their gender role expectations by race, class, age, sexual orientation, ethnicity, region, and nationality.

The research on men and masculinity is now entering a new stage, in which the variations among men are seen as central to the understanding of men's lives. The unexamined assumption in earlier studies had been that one version of masculinity—white, middle-aged, middle-class, heterosexual—was the sex role into which all men were struggling to fit in our society. Thus, working-class men, men of color, gay men, and younger and older men were all observed as departing in significant ways from the traditional definitions of masculinity. Therefore, it was easy to see these men as enacting "problematic" or "deviant" versions of masculinity. Such theoretical assertions, however, reproduce precisely the power relationships that keep these men in subordinate positions in our society. Not only does middle-class, middle-aged, heterosexual white masculinity become the standard against which all men are measured, but this definition, itself, is used against those who do not fit as a way to keep them down. The normative definition of masculinity is not the "right" one, but it is the one that is dominant.

The challenge to the hegemonic definition of masculinity came from men whose masculinity was cast as deviant: men of color, gay men, and ethnic men. We understand now that we cannot speak of "masculinity" as a singular term, but must examine *masculinities:* the ways in which different men construct different versions of masculinity. Such a perspective can be seen in several recent works, such as Harry Brod's *The Making of Masculinities* (1987), Michael Kimmel's *Changing Men: New Directions in Research on Men and Masculinity* (1987), and Tim Carrigan, R. W. Connell, and John Lee's "Toward a New Sociology of Masculinity" (1985). R. W. Connell's *Gender and Power* (1987) and Jeff Hearn's *The Gender of Oppression* (1987) represent the most sophisticated theoretical statements of this perspective. Connell argues that the oppression of women is a chief mechanism that links the various masculinities, and that the marginalization of certain masculinities is an important component of the reproduction of male power over women. This critique of the hegemonic definition of masculinity as a perspective on men's lives is one of the organizing principles of our book, which is the first college-level text in this second generation of work on men and masculinities.

Now that we have reviewed some of the traditional explanations for gender relations and have situated this book within the research on gender in general, and men in particular, let us briefly outline exactly the theoretical perspective we have employed in the book.

THE SOCIAL CONSTRUCTION OF MASCULINITIES

Men are not born, growing from infants through boyhood to manhood, to follow a predetermined biological imperative encoded in their physical organization. To be a man is to participate in social life as a man, as a gendered being. Men are not born; they are made. And men make themselves, actively constructing their masculinities within a social and historical context.

This book is about how men are made and how men make themselves in contemporary U.S. society. It is about what masculinity means, about how masculinity is organized, and about the social institutions that sustain and elaborate it. It is a book in which we will trace what it means to be a man over the course of men's lives.

Men's Lives revolves around three important themes that are part of a social scientific perspective. First, we have adopted a *social constructionist* perspective. By this, we mean that the important fact of men's lives is not that they are biological males, but that they become men. Our sex may be male, but our identity as men is developed through a complex process of interaction with the culture in which we both learn the gender scripts appropriate to our culture and attempt to modify those scripts to make them more palatable. The second axis around which the book is organized follows from our social constructionist perspective. As we have argued, the experience of masculinity is not uniform and universally generalizable to all men in our society. Masculinity differs dramatically in our society, and we have organized the book to illustrate the *variations* among men in the construction of masculinity. Third, we have adopted a *life course* perspective, to

chart the construction of these various masculinities in men's lives and to examine pivotal developmental moments or institutional locations during a man's life in which the meanings of masculinity are articulated. Social constructionism, variations among men, and the life course perspective define the organization of this book and the criteria we have used to select the articles included.

The Social Constructionist Model

The social constructionist perspective argues that the meaning of masculinity is neither transhistorical nor culturally universal, but rather varies from culture to culture and within any one culture over time. Thus, males become men in the United States in the early twenty-first century in a way that is very different from men in Southeast Asia, or Kenya, or Sri Lanka.

Men's lives also vary within any one culture over time. The experience of masculinity in the contemporary United States is very different from that experience 150 years ago. Who would argue that what it meant to be a "real man" in seventeenth-century France (at least among the upper classes)—high-heeled patent leather shoes, red velvet jackets covering frilly white lace shirts, lots of rouge and white powder makeup, and a taste for the elegant refinement of ornate furniture—bears much resemblance to the meaning of masculinity among a similar class of French men today?

A perspective that emphasizes the social construction of gender is, therefore, both *historical* and *comparative*. It allows us to explore the ways in which the meanings of gender vary from culture to culture, and how they change within any one culture over historical time.

Variations among Men

Masculinity also varies *within* any one society according to the various types of cultural groups that compose it. Subcultures are organized around other poles, which are the primary way in which people organize themselves and by which resources are distributed. And men's experiences differ from one another according to what social scientists have identified as the chief structural mechanisms along which power and resources are distributed. We cannot speak of masculinity in the United States as if it were a single, easily identifiable commodity. To do so is to risk positing one version of masculinity as normative and making all other masculinities problematic.

In the contemporary United States, masculinity is constructed differently by class culture, by race and ethnicity, and by age. And each of these axes of masculinity modifies the others. Black masculinity differs from white masculinity, yet each of them is also further modified by class and age. A 30-year-old middle-class black man will have some things in common with a 30-year-old middle-class white man that he might not share with a 60-year-old working-class black man, although he will share with him elements of masculinity that are different from those of the white man of his class and age. The resulting matrix of *masculinities* is complicated by cross-cutting elements; without understanding this, we risk collapsing all masculinities into one hegemonic version.

The challenge to a singular definition of masculinity as the normative definition is the second axis around which the readings in this book revolve.

The Life Course Perspective

The meaning of masculinity is not constant over the course of any man's life but will change as he grows and matures. The issues confronting a man about proving himself and feeling successful and the social institutions in which he will attempt to enact his definitions of masculinity will change throughout his life. Therefore, we have adopted a *life course perspective* to discuss the ways in which different issues will emerge for men at different times of their lives and the ways in which men's lives, themselves, change over time. The life course perspective that we have employed will examine men's lives at various pivotal moments in their development from young boys to adults. As in a slide show, these points will freeze the action for a short while, to afford us the opportunity to examine in more detail the ways in which different men in our culture experience masculinity at any one time.

The book's organization reflects these three concerns. Part One sets the context through which we shall examine men's lives. Parts Two through Ten follow those lives through their full course, examining central moments experienced by men in the United States today. Specifically, Parts Two and Three touch on boyhood and adolescence, discussing some of the institutions organized to embody and reproduce masculinities in the United States, such as fraternities, the Boy Scouts, and sports groups. Part Four, "Men and Work," explores the ways in which masculinities are constructed in relation to men's occupations. Part Five, "Men and Health," deals with heart attacks, stress, AIDS, and other health problems among men. Part Six, "Men in Relationships," describes men's emotional and sexual relationships. We deal with heterosexuality and homosexuality, mindful of the ways in which variations are based on specific lines (class, race, ethnicity). Part Seven, "Male Sexualities," studies the normative elements of heterosexuality and probes the controversial political implications of pornography as a source of both straight and gay men's sexual information. Part Eight, "Men in Families," concentrates on masculinities within the family and the role of men as husbands, fathers, and senior citizens. Part Nine, "Masculinities in Religion" explores several different approaches to thinking about the relationship between masculinity and religion. Part Ten, "Masculinities in the Media and Popular Culture," explores the different ways the media present modes of masculinity. Part Eleven, "Violence and Masculinities," looks at violence as the most obdurate, intractable behavioral gender difference. Part Twelve, "Men, Movements, and the Future," examines some of the ways in which men are changing and points to some directions in which men might continue to change.

Our perspective, stressing the social construction of masculinities over the life course, will, we believe, allow a more comprehensive understanding of men's lives in the United States today.

REFERENCES

Brod, Harry, ed. *The Making of Masculinities.* Boston: Unwin, Hyman, 1987.

Carrigan, Tim, Bob Connell, and John Lee. "Toward a New Sociology of Masculinity" in *Theory and Society,* 1985, 5(14).

Chodorow, Nancy. *The Reproduction of Mothering.* Berkeley: University of California Press, 1978.

Connell, R. W. *Gender and Power.* Stanford, CA: Stanford University Press, 1987.

David, Deborah, and Robert Brannon, eds. *The Forty-Nine Percent Majority.* Reading, MA: Addison-Wesley, 1976.

Elliott, J. H. *Richelieu and Olivares.* New York: Cambridge University Press, 1984.

Epstein, Cynthia Fuchs. "Inevitability of Prejudice" in *Society,* Sept./Oct., 1986.

Farrell, Warren. *The Liberated Man.* New York: Random House, 1975.

Feigen-Fasteau, Marc. *The Male Machine.* New York: McGraw-Hill, 1974.

Gilligan, Carol. *In a Different Voice.* Cambridge, MA: Harvard University Press, 1982.

Glider, George. *Men and Marriage.* Gretna, LA: Pelican Publishers, 1986.

Goldberg, Steven. *The Inevitability of Patriarchy.* New York: William Morrow & Co., 1975.

_____ "Reaffirming the Obvious" in *Society,* Sept./Oct., 1986.

Hearn, Jeff. *The Gender of Oppression.* New York: St. Martin's Press, 1987.

Hrdy, Sandra Blaffer. *The Woman That Never Evolved.* Cambridge, MA: Harvard University Press, 1981.

Kimmel, Michael S., ed. *Changing Men: New Directions in Research on Men and Masculinity.* Newbury Park, CA: Sage Publications, 1987.

Mead, Margaret. *Sex and Temperament in Three Primitive Societies.* New York: McGraw-Hill, 1935.

Pleck, Elizabeth, and Joseph Pleck, eds. *The American Man.* Englewood Cliffs, NJ: Prentice-Hall, 1980.

Pleck, Joseph. *The Myth of Masculinity.* Cambridge, MA: M.I.T. Press, 1981.

_____ and Jack Sawyer, eds. *Men and Masculinity.* Englewood Cliffs, NJ: Prentice-Hall, 1974.

Tiger, Lionel, and Robin Fox. *The Imperial Animal.* New York: Holt, Rinehart & Winston, 1984.

Trivers, Robert. "Parental Investment and Sexual Selection" in *Sexual Selection and the Descent of Man.* (B. Campbell, ed.). Chicago: Aldine Publishers, 1972.

Wilkinson, Rupert. *American Tough: The Tough Guy Tradition and American Character.* New York: Harper & Row, 1986.

Wilson, E. O. *Sociobiology: The New Synthesis.* Cambridge, MA: Harvard University Press, 1976.

Source: Jules Feiffer

PART ONE

PERSPECTIVES ON MASCULINITIES

A quick glance at any magazine rack or television talk show is enough to make you aware that these days, men are confused. What does it mean to be a "real man"? How are men supposed to behave? What are men supposed to feel? How are men to express their feelings? Who are we supposed to be like: Eminem or Boyz II Men? Jimmy Kimmel or Carson Kressley? Derek Jeter or Kobe Bryant? Rhett Butler or Ashley Wilkes?

We are bombarded daily with images and handy rules to help us negotiate our way through a world in which all the rules seem to have suddenly vanished or changed. Some tell us to reassert traditional masculinity against all contemporary challenges. But a strength that is built only on the weakness of others hardly feels like strength at all. Others tell us that men are in power, the oppressor. But if men are in power as a group, why do individual men often feel so powerless? Can men change?

These questions will return throughout this book. The articles in Part One begin to unravel the "masculine mystique" and suggest various dimensions of men's position in society, their power, their powerlessness, and their confusion.

But we cannot speak of "masculinity" as some universal category that is experienced in the same ways by each man. "All men are alike" runs a popular saying. But are they really? Are gay men's experiences with work, relationships, love, and politics similar to those of heterosexual men? Do black and Chicano men face the same problems and conflicts in their daily lives that white men face? Do middle-class men have the same political interests as blue-collar men? The answers to these questions, as the articles in this part suggest, are not simple.

Although earlier studies of men and masculinity focused on the apparently universal norms of masculinity, recent works have attempted to demonstrate how different the worlds of various men are. Men are divided along the same lines that divide any other group: race, class, sexual orientation, ethnicity, age, and geographic region. Men's lives vary in crucial ways, and understanding these variations will take us a long way toward understanding men's experiences.

Earlier studies that suggested a single universal norm of masculinity reproduced some of the problems they were trying to solve. To be sure, *all* men benefit from the inequality between women and men; for example, think of how male-exclusive sports culture or rape jokes provide contexts for the bonding of men across class, race, and ethnic lines while denying full public participation to women.

But the single, seemingly universal masculinity obscured ways in which some men hold and maintain power over other men in our society, hiding the fact that men do not all share equally in the fruits of gender inequality.

Here is how sociologist Erving Goffman put it in his important book *Stigma* (New York: Double-day, 1963, p. 128):

> In an important sense there is only one complete unblushing male in America: a young, married, white, urban, northern, heterosexual Protestant father of college education, fully employed, of good complexion, weight, and height, and a recent record in sports. Every American male tends to look out upon the world from this perspective, this constituting one sense in which one can speak of a common value system in America.

1

"Actually, Lou, I think it was more than just my being in the right place at the right time. I think it was my being the right race, the right religion, the right sex, the right socioeconomic group, having the right accent, the right clothes, going to the right schools..."

Source: Warren Miller / The New Yorker Collection / www.cartoonbank.com

Any male who fails to qualify in any one of these ways is likely to view himself—during moments at least—as unworthy, incomplete, and inferior.

As Goffman suggests, middle-class, white, heterosexual masculinity is used as the marker against which other masculinities are measured, and by which standard men may be found wanting. What is *normative* (prescribed) becomes translated into what is *normal*. In this way, heterosexual men maintain their status by the oppression of gay men; middle-aged men can maintain their dominance over older and younger men; upper-class men can exploit working-class men; and white men can enjoy privileges at the expense of men of color.

The articles in this part explore this idea of masculinities as plural. Edward Flores, Hernan Ramirez, and Yen Le Espiritu focus on the different ways in which different groups of men (Latino and Asian American) experience masculinity. They suggest that an understanding

of class differences and ethnic and racial minorities requires an understanding of how political, legal, and economic factors shape and constrain the employment possibilities as well as the personal lifestyle choices of different groups of men. Calls for "changing masculinities," which the articles in this part suggest, must involve an emphasis on *institutional* transformations.

And yet despite these differences, don't all men share some common experiences? Martha McCaughey shows how the new "science" of evolutionary psychology supports a resurgent public belief of biologically based male superiority. Paul Kivel suggests that there is a widely accepted definition of manhood that includes the promise of male privilege for boys and men who conform with what's inside the "be a man box." However, Jewell Woods' "black male privilege checklist" suggests that we show caution in making universal declarations about men: not all men share equal access to the sorts of privileges that white, class-privileged heterosexual men historically took for granted.

CAVEMAN MASCULINITY: FINDING AN ETHNICITY IN EVOLUTIONARY SCIENCE

timely
repetitive
theoretically thick
in parts

Martha McCaughey

THE CAVEMAN AS RETROSEXUALITY

Most of us can call up some image of prehistoric man and his treatment of women. He's a shaggy, well-muscled caveman, whose name is Thor, and we might picture him, club in hand, approaching a scrawny but curvaceous woman, whom he bangs over the head and drags by the hair into a cave to mate. I'm sure the majority of readers recognize this imagery. Indeed, today an image of modern men as guided by such prehistoric tendencies is even celebrated on T-shirts sold to American men on websites that allow people to post and sell their own designs. One such image for sale on the cafepress website features a version of Thor, wearing a fur pelt and holding a club, accompanied by the slogan "ME FIND WOMAN!" Another image available for T-shirts, boxer shorts, baseball caps, and coffee mugs features a man dressed in a one-shoulder fur pelt, with his club, smiling behind a cavewoman who is wearing a fur bikini outfit and cooking a skinned animal on a spit, with the saying "MEN'S PRIORITYS [*sic*]: 10,000 YEARS LATER AND STILL ON THE HUNT FOR FOOD AND SEX!" Another image features only the club, with the saying, "caveman: primitive pimpin'."

Everywhere we look we can find applications of an increasingly fashionable academic exercise—the invocation of evolutionary theory to explain human male behaviors, particularly deplorable behaviors such as sexual harassment, rape, and

aggression more generally. The familiar portrayals of sex differences based in evolution popularize and legitimize an academic version of evolutionary thought known increasingly as evolutionary psychology, a field referred to as the "science of the mind."[1] The combination of scholarly and popular attention to evolution and human male sexuality has increasingly lodged American manhood in an evolutionary logic. The discourse of evolutionary science has become part of popular consciousness, a sort of cultural consensus about who men are.

The evolutionary theory is that our human male ancestors were in constant competition with one another for sexual access to fertile women, who were picky about their mate choices given the high level of parental investment required of the human female for reproduction—months of gestation, giving birth, and then years of lactation and care for a dependent child. The human male's low level of parental investment required for reproduction, we are told, resulted in the unique boorishness of the hairier sex: He is sexually promiscuous; he places an enormous emphasis on women's youth and beauty, which he ogles every chance he gets; he either cheats on his wife or wants to; and he can be sexually aggressive to the point of criminality.

We find references to man's evolutionary heritage not only on T-shirts but in new science textbooks, pop psychology books on relationships, men's magazine, and Broadway shows. There are caveman fitness plans and caveman diets. *Saturday Night Live*'s hilarious "Unfrozen Caveman Lawyer" and the affronted caveman of the Geico car insurance ads joke about the ubiquity of caveman narratives. More disturbingly, the Darwinian discourse also crops up when men need an excuse for antisocial behavior. One man, who was caught on amateur video participating in the Central Park group sexual assaults in the summer of 2000, can be heard on video telling his sobbing victim, "Welcome back to the caveman times." How does a man come to think of himself as a caveman when he attacks a woman? What made so many American men decide that it's the DNA, rather than the devil, that makes them do it?

Using the late sociologist Pierre Bourdieu's theory of habitus, or the account of how cultural ideas are taken up in the form of bodily habits and tastes that reinforce behavioral norms and social inequality, I suggest that scientific theories find their way into both popular culture and men's corporeal habits and attitudes. Evolution has become popular culture, where popular culture is more than just media representations but refers to the institutions of everyday life: family, marriage, school, work—all sites where gender and racial knowledges are performed according to images people have available to them in actionable repertoires, scripts, and narratives. As popular culture, evolutionary narratives offer men a way to embody male sexuality.

That an evolutionary account of heterosexual male desire has captured the popular imagination is obvious from *Muscle & Fitness* magazine's article "Man the visual animal," which explains why men leer at women. Using a theory of the evolved difference between human male and female sexual psychologies developed by leading evolutionary psychologist Donald Symons, the article offers the following explanation under the subheading "Evolution Happens":

> Not much has changed in human sexuality since the Pleistocene. In his landmark book *The Evolution of Human Sexuality* (Oxford University Press, 1979), Symons hypothesizes that the male's sexual response to visual cues has been so rewarded by evolution that it's become innate.[2]

Such stories provide a means by which heterosexual male readers can experience their sexuality as acultural, primal[3] "The desire to ogle is your biological destiny."

Evolution may happen (or may have happened), but these stories do not just happen. Their appeal seems to lie precisely in the sense of security provided by the imagined inevitability of heterosexual manhood. In a marketplace of masculine identities, the caveman ethos is served up as Viagra for the masculine soul. Just as the 1950s women suffering what Betty Friedan famously called the "feminine mystique" were supposed to seek satisfaction in their Tupperware collections and their feminine figures, men today have been offered a way to think of their masculinity as powerful, productive, even aggressive—in a new economic and political climate where real opportunities to be rewarded for such traits have slipped away.[4]

It's hardly that most men today find themselves raising children at home while female partners bring home the bacon. But, like the fifties housewife, more men must now find satisfaction despite working below their potential (given that their job skills have lost their position to technology or other labor sources) in a postindustrial service economy that is less rewarding both materially and morally. As Susan Faludi puts it in her book *Stiffed*: "The fifties housewife, stripped of her connections to a wider world and invited to fill the void with shopping and the ornamental display of her ultrafemininity, could be said to have morphed into the nineties man, stripped of his connections to a wider world and invited to fill the void with consumption and a gym-bred display of his ultra-masculinity."[5]

On top of the economic changes affecting men, during the 1990s a growing anti-rape movement also challenged men, taking them to task for the problem of violence against women. More state and federal dollars supported efforts to stop such violence, and men increasingly feared complaints and repercussions for those complaints. The rape trials of Mike Tyson and William Kennedy Smith, Jr., the increasingly common school shootings (executed overwhelmingly by boys), the sexual harassment of women by men at the Citadel, the media attention given to the notorious Spurr Posse (a gang of guys who sought sex for "points" at almost all costs), the local sexual assault trials of countless high school and college athletic stars, the sexual harassment allegations against Supreme Court Justice nominee Clarence Thomas, and the White House sex scandals involving Bill Clinton meant more lost ground. Indeed, the 1990s saw relentless—though not necessarily ill-founded—criticism of men's sexual violence and other forms of aggression.

Right-wing leaders were as upset with men as feminists and other progressives. Those opposing abortion rights argued that sexual intercourse without procreation was undermining male responsibility, and those opposing women's equal-rights legislation argued that women's liberation would only allow men to relinquish their economic obligations to their families, sending women and children into divorce-induced poverty. Considering that critics of men came from the political right and left, and from among men as well as women, it seems fair to say that in turn-of-the-century America, moral disdain for men, whatever their age, race, or economic rank, had reached an all-time high.

For some men, the response was to cultivate a rude-dude attitude—popularized by Howard Stern, *The Man Show*, and MTV's endless shows about college spring break vacations. For some others, the response was to face, with a sense of responsibility and urgency, men's animal natures and either accept or reform their caveman ways. While some men were embracing the role of consumers and becoming creatures of ornamentation—the "metrosexuals"—other men revolted against metrosexuality, embracing a can-do virility that Sara Stewart in *The New York Post* referred to as "retrosexuality," or that "cringe-inducing backlash of beers and leers."[6] Caveman masculinity, with its focus on men's irrepressible heterosexuality and natural vigor, is a scientifically authorized form of retrosexuality.

THE CAVEMAN AS POPULAR SCIENTIFIC STORY

Popular culture is a political Petri dish for Darwinian ideas about sex. Average American guys don't read academic evolutionary science, but many do read about science in popular magazines and in best-selling books about the significance of the latest scientific ideas. As such, it is worth examining—even when magazine writers and television producers intentionally "dumb down" relatively sophisticated academic claims. In this section, I look at the way some popular texts make sense of evolutionary claims about men. Later I suggest that the caveman ideology, much of which centers on men's aggressive heterosexuality, gets embodied and thereby reproduced.[7]

In September of 1999, *Men's Health* magazine featured a caveman fitness program. Readers are shown an exercise routine that corresponds to the physical movements their ancestors would have engaged in: throwing a spear, hauling an animal carcass, honing a stone. A nice looking clean-shaven young man is shown exercising, his physical posture mirrored by a scruffy animal skin–clad caveman behind him in the photo. Each day of the week-long routine is labeled according to the caveman mystique: building the cave home; the hunt; the chase; the kill; the long trek home; preparing for the feast; and rest. That an exercise plan is modeled after man-as-caveman reveals the common assumption that being a caveman is good for a man, a healthy existence.

Another issue of *Men's Health* magazine explains "the sex science facts" to male readers interested in "the biology of attraction." We follow the steps of a mating dance, but don't quite understand that's what we're doing. Indeed, we must learn the evolutionary history of sex to see why men feel the way they do when they notice a beautiful woman walking down the street:

> Of course, out there in the street, you have no thoughts about genetic compatibility or childbearing. Probably the farthest thing from your mind is having a child with that beautiful woman.

But that doesn't matter. What you think counts for almost nothing. In the environment that crafted your brain and body, an environment in which you might be dead within minutes of spotting this beauty, the only thing that counted was that your clever neocortex—your seat of higher reason—be turned off so that you could quickly select a suitable mate, impregnate her, and succeed in passing on your genes to the next generation.[8]

The article proceeds to identify the signals of fertility that attract men: youth, beauty, big breasts, and a small waistline. Focusing on the desire for youth in women, the article tells men that "the reason men of any age continue to like young girls is that we were designed to get them pregnant and dominate their fertile years by keeping them that way. . . . When your first wife has lost the overt signals of reproductive viability, you desire a younger woman who still has them all."[9] And, of course, male readers are reminded that "your genes don't care about your wife or girlfriend or what the neighbors will say."[10]

Amy Alkon's *Winston-Salem Journal* advice column, "The Advice Goddess," uses an evolutionary theory of men's innate loutishness to comfort poor "Feeling Cheated On," who sent a letter complaining that her boyfriend fantasizes about other women during their lovemaking. The Advice Goddess cited a study by Bruce J. Ellis and Donald Symons (whose work was also mentioned in *Muscle & Fitness*) to conclude that "male sexuality is all about variety. Men are hard-wired to want you, the entire girls' dorm next door, and the entire girls' dorm next to that."[11]

Popular magazines tell men that they have a biological propensity to favor women with the faces of 11½ year-old girls (where the eyes and chin are close together) and a waist-to-hip ratio of .7 (where the waist measures 70% that of the hips). Men are told that their sexist double standard concerning appearance is evolutionary. Some of this research is very speculative—for instance, in some studies, men are simply shown photos of women with specific waist-to-hip ratios and then asked, "Would you like to spend the rest of your life with this woman?"—as though such staged answers reveal something about the individuals' real-life choices (or genes). But the results of this research make great copy.

Men's Health magazine in 1999 offers an article called "The Mysteries of Sex . . . Explained!" and relies on evolutionary theory, quoting several professors in the field, to explain "why most women won't sleep with you." The article elucidates:

> Stop blaming your wife. The fault lies with Mother Nature, the pit boss of procreation. Neil M. Malamuth, Ph.D., professor of psychology at UCLA, explains. "You're in Las Vegas with 10 grand. Your gambling strategy will depend on which form your money takes. With 10 chips worth $1,000 each, you'd weigh each decision cautiously. With 10,000 $1 chips, you'd throw them around." That's reproductive strategy in a nutshell.[12]

Popular magazine articles like this follow a standard formula. They quote the scientists, reporting on the evolutionary theorists' research, and offer funny anecdotes about male sexuality to illustrate the research findings. This *Men's Health* article continues to account for men's having fetishes: "Men are highly sexed creatures, less interested in relationship but highly hooked on visuals, says David Givens, Ph.D., an anthropologist. 'Because sex carries fewer consequences for men, it's easier for us to use objects as surrogate sexual partners.' Me? I've got my eye on a Zenith, model 39990."[13]

It's not just these popular and often humorous accounts of men that are based in some version of evolutionary theory. Even serious academic arguments rely on evolutionary theories of human behavior. For example, Steven Rhoads, a member of the University of Virginia faculty in public policy, has written *Taking Sex Differences Seriously* (2004), a book telling us why gender equity in the home and the workplace is a feminist pipedream. Rhoads argues that women are wrong to expect men to take better care of children, do more housework, and make a place for them as equals at work because, he states, "men and women still have different natures and, generally speaking, different preferences, talents and interests."[14] He substantiates much of his argument about the divergent psychological predispositions in men and women with countless references to studies done by evolutionary scholars.

News magazines and television programs have also spent quite a bit of time popularizing evolutionary science and its implications for understanding human sex differences. The ABC news program *Day One* reported in 1995 on evolutionary psychologist David Buss's new book, *The Evolution of Desire*.[15] Buss appeared on the show, which elaborated his theory by presenting us with super model Cindy Crawford and Barbie (the doll), presumably as representations of what men are wired to find desirable. As Buss explained in the interview, our evolutionary fore-brothers who did not prefer women with high cheekbones, big eyes, lustrous hair, and full lips did not reproduce. As Buss puts it, those men who happened to like someone who was older, sicker, or infertile "are not our ancestors. We are all the descendants of those men who preferred young healthy women and so as offspring, as descendants of those men, we carry with us their desires."[16] On that same television show, *Penthouse* magazine publisher Bob Guccioni was interviewed and explained that men are simply biologically designed to enjoy looking at sexy women: "This may be very politically incorrect but that's the way it is. . . . It's all part of our ancestral conditioning."[17] Evolutionary narratives clearly work for publishers of pornography marketed to men.

Newsweek's 1996 cover story, "The Biology of Beauty: What Science has Discovered about Sex Appeal," argues that the beautylust humans exhibit "is often better suited to the Stone Age than to the Information Age; the qualities we find alluring may be powerful emblems of health, fertility and resistance to disease. . . ."[18] Though "beauty isn't all that matters in life," the article asserts, "our weakness for 'biological quality' is the cause of endless pain and injustice."[19]

Sometimes the magazines and TV shows covering the biological basis of sexual desire give a nod to the critics. The aforementioned *Newsweek* article, for instance, quotes feminist writer Katha Pollitt, who insists that "human beings cannot be reduced to DNA packets."[20] And then, as if to affirm Pollitt's claim, homosexuality is invoked as an example of the countless non-adaptive delights we desire: "Homosexuality is hard to explain as a biological adaptation. So is stamp collecting. . . . We pursue countless passions that have no direct bearing on survival."[21] So when there is a nod to ways humans are not hardwired, homosexual desires are framed as oddities having no basis in nature, while heterosexual attraction along the lines of stereotypical heterosexual male fantasy is framed as biological. Heterosexual desire enjoys a *biologically correct* status.

Zoologist Desmond Morris explains how evolutionary theory applies to humans in his 1999 six-part television series, *Desmond Morris' The Human Animal: A Personal View of the Human Species*.[22] The first show in the series draws from his book, *The Naked Ape*, explaining that humans are relatively hairless with little to protect themselves besides their big brains.[23] This is stated as we watch two naked people, one male and one female, walk through a public place where everyone else is dressed in modern-day clothing. Both are white, both are probably 25 to 30 years old, both look like models (the man with well-chiseled muscles, a suntan, and no chest hair, the woman thin, yet shapely with larger than average breasts, shaved legs, and a manicured pubic region). This presentation of man and woman in today's aesthetically ideal form as the image of what all of us were once like is *de rigueur* for any popular representation of evolutionary theory applied to human sexuality. No woman is flabby, flat chested, or has body hair, no man has pimples or back hair. These culturally mandated ideal body types are presented as the image of what our human ancestors naturally looked like. In this way and others, such shows posit modern aesthetic standards as states of nature.

Time magazine's 1994 cover story on "Our Cheating Hearts" reports that "the emerging field known as evolutionary psychology" gives us "fresh detail about the feelings and thoughts that draw us into marriage—or push us out."[24] After explaining the basics about men being less discriminating about their sexual partners than women, the article moves on to discuss why people divorce, anticipating resistance to the evolutionary explanation:

> Objections to this sort of analysis are predictable: "But people leave marriages for emotional reasons. They don't add up their offspring and pull out their calculators." But emotions are just evolution's executioners. Beneath the thoughts and feelings and temperamental differences marriage counselors spend their time sensitively assessing are the stratagems of the genes—cold, hard equations composed of simple variables: social status, age of spouse, number of children, their ages, outside romantic opportunities, and so on. Is the wife really duller and more nagging than she was 20 years ago? Maybe, but maybe the husband's tolerance for nagging has dropped now that she is 45 and has no reproductive future.[25]

In case *Time* readers react to the new evolutionary psychology as part of a plot to destroy the cherished nuclear family, they are told that "progress will also depend on people using the explosive insight of evolutionary psychology in a morally responsible way. . . . We are potentially moral animals—which is more than any other animal can say—but we are not naturally moral animals. The first step to being moral is to realize how thoroughly we aren't."[26]

While many accounts of evolution's significance for male sexuality seem simply to rationalize sexist double standards and wallow in men's loutishness, a number of pop-Darwinist claims have the moral purpose of liberating men from being controlled by their caveman natures. Their message: Men can become enlightened cavemen. These popular versions of man as caveman make an attempt to liberate men by getting them to see themselves differently. They tell men that they are cavemen with potential. They either make fun of men's putatively natural shortcomings or encourage them to cage the caveman within through a kind of scientific consciousness-raising.

Rob Becker's one-man show, *Defending the Caveman*, played Broadway and elsewhere from 1993 to 2005. This performance piece poking fun at sex differences is the longest running solo play in Broadway

history. It relies on a longstanding man-the-hunter and woman-the-gatherer framework, from which modern sex differences follow. Cavemen hunted and focused on their prey until killing it. Cavewomen gathered things to use in the cave home. Men are thus strong silent types while women are into communication and togetherness. More significantly, *Defending the Caveman*'s creator and performer believes men have a bad rap. Becker points out that women say "men are all assholes" with a kind of feminist cultural authority men no longer enjoy when they make derogatory remarks about women. Rob Becker thus echoes the common sentiment among American men today that men are in the untenable position of being both hated and ignorant. They may want to try but they are unable to succeed. The show validates many people's observations of the behavior patterns and sex battles in their daily lives, and seems to poke fun at men's shortcomings—all the while affirming a vision of men as being as similar as peas in a primordial pea soup.

EVOLUTION AS IDEOLOGY

A critical examination of evolutionary science in its popular cultural manifestations over the past 15 to 20 years—the way most men come to know of the theory about their sexuality—allows us to ask how men come to know what they know about themselves. This type of analysis assumes that evolution is an ideology—which is not to suggest that humans got here via God's creation or some means other than evolution by natural selection. Positioning evolutionary arguments about human nature as an ideology is to understand that people think and act in ways that take evolutionary theory, however they construe it, as a self-evident truth. Furthermore, positioning evolutionary theory applied to humans as an ideology allows us to examine the way evolutionary ideas about male sexuality circulate in our culture. It is on this basis that I challenge the convenient innocence with which men invoke science to explain their bodies and their actions.

The caveman is certainly not the only form of masculine identity in our times. But the emergence of a caveman masculinity tells us much about the authority of science, the flow of scientific ideas in our culture, and the embodiment of those ideas. In *Science, Culture and Society* Mark Erickson explains the connection between science and society in our times:

> We live with science: science surrounds us, invades our lives, and alters our perspective on the world. We see things from a scientific perspective, in that we use science to help us make sense of the world—regardless of whether or not that is an appropriate thing to do—and to legitimize the picture of the world that results from such investigations.[27]

In a culture so attached to scientific authority and explication, it is worth examining the popular appeal of evolutionary theory and its impact on masculine embodiment. The popularity of the scientific story of men's evolved desires—however watered down or distorted the science becomes as enthusiasts popularize it—can tell us something about the appeal and influence of that story.

THE CAVEMAN AS EMBODIED ETHOS

If the evolutionary stories appeal to many men, and it seems they do indeed, it's because they ring true. Many men feel like their bodies are aggressive. They feel urges, at a physical level, in line with evolutionary theoretical predictions. With a naive understanding of experience, men can see affect as having an authenticity and empirical validity to it. In other words, the men who feel like cavemen do not see their identity as a fiction; it is their bodily reality and is backed by scientific study.

Certainly, evolutionary scholars would argue that the actual evolved psychologies make men feel like cavemen, or at least make those feelings emerge or affect behavior in particular environments. I argue that this explanation too simplistically separates men's bodies from discourse.

The work of Pierre Bourdieu provides a tool for understanding how power is organized at the level of unconscious embodiment of cultural forces. I suggest that popular manifestations of scientific evolutionary narratives about men's sexuality have

a real material effect on many men. Bourdieu's theory of practice develops the concepts of *habitus* and *field* to describe a reciprocally constitutive relationship between bodily dispositions and dominant power structures. Bourdieu concerned himself primarily with the ways in which socioeconomic class is incorporated at the level of the body, including class-based ways of speaking, postures, lifestyles, attitudes, and tastes.

Significant for Bourdieu is that people acquire tastes that mark them as members of particular social groups and particular social levels.[28] Membership in a particular social class produces and reproduces a class sensibility, what Bourdieu (1990) called "practical sense."[29] Habitus is "a somatized social relationship, a social law converted into an embodied law."[30] The process of becoming competent in the everyday life of a society or group constitutes habitus. Bourdieu's notion of embodiment can be extended to suggest that habitus, as embodied field, amounts to "the pleasurable and ultimately erotic constitution of [the individual's] social imaginary."[31]

Concerning the circulation of evolutionary narratives, we can see men taking erotic pleasure in the formation of male identity and the performance of accepted norms of heterosexual masculinity using precisely these tools of popular evolutionary science. Put differently, pop-Darwinism is a discourse that finds its way into men's bones and boners. The caveman story can become a man's practical sense of who he is and what he desires. This is so because masculinity is a dimension of embodied and performative practical sensibility—because men carry themselves with a bodily comportment suggestive of their position as the dominant gender, and they invest themselves in particular lifestyle practices, consumption patterns, attire, and bodily comportment. Evolutionary narratives thus enter the so-called habitus, and an aestheticized discourse and image of the caveman circulates through popular culture becoming part of natural perception, and consequently is reproduced by those embodying it.

In his study of the overwhelmingly white and male workspace of the Options Exchange floor, sociologist Richard Widick uses Bourdieu's theory to explain the traders' physical and psychical engagement with their work. Widick holds that "the traders' inhabitation and practical mastery of the trading floor achieves the bio-physical psycho-social state of a natural identity."[32] Hence the traders describe their manner as a "trading instinct." In a similar way, American men with what we might call a caveman instinct can be said to have acquired a "pre-reflexive practical sense" of themselves as heterosexually driven.[33]

Bourdieu gives the name "symbolic violence" to that process by which we come to accept and embody power relations without ever accepting them in the conscious sense of knowing them and choosing them. We hold beliefs that don't need to be thought—the effects of which can be "durably and deeply embedded in the body in the form of dispositions."[34] From this perspective, the durable dispositions of evolutionary discourse are apparent in our rape culture, for example, when a member of the group sexual assault in New York tells the woman he's attacking, "Welcome back to the caveman times." Embodying the ideology of irrepressible heterosexual desire makes such aggression appear to be natural.

Bourdieu's theory allows us to see that both cultural and material forces reveal themselves in the lived reality of social relations.[35] We can see on men's bodies the effects of their struggle with slipping economic privilege and a sense of entitlement to superiority over women. If men live out power struggles in their everyday experiences, then caveman masculinity can be seen as an imagined compensation for men's growing sense of powerlessness.[36] To be sure, some men have more social and economic capital than others. Those with less might invest even more in their bodies and appearances.[37]

Sociologist R. W. Connell discusses the significance of naturalizing male power. He states:

> The physical sense of maleness is not a simple thing. It involves size and shape, habits of posture and movement, particular physical skills and the lack of others, the image of one's own body, the way it is presented to other people and the ways they respond to it, the way it operates at work and in sexual relations In no sense is all this

a consequence of XY chromosomes, or even of the possession on which discussions of masculinity have so lovingly dwelt, the penis. The physical sense of maleness grows through a personal history of social practice, a life-history-in-society.[38]

We see and believe that men's power over women is the order of nature because "power is translated not only into mental body-images and fantasies, but into muscle tensions, posture, the feel and texture of the body"[39] Scientific discourse constitutes the field for some men in the constructed figure of the caveman, enabling those men to internalize such an identity. The caveman thus becomes an imaginative projection that is experienced and lived as real biological truth.

In his book, *Cultural Boundaries of Science*, Thomas Gieryn comments on the cultural authority of science, suggesting that "if 'science' says so, we are more often than not inclined to believe it or act on it—and to prefer it to claims lacking this epistemic seal of approval."[40] To his observation I would add that we are also more likely to *live* it. Ideas that count as scientific, regardless of their truth value, become lived ideologies. It's how modern American men have become cavemen and how the caveman ethos enjoys reproductive success.

Cultural anthropologist Paul Rabinow gives the name "biosociality" to the formation of new group and individual identities and practices that emerge from the scientific study of human life.[41] Rabinow offers the example of neurofibromatosis groups whose members have formed to discuss their experiences, educate their children, lobby for their disease, and "understand" their fate. And in the future, he points out, " . . . [i]t is not hard to imagine groups formed around the chromosome 17, locus 16,256, site 654,376 allele variant with a guanine substitution."[42] Rabinow's concept of biosociality is instructive here; for the discourse of the caveman offers this form of biosociality. The caveman constitutes an identity based on new scientific "facts" about one's biology.

Of course, evolutionary psychologists would have us think that men's desires are, in some final instance, biological properties of an internal psyche or sexual psychology. I am suggesting, in line with

Bourdieu, that men's desires are always performed in relation to the dominant discourses in circulation within their cultural lifeworlds, either for or against the representations that permeate those lifeworlds. We can see that a significant number of men are putting the pop-Darwinian rhetoric to good use in social interactions. The scientific discourse of the caveman (however unscientific we might regard it by the time it gets to everyday guys reading magazines and watching TV) is corporealized, quite literally incorporated into living identities, deeply shaping these men's experience of being a man.

THE CAVEMAN AS ETHNICITY

I recognize the lure of the caveman narrative. After all, it provides an explanation for patterns we do see and for how men do feel in contemporary society, tells men that they are beings who are the way they are for a specific reason, offers them an answer about what motivates them, and carries the authority of scientific investigation about their biological makeup. Evolutionary theory offers an origin story. Plus, it's fun: thinking of the reasons you might feel a certain way because such feelings might have been necessary for your ancestors to survive a hostile environment back in the Pleistocene can be a satisfying intellectual exercise.

In telling men a story about who they are, naturally, pop-Darwinism has the normalizing, disciplinary effect of forging a common, biological identity among men. Embodying ideology allows men to feel morally exonerated while they reproduce that very ideology. The discourse of male biological unity suppresses many significant differences among men, and of course many ways in which men would otherwise identify with women's tastes and behaviors. The evolutionary explanation of men's sexual behavior is an all-encompassing narrative enabling men to frame their own thoughts and experiences through it. As such it's a *grand narrative*, a totalizing theory explaining men's experiences as though all men act and feel the same ways, and as though the ideas of Western science provide a universal truth about those actions and feelings.

I'm skeptical of this kind of totalizing narrative about male sexuality because evolution applied to human beings does not offer that sort of truth. The application of evolutionary theory to human behavior is not as straightforwardly scientific as it might seem, even for those of us who believe in the theory of evolution by natural selection. It is a partial, political discourse that authorizes certain prevalent masculine behaviors and a problematic acceptance of those behaviors. I think there are better—less totalizing, and differently consequential—discourses out there that describe and explain those same behaviors. I'm also skeptical of men's use of the evolutionary narrative because, at its best, it can only create "soft patriarchs"—kinder, gentler cavemen who resist the putative urges of which evolutionary science makes them aware.[43]

Caveman masculinity has become an "ethnic option," a way of identifying and living one's manhood. Mary C. Waters explains that ethnic identity is "far from the automatic labeling of a primordial characteristic"[44] but instead is a complex, socially created identity. As an ethnicity, caveman masculinity is seen as not only impossible but also undesirable to change.[45] The caveman as an ethnicity reveals an embrace of biology as a reaction to social constructionist understandings of masculinity, feminist demands on men, and the changing roles of men at work and in families.

To repeat: My quarrel is not limited to evolutionary theorists alone. Darwinian ideas are often spread by enthusiasts—secondary school teachers, science editors of various newspapers and magazines, and educational television show producers—who take up evolutionary theorists' ideas and convey them to mass audiences. Evolutionary thinking has become popular in part because it speaks to a publicly recognized predicament of men. Changing economic patterns have propelled men's flight from marriage and bread-winning, in conjunction with women's increased (albeit significantly less prosperous) independence. If a man today wants multiple partners with as little commitment as possible, evolutionary rhetoric answers why this is so.

Evolutionary science doesn't tell a flattering story about men. But more significantly, many people don't understand that it's *a story*. Evolution has become not only a grand narrative but also a lived ideology. Maleness and femaleness, like heterosexuality and homosexuality, are not simply identities but *systems of knowledge*.[46] And those systems of knowledge inform thinking and acting. Bourdieu's concept of habitus explains the ways in which culture and knowledge, including evolutionary knowledge, implant themselves at the level of the body, becoming a set of attitudes, tastes, perceptions, actions, and reactions. The status of science as objective, neutral knowledge helps make evolution a lived ideology because it feels truthful, natural, real.

Taking the historical and cultural changes affecting men seriously and embracing the diversity among men demand new understandings of masculinity, identity, and science. In gaining such a sociological perspective, men might resist making gender a new ethnicity and instead take a great leap forward to become new kinds of men.

NOTES

1. For defenses of the study of the popularization of scientific discourse, and exemplary studies of the popularization of Darwinian discourse in different eras, see Alfred Kelly, *The Descent of Darwin: The Popularization of Darwinism in Germany, 1860–1914* (Chapel Hill: University of North Carolina Press, 1981) and Alvar Ellegård, *Darwin and the General Reader: The Reception of Darwin's Theory of Evolution in the British Press, 1859–1872* (Chicago: University of Chicago Press, 1990).

2. Mary Ellen Strote, "Man the Visual Animal," *Muscle & Fitness* (February 1994): 166.

3. Ibid., 166.

4. Betty Friedan, *The Feminine Mystique* (New York: Dell Publishing Company, 1963).

5. Susan Faludi, *Stiffed: The Betrayal of the American Man* (New York: HarperCollins, 1999), 40.

6. Sara Stewart, "Beasty Boys—'Retrosexuals' Call for Return of Manly Men; Retrosexuals Rising," *The New York Post*, July 18, 2006.

7. My argument here parallels a study of the pervasive iconography of the gene in popular culture. In *The DNA*

Mystique: The Gene As a Cultural Icon, Dorothy Nelkin and M. Susan Lindee (New York: W. H. Freeman and Company, 1995, 11) explain that popular culture provides "narratives of meaning." Those narratives filter complex ideas, provide guidance, and influence how people see themselves and evaluate other people, ideas, and policies. In this way, Nelkin and Lindee argue, DNA works as an ideology to justify boundaries of identity and legal rights, as well as to explain criminality, addiction, and personality. Of course addict genes and criminal genes are misnomers—the definitions of what counts as an addict and what counts as a crime have shifted throughout history. Understanding DNA stories as ideological clarifies why, for example, people made sense of Elvis's talents and shortcomings by referring to his genetic stock (Ibid., 79–80). To call narratives of DNA ideological, then, is *not* to resist the scientific argument that deoxyribonucleic acid is a double-helix structure carrying information forming living cells and tissues, but to look at the way people make sense of DNA and use DNA to make sense of people and events in their daily lives.

8. Laurence Gonzales, "The Biology of Attraction," *Men's Health* 20.7 (2005): 186–93.

9. Ibid., 192.

10. Ibid., 193.

11. Amy Alkon, "Many Men Fantasize During Sex, But It Isn't a Talking Point," *Winston-Salem Journal*, 29 September 2005, p. 34.

12. Greg Gutfeld, "The Mysteries of Sex . . . Explained!," *Men's Health* April: 1999, 76.

13. Ibid., 76.

14. Steven E. Rhoads, *Taking Sex Differences Seriously* (San Francisco: Encounter Books, 2004), 4.

15. David M. Buss, *The Evolution of Desire: Strategies of Human Mating* (New York: BasicBooks, 1994).

16. *Day One* reported in 1995. ABC News.

17. Ibid.

18. Geoffrey Cowley, "The Biology of Beauty," *Newsweek* 127 (1996): 62.

19. Ibid., 64.

20. Ibid., 66.

21. Ibid.

22. *Desmond Morris' The Human Animal: A Personal View of the Human Species* ["Beyond Survival"]. Clive Bromhall, dir. (Discovery Communication/TLC Video, 1999).

23. Desmond Morris, *The Naked Ape* (New York: Dell Publishing, 1967).

24. Robert Wright, *The Moral Animal: Evolutionary Psychology and Everyday Life* (New York: Pantheon Books, 1994), 45.

25. Ibid., 50.

26. Ibid., 52.

27. Mark Erickson, *Science, Culture and Society* (Cambridge: Polity Press, 2005), 224.

28. Pierre Bourdieu, *Distinction: A Social Critique of the Judgment of Taste* (Cambridge: Harvard University Press, 1984).

29. Pierre Bourdieu, *The Logic of Practice* (Stanford: Stanford University Press, 1990).

30. Pierre Bourdieu, *Masculine Domination* (Stanford: Sanford University Press, 2001).

31. Richard Widick, "Flesh and the Free Market: (On Taking Bourdieu to the Options Exchange)," *Theory and Society* 32 (2003): 679–723, 716.

32. Widick, 701.

33. Ibid.

34. Bourdieu, *Masculine*, 39.

35. Lois McNay, "Agency and Experience: Gender As a Lived Relation," in *Feminism After Bourdieu*, ed. Lisa Adkins and Bev Skeggs (Oxford: Blackwell, 2004), 177.

36. See McNay 175–90 for a discussion of emotional compensation and lived experience.

37. See Beverley Skeggs, *Formations of Class and Gender: Becoming Respectable* (London: Sage, 1997) for a study pointing this out about working class women.

38. R. W. Connell, *Gender and Power: Society, the Person and Sexual Politics* (Cambridge: Polity Press, 1987), 84.

39. Ibid., 85.

40. Thomas F. Gieryn, *Cultural Boundaries of Science: Credibility on the Line* (Chicago: University of Chicago Press, 1999), 1.

41. Paul Rabinow, *Making PCR, A Story of Biotechnology* (Chicago: University of Chicago Press, 1996), 101–102.

42. Ibid., 102.

43. I am appropriating W. Bradford Wilcox's term, from his book *Soft Patriarchs, New Men: How Christianity Shapes Fathers and Husbands* (Chicago: University of Chicago Press, 2004). Wilcox argues that the Christian men's movement known as the Promise Keepers encourages men to spend more time with their wives and children without ever challenging the fundamental patriarchal family structure that places men at the top.

44. Mary C. Waters, *Ethnic Options: Choosing Identities in America,* (Berkeley: University of California Press, 1990), 16.

45. See Michael S. Kimmel, *Manhood in America: A Cultural History* (New York: Free Press, 1996), 127–137.

46. Steven Seidman, *Difference Troubles: Queering Social Theory and Sexual Politics* (Cambridge, UK: Cambridge University Press, 1997), 93.

THE ACT-LIKE-A-MAN BOX

belabors the obvious diagram not explained well

Paul Kivel

How are boys trained in the United States? What is the predominant image of masculinity that boys must deal with while growing up?

From a very early age, boys are told to "Act Like a Man." Even though they have all the normal human feelings of love, excitement, sadness, confusion, anger, curiosity, pain, frustration, humiliation, shame, grief, resentment, loneliness, low self-worth, and self-doubt, they are taught to hide the feelings and appear to be tough and in control. They are told to be aggressive, not to back down, not to make mistakes, and to take charge, have lots of sex, make lots of money, and be responsible. Most of all, they are told not to cry.

My colleagues and I have come to call this rigid set of expectations the "Act-Like-a-Man" box because it feels like a box, a 24-hour-a-day, seven-day-a-week box that society tells boys they must fit themselves into. One reason we know it's a box is because every time a boy tries to step out he's pushed back in with names like wimp, sissy, mama's boy, girl, fag, nerd, punk, mark, bitch, and others even more graphic. Behind those names is the threat of violence.

These words are little slaps, everyday reminders designed to keep us in the box. They are also fighting words. If someone calls a boy a "wimp" or a "fag," he is supposed to fight to prove that he is not. Almost every adult man will admit that as a kid, he had to fight at least once to prove he was in the box.

The columns on either side of the box show the expectations our society holds for men. The abuse, pressure, and training boys receive to meet these expectations and stay in the box produce a lot of feelings. Yet they have to cover over those feelings and try to act like a man because one of the strictures of being a man is not to show your feelings.

Notice that many of the words we get called refer to being gay or feminine. This feeds into two things we're taught to fear: (1) that we are not manly enough and (2) that we might be gay. Homophobia, the fear of gays or of being taken for gay, is an incredibly strong fear we learn as boys and carry with us throughout our lives. Much too often we try to relieve our fears of being gay or effeminate by attacking others.

There is other training that keeps us in the box. Besides getting into fights, we are ostracized and teased, and girls don't seem to like us when we step out of the box. Many adults keep pushing us to be tough, and that process begins early. They seem convinced that if they "coddle" us, we will be weak and vulnerable. Somehow, withdrawal of affection is supposed to toughen us and prepare us for the "real" world. Withdrawal of affection is emotional abuse. And that's bad enough. But it often does not stop there. One out of every six of us is sexually abused as a child. Often, the verbal, physical, and sexual abuse continues throughout our childhood.

There are many cultural variations of this theme, but its prevalence in Western cultures is striking. All boys have different strategies for trying to survive in the box. Some might even sneak out of it at times, but the scars from living within the walls of the box are long-lasting and painful.

"Act-Like-a-Man" Box

VERBAL ABUSE:

wimp ▲
girl ▲
sissy ▲
mama's boy ▲
nerd ▲
fag ▲
punk ▲
mark ▲
bitch ▲

PHYSICAL ABUSE:

▲ hit/beat up
▲ teased
▲ isolated
▲ rejected
▲ forced to play sports
▲ sexual assault

tough		have money
aggressive	anger	never ask for help
competitive	sadness	angry
	love	
in control	connection	yell
no feelings	confusion	intimidate
	low self-worth	
don't cry	resentment	responsible
	curiosity	
take charge	excitement	take it
	isolation	
don't make mistakes		don't back down
succeed		have sex with women

If we pay attention we can easily see the box's effects on boys. Just watch a group of them together. They are constantly challenging each other, putting each other down, hitting each other, testing to see who is in the box. They are never at ease, always on guard. At an early age they start to hide their feelings, toughen up, and will make a huge emotional effort not to cry. They stop wearing colorful clothing or participating in activities that they think might make them vulnerable to being labeled gay. They walk more stiffly, talk more guardedly, move more aggressively. Behind this bravura they are often confused, scared, angry, and wanting closeness with others. But being in the box precludes closeness and makes intimacy unlikely.

The key to staying in the box is control. Boys are taught to control their bodies, control their feelings, control their relationships—to protect themselves from being vulnerable. Although the box is a metaphor for the pressures all boys must respond to, the possibility that a boy will have control over the conditions of his life varies depending on his race, class, and culture.

Being in control is not the same as being violent. In Western societies hitting people is frowned upon except in particular sports or military settings. It is deemed much more refined to retain control by using verbal, emotional, or psychological means rather than physical force. Financial manipulation, coercion and intimidation, and sexual pressure are also condoned as long as no one is physically injured.

Clearly, the more money, education, and connections a man has, the easier it is for him to buy or manipulate what he wants. Wealthy and upper- or middle-class white men are generally promoted and celebrated for being in control and getting what they want. Poor or working-class men and men of color are usually punished for these same behaviors, especially, but not only, if they use physical force.

Why are boys trained to be in control? Most boys will end up with one of three roles in society—to be workers, consumers, or enforcers. A small percentage of boys are trained to give orders—to be bosses, managers, or officers. The box trains boys for the roles they will play, whether they will make decisions governing the lives of others or carry out the decisions made by those at the top. The box prepares boys to be police officers, security cops, deans, administrators, soldiers, heads of families, probation officers, prison guards—the roles that men, primarily white men, are being trained to fill. Men of

color, along with women and young people, are the people more often being controlled.

Many men are under the illusion that being in the box is like being in an exclusive club. No girls allowed. All men are equal. For working- and middle-class white men and for those men of color who aspire to be accepted by them, the box creates a false feeling of solidarity with men in power and misleads many of them into thinking they have more in common with the corporate executives, political and religious leaders, generals, and bosses than they have with women.

Nobody is born in the Act-Like-a-Man box. It takes years and years of enforcement, name-calling, fights, threats, abuse, and fear to turn us into men who live in this box. By adolescence we believe that there are only two choices—we can be a man or a boy, a winner or a loser, a bully or a wimp, a champ or a chump.

Nobody wants to live in a box. It feels closed in; much of us is left out. It was a revelation to realize how I had been forced into the box. It was a relief to understand how it had been accomplished and to know it didn't have to be that way. Today, it inspires me to see adult men choose to live outside the box. It is a choice each of us can, and must make—to step outside the box and back into our families and communities.

ALL MEN ARE *NOT* CREATED EQUAL: ASIAN MEN IN U.S. HISTORY

Skimmed

Yen Le Espiritu

Today, virtually every major metropolitan market across the United States has at least one Asian American female newscaster. In contrast, there is a nearly total absence of Asian American men in anchor positions (Hamamoto, 1994, p. 245; Fong-Torres, 1995). This gender imbalance in television news broadcasting exemplifies the racialization of Asian American manhood: Historically, they have been depicted as either asexual or hypersexual; today, they are constructed to be less successful, assimilated, attractive, and desirable than their female counterparts (Espiritu, 1996, pp. 95–98). The exclusion of Asian men from Eurocentric notions of the masculine reminds us that not all men benefit—or benefit equally—from a patriarchal system designed to maintain the unequal relationship that exists between men and women. The feminist mandate for gender solidarity tends to ignore power differentials among men, among women, and between white women and men of color. This exclusive focus on gender bars traditional feminists from recognizing the oppression of men of color: the fact that there are men, and not only women, who have been "feminized" and the fact that some white middle-class women hold cultural power and class power over certain men of color (Cheung, 1990, pp. 245–246; Wiegman, 1991, p. 311). Presenting race and gender as relationally constructed, King-Kok Cheung (1990) exhorted white scholars to acknowledge that, like female voices, "the voices of many men of color have been historically silenced or dismissed"

Yen Le Espiritu, "All Men Are *Not* Created Equal: Asian Men in U.S. History." Reprinted by permission of the author.

(p. 246). Along the same line, black feminists have referred to "racial patriarchy"—a concept that calls attention to the white/patriarch master in U.S. history and his dominance over the black male as well as the black female (Gaines, 1990, p. 202).

Throughout their history in the United States, Asian American men, as immigrants and citizens of color, have faced a variety of economic, political, and ideological racism that have assaulted their manhood. During the pre–World War II period, racialized and gendered immigration policies and labor conditions emasculated Asian men, forcing them into womanless communities and into "feminized" jobs that had gone unfilled due to the absence of women. During World War II, the internment of Japanese Americans stripped *Issei* (first generation) men of their role as the family breadwinner, transferred some of their power and status to the U.S.-born children, and decreased male dominance over women. In the contemporary period, the patriarchal authority of Asian immigrant men, particularly those of the working class, has also been challenged due to the social and economic losses that they suffered in their transition to life in the United States. As detailed below, these three historically specific cases establish that the material existences of Asian American men have historically contradicted the Eurocentric, middle-class constructions of manhood.

ASIAN MEN IN DOMESTIC SERVICE

Feminist scholars have argued accurately that domestic service involves a three-way relationship between privileged white men, privileged white women, and poor women of color (Romero, 1992). But women have not been the only domestic workers. During the pre–World War II period, racialized and gendered immigration policies and labor conditions forced Asian men into "feminized" jobs such as domestic service, laundry work, and food preparation.[1] Due to their non-citizen status, the closed labor market, and the shortage of women, Asian immigrant men, first Chinese and later Japanese, substituted to some extent for female labor in the American West. David Katzman (1978) noted the peculiarities of the domestic labor situation in the West in this period: "In 1880, California and Washington were the only states in which a majority of domestic servants were men" (p. 55).

At the turn of the twentieth century, lacking other job alternatives, many Chinese men entered into domestic service in private homes, hotels, and rooming houses (Daniels, 1988, p. 74). Whites rarely objected to Chinese in domestic service. In fact, through the 1900s, the Chinese houseboy was the symbol of upper-class status in San Francisco (Glenn, 1986, p. 106). As late as 1920, close to 50 percent of the Chinese in the United States were still occupied as domestic servants (Light, 1972, p. 7). Large numbers of Chinese also became laundrymen, not because laundering was a traditional male occupation in China, but because there were very few women of any ethnic origin—and thus few washerwomen—in gold-rush California (Chan, 1991, pp. 33–34). Chinese laundrymen thus provided commercial services that replaced women's unpaid labor in the home. White consumers were prepared to patronize a Chinese laundryman because as such he "occupied a status which was in accordance with the social definition of the place in the economic hierarchy suitable for a member of an 'inferior race'" (cited in Siu, 1987, p. 21). In her autobiographical fiction *China Men*, Maxine Hong Kingston presents her father and his partners as engaged in their laundry business for long periods each day—a business considered so low and debased that, in their songs, they associate it with the washing of menstrual blood (Goellnicht, 1992, p. 198). The existence of the Chinese

houseboy and launderer—and their forced "bachelor" status—further bolstered the stereotype of the feminized and asexual or homosexual Asian man. Their feminization, in turn, confirmed their assignment to the state's labor force which performed "women's work."

Japanese men followed Chinese men into domestic service. By the end of the first decade of the twentieth century, the U.S. Immigration Commission estimated that 12,000 to 15,000 Japanese in the western United States earned a living in domestic service (Chan, 1991, pp. 39–40). Many Japanese men considered housework beneath them because in Japan only lower-class women worked as domestic servants (Ichioka, 1988, p. 24). Studies of Issei occupational histories indicate that a domestic job was the first occupation for many of the new arrivals, but unlike Chinese domestic workers, most Issei eventually moved on to agricultural or city trades (Glenn, 1986, p. 108). Filipino and Korean boys and men likewise relied on domestic service for their livelihood (Chan, 1991, p. 40). In his autobiography *East Goes West*, Korean immigrant writer Younghill Kang (1937) related that he worked as a domestic servant for a white family who treated him "like a cat or a dog" (p. 66).

Filipinos, as stewards in the U.S. Navy, also performed domestic duties for white U.S. naval officers. During the ninety-four years of U.S. military presence in the Philippines, U.S. bases served as recruiting stations for the U.S. armed forces, particularly the navy. Soon after the United States acquired the Philippines from Spain in 1898, its navy began actively recruiting Filipinos—but only as stewards and mess attendants. Barred from admissions to other ratings, Filipino enlistees performed the work of domestics, preparing and serving the officers' meals, and caring for the officers' galley, wardroom, and living spaces. Ashore, their duties ranged from ordinary housework to food services at the U.S. Naval Academy hall. Unofficially, Filipino stewards also have been ordered to perform menial chores such as walking the officers' dogs and acting as personal servants for the officers' wives (Espiritu, 1995, p. 16).

As domestic servants, Asian men became subordinates of not only privileged white men but also privileged white women. The following testimony from a Japanese house servant captures this unequal relationship:

> Immediately the ma'am demanded me to scrub the floor. I took one hour to finish. Then I had to wash windows. That was very difficult job for me. Three windows for another hour! . . . The ma'am taught me how to cook. . . . I was sitting on the kitchen chair and thinking what a change of life it was. The ma'am came into the kitchen and was so furious! It was such a hard work for me to wash up all dishes, pans, glasses, etc., after dinner. When I went into the dining room to put all silvers on sideboard, I saw the reflection of myself on the looking glass. In a white coat and apron! I could not control my feelings. The tears so freely flowed out from my eyes, and I buried my face with my both arms (quoted in Ichioka, 1988, pp. 25–26).

The experiences of Asian male domestic service workers demonstrate that not all men benefit equally from patriarchy. Depending on their race and class, men experience gender differently. While male domination of women may tie all men together, men share unequally in the fruits of this domination. For Asian American male domestic workers, economic and social discriminations locked them into an unequal relationship with not only privileged white men but also privileged white women (Kim, 1990, p. 74).

The racist and classist devaluation of Asian men had gender implications. The available evidence indicates that immigrant men reasserted their lost patriarchal power in racist America by denigrating a weaker group: Asian women. In *China Men*, Kingston's immigrant father, having been forced into "feminine" subject positions, lapses into silence, breaking the silence only to utter curses against women (Goellnicht, 1992, pp. 200–201). Kingston (1980) traces her father's abuse of Chinese women back to his feeling of emasculation in America: "We knew that it was to feed us you had to endure demons and physical labor" (p. 13). On the other hand, some men brought home the domestic skills they learned on the jobs. Anamaria Labao Cabato relates that her Filipino-born father, who spent twenty-eight years in the navy as a steward, is "one of the best cooks around" (Espiritu, 1995, p. 143). Leo Sicat, a retired U.S. Navy man, similarly reports that "we learned how to cook in the Navy, and we brought it home. The Filipino women are very fortunate because the husband does the cooking. In our household, I do the cooking, and my wife does the washing" (Espiritu, 1995, p. 108). Along the same line, in some instances, the domestic skills which men were forced to learn in their wives' absence were put to use when husbands and wives reunited in the United States. The history of Asian male domestic workers suggests that the denigration of women is only one response to the stripping of male privilege. The other is to institute a revised domestic division of labor and gender relations in the families.

CHANGING GENDER RELATIONS: THE WARTIME INTERNMENT OF JAPANESE AMERICANS

Immediately after the bombing of Pearl Harbor, the incarceration of Japanese Americans began. On the night of 7 December 1941, working on the principle of guilt by association, the Federal Bureau of Investigation (FBI) began taking into custody persons of Japanese ancestry who had connections to the Japanese government. On 19 February 1942, President Franklin Delano Roosevelt signed Executive Order 9066, arbitrarily suspending civil rights of U.S. citizens by authorizing the "evacuation" of 120,000 persons of Japanese ancestry into concentration camps, of whom approximately 50 percent were women and 60 percent were U.S.-born citizens (Matsumoto, 1989, p. 116).

The camp environment—with its lack of privacy, regimented routines, and new power hierarchy—inflicted serious and lasting wounds on Japanese American family life. In the crammed twenty-by-twenty-five-foot "apartment" units, tensions were high as men, women, and children struggled to recreate family life under very trying conditions. The internment also transformed the balance of power in families: husbands lost some of their power over wives, as did parents over children. Until the internment, the Issei man had been the undisputed authority over his wife and children: he was both the breadwinner and the decision maker for the entire family. Now "he had no rights, no home, no control over his own life" (Houston and Houston, 1973, p. 62). Most important, the internment reverted the economic roles—and thus the status and authority—of family members. With their means of livelihood cut off indefinitely, Issei men lost their role as breadwinners. Despondent over the loss of almost everything they had worked so hard to acquire, many Issei men felt useless and frustrated, particularly as their wives and children became less dependent on them. Daisuke Kitagawa (1967) reports that in the Tule Lake relocation center, "the [Issei] men looked as if they had suddenly aged ten years. They lost the capacity to plan for their own futures, let alone those of their sons and daughters" (p. 91).

Issei men responded to this emasculation in various ways. By the end of three years' internment, formerly enterprising, energetic Issei men had become immobilized with feelings of despair, hopelessness, and insecurity. Charles Kikuchi remembers his father—who "used to be a perfect terror and dictator"—spending all day lying on his cot: "He probably realizes that he no longer controls the family group and rarely exerts himself so that there is little family conflict as far as he is concerned" (Modell, 1973, p. 62). But others, like Jeanne Wakatsuki Houston's father, reasserted their patriarchal power by abusing their wives and children. Stripped of his roles as the protector and provider for his family, Houston's father "kept pursuing oblivion through drink, he kept abusing Mama, and there seemed to be no way out of it for anyone. You couldn't even run" (Houston and Houston, 1973, p. 61). The experiences of the Issei men underscore the intersections of racism and sexism—the fact that men of color live in a society that creates sex-based norms and expectations (i.e., man as breadwinner) which racism operates simultaneously to deny (Crenshaw, 1989, p. 155).

Camp life also widened the distance and deepened the conflict between the Issei and their U.S.-born children. At the root of these tensions were growing cultural rifts between the generations as well as a decline in the power and authority of the Issei fathers. The cultural rifts reflected not only a general process of acculturation, but were accelerated by the degradation of everything Japanese and the simultaneous promotion of Americanization in the camps (Chan, 1991, p. 128; see also Okihiro, 1991, pp. 229–232). The younger *Nisei* also spent much more time away from their parents' supervision. As a consequence, Issei parents gradually lost their ability to discipline their children, whom they seldom saw during the day. Much to the chagrin of the conservative parents, young men and women began to spend more time with each other unchaperoned—at the sports events, the dances, and other school functions. Freed from some of the parental constraints, the Nisei women socialized more with their peers and also expected to choose their own husbands and to marry for "love"—a departure from the old customs of arranged marriage (Matsumoto, 1989, p. 117). Once this occurred, the prominent role that the father plays in marriage arrangements—and by extension in their children's lives—declined (Okihiro, 1991, p. 231).

Privileging U.S. citizenship and U.S. education, War Relocation Authority (WRA) policies regarding camp life further reverted the power hierarchy between the Japan-born Issei and their U.S.-born children. In the camps, only Nisei were eligible to vote and to hold office in the Community Council; Issei were excluded because of their alien status. Daisuke Kitagawa (1967) records the impact of this policy on parental authority: "In the eyes of young children, their parents were definitely inferior to their grown-up brothers and sisters, who as U.S. citizens could elect and be elected members of the Community Council. For all these reasons many youngsters lost confidence in, and respect for, their parents" (p. 88). Similarly, the WRA salary scales were based on English-speaking ability and on citizenship status. As a result, the Nisei youths and young adults could earn relatively higher wages than their fathers. This shift in earning abilities eroded the economic basis for parental authority (Matsumoto, 1989, p. 116).

At war's end in August 1945, Japanese Americans had lost much of the economic ground that they had gained in more than a generation. The majority of Issei women and men no longer had their farms, businesses, and financial savings; those who still owned property found their homes dilapidated and vandalized and their personal belongings stolen or destroyed (Broom and Riemer, 1949). The internment also ended Japanese American concentration in agriculture and small businesses. In their absence, other groups had taken over these ethnic niches. This loss further eroded the economic basis of parental authority since Issei men no longer had businesses to hand down to their Nisei sons (Broom and Riemer, 1949, p. 31). Historian Roger Daniels (1988) declared that by the end of World War II, "the generational struggle was over: the day of the Issei had passed" (286). Issei men, now in their sixties, no longer had the vigor to start over from scratch. Forced to find employment quickly after the war, many Issei couples who had owned small businesses before the war returned to the forms of manual labor in which they began a generation ago. Most men found work as janitors, gardeners, kitchen helpers, and handymen; their wives toiled as domestic servants, garment workers, and cannery workers (Yanagisako, 1987, p. 92).

CONTEMPORARY ASIAN AMERICA: THE DISADVANTAGED

Relative to earlier historical periods, the economic pattern of contemporary Asian America is considerably more varied, a result of both the postwar restructured economy and the 1965 Immigration Act.[2] The dual goals of the 1965 Immigration Act—to facilitate family reunification and to admit educated workers needed by the U.S. economy—have produced two distinct chains of emigration from Asia: one comprising the relatives of working-class Asians who had immigrated to the United States prior to 1965; the other of highly trained immigrants

who entered during the late 1960s and early 1970s (Liu, Ong, and Rosenstein, 1991). Given their dissimilar backgrounds, Asian Americans "can be found throughout the income spectrum of this nation" (Ong, 1994, p. 4). In other words, today's Asian American men both join whites in the well-paid, educated, white collar sector of the workforce *and* join Latino immigrants in lower-paying secondary sector jobs (Ong and Hee, 1994). This economic diversity contradicts the model minority stereotype—the common belief that most Asian American men are college educated and in high-paying professional or technical jobs.

The contemporary Asian American community includes a sizable population with limited education, skills, and English-speaking ability. In 1990, 18 percent of Asian men and 26 percent of Asian women in the United States, age 25 and over, had less than a high school degree. Also, of the 4.1 million Asians 5 years and over, 56 percent did not speak English "very well" and 35 percent were linguistically isolated (U.S. Bureau of the Census, 1993, Table 2). The median income for those with limited English was $20,000 for males and $15,600 for females; for those with less than a high school degree, the figures were $18,000 and $15,000, respectively. Asian American men and women with both limited English-speaking ability and low levels of education fared the worst. For a large portion of this disadvantaged population, even working full-time, full-year brought in less than $10,000 in earnings (Ong and Hee, 1994, p. 45).

The disadvantaged population is largely a product of immigration: Nine tenths are immigrants (Ong and Hee, 1994). The majority enter as relatives of the pre-1956 working-class Asian immigrants. Because immigrants tend to have socioeconomic backgrounds similar to those of their sponsors, most family reunification immigrants represent a continuation of the unskilled and semiskilled Asian labor that emigrated before 1956 (Liu, Ong, and Rosenstein, 1991). Southeast Asian refugees, particularly the second-wave refugees who arrived after 1978, represent another largely disadvantaged group.

This is partly so because refugees are less likely to have acquired readily transferable skills and are more likely to have made investments (in training and education) specific to the country of origin (Chiswick, 1979; Montero, 1980). For example, there are significant numbers of Southeast Asian military men with skills for which there is no longer a market in the United States. In 1990, the overall economic status of the Southeast Asian population was characterized by unstable, minimum-wage employment, welfare dependency, and participation in the informal economy (Gold and Kibria, 1993). These economic facts underscore the danger of lumping all Asian Americans together because many Asian men do not share in the relatively favorable socioeconomic outcomes attributed to the "average" Asian American.

Lacking the skills and education to catapult them into the primary sector of the economy, disadvantaged Asian American men and women work in the secondary labor market—the labor-intensive, low-capital service, and small manufacturing sectors. In this labor market, disadvantaged men generally have fewer employment options than women. This is due in part to the decline of male-occupied manufacturing jobs and the concurrent growth of female-intensive industries in the United States, particularly in service, microelectronics, and apparel manufacturing. The garment industry, microelectronics, and canning industries are top employers of immigrant women (Mazumdar, 1989, p. 19; Takaki, 1989, p. 427; Villones, 1989, p. 176; Hossfeld, 1994, pp. 71–72). In a study of Silicon Valley (California's famed high-tech industrial region), Karen Hossfeld (1994) reported that the employers interviewed preferred to hire immigrant women over immigrant men for entry-level, operative jobs (p. 74). The employers' "gender logic" was informed by the patriarchal and racist beliefs that women can afford to work for less, do not mind dead-end jobs, and are more suited physiologically to certain kinds of detailed and routine work. As Linda Lim (1983) observes, it is the *"comparative disadvantage* of women in the wage-labor market that gives them a comparative

advantage vis-à-vis men in the occupations and industries where they are concentrated—so-called female ghettoes of employment" (p. 78). A white male production manager and hiring supervisor in a California Silicon Valley assembly shop discusses his formula for hiring:

> Just three things I look for in hiring [entry-level, high-tech manufacturing operatives]: small, foreign, and female. You find those three things and you're pretty much automatically guaranteed the right kind of work force. These little foreign gals are grateful to be hired—very, very grateful—no matter what (Hossfeld, 1994, p. 65).

Refugee women have also been found to be more in demand than men in secretarial, clerical, and interpreter jobs in social service work. In a study of Cambodian refugees in Stockton, California, Shiori Ui (1991) found that social service agency executives preferred to hire Cambodian women over men when both had the same qualifications. One executive explained his preference, "It seems that some ethnic populations relate better to women than men. . . . Another thing is that the pay is so bad" (cited in Ui, 1991, p. 169). As a result, in the Cambodian communities in Stockton, it is often women—and not men—who have greater economic opportunities and who are the primary breadwinners in their families (Ui, 1991, p. 171).

Due to the significant decline in the economic contributions of Asian immigrant men, women's earnings comprise an equal or greater share of the family income. Because the wage each earns is low, only by pooling incomes can a husband and wife earn enough to support a family (Glenn, 1983, p. 42). These shifts in resources have challenged the patriarchal authority of Asian men. Men's loss of status and power—not only in the public but also in the domestic arena—places severe pressure on their sense of well-being. Responding to this pressure, some men accepted the new division of labor in the family (Ui, 1991, pp. 170–173); but many others resorted to spousal abuse and divorce (Luu, 1989, p. 68). A Korean immigrant man describes his frustrations over changing gender roles and expectations:

> In Korea [my wife] used to have breakfast ready for me. . . . She didn't do it any more because she said she was too busy getting ready to go to work. If I complained she talked back at me, telling me to fix my own breakfast. . . . I was very frustrated about her, started fighting and hit her (Yim, 1978, quoted in Mazumdar, 1989, p. 18).

Loss of status and power has similarly led to depression and anxieties in Hmong males. In particular, the women's ability—and the men's inability—to earn money for households "has undermined severely male omnipotence" (Irby and Pon, 1988, p. 112). Male unhappiness and helplessness can be detected in the following joke told at a family picnic, "When we get on the plane to go back to Laos, the first thing we will do is beat up the women!" The joke—which generated laughter by both men and women—drew upon a combination of "the men's unemployability, the sudden economic value placed on women's work, and men's fear of losing power in their families" (Donnelly, 1994, pp. 74–75). As such, it highlights the interconnections of race, class, and gender—the fact that in a racist and classist society, working-class men of color have limited access to economic opportunities and thus limited claim to patriarchal authority.

CONCLUSION

A central task in feminist scholarship is to expose and dismantle the stereotypes that traditionally have provided ideological justifications for women's subordination. But to conceptualize oppression only in terms of male dominance and female subordination is to obscure the centrality of classism, racism, and other forms of inequality in U.S. society (Stacey and Thorne, 1985, p. 311). The multiplicities of Asian men's lives indicate that ideologies of manhood and womanhood have as much to do with class and race as they have to do with sex. The intersections of race, gender, and class mean that there are also hierarchies among women and among men and that some women hold power over certain groups of men. The task for feminist scholars, then, is to develop paradigms that articulate the complicity among these categories of oppression, that strengthen the alliance between gender and ethnic studies, and that reach out not only to women, but also to men, of color.

NOTES

1. One of the most noticeable characteristics of pre–World War II Asian America was a pronounced shortage of women. During this period, U.S. immigration policies barred the entry of most Asian women. America's capitalist economy also wanted Asian male workers but not their families. In most instances, families were seen as a threat to the efficiency and exploitability of the workforce and were actively prohibited.

2. The 1965 Immigration Act ended Asian exclusion and equalized immigration rights for all nationalities. No longer constrained by exclusion laws, Asian immigrants began arriving in much larger numbers than ever before. In the 1980s, Asia was the largest source of U.S. legal immigrants, accounting for 40 percent to 47 percent of the total influx (Min, 1995, p. 12).

REFERENCES

Broom, Leonard and Ruth Riemer. 1949. *Removal and Return: The Socio-Economic Effects of the War on Japanese Americans.* Berkeley: University of California Press.

Chan, Sucheng. 1991. *Asian Americans: An Interpretive History.* Boston: Twayne.

Cheung, King-Kok. 1990. "The Woman Warrior Versus the Chinaman Pacific: Must a Chinese American Critic Choose Between Feminism and Heroism?" In *Conflicts in Feminism,* edited by Marianne Hirsch and Evelyn Fox Keller (pp. 234–251). New York and London: Routledge.

Chiswick, Barry. 1979. "The Economic Progress of Immigrants: Some Apparently Universal Patterns." In *Contemporary Economic Problems* edited by W. Fellner (pp. 357–399). Washington, DC: American Enterprise Institute.

Crenshaw, Kimberlee. 1989. "Demarginalizing the Intersection of Race and Sex: A Black Feminist Critique of Antidiscrimination Doctrine, Feminist Theory and Antiracist Politics." In *University of Chicago Legal Forum: Feminism in the Law: Theory, Practice, and Criticism* (pp. 139–167). Chicago: University of Chicago Press.

Daniels, Roger. 1988. *Asian America: Chinese and Japanese in the United States Since 1850.* Seattle: University of Washington Press.

Donnelly, Nancy D. 1994. *Changing Lives of Refugee Hmong Women.* Seattle: University of Washington Press.

Espiritu, Yen Le. 1995. *Filipino American Lives.* Philadelphia: Temple University Press.

Espiritu, Yen Le. 1996. *Asian American Women and Men: Labor, Laws, and Love.* Thousand Oaks, CA: Sage.

Fong-Torres, Ben. 1995. "Why Are There No Male Asian Anchor*men* on TV?" In *Men's Lives,* 3rd ed., edited by Michael S. Kimmel and Michael A. Messner (pp. 208–211). Boston: Allyn and Bacon.

Gaines, Jane. 1990. "White Privilege and Looking Relations: Race and Gender in Feminist Film Theory." In *Issues in Feminist Film Criticism,* edited by Patricia Erens (pp. 197–214). Bloomington: Indiana University Press.

Glenn, Evelyn Nakano. 1983. "Split Household, Small Producer and Dual Wage Earner: An Analysis of Chinese-American Family Strategies.*" Journal of Marriage and the Family,* February: 35–46.

Glenn, Evelyn Nakano. 1986. *Issei, Nisei, War Bride: Three Generations of Japanese American Women at Domestic Service.* Philadelphia: Temple University Press.

Goellnicht, Donald C. 1992. "Tang Ao in America: Male Subject Positions in *China Men.*" In *Reading the Literatures of Asian America,* edited by Shirley Geok-lin-Lim and Amy Ling (pp. 191–212). Philadelphia: Temple University Press.

Gold, Steve and Nazli Kibria. 1993. "Vietnamese Refugees and Blocked Mobility." *Asian and Pacific Migration Review* 2:27–56.

Hamamoto, Darrell. 1994. *Monitored Peril: Asian Americans and the Politics of Representation.* Minneapolis: University of Minnesota Press.

Hossfeld, Karen J. 1994. "Hiring Immigrant Women: Silicon Valley's 'Simple Formula'". In *Women of Color in U.S. Society,* edited by Maxine Baca Zinn and Bonnie Thornton Dill (pp. 65–93). Philadelphia: Temple University Press.

Houston, Jeanne Wakatsuki and James D. Houston. 1973. *Farewell to Manzanar.* San Francisco: Houghton Mifflin.

Ichioka, Yuji. 1988. *The Issei: The World of the First Generation Japanese Immigrants, 1885–1924.* New York: The Free Press.

Irby, Charles and Ernest M. Pon. 1988. "Confronting New Mountains: Mental Health Problems Among Male Hmong and Mien Refugees. *Amerasia Journal* 14: 109–118.

Kang, Younghill. 1937. *East Goes West.* New York: C. Scribner's Sons.

Katzman, David. 1978. "Domestic Service: Women's Work." In *Women Working: Theories and Facts in Perspective,* edited by Ann Stromberg and Shirley Harkess (pp. 377–391). Palo Alto: Mayfield.

Kim, Elaine. 1990. " 'Such Opposite Creatures': Men and Women in Asian American Literature." *Michigan Quarterly Review,* 68–93.

Kingston, Maxine Hong. 1980. *China Men.* New York: Knopf.

Kitagawa, Daisuke. 1967. *Issei and Nisei: The Internment Years.* New York: Seabury Press.

Light, Ivan. 1972. *Ethnic Enterprise in America: Business and Welfare Among Chinese, Japanese, and Blacks.* Berkeley and Los Angeles: University of California Press.

Lim, Linda Y. C. 1983. "Capitalism, Imperialism, and Patriarchy: The Dilemma of Third-World Women Workers in Multinational Factories." In *Women, Men, and the International Division of Labor,* edited by June Nash and Maria Patricia Fernandez-Kelly (pp. 70–91). Albany: State University of New York.

Liu, John, Paul Ong, and Carolyn Rosenstein. 1991. "Dual Chain Migration: Post-1965 Filipino Immigration to the United States." *International Migration Review* 25 (3): 487–513.

Luu, Van. 1989. "The Hardships of Escape for Vietnamese Women." In *Making Waves: An Anthology of Writings by and About Asian American Women,* edited by Asian Women United of California (pp. 60–72). Boston: Beacon Press.

Matsumoto, Valerie. 1989. "Nisei Women and Resettlement During World War II." In *Making Waves: An Anthology of Writings by and about Asian American Women,* edited by Asian Women United of California (pp. 115–126). Boston: Beacon Press.

Mazumdar, Sucheta. 1989. "General Introduction: A Woman-Centered Perspective on Asian American

History." In *Making Waves: An Anthology by and about Asian American Women*, edited by Asian Women United of California (pp. 1–22). Boston: Beacon Press.

Min, Pyong Gap. 1995. "Korean Americans." In *Asian Americans: Contemporary Trends and Issues*, edited by Pyong Gap Min (pp. 199–231). Thousand Oaks, CA: Sage.

Modell, John, ed. 1973. *The Kikuchi Diary: Chronicle from an American Concentration Camp*. Urbana: University of Illinois Press.

Montero, Darrell. 1980. *Vietnamese Americans: Patterns of Settlement and Socioeconomic Adaptation in the United States*. Boulder, CO: Westview.

Okihiro, Gary Y. 1991. *Cane Fires: The Anti-Japanese Movement in Hawaii, 1865–1945*. Philadelphia: Temple University Press.

Ong, Paul. 1994. "Asian Pacific Americans and Public Policy." In *The State of Asian Pacific America: Economic Diversity, Issues, & Policies*, edited by Paul Ong (pp. 1–9). Los Angeles: LEAP Asian Pacific American Public Policy Institute and UCLA Asian American Studies Center.

Ong, Paul and Suzanne Hee. 1994. "Economic Diversity." In *The State of Asian Pacific America: Economic Diversity, Issues, & Policies*, edited by Paul Ong (pp. 31–56). Los Angeles: LEAP Asian Pacific American Public Policy Institute and UCLA Asian American Studies Center.

Romero, Mary. 1992. *Maid in the U.S.A.* New York: Routledge.

Siu, Paul. 1987. *The Chinese Laundryman: A Study in Social Isolation*. New York: New York University Press.

Stacey, Judith and Barrie Thorne. 1985. "The Missing Feminist Revolution in Sociology." *Social Problems* 32: 301–316.

Takaki, Ronald. 1989. *Strangers from a Different Shore: A History of Asian Americans*. Boston: Little, Brown.

Ui, Shiori. 1991. "'Unlikely Heroes': The Evolution of Female Leadership in a Cambodian Ethnic Enclave." In *Ethnography Unbound: Power and Resistance in the Modern Metropolis*, edited by Michael Burawoy et al. (pp. 161–177). Berkeley: University of California Press.

U.S. Bureau of the Census. 1993. *We the American Asians*. Washington, DC: U.S. Government Printing Office.

Villones, Rebecca. 1989. "Women in the Silicon Valley." In *Making Waves: An Anthology of Writings by and About Asian American Women*, edited by Asian Women United of California (pp. 172–176). Boston: Beacon Press.

Wiegman, Robyn. 1991. "Black Bodies/American Commodities: Gender, Race, and the Bourgeois Ideal in Contemporary Film." In *Unspeakable Images: Ethnicity and the American Cinema*, edited by Lester Friedman (pp. 308–328). Urbana and Chicago: University of Illinois Press.

Yanagisako, Sylvia Junko. 1987. "Mixed Metaphors: Native and Anthropological Models of Gender and Kinship Domains." In *Gender and Kinship: Essays Toward a Unified Analysis*, edited by Jane Fishburne Collier and Sylvia Junko Yanagisako (pp. 86–118). Palo Alto, CA: Stanford University Press.

THE BLACK MALE PRIVILEGES CHECKLIST

Jewel Woods

What does "privilege" have to do with Black men?[1] We understand some kinds of privilege. The twentieth-century white privilege to call a black man "boy" even if that black man happens to be sixty years old or older. The white privilege to drive a car and never have to worry about racial profiling. These are privileges that have nothing to do with what a person has earned but rather are based entirely on race. As African Americans, we have the ability to critique and condemn these types of "unearned assets" because we recognize that these privileges come largely at our expense. We have also learned from social and political movements that have sought to redress these privileges and academic disciplines that have provided us with the tools to critically examine and explore them.

However, there is another type of privilege that has caused untold harm to both black men and women, but our community has not had the benefit of that privilege being challenged by a social and political movement from within, nor has it been given adequate attention within our academic community. The privilege that I am referring to is male privilege. Male privilege is a "double standard" because it is based on attitudes or actions that come at the expense of women—that is, even while some black males challenge white racism, they do not address their male privilege vis-à-vis

Jewel Woods, "The Black Male Privileges Checklist" from the website www.renaissancemaleproject.com. Reprinted by permission.

[1]Please visit our website, http://renaissancemaleproject.com, to view our Teen and Male Youth Privileges Checklist, a historic tool for all young males, schools, community organizations, youth groups, sports teams, and families that can be used to assist our young males in becoming the type of adult men we want them to be.

women. Just as white privilege comes at the expense of African Americans and other people of color, male privilege comes at the expense of women.

Given the devastating history of racism in this country, it is understandable that getting black men to identify with the concept of male privilege isn't easy! For many black men, the phrase "black male privilege" seems like an oxymoron—three words that simply do not go together. Although it is understandable that some black men are hesitant or reluctant to examine the concept of male privilege, the African American community will never be able to overcome the serious issues we face if we as black men do not confront their role in promoting and sustaining male supremacist attitudes and actions.

Inviting black men and boys into a conversation about male privilege does not deny centuries of discrimination or the burden of racism that we continue to suffer today. As long as a black man can be tasered nine times in fourteen minutes, shot at fifty times on the morning of his wedding night, or receive fewer call-backs for a job than a white man with a felony record, we know that racism that targets black men is alive and kicking.

But race is not the only factor. Examining black male privileges offers black men and boys an opportunity to go beyond old arguments of "personal responsibility" or "blaming the man" to gain a deeper level of insight into how issues of class and race are shaped by gender. *Often times the focus on our experiences of racial oppression remove gender-based domination from the analytical—and the political—eye.*

The items presented on the Black Male Privileges Checklist reflect aspects of black men's lives we take for granted, male privileges that come at the expense of women in general and African American women in particular. I offer this checklist based on years of experience working with men and the profound influence of black woman activists and intellectuals such as bell hooks, Angela Davis, Patricia Hill-Collins, Kimberly Crenshaw, and numerous others. I have faith that we as men have far more to gain than we have to lose by challenging our male privileges.

I believe there are more similarities between men than there are differences. Therefore, many items on the Black Male Privilege Checklist apply to men generally, and others might apply to all men of color. However, because of the specific privileges black men possess in relationship to black women, certain items apply only to black men. *I will leave it up to the reader to determine which items apply only to black men and which items apply to all men of color or men in general.*

THE BLACK MALE PRIVILEGES CHECKLIST

Leadership and Politics

1. I don't have to choose my race over my sex in political matters.
2. When I read African American history textbooks, I will learn mainly about black men.
3. When I learn about the Civil Rights and Black Power movements, most of the leaders that I will learn about will be black men.
4. I can rely on the fact that in the nearly 100-year history of national civil rights organizations such as the NAACP and the Urban League, virtually all of the executive directors have been men.
5. I will be taken more seriously as a political leader than black women.
6. I can be pretty sure that all of the "race leaders" I see featured in the media will be men like me.
7. I can live my life without ever having read black feminist authors or knowing about black women's history or black women's issues.
8. I could be a member or an admirer of a black liberation organization such as the Black Panther Party, where an "out" rapist like Eldridge Cleaver could assume a leadership position, without feeling threatened or demeaned because of my sex.
9. I will make more money than black women at equal levels of education and occupation.
10. I know that most of the national "opinion framers" in black America, including talk show hosts and politicians, are men.

Beauty

11. I have the ability to define black women's beauty by European standards in terms of skin tone, hair, and body size. In comparison, black women rarely define me by European standards of beauty in terms of skin tone, hair, or body size.
12. I do not have to worry about the daily hassles of having my hair conform to some standard image of beauty the way black women do.
13. I do not have to worry about the daily hassles of being terrorized by the fear of gaining weight. In fact, in many instances bigger is better for my sex.
14. My looks will not be the central standard by which my worth is valued by members of the opposite sex.

Sex and Sexuality

15. I can purchase pornography that typically shows men defiling women by the common practice of the "money shot."
16. I can believe that causing pain during sex is connected with a woman's pleasure without ever asking her.
17. When it comes to sex, if I say "No," chances are that it will not be mistaken for "Yes."
18. If I am raped, no one will assume that "I should have known better" or suggest that my being raped had something to do with how I was dressed.
19. I can use sexist language like bonin', laying the pipe, hittin' it, and banging that convey

images of sexual acts based on dominance and performance.

20. I live in a world where polygamy is still an option for men in some countries.

21. I can be involved with younger women socially and sexually and it will be considered normal.

22. In general, the more sexual partners that I have the more stature I receive among my peers.

23. I have easy access to pornography that involves virtually any category of sex where men degrade women, often young women.

24. When I consume pornography, I can gain pleasure from images and sounds of men causing women pain.

Popular Culture

25. I have the privilege of coming from a tradition of humor based largely on insulting and disrespecting women; especially mothers.

26. I have the privilege of not having black women dress up and play funny characters—often overweight—that are supposed to look like me, for the entire nation to laugh at.

27. When I go to the movies, I know that most of the leads in black films will be men. I can also be confident that all of the action heroes in black film[s] will be men.

28. I can easily assume that most of the artists in hip-hop are members of my sex.

29. I can rest assured that most of the women that appear in hip-hop videos are there solely to please men.

30. Most of lyrics I listen to in popular hip-hop perpetuate the ideas of men dominating women, sexually and socially.

31. I can consume and popularize the word pimp, which is based on the exploitation of women, with virtually no opposition from other men.

32. I can hear and use language that refers to women as bitches and ho's that demean women, with virtually no opposition from men.

33. I can wear a shirt that others and I commonly refer to as a "wife beater" and never have the language challenged.

34. Many of my favorite movies include images of strength that do not include women and often are based on violence.

35. Many of my favorite genres of films, such as martial arts, are based on male violence.

Attitudes/Ideology

36. I have the privilege to define black women as having "an attitude" without referencing the range of attitudes that black women have.

37. I have the privilege of defining black women's attitudes without defining my attitudes as a black man.

38. I can believe that the success of the black family is dependent on men serving as the head of the family rather than in promoting policies that strengthen black women's independence or that provide social benefits to black children.

39. I have the privilege of believing that a black woman cannot raise a black son to be a man.

40. I have the privilege of believing that a woman must submit to her man.

41. I have the privilege of believing that before slavery, gender relationships between black men and women were perfect.

42. I have the privilege to define ideas such as feminism as being anti-black.

43. I have the privilege of believing that the failure of the black family is due in part to black women not allowing black men to be men.

44. I have the privilege of defining gender roles within the household.

45. I have the privilege of believing that black women are different sexually than other women and judging them negatively based on this belief.

Sports

46. I will make significantly more money as a professional athlete than women will.

47. My financial success or popularity as a professional athlete will not be associated with my looks.

48. I can talk about sports or spend large portions of the day playing video games while women are most likely tending household chores or child care duties.
49. I have the privilege to restrict my displays of emotion to certain spheres, such as sports.
50. If I am a coach, I can motivate, punish, or embarrass a player by saying that the player plays like a girl.
51. Most sports talk show hosts that are members of my race are men.
52. I can rest assured that most of the coaches—even in predominately female sports within my race—are male.
53. I am able to play sports outside without my shirt on and not worry it will be considered a problem.
54. I am essentially able to do anything inside or outside without my shirt on, whereas women are always required to cover up.

Diaspora/Global

55. I have the privilege of not being concerned that I am a member of a sex subjected to mutilation and disfigurement to deny our sexual sensations or to protect our virginity for males.
56. I have the privilege of not having rape be used as a primary tactic or tool to terrorize my sex during war and times of conflict.
57. I have the privilege of not being able to name one female leader in Africa or Asia, past or present, that I pay homage to the way I do male leaders in Africa and/or Asia.
58. I have the ability to travel around the world and have access to women in developing countries both sexually and socially.
59. I have the privilege of being a part of the sex that starts wars and that wields control of almost all the existing weapons of war and mass destruction.

College

60. In college, I will have the opportunity to date outside of the race at a much higher rate than black women will.

61. I have the privilege of having the phrase "sowing my wild oats" apply to my sex as if it were natural.
62. I know that the further I go in education the more success I will have with women.
63. By the time I enter college, and even through college, I have the privilege of not having to worry whether I will be able to marry a black woman.
64. In college, I will experience a level of status and prestige that is not offered to black women even though black women may outnumber me and outperform me academically.

Communication/Language

65. What is defined as "news" in black America is defined by men.
66. I can choose to be emotionally withdrawn and not communicate in a relationship and it may be considered unfortunate, yet normal.
67. I have the privilege of not knowing what words and concepts like patriarchy, misogyny, phallocentric, complicity, colluding, and obfuscation mean.

Relationships

68. I have the privilege of marrying outside my race at a much higher rate than black women.
69. My "strength" as a man is never connected with the failure of the black family, whereas the strength of black women is routinely associated with the failure of the black family.
70. If I am considering a divorce, I know that I have substantially more marriage and cohabitation options than my spouse.
71. Chances are I will be defined as a "good man" by things I do not do as much as what I do. If I don't beat, cheat, or lie, then I am a considered a "good man." In comparison, women are rarely defined as "good women" based on what they do not do.
72. I have the privilege of not having to assume most of the household or child care responsibilities.

Church and Religious Traditions

73. In the black church, the majority of the pastoral leadership is male.
74. In the black church tradition, most of the theology has a male point of view. For example, most will assume that the man is the head of household.

Physical Safety

75. I do not have to worry about being considered a traitor to my race if I call the police on a member of the opposite sex.
76. I have the privilege of knowing men who are physically or sexually abusive to women and yet I still call them friends.
77. I can videotape women in public—often without their consent—with male complicity.
78. I can be courteous to a person of the opposite sex that I do not know and say "hello" or "hi" and not fear that it will be taken as a come-on or fear being stalked because of it.
79. I can use physical violence or the threat of physical violence to get what I want when other tactics fail in a relationship.
80. If I get into a physical altercation with a person of the opposite sex, I will most likely be able to impose my will physically on that person.
81. I can go to parades or other public events and not worry about being physically and sexually molested by persons of the opposite sex.
82. I can touch and physically grope women's bodies in public—often without their consent—with male complicity.
83. In general, I have the freedom to travel in the night without fear of rape or sexual assault.
84. I am able to be out in public without fear of being sexually harassed by individuals or groups of the opposite sex.

BACKGROUND

The Black Male Privileges Checklist was born out of years of organizing men's groups and the numerous—often heated—conversations I have had with men while using Barry Deutsch's Male Privilege Checklist.[2] In my experience, most men raise objections to at least some items on the Male Privilege Checklist. However, "men of color," especially African American men, often have the sharpest criticisms of the Male Privilege Checklist and the greatest difficulty connecting to the idea of male privilege.

There are many reasons black men are reluctant to identify with the concept of male privilege. One of the most important reasons is that our experience with privilege has largely focused specifically on race, based on a history of political, economic, and military power whites have historically exercised over black life. This conceptualization of privilege has not allowed us to see ourselves as privileged because the focus has been placed largely on white domination. Our inability to have a more expansive understanding of privilege and power has foreclosed important insights into virtually every aspect of black men's lives and as well as the lives of other men of color.

As black men, we have also been skeptical of profeminist males, most of whom were (and still are) white and middle class. Black men who fought for freedom during the Civil Rights and the Black Power movement were suspicious—to say the least—of the motives of white men requesting that black men give up the privileges they never felt they had. Given the timing of the profeminist male movement and the demographics of these men, it has not been easy to separate the message from the messenger. Black men had a similar reaction to the voices of black feminists, whom we viewed as being influenced by white middle-class feminism. In addition, many of the items on the Male Privilege Checklist simply did not apply to black men and other men

[2]Barry Deutsch, http://www.amptoons.com/blog/the-male-privilege-checklist, September 15, 2004 (retrieved May 29, 2009). Barry Deutsch's list was inspired by Peggy McIntosh's 1988 article "White Privilege and Male Privilege: A Personal Account of Coming to See Correspondences through Work in Women's Studies" (Working Paper 189, Wellesley Center for Women, Wellesley, Massachusetts), available at mmcintosh@wellesley.edu.

of color. As a result, many black men argued that the list should have been called the White Male Privilege Checklist. In light of these considerations, the Black Male Privileges Checklist differs from the Male Privilege Checklist in several respects.

First, it departs from an "either/or" view of privilege that suggests that an individual or a group can only be placed into one category, isolating race or gender and ignoring the ways in which these traits interact in shaping our lives. Therefore, the focus is on privilege(s) and not privilege. It also highlights belief systems that often serve as the basis for justifications and rationalizations of exploitation and discrimination. Second, the Black Male Privileges Checklist takes a life-course perspective, acknowledging the fact that privilege takes on different forms at various points in men's lives. Third, it takes a global perspective to highlight the privilege that black males have as Americans, and the privileges black men share with other men of color worldwide. African American men rarely acknowledge the privilege we have in relationship to people in developing countries—especially women. Too often, our conception of privilege is limited to white men and does not lead us to reflect on the power that men of color in Africa, Asia, and Latin America exercise over women. Finally, it calls for action, not just awareness. We need men of color to be actively involved in social welfare and social justice movements.

As men of color, we have a responsibility to acknowledge that we participate in this sex/gender system even though it offers us little reward. Most African Americans, for example, take for granted the system of capitalism that we all participate in, even though we know that it does not offer us the same rewards that it does to whites. The sex/gender system, which privileges men over women, operates in similar ways for all men. However, black men and other men of color participate in the sex/gender system without receiving the same material and nonmaterial rewards white men do. More importantly, the participation of black men and other men of color in the sex/gender system further weakens communities of color, which already suffer under the weight of racial and class oppression.

Finally, the Black Male Privileges Checklist is a tool that can be used by any individual, group, organization, family, or community interested in black males having greater insight into their individual lives and the collective lives of black women and girls. It is also a living tool that will grow and be amended as more discussion and dialogue occurs. This is the first edition of the Black Male Privileges Checklist, and it will be updated regularly. This checklist was created with black men in mind and does not necessarily capture the experiences and cultural references of other ethnic minority males. I would welcome dialogue with others who are concerned about these constituencies as well.

LATINO MASCULINITIES IN THE POST-9/11 ERA

Hernan Ramirez   Edward Flores

American television, movies and magazines depict Latino[1] men in contradictory ways, as dangerous gun-toting hardened criminals and as family-oriented, low-wage laborers. The subordinate, "sleepy Mexican" still circulates in satirical form, as we saw in the 2009 film *Brüno*, which featured a talk show where Mexican gardeners kneel on all fours, substituting as chairs for the guests. Meanwhile, the image of Latino men as foreign, dangerous, and subversive appears more frequently in news reports of drug traffickers and gang members. The *Los Angeles Times* recently reported on military-style gang sweeps involving over one thousand law enforcement officials, assault rifles, and tanks. Readers posted racist comments online, such as, "They don't get deported and we taxpayers have to support them."

These two popular images of Latino men—as violently subversive foreign threats, or as docile low-wage workers—reflect sociologist Alfredo Mirande's (1997) analysis of Latino masculinity as rooted in dualistic cultural expressions of honor and dishonor. Over time, these dualistic images have had tremendous staying power. The mid-twentieth century movie image of Joaquin Murrieta's Mexican bandits marauding on horseback, killing lawmen, and stealing gold has morphed today into stereotypical portrayals of the violent urban Latino gang. The past image of the sleepy Mexican in a poncho and a sombrero has today become that of the docile Latino gardener. Mirande would argue that together, these two images have their origins in Mexican men's

compensatory reactions to colonial subordination. The cultural meanings of "macho," Mirande emphasizes, are best understood not as an attempt by Latino men to dominate women, but rather, as Latino men's multifaceted attempts to forge a respected and honored position in a context of cultural subordination.

Alternatively, gender scholars have located Latino masculinities within shifting political-economic relations in the United States. Maxine Baca Zinn (1982) argues that "manhood takes on greater importance for those who do not have access to socially valued roles," and that "to be 'hombre'. . . may take on greater significance when other roles and sources of masculine identity are structurally blocked." This view emphasizes that Latino men's masculine expressions are a result of contemporary structural conditions. Blocked economic mobility, poor schools, and dangerous urban neighborhoods compromise Latinos' and Blacks' access to conventional masculine expressions (i.e., Smith 2006; Lopez 2003; Bourgois 1995; Anderson 1990; Ferguson 2000).

In this article we report on our in-depth ethnographic research with Latino men behind these two images, the gardener and the gangster. Hernan Ramirez's research highlights Mexican immigrant gardeners' experience with low-wage labor and economic mobility, and the masculinities that organize, and are organized by, such a precarious social position. Edward Flores's research focuses on recovering gang members' experiences with rehabilitation, and the way in which masculinity organizes such rehabilitation. Our research is based in Los Angeles, and highlights how nativist backlash and persisting structural obstacles shape Latino men's masculine expressions.

We begin by considering the larger political and economic conditions in which the masculinity of Latino gang members and gardeners is embedded and expressed. By understanding some of the structural conditions that funnel Chicano men into gang activity and Mexican immigrant men into suburban maintenance gardening, respectively, we can enlarge our inquiry into contemporary Latino men and masculinities beyond the cultural stereotype of machismo.

CONTEXT

In the 1970s and 1980s, the effects of economic restructuring and deindustrialization were evident in major cities throughout the United States, as stable, relatively well-paid manufacturing jobs disappeared while low-wage service sector jobs grew (Kasarda 1995). In global cities (Sassen 1991) such as New York and Los Angeles, this decline in manufacturing was accompanied by an expanding high-income professional and managerial class. Problems endemic to America's inner cities—including gangs, drugs, unemployment, and violent crime—were linked to the disappearance of blue-collar jobs in the wake of deindustrialization (Wilson 1987, 1996). Moreover, with changes to U.S. immigration law in 1965, large numbers of immigrants from Asia and Latin America began entering the United States. By the 1990s, these new immigrants were increasingly present in retail and service employment (Lamphere et al. 1994), as exploited workers in hotels and restaurants, and in other jobs where wages are low and career ladders are short (Bobo et al. 2000). These structural transformations, coupled with years of disinvestment in our nation's public school systems, have left many young, urban Latino men at a marked economic disadvantage. Today, Mexican immigrant and Chicano men often find themselves on insecure economic ground, relying on casual work and a growing informal economy (i.e., one largely outside of formal regulations, union contracts, and guaranteed benefits) for their livelihoods.

Against this backdrop of swirling economic changes, the political climate faced by post-1965 Mexican immigrants has been ambivalent at best, and outright xenophobic at worst. For example, a 2001 *Time* magazine cover featured the word "Amexica," with colors from the national Mexican and American flags, and a statement about the vanishing border. Anthropologist Leo Chavez (2008) argues that by juxtaposing foreign images onto familiar American icons, media representations of Latinos suggest that post-1965 immigrants are unlike those of previous generations and will soon alter the nation's landscape. Similarly, the *Los Angeles Times* article on the gang sweep was presented in ways that meshed racist/sexist constructions of Latino males as foreigners and subversive.

The image of Latino men as foreign invaders has grown in the post-9/11 era. The USA PATRIOT Act of 2001 enhanced the discretion of law enforcement and immigration authorities in detaining and deporting immigrants suspected of terrorism-related acts, and it also added a looser definition of "domestic terrorism," now vague enough to apply not just to anti-American militia groups but urban gang members (Brotherton and Kretsedemas 2008). Although the FBI found no established link between gang members and international terrorism, these fears of urban gang members as foreign and subversive coalesced when the FBI investigated suspicions that Jose Padilla, an arrested Al-Qaeda operative, had gang ties in the United States (Brotherton and Kretsedemas 2008).

At the same time that this debate has unfolded, there has been an upswing in the number of right-wing pundits and politicians who characterize Latino immigrant men as a threat. Espousing a fear of immigrants as potential "terrorist" intruders, criminals, and threats to national security, radio and television hosts such as Lou Dobbs, Rush Limbaugh, and Glenn Beck rally support for restrictive immigration policies, increased federal funding for Border Patrol/ICE activities, and the building of a fence along the U.S.–Mexico border. The degree of virulent, xenophobic rhetoric leveled against Mexican immigrant men can be explained as an outgrowth of the post-9/11 fear of brown-skinned "outsiders" as well as a continuation of decades-old patterns of anti-Latino immigrant hysteria and discrimination. Since 9/11, cities across the United States have formulated anti-day laborer ordinances that have had the indirect—but intended—effect of excluding undocumented immigrants from their jurisdictions (Varsanyi 2008). One extreme right-wing nativist website claims that "some of the most violent murderers, rapists, and child molesters are illegal aliens who work as day laborers" (daylaborers.org), even though the social scientific literature indicates that most day laborers attend church regularly, and that nearly two-thirds of them have children (Valenzuela et al. 2006). These are certainly not characteristics one would expect to find among a population of men purportedly out to prey upon America's women and children.

In reality, the large concentrations of Latino immigrant men who work in the construction and home improvement trades, including roofers, painters, and dry-wall installers, as well as landscapers and gardeners, have become integral pistons in America's economic engine. Remarkably, one out of every eight Mexican immigrants in the United States currently works in the construction industry (Siniavskaia 2005). In New Orleans, post–Hurricane Katrina reconstruction efforts were spearheaded by thousands of immigrant men from Mexico and Central America (Quiñones 2006). This reliance on Mexican immigrant men to fill the nation's labor needs has historical precedence, as evidenced by the Bracero Program of the mid-twentieth century. Nevertheless, the link between images of Latino men, immigration, and crime has crystallized in the post-9/11 era. This has spurred a heightened fear of Latinos and has renewed interest in militarization of the border and the deportation of undocumented immigrants.

The political and economic transformations outlined have placed Chicano and Mexican immigrant men in a precarious situation vis-à-vis access to jobs and resources. Moreover, they have been subjected to discriminatory treatment and vilified as dangerous "outsiders" and potential criminal threats in the wake of 9/11. We can now take a closer look at a specific group of Latino men, *jardineros*—or Mexican immigrant gardeners—and think about how their masculinity is a response to structural inequality, exclusion, and discrimination.

LATINO MASCULINITY AT WORK: *JARDINERO* MASCULINITY

Gendered divisions of labor are well established and found throughout the economy. In fact, scholars of gender and work have long been concerned with understanding the ways in which gender itself is constructed on the job. While our knowledge of masculinity in blue-collar work settings has been growing (Ouellet 1994; Paap 2006; Desmond 2007), less is known about Latino immigrant men's work and how predominantly Latino immigrant workplaces serve as an arena for the construction and negotiation of Latino working-class masculinities. Although it was historically associated with the labor of Japanese American men in Pacific Coast cities (Tsuchida 1984; Tsukashima 1991), suburban maintenance gardening is today institutionalized as a Mexican man's job. Particularly large concentrations of Mexican immigrant men can be found working in the sunny climes of Los Angeles and Southern California more generally, mowing lawns, pruning trees, and maintaining the lush, leafy landscapes with which the region is so often associated.

As Smith (2003) notes, much of the literature on immigration is too quick to treat men as thoughtlessly embracing a traditional "ranchero" masculinity they may have been raised on in their rural villages of origin, one which legitimizes men's dominant and women's subordinate position. In reality, some migrant men pragmatically adapt to their new environment and engage in an ongoing critique of traditional masculinity (Smith 2006). Most *jardineros* come from ranches or rural villages in central-western Mexico, yet their displays of masculinity are influenced and shaped by their immigration experiences and by their structural position as low-wage laborers in the U.S. informal economy.

Jardinero masculinity refers to the distinctly working-class form of masculinity that Mexican immigrant men construct through their daily work activities in residential maintenance gardening, a male-dominated occupational niche, and in their daily on-the-job interactions with their fellow workers. This particular version of masculinity is unique in that it unfolds in the specific, working-class occupational and regional context of Southern Californian maintenance gardening and is deployed against a backdrop of racialized nativism and citizenship hierarchy in the United States. It finds its expression on the ground level, as *jardineros* engage in hard, dirty work on a daily basis to provide sustenance for their family members; as they engage in on-the-job conversations with their co-workers that can range from measured talk to friendly verbal banter; and as they put their bodies to the test in the course of their daily work routines.

Understanding *jardinero* masculinity requires sensitivity both to culture and to social structure. Moving beyond a sort of reiteration of a one-dimensional, cultural concept of "machismo," one culturally grounded in Mexico and simply re-articulated in the United States, *jardinero* masculinity stresses a more nuanced structural understanding of Mexican immigrant men's masculinity and how it is intertwined with their daily performance of masculinized "dirty" work in private residences. Yes, *jardineros* sometimes engage in on-the-job drinking and catcalling, traditionally "machista" modes of behavior. But the better part of these men's days is not spent in those activities, but rather with backbreaking, dangerous, physically hard manual work.

Like most men, *jardineros* derive their status primarily from their control of subsistence, through which they fulfill their primary cultural obligation, the economic support of their wives and children (Stone and McKee 2002: 129). The ideal man, one who is truly "manly," will provide for all of his family's needs. In practice, though, this ideal of male behavior may be very difficult for Mexican immigrant *jardineros* to achieve in the public world. This is especially true for *ayudantes*, young, apprentice gardeners who—unlike more experienced, self-employed owners of gardening routes—tend to be recently arrived, undocumented immigrants. *Ayudantes* typically share crowded apartments with other undocumented *paisanos* who are in a similar situation. They must work long hours while making low wages and evading the gaze of the authorities. *Ayudantes* present us with one type of *jardinero* masculinity, in which men's ability to fulfill socially valued breadwinner roles is severely limited by an important structural barrier: undocumented status.

Mexican immigrant gardeners express their masculinity in subtle ways, through their words and actions. While on the job, they often use humor as a "male bonding" mechanism, playfully teasing each other in order to alleviate the tedium of working together for long hours under the sun. Their workplace is where the *jardineros* develop the strong bodies and weathered hands that are a hallmark of their masculinity. Although they are readily available, *jardineros* often prefer to work without protective gloves. This can be explained in part by one *jardinero*'s observation that it is better to develop a pair of rough and callused hands because they are "manos de hombre," or "man hands," an outward symbol of their working-class masculinity.

Through their hard work cleaning and maintaining other people's properties, Mexican immigrant gardeners are able to provide for their families, but they are also able to gain the respect and esteem of their co-workers, projecting a masculinity that is honored by their fellow working-class men. For instance, as Carlos, a very young, recently arrived *ayudante*, proclaimed that he had entered the United States in order "to work hard, not to be lazy"("a trabajar duro, no a estar de huevon"), his older co-workers nodded in approval.

The difficulties faced by undocumented *jardineros* who hope to better provide for their loved ones by becoming self-employed route owners are described by Jose, a *veteran jardinero* with more than 20 years of experience:

> Well, there are obstacles that make things more difficult, really, because if a guy doesn't have a driver's license nowadays, how can he start his business? Without "papeles" (legal papers), you can't get a license. What do you do? Nobody knows you. How do you charge your clients? They give you a check, where do you cash it? It's tough, it's really tough without a license, because how are you going to go ahead and invest money in a truck and in equipment and everything, if later they're

going to take everything away? The police will catch you driving without a license and will take everything away from you. That's what happened to a guy that I know.

Once again we are reminded of the importance of understanding the structural constraints faced by Mexican immigrant men and how these impinge on their masculinity. Nationwide, many states have banned the issuance of driver's licenses to undocumented immigrants (Vock 2007; Seif 2003). This has had a deleterious effect on the livelihoods of undocumented Mexican immigrant men who work in gardening and landscaping, as well as in other jobs that require driving from jobsite to jobsite on a daily basis.

Many people believe that since Mexican immigrant gardeners wear dirty clothes, do dirty jobs, and have little formal education, they are necessarily drains on social services and the economy. Yet things are not as they appear to outsiders, as the maintenance gardening sector has allowed some *veteran jardineros* to achieve financial success and upward mobility (Ramirez and Hondagneu-Sotelo 2009). Most self-employed, independent owners of gardening routes entered the United States as undocumented immigrants some 20 or 30 years ago, speaking little or no English, but have since gone on to become legal residents or U.S. citizens, purchasing homes in the United States and even putting their children through college. Such men are *worker-entrepreneurs* who have worked hard day in and day out alongside their *ayudantes*, but who have done quite well for themselves by building and looking after gardening routes that can generate six-figure incomes. These financially solvent, self-employed owners of gardening routes (or "rutas") present us with a second type of *jardinero* masculinity: as *worker-entrepreneurs*, gardening route owners enjoy a great deal of autonomy and are able to fulfill the masculine ideal of providing for their families.

While *ayudantes* might fit the public's conception of Mexican immigrant men as "docile" low-wage workers, gardening route owners are essentially small entrepreneurs who display a remarkable degree of business acumen. However, behind the potential for economic success and mobility that comes with running one's own business there lay some hidden costs. Gardening route owners typically work very long hours, six days a week. Consequently, the amount of "quality time" they are able to spend with their spouses and children is very limited. Miguel, a gardening route owner, poignantly describes his situation:

> I would want the best for my kids. That they wouldn't . . . well, that they wouldn't have to work like I've had to work. I'd want them to have a better life. Better for them. Less backbreaking. I also get home late. I get home late from work, tired. Sometimes, I can't describe what I feel—[My kids] even tell me, "You don't want to play with us, papi. I tell them, "No, son, it's because I get back home really tired. You want me to start playing with you, to play, to run, to play basketball . . . Son, don't you know how tired I am when I return home from work? And you still want to keep playing . . . [laughs]. I tell them, "No, it's because I can't."

Gardening route owners must thus grapple with work-family conflicts that can diminish their ability to be as present in the lives of their children and spouses as they would like to be. Unlike *ayudantes*, who are low-wage workers, gardening route owners are a hybrid form of worker and entrepreneur; as such, they must spend long days toiling under the sun while constantly strategizing and thinking about ways of keeping their businesses afloat, even if it detracts from the amount—and quality—of time they spend with their family members. The work takes a physical toll on them, but it also takes a toll on their ability to fulfill their masculine roles as husbands and fathers.

Having considered the case of masculinity among Mexican immigrant gardeners, encompassing the experiences of young *ayudantes* and veteran gardening route owners, let us turn now to an examination of masculinity among another group of Latino men in Los Angeles: recovering gang members.

LATINO MASCULINITY IN RECOVERY: REFORMED BARRIO MASCULINITY

In contrast to immigrant Latino men employed in the densely concentrated maintenance gardening sector, men who have spent the majority of their life in the United States express different types of masculinities. Male Latinos are exposed to a particular type of masculine socialization in the barrio that makes them vulnerable to join gangs (Vigil 1988; Moore 1991; Yablonski 1997; Smith 2006). Three activities form the core of male Latino gang life, or *deviant barrio masculinity*: substance abuse, gang violence, and extramarital affairs. These three activities are embodied in a gang member's clothes, speech, and swagger. As one man said, "My role model was a gang member, all tattoos, coming out of prison, being buff, having all kinds of women, that's what I wanted to grow up to be" (Flores 2009).

Nevertheless, some Chicano gang members do want to exit from gang lifestyle, and do so by reconstructing notions of what it means to be a man. Gang members in recovery have conventional aspirations, such as getting married and having children, working in the formal labor market, and owning a home (Flores 2009). The young man quoted above said he had converted to Christianity the night he attended a play in which a Pentecostal church performed a drama with ex-gang members, "So I seen all that in the play, I see nothing but homeys with big ole' whips, tattoos, in the play talking about God, and that they're not using drugs, and they're not in prison no more, and I say, 'ey, cool.'"

Masculinity is central to faith-based rehabilitation, as leaders facilitate the process of recovery by transforming gang members' gendered expressions from deviant barrio masculinity to *reformed barrio masculinity* (Brusco 1995). Pastors frequently chastise members for abusing substances, not holding down a job, or engaging in extramarital affairs. Recovering gang members, instead of desiring to be like the leaders of the gang hierarchy, desire to become more like the leaders in the organization facilitating rehabilitation. Yablonski (1997) corroborates this and finds that ex-gang members often

find meaning by becoming counselors in a therapeutic community. In such communities men are instructed to make social and economic contributions to their household and to abstain from substance abuse, gang violence, and extramarital affairs.

At sites such as Victory Outreach, a highly spiritual Pentecostal church, and Homeboy Industries, a nondenominational nonprofit, leaders and members contest the notion that urban gang members are unable to change. The Latino men at these organizations approach this process in different ways. Spiritual worship plays an important role in the process of gendered recovery. At Homeboy Industries, Latino ex-gang members make use of Native American spiritual practices, such as sweat lodges, or Eastern spiritual practices, such as meditation and yoga, to symbolically expel cravings for drugs or violence. They get involved in 12-step programs, such as Alcoholics Anonymous, Substance Abuse, or Criminals and Gang Members Anonymous. The class moderators use the clinical language of therapeutic rehabilitation to encourage respect and honesty among class participants. They also juxtapose social critiques of the United States as an unequal society, such as the heightened sentencing handed out to gang members, with personal narratives that ask for redemption and seek personal change.

At Victory Outreach, a Latino pastor makes an altar call at the end of each sermon, proclaiming the opportunity for persons who are "serious" about "changing" or "rededicating" their life to God. Often, many members of the congregation gather in front of the pastor, worshipping in a tightly congested space, placing hands on each other, and speaking stream-of-thought prayers. During the regular sermon, a band plays loud, fast-paced Christian music that members clap and move to, and this alternates with soft music and prayer for roughly 45 minutes. A Victory Outreach pastor then allows men in recovery to "take the pulpit" and give announcements, recaps of important events, share testimonies, or even give a guest sermon. They also juxtapose biblical references of helping persons in need, such as that found in the Book of Mark, with their personal narratives of redemption and change. In these spiritually-based social interactions, men repeatedly frame the meaning of "being a man."

The patriarchal characteristics of reformed barrio masculinity motivate many Latino men to continue with recovery. Members at Victory Outreach often voice their ambition to be a "man of God," to one day get "launched out," or to "take a city" as the pastor of a new church.

Members aspire not only to recover from gang life, but to fulfill the ideals of the patriarchal American dream: to get married, hold a good job, and own a home. Several claim to have faith in God and to want to follow in the footsteps of their leaders because God "blessed" their pastor with a wife and children and a home. Members at Homeboy Industries talk about wanting to experience rehabilitation in order to provide for their mothers, partners, and children. Members that experienced close relationships with Father Greg, during the early years of a much smaller Homeboy Industries, say they aspire to be like Father Greg.

Unfortunately, the process of recovery is not a straight-line trajectory; many Latino gang members oscillate between recovery and sometimes the elements of gang lifestyle, such as smoking marijuana, drinking, or socializing with old acquaintances in the gang's neighborhood, that can spur a complete relapse. Several men became weary of placing themselves in situations that could escalate to a full relapse. Chris, a member of Victory Outreach who has been in recovery for four years, expressed a fear that he could easily engage in the same types of destructive social interactions by simply being around old gang members. As he put it, "I was really afraid to run into my old homies, because I know they were a big influence on me . . . it would just take a couple of hours for me to start drinking, or start getting high . . . you never know what could happen. You could get into a fight, you could get shot. [I]t doesn't take very long for you to go all the way back into your whole lifestyle." In order to prevent from engaging in gang behavior, Chris must now make his therapeutic community (Victory Outreach) his

primary sphere of socialization. He hopes to become a leader, possibly even a pastor, within the Victory Outreach hierarchy.

Some men also admitted to relapsing into gang activity. Matthew, a 20-year-old member of Homeboy Industries, asked if I knew of any vocational programs that could lead to stable employment. He said he had recently called a well-known vocational school but that they were reluctant to answer his questions after they found out he had two felonies on his record. A week later, I read in the *Los Angeles Times* that Matthew was picked up in a major gang sweep. I scanned through the photos of the military-style operation and read that a police officer alleged he had been selling drugs; the evidence—FBI wiretaps linking Matthew's involvement to his gang—however was four to five years old, predating his entry into rehabilitation. For carrying a gun during drug deals several years ago, Matthew is now facing a third felony. Under California law, this carries a mandatory sentence of life in prison without the possibility of parole.

CONCLUSION

The true diversity and complexity of Latino masculinities in the post-9/11 era goes well beyond the images that circulate in American television, movies, and magazines. Two dominant media images of Latino men, that of the docile low-wage worker and the hyper-masculine, criminal gang member, reiterate Mirande's (1997) views of machismo: It is a strictly cultural response to colonization and European domination, wherein the docile worker is colonized and the gangster remains defiant. Our ethnographic research with the real men behind these two images reveals an array of masculinities that, taken together, highlight the deficiencies of thinking about Latino men strictly in terms of traditional machismo, or a rigid cult of masculinity. Instead, our approach follows the lead of Baca Zinn (1982), who calls on students of Latino masculinity to view it as a response to structural inequality, exclusion, and discrimination. Culture plays a role, but structural constraints that keep men from living up to dominant masculine ideals must also be taken into consideration. As we saw, recent political and economic transformations have placed Chicano and Mexican immigrant men in an especially difficult situation vis-à-vis access to jobs and resources. Moreover, they have been vilified as brown-skinned "outsiders" and potential criminal threats in the wake of the terrorist attacks of 9/11.

Against this structural context, *jardinero masculinity* has developed as a distinctly working-class form of masculinity that Mexican immigrant men construct through their daily work activities in residential maintenance gardening, a male occupational niche. Its very expression is linked to their daily performance of hard, dirty, manual labor. In addition, while young apprentice gardeners, or *ayudantes*, find their ability to fulfill traditional masculine roles blocked by their undocumented status, upwardly mobile owners of gardening routes face unique constraints on their ability to balance work and family life. With *jardineros* as with gang members, looks can be deceiving. Just as it may be difficult to tell an *ayudante* from a successful gardening route owner based strictly on their appearance, it may also be difficult to tell an active gang member from a recovering one. But by looking closely at recovering gang members in two faith-based out-reach organizations, Homeboy Industries and Victory Outreach, we can see men leaving behind a life of substance abuse and gang violence, and actively embracing a *reformed barrio masculinity*, characterized by more conventional aspirations, such as getting married and starting a family. In the post-9/11 era, it is imperative that we continue to explore the structural conditions that are linked to multiplicities of Latino masculinities.

NOTE

1. Although this article is concerned with both native and foreign-born Latino men living in the United States, its primary emphasis is on first-generation Mexican immigrant men and Chicano, or Mexican American, men in the Los Angeles area.

REFERENCES

Anderson, Elijah. 1990. *Streetwise: Race, Class, and Change in an Urban Community.* Chicago: University of Chicago Press.

Baca Zinn, Maxine. 1982. "Chicano Men and Masculinity." *Journal of Ethnic Studies* 10(2):29–144.

Bobo, Lawrence D., Melvin L. Oliver, James H. Johnson, Jr., and Abel Valenzuela, Jr. 2000. "Analyzing Inequality in Los Angeles." pp. 3–50 in *Prismatic Metropolis: Inequality in Los Angeles.* New York: Russell Sage Foundation.

Bourgois, Philippe. 1995. *In Search of Respect: Selling Crack in El Barrio.* Cambridge: Cambridge University Press.

Brotherton, David C., and Philip Kretsedemas (eds.). 2008. *Keeping Out the Other: A Critical Introduction to Immigration Enforcement Today.* New York: Columbia University Press.

Brusco, Elizabeth. 1995. *The Reformation of Machismo: Evangelical Conversion and Gender in Colombia.* Austin: University of Texas Press.

Chavez, Leo R. 2008. *The Latino Threat: Constructing Immigrants, Citizens, and the Nation.* Stanford, CA: Stanford University Press.

Desmond, Matthew. 2007. *On the Fireline: Living and Dying with Wildland Firefighters.* Chicago: University of Chicago Press.

Ferguson, Ann Arnett. 2000. *Bad Boys: Public Schools in the Making of Black Masculinity.* Ann Arbor: University of Michigan Press.

Flores, Edward. 2009. "I Am Somebody: Barrio Pentecostalism and Gendered Acculturation among Chicano Ex-Gang Members." *Ethnic and Racial Studies* 32:6.

Kasarda, John. 1995. "Industrial Restructuring and the Changing Location of Jobs." pp. 215–267 in *State of the Union: America in the 1990s,* edited by Reynolds Farley. New York: Russell Sage Foundation.

Lamphere, Louise, Alex Stepick, and Guillermo Grenier. 1994. *Newcomers in the Workplace: Immigrants and the Restructuring of the U.S. Economy.* Philadelphia: Temple University Press.

Lopez, Nancy. 2003. *Hopeful Girls, Troubled Boys: Race and Gender Disparity in Urban Education.* New York: Routledge.

Mirande, Alfredo. 1997. *Hombres y Machos: Masculinity and Latino Culture.* Boulder: Westview Press.

Moore, Joan. 1991. *Going Down to the Barrio: Homeboys and Homegirls in Change.* Philadelphia: Temple University Press.

Ouellet, Lawrence J. 1994. *Pedal to the Metal: The Work Lives of Truckers*. Philadelphia: Temple University Press.

Paap, Kris. 2006. *Working Construction: Why White Working-Class Men Put Themselves—and the Labor Movement—in Harm's Way*. Ithaca, NY: Cornell University Press.

Quiñones, Sam. 2006. "Migrants Find a Gold Rush in New Orleans." *Los Angeles Times*, April 4.

Ramirez, Hernan, and Pierrette Hondagneu-Sotelo. 2009. "Mexican Immigrant Gardeners: Entrepreneurs or Exploited Workers?" *Social Problems* 56(1):70–88.

Sassen, Saskia. 1991. *The Global City: New York, London, Tokyo*. Princeton: Princeton University Press.

Seif, Hinda. 2003. "'Estado de Oro'o 'Jaula de Oro'? Undocumented Mexican Immigrant Workers, the Driver's License, and Subnational legalization in California." UC San Diego, Working Papers, The Center for Comparative Immigration Studies.

Siniavskaia, Natalia. 2005. "Immigrant Workers in Construction." National Association of Home Builders. Available at: http://www.nahb.org/generic.aspx?genericContentID=49216) (accessed October 2009).

Smith, Robert C. 2003. "Gender Strategies, Settlement and Transnational Life." Paper presented at the 2003 Meetings of the American Sociological Association. Atlanta, GA.

———. 2006. *Mexican New York: Transnational Lives of New Immigrants*. Berkeley: University of California Press.

Stone, Linda, and Nancy P. McKee. 2002. *Gender and Culture in America*. 2nd edition. Upper Saddle River, NJ: Prentice Hall.

Tsuchida, Nobuya. 1984. "Japanese Gardeners in Southern California, 1900–1941." pp. 435–469 in *Labor Immigration Under Capitalism: Asian Workers in the United States Before World War II*, edited by Lucie Cheng and Edna Bonacich. Berkeley: University of California Press.

Tsukashima, Ronald Tadao. 1991. "Cultural Endowment, Disadvantaged Status and Economic Niche: The Development of an Ethnic Trade." *International Migration Review* 25(2):333–354.

Valenzuela, Abel, Nik Theodore, Edwin Melendez, and Ana Luz Gonzalez. 2006. "On the Corner: Day Labor in the United States." UCLA Center for the Study of Urban Poverty.

Varsanyi, Monica W. 2008. "Immigration Policing through the Backdoor: City Ordinances, the 'Right to the City,' and the Exclusion of Undocumented Day Laborers." *Urban Geography* 29(1):29–52.

Vigil, James Diego. 1988. *Barrio Gangs: Street Life and Identity in Southern California*. Austin: University of Texas Press.

Vock, Daniel C. 2007. "Tighter License Rules Hit Illegal Immigrants." *Stateline*. August 24. Available at: http://www.stateline.org/live/details/story?contentId=234828 (accessed October 2009).

Wilson, William Julius. 1987. *The Truly Disadvantaged*. Chicago: University of Chicago Press.

———. 1996. *When Work Disappears: The World of the New Urban Poor*. New York: Vintage Books.

Yablonski, Lewis. 1997. *Gangsters: Fifty Years of Madness, Drugs, and Death on the Streets of America*. New York: New York University Press.

PART TWO

BOYHOOD

"One is not born, but rather becomes, a woman," wrote the French feminist Simone de Beauvoir in her ground-breaking book *The Second Sex* (New York: Vintage, 1958). The same is true for men. And the social processes by which boys become men are complex and important. How does early childhood socialization differ for boys and girls? What specific traits are emphasized for boys that mark their socialization as different? What types of institutional arrangements reinforce those traits? How do the various institutions in which boys find themselves—school, family, and circles of friends—influence their development? What of the special institutions that promote "boys' life" or an adolescent male subculture?

During childhood and adolescence, masculinity becomes a central theme in a boy's life. *New York Times* editor A. M. Rosenthal put the dilemma this way: "So there I was, 13 years old, the smallest boy in my freshman class at DeWitt Clinton High School, smoking a White Owl cigar. I was not only little, but I did not have longies—long trousers—and was still in knickerbockers. Obviously, I had to do something to project my fierce sense of manhood" (*New York Times*, April 26, 1987). That the assertion of manhood is part of a boy's natural development is suggested by Roger Brown in his textbook *Social Psychology* (New York: Free Press, 1965, p. 161):

> In the United States, a real boy climbs trees, disdains girls, dirties his knees, plays with soldiers, and takes blue for his favorite color. When they go to school, real boys prefer manual training, gym, and arithmetic. In college the

boys smoke pipes, drink beer, and major in engineering or physics. The real boy matures into a "man's man" who plays poker, goes hunting, drinks brandy, and dies in the war.

The articles in this part address the question of how boys develop, focusing on the institutions that shape boys' lives. Ellen Jordan and Angela Cowan describe how professional-class ideas of masculinity shape and constrain the experiences of young boys, in the kindergarten classroom. Families are also powerful sites of gender construction. As Emily Kane shows in her article, when boys show early signs of gender nonconformity in families, heterosexual fathers are most likely to attempt to press these boys into conformity with narrow definitions of masculinity, while heterosexual mothers and gay and lesbian parents show somewhat more flexibility.

In schools too, one of the key policing mechanisms of masculinity is homophobia. C. J. Pascoe argues that "fag discourse"—a ubiquity of homophobic slurs in schools—places powerful constraints on boys, while helping to reinforce the higher status of (apparently) heterosexual boys. There's little softening of masculinity in the tough, ritual performances of masculine fighting that Ann Ferguson found in the black working class and poor school that she studied. Michael Kimmel closes out this part with a general call for thinking sociologically, critically, and compassionately about the lives of boys.

Together, these studies of boys suggest that institutional contexts—what kinds of schools, what kinds of families—matter greatly in how boys' identities and relationships are shaped and constrained.

Source: Mike Messner

WARRIOR NARRATIVES IN THE KINDERGARTEN CLASSROOM: RENEGOTIATING THE SOCIAL CONTRACT?

Ellen Jordan   Angela Cowan

Since the beginning of second wave feminism, the separation between the public (masculine) world of politics and the economy and the private (feminine) world of the family and personal life has been seen as highly significant in establishing gender difference and inequality (Eisenstein 1984). Twenty years of feminist research and speculation have refined our understanding of this divide and how it has been developed and reproduced. One particularly striking and influential account is that given by Carole Pateman in her book *The Sexual Contract* (1988).

Pateman's broad argument is that in the modern world, the world since the Enlightenment, a "civil society" has been established. In this civil society, patriarchy has been replaced by a fratriarchy, which is equally male and oppressive of women. Men now rule not as fathers but as brothers, able to compete with one another, but presenting a united front against those outside the group. It is the brothers who control the public world of the state, politics, and the economy. Women have been given token access to this world because the discourses of liberty and universalism made this difficult to refuse, but to take part they must conform to the rules established to suit the brothers.

This public world in which the brothers operate together is conceptualized as separate from the personal and emotional. One is a realm where there

is little physicality—everything is done rationally, bureaucratically, according to contracts that the brothers accept as legitimate. Violence in this realm is severely controlled by agents of the state, except that the brothers are sometimes called upon for the supreme sacrifice of dying to preserve freedom. The social contract redefines the brawling and feuding long seen as essential characteristics of masculinity as deviant, even criminal, while the rest of physicality—sexuality, reproduction of the body, daily and intergenerationally—is left in the private sphere. Pateman quotes Robert Unger, "The dichotomy of the public and private life is still another corollary of the separation of understanding and desire. . . . When reasoning, [men] belong to a public world. . . . When desiring, however, men are private beings" (Pateman 1989, 48).

This is now widely accepted as the way men understand and experience their world. On the other hand, almost no attempt has been made to look at how it is that they take these views on board, or why the public/private divide is so much more deeply entrenched in their lived experience than in women's. This article looks at one strand in the complex web of experiences through which this is achieved. A major site where this occurs is the school, one of the institutions particularly characteristic of the civil society that emerged with the Enlightenment (Foucault 1980, 55–57). The school does not deliberately condition boys and not girls into this dichotomy, but it is, we believe, a site where what Giddens (1984, 10–13) has called a cycle of practice introduces little boys to the public/private division.

The article is based on weekly observations in a kindergarten classroom. We examine what happens in the early days of school when the children encounter the expectations of the school with their already established conceptions of gender. The early months of school are a period when a great deal of negotiating between the children's personal agendas and the teacher's expectations has to take place, where a great deal of what Genovese (1972) has described as accommodation and resistance must be involved.

In this article, we focus on a particular contest, which, although never specifically stated, is central to the children's accommodation to school: little boys' determination to explore certain narratives of masculinity with which they are already familiar—guns, fighting, fast cars—and the teacher's attempts to outlaw their importation into the classroom setting. We argue that what occurs is a contest between two definitions of masculinity: what we have chosen to call "warrior narratives" and the discourses of civil society—rationality, responsibility, and decorum—that are the basis of school discipline.

By "warrior narratives," we mean narratives that assume that violence is legitimate and justified when it occurs within a struggle between good and evil. There is a tradition of such narratives, stretching from Hercules and Beowulf to Superman and Dirty Harry, where the male is depicted as the warrior, the knight-errant, the superhero, the good guy (usually called a "goody" by Australian children), often supported by brothers in arms, and always opposed to some evil figure, such as a monster, a giant, a villain, a criminal, or, very simply, in Australian parlance, a "baddy." There is also a connection, it is now often suggested, between these narratives and the activity that has come to epitomize the physical expression of masculinity in the modern era: sport (Duthie 1980, 91–94; Crosset 1990; Messner 1992, 15). It is as sport that the physicality and desire usually lived out in the private sphere are permitted a ritualized public presence. Even though the violence once characteristic of the warrior has, in civil society and as part of the social contract, become the prerogative of the state, it can still be re-enacted symbolically in countless sporting encounters. The mantle of the warrior is inherited by the sportsman.

The school discipline that seeks to outlaw these narratives is, we would suggest, very much a product of modernity. Bowles and Gintis have argued that "the structure of social relations in education not only inures the student to the discipline of the work place, but develops the types of personal demeanor, modes of self-presentation, self-image, and social-class identifications which are the crucial ingredients of job adequacy" (1976, 131). The school is seeking to introduce the children to the behavior appropriate to the civil society of the modern world.

An accommodation does eventually take place, this article argues, through a recognition of the split between the public and the private. Most boys learn to accept that the way to power and respectability is through acceptance of the conventions of civil society. They also learn that warrior narratives are not a part of this world; they can only be experienced symbolically as fantasy or sport. The outcome, we will suggest, is that little boys learn that these narratives must be left behind in the private world of desire when they participate in the public world of reason.

THE STUDY

The school where this study was conducted serves an old-established suburb in a country town in New South Wales, Australia. The children are predominantly Australian born and English speaking, but come from socioeconomic backgrounds ranging from professional to welfare recipient. We carried out this research in a classroom run by a teacher who is widely acknowledged as one of the finest and most successful kindergarten teachers in our region. She is an admired practitioner of free play, process writing, and creativity. There was no gender definition of games in her classroom. Groups composed of both girls and boys had turns at playing in the Doll Corner, in the Construction Area, and on the Car Mat.

The research method used was nonparticipant observation, the classic mode for the sociological study of children in schools (Burgess 1984; Thorne

1986; Goodenough 1987). The group of children described came to school for the first time in February 1993. The observation sessions began within a fortnight of the children entering school and were conducted during "free activity" time, a period lasting for about an hour. At first we observed twice a week, but then settled to a weekly visit, although there were some weeks when it was inconvenient for the teacher to accommodate an observer.

The observation was noninteractive. The observer stationed herself as unobtrusively as possible, usually seated on a kindergarten-sized chair, near one of the play stations. She made pencil notes of events, with particular attention to accurately recording the words spoken by the children, and wrote up detailed narratives from the notes, supplemented by memory, on reaching home. She discouraged attention from the children by rising and leaving the area if she was drawn by them into any interaction.

This project thus employed a methodology that was ethnographic and open-ended. It was nevertheless guided by certain theories, drawn from the work on gender of Jean Anyon, Barrie Thorne, and R. W. Connell, of the nature of social interaction and its part in creating personal identity and in reproducing the structures of a society.

Anyon has adapted the conceptions of accommodation and resistance developed by Genovese (1972) to understanding how women live with gender. Genovese argued that slaves in the American South accommodated to their contradictory situation by using certain of its aspects, for example, exposure to the Christian religion, to validate a sense of self-worth and dignity. Christian beliefs then allowed them to take a critical view of slavery, which in turn legitimated certain forms of resistance (Anyon 1983, 21). Anyon lists a variety of ways in which women accommodate to and resist prescriptions of appropriate feminine behavior, arguing for a significant level of choice and agency (Anyon 1983, 23–26).

Thorne argues that the processes of social life, the form and nature of the interactions, as well as the choices of the actors, should be the object of analysis. She writes, "In this book I begin not with individuals, although they certainly appear in the

account, but with *group life*—with social relations, the organization and meanings of social situations, the collective practices through which children and adults create and recreate gender in their daily interactions" (1993, 4).

These daily interactions, Connell (1987, 139–141) has suggested, mesh to form what Giddens (1984, 10–13) has called "cyclical practices." Daily interactions are neither random nor specific to particular locations. They are repeated and recreated in similar settings throughout a society. Similar needs recur, similar discourses are available, and so similar solutions to problems are adopted; thus, actions performed and discourses adopted to achieve particular ends in particular situations have the unintended consequence of producing uniformities of gendered behavior in individuals.

In looking at the patterns of accommodation and resistance that emerge when the warrior narratives that little boys have adapted from television encounter the discipline of the classroom, we believe we have uncovered one of the cyclical practices of modernity that reveal the social contract to these boys.

WARRIOR NARRATIVES IN THE DOLL CORNER

In the first weeks of the children's school experience, the Doll Corner was the area where the most elaborate acting out of warrior narratives was observed. The Doll Corner in this classroom was a small room with a door with a glass panel opening off the main area. Its furnishings—stove, sink, dolls' cots, and so on—were an attempt at a literal re-creation of a domestic setting, revealing the school's definition of children's play as a preparation for adult life. It was an area where the acting out of "pretend" games was acceptable.

Much of the boys' play in the area was domestic:

> Jimmy and Tyler were jointly ironing a tablecloth. "Look at the sheet is burnt, I've burnt it," declared Tyler, waving the toy iron above his head. "I'm

telling Mrs. Sandison," said Jimmy worriedly. "No, I tricked you. It's not really burnt. See," explained Tyler, showing Jimmy the black pattern on the cloth. (February 23, 1993)

"Where is the baby, the baby boy?" Justin asked, as he helped Harvey and Malcolm settle some restless teddy babies. "Give them some potion." Justin pretended to force feed a teddy, asking "Do you want to drink this potion?" (March 4, 1993)

On the other hand, there were attempts from the beginning by some of the boys and one of the girls to use this area for nondomestic games and, in the case of the boys, for games based on warrior narratives, involving fighting, destruction, goodies, and baddies.

The play started off quietly, Winston cuddled a teddy bear, then settled it in a bed. Just as Winston tucked in his bear, Mac snatched the teddy out of bed and swung it around his head in circles. "Don't hurt him, give him back," pleaded Winston, trying vainly to retrieve the teddy. The two boys were circling the small table in the center of the room. As he ran, Mac started to karate chop the teddy on the arm, and then threw it on the floor and jumped on it. He then snatched up a plastic knife, "This is a sword. Ted is dead. They all are." He sliced the knife across the teddy's tummy, repeating the action on the bodies of two stuffed dogs. Winston grabbed the two dogs, and with a dog in each hand, staged a dog fight. "They are alive again." (February 10, 1993)

Three boys were busily stuffing teddies into the cupboard through the sink opening. "They're in jail. They can't escape," said Malcolm. "Let's pour water over them." "Don't do that. It'll hurt them," shouted Winston, rushing into the Doll Corner. "Go away, Winston. You're not in our group," said Malcolm. (February 12, 1993)

The boys even imported goodies and baddies into a classic ghost scenario initiated by one of the girls:

"I'm the father," Tyler declared. "I'm the mother," said Alanna. "Let's pretend it's a stormy night and I'm afraid. Let's pretend a ghost

has come to steal the dog." Tyler nodded and placed the sheet over his head. Tyler moaned, "ooooOOOOOOOOAHHHH!!!" and moved his outstretched arms toward Alanna. Jamie joined the game and grabbed a sheet from the doll's cradle, "I'm the goody ghost." "So am I," said Tyler. They giggled and wrestled each other to the floor. "No! you're the baddy ghost," said Jamie. Meanwhile, Alanna was making ghostly noises and moving around the boys. "Did you like the game? Let's play it again," she suggested. (February 23, 1993)

In the first two incidents, there was some conflict between the narratives being invoked by Winston and those used by the other boys. For Winston, the stuffed toys were the weak whom he must protect knight-errant style. For the other boys, they could be set up as the baddies whom it was legitimate for the hero to attack. Both were versions of a warrior narrative.

The gender difference in the use of these narratives has been noted by a number of observers (Paley 1984; Clark 1989, 250–252; Thorne 1993, 98–99). Whereas even the most timid, least physically aggressive boys—Winston in this study is typical—are drawn to identifying with the heroes of these narratives, girls show almost no interest in them at this early age. The strong-willed and assertive girls in our study, as in others (Clark 1990, 83–84; Walkerdine 1990, 10–12), sought power by commandeering the role of mother, teacher, or shopkeeper, while even the highly imaginative Alanna, although she enlivened the more mundane fantasies of the other children with ghosts, old widow women, and magical mirrors, seems not to have been attracted by warrior heroes.[1]

Warrior narratives, it would seem, have a powerful attraction for little boys, which they lack for little girls. Why and how this occurs remains unexplored in early childhood research, perhaps because data for such an explanation are not available to those doing research in institutional settings. Those undertaking ethnographic research in preschools find the warrior narratives already in possession in these sites (Paley 1984, 70–73, 116; Davies 1989, 91–92). In this research, gender difference in the appeal of warrior narratives has to be taken as a given—the data gathered are not suitable for constructing theories of origins; thus, the task of determining an explanation would seem to lie within the province of those investigating and theorizing gender differentiation during infancy, and perhaps, specifically, of those working in the tradition of feminist psychoanalysis pioneered by Dinnerstein (1977) and Chodorow (1978). Nevertheless, even though the cause may remain obscure, there can be little argument that in the English-speaking world for at least the last hundred years—think of Tom Sawyer playing Robin Hood and the pirates and Indians in J. M. Barrie's *Peter Pan*—boys have built these narratives into their conceptions of the masculine.

ACCOMMODATION THROUGH *BRICOLAGE*

The school classroom, even one as committed to freedom and self-actualization as this, makes little provision for the enactment of these narratives. The classroom equipment invites children to play house, farm, and shop, to construct cities and roads, and to journey through them with toy cars, but there is no overt invitation to explore warrior narratives.

In the first few weeks of school, the little boys un-self-consciously set about redressing this omission. The method they used was what is known as *bricolage*—the transformation of objects from one use to another for symbolic purposes (Hebdige 1979, 103). The first site was the Doll Corner. Our records for the early weeks contain a number of examples of boys rejecting the usages ascribed to the various Doll Corner objects by the teacher and by the makers of equipment and assigning a different meaning to them. This became evident very early with their use of the toy baby carriages (called "prams" in Australia). For the girls, the baby carriages were just that, but for many of the boys they very quickly became surrogate cars:

Mac threw a doll into the largest pram in the Doll Corner. He walked the pram out past a group of

his friends who were playing "crashes" on the Car Mat. Three of the five boys turned and watched him wheeling the pram toward the classroom door. Mac performed a sharp three-point turn, raced his pram past the Car Mat group, striking one boy on the head with the pram wheel. (February 10, 1993)

"Brrrrmmmmmm, brrrrrmmmmm," Tyler's revving engine noises grew louder as he rocked the pram back and forth with sharp jerking movements. The engine noise grew quieter as he left the Doll Corner and wheeled the pram around the classroom. He started to run with the pram when the teacher could not observe him. (March 23, 1993)

The boys transformed other objects into masculine appurtenances: knives and tongs became weapons, the dolls' beds became boats, and so on.

Mac tried to engage Winston in a sword fight using Doll Corner plastic knives. Winston backed away, but Mac persisted. Winston took a knife but continued to back away from Mac. He then put down the knife, and ran away half-screaming (semi-seriously, unsure of the situation) for his teacher. (February 10, 1993)

In the literature on youth subcultures, bricolage is seen as a characteristic of modes of resistance. Hebdige writes:

It is through the distinctive rituals of consumption, through style, that the subculture at once reveals its "secret" identity and communicates its forbidden meanings. It is predominantly the way commodities are used in subculture which mark the subculture off from more orthodox cultural formations. . . . The concept of *bricolage* can be used to explain how subcultural styles are constructed. (1979, 103)

In these early weeks, however, the boys did not appear to be aware that they were doing anything more than establishing an accommodation between their needs and the classroom environment.

This mode of accommodation was rejected by the teacher, however, who practiced a gentle, but steady, discouragement of such bricolage. Even though the objects in this space are not really irons, beds, and cooking pots, she made strong efforts to assert their cultural meaning, instructing the children in the "proper" use of the equipment and attempting to control their behavior by questions like "Would you do that with a tea towel in your house?" "Cats never climb up on the benches in *my* house." It was thus impressed upon the children that warrior narratives were inappropriate in this space.

The children, our observations suggest, accepted her guidance, and we found no importation of warrior narratives into the Doll Corner after the first few weeks. There were a number of elaborate and exciting narratives devised, but they were all to some degree related to the domestic environment. For example, on April 20, Justin and Nigel used one of the baby carriages as a four-wheel drive, packed it with equipment and went off for a camping trip, setting out a picnic with Doll Corner tablecloths, knives, forks, and plates when they arrived. On May 18, Matthew, Malcolm, Nigel, and Jonathan were dogs being fed in the Doll Corner. They then complained of the flies, and Jonathan picked up the toy telephone and said, "Flycatcher! Flycatcher! Come and catch some flies. They are everywhere." On June 1, the following was recorded:

> "We don't want our nappies [diapers] changed," Aaron informed Celia, the mum in the game. "I'm poohing all over your clothes mum," Mac declared, as he grunted and positioned himself over the dress-up box. Celia cast a despairing glance in Mac's direction, and went on dressing a doll. "I am too; poohing all over your clothes mum," said Aaron. "Now mum will have to clean it all up and change my nappy," he informed Mac, giggling. He turned to the dad [Nigel], and said in a baby voice, "Goo-goo, give him [Mac] the feather duster." "No! give him the feather duster, he did the longest one all over the clothes," Mac said to Nigel. (June 1, 1993)

Although exciting and imaginative games continued, the bricolage virtually disappeared from the Doll Corner. The intention of the designer of the Doll Corner equipment was increasingly respected. Food for the camping trip was bought from the shop the teacher had set up and consumed using the Doll Corner equipment. The space invaded by flies was a domestic space, and appropriate means, calling in expert help by telephone, were used to deal with the problem. Chairs and tables were chairs and tables, clothes were clothes and could be fouled by appropriate inhabitants of a domestic space, babies. Only the baby carriages continued to have an ambiguous status, to maintain the ability to be transformed into vehicles of other kinds.

The warrior narratives—sword play, baddies in jail, pirates, and so on—did not vanish from the boys' imaginative world, but, as the later observations show, the site gradually moved from the Doll Corner to the Construction Area and the Car Mat. By the third week in March (that is, after about six weeks at school), the observer noticed the boys consistently using the construction toys to develop these narratives. The bricolage was now restricted to the more amorphously defined construction materials.

> Tyler was busy constructing an object out of five pieces of plastic straw (clever sticks). "This is a water pistol. Everyone's gonna get wet," he cried as he moved into the Doll Corner pretending to wet people. The game shifted to guns and bullets between Tyler and two other boys. "I've got a bigger gun," Roger said, showing off his square block object "Mine's more longer Ehehehehehehehehe, got you," Winston yelled to Roger, brandishing a plastic straw gun. "I'll kill your gun," Mac said, pushing Winston's gun away. "No Mac You broke it. No," cried Winston. (March 23, 1993)

> Two of the boys picked up swords made out of blue- and red-colored plastic squares they had displayed on the cupboard. "This is my sword," Jamie explained to Tyler. "My jumper [sweater] holds it in. Whichever color is at the bottom, well that's the color it shoots out. Whoever is bad, we shoot with power out of it." "Come on Tyler," he went on. "Get your sword. Let's go get some baddies." (March 30, 1993)

The toy cars on the Car Mat were also pressed into the service of warrior narratives:

> Justin, Brendan, and Jonathan were busy on the Car Mat. The game involved police cars that were chasing baddies who had drunk "too much beers." Justin explained to Jonathan why his car had the word "DOG" written on the front. "These are different police cars, for catching robbers taking money." (March 4, 1993)

> Three boys, Harvey, Maurice, and Marshall, were on the Car Mat. "Here comes the baddies," Harvey shouted, spinning a toy car around the mat. "Crasssshhhhh everywhere." He crashed his car into the other boys' cars and they responded with laughter. "I killed a baddie everyone," said Maurice, crashing his cars into another group of cars. (May 24, 1993)

A new accommodation was being proposed by the boys, a new adaptation of classroom materials to the needs of their warrior narratives.

CLASSROOM RULES AND RESISTANCE

Once again the teacher would not accept the accommodation proposed. Warrior narratives provoked what she considered inappropriate public behavior in the miniature civil society of her classroom. Her aim was to create a "free" environment where children could work independently, learn at their own pace, and explore their own interests, but creating such an environment involved its own form of social contract, its own version of the state's appropriation of violence. From the very first day, she began to establish a series of classroom rules that imposed constraints on violent or disruptive activity.

The belief underlying her practice was that firmly established classroom rules make genuine free play possible, rather than restricting the range of play opportunities. Her emphasis on "proper" use of equipment was intended to stop it being damaged and consequently withdrawn from use. She had rules of "no running" and "no shouting" that allowed children to work and play safely on the floor of the classroom, even though other children

were using equipment or toys that demanded movement, and ensured that the noise level was low enough for children to talk at length to one another as part of their games.

One of the outcomes of these rules was the virtual outlawing of a whole series of games that groups of children usually want to initiate when they are playing together, games of speed and body contact, of gross motor self-expression and skill. This prohibition affected both girls and boys and was justified by setting up a version of public and private spaces: The classroom was not the proper place for such activities, they "belong" in the playground.[2] The combined experience of many teachers has shown that it is almost impossible for children to play games involving car crashes and guns without violating these rules; therefore, in this classroom, as in many others (Paley 1984, 71, 116), these games were in effect banned.

These rules were then policed by the children themselves, as the following interchange shows:

> "Eeeeeeheeeeeeeheeeeh!" Tyler leapt about the room. A couple of girls were saying, "Stop it Tyler" but he persisted. Jane warned, "You're not allowed to have guns." Tyler responded saying, "It's not a gun. It's a water pistol, and that's not a gun." "Not allowed to have water pistol guns," Tony reiterated to Tyler. "Yes, it's a water pistol," shouted Tyler. Jane informed the teacher, who responded stating, "NO GUNS, even if they are water pistols." Tyler made a spear out of Clever Sticks, straight after the banning of gun play. (March 23, 1993)

The boys, however, were not prepared to abandon their warrior narratives. Unlike gross motor activities such as wrestling and football, they were not prepared to see them relegated to the playground, but the limitations on their expression and the teacher disapproval they evoked led the boys to explore them surreptitiously; they found ways of introducing them that did not violate rules about running and shouting.

As time passed, the games became less visible. The warrior narratives were not so much acted out as talked through, using the toy cars and the construction materials as a prompt and a basis:

> Tyler was showing his plastic straw construction to Luke. "This is a Samurai Man and this is his hat. A Samurai Man fights in Japan and they fight with the Ninja. The bad guys who use cannons and guns. My Samurai is captain of the Samurai and he is going to kill the sergeant of the bad guys. He is going to sneak up on him with a knife and kill him." (June 1, 1993)

> Malcolm and Aaron had built boats with Lego blocks and were explaining the various components to Roger. "This ship can go faster," Malcolm explained. "He [a plastic man] is the boss of the ship. Mine is a goody boat. They are not baddies." "Mine's a steam shovel boat. It has wheels," said Aaron. "There it goes in the river and it has to go to a big shed where all the steam shovels are stopping." (June 11, 1993)

It also became apparent that there was something covert about this play. The cars were crashed quietly. The guns were being transformed into water pistols. Swords were concealed under jumpers and only used when the teacher's back was turned. When the constructed objects were displayed to the class, their potential as players in a fighting game was concealed under a more mundane description. For example:

> Prior to the free play, the children were taking turns to explain the Clever Stick and Lego Block constructions they had made the previous afternoon. I listened to Tyler describe his Lego robot to the class: "This is a transformer robot. It can do things and turn into everything." During free play, Tyler played with the same robot explaining its capacities to Winston: "This is a terminator ship. It can kill. It can turn into a robot and the top pops off." (March 23, 1993)

Children even protested to one another that they were not making weapons, "This isn't a gun, it's a lookout." "This isn't a place for bullets, it's for petrol."

The warrior narratives, it would seem, went underground and became part of a "deviant" masculine subculture with the characteristic "secret" identity and hidden meanings (Hebdige 1979, 103). The boys were no longer seeking accommodation but practicing hidden resistance. The classroom, they were learning, was not a place where it was acceptable to explore their gender identity through fantasy.

This, however, was a message that only the boys were receiving. The girls' gender-specific fantasies (Paley 1984, 106–108; Davies 1989, 118–122) of nurturing and self-display—mothers, nurses, brides, princesses—were accommodated easily within the classroom. They could be played out without contravening the rules of the miniature civil society. Although certain delightful activities—eating, running, hugging, and kissing (Best 1983, 110)—might be excluded from this public sphere, they were not ones by means of which their femininity, and thus their subjectivity, their conception of the self, was defined.

MASCULINITY, THE SCHOOL REGIME, AND THE SOCIAL CONTRACT

We suggest that this conflict between warrior narratives and school rules is likely to form part of the experience of most boys growing up in the industrialized world. The commitment to such narratives was not only nearly 100 percent among the boys we observed, but similar commitment is, as was argued above, common in other sites. On the other hand, the pressure to preserve a decorous classroom is strong in all teachers (with the possible exception of those teaching in "alternative" schools) and has been since the beginnings of compulsory education. Indeed, it is only in classrooms where there is the balance of freedom and constraint we observed that such narratives are likely to surface at all. In more formal situations, they would be defined as deviant and forced underground from the boys' first entry into school.

If this is a widely recurring pattern, the question then arises: Is it of little significance or is it what Giddens (1984, 10–3) would call one of the "cyclical practices" that reproduce the structures of our society? The answer really depends on how little boys "read" the outlawing of their warrior narratives. If they see it as simply one of the broad constraints of school against which they are continually negotiating, then perhaps it has no significance. If, on the other hand, it has in their minds a crucial connection to the definition of gender, to the creation of their own masculine identity, to where they position particular sites and practices on a masculine to feminine continuum, then the ostracism of warrior narratives may mean that they define the school environment as feminine.

There is considerable evidence that some primary school children do in fact make this categorization (Best 1983, 14–15; Brophy 1985, 118; Clark 1990, 36), and we suggest here that the outlawry of the masculine narrative contributes to this. Research by Willis (1977) and Walker (1988) in high schools has revealed a culture of resistance based on definitions of masculinity as antagonistic to the demands of the school, which are construed as feminine by the resisters. It might therefore seem plausible to see the underground perpetuation of the warrior narrative as an early expression of this resistance and one that gives some legitimacy to the resisters' claims that the school is feminine.

Is the school regime that outlaws the warrior narratives really feminine? We would argue, rather, that the regime being imposed is based on a male ideal, an outcome of the Enlightenment and compulsory schooling. Michel Foucault has pointed out that the development of this particular regime in schools coincided with the emergence of the prison, the hospital, the army barracks, and the factory (Foucault 1980, 55–57). Although teachers in the first years of school are predominantly female, the regime they impose is perpetuated by male teachers (Brophy 1985, 121), and this preference is endorsed by powerful and influential males in the society at large. The kind of demeanor and self-management that teachers are trying to inculcate in the early school years is the behavior expected in male-dominated public arenas like boardrooms, courtrooms, and union mass meetings.[3]

Connell (1989, 291) and Willis (1977, 76, 84) provide evidence that by adolescence, boys from all classes, particularly if they are ambitious, come to regard acquiescence in the school's demands as compatible with constructing a masculine identity. Connell writes:

> Some working class boys embrace a project of mobility in which they construct a masculinity organized around themes of rationality and responsibility. This is closely connected with the "certification" function of the upper levels of the education system and to a key form of masculinity among professionals. (1989, 291)

Rationality and responsibility are, as Weber argued long ago, the primary characteristics of the modern society theorized by the Enlightenment thinkers as based on a social contract. This prized rationality has been converted in practice into a bureaucratized legal system where "responsible" acceptance by the population of the rules of civil society obviates the need for individuals to use physical violence in gaming their ends or protecting their rights, and where, if such violence is necessary, it is exercised by the state (Weber 1978, 341–354). In civil society, the warrior is obsolete, his activities redefined bureaucratically and performed by the police and the military.

The teacher in whose classroom our observation was conducted demonstrated a strong commitment to rationality and responsibility. For example, she devoted a great deal of time to showing that there was a cause and effect link between the behavior forbidden by her classroom rules and classroom accidents. Each time an accident occurred, she asked the children to determine the cause of the accident, its result, and how it could have been prevented. The implication throughout was that children must take responsibility for the outcomes of their actions.

> Mac accidentally struck a boy who was lying on the floor, in the head with a pram wheel. He was screaming around with a pram, the victim was playing on the Car Mat and lying down to obtain a bird's eye view of a car crash. Mac rushed past the group and struck Justin on the side of the head. Tears and confusion ensued. The teacher's

reaction was to see to Justin, then stop all play and gain children's attention, speaking first to Mac and Justin plus Justin's group:

T. How did Justin get hurt?
M. [No answer]
T. Mac, what happened?
M. I was wheeling the pram and Justin was in the way.
T. Were you running?
M. I was wheeling the pram.

The teacher now addresses the whole class:

T. Stop working everyone, eyes to me and listen. Someone has just been hurt because someone didn't remember the classroom rules. What are they, Harvey?

(Harvey was listening intently and she wanted someone who could answer the question at this point.)

H. No running in the classroom.
T. Why?

Other children offer an answer.

CHN. Because someone will get hurt.
T. Yes, and that is what happened. Mac was going too quickly with the pram and Justin was injured. Now how can we stop this happening next time?
CHN. No running in the classroom, only walk. (February 10, 1993)

Malcolm, walking, bumped Winston on the head with a construction toy. The teacher intervened:

T. [To Malcolm and Winston] What happened?
W. Malcolm hit me on the head.
M. But it was an accident I didn't mean it. I didn't really hurt him.
T. How did it happen?
M. It was an accident.
W. He [Malcolm] hit me.
T. Malcolm, I know you didn't mean to hurt Winston, so how did it happen?
M. I didn't mean it.
T. I know you didn't mean it, Malcolm, but why did Winston get hurt?
CHN. Malcolm was running.
M. No I wasn't.
T. See where everyone was sitting? There is hardly enough room for children to walk. Children working on the floor must remember to leave a walking path so that other children

can move safely around the room. Otherwise someone will be hurt, and that's what has happened today. (February 23, 1993)

This public-sphere masculinity of rationality and responsibility, of civil society, of the social contract is not the masculinity that the boys are bringing into the classroom through their warrior narratives. They are using a different, much older version—not the male as responsible citizen, the producer and consumer who keeps the capitalist system going, the breadwinner, and caring father of a family. Their earliest vision of masculinity is the male as warrior, the bonded male who goes out with his mates and meets the dangers of the world, the male who attacks and defeats other males characterized as baddies, the male who turns the natural products of the earth into weapons to carry out these purposes.

We would argue, nevertheless, that those boys who aspire to become one of the brothers who wield power in the public world of civil society ultimately realize that conformity to rationality and responsibility, to the demands of the school, is the price they must pay. They realize that although the girls can expect one day to become the brides and mothers of their pretend games, the boys will never, except perhaps in time of war, be allowed to act out the part of warrior hero in reality.

On the other hand, the school softens the transition for them by endorsing and encouraging the classic modern transformation and domestication of the warrior narrative, sport (Connell 1987, 177; Messner 1992, 10–12). In the school where this observation was conducted, large playground areas are set aside for lunchtime cricket, soccer, and basketball; by the age of seven, most boys are joining in these games. The message is conveyed to them that if they behave like citizens in the classroom, they can become warriors on the sports oval.

Gradually, we would suggest, little boys get the message that resistance is not the only way to live out warrior masculinity. If they accept a public/private division of life, it can be accommodated within the private sphere; thus, it becomes possible for those boys who aspire to respectability, figuring in civil society as one of the brothers, to accept that the school regime and its expectations are masculine and to reject the attempts of the "resisters" to define it (and them) as feminine. They adopt the masculinity of rationality and responsibility as that appropriate to the public sphere, while the earlier, deeply appealing masculinity of the warrior narratives can still be experienced through symbolic reenactment on the sports field.

CONCLUSION

We are not, of course, suggesting that this is the only way in which the public/private division becomes part of the lived awareness of little boys. We do, however, believe that we have teased out one strand of the manner in which they encounter it. We have suggested that the classroom is a major site where little boys are introduced to the masculinity of rationality and responsibility characteristic of the brothers in civil society; we have been looking at a "cycle of practice" where, in classroom after classroom, generation after generation, the mode of masculinity typified in the warrior narratives is first driven underground and then transferred to the sports field. We are, we would suggest, seeing renegotiated for each generation and in each boy's own life the conception of the "social contract" that is characteristic of the era of modernity, of the Enlightenment, of democracy, and of capitalism. We are watching reenacted the transformation of violence and power as exercised by body over body, to control through surveillance and rules (Foucault 1977, 9; 1984, 66–67), the move from domination by individual superiors to acquiescence in a public sphere of decorum and rationality (Pateman 1988).

Yet, this is a social *contract*, and there is another side to the bargain. Although they learn that they must give up their warrior narratives of masculinity in the public sphere, where rationality and responsibility hold sway, they also learn that in return they may preserve them in the private realm of desire as fantasy, as bricolage, as a symbolic survival that is appropriate to the spaces of leisure and self-indulgence, the playground, the backyard, the television set, the sports field. Although this is too large an issue to be explored in detail here, there may even be a reenactment in the school setting of what Pateman (1988, 99–115) has defined as the sexual contract, the male right to dominate women in return for accepting the constraints of civil society. Is this, perhaps, established for both boys and girls by means of the endemic misogyny—invasion of girls' space (Thorne 1986, 172; 1993, 63–88), overt expressions of aversion and disgust (Goodenough 1987, 422; D'Arcy 1990, 81), disparaging sexual innuendo (Best 1983, 129; Goodenough 1987, 433; Clark 1990, 38–46)—noted by so many observers in the classrooms and playgrounds of modernity? Are girls being contained by the boys' actions within a more restricted, ultimately a private, sphere because, in the boys' eyes, they have not earned access to the public sphere by sharing their ordeal of repression, resistance, and ultimate symbolic accommodation of their gender-defining fantasies?

AUTHOR'S NOTE

The research on which this article is based was funded by the Research Management Committee of the University of Newcastle. The observation was conducted at East Maitland Public School, and the authors would like to thank the principal, teachers, and children involved for making our observer so welcome.

NOTES

1. Some ethnographic studies describe a "tomboy" who wants to join in the boys' games (Best 1983, 95–97; Davies 1989, 93, 123; Thorne 1993, 127–129), although in our experience, such girls are rare, rarer even than the boys who play by choice with girls. The girls' rejection of the warrior narratives does not appear to be simply the result of the fact that the characters are usually men. Bronwyn Davies, when she read the role-reversal story *Rita the Rescuer* to preschoolers, found that many boys identified strongly with Rita ("they flex their muscles to show how strong they are and fall to wrestling each other on the floor to display their strength"), whereas for most girls, Rita remained "other" (Davies 1989, 57–58).

2. This would seem to reverse the usual parallel of out-door/indoor with public/private. This further suggests that the everyday equation of "public" with "visible" may not be appropriate for the specialized use of the term in sociological discussions of the public/private division. Behavior in the street may be more visible than what goes on in a courtroom, but it is nevertheless acceptable for the street behavior to be, to a greater degree, personal, private, and driven by "desire."

3. There are some groups of men who continue to reject these modes of modernity throughout their lives. Andrew Metcalfe, in his study of an Australian mining community, has identified two broad categories of miner, the "respectable," and the "larrikin" (an Australian slang expression carrying implications of nonconformism, irreverence, and impudence). The first are committed to the procedural decorums of union meetings, sporting and hobby clubs, welfare groups, and so on; the others relate more strongly to the less disciplined masculinity of the pub, the brawl, and the racetrack (Metcalfe 1988, 73–125). This distinction is very similar to that noted by Paul Willis in England between the "ear'oles" and the "lads" in a working-class secondary school (Willis 1977). It needs to be noted that this is not a *class* difference and that demographically the groups are identical. What distinguishes them is, as Metcalfe points out, their relative commitment to the respectable modes of accommodation and resistance characteristic of civil society of larrikin modes with a much longer history, perhaps even their acceptance or rejection of the social contract.

REFERENCES

Anyon, Jean. 1983. Intersections of gender and class: Accommodation and resistance by working-class and affluent females to contradictory sex-role ideologies. In *Gender, class and education,* edited by Stephen Walker and Len Barton. Barcombe, Sussex: Falmer.

Best, Raphaela. 1983. *We've all got scars: What girls and boys learn in elementary school.* Bloomington: Indiana University Press.

Bowles, Samuel, and Herbert Gintis. 1976. *Schooling in capitalist America: Educational reform and the contradictions of economic life.* London: Routledge and Kegan Paul.

Brophy, Jere E. 1985. Interactions of male and female students with male and female teachers. In *Gender influences in classroom interaction,* edited by L. C. Wilkinson and C. B. Marrett. New York: Academic Press.

Burgess, R. G., ed. 1984. *The research process in educational settings: Ten case studies.* Lewes: Falmer.

Chodorow, Nancy. 1978. *The reproduction of mothering: Psychoanalysis and the sociology of gender.* Berkeley: University of California Press.

Clark, Margaret. 1989. Anastasia is a normal developer because she is unique. *Oxford Review of Education* 15: 243–255.

————. 1990. *The great divide: Gender in the primary school.* Melbourne: Curriculum Corporation.

Connell, R. W. 1987. *Gender and power: Society, the person and sexual politics.* Sydney: Allen and Unwin.

————. 1989. Cool guys, swots and wimps. The interplay of masculinity and education. *Oxford Review of Education* 15:291–303.

Crosset, Todd. 1990. Masculinity, sexuality, and the development of early modern sport. In *Sport, men and the gender order,* edited by Michael E. Messner and Donald F. Sabo. Champaign, IL: Human Kinetics Books.

D'Arcy, Sue. 1990. Towards a non-sexist primary classroom. In *Dolls and dungarees: Gender issues in the primary school curriculum,* edited by Eva Tutchell. Milton Keynes: Open University Press.

Davies, Bronwyn. 1989. *Frogs and snails and feminist tales: Preschool children and gender.* Sydney: Allen and Unwin.

Dinnerstein, Myra. 1977. *The mermaid and the minotaur: Sexual arrangements and human malaise.* New York: Harper and Row.

Duthie, J. H. 1980. Athletics: The ritual of a technological society? In *Play and culture,* edited by Helen B. Schwartzman. West Point, NY: Leisure.

Eisenstein, Hester. 1984. *Contemporary feminist thought.* London: Unwin Paperbacks.

Foucault, Michel. 1977. *Discipline and punish: The birth of the prison.* Translated by Alan Sheridan. New York: Pantheon.

————. 1980. Body/power. In *power/knowledge: Selected interviews and other writings 1972–1977,* edited by Colin Gordon. Brighton: Harvester.

————. 1984. Truth and power. In *The Foucault reader,* edited by P. Rabinow. New York: Pantheon.

Genovese, Eugene E. 1972. *Roll, Jordan, roll: The world the slaves made.* New York: Pantheon.

Giddens, Anthony. 1984. *The constitution of society: Outline of the theory of structuration.* Berkeley: University of California Press.

Goodenough, Ruth Gallagher. 1987. Small group culture and the emergence of sexist behaviour: A comparative study of four children's groups. In *Interpretive ethnography of education*, edited by G. Spindler and L. Spindler. Hillsdale, NJ: Lawrence Erlbaum.

Hebdige, Dick. 1979. *Subculture: The meaning of style.* London: Methuen.

Messner, Michael E. 1992. *Power at play: Sports and the problem of masculinity.* Boston: Beacon.

Metcalfe, Andrew. 1988. *For freedom and dignity: Historical agency and class structure in the coalfields of NSW.* Sydney: Allen and Unwin.

Paley, Vivian Gussin. 1984. *Boys and girls: Superheroes in the doll corner.* Chicago: University of Chicago Press.

Pateman, Carole. 1988. *The sexual contract.* Oxford: Polity.

———. 1989. The fraternal social contract. In *The disorder of women.* Cambridge: Polity.

Thorne, Barrie. 1986. Girls and boys together . . . but mostly apart: Gender arrangements in elementary schools. In *Relationships and development*, edited by W. W. Hartup and Z. Rubin. Hillsdale, NJ: Lawrence Erlbaum.

———. 1993 *Gender play: Girls and boys in school.* New Brunswick, NJ: Rutgers University Press.

Walker, J. C. 1988. *Louts and legends: Male youth culture in an inner-city school.* Sydney: Allen and Unwin.

Walkerdine, Valerie. 1990. *Schoolgirl fictions.* London: Verso.

Weber, Max. 1978. *Selections in translation.* Edited by W. G. Runciman and translated by Eric Matthews. Cambridge: Cambridge University Press.

Willis, Paul. 1977. *Learning to labour: How working class kids get working class jobs.* Farnborough: Saxon House.

"NO WAY MY BOYS ARE GOING TO BE LIKE THAT!": PARENTS' RESPONSES TO CHILDREN'S GENDER NONCONFORMITY

Emily W. Kane

Parents begin gendering their children from their very first awareness of those children, whether in pregnancy or while awaiting adoption. Children themselves become active participants in this gendering process by the time they are conscious of the social relevance of gender, typically before the age of two. I address one aspect of this process of parents doing gender, both for and with their children, by exploring how parents respond to gender nonconformity among preschool-aged children. As West and Zimmerman (1987, 136) note, "to 'do' gender is not always to live up to normative conceptions of femininity or masculinity; it is to engage in behavior *at the risk of gender assessment.*" I argue that many parents make efforts to stray from and thus expand normative conceptions of gender. But for their sons in particular, they balance this effort with conscious attention to producing a masculinity approximating hegemonic ideals. This balancing act is evident across many parents I interviewed regardless of gender, race/ethnicity, social class, sexual orientation, and partnership status. But I also argue that within that broader pattern are notable variations. Heterosexual fathers play a particularly central role in accomplishing their sons' masculinity and, in the process, reinforce their own as well. Their

expressed motivations for that accomplishment work often involve personal endorsement of hegemonic masculinity. Heterosexual mothers and gay parents, on the other hand, are more likely to report motivations that invoke accountability to others for crafting their sons' masculinity in accordance with hegemonic ideals.

Three bodies of literature provide foundations for this argument. Along with the body of work documenting parental behaviors in relation to gendering children, I draw on interactionist approaches that view gender as a situated accomplishment and scholarship outlining the contours of normative conceptions of masculinity. These latter two literatures offer a framework for understanding the significance of the patterns evident in my analysis of interview data.

PARENTS AND THE SOCIAL CONSTRUCTION OF GENDER

Scholars of gender and childhood are increasingly interested in the role of peers in the process of gendering children, viewing children themselves as active agents rather than passive recipients of adult influence. However, they also continue to recognize parents as important in the gendering of children (Coltrane and Adams 1997; Maccoby 1998). Lytton and Romney's (1991) meta-analysis of the substantial quantitative and experimental literature on gender and parents' behavior toward their sons and daughters documents that parents do not always enforce gendered expectations for their children, nor do they consistently treat sons and daughters differently. Some researchers have highlighted subgroups of parents who actively seek to disrupt traditional gendered expectations for their children (Quoss, Ellis, and Stromberg 1987; Risman 1998; Risman and Myers 1997; Stacey and Biblarz 2001). But as a whole, the literature documents definite parental tendencies toward gendered treatment of children. These tendencies are evident beginning at birth and in the early childhood years. For example, the literature indicates differential treatment of sons and daughters in terms of parental selection of toys (Etaugh and Liss 1992; Pomerleau et al. 1990), clothing (Cahill 1989), and décor for children's rooms (Pomerleau et al. 1990), as well as parental emphasis on emotions versus autonomy in family stories (Fiese and Skillman 2000; Reese, Haden, and Fivush 1996). Across this literature, gender typing by parents is well documented, as are two patterns within that gender typing. First, fathers appear to engage in more differential treatment of sons and daughters and more enforcement of gender boundaries than do mothers; second, for both mothers and fathers, such boundary maintenance appears to be more evident in the treatment of sons than daughters (Antill 1987; Coltrane and Adams 1997; Maccoby 1998).

The large literature on gender typing by parents is predominantly quantitative and often based on experiments, closed-ended surveys, and/or counting the frequency of various parental behaviors. This literature is valuable in documenting the role that parents play in gendering their children. However, it does less to explore the nuances of how parents make meaning around gender, to document in detail what kinds of attributes and behaviors are accepted and sanctioned by parents of young children, to reveal what motivates parents as they participate in the social construction of their children's gender, or to illuminate how aware parents are of their role in these processes. Parents are clearly gendering their children, but what are the subtleties of the gendered outcomes they seek to construct, why do they seek to construct those, and how aware are they of that construction process?

DOING GENDER: ACCOMPLISHMENT AND ACCOUNTABILITY

The interactionist approach to gender as accomplishment (West and Fenstermaker 1993, 1995; West and Zimmerman 1987) provides a powerful framework for understanding what I heard about gender nonconformity in my interviews with parents of young children. This approach allows us to view parents not simply as agents of gender socialization but rather as actors involved in a more complex process of accomplishing gender with and for their children. Along with the notion of gender as accomplished, equally central is the concept of accountability. Accountability is relevant not only when people are doing gender in accordance with the expectations of others but also when they resist or stray from such expectations. This claim, present in West and Zimmerman's (1987) earlier formulation, is one to which Fenstermaker and West (2002) return in defending the approach against criticism that it does not allow for resistance and social change. They note that their focus on the process by which gender is accomplished places activity, agency, and the possibility of resistance in the foreground. But the accomplishment of such change takes place within the context of, and is constrained by, accountability to gendered assessment. Fenstermaker and West (2002, 212) have recently argued that accountability is "the most neglected aspect of our formulation. . . . Few of those who have used our approach have recognized the essential contribution that accountability makes to it."

While accomplishment and accountability are key concepts framing my analysis of parents' responses to their children's gender nonconformity, it is also crucial to note the importance of normative conceptions. Fenstermaker and West (2002) have extended their approach to address not only gender but other categories of difference. "In the accomplishment of difference [including gender], accountability is the driving motivator; the specifics of the normative order provide the content, with social interaction the medium" (Fenstermaker and West 2002, 213–14). They refer to the "content" provided by the normative order as *normative conceptions* and view these as historically and locally variable. Normative conceptions of appropriate masculine conduct are particularly relevant to my analysis, and to explore that domain, I turn briefly to scholarship on the history of masculinity as a social construct.

NORMATIVE CONCEPTIONS OF MASCULINITY: HEGEMONIC MASCULINITY

Connell (1995, 77) has argued persuasively that "at any given time, one form of masculinity rather than others is culturally exalted." This hegemonic masculinity is cross-culturally and historically variable and offers a clear example of a locally specific normative conception of gender. It stands as a normative conception to which men are accountable, a form of masculinity in relation to which subordinated masculinities, as well as femininities, are defined. Connell (1987, 187) argues that there is no need for a concept of hegemonic femininity, because the fundamental purpose of hegemonic masculinity is to legitimate male domination. The subordination of nonhegemonic masculinities is crucial as well, as it allows hegemonic masculinity to legitimate not only male privilege but also race, class, and sexual orientation–based privileges as well.

Several elements of Connell's theory are especially relevant to my analysis of how parents think about their preschool sons' gender nonconformity. He argues that among the features of hegemonic masculinity in this particular time and place are aggression, limited emotionality, and heterosexuality. In addition, he and other scholars interested in the social construction of masculinity emphasize its relational meaning: "'masculinity' does not exist except in contrast with 'femininity'" (Connell 1995, 68). As Kimmel notes, the "notion of anti-femininity lies at the heart of contemporary and historical constructions of manhood, so that masculinity is defined more by what one is not rather than who one is" (1994, 119). Passivity and excessive emotionality, as well as more material adornments of

femininity, are precisely what must be avoided in this hegemonic version of masculinity. Both Connell and Kimmel view homophobia as central to this rejection of femininity. Connell (1987, 186) states this bluntly when he notes that "the most important feature of contemporary hegemonic masculinity is that it is heterosexual. . . . Contempt for homosexuality and homosexual men . . . is part of the ideological package of hegemonic masculinity."

DATA AND METHOD

Participants and Interviewing

The analyses presented here are based on data from 42 interviews with a diverse sample of parents, each of whom has at least one preschool-aged child (three to five years old). Interviews focused on parents' perceptions of their children's gendered attributes and behaviors. The preschool age range is emphasized because this is the period when most children begin to develop a clear understanding of the gender expectations around them, as evidenced in the development of gender identity and the tendency to engage in more gender-typed patterns of behavior (Maccoby 1998; Weinraub et al. 1984).

Interviews were conducted primarily in southern and central Maine (with a small number conducted elsewhere in New England), over a period ranging from the summer of 1999 to the fall of 2002. Participants were recruited through postings in local child care centers, parents' resource organizations, community colleges, local businesses, and public housing projects and through personal networks (though none of the participants were people I knew prior to the interviews). Recruiting materials included general reference to "parents' experiences raising sons and daughters" and did not emphasize gender conformity or nonconformity. Thus, recruitment was focused not on trying to find parents struggling with significant gender-related issues but rather on finding a cross-section of parents. None of those eventually participating reported seeking any professional intervention related to their children's gender identity or gendered behaviors.

The process of participation began with a brief written questionnaire, which was followed by a semistructured interview. Particular emphasis was on a focal child between the ages of three and five, although questions were asked about any other children the respondents lived with as well. The major focus of the interview questions was on the current activities, toys, clothes, behaviors, and gender awareness of the focal child and the parents' perceptions of the origins of these outcomes, as well as their feelings about their children's behaviors and characteristics in relation to gendered expectations. Interviews ended with some general questions about the desirability and feasibility of gender neutrality in childhood. The interviews were taped and transcribed, although some minor smoothing of quotes used in the analyses presented below was conducted to increase clarity. The length of interviews was generally from one to two hours. Most interviews were conducted in the interviewees' homes, but 7 of the 42 interviewees preferred their place of employment or some other neutral site such as a restaurant or my office. Even for those interviews conducted in the home, it is important to note that sometimes a child or children were present and other times not. Therefore, I had no consistent opportunity to observe parents' behavior with their children. The project focuses on parents' perceptions and self-reports, and I am not able to compare those to evidence on actual parental behavior. Interviews were conducted either by myself or by a research assistant. Participants were paid a modest honorarium ($25 to $35, depending on the year of the interview) for their time and participation, funded by a series of small internal research grants, and were ensured complete confidentiality.

The 42 interviewees include 24 mothers and 18 fathers. Four of the fathers are married to women interviewed for the study as mothers. Although geographically specific primarily to northern New England, interviewees come from a relatively diverse range of family types (single-parent and two-parent families, with some of the latter being blended families), class locations (ranging from those self-identifying as poor/low income to upper middle class), racial/ethnic groups (including white, Asian American, and African American interviewees), and sexual orientations (including heterosexual and gay parents).[1] These parents' children include biological children, adopted children, step-children, and foster children. Interviewees' educational backgrounds range from having completed less than a high school education to holding a doctorate, with the average years of formal schooling falling between high school graduate and college graduate. Ages range from 23 to 49 years, with the average age at 35 years. All of the men interviewed work outside the home for pay; among those in heterosexual partnerships, their female partners were roughly equally split among full-time home-makers, those employed part-time in the paid labor force, and those employed full-time. Among the mothers interviewed, about one in three are full-time home-makers, with the remainder employed part-time or full-time in the paid labor force. Interviewees average 2.5 children (with the mode being 2) and are split among those having only daughters (11), only sons (12), or at least one of each (23). The focal children on whom interviews focused include 22 sons and 20 daughters.

Coding and Analysis

I began with a general interest in how parents responded to gender nonconformity, but otherwise my reading and rereading of the transcripts was inductive, coding for issues addressed by all interviewees in response to the structure of the questions as well as for other themes that arose. For the particular focus of this analysis, parental responses to perceived gender nonconformity, I began by identifying all instances in which a parent commented on items, activities, attributes, or behaviors—whether actual or hypothetical—of one of their children as more typical of a child of the other sex. Given that many of the interview questions specifically addressed whether the parent considers their child(ren)'s toys, clothes, activities, and attributes stereotypically gender linked, much of the interview focused on the parents' perception of gender typicality and atypicality. As a result, for the coding relevant to this analysis, I did not identify particular activities or attributes as stereotypically male or female. Instead, I was able to focus only on instances in which the parent himself or herself explicitly noted something as more typical of the other sex, allowing me to document what parents themselves view as atypical. Most of these mentions involved actual instances of perceived nonconformity, but some involved hypothetical outcomes.

Among these mentions of gender atypicality or nonconformity, I then narrowed my focus to just those quotes addressing a parental response. Such responses fell into two broad groups: feelings and actions related to gender nonconformity. Parental feelings were defined as any reported emotional response and were further divided into positive/neutral (e.g., "I love it," "I think it's great," "it's fine with me") versus negative (e.g., "I worry about. . . . ," "it bothers me when. . . ."). Actions were defined as reports of actually doing something about gender nonconformity, acting in some way to either encourage or discourage it. These too were coded as positive/neutral versus negative. Examples of positive and neutral actions include actively encouraging use of an atypical toy or just allowing something atypical because the child really wanted it. Negative actions included a range of reported efforts to discourage or even forbid gender-atypical choices. Once I had coded all of the transcripts for these categories, I coded each interviewee for whether his or her responses to perceived gender nonconformity were all positive/neutral, all negative, or a combination of both. This coding was done separately for sons and daughters because the patterns of positive/neutral and negative responses varied markedly by the child's gender. On the basis of that coding, I decided to focus this article primarily on parents' responses regarding their sons.

Combinations of positive/neutral and negative responses toward children's gender nonconformity varied by gender of child and gender of parent. But they did not vary consistently by parents' racial/ethnic background or class location, perhaps indicating that geographic similarity outweighs such variation

in my particular sample. Scholars of gender have clearly documented the inseparability of race, class, gender, and sexual orientation, and I endeavor to consider each within the context of my interview data. But it is also important to note that the size of my interview sample limits my ability to fully consider those intersections. While some variations by race and class are evident within the broader interview project from which this particular analysis is drawn, such variations are generally absent in terms of parental responses to gender nonconformity. Therefore, although I indicate the race, class, and sexual orientation of each parent quoted, I analyze variations only by sexual orientation, and only when those are evident.

RESPONSES TO GENDER NONCONFORMITY

Mothers and fathers, across a variety of social locations, often celebrated what they perceived as gender nonconformity on the part of their young daughters. They reported enjoying dressing their daughters in sports-themed clothing, as well as buying them toy cars, trucks, trains, and building toys. Some described their efforts to encourage, and pleased reactions to, what they considered traditionally male activities such as t-ball, football, fishing, and learning to use tools. Several noted that they make an effort to encourage their young daughters to aspire to traditionally male occupations and commented favorably on their daughters as "tomboyish," "rough and tumble," and "competitive athletically." These positive responses were combined with very little in the way of any negative response. The coding of each interviewee for the combination of positive/neutral and negative responses summarizes this pattern clearly: Among parents commenting about daughter(s), the typical combination was to express only positive responses. For example, a white, middle-class, heterosexual mother noted approvingly that her five-year-old daughter "does a lot of things that a boy would do, and we encourage that," while a white, upper-middle-class, lesbian mother reported that she and her partner intentionally "do [a lot] of stuff that's not stereo-typically female" with their daughter. Similarly, a white, upper-middle-class, heterosexual father indicated with relief that his daughter is turning out to be somewhat "boyish": "I never wanted a girl who was a little princess, who was so fragile. . . . I want her to take on more masculine characteristics." An African American, working-class, heterosexual father also noted this kind of preference: "I don't want her just to color and play with dolls, I want her to be athletic."

A few parents combined these positive responses with vague and general negative responses. But these were rare and expressed with little sense of concern, as in the case of an African American, low-income, heterosexual mother who offered positive responses but also noted limits regarding her daughter: "I wouldn't want her to be too boyish, because she's a girl." In addition, no parents expressed only negative responses. These various patterns suggest that parents made little effort to accomplish their daughters' gender in accordance with any particular conception of femininity, nor did they express any notable sense of accountability to such a conception. Instead, parental responses may suggest a different kind of gendered phenomenon closely linked to the pattern evident in responses toward sons: a devaluing of traditionally feminine pursuits and qualities. Although many parents of daughters reported positive responses to what they consider typical interests and behaviors for a girl, most also celebrated the addition of atypical pursuits to their daughters' lives, and very few noted any negative response to such additions.

It is clear in the literature that there are substantial gendered constraints placed on young girls, and any devaluation of the feminine is potentially such a constraint. But the particular constraint of negative responses by parents to perceived gender nonconformity was not evident in my interview results. It is possible that negative response from parents to perceived departures from traditional femininity would be more notable as girls reach adolescence. Pipher (1998, 286) argues that parents of young girls resist gender stereotypes for their daughters but

that "the time to really worry is early adolescence. That's when the gender roles get set in cement, and that's when girls need tremendous support in resisting cultural definitions of femininity." Thorne (1994, 170) invokes a similar possibility, claiming that girls are given more gender leeway than boys in earlier childhood, "but the lee-way begins to tighten as girls approach adolescence and move into the heterosexualized gender system of teens and adults." The question of whether negative parental responses might be less gender differentiated in adolescence cannot be addressed with my interview data and remains instead an intriguing question for future research.

In stark contrast to the lack of negative response for daughters, 23 of 31 parents of sons expressed at least some negative responses, and 6 of these offered only negative responses regarding what they perceived as gender nonconformity. Of 31 parents, 25 did indicate positive responses as well, but unlike references to their daughters, they tended to balance those positive feelings and actions about sons with negative ones as well.[2] The most common combination was to indicate both positive and negative responses.

DOMESTIC SKILLS, NURTURANCE, AND EMPATHY

Parents accepted, and often even celebrated, their sons' acquisition of domestic abilities and an orientation toward nurturance and empathy. Of the 25 parents of sons who offered positive/neutral responses, 21 did so in reference to domestic skills, nurturance, and/or empathy. For example, they reported allowing or encouraging traditionally girl toys such as dolls, doll houses, kitchen centers, and tea sets, with that response often revolving around a desire to encourage domestic competence, nurturance, emotional openness, empathy, and nonviolence as attributes they considered nontraditional but positive for boys. These parents were reporting actions and sentiments oriented toward accomplishing gender in what they considered a less conventional manner. One white, low-income, heterosexual mother taught her son to cook, asserting that "I want my son to know how to do more than boil water, I want him to know how to take care of himself." Another mother, this one a white, working-class, heterosexual parent, noted that she makes a point of talking to her sons about emotions: "I try to instill a sense of empathy in my sons and try to get them to see how other people would feel." And a white, middle-class, heterosexual father emphasized domestic competence when he noted that it does not bother him for his son to play with dolls at his cousin's house: "How then are they going to learn to take care of their children if they don't?" This positive response to domestic activities is consistent with recent literature on parental coding of toys as masculine, feminine, or neutral, which indicates that parents are increasingly coding kitchens and in some cases dolls as neutral rather than exclusively feminine (Wood, Desmarais, and Gugula 2002).

In my study, mothers and fathers expressed these kinds of efforts to accomplish gender differently for their sons with similar frequency, but mothers tended to express them with greater certainty, while fathers were less enthusiastic and more likely to include caveats. For example, this mother described her purchase of a variety of domestic toys for her three-year-old son without ambivalence: "One of the first big toys [I got him] was the kitchen center. . . . We cook, he has an apron he wears. . . . He's got his dirt devil vacuum and he's got his baby [doll]. And he's got all the stuff to feed her and a highchair" (white, low-income, heterosexual mother).

Some mothers reported allowing domestic toys but with less enthusiasm, such as a white, low-income, heterosexual mother who said, regarding her three-year-old son, "He had been curious about dolls and I just said, you know, usually girls play with dolls, but it's okay for you to do it too." But this kind of caution or lack of enthusiasm, even in a response coded as positive or neutral due to its allowance of gender-atypical behavior, was more evident among fathers, as the following quote

illustrates: "Occasionally, if he's not doing something, I'll encourage him to maybe play with his tea cups, you know, occasionally. But I like playing with his blocks better anyway" (white, middle-class, heterosexual father).

Thus, evident among both mothers and fathers, but with greater conviction for mothers, was widespread support among parents for working to "undo" gender at the level of some of their sons' skills and values. However, this acceptance was tempered for many parents by negative responses to any interest in what I will refer to as iconic feminine items, attributes, or activities, as well as parental concern about homosexuality.

ICONS OF FEMININITY

A range of activities and attributes considered atypical for boys were met with negative responses, and for a few parents (3 of 31 parents of sons) this even included the kind of domestic toys and nurturance noted above. But more common were negative responses to items, activities, or attributes that could be considered icons of femininity. This was strikingly consistent with Kimmel's (1994, 119) previously noted claim that the "notion of antifemininity lies at the heart of contemporary and historical constructions of manhood," and it bears highlighting that this was evident among parents of very young children. Parents of sons reported negative responses to their sons' wearing pink or frilly clothing; wearing skirts, dresses, or tights; and playing dress up in any kind of feminine attire. Nail polish elicited concern from a number of parents too, as they reported young sons wanting to have their fingernails or toenails polished. Dance, especially ballet, and Barbie dolls were also among the traditionally female activities often noted negatively by parents of sons. Of the 31 parents of sons, 23 mentioned negative reactions to at least one of these icons.

In relation to objects such as clothing and toys, the following responses are typical of the many concerns raised and the many indications of actions parents had taken to accomplish gender with and for their sons:

> He's asked about wearing girl clothes before, and I said no. . . . He likes pink, and I try not to encourage him to like pink just because, you know, he's not a girl. . . . There's not many toys I wouldn't get him, except Barbie, I would try not to encourage that. (white, low-income, heterosexual mother)

> If we go into a clothing store. . . . I try to shy my son away from the Power Puff Girls shirt or anything like that. . . . I would steer him away from a pink shirt as opposed to having him wear a blue shirt. (Asian American, middle-class, heterosexual father)

These quotes are typical of many instances in which parents not only specify the items that strike them as problematic but clearly indicate the actions they take in accomplishing gender. In the first quote, the mother indicates her actions in encouraging and discouraging various outcomes, while in the second, the father reports "shying away" and "steering" his young son.

Playing with nail polish and makeup, although tolerated by some parents, more often evoked negative responses like this one, from a white, upper-middle-class, gay father, speaking about his four-year-old son's use of nail polish: "He put nail polish on himself one time, and I said 'No, you can't do that, little girls put nail polish on, little boys don't.'"

Barbie dolls are an especially interesting example in that many parents reported positive responses to baby dolls, viewing these as encouraging nurturance and helping to prepare sons for fatherhood. Barbie, on the other hand, an icon of femininity, struck many parents of sons as more problematic. Barbie was often mentioned when parents were asked whether their child had ever requested an item or activity more commonly associated with the other gender. Four parents—three mothers and one father—indicated that they had purchased a Barbie at their son's request, but more often parents of sons noted that they would avoid letting their son have or play with Barbie dolls. Sometimes this negative response was categorical, as in the quote above in which a mother

of a three-year-old son noted that "there's not many toys I wouldn't get him, except Barbie." A father offers a similar negative reaction to Barbie in relation to his two young sons: "If they asked for a Barbie doll, I would probably say no, you don't want [that], girls play with [that], boys play with trucks" (white, middle-class, heterosexual father).

In other cases, parents reported that they would compromise in ways that strike me as designed to minimize Barbie's iconic status. These instances are particularly pointed examples of carefully crafted parental accomplishment of gender: "I would ask him 'What do you want for your birthday?'. . . . and he always kept saying Barbie. . . . So we compromised, we got him a NASCAR Barbie" (white, middle-class, heterosexual mother).

Another father reported that his five-year-old son likes to play Barbies with his four-year-old sister and expressed relief that his son's interest is more in Ken than Barbie: "He's not interested in Barbie, he's interested in Ken. . . . He plays with Ken and does boy things with him, he has always made clear that he likes Ken. . . . If he was always playing with dolls and stuff like this then I would start to worry and try to do something to turn it around. But he plays with Ken and it doesn't go much further than that, so I'm fine" (white, upper-middle-class, heterosexual father).

Notable throughout these comments is the sense that parents are carefully balancing an openness to some crossing of gender boundaries but only within limits, as the father in the final quote indicated when he said that he would "do something to turn it around" if his son's interest were in Barbie rather than Ken. A similar balancing act in the accomplishment of masculinity is evident for a white, middle-class, heterosexual father who noted that if his son "really wanted to dance, I'd let him. . . . , but at the same time, I'd be doing other things to compensate for the fact that I signed him up for dance."

Along with material markers of femininity, many parents expressed concern about excessive emotionality (especially frequent crying) and passivity in their sons. For example, a white, upper-middle-class, heterosexual father, concerned about public crying, said about his five-year-old son, "I don't want him to be a sissy. . . . I want to see him strong, proud, not crying like a sissy." Another father expressed his frustration with his four-year-old son's crying over what the father views as minor injuries and indicated action to discourage those tears: "Sometimes I get so annoyed, you know, he comes [crying], and I say, 'you"re not hurt, you don't even know what hurt is yet,' and I'm like 'geez, sometimes you are such a little wean,' you know?" (white, middle-class, heterosexual father).

Passivity was also raised as a concern, primarily by fathers. For example, one white, middle-class, heterosexual father of a five-year-old noted that he has told his son to "stop crying like a girl," and also reported encouraging that son to fight for what he wants: "You just go in the corner and cry like a baby. I don't want that. If you decide you want [some] thing, you are going to fight for it, not crying and acting like a baby and hoping that they're going to feel guilty and give it to you."

A mother who commented negatively about passivity even more directly connected her concern to how her son might be treated: "I do have concerns. . . . He's passive, not aggressive. . . . He's not the rough and tumble kid, and I do worry about him being an easy target" (white, working-class, heterosexual mother).

Taken together, these various examples indicate clearly the work many parents are doing to accomplish gender with and for their sons in a manner that distances those sons from any association with femininity. This work was not evident among all parents of sons. But for most parents, across racial, class, and sexual orientation categories, it was indeed evident.

HOMOSEXUALITY

Along with these icons of feminine gender performance, and arguably directly linked to them, is the other clear theme evident among some parents' negative responses to perceived gender nonconformity on the part of their sons: fear that a son either would be or would be perceived as gay. Spontaneous connections of gender nonconformity and sexual orientation were not evident in parents' comments about daughters, nor among gay and lesbian parents, but arose for 7 of the 27 heterosexual parents who were discussing sons. The following two examples are typical of responses that invoked the possibility of a son being gay, with explicit links to performance of femininity and to the parents' own role in accomplishing heterosexuality:

> If he was acting feminine, I would ask and get concerned on whether or not, you know, I would try to get involved and make sure he's not gay. (white, low-income, heterosexual mother)

> There are things that are meant for girls, but why would it be bad for him to have one of them? I don't know, maybe I have some deep, deep, deep buried fear that he would turn out, well, that his sexual orientation may get screwed up. (white, middle-class, heterosexual father)

The first comment explicitly indicates that feminine behavior, even in a three-year-old boy, might be an indicator of an eventual nonheterosexual orientation. The second comment raises another possibility: that playing with toys "that are meant for girls" might not indicate but rather shape the son's eventual sexual orientation. In both cases, though, the parent is reporting on actions, either actual or hypothetical, taken to discourage homosexuality and accomplish heterosexuality. Another quote from a father raises a similar concern and further exemplifies parental responsibility for the accomplishment of masculinity as linked to heterosexuality. This father had noted throughout the interview that his five-year-old son tends to show some attributes he considers feminine. At one point, he mentioned that he sometimes wondered if his son might be gay, and he explained his reaction to that possibility in the following terms: "If [he] were to be gay, it would not make me happy at all. I would probably see that as a failure as a dad. . . , as a failure because I'm raising him to be a boy, a man" (white, upper-middle-class, heterosexual father). This comment suggests that the parent does not view masculinity as something that naturally unfolds but rather as something he feels responsible for crafting, and he explicitly links heterosexual orientation to the successful accomplishment of masculinity.

The fact that the connection between gender performance and sexual orientation was not raised for daughters, and that fear of homosexuality was not spontaneously mentioned by parents of daughters whether in connection to gender performance or not, suggests how closely gender conformity and heterosexuality are linked within hegemonic constructions of masculinity. Such connections might arise more by adolescence in relation to daughters, as I noted previously regarding other aspects of parental responses to gender nonconformity. But for sons, even among parents of very young children, heteronormativity appears to play a role in shaping parental responses to gender nonconformity, a connection that literature on older children and adults indicates is made more for males than females (Antill 1987; Hill 1999; Kite and Deaux 1987; Sandnabba and Ahlberg 1999). Martin's (2005) recent analysis also documents the importance of heteronormativity in the advice offered to parents by experts. She concludes that expert authors of child-rearing books and Web sites are increasingly supportive of gender-neutral child rearing. But especially for sons, that expert support is limited by implicit and even explicit invocations of homosexuality as a risk to be managed. As McCreary (1994, 526) argues on the basis of experimental work on responses to older children and adults, "the asymmetry in people's responses to male and female gender role deviations is motivated, in part, by the implicit assumption that male transgressions are symptomatic of a homosexual orientation." This implicit assumption appears to motivate at least some parental gender performance management among heterosexual parents, even for children as young as preschool age. Given the connections between male heterosexuality and the rejection of femininity noted previously as evident in theories of hegemonic masculinity, the tendency for parents to associate gender performance and sexual orientation for sons more than daughters may also reflect a more general devaluation of femininity.

MOTHERS VERSUS FATHERS IN THE ACCOMPLISHMENT OF MASULINITY

In documenting parental work to accomplish masculinity with and for young sons, I have focused on the encouragement of domestic skills, nurturance, and empathy; discouragement of icons of femininity; and heterosexual parents' concerns about homosexuality. Within all three of these arenas, variation by parental gender was evident. Although both mothers and fathers were equally likely to express a combination of positive and negative responses to their sons' perceived gender nonconformity, with domestic skills and empathy accepted and icons of femininity rejected, the acceptance was more pointed for mothers, and the rejection was more pointed for fathers. More fathers (11 of 14) than mothers (12 of 17) of sons indicated negative reactions to at least one of the icons discussed. Fathers also indicated more categorically negative responses: 7 of the 14 fathers but only 2 of the 17 mothers reported simply saying "no" to requests for things such as Barbie dolls, tea sets, nail polish, or ballet lessons, whether actual requests or hypothetical ones. Although fewer parents referred to excessive emotionality and passivity as concerns, the 6 parents of sons who did so included 4 fathers and 2 mothers, and here too, the quotes indicate a more categorical rejection by fathers.

Another indication of more careful policing of icons of femininity by fathers is evident in comments that placed age limitations on the acceptability of such icons. Four fathers (but no mothers) commented with acceptance on activities or interests that they consider atypical for boys but went on to note that these would bother them if they continued well past the preschool age range. The following quote from a father is typical of these responses. After noting that his four-year-old son sometimes asks for toys he thinks of as "girl toys," he went on to say, "I don't think it will ruin his life at this age but. . . . if he was 12 and asking for it, you know, My Little Pony or Barbies, then I think I'd really worry" (white, middle-class, heterosexual father). While comments like this one were not coded as negative responses, since they involved acceptance, I mention them here as they are consistent with the tendency for fathers to express particular concern about their sons' involvement with icons of femininity.

Three of 15 heterosexual mothers and 4 of 12 heterosexual fathers of sons responded negatively to the possibility of their son's being, or being perceived as, gay. These numbers are too small to make conclusive claims comparing mothers and fathers. But this pattern is suggestive of another arena in which fathers—especially heterosexual fathers—may stand out, especially taken together with another pattern. Implicit in the quotes offered above related to homosexuality is a suggestion that heterosexual fathers may feel particularly responsible for crafting their sons' heterosexual orientation. In addition, in comparison to mothers, their comments are less likely to refer to fears for how their son might be treated by others if he were gay and more likely to refer to the personal disappointment they anticipate in this hypothetical scenario. I return to consideration of these patterns in my discussion of accountability below.

PARENTAL MOTIVATIONS FOR THE ACCOMPLISHMENT OF MASCULINITY

The analysis I have offered thus far documents that parents are aware of their role in accomplishing gender with and for their sons. Although some parents did speak of their sons as entirely "boyish" and "born that way," many reported efforts to craft a hegemonic masculinity. Most parents expressed a very conscious awareness of normative conceptions of masculinity (whether explicitly or implicitly). Many, especially heterosexual mothers and gay parents, expressed a sense that they felt accountable to others in terms of whether their sons live up to those conceptions. In numerous ways, these parents indicated their awareness that their sons' behavior was at risk of gender assessment, an awareness rarely noted with regard to daughters. Parents varied in terms of their expressed motivations for crafting their sons' masculinity, ranging from a sense of measuring their sons against their own preferences

for normative masculinity (more common among heterosexual fathers) to concerns about accountability to gender assessment by peers, other adults, and society in general (more common among heterosexual mothers and gay parents, whether mothers or fathers).

Heterosexual Fathers

Some parents expressed negative feelings about a son's perceived gender nonconformity that were personal, invoking a sense of accountability not so much to other people as to their own moral or normative framework. Among fathers, twice as many expressed personal accountability than accountability toward others (six versus three). Some references that were personal did arise among mothers, such as this response from a white, working-class, heterosexual mother talking about how she would feel if one of her sons asked for a toy more typically associated with girls: "I'd rather have my girls playing with bows and arrows and cowboys and Indians than the boys to play with dolls and dresses and stuff, you know? . . . . I don't think it's normal that boys play with dolls and Barbies and dress them, it's not in their gender."

But, as noted, such references to a personal normative framework dominated the negative responses offered by fathers. Among fathers, this was the case for the two major themes documented previously as eliciting negative response: icons of feminine gender performance and homosexuality. For example, one white, middle-class, heterosexual father referred to this general issue in two separate portions of the interview. These comments were in relation to his four-year-old son's interest in what he considered "girly" toys.

> FATHER: I don't want him to be a little "quiffy" thing, you know. . . . It's probably my own insecurities more than anything. I guess it won't ruin his life. . . . It's probably my own selfish feeling of like "no way, no way my kids, my boys, are going to be like that."
>
> INTERVIEWER: Is it a reflection on you as a parent, do you think?
>
> FATHER: As a male parent, yeah, I honestly do.

This comment suggests the interviewee's belief that fathers are responsible for crafting appropriately masculine sons. A similar sense of responsibility is evident in relation to homosexuality in a quote presented earlier, from the father who indicated that he would see himself as a failure if his son were gay because "he is raising him to be a boy, a man." Sometimes this invocation of a father's own sense of normative gender for his son was offered more casually, as in the case of an Asian American, middle-class, heterosexual father who said regarding his four-year-old son, "I wouldn't encourage him to take ballet or something like that, 'cause I guess in my own mind that's for a girl."

Although not all heterosexual fathers made these kinds of comments, they were more likely than heterosexual mothers or gay and lesbian parents to situate themselves as the reference point in their concerns about gender nonconformity among their sons. Their motivation for accomplishing hegemonic masculinity with and for their sons is more often expressed as personal, a pattern consistent with the role both Connell and Kimmel argue heterosexual men play in maintaining hegemonic masculinity. In some cases, these heterosexual fathers even explicitly judge their success as a father based on the degree to which they are raising adequately masculine sons. This suggests that passing along that normative conception to their sons may be part of how they accomplish their own masculinity. Not just their sons but their own execution of fatherhood in raising those sons are at risk of gender assessment if they do not approximate the ideal of hegemonic masculinity.

Heterosexual Mothers, Lesbian Mothers, and Gay Fathers

Heterosexual mothers, lesbian mothers, and gay fathers were involved in the same balancing act in accomplishing gender with and for their sons, but their expressed motivations tended to invoke accountability to others. Rather than expressing a sense of commitment directly to the ideal of hegemonic masculinity, they were more likely to express fear for how their sons would be assessed by others

if they did not approximate that ideal. The focus was more often on the child and the others to whom they assumed their son's gender performance would be accountable rather than on the parent. Some heterosexual fathers did express concern about accountability to others, but as noted previously, such concerns were outnumbered two to one by their references to their own normative framework. But for heterosexual mothers and gay and lesbian parents, explanations for concern more often invoked accountability in terms of how others might react to breaches both of the icons of femininity and of heteronormativity. It is also worth noting that very few of the parents reported experiencing any specific problems for their young sons. Instead, they seemed to view this preschool age as an important, foundational moment in accomplishing their sons' gender, often projecting into the future as they expressed concern about the risk of gender assessment.

Among both heterosexual and lesbian mothers, a substantial number (11 of 17 mothers of sons) expressed fear that their sons might be treated negatively by adults and/or their peers if they did not approximate hegemonic masculinity. One mother indicated that she would encourage her three-year-old son to wear styles and colors of clothing typically associated with boys, explaining her reasoning in terms of her fear for how her son would feel if others treated him negatively: "This stupid world cares about what we look like, unfortunately. . . . You know, it shouldn't, probably shouldn't matter. It's a piece of cloth, but that's the way the world is and I wouldn't want him to feel out of place" (white, low-income, heterosexual mother).

About half of such comments by mothers referred in this way to society in general, or the adult world, while the other half referred to peers. Six mothers of sons referred to peers, whether through explicit mention of other children or more implicitly through the use of language suggestive of children's peer groups, while only two fathers did so. The following quote is typical of the various responses invoking the risk of gender assessment within a son's peer group: "I would worry if he had too many feminine characteristics, that would worry me. I just want him to be a boy and play with the boys, not to like girl things. If he did that, the boys would think he's weird, and then he'd be lonely" (African American, low-income, heterosexual mother).

Another mother offered a particularly dramatic example of her sense of accountability to others, in this case with concern expressed both for her son and herself, when describing an incident that occurred about a year before the interview. Her son was two years old at the time and sustained an injury while playing dress up with his older sister. He was dressed in a pink princess costume, and once they arrived at the hospital, the mother began to feel concerned about gender assessment:

> People can be so uptight about things, I was worried they were going to think I was some kind of nut and next thing you know, send a social worker in. . . . You never know what people will think, and in a hospital, someone has the power to go make a phone call to a social worker or someone, someone who doesn't realize he's two years old and it doesn't matter. . . . It was totally obvious that it was a little boy dressing up in silly clothing but there are people out there who would think that's really wrong, and I was afraid. (white, upper-middle-class, heterosexual mother)

A sense of accountability regarding the reactions of others was expressed in relation to sexual orientation as well. When heterosexual mothers raised the issue, they were more likely to invoke fear regarding the reactions of others. In fact, all three mothers who were coded as offering a negative response to the possibility of a son being gay or being perceived as gay included at least some reference to concern about the reactions that her child might have to face from others, while all four fathers who were coded in this category included at least some reference to their own personal negative reactions, as documented in the previous section.[3] Typical of mothers' concerns is the following quote, which refers to a son being perceived as gay if he does not conform to masculine expectations (but others also referred to fears for a son who actually does grow up to identify as gay): "If he's a nurse or

something he must be gay, you know, [people] label you instantly that there must be something wrong with you if you're doing this 'cause men should be like construction workers and women should be nurses and things like that. Yeah, it's very difficult in society. . . . I don't want people to think something of me that I'm not. I don't want them to think that on my children either, I don't want my children to be hurt by that in the future, you know?" (white, low-income, heterosexual mother). This comment, and others like it, demonstrates that parents—especially mothers—feel accountable to others in fulfilling heteronormative expectations for their sons and expect that gender nonconformity and sexual orientation will be linked in the assessments those others make of their sons.

Also notable among the comments expressing accountability to others were reports by gay and lesbian parents who felt under particular scrutiny in relation to their sons' (but not their daughters') gender performance. Although my sample is diverse in terms of parents' sexual orientation, all five of the gay and lesbian parents interviewed are white, partnered, and identify as middle or upper middle class. In most ways, their responses to gender nonconformity paralleled those of heterosexual parents. But there are two particular ways in which heterosexual parents differed from gay and lesbian parents. As noted previously, only heterosexual parents raised fears or concerns about their sons' eventual sexual orientation. In addition, four of the five gay and lesbian parents I interviewed had at least one son, and all four of those reported at least some concern that they were held accountable for their sons' gender conformity. One white, upper-middle-class, lesbian mother of two sons noted that she feels "under more of a microscope" and that her sons "don't have as much fluidity" because she has "loaded the dice. . . . in terms of prejudice they will face because of who their parents are." Similar sentiments are evident in the following quote from another interviewee: "I feel held up to the world to make sure that his masculinity is in check or something. . . . It's a big rap against lesbian parents, how can you raise sons without a masculine role model in the house, and that's something I always feel up against" (white, upper-middle-class, lesbian mother).

Although stated in less detail, a similar concern is invoked in the following quote from a gay father of a three-year-old son: "I mean I think we have to be a little bit conscious of going too far, you know, as gay men the last thing we want to do is put him in anything that's remotely girly" (white, middle-class, gay father).

Some past research has emphasized the lack of any variation in gender typing by sexual orientation of parents (Golombock and Tasker 1994; Gottman 1990; Patterson 1992). Stacey and Bibliarz (2001) have more recently offered a compelling case that gay and lesbian parents tend to allow their children more freedom in terms of gendered expectations. But the concern these parents express indicates yet another social price they pay in a homophobic society, and it is one that seems to arise for sons more so than for daughters. I cannot offer any conclusive claims about how gay and lesbian parents feel about gender conformity based on only four interviews. However, the fact that all of the gay and lesbian parents with sons spontaneously mentioned this sense of additional accountability regarding their sons' masculinity offers strong suggestive evidence that gay and lesbian parents feel under particular scrutiny.

Another intriguing pattern in terms of accountability was evident among heterosexual mothers, and this pattern further indicates the unique role that heterosexual fathers play in accomplishing gender for their sons. No specific questions were asked about each interviewee's partner or ex-partner, but 12 of the 15 heterosexual mothers of sons spontaneously mentioned either actual or potential negative reactions to a boy's gender nonconformity on the part of their son's father (while only 2 mentioned any such paternal reactions to a daughter's nonconformity, and of those, one was a positive response by the father). The negative responses these mothers reported are similar to those previously described in quotes from heterosexual fathers themselves. Sometimes these responses were hypothetical, as in the following example: "I love dance, and I would give

him the opportunity and let him decide. But I think my husband has a stereotype that boy dancers are more feminine. He definitely, you know, has said that. I don't think he would want his son in ballet" (white, upper-middle-class, heterosexual mother). Other references to fathers' negative responses were reports of actual situations: "My son, when he gets upset, he will cry at any child, boy or girl, and my husband has made the comment about that being, you know, a girl thing, crying like a girl" (white, low-income, heterosexual mother).

One comment offered by a nonpartnered mother resonates with this theme and is interesting in terms of what it suggests about partnership status for heterosexual women. She encourages her sons to play with a wide range of toys, both stereotypically male and stereotypically female ones. But she noted that many other people do not do this and that it would be difficult to encourage most people to relax gender constraints on their sons for the following reason: "I tend to think that you have the most difficulty when you have fathers around, they're the ones. . . . I have the final say here, but when you've got a husband to deal with it's harder" (white, low-income, heterosexual mother).

This notion is speculative, as it did not arise consistently among nonpartnered mothers. But taken together with the frequent mentions of male partners' reactions among heterosexually partnered mothers, it bolsters the contention that accountability to fathers is felt strongly by heterosexual mothers as they assess their sons' gender performance. This may influence their approach to accomplishing gender. For example, one white, middle-class, heterosexual mother recounted defending her clothing purchases to her husband after having a stranger assume her then-infant son was a girl: "I had a few people think the baby was a girl, which is kind of irritating, because I would think 'Oh my God, am I buying clothes that are too feminine looking?' The first time it happened I went right to [my husband] and said 'I bought this in the boys' department at Carter's, I'm telling you, I really did.'"

Another heterosexual mother, this one a white, working-class parent, reported not just defending her actions to her husband but changing a purchase decision based on what her husband might think. When her five-year-old son asked for a Barbie suitcase at the store, she told him, "No, you can't have that, your father wouldn't like it." This mother may be steering her son in a direction that avoids the need for his father to become aware of, or react to, gender-atypical preferences in his son. Direct actions to accomplish masculinity by fathers are certainly evident in my analyses, but accountability to fathers indicates an indirect path through which heterosexual men may further influence the accomplishment of their sons' gender.

CONCLUSION

The interviews analyzed here, with New England parents of preschool-aged children from a diverse array of backgrounds, indicate a considerable endorsement by parents of what they perceive as gender nonconformity among both their sons and their daughters. This pattern at first appears encouraging in terms of the prospects for a world less constrained by gendered expectations for children. Many parents respond positively to the idea of their children's experiencing a greater range of opportunities, emotions, and interests than those narrowly defined by gendered stereotypes, with mothers especially likely to do so. However, for sons, this positive response is primarily limited to a few attributes and abilities, namely, domestic skills, nurturance, and empathy. And it is constrained by a clear recognition of normative conceptions of masculinity (Connell 1987, 1995). Most parents made efforts to accomplish, and either endorsed or felt accountable to, an ideal of masculinity that was defined by limited emotionality, activity rather than passivity, and rejection of material markers of femininity. Work to accomplish this type of masculinity was reported especially often by heterosexual fathers; accountability to approximate hegemonic masculinity was reported especially often by heterosexual mothers, lesbian mothers, and gay fathers. Some heterosexual parents also invoked sexual orientation as part of this conception of masculinity, commenting

with concern on the possibility that their son might be gay or might be perceived as such. No similar pattern of well-defined normative expectations or accountability animated responses regarding daughters, although positive responses to pursuits parents viewed as more typically masculine may well reflect the same underlying devaluation of femininity evident in negative responses to gender nonconformity among sons.

In the broader study from which this particular analysis was drawn, many parents invoked biology in explaining their children's gendered tendencies. Clearly, the role of biological explanations in parents' thinking about gender merits additional investigation. But one of the things that was most striking to me in the analyses presented here is how frequently parents indicated that they took action to craft an appropriate gender performance with and for their preschool-aged sons, viewing masculinity as something they needed to work on to accomplish. These tendencies are in contrast to what Messner (2000) summarizes eloquently in his essay on a gender-segregated preschool sports program. He observes a highly gender-differentiated performance offered by the boys' and girls' teams during the opening ceremony of the new soccer season, with one of the girls' teams dubbing themselves the Barbie Girls, while one of the boys' teams called themselves the Sea Monsters. He notes that parents tended to view the starkly different approaches taken by the boys and girls as evidence of natural gender differences. "The parents do not seem to read the children's performances of gender as social constructions of gender. Instead, they interpret them as the inevitable unfolding of natural, internal differences between the sexes" (Messner 2000, 770).

I agree with Messner (2000) that this tendency is evident among parents, and I heard it articulated in some parts of the broader project from which the present analysis is drawn. I began this project expecting that parents accept with little question ideologies that naturalize gender difference. Instead, the results I have presented here demonstrate that parents are often consciously aware of gender as something that they must shape and construct, at least for their sons. This argument extends the literature on the routine accomplishment of gender in childhood by introducing evidence of conscious effort and awareness by parents as part of that accomplishment. This awareness also has implications for efforts to reduce gendered constraints on children. Recognition that parents are sometimes consciously crafting their children's gender suggests the possibility that they could be encouraged to shift that conscious effort in less gendered directions.

In addition to documenting this parental awareness, I am also able to extend the literature by documenting the content toward which parents' accomplishment work is oriented. The version of hegemonic masculinity I have argued underlies parents' responses is one that includes both change and stability. Parental openness to domestic skills, nurturance, and empathy as desirable qualities in their sons likely represents social change, and the kind of agency in the accomplishment of gender to which Fenstermaker and West (2002) refer. As Connell (1995) notes, hegemonic masculinity is historically variable in its specific content, and the evidence presented in this article suggests that some broadening of that content is occurring. But the clear limits evident within that broadening suggest the stability and power of hegemonic conceptions of masculinity. The parental boundary maintenance work evident for sons represents a crucial obstacle limiting boys' options, separating boys from girls, devaluing activities marked as feminine for both boys and girls, and thus bolstering gender inequality and heteronormativity.

Finally, along with documenting conscious awareness by parents and the content toward which their accomplishment work is oriented, my analysis also contributes to the literature by illuminating the process motivating parental gender accomplishment. The heterosexual world in general, and heterosexual fathers in particular, play a central role in that process. This is evident in the direct endorsement of hegemonic masculinity many heterosexual fathers expressed and in the accountability to others (presumably heterosexual others) many heterosexual mothers, lesbian mothers, and gay fathers

expressed. Scholarly investigations of the routine production of gender in childhood, therefore, need to pay careful attention to the role of heterosexual fathers as enforcers of gender boundaries and to the role of accountability in the process of accomplishing gender. At the same time, practical efforts to loosen gendered constraints on young children by expanding their parents' normative conceptions of gender need to be aimed at parents in general and especially need to reach heterosexual fathers in particular. The concern and even fear many parents—especially heterosexual mothers, lesbian mothers, and gay fathers— expressed about how their young sons might be treated if they fail to live up to hegemonic conceptions of masculinity represent a motivation for the traditional accomplishment of gender. But those reactions could also serve as a motivation to broaden normative conceptions of masculinity and challenge the devaluation of femininity, an effort that will require participation by heterosexual fathers to succeed.

NOTES

1. Details regarding key social locations are as follows: 7 of the interviewees are people of color, and a total of 12 come from families who are of color or are multiracial (including white parents who have adopted children of color); 4 interviewees are poor/low income, 13 working class, 17 middle class, and 8 upper middle class; 5 interviewees are gay, including 2 gay fathers and 3 lesbian mothers.

2. One explanation for the paucity of negative responses could be that a broader range of actions, objects, and attributes are considered appropriate for girls than for boys. But this seems unlikely given that a similar number of parents offered positive or neutral comments about sons and daughters, indicating that they were equally likely to identify a range of actions, attributes, and objects as atypical for each gender.

3. This pattern is also consistent with the results of the literature on heterosexual men's and women's attitudes toward homosexuality, which documents that heterosexual men tend to hold more negative attitudes (Kane and Schippers 1996) and that homophobic attitudes are especially notable toward gay men as compared with lesbians (Herek 2002).

REFERENCES

Antill, John K. 1987. Parents' beliefs and values about sex roles, sex differences, and sexuality. *Review of Personality and Social Psychology* 7:294–328.

Cahill, Spencer. 1989. Fashioning males and females. *Symbolic Interaction* 12:281–98.

Coltrane, Scott, and Michele Adams. 1997. Children and gender. In *Contemporary parenting*, edited by Terry Arendell. Thousand Oaks, CA: Sage.

Connell, R. W. 1987. *Gender and power.* Stanford, CA: Stanford University Press.

———. 1995. *Masculinities.* Berkeley: University of California Press.

Etaugh, Claire, and Marsha B. Liss. 1992. Home, school, and playroom: Training grounds for adult gender roles. *Sex Roles* 26:129–47.

Fenstermaker, Sarah, and Candace West, eds. 2002. *Doing gender, doing difference.* New York: Routledge.

Fiese, Barbara H., and Gemma Skillman. 2000. Gender differences in family stories. *Sex Roles* 43:267–83.

Golombock, Susan, and Fiona Tasker. 1994. Children in lesbian and gay families: Theories and evidence. *Annual Review of Sex Research* 5:73–100.

Gottman, Julie Schwartz. 1990. Children of gay and lesbian parents. *Marriage and Family Review* 14:177–96.

Herek, Gregory. 2002. Gender gaps in public opinion about lesbians and gay men. *Public Opinion Quarterly* 66:40–66.

Hill, Shirley A. 1999. *African American children.* Thousand Oaks, CA: Sage.

Kane, Emily W., and Mimi Schippers. 1996. Men's and women's beliefs about gender and sexuality. *Gender & Society* 10:650–65.

Kimmel, Michael S. 1994. Masculinity as homophobia. In *Theorizing masculinities*, edited by Harry Brod. Thousand Oaks, CA: Sage.

Kite, Mary E., and Kay Deaux. 1987. Gender belief systems Homosexuality and the implicit inversion theory. *Psychology of Women Quarterly* 11:83–96.

Lytton, Hugh, and David M. Romney. 1991. Parents' differential socialization of boys and girls. *Psychological Bulletin* 109:267–96.

Maccoby, Eleanor E. 1998. *The two sexes: Growing up apart, coming together.* Cambridge, MA: Harvard University Press.

Martin, Karin A. 2005. William wants a doll, can he have one? Feminists, child care advisors, and gender-neutral child rearing. *Gender & Society* 20:1–24.

McCreary, Donald R. 1994. The male role and avoiding femininity. *Sex Roles* 31:517–31.

Messner, Michael. 2000. Barbie girls versus sea monsters: Children constructing gender. *Gender & Society* 14:765–84.

Patterson, Charlotte J. 1992. Children of lesbian and gay parents. *Child Development* 63:1025–42.

Pipher, Mary. 1998. *Reviving Ophelia.* New York: Ballantine Books.

Pomerleau, Andree, Daniel Bolduc, Gerard Malcuit, and Louise Cossette. 1990. Pink or blue: Environmental gender stereotypes in the first two years of life. *Sex Roles* 22:359–68.

Quoss, Bernita, Godfrey J. Ellis, and Frances Stromberg. 1987. Sex-role preferences of young children reared by feminist parents and parents from the general population. *Free Inquiry in Creative Sociology* 15:139–44.

Reese, Elaine, Catherine Haden, and Robyn Fivush. 1996. Gender differences in autobiographical reminiscing. *Research on Language and Social Interaction* 29:27–56.

Risman, Barbara. 1998. *Gender vertigo.* New Haven, CT: Yale University Press.

Risman, Barbara J., and Kristen Myers. 1997. As the twig is bent: Children reared in feminist households. *Qualitative Sociology* 20:229–52.

Sandnabba, N. Kenneth, and Christian Ahlberg. 1999. Parents' attitudes and expectations about children's cross-gender behavior. *Sex Roles* 40:249–63.

Stacey, Judith, and Timothy J. Biblarz. 2001. (How) does the sexual orientation of parents matter? *American Sociological Review* 66:159–83.

Thorne, Barrie. 1994. *Gender play.* New Brunswick, NJ: Rutgers University Press.

Weinraub, Marsha, Lynda P. Clemens, Alan Sockloff, Teresa Ethridge, Edward Gracely, and Barbara Myers. 1984. The development of sex role stereotypes in the third year. *Child Development* 55:1493–1503.

West, Candace, and Don Zimmerman. 1987. Doing gender. *Gender & Society* 1:124–51.

West, Candace, and Sarah Fenstermaker. 1993. Power, inequality and the accomplishment of gender. In *Theory on gender/feminism on theory*, edited by Paula England. New York: Aldine de Gruyter.

———. 1995. Doing difference. *Gender & Society* 9:8–37.

Wood, Eileen, Serge Desmarais, and Sara Gugula. 2002. The impact of parenting experience on gender stereotyped toy play of children. *Sex Roles* 47:39–49.

"GUYS ARE JUST HOMOPHOBIC:" RETHINKING ADOLESCENT HOMOPHOBIA AND HETEROSEXUALITY

C. J. Pascoe

TEENAGE MASCULINITY

Kevin, a high school student in suburban San Francisco, sits at an IHOP, short money for dinner. His friend, Craig, agrees to lend him money, but only on the following condition—that Kevin repeat a series of confessional phrases which Craig can videotape and place on YouTube. Kevin buries his head in his hands asking, "You're going to take a video of this and post it on YouTube aren't you?!" Craig ignores Kevin's plea saying, "Anyway, repeat after me. 'I Kevin James Wong.'"

> KEVIN: I, Kevin James Wong
> CRAIG: 17 years old
> KEVIN (who at this point starts to giggle embarrassedly): 17 years old.
> CRAIG: Senior at Valley High School.
> KEVIN: Senior at Valley High School.
> CRAIG: In Santa Clarita.
> KEVIN: In Santa Clarita.
> CRAIG: Am now confessing.
> KEVIN: Am now confessing.
> CRAIG: That I, Kevin Wong.
> KEVIN: That I, Kevin Wong.
> CRAIG: Am a homosexual male.
> KEVIN: Am a homosexual male.

They devolve into laughter as their friend Jesse jumps into the frame behind Kevin. Craig posted

the video on YouTube and eagerly showed it to me as I interviewed him in a local Starbucks. He and his friends giggled as they continued to show me other YouTube videos, one of which featured them imitating men engaging in anal intercourse and then bursting into fits of laugher.

About two years before I watched Craig's video in that Santa Clarita coffee shop I found myself two hours away, at a high school in Riverton California, where a group of fifth graders had been bussed in for the day to participate in the local high school's performing arts day. As I looked around the outdoor quads decorated with student artwork and filled with choirs singing and bands playing, a student from River High, Brian, ran past me to the rear quad yelling to a group of the elementary school boys. He hollered at them, pointing frantically, "There's a faggot over there! There's a faggot over there! Come look!" The group of boys dashed after Brian as he ran down the hallway, towards the presumed "faggot." Peering down the hallway I saw Brian's friend, Dan, waiting for the boys. As the boys came into his view, Dan pursed his lips and began sashaying towards them. He swung his hips exaggeratedly and wildly waved his arms on the end of which his hands hung from limp wrists. To the boys Brian yelled, referring to Dan, "Look at the faggot! Watch out! He'll get you!" In response, the 10 year olds screamed in terror and raced back down the hallway. I watched Brian and Dan repeat this drama about the predatory faggot, each time with a new group of young boys.

Kevin, Craig, Brian and Dan enacted similar scenes containing similar messages: men or boys who do not conform to normative understandings of masculinity and sexuality should be mocked, humiliated and possibly feared. I have spent the better part of the last decade interviewing teens about and observing their behavior around definitions of masculinity and sexuality. Across a variety of geographic settings boys from a range of class and racial/ethnic backgrounds report sentiments much like those expressed by Kevin, Craig, Brian and Dan. Conversations with and observations of these boys indicate that homophobic taunts, jokes, teasing and harassment are central to the ways in which contemporary American boys come to think of themselves as men.

The homophobia articulated by Kevin, Craig, Brian and Dan seem representative of many American youth. Nationally, 93% of youth hear homophobic slurs at least occasionally and 51% hear them on a daily basis (National Mental Health Association 2002). Interestingly, in one state, 80% of youth who have been targeted with anti-gay harassment identify as heterosexual (Youth Risk Behavior Survey—Washington 1995). While this harassment is primarily directed at boys, girls suffer from sexualized harassment as well. The American Association of University Women documents that 83% of girls have been sexually harassed at school (2001). These cursory statistics point to an educational experience in adolescence characterized in part by sexualized and gendered aggression directed from boys at other boys *and* at girls.

This type of joking and teasing can have dire consequences. 90% of random school shootings have involved straight identified boys who have been relentlessly humiliated with homophobic remarks (Kimmel 2003). For instance, Michael Carneal and Andy Williams, both involved in rampage school shootings, had been harassed for being gay (Kimmel 2003; Newman et al. 2004). Michael Carneal's school newspaper actually published a report outing him as gay (though he did not self identify as such) (Newman et al. 2004). Eric Mohat, a 17 year old high school student in Ohio who enjoyed theater and playing music, shot himself in 2007 after hearing homophobic taunts. Similarly, Carl Joseph Walker Hoover, an 11 year old middle school student in Massachusetts, suffered homophobic harassment from his classmates for performing well academically. He hung himself in a desperate response to the teasing. In 2008 Lawrence King, having been bullied relentlessly since third grade for his non-traditional gender presentation, was shot and killed by a fellow student whom he had asked to be his Valentine.

While certainly the sort of joking and minor humiliation exhibited in the two opening stories does not match the level of violence in these examples, a problematic intersection of gender and sexuality undergirds all of them. Practices that seem to reflect basic homophobia—imitating same sex eroticism, calling someone queer, or mincing about with limp wrists—are also about policing gendered identities and practices. Through making homophobic jokes, calling other boys gay and imitating effeminate men boys attempt to assure themselves and others of their masculinity. For contemporary American boys, the definition of masculinity entails displaying power, competence, a lack of emotions, heterosexuality, and dominance. Says Kevin, for instance, to be masculine is to be "tough." The ideal man is "strong" and he "can't be too emotional" adds Erik. Maleness does not confer masculinity upon a given boy. Rather masculinity is the repeated signaling to self and others that one is powerful, competent, unemotional, heterosexual and dominant.

This signaling appears in two ways, through practices of repudiation and confirmation. Repudiatory practices take the form of a "fag discourse," consisting of homophobic jokes, taunts, and imitations through which boys publicly signal their rejection of that which is considered unmasculine. Boys confirm masculine selves through public enactments of compulsive heterosexuality which include practices of "getting girls," physically confining girls under the guise of flirtation, and sex talk. For many contemporary American boys masculinity must be repeatedly proven as one's identity as masculine is never fully secured. This essay unpacks adolescent boys' public enactments of homophobia and heterosexuality, examining them as sexualized as well as gendered processes which have ramifications for all teenagers—male, female, straight and gay.

THE FAG DISCOURSE

Boys repeatedly tell me that "fag" is the ultimate insult for a boy. Darnell stated, "Since you were little boys you've been told, 'hey, don't be a little faggot.'" Jeremy emphasized that this insult literally reduced a boy to nothing, "To call someone gay or fag is like the lowest thing you can call someone. Because that's like saying that you're nothing." Indeed, much like the boys terrorized by Brian and Craig, boys often learn long before adolescence that a "fag" was the worst thing a guy could be. Thus boys' daily lives often consist of interactions in which they frantically lob these epithets at one another and try to deflect them from themselves.

Many boys explained their frequent use of insults like queer, gay and fag by asserting that, as Keith put it, "guys are just homophobic." However, analyzing boys' homophobic practices as a "fag discourse" shows that their behavior reflects not just a fear of same sex desire, but a specific fear of *men*'s same sex desire. Many told me that homophobic insults applied primarily to boys, not to girls. While Jake told me that he didn't like gay people, he quickly added, "Lesbians, okay, that's good!" Now lesbians are not "good" because of some enlightened approach to sexuality, but because, as Ray, said, "To see two hot chicks banging bodies in a bed, that's like every guy's fantasy right there. It's the truth. I've heard it so many times." So their support of lesbians is more about heterosexual fantasy than about a progressive attitude (Jenefsky and Miller 1998).

Furthermore, several boys argued that fag, queer and gay had little to do with actual sexual practices or desires. Darnell told me "It doesn't have anything to do with being gay." Adding to this sentiment, J. L. said, "Fag, seriously, it has nothing to do with sexual preference at all. You could just be calling somebody an idiot, you know?" As David explained, "Being gay is just a lifestyle. It's someone you choose to sleep with. You can still throw a football around and be gay." David's final statement clarifies the distinction between popular understandings of these insults and teens' actual use of

them. That is, that they have to do with men's same sex eroticism, but at their core discipline gendered practices and identities (such as the ability, or lack thereof, to throw a football). In asserting the primacy of gender to the definition of these seemingly homophobic insults boys reflect what Riki Wilchins (2003) calls the Eminem Exception, in which Eminem explains that he doesn't call people "faggot" because of their sexual orientation, but because they are weak and unmanly. While it is not necessarily acceptable to be gay, if a man were gay *and* masculine, as in David's portrait of the football throwing gay man, he does not deserve the insult.

What renders a boy vulnerable to homophobic epithets often depends on local definitions of masculinity. Boys frequently cited exhibiting stupidity, femininity, incompetence, emotionality or same sex physicality as notoriously non-masculine practices. Chad, for instance, said that boys might be called a fag if they seemed "too happy or something" while another boy expounded on the dangers of being "too smiley." Ironically, these insults are pitched at boys who engage in seemingly heterosexual activities. Kevin, when describing his ideal girlfriend said, "I have to imagine myself singing, like serenading her. Okay, say we got in a fight and we broke up. I have to imagine myself as a make-up gift to her singing to her out of her window." Kevin laughed as he said that when he shares this scenario with his friends "the guys are like, 'dude you're gay!'"

Because so many activities could render a boy vulnerable to these insults perhaps it is little surprise that Ben asserted that one could be labeled for "anything, literally anything. Like you were trying to turn a wrench the wrong way, 'dude you're a fag.' Even if a piece of meat drops out of your sandwich, 'you fag!'" While my research shows that there are particular set of behaviors that could get a boy called the slur, it is no wonder that Ben felt a boy could be called it for "anything." In that statement he reveals the intensity and extent of the policing boys must do of their behaviors in order to avoid the epithet.

The sort of homophobic harassment detailed above has as much to do [with] definitions of masculinity as it does with actual fear of other gay men

(Corbett 2001, Kimmel 2001). Being subject to homophobic harassment has as much to do with failing at masculine tasks of competence, heterosexual prowess or in any way revealing weakness as it does with a sexual identity. Homophobic epithets such as fag have gendered meanings *and* sexual meanings. The insult is levied against boys who are not masculine, even momentarily, and boys who identify (or are identified by others) as gay. This sets up a very complicated daily ordeal in which boys continually strive to avoid being subject to the epithet, but are simultaneously constantly vulnerable to it.

This sort of homophobia appears frequently in boys' joking relationships. Sociologists have pointed out that joking is central to men's relationships in general (Kehily and Nayak 1997, Lyman 1998). Through aggressive joking boys cement friendship bonds with one another. Boys often draw laughs though imitating effeminate men or men's same sex desire. Emir frequently imitated effeminate men who presumably sexually desired other men to draw laughs from students in his introductory drama class. One day his teacher, disturbed by noise outside the classroom, turned to close the door saying, "We'll shut this unless anyone really wants to watch sweaty boys playing basketball." Emir lisped, "I wanna watch the boys play!" The rest of the class cracked up at his imitation. No one [in] the class actually though[t] Emir was gay, as he purposefully mocked both same-sex sexual desire and an effeminate gender identity. This sort of ritual reminded other youth that masculine men did not desire other men, nor did they lisp or behave in other feminine manners. It also reminded them that men who behaved in these ways were worthy of laughter and derision.

These everyday joking interchanges, however, were more than "just jokes." For some boys, such as Lawrence King, the intolerance for gender differences espoused by these joking rituals have serious, if not deadly, consequences. Ray and Peter underscore this in their conversation. Ray asserted "I can't stand fags. Like I've met a couple. I don't know. The way they rub you. Gay people I don't care. They do their thing in their bedroom and that's fine. Feminine guys bother me." Peter, his friend, continued "If they try to get up on you. I'll kill you." Ray and Peter illuminated the teenage boys' different responses to gay and unmasculine men as Ray espouses tolerance for the presumably gender normative former and Peter threatens violence against latter. In this sense the discourse runs a continuum from joking to quite violent harassment. While boys said that the "fag" insult was more about failing at masculinity than about actually being gay, it seemed that a gay and unmasculine boy suffered the most under this "gender regime" (Connell 1987).

As a talented dancer who frequently sported multicolored hair extensions, mascara and wore baggy pants, fitted tanktops and sometimes a skirt, Ricky violated these norms of gender *and* sexuality. He told me that harassment started early, in elementary school. "I'm talking like sixth grade, I started being called a fag. Fifth grade I was called a fag. Third grade I was called a fag." Though he moved schools every two years or so, this sort of harassment continued and intensified as he moved into high school. At his school's homecoming game (for which Ricky had choreographed the half time show) he was harassed until he left after hearing things like "there's that fucking fag" and "What the fuck is that fag doing here? That fag has no right to be here." When watching him dance with the school's all female dance team other boys reacted in revulsion. Nils said, "it's like a car wreck, you just can't look away." J. R., the captain of the football team, shook his head and muttered under his breath, "That guy dancing, it's just disgusting, Disgusting!" shaking his head and stomping off. Even though dancing is the most important thing in his life, Ricky did not attend school dances because he didn't like to "watch my back" the whole time. He had good reason for this fear. Brad said of prom, "I heard Ricky is going in a skirt, it's a hella short one." Sean responded with "I wouldn't even go if he's there." Topping Sean's response Brad claimed, "I'd probably beat him up outside."

The harassment suffered by Ricky featured none of the joking or laughter exhibited in other interchanges. Very real threats of violence under-girded boys' comments about him. Ricky told me that he walked with his eyes downcast, in order to avoid boys' eye contact fearing that they would see such eye contact as a challenge. Similarly he varied his route home from school each day and carried a rock in his hand to protect himself. For many boys, in order to maintain a sense of themselves as masculine, they felt they had to directly attack Ricky, a symbol of what they feared most.

COMPULSIVE HETEROSEXUALITY

If daily life for many boys entails running a gauntlet of homophobic insults, how do they avoid being permanently labeled as Ricky was? Boys defend against homophobic teasing and harassment by assuring others of their heterosexuality. In the same way that boys' homophobia is not specifically about a sexual identity, compulsive heterosexuality[1] is not only about expressing love, desire and intimacy, but about showing a sexualized dominance over girls' bodies. The sort of gendered teasing in which boys engage in takes a toll on girls as well as other boys. In my research I found three components of compulsive heterosexuality: rituals of getting girls, rituals of touch, and sex talk.

Perhaps the most obvious example of "getting girls" is having a girlfriend. Having a girlfriend seems a normal teen behavior. For boys who are identified as feminine and teased for unmasculine practices, having a girlfriend functions as some sort of protection against homophobic harassment. Justin told me that some boys have girlfriends "so they look like they're not losers or they're not gay." David told me that a lot of the kids at his high school think that he is gay because of his preppy clothing choices and his lisp such that for him "it's better to have a girlfriend . . . because people think I'm gay. I get that all the time." In order to defend against

teasing and harassment boys like David need to establish a short of baseline heterosexuality by proving they can "get a girl." Because of the difficulty in avoiding all of the behaviors that might render one vulnerable to teasing, having a girlfriend helps to inure one to accusations of the "fag discourse."

Similarly, cross gender touching rituals establish a given boy's heterosexuality. These physical interchanges may first appear as harmless flirtation, but upon closer inspection actually reinforce boys' dominance over girls['] bodies. The use of touch maintains a social hierarchy (Henley 1977). Superiors touch subordinates, invade their space and interrupt them in a way [that] subordinates [do] not to do [to] superiors and these superior inferior relationships are often gendered ones. Boys and girls often touch each other as part of daily interaction, communication and flirtation. In many instances cross-sex touching was lightly flirtations and reciprocal. But these touching rituals ranged from playfully flirtations to assault like interactions. Boys might physically constrain girls under the guise of flirtation. One time in a school hallway a boy wrapped his arms around a girl and started to "freak" her, or grind his pelvis into hers as she struggled to get away. This sort of behavior happened more often in primarily male spaces. One day for instance, in a school weight room, Monte wrapped his arms around a girl's neck as if to put her in a headlock and held her there while Reggie punched her in the stomach, albeit lightly and she squealed. A more dramatic example of this was during a passing period in which Keith rhythmically jabbed a girl in the crotch with his drumstick, while he yelled "Get raped! Get raped!" These examples show how the constraint and touch of female bodies gets translated as masculinity, embedding sexualized meanings in which heterosexual flirting is coded as female helplessness and male bodily dominance.

While people jokingly refer to boys' sex talk as "boys will be boys" or "locker room" talk, this sex talk plays a serious role in defending against acquiring an identity like Ricky's. Boys enact and naturalize their heterosexuality by asserting "guys are horndogs" or by claiming that it is "kind of

---

[1]This concept draws upon Adrienne Rich's (1986) influential concept of "compulsory heterosexuality" as well as Michael Kimmel's (1987) notion of "compulsive masculinity."

impossible for a guy" to not "think of sex every two minutes" as Chad does. Thinking about boys' sexual performance in terms of compulsive heterosexuality shows that asserting that one is a horndog and cannot help but think about sex is actually a gendered performance. Boys' sex talk often takes the form of "mythic story telling" in which they tell larger than life tales about their sexual adventures, their bodies and girls' bodies that do not reflect love, desire or sensuality, but rather dominance over girls' bodies. Pedro, for instance, laughed and acted out having sex with his girlfriend by leaning back up against the wall, legs and arms spread and head turning back and forth as he continued to say proudly "I did her so hard when I was done she was bleeding. I tore her walls!" The boys surrounding him cheered and oohed and aahhed in amazement. Violence frequently frames these stories. Much like the touching rituals in which boys establish dominance over girls' bodies these stories show what boys can make girls' bodies do. Rich, after finishing lifting weights in his school's weight room, sat on weight bench and five boys gathered around him as he told a story, after much urging, about sex with his now ex-girlfriend. He explained that they were having sex and "she said it started to hurt. I said we can stop and she said no. Then she said it again and she started crying. I told her to get off! Told her to get off! Finally I took her off," making a motion like he was lifting her off of him. He continued, there was "blood all over me! Blood all over her! Popped her wall! She had to have stitches." The boys started cracking up and moaning. Not to be outdone, the other boys in the circle began to chime in about their sexual exploits. Even those who didn't have stories about themselves, asserted their knowledge of sex through vicarious experiences. Troy joined the discussion with a story about his brother, a professional basketball player for a nearby city. He "brought home a 24 year old drunk chick! She *farted* the whole time they were doing it in the other room! It was *hella gross!*" All the boys cracked up again. Adam, not to be outdone, claimed "my friend had sex with a drunk chick. He did her in the butt! She s*** all over the place!" The boys all cracked up again and yelled

out things like "hella gross!" or "that's disgusting!" These graphic, quite violent stories detail what boys can make girls bodies do—rip, bleed, fart and poop.

To understand the role of sexuality in maintaining gender inequality, it is important to look at sexuality and specifically heterosexuality, not as a set of desires, identities or dispositions, but as an institution. Adrienne Rich (1986) does this when she argues that heterosexuality is an institution that systematically disempowers women. Similarly compulsive heterosexuality is a set of practices through which boys reinforce linkages between sexuality, dominance, and violence. This heterosexuality is a defensive heterosexuality, not necessarily a reflection of an internal set of emotions.

CONCLUSION

Many boys' school based lives involve running a daily gauntlet of sexualized insults, as they simultaneously try to lob homophobic epithets at others and defend themselves from the said epithets. In this sense masculinity becomes the daily interactional work of repudiating the labels of fag, queer or gay. Unpacking the definition of what appears to be homophobia clarifies the gender policing at the heart of boys' harassment of one another and of girls. Homophobic epithets may or may not have explicitly sexual meanings, but they always have gendered meanings. Many boys are terrified of being permanently labeled as gay, fag or queer since to them, such a label effectively negates their humanness. As a part of boys' defensive strategies, girls' bodies become masculinity resources deployed in order to stave off these labels.

The practices of compulsive heterosexuality indicate that control over girls' bodies and their sexuality is central to definitions of adolescent masculinity. If masculinity is, as boys told me, about competence, heterosexuality, being unemotional, and dominance, then girls' bodies provide boys the opportunity to ward off the fag discourse by demonstrating mastery and control over them. Engaging in compulsive heterosexuality also allows boys to display a lack of emotions by refusing to engage the empathy that might mitigate against such a use of girls and their bodies. It is important to note that many of these boys are not unrepentant sexists or homophobes. In private and in one on one conversations many spoke of sexual equality and of tender feelings for girls. For the most part these were social behaviors that boys engaged in when around other boys, precisely because they are less reflections of internal homophobic and sexist dispositions and more about constituting a masculine identity, something that is accomplished interactionally.

This gendered homophobia as well as sexualized and gendered defenses against it comprise contemporary adolescent masculinity. Fear of any sort of same-sex intimacy (platonic or not) polices boys' friendships with one another. The need to repudiate that which is not considered masculine leads to a very public renunciation of same-sex desire. Heterosexual flirtation becomes intertwined with gendered dominance. What this means is that the public face of adolescent sexuality is rife with reproduction of gender inequality, through processes of the fag discourse and compulsive heterosexuality.

REFERENCES

A.A.U.W. 2001. *Hostile Hallways*. Washington, D.C.: American Association of University Women.

Connell, R. W. 1987. *Gender and Power*. Stanford: Stanford University Press.

Corbett, Ken. 2001. "Faggot = Loser." *Studies in Gender and Sexuality* 2(1):3–28.

Henley, Nancy. 1977. *Body Politics: Power, Sex, and Nonverbal Communication*. Englewood Cliffs, N.J.: Prentice-Hall.

Jenefsky, Cindy and Diane H. Miller. 1998. "Phallic Intrusion: Girl-Girl Sex in Penthouse." *Women's Studies International Forum* 21(4):375–385.

Kehily, Mary J. and Anoop Nayak. 1997. "'Lads and Laughter': Humour and the Production of Heterosexual Masculinities." *Gender and Education* 9(1):69–87.

Kimmel, Michael. 1987. "The Cult of Masculinity: American Social Character and the Legacy of the Cowboy." pp. 235–249 in *Beyond Patriarchy: Essays by Men on Pleasure, Power and Change*, edited by M. Kaufman. New York: Oxford University Press.

——. 2001. "Masculinity as Homophobia: Fear, Shame, and Silence in the Construction of Gender Identity." pp. 266–287 in *The Masculinities Reader*, edited by S. Whitehead and F. Barrett. Cambridge: Polity.

Kimmel, Michael S. 2003. "Adolescent Masculinity, Homophobia, and Violence: Random School Shootings, 1982–2001." *American Behavioral Scientist* 46(10):1439–1458.

Lyman, Peter. 1998. "The Fraternal Bond as a Joking Relationship: A Case Study of the Role of Sexist Jokes in Male Group Bonding." pp. 171–193 in *Men's Lives*. Fourth ed, edited by M. Kimmel and M. Messner. Boston: Allyn and Bacon.

National Mental Health Association. 2002. *What Does Gay Mean? Teen Survey Executive Summary*.

Newman, Katherine, Cybelle Fox, David J. L. Harding, Jal Mehta and Wendy Roth. 2004. *Rampage: The Social Roots of School Shootings*. New York: Basic Books.

Rich, Adrienne. 1986. "Compulsory Heterosexuality and Lesbian Existence." pp. 23–74 in *Blood, Bread and Poetry*. New York: W.W. Norton & Company.

Wilchins, Riki. 2003. "Do You Believe in Fairies?" *The Advocate*, February 4, pp. 72.

Youth Risk Behavior Survey—Washington. 1995.

MAKING A NAME FOR YOURSELF: TRANSGRESSIVE ACTS AND GENDER PERFORMANCE

Ann Ferguson

Though girls as well as boys infringe the rules, the overwhelming majority of violations in every single category, from misbehavior to obscenity, are by males. In a disturbing tautology, transgressive behavior is that which constitutes masculinity. Consequently, African American males in the very act of identification, of signifying masculinity, are likely to be breaking rules.

I use the concept of sex/gender not to denote the existence of a stable, unitary category that reflects the presence of fundamental, natural biological difference, but as a socially constructed category whose form and meaning [vary] culturally and historically. We come to know ourselves and to recognize others as of a different sex through an overdetermined complex process inherent in every sphere of social life at the ideological and discursive level, through social structures and institutional arrangements, as well as through the micropolitics of social interactions.[1] We take sex difference for granted, as a natural form of difference as we look for it, recognize it, celebrate it; this very repetition of the "fact" of difference produces and confirms its existence. Indeed, assuming sex/gender difference and identifying as one or the other gender is a precursor of being culturally recognizable as "human."

While all these modes of constituting gender as difference were palpable in the kids' world, in the following analysis of sex/gender as a heightened and highly charged resource for self-fashioning and making a name for oneself, the phenomenological approach developed by ethnomethodologists and by poststructuralist feminist Judith Butler is the most productive one to build on. Here gender is conceptualized as something we do in a performance that is both individually and socially meaningful. We signal our gender identification through an ongoing performance of normative acts that are ritually specific, drawing on well-worked-over, sociohistorical scripts and easily recognizable scenarios.[2]

Butler's emphasis on the coerced and coercive nature of these performances is especially useful. Her work points out that the enactment of sex difference is neither voluntary nor arbitrary in form but is a compulsory requirement of social life. Gender acts follow sociohistorical scripts that are policed through the exercise of repression and taboo. The consequences of an inadequate or bad performance are significant, ranging from ostracism and stigmatization to imprisonment and death. What I want to emphasize in the discussion that follows are the rewards that attach to this playing out of roles; for males, the enactment of masculinity is also a thoroughly embodied display of physical and social power.

Identification as masculine through gender acts, within this framework, is not simply a matter of imitation or modeling, but is better understood as a highly strategic attachment to a social category that has political effects. This attachment involves narratives of the self and of Other, constructed within and through fantasy and imagination, as well as through repetitious, referential acts. The performance signals the individual as socially connected, embedded in a collective membership that always references relations of power.

African American boys at Rosa Parks School use three key constitutive strategies of masculinity in the embrace of the masculine "we" as a mode of self-expression. These strategies speak to and about power. The first is that of heterosexual power, always marked as male. Alain's graffiti become the centerpiece of this discussion. The second involves classroom performances that engage and disrupt the normal direction of the flow of power. The third strategy involves practices of "fighting." All three invoke a "process of iterability, a regularized and constrained repetition of norms," in doing gender, constitute masculinity as a natural, essential, corporeal style; and involve imaginary, fantasmatic identifications.[3]

These three strategies often lead to trouble, but by engaging them a boy can also make a name for himself as a real boy, the Good Bad Boy of a national fantasy. All three illustrate and underline the way that normative male practices take on a different, more sinister inflection when carried out by African American boys. Race makes a significant difference both in the form of the performance as well as its meaning for the audience of adult authority figures and children for whom it is played.

HETEROSEXUAL POWER: ALAIN'S GRAFFITI

One group of transgressions specifically involves behavior that expresses sexual curiosity and attraction. These offenses are designated as "personal violations" and given more serious punishment. Inscribed in these interactions are social meanings about relations of power between the sexes as well as assumptions about male and female difference at the level of the physical and biological as well as the representational. It is assumed that females are

sexually passive, unlikely to be initiators of sexual passes, while males are naturally active sexual actors with strong sexual drives. Another assumption is that the feminine is a contaminated, stigmatizing category in the sex/gender hierarchy.

Typically, personal violations involved physical touching of a heterosexual nature where males were the "perpetrators" and females the "victims." A few examples from the school files remind us of some of the "normal" displays of sexual interest at this age.

- Boy was cited with "chasing a girl down the hall" [punishment: two days in the Jailhouse].
- Boy pulled a female classmate's pants down during recess [punishment: one and a half days in the Jailhouse].
- Boy got in trouble for, "touching girl on private parts. She did not like" [punishment: a day in the Jailhouse].
- Boy was cited for "forcing girl's hand between his legs" [punishment: two and a half days in the Jailhouse].

In one highly revealing case, a male was cast as the "victim" when he was verbally assaulted by another boy who called him a girl. The teacher described the "insult" and her response to it on the referral form in these words:

During the lesson, Jonas called Ahmed a girl and said he wasn't staying after school for detention because "S" [another boy] had done the same thing. Since that didn't make it ok for anyone to speak this way I am requesting an hour of detention for Jonas. I have no knowledge of "S" saying so in my presence.

This form of insult is not unusual. When boys want to show supreme contempt for another boy they call him a girl or liken his behavior to female behavior. What is more troubling is that adults capitulate in this stigmatization. The female teacher takes for granted that a comment in which a boy is called a girl is a symbolic attack, sufficiently derogatory to merit punishment. All the participants in the classroom exchange witness the uncritical acknowledgment of adult authority to a gender order of female debasement.

Of course, this is not news to them. Boys and girls understand the meaning of being male and being female in the field of power; the binary opposition of male/female is always one that expresses a norm, maleness, and its constitutive outside, femaleness. In a conversation with a group of boys, one of them asserted and then was supported by others that "a boy can be a girl, but a girl can never be a boy." Boys can be teased, controlled, punished by being accused of being "a girl." A boy faces the degradation of "being sissified," being unmanned, transferred to the degraded category of female. Girls can be teased about being a tomboy. But this is not the same. To take on qualities of being male is the access to and performance of power. So females must now fashion themselves in terms of male qualities to partake of that power. Enactments of masculinity signal value, superiority, power.

Let us return to Alain, the 11-year-old boy who while cooling off and writing lines as a punishment in the antechamber of the Punishing Room, writes on the table in front of him: "Write 20 times. I will stop fucking 10 cent teachers and this five cent class. Fuck you. Ho! Ho! Yes Baby." Alain's message can be read in a number of ways. The most obvious way is the one of the school. A child has broken several rules in one fell swoop and must be punished: he has written on school property (punishable); he has used an obscenity (punishable); he has committed an especially defiant and disrespectful act because he is already in the Punishing Room and therefore knows his message is likely to be read (punishable). Alain is sent home both as a signal to him and to the other witnesses as well as to the students and adults who will hear it through the school grapevine that he cannot get away with such flagrant misbehavior.

An alternative reading looks at the content of the message itself and the form that Alain's anger takes at being sent to the Punishing Room. Alain's anger is being vented against his teacher and the school itself, expressing his rejection, his disidentification with school that he devalues as monetarily virtually worthless. His message expresses his anger through an assertion of sexual power—to fuck or

not to fuck—one sure way that a male can conjure up the fantasmatic as well as the physical specter of domination over a female of any age. His assertion of this power mocks the authority of the teacher to give him orders to write lines. His use of "baby" reverses the relations of power, teacher to pupil, adult to child; Alain allies himself through and with power as the school/teacher becomes "female," positioned as a sex object, as powerless, passive, infantilized. He positions himself as powerful through identification with and as the embodiment of male power as he disidentifies with school. At this moment, Alain is not just a child, a young boy, but taking the position of "male" as a strategic resource for enacting power, for being powerful. At the same time, this positioning draws the admiring, titillated attention of his peers.

These moments of sex trouble exemplify some of the aspects of the performance of sex/gender difference that is naturalized through what is deemed punishable as well as punishment practices. Judging from the discipline records, girls do not commit sexual violations. It is as if by their very nature they are incapable. To be female is to be powerless, victimizable, chased down the hallway, an object to be acted upon with force, whose hand can be seized and placed between male legs. To be female is also to be sexually passive, coy, the "chaste" rather than the chaser, in relation to male sexual aggressiveness. In reality, I observed girls who chased boys and who interacted with them physically. Girls, in fact, did "pants" boys, but these acts went unreported by the boys. For them to report and therefore risk appearing to be victimized by a girl publicly would be a humiliating outcome that would only undermine their masculinity. In the production of natural difference, boys' performances work as they confirm that they are active pursuers, highly sexualized actors who must be punished to learn to keep their burgeoning sexuality under control. There is a reward for the behavior even if it may be punished as a violation. In the case of African American boys, sex trouble is treated as egregious conduct.

African American males have historically been constructed as hypersexualized within the national imagination. Compounding this is the process of the adultification of their behavior. Intimations of sexuality on their part, especially when directed toward girls who are bused in—white girls from middle-class families—are dealt with as grave transgressions with serious consequences.

POWER REVERSALS: CLASS ACTS

Performance is a routine part of classroom work. Students are called upon to perform in classes by teachers to show off their prowess or demonstrate their ineptitude or lack of preparation. They are required to read passages aloud, for example, before a highly critical audience of their peers. This display is teacher initiated and reflects the official curricula; they are command performances with well-scripted roles, predictable in the outcome of who has and gets respect, who is in control, who succeeds, who fails.

Another kind of performance is the spontaneous outbreaks initiated by the pupils generally defined under the category of "disruption" by the school. These encompass a variety of actions that punctuate and disrupt the order of the day. During the school year about two-thirds of these violations were initiated by boys and a third by girls. Here are some examples from the discipline files of girls being "disruptive":

- Disruptive in class—laughing, provoking others to join her. Purposely writing wrong answers, being very sassy, demanding everyone's attention.
- Constantly talking; interrupting; crumpling paper after paper; loud.

Some examples of boys' disruption:

- Constant noise, indian whoops, face hiccups, rapping.
- Chanting during quiet time—didn't clean up during art [punishment: detention].
- Joking, shouting out, uncooperative, disruptive during lesson.

From the perspective of kids, what the school characterizes as "disruption" on the referral slips is often a form of performance of the self: comedy, drama, melodrama become moments for self-expression and display. Disruption adds some lively spice to the school day; it injects laughter, drama, excitement, a delicious unpredictability to the classroom routine through spontaneous, improvisational outbursts that add flavor to the bland events.

In spite of its improvisational appearance, most performance is highly ritualized with its own script, timing, and roles. Teachers as well as students engage in the ritual and play their parts. Some kids are regular star performers. Other kids are audience. However, when a substitute is in charge of the class and the risk of being marked as a troublemaker is minimal, even the most timid kids "act up." These rituals circulate important extracurricular knowledge about relations of power.

These dramatic moments are sites for the presentation of a potent masculine presence in the classroom. The Good Bad Boy of our expectations engages power, takes risks, makes the class laugh, and the teacher smile. Performances mark boundaries of "essential difference"—risk taking, brinkmanship. The open and public defiance of the teacher in order to get a laugh, make things happen, take center stage, be admired, is a resource for doing masculinity.

These acts are especially meaningful for those children who have already been marginalized as outside of the community of "good," hard-working students. For the boys already labeled as troublemakers, taking control of the spotlight and turning it on oneself so that one can shine, highlights, for a change, one's strengths and talents. Already caught in the limelight, these kids put on a stirring performance.

Reggie, one of the Troublemakers, prides himself on being witty and sharp, a talented performer. He aspires to two careers: one is becoming a Supreme Court justice, the other an actor. He had recently played the role of Caliban in the school production of *The Tempest* that he described excitedly to me:

> I always try to get the main characters in the story 'cause I might turn out to be an actor because I'm really good at acting and I've already did some acting. Shakespeare! See I got a good part. I was Caliban. I had to wear the black suit. Black pants and top. Caliban was a beast! In the little picture that we saw, he looks like the . . . the . . . [searching for image] the beast of Notre Dame. The one that rings the bells like *fing! fing! fing!*

Here is one official school activity where Reggie gets to show off something that he is "good at." He is also proud to point out that this is not just a role in any play, but one in a play by Shakespeare. Here his own reward, which is not just doing something that he is good at, but doing it publicly so that he can receive the attention and respect of adults and peers, coincides with the school's educational agenda of creating an interest in Shakespeare among children.

Reggie also plays for an audience in the classroom, where he gets in trouble for disruption. He describes one of the moments for me embellished with a comic imitation of the teacher's female voice and his own swaggering demeanor as he tells the story:

> The teacher says [he mimics a high-pitched fussy voice], "You not the teacher of this class." And then I say [adopts a sprightly cheeky tone], "Oh, yes I am." Then she say, "No, you're not, and if you got a problem, you can just leave." I say, "Okay" and leave.

This performance, like others I witnessed, are strategies for positioning oneself in the center of the room in a face-off with the teacher, the most powerful person up to that moment. Fundamental to the performance is engagement with power; authority is teased, challenged, even occasionally toppled from its secure heights for brief moments. Children-generated theatrics allow the teasing challenge of adult power that can expose its chinks and weaknesses. The staged moments heighten tension, test limits, vent emotions, perform acts of courage. For Reggie to have capitulated to the teacher's ultimatum would have been to lose what he perceives as the edge in the struggle. In addition, he has won his escape from the classroom.

Horace describes his challenge to the teacher's authority in a summer school math class:

> Just before the end of the period he wrote some of our names on the board and said, "Whoever taught these students when they were young must have been dumb." So I said, "Oh, I didn't remember that was you teaching me in the first grade." Everyone in the room cracked up. I was laughing so hard, I was on the floor. He sent me to the office.

Horace is engaging the teacher in a verbal exchange with a comeback to an insult rather than just passively taking it. In this riposte, Horace not only makes his peers laugh at the teacher, but he also defuses the insult through a quick reversal. The audience in the room, raised on TV sitcom repartee and canned laughter, is hard to impress, so the wisecrack, the rejoinder, must be swift and sharp. Not everyone can get a laugh at the teachers' expense, and to be topped by the teacher would be humiliating, success brings acknowledgment, confirmation, applause from one's peers. For Horace, this is a success story, a moment of gratification in a day that brings few his way.

The tone of the engagement with power and the identity of the actor is highly consequential in terms of whether a performance is overlooked by the teacher or becomes the object of punishment. In a study of a Texas high school, Foley documents similar speech performances.[4] He describes how both teacher and students collaborate to devise classroom rituals and "games" to help pass the time given the context of routinized, alienating classroom work. He observes that upper-middle-class male Anglo students derail boring lessons by manipulating teachers through subtle "making out" games without getting in trouble. In contrast, low-income male Hispanic students, who were more likely to challenge teachers openly in these games, were punished. Foley concluded that one of the important lessons learned by all participants in these ritual games was that the subtle manipulation of authority was a much more effective way of getting your way than openly confronting power.

Style becomes a decisive factor in who gets in trouble. I am reminded of comments made by one of the student specialists at Rosa Parks who explained the high rate of black kids getting in trouble by remarking on their different style of rule breaking: "The white kids are sneaky, black kids are more open."

So why are the black kids "more open" in their confrontations with power? Why not be really "smart" and adopt a style of masculinity that allows them to engage in these rituals that spice the school day and help pass time, but carry less risk of trouble because it is within certain mutually understood limits?

These rituals are not merely a way to pass time, but are also a site for constituting a gendered racial subjectivity. For African American boys, the performance of masculinity invokes cultural conventions of speech performance that draw on a black repertoire. Verbal performance is an important medium for black males to establish a reputation, make a name for yourself, and achieve status.[5] Smitherman points out that black talk in general is

> a functional dynamic that is simultaneously a mechanism for learning about life and the world and a vehicle for achieving group recognition. Even in what appears to be only casual conversation, whoever speaks is highly conscious of the fact that his personality is on exhibit and his status at stake.[6]

Oral performance has a special significance in black culture for the expression of masculinity. Harper points out that verbal performance functions as an identifying marker for masculinity only when it is delivered in the vernacular and that "a too-evident facility in white idiom can quickly identify one as a white-identified uncle Tom who must also be therefore weak, effeminate, and probably a fag."[7] Though the speech performances that I witnessed were not always delivered in the strict vernacular, the nonverbal, bodily component accompanying it was always delivered in a manner that was the flashy, boldly flamboyant popular style essential to a good performance. The body language and spoken idiom openly engage power in a provocative competitive way. To be indirect, "sly," would not be performing masculinity.

This nonstandard mode of self-representation epitomizes the very form the school seeks to exclude and eradicate. It is a masculine enactment of defiance played in a black key that is bound for punishment. Moreover, the process of adultification translates the encounter from a simple verbal clash with an impertinent child into one interpreted as an intimidating threat.

Though few white girls in the school were referred to the office for disruptive behavior, a significant number of African American girls staged performances, talked back to teachers, challenged authority, and were punished. But there was a difference with the cultural framing of their enactments and those of the boys. The bottom line of Horace's story was that "everyone in the room cracked up." He engaged authority through a self-produced public spectacle with an eye for an audience that is at home with the cultural icon of the Good Bad Boy as well as the "real black man." Boys expect to get attention. Girls vie for attention too, but it is perceived as illegitimate behavior. As the teacher described it in the referral form, the girl is "demanding attention." The prevailing cultural framework denies her the rights for dramatic public display.

Male and female classroom performance is different in another respect. Girls are not rewarded with the same kind of applause or recognition by peers or by teachers. Their performance is sidelined; it is not given center stage. Teachers are more likely to "turn a blind eye" to such a display rather than call attention to it, for girls are seen as individuals who operate in cliques at most and are unlikely to foment insurrection in the room. Neither the moral nor the pragmatic principle prods teachers to take action. The behavior is not taken seriously; it is rated as "sassy" rather than symptomatic of a more dangerous disorder. In some classrooms, in fact, risk taking and "feistiness" on the part of girls is subtly encouraged given the prevailing belief that what they need is to become more visible, more assertive in the classroom. The notion is that signs of self-assertion on their part should be encouraged rather than squelched.

Disruptive acts have a complex, multifaceted set of meanings for the male Troublemakers themselves. Performance as an expression of black masculinity is a production of a powerful subjectivity to be reckoned with, to be applauded; respect and ovation are in a context where none is forthcoming. The boys' anger and frustration as well as fear motivate the challenge to authority. Troublemakers act and speak out as stigmatized outsiders.

RITUAL PERFORMANCES OF MASCULINITY: FIGHTING

Each year a substantial number of kids at Rosa Parks get into trouble for fighting. It is the most frequent offense for which they are referred to the Punishing Room. Significantly, the vast majority of the offenders are African American males.[8]

The school has an official position on fighting; it is the wrong way to handle any situation, at any time, no matter what. Schools have good reasons for banning fights: kids can get hurt and when fights happen they sully the atmosphere of order, making the school seem like a place of danger, of violence.

The prescribed routine for schoolchildren to handle situations that might turn into a fight is to tell an adult who is then supposed to take care of the problem. This routine ignores the unofficial masculine code that if someone hits you, you should solve the problem yourself rather than showing weakness and calling an adult to intervene. However, it is expected that girls with a problem will seek out an adult for assistance. Girls are assumed to be physically weaker, less aggressive, more vulnerable, more needy of self-protection; they must attach themselves to adult (or male) power to survive. This normative gender distinction, in how to handle both problems of a sexual nature and physical aggression, operates as a "proof" of a physical and dispositional gender nature rather than behavior produced through discourses and practices that constitute sex difference.

Referrals of males to the Punishing Room, therefore, are cases where the unofficial masculine code for problem resolution has prevailed. Telling an adult is anathema to these youth. According to their own codes, the act of "telling" is dangerous for a number of reasons. The most practical of these sets it as a statement to the "whole world" that you are unable to deal with a situation on your own—to take care of yourself—an admission that can have disastrous ramifications when adult authority is absent. This is evident from the stance of a Troublemaker who questions the practical application of the official code by invoking knowledge of the

proper male response when one is "attacked" that is shared with the male student specialist charged with enforcing the regulation: "I said, 'Mr. B, if somebody came up and hit you, what would you do?' 'Well,' he says, 'We're not talking about me right now, see.' That's the kind of attitude they have. It's all like on you."

Another reason mentioned by boys for not relying on a teacher to take care of a fight situation is that adults are not seen as having any real power to effectively change the relations among kids:

> If someone keep messing with you, like if someone just keep on and you tell them to leave you alone, then you tell the teacher. The teacher can't do anything about it because, see, she can't hit you or nothing. Only thing she can do is tell them to stop. But then he keep on doing it. You have no choice but to hit 'em. You already told him once to stop.

This belief extends to a distrust of authority figures by these young offenders. The assumption that all the children see authority figures such as teachers, police, and psychologists as acting on their behalf and trust they will act fairly may be true of middle- and upper-class children brought up to expect protection from authority figures in society. This is not the case with many of the children at the school. Their mistrust of authority is rooted in the historical and locally grounded knowledge of power relations that come from living in a largely black and impoverished neighborhood.

Fighting becomes, therefore, a powerful spectacle through which to explore trouble as a site for the construction of manhood. The practice takes place along a continuum that ranges from play—spontaneous outbreaks of pummeling and wrestling in fun, ritualistic play that shows off "cool" moves seen on video games, on TV, or in movies—to serious, angry socking, punching, fistfighting. A description of some of these activities and an analysis of what they mean provides the opportunity for us to delve under the surface of the ritualized, discrete acts that make up a socially recognizable fight even into the psychic, emotional, sensuous aspects of gender performativity. The circular, interactive flow between

fantasmatic images, internal psychological processes, and physical acts suggest the dynamics of attachment of masculine identification.

Fighting is one of the social practices that
add tension, drama, and spice to the routine of
the school day. Pushing, grabbing, shoving, kicking, karate chopping, wrestling, fistfighting engage
the body and the mind. Fighting is about play and
games, about anger and pain, about hurt feelings,
about "messing around." To the spectator, a fight
can look like serious combat, yet when the combatants are separated by an adult, they claim, "We
were only playing." In fact, a single fight event can
move along the continuum from play to serious
blows in a matter of seconds. As one of the boys explained, "You get hurt and you lose your temper."

Fighting is typically treated as synonymous
with "aggression" or "violence," terms that already
encode the moral, definitional frame that obscures
the contradictory ways that the practice, in all its
manifestations, is used in our society. We, as good
citizens, can distance ourselves from aggressive and
violent behavior. "Violence" as discourse constructs
"fighting" as pathological, symptomatic of asocial,
dangerous tendencies, even though the practice of
"fighting" and the discourses that constitute this
practice as "normal," are in fact taken for granted as
ritualized resources for "doing" masculinity in the
contemporary United States.

The word *fighting* encompasses the "normal"
as well as the pathological. It allows the range of
meanings that the children, specifically the boys
whom I interviewed and observed, as well as some
of the girls, bring to the practice. One experience
that it is open to is the sensuous, highly charged
embodied experience before, during, and after fighting; the elating experience of "losing oneself" that I
heard described in fight stories.

WAR STORIES

I began thinking about fights soon after I started interviews with the Troublemakers and heard "fight
stories." Unlike the impoverished and reluctantly
told accounts of the school day, these stories were
vivid, elaborate descriptions of bodies, mental states,
and turbulent emotional feelings. They were stirring,
memorable moments in the tedious school routine.

Horace described a fight with an older boy who
had kept picking on him. He told me about the incident as he was explaining how he had broken a fin-
ger one day when we were trading "broken bones"
stories.

> When I broke this finger right here it really hurt.
> I hit somebody in the face. It was Charles. I hit
> him in the face. You know the cafeteria and how
> you walk down to go to the cafeteria. Right there.
> That's where it happened. Charles picked me up
> and put me on the wall, slapped me on the wall,
> and dropped me. It hurt. It hurt bad. I got mad
> because he used to be messing with me for a long
> time so I just swung as hard as I could, closed my
> eyes, and just *pow*, hit him in the face. But I did
> like a roundhouse swing instead of doing it straight
> and it got the index finger of my right hand. So it
> was right there, started right here, and all around
> this part [he is showing me the back of his hand]
> it hurt. It was swollen. Oooh! It was like this! But
> Charles, he got hurt too. The next day I came to
> school I had a cast on my finger and he had a ban-
> dage on his ear. It was kinda funny, we just looked
> at each other and smiled.

The thing that most surprised and intrigued
me about Horace's story was that he specifically recalled seeing Charles the next day and that they had
looked at each other and smiled. Was this a glance
of recognition, of humor, of recollection of something pleasing, of all those things? The memory of
the exchanged smile derailed my initial assumption
that fighting was purely instrumental. This original
formulation said that boys fight because they have
to fight in order to protect themselves from getting
beaten up on the playground. Fighting from this
instrumental perspective is a purely survival practice. Boys do fight to stave off the need to fight in
the future, to stop the harassment from other boys
on the playground and in the streets. However,
this explains only a small group of boys who live
in certain environments; it relegates fighting to the
realm of the poor, the deviant, the delinquent, the

pathological. This position fails to address these physical clashes as the central normative practice in the preparation of bodies, of mental stances, of self-reference for manhood and as the most effective form of conflict resolution in the realm of popular culture and international relations.

I listened closely to the stories to try to make sense of behavior that was so outside of my own experience, yet so familiar a part of the landscape of physical fear and vulnerability that I as a female walked around with every day. I asked school adults about their own memories of school and fighting. I was not surprised to find that few women seemed to recall physical fights at school, though they had many stories of boys who teased them or girlfriends whom they were always "fighting" with. This resonated with my own experience. I was struck, however, by the fact that all of the men whom I talked to had had to position themselves in some way with regard to fighting. I was also struck that several of these men framed the memory of fighting in their past as a significant learning experience.

Male adults in school recall fighting themselves, but in the context both of school rules and of hindsight argue that they now know better. One of the student specialists admitted that he used to fight a lot. I found it significant that he saw "fighting" as the way he "learned":

> I used to fight a lot. [Pause.] I used to fight a lot and I used to be real stubborn and silent. I wouldn't say anything to anybody. It would cause me a lot of problems, but that's just the way I learned.

The after-school martial arts instructor also admitted to fighting a lot when he was younger:

> There were so many that I had as a kid that it's hard to remember all of them and how they worked out. But yes, I did have a lot of arguments and fights. A lot of times I would lose my temper, which is what kids normally do, they lose their temper, and before they have a chance to work things out they begin punching and kicking each other. Right? Well I did a lot of those things so I know from experience those are not the best thing to do.

As I explored the meaning of fighting I began to wonder how I, as female, had come to be shaped so fighting was not a part of my own corporeal or mental repertoire. A conversation with my brother reminded me of a long forgotten self that could fight, physically, ruthlessly, inflict hurt, cause tears. "We were always fighting," he recalled "You used to beat me up." Memories of these encounters came back. I am standing with a tuft of my brother's hair in my hand, furious tears in my eyes. Full of hate for him. Kicking, scratching, socking, feeling no pain. Where had this physical power gone? I became "ladylike," repressing my anger, limiting my physical contact to shows of affection, fearful. I wondered about the meaning of being female in a society in which to be female is to be always conscious of men's physical power and to consciously chart one's everyday routines to avoid becoming a victim of this power, but to never learn the bodily and mental pleasure of fighting back.

BODILY PREPARATIONS: PAIN AND PLEASURE

Fighting is first and foremost a bodily practice. I think about fighting and physical closeness as I stand observing the playground at recess noticing a group of three boys, bodies entangled, arms and legs flailing. In another area, two boys are standing locked closely in a wrestling embrace. Children seem to gravitate toward physical contact with each other. For boys, a close, enraptured body contact is only legitimate when they are positioned as in a fight. It is shocking that this bodily closeness between boys would be frowned on, discouraged if it were read as affection. Even boys who never get in trouble for "fighting" can be seen engaging each other through the posturing and miming, the grappling of playfight encounters.

This play can lead to "real" fights. The thin line between play and anger is crossed as bodies become vulnerable, hurt, and tempers are lost. One of the white boys in the school who was in trouble for fighting describes the progression this way:

> Well we were messing with each other and when it went too far, he started hitting me and then I hit him back and then it just got into a fight. It was sorta like a game between me, him and Thomas. How I would get on Thomas's back an—he's a big guy—and Stephen would try to hit me and I would wanta hit him back. So when Thomas left it sorta continued and I forgot which one of us wanted to stop—but one of us wanted to stop and the other one wouldn't.

Fighting is about testing and proving your bodily power over another person, both to yourself and to others through the ability to "hurt" someone as well as to experience "hurt."

> HORACE: You know Claude. He's a bad boy in the school. When I was in the fifth grade, he was in the fifth grade. I intercepted his pass and he threw the ball at my head and then I said, "You're mad," and I twisted the ball on the floor. I said, "Watch this," and y'know spiraled it on the floor, and he kicked it and it hit my leg, and I said, "Claude, if you hit me one more time with the ball or anything I'm going to hurt you." He said. "What if you do?" I said, "Okay, you expect me not to do anything, right?" He said, "Nope." Then I just *pow, pow, pow*, and I got him on the floor and then I got him on his back. I wanted to hurt him badly but I couldn't.
>
> ANN: Why couldn't you?
>
> HORACE: I didn't want to get in trouble. And if I did really hurt him it wouldn't prove anything anyway. But it did. It proved that I could hurt him and he didn't mess with me anymore.

Pain is an integral part of fighting. Sometimes it is the reason for lashing out in anger. This description by Wendell also captures the loss of self-control experienced at the moment of the fight:

> Sometimes it starts by capping or by somebody slams you down or somebody throws a bullet at you. You know what a bullet is, don't you? [He chuckles delightedly because I think of a bullet from a gun.] The bullet I am talking about is a football! You throw it with all your might and it hits somebody. It just very fast and they call it bullets. You off-guard and they throw it at your head, and bullets they throw with all their might so it hurts. Then that sorta gets you all pissed off. Then what happens is, you kinda like, "Why you threw it?" "'Cause I wanted to. Like, so?" "So you not going to do that to me." Then: "So you going to do something about it?" Real smart. "Yeah!" And then you tap the person on the shoulder and your mind goes black and then *shweeeee* [a noise and hand signal that demonstrates the evaporation of thought] you go at it. And you don't stop until the teacher comes and stops it.

Fighting is a mechanism for preparing masculinized bodies through the playful exercise of bodily moves and postures and the routinized rehearsal of sequences and chains of stances of readiness, attack, and defense. Here it is crucial to emphasize that while many boys in the school never ever engage in an actual physical fight with another boy or girl during school hours, the majority engage in some form of body enactments of fantasized "fight" scenarios. They have observed boys and men on TV, in the movies, in video games, on the street, in the playground adopting these stances.

These drills simultaneously prepare and cultivate the mental states in which corporeal styles are grounded. So for instance, boys are initiated into the protocol of enduring physical pain and mental anguish—"like a man"—through early and small infusions of the toxic substance itself in play fights. The practice of fighting is the site for a hot-wiring together of physical pain and pleasure, as components of masculinity as play and bodily hurt inevitably coincide.

Consequently, it also engages powerful emotions. Lindsey described the feelings he experienced prior to getting into a fight:

> Sometimes it's play. And sometimes it's real. But that's only sometimes, because they can just suddenly make you angry and then, it's like they take control of your mind. Like they manipulate your mind if you angry. Little by little you just lose it and you get in a temper.

One of the white boys in the school who had gotten in trouble for fighting described his thoughts and feelings preceding a fight and the moment of "just going black" in a loss of self:

> My mind would probably be going through how I would do this. If I would stop it now or if I would follow through with it. But once the fight actually happens I sort of go black and just fight 'em.

Fighting is a practice, like sports, that is so symbolically "masculine" that expressions of emotion or behavior that might call one's manhood into question are allowed without danger of jeopardizing one's manliness. Even crying is a permissible expression of "masculinity" under these circumstances. One of the boys who told me he never cried, corrected himself:

> But if I be mad, I cry. Like if I get into a fight or something like that, I cry because I lose my temper and get so mad. But sometimes, I play football and if I cry that mean I'm ready to tumble—throw the ball to me because I'm going.

Fighting in school is a space in which boys can feel free to do emotional work.[9] In a social practice that is so incontrovertibly coded as masculine, behaviors marked as feminine, such as crying, can be called upon as powerful wellsprings for action.

One of the questions that I asked all the boys about fighting came out of my own ignorance. My query was posed in terms of identity work around the winning and losing of fights. Did you ever win a fight? Did you ever lose a fight? How did you feel when you lost? How did you feel when you won? I found the answers slippery, unexpected, contradictory. I had anticipated that winning would be described in proud and boastful ways, as success stories. But there seemed to be a surprising reluctance to embellish victory. I learned that I was missing the point by posing the question the way I had in terms of winning and losing. Trey enlightened me when he explained that what was at stake was not winning or losing per se but in learning about the self:

> I won a lot of fights. You know you won when they start crying and stuff or when they stop and leave. I lost fights. Then you feel a little okay.

At least you lost. I mean like you ain't goin' win every fight. At least you fought back instead of just standing there and letting them hit you.

Another boy expressed the function that fighting played in establishing yourself as being a particular kind of respectable person:

> It's probably like dumb, but if somebody wants to fight me, I mean, I don't care even if I know I can't beat 'em. I won't stop if they don't stop. I mean I'm not scared to fight anybody. I'm not a coward. I don't let anybody punk me around. If you let people punk you around, other peoples want to punk you around.

Proving yourself to others is like a game, a kind of competition:

> Me and Leslie used to fight because we used to be the biggest boys, but now we don't care anymore. We used to get friends and try and fight each other. I fought him at Baldwin school all the time. We stopped about the fifth grade [the previous year]. Just got tired, I guess.

Standing and proving yourself today can be insurance against future harassment in the yard as you make a name for yourself through readiness to fight: "Like if somebody put their hands on you, then you have to, you have to hit them back. Because otherwise you going be beat up on for the rest of your life."

Eddie, who has avoided fights because he does not want to get in trouble, is now seen as a target for anyone to beat up, according to one of his friends, who characterized Eddie's predicament this way: "He can't fight. *He can't fight.* Every girl, every boy in the whole school fixing to beat him up. Badly. They could beat him up badly."

Eddie explains his own perspective on how he has come to actually lose a reputation.

> Yeah, I won a fight in preschool. Like somebody this tall [his gesture indicates a very tall someone] I had to go like this [reaches up to demonstrate] so I could hit him. He was older than me. He was the preschool bully. Till I mess him up.

But Eddie's parents came down hard on him for getting in trouble for fighting in elementary school:

> Yeah, I lost fights. See when I got to Rosa Parks my parents told me not to fight unless I had to—so I lost my face. 'Cause I was so used to telling them to stop, don't fight, don't fight.

In constructing the self through fight stories, it is not admirable to represent oneself as the aggressor or initiator in a fight. All the boys whom I talked to about fighting presented themselves as responding to a physical attack that had to be answered in a decisive way. No one presented himself as a "bully," though I knew that Horace had that reputation. Yet he told me that "only fights I been in is if they hit me first."

There are, however, times when it is legitimate to be the initiator. When verbal provocation is sufficient. This is when "family" has been insulted. Talking about "your momma" is tantamount to throwing down the gauntlet:

> Mostly I get in fights if somebody talk about my grandfather because he's dead. And I loved my grandfather more than I love anybody and then he died. [Tears are in Jabari's eyes as we talk.] That's why I try to tell people before they get ready to say anything, I'm like, "Don't say anything about my grandfather, 'cause if you say something about him, I'm goin' hit you."

The boys talked about how they learned to fight. How one learns to fight and what one learns about the meaning of fighting—why fight, to fight or not to fight—involved both racial identity and class positioning. Ricky and Duane, two of the Schoolboys, have been enrolled by their parents in martial arts classes. Fighting remains a necessary accoutrement of masculinity that is "schooled," not a "natural" acquisition of doing. As such, it becomes a marker of higher class position. Fighting takes place in an institutionalized arena rather than spontaneously in just any setting. The mind seems to control the body here, rather than vice versa.

Horace, on the other hand, like the majority of boys with whom I talked, explained that he had learned to fight through observation and practice:

> I watched people. Like when I was younger, like I used to look up to people. I still do. I look up to people and they knew how to fight so I just watched them. I just like saw people fight on TV, you know. Boxing and stuff.

Another boy told me that he thought kids learned to fight "probably from theirselves. Like their mom probably say, if somebody hit you, hit them back." This advice about proper behavior is grounded in the socialization practices that are brought into school as ways of responding to confrontations.

GENDER PRACTICE AND IDENTIFICATION

Fighting acts reproduce notions of essentially different gendered natures and the forms in which this "difference" is grounded. Though class makes some difference in when, how, and under what conditions it takes place, fighting is the hegemonic representation of masculinity. Inscribed in the male body—whether individual males fight or not, abjure fighting or not—is the potential for this unleashing of physical power. By the same token, fighting for girls is considered an aberration, something to be explained.

Girls do get in fights at school. Boys asserted that girls can fight, even that "sometimes they get in fights easier. Because they got more attitude." Indeed, girls do make a name for themselves this way. One of the girls at Rosa Parks was in trouble several times during the school year for fighting. Most of her scrapes were with the boys who liked to tease her because she was very tall for her age. This, however, was not assumed to be reflective of her "femaleness" but of her individuality. Mr. Sobers, for example, when I asked him about her, made a point of this singularity rather than explaining her in terms of race, class, or gender: "Oh, Stephanie is just Stephanie."

NOTES

1. Here are a very few examples of the enormous body of work concerned with the production of gender differences in the last two decades. At the ideological and discursive level see Mullings, "Images, Ideology"; Teresa de Lauretis, *Technologies of Gender: Essays on Theory, Film, and Fiction* (Bloomington: Indiana University Press, 1987); and Michele Barrett, *Women's Oppression Today: Problems in Marxist Feminist Analysis* (London: New Left Books, 1980). For processes of social structure and institutional arrangements see R. W. Connell et al., *Making the Difference: Schools, Families, and Social Division* (London: George Allen and Unwin, 1982); Mariarosa Dalla Costa, "Women and the Subversion of the Community," in *The Power of Women and the Subversion of Community*, ed. Mariarosa Dalla Costa and Selma James (Bristol, England: Falling Wall Press, 1973); Catharine A. MacKinnon, *Feminism Unmodified: Discourses on Life and Law* (Cambridge: Harvard University Press, 1987). For micropolitics see Arlie Russell Hochschild, *The Second Shift: Working Parents and the Revolution at Home* (New York: Viking, 1989); Donna Eder, Catherine Colleen Evans, and Stephen Parker, *School Talk: Gender and Adolescent Culture* (New Brunswick, N.J.: Rutgers University Press, 1995); and Candace West and Don H. Zimmerman, "Doing Gender," *Gender & Society* 1, no. 2 (1987).

2. Judith Butler, "Performative Acts and Gender Constitution: An Essay in Phenomenology and Feminist Theory," *Theatre Journal* 40, no. 4 (1988).

3. Judith Butler, *Bodies That Matter: On the Discursive Limits of "Sex"* (New York: Routledge, 1993), 95.

4. Douglas E. Foley, *Learning Capitalist Culture: Deep in the Heart of Tejas* (Philadelphia: University of Pennsylvania, 1990).

5. Geneva Smitherman, *Talkin and Testifyin: Language of Black America* (Detroit: Wayne State University Press, 1977); Lawrence Levine, *Black Culture and Black Consciousness: Afro-American Folk Thought from Slavery to Freedom* (New York: Oxford University Press, 1977); Philip Brian Harper, *Are We Not Men? Masculine Anxiety and the Problem of African-American Identity* (New York: Oxford University Press, 1996); Keith Gilyard, *Voices of the Self: A Study of Language Competence* (Detroit: Wayne State University Press, 1991).

6. Smitherman, *Talkin and Testifyin*, 80.

7. Harper, *Are We Not Men?* 11.

8. One-quarter of the 1,252 referrals to the Punishing Room were for fighting; four-fifths of the incidents involved boys, nine out of ten of whom were African Americans. All except three of the girls who were in fights were black.

9. Arlie Russell Hochschild, *The Managed Heart: Commercialization of Human Feeling* (Berkeley and Los Angeles: University of California Press, 1983). Hochschild explores the feeling rules that guide and govern our own emotional displays as well as how we interpret the emotional expression of others.

A WAR AGAINST BOYS?

Michael Kimmel

Doug Anglin isn't likely to flash across the radar screen at an Ivy League admissions office. A seventeen-year-old senior at Milton High School, a suburb outside Boston, Anglin has a B-minus average and plays soccer and baseball. But he's done something that millions of other teenagers haven't: he's sued his school district for sex discrimination.

Anglin's lawsuit, brought with the aid of his father, a Boston lawyer, claims that schools routinely discriminate against males. "From the elementary level, they establish a philosophy that if you sit down, follow orders, and listen to what they say, you'll do well and get good grades," he told a journalist. "Men naturally rebel against this." He may have a point: overworked teachers might well look more kindly on classroom docility and decorum. But his proposed remedies—such as raising boys' grades retroactively—are laughable.

And though it's tempting to parse the statements of a mediocre high school senior—what's so "natural" about rebelling against blindly following orders, a military tactician might ask—Anglin's apparent admissions angle is but the latest skirmish of a much bigger battle in the culture wars. The current salvos concern boys. The "trouble with boys" has become a staple on talk-radio, the cover story in *Newsweek*, and the subject of dozens of columns in newspapers and magazines. And when the First Lady offers a helping hand to boys, you know something political is in the works. "Rescuing" boys actually translates into bashing feminism.

There is no doubt that boys are not faring well in school. From elementary schools to high schools they have lower grades, lower class rank, and fewer honors than girls. They're 50 percent more likely to repeat a grade in elementary school, one-third more likely to drop out of high school, and about six times more likely to be diagnosed with attention deficit and hyperactivity disorder (ADHD).

College statistics are similar—if the boys get there at all. Women now constitute the majority of students on college campuses, having passed men in 1982, so that in eight years women will earn 58 percent of bachelor's degrees in U.S. colleges. One expert, Tom Mortensen, warns that if current trends continue, "the graduation line in 2068 will be all females." Mortensen may be a competent higher education policy analyst but he's a lousy statistician. His dire prediction is analogous to predicting forty years ago that, if the enrollment of black students at Ol' Miss was one in 1964, and, say, two hundred in 1968 and one thousand in 1976, then "if present trends continue" there would be no white students on campus by 1982. Doomsayers lament that women now outnumber men in the social and behavioral sciences by about three to one, and that they've invaded such traditionally male bastions as engineering (where they now make up 20 percent) and biology and business (virtually par).

These three issues—declining numbers, declining achievement, and increasingly problematic behavior—form the empirical basis of the current debate. But its political origins are significantly older and ominously more familiar. Peeking underneath the empirical façade helps explain much of the current lineup.

WHY NOW?

If boys are doing worse, whose fault is it? To many of the current critics, it's women's fault, either as feminists, as mothers, or as both. Feminists, we read, have been so successful that the earlier "chilly classroom climate" has now become overheated to the detriment of boys. Feminist-inspired programs have enabled a whole generation of girls to enter the sciences, medicine, law, and the professions; to continue their education; to imagine careers outside the home. But in so doing, these same feminists have pathologized boyhood. Elementary schools are, we read, "anti-boy"—emphasizing reading and restricting the movements of young boys. They "feminize" boys, forcing active, healthy, and naturally exuberant boys to conform to a regime of obedience, "pathologizing what is simply normal for boys," as one psychologist puts it. Schools are an "inhospitable" environment for boys, writes Christina Hoff Sommers, where their natural propensities for rough-and-tumble play, competition, aggression, and rambunctious violence are cast as social problems in the making. Michael Gurian argues in *The Wonder of Boys*, that, with testosterone surging through their little limbs, we demand that they sit still, raise their hands, and take naps. We're giving them the message, he says, that "boyhood is defective." By the time they get to college, they've been steeped in anti-male propaganda. "Why would any self-respecting boy want to attend one of America's increasingly feminized universities?" asks George Gilder in *National Review*. The American university is now a "fluffy pink playpen of feminist studies and agitprop 'herstory,' taught amid a green goo of eco-motherism . . ."

Such claims sound tinnily familiar. At the turn of the last century, cultural critics were concerned that the rise of white-collar businesses meant increasing indolence for men, whose sons were being feminized by mothers and female teachers. Then, as now, the solutions were to find arenas in which boys could simply be boys, and where men could be men as well. So fraternal lodges offered men a homo-social sanctuary, and dude ranches and sports provided a place where these sedentary men

could experience what Theodore Roosevelt called the strenuous life. Boys could troop off with the Boy Scouts, designed as a fin-de-siècle "boys' liberation movement." Modern society was turning hardy, robust boys, as Boy Scouts' founder Ernest Thompson Seton put it, into "a lot of flat chested cigarette smokers with shaky nerves and doubtful vitality." Today, women teachers are once again to blame for boys' feminization. "It's the teacher's job to create a classroom environment that accommodates both male and female energy, not just mainly female energy," explains Gurian.

What's wrong with this picture? Well, for one thing, it creates a false opposition between girls and boys, assuming that educational reforms undertaken to enable girls to perform better hinder boys' educational development. But these reforms—new classroom arrangements, teacher training, increased attentiveness to individual learning styles—actually enable larger numbers of boys to get a better education. Though the current boy advocates claim that schools used to be more "boy friendly" before all these "feminist" reforms, they obviously didn't go to school in those halcyon days, the 1950s, say, when the classroom was far more regimented, corporal punishment common, and teachers far more authoritarian; they even gave grades for "deportment." Rambunctious boys were simply not tolerated; they dropped out.

Gender stereotyping hurts both boys and girls. If there is a zero-sum game, it's not because of some putative feminization of the classroom. The net effect of the No Child Left Behind Act has been zero-sum competition, as school districts scramble to stretch inadequate funding, leaving them little choice but to cut noncurricular programs so as to ensure that curricular mandates are followed. This disadvantages "rambunctious" boys, because many of these programs are after-school athletics, gym, and recess. And cutting "unnecessary" school counselors and other remedial programs also disadvantages boys, who compose the majority of children in behavioral and remedial educational programs. The problem of inadequate school funding lies not at feminists' door, but in the halls of Congress. This is further compounded by changes in the insurance industry, which often pressure therapists to put children on medication for ADHD rather than pay for expensive therapy.

Another problem is that the frequently cited numbers are misleading. More *people*—that is, males and females—are going to college than ever before. In 1960, 54 percent of boys and 38 percent of girls went directly to college; today the numbers are 64 percent of boys and 70 percent of girls. It is true that the *rate of increase* among girls is higher than the rate of increase among boys, but the numbers are increasing for both.

The gender imbalance does not obtain at the nation's most elite colleges and universities, where percentages for men and women are, and have remained, similar. Of the top colleges and universities in the nation, only Stanford sports a fifty-fifty gender balance. Harvard and Amherst enroll 56 percent men, Princeton and Chicago 54 percent men, Duke and Berkeley 52 percent, and Yale 51 percent. In science and engineering, the gender imbalance still tilts decidedly toward men: Cal Tech is 65 percent male and 35 percent female; MIT is 62 percent male, 38 percent female.

And the imbalance is not uniform across class and race. It remains the case that far more working-class women—of all races—go to college than do working-class men. Part of this is a seemingly rational individual decision: a college-educated woman still earns about the same as a high-school educated man, $35,000 to $31,000. By race, the disparities are more starkly drawn. Among middle-class, white, high school graduates going to college this year, half are male and half are female. But only 37 percent of black college students and 45 percent of Hispanic students are male. The numerical imbalance turns out to be more a problem of race and class than gender. It is what Cynthia Fuchs Epstein calls a "deceptive distinction"—a difference that appears to be about gender, but is actually about something else.

Why don't the critics acknowledge these race and class differences? To many who now propose to "rescue" boys, such differences are incidental because, in their eyes, all boys are the same aggressive, competitive, rambunctious little devils. They operate from a facile and inaccurate essentialist dichotomy between males and females. Boys must be allowed to be boys—so that they grow up to be men.

This facile biologism leads the critics to propose some distasteful remedies to allow these testosterone-juiced boys to express themselves. Gurian, for example, celebrates all masculine rites of passage, "like military boot camp, fraternity hazings, graduation day, and bar mitzvah" as "essential parts of every boy's life." He also suggests reviving corporal punishment, both at home and at school—but only when administered privately with cool indifference and never in the heat of adult anger. He calls it "spanking responsibly," though I suspect school boards and child welfare agencies might have another term for it.

But what boys need turns out to be pretty much what girls need. In their best-selling *Raising Cain*, Michael Thompson and Dan Kindlon describe *boys'* needs: to be loved, get sex, and not be hurt. Parents are counseled to allow boys their emotions; accept a high level of activity; speak their language; and treat them with respect. They are to teach the many ways a boy can be a man, use discipline to guide and build, and model manhood as emotionally attached. Aside from the obvious tautologies, what they advocate is exactly what feminists have been advocating for girls for some time.

BOYS' LIVES AND FATHERLESSNESS

However, those feminist women, many of whom are also involved mothers, are seen not as boys' natural allies in claiming a better education but as their enemies. Fears of "momism"—that peculiar cultural malady that periodically rears its head—have returned. Remember those World War II best sellers, like Philip Wylie's *Generation of Vipers*, David Levy's *Maternal Overprotection*, and Edward Strecker's *Their Mothers' Sons* that laid men's problems at the foot of overdominant mothers, who drained their boys of ambition and hardy manliness and led them straight to the summit of Brokeback Mountain?

Well, they're back. Now the problem with mothers is that they read *The Feminine Mystique* and ran out to pursue careers, which caused a mass exodus of fathers from the lives of their sons. Feminist women not only promoted girls at the expense of boys, but they kicked dad out of the house and left boys wallowing in an anomic genderless soup.

The cause of the boy crisis, we hear, is fatherlessness. Boys lack adequate role models because their fathers are either at work all the time or are divorced with limited custody and visitation privileges. Discussions of boys' problems almost invariably circle back to fathers or, rather the lack of them. But fatherlessness is not Dad's fault. It's Mom's. The debate about boys instantly morphs into a discussion of unwed mothers, single-parent families, babies having babies, and punitive and vindictive ex-wives (and their equally punitive and vindictive lawyers) who prevent men from being more present in their lives of their children. Women left the home in search of work and fulfillment, abandoning their natural role of taming men and rearing children. Feminism declares war against nature. The battle for boys is only the latest front.

This antifeminist political argument is best, and most simply, made by Harvey Mansfield, author of the recent *Manliness*, in a November 3, 1997, op-ed essay in the *Wall Street Journal*. "The protective element of manliness is endangered when women have equal access to jobs outside the home," he writes. "Women who do not consider themselves feminist often seem unaware of what they are doing to manliness when they work to support themselves. They think only that people should be hired and promoted on merit, regardless of sex." When Lionel Tiger argues that "the principal victims of moving toward a merit-based society have been male," one feels a certain resigned sadness. Imagine that: it's feminists who actually believe in meritocracy.

Fathers *would* be present in their sons' lives (in this debate, fathers don't seem to have daughters)— if only women would let them. "Fortunately," writes pro-fatherhood activist Steve Biddulph, "fathers are fighting their way back into family life." Fighting against whom exactly? Feminist women have been pleading with men to come home and share housework and child care—let alone to help raise their sons—for what, 150 years?

As role models, fathers could provide a model of decisiveness, discipline, and emotional control— which would be useful for their naturally aggressive, testosterone-juiced sons at school. But how do these same biologically driven, rambunctious boys magically grow up to be strong, silent, decisive, and controlled fathers?

It's easy—if women do what *they* are biologically programmed to do: stay home and raise boys (but not for too long) and constrain the natural predatory, aggressive, and lustful impulses of their men. In leaving the home and going to work, women abandoned their naturally prescribed role of sexual constraint. Presto: a debate about fatherhood and boyhood becomes a debate about feminism.

The boy crisis would be magically solved if fathers were not exiled from family life. The spate of works about fatherhood that appeared several years ago is now being recycled in the debate about boys. Fathers, by virtue of being men, bring something irreplaceable to the family, something "inherently masculine" notes Wade Horn, assistant secretary in the U.S. Department of Health and Human Services, Administration for Children and Families. (It is Horn who is promoting the backward idea that marriage-based programs will alleviate poverty when all available evidence suggests the opposite relationship, that alleviating poverty would actually lead to an increase in marriages.) That "inherently masculine" influence is a triumph of form over content. David Blankenhorn's catalog of specious correlations, *Fatherless America*, that saw fathers' absence as the source of virtually every social problem in America, doesn't call for a new fatherhood, based on emotional receptivity and responsiveness, compassion and patience, care and nurture. Instead he rails against such a father in this sarcastic passage:

> He is nurturing. He expresses his emotions. He is a healer, a companion, a colleague. He is a deeply involved parent. He changes diapers, gets up at 2:00 a.m. to feed the baby, goes beyond "helping out" . . . to share equally in the work, joys, and responsibilities of domestic life.

How utterly "selfish" of him. This "reflects the puerile desire for human omnipotentiality in the form of genderless parenthood, a direct repudiation of fatherhood as a gendered social role for men." What he means is that the real father is neither nurturing nor expressive; he is neither a partner nor a friend to his wife, and he sleeps through most of the young baby's infantile helplessness, oblivious to the needs of his wife and child. This guy is a father simply because he has a Y chromosome. Men are fathers, but they are not required to do any real parenting. The father "protects his family, provides for its material needs, devotes himself to the education of his children, and represents his family's interests in the larger world"—all valuable behaviors, to be sure. But he need not ever set foot in his child's room.

The notion that men should be exempt from mundane housework and child care, which should be left to their wives, is deeply insulting to women. Feminism taught us that. But it's also deeply insulting to men, because it assumes that the nurturing of life itself cannot be our province; given how clumsy and aggressive we are, it had better be done at a distance.

MASCULINITY: THE MISSING PIECE

What, then, is missing from the debate about boys? In a word, the boys themselves—or rather, what the boys feel, think, and believe—especially what they believe will make them men. None of the antifeminist pundits who seek to rescue boys from the emasculating clutches of feminism ever talks about what masculinity means to boys. The beliefs, attitudes, and traits that form the foundation of gender identity and ideology are nowhere to be found—except as some mythic endocrine derivative. "Males" are the topic, not "masculinity." Countless surveys suggest that young boys today subscribe to a traditional definition of masculinity, stressing the suppression of emotion, stoic resolve, aggression, power, success, and other stereotypic features. Indeed, the point of such successful books as William Pollack's *Real Boys* and Thompson and Kindlon's *Raising Cain* is to expand the emotional and psychological

repertoire of boys, enabling them to express a wider emotional and creative range.

How does a focus on the ideology of masculinity explain what is happening to boys in school? Consider the parallel for girls. Carol Gilligan's work on adolescent girls describes how these assertive, confident, and proud young girls "lose their voices" when they hit adolescence. At that same moment, Pollack notes, boys become *more* confident, even beyond their abilities. You might even say that boys *find* their voices, but it is the inauthentic voice of bravado, posturing, foolish risk-taking, and gratuitous violence. He calls it "the boy code." The boy code teaches them that they are supposed to be in power, and so they begin to act as if they are. They "ruffle in a manly pose," as William Butler Yeats once put it, "for all their timid heart."

In adolescence, both boys and girls get their first real dose of gender inequality: girls suppress ambition, boys inflate it. Recent research on the gender gap in school achievement bears this out. Girls are more likely to undervalue their abilities, especially in the more traditionally "masculine" educational arenas such as math and science. Only the most able and most secure girls take courses in those fields. Thus, their numbers tend to be few, and their mean test scores high. Boys, however, possessed of this false voice of bravado (and facing strong family pressure) are likely to *overvalue* their abilities, to remain in programs though they are less capable of succeeding.

This difference, and not some putative discrimination against boys, is the reason that girls' mean test scores in math and science are now, on average, approaching that of boys. Too many boys remain in difficult math and science courses longer than they should; they pull the boys' mean scores down. By contrast, the smaller number of girls, whose abilities and self-esteem are sufficient to enable them to "trespass" into a male domain, skew female data upward.

A parallel process is at work in the humanities and social sciences. Girls' mean test scores in English and foreign languages, for example, outpace those of boys. But this is not the result of "reverse discrimination"; it is because the boys bump up against the norms of masculinity. Boys regard English as a "feminine" subject. Pioneering research by Wayne Martino in Australia and Britain found that boys avoid English because of what it might say about their (inauthentic) masculine pose. "Reading is lame, sitting down and looking at words is pathetic," commented one boy. "Most guys who like English are faggots." The traditional liberal arts curriculum, as it was before feminism, is seen as feminizing. As Catharine Stimpson recently put it, "Real men don't speak French."

Boys tend to hate English and foreign languages for the same reasons that girls love them. In English, they observe, there are no hard-and-fast rules, one expresses one's opinion about the topic and everyone's opinion is equally valued. "The answer can be a variety of things, you're never really wrong," observed one boy. "It's not like maths and science where there is one set answer to everything." Another boy noted:

I find English hard. It's because there are no set rules for reading texts. . . . English isn't like maths where you have rules on how to do things and where there are right and wrong answers. In English you have to write down how you feel and that's what I don't like.

Compare this to the comments of girls in the same study:

I feel motivated to study English because . . . you have freedom in English—unlike subjects such as maths and science—and your view isn't necessarily wrong. There is no definite right or wrong answer, and you have the freedom to say what you feel is right without it being rejected as a wrong answer.

It is not the school experience that "feminizes" boys, but rather the ideology of traditional masculinity that keeps boys from wanting to succeed. "The work you do here is girls' work," one boy commented to a researcher. "It's not real work."

"Real work" involves a confrontation—not with feminist women, whose sensible educational reforms have opened countless doors to women while closing off none to men—but with an anachronistic definition of masculinity that stresses many of its vices (anti-intellectualism, entitlement, arrogance, and aggression) but few of its virtues. When the self-appointed rescuers demand that we accept boys' "hardwiring," could they possibly have such a monochromatic and relentlessly negative view of male biology? Maybe they do. But simply shrugging our collective shoulders in resignation and saying "boys will be boys" sets the bar much too low. Boys can do better than that. They can be men.

Perhaps the real "male bashers" are those who promise to rescue boys from the clutches of feminists. Are males not also "hardwired" toward compassion, nurturing, and love? If not, would we allow males to be parents? It is never a biological question of whether we are "hardwired" for some behavior; it is, rather, a political question of which "hardwiring" we choose to respect and which we choose to challenge.

The antifeminist pundits have an unyielding view of men as irredeemably awful. We men, they tell us, are savage, lustful, violent, sexually omnivorous, rapacious, predatory animals, who will rape, murder, pillage, and leave towels on the bathroom floor—unless women fulfill their biological duty and constrain us. "Every society must be wary of the unattached male, for he is universally the cause of numerous ills," writes David Popenoe. Young males, says Charles Murray, are "essentially barbarians for whom marriage . . . is an indispensable civilizing force."

By contrast, feminists believe that men are better than that, that boys can be raised to be competent and compassionate, ambitious and attentive, and that men are fully capable of love, care, and nurturance. It's feminists who are really "pro-boy" and "pro-father"—who want young boys and their fathers to expand the definition of masculinity and to become fully human.

PART THREE

COLLEGIATE MASCULINITIES: PRIVILEGE AND PERIL

The old social science orthodoxy about sex role socialization, from the 1950s until today, held that three institutions—family, church, and school—formed the primary sites of socialization, and the impact of education, family values, and religious training was decisive in shaping people's lives. This view tended to emphasize the centrality of adults in boys' lives. Because adults themselves were constructing the models of socialization, this conclusion seems understandable. But as social scientists began to ask boys and girls about the forces that influenced them, they heard about the increasing importance of peer groups and the media—two arenas where adults had far less reach. In recent years, researchers have begun to explore how homosocial peer groups affect men's lives.

The articles in Part Three focus on masculinities in college, a place Michael Kimmel calls "Guyland," where the all-male peer group is especially salient. How does collegiate life organize and reproduce the definitions of masculinity that we learn as young boys? How do specific all-male subcultures develop within these institutions, and what roles do they play?

Frank Harris discusses the particular challenges that African American men face in college life. Rocco Capraro provides a fascinating gender analysis of male drinking culture in college. And Greg Bortnichak describes how, while working as a barista in a local Starbucks, he decided to do something about what he saw.

GUYLAND: GENDERING THE TRANSITION TO ADULTHOOD

Michael Kimmel

The period between childhood and adulthood has been expanding for centuries. "Our society has passed from a period which was ignorant of adolescence to a period in which adolescence is the favorite age," wrote the French historian Philippe Aires (1962: 30). "We now want to come to it early and linger in it as long as possible."

Recently a body of research has emerged that expands this stage of development beyond the boundaries of what had been considered adolescence. Drawing on current empirical research on postadolescent development, a new group of social and behavioral scientists have identified what they call the "transition to adulthood." Although this new body of research has mapped the broadest parameters of this stage of development, the initial analytic forays have been astonishingly lacking in any analysis of gender. This lacuna is more striking because it is during the transition to adulthood that gender plays perhaps its most central role. To understand this new stage and to better map its gendered topography, it makes some sense to begin by remembering how deeply gendered was the initial study of adolescence.

THE INVENTION OF ADOLESCENCE

In 1904, G. Stanley Hall published his massive two-volume tome, *Adolescence: Its Psychology and Its Relations to Physiology, Anthropology, Sociology, Sex, Crime,*

Religion, and Education. Almost immediately, the word *adolescence* entered the common vocabulary to describe a stage of development poised anxiously between childhood puerility and adult virility. Hall saw adolescence, roughly coincident with the biological changes of puberty (ages 12–15), as a time of transition—a time when boys and girls develop their adult identity, test themselves, and find out who they really are.

No one could accuse Hall of failing to pay attention to gender. He was preoccupied with it. While he was generally eager to shield adolescents from entering the adult world prematurely, his chief interest was in boys' development. Concerned that boys were becoming feminized, in part by overprotective mothers and largely because of the increasingly coeducational environment of school and church, Hall wanted to rescue boys—from both the feminizing tendencies of girls and the enervating world of work, hoping that adolescent boys could be immersed in supportive, controlled, adult-monitored homosocial environments. Hall opposed coeducation, which he believed turned boys gay as it "diluted the mystic attraction of the opposite sex," and proposed a host of masculinity-building activities like sports, vigorous exertion in the outdoors, and even fighting and bullying others. He championed the Boy Scouts (founded in 1910) and the YMCA (founded in 1844 and revamped in the early 1900s) as vehicles to stem the tide of enervation.[1]

Hall generalized to all adolescents from only a tiny fraction of America's youth. When his book was published, only 6% of American teenagers actually graduated from high school. By contrast, 18%

of youth between 10 and 14 worked in factories or stores, and millions more were working on family farms. But Hall was on to something important. In the first decades of the twentieth century, the structural foundations of a prolonged adolescence were established, as an industrializing nation sought to stabilize its progress. Apprenticeships declined and child labor laws pushed young people out of the labor force. Compulsory education laws gave them someplace else to go if they couldn't work.

High school became the single defining experience for children of the middle and professional classes. While as late as 1920, only 16% of 17-year-old males had graduated from high school, by 1936 the majority of American teenagers attended high school. A new high school opened every day for the first 30 years of the century.[2]

With the increased universality of high school, a new word, "teenager," entered the American vocabulary in 1941, on the eve of our entrance into World War II. Critics worried that this "sudden and dramatic prolongation of adolescence" meant that over half of those who had "passed the terminal age of adolescence" were not acting as adults—physically, socially, economically, as E. C. Cline, the high school principal in Richmond, Indiana, worried.[3]

And Americans have been worrying about teenagers ever since. Some worried about teen sexuality, especially after the publication of the two volumes of Kinsey's studies of American sexual behavior. Some worried about "juvenile delinquency," another new term from the era—lonely, disaffected boys who sought the approval of their fellows by participating in increasingly dangerous stunts and petty crime. "Let's Face It" read the cover of *Newsweek* in 1956, "Our Teenagers Are Out of Control." Many youths, the magazine reported, "got their fun" by "torturing helpless old men and horsewhipping girls they waylaid in public parks."

By the 1950s, many cultural critics followed Hall's lead and blamed mothers—works by Philip Wylie and Edward Strecker identified "momism" as the cultural illness that resulted in emasculated boys and henpecked husbands. Others blamed the absent or emasculated fathers, the men in the grey flannel suits, like Jim Backus in *Rebel without a Cause*; its author, Robert Lindner, argued that "almost every symptom that delineates the psychopath clinically is to be found increasingly in the contemporary adolescent."[4]

TWO BREAKTHROUGHS IN PSYCHOLOGY AND SOCIOLOGY

Into this cultural controversy stepped psychologist Erik H. Erikson and sociologist James Coleman. Taken together, their writings helped to normalize adolescence, to neutralize and naturalize it. In his path-breaking book, *Childhood and Society* (1950) and later in *Identity: Youth and Crisis* (1968), Erikson identified the seven life-stages of individual psychological development that became a mantra in Developmental Psychology classes for decades. By labeling adolescence as a "moratorium"—a sort of prolonged time-out between childhood and adulthood—Erikson tamed and sanitized Hall's fears that adolescence was a maelstrom, a chaos of uncontrolled passions.

To Erikson, the moratorium of adolescence was a time for regrouping, reassessing, and regenerating oneself before undertaking the final quest for adult identity, "a vital regenerator in the process of social evolution," as he put it. Rather than rushing headlong into work and family lives, as children did in earlier societies, adolescents slow down the process to accomplish certain identity tasks. The venerable institutions that structured a young person's socialization—family, church, school—began to recede in their importance as the adolescent began to strike out on his or her own, plagued by doubts, taking tentative steps towards autonomy, and faced with a set of adult responsibilities looming ominously ahead.[5]

In his treatise, *The Adolescent Society* (1961), sociologist James Coleman had a somewhat less sanguine view of the displacement of education, religion, and family as the primary institutions of socialization. He noticed in high schools that teachers and administrators had lost most of their credibility as agents of socialization—they were more like agents of repression, as far as the kids were concerned. Parental scrutiny waned, and the influence of religion dissipated. As a result, he argued, adolescents developed a distinct peer culture, toward which they oriented their activities and from which they derived their sense of identity. Anti-intellectualism abounded, sports reigned supreme, and everyone wanted to be popular! Hardly tremulous individualists, Coleman saw adolescents as frighteningly dependent on peer culture, and boys, especially, desperate to prove their masculinity in the eyes of other boys.[6]

By the 1960s and 1970s, observers had a more optimistic view of late adolescence. While many shared Coleman's sense that peer groups had replaced parents as the primary source of socialization, they saw this simply as the attenuation of socialization, not its resolution. Indeed, Yale psychoanalyst Kenneth Keniston warned in 1971 that if the "conformity to peer group norms merely replaces conformity to parental norms . . . adolescent development is foreclosed before real self-regulation and independence are achieved." Reliance on peers was just another late hurdle on the way to autonomy and adulthood.[7]

As we will see, contemporary psychologists have tended to follow Erikson and Keniston. And, as we will see, Coleman was far more prescient.

POSTWAR ADOLESCENCE AS ANOMALY

One problem with Erikson and others' theories of adolescence was that although they insisted that they described eternal—or at least reliably consistent historical—trajectories, they were written during a period that is now understood to have been anomalous. The immediate postwar era was, in many ways, an era utterly unlike our own. It's the stuff of nostalgic longings, and the screen against which we often project our anxieties about the contemporary era.[8]

For adolescents, the period was no less anomalous. It was the only time when all the developmental markers were in perfect alignment with all the social and institutional frameworks in which development takes place. Those developmental psychological indicators—increased autonomy, the capacity for intimacy, a commitment to a career and the development of a life plan—all coincided with the social and cultural markers that have typically denoted adulthood.

How different that world seems now—and how different were the motivations of men and women who were in the 18–26 age group. For one thing, Americans had just emerged from a calamitous war, in which millions of young men had been killed or wounded. The generation of men that came of age in 1950 had just experienced the horrors of the beaches in Normandy or the South Pacific, the randomness of death and destruction as the guys next to them were gunned down. They couldn't wait to get married, settle down into stable adulthood, to forget the terrors of war, to silence their nightmares. They rushed into careers, married their high schools sweethearts, moved to the suburbs, and started their families. The housing boom spurred by rapid suburbanization was accompanied by an education boom and a baby boom. No wonder the "Greatest Generation" almost instantly morphed into the bland conformity of the "man in the gray flannel suit."

ADOLESCENCE STARTS EARLIER AND ENDS LATER

Adolescence today stretches out in both directions; it starts earlier and ends later. Children are becoming adolescents earlier and earlier, both biologically and socially. Typically we mark adolescence by the onset of puberty—which today occurs 4–5 years earlier than it did in the mid-nineteenth century. Improvements in nutrition, sanitation, and health care have lowered the average age of puberty about one year for every 25 years of development. Each generation enters puberty about a year earlier than its predecessor. In the years just before the Civil War, the average age for the onset of puberty was 16 for girls and 18 for boys; today it is about 12 for girls and 14 for boys.

Since the average age of marriage in the mid-nineteenth century was about the same—16 for girls and 18 for boys—there was really no "stage of development" during which time a youth was both single and sexually active. It wouldn't be farfetched to say that before the twentieth century, there were no "teenagers" in America.

But just as adolescence reaches us earlier and earlier, it also seems to stretch longer and longer. Biologically, just as puberty is beginning at earlier ages, full physiological maturation doesn't take place until well into our 20s. At 18, neuropsychological development is far from complete; the brain continues to grow and develop into the early 20s. In a bit of a stretch, one biologist suggests that this immature brain lacks the "wiring" for placing long-term benefits over shorter-term gains, which explains how we are "hard-wired" for high-risk behaviors like drug taking, smoking, and drinking.[9]

Young people today seem almost determined not to grow up too fast, to give the lie to George Bernard Shaw's famous dictum that "youth is wasted on the young." They may move directly from the "crisis" of adolescence to their "quarter-life crisis" and right into a "mid-life crisis" without ever having settled into a stage of life that wasn't a crisis!

Over the past two years, I interviewed about 400 college students at more than 40 colleges and universities across the United States. While in no way a nationally representative sample, my interviews provide compelling empirical evidence of the transition to adulthood as a new and previously unnoticed stage of development poised between adolescence and adulthood, and the ways that it is deeply and determinatively gendered.

"I feel like my whole life has been one long exercise in delayed gratification," says Matt, a graduate student in psychology at University of Wisconsin:

> I mean, in high school, I had to get good grades, study hard, and do a bunch of extracurricular things so I could get into a good college. OK, I did that. Went to Brown. Then, in college, I had to work really hard and get good grades so I could get into a good graduate school. OK, I did that. I'm here at Wisconsin. Now, though, I have to work really hard, publish my research, so I can get a good tenure track job somewhere. And then, I'll have to work really hard for six years just to get tenure. I mean, by the time I can exhale and have a little fun, I'll be in my mid-30s—and that's too old to have fun anymore!

When do young people become adults? How do they know? What are the markers of adulthood now? Is it when you can legally drink? Get married? Drive a car? Rent a car? Vote? Serve in the military? Have an abortion without parental consent? Consider how disparate these ages are. More than 50,000 Americans get married each year before their 18th birthday—that is, they are legally allowed to have sex before they can legally watch it on a video. We can buy cars before we are legally allowed to drive them and long before we can rent them.

MARKERS OF ADULTHOOD

Demographers today typically cite five life-stage events to mark the transition to adulthood: leaving home, completing one's education, starting work, getting married, and becoming a parent. Just about all adolescents live at home, go to high school, experience puberty, and are unmarried. "Adults," by contrast, have completed their educations, live away from home, are married, and have children and stable careers. (Of course, not all adults would actually check off all those markers, but they represent a pattern, a collection of indicators.) In 1950, when Erikson and Coleman wrote, all those markers clicked at almost exactly the same time.

Let's look at what happened to each of those markers of the transition from adolescence to adulthood. Let's begin with the narrative of one baby boomer:

> My parents married in 1948, after my father returned from the wartime Navy, and both he and my mother began their careers. At first, like so many of their generation, they lived in the bottom floor of my grandparents' home, saving their

money to flee the city and buy a house in the New York suburbs—part of the great wave of suburban migration of the early to mid-1950s. My mother, and her five closest lifelong friends, all had their first children within two years of their weddings, and their second child three years later—all within five years of graduating from college. And all of their friends did the same.

That baby boomer is me. And that pattern is a distant memory today. Baby boomers began to expand the timeframe of these markers of adulthood, attenuating education, prolonging singlehood as a permanent life stage, and drifting toward settled careers. The U.S. census shows a steady and dramatic decline in the percentage of young adults, under 30, who have finished school, left home, gotten married, had a child, and entered the labor force sufficiently to develop financial independence of their parents. In 2000, 46% of women and 31% of men had reached those markers by age 30. In 1960, just forty years earlier, 77% of women and 65% of men had reached them.[10]

MARRIAGE AND FAMILY LIFE

In 1950, the average age of marriage was 20.3 for women and 22.8 for men. Close to half of all women were married by age 20. Even by 1975, the median age for marriage was 21.1 for women and 23.5 for men. The age of marriage has climbed steadily and today, the median age of marriage is 27.1 for men and 25.3 for women.[11]

And young people are having their first child four years later than they did in 1970. In 1970, the average age at which people had their first child was 21.4 years. By 2000, it was 24.9. (Massachusetts had the highest mean age for first birth; Mississippi had the lowest.)[12]

Today's young people live much less stable and settled family lives than their own parents did. They're far more likely to have been raised in a single-parent home. Their reticence is the result of high expectations for their own relationships and fears that their love lives will resemble those of their parents. Afraid to commit and desperate to do

so, they make great cross-sex friends and casually hook up sexually. Their parents understand neither phenomenon.

"SERIAL JOBOGAMY"

They feel similarly about their careers. They know that their career is supposed to be more than a job, that it is supposed to be financially rewarding, be emotionally rich and satisfying, and offer them a sense of accomplishment and inner satisfaction. Work, for them, is an "identity quest." "Emerging adults want more out of work than a decent wage and a steady paycheck. They want their work to be an expression of themselves, to fit well their interests and abilities, to be something they find satisfying and enjoyable," writes Arnett.[13] And they expect that; they feel *entitled* to it. And why shouldn't they? They put up with four years of college, and maybe even some years of professional or graduate school, just to enhance their career prospects. Many have utterly unrealistic expectations about the range of jobs they might find satisfying. They all seem to want to write for television, become famous actors, or immediately become dot.com entrepreneurs. One employment recruiter calls them "the Entitlement Generation" since they have such "shockingly high expectations for salary, job flexibility, and duties but little willingness to take on grunt work or remain loyal to a company."[14]

But in a way, their bloated expectations may be a response to the very different economic climate in which they're coming of age. For one thing, the secure economic foundation on which previous generations have come of age has eroded. Globalization, the decline in manufacturing jobs, the decline in union protections for workers, and the increase in the supply of service sector jobs has changed all that. They know that corporations are no longer loyal to their employees—just consider all those companies that picked up and moved out of towns they had helped to build, watching indifferently as entire communities unraveled. So why should they be loyal to the company?

They're lucky to find a job at all. In 2000, 72.2% of Americans aged 20–24 were employed;

four years later it was barely two-thirds (67.9%). "Younger workers have just been crushed," commented Andrew Sum, the director of the Center for Labor Market Studies at Northeastern University.[15] Unlike virtually every single previous generation of Americans, the income trajectory for the current generation of young people is downwards. Between 1949 and 1973, during that postwar economic boom, men's earnings doubled and the income gap narrowed. But since the early 1970s, annual earnings for men, aged 25–34 with full-time jobs has steadily declined, dropping 17% from 1971 to 2002. Of male workers with only a high school diploma, the average wage decline from 1975 to 2002 was 11%. Only half of all Americans in their mid-20s earn enough to support a family. Two-thirds of this current generation "are not living up to their parents' standard of living," commented Professor Sum.[16]

And the gap between college-educated and non-college-educated has increased as well. In the late 1970s, male college graduates earned about 33% more than high school graduates; by the end of the 1980s, that gap had increased to 53%.[17] Nor do they have much protection. Once they're 18 or 19, young people are rarely covered as dependents on their parents' health and medical care plans. And many work at low-wage, temporary, low-benefit jobs, or remain dependent on their parents. As a result, in 1999, over half (53%) of all young adults (aged 18–21) had no health insurance at all—all the more striking when compared with those 35–44 (16.5% had no health care) and 45–54 (13.4% uninsured), according to the General Accounting Office. Another 12.9% are covered by Medicare or other public insurance. Fewer than 10% (8.8%) were covered by their employer.

This generation of young people is downwardly mobile. Gen Xers and Gen Yers will earn less than their parents did—at every single age marker. Of all age groups, the 18–25 year olds are the lowest ranked in earned income of all age groups. Their household income is the second lowest (right above 65 and older). "On most socioeconomic measures, the young were the worst off age group in 1997—and the gap has widened since," notes Tom Smith, the director of the General Social Survey.[18]

The only economic sector in which jobs are being created is entry-level service and sales. In *Generation X*, author Douglas Coupland calls it "McJob"—"low paying, low-prestige, low-dignity, no future job in the service sector. Frequently considered a satisfying career choice by people who have never held one."[19] Young people, along with immigrants, minorities, and the elderly, are the bulk of workers in the new service economy. Half of all workers in restaurants, grocery stores, and department stores are under 24. As one journalist recently put it, "hundred of thousands of young people are spending hours making decaf lattes, folding jeans, grilling burgers or unpacking boxes of books and records for minimum wage." And their poverty rates are twice the national average.[20]

As a result, young people rarely commit to a career right out of college. They don't have their eyes on the prize; it's really more like their "eyes on the fries," as a recent documentary film put it. The increased instability of their employment prospects coupled with their sense that jobs must be emotionally and financially fulfilling leads to a volatile career trajectory. Many experience the "two-month itch" and switch jobs as casually as they change romantic partners. They take "stopgap jobs," engaging in what I like to call "serial jobogamy." Listen to Jon, a 1992 Rutgers grad, who told a journalist about his career cluelessness:

> I had absolutely no idea what I wanted to do right out of college. I was clueless and fell blindly into a couple of dead-end jobs, which were just there for me to make money and figure out what I wanted to do. When I had no idea what I wanted to do, I couldn't even picture myself doing anything because I was so clueless about what was out there. I had so little direction. I was hanging on to these completely dead-end jobs thinking that maybe something would turn up. I was unhappy about the situation, and the only thing that made it better was that all of my friends out of college were in the same boat. We would all come home and complain about our jobs together. We were all still drunks back then.[21]

And remember, this is the kid who is moving back home after graduation!

EDUCATION FOR WHAT?

In 1900, only a small fraction of male teens attended secondary schools. About half were involved in agricultural labor and the rest were employed in resource, manufacturing, or the service sector, making nearly a living wage. Many lived with their families, and when they did, they made considerable financial contributions to family income. In fact, for many working-class families, the family's most prosperous years were the years their children were living at home with them.[22]

A century later, in most western nations, the vast majority of teens attended secondary school. In 2000, over 88% of all people aged 25–29 had completed high schools and nearly 30% (29.1%) had a BA—up from 17% only thirty years ago. This is the most highly educated group of young people in history.[23]

But they're taking their time getting that education. Four years after high school, 15% of the high school graduating class of 1972 had obtained their degree. Ten years later, the percentage had been cut by more than half—less than 7% had obtained a degree. Today, it's closer to 4%.

And also the least financially independent generation. Two-thirds of all college graduates owe more than $10,000 when they graduate; the average debt is nearly $20,000 and 5% owe more than $100,000. Recent college graduates owe 85% more in student loans alone than graduates a decade ago according to the Center for Economic and Policy research. Credit card debt for the age group 18–24 more than doubled between 1992 and 2001.[24]

The twentieth century has seen these kids move from being productive citizens to dependents on their families, the educational system, and the state. Less than one-third of this age group are employed enough to make them potentially financially independent. Those who live with their parents make virtually no contribution to family income. More than one-third of youth aged 18–34 receive cash

from their parents, and nearly half (47%) receive time-help from their parents in any given year—averaging about $3,410 in cash and about 367 hours of help from their parents. At home, adolescents in many families are not treated as equal adults but as "indulged guests," writes psychologist Jeffrey Arnett. And away, young people who "swim" are able to do so "because families provide significant material and emotional support."[25]

No wonder two-thirds of all young people 18 to 24 live with their parents or other relatives and one-fifth of all 25-year-old Americans still live at home. And no wonder that 40% of all college graduates return to live with their parents for at least some period of time in that age span. Only 25% of men aged 25 live independently; 38% of women do. Eighteen million Americans between 20 and 34 live with their parents. Forget the empty nest syndrome—for one in five American families, it's still a "full nest."

And we're not the only country where this is happening. In Britain, for example, they're talking about nesters, boomerang children, co-resident adults, or "kippers"—Kids In Pockets, Eroding Retirement Savings, which pretty much sums up what their parents think of the 50% of college graduates who have returned home. In Japan, 70% of women between age 30 and 35 live with their parents, and in Australia, only 14% of people in their early 20s are independent.[26]

THE UPWARD AGE SPIRAL

These five classic demographic markers—education, marriage, parenthood, career and residential independence—have not simply shifted over the past generation. They've exploded, scattered across a time span that now stretches to more than a decade for a large swath of American youth. And they feed back on each other, reinforcing their separation and pushing the boundaries even further. "Because people are delaying marriage, they're living with their parents longer," writes Farnsworth Riche, in an article in *American Demographics*. "They are delaying marriage longer because they are going to school. They're going to school because most well-paying jobs now require a college degree." The National Marriage Project found that 86% of 20–29 year olds agree that "it is extremely important to be economically set before you get married."

Surely, then, it makes little sense to speak of this entire period, from early teens to late 20s, as a single identifiable period called "adolescence." The developmental tasks of a 13 year old are just too different from those of a 23 year old—even if they both are single, unemployed, and live with their parents. We need to identify this new stage of development, between adolescence and adulthood, that both captures the developmental characteristics of this life stage and locates it within important social and cultural shifts in American life, including the historical decrease in the number of males under 25 who are married or fathers; the increased number of young males who are extending their educations beyond college, to professional or graduate school; and, the increased percentage of young males under 25 who are living with their parents.

We need to see the stage from 18–26 as a distinct stage of development, a unique period. We need to map its contours, explore its boundaries, and understand its meaning. "In another 10 or 20 years, we're not going to be talking about this as a delay," says Tom Smith, director of the General Social Survey. "We're going to be talking about this as a normal trajectory."[27]

THIRTY IS THE NEW TWENTY

Recently, some social scientists have begun to pay attention to this period between the end of adolescence and the beginning of adulthood. In September, 2004, a front page story in *USA Today* noticed that something was happening; a few months later, *Time* made it their cover story, calling them "twixters"—neither kids nor adults, but betwixt and between.[28]

The *Time* story, and the subsequent letters the magazine published offer a glimpse of our national confusion about this age. The twixters wrote eloquently about their situation. One moved back home after college because she couldn't find a job

that paid enough to live on her own—only to find that "the majority of my high school class had done the same thing." But, she insisted, "we are not lazy. We want to work and make our way in the world." Another pointed out that her generation is "overwhelmed by indecision. We have the necessary tools, but now have too many options and not enough options at the same time. We are stuck." Another painted a nearly inspirational picture. Given that half their "parents are divorced, have financial problems or are stuck in jobs they loathe," she wrote, the twixters might instead be seen as "a generation that refuses to fall into the same archaic conventions that have led to so many dysfunctional families."

Adult letter writers were uniformly unsympathetic. They blamed the kids themselves, as if somehow the disastrous economy, sky-high housing costs, and high aspirations with no ways to fulfill them were somehow the fault of job seekers, not job suppliers—namely the adults themselves. "If only their parents had cut the golden apron strings and left them to their own devices, they would have learned to be more independent," wrote one. "There's not a single thing wrong with the young adults who live off their parents that a stint in the U.S. Marine Corps couldn't fix," wrote another. "Why do we need to come up with a new label for kids who stay home with their parents while figuring out what to do?" asked another, before reminding us that "we've had a name for that for years: moocher."[29]

Ironically, *all* of the twixter letters were from women, and *all* of the adult respondents were male. (*Time* did not seem to notice this interesting gender difference.) But it's an important element in our conversation: it is fathers—far more than mothers—who deeply resent the return of their college graduate children. The empty nest is experienced differently by fathers and mothers. Mothers may, for a time, mourn the absence of their children, as if their world has suddenly lost its center of gravity and spins aimlessly off its axis. Fathers, by contrast, often celebrate their new freedom from child-care responsibilities—they buy new golf clubs, load up on Viagra, and talk about this being, finally, their "turn." Similarly, mothers may be ambivalent about the "full nest" syndrome, but their husbands seem to be universally unhappy about it.

Developmental psychologists and sociologists have also tried to map this newly emerging stage of life. Sociologist James Cote calls the period "youthhood," while Terri Apter, a British social psychologist calls them "thresholders," who suffer from the neglect and scorn from parents who mistake their need for support and guidance as irresponsibility and immaturity. Recently, the John D. and Catherine T. MacArthur Foundation convened an academic panel on the "Transition to Adulthood."

Perhaps the most ambitious effort to map this postadolescent terra incognita has been Jeffrey Arnett's studies of what he calls "emerging adulthood." Following Erikson, Arnett sees this developmental stage as a gradual unfolding of a life plan, a "time for serious self-reflection, for thinking about what kind of life you want to live and what your Plan should be for your life" (p. 181). It's a period of increased independence—including independence from the preordained roles that they inherited from their elders. So, "they are not constrained by gender roles that prescribe strict rules for how they may meet and get to know each other" (p. 94). They are moving deliberately if unevenly toward intimate relationships, a steady and stable career path, and family lives, and along the way they are developing closer friendships with their parents, since the old issues of adolescent rebellion have been resolved by time and experience.

Yet Arnett's view of this stage of life is so sanguine, so sanitized, it's hardly recognizable. It's hard to square becoming better friends with your parents and an increasing sense of autonomy (and a decreasing reliance on peer groups for validation) with the fraternity initiations, binge drinking, athletic hazing, and date rape and other forms of sexual predation that often fill the exposés of campus life.

It's also hard to square this gradual easing into adulthood with the observations of other cultural critics. For example, Christopher Lasch observed more than twenty years ago that college students have a "certain protective shallowness, a fear of binding commitments, a willingness to pull up roots whenever the need arises, a dislike of depending on anyone, an incapacity for loyalty or gratitude."[30]

So, what do psychologists and sociologists know about this stage of development? For one thing, it's a stage of life characterized by indeterminacy. Many young adults feel they are just treading water, waiting to find the right job, the right person, the right situation, to reveal itself. "I'm just sitting around waiting for my life to begin, while it's all just slippin' away," sings Bruce Springsteen on "Better Days."

All the established markers of adulthood feel more ephemeral, more transient, and less reliable—both as events and as markers of adulthood. They're children of divorce, of family instability or dysfunction. They're unsure what to think about their parents. Some, mostly young women, describe their parents (mothers) as their best friend, others see their parents as exactly who they don't want to end up like.

"I'm in no rush to get married, and even less in a rush to have a kid," says Jeff, a 22-year-old senior at Indiana University interviewed 2/23/05. "I watched my own parents divorce, and it became pretty clear that they got married and started having kids—namely me—before they were ready. I'm not going to make that mistake."

It's a time of perhaps the greatest mismatch between their ambitions and their accomplishments. They graduate from college filled with ideas about changing the world, making their contribution, finding their place, and they enter a job market at the bottom, where work is utterly unfulfilling, boring, and badly paid. "It concerns me that of the many gifted people I went to school with, so few of them are actually doing what they really want to do," said one.[31] They are among the most entitled and underappreciated people in America. This was a generation that was told from the get-go that each of them was special, in which their self-esteem was so inflated they became light-headed, in which they were rewarded for every normal developmental milestone as if they were Mozart.

They're extremely other-directed, taking their cues from outside. They perform to please grown-ups—parents, teachers—but exhibit little capacity for self-reflection or internal motivation. They have high self-esteem, but little self-awareness. Many suspect that their self-esteem, so disconnected from actual achievement, is a bit of a fraud. Many lack a moral compass to help negotiate their way in the world.

It's unstable and uncertain. They drink more than they think they should, take more drugs, and probably get involved in more hook ups and bad relationships than they think they should. And they also get more down on themselves, because at this stage they also think they should know better. Their suicide rate is the highest for any age group except men over 70.[32]

As a result, they're more disconnected. They are less likely to read a newspaper, attend church, belong to a religion or a union, vote for president, or identify with a political party than any other age group, according to the General Social Survey. They're more cynical or negative about other people and less trusting. They are less likely to believe that people are basically trustworthy, helpful, fair, or that human beings are naturally good.[33]

Nor do they have any particular confidence in social, economic, or political institutions. They don't trust corporations, the way their parents did, because they've seen how such loyalty is rewarded with layoffs, downsizing, outsourcing, and moving overseas. They've watched as corporate executives lined their pockets with the pension funds of their own employees. They believe the only way to get rich in this culture is not by working hard, saving, and sacrificing, but by winning the lottery. And they don't trust the government, which they believe is filled with people who are venal and self-aggrandizing, out of touch with the needs of their constituents.

On the other hand, there is plenty of good news. For one thing, they're developing friendships, especially across sex, the likes of which their parents do not understand. Young people constantly told me of trying to explain their cross-sex friendships to their parents. "My father just doesn't get it," said Kim, a 21-year-old senior at Oakland University in suburban Detroit. "I keep saying that they're my 'guy friends' and he's like, 'Wait. He's a boy and he's your friend, but he's not your boyfriend?' And I'm like 'Dad, chill. He's a boy. He's my friend. He is not my boyfriend.' And so he asks 'Does Jeff [her boyfriend] know?' "

Young adults go out in groups, hang out together, maybe even hook up. But they are friends first. And this bodes well in two ways. First, friendships are based on mutuality and equality, which assumes, at least in part, a more equal relationship between women and men than is offered either by the sexual predatory conquest model and its corollary, the passionate-swept-off-the-feet model, or even the chivalric code of gentlemen and ladies. And second, gender equality in marriage—marriages based on models of friendship and partnership—are far sturdier and more successful than those based on those other sexual passion-attractiveness models, according to psychologist John Gottman.

For some, friends are the new family. Think, actually, of the hit television sit-com *Friends*. Six friends share their mutual befuddlement about being grown-ups, relationships, careers, and life in general until they suddenly realize that everything they ever wanted in a life partner is right there next to them. And they then spend the next two seasons sorting out which one goes with whom. Or consider the HBO show, *Sex and the City*, the story of a quartet of single, sexually active women on the loose in New York City, each one hoping and struggling through relationships with the opposite sex, all the while aware that their real "family" was each other.

For others, our families become friends. Arnett suggests that some young adults become closer to their parents, and develop cross-generational friendships that surprise both parent and child. Over half of all Americans aged 18–29 talk to their parents every day, according to a January, 2005, article in *Time*. But it is also true that the half who do speak to their parents every day are daughters—and the parents they are speaking to are their mothers.

There is more potentially good news. Students of domestic violence have recently noted a significant downward trend—lower and lower rates of domestic violence seem to be popping up in the United States, Canada, and Britain. For a long time, social scientists worried that a host of factors—increasing attention to the problem, better reporting of the crimes, better police and hospital evaluations, more stringent arrest mandates—would actually drive the rates higher, creating the irony that the more we talked about it, the more it seemed to increase. But the decrease in domestic violence seems to come less from the increased constraints placed on men, or even the increased deterrence of stronger laws, better enforced with mandatory sentencing. It seems to stem, instead, from the increased age of women entering into marriage (younger women are battered more often than older women) and the host of dramatic changes in women's lives (work outside the home leads to increased economic resources to leave a dangerous situation; women feel entitled not to be battered; playing sports and working outside the home correlate with higher self-esteem, which leads them to put up with less, etc.). It may be that the older women are when they marry, the lower their chances of being battered when they do.

SITUATIONAL MATURITY

If the demographic markers of adulthood have scattered across a decade or more, young people today are turning to more attitudinal indicators of when they become adults. In a 1994 study, Jeffrey Arnett asked students at a large Midwestern university "Do you think you have reached adulthood?" Twenty-seven per cent said "yes," 10% said "no" and 63% said "in some respects yes, in some respects no." Interestingly, the students no longer used traditional markers to categorize themselves. Completing education, entering the labor force, marriage, and parenthood all got low ratings, from 14% for parenthood to 27% for entering the labor force. Marriage and completing education were only identified by 15%, having a child by 14% as indicators of adulthood.

On the other hand, psychological criteria received much higher endorsements. "Accept responsibility for the consequences of your actions" led the list at 93%. Being able to "decide on personal beliefs and values independently of parents or other influences" was noted by 81%, the same percentage that identified becoming "less self-oriented, develop greater consideration for others."[34]

They become adults when they *feel* like adults. They experience a "situational maturity." Sometimes they want to be treated like adults, sometimes they want to be treated like children. "You don't get lectures about what life is like after college," comments Brandon to journalist Alexandra Robbins. "You don't have a textbook that tells you what you need to do to find success." "People have to invent their own road map," commented another.[35]

And they don't experience a calamitous break with their childhoods, since there is no one time when all five transitional indicators are achieved. By spreading them out, adulthood becomes a gradual process, a series of smaller decisions. One looks back suddenly and realizes one is actually an adult. The General Social Survey found that most people believe the transition to adulthood should be completed by age 26, a number that seems to rise every year.

THE MISSING CONVERSATION: GENDER

Perhaps one reason Arnett and his colleagues are so sanguine about emerging adulthood is because there is nary a word about gender in their work. The word *masculinity*—or, for that matter *femininity*—does not appear in his book's index; there's scant mention of gender gaps in attitudes. And that's about it.[36]

How can one possibly discuss the age group 16–26 and not talk about gender? In fact, this is perhaps the most gendered stage of a person's development—for one simple reason: It is a time that is utterly unmapped. The older institutions of socialization exert far less influence, although same-sex peers and media often pick up some of the slack. It is a time when there are no road maps, no blueprints, no primers that tell the young person what to do, how to understand this period. That's why none of the terms given to this stage of development—"emergent adulthood," "transition to adulthood," "twixters," "thresholders," and the like—have any resonance whatever to the young men and women I speak to on college campuses and in workplaces around the country.

Almost all of them call themselves—and call each other—"guys." It's both a generic catch-all term that goes beyond this age group and a specific term demarcating it from "kids" and "grown-ups." While it's gender-specific, women use it too. Watch a group of college women sitting around wondering what to do that evening: "What do you guys want to do?" "I don't know, what do you guys want to do?" One hardly needs a man around to whom the term would refer. (This "generic" term is also gender-specific, and we'll look at the ways that the term itself implies the gender inequality that characterizes this stage of life. Girls live in Guyland—*not* the other way around.)

In fact, this is a period of what sociologists James Cote and Anton Allahar call "gender intensification"—the assertion of "exaggerated notions associated with the different roles that still hold many men and women in separate spheres of endeavor."[37] It's when the struggle to prove manhood becomes even more intense—in part because it is only peers who are watching—and judging.

That the territory remains so unmapped actually exacerbates the emphasis on gender. Part of the definition of masculinity is, after all, to act as if one knows exactly where one is going. If men have a difficult time asking for directions when they get lost driving their cars, imagine what they'll do when they feel lost and adrift on the highway of life! One acts as if one knows where one is going, even if it isn't true. And it's this posture, and the underlying sense that one is a fraud, that leaves young men most vulnerable to manipulation by the media and by their peers. If I just follow along and don't ask any questions, everyone will assume I have it all together—and I won't be exposed.

Guyland thus becomes the terrain in which young men so relentlessly seem to act out, seem to take the greatest risks, and do the stupidest things. It's also the time when they need the involvement of their parents—especially their fathers. Fathers often fade out of the picture, thinking their job of child-rearing and role-modeling is over once their offspring graduate from high school. For many guys, their fathers are a "shadowy presence."[38] Their kids have survived, so now, fathers seem to say, it's time for "us."

It's not entirely true that fathers are just selfish; they're also encouraged to think selfishly for the first time in a long time, by an advertising industry that has recently discovered empty nesters as an emerging market—they've finally shed all the financial responsibilities of child-rearing and college, giving them some disposable income for the first time in decades. And they're ready to find something other than their children to fulfill them.

All the advice books about boys' development offer little guidance here. Although they may be useful when they discuss boys' development until they turn 16 or so, they all end just at the cusp of "guyland." It's pretty difficult to talk to a 17- or 22-year-old guy about what the books say about being a man when the books top out at 16!

And so, directionless and clueless, we come to rely increasingly on our peers. And our peers often have some interesting plans for what we have to endure to prove to them that we are real men. The "penalty for not living up to the norms of being tough, being 'cool' is severe," writes Marie Richmond-Abbott.[39] Is it "rejection or simply being ignored?"

BEYOND GUYLAND

Guyland is both a social space and a stage of life. It's unlikely to disappear. If anything, the stage of life is likely to become more firmly entrenched. There are positive reasons for delaying marriage, exploring different career paths, playing the field, traveling, hanging out, exploring one's self and who one wants to be, and become, in this lifetime. But it must be time well spent.

Most guys drift out of Guyland by their late 20s, as they commit to careers or girlfriends, and begin to enter the world of responsible adulthood. But still, they do so with few rules and fewer signposts to help them on their journeys.

Our task, as a society, is to disengage the stage of life with that social space—to enable young men to live through this stage more consciously, more honorably, and with greater resilience—to inject into that anomic and anarchic space called Guyland a code of ethics, of emotional responsiveness, and of wholesome occasional irresponsibility.

Some of Guyland's most celebrated inhabitants seem to be getting that message—and passing it on. In response to the death of Scott Krueger (a pledge at MIT) during a drinking and hazing ritual, the national office of Phi Gamma Delta has produced a well-conceived video about high-risk drinking that is required for all their chapters. The local chapter of another fraternity accepts openly gay men and then works to make other brothers' homophobia the problem to be addressed. Sigma Phi Epsilon has embraced a new "balanced man program," which the fraternity developed in the 1990s to combat a culture of "boozing, drugging and hazing." They've simply and unilaterally done away with the pledge system; new members have virtually all the rights and privileges of brothers. The brothers are *presumed* to be men when they begin; they don't have to prove their manhood to their peers. Scott Thompson, the fraternity's national spokesman, told a journalist:

> New members don't pledge for a certain period of time, get hazed, get initiated, and then show up for parties until they graduate. In the Balanced Man Program, men join, and they are developed from the time they join until the time they graduate. Part of that development focuses on building a sound mind and sound body, a simple philosophy that we took from the ancient Greeks.[40]

Here, in the words of a former frat guy, lies the hope of guys everywhere: that the culture of entitlement can become a culture of integrity—in which guys know that each person's integrity is equal to his own. That guys can be valued for their integrity and encouraged to be good, whole human beings. That the culture of silence can become a culture of honor, in which each guy feels honor bound to speak up, to act ethically, and to defend his core beliefs with respect for the simple dignity of his friends. That the culture of protection can become a culture of love, in which each guy feels surrounded by support and care, knows that he is not alone, and that having left Guyland far behind, he has nothing left to prove.

NOTES

1. G. Stanley Hall, *Adolescence: Its Psychology and Its Relations to Physiology, Anthropology, Sociology, Sex, Crime, Religion, and Education* (New York: Appleton, 1904). In an earlier essay, he explained that "the boy's bullying is the soul-germ of the man's independence." He defended one boy who was "overbearing and cruel" to his sister, whom he had "perfectly terrorized."

2. See Steven Mintz, "Adolescence's Neglected Anniversary" op-ed at Ascribe Newswire, January 10, 2005; archived at www.contemporaryfamilies.org/media/news%2099.htm

3. E. C. Cline, "Social Implications of Modern Adolescent Problems" in *The School Review*, September 1941, pp. 511–514.

4. Edward Strecker, *Their Mothers' Sons: The Psychiatrist Examines an American Problem* (Philadelphia: Lippincott, 1946) and Philip Wylie, *Generation of Vipers* (New York: Rinehart, 1942).

5. Erik Erikson, *Childhood and Society* (New York: W. W. Norton, 1950) and *Identity: Youth and Crisis* (New York: W.W. Norton, 1968).

6. James Coleman, *The Adolescent Society* (New York: The Free Press, 1961). See also James Coleman, *Adolescents and Schools* (New York: Basic Books, 1965).

7. Kenneth Keniston, *Young Radicals: Notes on a Committed Youth* (New York: Harcourt, 1968).

8. See Stephanie Coontz, *The Way We Never Were* (New York: Basic, 1992).

9. See Caroline Stanley, "Why Teens Do Dumb Things" in www.healthykids.com, accessed October 23, 2004, describing the research of Dr. James Bjork.

10. Sharon Jayson, "It's Time to Grow Up—Later" in *U.S.A. Today*, September 30, 2004, p. 1D.

11. U.S. Bureau of the Census, Table MS-2: "Estimated Median Age at First Marriage by Sex, 1890 to Present"

released September 15, 2004. In the first part of the century, the median age of first marriage fluctuated as the economy expanded and contracted; now, however, the median age creeps up steadily, seemingly disconnected from and uninfluenced by external factors.

12. T. J. Mathews, and Brady Hamilton, "Mean Age of Mother, 1970–2000" in *National Vital Statistics Reports*, 51 (1), December, 2002.

13. Jeffrey Jensen Arnett, *Emerging Adulthood: The Winding Road from the Late Teens through the Twenties* (New York: Oxford University Press, 2004), p. 162.

14. Martha Irvine, "Young Workers Want It All, Now" in *Seattle-Post-Intelligencer*, June 27, 2005; available at: http://seattlepi.nwsource.com/business/230177_entitlement27.html (accessed 6/28/05).

15. Bob Herbert, "The Young and the Jobless" in *New York Times*, May 12, 2005.

16. Cited in Herbert, "The Young and the Jobless," *ibid.*

17. Mary Corcoran and Jordan Matsudaira, "Is It Getting Harder to Get Ahead? Economic Attainment in Early Adulthood for Two Cohorts" in *On the Frontier of Adulthood: Theory, Research and Public Policy*, Richard Settersten, Jr., Frank F. Furstenberg, Jr., and Ruben G. Rumbaut, eds. (Chicago: University of Chicago Press, 2005), p. 357.

18. Tom Smith, "Generation Gaps in Attitudes and Values from the 1970s to the 1990s" in *On the Frontier of Adulthood: Theory, Research and Public Policy*, Richard Settersten, Jr., Frank F. Furstenberg, Jr., and Ruben G. Rumbaut, eds. (Chicago: University of Chicago Press, 2005), p. 182.

19. Douglas Coupland, *Generation X: Tales for an Accelerated Culture* (New York: St Martin's Press, 1991).

20. Elana Berkowitz, "Eyes on the Fries: Young People are Coming of Age in the Era of the McJob," published by CampusProgress.org on March 31, 2005.

21. Cited in Alexandra Robbins and Abby Wilner, *Quarterlife Crisis* (New York: Jeremy Tarcher, 2001), p. 113.

22. William Reese, *The Origins of the American High School* (New Haven: Yale University Press, 1995).

23. Elizabeth Fussell and Frank F. Furstenberg, Jr., "The Transition to Adulthood during the Twentieth Century: Race, Nativity and Gender" in *On the Frontier of Adulthood*, p. 38.

24. Lou Dobbs, "The Generation Gap" in *U.S. News and World Report*, May 23, 2005, p. 58.

25. Schoeni and Ross, 402; Settersten, 2005, p. 535; Jeffrey Jensen Arnett, "Are College Students Adults? Their Conceptions of the Transition to Adulthood" in *Journal of Adult Development* 1, 1994, p. 162.

26. Edi Smockum, "Done with College? Come back to the Fold" in *Financial Times*, September 10, 2005, p. 23.

27. As cited in Tom Smith, "Generation Gaps in Attitudes and Values from the 1970s to the 1990s" in *On the Frontier of Adulthood: Theory, Research, and Public Policy*, edited by Richard Settersten, Frank Furstenberg and Ruben Rumbaut (Chicago: University of Chicago Press, 2005), p. 182.

28. Sharon Jayson, "It's Time to Grow Up—Later" in *USA Today*, September 30, 2004, p. 1D; Lev Grossman, "Grow Up? Not So Fast" in *Time*, January 24, 2005, p. 42–54.

29. Letters, *Time*, February 14, 2005, p. 6.

30. Christopher Lasch, *Haven in a Heartless World*, (New York:Basic Books, 1977, no page given

31. In Jeffrey Arnett, *Emerging Adulthood*, p. 41.

32. James E. Cote and Anton L. Allahar, *Generation on Hold: Coming of Age in the Late Twentieth Century* (New York: New York University Press, 1996), p. 59.

33. Tom Smith, "Generation Gaps in Attitudes and Values from the 1970s to the 1990s" in *On the Frontier of Adulthood: Theory, Research, and Public Policy*, edited by Richard Settersten, Frank Furstenberg and Ruben Rumbaut (Chicago: University of Chicago Press, 2005), p. 182.

34. Jeffrey Jensen Arnett, "Are College Students Adults?"; see also Arnett, *Emerging Adulthood*, p. 210.

35. Alexandra Robbins and Amy Willner, *Quarterlife Crisis*, p. 121, 6.

36. Neither of the two major works cited here—Arnett's *Emerging Adulthood* and the MacArthur-sponsored *On the Frontier of Adulthood*—has a single reference to "masculinity," "manhood," or even "men" in the index.

37. James Cote and Anton Allahar, *Generation on Hold*, p. 84.

38. Larson and Richard, 1994, p. 164.

39. Marie Richmond-Abbott, *Masculine and Feminine: Gender Roles over the Life Cycle* (2nd ed). McGraw-Hill, 1992, p. 121.

40. Benoit Denizet-Lewis, "Ban of Brothers" in *New York Times Magazine*, January 9, 2005, p. 74.

COLLEGE MEN'S MEANINGS OF MASCULINITIES AND CONTEXTUAL INFLUENCES: TOWARD A CONCEPTUAL MODEL

Frank Harris III

Recent behavioral trends involving male students on college campuses have led to increased scholarly attention to masculinities in higher education. For example, recent inquiries have concluded that college men comprise the majority of students who are cited for nonacademic violations of campus judicial policies (Harper, Harris, & Mmeje, 2005) and more than 90 percent of students who are accused of sexual assault, relationship violence, and sexual harassment on college campuses (Foubert, Newberry, & Tatum, 2007; Hong, 2000). Others report academic underachievement (Kellom, 2004; Sax, 2008), disengagement in campus programs and activities (Davis & Laker, 2004), alcohol and substance abuse (Capraro, 2000; Courtenay, 1998; Kuh & Arnold, 1993), homophobia (Harris, 2008; Rhoads, 1995), depression (Good & Mintz, 1990), and poor coping (Good & Wood, 1995) among college men. Similarly, Sax's longitudinal quantitative study revealed that, in comparison to women, men reportedly spent more time watching television, playing video games, consuming alcohol, and partying while in college.

The widening gender gap in college student enrollment has also been an area of focus in much of the recent scholarly discourse concerning college men.

In 2003–2004, men comprised 42 percent of the total undergraduate enrollment in the United States (King, 2006). The college enrollment gap widens when these data are disaggregated by race/ethnicity where the largest percentage gaps are among African American, Native American, and Hispanic students where men accounted for 36 percent, 39 percent, and 41 percent of 2004 undergraduate enrollees, respectively (KewalRamani, Gilbertson, Fox, & Provasnik, 2007).

Despite this recent scholarly attention, college educators still know little about the gender identity development process for college men. Consequently, educators who aim to implement theoretically based interventions to facilitate college men's healthy and productive gender identity development must rely on frameworks that were not created for this purpose. Theories and frameworks have been proposed to explain the identity development of women (Josselson, 1987); persons who are lesbian, gay, and bisexual (D'Augelli, 1994); African Americans (Cross, 1995; Taylor & Howard-Hamilton, 1995); Asian Americans (Kim, 2001); Latinos (Torres, 2003); multiracial persons (Renn, 2003); and students with learning disabilities (Troiano, 2003); to name a few. Yet, models that seek to explain college men's gender identity development are largely absent in the published college student development research. Even recent studies that aim to understand men as gendered beings (e.g., Davis, 2002; Harris, 2008; Hong, 2000; Martin & Harris, 2006) focus primarily on describing

2009 or so

gender-related conflicts and challenges among college men rather than a process of masculine identity development in college. Classic theories of identity and psychosocial development (e.g., Chickering, 1969; Erikson 1968; Marcia, 1980) were based largely on the experiences of men (Evans, Forney & Guido-DiBrito, 1998). However, the construct of gender was not purposefully explored in the research used to develop and validate these theories (Davis; Davis & Laker, 2004; Evans et al.). Thus, the extent to which these theories, in and of themselves, provide insight into the gender identity development of college men is questionable.

Harper et al. (2005) was one of the first studies in which a model describing the interactions between masculinities and college environments was proposed. Yet, despite the model's utility in understanding the developmental experiences of men on college campuses, it is limited in two respects. First, it focuses exclusively on male judicial offenders. Therefore, the extent to which the model accounts for the experiences of college men who are not cited for violations of campus judicial policies is unknown. Second, the model was developed theoretically and has yet to be empirically validated.

Edwards and Jones (2009) offered much-needed insight into the experiences of college men by proposing an empirically derived model of men's gender identity development. Based on multiple interviews with a diverse sample of 10 undergraduate men, Edwards and Jones used grounded theory to explore "the process by which the participants came to understand themselves as men" (p. 214) and proposed a three-phase model that described the participants' gender identity development. Edwards and Jones described masculine identity development as an interactive process involving men's awareness of society's expectations of performing masculinities, challenges men experience in meeting societal expectations, and men's efforts to transcend societal expectations by redefining what it means to be a man and performing masculinities according to their own beliefs and values. Given that Edwards and Jones's study was situated at one large public university on the East Coast one question that emerged was: How might these findings transfer to other institutional contexts, such as a large private university or a campus in another region of the country? In addition, Edwards and Jones called for more studies of masculinities involving a larger group of men "representing other social group identities and college experiences" (p. 226).

In response to the aforementioned knowledge gaps in the published research on college men and masculinities, I conducted a qualitative study to: (a) examine shared masculine conceptualizations among college men who represented a range of identities and experiences, (b) understand how contextual factors (e.g., socialization, campus culture, peer group interactions) shape and reinforce college men's gender identity development and gender performance, and (c) propose a conceptual model of the meanings college men make of masculinities. The primary research question that guided this study was, "What are the shared meanings of masculinities among men who represent diverse backgrounds, experiences, and identities?" Additional questions that informed this study were: (a) How do these meanings influence college men's gender-related attitudes and behaviors? and (b) From the participants' perspectives, what are the dominant and negotiable boundaries of masculinities on a university campus?

The purpose of this article is to present the conceptual model that emerged from this study. Before presenting the findings and the conceptual model, I briefly discuss the study's theoretical underpinnings and research methodology. Please note that although this article focuses exclusively on the social construction of masculinities, I use the terms "male" and "man" interchangeably. Therefore, it's important to acknowledge that the term "male" applies specifically to a biological sex role whereas "man" is a socially constructed concept that encompasses the social and cultural meanings that are associated with the male sex role.

THEORETICAL UNDERPINNINGS

I approached this study from a constructionist epistemological perspective. Constructionist epistemology is fundamentally concerned with the meanings individuals derive from their lived experiences and social interactions (Arminio & Hultgren, 2002). Constructionist researchers also challenge the objectivist assumption that a "knowable, singular reality" exists independent of human experiences and can be captured empirically (Broido & Manning, 2002, p. 435). As such, a major theoretical assumption of constructionist epistemology is that empirical knowledge is produced in partnership between researchers and participants through their collective involvement in the inquiry process (Arminio & Hultgren).

Consistent with constructionist epistemology, an interdisciplinary conceptual framework comprising theories and perspectives regarding the social construction of masculinities and the identity development of college students informed the design and execution of this study. Key assumptions of the two theories that were most influential in guiding this study are discussed in the sections that follow.

The Social Construction of Masculinities

The social construction of masculinities—a perspective that was proposed by pro-feminist men's studies scholars (e.g., Connell, 1995; Kimmel & Messner, 2007; Levant, 1996; Pleck, 1981)—emphasizes the influence of social interactions, social structures, and social contexts in producing and reinforcing so-called normative expectations of masculine behavior. This perspective challenged the earlier research on men, which assumed that biological differences between men and women were explanatory factors for men's aggressiveness, toughness, competitiveness, and other stereotypically masculine behaviors.

Scholars who examine masculinities from a social constructionist perspective view gender as a performed social identity and are fundamentally concerned with the consequences of traditional patterns of male gender socialization and of performing masculinities according to prevailing societal norms. Another key assumption of this perspective is that no one dominant masculine form persists across all social settings but rather *multiple masculinities* that are situated in sociocultural contexts. In addition, although acknowledging that men occupy

a privileged space in society, this perspective also recognizes that some masculinities (e.g., White, heterosexual, able-bodied) are prioritized and situated as dominant above others (e.g., gay, feminine, racial/ethnic minority, physically disabled, working class). Lastly, as Kimmel and Messner (2007) noted in their discussion, because gender is a performed social identity, one can assume that the ways in which individuals conceptualize and express masculinities will change as they "grow and mature" throughout their lives (p. xxii).

Multiple Dimensions of Identity

The social construction of masculinities perspective described in the previous section recognizes the existence of multiple masculinities among men. Issues of race/ethnicity, class, religion, and sexual orientation interact and influence the development of these multiple masculinities—some of which challenge dominant and traditional social constructions. A framework that has proven useful in making sense of the intersection of identities is Jones and McEwen's (2000) multiple dimensions of identity (MDI) model. The main components of the MDI model are: (a) the core sense of self, (b) identity dimensions, and (c) contextual influences.

At the center of the model is the core sense of self, which is derived from an individual's personal attributes, characteristics, and personal identity. The core comprises a person's "inner identity" and internal qualities, such as intelligence, kindness, loyalty, compassion, and independence (Jones & McEwen, 2000). Surrounding the core are intersecting dimensions that contribute to an individual's overall identity. These include: sexual orientation, race/ethnicity, culture, gender, class, religion, and other socially constructed dimensions. The concept of "salience" is used in the model to describe the proximity of an identity dimension to the core. Identity dimensions that are positioned closest to the core are deemed to be more salient or important to the individual at a particular time. Jones and McEwen noted, "the salience of identity dimensions [is] rooted in internal awareness and external scrutiny" (p. 410). In other words, individuals are typically more internally aware of their marginalized identities, such as being a woman in a male-dominated setting or a racial/ethnic minority. Thus, these identity dimensions are usually more salient than are those that are often privileged in society. Contextual influences make up the third component of the MDI model. Because individuals interact in a larger social context, the model accounts for factors such as family background, significant life experiences, and the sociocultural conditions that influence identity development and expression.

In sum the social construction of masculinities perspective and the MDI model recognize the fluidity of gender identity, highlight the ways in which gender intersects other identity dimensions, and emphasize the influence of social contexts on identity development and gender performance. Collectively, these theories provided a heuristic conceptual framework for examining masculinities in college environments from a social constructionist perspective.

METHODOLOGY

Given the study's research questions, stated purposes, and that the gender identity development of college men is a phenomenon that has not been fully explored, I used grounded theory as the methodological approach. Originally developed by Glaser and Strauss in 1967, grounded theory offers a set of analytic guidelines for building theories through successive levels of data analysis and conceptual development (Charmaz, 2006). To this end, researchers develop increasingly abstract ideas about research participants' meanings, actions, and worlds and seek specific data to refine and check emerging conceptual categories (Charmaz). The grounded theory approach has undergone several modifications in recent years, most notably by Strauss and Corbin (1990, 1998) and Charmaz. Charmaz's approach, "constructivist grounded theory," provides space for researchers to situate themselves in the research process by being reflexive and transparent about the biases and assumptions they bring to the inquiry—a sharp contrast from Glaser and Strauss's

approach that calls for strict objectivity on the part of researchers.

Grounded theory has been employed successfully in previous studies that have examined the identity development of college students (e.g., Abes, Jones, & McEwen, 2007; Edwards & Jones, 2009; Jones & McEwen, 2000; Renn, 2000; Renn & Bilodeau, 2005; Torres, 2003; Troiano, 2003). In fact, Brown, Stevens, Troiano, and Schneider (2002) argued that grounded theory is particularly useful for inquiries seeking to explore the experiences of college students when little is known about the phenomenon being studied.

Research Setting and Context

The research site for the study was Wallbrook University (a pseudonym), a large, selective private research institution. Wallbrook is an urban institution situated in the western region of the United States. When the data were collected for this study, men comprised nearly half (49%) of the undergraduates at Wallbrook. Among undergraduate men, White students were most represented (49%), followed by Asian American/Pacific Islanders (21%), Latinos (12%), African Americans (5%), and Native Americans (less than 1%). International students comprised nearly 10% of Wallbrook's undergraduate men. The race/ethnicity was "unknown" for nearly 3% of Wallbrook's undergraduate men. Sixty-one percent of all undergraduates at Wallbrook were 21 years old or younger.

Wallbrook offered a rich context for examining college masculinities. It has a diverse male student population, a culture of "big-time" NCAA Division I athletics, and a highly visible fraternity system. The published literature on college men and masculinities suggest that these factors may have observable effects on male behavioral norms and the ways in which college men perform masculinities (Harris & Struve, 2009; Martin & Harris, 2006; Messner, 2001; Whitson, 1990).

A total of 68 undergraduate men participated in this study. The men were selected according to the theoretical assumptions of the social construction of masculinities and the MDI model, notably that men are not a homogenous group and that gender is intersected by other salient identity dimensions (e.g., race/ethnicity, sexual orientation, age, [dis]ability, and socioeconomic status). Thus, the participants were selected purposefully to capture a participant pool comprising information-rich cases (Brown et al., 2002; Jones, 2002; Patton, 2002). To recruit the participants, I asked campus administrators in student affairs, religious life, and athletics at Wallbrook to nominate men with whom they worked to participate in this study. I contacted each nominated student to describe the goals and purposes of the study, confirm his willingness to participate, and to address any questions or concerns. Students were informed that they were recommended for participation by a campus administrator, but their participation in the study was strictly voluntary.

The participant pool for this study included 22 seniors, 14 juniors, 12 sophomores, and 20 first-year students. Twenty-two of the participants were African American, 21 were White, 11 were Latino, 7 were Asian/Pacific Islander, and 7 identified as biracial/multiethnic. Thirteen of the 68 men in the study identified as nonheterosexual (gay or bisexual). Fifteen of the participants were involved in varsity athletics at Wallbrook. Fifteen also held membership in a Wallbrook fraternity. Fifty-three of the 68 participants were raised in "two parent" (mother and father) homes. A majority of the participants (40 of the 68) described their socioeconomic backgrounds as "middle-class." Of the remaining participants, 18 identified as "affluent" whereas 8 came from "low-income" backgrounds. Two participants did not disclose their socioeconomic backgrounds.

Data Collection

I collected data for this study in two phases. In phase one I conducted face-to-face, semi-structured individual interviews with 12 of the 68 participants— each representing one of nine identity groups (described later in this section). The duration of the interviews ranged from 60 to 90 minutes. During the interviews I asked the participants to reflect on and discuss experiences and interactions that had

significant influences on their conceptualizations of masculinities and the way they viewed themselves as men. For example, some of the questions I asked during the interviews were: "What defining characteristics would you use to describe what it means to be a man?" "How did you come to learn what it means to be a man?" and "What were some messages about masculinities that were communicated and reinforced by your parents?" I also asked the participants to share stories and details about their interactions with male peers in college.

Each interview was audio taped, fully transcribed, and analyzed using the Atlas.Ti qualitative data analysis program. My analysis of the data from the interviews allowed me to identify a set of preliminary concepts and categories relating to the participants' masculine conceptualizations and gender-related experiences. I used these concepts and categories to develop a protocol that guided my inquiry in phase two of the data collection.

During phase two of the data collection, nine focus groups with a total of 56 participants who represented the following male student subgroups were convened: (a) members of predominantly White fraternities, (b) members of historically Black fraternities, (c) Asian American students, (d) Latino men, (e) first-year students, (f) openly gay and bisexual students, (g) Jewish men, (h) White student–athletes, and (i) African American student–athletes. These groups were selected because they are largely reflective of the diversity of undergraduate male student populations at Wallbrook. Recognizing the interconnectedness and fluidity of the dimensions that make up an individual's identity, I contextualized the questions in ways that allowed the participants to reflect on and speak to the salience of a particular identity dimension (e.g., "During your interactions with your Latino male peers . . ."). This strategy proved useful in scaffolding the reflection of participants who represented multiple identities (e.g., African American men who were also openly gay or bisexual). The focus groups lasted 45 to 60 minutes. All nine focus groups were audio taped, fully transcribed, and analyzed using the Atlas.Ti qualitative data analysis program.

Data Analysis

Data analysis for this study followed the techniques and procedures proposed by Strauss and Corbin (1998) and Charmaz (2006) for developing grounded theory. Specifically, I used open, axial, and selective coding to deconstruct, interpret, and reassemble the data in ways that provided insight into the participants' meanings of masculinities. During the open-coding phase, I took my first look at the transcripts, identified significant concepts and incidents that emerged, and assigned a word or phrase to capture my initial interpretations of the data. I recorded in writing the thoughts and reflections that came to mind as I read through and made sense of the data.

After all of the transcripts were initially coded, I used axial coding to group the coded incidents and concepts into categories based on their shared properties and relationships to the participants' masculine conceptualizations. This process began as I reread the fully coded transcripts along with the initial codes and analytic reflections that I had applied during the open-coding phase. Concepts and incidents that appeared to be related to the same phenomenon were grouped together and given a code that captured the essence of this phenomenon. For example, the concepts, "getting drunk," "playing video games," "watching sports," and "locker room talk" were grouped under the category "male bonding" (which was eventually renamed "activities that facilitate male bonding"). Likewise, "parental influences," "peer interactions," and "sports participation" were concepts that comprised the category "precollege gender socialization." All categories and concepts were considered "emerging" until I compared them across all of the interview and focus group transcripts.

Finally, I used selective coding to understand the relationships between the categories that emerged during the axial coding phase. Charmaz (2006) emphasized three guiding questions in making sense of the relationships between categories: (a) What are the conditions or circumstances under which the phenomenon takes place? (b) What actions or strategies are employed by the participants

in response to the phenomenon? and (c) What were the consequences or outcomes of the strategies or actions taken? In applying these questions to the current study, I sought insight into the participants' conceptualizations of masculinities, the contextual and environmental factors that influenced the participants' conceptualizations, and the behavioral norms and expectations that emerged as a result of the interactions between these variables. Again, I compared these relationships across the data to ensure saturation. The aforementioned analyses and interpretations of the data allowed me to develop a conceptual model (see Figure 12.1) that captured the participants' meanings of masculinities and the contextual factors that influenced these meanings.

Trustworthiness and Quality Assurance

Several strategies prescribed by Lincoln and Guba (1985) were used to establish trustworthiness in this study. First, I relied on a peer debriefing team, comprising informed colleagues with expertise in qualitative research, college student development, and masculinities with whom I shared the process I used for data collection and analysis. I also furnished a complete write-up of the findings, which reflected my interpretations of the students' experiences. The roles of peer debriefers were to scrutinize the methods that were used to conduct the study and to both challenge and confirm my interpretations of the data. When questions were raised by a debriefer, I returned to the data to ensure that my interpretations were grounded in the data.

I also used member checking to establish trustworthiness in this study. In so doing, I held a feedback session where I presented the conceptual model to men who participated in the study. During the feedback session, I asked the participants to comment on the degree to which the model accurately captured their perspectives on masculinities and the gender-related experiences they shared. Overall, the participants confirmed that the model reflected their experiences and perspectives.

In addition, the criteria proposed by Strauss and Corbin (1998) provided a framework for evaluating the trustworthiness of this research. The

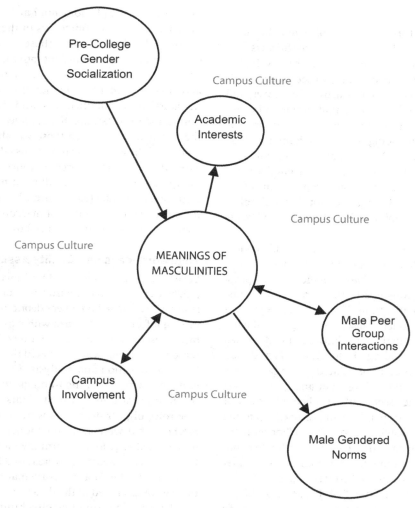

Pre-College Gender Socialization

Campus Culture

Academic Interests

Campus Culture

Campus Culture

MEANINGS OF MASCULINITIES

Male Peer Group Interactions

Campus Involvement

Campus Culture

Male Gendered Norms

■ **FIGURE 12.1**
A Conceptual Model of the Meanings College Men Make of Masculinities

conceptual model meets Strauss and Corbin's (1998) criteria in that: (a) Its concepts and categories were generated systematically and are grounded in the data; (b) there are clear conceptual linkages between the central phenomenon, concepts, and categories of the model; (c) the model describes the central phenomenon as a process that operates under a set of conditions with variation; and (d) new

insights about masculinities emerging from the research are reflected in the model.

Lastly, as advised by Torres and Baxter Magolda (2002) and Charmaz (2006) in their discussions of constructivist research studies, I routinely reflected on my own salient identities as a college-educated heterosexual African American man while conducting this study. Doing so allowed me to recognize how these identity dimensions informed my beliefs and assumptions about college men and masculinities and shaped my interactions with the participants. Being reflexive also helped to ensure that my gender identity and experiences did not lead to hasty or shallow interpretations of the data.

Findings

From the data analysis emerged a conceptual model that represented the participants' meanings of masculinities and the corresponding contextual influences (see Figure 12.1). The key variables of the model are: (a) meanings of masculinities, which reflected the participants' gender-related attitudes, beliefs, and assumptions; (b) contextual influences that shaped, reinforced, and challenged the participants' meanings; and (c) male gendered norms that represent the outcomes of the interactions between the aforementioned variables of the model. In this section of the article, each variable of the model is discussed and supported with representative quotes and reflections from the interviews and focus groups.

Meanings of Masculinities

The "meanings of masculinities" variable represents the core category or central phenomenon of the model. The core category captures the essence of the findings and summarizes "in a few words what the research is all about" (Strauss & Corbin, 1998, p. 146). As displayed in Figure 12.1, the core category is situated in the center of the model and is surrounded by three smaller circles and a series of arrows indicating interactions with the other variables of the model. Several concepts emerged from the data as meanings the participants ascribed to masculinities. These included: "being respected," "being confident and self-assured," "assuming responsibility," and "embodying physical prowess." According to the participants, these were some "defining characteristics" of men and reflected the attitudes and behaviors about masculinities that they learned and were reinforced before they enrolled in college.

"Being respected," according to the participants, entailed "being willing to stand up for yourself" as well as earning the deference and admiration of other men. For instance, a Latino focus group participant asserted, "I think as long as you stand up for yourself [and] for what you believe in and not being ashamed when someone challenges you, then that defines masculinity." A first-year student interviewee offered a similar perspective: "You [have to] stand up for what you believe in. You [have to] be strong-willed and [not] let people push you around and that kind of stuff." The participants also shared examples of men on campus who were respected by male peers for their "hard work." Specifically, guys who were "well-rounded" and able to successfully balance the demands of academics, campus involvement (which includes participation in athletics), and an active social life are examples of the type of men who were respected at Wallbrook. This was a recurring theme among the men in the study as they offered numerous examples of men who were well-respected for their abilities to manage multiple demands successfully.

"Being confident and self-assured" was another concept the participants associated with masculinities. The men in the study spoke of rejecting masculine stereotypes and making conscious decisions to perform masculinities based on what they themselves deemed appropriate, rather than simply conforming to popular notions or others' expectations. They also reported that self-assured men are able to engage in activities and exhibit behaviors that may be perceived as contradictory to masculine norms without being concerned about raising suspicions about their sexual orientations. Interestingly, some of the men recalled arriving at these decisions prior to matriculating to college. For example, during a discussion about factors that influenced their beliefs and ideas about masculinities a participant in the focus group with openly gay and bisexual men shared that he developed his own ideas about "what a male should be" as early as age 16 and since that time decided he was going to express his gender in ways that were consistent with these ideas. He noted:

> I was just so much more comfortable just being who I was rather than trying to pretend to have a deeper voice all the time, dress a certain way, walk a certain way. Like you just come to be a

lot more comfortable with yourself and you just accept yourself for who you are and you don't feel like you have to fit into a certain type of mold. So I came into Wallbrook with that notion already. I was going to come [to Wallbrook] and I was still going to be who I was, regardless of what the notions of masculinity were here.

Similarly, a student–athlete spoke of participating in the band in middle school, which required him to forgo some of his time playing sports with male friends at lunch time. "I did something that was considered uncool [by male peers], but I didn't mind it because it wasn't about that. It was about what I wanted to do."

The men also associated masculinities with "assuming responsibility." This meaning seemed to relate primarily to men who "took care of their families" by successfully fulfilling "breadwinner" roles and expectations in their homes. The participants often referenced their fathers and other adult male role models in discussing the nexus between responsibility and masculinities. One of the first-year participants shared how he learned to equate masculinities with responsibility from a group of older, "blue-collar" men he observed during a summer job in his hometown:

> I worked this summer at a rock yard. [The men I worked with were] blue-collar workers, they chew tobacco and they spit and they cuss and they only drive American trucks, stuff like that. [I] definitely learned a lot about being a man. I was working about three-fourths of the day as a lot of the guys. They worked seven days a week, nine hours a day, and they do it because they have families and wives to support. I think that's a big thing, is just being responsible and doing what it takes.

The concept of responsibility also underscored the participants' reflections on their leadership experiences. The participants assumed that men were "groomed" or socialized to assume positions of leadership and authority. For example, one participant made the following connection between masculinities, responsibility, and leadership: "[Leadership] is really being in the forefront

[which] goes back to how we view men personally. Women play the background and men are more in the forefront. So I think that goes along with traditional views of masculinity." The participants also recognized that leadership involves "making tough decisions"—a behavior they also associated with masculinities.

Finally, the participants confirmed that men's bodies factored into their meanings of masculinities, primarily as they relate to men's physical statures and the extent to which they engaged in heterosexual sex with women. Simply stated, the participants assumed that men who had large, muscular builds; displayed physical prowess (by way of sports, weight lifting, etc.); and captured the attention and attraction of women were "more masculine" than were men who were less competitive in these regards. Reflecting on the nexus between physical prowess and masculinities, a Jewish participant exclaimed: "Look at [name], a middle linebacker on the [Wallbrook] football team. The guy has to be 6'6", 250, looks like a brick wall walking. The guy's fucking gigantic and nobody would ever question that guy's masculinity." The following exchange that took place during the focus group with Asian American students illustrates the ways in which the participants viewed women and objects of expressing masculinities:

> If I could define masculinity in any one way, I think the most . . . the strongest thing would be towards appealing to women because the idea of getting a girlfriend or hooking up or whatever it is you're interested in, getting that would make you more masculine than not having it. Right, exactly, for instance, if I was interested in hooking up and I was unable to, I would not consider myself as masculine as I would if I had when I woke up the next morning after hooking up with a girl.

Interestingly, many of the participants declared that these meanings of masculinities were not nearly as important as the aforementioned concepts of respect, self-assurance, and responsibility. The following reflection that was offered by a student–athlete focus group participant provides an example of the ways in which the men sought to make these distinctions: "Not to say that my masculinity isn't defined by women—it is. But it's so low on the list of overall things in my definition of what masculinity means compared to respect, responsibility, and things like that."

Contextual Influences

Several interactive sociocultural factors emerged as contextual influences on both the meanings the participants ascribed to masculinities as well as the ways in which they expressed masculinities in the campus context: precollege gender socialization, the campus culture, campus involvement, academic interests, and male peer group interactions. These variables of the model capture the experiences and interactions that: (a) reinforced previously learned lessons about masculinities or (b) challenged the participants to acknowledge other ideas and expressions of masculinities and reconsider their own beliefs, attitudes, and assumptions about masculinities. Each of these contextual influences and interactions with the core category are discussed throughout this section.

Precollege Gender Socialization. The participants' precollege gender socialization emerged as a contextual factor that influenced the ways in which they conceptualized and expressed masculinities in college. This variable is situated at the very top of the model. The unidirectional arrow that points to the core category denotes that this variable led to the development of the participants' meanings of masculinities. Three factors were consistently identified by the participants as having significant influences on the beliefs and attitudes about masculinities they learned prior to their matriculation to college: (a) parental influences, (b) male peer interactions, and (c) participating in sports and other "masculinizing" activities.

Parents, especially fathers, socialized the participants to behave and interact in ways that were deemed acceptable by traditional expectations of masculinities. Avoiding feminine behaviors and attitudes as well as expressing masculinities through physicality and toughness were notable in this regard. One student shared that, unlike his mother, his father was very purposeful in ensuring that he expressed his gender in ways that were deemed socially acceptable for young boys:

> There were times when I was younger where maybe I was playing with my sister or putting on makeup or something . . . and usually the person that would . . . not really reprimand, but correct that would be my father . . . because my mother, she'd play along, "Oh, that's cute," and all that sort of stuff, but my dad always tried to make sure . . . like he'd toughen me up and prepare . . . kind of condition me to have that mentality as being masculine and trying to be strong and doing manly things, you know.

The messages about masculinities that were communicated by the participants' mothers differed somewhat from those that were reinforced by their fathers. Mothers reportedly encouraged relational, sensitive, and well-rounded masculinities. "My mom always taught me how to be sensitive and express my feelings," noted one of the participants. Another recalled: "She really wanted to instill fairness and make sure that I respected other people and treated them the way I would want to be treated."

There was one notable exception to this finding regarding messages that were reinforced by mothers. One of the focus group participants, who happened to be raised in a single-parent family that was headed by his mother, shared that "crying" and other behaviors that were not considered masculine were not accepted in his home: "My mother was always like, 'You should be a man about it.' [She had] a 'take-it-like-a-man' kind of [mentality]."

The participants also reported that, much like their fathers, their middle and high school male peers reinforced stereotypically masculine behavioral norms. For example, an Asian American interviewee shared some of the lessons and behaviors that were reinforced as early as elementary school by his male peers:

> During elementary school there was a group of peers that I looked to for any sense of what a boy is supposed to be and do. . . . You're supposed to

play tackle football, not touch, that kind of a thing, and cursing a lot as well. I learned predominantly through them that you're going to play football, you're going to curse, and that's what all the other guys are doing, you should be doing that too.

As they reflected on the experiences and interactions with male peers that influenced their conceptualizations of masculinities, the participants recalled many instances in which they felt compelled to engage in behaviors they would have otherwise avoided. Getting into the physical fights, vandalizing property, lying about having sex with their girlfriends, consuming alcohol, and using profanity were offered as examples of the behaviors in which they engaged in order to assert and affirm their masculinities with male peers. Likewise, some participants reportedly downplayed their academic success and hid their involvement in activities that were not considered masculine by peers, such as playing tennis, piano, and singing in the choir. Again, the participants' desires to be accepted by male peers and to not be perceived as feminine were the primary reasons why they performed gender in these ways.

Youth sports and other traditionally masculine activities, such as martial arts and boy scouts, also provided a context in which traditional notions of masculinities were infused and reinforced during the participants' precollege gender socialization. Expressing masculinities through toughness, physical aggression, and by not showing weakness were some of the key lessons about masculinities the participants recalled learning by way of their involvement in these activities. For example, one of the gay participants in the study shared that his youth football coach reinforced a very rigid definition of masculinities and did not allow members of the team to express behaviors that were socially constructed as feminine:

Well, I was in football, and our coach had a very, very strict definition of what masculinity was, and he very much tried to press that view on all of us, mostly because he believed that it was important and part of his job to make sure that we all turned

out to be men, as opposed to boys, I guess, and so it was very important that we not be feminine, not exhibit any feminine traits at all.

An African American participant who also grew up playing football reflected on the ways in which his involvement in sports informed his ideas about masculinities. Through sports, he learned that "men were supposed to be kind of rough and tumble, be out there on the field hitting people and stuff and acting crazy and running around." This same participant further declared that this rough and tumble image of masculinity has remained "embedded in [his] mind."

Sports and similar activities in which the gender socialization of boys was prioritized were also key contexts in which the participants had meaningful interactions with their fathers. A critical mass of the participants, even those who were not student–athletes at Wallbrook, shared that their fathers encouraged, and at times demanded, their participation in these activities. Some participants felt that their fathers pushed too far in this regard, which resulted in strained and conflicted relationships between them and their fathers.

Campus Culture. The campus culture variable of the model represents the "context" or the "location of events and incidents that influence the central category or related phenomena" (Strauss & Corbin, 1990, p. 96). This variable is situated in the background of the model and surrounds the other variables of the model. The positioning of the campus culture variable of the model suggests that the interactions between variables that are depicted in the model are situated in the Wallbrook campus context. The participants described the campus culture in three meaningful ways and discussed the corresponding effects on the expression of masculinities: "diverse," "patriarchal," and "competitive."

The diversity described by the participants provided space for a wide range of masculine expressions, particularly among men who did not express masculinities according to traditional expectations. The diversity among men at Wallbrook not only allowed for the expression of a wide range of masculinities but, according to the participants, it also afforded them opportunities for sustained contact and crosscultural interaction with men who represented diverse backgrounds and experiences. As a result, the participants reported gaining richer and more complex ideas about masculinities that challenged some of the conceptualizations that were infused during their gender socialization prior to college.

Despite having a very diverse campus culture that provided a context for a range of masculinities, the participants also described Wallbrook as "patriarchal." This characterization stemmed from the assumption that men who embodied traditional masculinities, notably fraternity members and male student–athletes, were privileged and maintained a higher social status than did the other men on campus who did not hold membership in these groups. They noted that because of their visibility and popularity among men at Wallbrook, fraternity members and student–athletes had substantial influences on the ways in which other men were judged. Being in good physical shape, being competitive, and "hooking up with lots of women"—characteristics of masculinities that were associated with fraternity members and male student–athletes—were prioritized among men at Wallbrook.

Lastly, the participants described the campus culture as competitive in that they felt constant pressure to compete with other men for status, attention, and popularity. Perhaps not surprisingly, much of the competition the participants described was centered on traditionally masculine pursuits and activities like consuming alcohol, playing video games, working out in the gym, participating in sports, and having sex with women. However, the participants also acknowledged that competition among men was not restricted to the traditional masculine activities that were described earlier. They indicated that the competition to outperform each other academically by having the most rigorous course loads or the toughest majors was almost as intense as the competition around drinking, hooking up, and similar pursuits. As one participant explained, "There is a level of competition in terms of who is taking the

hardest course load or who's got the highest GPA." Later in the interview, this same participant recalled some of the conversations he and some of his male peers often have when discussing their academic workload and shared, "Sometimes there is sort of the idea of trying to outdo the other person, like, 'I had this really hard 20 page paper that I had to [write.]' 'Well, mine was 30 pages. It was harder.' " (See Harris & Struve, 2009, for an expanded discussion of the campus culture variable of the model).

Academic Interests. The participants' academic interests are represented as a contextual influence in the model. Note that the interaction between this variable and the core category is depicted with a unidirectional arrow because evidence of the participants' academic interests influencing their meanings of masculinities did not emerge from the data. I inquired purposefully into the participants' perceptions of academic success and connections to their conceptualizations of masculinities. For example, I asked the participants to what extent was academic success valued and celebrated among their male peers and if it was possible for men to be perceived as both smart and masculine at Wallbrook. There was widespread agreement across the subgroups that men indeed could achieve academic success and still be perceived as masculine at Wallbrook. A student–athlete in the sample shared: "[Academic success] is never negative. I've never had anybody look at me negatively for being smart. If anything, it's been like, 'Man, I wish I could do that.' " Similarly, a Jewish focus group participant offered the following response: "Yeah, it's like, 'Wow! This guy's buff, he has a bunch of girls, he's at [Wallbrook] now but next semester, he's going to community college because he's flunking out.' That's not success." However, what was especially interesting is that these perceptions were qualified with the caveat that men who achieved academic success had to be "well-rounded," which was defined by the participants as displaying competence in multiple domains (including academics) such as physical prowess, leadership, and popularity.

Another finding that emerged regarding the participants' academic interests was the extent to which their chosen fields of study were informed by their conceptualizations of masculinities. Many of the men in the study indicated a desire to pursue careers in traditionally masculine fields (e.g., law, medicine, real estate, engineering) after graduating from college, which influenced their choices of classes and majors. These participants assumed that these fields would lead to high paying jobs and allow them to fulfill traditional "breadwinner" roles that are culturally defined as masculine in American families. As such, many of the participants believed men had to be purposeful in choosing a major or a career path because making the wrong choice could limit their earning potential thereby making it more difficult to fulfill the breadwinner role. They also assumed that women did not face these same pressures because, despite earning a college degree, most would settle down, get married, and stay at home to raise their children. To this point, one participant declared,

> The game steps up a lot in college and serious things like providing for a family become a man's issue. You don't really hear women say, "I need to go get a business degree so I can provide for my family." I'll ask them, "What do you want to do after college?" They don't say, "I need to provide for my family." You talk to most guys, "I want to make some money so I can provide for a family." That's a genuine issue for a lot of guys and I think that's just society's impact on everyone. It's just a natural progression, men provide for a family.

Most of the participants confirmed that having access to financial resources, being successful in respected and well-paying careers, and taking care of their families were central to how they viewed masculinities and would define themselves as men later in life. There was agreement among the men in the study that taking care of a family and achieving some financial security were important indicators of masculinities. For example, in the focus group with fraternity members, one student exclaimed:

> I'm a political science major, like, I'm going to law school, I'm going to become a lawyer and that's just what's going to happen, and I do well in

school because I want to go to a good law school so that I can get rich. It's not a secret to anybody that I want to be rich. I mean, when my kid turns 16, I want to buy him a BMW and I just want to have a ridiculous amount of money.

Campus Involvement. The participants' campus involvement was another contextual factor that interacted with their conceptualizations of masculinities. The participants reported being involved in a range of campus activities—some of which were traditionally masculine (e.g., sports teams, student government, fraternities) whereas others were gender neutral (e.g. political science undergraduate association, residence hall council, ethnic student organizations). Many of the students held leadership positions in their respective organizations and made connections between these roles and their beliefs about masculinities. When I asked a group of African American focus group participants if there was a connection between their masculinities and their pursuit of campus leadership, one student affirmed,

> [Yes], men should be leaders, heads of organizations. There's nothing wrong with having a cute vice president or a cute secretary, or a cute treasurer, but . . . don't laugh, I'm real serious . . . men tend to believe . . . like we are supposed to be leaders, so when you go into organizations, you expect to see a male president . . . . There shouldn't be a vacant slot because no man wants to step up.

Although some participants focused on the ways in which their leadership and involvement allowed them to perform traditional expectations of masculinities, others discussed how their involvement provided opportunities for meaningful interactions with male peers from different backgrounds and encouraged them to be more accepting of masculinities that were different from their own. Serving on student organizational boards and committees and attending campus retreats with men who represented different backgrounds provided these cross-cultural engagement opportunities. What was most compelling about this finding was that the men confirmed that had it not been for their involvement in activities outside of class, it was unlikely that they would have had these opportunities to get to know men who were different from themselves in some meaningful way.

Male Peer Group Interactions. The data provided evidence of interaction between the participants' involvement in exclusively male subgroups and the meanings they ascribed to masculinities. The men in the study spoke of the interactions and conversations that often took place within their respective male peer groups and made very clear connections regarding the ways in which these interactions influenced their behavioral expressions of masculinities. One of the most illustrative examples of the connections the participants made between their masculinities and their interactions with male peers was offered by one of the fraternity men in the study who proudly proclaimed:

> I really give in to the male stereotypes by being in a fraternity. I curse, I drink a lot, I smoke cigars. Like we do the things that men are supposed to do. We entertain women, we drink a lot, and for me, that's what it is and I act that same way.

Other participants reported that their masculine expression with close male peers is noticeably different than it is in mixed-gender groups. For instance, talking sexually about women was a popular pastime among the majority of the heterosexual men who participated in the study. These men noted that the ways in which they talked about women in the presence of another woman was far more respectful and less sexual than what could be observed during their discussions about women when only men were around. Interestingly, some of the participants confirmed that, at times, they did not approve of the way they and their male peers talked about women. Yet, they partook in these discussions anyhow as to not disrupt the dynamics of the group and to maintain their status and acceptance within the group.

Male Gendered Norms

The last variable of the model, "male gendered norms," represents the "consequences" (Strauss & Corbin, 1998) or the outcomes of the interactions between the participants' meanings of masculinities

and the contextual influences that were discussed in previous sections of this article (precollege gender socialization, campus culture, academic interests, campus involvement, and male peer group interactions). Here I discuss three shared gendered norms that resonated across the groups of men in the study: (a) having "work hard–play hard mentalities, (b) hypermasculine performance, and (c) male bonding.

Work Hard–Play Hard. The "work hard–play hard" concept describes the ongoing challenge men faced of having a visible and fulfilling social life while privately balancing intense academic expectations and out-of-class responsibilities. This gendered norm is perhaps best described by one of the first-year students who offered the following perspective during a discussion about the challenges of being a male student at Wallbrook: "Being cool enough to stay up all night playing poker with them [other male peers] and still turn in your paper by eight o'clock [the next morning]."

The participants felt that college would be their last opportunity to take advantage of the wide range of freedom without the demanding responsibilities of managing their careers and taking care of their families. One of the African American students offered his perspective on the importance of balancing work and play in college:

> I know there's a lot expected of me after I leave here [Wallbrook] . . . I mean, the opportunities for the pleasurable stuff and whatever might not be as abundant once I go out into the real world and have to pay bills and all that stuff. So it's like . . . you have to make the memories now so that once you work hard, get to a certain level, then you're [not] going to look back and be like, "Damn, I missed out on everything." So you kind of got to [balance] doing your work and your pleasure, but they should both be very strong, in my opinion.

Participants also attributed this shared work hard—play hard mentality among men to the campus culture and suggested that Wallbrook offered "the best of both worlds," given its thriving academic and social cultures for students. The participants also acknowledged some of the consequences of not maintaining an appropriate balance between work and play, especially when the latter becomes the priority. "Missing assignments" and "pulling all-nighters to get the work done" were offered as consequences.

Hypermasculine Performance. The participants' hypermasculine performance, or the behaviors they employed strategically to express themselves as men in ways that were consistent with stereotypical expectations, was also a shared gendered norm among the men in the study. Several of the behaviors that have been discussed in detail throughout this article—notably their abuse of alcohol, objectification of women, and pursuit of exclusively sexual relationships—characterize the participants' hypermasculine performance. In addition, there was generalized fear of femininity among the heterosexual participants, which was manifested most strongly during discussions about their interactions with openly gay men. These participants admitted that they would find it difficult to embrace a gay friend, teammate, or fraternity brother out of fear that others would assume they were also gay if they were seen interacting publicly with these men. They also expressed anxiety and discomfort about being the object of a gay peer's affection, which can also be linked to their fear of femininity and hypermasculine performance.

Male Bonding. Finally, despite the stereotypical norms and expectations that governed the expression of masculinities at Wallbrook, cultivating bonding relationships with male peers, particularly those who held similar interests and perspectives, was a shared norm among the men. The participants spoke of the importance of having "a group of close male friends to share memorable experiences in college" and to rely on for support during challenging times. Most of the men described their bonding relationships with other men as "healthy" and "necessary" to have a fulfilled college experience. For instance, a participant from the Latino focus group shared, "For me, the aspect of masculinity comes from as a guy, you could act however you want, but

you need a strong group of guy friends with you because it's important to have them there to share the experience." Likewise, a participant from the focus group with gay and bisexual students asserted, "I think it's a healthy thing to do, to socialize, psychologically and just getting away from being alone, by yourself, and to be with friends and have friends to socialize with. It's a healthy thing."

Participants also believed these relationships with a core group of male friends were necessary given the intensity and competitiveness of the Wallbrook campus culture for men. Regarding life challenges, several of the participants shared personal crises they have faced while in college, such as parental divorces and the death of family members. These men believed they would not have made it through these difficult times had it not been for the support of their closest male friends. "When my mom passed away, my friends were the ones there for me, so it was like, 'I gotta open up to these people,' and it was never a problem and I'm really, really happy that I did it," noted one of the men in the study.

LIMITATIONS

Despite the aforementioned steps I took to establish trustworthiness in this study, several limitations are worth noting. First, given the study's qualitative design, the findings should not be generalized beyond the site and the men who participated. Second, the purpose of this study was to identify meanings of masculinities that were salient across the 68 men in the study. Thus, group-specific meanings and comparisons were not considered in the analysis on which this article is based. This is a potentially rich area for future analyses of the data that were collected for this study. Lastly, the overrepresentation of African American, White, and heterosexual men among the participants in this study is also important to note. These limitations notwithstanding, the conceptual model presented herein offers much-needed insight into the gender identity development and related experiences of college men. This study may also inform future inquires on college men, masculinities, and college student development.

DISCUSSION AND IMPLICATIONS

This study confirms that men are arriving on college campuses having been socialized to embrace traditional notions of masculinities. Many of the meanings the participants reportedly ascribed to masculinities serve to privilege men who perform masculinities according to culturally dominant expectations. Therefore, the findings of this study call for institutional efforts that help men to: (a) see the range of healthy options that are available to them in expressing their masculinities and (b) recognize how developing less-conflicted gender identities leads to a host of productive outcomes that will serve them well throughout their lives. For example, student affairs educators working on campuses like Wallbrook may find the conceptual model useful in designing programs and services to support men in their transition from high school to college, in academic advisement with college men, and in supporting men in their career development. Myers-Briggs, StrengthsQuests, and other assessments can be used to help college men make better-informed choices about their career paths and majors. Likewise, data that are collected using the National Survey of Student Engagement (NSSE), the College Student Experiences Questionnaire (CSEQ), and the National College Health Assessment (NCHA) should be routinely disaggregated and analyzed using gender frameworks to recognize and make sense of gendered trends that may exist and warrant further examination (see Sax, 2008, for example).

The study's findings support Jones and McEwen's (2000) assertions regarding the salience of identity dimensions. The participants in the study who were not student–athletes or members of a fraternity believed they did not have as much status as their peers who belonged to these groups. In relation to the larger male student population at Wallbrook, student–athletes represented a small minority of men on the campus; yet the participants agreed that these men were the most popular men at Wallbrook. Likewise, fraternity members did not constitute a quantitative majority of Wallbrook's undergraduate men. However, these subgroups were highly visible and occupied a privileged space among men at Wallbrook, which made the differences between these men and those who were not privileged in these regards more obvious and transparent. These findings are also consistent with claims by Connell (1995), Kimmel and Messner (2007), and other scholars who argued that within a given context, there will be a hierarchy of masculinities in which some will have more privilege than others. Therefore, campus administrators may be well-served by recognizing men who exhibit excellence in areas other than fraternity involvement and athletics.

With respect to campus culture, perhaps the most insightful finding from this study was the ways in which campus diversity influenced the participants' meanings of masculinities. Sax (2008) found that experiences with diversity are "liberalizing, motivating, and eye opening" for college men (p. 234). This study's findings support Sax's conclusion. Meaningful and sustained cross-cultural interaction among men who represent diverse backgrounds, identities, and experiences challenged prevailing assumptions about masculinities and motivated the participants to consider new meanings. The connections the participants made between these interactions and their involvement outside of the classroom are also significant and confirm what scholars have consistently concluded regarding the impact of campus environments on college student identity development. Therefore, educators should be mindful of the extent to which campus services, programs, and activities facilitate cross-cultural engagement among the men on their campuses. If these opportunities are not readily available, educators should consider collaborating with male student leaders to identify innovative strategies to facilitate this type of engagement for the men on their campuses. For example, collaboration between predominantly White, historically Black, and multicultural fraternities may offer opportunities for cross-cultural engagement given the roles fraternities play in bringing men from their respective communities together.

The overwhelming majority of the published research on college men and masculinities focuses on problematic trends, issues, and conflicts involving college men. These issues are important and warrant ongoing attention. Nevertheless, the key findings from this study suggest that these issues do not fully capture the developmental experiences of college men. Men in this study showed some evidence, albeit modest, of productive identity development. For instance, meanings of masculinities that encouraged the men to develop their competencies in multiple domains, like leadership and academics, may offer some potentially promising starting points for educators to encourage men to engage in campus service activities and pursue nonhierarchal leadership opportunities.

The participants' reliance on other men for emotional support during challenging times is also an interesting and somewhat surprising finding given the multiple published reports that confirm that college men invest significant efforts toward hiding their vulnerabilities from other men. In fact, most of what is known about the expression of emotions other than anger among college men revolves around the difficulties they face in doing so because this behavior is socially constructed as feminine. The factors that facilitate the level of trust and rapport-building necessary for men to feel safe opening up to each other warrant further empirical consideration.

Several key themes from Edwards and Jones's (2009) study of college men's gender identity are reflected in the conceptual model that emerged from this study. The participants in both studies embraced similar conceptualizations of men: being confident and self-assured, being respected, and being tough. They also relied heavily on hypermasculine performance to express themselves as men. The participants in both studies also reported ongoing fear and anxiety of being perceived as gay or feminine by their peers, which exacerbated their hypermasculine performance. These consistencies in the findings are especially notable considering the differences in the institutional contexts and data collection strategies that were employed in the two studies. Interestingly, unlike the present study, academic interests, campus involvement, and campus

culture did not emerge as significant influences on gender performance among the men in Edwards and Jones's study.

The hypermasculine performance variable of the conceptual model also supports O'Neil's (1981) male gender role conflict model, which identifies "fear of femininity" as an explanatory factor for homophobia, sexism, restrictive emotionality, competitiveness, and other unhealthy behaviors that are commonly observed among college men. Fear of femininity also emerged as a central theme in Davis's (2002) study of college men and masculinities.

The findings of this study raise several questions that can be explored in future studies of college men and masculinities. The conceptual model presented herein represents a snapshot or moment in time in the participants' gender identity development. Thus, the extent to which the meanings the participants ascribed to masculinities changed between the time the study was conducted and their departure from Wallbrook is unknown, which raises the question, "How do meanings of masculinities change and develop between men's initial enrollment and graduation from the institution?" Engaging in longitudinal studies similar to those conducted by Josselson (1987), Baxter Magolda (2001), and Torres (1999) may help to capture the long-term effects attending college may have on men's gender identity development.

Meanings the participants learned to associate with masculinities during their precollege gender socialization were also revealed in this study. It would be interesting to know what meanings of masculinities that are learned and reinforced in college persist beyond their departure from the institution. A related question is: "How do life experiences, like becoming a parent, being engaged in a marriage or life partnership, or committing to a career influence the meanings men ascribe to masculinities?" If one accepts Kimmel and Messner's (2007) assertion that the ways in which men perform masculinities will change as they grow and mature throughout their lives, one can reasonably assume that meanings of masculinities will be shaped by these experiences.

Given that campus culture was a contextual influence in this study, one can expect that men who are enrolled at institutions with cultures that differ from Wallbrook's will express masculinities in different ways. Replicating this study in an institutional setting that is less competitive, has a more homogenous male student population, and does not prioritize men's sports and fraternities would likely yield new insights about masculinities. Some questions to consider are: "What meanings do men who are enrolled at small liberal arts institutions, community colleges, religiously affiliated institutions, or historically Black institutions ascribe to masculinities?" and "What factors that are situated in these campus contexts influence the meanings and gender identity development of college men?"

As noted previously in this article, the purpose of this study was to identify meanings that were salient across the subgroups that were represented in this study. A goal of future studies should be to identify group-specific meanings that are situated within male subgroups. Because gender is intersected and influenced by other identity dimensions, it is very likely that some meanings can be linked to men's race/ethnicities, sexual orientations, spirituality, [dis]ability, and other salient aspects of their identities.

Lastly, postsecondary educators should not allow their efforts to support the gender identities of college men to detract attention and resources away from supporting the women on their campuses. Campus safety, academic segregation, disordered eating, and depression are but a few examples of the critical issues that challenge the psychosocial development and achievement of successful outcomes for college women. These issues demand the ongoing attention and support of all college and university educators.

REFERENCES

Abes, E. S., Jones, S. R., & McEwen, M. K. (2007). Reconceptualizing the model of multiple dimensions of identity: The role of meaning-making capacity in the construction of multiple identities. *Journal of College Student Development, 48*(1), 1–22.

Arminio, J. L., & Hultgren, F. H. (2002). Breaking out from the shadow: The question of criteria in qualitative research. *Journal of College Student Development, 43*(4), 446–473.

Baxter Magolda, M. B. (2001). *Making their own way: Narrative for transforming higher education to promote self development.* Sterling, VA: Stylus.

Broido, E. M., & Manning, K. (2002). Philosophical foundations and current theoretical perspectives in qualitative research. *Journal of College Student Development, 43*(4), 434–445.

Brown, S. C., Stevens, R. A., Jr., Troiano, P. F., & Schneider, M. K. (2002). Exploring complex phenomena: Grounded theory in student affairs research. *Journal of College Student Development, 43*(2), 1–11.

Capraro, R. L. (2000). Why college men drink: Alcohol, adventure, and the paradox of masculinity. *Journal of American College Health, 48*, 307–315.

Charmaz, K. (2006). *Constructing grounded theory: A practical guide through qualitative analysis.* Thousand Oaks, CA: Sage.

Chickering, A. W. (1969). *Education and identity.* San Francisco: Jossey-Bass.

Connell, R. W. (1995). *Masculinities.* Berkeley: University of California Press.

Courtenay, W. H. (1998). College men's health: An overview and call to action. *Journal of American College Health, 46*(6), 279–290.

Cross, W. E., Jr. (1995). The psychology of Nigrescence: Revising the Cross model. In J. G. Ponterotto, J. M. Casas, L. A. Suzuki, & C. M. Alexander (Eds.), *Handbook of multicultural counseling* (pp. 93–122). Thousand Oaks, CA: Sage.

D'Augelli, A. R. (1994). Identity development and sexual orientation: Toward a model of lesbian, gay, and bisexual development. In E. J. Trickett, R. Watts, & D. Birman (Eds.), *Human diversity: Perspectives on people in context* (pp. 312–333). San Francisco: Jossey-Bass.

Davis, T. (2002). Voices of gender role conflict: The social construction of college men's identity. *Journal of College Student Development, 43*(4), 508–521.

Davis, T., & Laker, J. A. (2004). Connecting men to academic and student affairs programs and services. *Developing effective programs and services for college men: New directions for student services* (Vol. 107, pp. 47–57). San Francisco: Jossey-Bass.

Edwards, K. E., & Jones, S. R. (2009). "Putting my man face on": A grounded theory of college men's gender identity development. *Journal of College Student Development, 50*(2), 210–228.

Erikson, E. (1968). *Identity: Youth and crisis.* New York: Norton.

Evans, N. J., Forney, D. S., & Guido-DiBrito, F. (1998). *Student development in college: Theory, research, and practice.* San Francisco: Jossey-Bass.

Foubert, J. D., Newberry, J. T., & Tatum, J. (2007). Behavior differences seven months later: Effects of a rape prevention program. *NASPA Journal, 44*(4), 728–749.

Glaser, B. G., & Strauss, A. L. (1967). *The discovery of grounded theory.* Chicago: Aldine.

Good, G. E., & Mintz, L. B. (1990). Gender role conflict and depression in college men: Evidence for compounded risk. *Journal of Counseling and Development, 69*(1), 17–21.

Good, G. E., & Wood, P. K. (1995). Male gender role conflict, depression, and help seeking: Do college men face double jeopardy? *Journal of Counseling & Development, 74,* 70–75.

Harper, S. R., Harris III, F., & Mmeje, K. (2005). A theoretical model to explain the overrepresentation of college men among campus judicial offenders: Implications for campus administrators. *NASPA Journal, 42*(4), 565–588.

Harris III, F. (2008). Deconstructing masculinity: A qualitative study of college men's masculine conceptualizations and gender performance. *NASPA Journal, 45*(4), 453–474.

Harris III, F., & Struve, L. E. (2009). Gents, jerks, and jocks: What men learn about masculinity in college. *About Campus, 14*(3), 2–9.

Hong, L. (2000). Toward a transformed approach to prevention: Breaking the link between masculinity and violence. *Journal of American College Health, 48,* 269–282.

Jones, S. R. (2002). (Re)Writing the word: Methodological strategies and issues in qualitative *research. Journal of College Student Development, 43*(4), 461–472.

Jones, S. R., & McEwen, M. K. (2000). A conceptual model of multiple dimensions of identity. *Journal of College Student Development, 41*(4), 405–414.

Josselson, R. (1987). *Finding herself: Pathways to identity development in women.* San Francisco: Jossey-Bass.

Kellom, G. E. (Ed.). (2004). *Developing effective programs and services for college men: New directions for student services* (Vol. 107). San Francisco: Jossey-Bass.

KewalRamani, A., Gilbertson, L., Fox, M., & Provasnik, S. (2007). *Status and trends in the education of racial and ethnic minorities* (NCES 2007–039). Washington, DC: National Center for Education Statistics, Institute of Education Sciences, U.S. Department of Education.

Kim, J. (2001). Asian American identity development. In C. L. Wijeyesinghe & B. W. Jackson (Eds.), *New perspectives on racial identity development: A theoretical and practical anthology* (pp. 67–90). New York: New York University Press.

Kimmel, M. S., & Messner, M. A. (Eds.). (2007). *Men's lives* (7th ed.). Boston: Allyn & Bacon.

King, J. E. (2006). *Gender equity in higher education: 2006.* Washington, DC: American Council on Education.

Kuh, G. D., & Arnold, J. C. (1993). Liquid bonding: A cultural analysis of the role of alcohol in fraternity pledgeship. *Journal of College Student Development, 34,* 327–334.

Levant, R. F. (1996). The new psychology of men. *Professional Psychology: Research and Practice, 27*(3), 259–265.

Lincoln, Y. S., & Guba, E. G. (1985). *Naturalistic inquiry.* Newbury Park, CA: Sage.

Martin, B. E., & Harris, F., III. (2006). Examining productive conceptions of masculinities: Lessons learned from academically driven African American male student-athletes. *Journal of Men's Studies, 14*(3), 359–378.

Messner, M. A. (2001). Friendship, intimacy, and sexuality. In S. M. Whitehead & F. J. Barrett (Eds.), *The masculinities reader* (pp. 253–265). Malden, MA: Blackwell.

Marcia, J. E. (1980). Identity in adolescence. In J. Adelson (Ed.), *Handbook of adolescent psychology* (pp. 159–187). New York: Wiley.

O'Neil, J. M. (1981). Patterns of gender role conflict and strain: Sexism and fear of femininity in men's lives. *Personnel and Guidance Journal, 60,* 203–210.

Patton, M. Q. (2002). *Qualitative research & evaluation methods* (3rd ed.). Thousand Oaks, CA: Sage.

Pleck, J. H. (1981). *The myth of masculinity.* Cambridge, MA: MIT Press.

Renn, K. A. (2000). Patterns of situational identity among biracial and multiracial college students. *Review of Higher Education, 23*(4), 399–420.

Renn, K. A. (2003). Understanding the identities of mixed race college students through a developmental ecology lens. *Journal of College Student Development*, *44*(3), 383–403.

Renn, K. A., & Bilodeau, B. L. (2005). Leadership identity development among lesbian, gay, bisexual, and transgender student leaders. *NASPA Journal*, *42*(5), 342–367.

Rhoads, R. A. (1995). The cultural politics of coming out in college: Experiences of male students. *Review of Higher Education*, *19*(2), 1–22.

Sax, L. J. (2008). *The gender gap in college: Maximizing the developmental potential of women and men*. San Francisco: Jossey-Bass.

Strauss, A., & Corbin, J. (1990). *Basics of qualitative research: Grounded theory procedures and techniques*. Thousand Oaks, CA: Sage.

Strauss, A., & Corbin, J. (1998). *Basics of qualitative research: Techniques and procedures for developing grounded theory* (2nd ed.). Thousand Oaks, CA: Sage.

Taylor, C. M., & Howard-Hamilton, M. F. (1995). Student involvement and racial identity attitudes among African American males. *Journal of College Student Development*, *36*, 330–336.

Torres, V. (1999). Validation of a bicultural orientation model for Hispanic college students. *Journal of College Student Development*, *40*(3), 285–299.

Torres, V. (2003). Influences on ethnic identity development of Latino college students in the first two years of college. *Journal of College Student Development*, *44*(4), 532–547.

Torres, V., & Baxter Magolda, M. B. (2002). The evolving role of the researcher in constructivist longitudinal studies. *Journal of College Student Development*, *43*(4), 474–489.

Troiano, P. F. (2003). College students and learning disability: Elements of self-style. *Journal of College Student Development*, *44*(3), 404–419.

Whitson, D. (1990). Sport in the social construction of masculinity. In M. Messner & D. Sabo (Eds.), *Sport, men, and the gender order: Critical feminist perspectives* (pp. 19–29). Champaign, IL: Human Kinetics.

WHY COLLEGE MEN DRINK: ALCOHOL, ADVENTURE, AND THE PARADOX OF MASCULINITY

Rocco L. Capraro

And you drink this burning liquor like your life
Your life you drink like an eau-de-vie.

Apollinaire[1]

Though terror speaks to life and death and distress makes of the world a vale of tears,
yet shame strikes deepest into the heart of man.

Tomkins[2]

Given the magnitude of the negative consequences of some college men's drinking—for themselves and for those around them—on campuses across the nation,[3] college health professionals and alcohol prevention educators might well wonder: "Why *do* college men drink?" Because most college men drink in unproblematic ways and only to be sociable,[4] those men who drink in a way that is likely to be harmful to themselves or others are actually the central focus of this article—that is, those men "for whom drinking has become a central activity in their way of life" (p. 100).[5]

Writing from a men's health studies perspective, I articulate what is necessarily only a tentative answer to the question of men's problem drinking

Rocco L. Capraro, "Why College Men Drink: Alcohol, Adventure, and the Paradox of Masculinity," *Journal of American College Health*, 48(6), 307–315. Copyright © 2000. Reprinted by permission of the Taylor & Francis Group, http://www.informaworld.com.

by offering a model for conceptualizing the complex connections between college men and alcohol. Men's health studies, a subfield of men's studies, describes and analyzes men's experience of health, injury, morbidity, and mortality in the context of masculinity.[6,7] I also suggest an answer to the companion question that immediately presents itself to us: "What can we do about it?"

Part one of this article discusses the connections between alcohol, men, and masculinity generally; part two, the cultural and developmental aspects of men in a college setting; and part three, conceptual and programmatic responses to the men's problem drinking.

In general, I conclude that when college men drink, they are simply *being* men in college: that is the best context for understanding why they drink. I further conclude, in what is perhaps my central insight in this article, that college men's drinking appears to be profoundly paradoxical in a way that seems to replicate a larger paradox of masculinity itself: that men's alcohol use is related to both men's power and men's powerlessness. Stated most succinctly, my interpretation of a variety of evidence suggests that many college men may be drinking not only to enact male privilege but also to help them negotiate the emotional hazards of being a man in the contemporary American college.

ALCOHOL AND MASCULINITY

Drinking as a Male Domain

If we want to understand why college men drink, then we might embed drinking and college in masculinity and ask in what ways each might be seen as a specific male experience.[6] When we look for connections between drinking, men, and masculinity, we observe that the most prominent feature on the social landscape of drinking is that drinking is a "male domain" (p. 6).[3] By *male domain*, I suggest that drinking is male dominated, male identified, and male centered.[8]

Men outnumber women in virtually every category of drinking behavior used in research for comparison—prevalence, consumption, frequency of drinking and intoxication, incidence of heavy and problem drinking, alcohol abuse and dependence, and alcoholism.[4,9–12] Although most college men and women say they drink to be sociable, men are more likely than women to say they drink for escapism or to get drunk (p. 125).[4]

These findings hold true for the categories of age, ethnicity, geographic region, religion, education, income, and marital status.[9] Although there has been some speculation that changing gender roles may be narrowing the gap between women and men vis-á-vis alcohol, discussed by scholars as the *convergence hypothesis*, research tends to reject that proposition.[3]

In a classic and often-cited article, Lemle and Mishkind[9] asked, "Why should it be that males drink and abuse alcohol in such magnitude and in such marked contrast to females?" Citing empirical research that placed men mostly in the company of other men in the life course of their drinking, they suggested that drinking was a symbol of masculinity and speculated that men may drink to be manly (p. 215). They found little or no empirical evidence to support many of the theoretical possibilities they discussed, particularly for any theories concerned with men's abusive drinking, yet they remained intrigued with the idea that men were affirming their manliness by drinking.

More recently, McCreary et al.[10] ask what *specific* aspects of the male gender role correlate with alcohol involvement. In addition to the personality traits of instrumentality and expressiveness, they explore the traits of traditional male-role attitudes and masculine gender-role stress. For their research, traditional male-role attitudes represent a "series of beliefs and assumptions that men should be in high-status positions in society, act in physically and emotionally toughened ways, and avoid anything stereotypically feminine." *Masculine gender-role stress* is a term used to "describe the stress resulting from a man's belief that he is unable to meet society's demands of what is expected from men or the male role or from having to respond to a situation in a feminine-typed manner" (pp. 111–112).

McCreary et al.[10] identify traditional male-role attitudes as the *one* aspect of the male gender role they studied that predicts alcohol *use* among men. Alcohol use itself correlates with alcohol problems. However, masculine gender-role stress, while statistically unrelated to alcohol *use*, does predict alcohol *problems* for men (p. 121). In short, this study suggests that, from the point of view of masculinity or culture of manhood as a factor among many others, men *qua* men might arrive at alcohol problems by two routes: one route starts at traditional male-role attitudes, passes through alcohol use, and ends in alcohol problems; another route starts at masculine gender-role stress and ends directly in alcohol problems.

Variations on a Theme: Conflict and Strain, Shame and Fear, Depression, and the Paradox of Masculinity

The Paradox of Masculinity. Traditional male-role attitudes and masculine gender-role stress are actually not very far apart; in some aspects, they are correlated.[10,13] Their correlation reveals the contradictory nature of masculinity.[14] Reflecting upon the contradictory nature of the male role, researchers in the field of men's studies have articulated the paradox of masculinity, or the paradox of men's power, as follows: *men are powerful and powerless.*[15-18]

What is the resolution of the apparent contradiction that constitutes the paradox? How can men be both powerful and powerless? Men's studies observe two aspects of men's lives. First, in objective social analysis, *men as a group have power over women as a group*: but, in their subjective experience of the world, *men as individuals do not feel powerful.* In fact, they feel powerless. As at first articulated, and then later resolved by men's studies, the concept of a paradox of men's power offers an important insight into men's lives, one that seems to capture and to explain many of the contradictory claims made by and about men.

Ironically, it is men themselves who make the "rules of manhood" by which men as individuals are "disempowered" (p. 138).[17] Kaufman[16] aptly concludes that men's power is actually the cause of men's pain: "men's social power is the source of individual power and privilege . . . it is also the source of the individual experience of pain and alienation" (pp. 142, 143).

The paradoxical nature of masculinity is further illuminated in other men's studies research on at least three critical psychosocial aspects of masculinity: gender-role conflict and strain, shame and fear, and depression. Interestingly, those same aspects of masculinity are themselves important possible connections between men and alcohol. Consequently, the concept of the paradox of men's power draws us to an important conceptual understanding of some men's connections to alcohol.

Conflict and Strain. O'Neil[19] provides a useful series of interlocking definitions that locate gender-role conflict and strain in relation to the gender role itself. Gender roles are "behaviors, expectations, and values defined by society as masculine or feminine," or "as appropriate behavior for men and women." Gender-role conflict is "a psychological state in which gender roles have negative consequences on the individual or others" through the restriction, devaluation, or violation of oneself or others. Gender-role strain is "physical or psychological tension experienced as an outcome of gender-role conflict." At the bottom of gender-role strain is a "discrepancy between the real self and the gender role" (pp. 24, 25). Strain can follow from both conformity and nonconformity to the male role.

In his writings on strain, Pleck[14,20] provides additional insight into the relation between the masculine gender role and conflict or strain. Pleck maintains that the masculine gender role itself is "dysfunctional," (p. 147)[14] fraught with contradictions and negative consequences. Even when men live up to the role, they suffer well-documented adverse consequences. But, very often, men do not live up to the role. In fact, conflict and strain are inherent in the role, and they are actually the best rubrics under which to understand most men's identity and experience.

In Pleck's[14] role-strain paradigm, social approval and situational adaptation replace innate psychological need as the social and psychological mechanisms by which men achieve manhood. Violating gender roles (norms and stereotypes) results in social condemnation, a negative consequence experienced as sex-role strain and anxiety, a negative psychological consequence (pp. 145, 146). At least one study has connected role conflict and alcohol use. Blazina and Watkins[21] found that masculine gender-role conflict, in particular the factor cluster of "success, power, and competition," were significantly related to college men's reported use of alcohol.

Shame and Fear. Krugman,[22] reflecting on Pleck's foundational work on gender-role strain, characterizes male-role strain, with its grounding in feelings of inadequacy and inferiority, as a shame-based experience. "Role strain generates shame affect as males fail to live up to the cultural and peer group standards they have internalized" (p. 95). The essence of shame for Krugman is "painful self-awareness" or "a judgment against the self" (p. 99).

He advises that shame is active in both male gender-role strain and normal male socialization.

Recent research suggests that normative male socialization employs shame to shape boys' and men's behaviors and attitudes.[22,23] In common and nonpathological forms, shame becomes integrated into the self and transformed into a cue that tells us when to modify our behaviors and feelings in response to shame's messages about their appropriateness. But although shame may be the powerful leverage to enforce boys' and men's conformity to the male role, men are less likely than women to transform shame because they find shame to be *repugnant* to their masculinity. Consequently, for Krugman,[22] boys and men internalize male gender roles to avoid shame; but they also learn that dependency needs, for example, are shameful, especially under the gaze of their peer group.

Shame is related to fear.[2] Shame can magnify fear by linking similar episodes of fear into what Tomkins refers to as a family of episodes, creating a behavioral template in which fear can be anticipated and become more pervasive. In adversarial cultures, and I would include our own society generally in that category, fear and shame are conjoined, resulting in the mutually reinforcing "fear of shame" and "shame of fear" (p. 538).

Kimmel[17] places fear and shame at the very center of the social construction of men's identity. For him, men "fear that other men will unmask us, emasculate us, reveal to us and the world that we do not measure up, that we are not real men. Fear makes us ashamed" (p. 131). To avoid shame, Kimmel writes, men distance themselves from the feminine and all associations with it, including mothers, the world of feelings, nurturing, intimacy, and vulnerability.

Without the transformation of shame, men learn to manage shame in other ways. Alcohol is one of the significant ways men manage shame: drinking is a "maladaptive male solution to the pressure of undischarged shame" (p. 120).[22] Speaking metaphorically, Krugman observes that alcohol "dissolves acute shame" (p. 94). Referring to Lansky's study of shame in families, Krugman reports

that alcohol, as a disinhibitor, is used by some men "to handle vulnerable and exposed states that generate shameful feelings." Krugman, citing M. Horowitz, advises that alcohol "softens ego criticism" and "facilitates interpersonal connections and self-disclosures" (p. 120). Drinking may also reduce fear.[2] It seems to me that shame may also be the mechanism that leads men directly to alcohol, which is used to instill conformity to the dictates of traditional masculinity that encourage men to drink.

Depression. In addition to anxiety and shame, male gender-role strain and conflict make themselves known in the lives of men in depression. Depression is significantly related to all four aspects of gender-role conflict: (a) success, power, and competition; (b) restrictive emotionality; (c) restrictive affectionate behavior between men; and (d) conflicts between work and family relations.[13,24] Traditional masculinity insidiously puts men at risk for depression and also masks the depression, should it actually develop.[25-26]

Whereas Kaufman[16] uses a discourse of power to explain men's unacknowledged emotions, Lynch and Kilmartin[25] offer an alternative approach to the pitfalls of masculinity drawn from the point of view of social relations. Men's socialization encourages them to disconnect, or dissociate, from their feelings. An emotionally restrictive masculinity permits men to show their feelings only "in disguised form," and so they become "mostly unrecognized, unexpressed, and misunderstood by self and others" (p. 45). Men, instead, express their feelings in indirect ways, often through behavior that is destructive to themselves or others. Dissociation from feelings and destructive behavior are the two major characteristics of what Lynch and Kilmartin refer to as "masculine depression" (pp. 9, 10).

Heavy drinking, or binge drinking, is one of the ways some depressed men may act out, or manifest, their depression.[4] Lynch and Kilmartin[25] cite research indicating that depression is a strong risk factor for substance abuse problems. Krugman[22] notes a study showing strong correlations between alcohol abuse and major depression, especially among men.

Although they do not cite empirical evidence for it, Blazina and Watkins[21] speculate that traditional men may "self-medicate their pain and depression with alcohol" (p. 461). Although research findings suggest only a possible correlation between alcohol use or abuse and depression, perhaps alcohol use or abuse may actually precede depression. Alcohol and depression are certainly connected in the lives of some men.

Alcohol and the Paradox of Men's Power

Men in our society are supposed to be powerful.[27] According to the empirical findings of McClelland et al.,[28] when men are not powerful, they may often compensate for their lack of power or seek an "alternative to obtaining social power" with alcohol. Stated most dramatically by McClelland, drinking is "part of a cluster of actions which is a principal manifestation of the need for power" (p. 119). For this research, feeling powerful means "feeling that one is vigorous and can [have] an impact on others" (p. 84). But men's power motivation can be personalized (i.e., for "the greater glory or influence of the individual") or socialized for "the good of others" (p. 137).

According to McClelland,[28] a few drinks will stimulate socialized power thoughts for most men, and that is one of the reasons they like to drink. Higher levels of drinking tend to decrease inhibitions and stimulate personalized power thoughts. Heavy drinking in men is uniquely associated with personalized power, McClelland says. Heavy drinking makes men feel strong and assertive and, I would argue, the way they are supposed to feel.

Drinking may be related to men's power in a more profound and paradoxical way. In the aggregate, the connection between some men and heavy or problem drinking appears to be of two sorts: (a) that which follows from simple, apparently uncomplicated, conformity to traditional masculinity—drinking simply because men are supposed to drink; and (b) that which is informed by complex, perceived inadequacy as men, either from men's own point of view, or from that of society. If they do not feel inadequate, then at least they experience a kind of doubt, or a sense of falling short of the cultural ideal of manhood—drinking because of gender-role conflicts.

This distinction may be, after all, only a conceptual, or theoretical, distinction; in practice, the two sorts of connection co-occur. I wonder if traditional masculinity does not contain within it, socially constructed over time in the course of men's history, the use of alcohol to accommodate gender-role conflict. Given the way traditional masculinity has been constructed, is not gender-role conflict of the sort described by Pleck[14] and O'Neil[19] and documented in the lives of the men studied by Tomkins,[2] Krugman,[21] Lynch and Kilmartin,[25] Real,[26] and Kimmel[17] inherent in most men's lives? Have not men as historical agents, therefore, made provision for taking care of their own? If so, traditional masculine drinking would encompass conflicted drinking; certainly, in the culture of manhood, it does.

If heavy and problem drinking is associated with conformity, overconformity, or conflicted or strained resistance to the imperatives of traditional masculinity, why should this be the case? It would appear that drinking is a kind of fatally flawed defense mechanism, or compensatory behavior. It protects men's objective power as a group, even as it reveals men's subjective powerlessness as individuals and results in a diminution of men's power, particularly through the loss of control of emotions, health, and a variety of other negative consequences.

If this is the case, then drinking would have much in common with other documented psychological defense mechanisms that correlate with male gender-role conflict. And gender-role conflict, following from either conformity or nonconformity, might itself be seen as a defense mechanism that "protects a man's sense of well-being" (p. 253).[29] Like men's silence,[30] men's drinking turns out to be in the interest of men's power, even as it disempowers individual men. And alcohol, in my view, is the paradoxical drug that is a part of the larger whole, a trope, of a paradoxical masculinity.

As I ponder this material, then, it seems to me that a significant part of men's drinking, like male gender-role stress and strain, men's shame, and masculine depression themselves, is a reflection of both *risk ?*

men's power and men's powerlessness about men's privilege and men's pain. Heavy and problem drinking join other aspects of masculinity as they, too, come to be seen as manifestations of the paradox of masculinity. Drinking thus falls into a line of masculine icons, including body building, sexual assault, and pornography, that reveal the paradoxical nature of masculinity itself.[31–34] As I review those icons, it strikes me that at those times men *appear* most powerful socially, they *feel* most powerless personally.

COLLEGE AND MASCULINITY

College Drinking

What happens when we look at *college* men? College students, mostly men, are among the heavy drinkers in Rorabaugh's[35] history of drinking in early American society. Contemporary college men drink more than they did in high school and more heavily than their noncollege counterparts, and the gap is widening.[3,36–38] Men have been the primary public purveyors of alcohol to the college campus. All of the differences in drinking behavior for men and women generally hold true for college men and women.[3,4]

Given today's college students' preference for alcohol, one could not really imagine most colleges void of alcohol.[39] However, given the great variety of colleges and universities, the diversity of today's student populations, and the sweeping nature of the concerns I express in this article, most of what follows must necessarily speak primarily to an ideal type, represented for me by the relatively small, residential liberal arts college, occupied by a mostly traditionally aged student population.[40] In the following pages, I shall discuss critical aspects of college that seem to define college men's experience and help explain much of the presence of alcohol on college campuses: adventure, adult development, and permissiveness.

College as Adventure

Green[41] conceptualizes adventure as a domain of transgression. For Green, adventure takes shape around the themes of "eros" and "potestas"—love and power. Following Bataille, Green asks us to

think about civil society "as based on the purposes and values of work, which means the denial of all activities hostile to work, such as both the ecstasies of eroticism and those of violence." Adventure lies in the conceptual space where heroes, "men acting with power," break free of ordinary restraints and "sample the repressed pleasures of sex and violence" (p. 17).[42]

Although Green[41] makes no reference to drinking in his essays on adventure, we can easily recognize that the terrain of adventure is the same terrain as that of alcohol: "a boy's first drink, first prolonged drinking experience, and first intoxication tend to occur with other boys away from home" (p. 214).[9] Sports and the military are contexts for both adventure and drinking. Drinking games "are an important factor in the socialization of new students into heavy use," particularly for men (p. 105).[42] Drinking, in general, can be an adventure, insofar as it takes men through a "breach" of the social contract and into the realms of violence, sex, and other adventure motifs.

In what way might college be conceptualized as an adventure? College is not literally, or predominantly, a scene of eros and potestas. It is, however, a time and place of an imaginative assertion of manhood outside of civil society, away from home and family, where a kind of heroism is possible. By analogy, we can observe that student life in 19th-century American colleges developed outside of the civil society represented by the faculty and administration in what I would regard as the realm of adventure. Horowitz[43] argues that what we think of as student life was actually "born in revolt" (p. 23) against the faculty and administration. It is a "world made by the undergraduates," she says (p. 3).

Levine and Cureton[39] find that colleges today are occupied by a transitional generation that reflects the changing demographics of contemporary American society. Horowitz's history, however, employs a simple tripartite typology of college students that is still largely applicable as a model for understanding students on many campuses in more recent times. That typology deeply resonates with my own many years of experience in student affairs: (a) college men—affluent men in revolt against the faculty and administration who created campus life as "the culture of the college man" (p. 32); (b) outsiders—hardworking men who identify with the faculty (p. 14); and (c) rebels—creative, modernist, and expressive men who conform neither to campus life nor to the faculty (p. 15). Horowitz[43] observes that these three student types were distinctly *male* when they first made their appearance, but their female counterparts eventually found their place alongside the men.

Nuwer[44] argues that there are historical links between traditional male undergraduate life and danger, a key adventure motif. Social interactions initiating students into various campus communities have continuously subjected college men to high risk. Acceptance by their peers is granted in exchange for successfully undertaking the risk involved. A variety of college rituals and traditions often mix danger and alcohol.[44] Alcohol, itself, is associated with risk in men's lives.[9] Seen this way, college and campus life become an adventure-scape, where young men (college men) imagine their manhood in a developmental moment that is socially dominated by alcohol.

Green[41] identifies a number of arenas or institutions of adventure: manhood before marriage, hunting, battle, travel, sports, and politics, to name a few. Although there may be feminine variants, Green links adventure to masculinity because society gives men the freedom to "apply forces to the world to assert power and identity." Adventure is an act of assertion by which men "imagine themselves" in "a breach of the social contract" (p. 19).

College as a Male Developmental Moment

Beyond seeing the sociology of college and student life organized as adventure, we must also consider the role of individual developmental psychology in the college environment. Paradoxically, just at the moment the great adventure begins, college men feel the most vulnerable. Rotundo[45] observes that in the 19th century, "male youth culture" made its appearance in men's development as the vehicle for the transition from boyhood to manhood.

Boys' principal developmental task was disengagement from home, which created conflict between the imperatives of worldly ambition young men's psychological needs for attachment. Young men of Rotundo's period gathered in business districts and colleges. Wherever they gathered, a "special culture" developed to support them in a time of need (pp. 56–62).

Lyman[46] carries us forward from Rotundo's[45] historical analysis to the present. In his essay on male bonding in fraternities, he locates college as a developmental time and place between the authority of home and family (in the high school years), and that of work and family (after graduation). He identifies college men's anger, their "latent anger about the discipline that middle-class male roles impose upon them, both marriage rules and work rules" (p. 157). Their great fear is loss of control and powerlessness. Lyman concludes that joking relationships (banter, sexual humor, etc.) among men allow a needed connection without being self-disclosive or emotionally intimate, that is, with little vulnerability. Recent research on first-year college men has characterized their transition to college as often involving separation anxiety and loss, followed by grieving. Among the significant responses that may manifest some college men's grief, we find self-destructive behaviors, including alcohol use.[47]

Shame theory advises that to avoid shame, boys need to distance themselves from their mothers because of the "considerable discomfort with dependency needs at the level of the peer group" (p. 107).[22] College men in groups, such as Lyman's fraternity men, perceive homosexuality and intimate emotional relationships with women to be a threat to their homosocial world. Thus, men are encouraged to treat women as sexual objects, which confirms their heterosexuality, but prevents true intimacy with women.

Alcohol plays a role in men's emotional management under these conditions. Drinking remains a "socially acceptable way for men to satisfy their dependency needs while they maintain a social image of independence" (p. 187),[48] even as it masks those needs. For example, recent research on drinking games suggests they are actually an environmental context for drinking where a variety of students' social and psychological needs come into play.[49] When men (and women) give reasons for playing drinking games, they are likely to be "tapping into more general motives for drinking" (p. 286). Alcohol may be an effective way to cope in the short term, but it is ultimately "self-destructive" (p. 191).[48]

For Nuwer,[44] as was true for Horowitz,[43] fraternities are the quintessential emblems of traditional college life. They provide a "feeling of belonging" for students who "crave relationships and acceptance" in their college years (p. 38). They are also the riskiest environments for heavy and problem drinking.[4] Nationally, just over 80 percent of fraternity residents binge drink, whereas just over 40 percent of all college students binge.[50] Drinking in fraternities is perhaps best understood as an extreme on a continuum of college men's drinking, dramatizing what may be going on to a lesser extent in traditional student life among a range of men. From the point of view of men's needs assessments, we have much to learn from the psychology of brotherhood.

Permissiveness—Real and Imagined

Alcohol is "one of the oldest traditions in the American college," and alcohol-related problems have also been a benchmark of campus life. Until very recently, though, college administrations have been permissive about alcohol, voicing "official condemnation tempered by tacit toleration" (pp. 81–83).[51] Myers[52] provides a model for "institutional (or organizational) denial" of the presence (or extent) of alcohol abuse that could easily apply to college campuses nationally (p. 43). In 1995, Wechsler[11] was explicit about the widespread denial about alcohol on college campuses.

With the increase in the drinking age from 18 to 21 years and increased awareness of the dangers of alcohol abuse, colleges now "typically have policies which promote responsible drinking" and attempt the "management of student drinking and its consequences" (pp. 84–88).[51] My own informal

observations are that liability case law, awareness of the negative impact of alcohol on the achievement of educational mission, and enrollment management concerns for retention have also encouraged colleges to be more vigilant about the role of alcohol in campus cultures.

But among students, permissiveness persists, both in drinking behavior and in attitudes toward drinking. Permissiveness itself is, in part, the result of students' own misperceptions of campus norms for alcohol behavior and attitudes.[53,54] With reference to the consumption of alcohol and the acceptability of intoxication, students generally perceive themselves to be in a permissive environment. In reality, the environment is not as permissive as they think. Misperceiving the norm leads students who are inclined to drink to consume more alcohol than they otherwise would drink were they to perceive the norm correctly.[55] This social norms research indicates that correcting the misperception through public information campaigns can reduce both problem drinking and binge drinking on college campuses.[56,57]

How well do social norms approaches work with college men who are heavy drinkers? How are masculinity, permissive attitudes about drinking, and misperceptions of the norm related? How accurately do college men perceive their campus norms? For social norms theory and research, the heaviest drinking results from the interaction of the most permissive personal attitudes toward alcohol and the greatest misperception of the norm as more permissive than it actually is. Men as a group are the heaviest drinkers on campus. We might conclude that the heaviest drinking men have the most permissive attitudes about drinking and that they misperceive the norm at the greatest rates. But, theoretically, they should also be most susceptible to the benefits of social norms approaches.

However, in one study, the heaviest drinking college men proved to be the least susceptible to social norms interventions. From 1995 to 1998 Western Washington University implemented a campus-wide social norms approach. Although most students on the campus changed their patterns of drinking in positive ways, the "students reporting they had seven or more drinks on peak occasions [the most consumed at one time in the past month] remained virtually unchanged [at about 35 percent]." The most recalcitrant students at Western Washington were underage men: "nearly two thirds of the underage men still reported having seven or more drinks on a peak occasion. Only one third of the underage women reported the same" (p. 3)[56] level of consumption.

In view of the significance of personal attitudes toward alcohol,[55] permissive personal attitudes about alcohol in the group of recalcitrant underage men might have been so robust that they simply overwhelmed any other perceptions of the environment. Prentice and Miller[58] found that men and women in their study did respond differently to corrections of misperceptions. Perhaps, in the case of at least some college men, personal attitudes about drinking and misperception of the campus norm are so inextricably linked that research and prevention work that addresses the one (personal attitudes) must necessarily be done in conjunction with the same kind of work on the other (misperception of the norm).

Perkins once characterized "the perceived male stereotype of heavy use as a misperception to which males do not need to conform" (p. 6).[3] Some college men's misperceptions of their campus alcohol norms may be "contained" in their personal attitudes about drinking. Baer found that differences in the perception of campus drinking norms among students in different housing situations on one campus "*already existed prior to college enrollment*" (p. 98)[42] [emphasis mine]. Certainly, if "the impact of public behavior and conversation" on campus can generate misperceptions of the norm (p. 17),[54] a lifetime of powerful messages about the connection between alcohol and manhood would produce great distortions of its own.

Social norms theory, research, and strategies would be enhanced by a closer look at gender in the creation of drinking attitudes and behaviors, in possible differences in the misperception of norms, and in the social mechanisms that lie behind the actual norms. Social norms research surveys should include measures of traditional masculine role strain and should look for correlations between attitudes and perceptions of the norm and actual drinking behavior.

In addition, surveys should replace the generic "college student" with "male student" or "female student" when asking college students about how much students are drinking and asking about their attitudes toward drinking. So, for example, we should ask, "How many drinks does a *male* [or *female*] student typically have at a party on this campus?" instead of "do *students* typically have" or "Is it acceptable for men [or women] to drink with occasional intoxication as long as it does not interfere with other responsibilities?" (p. 15).[54]

The results would have implications for norms-based prevention programs. It would make sense if, in fact, masculinity were found to predispose men to misperceive the norm because assumptions and attitudes about drinking and how drinking relates to manhood are built into masculinity. It would also make sense that the actual and perceived social norms be gender specific.

WHAT IS TO BE DONE?

Concrete Responses

Men, alcohol, and college are connected by the paradoxical nature of men's power. What can we do about college men's frequent, heavy, and problem drinking? Following from the model that has been developed in this essay, nothing short of radical reconstruction of masculinity and a reimagining of the college experience are likely to bring about significant change in college men's drinking. The same paradox that characterizes college men's drinking also provides a pedagogy for change. This is because, while the paradox acknowledges men's pain and powerlessness, it also discourages men from seeing themselves simply as victims, and it insists that men take responsibility for their actions.

Colleges, in collaboration with high schools and community agencies, should integrate gender awareness into alcohol education, prevention, and risk-reduction programs. For men, I recommend a comprehensive educational program that addresses four central themes in men's lives: friendship, health, life/work/family, and sexual ethics (see also Good and Mintz (p. 20)[24]).

As in the case of effective rape prevention education workshops for men, the pedagogy should be workshops that are all male, small group, interactive, and peer facilitated. Such programs have been shown to change some men's attitudes and values that are associated with the perpetration of rape.[59] It may be that the rape prevention workshops are changing attitudes because they correct men's misperceived norm of other men's attitudes about women, or vice versa.[60]

Attitudes and values associated with problem drinking could be similarly changed. Developing what Lynch and Kilmartin[25] refer to as "healthy masculinity" that connects men in healthy relationships with other men, family, and intimate partners would be a succinct statement of the goal of such programming (pp. 46, 47).

The transition to college is a critical juncture in the consumption of alcohol.[4] Programming should therefore begin early in the first year and continue well beyond orientation week. Broad-based, fully integrated, social norms educational programs, interventions, and public information initiatives should be implemented.[55] I would add that such programs should be gender-informed along the lines I have suggested in this article. College men should understand how the paradoxical masculinity I have discussed may orient them to alcohol use and abuse.

College students should be strongly encouraged to get involved in clubs and organizations on campus, to run for office, and to be involved in sports as ways of meeting power orientation needs in socially responsible ways.[23] Those activities themselves must have alcohol education components; otherwise, involvement could have the ironic consequence of promoting heavier drinking.[3] Associations between men and beer in campus media should be discouraged.[61,62] Given their powerful influence over men's drinking in the first year,[43] the hazards of drinking games should be especially discussed in educational programming.

In general, college as adventure is a theme that should be discouraged. A "boys will be boys" permissiveness should be rejected. Recognizing and affirming that alcohol does harm, colleges must assert themselves as "moral communities" and move from permissive to restrictive stances on alcohol by first articulating what the harm is, then establishing policies to prevent college community members from harming themselves or others (pp. 135, 150–159).[51] Wechsler and associates[63] recommend a comprehensive approach to alcohol use on college campuses, including scrutiny of alcohol marketing, more alcohol-free events and activities, and more restrictive policies that control the flow of alcohol on campus. Their recommendation would benefit from more deeply gendered approaches to the problem because the problem, itself, is deeply gendered.[64,65]

In addition to promoting social norms approaches, preventive education, and risk-reduction education, college administrators should require that frequent violators of alcohol policy seek treatment or seek their education elsewhere. Although critics of treatment may say it addresses the symptoms and not the real problem, which is the campus culture itself, colleges must offer treatment as part of a comprehensive program for renewed campus life. Treatment should seamlessly integrate men's health studies approaches.[66,67] Unfortunately, some college men will be untouched and untouchable by education or treatment, and they must lose the privilege of attending their chosen college and be asked to leave.

Conceptual Responses

Speaking most globally about solving the problem of college men's drinking and solving the problem of the connections between alcohol and masculinity, I would paraphrase what I have previously written about the problem of rape: Our understanding of the specific act of drinking should be embedded in our understanding of masculinity. Drinking is not an isolated behavior; it is a behavior linked to larger systems of attitudes, values, and modalities of conduct in men's lives that constitute masculinity and men's social position relative to women. In this model, alcohol prevention work with men begins with them *as* men, and with men's questioning of prevailing assumptions about masculinity and what it means to be a man. I am extremely skeptical of any alcohol prevention work that proposes solutions to the problem of drinking that leave masculinity, as we know it, largely intact (p. 22).[68]

The educational challenge, which is really the psychological and political resistance to this solution, lies in the fact that alcohol benefits men as a group, even as it injures men as individuals. Men are likely to resist this global approach because we fear losing the benefits of masculinity conferred upon the group. The path to a reconstructed masculinity or alternatives to the dominant masculinity that includes more variety of men's identities and experiences may look something like Helms's[69] stage-development model for a positive racial-cultural identity for minority groups. It will not be easy getting there.

In the meantime, in our work with college men who drink, we must look to the bottom of their glasses and find the *men* inside. For when college men drink, they are simply being men at college, or what they perceive men at college to be. By this I mean that the most useful way to interpret their behavior is not so much in its *content*, but in its *context*—first, the imperatives of manhood, then the psychosocial particulars of college life, both of which put men at risk for drinking. Basically, at the bottom of heavy and problematic drinking among college men are the paradoxical nature of masculinity and the corresponding paradoxical nature of alcohol in men's lives. Once we know college men *as* men, we will know more about why they drink and what we can do about it.

REFERENCES

1. Apollinaire G. Zone. In: *Selected Writings of Guillaume Apollinaire* (trans. Roger Shattuck). New York: New Directions, 1971.

2. Tomkins S. *Affect, Imagery, Consciousness*. Vol 3, 1962–1992. New York: Springer, 1991.

3. Perkins H. W. Gender patterns in consequences of collegiate alcohol abuse: A 10-year study of trends in an undergraduate population. *J Stud Alcohol*. 1992, September: 458–462.

4. Berkowitz A. D., Perkins H. W. Recent research on gender differences in collegiate alcohol use. *J Am Coll Health*. 1987, 36: 123–129.

5. Fingarette H. *Heavy Drinking: The Myth of Alcoholism as a Disease*. Berkeley, CA: University of California Press, 1989.

6. Brod H. The case for men's studies. In: Brod H., ed. *The Making of Masculinities: The New Men's Studies*. Boston: Allen Unwin, 1987.

7. Sabo D., Gordon D. F. Rethinking men's health and illness. In: Sabo D., Gordon D. F. eds. *Men's Health and Illness: Gender, Power, and the Body*. Thousand Oaks, CA: Sage, 1995.

8. Johnson A. G. *The Gender Knot: Unraveling Our Patriarchal Legacy*. Philadelphia: Temple University Press, 1997.

9. Lemle R., Mishkind M. E. Alcohol and masculinity. *Journal of Substance Abuse Treatment*. 1989, 6:213–222.

10. McCreary D. R., Newcomb M. D., Sadave S. The male role, alcohol use, and alcohol problems. *Journal of Counseling Psychology*. 1999, 46(1): 109–124.

11. Wechsler H., Deutsch C., Dowdell G. Too many colleges are still in denial about alcohol abuse. (1995). http://www.hsph.harvard.edu/cas/test/articles/chronicle2.shtm/.

12. Courtenay W. H. Behavioral factors associated with disease, injury, and death among men: Evidence and implications for prevention. *The Journal of Men's Studies*. In press.

13. Sharpe M. J. Heppner P. P. Gender role, gender-role conflict, and psychological well-being in men. *Journal of Counseling Psychology*. 1991, 39(3): 323–330.

14. Pleck J. H. *The Myth of Masculinity*. Cambridge, MA: The MIT Press, 1981.

15. Pleck J. Men's power with women, other men, and society: A men's movement analysis. In: Kimmel M. S., Messner M. A. eds. *Men's Lives*. New York: Macmillan, 1989.

16. Kaufman M. Men, feminism, and men's contradictory experiences of power. In: Brod H., Kaufman M., eds. *Theorizing Masculinities*. Newbury Park, CA: Sage, 1994.

17. Kimmel M. S. Masculinity as homophobia: Fear, shame, and silence in the construction of gender identity. In: Brod H., Kaufman M., eds. *Theorizing Masculinities*. Newbury Park, CA: Sage, 1994.

18. Capraro R. L. Review of *Theorizing Masculinities*. Brod H., Kaufman M., eds. Sage; 1994. *Journal of Men's Studies*. 1995, 4(2):169–172.

19. O'Neil J. Assessing men's gender role conflict. In: Moore D., Leafgren F., eds. *Problem Solving Strategies and Interventions for Men in Conflict.* Alexandria, VA: American Association for Counseling and Development, 1990.

20. Pleck J. The gender role strain paradigm: An update. In: Levant R. L., Pollack W. S., eds. *A New Psychology of Men.* New York: Basic, 1995.

21. Blazina C., Watkins C. E. Masculine gender role conflict: Effects on college men's psychological well-being, chemical substance usage, and attitudes toward help-seeking. *Journal of Counseling Psychology.* 1995, 43(4): 461–465.

22. Krugman S. Male development and the transformation of shame. In: Levant R. F., Pollack W. S., eds. *A New Psychology of Men.* New York: Basic, 1995.

23. Pollack W. *Real Boys.* New York: Henry Holt, 1999.

24. Good G. E., Mintz L. Gender role conflict and depression in college men: Evidence for compounded risk. *Journal of Counseling and Development.* 1990, 69 (September/October): 17–21.

25. Lynch J., Kilmartin C. *The Pain Behind the Mask: Overcoming Masculine Depression.* New York: Haworth, 1999.

26. Real T. *I Don't Want to Talk About It.* New York: Simon & Schuster, 1997.

27. David D. S., Brannon R., eds. *The Forty-Nine Percent Majority: The Male Sex Role.* New York: Random House, 1976.

28. McClelland D. C., David W. N., Kalin R., Wanner E. *The Drinking Man.* New York: The Free Press, 1972.

29. Mahalik J. R., Cournoyer R. J., DeFran W., Cherry M., Napolitano J. M. Men's gender role conflict in relation to their use of psychological defenses. *Journal of Counseling Psychology.* 1998, 45(3): 247–255.

30. Sattel J. W. Men, inexpressiveness, and power. In: Thorne K. H. *Language, Gender and Society.* Newbury House, 1983.

31. Fussell W. S. *Muscle: Confessions of an Unlikely Bodybuilder.* New York: Avon Books, 1991.

32. Berkowitz A. D., Burkhart B. R., Bourg S. E. *Research on College Research and Prevention Education in Higher Education.* San Francisco: Jossey-Bass, 1994.

33. Brod H. Pornography and the alienation of male sexuality. In: Hearn J., Morgan D., eds. *Men, Masculinities and Social Theory.* London: Unwin Hyman, 1990.

34. Kimmel M. S. *Men Confront Pornography.* New York: Crown, 1990.

35. Rorabaugh W. J. *The Alcoholic Republic: An American Tradition.* New York: Oxford University Press, 1981.

36. Maddox G. L., ed. *The Domesticated Drug: Drinking Among Collegians.* New Haven: College and University Press, 1970.

37. Bacon S. D., Strauss R. *Drinking in College.* New Haven: Yale University Press, 1953.

38. Johnston L., Bachman J. G., O'Malley P. M. *Monitoring the Future.* Health and Human Services Dept., US Public Health Service, National Institutes of Health, National Institute of Drug Abuse, 1996.

39. Levine A., Cureton J. S. *When Hope and Fear Collide: A Portrait of Today's College Student.* San Francisco: Jossey-Bass, 1998.

40. *Daedalus.* Distinctively American: The residential liberal arts colleges. Winter 1999.

41. Green M. *The Adventurous Male: Chapters in the History of the White Male Mind.* University Park, PA: The Pennsylvania State University Press, 1993.

42. Adams C. E., Nagoshi C. T. Changes over one semester in drinking game playing and alcohol use and problems in a college sample. *Subst Abuse.* 1999, 20(2): 97–106.

43. Horowitz H. L. *Campus Life: Undergraduate Cultures from the End of the Eighteenth Century to the Present.* Chicago: University of Chicago Press, 1987.

44. Nuwer H. *Wrongs of Passage: Fraternities, Sororities, Hazing, and Binge Drinking.* Bloomington, IN: Indiana University Press, 1999.

45. Rotundo E. A. *American Manhood: Transformations in Masculinity from the Revolution to the Modern Era.* New York: HarperCollins, 1993.

46. Lyman P. The fraternal bond as a joking relationship. In: Kimmel M. S., ed. *Changing Men: New Directions in Research on Men and Masculinity.* Newbury Park, CA: Sage, 1987.

47. Gold J., Neururer J., Miller M. Disenfranchised grief among first-semester male university students: Implications for systemic and individual interventions. *Journal of the First Year Experience.* 2000, 12(1): 7–27.

48. Burda P. C., Tushup R. J., Hackman P. S. Masculinity and social support in alcoholic men. *Journal of Men's Studies.* 1992, 1(2): 187–193.

49. Johnson T. J., Hamilton S., Sheets V. L. College students' self-reported reasons for playing drinking games. *Addict Behav.* 1999, 24(2): 279–286.

50. Wechsler H., Dowdall G. W., Maener G., Gledhill-Hoyt J., Lee H. Changes in binge drinking and related problems among American college students between 1993 and 1997. *J Am Coll Health.* 1998, 47: 57–68.

51. Hoekema D. A. *Campus Rules and Moral Community: In Place of In Loco Parentis.* Lanham, MD: Rowman & Littlefield, 1994.

52. Myers P. L. Sources and configurations of institutional denial. *Employee Assistance Quarterly.* 1990, 5(3): 43–53.

53. Berkowitz, A. D. From reactive to proactive prevention: Promoting an ecology of health on campus. In: Rivers P. C., Shore E. R., eds. *Substance Abuse on Campus: A Handbook for College and University Personnel.* Westport, CT: Greenwood Press, 1997.

54. Perkins H. W. Confronting misperceptions of peer drug use norms among college students: An alternative approach for alcohol and other drug education programs. In: *The Higher Education Leaders/Peer Network Peer Prevention Resource Manual.* US Dept. of Education, FIPSE Drug Prevention Program, 1991.

55. Perkins H. W., Wechsler H. Variation in perceived college drinking norms and its impact on alcohol abuse: A nationwide study. *Journal of Drug Issues.* 1996, 26(4): 961–974.

56. Fabiano P. M., McKinney G. R., Hyun Y.-R., Mertz H. K., Rhoads K. Lifestyles, 1998: Patterns of alcohol and drug consumption and consequences among Western Washington University students—An extended executive study. *Focus: A Research Summary.* 1999, 4(3): 1–8.

57. Haines M. *A Social Norms Approach to Preventing Binge Drinking at Colleges and Universities.* Newton, MA: The Higher Education Center for Alcohol and Other Drug Prevention, 1998.

58. Prentice D. A., Miller D. T. Pluralistic ignorance and alcohol use on campus: Some consequences of misperceiving the social norms. *J Pers Soc Psychol.* 1993, 65: 243–256.

59. Berkowitz A. D. A model acquaintance rape prevention program for men. In: Berkowitz A. D., ed. *Men and Rape: Theory, Research, and Prevention Education in Higher Education.* San Francisco: Jossey-Bass, 1994.

60. Berkowitz A. D. Applications of social norms theory to other health and social justice issues. Paper presented at: Annual Social Norms Conference. July 28–30, 1999, Big Sky, Mont.

61. Postman N., Nystrom C., Strate L., Weingartner C. *Myths, Men, and Beer: An Analysis of Beer Commercials on Broadcast Television, 1987.* Washington, DC: AAA Foundation for Traffic Safety, undated.

62. Courtenay W. H. Engendering health: A social constructionist examination of men's health beliefs and behaviors. *Psychology of Men and Masculinity.* In press.

63. Wechsler H., Kelley K., Weitzman E. R., San Giovanni J. P., Seebring M. What colleges are doing about student binge drinking: A survey of college administrators. (March 2000) http://www.hsph.Harvard.edu/cas/test/alcohol/surveyrpt.shtm/

64. Scher M., Steven M., Good G., Eichenfield G. A. *Handbook of Counseling and Psychotherapy with Men.* Newbury Park, CA: Sage, 1987.

65. Moore D., Leafgren F., eds. *Problem Solving Strategies and Intervention for Men in Conflict.* Alexandria, VA: American Association for Counseling and Development, 1990.

66. Levant R. F., Pollack, W. S., eds. *A New Psychology of Men.* New York: Basic, 1995.

67. Mahalik M. R. Incorporating a gender role strain perspective in assessing and treating men's cognitive distortions. *Professional Psychology: Research and Practice.* 1999, 30(4): 333–340.

68. Capraro R. L. Disconnected lives: Men, masculinity, and rape prevention. In Berkowitz A. D., ed. *Men and Rape: Theory, Research, and Prevention Programs in Higher Education.* San Francisco: Jossey-Bass, 1994.

69. Helms J. An Update of Helms' *White and People of Color Racial Identity Models.* In: Ponterretto J., et al., eds. *Handbook of Multicultural Counseling.* Newbury Park, CA: Sage, 1995.

THE STARBUCKS INTERVENTION

Greg Bortnichak

I'm the kind of twenty-something guy you would expect to work in a coffee shop. I play guitar and cello in an experimental punk band and have some cool downloads on MySpace. I'm tall and lean, with an explosive mess of dark hair that makes me look like the love child of Edward Scissorhands and Blacula. Most people correctly guess that I'm artistic and a bit to the political left. What they may not realize is that I am a self-defined male feminist. Being a feminist is mighty powerful stuff because staying true to ideals about equality and justice involves consciously altering the way I behave. The bottom line is that I try to reject personal acts of subjugation, and I do my best to combat the systems that enable others to be oppressive. As the saying goes, the personal is political.

My brand of feminism is all about not imposing patriarchal power on the women in my life, and hoping to set an example for the boys and men I meet. From the time I was 7 and too short to play ball with big kids, to the time I was 13 and too sensitive to party with the cool kids, to now when I struggle with masculinist ideology, I have always felt that the dominant culture only truly benefits a select few. So I do my best to reject it. I do it for me. I do it for my partner, and for every man who feels alienated by the expectations that culture places on guys who do not quite fit the "man's man" mold. I do it for anyone who feels constrained by the music videos on MTV because they see both women and men reduced to sexual commodities. But the question remains, how do I do my feminism? And, more important, how am I a male feminist?

It's tricky. And the truth is that a lot of the time I feel friction between being a man and being a feminist. Problems come up when I want more than anything to take feminist action—to act in defense of someone who is being victimized by patriarchal power—but my aid is unwelcome or inappropriate or potentially does more political harm than good.

Allow me to illustrate: I work at Starbucks. I spend roughly 20 hours each week serving coffee to strangers, sometimes as many as several hundred each day. And you better believe I see it all. Customers reveal all kinds of personal details. So do my coworkers. I put up with a lot from them: sexist and racist jokes, routine descriptions of masculinist sexploitation, flat-out ridicule for my feminist views. And at the end of the day when my feet feel like they're ready to fall off and my entire body reeks of espresso grinds, I think back and try to make sense of it.

One day a customer comes in and begins telling us about this scheme he has to buy a wife. What he really wants to do is hire a housekeeper, but he thinks it's funnier if he tells us that he's "wife shopping" today. He complains about doing housework, saying he'd pay a cute, young girl 20 bucks an hour to do his chores for him rather than do them himself, or worse, get remarried to have yet another woman sit at home all day, take his money, and bitch at him when [he] gets home from work. He keeps saying there is nothing worse than married life, to which the guys I'm working with chuckle in agreement. The only girl working at the time, Joy, is offended. She tells the customer that marriage won't be bad at all for her husband—she will do all the housework and more (wink, wink). For free. Joy wants to be a housewife, and she gives me a hard time for being feminist. The customer tells Joy that she's sweet but that she won't be sweet forever. He's expecting his purchased "wife" to be totally obedient and pleasant every hour of every day. Then, as an afterthought, he mentions that he has no problem getting his "non-domestic" (wink, wink) needs met elsewhere for not much more than it's going to cost him to buy this wife of his.

Later, my girlfriend, Ana, decides to come by and do some homework, keeping me company as I work. She is sitting alone in a far corner, completely engrossed in her studies. A man with slicked-back silver hair, white guy, probably in his fifties, and appearing to be quite wealthy (gold jewelry, designer golf shirt, the works) steps into line and begins staring at Ana. He makes no effort to hide this, and gets out of line to walk around behind her and get a better look. Then he gets back into line and cranes his neck to see down her shirt and up her dress. I see all of this, and I'm simultaneously disgusted and pissed off. He's such trash. I would love to call him out, or lay him out right then and there, but I risk losing my job if I'm rude to the customers. So I bite my tongue. It gets to be his turn in line and he still won't stop staring at her, not even to place his order. He's holding up the line, people behind him are starting to get flustered, and I lose it.

"What's so interesting over there, sir? You seem to be looking very intently at something," I ask as innocently as I possibly can. "That girl in the corner," he says like he's ready to eat her. He doesn't take his eyes off Ana once. "Oh yeah, what do you think?" I'm trying now to sound as sleazy as I possibly can in an attempt to lead him to believe that I'm going along with the shameless objectification of Ana. "I think she's a real pretty girl in that little dress of hers." He licks his ugly thin lips and makes a face that screams "pervert." I've caught him red-handed at his patriarchal bullshit, and at this point, I'm done "Well, I think she's a friend

of mine, and I think she'd feel violated if she knew you were staring at her like that." I say it low and threateningly beneath my breath so as not to cause a scene. "I think she should get used to it," he replies. There is no hint of apology in his tone. It's like I'm wrong for telling him not to lech at a girl who could be his fucking granddaughter! I glare at him like I want to burn a hole in his face with my eyes and growl, "I think you need to learn a little respect." He leaves. I'm shaking.

I go to Ana and ask her if she saw what just transpired. She says no, that she was completely unaware. When I tell her what happened she is visibly upset. She thanks me for sticking up for her and waits for me to finish my shift without returning to her homework. The woman in line behind the silver-haired man approaches me before leaving and wishes me goodnight, smiling at me in a way that I could only interpret as solidarity.

That night I had nightmares about the silver-haired man. He was so ruthless in how he visually dismembered Ana that he put me in touch with a very distinct fear. No one had ever made me so mad, or provoked such a reaction from me. But was it even my place to step in on Ana's behalf? Was I being overprotective?

Despite Ana's appreciation for my fast action, I still could not get this encounter out of my mind. The silver-haired man obviously saw nothing wrong with what he did. I even had a coworker poke fun at me for bothering that "poor old man." The woman in line behind the silver-haired man was my best assurance—as iffy as it was—that speaking up was the right thing to do. Yet I could not help but feel unsettled about how I chose to respond. After all, I don't doubt that if Ana looked up at the right time, she would have reacted more strongly and defended herself far better than I. And if Ana had been the one to terminate the encounter, perhaps she would have a stronger feeling of closure or justice. I had to wonder what it meant that I defended Ana instead of simply bringing her attention to what was happening. Did my chivalrous feminism reflect some duty I feel to protect her? And if so, does that mean that on some level I think she is incapable of protecting herself? Even worse, what if my actions actually revealed a sense of possession or ownership over Ana? And what about that burst of anger I felt? How stereotypically masculine to feel angry in light of something another man did to my girlfriend.

This encounter with the silver-haired man raises so many difficult questions for me about whether profeminist men ought to step in to help women or instead focus our efforts on enabling women to protect themselves. On the night of the scuffle in Starbucks, Ana happened to be wearing a gorgeous dress that was short, with a very low neckline. She has gotten upset in the past over men leering at her when she wears this dress. Sometimes I think about gently suggesting to Ana that she shelve the dress, but I don't think it's my place to say so. I do not want Ana to continue feeling violated by these tactless creeps but, at the same time, I do not want her to compromise her own sense of beauty, self-expression, and sexuality. I also don't want to be perceived as controlling or paternalistic. It is not Ana's fault that some men feel it's their right to stare crudely at young women. But still, it upsets Ana, and it happens less when she does not wear this particular dress. It is clear who is at fault. It's the voyeurs like that silver-haired man at Starbucks. But if men like that deny responsibility, and if women have the right to wear whatever they damn well please, and if I happen to see what's going on, then shouldn't I step in and speak my mind?

I've run into a dilemma: It's true that men can deflect unwanted attention, but in doing so we risk offending or patronizing women who are capable of protecting themselves, or insulting women who like this sort of thing. I know that some women rely on the male gaze to feel attractive and some may dress in ways to get attention on purpose. Women have the right to express themselves through their clothes and demeanor in any way they see fit. But I risk sounding sexist if I advise a woman not to go to certain parts of the city looking a certain way, and I risk feeling guilty knowing someone could get hurt if I don't speak up.

The problem lies in knowing when it's okay to intervene; in knowing when to act on my personal feminist beliefs, and knowing when to hold back. Mastering this discretion is something I grapple with each day. Sometimes I get to thinking that I'm setting myself up for an unconquerable task by trying to live the life of an active male feminist. Sometimes it feels so daunting that I consider giving up. But then I remember what got me here in the first place, and it gives me hope. Feminism is something I embrace because it helps me think more clearly about who I am and how I behave as a man in this society. When I keep this in mind, I understand that I'm not about to defeat the patriarchy overnight, but that I can feel a little better knowing I'm not letting it defeat me little by little, each and every day.

PART FOUR

MEN AND WORK

In what ways is work tied to male identity? Do men gain a sense of fulfillment from their work, or do they view it as necessary drudgery? How might the organization of workplaces play on, reinforce, or sometimes threaten the types of masculinity that males have already learned as youngsters? How does the experience of work (or of not having work) differ for men of different social classes, ethnicities, and sexual preference groups? And how do recent structural changes in society affect the masculinity–work relationship? The articles in this part address these issues and more.

The rise of urban industrial capitalism saw the creation of separate "public" and "domestic" spheres of social life. As women were increasingly relegated to working in the home, men were increasingly absent from the home, and the male "breadwinner role" was born. The sexual division of labor, this gendered split between home and workplace, has led to a variety of problems and conflicts for women and for men. Women's continued movement into the paid labor force, higher levels of unemployment, and the rise of a more service-oriented economy have led to dramatic shifts in the quality and the quantity of men's experiences in their work.

Sociologists have long noted that when men work in female-dominated occupations, they often receive unearned privileges, like the "glass escalator effect" for male elementary teachers noted by sociologist Christine Williams. However, as this part's second article by Adia Harvey Wingfield illustrates, men's gender privilege in workplaces largely evaporates when race is taken into account: there is no glass escalator for black males. Deploying yet another angle on intersectional studies of men in workplaces, Kristen Schilt shows how the experience of transgendered (female to male) people illuminates the informal workings of men's continued privilege in workplaces. Finally, Beth Quinn's discussion of the gender dynamics of "girl watching" sheds light on the continuing debates about sexual harassment in workplaces.

Source: Leo Cullum / The New Yorker Collection / www.cartoonbank.com

THE GLASS ESCALATOR: HIDDEN ADVANTAGES FOR MEN IN THE "FEMALE" PROFESSIONS

Christine L. Williams

The sex segregation of the U.S. labor force is one of the most perplexing and tenacious problems in our society. Even though the proportion of men and women in the labor force is approaching parity (particularly for younger cohorts of workers) (U.S. Department of Labor 1991:18), men and women are still generally confined to predominantly single-sex occupations. Forty percent of men or women would have to change major occupational categories to achieve equal representation of men and women in all jobs (Reskin and Roos 1990:6), but even this figure underestimates the true degree of sex segregation. It is extremely rare to find specific jobs where equal numbers of men and women are engaged in the same activities in the same industries (Bielby and Baron 1984).

Most studies of sex segregation in the work force have focused on women's experiences in male-dominated occupations. Both researchers and advocates for social change have focused on the barriers faced by women who try to integrate predominantly male fields. Few have looked at the "flip-side" of occupational sex segregation: the exclusion of men from predominantly female occupations (exceptions include Schreiber 1979; Zimmer 1988; Williams 1989). But the fact is that men are less likely to enter

female sex-typed occupations than women are to enter male-dominated jobs (Jacobs 1989). Reskin and Roos, for example, were able to identify 33 occupations in which female representation increased by more than nine percentage points between 1970 and 1980, but only three occupations in which the proportion of men increased as radically (1990:20–21).

In this article, I examine men's underrepresentation in four predominantly female occupations—nursing, librarianship, elementary school teaching, and social work. Throughout the twentieth century, these occupations have been identified with "women's work"—even though prior to the Civil War, men were more likely to be employed in these areas. These four occupations, often called the female "semi-professions" (Hodson and Sullivan 1990), today range from 5.5 percent male (in nursing) to 32 percent male (in social work). (See Table 15.1.) These percentages have not changed substantially in decades. In fact, as Table 15.1 indicates, two of these professions—librarianship and social work—have experienced declines in the proportions of men since 1975. Nursing is the only one of the four experiencing noticeable changes in sex composition, with the proportion of men increasing 80 percent between 1975 and 1990. Even so, men continue to be a tiny minority of all nurses.

Although there are many possible reasons for the continuing preponderance of women in these fields, the focus of this paper is discrimination. Researchers examining the integration of women into "male fields" have identified discrimination as a major barrier to women (Reskin and Hartmann

Percent Male in Selected Occupations,
Selected Years

Profession	1990	1980	1975
Nurses	5.5	3.5	3.0
Elementary teachers	14.8	16.3	14.6
Librarians	16.7	14.8	18.9
Social workers	31.8	35.0	39.2

Source: U.S. Department of Labor. Bureau of Labor Statistics. *Employment and Earnings* 38:1 (January 1991), Table 22 (Employed civilians by detailed occupation), 185; 28:1 (January 1981), Table 23 (Employed persons by detailed occupation), 180; 22:7 (January 1976), Table 2 (Employed persons by detailed occupation), 11.

1986; Reskin 1988; Jacobs 1989). This discrimination has taken the form of laws or institutionalized rules prohibiting the hiring or promotion of women into certain job specialties. Discrimination can also be "informal," as when women encounter sexual harassment, sabotage, or other forms of hostility from their male coworkers resulting in a poisoned work environment (Reskin and Hartmann 1986). Women in nontraditional occupations also report feeling stigmatized by clients when their work puts them in contact with the public. In particular, women in engineering and blue-collar occupations encounter gender-based stereotypes about their competence which undermine their work performance (Martin 1980; Epstein 1988). Each of these forms of discrimination—legal, informal, and cultural—contributes to women's underrepresentation in predominantly male occupations.

The assumption in much of this literature is that any member of a token group in a work setting will probably experience similar discriminatory treatment. Kanter (1977), who is best known for articulating this perspective in her theory of tokenism, argues that when any group represents less than 15 percent of an organization, its members will be subject to predictable forms of discrimination. Likewise, Jacobs argues that "in some ways, men in female-dominated occupations experience the same

difficulties that women in male-dominated occupations face" (1989:167), and Reskin contends that any dominant group in an occupation will use their power to maintain a privileged position (1988:62).

However, the few studies that have considered men's experience in gender-atypical occupations suggest that men may not face discrimination or prejudice when they integrate [into] predominantly female occupations. Zimmer (1988) and Martin (1988) both contend that the effects of sexism can outweigh the effects of tokenism when men enter nontraditional occupations. This study is the first to systematically explore this question using data from four occupations. I examine the barriers to men's entry into these professions; the support men receive from their supervisors, colleagues, and clients; and the reactions they encounter from the public (those outside their professions).

METHODS

I conducted in-depth interviews with 76 men and 23 women in four occupations from 1985–1991. Interviews were conducted in four metropolitan areas: San Francisco/Oakland, California; Austin, Texas; Boston, Massachusetts; and Phoenix, Arizona. These four areas were selected because they show considerable variation in the proportions of men in the four professions. For example, Austin has one of the highest percentages of men in nursing (7.7 percent), whereas Phoenix's percentage is one of the lowest (2.7 percent) (U.S. Bureau of the Census 1980). The sample was generated using "snowballing" techniques. Women were included in the sample to gauge their feelings and responses to men who enter "their" professions.

Like the people employed in these professions generally, those in my sample were predominantly white (90 percent).[1] Their ages ranged from 20 to 66 and the average age was 38. The interview questionnaire consisted of several open-ended questions on four broad topics: motivation to enter the profession; experiences in training; career progression; and general views about men's status and prospects within these occupations. I conducted all the interviews, which generally lasted between one and two hours. Interviews took place in restaurants, my home or office, or the respondent's home or office. Interviews were tape-recorded and transcribed for the analysis.

Data analysis followed the coding techniques described by Strauss (1987). Each transcript was read several times and analyzed into emergent conceptual categories. Likewise, Strauss's principle of theoretical sampling was used. Individual respondents were purposively selected to capture the array of men's experiences in these occupations. Thus, I interviewed practitioners in every specialty, oversampling those employed in the *most* gender atypical areas (e.g., male kindergarten teachers). I also selected respondents from throughout their occupational hierarchies—from students to administrators to retirees. Although the data do not permit within-group comparisons, I am reasonably certain that the sample does capture a wide range of experiences common to men in these female-dominated professions. However, like all findings based on qualitative data, it is uncertain whether the findings generalize to the larger population of men in nontraditional occupations.

In this paper, I review individuals' responses to questions about discrimination in hiring practices, on-the-job rapport with supervisors and coworkers, and prejudice from clients and others outside their profession.

DISCRIMINATION IN HIRING

Contrary to the experience of many women in the male-dominated professions, many of the men and women I spoke to indicated that there is a *preference* for hiring men in these four occupations. A Texas librarian at a junior high school said that his school district "would hire a male over a female."

> I: Why do you think that is?
>
> R: Because there are so few, and the . . . ones that they do have, the library directors seem to . . . really think they're doing great jobs. I don't know,

maybe they just feel they're being progressive or something, [but] I have had a real sense that they really appreciate having a male, particularly at the junior high . . . . As I said, when seven of us lost our jobs from the high schools and were redistributed, there were only four positions at the junior high, and I got one of them. Three of the librarians, some who had been here longer than I had with the school district, were put down in elementary school as librarians. And I definitely think that being male made a difference in my being moved to the junior high rather than an elementary school.

Many of the men perceived their token status as males in predominantly female occupations as an *advantage* in hiring and promotions. I asked an Arizona teacher whether his specialty (elementary special education) was an unusual area for men compared to other areas within education. He said,

> Much more so. I am extremely marketable in special education. That's not why I got into the field. But I am extremely marketable because I am a man.

In several cases, the more female-dominated the specialty, the greater the apparent preference for men. For example, when asked if he encountered any problem getting a job in pediatrics, a Massachusetts nurse said,

> No, no, none. . . . I've heard this from managers and supervisory-type people with men in pediatrics: "It's nice to have a man because it's such a female-dominated profession."

However, there were some exceptions to this preference for men in the most female-dominated specialties. In some cases, formal policies actually barred men from certain jobs. This was the case in some rural Texas school districts, which refused to hire men in the youngest grades (K–3). Some nurses also reported being excluded from positions in obstetrics and gynecology wards, a policy encountered more frequently in private Catholic hospitals.

But often the pressures keeping men out of certain specialties were more subtle than this. Some men described being "tracked" into practice areas within their professions which were considered more legitimate for men. For example, one Texas man described how he was pushed into administration and planning in social work, even though "I'm not interested in writing policy; I'm much more interested in research and clinical stuff." A nurse who is interested in pursuing graduate study in family and child health in Boston said he was dissuaded from entering the program specialty in favor of a concentration in "adult nursing." A kindergarten teacher described the difficulty of finding a job in his specialty after graduation: "I was recruited immediately to start getting into a track to become an administrator. And it was men who recruited me. It was men that ran the system at that time, especially in Los Angeles."

This tracking may bar men from the most female-identified specialties within these professions. But men are effectively being "kicked upstairs" in the process. Those specialties considered more legitimate practice areas for men also tend to be the most prestigious, better paying ones. A distinguished kindergarten teacher, who had been voted city-wide "Teacher of the Year," told me that even though people were pleased to see him in the classroom, "there's been some encouragement to think about administration, and there's been some encouragement to think about teaching at the university level or something like that, or supervisory-type position." That is, despite his aptitude and interest in staying in the classroom, he felt pushed in the direction of administration.

The effect of this "tracking" is the opposite of that experienced by women in male-dominated occupations. Researchers have reported that many women encounter a "glass ceiling" in their efforts to scale organizational and professional hierarchies. That is, they are constrained by invisible barriers to promotion in their careers, caused mainly by sexist attitudes of men in the highest positions (Freeman 1990).[2] In contrast to the "glass ceiling," many of the men I interviewed seem to encounter a "glass escalator." Often, despite their intentions, they face invisible pressures to move up in their professions.

As if on a moving escalator, they must work to stay in place.

A public librarian specializing in children's collections (a heavily female-dominated concentration) described an encounter with this "escalator" in his very first job out of library school. In his first six-months' evaluation, his supervisors commended him for his good work in storytelling and related activities, but they criticized him for "not shooting high enough."

> Seriously. That's literally what they were telling me. They assumed that because I was a male—and they told me this—and that I was being hired right out of graduate school, that somehow I wasn't doing the kind of management-oriented work that they thought I should be doing. And as a result, really they had a lot of bad marks, as it were, against me on my evaluation. And I said I couldn't believe this!

Throughout his ten-year career, he has had to struggle to remain in children's collections.

The glass escalator does not operate at all levels. In particular, men in academia reported some gender-based discrimination in the highest positions due to their universities' commitment to affirmative action. Two nursing professors reported that they felt their own chances of promotion to deanships were nil because their universities viewed the position of nursing dean as a guaranteed female appointment in an otherwise heavily male-dominated administration. One California social work professor reported his university canceled its search for a dean because no minority male or female candidates had been placed on their short list. It was rumored that other schools on campus were permitted to go forward with their searches—even though they also failed to put forward names of minority candidates—because the higher administration perceived it to be "easier" to fulfill affirmative action goals in the social work school. The interviews provide greater evidence of the "glass escalator" at work in the lower levels of these professions.

Of course, men's motivations also play a role in their advancement to higher professional positions. I do not mean to suggest that the men I talked to all resented the informal tracking they experienced. For many men, leaving the most female-identified areas of their professions helped them resolve internal conflicts involving their masculinity. One man left his job as a school social worker to work in a methadone drug treatment program not because he was encouraged to leave by his colleagues, but because "I think there was some macho shit there, to tell you the truth, because I remember feeling a little uncomfortable there . . . ; it didn't feel right to me." Another social worker, employed in the mental health services department of a large urban area in California, reflected on his move into administration:

> The more I think about it, through our discussion, I'm sure that's a large part of why I wound up in administration. It's okay for a man to do the administration. In fact, I don't know if I fully answered a question that you asked a little while ago about how did being male contribute to my advancing in the field. I was saying it wasn't because I got any special favoritism as a man, but . . . I think . . . because I'm a man, I felt a need to get into this kind of position. I may have worked harder toward it, may have competed harder for it, than most women would do, even women who think about doing administrative work.

Elsewhere I have speculated on the origins of men's tendency to define masculinity through single-sex work environments (Williams 1989). Clearly, personal ambition does play a role in accounting for men's movement into more "male-defined" arenas within these professions. But these occupations also structure opportunities for males independent of their individual desires or motives.

The interviews suggest that men's underrepresentation in these professions cannot be attributed to discrimination in hiring or promotions. Many of the men indicated that they received preferential treatment because they were men. Although men mentioned gender discrimination in the hiring process, for the most part they were channeled into the more "masculine" specialties within these professions, which ironically meant being "tracked" into better paying and more prestigious specialties.

SUPERVISORS AND COLLEAGUES: THE WORKING ENVIRONMENT

Researchers claim that subtle forms of workplace discrimination push women out of male-dominated occupations (Reskin and Hartmann 1986; Jacobs 1989). In particular, women report feeling excluded from informal leadership and decision-making networks, and they sense hostility from their male co-workers, which makes them feel uncomfortable and unwanted (Carothers and Crull 1984). Respondents in this study were asked about their relationships with supervisors and female colleagues to ascertain whether men also experienced "poisoned" work environments when entering gender atypical occupations.

A major difference in the experience of men and women in nontraditional occupations is that men in these situations are far more likely to be supervised by a member of their own sex. In each of the four professions I studied, men are overrepresented in administrative and managerial capacities, or, as in the case of nursing, their positions in the organizational hierarchy are governed by men (Grimm and Stern 1974; Phenix 1987; Schmuck 1987; York, Henley, and Gamble 1987; Williams 1989). Thus, unlike women who enter "male fields," the men in these professions often work under the direct supervision of other men.

Many of the men interviewed reported that they had good rapport with their male supervisors. Even in professional school, some men reported extremely close relationships with their male professors. For example, a Texas librarian described an unusually intimate association with two male professors in graduate school:

> I can remember a lot of times in the classroom there would be discussions about a particular topic or issue, and the conversation would spill over into their office hours, after the class was over. And even though there were . . . a couple of the other women that had been in on the discussion, they weren't there. And I don't know if that was preferential or not . . . it certainly carried over into personal life as well. Not just at the school and that sort of thing. I mean, we would get together for dinner . . .

These professors explicitly encouraged him because he was male:

I: Did they ever offer you explicit words of encouragement about being in the profession by virtue of the fact that you were male? . . .

R: Definitely. On several occasions. Yeah. Both of these guys, for sure, including the Dean who was male also. And it's an interesting point that you bring up because it was, oftentimes, kind of in a sign, you know. It wasn't in the classroom, and it wasn't in front of the group, or if we were in the student lounge or something like that. It was . . . if it was just myself or maybe another one of the guys, you know, and just talking in the office. It's like . . . you know, kind of an opening-up and saying, "You know, you are really lucky that you're in the profession because you'll really go to the top real quick, and you'll be able to make real definite improvements and changes. And you'll have a real influence," and all this sort of thing. I mean, really, I can remember several times.

Other men reported similar closeness with their professors. A Texas psychotherapist recalled his relationships with his male professors in social work school:

I made it a point to make a golfing buddy with one of the guys that was in administration. He and I played golf a lot. He was the guy who kind of ran the research training, the research part of the master's program. Then there was a sociologist who ran the other part of the research program. He and I developed a good friendship.

This close mentoring by male professors contrasts with the reported experience of women in nontraditional occupations. Others have noted a lack of solidarity among women in nontraditional occupations. Writing about military academies, for example, Yoder describes the failure of token women to mentor succeeding generations of female cadets. She argues that women attempt to play down their gender difference from men because it is the source of scorn and derision.

Because women felt unaccepted by their male colleagues, one of the last things they wanted to do was to emphasize their gender. Some women thought that, if they kept company with other women, this would highlight their gender and would further isolate them from male cadets. These women desperately wanted to be accepted as cadets, not as *women* cadets Therefore, they did everything from not wearing skirts as an option with their uniforms to avoiding being a part of a group of women (Yoder 1989:532).

Men in nontraditional occupations face a different scenario—their gender is construed as a *positive* difference. Therefore, they have an incentive to bond together and emphasize their distinctiveness from the female majority.

Close, personal ties with male supervisors were also described by men once they were established in their professional careers. It was not uncommon in education, for example, for the male principal to informally socialize with the male staff, as a Texas special education teacher describes:

Occasionally I've had a principal who would regard me as "the other man on the campus" and "it's us against them," you know? I mean, nothing really that extreme, except that some male principals feel like there's nobody there to talk to except the other man. So I've been in that position.

These personal ties can have important consequences for men's careers. For example, one California nurse, whose performance was judged marginal by his nursing supervisors, was transferred to the emergency room staff (a prestigious promotion) due to his personal friendship with the physician in charge. A Massachusetts teacher acknowledged that his principal's personal interest in him landed him his current job.

I: You had mentioned that your principal had sort of spotted you at your previous job and had wanted to bring you here [to this school]. Do you think that has anything to do with the fact that you're a man, aside from your skills as a teacher?

R: Yes, I would say in that particular case, that was part of it . . . . We have certain things in common, certain interests that really lined up.

I: Vis-à-vis teaching?

R: Well, more extraneous things—running specifically, and music. And we just seemed to get along real well right off the bat. It is just kind of a guy thing; we just liked each other . . .

Interviewees did not report many instances of male supervisors discriminating against them, or refusing to accept them because they were male. Indeed, these men were much more likely to report that their male bosses discriminated against the *females* in their professions. When asked if he thought physicians treated male and female nurses differently, a Texas nurse said:

I think yeah, some of them do. I think the women seem like they have a lot more trouble with the physicians treating them in a derogatory manner. Or, if not derogatory, then in a very paternalistic way than the men [are treated]. Usually if a physician is mad at a male nurse, he just kind of yells at him. Kind of like an employee. And if they're mad at a female nurse, rather than treat them on an equal basis, in terms of just letting their anger out at them as an employee, they're more paternalistic or there's some sexual harassment component to it.

A Texas teacher perceived a similar situation where he worked:

I've never felt unjustly treated by a principal because I'm a male. The principals that I've seen that I felt are doing things that are kind of arbitrary or not well thought out are doing it to everybody. In fact, they're probably doing it to the females worse than they are to me.

Openly gay men may encounter less favorable treatment at the hands of their supervisors. For example, a nurse in Texas stated that one of the physicians he worked with preferred to staff the operating room with male nurses exclusively—as long as they weren't gay. Stigma associated with homosexuality leads some men to enhance, or even exaggerate their "masculine" qualities, and may be another factor pushing men into more "acceptable" specialties for men.

Not all men who work in these occupations are supervised by men. Many of the men interviewed who had female bosses also reported high levels of acceptance—although levels of intimacy with women seemed lower than with other men. In some cases, however, men reported feeling shut-out from decision making when the higher administration was constituted entirely by women. I asked an Arizona librarian whether men in the library profession were discriminated against in hiring because of their sex:

Professionally speaking, people go to considerable lengths to keep that kind of thing out of their [hiring] deliberations. Personally, is another matter. It's pretty common around here to talk about the "old girl network." This is one of the few libraries that I've had any intimate knowledge of which is actually controlled by women . . . . Most of the department heads and upper level administrators are women. And there's an "old girl network" that works just like the "old boy network," except that the important conferences take place in the women's room rather than on the golf course. But the political mechanism is the same, the exclusion of the other sex from decision making is the same. The reasons are the same. It's somewhat discouraging . . .

Although I did not interview many supervisors, I did include 23 women in my sample to ascertain their perspectives about the presence of men in their professions. All of the women I interviewed claimed to be supportive of their male colleagues, but some conveyed ambivalence. For example, a social work professor said she would like to see more men enter the social work profession, particularly in the clinical specialty (where they are underrepresented). Indeed, she favored affirmative action hiring guidelines for men in the profession. Yet, she resented the fact that her department hired "another white male" during a recent search. I questioned her about this ambivalence:

I: I find it very interesting that, on the one hand, you sort of perceive this preference and perhaps even sexism with regard to how men are evaluated and how they achieve higher positions within the profession, yet, on the other hand, you would be encouraging of more men to enter the field. Is that contradictory to you, or . . . ?

R: Yeah, it's contradictory.

It appears that women are generally eager to see men enter "their" occupations. Indeed, several men noted that their female colleagues had facilitated their careers in various ways (including mentorship in college). However, at the same time, women often resent the apparent ease with which men advance within these professions, sensing that men at the higher levels receive preferential treatment which closes off advancement opportunities for women.

But this ambivalence does not seem to translate into the "poisoned" work environment described by many women who work in male-dominated occupations. Among the male interviewees, there were no accounts of sexual harassment. However, women do treat their male colleagues differently on occasion. It is not uncommon in nursing, for example, for men to be called upon to help catheterize male patients, or to lift especially heavy patients. Some librarians also said that women asked them to lift and move heavy boxes of books because they were men. Teachers sometimes confront differential treatment as well, as described by this Texas teacher:

> As a man, you're teaching with all women, and that can be hard sometimes. Just because of the stereotypes, you know I'm real into computers . . . and all the time people are calling me to fix their computer. Or if somebody gets a flat tire, they come and get me. I mean, there are just a lot of stereotypes. Not that I mind doing any of those things, but it's . . . you know, it just kind of bugs me that it is a stereotype, "A man should do that." Or if their kids have a lot of discipline problems, that kiddo's in your room. Or if there are kids that don't have a father in their home, that kid's in your room. Hell, nowadays that'd be half the school in my room (laughs). But you know, all the time I hear from the principal or from other teachers, "Well, this child really needs a man . . . a male role model" (laughs). So there are a lot of stereotypes that . . . men kind of get stuck with.

This special treatment bothered some respondents. Getting assigned all the "discipline problems" can make for difficult working conditions, for example. But many men claimed this differential treatment

did not cause distress. In fact, several said they liked being appreciated for the special traits and abilities (such as strength) they could contribute to their professions.

Furthermore, women's special treatment sometimes enhanced—rather than poisoned—the men's work environments. One Texas librarian said he felt "more comfortable working with women than men" because "I think it has something to do with control. Maybe it's that women will let me take control more than men will." Several men reported that their female colleagues often cast them into leadership roles. Although not all savored this distinction, it did enhance their authority and control in the workplace. In subtle (and not-too-subtle) ways, then, differential treatment contributes to the "glass escalator" men experience in nontraditional professions.

Even outside work, most of the men interviewed said they felt fully accepted by their female colleagues. They were usually included in informal socializing occasions with the women—even though this frequently meant attending baby showers or Tupperware parties. Many said that they declined offers to attend these events because they were not interested in "women's things," although several others claimed to attend everything: The minority men I interviewed seemed to feel the least comfortable in these informal contexts. One social worker in Arizona was asked about socializing with his female colleagues:

> I: So in general, for example, if all the employees were going to get together to have a party, or celebrate a bridal shower or whatever, would you be invited along with the rest of the group?
>
> R: They would invite me, I would say, somewhat reluctantly. Being a black male, working with all white females, it did cause some outside problems. So I didn't go to a lot of functions with them . . .
>
> I: You felt that there was some tension there on the level of your acceptance . . . ?
>
> R: Yeah. It was OK working, but on the outside, personally, there was some tension there. It never came out, that they said, "Because of who you are we can't invite you" (laughs), and I wouldn't

have done anything anyway. I would have probably respected them more for saying what was on their minds. But I never felt completely in with the group.

Some single men also said they felt uncomfortable socializing with married female colleagues because it gave the "wrong impression." But in general, the men said that they felt very comfortable around their colleagues and described their workplaces as very congenial for men. It appears unlikely, therefore, that men's underrepresentation in these professions is due to hostility toward men on the part of supervisors or women workers.

DISCRIMINATION FROM "OUTSIDERS"

The most compelling evidence of discrimination against men in these professions is related to their dealings with the public. Men often encounter negative stereotypes when they come into contact with clients or "outsiders"—people they meet outside of work. For instance, it is popularly assumed that male nurses are gay. Librarians encounter images of themselves as "wimpy" and asexual. Male social workers describe being typecast as "feminine" and "passive." Elementary school teachers are often confronted by suspicions that they are pedophiles. One kindergarten teacher described an experience that occurred early in his career which was related to him years afterwards by his principal:

> He indicated to me that parents had come to him and indicated to him that they had a problem with the fact that I was a male . . . . I recall almost exactly what he said. There were three specific concerns that the parents had: One parent said, "How can he love my child, he's a man." The second thing that I recall, he said the parent said, "He has a beard." And the third thing was, "Aren't you concerned about homosexuality?"

Such suspicions often cause men in all four professions to alter their work behavior to guard against sexual abuse charges, particularly in those specialties requiring intimate contact with women and children.

Men are very distressed by these negative stereotypes, which tend to undermine their self-esteem and to cause them to second-guess their motivations for entering these fields. A California teacher said,

> If I tell men that I don't know, that I'm meeting for the first time, that that's what I do, . . . sometimes there's a look on their faces that, you know, "Oh, couldn't get a real job?"

When asked if his wife, who is also an elementary school teacher, encounters the same kind of prejudice, he said,

> No, it's accepted because she's a woman . . . . I think people would see that as a . . . step up, you know. "Oh, you're not a housewife, you've got a career. That's great . . . that you're out there working. And you have a daughter, but you're still out there working. You decided not to stay home, and you went out there and got a job." Whereas for me, it's more like I'm supposed to be out working anyway, even though I'd rather be home with [my daughter].

Unlike women who enter traditionally male professions, men's movement into these jobs is perceived by the "outside world" as a step down in status. This particular form of discrimination may be most significant in explaining why men are underrepresented in these professions. Men who otherwise might show interest in and aptitudes for such careers are probably discouraged from pursuing them because of the negative popular stereotypes associated with the men who work in them. This is a crucial difference from the experience of women in nontraditional professions: "My daughter, the physician," resonates far more favorably in most people's ears than "My son, the nurse."

Many of the men in my sample identified the stigma of working in a female-identified occupation as the major barrier to more men entering their professions. However, for the most part, they claimed that these negative stereotypes were not a factor in their own decisions to join these occupations. Most respondents didn't consider entering these fields until well into adulthood, after working in some related occupation. Several social workers and librarians even claimed they were not aware that men were a minority in their chosen professions. Either they had no well-defined image or stereotype, or their contacts and mentors were predominantly men. For example, prior to entering library school, many librarians held part-time jobs in university libraries, where there are proportionally more men than in the profession generally. Nurses and elementary school teachers were more aware that mostly women worked in these jobs, and this was often a matter of some concern to them. However, their choices were ultimately legitimized by mentors, or by encouraging friends or family members who implicitly reassured them that entering these occupations would not typecast them as feminine. In some cases, men were told by recruiters there were special advancement opportunities for men in these fields, and they entered them expecting rapid promotion to administrative positions.

> I: Did it ever concern you when you were making the decision to enter nursing school, the fact that it is a female-dominated profession?
>
> R: Not really. I never saw myself working on the floor. I saw myself pretty much going into administration, just getting the background and then getting a job someplace as a supervisor and then working, getting up into administration.

Because of the unique circumstances of their recruitment, many of the respondents did not view their occupational choices as inconsistent with a male gender role, and they generally avoided the negative stereotypes directed against men in these fields.

Indeed, many of the men I interviewed claimed that they did not encounter negative professional stereotypes until they had worked in these fields for several years. Popular prejudices can be damaging to self-esteem and probably push some men out of these professions altogether. Yet, ironically, they sometimes contribute to the "glass escalator" effect I have been describing. Men seem to encounter the most vituperative criticism from the public when they are in the most female-identified specialties. Public concerns sometimes result in their being shunted into more "legitimate" positions for men.

A librarian formerly in charge of a branch library's children's collection, who now works in the reference department of the city's main library, describes his experience:

> R: Some of the people [who frequented the branch library] complained that they didn't want to have a man doing the storytelling scenario. And I got transferred here to the central library in an equivalent job . . . I thought that I did a good job. And I had been told by my supervisor that I was doing a good job.
>
> I: Have you ever considered filing some sort of lawsuit to get that other job back?
>
> R: Well, actually, the job I've gotten now . . . well, it's a reference librarian; it's what I wanted in the first place. I've got a whole lot more authority here. I'm also in charge of the circulation desk. And I've recently been promoted because of my new stature, so . . . no, I'm not considering trying to get that other job back.

The negative stereotypes about men who do "women's work" can push men out of specific jobs. However, to the extent that they channel men into more "legitimate" practice areas, their effects can actually be positive. Instead of being a source of discrimination, these prejudices can add to the "glass escalator effect" by pressuring men to move *out* of the most female-identified areas, and *up* to those regarded as more legitimate and prestigious for men.

CONCLUSION: DISCRIMINATION AGAINST MEN

Both men and women who work in nontraditional occupations encounter discrimination, but the forms and consequences of this discrimination are very different. The interviews suggest that unlike "nontraditional" women workers, most of the discrimination and prejudice facing men in the "female professions" emanates from outside those professions. The men and women interviewed for the most part believed that men are given fair—if not preferential—treatment in hiring and promotion decisions, are accepted by supervisors and colleagues, and are well-integrated into the workplace subculture. Indeed, subtle mechanisms seem to enhance men's position in these professions—a phenomenon I refer to as the "glass escalator effect."

The data lend strong support for Zimmer's (1988) critique of "gender neutral theory" (such as Kanter's [1977] theory of tokenism) in the study of occupational segregation. Zimmer argues that women's occupational inequality is more a consequence of sexist beliefs and practices embedded in the labor force than the effect of numerical underrepresentation per se. This study suggests that token status itself does not diminish men's occupational success. Men take their gender privilege with them when they enter predominantly female occupations: this translates into an advantage in spite of their numerical rarity.

This study indicates that the experience of tokenism is very different for men and women. Future research should examine how the experience of tokenism varies for members of different races and classes as well. For example, it is likely that informal workplace mechanisms similar to the ones identified here promote the careers of token whites in predominantly black occupations. The crucial factor is the social status of the token's group—not their numerical rarity—that determines whether the token encounters a "glass ceiling" or a "glass escalator."

However, this study also found that many men encounter negative stereotypes from persons not directly involved in their professions. Men who enter these professions are often considered "failures" or sexual deviants. These stereotypes may be a major impediment to men who otherwise might consider careers in these occupations. Indeed, they are likely to be important factors whenever a member of a relatively high status group crosses over into a lower status occupation. However, to the extent that these stereotypes contribute to the "glass escalator effect" by channeling men into more "legitimate" (and higher paying) occupations, they are not discriminatory.

Women entering traditionally "male" professions also face negative stereotypes suggesting they are not "real women" (Epstein 1981; Lorber 1984; Spencer and Podmore 1987). However, these stereotypes do not seem to deter women to the same degree that they deter men from pursuing nontraditional professions. There is ample historical evidence that women flock to male-identified occupations once opportunities are available (Cohn 1985; Epstein 1988). Not so with men. Examples of occupations changing from predominantly female to predominantly male are very rare in our history. The few existing cases—such as medicine—suggest that redefinition of the occupations as appropriately "masculine" is necessary before men will consider joining them (Ehrenreich and English 1978).

Because different mechanisms maintain segregation in male- and female-dominated occupations, different approaches are needed to promote their integration. Policies intended to alter the sex composition of male-dominated occupations—such as affirmative action—make little sense when applied to the "female professions." For men, the major barriers to integration have little to do with their treatment once they decide to enter these fields. Rather, we need to address the social and cultural sanctions applied to men who do "women's work" which keep men from even considering these occupations.

One area where these cultural barriers are clearly evident is in the media's representation of men's occupations. Women working in traditionally male professions have achieved an unprecedented acceptance on popular television shows. Women are portrayed as doctors ("St. Elsewhere"), lawyers ("The Cosby Show," "L.A. Law"), architects ("Family Ties"), and police officers ("Cagney and Lacey"). But where are the male nurses, teachers, and secretaries? Television rarely portrays men in nontraditional work roles, and when it does, that anomaly is made the central focus—and joke—of the program. A comedy series (1991–1992) about a male elementary school teacher ("Drexell's Class") stars a lead character who *hates children*! Yet even this negative portrayal is exceptional. When a prime-time hospital drama series ("St Elsewhere") depicted a male orderly striving for upward mobility, the show's writers made him a "physician's assistant," not a nurse or nurse practitioner—the much more likely "real life" possibilities.

Presenting positive images of men in nontraditional careers can produce limited effects. A few social workers, for example, were first inspired to pursue their careers by George C. Scott, who played a social worker in the television drama series, "Eastside/Westside." But as a policy strategy to break down occupational segregation, changing media images of men is no panacea. The stereotypes that differentiate masculinity and femininity, and degrade that which is defined as feminine, are deeply entrenched in culture, social structure, and personality (Williams 1989). Nothing short of a revolution in cultural definitions of masculinity will effect the broad scale social transformation needed to achieve the complete occupational integration of men and women.

Of course, there are additional factors besides societal prejudice contributing to men's underrepresentation in female-dominated professions. Most notably, those men I interviewed mentioned as a deterrent the fact that these professions are all underpaid relative to comparable "male" occupations, and several suggested that instituting a "comparable worth" policy might attract more men. However, I am not convinced that improved salaries will substantially alter the sex composition of these professions unless the cultural stigma faced by men in these occupations diminishes. Occupational sex segregation is remarkably resilient, even in the face of devastating economic hardship. During the Great Depression of the 1930s, for example, "women's jobs" failed to attract sizable numbers of men (Blum 1991:154). In her study of American Telephone and Telegraph (AT&T) workers, Epstein (1989) found that some men would rather suffer unemployment than accept relatively high paying "women's jobs" because of the damage to their identities this would cause. She quotes one unemployed man who refused to apply for a female-identified telephone operator job:

> I think if they offered me $1000 a week tax free, I wouldn't take that job. When I . . . see those guys sitting in there [in the telephone operating room], I wonder what's wrong with them. Are they pansies or what? (Epstein 1989: 577)

This is not to say that raising salaries would not affect the sex composition of these jobs. Rather, I am suggesting that wages are not the only—or perhaps even the major—impediment to men's entry into these jobs. Further research is needed to explore the ideological significance of the "woman's wage" for maintaining occupational stratification.[3]

At any rate, integrating men and women in the labor force requires more than dismantling barriers to women in male-dominated fields. Sex segregation is a two-way street. We must also confront and dismantle the barriers men face in predominantly female occupations. Men's experiences in these nontraditional occupations reveal just how culturally embedded the barriers are, and how far we have to travel before men and women attain true occupational and economic equality.

AUTHOR'S NOTE

This research was funded in part by a faculty grant from the University of Texas at Austin. I also acknowledge the support of the sociology departments of the University of California, Berkeley; Harvard University; and Arizona State University. I would like to thank Judy Auerbach, Martin Button, Robert Nye, Teresa Sullivan, Debra Umberson, Mary Waters, and the reviewers at *Social Problems* for their comments on earlier versions of this paper.

NOTES

1. According to the U.S. Census, black men and women comprise 7 percent of all nurses and librarians, 11 percent of all elementary school teachers, and 19 percent of all social workers (calculated from U.S. Census 1980: Table 278, 1–197). The proportion of blacks in social work may be exaggerated by these statistics. The occupational definition of "social worker" used by the Census Bureau includes welfare workers and pardon and parole officers, who are not considered "professional" social workers by the National Association of Social Workers. A study of degreed professionals found that 89 percent of practitioners were white (Hardcastle 1987).

2. In April 1991, the Labor Department created a "Glass Ceiling Commission" to "conduct a thorough study of the underrepresentation of women and minorities in executive, management, and senior decision-making positions in business" (U.S. House of Representatives 1991:20).

3. Alice Kessler-Harris argues that the lower pay of traditionally female occupations is symbolic of a patriarchal order that assumes female dependence on a male breadwinner. She writes that pay equity is fundamentally threatening to the "male worker's sense of self, pride, and masculinity" because it upsets his individual standing in the hierarchical ordering of the sexes (1990:125). Thus, men's reluctance to enter these occupations may have less to do with the actual dollar amount recorded in their paychecks, and more to do with the damage that earning "a woman's wage" would wreak on their self-esteem in a society that privileges men. This conclusion is supported by the interview data.

REFERENCES

Bielby, William T., and James N. Baron 1984. "A woman's place is with other women: Sex segregation within organizations." In *Sex Segregation in the Workplace: Trends, Explanations, Remedies*, ed. Barbara Reskin, 27–55. Washington, D.C.: National Academy Press.

Blum, Linda M. 1991. *Between Feminism and Labor: The Significance of the Comparable Worth Movement*. Berkeley and Los Angeles: University of California Press.

Carothers, Suzanne C., and Peggy Crull 1984. "Contrasting sexual harassment in female-dominated and male-dominated occupations." In *My Troubles Are Going to have Trouble with Me: Everyday Trials and Triumphs of Women Workers*, ed. Karen B. Sacks and Dorothy Remy, 220–227. New Brunswick, N.J.: Rutgers University Press.

Cohn, Samuel 1985. *The Process of Occupational Sex-Typing*. Philadelphia: Temple University Press.

Ehrenreich, Barbara, and Deirdre English 1978. *For Her Own Good: 100 Years of Expert Advice to Women*. Garden City, N.Y.: Anchor Press.

Epstein, Cynthia Fuchs 1981. *Women in Law*. New York: Basic Books.

1988. *Deceptive Distinctions: Sex, Gender and the Social Order*. New Haven: Yale University Press.

1989. "Workplace boundaries: Conceptions and creations." *Social Research* 56: 571–590.

Freeman, Sue J. M. 1990. *Managing Lives: Corporate Women and Social Change*. Amherst, Mass.: University of Massachusetts Press.

Grimm, James W., and Robert N. Stern 1974. "Sex roles and internal labor market structures: The female semi-professions." *Social Problems* 21: 690–705.

Hardcastle, D. A. 1987. "The social work labor force." Austin, Tex.: School of Social Work, University of Texas.

Hodson, Randy, and Teresa Sullivan 1990. *The Social Organization of Work*. Belmont, Calif.: Wadsworth Publishing Co.

Jacobs, Jerry 1989. *Revolving Doors: Sex Segregation and Women's Careers*. Stanford, Calif.: Stanford University Press.

Kanter, Rosabeth Moss 1977. *Men and Women of the Corporation*. New York: Basic Books.

Kessler-Harris, Alice 1990. *A Woman's Wage: Historical Meanings and Social Consequences*. Lexington, Ky: Kentucky University Press.

Lorber, Judith 1984. *Women Physicians: Careers, Status, and Power*. New York: Tavistock.

Martin, Susan E. 1980. *Breaking and Entering: Police Women on Patrol*. Berkeley, Calif.: University of California Press.

1988. "Think like a man, work like a dog, and act like a lady: Occupational dilemmas of policewomen." In *The Worth of Women's Work: A Qualitative Synthesis*, ed. Anne Statham, Eleanor M. Miller, and Hans O. Mauksch, 205–223. Albany, N.Y.: State University of New York Press.

Phenix, Katharine 1987. "The status of women librarians." *Frontiers* 9: 36–40.

Reskin, Barbara 1988. "Bringing the men back in: Sex differentiation and the devaluation of women's work." *Gender & Society* 2: 58–81.

Reskin, Barbara, and Heidi Hartmann 1986. *Women's Work, Men's Work: Sex Segregation on the Job*. Washington, D.C.: National Academy Press.

Reskin, Barbara, and Patricia Roos 1990. *Job Queues, Gender Queues: Explaining Women's Inroads into Male Occupations*. Philadelphia: Temple University Press.

Schmuck, Patricia A. 1987. "Women school employees in the United States." In *Women Educators: Employees of Schools in Western Countries*, ed. Patricia A. Schmuck, 75–97. Albany, N.Y.: State University of New York Press.

Schreiber, Carol 1979. *Men and Women in Transitional Occupations.* Cambridge, Mass.: MIT Press.

Spencer, Anne, and David Podmore 1987. *In a Man's World: Essays on Women in Male-Dominated Professions.* London: Tavistock.

Strauss, Anselm L. 1987. *Qualitative Analysis for Social Scientists.* Cambridge, England: Cambridge University Press.

U.S. Bureau of the Census 1980. *Detailed Population Characteristics*, Vol. 1, Ch. D. Washington, D.C.: Government Printing Office.

U.S. Congress House 1991. *Civil Rights and Women's Equity in Employment Act of 1991.* Report. (Report 102-40, Part I.) Washington, D.C.: Government Printing Office.

U.S. Department of Labor. Bureau of Labor Statistics 1991. *Employment and Earnings.* January. Washington, D.C.: Government Printing Office.

Williams, Christine L. 1989. *Gender Differences at Work: Women and Men in Nontraditional Occupations.* Berkeley, Calif.: University of California Press.

Yoder, Janice D. 1989. "Women at West Point: Lessons for token women in male-dominated occupations." In *Women: A Feminist Perspective*, ed. Jo Freeman, 523–537. Mountain View, Calif.: Mayfield Publishing Company.

York, Reginald O., H. Carl Henley, and Dorothy N. Gamble 1987. "Sexual discrimination in social work: Is it salary or advancement?" *Social Work* 32: 336–340.

Zimmer, Lynn 1988. "Tokenism and women in the workplace." *Social Problems* 35: 64–77.

RACIALIZING THE GLASS ESCALATOR: RECONSIDERING MEN'S EXPERIENCES WITH WOMEN'S WORK

Adia Harvey Wingfield

Sociologists who study work have long noted that jobs are sex segregated and that this segregation creates different occupational experiences for men and women (Charles and Grusky 2004). Jobs predominantly filled by women often require "feminine" traits such as nurturing, caring, and empathy, a fact that means men confront perceptions that they are unsuited for the requirements of these jobs. Rather than having an adverse effect on their occupational experiences, however, these assumptions facilitate men's entry into better paying, higher status positions, creating what Williams (1995) labels a "glass escalator" effect.

The glass escalator model has been an influential paradigm in understanding the experiences of men who do women's work. Researchers have identified this process among men nurses, social workers, paralegals, and librarians and have cited its pervasiveness as evidence of men's consistent advantage in the workplace, such that even in jobs where men are numerical minorities they are likely to enjoy higher wages and faster promotions (Floge and Merrill 1986; Heikes 1991; Pierce 1995; Williams 1989, 1995). Most of these studies implicitly assume a racial homogenization of men workers in women's professions, but this supposition is problematic for several reasons. For one, minority men are not only present but are actually overrepresented in certain areas of reproductive work that have historically been dominated by white women (Duffy 2007). Thus, research that focuses primarily on white men in women's professions ignores a key segment of men who perform this type of labor. Second, and perhaps more important, conclusions based on the experiences of white men tend to overlook the ways that intersections of race and gender create different experiences for different men. While extensive work has documented the fact that white men in women's professions encounter a glass escalator effect that aids their occupational mobility (for an exception, see Snyder and Green 2008), few studies, if any, have considered how this effect is a function not only of gendered advantage but of racial privilege as well.

In this article, I examine the implications of race–gender intersections for minority men employed in a female-dominated, feminized occupation, specifically focusing on Black men in nursing. Their experiences doing "women's work" demonstrate that the glass escalator is a racialized as well as gendered concept.

THEORETICAL FRAMEWORK

In her classic study *Men and Women of the Corporation*, Kanter (1977) offers a groundbreaking analysis of group interactions. Focusing on high-ranking women executives who work mostly with men, Kanter argues that those in the extreme numerical minority are tokens who are socially isolated, highly visible, and adversely stereotyped. Tokens have difficulty forming relationships with colleagues and often are excluded from social networks that provide mobility. Because of their low numbers, they are also highly visible as people who are different from the majority, even though they often feel invisible when they are ignored or overlooked in social settings. Tokens are also stereotyped by those in the majority group and frequently face pressure to behave in ways that challenge and undermine these stereotypes. Ultimately, Kanter argues that it is harder for them to blend into the organization and to work effectively and productively, and that they face serious barriers to upward mobility.

Kanter's (1977) arguments have been analyzed and retested in various settings and among many populations. Many studies, particularly of women in male-dominated corporate settings, have supported her findings. Other work has reversed these conclusions, examining the extent to which her conclusions hold when men were the tokens and women the majority group. These studies fundamentally challenged the gender neutrality of the token, finding that men in the minority fare much better than do similarly situated women. In particular, this research suggests that factors such as heightened visibility and polarization do not necessarily disadvantage men who are in the minority. While women tokens find that their visibility hinders their ability to blend in and work productively, men tokens find that their conspicuousness can lead to greater opportunities for leadership and choice assignments (Floge and Merrill 1986; Heikes 1991). Studies in this vein are important because they emphasize organizations—and occupations—as gendered institutions that subsequently create dissimilar experiences for men and women tokens (see Acker 1990).

In her groundbreaking study of men employed in various women's professions, Williams (1995) further develops this analysis of how power relationships shape the ways men tokens experience work in women's professions. Specifically, she introduces the concept of the glass escalator to explain men's experiences as tokens in these areas. Like Floge and Merrill (1986) and Heikes (1991), Williams finds that men tokens do not experience the isolation, visibility, blocked access to social networks, and stereotypes in the same ways that women tokens do. In contrast, Williams argues that even though they are in the minority, processes are in place that actually facilitate their opportunity and advancement. Even in culturally feminized occupations, then, men's advantage is built into the very structure and everyday interactions of these jobs so that men find themselves actually struggling to remain in place. For these men, "despite their intentions, they face invisible pressures to move up in their professions. Like being on a moving escalator, they have to work to stay in place" (Williams 1995, 87).

The glass escalator term thus refers to the "subtle mechanisms in place that enhance [men's] positions in [women's] professions" (Williams 1995, 108). These mechanisms include certain behaviors, attitudes, and beliefs men bring to these professions as well as the types of interactions that often occur between these men and their colleagues, supervisors, and customers. Consequently, even in occupations composed mostly of women, gendered perceptions about men's roles, abilities, and skills privilege them and facilitate their advancement. The glass escalator serves as a conduit that channels men in women's professions into the uppermost levels of the occupational hierarchy. Ultimately, the glass escalator effect suggests that men retain consistent occupational advantages over women, even when women are numerically in the majority (Budig 2002; Williams 1995).

Though this process has now been fairly well established in the literature, there are reasons to question its generalizability to all men. In an early critique of the supposed general neutrality of the token, Zimmer (1988) notes that much research on race comes to precisely the opposite of Kanter's conclusions, finding that as the numbers of minority group members increase (e.g., as they become less likely to be "tokens"), so too do tensions between the majority and minority groups. For instance, as minorities move into predominantly white neighborhoods, increasing numbers do not create the likelihood of greater acceptance and better treatment. In contrast, whites are likely to relocate when neighborhoods become "too" integrated, citing concerns about property values and racialized ideas about declining neighborhood quality (Shapiro 2004). Reinforcing, while at the same time tempering, the findings of research on men in female-dominated occupations, Zimmer (1988, 71) argues that relationships between tokens and the majority depend on understanding the underlying power relationships between these groups and "the status and power differentials between them." Hence, just as men who are tokens fare better than women, it also follows that the experiences of Blacks and whites as tokens should differ in ways that reflect their positions in hierarchies of status and power.

The concept of the glass escalator provides an important and useful framework for addressing men's experiences in women's occupations, but so far research in this vein has neglected to examine whether the glass escalator is experienced among all men in an identical manner. Are the processes that facilitate a ride on the glass escalator available to minority men? Or does race intersect with gender to affect the extent to which the glass escalator offers men opportunities in women's professions? In the next section, I examine whether and how the mechanisms that facilitate a ride on the glass escalator might be unavailable to Black men in nursing.[1]

Relationships with Colleagues and Supervisors

One key aspect of riding the glass escalator involves the warm, collegial welcome men workers often receive from their women colleagues. Often, this reaction is a response to the fact that professions dominated by women are frequently low in salary and status and that greater numbers of men help improve prestige and pay (Heikes 1991). Though

some women workers resent the apparent ease with which men enter and advance in women's professions, the generally warm welcome men receive stands in stark contrast to the cold reception, difficulties with mentorship, and blocked access to social networks that women often encounter when they do men's work (Roth 2006; Williams 1992). In addition, unlike women in men's professions, men who do women's work frequently have supervisors of the same sex. Men workers can thus enjoy a gendered bond with their supervisor in the context of a collegial work environment. These factors often converge, facilitating men's access to higher-status positions and producing the glass escalator effect.

The congenial relationship with colleagues and gendered bonds with supervisors are crucial to riding the glass escalator. Women colleagues often take a primary role in casting these men into leadership or supervisory positions. In their study of men and women tokens in a hospital setting, Floge and Merrill (1986) cite cases where women nurses promoted men colleagues to the position of charge nurse, even when the job had already been assigned to a woman. In addition to these close ties with women colleagues, men are also able to capitalize on gendered bonds with (mostly men) supervisors in ways that engender upward mobility. Many men supervisors informally socialize with men workers in women's jobs and are thus able to trade on their personal friendships for upward mobility. Williams (1995) describes a case where a nurse with mediocre performance reviews received a promotion to a more prestigious specialty area because of his friendship with the (male) doctor in charge. According to the literature, building strong relationships with colleagues and supervisors often happens relatively easily for men in women's professions and pays off in their occupational advancement.

For Black men in nursing, however, gendered racism may limit the extent to which they establish bonds with their colleagues and supervisors. The concept of gendered racism suggests that racial stereotypes, images, and beliefs are grounded in gendered ideals (Collins 1990, 2004; Espiritu

2000; Essed 1991; Harvey Wingfield 2007). Gendered racist stereotypes of Black men in particular emphasize the dangerous, threatening attributes associated with Black men and Black masculinity, framing Black men as threats to white women, prone to criminal behavior, and especially violent. Collins (2004) argues that these stereotypes serve to legitimize Black men's treatment in the criminal justice system through methods such as racial profiling and incarceration, but they may also hinder Black men's attempts to enter and advance in various occupational fields.

For Black men nurses, gendered racist images may have particular consequences for their relationships with women colleagues, who may view Black men nurses through the lens of controlling images and gendered racist stereotypes that emphasize the danger they pose to women. This may take on a heightened significance for white women nurses, given stereotypes that suggest that Black men are especially predisposed to raping white women. Rather than experiencing the congenial bonds with colleagues that white men nurses describe, Black men nurses may find themselves facing a much cooler reception from their women coworkers.

Gendered racism may also play into the encounters Black men nurses have with supervisors. In cases where supervisors are white men, Black men nurses may still find that higher-ups treat them in ways that reflect prevailing stereotypes about threatening Black masculinity. Supervisors may feel uneasy about forming close relationships with Black men or may encourage their separation from white women nurses. In addition, broader, less gender-specific racial stereotypes could also shape the experiences Black men nurses have with white men bosses. Whites often perceive Blacks, regardless of gender, as less intelligent, hardworking, ethical, and moral than other racial groups (Feagin 2006). Black men nurses may find that in addition to being influenced by gendered racist stereotypes, supervisors also view them as less capable and qualified for promotion, thus negating or minimizing the glass escalator effect.

Suitability for Nursing and Higher-Status Work

The perception that men are not really suited to do women's work also contributes to the glass escalator effect. In encounters with patients, doctors, and other staff, men nurses frequently confront others who do not expect to see them doing "a woman's job." Sometimes this perception means that patients mistake men nurses for doctors; ultimately, the sense that men do not really belong in nursing contributes to a push "*out* of the most feminine-identified areas and *up* to those regarded as more legitimate for men" (Williams 1995, 104). The sense that men are better suited for more masculine jobs means that men workers are often assumed to be more able and skilled than their women counterparts. As Williams writes (1995, 106), "Masculinity is often associated with competence and mastery," and this implicit definition stays with men even when they work in feminized fields. Thus, part of the perception that men do not belong in these jobs is rooted in the sense that, as men, they are more capable and accomplished than women and thus belong in jobs that reflect this. Consequently, men nurses are mistaken for doctors and are granted more authority and responsibility than their women counterparts, reflecting the idea that, as men, they are inherently more competent (Heikes 1991; Williams 1995).

Black men nurses, however, may not face the presumptions of expertise or the resulting assumption that they belong in higher-status jobs. Black professionals, both men and women, are often assumed to be less capable and less qualified than their white counterparts. In some cases, these negative stereotypes hold even when Black workers outperform white colleagues (Feagin and Sikes 1994). The belief that Blacks are inherently less competent than whites means that, despite advanced education, training, and skill, Black professionals often confront the lingering perception that they are better suited for lower-level service work (Feagin and Sikes 1994). Black men in fact often fare better than white women in blue-collar jobs such as policing and corrections work (Britton 1995), and this may be, in part, because they are viewed as more appropriately suited for these types of positions.

For Black men nurses, then, the issue of perception may play out in different ways than it does for white men nurses. While white men nurses enjoy the automatic assumption that they are qualified, capable, and suited for "better" work, the experiences of Black professionals suggest that Black men nurses may not encounter these reactions. They may, like their white counterparts, face the perception that they do not belong in nursing. Unlike their white counterparts, Black men nurses may be seen as inherently less capable and therefore better suited for low-wage labor than a professional, feminized occupation such as nursing. This perception of being less qualified means that they also may not be immediately assumed to be better suited for the higher-level, more masculinized jobs within the medical field.

As minority women address issues of both race and gender to negotiate a sense of belonging in masculine settings (Ong 2005), minority men may also face a comparable challenge in feminized fields. They may have to address the unspoken racialization implicit in the assumption that masculinity equals competence. Simultaneously, they may find that the racial stereotype that Blackness equals lower qualifications, standards, and competence clouds the sense that men are inherently more capable and adept in any field, including the feminized ones.

Establishing Distance from Femininity

An additional mechanism of the glass escalator involves establishing distance from women and the femininity associated with their occupations. Because men nurses are employed in a culturally feminized occupation, they develop strategies to disassociate themselves from the femininity associated with their work and retain some of the privilege associated with masculinity. Thus, when men nurses gravitate toward hospital emergency wards rather than obstetrics or pediatrics, or emphasize that they are only in nursing to get into hospital administration, they distance themselves from the femininity of their profession and thereby preserve their status as men despite the fact that they do "women's work." Perhaps more important, these strategies also place men in a prime position to experience the glass escalator effect, as they situate themselves to move upward into higher-status areas in the field.

Creating distance from femininity also helps these men achieve aspects of hegemonic masculinity, which Connell (1989) describes as the predominant and most valued form of masculinity at a given time. Contemporary hegemonic masculine ideals emphasize toughness, strength, aggressiveness, heterosexuality, and, perhaps most important, a clear sense of femininity as different from and subordinate to masculinity (Kimmel 2001; Williams 1995). Thus, when men distance themselves from the feminized aspects of their jobs, they uphold the idea that masculinity and femininity are distinct, separate, and mutually exclusive. When these men seek masculinity by aiming for the better paying or most technological fields, they not only position themselves to move upward into the more acceptable arenas but also reinforce the greater social value placed on masculinity. Establishing distance from femininity therefore allows men to retain the privileges and status of masculinity while simultaneously enabling them to ride the glass escalator.

For Black men, the desire to reject femininity may be compounded by racial inequality. Theorists have argued that as institutional racism blocks access to traditional markers of masculinity such as occupational status and economic stability, Black men may repudiate femininity as a way of accessing the masculinity—and its attendant status—that is denied through other routes (hooks 2004; Neal 2005). Rejecting femininity is a key strategy men use to assert masculinity, and it remains available to Black men even when other means of achieving masculinity are unattainable. Black men nurses may be more likely to distance themselves from their women colleagues and to reject the femininity associated with nursing, particularly if they feel that they experience racial discrimination that renders occupational advancement inaccessible. Yet if they encounter strained relationships with women colleagues and men supervisors because of gendered racism or racialized stereotypes, the efforts to distance themselves from femininity still may not result in the glass escalator effect.

On the other hand, some theorists suggest that minority men may challenge racism by rejecting hegemonic masculine ideals. Chen (1999) argues that Chinese American men may engage in a strategy of repudiation, where they reject hegemonic masculinity because its implicit assumptions of whiteness exclude Asian American men. As these men realize that racial stereotypes and assumptions preclude them from achieving the hegemonic masculine ideal, they reject it and dispute its racialized underpinnings. Similarly, Lamont (2000, 47) notes that working-class Black men in the United States and France develop a "caring self" in which they emphasize values such as "morality, solidarity, and generosity." As a consequence of these men's ongoing experiences with racism, they develop a caring self that highlights work on behalf of others as an important tool in fighting oppression. Although caring is associated with femininity, these men cultivate a caring self because it allows them to challenge racial inequality. The results of these studies suggest that Black men nurses may embrace the femininity associated with nursing if it offers a way to combat racism. In these cases, Black men nurses may turn to pediatrics as a way of demonstrating sensitivity and therefore combating stereotypes of Black masculinity, or they may proudly identify as nurses to challenge perceptions that Black men are unsuited for professional, white-collar positions.

Taken together, all of this research suggests that Black men may not enjoy the advantages experienced by their white men colleagues, who ride a glass escalator to success. In this article, I focus on the experiences of Black men nurses to argue that the glass escalator is a racialized as well as a gendered concept that does not offer Black men the same privileges as their white men counterparts.

DATA COLLECTION AND METHOD

I collected data through semistructured interviews with 17 men nurses who identified as Black or African American. Nurses ranged in age from 30 to 51 and lived in the southeastern United States. Six worked in suburban hospitals adjacent to major cities, six were located in major metropolitan urban care centers, and the remaining five worked in rural hospitals or clinics. All were registered nurses or licensed practical nurses. Six identified their specialty as oncology, four were bedside nurses, two were in intensive care, one managed an acute dialysis program, one was an orthopedic nurse, one was in ambulatory care, one was in emergency, and one was in surgery. The least experienced nurse had worked in the field for five years; the most experienced had been a nurse for 26 years. I initially recruited participants by soliciting attendees at the 2007 National Black Nurses Association annual meetings and then used a snowball sample to create the remainder of the data set. All names and identifying details have been changed to ensure confidentiality (see Table 16.1).

I conducted interviews during the fall of 2007. They generally took place in either my campus office or a coffee shop located near the respondent's home or workplace. The average interview lasted about an hour. Interviews were tape-recorded and transcribed. Interview questions primarily focused on how race and gender shaped the men's experiences as nurses. Questions addressed respondents' work history and current experiences in the field, how race and gender shaped their experiences as nurses, and their future career goals. The men discussed their reasons for going into nursing, the reactions from others on entering this field, and the particular challenges, difficulties, and obstacles Black men nurses faced. Respondents also described their work history in nursing, their current jobs, and their future plans. Finally, they talked about stereotypes of nurses in general and of Black men nurses in particular and their thoughts about and responses to these stereotypes. I coded the data according to key themes that emerged: relationships with white patients versus minority patients, personal bonds with colleagues versus lack of bonds, opportunities for advancement versus obstacles to advancement.

The researcher's gender and race shape interviews, and the fact that I am an African American woman undoubtedly shaped my rapport and the interactions with interview respondents. Social

■ **TABLE 16.1**
Respondents

Name	Age	Specialization	Years of Experience	Years at Current Job
Chris	51	Oncology	26	16
Clayton	31	Emergency	6	6
Cyril	40	Dialysis	17	7
Dennis	30	Bedside	7	7 (months)
Evan	42	Surgery	25	20
Greg	39	Oncology	10	3
Kenny	47	Orthopedics	23	18 (months)
Leo	50	Bedside	20	18
Ray	36	Oncology	10	5
Ryan	37	Intensive care	17	11
Sean	46	Oncology	9	9
Simon	36	Oncology	5	5
Stuart	44	Bedside	6	4
Terrence	32	Bedside	10	6
Tim	39	Intensive care	20	15 (months)
Tobias	44	Oncology	25	7
Vern	50	Ambulatory care	7	7

desirability bias may compel men to phrase responses that might sound harsh in ways that will not be offensive or problematic to the woman interviewer. However, one of the benefits of the interview method is that it allows respondents to clarify comments diplomatically while still giving honest answers. In this case, some respondents may have carefully framed certain comments about working mostly with women. However, the semistructured interview format nonetheless enabled them to discuss in detail their experiences in nursing and how these experiences are shaped by race and gender. Furthermore, I expect that shared racial status also facilitated a level of comfort, particularly as respondents frequently discussed issues of racial bias and mistreatment that shaped their experiences at work.

FINDINGS

The results of this study indicate that not all men experience the glass escalator in the same ways. For Black men nurses, intersections of race and gender create a different experience with the mechanisms that facilitate white men's advancement in women's professions. Awkward or unfriendly interactions with colleagues, poor relationships with supervisors, perceptions that they are not suited for nursing, and an unwillingness to disassociate from "feminized" aspects of nursing constitute what I term *glass barriers* to riding the glass escalator.

Reception from Colleagues and Supervisors

When women welcome men into "their" professions, they often push men into leadership roles that ease their advancement into upper-level positions. Thus, a positive reaction from colleagues is critical to riding the glass escalator. Unlike white men nurses, however, Black men do not describe encountering a warm reception from women colleagues (Heikes 1991). Instead, the men I interviewed find that they often have unpleasant interactions with women coworkers who treat them rather coldly and attempt to keep them at bay. Chris is a 51-year-old oncology nurse who describes one white nurse's attempt to isolate him from other white women nurses as he attempted to get his instructions for that day's shift:

> She turned and ushered me to the door, and said for me to wait out here, a nurse will come out and give you your report. I stared at her hand on my arm, and then at her, and said, "Why? Where do you go to get your reports?" She said, "I get them in there." I said, "Right. Unhand me." I went right back in there, sat down, and started writing down my reports.

Kenny, a 47-year-old nurse with 23 years of nursing experience, describes a similarly and particularly painful experience he had in a previous job where he was the only Black person on staff:

> [The staff] had nothing to do with me, and they didn't even want me to sit at the same area where they were charting in to take a break. They wanted me to sit somewhere else . . . . They wouldn't even sit at a table with me! When I came and sat down, everybody got up and left.

These experiences with colleagues are starkly different from those described by white men in professions dominated by women (see Pierce 1995; Williams 1989). Though the men in these studies sometimes chose to segregate themselves, women never systematically excluded them. Though I have no way of knowing why the women nurses in Chris's and Kenny's workplaces physically segregated themselves, the pervasiveness of gendered racist images that emphasize white women's vulnerability to dangerous Black men may play an important role. For these nurses, their masculinity is not a guarantee that they will be welcomed, much less pushed into leadership roles. As Ryan, a 37-year-old intensive care nurse says, "[Black men] have to go further to prove ourselves. This involves proving our capabilities, *proving to colleagues that you can lead,* be on the forefront" (emphasis added). The warm welcome and subsequent opportunities for leadership cannot be taken for granted. In contrast, these men describe great challenges in forming congenial

relationships with coworkers who, they believe, do not truly want them there.

In addition, these men often describe tense, if not blatantly discriminatory, relationships with supervisors. While Williams (1995) suggests that men supervisors can be allies for men in women's professions by facilitating promotions and upward mobility, Black men nurses describe incidents of being overlooked by supervisors when it comes time for promotions. Ryan, who has worked at his current job for 11 years, believes that these barriers block upward mobility within the profession:

> The hardest part is dealing with people who don't understand minority nurses. People with their biases, who don't identify you as ripe for promotion. I know the policy and procedure, I'm familiar with past history. So you can't tell me I can't move forward if others did. [How did you deal with this?] By knowing the chain of command, who my supervisors were. Things were subtle. I just had to be better. I got this mostly from other nurses and supervisors. I was paid to deal with patients, so I could deal with [racism] from them. I'm not paid to deal with this from colleagues.

Kenny offers a similar example. Employed as an orthopedic nurse in a predominantly white environment, he describes great difficulty getting promoted, which he primarily attributes to racial biases:

> It's almost like you have to, um, take your ideas and give them to somebody else and then let them present them for you and you get no credit for it. I've applied for several promotions there and, you know, I didn't get them. . . . When you look around to the, um, the percentage of African Americans who are actually in executive leadership is almost zero percent. Because it's less than one percent of the total population of people that are in leadership, and it's almost like they'll go outside of the system just to try to find a Caucasian to fill a position. Not that I'm not qualified, because I've been master's prepared for 12 years and I'm working on my doctorate.

According to Ryan and Kenny, supervisors' racial biases mean limited opportunities for promotion and upward mobility. This interpretation is consistent with research that suggests that even with stellar performance and solid work histories, Black workers may receive mediocre evaluations from white supervisors that limit their advancement (Feagin 2006; Feagin and Sikes 1994). For Black men nurses, their race may signal to supervisors that they are unworthy of promotion and thus create a different experience with the glass escalator.

Strong relationships with colleagues and supervisors are a key mechanism of the glass escalator effect. For Black men nurses, however, these relationships are experienced differently from those described by their white men colleagues. Black men nurses do not speak of warm and congenial relationships with women nurses or see these relationships as facilitating a move into leadership roles. Nor do they suggest that they share gendered bonds with men supervisors that serve to ease their mobility into higher-status administrative jobs. In contrast, they sense that racial bias makes it difficult to develop ties with coworkers and makes superiors unwilling to promote them. Black men nurses thus experience this aspect of the glass escalator differently from their white men colleagues. They find that relationships with colleagues and supervisors stifle, rather than facilitate, their upward mobility.

Perceptions of Suitability

Like their white counterparts, Black men nurses also experience challenges from clients who are unaccustomed to seeing men in fields typically dominated by women. As with white men nurses, Black men encounter this in surprised or quizzical reactions from patients who seem to expect to be treated by white women nurses. Ray, a 36-year-old oncology nurse with 10 years of experience, states,

> Nursing, historically, has been a white female's job [so] being a Black male it's a weird position to be in. . . . I've, several times, gone into a room and a male patient, a white male patient has, you know, they'll say, "Where's the pretty nurse? Where's the pretty nurse? Where's the blonde nurse?." . . . "You don't have one. I'm the nurse."

Yet while patients rarely expect to be treated by men nurses of any race, white men encounter statements and behaviors that suggest patients expect them to be doctors, supervisors, or other higher-status, more masculine positions (Williams 1989, 1995). In part, this expectation accelerates their ride on the glass escalator, helping to push them into the positions for which they are seen as more appropriately suited.

(White) men, by virtue of their masculinity, are assumed to be more competent and capable and thus better situated in (nonfeminized) jobs that are perceived to require greater skill and proficiency. Black men, in contrast, rarely encounter patients (or colleagues and supervisors) who immediately expect that they are doctors or administrators. Instead, many respondents find that even after displaying their credentials, sharing their nursing experience, and, in one case, dispensing care, they are still mistaken for janitors or service workers. Ray's experience is typical:

> I've even given patients their medicines, explained their care to them, and then they'll say to me, "Well, can you send the nurse in?"

Chris describes a somewhat similar encounter of being misidentified by a white woman patient:

> I come [to work] in my white uniform, that's what I wear—being a Black man, I know they won't look at me the same, so I dress the part— I said good evening, my name's Chris, and I'm going to be your nurse. She says to me, "Are you from housekeeping?" . . . I've had other cases. I've walked in and had a lady look at me and ask if I'm the janitor.

Chris recognizes that this patient is evoking racial stereotypes that Blacks are there to perform menial service work. He attempts to circumvent this very perception through careful self-presentation, wearing the white uniform to indicate his position as a nurse. His efforts, however, are nonetheless met with a racial stereotype that as a Black man he should be there to clean up rather than to provide medical care.

Black men in nursing encounter challenges from customers that reinforce the idea that men are not suited for a "feminized" profession such as nursing. However, these assumptions are racialized as well as gendered. Unlike white men nurses who are assumed to be doctors (see Williams 1992), Black men in nursing are quickly taken for janitors or housekeeping staff. These men do not simply describe a gendered process where perceptions and stereotypes about men serve to aid their mobility into higher-status jobs. More specifically, they describe interactions that are simultaneously raced *and* gendered in ways that reproduce stereotypes of Black men as best suited for certain blue-collar, unskilled labor.

These negative stereotypes can affect Black men nurses' efforts to treat patients as well. The men I interviewed find that masculinity does not automatically endow them with an aura of competency. In fact, they often describe interactions with white women patients that suggest that their race minimizes whatever assumptions of capability might accompany being men. They describe several cases in which white women patients completely refused treatment. Ray says,

> With older white women, it's tricky sometimes because they will come right out and tell you they don't want you to treat them, or can they see someone else.

Ray frames this as an issue specifically with older white women, though other nurses in the sample described similar issues with white women of all ages. Cyril, a 40-year-old nurse with 17 years of nursing experience, describes a slightly different twist on this story:

> I had a white lady that I had to give a shot, and she was fine with it and I was fine with it. But her husband, when she told him, he said to me, I don't have any problem with you as a Black man, but I don't want you giving her a shot.

While white men nurses report some apprehension about treating women patients, in all likelihood this experience is compounded for Black men (Williams

1989). Historically, interactions between Black men and white women have been fraught with complexity and tension, as Black men have been represented in the cultural imagination as potential rapists and threats to white women's security and safety—and, implicitly, as a threat to white patriarchal stability (Davis 1981; Giddings 1984). In Cyril's case, it may be particularly significant that the Black man is charged with giving a shot and therefore literally penetrating the white wife's body, a fact that may heighten the husband's desire to shield his wife from this interaction. White men nurses may describe hesitation or awkwardness that accompanies treating women patients, but their experiences are not shaped by a pervasive racial imagery that suggests that they are potential threats to their women patients' safety.

This dynamic, described primarily among white women patients and their families, presents a picture of how Black men's interactions with clients are shaped in specifically raced and gendered ways that suggest they are less rather than more capable. These interactions do not send the message that Black men, because they are men, are too competent for nursing and really belong in higher-status jobs. Instead, these men face patients who mistake them for lower-status service workers and encounter white women patients (and their husbands) who simply refuse treatment or are visibly uncomfortable with the prospect. These interactions do not situate Black men nurses in a prime position for upward mobility. Rather, they suggest that the experience of Black men nurses with this particular mechanism of the glass escalator is the manifestation of the expectation that they should be in lower-status positions more appropriate to their race and gender.

Refusal to Reject Femininity

Finally, Black men nurses have a different experience with establishing distance from women and the feminized aspects of their work. Most research shows that as men nurses employ strategies that distance them from femininity (e.g., by emphasizing nursing as a route to higher-status, more masculine jobs), they place themselves in a position for upward mobility and the glass escalator effect (Williams 1992). For Black men nurses, however, this process looks different. Instead of distancing themselves from the femininity associated with nursing, Black men actually embrace some of the more feminized attributes linked to nursing. In particular, they emphasize how much they value and enjoy the way their jobs allow them to be caring and nurturing. Rather than conceptualizing caring as anathema or feminine (and therefore undesirable), Black men nurses speak openly of caring as something positive and enjoyable.

This is consistent with the context of nursing that defines caring as integral to the profession. As nurses, Black men in this line of work experience professional socialization that emphasizes and values caring, and this is reflected in their statements about their work. Significantly, however, rather than repudiating this feminized component of their jobs, they embrace it. Tobias, a 44-year-old oncology nurse with 25 years of experience, asserts,

> The best part about nursing is helping other people, the flexibility of work hours, and the commitment to vulnerable populations, people who are ill.

Simon, a 36-year-old oncology nurse, also talks about the joy he gets from caring for others. He contrasts his experiences to those of white men nurses he knows who prefer specialties that involve less patient care:

> They were going to work with the insurance industries, they were going to work in the ER where it's a touch and go, you're a number literally. I don't get to know your name, I don't get to know that you have four grandkids, I don't get to know that you really want to get out of the hospital by next week because the following week is your birthday, your 80th birthday and it's so important for you. I don't get to know that your cat's name is Sprinkles, and you're concerned about who's feeding the cat now, and if they remembered to turn the TV on during the day so that the cat can watch *The Price is Right*. They don't get into all that kind of stuff. OK, I actually need to remember the name of your cat so that tomorrow morning when

I come, I can ask you about Sprinkles and that will make a world of difference. I'll see light coming to your eyes and the medicines will actually work because your perspective is different.

Like Tobias, Simon speaks with a marked lack of self-consciousness about the joys of adding a personal touch and connecting that personal care to a patient's improvement. For him, caring is important, necessary, and valued, even though others might consider it a feminine trait.

For many of these nurses, willingness to embrace caring is also shaped by issues of race and racism. In their position as nurses, concern for others is connected to fighting the effects of racial inequality. Specifically, caring motivates them to use their role as nurses to address racial health disparities, especially those that disproportionately affect Black men. Chris describes his efforts to minimize health issues among Black men:

> With Black male patients, I have their history, and if they're 50 or over I ask about the prostate exam and a colonoscopy. Prostate and colorectal death is so high that that's my personal crusade.

Ryan also speaks to the importance of using his position to address racial imbalances:

> I really take advantage of the opportunities to give back to communities, especially to change the disparities in the African American community. I'm more than just a nurse. As a faculty member at a major university, I have to do community hours, services. Doing health fairs, in-services on research, this makes an impact in some disparities in the African American community. [People in the community] may not have the opportunity to do this otherwise.

As Lamont (2000) indicates in her discussion of the "caring self," concern for others helps Chris and Ryan to use their knowledge and position as nurses to combat racial inequalities in health. Though caring is generally considered a "feminine" attribute, in this context it is connected to challenging racial health disparities. Unlike their white men colleagues, these nurses accept and even embrace certain aspects of femininity rather than rejecting them. They thus reveal yet another aspect of the glass escalator process that differs for Black men. As Black men nurses embrace this "feminine" trait and the avenues it provides for challenging racial inequalities, they may become more comfortable in nursing and embrace the opportunities it offers.

CONCLUSIONS

Existing research on the glass escalator cannot explain these men's experiences. As men who do women's work, they should be channeled into positions as charge nurses or nursing administrators and should find themselves virtually pushed into the upper ranks of the nursing profession. But without exception, this is not the experience these Black men nurses describe. Instead of benefiting from the basic mechanisms of the glass escalator, they face tense relationships with colleagues, supervisors' biases in achieving promotion, patient stereotypes that inhibit caregiving, and a sense of comfort with some of the feminized aspects of their jobs. These "glass barriers" suggest that the glass escalator is a racialized concept as well as a gendered one. The main contribution of this study is the finding that race and gender intersect to determine which men will ride the glass escalator. The proposition that men who do women's work encounter undue opportunities and advantages appears to be unequivocally true only if the men in question are white.

This raises interesting questions and a number of new directions for future research. Researchers might consider the extent to which the glass escalator is not only raced and gendered but sexualized as well. Williams (1995) notes that straight men are often treated better by supervisors than are gay men and that straight men frequently do masculinity by strongly asserting their heterosexuality to combat the belief that men who do women's work are gay. The men in this study (with the exception of one nurse I interviewed) rarely discussed sexuality except to say that they were straight and were not bothered by "the gay stereotype." This is consistent with Williams's findings. Gay men, however, may

also find that they do not experience a glass escalator effect that facilitates their upward mobility. Tim, the only man I interviewed who identified as gay, suggests that gender, race, and sexuality come together to shape the experiences of men in nursing. He notes,

> I've been called awful things—you faggot this, you faggot that. I tell people there are three *F*s in life, and if you're not doing one of them it doesn't matter what you think of me. They say, "Three *F*s?" and I say yes. If you aren't feeding me, financing me, or fucking me, then it's none of your business what my faggot ass is up to.

Tim's experience suggests that gay men—and specifically gay Black men—in nursing may encounter particular difficulties establishing close ties with straight men supervisors or may not automatically be viewed by their women colleagues as natural leaders. While race is, in many cases, more obviously visible than sexuality, the glass escalator effect may be a complicated amalgam of racial, gendered, and sexual expectations and stereotypes.

It is also especially interesting to consider how men describe the role of women in facilitating—or denying—access to the glass escalator. Research on white men nurses includes accounts of ways white women welcome them and facilitate their advancement by pushing them toward leadership positions (Floge and Merrill 1986; Heikes 1991; Williams 1992, 1995). In contrast, Black men nurses in this study discuss white women who do not seem eager to work with them, much less aid their upward mobility. These different responses indicate that shared racial status is important in determining who rides the glass escalator. If that is the case, then future research should consider whether Black men nurses who work in predominantly Black settings are more likely to encounter the glass escalator effect. In these settings, Black men nurses' experiences might more closely resemble those of white men nurses.

Future research should also explore other racial minority men's experiences in women's professions to determine whether and how they encounter the processes that facilitate a ride on the glass escalator.

With Black men nurses, specific race or gender stereotypes impede their access to the glass escalator; however, other racial minority men are subjected to different race or gender stereotypes that could create other experiences. For instance, Asian American men may encounter racially specific gender stereotypes of themselves as computer nerds, sexless sidekicks, or model minorities and thus may encounter the processes of the glass escalator differently than do Black or white men (Espiritu 2000). More focus on the diverse experiences of racial minority men is necessary to know for certain.

Finally, it is important to consider how these men's experiences have implications for the ways the glass escalator phenomenon reproduces racial and gendered advantages. Williams (1995) argues that men's desire to differentiate themselves from women and disassociate from the femininity of their work is a key process that facilitates their ride on the glass escalator. She ultimately suggests that if men reconstruct masculinity to include traits such as caring, the distinctions between masculinity and femininity could blur and men "would not have to define masculinity as the negation of femininity" (Williams 1995, 188). This in turn could create a more equitable balance between men and women in women's professions. However, the experiences of Black men in nursing, especially their embrace of caring, suggest that accepting the feminine aspects of work is not enough to dismantle the glass escalator and produce more gender equality in women's professions. The fact that Black men nurses accept and even enjoy caring does not minimize the processes that enable *white* men to ride the glass escalator. This suggests that undoing the glass escalator requires not only blurring the lines between masculinity and femininity but also challenging the processes of racial inequality that marginalize minority men.

AUTHOR'S NOTE

Special thanks to Kirsten Dellinger, Mindy Stombler, Ralph LaRossa, Cindy Whitney, Laura Logan, Dana Britton, and the anonymous reviewers for their insights and helpful feedback. Thanks also to Karyn Lacy, Andra Gillespie, and Isabel Wilkerson for their comments and support. Correspondence concerning this article should be addressed to Adia Harvey Wingfield, Department of Sociology, Georgia State University, P.O. Box 5020, Atlanta, GA 30302-5020; phone: 404-413-6509; e-mail: aharvey@gsu.edu.

NOTE

1. I could not locate any data that indicate the percentage of Black men in nursing. According to 2006 census data, African Americans compose 11 percent of nurses, and men are 8 percent of nurses (http://www.census.gov/compendia/statab/tables/08s0598.pdf). These data do not show the breakdown of nurses by race and sex.

REFERENCES

Acker, Joan. 1990. Hierarchies, jobs, bodies: A theory of gendered organizations. *Gender & Society* 4:139–58.

Britton, Dana. 1995. *At work in the iron cage.* New York: New York University Press.

Budig, Michelle. 2002. Male advantage and the gender composition of jobs: Who rides the glass escalator? *Social Forces* 49 (2): 258–77.

Charles, Maria, and David Grusky. 2004. *Occupational ghettos: The worldwide segregation of women and men.* Palo Alto, CA: Stanford University Press.

Chen, Anthony. 1999. Lives at the center of the periphery, lives at the periphery of the center: Chinese American masculinities and bargaining with hegemony. *Gender & Society* 13:584–607.

Collins, Patricia Hill. 1990. *Black feminist thought.* New York: Routledge.

———. 2004. *Black sexual politics.* New York: Routledge.

Connell, R. W. 1989. *Gender and power.* Sydney, Australia: Allen and Unwin.

Davis, Angela. 1981. *Women, race, and class.* New York: Vintage.

Duffy, Mignon. 2007. Doing the dirty work: Gender, race, and reproductive labor in historical perspective. *Gender & Society* 21:313–36.

Espiritu, Yen Le. 2000. *Asian American women and men: Labor, laws, and love.* Walnut Creek, CA: AltaMira.

Essed, Philomena. 1991. *Understanding everyday racism.* New York: Russell Sage.

Feagin, Joe. 2006. *Systemic racism.* New York: Routledge.

Feagin, Joe, and Melvin Sikes. 1994. *Living with racism.* Boston: Beacon Hill Press.

Floge, Liliane, and Deborah M. Merrill. 1986. Tokenism reconsidered: Male nurses and female physicians in a hospital setting. *Social Forces* 64:925–47.

Giddings, Paula. 1984. *When and where I enter: The impact of Black women on race and sex in America.* New York: HarperCollins.

Harvey Wingfield, Adia. 2007. The modern mammy and the angry Black man: African American professionals' experiences with gendered racism in the workplace. *Race, Gender, and Class* 14 (2): 196–212.

Heikes, E. Joel. 1991. When men are the minority: The case of men in nursing. *Sociological Quarterly* 32:389–401.

hooks, bell. 2004. *We real cool.* New York: Routledge.

Kanter, Rosabeth Moss. 1977. *Men and women of the corporation.* New York: Basic Books.

Kimmel, Michael. 2001. Masculinity as homophobia. In *Men and masculinity*, edited by Theodore F. Cohen. Belmont, CA: Wadsworth.

Lamont, Michelle. 2000. *The dignity of working men.* New York: Russell Sage.

Neal, Mark Anthony. 2005. *New Black man.* New York: Routledge.

Ong, Maria. 2005. Body projects of young women of color in physics: Intersections of race, gender, and science. *Social Problems* 52 (4): 593–617.

Pierce, Jennifer. 1995. *Gender trials: Emotional lives in contemporary law firms.* Berkeley: University of California Press.

Roth, Louise. 2006. *Selling women short: Gender and money on Wall Street.* Princeton, NJ: Princeton University Press.

Shapiro, Thomas. 2004. *Hidden costs of being African American: How wealth perpetuates inequality.* New York: Oxford University Press.

Snyder, Karrie Ann, and Adam Isaiah Green. 2008. Revisiting the glass escalator: The case of gender segregation in a female dominated occupation. *Social Problems* 55 (2): 271–99.

Williams, Christine. 1989. *Gender differences at work: Women and men in non-traditional occupations.* Berkeley: University of California Press.

———. 1992. The glass escalator: Hidden advantages for men in the "female" professions. *Social Problems* 39 (3): 253–67.

———. 1995. *Still a man's world: Men who do women's work.* Berkeley: University of California Press.

Zimmer, Lynn. 1988. Tokenism and women in the workplace: The limits of gender neutral theory. *Social Problems* 35 (1): 64–77.

SEXUAL HARASSMENT AND MASCULINITY: THE POWER AND MEANING OF "GIRL WATCHING"

Beth A. Quinn

Confronted with complaints about sexual harassment or accounts in the media, some men claim that women are too sensitive or that they too often misinterpret men's intentions (Buckwald 1993; Bernstein 1994). In contrast, some women note with frustration that men just "don't get it" and lament the seeming inadequacy of sexual harassment policies (Conley 1991; Guccione 1992). Indeed, this ambiguity in defining acts of sexual harassment might be, as Cleveland and Kerst (1993) suggested, the most robust finding in sexual harassment research.

Using in-depth interviews with 43 employed men and women, this article examines a particular social practice—"girl watching"—as a means to understanding one way that these gender differences are produced. This analysis does not address the size or prevalence of these differences, nor does it present a direct comparison of men and women; this information is essential but well covered in the literature.[1] Instead, I follow Cleveland and Kerst's (1993) and Wood's (1998) suggestion that the question may best be unraveled by exploring how the "subject(ivities) of perpetrators, victims, and resistors of sexual harassment" are "discursively produced, reproduced, and altered" (Wood 1998, 28).

This article focuses on the subjectivities of the perpetrators of a disputable form of sexual harassment,

"girl watching." The term refers to the act of men's sexually evaluating women, often in the company of other men. It may take the form of a verbal or gestural message of "check it out," boasts of sexual prowess, or explicit comments about a woman's body or imagined sexual acts. The target may be an individual woman or group of women or simply a photograph or other representation. The woman may be a stranger, coworker, supervisor, employee, or client. For the present analysis, girl watching within the workplace is [the focus].

The analysis is grounded in the work of masculinity scholars such as Connell (1987, 1995) in that it attempts to explain the subject positions of the interviewed men—not the abstract and genderless subjects of patriarchy but the gendered and privileged subjects embedded in this system. Since I am attempting to delineate the gendered worldviews of the interviewed men, I employ the term "girl watching," a phrase that reflects their language ("they watch girls").

I have chosen to center the analysis on girl watching within the workplace for two reasons. First, it appears to be fairly prevalent. For example, a survey of federal civil employees (U.S. Merit Systems Protection Board 1988) found that in the previous 24 months, 28 percent of the women surveyed had experienced "unwanted sexual looks or gestures," and 35 percent had experienced "unwanted sexual teasing, jokes, remarks, or questions." Second, girl watching is still often normalized and trivialized as only play, or "boys will be boys." A man watching girls—even in his workplace—is frequently accepted as a natural and commonplace activity, especially if he is in the presence of other men.[2] Indeed, it may be required (Hearn 1985). Thus, girl watching sits on the blurry edge between fun and harm, joking and harassment. An understanding of the process of identifying behavior as sexual harassment, or of rejecting this label, may be built on this ambiguity.

Girl watching has various forms and functions, depending on the context and the men involved. For example, it may be used by men as a directed act of power against a particular woman or women. In this, girl watching—at least in the workplace—is most clearly identified as harassing by both men and women. I am most interested, however, in the form where it is characterized as only play. This type is more obliquely motivated and, as I will argue, functions as a game men play to build shared masculine identities and social relations.

Multiple and contradictory subject positions are also evidenced in girl watching, most notably that between the gazing man and the woman he watches. Drawing on Michael Schwalbe's (1992) analysis of empathy and the formation of masculine identities, I argue that girl watching is premised on the obfuscation of this multiplicity through the objectification of the woman watched and a suppression of empathy for her. In conclusion, the ways these elements operate to produce gender differences in interpreting sexual harassment and the implications for developing effective policies are discussed.

PREVIOUS RESEARCH

The question of how behavior is or is not labeled as sexual harassment has been studied primarily through experimental vignettes and surveys.[3] In both methods, participants evaluate either hypothetical scenarios or lists of behaviors, considering whether, for example, the behavior constitutes sexual harassment, which party is most at fault, and what consequences the act might engender. Researchers manipulate factors such as the level of "welcomeness" the target exhibits, and the

relationship of the actors (supervisor–employee, coworker–coworker).

Both methods consistently show that women are willing to define more acts as sexual harassment (Gutek, Morasch, and Cohen 1983; Padgitt and Padgitt 1986; Powell 1986; York 1989; but see Stockdale and Vaux 1993) and are more likely to see situations as coercive (Garcia, Milano, and Quijano 1989). When asked who is more to blame in a particular scenario, men are more likely to blame, and less likely to empathize with, the victim (Jensen and Gutek 1982; Kenig and Ryan 1986). In terms of actual behaviors like girl watching, the U.S. Merit Systems Protection Board (1988) survey found that 81 percent of the women surveyed considered "uninvited sexually suggestive looks or gestures" from a supervisor to be sexual harassment. While the majority of men (68 percent) also defined it as such, significantly more men were willing to dismiss such behavior. Similarly, while 40 percent of the men would not consider the same behavior from a coworker to be harassing, more than three-quarters of the women would.

The most common explanation offered for these differences is gender role socialization. This conclusion is supported by the consistent finding that the more men and women adhere to traditional gender roles, the more likely they are to deny the harm in sexual harassment and to consider the behavior acceptable or at least normal (Pryor 1987; Malovich and Stake 1990; Popovich et al. 1992; Gutek and Koss 1993; Murrell and Dietz-Uhler 1993; Tagri and Hayes 1997). Men who hold predatory ideas about sexuality, who are more likely to believe rape myths, and who are more likely to self-report that they would rape under certain circumstances are less likely to see behaviors as harassing (Pryor 1987; Reilly et al. 1992; Murrell and Dietz-Uhler 1993).

These findings do not, however, adequately address the between-group differences The more one is socialized into traditional notions of sex roles, the more likely it is for both men and women to view the behaviors as acceptable or at least unchangeable. The processes by which gender roles operate to produce these differences remain underexamined.

Some theorists argue that men are more likely to discount the harassing aspects of their behavior because of a culturally conditional tendency to misperceive women's intentions. For example, Stockdale (1993, 96) argued that "patriarchal norms create a sexually aggressive belief system in some people more than others, and this belief system can lead to the propensity to misperceive." Gender differences in interpreting sexual harassment, then, may be the outcome of the acceptance of normative ideas about women's inscrutability and indirectness and men's role as sexual aggressors. Men see harmless flirtation or sexual interest rather than harassment because they misperceive women's intent and responses.

Stockdale's (1993) theory is promising but limited. First, while it may apply to actions such as repeatedly asking for dates and quid pro quo harassment,[4] it does not effectively explain motivations for more indirect actions, such as displaying pornography and girl watching. Second, it does not explain why some men are more likely to operate from these discourses of sexual aggression contributing to a propensity to misperceive.

Theoretical explanations that take into account the complexity and diversity of sexually harassing behaviors and their potentially multifaceted social etiologies are needed. An account of the processes by which these behaviors are produced and the active construction of their social meanings is necessary to unravel both between- and within-gender variations in behavior and interpretation. A fruitful framework from which to begin is an examination of masculine identities and the role of sexually harassing behaviors as a means to their production.

METHOD

I conducted 43 semistructured interviews with currently employed men and women between June 1994 and March 1995. Demographic characteristics of the participants are reported in Table 17.1. The interviews ranged in length from one to three hours. With one exception, interviews were audiotaped and transcribed in full.

Participants were contacted in two primary ways. Twenty-five participants were recruited from "Acme Electronics," a Southern California electronic design and manufacturing company. An additional 18 individuals were recruited from an evening class at a community college and a university summer school class, both in Southern California. These participants referred three more individuals. In addition to the interviews, I conducted participant observation for approximately one month while on site at Acme. This involved observations of the public and common spaces of the company.

At Acme, a human resources administrator drew four independent samples (salaried and hourly women and men) from the company's approximately 300 employees. Letters of invitation were sent to 40 individuals, and from this group, 13 women and 12 men agreed to be interviewed.[5]

The strength of organizationally grounded sampling is that it allows us to provide context for individual accounts. However, in smaller organizations and where participants occupy unique positions, this method can compromise participant anonymity when published versions of the research are accessed by participants. Since this is the case with Acme, and since organizational context is not particularly salient for this analysis, the identity of the participant's organization is sometimes intentionally obscured.

The strength of the second method of recruitment is that it provides access to individuals employed in diverse organizations (from self-employment to multinational corporations) and in a range of occupations (e.g., nanny, house painter, accounting manager). Not surprisingly, drawing from college courses resulted in a group with similar educational backgrounds; all participants from this sample had some college, with 22 percent holding college degrees. Student samples and snowball sampling are not particularly robust in terms of generalizability. They are, nonetheless, regularly employed

■ TABLE 17.1
Participant Demographic Measures

Variable	Men		Women		Total	
	n	%	n	%	n	%
Student participants and referrals	6	33	12	67	18	42
Racial/ethnic minority	2	33	2	17	4	22
Mean age	27.2		35		32.5	
Married	3	50	3	25	6	33
Nontraditional job	1	17	4	33	5	28
Supervisor	0	0	6	50	6	33
Some college	6	100	12	100	18	100
Acme participants	12	48	13	52	25	58
Racial/ethnic minority	2	17	3	23	5	20
Mean age	42.3		34.6		38.6	
Married	9	75	7	54	16	64
Nontraditional job	0	0	4	31	4	16
Supervisor	3	25	2	15	5	20
Some college	9	75	9	69	18	72
All participants	18	42	25	58	43	100
Racial/ethnic minority	4	22	5	20	9	21
Mean age	37.8		34.9		36.2	
Married	12	67	10	40	22	51
Nontraditional job	1	6	8	32	9	21
Supervisor	3	17	8	32	11	26
Some college	15	82	21	84	36	84

in qualitative studies (Connell 1995; Chen 1999) when the goal is theory development—as is the case here—rather than theory testing.

The interviews began with general questions about friendships and work relationships and progressed to specific questions about gender relations, sexual harassment, and the policies that seek to address it.[6] Since the main aim of the project was to explore how workplace events are framed as sexual harassment (and as legally bounded or not), the term "sexual harassment" was not introduced by the interviewer until late in the interview.

While the question of the relationship between masculinity and sexual harassment was central, I did not come to the research looking expressly for girl watching. Rather, it surfaced as a theme across several men's interviews in the context of a gender reversal question:

It's the end of an average day. You get ready for bed and fall to sleep. In what seems only a moment, the alarm goes off. As you awake, you find your body to be oddly out of sorts. . . . To your surprise, you find that you have been transformed into the "opposite sex." Even stranger, no one in your life seems to remember that you were ever any different.

Participants were asked to consider what it would be like to conduct their everyday work life in this transformed state. I was particularly interested in their estimation of the impact it would have on their interactions with coworkers and supervisors. Imagining themselves as the opposite sex, participants were forced to make explicit the operation of gender in their workplace, something they did not do in their initial discussions of a typical workday.

Interestingly, no man discussed girl watching in initial accounts of his workplace. I suspect that they did not consider it to be relevant to a discussion of their average *work* day, even though it became apparent that it was an integral daily activity for some groups of men. It emerged only when men were forced to consider themselves as explicitly gendered workers through the hypothetical question, something they were able initially to elide.[7]

Taking guidance from Glaser and Strauss's (1967) grounded theory and the methodological insights of Dorothy Smith (1990), transcripts were analyzed iteratively and inductively, with the goal of identifying the ideological tropes the speaker used to understand his or her identities, behaviors, and relationships. Theoretical concepts drawn from previous work on the etiology of sexual harassment (Bowman 1993; Cleveland and Kerst 1993), the construction of masculine identities (Connell 1995, 1987), and sociolegal theories of disputing and legal consciousness (Bumiller 1988; Conley and O'Barr 1998) guided the analysis.

Several related themes emerged and are discussed in the subsequent analysis. First, girl watching appears to function as a form of gendered play among men. This play is productive of masculine identities and premised on a studied lack of empathy with the feminine other. Second, men understand the targeted woman to be an object rather than a player in the game, and she is most often not the intended audience. This obfuscation of a woman's subjectivity, and men's refusal to consider the effects of their behavior, means men are likely to be confused when a woman complains. Thus, the production of masculinity through girl watching, and its compulsory disempathy, may be one factor in gender differences in the labeling of harassment.

FINDINGS: GIRL WATCHING AS "HOMMO-SEXUALITY"

[They] had a button on the computer that you pushed if there was a girl who came to the front counter. . . . It was a code and it said "BAFC"— Babe at Front Counter. . . . If the guy in the back looked up and saw a cute girl come in the station, he would hit this button for the other dispatcher to [come] see the cute girl.

—Paula, police officer

In its most serious form, girl watching operates as a targeted tactic of power. The men seem to want everyone—the targeted woman as well as coworkers, clients, and superiors—to know they are looking. The gaze demonstrates their right, as men, to sexually evaluate women. Through the gaze, the targeted woman is reduced to a sexual object, contradicting her other identities, such as that of competent worker or leader. This employment of the discourse of asymmetrical heterosexuality (i.e., the double standard) may trump a woman's formal organizational power, claims to professionalism, and organizational discourses of rationality (Collinson and Collinson 1989; Yount 1991; Gardner 1995).[8] As research on rape has demonstrated (Estrich 1987), calling attention to a woman's gendered sexuality can function to exclude recognition of her competence, rationality, trustworthiness, and even humanity. In contrast, the overt recognition of a man's (hetero)sexuality is normally compatible with other aspects of his identity; indeed, it is often required (Hearn 1985; Connell 1995). Thus, the power of sexuality is asymmetrical, in part, because being seen as sexual has different consequences for women and men.

But when they ogle, gawk, whistle and point, are men always so directly motivated to disempower their women colleagues? Is the target of the gaze also the intended audience? Consider, for example, this account told by Ed, a white, 29-year-old instrument technician.

When a group of guys goes to a bar or a nightclub and they try to be manly. . . . A few of us always found [it] funny [when] a woman would walk by and a guy would be like, "I can have her." [pause] "Yeah, OK, we want to see it!" [laugh]

In his account—a fairly common one in men's discussions—the passing woman is simply a visual cue for their play. It seems clear that it is a game played by men for men; the woman's participation and awareness of her role seem fairly unimportant.

As Thorne (1993) reminded us, we should not be too quick to dismiss games as "only play." In her study of gender relations in elementary schools, Thorne found play to be a powerful form of gendered social action. One of its "clusters of meaning" most relevant here is that of "dramatic performance." In this, play functions as both a source of fun and a mechanism by which gendered identities, group boundaries, and power relations are (re)produced.

The metaphor of play was strong in Karl's comments. Karl, a white man in his early thirties who worked in a technical support role in the Acme engineering department, hoped to earn a degree in engineering. His frustration with his slow progress—which he attributed to the burdens of marriage and fatherhood—was evident throughout the interview. Karl saw himself as an undeserved outsider in his department and he seemed to delight in telling on the engineers.

Girl watching came up as Karl considered the gender reversal question. Like many of the men I interviewed, his first reaction was to muse about premenstrual syndrome and clothes. When I inquired about the potential social effects of the transformation (by asking him, would it "be easier dealing with the engineers or would it be harder?") he haltingly introduced the engineers' "game."

> KARL: Some of the engineers here are very [pause] they're not very, how shall we say? [pause] What's the way I want to put this? They're not very, uh [pause] what's the word? Um. It escapes me.
>
> RESEARCHER: Give me a hint?
>
> KARL: They watch women but they're not very careful about getting caught.

> RESEARCHER: Oh! Like they ogle?
>
> KARL: Ogle or gaze or [pause] stare even, or [pause] generate a commotion of an unusual nature.

His initial discomfort in discussing the issue (with me, I presume) is evident in his excruciatingly formal and hesitant language. The aspect of play, however, came through clearly when I pushed him to describe what generating a commotion looked like: " 'Oh! There goes so-and-so. Come and take a look! She's wearing this great outfit today!' Just like a schoolboy. They'll rush out of their offices and [cranes his neck] and check things out." That this is a form of play was evident in Karl's boisterous tone and in his reference to schoolboys. This is not a case of an aggressive sexual appraising of a woman coworker but a commotion created for the benefit of other men.

At Acme, several spatial factors facilitated this form of girl watching. First, the engineering department is designed as an open-plan office with partitions at shoulder height, offering a maze-like geography that encourages group play. As Karl explained, the partitions offer both the opportunity for sight and cover from being seen. Although its significance escaped me at the time, I was directly introduced to the spatial aspects of the engineers' game of girl watching during my first day on site at Acme. That day, John, the current human resources director, gave me a tour of the facilities, walking me through the departments and offering informal introductions. As we entered the design engineering section, a rhythm of heads emerged from its landscape of partitions, and movement started in our direction. I was definitely aware of being on display as several men gave me obvious once-overs.

Second, Acme's building features a grand stairway that connects the second floor—where the engineering department is located—with the lobby. The stairway is enclosed by glass walls, offering a bird's eye view to the main lobby and the movements of visitors and the receptionists (all women). Robert, a senior design engineer, specifically noted the importance of the glass walls in his discussion of the engineers' girl watching.

There's glass walls around the upstairs right here by the lobby. So when there's an attractive young female . . . someone will see the girl in the area and they will go back and inform all the men in the area. "Go check it out." [laugh] So we'll walk over to the glass window, you know, and we'll see who's down there.

One day near the end of my stay at Acme, I was reminded of his story as I ventured into the first-floor reception area. Looking up, I saw Robert and another man standing at the top of the stairs watching and commenting on the women gathered around the receptionist's desk. When he saw me, Robert gave me a sheepish grin and disappeared from sight.

PRODUCING MASCULINITY

I suggest that girl watching in this form functions simultaneously as a form of play and as a potentially powerful site of gendered social action. Its social significance lies in its power to form identities and relationships based on these common practices for, as Cockburn (1983, 123) has noted, "patriarchy is as much about relations between man and man as it is about relations between men and women." Girl watching works similarly to the sexual joking that Johnson (1988) suggested is a common way for heterosexual men to establish intimacy among themselves.

In particular, girl watching works as a dramatic performance played to other men, a means by which a certain type of masculinity is produced and heterosexual desire displayed. It is a means by which men assert a masculine identity to other men, in an ironic "hommo-sexual" practice of heterosexuality (Butler 1990).[9] As Connell (1995) and others (West and Zimmerman 1987; Butler 1990) have aptly noted, masculinity is not a static identity but rather one that must constantly be reclaimed. The content of any performance—and there are multiple forms—is influenced by a hegemonic notion of masculinity. When asked what "being a man" entailed, many of the men and women I interviewed triangulated toward notions of strength (if not in muscle, then in character and job performance), dominance, and a marked sexuality, overflowing and uncontrollable to some degree and

natural to the male "species." Heterosexuality is required, for just as the label "girl" questions a man's claim to masculine power, so does the label "fag" (Hopkins 1992; Pronger 1992). I asked Karl, for example, if he would consider his sons "good men" if they were gay. His response was laced with ambivalence; he noted only that the question was "a tough one."

The practice of girl watching is just that—a practice—one rehearsed and performed in everyday settings. This aspect of rehearsal was evident in my interview with Mike, a self-employed house painter who used to work construction. In locating himself as a born-again Christian, Mike recounted the girl watching of his fellow construction workers with contempt. Mike was particularly disturbed by a man who brought his young son to the job site one day. The boy was explicitly taught to catcall, a practice that included identifying the proper targets: women and effeminate men.

Girl watching, however, can be somewhat tenuous as a masculine practice. In their acknowledgment (to other men) of their supposed desire lies the possibility that in being too interested in women the players will be seen as mere schoolboys giggling in the playground. Taken too far, the practice undermines rather than supports a masculine performance. In Karl's discussion of girl watching, for example, he continually came back to the problem of men not being careful about getting caught. He referred to a particular group of men who, though "their wives are [pause] very attractive—very much so," still "gawk like schoolboys." Likewise, Stephan explained that men who are obvious, who "undress [women] with their eyes" probably do so "because they don't get enough women in their lives. Supposedly." A man must be interested in women, but not too interested; they must show their (hetero)sexual interest, but not overly so, for this would be to admit that women have power over them.

THE ROLE OF OBJECTIFICATION AND (DIS)EMPATHY

As a performance of heterosexuality among men, the targeted woman is primarily an object onto which men's homosocial sexuality is projected.

The presence of a woman in any form—embodied, pictorial, or as an image conjured from words—is required, but her subjectivity and active participation is not. To be sure, given the ways the discourse of asymmetrical sexuality works, men's actions may result in similarly negative effects on the targeted woman as that of a more direct form of sexualization. The crucial difference is that the men's understanding of their actions differs. This difference is one key to understanding the ambiguity around interpreting harassing behavior.

When asked about the engineers' practice of neck craning, Robert grinned, saying nothing at first. After some initial discussion, I started to ask him if he thought women were aware of their game ("Do you think that the women who are walking by . . . ?"). He interrupted, misreading my question. What resulted was a telling description of the core of the game:

> It depends. No. I don't know if they enjoy it. When I do it, if I do it, I'm not saying that I do. [big laugh] . . . If they do enjoy it, they don't say it. If they don't enjoy it—wait a minute, that didn't come out right. I don't know if they enjoy it or not [pause]; that's not the purpose of us popping our heads out.

Robert did not want to admit that women might not enjoy it ("that didn't come out right") but acknowledged that their feelings were irrelevant. Only subjects, not objects, take pleasure or are annoyed. If a woman did complain, Robert thought "the guys wouldn't know what to say." In her analysis of street harassment, Gardner (1995, 187) found a similar absence, in that "men's interpretations seldom mentioned a woman's reaction, either guessed at or observed."

The centrality of objectification was also apparent in comments made by José, a Hispanic man in his late 40s who worked in manufacturing. For José, the issue came up when he considered the topic of compliments. He initially claimed that women enjoy compliments more than men do. In reconsidering, he remembered girl watching and the importance of intent.

There is [pause] a point where [pause] a woman can be admired by [pause] a pair of eyes, but we're talking about "that look." Where, you know, you're admiring her because she's dressed nice, she's got a nice figure, she's got nice legs. But then you also have the other side. You have an animal who just seems to undress you with his eyes and he's just [pause], there's those kind of people out there too.

What is most interesting about this statement is that in making the distinction between merely admiring and an animal look that ravages, José switched subject position. He spoke in the second person when describing both forms of looking, but his consistency in grammar belies a switch in subjectivity: you (as a man) admire, and you (as a woman) are undressed with his eyes. When considering an appropriate, complimentary gaze, José described it from a man's point of view; the subject who experiences the inappropriate, violating look, however, is a woman. Thus, as in Robert's account, José acknowledged that there are potentially different meanings in the act for men and women. In particular, to be admired in a certain way is potentially demeaning for a woman through its objectification.

The switch in subject position was also evident in Karl's remarks. Karl mentioned girl watching while imagining himself as a woman in the gender reversal question. As he took the subject position of the woman watched rather than the man watching, his understanding of the act as a harmless game was destabilized. Rather than taking pleasure in being the object of such attention, Karl would take pains to avoid it.

So with these guys [if I were a woman], I would probably have to be very concerned about my attire in the lab. Because in a lot of cases, I'm working at a bench and I'm hunched over, in which case your shirt, for example, would open at the neckline, and I would just have to be concerned about that.

Thus, because the engineers girl watch, Karl feels that he would have to regulate his appearance if he were a woman, keeping the men from using him in their game of girl watching. When he considered the act from the point of view of a man, girl watching was simply a harmless antic and an act of appreciation. When he was forced to consider the subject position of a woman, however, girl watching was something to be avoided or at least carefully managed.

When asked to envision himself as a woman in his workplace, like many of the individuals I interviewed, Karl believed that he did not "know how to be a woman." Nonetheless, he produced an account that mirrored the stories of some of the women I interviewed. He knew the experience of girl watching could be quite different—in fact, threatening and potentially disempowering—for the woman who is its object. As such, the game was something to be avoided. In imagining themselves as women, the men remembered the practice of girl watching. None, however, were able to comfortably describe the game of girl watching from the perspective of a woman and maintain its (masculine) meaning as play.

In attempting to take up the subject position of a woman, these men are necessarily drawing on knowledge they already hold. If men simply "don't get it"—truly failing to see the harm in girl watching or other more serious acts of sexual harassment—then they should not be able to see this harm when envisioning themselves as women. What the interviews reveal is that many men—most of whom failed to see the harm of many acts that would constitute the hostile work environment form of sexual harassment—did in fact understand the harm of these acts when forced to consider the position of the targeted woman.

I suggest that the gender reversal scenario produced, in some men at least, a moment of empathy. Empathy, Schwalbe (1992) argued, requires two things. First, one must have some knowledge of the other's situation and feelings. Second, one must be motivated to take the position of the other. What the present research suggests is that gender differences in interpreting sexual harassment stem not so much from men's not getting it (a failure of the first element) but from a studied, often compulsory, lack of motivation to identify with women's experiences.

In his analysis of masculinity and empathy, Schwalbe (1992) argued that the requirements of masculinity necessitate a "narrowing of the moral self." Men learn that to effectively perform masculinity and to protect a masculine identity, they must, in many instances, ignore a woman's pain and obscure her viewpoint. Men fail to exhibit empathy with women because masculinity precludes them from taking the position of the feminine other, and men's moral stance vis-à-vis women is attenuated by this lack of empathy.

As a case study, Schwalbe (1992) considered the Thomas–Hill hearings, concluding that the examining senators maintained a masculinist stance that precluded them from giving serious consideration to Professor Hill's claims. A consequence of this masculine moral narrowing is that "charges of sexual harassment . . . are often seen as exaggerated or as fabricated out of misunderstanding or spite" (Schwalbe 1992, 46). Thus, gender differences in interpreting sexually harassing behaviors may stem more from acts of ignoring than states of ignorance.

THE PROBLEM WITH GETTING CAUGHT

But are women really the untroubled objects that girl watching—viewed through the eyes of men—suggests? Obviously not; the game may be premised on a denial of a woman's subjectivity, but an actual erasure is beyond men's power! It is in this multiplicity of subjectivities, as Butler (1990, ix) noted, where "trouble" lurks, provoked by "the unanticipated agency of a female 'object' who inexplicably returns the glance, reverses the gaze, and contests the place and authority of the masculine position." To face a returned gaze is to get caught, an act that has the power to undermine the logic of girl watching as simply a game among men. Karl, for example, noted that when caught, men are often flustered, a reaction suggesting that the boundaries of usual play have been disturbed.[10]

When a woman looks back, when she asks, "What are you looking at?" she speaks as a subject, and her status as mere object is disturbed. When the game is played as a form of hommosexuality,

the return gaze can be interpreted as engagement or approval

the confronted man may be baffled by her response. When she catches them looking, when she complains, the targeted woman speaks as a subject. The men, however, understand her primarily as an object, and objects do not object.

The radical potential of sexual harassment law is that it centers women's subjectivity, an aspect prompting Catharine MacKinnon's (1979) unusual hope for the law's potential as a remedy. For men engaged in girl watching, however, this subjectivity may be inconceivable. From their viewpoint, acts such as girl watching are simply games played with objects: women's bodies. Similar to Schwalbe's (1992) insight into the senators' reaction to Professor Hill, the harm of sexual harassment may seem more the result of a woman's complaint (and the law's "illegitimate" encroachment into the everyday work world) than men's acts of objectification. For example, in reflecting on the impact of sexual harassment policies in the workplace, José lamented that "back in the '70s, [it was] all peace and love then. Now as things turn around, men can't get away with as much as what they used to." Just whose peace and love are we talking about?

REACTIONS TO ANTI-SEXUAL HARASSMENT TRAINING PROGRAMS

The role that objectification and disempathy play in men's girl watching has important implications for sexual harassment training. Consider the following account of a sexual harassment training session given in Cindy's workplace. Cindy, an Italian American woman in her early 20s, worked as a recruiter for a small telemarketing company in Southern California.

[The trainer] just really laid down the ground rules, um, she had some scenarios. Saying, "OK, would you consider this sexual harassment?" "Would you . . . " this, this, this? "What level?" Da-da-da. So, um, they just gave us some real numbers as to lawsuits and cases. Just that "you guys better be careful" type of a thing.

From Cindy's description, this training is fairly typical in that it focuses on teaching participants definitions of sexual harassment and the legal ramifications of accusations. The trainer used the common strategy of presenting videos of potentially harassing situations and asking the participants how they would judge them. Cindy's description of the men's responses to these videos reveals the limitation of this approach.

We were watching [the TV] and it was [like] a studio audience. And [men] were getting up in the studio audience making comments like "Oh well, look at her! I wouldn't want to do that to her either!" "Well, you're darn straight, look at her!"

Interestingly, the men successfully used the training session videos as an opportunity for girl watching through their public sexual evaluations of the women depicted. In this, the intent of the training session was doubly subverted. The men interpreted scenarios that Cindy found plainly harassing into mere instances of girl watching and sexual (dis) interest. The antiharassment video was ironically transformed into a forum for girl watching, effecting male bonding and the assertion of masculine identities to the exclusion of women coworkers. Also, by judging the complaining women to be inferior as women, the men sent the message that women who complain are those who fail at femininity.

Cindy conceded that relations between men and women in her workplace were considerably strained after the training ("That day, you definitely saw the men bond, you definitely saw the women bond, and there was a definite separation"). The effect of the training session, rather than curtailing the rampant sexual harassment in Cindy's workplace, operated as a site of masculine performance, evoking manly camaraderie and reestablishing gender boundaries.

To be effective, sexual harassment training programs must be grounded in a complex understanding of the ways acts such as girl watching operate in the workplace and the seeming necessity of a culled empathy to some forms of masculinity. Sexually harassing behaviors are produced from more than a lack of knowledge, simple sexist attitudes, or misplaced sexual desire. Some forms of sexually harassing behaviors—such as girl watching—are mechanisms through which gendered boundaries are patrolled and evoked and by which deeply held identities are established. This complexity requires complex interventions and leads to difficult questions about the possible efficacy of any workplace training program mandated in part by legal requirements.

CONCLUSIONS

In this analysis, I have sought to unravel the social logic of girl watching and its relationship to the question of gender differences in the interpretation of sexual harassment. In the form analyzed here, girl watching functions simultaneously as only play and as a potent site where power is played. Through the objectification on which it is premised and in the nonempathetic masculinity it supports, this form of girl watching simultaneously produces both the harassment and the barriers to men's acknowledgment of its potential harm.

The implications these findings have for antisexual harassment training are profound. If we understand harassment to be the result of a simple lack of knowledge (of ignorance), then straightforward informational sexual harassment training may be effective. The present analysis suggests, however, that the etiology of some harassment lies elsewhere. While they might have quarreled with it, most of the men I interviewed had fairly good abstract understandings of the behaviors their companies' sexual harassment policies prohibited. At the same time, in relating stories of social relations in their workplaces, most failed to identify specific behaviors as sexual harassment when they matched the abstract definition. As I have argued, the source of this contradiction lies not so much in ignorance but in acts of ignoring. Traditional sexual harassment training programs address the former rather than the latter. As such, their effectiveness against sexually harassing behaviors born out of social practices of masculinity like girl watching is questionable.

Ultimately, the project of challenging sexual harassment will be frustrated and our understanding distorted unless we interrogate hegemonic, patriarchal forms of masculinity and the practices by which they are (re)produced. We must continue to research the processes by which sexual harassment is produced and the gendered identities and subjectivities on which it poaches (Wood 1998). My study provides a first step toward a more process-oriented understanding of sexual harassment, the ways the social meanings of harassment are constructed, and ultimately, the potential success of antiharassment training programs.

AUTHOR'S NOTE

I would like to thank the members of my faculty writing group—Lisa Aldred, Susan Kollin, and Colleen Mack-Canty—who prove again and again that cross-disciplinary feminist dialogue is not only possible but a powerful reality, even in the wilds of Montana. In addition, thanks to Lisa Jones for her thoughtful reading at a crucial time and to the anonymous reviewers who offered both productive critiques and encouragement.

NOTES

1. See Welsh (1999) for a review of this literature.

2. For example, Maria, an administrative assistant I interviewed, simultaneously echoed and critiqued this understanding when she complained about her boss's girl watching in her presence: "If he wants to do that in front of other men . . . you know, that's what men do."

3. Recently, more researchers have turned to qualitative studies as a means to understand the process of labeling behavior as harassment. Of note are Collinson and Collinson (1996), Giuffre and Williams (1994), Quinn (2000), and Rogers and Henson (1997).

4. Quid pro quo ("this for that") sexual harassment occurs when a person with organizational power attempts to coerce an individual into sexual behavior by threatening adverse job actions.

5. This sample was not fully representative of the company's employees; male managers (mostly white) and

minority manufacturing employees were underrepresented. Thus, the data presented here best represent the attitudes and workplace tactics of white men working in white-collar, technical positions and white and minority men in blue-collar jobs.

6. Acme employees were interviewed at work in an office off the main lobby. Students and referred participants were interviewed at sites convenient to them (e.g., an office, the library).

7. Not all the interviewed men discussed girl watching. When asked directly, they tended to grin knowingly, refusing to elaborate. This silence in the face of direct questioning—by a female researcher—is also perhaps an instance of getting caught.

8. I prefer the term "asymmetrical heterosexuality" over "double standard" because it directly references the dominance of heterosexuality and more accurately reflects the interconnected but different forms of acceptable sexuality for men and women. As Estrich (1987) argued, it is not simply that we hold men and women to different standards of sexuality but that these standards are (re)productive of women's disempowerment.

9. "Hommo" is a play on the French word for man, *homme.*

10. Men are not always concerned with getting caught, as the behavior of catcalling construction workers amply illustrates; that a woman hears is part of the thrill (Gardner 1995). The difference between the workplace and the street is the level of anonymity the men have vis-à-vis the woman and the complexity of social rules and the diversity of power sources an individual has at his or her disposal.

REFERENCES

Bernstein, R. 1994. Guilty if charged. *New York Review of Books,* 13 January.

Bowman, C. G. 1993. Street harassment and the informal ghettoization of women. *Harvard Law Review* 106: 517–580.

Buckwald, A. 1993. Compliment a woman, go to court. *Los Angeles Times,* 28 October.

Bumiller, K. 1988. *The civil rights society: The social construction of victims.* Baltimore: Johns Hopkins University Press.

Butler, J. 1990. *Gender trouble: Feminism and the subversion of identity.* New York: Routledge.

Chen, A. S. 1999. Lives at the center of the periphery, lives at the periphery of the center: Chinese American masculinities and bargaining with hegemony. *Gender & Society* 13: 584–607.

Cleveland, J. N., and M. E. Kerst. 1993. Sexual harassment and perceptions of power: An under-articulated relationship. *Journal of Vocational Behavior* 42 (1): 49–67.

Cockburn, C. 1983. *Brothers: Male dominance and technological change.* London: Pluto Press.

Collinson, D. L., and M. Collinson. 1989. Sexuality in the workplace: The domination of men's sexuality. In *The sexuality of organizations,* edited by J. Hearn and D. L. Sheppard. Newbury Park, CA: Sage.

———. 1996. "It's only Dick": The sexual harassment of women managers in insurance sales. *Work, Employment & Society* 10(1): 29–56.

Conley, F. K. 1991. Why I'm leaving Stanford: I wanted my dignity back. *Los Angeles Times,* 9 June.

Conley, J., and W. O'Barr. 1998. *Just words.* Chicago: University of Chicago Press.

Connell, R. W. 1987. *Gender and power.* Palo Alto, CA: Stanford University Press.

———. 1995. *Masculinities.* Berkeley: University of California Press.

Estrich, S. 1987. *Real rape.* Cambridge, MA: Harvard University Press.

Garcia, L., L. Milano, and A. Quijano. 1989. Perceptions of coercive sexual behavior by males and females. *Sex Roles* 21(9/10): 569–577.

Gardner, C. B. 1995. *Passing by Gender and public harassment.* Berkeley: University of California Press.

Giuffre, P., and C. Williams. 1994. Boundary lines: Labeling sexual harassment in restaurants. *Gender & Society* 8: 378–401.

Glaser, B., and A. L. Strauss. 1967. *The discovery of grounded theory: Strategies for qualitative research.* Chicago: Aldine.

Guccione, J. 1992. Women judges still fighting harassment. *Daily Journal,* 13 October, 1.

Gutek, B. A., and M. P. Koss. 1993. Changed women and changed organizations: Consequences of and coping with sexual harassment. *Journal of Vocational Behavior* 42(1): 28–48.

Gutek, B. A., B. Morasch, and A. G. Cohen. 1983. Interpreting social-sexual behavior in a work setting. *Journal of Vocational Behavior* 22(1): 30–48.

Hearn, J. 1985. Men's sexuality at work. In *The sexuality of men,* edited by A. Metcalf and M. Humphries. London: Pluto Press.

Hopkins, P. 1992. Gender treachery: Homophobia, masculinity, and threatened identities. In *Rethinking masculinity: Philosophical explorations in light of feminism,* edited by L. May and R. Strikwerda. Lanham, MD: Littlefield, Adams.

Jensen, I. W., and B. A. Gutek. 1982. Attributions and assignment of responsibility in sexual harassment. *Journal of Social Issues* 38(4): 121–136.

Johnson, M. 1988. *Strong mothers, weak wives.* Berkeley: University of California Press.

Kenig, S., and J. Ryan. 1986. Sex differences in levels of tolerance and attribution of blame for sexual harassment on a university campus. *Sex Roles* 15 (9/10): 535–549.

MacKinnon, C. A. 1979. *The sexual harassment of working women.* New Haven: Yale University Press.

Malovich, N. J., and J. E. Stake. 1990. Sexual harassment on campus: Individual differences in attitudes and beliefs. *Psychology of Women Quarterly* 14(1): 63–81.

Murrell, A. J, and B. L. Dietz-Uhler. 1993. Gender identity and adversarial sexual beliefs as predictors of attitudes toward sexual harassment. *Psychology of Women Quarterly* 17(2): 169–175.

Padgitt, S. C., and J. S. Padgitt. 1986. Cognitive structure of sexual harassment: Implications for university policy. *Journal of College Students Personnel* 27: 34–39.

Popovich, P. M., D. N. Gehlauf, J. A. Jolton, J. M. Somers, and R. M. Godinho. 1992. Perceptions of sexual harassment as a function of sex of rater and incident form and consequent. *Sex Roles* 27(11/12): 609–625.

Powell, G. N. 1986. Effects of sex-role identity and sex on definitions of sexual harassment. *Sex Roles* 14: 9–19.

Pronger, B. 1992. Gay jocks: A phenomenology of gay men in athletics. In *Rethinking masculinity: Philosophical explorations in light of feminism,* edited by L. May and R. Strikwerda. Lanham, MD: Littlefield Adams.

Pryor, J. B. 1987. Sexual harassment proclivities in men. *Sex Roles* 17(5/6): 269–290.

Quinn, B. A. 2000. The paradox of complaining: Law, humor, and harassment in the everyday work world. *Law and Social Inquiry* 25(4): 1151–1183.

Reilly M. E., B. Lott, D. Caldwell, and L. DeLuca. 1992. Tolerance for sexual harassment related to self-reported sexual victimization. *Gender & Society* 6: 122–138.

Rogers, J. K., and K. D. Henson. 1997. "Hey, why don't you wear a shorter skirt?" Structural vulnerability and the organization of sexual harassment in temporary clerical employment. *Gender & Society* 11: 215–238.

Schwalbe, M. 1992. Male supremacy and the narrowing of the moral self. *Berkeley Journal of Sociology* 37: 29–54.

Smith, D. 1990. *The conceptual practices of power: A feminist sociology of knowledge.* Boston: Northeastern University Press.

Stockdale, M. S. 1993. The role of sexual misperceptions of women's friendliness in an emerging theory of sexual harassment. *Journal of Vocational Behavior* 42 (1): 84–101.

Stockdale, M. S. and A. Vaux. 1993. What sexual harassment experiences lead respondents to acknowledge being sexually harassed? A secondary analysis of a university survey. *Journal of Vocational Behavior* 43(2): 221–234.

Tagri, S., and S. M. Hayes. 1997. Theories of sexual harassment. In *Sexual harassment: Theory, research and treatment,* edited by W. O'Donohue. New York: Allyn and Bacon.

Thorne, B. 1993. *Gender play: Girls and boys in school.* Buckingham, UK: Open University Press.

U.S. Merit Systems Protection Board. 1988. *Sexual harassment in the federal government: An update.* Washington, DC: Government Printing Office.

Welsh, S. 1999. Gender and sexual harassment. *Annual Review of Sociology* 1999: 169–190.

West, C., and D. H. Zimmerman. 1987. Doing gender. *Gender & Society* 1: 125–151.

Wood, J. T. 1998. Saying makes it so: The discursive construction of sexual harassment. In *Conceptualizing sexual harassment as discursive practice,* edited by S. G. Bingham. Westport, CT: Praeger.

York, K. M. 1989. Defining sexual harassment in workplaces: A policy-capturing approach. *Academy of Management Journal* 32: 830–850.

Yount, K. R. 1991. Ladies, flirts, tomboys: Strategies for managing sexual harassment in an underground coal mine. *Journal of Contemporary Ethnography* 19: 396–422.

JUST ONE OF THE GUYS?: HOW TRANSMEN MAKE GENDER VISIBLE AT WORK

Kristen Schilt

Theories of gendered organizations argue that cultural beliefs about gender difference embedded in workplace structures and interactions create and reproduce workplace disparities that disadvantage women and advantage men (Acker 1990; Martin 2003; Williams 1995). As Martin (2003) argues, however, the practices that reproduce gender difference and gender inequality at work are hard to observe. As these gendered practices are citations of established gender norms, men and women in the workplace repeatedly and unreflectively engage in "doing gender" and therefore "doing inequality" (Martin 2003; West and Zimmerman 1987). This repetition of well-worn gender ideologies naturalizes workplace gender inequality, making gendered disparities in achievements appear to be offshoots of "natural" differences between men and women, rather than the products of dynamic gendering and gendered practices (Martin 2003). As the active reproduction of gendered workplace disparities is rendered invisible, gender inequality at work becomes difficult to document empirically and therefore remains resistant to change (Acker 1990; Martin 2003; Williams 1995).

The workplace experiences of female-to-male transsexuals (FTMs), or transmen, offer an opportunity to examine these disparities between men and women at work from a new perspective. Many

FTMs enter the workforce as women and, after transition, begin working as men.[1] As men, they have the same skills, education, and abilities they had as women; however, how this "human capital" is perceived often varies drastically once they become men at work. This shift in gender attribution gives them the potential to develop an "outsider-within" perspective (Collins 1986) on men's advantages in the workplace. FTMs can find themselves benefiting from the "patriarchal dividend" (Connell 1995, 79)—the advantages men in general gain from the subordination of women—after they transition. However, not being "born into it" gives them the potential to be cognizant of being awarded respect, authority, and prestige they did not have working as women. In addition, the experiences of transmen who fall outside of the hegemonic construction of masculinity, such as FTMs of color, short FTMs, and young FTMs, illuminate how the interplay of gender, race, age, and bodily characteristics can constrain access to gendered workplace advantages for some men (Connell 1995).

In this article, I document the workplace experiences of two groups of FTMs, those who openly transition and remain in the same jobs (open FTMs) and those who find new jobs posttransition as "just men" (stealth FTMs).[2] I argue that the positive and negative changes they experience when they become men can illuminate how gender discrimination and gender advantage are created and maintained through workplace interactions. These experiences also illustrate that masculinity is not a fixed character type that automatically commands privilege but rather that the relationships between competing hegemonic and marginalized masculinities give men differing abilities to access gendered workplace advantages (Connell 1995).

THEORIES OF WORKPLACE GENDER DISCRIMINATION

Sociological research on the workplace reveals a complex relationship between the gender of an employee and that employee's opportunities for advancement in both authority and pay. While white-collar men and women with equal qualifications can begin their careers in similar positions in the workplace, men tend to advance faster, creating a gendered promotion gap (Padavic and Reskin 2002; Valian 1999). When women are able to advance, they often find themselves barred from attaining access to the highest echelons of the company by the invisible barrier of the "glass ceiling" (Valian 1999). Even in the so-called women's professions, such as nursing and teaching, men outpace women in advancement to positions of authority (Williams 1995). Similar patterns exist among blue-collar professions, as women often are denied sufficient training for advancement in manual trades, passed over for promotion, or subjected to extreme forms of sexual, racial, and gender harassment that result in women's attrition (Byrd 1999; Miller 1997; Yoder and Aniakudo 1997). These studies are part of the large body of scholarly research on gender and work finding that white- and blue-collar workplaces are characterized by gender segregation, with women concentrated in lower-paying jobs with little room for advancement.

Among the theories proposed to account for these workplace disparities between men and women are human capital theory and gender role socialization. Human capital theory posits that labor markets are neutral environments that reward workers for their skills, experience, and productivity. As women workers are more likely to take time off from work for child rearing and family obligations, they end up with less education and work experience than men. Following this logic, gender segregation in the workplace stems from these discrepancies in skills and experience between men and women, not from gender discrimination. However, while these differences can explain some of the disparities in salaries and rank between women and men, they fail to explain why women and men with comparable prestigious degrees and work experience still end up in different places, with women trailing behind men in advancement (Valian 1999; Williams 1995).

A second theory, gender socialization theory, looks at the process by which individuals come to learn, through the family, peers, schools, and the media, what behavior is appropriate and inappropriate for their gender. From this standpoint, women seek out jobs that reinforce "feminine" traits such as caring and nurturing. This would explain the predominance of women in helping professions such as nursing and teaching. As women are socialized to put family obligations first, women workers would also be expected to be concentrated in part-time jobs that allow more flexibility for family schedules but bring in less money. Men, on the other hand, would be expected to seek higher-paying jobs with more authority to reinforce their sense of masculinity. While gender socialization theory may explain some aspects of gender segregation at work, however, it leaves out important structural aspects of the workplace that support segregation, such as the lack of workplace child care services, as well as employers' own gendered stereotypes about which workers are best suited for which types of jobs (Padavic and Reskin 2002; Valian 1999; Williams 1995).

A third theory, gendered organization theory, argues that what is missing from both human capital theory and gender socialization theory is the way in which men's advantages in the workplace are maintained and reproduced in gender expectations that are embedded in organizations and in interactions between employers, employees, and coworkers (Acker 1990; Martin 2003; Williams 1995). However, it is difficult to study this process of reproduction empirically for several reasons.

First, while men and women with similar education and workplace backgrounds can be compared to demonstrate the disparities in where they end up in their careers, it could be argued that differences in achievement between them can be attributed to personal characteristics of the workers rather than to systematic gender discrimination. Second, gendered expectations about which types of jobs women and men are suited for are strengthened by existing occupational segregation; the fact that there are more women nurses and more men doctors comes to be seen as proof that women are better suited for helping professions and men for rational professions. The normalization of these disparities as natural differences obscures the actual operation of men's advantages and therefore makes it hard to document them empirically. Finally, men's advantages in the workplace are not a function of simply one process but rather a complex interplay between many factors, such as gender differences in workplace performance evaluation, gendered beliefs about men's and women's skills and abilities, and differences between family and child care obligations of men and women workers.

The cultural reproduction of these interactional practices that create and maintain gendered workplace disparities often can be rendered more visible, and therefore more able to be challenged, when examined through the perspective of marginalized others (Collins 1986; Martin 1994, 2003; Yoder and Aniakudo 1997). As Yoder and Aniakudo note, "marginalized others offer a unique perspective on the events occurring within a setting because they perceive activities from the vantages of both nearness (being within) and detachment (being outsiders)" (1997, 325–26). This importance of drawing on the experiences of marginalized others derives from Patricia Hill Collins's theoretical development of the "outsider-within" (1986, 1990). Looking historically at the experience of Black women, Collins (1986) argues that they often have become insiders to white society by virtue of being forced, first by slavery and later by racially bounded labor markets, into domestic work for white families. The

insider status that results from being immersed in the daily lives of white families carries the ability to demystify power relations by making evident how white society relies on racism and sexism, rather than superior ability or intellect, to gain advantage; however, Black women are not able to become total insiders due to being visibly marked as different. Being a marginalized insider creates a unique perspective, what Collins calls "the outsider-within," that allows them to see "the contradictions between the dominant group's actions and ideologies" (Collins 1990, 12), thus giving a new angle on how the processes of oppression operate. Applying this perspective to the workplace, scholars have documented the production and reproduction of gendered and racialized workplace disparities through the "outsider-within" perspective of Black women police officers (Martin 1994) and Black women firefighters (Yoder and Aniakudo 1997).

In this article, I posit that FTMs' change in gender attribution, from women to men, can provide them with an outsider-within perspective on gendered workplace disparities. Unlike the Black women discussed by Collins, FTMs usually are not visibly marked by their outsider status, as continued use of testosterone typically allows for the development of a masculine social identity indistinguishable from "bio men."[3] However, while both stealth and open FTMs can become social insiders at work, their experience working as women prior to transition means they maintain an internalized sense of being outsiders to the gender schemas that advantage men. This internalized insider/outsider position allows some transmen to see clearly the advantages associated with being men at work while still maintaining a critical view to how this advantage operates and is reproduced and how it disadvantages women. I demonstrate that many of the respondents find themselves receiving more authority, respect, and reward when they gain social identities as men, even though their human capital does not change. This shift in treatment suggests that gender inequality in the workplace is not continually reproduced only because women make different education and workplace choices than men but rather because coworkers and employers often rely on gender stereotypes to evaluate men's and women's achievements and skills.

METHOD

I conducted in-depth interviews with 29 FTMs in the Southern California area from 2003 to 2005. My criteria for selection were that respondents were assigned female at birth and were currently living and working as men or open transmen. These selection criteria did exclude female-bodied individuals who identified as men but had not publicly come out as men at work and FTMs who had not held any jobs as men since their transition, as they would not be able to comment about changes in their social interactions that were specific to the workplace. My sample is made up of 18 open FTMs and 11 stealth FTMs.

At the onset of my research, I was unaware of how I would be received as a non-transgender person doing research on transgender workplace experiences, as well as a woman interviewing men. I went into the study being extremely open about my research agenda and my political affiliations with feminist and transgender politics. I carried my openness about my intentions into my interviews, making clear at the beginning that I was happy to answer questions about my research intentions, the ultimate goal of my research, and personal questions about myself. Through this openness, and the acknowledgment that I was there to learn rather than to be an academic "expert," I feel that I gained a rapport with my respondents that bridged the "outsider/insider" divide (Merton 1972).

Generating a random sample of FTMs is not possible as there is not an even dispersal of FTMs throughout Southern California, nor are there transgender-specific neighborhoods from which to sample. I recruited interviewees from transgender activist groups, transgender listservers, and FTM support groups. In addition, I participated for two years in Southern California transgender community events, such as conferences and support group meetings. Attending these community events gave me an opportunity not only to demonstrate long-term political commitment to the transgender community but also to recruit respondents who might not be affiliated with FTM activist groups. All the interviews were conducted in the respondents' offices, in their homes, or at a local café or restaurant. The interviews ranged from one and a half to four hours. All interviews were audio recorded, transcribed, and coded.

Drawing on sociological research that reports long-standing gender differences between men and women in the workplace (Reskin and Hartmann 1986; Reskin and Roos 1990; Valian 1999; Williams 1995), I constructed my interview schedule to focus on possible differences between working as women and working as men. I first gathered a general employment history and then explored the decision to openly transition or to go stealth. At the end of the interviews, I posed the question, "Do you see any differences between working as a woman and working as a man?" All but a few of the respondents immediately answered yes and began to provide examples of both positive and negative differences. About half of the respondents also, at this time, introduced the idea of male privilege, addressing whether they felt they received a gender advantage from transitioning. If the concept of gender advantage was not brought up by respondents, I later introduced the concept of male privilege and then posed the question, saying, "Do you feel that you have received any male privilege at work?" The resulting answers from these two questions are the framework for this article.

In reporting the demographics of my respondents, I have opted to use pseudonyms and general categories of industry to avoid identifying my respondents. Respondents ranged in age from 20 to 48. Rather than attempting to identify when they began their gender transition, a start date often hard to pinpoint as many FTMs feel they have been personally transitioning since childhood or adolescence, I recorded how many years they had been working as men (meaning they were either hired as men or had openly transitioned from female to male and remained in the same job). The average time of working as a man was seven years. Regarding race and ethnicity, the sample was predominantly white (17), with 3 Asians, 1 African American, 3 Latinos, 3 mixed-race individuals, 1 Armenian American, and 1 Italian American. Responses about sexual identity fell into four main categories, heterosexual (9), bisexual (8), queer (6), and gay (3). The remaining 3 respondents identified their sexual identity as celibate/asexual, "dating women," and pansexual. Finally, in terms of region, the sample included a mixture of FTMs living in urban and suburban areas. (See Table 18.1 for sample characteristics.)

The experience of my respondents represents a part of the Southern California FTM community from 2003 to 2005. As Rubin (2003) has demonstrated, however, FTM communities vary greatly from city to city, meaning these findings may not be representative of the experiences of transmen in Austin, San Francisco, or Atlanta. In addition, California passed statewide gender identity protection for employees in 2003, meaning that the men in my study live in an environment in which they cannot legally be fired for being transgender (although most of my respondents said they would not wish to be a test case for this new law). This legal protection means that California transmen might have very different workplace experiences than men in states without gender identity protection. Finally, anecdotal evidence suggests that there are a large number of transgender individuals who transition and then sever all ties with the transgender community, something known as being "deep stealth." This lack of connection to the transgender community means they are excluded from research on transmen but that their experiences with the workplace may be very different than those of men who are still connected, even slightly, to the FTM community.

TRANSMEN AS OUTSIDERS WITHIN AT WORK

In undergoing a physical gender transition, transmen move from being socially gendered as women to being socially gendered as men (Dozier 2005).

This shift in gender attribution gives them the potential to develop an "outsider-within" perspective (Collins 1986) on the sources of men's advantages in the workplace. In other words, while they may find themselves, as men, benefiting from the "patriarchal dividend"(Connell 1995, 79), not being "born into it" can make visible how gendered workplace disparities are created and maintained through interactions. Many of the respondents note that they can see clearly, once they become "just one of the guys," that men succeed in the workplace at higher rates than women because of gender stereotypes that privilege masculinity, not because they have greater skill or ability. For transmen who do see how these cultural beliefs about gender create gendered workplace disparities, there is an accompanying sense that these experiences are visible to them only because of the unique perspective they gain from undergoing a change in gender attribution. Exemplifying this, Preston reports about his views on gender differences at work posttransition: "I swear they let the guys get away with so much stuff! Lazy ass bastards get away with so much stuff and the women who are working hard, they just get ignored . . . . I am really aware of it. And that is one of the reasons that I feel like I have become much more of a feminist since transition. I am just so aware of the difference that my experience has shown me." Carl makes a similar point, discussing his awareness of blatant gender discrimination at a hardware/home construction store where he worked immediately after his transition: "Girls couldn't get their forklift license or it would take them forever. They wouldn't make as much money. It was so pathetic. I would have never seen it if I was a regular guy. I would have just not seen it . . . . I can see things differently because of my perspective. So in some ways I am a lot like a guy because I transitioned younger but still, you can't take away how I was raised for 18 years." These comments illustrate how the outsider-within perspective of many FTMs can translate into a critical perspective on men's advantages at work. The idea that a "regular guy," here meaning a bio man, would not be able to see how women were passed over in favor

■ TABLE 18.1
Sample Characteristics

Pseudonym	Age	Race/Ethnicity	Sexual Identity	Approximate Number of Years Working as Male	Industry	Status at Work
Aaron	28	Black/White	Queer	5	Semi-Professional	Open
Brian	42	White	Bisexual	14	Semi-Professional	Stealth
Carl	34	White	Heterosexual	16	Higher Professional	Stealth
Christopher	25	Asian	Pansexual	3	Semi-Professional	Open
Colin	31	White	Queer	1	Lower Professional	Open
Crispin	42	White	Heterosexual	2	Blue-Collar	Stealth
David	30	White	Bisexual	2	Higher Professional	Open
Douglas	38	White	Gay	5	Semi-Professional	Open
Elliott	20	White	Bisexual	1	Retail/Customer Service	Open
Henry	32	White	Gay	5	Lower Professional	Open
Jack	30	Latino	Queer	1	Semi-Professional	Open
Jake	45	White	Queer	9	Higher Professional	Open
Jason	48	White/Italian	Celibate	20	Retail/Customer Service	Stealth
Keith	42	Black	Heterosexual	1	Blue-Collar	Open
Kelly	24	White	Bisexual	2	Semi-Professional	Open
Ken	26	Asian/White	Queer	6 months	Semi-Professional	Open
Paul	44	White	Heterosexual	2	Semi-Professional	Open
Peter	24	White/Armenian	Heterosexual	4	Lower Professional	Stealth
Preston	39	White	Bisexual	2	Blue-Collar	Open
Riley	37	White	Dates women	1	Lower Professional	Open
Robert	23	Asian	Heterosexual	2	Retail/Customer Service	Stealth
Roger	45	White	Bisexual	22	Lower Professional	Stealth
Sam	33	Latino	Heterosexual	15	Blue-Collar	Stealth
Simon	42	White	Bisexual	2	Semi-Professional	Open
Stephen	35	White	Heterosexual	1	Retail/Customer Service	Stealth
Thomas	42	Latino	Queer	13	Higher Professional	Open
Trevor	35	White	Gay/Queer	6	Semi-Professional	Open
Wayne	44	White/Latino	Bisexual	22	Higher Professional	Stealth
Winston	40	White	Heterosexual	14	Higher Professional	Stealth

of men makes clear that for some FTMs, there is an ability to see how gender stereotypes can advantage men at work.

However, just as being a Black woman does not guarantee the development of a Black feminist perspective (Collins 1986), having this critical perspective on gender discrimination in the workplace is not inherent to the FTM experience. Respondents who had held no jobs prior to transition, who were highly gender ambiguous prior to transition, or who worked in short-term, high-turnover retail jobs, such as food service, found it harder to identify gender differences at work. FTMs who transitioned in their late teens often felt that they did not have enough experience working as women to comment on any possible differences between men and women at work. For example, Sam and Robert felt they could not comment on gender differences in the workplace because they had begun living as men at the age of 15 and, therefore, never had been employed as women. In addition, FTMs who reported being very "in-between" in their gender appearance, such as Wayne and Peter, found it hard to comment on gender differences at work, as even when they were hired as women, they were not always sure how customers and coworkers perceived them. They felt unable to speak about the experience of working as a woman because they were perceived either as androgynous or as men.

The kinds of occupations FTMs held prior to transition also play a role in whether they develop this outsider-within perspective at work. Transmen working in blue-collar jobs—jobs that are predominantly staffed by men—felt their experiences working in these jobs as females varied greatly from their experiences working as men. This held true even for those transmen who worked as females in blue-collar jobs in their early teens, showing that age of transition does not always determine the ability to see gender discrimination at work. FTMs working in the "women's professions" also saw a great shift in their treatment once they began working as men. FTMs who transitioned in their late teens and worked in marginal "teenage" jobs, such as fast food, however, often reported little sense of change

posttransition, as they felt that most employees were doing the same jobs regardless of gender. As a gendered division of labor often does exist in fast food jobs (Leidner 1993), it may be that these respondents worked in atypical settings, or that they were assigned "men's jobs" because of their masculine appearance.

Transmen in higher professional jobs, too, reported less change in their experiences posttransition, as many of them felt that their workplaces guarded against gender-biased treatment as part of an ethic of professionalism. The experience of these professional respondents obviously runs counter to the large body of scholarly research that documents gender inequality in fields such as academia (Valian 1999), law firms (Pierce 1995), and corporations (Martin 1992). Not having an outsider-within perspective, then, may be unique to these particular transmen, not the result of working in a professional occupation.

Thus, transitioning from female to male can provide individuals with an outsider-within perspective on gender discrimination in the workplace. However, this perspective can be limited by the age of transition, appearance, and type of occupation. In addition, as I will discuss at the end of this article, even when the advantages of the patriarchal dividend are seen clearly, many transmen do not benefit from them. In the next section, I will explore in what ways FTMs who expressed having this outsider-within perspective saw their skills and abilities perceived more positively as men. Then, I will explore why not all of my respondents received a gender advantage from transitioning.

TRANSITION AND WORKPLACE GENDER ADVANTAGES[4]

A large body of evidence shows that the performance of workers is evaluated differently depending on gender. Men, particularly white men, are viewed as more competent than women workers (Olian, Schwab, and Haberfeld 1988; Valian 1999). When men succeed, their success is seen as stemming from their abilities while women's success often is attributed to luck (Valian 1999). Men are rewarded more than women for offering ideas and opinions and for taking on leadership roles in group settings (Butler and Geis 1990; Valian 1999). Based on these findings, it would be expected that stealth transmen would see a positive difference in their workplace experience once they have made the transition from female to male, as they enter new jobs as just one of the guys. Open FTMs, on the other hand, might find themselves denied access to these privileges, as they remain in the same jobs in which they were hired as women. Challenging these expectations, two-thirds of my respondents, both open and stealth, reported receiving some type of posttransition advantage at work. These advantages fell into four main categories: gaining competency and authority, gaining respect and recognition for hard work, gaining "body privilege," and gaining economic opportunities and status.

AUTHORITY AND COMPETENCY

Illustrating the authority gap that exists between men and women workers (Elliott and Smith 2004; Padavic and Reskin 2002), several of my interviewees reported receiving more respect for their thoughts and opinions posttransition. For example, Henry, who is stealth in a professional workplace, says of his experiences, "I'm right a lot more now . . . . Even with folks I am out to [as a transsexual], there is a sense that I know what I am talking about." Roger, who openly transitioned in a retail environment in the 1980s, discussed customers' assumptions that as a man, he knew more than his boss, who was a woman: "People would come in and they would go straight to me. They would pass her and go straight to me because obviously, as a male, I knew [sarcasm]. And so we would play mind games with them . . . . They would come up and ask me a question, and then I would go over to her and ask her the same question, she would tell me the answer, and I would go back to the customer and tell the customer the answer." Revealing how entrenched these stereotypes about masculinity and authority are, Roger added that none of the customers ever recognized the sarcasm behind his

actions. Demonstrating how white men's opinions are seen to carry more authority, Trevor discusses how, posttransition, his ideas are now taken more seriously in group situations—often to the detriment of his women coworkers: "In a professional workshop or a conference kind of setting, a woman would make a comment or an observation and be overlooked and be dissed essentially. I would raise my hand and make the same point in a way that I am trying to reinforce her and it would be like [directed at me], 'That's an excellent point!' I saw this shit in undergrad. So it is not like this was a surprise to me. But it was disconcerting to have happen to me." These last two quotes exemplify the outsider-within experience. Both men are aware of having more authority simply because of being men, an authority that happens at the expense of women coworkers.

Looking at the issue of authority in the women's professions, Paul, who openly transitioned in the field of secondary education, reports a sense of having increased authority as one of the few men in his work environment:

> I did notice [at] some of the meetings I'm required to attend, like school district or parent involvement [meetings], you have lots of women there. And now I feel like there are [many times], mysteriously enough, when I'm picked [to speak] . . . . I think, well, why me, when nobody else has to go to the microphone and talk about their stuff? That I did notice and that [had] never happened before. I mean there was this meeting . . . a little while ago about domestic violence where I appeared to be the only male person between these 30, 40 women and, of course, then everybody wants to hear from me.

Rather than being alienated by his gender tokenism, as women often are in predominantly male workplaces (Byrd 1999), he is asked to express his opinions and is valued for being the "male" voice at the meetings, a common situation for men in "women's professions" (Williams 1995). The lack of interest paid to him as a woman in the same job demonstrates how women in predominantly female workspaces can encourage their coworkers who are men to take more authority and space in these careers, a situation that can lead to the promotion of men in women's professions (Williams 1995).

Transmen also report a positive change in the evaluation of their abilities and competencies after transition. Thomas, an attorney, relates an episode in which an attorney who worked for an associated law firm commended his boss for firing Susan, here a pseudonym for his female name, because she was incompetent—adding that the "new guy" [i.e., Thomas] was "just delightful." The attorney did not realize that Susan and "the new guy" were the same person with the same abilities, education, and experience. This anecdote is a glaring example of how men are evaluated as more competent than women even when they do the same job in careers that are stereotyped requiring "masculine" skills such as rationality (Pierce 1995; Valian 1999). Stephen, who is stealth in a predominantly male customer-service job, reports, "For some reason just because [the men I work with] assume I have a dick, [they assume] I am going to get the job done right, where, you know, they have to second guess that when you're a woman. They look at [women] like well, you can't handle this because you know, you don't have the same mentality that we [men] do, so there's this sense of panic . . . and if you are a guy, it's just like, oh, you can handle it." Keith, who openly transitioned in a male-dominated blue-collar job, reports no longer having to "cuddle after sex," meaning that he has been able to drop the emotional labor of niceness women often have to employ when giving orders at work. Showing how perceptions of behavior can change with transition, Trevor reports, "I think my ideas are taken more seriously [as a man]. I had good leadership skills leaving college and um . . . I think that those work well for me now . . . . Because I'm male, they work better for me. I was 'assertive' before. Now I'm 'take charge.'" Again, while his behavior has not changed, his shift in gender attribution translates into a different kind of evaluation. As a man, being assertive is consistent with gendered expectations for men, meaning his same leadership skills have more worth in the workplace because of his transition. His experience underscores how women who take on leadership

roles are evaluated negatively, particularly if their leadership style is perceived as assertive, while men are rewarded for being aggressive leaders (Butler and Geis 1990; Valian 1999).[5]

This change in authority is noticeable only because FTMs often have experienced the reverse: being thought, on the basis of gender alone, to be less competent workers who receive less authority from employers and coworkers. This sense of a shift in authority and perceived competence was particularly marked for FTMs who had worked in blue-collar occupations as women. These transmen report that the stereotype of women's incompetence often translated into difficulty in finding and maintaining employment. For example, Crispin, who had worked as a female construction worker, reports being written up by supervisors for every small infraction, a practice Yoder and Aniakudo (1997, 330) refer to as "pencil whipping." Crispin recounts, "One time I had a field supervisor confront me about simple things, like not dotting i's and using the wrong color ink . . . . Anything he could do, he was just constantly on me . . . . I ended up just leaving." Paul, who was a female truck driver, recounts, "Like they would tell [me], 'Well we never had a female driver. I don't know if this works out.' Blatantly telling you this. And then [I had] to go, 'Well let's see. Let's give it a chance, give it a try. I'll do this three days for free and you see and if it's not working out, well then that's fine and if it works out, maybe you want to reconsider [not hiring me].'" To prove her competency, she ended up working for free, hoping that she would eventually be hired.

Stephen, who was a female forklift operator, described the resistance women operators faced from men when it came to safety precautions for loading pallets:

> [The men] would spot each other, which meant that they would have two guys that would closedown the aisle . . . so that no one could go on that aisle while you know you were up there [with your forklift and load] . . . and they wouldn't spot you if you were a female. If you were a guy . . . they got the red vests and the safety cones out and it's like you

know—the only thing they didn't have were those little flashlights for the jets. It would be like God or somebody responding. I would actually have to go around and gather all the dykes from receiving to come out and help and spot me. And I can't tell you how many times I nearly ran over a kid. It was maddening and it was always because [of] gender.

Thus, respondents described situations of being ignored, passed over, purposefully put in harm's way, and assumed to be incompetent when they were working as women. However, these same individuals, as men, find themselves with more authority and with their ideas, abilities, and attributes evaluated more positively in the workforce.

RESPECT AND RECOGNITION

Related to authority and competency is the issue of how much reward workers get for their workplace contributions. According to the transmen I interviewed, an increase in recognition for hard work was one of the positive changes associated with working as a man. Looking at these stories of gaining reward and respect, Preston, who transitioned openly and remained at his blue-collar job, reports that as a female crew supervisor, she was frequently short staffed and unable to access necessary resources yet expected to still carry out the job competently. However, after his transition, he suddenly found himself receiving all the support and materials he required:

I was not asked to do anything different [after transition]. But the work I did do was made easier for me. [Before transition] there [were] periods of time when I would be told, "Well, I don't have anyone to send over there with you." We were one or two people short of a crew or the trucks weren't available. Or they would send me people who weren't trained. And it got to the point where it was like, why do I have to fight about this? If you don't want your freight, you don't get your freight. And, I swear it was like from one day to the next of me transitioning [to male], I need this, this is what I want and [snaps his fingers]. I have not had to fight about anything.

He adds about his experience, "The last three [performance] reviews that I have had have been the absolute highest that I have ever had. New management team. Me not doing anything different than I ever had. I even went part-time." This comment shows that even though he openly transitioned and remained in the same job, he ultimately finds himself rewarded for doing less work and having to fight less for getting what he needs to effectively do his job. In addition, as a man, he received more positive reviews for his work, demonstrating how men and women can be evaluated differently when doing the same work.

As with authority and competence, this sense of gaining recognition for hard work was particularly noticeable for transmen who had worked as women in blue-collar occupations in which they were the gender minority. This finding is not unexpected, as women are also more likely to be judged negatively when they are in the minority in the workplace, as their statistical minority status seems to suggest that women are unsuited for the job (Valian 1999). For example, Preston, who had spent time in the ROTC as a female cadet, reported feeling that no matter how hard she worked, her achievements were passed over by her men superiors: "On everything that I did, I was the highest. I was the highest-ranking female during the time I was there .... I was the most decorated person in ROTC. I had more ribbons, I had more medals, in ROTC and in school. I didn't get anything for that. There was an award every year called Superior Cadet, and guys got it during the time I was there who didn't do nearly what I did. It was those kinds of things [that got to me]." She entered a blue-collar occupation after ROTC and also felt that her workplace contributions, like designing training programs for the staff, were invisible and went unrewarded.

Talking about gender discrimination he faced as a female construction worker, Crispin reports,

I worked really hard .... I had to find myself not sitting ever and taking breaks or lunches because I felt like I had to work more to show my worth. And though I did do that and I produced typically more than three males put together—and that is really a statistic—what it would come down to a lot of times was, "You're single. You don't have a family." That is what they told me. "I've got guys here who have families." ... And even though my production quality [was high], and the customer was extremely happy with my work ... I was passed over lots of times. They said it was because I was single and I didn't have a family and they felt bad because they didn't want Joe Blow to lose his job because he had three kids at home. And because I was intelligent and my qualities were very vast, they said, "You can just go get a job anywhere." Which wasn't always the case. A lot of people were—it was still a boy's world and some people were just like, uh-uh, there aren't going to be any women on my job site. And it would be months ... before I would find gainful employment again.

While she reports eventually winning over many men who did not want women on the worksite, being female excluded her from workplace social interactions, such as camping trips, designed to strengthen male bonding.

These quotes illustrate the hardships that women working in blue-collar jobs often face at work: being passed over for hiring and promotions in favor of less productive male coworkers, having their hard work go unrecognized, and not being completely accepted.[6] Having this experience of being women in an occupation or industry composed mostly of men can create, then, a heightened appreciation of gaining reward and recognition for job performance as men.

Another form of reward that some transmen report receiving posttransition is a type of bodily respect in the form of being freed from unwanted sexual advances or inquiries about sexuality. As Brian recounts about his experience of working as a waitress, that customer service involved "having my boobs grabbed, being called 'honey' and 'babe.' " He noted that as a man, he no longer has to worry about these types of experiences. Jason reported being constantly harassed by men bosses for sexual favors in the past. He added, "When I transitioned it was like a relief! [laughs] ... I swear to God! I am not saying I was beautiful or sexy but I was always

attracting something." He felt that becoming a man meant more personal space and less sexual harassment. Finally, Stephen and Henry reported being "obvious dykes," here meaning visibly masculine women, and added that in blue-collar jobs, they encountered sexualized comments, as well as invasive personal questions about sexuality, from men uncomfortable with their gender presentation, experiences they no longer face posttransition. Transitioning for stealth FTMs can bring with it physical autonomy and respect, as men workers, in general, encounter less touching, groping, and sexualized comments at work than women. Open FTMs, however, are not as able to access this type of privilege, as coworkers often ask invasive questions about their genitals and sexual practices.

ECONOMIC GAINS

As the last two sections have shown, FTMs can find themselves gaining in authority, respect, and reward in the workplace posttransition. Several FTMs who are stealth also reported a sense that transition had brought with it economic opportunities that would not have been available to them as women, particularly as masculine women.

Carl, who owns his own company, asserts that he could not have followed the same career trajectory if he had not transitioned:

> I have this company that I built, and I have people following me; they trust me, they believe in me, they respect me. There is no way I could have done that as a woman. And I will tell you that as just a fact. That when it comes to business and work, higher levels of management, it is different being a man. I have been on both sides [as a man and a woman], younger obviously, but I will tell you, man, I could have never done what I did [as a female]. You can take the same personality and it wouldn't have happened. I would have never made it.

While he acknowledges that women can be and are business entrepreneurs, he has a sense that his business partners would not have taken his business venture idea seriously if he were a woman or that he might not have had access to the type of social networks that made his business venture possible. Henry feels that he would not have reached the same level in his professional job if he were a woman because he had a nonnormative gender appearance:

> If I was a gender normative woman, probably. But no, as an obvious dyke, I don't think so … which is weird to say but I think it's true. It is interesting because I am really aware of having this job that I would not have had if I hadn't transitioned. And [gender expression] was always an issue for me. I wanted to go to law school but I couldn't do it. I couldn't wear the skirts and things females have to wear to practice law. I wouldn't dress in that drag. And so it was very clear that there was a limit to where I was going to go professionally because I was not willing to dress that part. Now I can dress the part and it's not an issue. It's not putting on drag; it's not an issue. I don't love putting on a tie, but I can do it. So this world is open to me that would not have been before just because of clothes. But very little has changed in some ways. I look very different but I still have all the same skills and all the same general thought processes. That is intense for me to consider.

As this response shows, Henry is aware that as an "obvious dyke," meaning here a masculine-appearing woman, he would have the same skills and education level he currently has, but those skills would be devalued due to his nonnormative appearance. Thus, he avoided professional careers that would require a traditionally feminine appearance. As a man, however, he is able to wear clothes similar to those he wore as an "obvious dyke," but they are now considered gender appropriate. Thus, through transitioning, he gains the right to wear men's clothes, which helps him in accessing a professional job.

Wayne also recounts negative workplace experiences in the years prior to his transition due to being extremely ambiguous or "gender blending" (Devor 1987) in his appearance. Working at a restaurant in his early teens, he had the following experience:

The woman who hired me said, "I will hire you only on the condition that you don't ever come in the front because you make the people uncomfortable." 'Cause we had to wear like these uniforms or something and when I would put the uniform on, she would say, "That makes you look like a guy." But she knew I was not a guy because of my name that she had on the application. She said, "You make the customers uncomfortable." And a couple of times it got really busy, and I would have to come in the front or whatever, and I remember one time she found out about it and she said, "I don't care how busy it gets, you don't get to come up front." She said I'd make people lose their appetite.

Once he began hormones and gained a social identity as a man, he found that his work and school experiences became much more positive. He went on to earn a doctoral degree and become a successful professional, an economic opportunity he did not think would be available had he remained highly gender ambiguous.

In my sample, the transmen who openly transitioned faced a different situation in terms of economic gains. While there is an "urban legend" that FTMs immediately are awarded some kind of "male privilege" posttransition (Dozier 2005), I did not find that in my interviews. Reflecting this common belief, however, Trevor and Jake both recount that women colleagues told them, when learning of their transition plans, that they would probably be promoted because they were becoming white men. While both men discounted these comments, both were promoted relatively soon after their transitions. Rather than seeing this as evidence of male privilege, both respondents felt that their promotions were related to their job performance, which, to make clear, is not a point I am questioning. Yet these promotions show that while these two men are not benefiting undeservedly from transition, they also are not disadvantaged.[7] Thus, among the men I interviewed, it is common for both stealth and open FTMs to find their abilities and skills more valued posttransition, showing that human capital can be valued differently depending on the gender of the employee.

IS IT PRIVILEGE OR SOMETHING ELSE?

While these reported increases in competency and authority make visible the "gender schemas" (Valian 1999) that often underlie the evaluation of workers, it is possible that the increases in authority might have a spurious connection to gender transitions. Some transmen enter a different work field after transition, so the observed change might be in the type of occupation they enter rather than a gender-based change. In addition, many transmen seek graduate or postgraduate degrees posttransition, and higher education degrees afford more authority in the workplace. As Table 18.2 shows, of the transmen I interviewed, many had higher degrees working as men than they did when they worked as women. For some, this is due to transitioning while in college and thus attaining their bachelor's degrees as men. For others, gender transitions seem to be accompanied by a desire to return to school for a higher degree, as evidenced by the increase in master's degrees in the table.

A change in educational attainment does contribute to getting better jobs with increased authority, as men benefit more from increased human capital in the form of educational attainment (Valian 1999). But again, this is an additive effect, as higher education results in greater advantages for men than for women. In addition, gender advantage alone also is apparent in these experiences of

increased authority, as transmen report seeing an increase in others' perceptions of their competency outside of the workplace where their education level is unknown. For example, Henry, who found he was "right a lot more" at work, also notes that in daily, nonworkplace interactions, he is assumed, as a man, to know what he is talking about and does not have to provide evidence to support his opinions. Demonstrating a similar experience, Crispin, who had many years of experience working in construction as a woman, relates the following story:

> I used to jump into [situations as a woman]. Like at Home Depot, I would hear … [men] be so confused, and I would just step over there and say, "Sir, I work in construction and if you don't mind me helping you." And they would be like, "Yeah, yeah, yeah" [i.e., dismissive]. But now I go [as a man] and I've got men and women asking me things and saying, "Thank you so much," like now I have a brain in my head! And I like that a lot because it was just kind of like, "Yeah, whatever." It's really nice.

His experience at Home Depot shows that as a man, he is rewarded for displaying the same knowledge about construction—knowledge gendered as masculine—that he was sanctioned for offering when he was perceived as a woman. As a further example of this increased authority outside of the workplace, several FTMs report a difference in their treatment at the auto shop, as they are not assumed

■ **TABLE 18.2**
Highest Level of Education Attained

Highest Degree Level	Stealth FTMs		Open FTMs	
	As Female	As Male	As Female	As Male
High school/GED	7	2	3	2
Associate's degree	2	3	3	3
Bachelor's degree	2	4	7	4
Master's degree	0	1	2	4
Ph.D.	0	1	1	2
J.D.	0	0	1	2
Other	0	0	1	1
Total	11	11	18	18

Note: FTMs = female-to-male transsexuals.

to be easy targets for unnecessary services (though this comes with an added expectation that they will know a great deal about cars). While some transmen report that their "feminine knowledge," such as how to size baby clothes in stores, is discounted when they gain social identities as men, this new recognition of "masculine knowledge" seems to command more social authority than prior feminine knowledge in many cases. These stories show that some transmen gain authority both in and out of the workplace. These findings lend credence to the argument that men can gain a gender advantage, in the form of authority, reward, and respect.

BARRIERS TO WORKPLACE GENDER ADVANTAGES

Having examined the accounts of transmen who feel that they received increased authority, reward, and recognition from becoming men at work, I will now discuss some of the limitations to accessing workplace gender advantages. About one-third of my sample felt that they did not receive any gender advantage from transition. FTMs who had only recently begun transition or who had transitioned without using hormones ("no ho") all reported seeing little change in their workplace treatment. This group of respondents felt that they were still seen as women by most of their coworkers, evidenced by continual slippage into feminine pronouns, and thus were not treated in accordance with other men in the workplace. Other transmen in this group felt they lacked authority because they were young or looked extremely young after transition. This youthful appearance often is an effect of the beginning stages of transition. FTMs usually begin to pass as men before they start taking testosterone. Successful passing is done via appearance cues, such as hairstyles, clothes, and mannerisms. However, without facial hair or visible stubble, FTMs often are taken to be young boys, a mistake that intensifies with the onset of hormone therapy and the development of peach fuzz that marks the beginning of facial hair growth. Reflecting on how this youthful appearance, which can last several years depending on the effects of hormone therapy, affected his work experience immediately after transition, Thomas reports, "I went from looking 30 to looking 13. People thought I was a new lawyer so I would get treated like I didn't know what was going on." Other FTMs recount being asked if they were interns, or if they were visiting a parent at their workplace, all comments that underscore a lack of authority. This lack of authority associated with looking youthful, however, is a time-bounded effect, as most FTMs on hormones eventually "age into" their male appearance, suggesting that many of these transmen may have the ability to access some gender advantages at some point in their careers.

Body structure was another characteristic some FTMs felt limited their access to increased authority and prestige at work. While testosterone creates an appearance indistinguishable from bio men for many transmen, it does not increase height. Being more than 6 feet tall is part of the cultural construction for successful, hegemonic masculinity. However, several men I interviewed were between 5′1″ and 5′5″, something they felt put them at a disadvantage in relation to other men in their workplaces. Winston, who managed a professional work staff who knew him only as a man, felt that his authority was harder to establish at work because he was short. Being smaller than all of his male employees meant that he was always being looked down on, even when giving orders. Kelly, who worked in special education, felt his height affected the jobs he was assigned: "Some of the boys, especially if they are really aggressive, they do much better with males that are bigger than they are. So I work with the little kids because I am short. I don't get as good of results if I work with [older kids]; a lot of times they are taller than I am." Being a short man, he felt it was harder to establish authority with older boys. These experiences demonstrate the importance of bringing the body back into discussions of masculinity and gender advantage, as being short can constrain men's benefits from the "patriarchal dividend" (Connell 1995).

In addition to height, race/ethnicity can negatively affect FTMs' workplace experience post-transition. My data suggest that the experiences of FTMs of color is markedly different than that of their white counterparts, as they are becoming not just men but Black men, Latino men, or Asian men, categories that carry their own stereotypes. Christopher felt that he was denied any gender advantage at work not only because he was shorter than all of his men colleagues but also because he was viewed as passive, a stereotype of Asian men (Espiritu 1997). "To the wide world of America, I look like a passive Asian guy. That is what they think when they see me. Oh Asian? Oh passive.... People have this impression that Asian guys aren't macho and therefore they aren't really male. Or they are not as male as [a white guy]." Keith articulated how his social interactions changed with his change in gender attribution in this way: "I went from being an obnoxious Black woman to a scary Black man." He felt that he has to be careful expressing anger and frustration at work (and outside of work) because now that he is a Black man, his anger is viewed as more threatening by whites. Reflecting stereotypes that conflate African Americans with criminals, he also notes that in his law enforcement classes, he was continually asked to play the suspect in training exercises. Aaron, one of the only racial minorities at his workplace, also felt that looking like a Black man negatively affected his workplace interactions. He told stories about supervisors repeatedly telling him he was threatening. When he expressed frustration during a staff meeting about a new policy, he was written up for rolling his eyes in an "aggressive" manner. The choice of words such as "threatening" and "aggressive," words often used to describe Black men (Ferguson 2000), suggests that racial identity and stereotypes about Black men were playing a role in his workplace treatment. Examining how race/ethnicity and appearance intersect with gender, then, illustrates that masculinity is not a fixed construct that automatically generated privilege (Connell 1995), but that white, tall men often see greater returns from the patriarchal dividend than short men, young men, and men of color.

CONCLUSION

Sociological studies have documented that the workplace is not a gender-neutral site that equitably rewards workers based on their individual merits (Acker 1990; Martin 2003; Valian 1999; Williams 1995); rather "it is a central site for the creation and reproduction of gender differences and gender inequality" (Williams 1995, 15). Men receive greater workplace advantages than women because of cultural beliefs that associate masculinity with authority, prestige, and instrumentality (Martin 2003; Padavic and Reskin 2002; Rhode 1997; Williams 1995)—characteristics often used to describe ideal "leaders" and "managers" (Valian 1999). Stereotypes about femininity as expressive and emotional, on the other hand, disadvantage women, as they are assumed to be less capable and less likely to succeed than men with equal (or often lesser) qualifications (Valian 1999). These cultural beliefs about gender difference are embedded in workplace structures and interactions, as workers and employers bring gender stereotypes with them to the workplace and, in turn, use these stereotypes to make decisions about hiring, promotions, and rewards (Acker 1990; Martin 2003; Williams 1995). This cultural reproduction of gendered workplace disparities is difficult to disrupt, however, as it operates on the level of ideology and thus is rendered invisible (Martin 2003; Valian 1999; Williams 1995).

In this article, I have suggested that the "outsider-within" (Collins 1986) perspective of many FTMs can offer a more complex understanding of these invisible interactional processes that help maintain gendered workplace disparities. Transmen are in the unique position of having been socially gendered as both women and men (Dozier 2005). Their workplace experiences, then, can make the underpinnings of gender discrimination visible, as well as illuminate the sources of men's workplace advantages. When FTMs undergo a change in gender attribution, their workplace treatment often varies greatly—even when they continue to interact with coworkers who knew them previously as women. Some posttransition FTMs, both stealth and open, find that their coworkers, employers, and customers attribute more authority, respect, and prestige to them. Their experiences make glaringly visible the process through which gender inequality is actively created in informal workplace interactions. These informal workplace interactions, in turn, produce and reproduce structural disadvantages for women, such as the glass ceiling (Valian 1999), and structural advantages for men, such as the glass escalator (Williams 1995).

However, as I have suggested, not all of my respondents gain authority and prestige with transition. FTMs who are white and tall received far more benefits posttransition than short FTMs or FTMs of color. This demonstrates that while hegemonic masculinity is defined against femininity, it is also measured against subordinated forms of masculinity (Connell 1995; Messner 1997). These findings demonstrate the need for using an intersectional approach that takes into consideration the ways in which there are cross-cutting relations of power (Calasanti and Slevin 2001; Collins 1990; Crenshaw 1989), as advantage in the workplace is not equally accessible for all men. Further research on FTMs of color can help develop a clearer understanding of the role race plays in the distribution of gendered workplace rewards and advantages.[8]

The experiences of this small group of transmen offer a challenge to rationalizations of workplace inequality. The study provides counterevidence for human capital theories: FTMs who find themselves receiving the benefits associated with being men at work have the same skills and abilities they had as women workers. These skills and abilities, however, are suddenly viewed more positively due to this change in gender attribution. FTMs who may have been labeled "bossy" as women become "go-getting" men who seem more qualified for managerial positions. While FTMs may not benefit at equal levels to bio men, many of them do find themselves receiving an advantage to women in the workplace they did not have prior to transition. This study also challenges gender socialization theories that account for inequality in the workplace. Although all of my respondents were subjected to gender socialization as girls, this background did not impede their success as men. Instead, by undergoing

a change in gender attribution, transmen can find that the same behavior, attitudes, or abilities they had as females bring them more reward as men. This shift in treatment suggests that gender inequality in the workplace is not continually reproduced only because women make different education and workplace choices than men but rather because co-workers and employers often rely on gender stereotypes to evaluate men and women's achievements and skills.

It could be argued that because FTMs must overcome so many barriers and obstacles to finally gain a male social identity, they might be likely to overreport positive experiences as a way to shore up their right to be a man. However, I have reasons to doubt that my respondents exaggerated the benefits of being men. Transmen who did find themselves receiving a workplace advantage posttransition were aware that this new conceptualization of their skills and abilities was an arbitrary result of a shift in their gender attribution. This knowledge often undermined their sense of themselves as good workers, making them continually second-guess the motivations behind any rewards they receive. In addition, many transmen I interviewed expressed anger and resentment that their increases in authority, respect, and recognition came at the expense of women colleagues. It is important to keep in mind, then, that while many FTMs can identify privileges associated with being men, they often retain a critical eye to how changes in their treatment as men can disadvantage women.

This critical eye, or "outsider-within" (Collins 1986) perspective, has implications for social change in the workplace. For gender equity at work to be achieved, men must take an active role in challenging the subordination of women (Acker 1990; Martin 2003; Rhode 1997; Valian 1999; Williams 1995). However, bio men often cannot see how women are disadvantaged due to their structural privilege (Rhode 1997; Valian 1999). Even when they are aware that men as a group benefit from assumptions about masculinity, men typically still "credit their successes to their competence" (Valian 1999, 284) rather than to gender stereotypes. For many transmen, seeing how they stand to benefit at work to the detriment of women workers creates a sense of increased responsibility to challenge the gender discrimination they can see so clearly. This challenge can take many different forms. For some, it is speaking out when men make derogatory comments about women. For others, it means speaking out about gender discrimination at work or challenging supervisors to promote women who are equally qualified as men. These challenges demonstrate that some transmen are able, at times, to translate their position as social insiders into an educational role, thus working to give women more reward and recognition at these specific work sites. The success of these strategies illustrates that men have the power to challenge workplace gender discrimination and suggests that bio men can learn gender equity strategies from the outsider-within at work.

NOTES

1. Throughout this article, I endeavor to use the terms "women" and "men" rather than "male" and "female" to avoid reifying biological categories. It is important to note, though, that while my respondents were all born with female bodies, many of them never identified as women but rather thought of themselves as always men, or as "not women." During their time as female workers, however, they did have social identities as women, as coworkers and employers often were unaware of their personal gender identities. It is this social identity that I am referencing when I refer to them as "working as women," as I am discussing their social interactions in the workplace. In referring to their specific work experiences, however, I use "female" to demonstrate their understanding of their work history. I also do continue to use "female to male" when describing the physical transition process, as this is the most common term employed in the transgender community.

2. I use "stealth," a transgender community term, if the respondent's previous life as female was not known at work. It is important to note that this term is not analogous with "being in the closet," because stealth female-to-male transsexuals (FTMs) do not have "secret" lives as women outside of working as men. It is used to describe two different workplace choices, not offer a value judgment about these choices.

3. "Bio" man is a term used by my respondents to mean individuals who are biologically male and live

socially as men throughout their lives. It is juxtaposed with "transman" or "FTM."

4. A note on pronoun usage: This article draws from my respondents' experiences working as both women and men. While they now live as men, I use feminine pronouns to refer to their female work histories.

5. This change in how behavior is evaluated can also be negative. Some transmen felt that assertive communication styles they actively fostered to empower themselves as lesbians and feminists had to be unlearned after transition. Because they were suddenly given more space to speak as men, they felt they had to censor themselves or they would be seen as "bossy white men" who talked over women and people of color. These findings are similar to those reported by Dozier (2005).

6. It is important to note that not all FTMs who worked blue-collar jobs as women had this type of experience. One respondent felt that he was able to fit in, as a butch, as "just one of the guys." However, he also did not feel he had an outsider-within perspective because of this experience.

7. Open transitions are not without problems, however. Crispin, a construction worker, found his contract mysteriously not renewed after his announcement. However, he acknowledged that he had many problems with his employers prior to his announcement and had also recently filed a discrimination suit. Aaron, who announced his transition at a small, medical site, left after a few months as he felt that his employer was trying to force him out. He found another job in which he was out as a transman. Crispin unsuccessfully attempted to find work in construction as an out transman. He was later hired, stealth, at a construction job.

8. Sexual identity also is an important aspect of an intersectional analysis. In my study, however, queer and gay transmen worked either in lesbian, gay, bisexual, transgender work sites, or were not out at work. Therefore, it was not possible to examine how being gay or queer affected their workplace experiences.

REFERENCES

Acker, Joan. 1990. Hierarchies, jobs, bodies: A theory of gendered organizations. *Gender & Society* 4: 139–58.

Butler, D., and F. L. Geis. 1990. Nonverbal affect responses to male and female leaders: Implications for leadership evaluation. *Journal of Personality and Social Psychology* 58: 48–59.

Byrd, Barbara. 1999. Women in carpentry apprenticeship: A case study. *Labor Studies Journal* 24 (3): 3–22.

Calasanti, Toni M., and Kathleen F. Slevin. 2001. *Gender, social inequalities, and aging.* Walnut Creek, CA: Alta Mira Press.

Collins, Patricia Hill. 1986. Learning from the outsider within: The sociological significance of Black feminist thought. *Social Problems* 33 (6): S14–S31.

———. 1990. *Black feminist thought.* New York: Routledge.

Connell, Robert. 1995. *Masculinities.* Berkeley: University of California Press.

Crenshaw, Kimberle. 1989. Demarginalizing the intersection of race and sex: A Black feminist critique of antidiscrimination doctrine, feminist theory, and antiracist politics. *University of Chicago Legal Forum* 1989: 139–67.

Devor, Holly. 1987. Gender blending females: Women and sometimes men. *American Behavioral Scientist* 31 (1): 12–40.

Dozier, Raine. 2005. Beards, breasts, and bodies: Doing sex in a gendered world. *Gender & Society* 19: 297–316.

Elliott, James R., and Ryan A. Smith. 2004. Race, gender, and workplace power. *American Sociological Review* 69: 365–86.

Espiritu, Yen. 1997. *Asian American women and men.* Thousand Oaks, CA: Sage.

Ferguson, Ann Arnett. 2000. *Bad boys: Public schools in the making of Black masculinity.* Ann Arbor: University of Michigan Press.

Leidner, Robin. 1993. *Fast food, fast talk: Service work and the routinization of everyday life.* Berkeley: University of California Press.

Martin, Patricia Yancy. 1992. Gender, interaction, and inequality in organizations. In *Gender, interaction, and inequality,* edited by Cecelia L. Ridgeway. New York: Springer-Verlag.

———. 2003 "Said and done" versus "saying and doing": Gendering practices, practicing gender at work. *Gender & Society* 17: 342–66.

Martin, Susan. 1994. "Outsiders-within" the station house: The impact of race and gender on Black women police officers. *Social Problems* 41: 383–400.

Merton, Robert. 1972. Insiders and outsiders: A chapter in the sociology of knowledge. *American Journal of Sociology* 78 (1): 9–47.

Messner, Michael. 1997. *The politics of masculinities: Men in movements.* Thousand Oaks, CA: Sage.

Miller, Laura. 1997. Not just weapons of the weak: Gender harassment as a form of protest for army men. *Social Psychology Quarterly* 60 (1): 32–51.

Olian, J. D., D. P. Schwab, and Y. Haberfeld. 1988. The impact of applicant gender compared to qualifications on hiring recommendations: A meta-analysis of experimental studies. *Organizational Behavior and Human Decision Processes* 41: 180–95.

Padavic, Irene, and Barbara Reskin. 2002. *Women and men at work.* 2nd ed. Thousand Oaks, CA: Pine Forge Press.

Pierce, Jennifer. 1995. *Gender trials: Emotional lives in contemporary law firms.* Berkeley: University of California Press.

Reskin, Barbara, and Heidi Hartmann. 1986. *Women's work, men's work: Sex segregation on the job.* Washington, DC: National Academic Press.

Reskin, Barbara, and Patricia Roos. 1990. *Job queues, gender queues.* Philadelphia: Temple University Press.

Rhode, Deborah L. 1997. *Speaking of sex: The denial of gender inequality.* Cambridge, MA: Harvard University Press.

Rubin, Henry. 2003. *Self-made men: Identity and embodiment among transsexual men.* Nashville, TN: Vanderbilt University Press.

Valian, Virginia. 1999. *Why so slow? The advancement of women.* Cambridge, MA: MIT Press.

West, Candace, and Don Zimmerman. 1987. Doing gender. *Gender & Society* 1: 13–37.

Williams, Christine. 1995. *Still a man's world: Men who do "women's" work.* Berkeley: University of California Press.

Yoder, Janice, and Patricia Aniakudo. 1997. Outsider within the firehouse: Subordination and difference in the social interactions of African American women firefighters. *Gender & Society* 11: 324–41.

PART FIVE

MEN AND HEALTH

The gap between male and female life expectancy was 2 years in 1900. Why is it more than 5 years today? Why do men suffer heart attacks and ulcers at such a consistently higher rate than women do? Why are auto insurance rates so much higher for young males than for females of the same age? Are mentally and emotionally "healthy" males those who conform more closely to the dominant cultural prescriptions for masculinity, or those who resist those dominant ideals?

The articles in this part examine the "embodiment" of masculinity, the ways in which men's mental health and physical health express and reproduce the definitions of masculinity we have ingested in our society. Don Sabo offers a compassionate account of how men will invariably confront traditional stereotypes as they look for more nurturing roles. Gloria Steinem pokes holes in the traditional definitions of masculinity, especially the putative biological basis for gender expression.

Kathleen Slevin and Thomas Linneman examine the specifically gendered experiences of gay men as they age. In a project that complements feminist discussions of women's health, Shari Dworkin reframes the discussion of men's health in terms of global human rights. And Tristan Bridges returns our focus to a close-up examination of the often-contradictory meaning of muscles in building the masculinity of male body builders.

"Gotta be an implant."

Source: Alex Gregory/The New Yorker Collection/www.cartoonbank.com

MASCULINITIES AND MEN'S HEALTH: MOVING TOWARD POST-SUPERMAN ERA PREVENTION

Don Sabo

My grandfather used to smile and say, "Find out where you're going to die and stay the hell away from there." Grandpa had never studied epidemiology (i.e., the study of variations in health and illness in society) but he understood that certain behaviors, attitudes, and cultural practices can put individuals at risk for accidents, illness, or death. This chapter presents an overview of men's health that proceeds from the basic assumption that aspects of traditional masculinity can be dangerous for men's health (Sabo & Gordon, 1995; Harrison, Chin, & Ficarrotto, 1992). First, I identify some gender differences in relation to morbidity (i.e., sickness) and mortality (i.e., death). Next, I examine how the risk for illness varies from one male group to another. I then discuss an array of men's health issues and a preventive strategy for enhancing men's health.

GENDER DIFFERENCES IN HEALTH AND ILLNESS

When British sociologist, Ashley Montagu, put forth the thesis in 1953 that women were biologically superior to men, he shook up the prevailing chauvinistic beliefs that men were stronger, smarter, and better than women. His argument was partly based on epidemiological data that show males are more vulnerable to mortality than females from before birth and throughout the life span.

MORTALITY AND LIFE EXPECTANCY

From the time of conception, men are more likely to succumb to prenatal and neonatal death than females. Men's chances of dying during the prenatal stage of development and also the neonatal (newborn) stage are greater than those of females. A number of neonatal disorders are common to males but not females, such as bacterial infections, respiratory illness, digestive diseases, and some circulatory disorders of the aorta and pulmonary artery. Table 19.1 illustrates the disparities between male and female infant mortality rates (i.e., death during the first year of life) across a 50-year span of the 20th century (Centers for Disease Control and Prevention [CDC], 1992). Men's greater mortality rates persist through the "age 85" subgroup and, as Table 19.2 shows, male death rates are higher than female rates

■ **TABLE 19.1**
Gender and Infant Mortality Rates for the United States, 1940–1989

Year	Both Sexes	Males	Females
1940	47.0	52.5	41.3
1950	29.2	32.8	25.5
1960	26.0	29.3	22.6
1970	20.0	22.4	17.5
1980	12.6	13.9	11.2
1989	9.8	10.8	8.8

Source: Adapted from Centers for Disease Control and Prevention, *Monthly Vital Statistics Report, 40*(8, Suppl. 2), p. 41.
Note: Rates are for infant (under 1 year) deaths per 1,000 live births for all races.

for 12 of the 15 leading causes of death in the United States (National Center for Health Statistics, 2002). Females have greater life expectancy than males in the United States, Canada, and post-industrial societies (Payne, 2006).

These facts suggest a female biological advantage, but a closer analysis of changing trends in the gap between women's and men's life expectancy indicates that social and cultural factors related to lifestyle, gender identity, and behavior are operating as well. Life expectancy among American females in 2004 was about 80.4 but 75.2 for males (National Center for Health Statistics, 2006). While life expectancy for U.S. citizens is now the highest in history, it has shifted a lot during the 20th century. Women's relative advantage in life expectancy over men was rather small at the beginning of the 20th century (Waldron, 1995). During the mid-20th century, female mortality declined more rapidly than male mortality, thereby increasing the gender gap in life expectancy. Whereas women benefited from the decreased maternal mortality, the mid-century trend toward elevating men's life expectancy was slowed by increasing mortality from coronary heart disease and lung cancer that were, in turn, mainly due to higher rates of cigarette smoking among males.

The recent trends show that differences between U.S. women's and men's mortality have decreased. Female life expectancy was 7.9 years greater than males in 1979, 6.9 years in 1989 (National Center for Health Statistics, 1992), and 5.2 years in 2004. Some changes in behavior between the sexes, such as increased smoking among women, have narrowed the gap between men's formerly higher mortality rates from lung cancer, chronic obstructive pulmonary disease, and ischemic heart disease (Waldron, 1995). Figures 19.1 and 19.2 illustrate shifting patterns of life expectancy by race and gender across the past four decades (Kung, Hoyert, Xu, & Murphy, 2008). In summary, both biological and

■ **TABLE 19.2**
Ratio of Male to Female Age-Adjusted Death Rates, for the 15 Leading Causes of Death for the Total U.S. Population in 2002

Rank	Cause of Death	Number of Total Deaths	Percentage	Male to Female Ratio
1	Diseases of heart	710,760	29.6	1.4
2	Malignant neoplasms	553,091	23.0	1.5
3	Cerebrovascular diseases	167,661	7.0	1.0
4	Chronic lower respiratory diseases	122,009	5.1	1.4
5	Accidents (unintentional injuries)	97,900	4.1	2.2
6	Diabetes	69,301	2.9	1.2
7	Influenza and pneumonia	65,313	2.7	1.3
8	Alzheimer's disease	49,558	2.1	0.8
9	Nephritis, nephritic syndrome, nephrosis	37,251	1.5	1.4
10	Septicemia	31,224	1.3	1.2
11	Intentional harm (suicide)	29,350	1.2	4.5
12	Chronic liver disease and cirrhosis	26,552	1.1	2.2
13	Essential hypertension and hypertensive renal disease	18,073	0.8	1.0
14	Assault (homicide)	16,765	0.7	3.3
15	Pneumonitis due to solids and liquids	16,636	0.7	1.8

Source: Adapted from National Center for Health Statistics, *National Vital Statistics Report,* 50(15), September 16, 2002, Table C.

sociocultural processes help to shape patterns of men's and women's mortality.

MORBIDITY

While females generally outlive males, females report higher morbidity (or sickness) rates even after controlling for maternity. U.S. National Health surveys show that females experience acute illnesses, such as respiratory conditions, infective and parasitic conditions, and digestive system disorders, at higher rates than males do, with the exception of injuries (Cypress, 1981; Dawson & Adams, 1987). Men's higher injury rates are partly owed to gender differences in socialization and lifestyle; for example, learning to prove manhood through recklessness, involvement in contact sports, working in risky blue-collar occupations. Women are generally more likely than males to experience chronic conditions such as anemia, chronic enteritis and colitis, migraine headaches, arthritis, diabetes, and thyroid disease. However, males are more prone to develop chronic illnesses such as coronary heart disease, emphysema, and gout. While chronic conditions do not ordinarily cause death, they often limit activity

or cause disability. Finally, a lot of pharmaceutical advertising aims to convince people that they are sick or need to see a doctor when, in fact, they are not clinically ill (Brownlee, 2007). Much of this type of "direct to consumer" advertising has been geared to women, but greater marketing efforts are now geared to men. Men's rate of "morbidity" may be increasing as a result.

Biology + Society + Culture = Complexity

In addition to gender, a highly complex set of global, social, cultural, psychological, racial, and ethnic factors influence variations in men's and women's health (Payne, 2006). Understanding the disparate mortality and morbidity rates between men and women is further complicated by the emphasis on gender differences itself, which, ironically, has been part of traditional patriarchal beliefs *and* much Second Wave feminist thought (Sabo, 2005). Whereas patriarchal culture exaggerated differences between men and women, and masculinity and femininity, Second Wave feminists theorized a "presumed oppositionality" between men and women, and masculinity and femininity (Digby, 1998). Epidemiologically, however, the emphasis

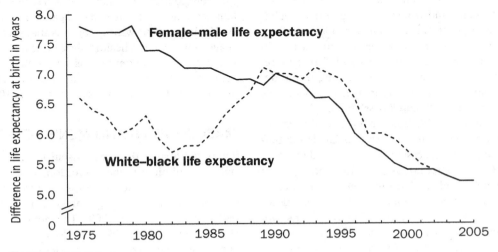

■ FIGURE 19.1

Difference in Life Expectancy between Males and Females, and between Black and White: United States, 1975–2005

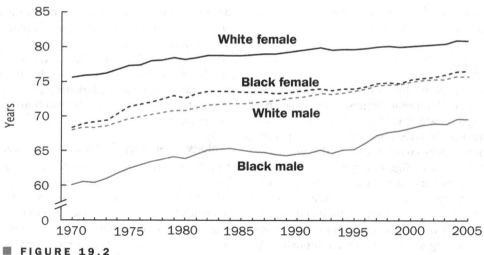

FIGURE 19.2
Life Expectancy by Race and Sex: United States, 1970–2005

on *differences* can sometimes hide *similarities*. For example, MacIntyre, Hunt, and Sweeting (1996) questioned the conventional wisdom that in industrialized countries men die earlier than women, and that women get sick more often than men. They studied health data sets from both Scotland and the United Kingdom and found that, after controlling for age, statistically significant differences between many of men's and women's self-reported psychological and physical symptoms disappeared. They concluded that *both* differences and similarities in men's and women's health exist and, furthermore, that changes in gender relations during recent decades "may produce changes in men's and women's experiences of health and illness" (p. 623).

In summary, although some gender differences in mortality and morbidity are associated with biological or genetic processes, or with reproductive biology (e.g., testicular or prostate cancer), it is increasingly evident that the largest variations in men's and women's health are related to shifting social, economic, cultural, and behavioral factors (Courtenay, McCreary, & Merighi, 2002; Kandrack, Grant, & Segall, 1991). For this reason, Schofield et al. (2000) critiqued the prevailing "men's health discourse," which too often equates "men's health"

to the delivery of biomedical services to men, or to private sector marketing services or products designed to enhance "men's health." They reject lumping "all men" into statistical comparisons between men's and women's health outcomes because, mainly, it is disadvantaged men (e.g., poor men, men of color, uninsured men, gay men) who disproportionately contribute to men's collective higher mortality and morbidity rates in comparison to women. As Keeling (2000) writes, "So it is that there is no single, unitary men's health—instead, sexual orientation, race, socioeconomic status, and culture all intervene to affect the overall health status of each man and of men of various classes or groups" (p. 101).

MASCULINITIES AND MEN'S HEALTH

There is no such thing as masculinity, there are only masculinities (Sabo & Gordon, 1995). A limitation of early gender theory was its treatment of "all men" as a single, large category in relation to "all women" (Connell, 2000). The fact is, however, that all men are not alike, nor do all male groups share the same stakes in the gender order. At any given historical moment, there are competing masculinities—some dominant, some marginalized, and some stigmatized—each with their respective structural, psychosocial, and cultural moorings. There are substantial differences between the health options of homeless men, working-class men, underclass men, gay men, men with AIDS, prison inmates, men of color, and their comparatively advantaged middle- and upper-class, Caucasian, professional male counterparts. Similarly, there exists a wide range of individual differences between the ways that men and women act out "femininity" and "masculinity" in their everyday lives. A health profile of several male groups is discussed below.

Adolescent Males

Pleck, Sonenstein, and Ku (1992) applied critical feminist perspectives to their research on problem behaviors and health among adolescent males. A national sample of adolescent males, never-married males aged 15–19 were interviewed in 1980 and 1988. They tested whether the extent that young men identified with traditionally masculine attitudes increased their risk for an array of problem behaviors. The findings showed a significant, independent association with seven of ten problem behaviors. Specifically, traditionally masculine attitudes were associated with being suspended from school, drinking and use of street drugs, frequency of being picked up by the police, being sexually active, the number of heterosexual partners in the last year, and tricking or forcing someone to have sex. These kinds of behaviors, which are in part expressions of the pursuit of traditional masculinity, elevate boys' risk for sexually transmitted diseases, HIV transmission, and early death by accident or homicide. At the same time, however, these same behaviors can also encourage victimization of women through men's violence, sexual assault, unwanted teenage pregnancy, and sexually transmitted diseases.

Today not as many young men may buy into traditional "macho" identities. But traditional masculinities remain plentiful in media, school subcultures, locker rooms, advertising, gangs, the military, and other institutions. We can only speculate about the links between traditional masculinities and the health risk behaviors of 10–24 year-old males in the United States, for whom four main causes are responsible for 72% of their deaths: homicide, motor-vehicle accidents, suicide, and unintentional injuries (Eaton et al., 2006).

Finally, adolescence is a phase of accelerated physiological development and, contrary to many people's beliefs, more boys than girls are classified as "obese." Obesity puts adults at risk for a variety of diseases such as coronary heart disease, diabetes mellitus, joint disease, and certain cancers. Obese adolescents often become obese adults, thus elevating long-term risk for illness. Obesity among *both* boys and girls has been increasing; for example, the percentage of overweight children aged 12–19 moved from 5% in 1970 to 14% in 1999 (National Health and Nutrition Examination Survey [NHANES], 2003). Between 1988 and 1994, about 11.3% of all boys in this age group were overweight compared with 9.7% of all girls. Adolescents from racial/ethnic minorities were especially likely to be overweight. Among non-Hispanic blacks, 10.7% of boys and 16.3% of girls were overweight, and among Mexican Americans, the corresponding proportions were 14.1% for boys and 13.5% for girls (NHANES, 2003). In 2007, 16.3% of high school males were obese compared with 9.6% of females (Eaton et al., 2006).

Men of Color

Patterns of health and illness among men of color can be partly understood against the historical and social context of economic inequality. Generally, because African Americans, Hispanics, and Native Americans are disproportionately poor, they are more apt to work in low-paying and dangerous occupations, live in polluted environments, be exposed to toxic substances, experience the threat and reality of crime, and worry about meeting basic needs. Cultural barriers can also complicate their access to available health care. Poverty is correlated with lower educational attainment which, in turn, works against adoption of preventive health behaviors.

Compared with Caucasians, African Americans experience twice as much infant mortality, are twice as likely to die from diabetes-related complications, have 80% more strokes, have 20–40% higher rates of cancer, and have 5–7 years less life expectancy (Burrus, Liburd, & Burroughs, 1998; Chin, Zhang, & Merrell, 1998; Straub, 1994; Wingo et al., 1996). The age-adjusted death rate is greater for men in all racial/ ethnic groups: 1.7 times greater among African Americans, 1.8 times greater among Asians, and 1.5 times greater among Latinos/Hispanics (Collins, Hall, & Neuhaus, 1999; Courtenay, McCreary & Merighi, 2002).

The neglect of the public health in the United States is particularly pronounced in relation to African Americans (Polych & Sabo, 2001). Even though African American men have higher rates of alcoholism, infectious diseases, and drug-related conditions, for example, they are less apt to receive health care and, when they do, they are more apt to receive inferior care (Bullard, 1992). The statistics below document the woeful state of African American men's health.

- The leading cause of death among 18–34 year-old African American males is homicide (National Vital Statistics Reports, 2006).
- While 21% of nonelderly Asian men and 16% of non-Hispanic Caucasian men had no health insurance in 2005, 25% of African American men had no coverage (CDC, April 2, 2006).
- When it comes to HIV/AIDS, heart disease, prostate cancer, colon cancer, and lung cancer, African American males have higher death rates than men from other racial groups (Kaiser Family Foundation, 2007).

The health profile of many other men of color is also poor. Compared to the "all race" population, for example, Native American youth exhibit more serious problems in the areas of depression, suicide, anxiety, alcohol and substance use, and general health status (Blum et al., 1992). The health problems facing American and Canadian natives are correlates of poverty and social marginalization such as school drop-out, sense of hopelessness, experience of prejudice, poor nutrition, and lack of regular health care. Hispanic males also show more signs of ill health than their Caucasian counterparts. One explanation is that the growing

numbers of both documented and undocumented Hispanic males in the U.S. work force in recent decades, particularly in blue-collar jobs (e.g., construction, agriculture, warehousing), contributed to high rates of work-related injuries and deaths between 1992–2006 (Mortality and Morbidity Weekly Report [MMWR], 2008). Those who care about men's health, therefore, need to be attuned to the interplay between gender, race/ethnicity, cultural differences, and economic conditions when working with diverse populations.

Gay and Bisexual Men

Gay and bisexual men are estimated to be anywhere from 5 to 10 percent of the male population. In the past, gay men have been viewed as evil, sinful, sick, emotionally immature, and socially undesirable. Many health professionals and the wider public have harbored mixed feelings and homophobic attitudes toward gay and bisexual men. Gay men's identity, their lifestyles, and the social responses to homosexuality can impact the health of gay and bisexual men. Stigmatization and marginalization, for example, may lead to emotional confusion and suicide among gay male adolescents. For gay and bisexual men who are "in the closet," anxiety and stress can tax emotional and physical health. When seeking medical services, gay and bisexual men must often cope with the homophobia of health care workers or deal with the threat of losing health care insurance if their sexual orientation is made known.

Whether they are straight or gay, men tend to have more sexual contacts than women do, which heightens men's risk for STD's. Men's sexual attitudes and behaviors are closely tied to the way masculinity has been socially constructed. For example, "real" men are taught to suppress their emotions, which can lead to a separation of sex from feeling. Traditionally, men are also encouraged to be daring, which can lead to risky sexual decisions. In addition, contrary to common myths about gay male effeminacy, masculinity also plays a powerful role in shaping gay and bisexual men's identity and behavior. To the extent that traditional masculinity informs sexual activity of men, masculinity can be a barrier to safer sexual behavior among men.

Although rates of sexually transmitted disease declined in the 1980s among American men who had sex with men (MSM), data gathered in some cities indicate a resurgent trend toward increased prevalence rates since 1993 (Fox et al., 2001). These latter data may mean that more MSM are engaging in sexual behaviors that elevate risk for contagion, such as unprotected anal and oral sex. Other researchers suggest that some risky sexual behaviors among MSM are related to polysubstance abuse. One American Medical Association council report (1996) estimated the prevalence of substance abuse among gay men and lesbians at 28–35%, compared with a 10–21% rate for heterosexuals. Some studies of gay communities have found higher rates of substance use (e.g., heavy drinking, amphetamines, heroin, and Ecstasy) than among heterosexual males (Crosby, Stall, Paul, & Barrett, 1998; Klitzman, Pope, & Hudson, 2000).

In the United States and Canada, MSM remain a large risk group for HIV transmission (especially among Caucasian men). For gay and bisexual men who are infected by the HIV virus, the personal burden of living with an AIDS diagnosis is made heavier by the stigma associated with homosexuality. The cultural meanings associated with AIDS can also filter into gender and sexual identities. Tewksbury's (1995) interviews with 45 HIV+ gay men showed how masculinity, sexuality, stigmatization, and interpersonal commitment mesh in the decision making around risky sexual behavior. Most of the men practiced celibacy in order to prevent others from contracting the disease, others practiced safe sex, and a few went on having unprotected sex.

Prison Inmates

In 2006, there were 2,258,983 prisoners in federal or state prisons or in local jails (U.S. Department of Justice, 2006). The United States has the highest rate of incarceration of any nation in the world, and racial and ethnic minorities are over-represented among those behind bars. In many states, black and Hispanic males comprise the majority of prisoners

(Mauer, 1999). Among African American males born between 1965 and 1969, for example, 20% spent time in prison in their teens or twenties (Treadwell & Nottingham, 2005).

The prison system acts as a pocket of risk, within which men already at greater risk of a preexisting Acquired Immune Deficiency Syndrome (AIDS) infection, are, because of prison conditions, yet again exposed to heightened risk of contracting Human Immunodeficiency Virus (HIV) or other infections such as tuberculosis (TB) or hepatitis (Polych & Sabo, 2001). The corrections system is part of an institutional chain that facilitates transmission of HIV and other infections in certain North American populations, particularly among poor, inner-city, men of color. Prisoners are burdened not only by social disadvantage but also by high rates of physical illness, mental disorder, and substance use that jeopardize their health.

HIV/AIDS prevalence is markedly higher among state and federal inmates than in the general U.S. population (Maruschak, 2003; McQuillan, Kottiri, & Kruszon-Moran, 2007). Many men already have AIDS at the time of admission (Mumola, 2007). Inside prisons, the HIV virus is primarily transmitted between adults by unprotected penetrative sex, or needle sharing without bleaching, with an infected partner. Sexual contacts between prisoners occur mainly through consensual unions and secondarily through sexual assault and rape (Kupers, 2001). The amount of IV drug use behind prison walls is unknown, although it is known to be prevalent, and that the scarcity of needles often leads to needle and sharps sharing.

The failure to provide comprehensive health education and treatment interventions in prisons is not only putting more inmates at risk for HIV infections, but also the public at large. Prisons are not hermetically sealed enclaves set apart from the community, but an integral part of society. Prisoners regularly move in and out of the prison system, and this means that they often return to their communities after having served their sentences. Indeed, several hundred thousand prisoners are released each year, while hundreds of thousands return to the prison system. The extent to which the drug-related social practices and sexual activities of released and/or paroled inmates who are HIV positive is putting others at risk upon return to their communities is unresearched and unknown (Polych & Sabo, 2001).

Many prison sentences became longer during the past few decades. One consequence is that more prisoners are now age 50 or older. The "graying" of the prison population is placing more demands on the system to attend to both the physical and mental health needs of men behind bars (Day, 2003). Heart disease, cancer, and liver diseases are likely to top the list of ailments for this aging population (Mumola, 2007). Many older men will also be among the more than half of U.S. prison and jail prisoners who are dealing with a mental illness (James & Glaze, 2006).

Male Athletes

Injury is everywhere in sport. It is evident in the lives and bodies of athletes who regularly experience bruises, torn ligaments, broken bones, aches, lacerations, muscle tears, and so forth. There were an estimated 1,442,533 injuries to U.S. high school athletes in nine popular sports during the 2005–06 school year (MMWR, Sept. 29, 2006a). Football players and wrestlers had the highest injury rates. Critics of violent contact sports claim that athletes are paying too high a physical price for their participation. George D. Lundberg (1994), former editor of the *Journal of the American Medical Association,* called for a ban on boxing in the Olympics and in the United States military. His editorial entreaty, while based on clinical evidence for neurological harm from boxing, was also couched in a wider critique of the exploitative economics of the sport.

Injuries are basically unavoidable in sports but, in traditional men's sports, there has been a tendency to glorify pain and injury, to inflict injury on others, and to sacrifice one's body in order to "win at all costs." Some men's sport subcultures such as football, hockey, and rodeo raise risk-taking to the level of male heroism (Frey, Preston, & Bernhard, 2004). The "no pain, no gain" philosophy, which

is rooted in traditional cultural equations between masculinity and sports, can jeopardize the health of athletes who conform to its ethos (Sabo, 2004). It is often difficult for injured athletes to figure out when to push themselves to compete or to back off and heal. For example, Tiger Woods played in pain and won the 2008 U.S. Open only weeks after knee surgery. Right after the event, he admitted that doctors had told him it might not be a good idea to play. When asked why he played in spite of the pain and risks for complication, he explained, "You just keep playing. Like one of my buddies, we always used to joke 'How many reps you got?' And we used to say 'Four? No, it's forever'." (Golf Channel & Yahoo.com videoclip, June 17, 2008). Hopefully, his decision will not contribute to serious future medical complications. But for some young athletes the mind-over-matter and macho-over-medicine credo of "hang tough" leads to permanent damage and a sad end to their dreams.

The connections between sport, masculinity, and health risks are also evident in Klein's (1993) study of how bodybuilders use anabolic steroids, overtrain, and engage in extreme dietary practices. He spent years as an ethnographic researcher in the muscled world of the bodybuilding subculture, where masculinity is equated to maximum muscularity and men's striving for bigness and physical strength hide emotional insecurity and low self-esteem. Klein lays bare a tragic irony in American culture; that is, that the powerful male athlete, a symbol of strength and health, has often sacrificed his health in pursuit of ideal masculinity (Messner & Sabo, 1994).

An early nationwide survey of American male high school seniors found that 6.6% used or had used anabolic steroids. About two-thirds of the steroid users were athletes (Buckley et al., 1988). Since that time extensive use of anabolic steroids has been uncovered in professional baseball and football, Olympic weight lifting, and international cycling. Anabolic steroid use is now also happening among boys (and girls) involved with youth and recreational sports (Bahrke et al., 2000). Anabolic steroid use has been linked to physical health risks such as liver disease, kidney problems, atrophy of the testicles, elevated risk for injury, and premature skeletal maturation. The use of anabolic steroid by young males makes it more likely that they engage in other health risk behaviors such as fighting, driving without a seatbelt, drug and alcohol use, and suicide (Miller et al., 2002).

Finally, high school athletic participation is associated with a variety of health benefits for boys. Male high school athletes are less likely than nonathletes to use marijuana, cocaine, crack cocaine, and inhalants (Miller et al., 2001). Fewer athletes than nonathletes start smoking cigarettes (Melnick et al., 2001). High school athletes also have higher odds of using seatbelts than their nonathletic counterparts (Melnick et al., 2005). A key question for men's health is whether youthful involvement with sport gets translated into greater physical activity in older men's lives. Physical activity helps adult males (and females) reduce their overall risk for heart disease and certain cancers. Regretfully, however, little is known about the extent that youthful involvement with sports contributes to a physically active lifestyle among adults.

Infertile Men

Millions of American couples experience difficulty conceiving a pregnancy. Although factors related to infertility can be found in both sexes, the bulk of extant research focuses on the psychosocial aspects of women's experiences with involuntary childlessness and in vitro fertilization (Daniluk, 1997; Nachtigall, Becker, & Wozny, 1992). In one of the few studies of men's experiences, Webb and Daniluk (1999) interviewed men who had never biologically fathered a child and were the sole cause of the infertility in their marriages. They found that men experienced a "tremendous blow to their masculine identities" (p. 21), profound grief and loss, loss of control, personal inadequacy, isolation, a sense of foreboding, and a desire to overcome and survive. They recommend that both "infertile men and women receive compassionate support when faced with negotiating this challenging life transition" (p. 23).

MEN'S HEALTH ISSUES

Advocates for men's health have identified a variety of issues that impact directly on men's lives. Some of these issues may concern you or men you care about.

Testicular Cancer

Though relatively rare in the general population (1% of all cancers in men), it is the most common cancer among 15–34 year-old males (American Cancer Society, 2005). The incidence of testicular cancer is increasing, doubling during the past 40 years, and accounting for about 8,000 new cases and 390 deaths per year (Ibid.). If detected early, the cure rate is high, while delayed diagnosis can be life-threatening. Regular testicular self-examination (TSE), therefore, is a potentially effective preventive means for insuring early detection and successful treatment. Regretfully, however, most physicians do not teach TSE techniques.

Although testicular cancer rates are increasing in many countries, mortality rates have declined in the European Union, Eastern Europe, Japan, the United States, and Canada (Levi, LaVecchia, Boyle, Lucchini, & Negri, 2001). Declining mortality is likely due to advances in medical diagnosis and treatment, early detection, TSE, and greater educational awareness among males. Finally, survivors of testicular cancer generally go on to have physically and emotionally healthy lives (Rudberg, Nilsson, & Wikblad, 2000).

Denial may influence men's perceptions of testicular cancer and TSE (Blesch, 1986). Studies show that most males are not aware of testicular cancer and, even among those who are aware, many are reluctant to examine their testicles as a preventive measure. Even when symptoms are recognized, men sometimes postpone seeking treatment. Moreover, men who are taught TSE are often initially receptive, but the practice of TSE decreases over time. Men's resistance to TSE has been linked to awkwardness about touching themselves, associating touching genitals with homosexuality or masturbation, or the idea that TSE is not a manly behavior. And finally, men's individual reluctance to discuss testicular cancer partly derives from the widespread cultural silences that envelope it. The penis is a cultural symbol of male power, authority, and sexual domination. Its symbolic efficacy in traditional, male-dominated gender relations, therefore, would be eroded or neutralized by the realities of testicular cancer.

Diseases of the Prostate

Middle-aged and elderly men are likely to develop medical problems with the prostate gland. The older men get, the more likely it is that they will develop prostate cancer. Some men may experience benign prostatic hyperplasia, an enlargement of the prostate gland that is associated with symptoms such as dribbling after urination, frequent urination, or incontinence. Others may develop infections (prostatitis) or malignant prostatic hyperplasia (prostate cancer). Prostate cancer is diagnosed more frequently in Canada and the United States than any other cancer (McDavid, Lee, Fulton, Tonita, & Thompson, 2004). One in six men develop this cancer during their lifetime, with African American males showing a higher prevalence rate than their Caucasian counterparts (American Cancer Society, 2007; Jones et al., 2007). While the incidence of prostate cancer has been increasing in recent decades, earlier diagnosis and treatment have reduced mortality.

Treatments for prostate problems depend on the specific diagnosis and may range from medication to radiation and surgery. As is the case with testicular cancer, survival from prostate cancer is enhanced by early detection. Raising men's awareness about the health risks associated with the prostate gland, therefore, may prevent unnecessary morbidity and mortality. Finally, more invasive surgical treatments for prostate cancer can produce incontinence and impotence, so men should diligently explore their medical options. Men are also beginning to talk about their physical, emotional, and sexual experiences following treatment for prostate cancer (Gray, 2005).

Alcohol Use

While social and medical problems stemming from alcohol abuse involve both sexes, males comprise the largest segment of alcohol abusers. Some researchers have begun exploring the connections between traditional masculinity and alcohol abuse. Mass media often sensationalize links between booze and male bravado. For decades, male stereotypes have been used in beer commercials to promote beer drinking as a reward for a job well done or to glorify daring, male friendship, or romantic success with women (Postman, Nystrom, Strate, & Weingartner, 1987). The combination of beer and liquor ads with sports imagery is a common advertising ploy to entice males to consume alcohol products (Messner & Montez de Oca, 2005).

Alcohol use is now highly prevalent among U.S. teenagers. More than half (55%) of youth in 2007 reported they had gotten drunk "at least once" in their lives by 12th grade, compared to about 1 in 5 (18%) of 8th graders (Johnston, O'Malley, Bachman, & Schulenberg, 2008). While boys typically have showed higher rates of heavy drinking in the past, 8th and 10th grade girls now match boys' rates (Ibid).

Findings from a 1999 Harvard School of Public Health nationwide survey of U.S. college students found that 44% engaged in "binge drinking," defined as drinking five drinks in rapid succession for males and four drinks for females (Wechsler, 2005). Males were more apt to report binge drinking during the past two weeks than females; 51% and 40% respectively. Males who were frequent binge drinkers were more likely than non-binge-drinking males to report driving after drinking, missing class, engaging in unplanned sexual behavior, falling behind in school work, being hurt or injured and having trouble with campus police.

Between 1999 and 2005, about twice as many men as women died from alcohol-induced causes (National Vital Statistics Reports, 2006). Alcohol-related automobile accidents are the top cause of death among 16–24 year-olds. The number of automobile fatalities among male adolescents that result from a mixture of alcohol abuse and masculine daring is unknown. Alcohol use is frequently involved with the four leading causes of death among youth and young adults—motor vehicle accidents, unintentional injuries, homicide, and suicide (Eaton et al., 2006). However, readers can assess the links between alcohol use and men's greater risks for accidents in this context. Even though heart disease is the leading health risk for U.S. men *across all* age groups, from childhood through age 44 it is unintentional injuries that are the greatest threats to men's lives (Mayo Clinic, 2008).

MEN AND HIV/AIDS

Human immunodeficiency virus (HIV) infection became a major cause of death among U.S. males in the 1980s. By 1990, among men aged 25–44, HIV infection was the second leading cause of death, compared to the sixth leading cause of death among same-age women (MMWR, 1993a). It is now estimated that about one million persons in the United States live with HIV. Among reported cases of acquired immunodeficiency syndrome (AIDS) for adolescent and adult men at the end of 2006, 59% were men who had sex with other men, 20% were injecting drug users, 11% were exposed through heterosexual sexual contact, 8% were men who had sex with men and injected drugs (Noble, 2008). Among U.S. adolescent and adult women living with AIDS in 2006, 65% were exposed through heterosexual contact, 33% were injecting drug users, and 3% had other or unknown risks (MMWR, 2006b).

Because most AIDS cases have been among men who have sex with other men, perceptions of the epidemic and its victims have been tinctured by sexual attitudes. In North American cultures, the stigma associated with AIDS is fused with stigma complicated by homophobia. Thoughts and feelings about men with AIDS are also influenced by attitudes toward race, ethnicity, drug abuse, and social marginality. CDC data show, for example, that African Americans, who are about 14% of the total U.S. population, comprised 49% of both new HIV cases and new AIDS diagnoses in 2006 (Noble, 2008). African Americans (not Hispanic) were 38.2% of all the estimated adult and adolescent males living with AIDS between 1981 and 2006 (MMWR, 2006b). (The corresponding estimate for African American (not Hispanic) females is 62%.)

Courtenay (2008) reports that one in four males who die from HIV infection is African American, and among college-age African American men, the HIV infection rate is three times greater than the rate of their Caucasian American counterparts. The high rate of AIDS among racial and ethnic minorities can kindle racial prejudices in some minds, and AIDS is sometimes seen as a "minority disease." While African American or Hispanic males may be at greater risk of contracting HIV/AIDS, just as yellow fingers do not cause lung disease, it is not their race or ethnicity that confers risk, but the behaviors they engage in and the social circumstances of their lives (Polych & Sabo, 2001).

Perceptions of HIV/AIDS can also be influenced by attitudes toward poverty and poor people (Zierler & Krieger, 1997). HIV infection is linked to economic problems that include community disintegration, unemployment, homelessness, eroding urban tax bases, mental illness, substance use, and criminalization (Wallace, 1991). For example, males comprise the majority of homeless persons and runaway children. Poverty and adult homelessness and running away from home among children overlap with drug addiction and sexual victimization which, in turn, are linked to HIV infection.

Suicide

Centers for Disease Control data show that males are more likely than females to commit suicide (Suicide.org, 2008). In 2001 an estimated 1.3% of all deaths were due to suicide, with one 15–24 year-old dying by suicide every 97 minutes. Suicide is the eleventh leading cause of death among Americans, and the second leading cause of death for college students. For each one female to die by suicide, there are four males who do so. Among racial and ethnic groups, it is Caucasian males [who] are most likely to commit suicide, especially if they are elderly, accounting for 73% of all suicide deaths during 2001. During 2004, elderly males (65+) in the United States committed suicide more than seven times more often than elderly females (respectively, 29 suicides per 100,000 versus 3.8 per 100,000) (Suicide.org, 2008). Compared to females, males typically deploy more violent means of attempting suicide (e.g., guns or hanging versus pills) and are more likely to complete the act. Men's selection of more violent methods to kill themselves is consistent with traditionally masculine behavior.

Canetto (1995) interviewed male survivors of suicide attempts in order to better understand sex differences in suicidal behavior. While she recognizes that men's psychosocial reactions and adjustments to nonfatal suicide vary by race/ethnicity, socioeconomic status, and age, she also finds that gender identity is an important factor in men's experiences. Suicide data show that men attempt suicide less often than women but are more likely to die than women. Canetto indicates that men's comparative "success" rate points toward a tragic irony in that, consistent with gender stereotypes, men's failure even at suicide undercuts the cultural mandate that men are supposed to succeed at everything. A lack of embroilment in traditionally masculine expectations, she suggests, may actually increase the likelihood of surviving a suicide attempt for some men.

Erectile Dysfunction

Erectile Dysfunction is basically a partial or complete inability to get and maintain an erection. Men often joke about their penises or tease one another about penis size and erectile potency (i.e., "not getting it up"). In contrast, they rarely discuss their concerns about erectile dysfunction (ED) in a serious way. Men's silences about ED are regrettable in that many men, both young and old, experience recurrent or periodic difficulties getting or maintaining an erection. ED usually has physical causes, happens mostly to older men, and is frequently treatable. Estimates of the number of American men with erectile disorders range from 10 million to 30 million (Minnesota Men's Health Center, 2008). Some main risk factors for ED are diabetes, smoking, and aging.

During the 1960s and 1970s, erectile disorders were largely thought to stem from psychological problems such as depression, financial worries, or work-related stress. Masculine stereotypes about male sexual prowess, phallic power, or being in charge of lovemaking were also said to put too much pressure on some males to perform. Today, however, physiological explanations of ED and medical treatments have been increasingly emphasized.

Finally, the marketing and availability of drugs like Viagra to treat ED have inadvertently spawned a wave of recreational drug use (Brownlee, 2007). Younger men may mix Viagra with other club drugs at rave parties or for all-night sex. Some evidence shows that Viagra use is greater among MSMs and heterosexuals who use other kinds of drugs during sex which, in turn, can lead to other forms of sexual risk taking (Fisher et al., 2006).

MEN'S VIOLENCE

Men's violence is a major public health problem. The traditional masculine ideal calls on males to be aggressive and tough. Anger is a by-product of aggression and toughness and, ultimately, part of the inner terrain of traditional masculinity. Images of angry young men are compelling vehicles used by some males to separate themselves from women and to measure their status in respect to other males. Men's anger and violence derive, in part, from sex inequality. Men use the threat and/or application of violence to maintain their political and economic advantage over women and lower-status men. Male socialization reflects and reinforces these larger patterns of domination.

The homicide rate is highest among U.S. 15–19 year-old males (13/100,000 standard population) followed by 25–34 year-olds (11/ 8100,000) (Kung, Hoyert, Xu, & Murphy, 2008). In 2005 males were almost four times more likely than females to die from homicide (9.8/100,000 and 2.5/100,000, respectively). The convergence of race, ethnicity, and economic inequalities also shapes risk for death from homicide, with death rates among African American males at 39.7/100,000, Caucasian males at 5.4/100,000, and Hispanic males at 13.6/100,000. Finally, 65.3% of men's homicide victims in 2005 were *other men* (U.S. Department of Justice, 2008).

Women are especially victimized by men's anger and violence in the form of rape, date rape, wife beating, assault, sexual harassment on the job, and verbal harassment (Katz, 2006). That the reality and potential of men's violence impacts women's mental and physical health is safely assumed. However, men's violence also exacts a toll on men themselves in the forms of fighting, gang clashes, hazing, gay-bashing, intentional infliction of injury, homicide, suicide, and organized warfare.

War, a form of institutionalized violence, has always been a predominantly male activity (Malszecki & Carver, 2001) that exacted high rates of morbidity and mortality among its participants. Warriors were taught to conform to a type of traditional masculinity that embodies violence-proneness, toughness, and obedience to male authority. The negative health consequences of war for both sexes are painfully evident. Many boys and men, who are disproportionately enlisted to fight in wars, are killed or physically and psychologically maimed, whereas elite male groups may profit or solidify political power through warfare. Men's violence on the patriarchal battlefields also often spills over into civilian populations, where women and children are victimized (Brownmiller, 1975; Chang, 1997). As Sen (1997) observed, "Historically, wars between nations, classes, castes, races, have been fought on the battlefield on the bodies of men, and off the battlefield on the bodies of women" (p. 12). Recent expressions of the militarization of men's violence, partly inspired and fueled by traditional masculinities, can be found in the Taliban of Afghanistan, the Darfur region of Sudan, terrorist movements, and the war in Iraq.

MALE VICTIMS OF SEXUAL ASSAULT

Sexual violence typically involves a male perpetrator and female victim. Whereas researchers and public health advocates began to recognize the sexual victimization of women in Western countries during the late 1960s, it was not until the latter 1990s that the sexual abuse of males began to receive systematic scrutiny from human service professionals and gender researchers (O'Leary, 2001). Recognition of the issue in Canada was spurred by media coverage of the sexual abuse of youth hockey players by their coaches (Robinson, 1998). Prison reformers have recently decried man-on-man rape in North American prisons (see www.stopprisonrape.org). The alleged cover-ups by Catholic bishops in the United States, in relation to some priests' pedophilic exploitation of boys, and the activism and litigation of victims have expanded public awareness of the problem. Despite growing public recognition, research in this area is rare, and little is [known] about the prevalence of sexual abuse of boys and its psychosocial effects (Dhaliwal, Gauzas, Antonowicz, & Ross, 1996). Some studies show that males who suffer sexual victimization as children experience lasting self-blame, feelings of powerlessness and stigmatization, suspicion of others, and confusion about sexual identity, and some eventually repeat the cycle by victimizing others as adolescents and adults (Messerschmidt, 2000; O'Leary, 2001).

SUMMARY

Traditional images of muscled, invulnerable, daring, unemotional, and risk-taking masculinity are still a big part of the culture. Each summer Hollywood pumps old patriarchal blood into the newest cinemagraphic renderings of superheroes like the Hulk, Iron Man, Spiderman, the X-Men, and Fantastic Four. It is ironic, however, that two of the best known actors who portrayed Superman met with real-life disaster. George Reeves, who starred in the original black-and-white television show, committed suicide, and Christopher Reeve, who portrayed the "man of steel" in recent film versions, was paralyzed by an accident during a high-risk equestrian event. Perhaps, one lesson to be learned here is that, behind the cultural facade of mythic masculinity, men are vulnerable. Indeed, as we have seen in this chapter, some of the cultural messages sewn into the cloak of masculinity can put men at risk for illness and early death. A sensible preventive health strategy for men today is to critically evaluate the Superman legacy, that is, to challenge the negative aspects of traditional masculinity that endanger their health, while hanging on to the positive aspects of masculinity and men's lifestyles that heighten men's physical vitality. Hey guys, enjoy the movies, play with the myths, but don't buy into messages about masculinity that put your well-being at risk.

The promotion of men's health requires a sharper recognition that the sources of men's risks for many diseases do not strictly reside in men's psyches, gender identities, or the activities that they enact in daily life. Men's activities, routines, and relations with others are fixed in the historical and structural relations that constitute the larger gender order. As we have seen, not all men or male groups share the same access to social resources, educational attainment, and opportunity that, in turn, can influence their health options. Yes, men need to pursue personal change in order to enhance their health, but without changing the political, economic, and ideological structures of the gender order, the subjective gains and insights forged within individuals can easily erode and fade away. If men are going to pursue self-healing, therefore, they need to create an overall preventive strategy that at once seeks to change potentially harmful aspects of traditional masculinity as well as meeting the health needs of lower-status men.

NOTES

1. This overview of men's health issues and concerns was updated during the summer of 2008. Special thanks to Jill Church at D'Youville College for her library research expertise.

2. For a list of ten ways to stop men's violence go to http://www.jacksonkatz.com/topten.html

REFERENCES

American Cancer Society. (2005). *Cancer facts and figures 2005.* American Cancer Society, Inc. Available at www.cancer.org/downloads/STT/CAFF2005f4P-Wsecured.pdf

American Cancer Society. (2007). *Cancer facts and figures 2007.* Altanta, GA: Author.

American Medical Association. (1996). Health care needs of gay men and lesbians in the United States. *Journal of the American Medical Association, 275,* 1354–1359.

Bahrke, M. S., Yesalis, C. E., Kopstein, A. N., & Stephens, J. A. (2000). Risk factors associated with anabolic-androgenic steroid use among adolescents. *Sports Medicine, 29*(6): 397–405.

Blesch, K. (1986). Health beliefs about testicular cancer and self-examination among professional men. *Oncology Nursing Forum, 13*(1): 29–33.

Blum, R., Harman, B., Harris, L., Bergeissen, L., & Restrick, M. (1992). American Indian–Alaska native youth health. *Journal of American Medical Association, 267(12):* 1637–44.

Brownlee, S. (2007). *Overtreated: Why too much medicine is making us sicker and poorer.* New York: Bloomsbury.

Brownmiller, S. (1975). *Against our will: Men, women, and rape.* New York: Simon and Schuster.

Buckley, W. E., Yesalis, C. E., Friedl, K. E., Anderson, W. A., Streit, A. L., & Wright, J. E. (1988). Estimated prevalence of anabolic steroid use among male high school seniors. *Journal of the American Medical Association, 260*(23): 3441–46.

Bullard, R. D. (1992). Urban infrastructure: Social, environmental, and health risks to African-Americans. In Tidwell, B. J. (Ed.) *The state of Black America.* New York: National Urban League, pp. 183–196.

Burrus, B. B., Liburd, L. C, & Burroughs, A. (1998). Maximizing participation by Black Americans in population-based diabetes research: The Project Direct pilot experience. *Journal of Community Health, 23,* 15–37.

Canetto, S. S. (1995). Men who survive a suicidal act: Successful coping or failed masculinity? In D. Sabo & D. Gordon (Eds.) (1995). *Men's Health and Illness.* Newbury Park, CA: Sage.

Centers for Disease Control and Prevention. (1992). *Monthly Vital Statistics Report, 40*(8, Suppl. 2), p. 41.

Centers for Disease Control and Prevention. (2006). *HIV/AIDS Surveillance Report 2006, (Vol. 18).*

Chang, I. (1997). *The rape of Nanking: The forgotten holocaust of World War II.* New York: Penguin Books.

Chin, M. H., Zhang, J. X., & Merrell, K. (1998). Diabetes in the African-American Medicare population. *Diabetes Care, 21,* 1090–1095.

Collins, K. S., Hall, A., & Neuhaus, C. (1999). *U.S. minority health: A chartbook.* New York: The Commonwealth Fund.

Connell, R. W. (2000). *The men and the boys.* Berkeley, CA: University of California Press.

Courtenay, W. H. (2008). Men's Health Consulting website. See www.menshealth.org

Courtenay, W. H., McCreary, D. R., & Merighi, J. R. (2002). Gender and ethnic differences in health beliefs and behaviors. *Journal of Health Psychology,* *7*(3), 219–231.

Crosby, G. M., Stall, R. D., Paul, J. P., & Barrett, D. C. (1998). Alcohol and drug use patterns have declined between generations of younger gay-bisexual men in San Francisco. *Drug and Alcohol Dependence,* *52,* 177–182.

Cypress, B. (1981). *Patients' reasons for visiting physicians: National ambulatory medical care survey, U.S. 1977–78.* DHHS Publication No. (PHS) 82-1717, Series 13, No. 56. Hyattsville, MD: National Center for Health Statistics, December, 1981a.

Daniluk, J. C. (1997). Gender and infertility. In S. R. Leiblum (ed.), *Infertility: Psychological issues and counseling strategies* (pp. 103–125). New York: Wiley.

Dawson, D. A., & Adams, P. F. (1987). *Current estimates from the national health interview survey: U.S., 1986.* Vital Health Statistics Series, Series 10, No. 164. DHHS Publication No. (PHS) 87-1592, Public Health Service, Washington, D. C., U.S. Government Printing Office.

Day, R. H. (2003). *Aging prisoners: Crisis in American corrections.* New York: Praeger.

Dhaliwal, G. K., Gauzas, L., Antonowicz, D. H., & Ross, R. R. (1996). Adult male survivors of childhood sexual abuse: Prevalence, sexual abuse characteristics, and long-term effects. *Clinical Psychology Review, 16*(7), 616–639.

Digby, T. (Ed.) (1998). *Men doing feminism.* New York: Routledge.

Eaton, D. K., Kann, L., Kinchen, S., et al. (2006). Youth risk behavior survey surveillance—United States, 2005. *Journal of School Health, 76,* 353–372.

Fisher, G. F., Malow, R., Rosenberg, R., Reynolds, G. L., Farrell, N., & Jaffe, A. (2006). Recreational Viagra use and sexual risk among drug abusing men. *American Journal of Infectious Diseases, 2*(2): 107–114.

Fox, K. K., del Rio, C., Holmes, K. K., Hook, E. W. III, Judson, F. N., Knapp, J. S., Procop, G. W., Wang, S. A., Whittington, W. L., & Levine, W. C. (2001). Gonorrhea in the HIV era: A reversal in trends among men who have sex with men. *American Journal of Public Health, 91,* 959–964.

Frey, J. H., Preston, F. W., & Bernhard, B. J. (2004). Risk and injury: A comparison of football and rodeo subcultures. In Young, K. (Ed.) *Sporting bodies, damaged selves: Sociological studies of sports-related injury,* pp. 211–222. Boston: Elsevier.

Gray, R. E. (2005). *Prostate tales: Men's experiences with prostate cancer.* Harriman, TN: Men's Studies Press.

Harrison, J., Chin, J., & Ficarrotto, T. (1992). Warning: Masculinity may be dangerous to your health. In M. S. Kimmel & M. A. Messner (Eds.) *Men's Lives,* pp. 271–285. New York: Macmillan.

James, D. J., & Glaze, L. E. (2006). Mental health problems of prison and inmates. *Bureau of Justice Statistics Special Report.* September, NCJ 213600.

Johnston, L. D., O'Malley, P. M., Bachman, J. G., & Schulenberg, J. E. (2008). *Monitoring the future national results on adolescent drug use: Overview of key findings, 2007* (NIH Publication No. 08-6418). Bethesda, MD: National Institute on Drug Abuse.

Jones, R. A., Underwood, S. A., & Rivers, B. M. (2007). Reducing prostate cancer morbidity and mortality in African American men: Issues and challenges. *Clinical Journal of Oncology Nursing, 11*(6):865–872.

Kaiser Family Foundation. (2007). Race, ethnicity & health care fact sheet. Publication #7630 available on the Kaiser Family Foundation's website at www.kff.org.

Kandrack, M., Grant, K. R., & Segall, A. (1991). Gender differences in health-related behavior: Some unanswered questions. *Social Science & Medicine, 32*(5), 579–590.

Katz, J. (2006). *The macho paradox: Why some men hurt women and how all men can help.* Naperville, IL: Sourcebooks.

Keeling, R. R. (2000). College health: Biomedical and beyond. *Journal of American College Health, 49,* 101–104.

Klein, A. (1993). *Little Big Men: Bodybuilding Subculture and Gender Construction.* Albany, NY: SUNY Press.

Klitzman, R., Pope, H., & Hudson, J. (2000). Ecstasy abuse and high risk sexual behaviors among 169 gay and bisexual men. *American Journal of Psychiatry, 157,* 1162–1164.

Kupers, T. A. (2001). Rape and the prison code. In Sabo, D., Kupers, T. A., & London, W. (Eds.), *Prison Masculinities,* pp. 111–17. Philadelphia: Temple University Press.

Kung, H. C., Hoyert, D. L., Xu, J. & Murphy, S. L. (2008). Deaths: Final data for 2005. *National Vital Statistics Reports,* 56(10), April 24.

Levi, F, LaVecchia, C, Boyle, P., Lucchini, F, & Negri, E. (2001). Western and Eastern European trends in testicular cancer mortality. *Lancet, 357,* 1853–1854.

Lundberg, G. D. (1994). Let's stop boxing in the Olympics and the United States military. *Journal of the American Medical Association, 271* (22), p. 1790.

MacIntyre, S., Hunt, K., & Sweeting, H. (1996). Gender differences in health: Are things really as simple as they seem? *Social Science of Medicine, 42*(2), 617–624.

Malszecki, G., & Carver, T. (2001). Men, masculinities, war, and sport. In N. Mandell (Ed.), *Feminist issues: Race, class, and sexuality* (pp. 166–192). Toronto: Pearson Education Canada.

Malszecki, K. G., Blazer, D. G., & Woodbury, M. A. (1987). Suicide in middle age and later life: Sex and race specific life table and cohort analyses. *Journal of Gerontology, 42,* 219–227.

Maruschak, L. M. (2003). *HIV in prisons.* Bureau of Justice Statistics bulletin. Washington, DC: US Department of Justice, Office of Justice Programs; September 2005. Publication no. NCJ 210344.

Mauer, M. (1999). *Race to incarcerate.* New York: The New Press.

Mayo Clinic. (2008). *Men's top 10 health threats: Mostly preventable.* Retrieved online at http://www.mayoclinic.com/health/mens-health/MC00013

McDavid, K., Lee, J., Fulton, J. P., Tonita, J., & Thompson, T. D. (2004). *Prostate cancer incidence and mortality rates and trends in the United States and Canada.* U.S. Department of Health and Human Services; Public Health Report 2004: 119: 174–186.

McQuillan, G. M., Kottiri, B. J., & Kruszon-Moran, D. (2007). The prevalence of HIV in the United States household population: The national health and nutrition examination surveys, 1988 to 2002. Presented at the 12th Conference on Retroviruses and Opportunistic Infections, Boston, MA; Abstract no. 166.

Melnick, M., Miller, K., Sabo, D., Barnes, G., & Farrell, M. P. (2005). "Athletic Participation and Seat Belt Use Among U.S. Teenagers: A National Study." Paper presented at the Annual Conference of the North American Society for the Study of Sport, Winston-Salem, NC.

Melnick, M., Miller, K., Sabo, D., Farrell, M. P., & Barnes, G. (2001). Tobacco use among high school athletes and nonathletes: Results of the 1997 Youth Risk Behavior Survey. *Adolescence, 36*(144): 727–747.

Messerschmidt, J. W. (2000). *Nine lives: Adolescent masculinities, the body, and violence.* Boulder, CO: Westview.

Messner, M. A., & Montez de Oca, J. (2005). The male consumer as loser: Beer and liquor ads in mega sports media events. *Signs: Journal of Women in Culture and Society 30,* 1879–1909.

Messner, M. A., and Sabo, D. (1994). *Sex, violence, and power in sports: Rethinking masculinity.* Freedom, CA: Crossing Press.

Miller, K., Barnes, G., Sabo, D. F., Melnick, M. J., & Farrell, M. P. (2002). Anabolic-androgenic steroid use and other adolescent problem behaviors: Rethinking the male athlete assumption. *Sociological Perspectives, 44*(4):467–489.

Miller, K., Sabo, D., Melnick, M., Farrell, M. P., & Barnes, G. (2001). *The Women's Sports Foundation Report: Health risks and the teen athlete.* East Meadow, New York: The Women's Sports Foundation. See www.womenssportsfoundation.org

Minnesota Men's Health Center. (2008). *Facts about Erectile Dysfunction.* Retrieved online at http://www.mmhc-online.com/articles/impotency.html

Montagu, A. (1953). *The natural superiority of women.* New York: MacMillan.

Morbidity and Mortality Weekly Report. (2008). *Work-related injury deaths among Hispanics—United States, 1992–2006,* 57(22), June 6, pp. 597–600.

——— (2006a). *Sports-related injuries among high school athletes—United States, 2005–06 school year,* 55(38), September 29, retrieved online.

——— (2006b). *Twenty-five years of HIV/AIDS— United States, 1981–2006,* 55(21): 585–589.

——— (1993a). *Update: Mortality attributable to HIV infection/AIDS among persons aged 25–44 years— United States, 1990–91,* 42(25), July 2, pp. 481–486.

——— (1993b). *Summary of notifiable diseases United States, 1992,* 41 (55), September 24.

Mumola, C. J. (2007). *Medical causes of death in state prisons, 2001–2004.* Bureau of Justice Statistics Data Brief. January, NCJ 215340.

Nachtigall, R. D., Becker, G., & Wozny, M. (1992). The effects of gender-specific diagnosis on men's and women's response to infertility. *Fertility and Sterility, 57,* 113–121.

National Center for Health Statistics. (2006). *Deaths: Preliminary data for 2004.* Health e-stat. Retrieved online at www.cdc.gov/nchs/pressroom/06facts/preliminarydeaths04.htm

National Center for Health Statistics. (2002). *National Vital Statistics Report, 50*(15), September 16, 2002, Table C.

National Center for Health Statistics. (1992). Advance report of final mortality statistics, 1989. *Monthly Vital Statistics Report, 40* (8) supplement 2 (DHHS Publication No. (PHS) 92–1120).

National Health and Nutrition Examination Survey (NHANES). (2003). *Overweight among U.S. children and adolescents.* Hyattsville, MD: Department of Health and Human Services, Centers for Disease Control and Prevention. Retrieved from www.cdc.gov/nchs/nhanes.htm.

National Vital Statistics Reports. (2006). *Leading causes of death by age group, black males—United States, 2004.* Retrieved online at http://www.cdc gov/nchs/datawh/statab/unpubd/mortabs.htm

Noble, R. (2008). *AVERT (Averting HIV and AIDS), United States Statistics Summary.* Retrieved online at http://www.avert.org/statsum.htm

O'Leary, P. (2001). Working with males who have experienced childhood sexual abuse. In B. Pease & P. Camilleri (Eds.), *Working with men in the human services* (pp. 80–92). New South Wales, Australia: Allen & Unwin.

Payne, S. (2006). *The health of men and women.* Maiden, MA: Polity Press.

Pleck, J., Sonenstein, F. L., & Ku, L. C. (1992). In Ketterlinus, R. & Lamb, M. E. (Eds.). *Adolescent problem behaviors.* Hillsdale, NJ: Lawrence Erlbaum Associates.

Polych, C., & Sabo, D. (2001). Sentence—Death by lethal infection: IV-drug use and infectious disease transmission in North American prisons. In Sabo, D., Kupers, T. A., & London, W. *Prison masculinities.* Philadelphia: Temple University Press, pp 173–83.

Postman, N., Nystrom, C., Strate, L. & Weingartner, C. (1987). *Myths, men and beer: An analysis of beer commercials on broadcast television, 1987.* Falls Church, VA: Foundation for Traffic Safety.

Robinson, L. (1998). *Crossing the line: Violence and sexual assault in Canada's national sport.* Toronto: McClelland and Stewart.

Rudberg, L., Nilsson, S., & Wikblad, K. (2000). Health-related quality of life in survivors of testicular cancer 3 to 13 years after treatment. *Journal of Psychosocial Oncology, 18,* 19–31.

Sabo, D. (2005). The Study of Masculinities and Men's Health: An Overview (2005). In M. Kimmel, J. Hearn, & R. W. Connell (Eds.). *Handbook of men's studies.* Newbury Park, CA: Sage Publications, pp. 326–352.

Sabo, D. (2004). The politics of sports injury: Hierarchy, power, and the pain principle. In Young, K. (Ed.). *Sporting bodies, damaged selves: Sociological studies of sports-related injury.* Boston: Elsevier, pp. 59–79.

Sabo, D., & Gordon, D. (1995). *Men's health & illness: Gender, power & the body.* Newbury Park: Sage.

Schofield, T., Connell, R. W, Walker, L., Wood, J. F., & Butland, D. L. (2000). Understanding men's health and illness: A gender relations approach to policy, research and practice. *Journal of American College Health, 48*(6), 247–256.

Sen, G. (1997, June). *Globalization in the 21st century: Challenges for civil society.* The UVA Development Lecture, delivered at the University of Amsterdam.

Straub, N R. (1994, Winter). African Americans: Their health and the health care system. *The Pharos,* pp. 18–20.

Suicide.org (2008). U. S. Suicide Rates, 1950–2003. See http://www.suicide.org/suicide-statistics.html

Tewksbury, (1995). Sexual adaptation among gay men with HIV. In D. Sabo & D. Gordon, *Men's health & illness: Gender, power & the body.* Newbury Park: Sage, pp. 222–245.

Treadwell, H. M., & Nottingham, J. H. (2005). Editor's choice: Standing in the gap. *American Journal of Public Health, 95*(10): 1676.

U.S. Department of Justice (2008). Bureau of Justice Statistics, Homicide trends in the U.S.: Trends by gender. Retrieved online http://www.ojp.usdoj.gove/bjs/homicide/gender.htm

U.S. Department of Justice (2006). Bureau of Justice Statistics, Prison statistics, December 31, 2006. Retrieved online http://wwwojp.usdoj.gov/bjs/prisons.htm

Waldron, I. (1995). Contributions of changing gender differences in behavior and social roles to changing gender differences in mortality. In D. Sabo & D. Gordon (Eds.), *Men's health and illness,* Newbury Park, CA: Sage.

Wallace, R. (1991). Traveling waves of HIV infection on a low dimensional 'socio-geographic' network. *Social Science Medicine, 32*(7), 847–852.

Webb, R. E., & Daniluk, J. C. (1999). The end of the line: Infertile men's experiences of being unable to produce a child. *Men and Masculinities, 2*(1), 6–25.

Wechsler, H. (2005). *Harvard School of Public Health College Alcohol Study, 1999* [Computer file]. ICPSR03818-v2. Boston, MA: Harvard School of Public Health [producer], 2005. Ann Arbor, MI: Inter-university Consortium for Political and Social Research [distributor], 2005-11-22.

Wingo, P. A, Bolden, S., Tong, T., Parker, S. L., Martin, L. M. & Heath, C. W. (1996). Cancer statistics for African Americans, 1996. *CA: A Cancer Journal for Clinicians, 46,* 113–125.

Zierler, S., & Krieger, N. (1997). Reframing women's risk: Social inequalities and HIV infection. *Annual Review of Public Health, 18*(1), 401–436.

OLD GAY MEN'S BODIES AND MASCULINITIES

Kathleen F. Slevin   Thomas J. Linneman

INTRODUCTION

There is a relative lack of literature regarding old,[1] gay men. One reason is that this important population is not easily accessible to researchers. Another factor is the invisibility of these men—not only in society in general but also within gay communities themselves. Consequently, this paper addresses a much-needed topic for discussion—not only in the social science literature but also in the masculinities literature.

Within the growing literature on masculinities, several claims deserve note. First, given the focus of this paper, it is important to register that notions of masculinity are embodied: the body plays a critical role in how men understand and practice what it means to be a man (Connell 1995). Second, multiple forms of masculinity exist: there are many ways to be a man, based on the various intersections of race/ethnicity, age, class, and sexuality. Given this plurality of masculinities, it is also the case that some forms of manhood are more honored than others. Hence, hegemonic masculinity which, while not assumed to be statistically representative among populations of men, presents exalted ideals or exemplars of masculinity, of the ideal man (e.g., the professional sports star in contemporary U.S.). Yet, as Connell and Messerschmidt remind us in their recent historical review of the concept of hegemonic masculinity, scholars need to "eliminate any usage of hegemonic masculinity as a fixed, transhistorical

Kathleen F. Slevin and Thomas J. Linneman, "Old Gay Men's Bodies and Masculinities." Paper presented at the annual meetings of the American Sociological Association, New York, August 2008. Reprinted by permission of the authors.

model" (Connell and Messerschmidt 2005, 838). Accordingly, understanding masculinities requires that we acknowledge the complex ways that notions of manhood are dynamic. As well as being shaped by social locations, they are also influenced by local, regional, and global practices (Connell and Messerschmidt 2005). Thus, in any particular historical moment, men and boys construct, produce, negotiate, and re-negotiate what it means to be a man. Age relations are centrally important for at least two reasons: first, because hegemonic masculinity honors what is youthful and, second, notions of manhood are not only influenced by age but also are likely to change over an individual's life course. In addition, gender plays a powerful role in how men construct their notions of manhood; masculinity is invariably defined relationally, against the feminine (Hennen 2005). Also worthy of note is the recent documentation of subordinate or subaltern masculinities that are considered to be inferior variants of the masculine ideal: non-white masculinities, working-class masculinities, older masculinities, and gay masculinities (Chen 1999; Connell 1995; Nardi 2000). Often, researchers analyze each of these masculinities separately, examining how old men are demasculinized (Meadows and Davidson 2006), or how gay men are feminized (Linneman 2008). Increasingly, however, scholars are focusing on the intersections of these subaltern forms (Barrett 2000; Han 2000).

It is to this latter development that this paper contributes by studying the masculinities of old, white, privileged gay men. The use of an intersectionality perspective allows us to explore the complexities of how the intersections of various locations such as race, class, gender, sexuality and age shape the ways the men interviewed for this study experience what it means to be old men who are both advantaged and disadvantaged by these interlocking systems of power and oppression. Our attention to age relations and sexuality adds a new perspective to the traditional dominant statuses of race, class, and gender that typically represent intersectional analyses (Collins 2000; Crenshaw 1991). Indeed, age inequalities are widely ignored, even in feminist literatures (Calasanti and Slevin 2006).

Through narrative analysis, this paper explores how ten old gay men talk about their masculinities, and specifically the masculinities of their aging bodies. This qualitative approach, often missing in extant literature, allows these old gay men to tell us how they understand themselves as men. It also allows us to make explicit the connections between men's bodies and masculinity (Connell 1995). Thus, we draw attention to old men and their aging bodies—topics largely ignored by scholars (Katz 2005; Calasanti and King 2005; Faircloth 2003; Calasanti and Slevin 2001). Through a focus on this largely ignored group, we explore how the intersections of race, class, gender, and sexual orientation intersect with age to influence notions of masculinity and aging. We also uncover how old gay men talk about their self-identities as men who are both old and gay, as men with at least two negatively "marked identities" (Brekhus 2003, 11). Thus, through them we gain insights into how their notions of embodied masculinity are constructed within a cultural context that stigmatizes both being old and being gay while glorifying youthful and heterosexual notions of masculinity. Narrative analysis provides us a window through which we can glimpse "the contradictory and shifting nature of hegemonic discourse" (Chase 2005). Such analysis allows us to see how these men both create meaning and make sense of what it means to grow old and to be old gay men. It provides us a mechanism to explore the contradictions and messiness of lived experiences, uncovering how "hegemonic masculinity may not be the lived form of masculinity at all" despite the fact that it is a powerful, even dominant script, against which men judge themselves and others (Thompson and Whearty 2004, 6). As

well, these men's narratives allow us to illustrate the complicated nature of how old gay men who are privileged by class and race experience their aging bodies; through their voices we understand better how they work to create and sustain biographical continuity as they sort through and integrate the forces that shape and re-shape their lives. Finally, their stories reveal common threads among the men but they also highlight their diverse and unique experiences.

Old Masculinities

In our culture growing old and being old is nowadays constructed as a problem—albeit one that we are told is increasingly solvable (Cruikshank 2003). Nowadays consumer society targets the body as central to age-resisting practices and strategies; fighting aging, resisting growing old or looking old is big business (Slevin 2006; Calasanti and Slevin 2001; Gilleard and Higgs 2000). As well, the body is central to ageist notions and practices (Slevin 2006); and, as Laws (1995) reminds us, ageism is an embodied form of oppression. Yet, despite all attempts to fight aging, bodies are more than social constructions, they are subject to biological and physiological constraints and they decline (Turner 1996). The male body at the height of its productive capacities is held up as an ideal form of masculinity. This production occurs at a number of sites: economic, athletic, and sexual, to name a few. As men enter old age, their productivity within these sites decreases markedly. As Calasanti and Slevin point out "old age does in fact confer a loss of power, even for those advantaged by other social locations" (Calasanti and Slevin 2001, 191). A common cultural belief holds that men gain power and become men when they achieve the status of economic producers (Emslie et al. 2004). But, as men enter old age and face a new set of socially constructed gender norms, they find themselves increasingly moving from sites of economic production such as the workplace to the feminized sphere of the home (Meadows and Davidson 2006). Their contributions to the economy occur primarily through consumption and not through production (Calasanti and King 2005).

The sporting arena is another institution typically associated with masculinity (Messner 1992). The finely tuned male body is idealized both on the playing field and in advertisements. Though the aging male body indeed may successfully maintain some presence within certain sporting activities, men must take greater care as their bodies begin their inevitable physical decline (Calasanti 2004). As with economic production, their participation on the sporting field moves to the sidelines and towards consumption. Furthermore, approaches to inevitable physical decline are complicated by gender because seeking health care (a common need in old age) is inconsistent with hegemonic masculinity (McVittie and Willock 2006).

Just as male bodily performance decreases on the playing field, many men experience a similar decline in the bedroom. Sexual performance among old men certainly has entered the public consciousness through the development of Viagra and similar drugs that aim to re-sex the aging male body (Marshall 2006; Loe 2003). A multi-billion dollar industry has grown around the new expectation that aging men are expected now to "keep it up" as long as possible, and to age more "successfully" than previous generations of old men (Calasanti and King 2005). Recent survey data does show that the old have sex more frequently than previously believed (Lindau et al. 2007). However, loss of ability to perform sexually, and loss of interest in sex, remain key indicators of old age (Marshall and Katz 2002). As a consequence of these losses and declines the ability of old men to correspond to the widespread ideals of ideal manhood are both compromised and jeopardized.

At every turn, then, the aging male body faces the likelihood of demasculinization. Yet, as Spector-Mercel argues, scholars of masculinity, while focusing on the varied influences of, for example, race, class, culture and sexual orientation, have largely disregarded the critical role played by age and life course (Spector-Mersel 2006). She reminds us that the scripts for masculinity in old age are ambiguous and ill-formed; old men not only constitute an ambiguous social category, but also they "live in a hybrid-state" (Spector-Mercel 2006, 68). Thompson further concludes: "To many people, aging is a negation of masculinity, and thus older men become effeminate overtime" (Thompson 1994, 13). But, given the dearth of empirical literature on the lived bodily experiences of old people in general what all of this means for their *subjective* experiences of aging and aging bodies is quite unexplored (Slevin 2006). Indeed, we must be wary of assuming that dominant social values, such as those that characterize the aging body as negative, are synonymous with what old men and women actually experience (Oberg 2003).

Gay Masculinities

The hegemonic form of masculinity is youthful *and* heterosexual. Consequently, homosexuality is routinely associated with gender inversion (Rosenfeld 2003). When a man reveals his homosexuality, regardless of his gender performance, many question his masculinity because of his sexual desires (Kimmel 1996). Accordingly, much of the demasculinization associated with gay men takes the form of feminization. There is a long history of gay men's feminization. Indeed, the arbiters of this feminizing are often gay men themselves. In the introduction to his important volume on gay masculinities, Nardi titles his introduction "Anything for a Sis, Mary," quoting from the classic gay play "The Boys in the Band." Feminizing camp has a long tradition in gay male culture (Dyer 2002). Even today, the feminization of gay men remains prevalent. For example, the popular pro-gay show "Will & Grace" consistently engaged in feminizing its gay characters hundreds of times, often in moments of conflict where the goal was castigation of the gay men (Linneman 2008). It is important to maintain the distinction between feminization and demasculinization, for even if a gay man is not feminized, he still is often not considered able to live up to the true standards of masculinity. Indeed, openly gay men are virtually shut out of bastions of hegemonic masculinity, such as corporate boardrooms, professional sports teams, and the military. There are communities of gay men, such as the radical faeries and the bears, who actively disrupt the connections between homo-sexuality and femininity (Hennen 2008), but given that these groups are doubly marginalized (by het-erosexuals and by gay cultures), the effect of such efforts is minor.

As attention to gay masculinities has grown, researchers have begun to study various forms of gay masculinities. Nardi's volume contains pieces on the masculinities of working-class gay men (Bar-rett 2000), Latino gay men (Cantu 2000), and Asian American gay men (Han 2000). However, the mas-culinities of old gay men make no appearance. In fact, as Jones and Pugh point out, the oldest respon-dent in any of the studies in Nardi's volume was 56 (Jones and Pugh 2005).

The Masculinities of Old Gay Men

Reinforcing the need for studies such as our own, we note the limited research available on the masculini-ties of old gay men. Brekhus's seminal work on gay suburban men, while not focusing on old men, does suggest that the intersection of these identities cre-ates complicated identity work that requires various strategies and struggles to accomplish some sense of authenticity (Brekhus 2003). Yet, while acknowl-edging the role of stigma in old gay men's lives, it is equally important to note that cultural domination is never complete; those who are stigmatized—either by age or sexual orientation—may elect in various ways to resist ageist or homophobic messages and to create alternative notions of manhood. Managing multiple identities (positive and negative) requires much work and in exposing this on-going identity work, we begin to uncover how the old gay men in this study work hard to counteract and resist stig-matized identities. The fact that they are privileged by race and class provides them resources that most likely would be unavailable to men of color or those who are in lower social classes.

Another common theme in the literature on older gay men is that of "accelerated aging" (Wahler and Gabbay 1997). Indeed, some scholars argue that gay men become arbiters of their own op-pression (Chen 1999). Gay male culture, in many of its commodified forms, holds up as its masculine

ideal the young, muscular man, even more so than in heterosexual male culture. Because of this, gay men are considered old much sooner than in non-gay culture:

> Because of the gay community's emphasis on youth, homosexual men are considered middle-aged and elderly by other homosexual men at an earlier age than heterosexual men in the general community. Since these age-status norms occur earlier in the gay sub-culture, the homosexual man thinks of himself as middle-aged and old before his heterosexual counterpart does. (Bennett and Thompson 1991, 66)

A cursory look at gay culture corroborates this: glossy gay newsmagazines consistently feature young men on their covers, and gay pornography treats older men as a marginalized fetish. However, empirical data regarding how real gay men experi-ence this phenomenon are scarce and contradictory (Jones and Pugh 2005).

Also inconsistent are findings regarding the effects of involvement in gay communities. Quam and Whitford (1992) found that many of the older gay men they studied were both involved in gay communities and experienced high levels of life satisfaction. In contrast, one of the more provoca-tive findings of Hostetler's empirical research is that a high level of involvement in a gay community was associated with increased concern over aging (Hostetler 2004). However, the nature of the rela-tionship is uncertain, and the causal argument may go both ways. It could be that old gay men, through their involvement in the gay community, may ex-perience ageism as they interact with younger members of the community (Heaphy 2007). Alter-natively, concern over aging could prompt some gay men to seek involvement in their community. Further complicating the matter, it is necessary to keep in mind the multiplicity of gay communities and the wide variation among such communities with regard to the extent to which they stigmatize old age.

A prominent argument that highlights some positive consequences of being gay reminds us that at various points in their lives gay men learn to cope with stigma because they are denied the privileges that accompany normative notions of masculinity. Yet, of course, some gay men also benefit to a degree from the privileges of being white men who are relatively affluent. Indeed, gay men often can pass for heterosexual and thus insure that they are still beneficiaries of the privileges associated with being heteronormative men. That said, if they live their lives out of the closet, a loss of privilege is a distinct possibility. Thus, having learned to live with one marked identity (being gay), they are potentially positioned to adapt better to a second stigmatized or marked identity (being old). If this is the case, and their narratives lend some credence to this proposition, they might be less likely to miss these privileges when they are denied them in old age. Thus, by the time they reach their 60s and 70s, gay men have had decades of experience dealing with demasculinization and stigma, and therefore have a battery of coping skills at the ready:

> The gay man who has successfully navigated the coming-out process arrives at the knowledge that how he constructs his reality need most importantly be acceptable to himself, according to the dictates of his own needs. Gay men frequently report a greater sense of freedom from cultural norms. This may mean a highly adaptive flexibility in terms of which roles and role expectations are "acceptable." This translates into more flexibility in meeting the challenges of aging, and leads to individuals who may be better equipped to construct an interpersonal reality that meets their needs not just as gay people but as old people. (Wahler and Gabbay 1997, 14)

In contrast, aging heterosexual men experience demasculinization for perhaps the first time in their lives (Meadows and Davidson 2006). Thus, old gay men may indeed be ahead of their heterosexual peers in some ways as they face the daily challenges of inhabiting older bodies. In sum, exploring how being gay shapes men's embodied experiences of masculinity, and trying to understand how these notions are shaped by other intersecting social relations such as race, class, and age, is likely to reveal a complicated picture that differs for each man and reveals multiple, varying factors that shape their notions of what it means to be a man, to be gay, to be old, and to be an old gay man.

METHODS

Based on intensive interviews with ten gay men aged 60 to 85, this study explores the narrative accounts of how they conceive of embodied masculinity in old age. The study is part of a larger study in which the lead author, between 2002 and 2004, conducted intensive interviews with 26 men (16 heterosexual, 10 homosexual) and 31 women (22 heterosexual, 9 lesbian) in their 60s, 70s and 80s about how they experienced their bodies in old age. The researcher used a snowball sampling method to obtain interviewees from different backgrounds. Such a sampling method is very appropriate for locating this invisible population (Carpenter 2002). The intensive, exploratory interviews addressed a variety of topics related to aging and the body. Questions were broad and there were lots of invited opportunities to "think out loud" about the topics that were the focus of the interviews. This sort of narrative inquiry made sense for a number of reasons. First, because so little is known empirically about the topics under investigation, such inquiry is most likely to capture "retrospective meaning making—the shaping or ordering of past experience" (Chase 2005). Second, it allows the researcher to explore very broadly the lived experiences of individuals who are willing to talk about their own biographical particulars, and it allows for "the uniqueness of each human action and event rather than their common properties" (Chase 2005). As well, narrative inquiry provides us the opportunity to seek similarities and differences across narratives on topics that are difficult to explore. It is especially suited not only to the subject matter but also to recruitment of members of "hard to find" populations, especially those who are reluctant to reveal their sexual identities and, are often *only* accessible through person-to-person recruitment. Thus, the word-of-mouth support for this research (which was critical, given the snowball nature of the sample) was enhanced by the fact that future participants learned from those already interviewed that they would have an opportunity to "tell their story" to a sympathetic listener. Finally, narrative inquiry is particularly well suited for exploring and deepening our understanding of various oppressions but especially ageism, which (unlike racism, sexism, and homophobia) is "more often invoked than analyzed" (Cruikshank 2003, 135).

Topics addressed concerns about aging in general and specifically about looking and feeling old, preventing the aging process, body image issues, sexuality/ageism/attractiveness issues, masculinity/femininity issues, and the media and aging. In the case of these old gay men, they were asked at various times throughout the interviews to reflect upon how being gay shaped their responses to various issues. All interviews took place in the homes of the respondents and lasted between one and a half to two and a half hours. The interviews were taped and later transcribed. Interviews and transcripts were read and re-read to identify themes within the interviews.

All of the old gay interviewees lived in a mid-Atlantic state and the majority, seven, lived in mid-sized cities. The remaining three lived in small towns. All were born between 1922 and 1947 and all came of age when to be homosexual was to experience stigma and fear of reprisal on multiple fronts. Consequently, they were part of a cohort that grew up in especially stigmatized conditions. Two were previously married to heterosexual women and one had children during this marriage; both divorced and came out in their forties. The eight remaining men were "lifetime" gay men. Two were living with partners at the time of the interviews. All of the interviewees were white and very well educated: all had bachelor's degrees and the majority, seven, also had earned graduate degrees. While one man had spent his working life as a religious pastor, the majority, six, were employed in various fields of education: two were teachers, four held administrative positions. The remaining three interviewees were executives in various organizations. Eight of the men were formally retired from the workforce,

one was employed full-time, and one was working part-time. All of the men were financially secure and their lifetimes in professional jobs provide them with financial and health benefits that ensured secure retirements.

FINDINGS

The narratives of these ten gay men provided numerous insights about how they experience and make sense of their bodies as they age and as they relate to their masculinities, to their identities, and to the gay communities in which they interact. Below, we recount several themes that emerged from the interviews. All of these themes point to the complexities inherent in the relationships among masculinities and the intersections of race, class, gender, age, and sexualities.

Aging and Acceptance of Self/Body

While one interviewee, Bart (67),[2] claims that over the decades of his life there has been consistency in his sense of himself as masculine, the rest of the respondents talked about how they had changed over the years. Most talked about how they have, over time, become more accepting of who they are, both as men and as gay men. Taken-for-granted and totally unnoted in conversations, however, are the race and class privileges that provide them useful resources—social, educational, and financial—to address many of the disadvantages stemming from their sexual orientation and from growing old. For instance, these men have the time and financial resources to avail of therapy, and they are, by and large, surrounded by friends and others who value a therapeutic culture of self-reflection as well as individual therapy. Consequently, it is not surprising that most of the interviewees are very explicit about how they have worked hard to recognize, accept, and be comfortable with themselves as they are, not as others might have them be. In general, the interviewees appear to have reflected long and hard on who they are. In old age they have arrived, for the most part, at a notable level of comfort with themselves. Analysis of conversations about masculinity and changes over time, as well as about general life changes, reveals an interesting and complicated picture. In part, their conversations suggest that aging itself has contributed to a growing comfort level. Glen (85) captures this notion when he comments that "Most mature men have become more thoughtful." Raymond (67) reinforces this notion when he comments: "I'm so much wiser now . . . I like being where I am." Yet, the comments of Glen and Raymond, positive as they are, also illuminate an embedded ageism that manifests itself in notions of "sageism"—the idea that old people are wiser than young people simply because they are older.

Given their race and class privileges—and the fact that they are very well educated—it is hardly surprising that most of these men consciously explored these issues through therapy and through a growing political awareness or engagement in gay issues, and are cognizant of the fact that mainstream society has become significantly less anti-gay throughout their lives (Loftus 2001). In these ways class and race privilege intertwine with sexual orientation in shaping how these old men approach their identities and, for the most part, ensures that they are both thoughtful and articulate about who they are and about the identity shifts that have accompanied various life transitions and societal changes. Still, an intersectionality lens also requires that we account for disadvantages and that we recognize how structural inequalities create multiple (dis)advantages. Consequently, while our interviewees grew up as white, upper-middle-class men who were advantaged by those societal positions, it is also the case that they are disadvantaged by their sexual orientation. They grew up and lived many decades of their lives in a cultural milieu where being gay was both denigrated and dangerous. Their comments convey some of what they faced as they tried to make sense of their multiple identities and their narratives remind us of the complicated nature of identity construction. Aging, and especially retirement from a labor force where most had to hide their sexual identities, provides for different perspectives and allows us to glimpse how identities shift over the life course. For instance, Glen (85)

captures some of this identity struggle with these words, "Getting older has made me more real. . . . I am freer now to say 'Hey, I am not a gay, just a guy.' That does not fit me. I'm a man before I'm a gay man. . . ." Glen's words provide us a window into the tenuous and elastic interplay between identities, they hint at a blurring of boundaries, a blending of identities. His words remind us of the need to recognize how identities are nuanced and ambivalent. Indeed, they serve as a caution not to jump easily into classifying certain identities as fixed master statuses. Finally, his comments shed light on the tensions between his masculine and gay identities and they allow us to appreciate that old age has allowed him to find some authenticity in an accommodation of *both* identities.

Raymond (67) also alludes to a journey toward greater self-acceptance. His story underscores how identity work is an on-going and fluid process that reflects a larger cultural narrative that includes a growing emphasis on self-reflection, as well as shifting messages about masculinity and homosexuality. Thus, he spoke of how, in his early 40s, he shifted from Western to Eastern philosophies of life and how the shift had helped him become more self-accepting. He goes on to explain how his sense of masculinity changed as he grew older. For Raymond, the journey described is of a gay man keenly aware of his body's role in shaping masculine identity. His story is also one that highlights his aim to approximate the ideal images of masculinity that he grew up with. Here is how he talks about his 40s and how at that time he came closer to approximating ideal standards of masculine strength: "I filled out and so I was no longer emaciated looking. I began to look like all those men I guess I had seen [in] those movies and so, because I did, I no longer felt so bad about myself. I felt like a male." Raymond talks at considerable length about how, over the years, he grew to be much more accepting of himself. He is emphatic that he needs to see himself as masculine. Indeed, being masculine is critical to his overall well-being. Thus, it is hardly surprising that he claims to have "worked very hard over the years to make myself feel masculine." His journey ultimately has led to a more positive self-image of himself as a man: "My sense of masculinity now is very strong." Interestingly, coming to accept that he is gay was, in his own mind, critical to reaching a more positive image of himself as a man: "When I realized I was gay, I began to feel much better about myself as a male."

While on its face it may appear paradoxical that Raymond achieves a greater sense of himself as masculine once he accepts that he is gay, it is critical to consider Raymond's analysis of the shifts in his masculine identity over his life. Raymond's narrative reveals the struggles he has undergone over decades and it allows us to hear how he works to repair his identity. His is a story that also highlights the need to understand both how notions of masculinity shift with age as well as how gay men develop coping skills that help them manage the stigma of their sexual identity. Thus, with age and time he has negotiated the tensions between his notions of masculinity as heteronormative and his own sexual identity. Like Glen, getting older has also allowed him to develop notions of manhood that incorporate his masculine and gay identities. Indeed, he hints at this when he says "I felt so un-male for so many years growing up because my maleness was measured by all those things I could not achieve." Nowadays, Raymond has adopted a biological minimum for being a man: "If you have a penis and testicles, you're male." Such a biologically reductionist argument flattens the hierarchies of masculinities: Raymond is gay and old, but his male body speaks for itself. While this equation may seem at first overly simplistic, taking into account Raymond's long-standing work on his masculinity gives this statement a power that it otherwise might not have.

Constructing/Managing Identities

For several of the men interviewed, the secret to greater self-acceptance appears to lie in their abilities to negotiate what it means to be a man. Social class privileges provide them not only the material means to explore their identities (through therapy, supportive others, leisure time to think about these sorts of issues, etc.) but also provide them a language to communicate their identity work to others. Through their voices we glimpse the dynamics of how they construct notions of self; we learn how they reject exaggerated masculinity in favor of a more authentic masculinity or what Connell and Messerschmidt (2005, 848) refer to as "nonhegemonic patterns of masculinity." For instance, four of the interviewees are very explicit about the fact that they recognize that they combine both masculine and feminine traits. For example, Eric (60), talks about the need to recognize and accept the "ying-yang or balance" between masculinity and femininity in himself. Peter (62), who at various points in the interview refers to himself as "queenish," uses similar language to Eric and argues that masculine and feminine traits co-exist for him: "I know I have female points of view . . . I've always been a combination of the two. It won't shift. Well, it never has." Unlike Peter, Eric's acceptance of his masculine and feminine sides has come in mid-life. A level of comfort has developed over time, he claims. He goes on to register that he has "always been aware that I was not masculine—now [I am] more comfortable with it." Richard (69), who is very religious, talks about how he works with his spiritual director in order to "accept the feminine side of myself." Asked how he feels about his masculinity, he responds: "[I am] probably not the most masculine out there. [I] accept my femininity. [I am] OK with the blending—whatever that looks like I have no idea yet." Still, Richard's next observation illuminates how notions of masculinity are defined relationally: "When I am creative, I'm feminine. [I am] masculine when I do butch things at the gym." Richard ends his comments on the topic by suggesting that the very terms *masculine* and *feminine* become less important as one grows old. In keeping with his deep religiosity, he concludes that growing old makes one "more prepared for the next life, where being masculine and feminine don't matter." Gary (64) has a slightly different angle on this issue and his comments reinforce ageist notions of old men and women as sexless. He ascribes to the view that "men and women, as they get older, become . . . less feminine [and] . . . less masculine. They just become old people." Thus, Gary would have us believe that growing old makes gender matter less.

But even those who resisted rigid notions of what it means to be a man spoke of managing their public persona in order to avoid being perceived as what Freitas and others (1997, 329) refer to as "visual caricatures." Conversations about public presentations of self sensitize us to "the complicated work of appearance management and identity border construction" (Freitas et al., 1997, 325). Yet, we caution that this drive to distance themselves from "a perceived stereotypical aesthetic" (Freitas et al., 1997, 329) does not represent a desire to distance themselves from gay culture. Similarly, this disassociation from stereotypical effeminacy does not signal that these men embraced heterosexuality. When asked whether they presented themselves differently when spending time with gay men and lesbians versus heterosexuals, many told stories that illustrate that they manage their presentations of self very carefully. By contrast, all spoke in one way or another of being "more free," "more comfortable," "more open" around other gay people: free to dress as they wished, free to physically express themselves as they desired. Bart (67) captures a common sentiment when he claims that he has a "great sense of relaxation with other gays." Some talked of monitoring their physical presentations of self in public spaces, of being careful with their "non-verbal cues." For instance, Eric (60), who has a deep, male voice and who strikes the interviewer as "typically male" in his embodiment, illuminates how critical the body is to "reading" sexual orientation, specifically homosexuality. He spoke of being very aware that others look at body movement to assess masculinity and, by extension, to ascribe sexual orientation. Thus, he pays particular attention to not being seen to "flit around the grocery store." Similarly, he avoids public gestures that are seen as stereotypically feminine such as resting his hands on his hips. Yet, as Hennen (2005) reminds us, such attention to not being seen as effeminate signals more than concerns about the complex negotiations of gendered and sexed spaces, it also signals a rejection and devaluation of the feminine and demonstrates a

gendered hierarchy that remains central to the logic of hegemonic masculinity.

Achieving Masculinity

Gary (64) in some ways mirrors Raymond's lifetime battle to achieve a greater sense of himself as masculine. Both have struggled with heteronormative ideals and both have tried in some fundamental ways to aspire to those ideals while also accepting that being gay may compromise these ideals, if only in the eyes of others. Thus, Gary, like Raymond, talks at some length about the "long fight" to live up to dominant notions of manhood and to achieve some sense of normative masculinity. Both highlight how, in negotiating notions of effeminacy, they reject what is feminine and they shape their own masculine ideals by calling on the standards of hegemonic masculinity. For instance, Gary emphatically claims that he is "very much into masculinity and not being limp-wristed." Another interesting angle on issues of masculinity and sexual orientation is revealed in a story told by James (64). His partner of 22 years recently died and James, at one point in the discussion about masculinity, comments that the absence of his partner in his life has led to his feeling more masculine. Upon further discussion, James explains that his partner was more masculine than he was because "He could fix more things." Consequently, James's partner's death has caused him to be "more self-sufficient, to mow the lawn, to fix things." As this explanation suggests, James's notions of manhood are intimately tied to normative notions of the man as doer and fixer and his comments imply that his personal loss now allows him to embrace an identity that is more masculine.

The oldest interviewee, Glen (85), calls on classic notions of masculinity when he talks about what sorts of things make him feel masculine. He has already established that his best friend is a heterosexual man who loves to work on cars and his answer implies that heterosexual men define conventional masculinity. Indeed, he talks about how just being around heterosexual men shores up his own sense of masculinity—the very act of associating with a heterosexual man reinforces a sense of manhood that might otherwise be lacking. Thus, feeling masculine for Glen is about "football, phoning my best friend . . . [and] I feel most masculine when I watch him repair cars, when I have my car oiled and greased and I realize I'm with these [heterosexual] guys." As Glen's comments suggest, the essence of masculinity is embodied in his friend and his masculine activities; his friend is a sort of talisman for masculine ideals. As Connell and Messerschmidt remind us: "hegemony works in part through the production of exemplars of masculinity, symbols that have authority despite the fact that most men and boys do not fully live up to them" (2005, 846).

Disapproval/Distancing

Despite the fact that several of the men interviewed expressed a range of openness and acceptance for themselves when it came to androgynous or feminine traits and characteristics, it is especially interesting to explore what some of the interviewees have to say about masculinity and its perceived presence or absence in other men. This sort of analysis allows us to highlight the complicated ways that ambivalence manifests itself in the lives of most of these old gay men. In many ways, the uncovered ambivalence allows us to glimpse how these men use strategies of separation in order to establish who they are not. As Freitas and others (1997, 324) remind us, such attention also "fosters an awareness of actions and transaction that enables individuals to vie for preferred identities in the face of stigmatizing or discrediting social labels." Additionally, our analysis illuminates the insidiousness of hegemonic masculinity; it underscores how old gay men may contribute to their own oppression through their rejection of men who do not adhere to hegemonic ways of being male. Finally, we are reminded again of the importance of gender relations and how masculinity is defined relationally, against what is feminine.

Despite, or perhaps because of his own acknowledged struggles with masculinity, Gary (64) is among the most vocal in his disapproval of men who do not measure up to heteronormative ideals of masculinity. He is clear that he likes masculine-looking men those, as he says, who demonstrate a "lack of physical feminine characteristics." Gary also highlights another component of ideal masculinity when he identifies sexual activity and sexual attractiveness as important. Indeed, when asked what makes a man masculine, he responds by exclaiming that for him the epitome of masculinity is a "hot guy." He further elaborates in a way that highlights how notions of embodied masculinity shift when we consider sexual orientation. Thus, when asked to elaborate on his notion that "a guy who is hot is masculine," Gary obliges with this analysis wherein he objectifies and sexualizes the male body in ways similar to how heterosexual men often objectify female bodies: "It has to do with the way he moves, to a certain extent with the way he dresses." Gary seems to be criticizing here what Hennen describes as "kinesthetic effeminacy, wherein a man is judged by prevailing standards as either moving or using his voice 'like a woman'" (Hennen 2008). To be considered "hot" by Gary one must sufficiently discipline the body to comport to hegemonic standards of masculinity.

On the other hand, not all of the men interviewed were disapproving of gay men who did not uphold ideal notions of masculinity or who sometimes exhibited what some would describe as feminine characteristics. The story here is complicated, however. On one hand, the narratives underscore that these old men are not monolithic and also that we must consider context as important. Thus, some of the men interviewed spoke of responding one way in a particular context and another way when circumstances were different. For instance, Bart (67) responded to the question about whether masculinity was important to him with a loud "Oh, Yes," and even went on to exclaim that "[I] like my men to look like men." This claim describes Bart's personal desires about ideal partners and, as such, differs from his willingness to be accepting of more feminine men in contexts beyond those of personal desire. Consequently, he reinforces this distinction when he later talks openly and warmly about the gay world he inhabits where gay drag queens and "gay peacocks" are acceptable and welcome. Jake (78) also is very open about his own presentation of self, especially around other gays. He exclaims at one point: "I'm an effeminate person and more so with gays." At other times as we talk, he refers comfortably to himself as "an old queen." On the other hand, some men take a different approach and their comments illuminate the tensions and conflicts in how they negotiate their own notions of authentic masculinity. Victor (71) exemplifies this tension when he says that masculinity is not important to him and yet he is also clear that he dislikes "effeminacy" in men. Indeed, not only does he associate such characteristics with drag queens but his words suggest a negative association with things feminine. Thus, he claims that he has "never been comfortable with 'nelly queens.' [I] don't enjoy drag." At another point in the interview, Victor is more explicit in his negative connection of effeminacy in gay men with lower-class women. He talks about not liking gay men who are "slutty [and who wear] ridiculously tight pants." Conversations such as those with Victor, increase our awareness of how distancing strategies work. Accordingly, we see how some gay men protect their own identities by choosing to disidentify with gay men who represent "visual caricatures" (Freitas et al. 1997). Nonetheless, as we have argued already, Victor and others who use distancing tactics are not engaged in wholesale rejection of homosexuals or homosexuality. Rather, such responses illustrate the complicated work of stigma management. Such work brings to mind Goffman's seminal work on stigma and his insight about ambivalence toward similar others: "he can neither embrace his group nor let it go" (Goffman 1963, 109).

Ageism in Gay Communities

A predominant theme that interviewees cited repeatedly was the youth obsession of gay culture and of its consequences for themselves and others. Glen (85), for instance, talked at length when we first met about these issues and, as a political activist for gay issues, it is clear that he thinks a lot about these concerns. He is extremely well-networked and well-known in the gay communities of his city and well beyond. Asked to respond to what he sees as the level of ageism among gays, Glen puts

into words a sentiment that the others share "gays are much more ageist than straights." Eric (60) sees this ageism as having to do with how gay culture "really accentuates youth and body and physical conditions." Guy goes on to talk about gay social life and the dominance of "the bar scene" in urban areas, and he makes the point that "in many a bar, a man over 40 would not be looked at because he is too old." At least in part because they face ageism in this social setting, he argues that, in his experience many gay men become increasingly socially isolated. Here is how he responds to a question about what happens to gay men in their 60s, 70s, and 80s: "Well, such men stop going to bars, [they] become isolated, [they] become introverted, [they] become loners, [they] become peculiar people. From being in their 30s where they had a number of friends, as each decade comes they have fewer friends and go out less." Nevertheless, unmentioned in this narrative is the role that cohort plays in how these particular old gay men experience growing old. As well, what Glen is not explicit about at this point in the interview—although he later raises this issue—is the importance of having a partner and how this can mitigate the loneliness of being old and gay. Others raise this issue and underscore the varying strategies adopted by these old gay men to ensure a viable social or sexual life in the face of the ageism they see in the gay communities around them. For instance, Victor (71) talks about his current situation with his life partner of 22 years (who is 24 years younger than he is): "Well, if I had to go out and compete for sexual partners like I did years ago, that would be a definite concern. But I've got what I want and he accepts me as I am."

As well as having partners, some of the men interviewed are also involved with a group called "Prime Timers" which several describe as a social group for "older gay men and their [younger] admirers." The extent to which this organization is joined by men who are white, middle class and beyond is not known to us but comments made by the interviewees suggest that the chapters attended by these men predominantly meet these class and race profiles. On the international group's website, Prime

Timers are described as "Older gay or bisexual men (and younger men who admire mature men)" (www.primetimer-sww.org/about.htm). Glen, who is heavily involved with this national organization (which has numerous local chapters), tells us that these younger admirers are not ageist because they like men older than themselves. Yet, and several interviewees make this point, Prime Timers is an organization that in many ways highlights the ageism of gay culture by reinforcing hegemonic ideals of what constitutes an attractive man. Consequently, even if inadvertently, this organization reproduces the notion that youth and youthful attractiveness and sexual vitality are the coins of the realm. Here is what Victor (71) tells us in these regards:

> I think, like most aging or older gay men, I find younger men attractive. I think that's why a lot of Prime Timers don't get together with each other. The majority of them would say that they would love to have a partner and most of them don't . . . they want somebody younger and that's the way it is . . . I can walk into a room of 100 Prime Timers and I might be very fond of most of them but I don't want to go to bed with any of them . . . I think they are all very aware of that.

Gary (64) also tells a story that not only reinforces the ageism suggested above but also hints at his attempts to cover up his real age, to use the strategy of passing as younger than his chronological age. When asked if he is comfortable telling his age, he responds "It depends on the people . . . if I am trying to chat up some man I have to figure out 'Now, if I tell you the truth' is he going to find out that I'm too old." Thus, Gary illustrates his own internalization of ageist notions and his narrative also portrays the stigma older gay men experience when they seek to find partners—especially younger men—for sexual pleasure Victor and Gary's comments also underscore the importance of sex in the gay world, even among old men. These comments allow us to glimpse how they construct gayness. Indeed, Eric (60) is explicit in this regard: "Gays [are] defined in terms of sex. It's what defines us."

Richard (69), who has taken a vow of celibacy, is not as accepting as Victor and others of the ageist self-denigration within Prime Timers. He has recently decided not to attend their functions because "when an admirer [a young man] walks in [to the room] and everybody flocks around him, I can't stand this." Eric (60) also resists what he sees as the youth obsession of exclusively gay groups and allows: "I don't socialize just with gays." He has recently experienced a break up with his younger partner and learned from close friends that the partner saw Eric's being older as a negative. Yet, illustrating how pervasive is the social value placed on youthful attractiveness and how insidious ageism is, Eric admits that he does not date men over 50. He tells of how he has had several arguments with close lesbian friends who accuse him of being ageist in his choice of partners. He acknowledges his own ageism but still observes that he was recently "flattered to hell and back when a 27-year-old model wanted to see me."

Negotiating Old Bodies: Resisting Old Age

What can we learn from these gay men's masculinity and about how their various social locations shape how they inhabit and negotiate old bodies? How do they make sense of what it means to be physically old, and to look old, in a world that denigrates old age? How does being white and relatively affluent influence their experiences with old bodies? How do they negotiate and respond to masculinity scripts that glorify young bodies, especially in gay culture? The picture is far from being a straightforward one. The narratives of these men uncover the complications and ambivalences of managing stigmatized identities. What we learn is that in coping with the stigmas of being old gay men there is no one script that all follow. In some ways, as gay men who spend time in gay communities, they have had the experience of being defined as old for many more years than would be the case if they were heterosexual; they have learned to deal with this marked identity in a variety of ways.

High levels of education and other life privileges that accompany being white and economically secure provide these men with the wherewithal to resist aging and to be more positive about some aspects of being old. Coping with the stigmas of being gay has also taught them some valuable life lessons about oppression, how to manage it and, ideally, how to resist it. Nevertheless, there are commonalities among these men that illustrate the oppressive nature of age relations. Their accounts reveal strategies they employ to manage the ageism that shapes their responses to their own bodies and the bodies of others.

At age 64 Gary is a large, bearded man who lives alone but also within what he calls a "gay world, not community." Gary talks frequently throughout our interview about sex and his desire to have frequent sex. He is keenly aware that his age is a distinct disadvantage in the gay world he moves in, especially when seeking sex partners. For instance, when asked whether he is comfortable telling his age, he is the only man interviewed who suggests that he sometimes hides his age or, at the very least, avoids talking about it. Gary's motivation to avoid telling his age is intimately connected to his desire to find a sex partner and the fact that he feels it necessary to hide his real age underscores the ageism that exists within the gay world. Gary's strategy of passing or covering also illustrates how he works to minimize the impact of his stigmatized status as an old man.

As Gary's narrative demonstrates, ageism gets reinforced and reproduced through ideas that to be old is bad and to be seen as more youthful than one's chronological age is good. Covering or passively "passing" as younger than one's real age is a strategy sometimes used by our interviewees and they provide us evidence that they use this strategy specifically to accommodate the ageism they encounter in their daily lives. Thus, while in one voice they tell us that they are comfortable with where they are in their lives, that being old brings a measure of contentment, they also echo this sentiment of Peter: (62) "I do not feel old, so when I hear the word 'old' I can't relate to it." Put another way, Bart (67) says: "I don't like the term 'old.'. . . I hate [the term] 'senior citizens'." Gary (64) illustrates

another form of denial "I do not admit that my body has slowed down." Victor (71) also refuses to see himself as "old" and all of the negative things that that implies. Indeed, he exhibits a level of denial and ambivalence that is typical of almost all of the men interviewed. Unwilling to use the word "old" in reference to himself, he claims: "I do not see myself as an older person I do not feel like an older person. I don't feel much different than I can remember feeling 40 to 50 years ago. I am thrilled with that I'm so glad that is the case." At least for Victor, but we suspect for others too, acceptance of being gay comes more easily than acceptance of being old.

Illuminating the complex ways that gay culture reinforces youthful and hegemonic masculinity and how old gay men, even if unwittingly, adhere to such notions, several talk about how gay men age better than heterosexual men because they pay more attention to keeping youthful bodies through exercise and disciplining their bodies. Responses vary as to why this might be the case. For instance, Eric (60) makes a general claim that "appearance is more of a concern with gay men." Gary (64) who is, by his own assessment, 75 pounds overweight, supports this same notion by laughingly explaining that "straight men age quicker than gay men do. I think gay men take better care of themselves." This notion of paying attention to one's appearance, doing the work necessary to "look good" (meaning youthful) is also captured in this comment of Bart's (67): "Many, many heterosexual friends, some younger than I, look twice as old as I am because they have given up." Raymond is quite explicit about the ageism that underscores this obligatory dictate of keeping up appearances: "old gay men feel compelled to do everything they can to hide the ravages of their body. They dye their hair, they have facelifts, they wear clothing that they think makes them look younger . . . they do a lot of exercise." However, Raymond and others do not reflect upon how their social class (and race) privileges provide them with the means to consume more youthful lifestyles, to exercise, and to look younger for more years than their less affluent peers.

Peter (62) also claims that gay men age better than heterosexual men: "if you were to compare heterosexual men my age to homosexual men my age, the homosexual men are much more interested in what they look like. They have not gone to pot, to seed. They are snappy dressers . . . they are conscious of their physical appearance." Peter's comparison of older gay and heterosexual men's appearances highlights his ageist and class-specific notions of how gay men are more concerned than heterosexual men with embracing youthful bodies and youthful fashion as ways to avoid being seen as old. Yet, underscoring the often contradictory and ambivalent nature of such responses, Peter also claims that gay men do not chase youthful bodies as they age. Indeed, he decries such stereotypes—at least in his own circle of friends: "The gay men I know are not like that. They do not work out and wear youthful clothes. They are not in the 'silly old fool syndrome.' The gay people I know are content with their ages."

In keeping with the story above, others also told stories that left no doubt that they were ambivalent about growing old and especially about looking old. Their stories provide us a picture of the ambivalences and contradictions that are ongoing in the management of stigmatized identities. For instance, Raymond (67), who is generally very positive about being old, tells us of another strategy for coping with old age, one that highlights how old age is "contagious" and thus, must be avoided. Consequently, Raymond tells how he avoids others who are old: "All of the friends I have from the time that I was 40 are much younger than I am." Perhaps by associating with younger people, one can stave off the inevitable, because Raymond is also quite sure that getting older makes a man less masculine: "I think most men think that. Because most men tie masculinity to their physical prowess. And once they sit in a wheelchair and can't feed themselves anymore, I think they feel very . . . emasculated." Raymond's sentiment about embodied old age and the resulting diminution of masculinity is shared by James (64) who also sees masculinity and independence as inevitably compromised by old age. In

response to the question about whether of not being old makes men less masculine, he claims: "Yea, I think it does in that they become dependent. When you lose that element of dignity, I think of the product called 'Depends'."

For affluent consumers, especially those who are white, cosmetic surgery offers a way to regain or sustain a more youthful appearance, to cover signs of aging and to pass as younger than one's chronological age. Such surgery illuminates the strategies of ongoing appearance management that can be called upon in the face of "stigmatizing or discrediting social labels" (Freitas et al., 1997, 324). This analysis allows us to glimpse how some of these men actively work to acquire a preferred embodied identity of being not old—or at least not looking as old as they are. Seeking to maintain a youthful appearance through cosmetic surgery was something that four of these interviewees were willing to consider. For instance, James (64) claimed that "If I had lots of money, I guess I would. I'd have a body makeover." Eric (60) was similarly inclined and he admitted that he had been "seriously considering it for a year or two." He told how he had gone so far as to get the name of a local cosmetic surgeon; he was interested in both a facelift and liposuction around the abdominal area. Victor talked about how he had considered cosmetic eye surgery to reduce the bags under his eyes ten or fifteen years ago but had never gotten around to doing it. Cost was a disincentive but also "discomfort," plus the fact that "I don't trust it. I don't know that it's safe." Gary (64) had this to say about cosmetic surgery: "you've got to deal with what you've got . . . next time I go to Brazil, I'm going to have some face work done." "I have no interest in plastic surgery and tightening up and getting rid of wrinkles," he claimed. Instead, Gary wanted to remove some other signs of aging: "The liver spots I'll get removed and some of the moles." Using makeup provides a cheaper and less intrusive way to hide certain signs of aging, such as the liver or age spots referred to by Gary. Bart (67), for instance, talked openly about how "a good five years ago I tried to cover up some aging marks" by using makeup. He was especially proud of the fact that he was so adept at using it that "you'd never know I had it on." Yet, underscoring how complex and sometimes paradoxical are approaches to aging, Bart told of how he had stopped using makeup to hide his aging because "I am pretty much trying to be honest with myself and to others." By revealing his true physiological self, and accepting the embodied stigma(ta) of old age, Bart also moves himself away from engaging in feminine behavior (wearing makeup). Stories such as Bart's shed some light on the shifting and fluid nature of how some old gay men negotiate multiple stigmatized identities.

Even among this small number of old gay men, the reactions to the aging process are impressively wide-ranging: it is clear that there is no one way for gay men to grow old. In fact, given their widely varying life histories, the multiple forms of masculinity at play, and the variety of involvement in gay communities, it is quite possible that old gay men's experiences with aging may be even more diverse than those of their heterosexual peers.

CONCLUSIONS

This study gives voice to the experiences of a group of men who rarely have been heard. We trust that their voices will help illuminate the experiences of other old gay men like them, and provoke further discussion on the ways such men grapple with their sexuality, with aging, with masculinities, and with how their bodies are critical to their sense-making of all of these. Through the use of an intersectionality perspective that highlights not only race, class, and gender but also age and sexuality, we uncover how privileges and disadvantages are negotiated, we begin to understand how gender, race, and class privileges help mitigate forms of oppression stemming from sexuality and old age.

As well, the narrative analysis used in this paper allows us to explore in some depth how a small, privileged group of old, white, relatively affluent gay men experience key corporeal aspects of growing old in a culture that glorifies hegemonic masculinity and its key components of youthfulness and heterosexuality. Again, we come to understand

how they have forms of capital (through class, race, and gender privileges) that allow them to resist aging and, sometimes, to pass as younger than their chronological ages. Our focus on this marginalized population brings attention that is much needed in studies of masculinities. We learn firsthand how many struggle to live up to hegemonic ideals of what it means to be a man and to look like one. In addition, we also come to appreciate the diversity of their approaches to manhood as they strive to accomplish some sense of authenticity.

Additionally, we appreciate the complicated and contradictory nature of their approaches to being men who are old and gay. Narrative analysis proves particularly salient as a method that exposes the ways that the body is central to notions of masculinity; the voices of the interviewees allow us to glimpse the contradictions and messiness of how they grapple with embodied masculinity throughout the life course. As well, the narratives attest to a long-standing assumption about gay culture: ageism is prominent, and much of this ageism is related to the body. Indeed, their words lend credence to Laws's (1995) claim that ageism is an embodied form of oppression. This should come as no surprise, given that gay male culture puts a very specific body on a pedestal, and this body is in no way old. Regardless of their many successes in other areas of their lives, many of these men have experienced the stigmatization of their aging bodies.

We gain, too, a greater understanding of how age relations render the body a site of struggle and ambivalence. These struggles and ambivalences demonstrate themselves in myriad ways. For instance, we hear over and over again how, despite a declared comfort with themselves, that comfort has more to do with being gay than with being old; most subscribe to negative notions of being old and looking old. That they frequently enact these negative notions when they interact with other old gay men reinforces Chen's (1999) claim that gay men become arbiters of their own oppression. As relatively affluent retirees, most feel fairly keenly the continuous obligation to consume products and lifestyles (exercising, dieting, youthful clothes, etc.) that reinforce ageist notions of old bodies as undesirable bodies. Even though the men sometimes positively framed contrasts to heterosexual men, who they see as having "given up" on stopping their bodily declines, there is a subtext to the narratives, one that sees old age as something to avoid or resist. Indeed, they confirm what Cruikshank (2003) reminds us of old age is increasingly pathologized in our culture.

We suggest that the interviewees, as white professional men, have much in common with similarly situated heterosexual men, especially when they discuss their aging bodies (Slevin, forthcoming). As we argued in the introduction, in addition to the socially constructed nature of aging in all its permutations, a fact glares: the physical body ages and at some point begins to break down. An aching joint and a non-responsive penis know no sexual orientation. Nowadays, consumer society encourages all men to chase youthful ideals—whether they are 30 or 80. Class and race privileges allow some men to postpone the inevitabilities of aging bodies and to adhere to hegemonic masculine ideals for longer than less affluent men. Yet, there are some differences in the way gay men react to the bodily changes that accompany aging. For example, few heterosexual men would dare to use makeup, as Bart (67) admitted to doing. Though these men face little discrimination due to their sexual orientation, they do face significant discrimination as old men in gay communities. And in the bitterest of ironies, some of this discrimination is carried out by other old gay men as they continually attempt to construct positive identities through strategies that distance themselves from other old men.

We see fruitful possibilities for researchers interested in the lives of old gay men. The first and most promising avenue for research leads directly to the group Prime Timers. As noted, some of the interview respondents in this study had heated views of this organization, and questioned the role that it plays within the older gay male community. While some see the group as an oasis from invisibility, there are signs that Prime Timers chapters (or at least some of the men involved in them) perpetuate and reinforce the very ageism that they seek

to address. A large-scale, multi-site study of Prime Timers and its membership could make great strides in advancing our understanding of the complexities we identified above. Studying the membership experiences of men at a variety of stages of old age could help us to understand the various points at which these men develop problematic relationships with the organization. Do younger Prime Timers have more positive experiences than those who are at a more advanced stage of old age? What steps does the organization, or specific chapters within the organization, take to address these issues among its constituencies?

Those who "admire" old gay men (as some of the interviewees put it, and as the organization explicitly states) are also worthy of study. For example, we recounted a story from Ed (60), who had a 27-year-old admirer, and a male model at that. Who is this young man, and how does he conceive of his admiration for older men? If the goal is to decrease the ageism that old gay men face in gay communities, in-depth analyses of such young men certainly would be a place to start. In addition to delineating what they find attractive about older men, another topic of interest would be the stigma such men might themselves face from others in the gay community. The common, immediate assumption that such a man simply must be a gold-digger is yet another window into the ageism of the gay community.

In addition to Prime Timers, one might explore other options for old gay men to be involved in gay communities. Of course old gay men may (and do) become involved in all aspects of gay communities, but their presence in two subcultures is particularly striking: the bears and the sadomasochism communities. The bear community rejects the strict body norms (washboard abs, hairless torsos) that the broader gay community tends to value. Therefore, it should be no surprise that some old gay men find the bears a welcome respite, as their aging bodies will be treated with a greater level of admiration than elsewhere in the gay community. Some old gay men find a place in the SM community, serving in the role of a "daddy" to submissive (and usually younger) participants. This community actually may allow old gay men to turn their aging into a distinct advantage. A comparative study of these three communities (Prime Timers, bears, and SM), and why various men seek out each of these communities would offer some understanding of the way old gay men see themselves and their places within gay culture. Hennen's groundbreaking study of communities of faeries, bears, and leathermen (2008) is replete with insights about gay masculinities, but he does not deal with age in any in-depth fashion. Thus, these groups are worthy of much more attention.

A final possibility for continuing this line of research involves an expansion of the study to middle-aged gay men. Are these men indeed considered old within their gay communities, and do they in some ways buy into this perception? The rising generation of middle-aged gay men offers unique research opportunities, as these men are among the first to come of age in a culture with markedly less stigma attached to gay identities, as well as less imminent concern over AIDS. Their aging may look quite different from the aging of their gay brothers a generation before them. We should not pass up the opportunity to study this process as it occurs.

NOTES

1. Because "old" carries a unique stigma in our culture we want to reclaim its positive connotations, to naturalize and neutralize it. Thus, we use it throughout this article (rather than "older") in an activist manner. See Calasanti and Slevin 2001 (pp. 9–10) for a more detailed discussion.

2. Throughout the paper, we use pseudonyms to protect the identities of the respondents.

REFERENCES

Barrett, D. 2000. Masculinity among working-class gay males. In *Gay masculinities*, edited by P. Nardi, 176–205. Thousand Oaks, CA: Sage.

Bennett, K. C., and N. L. Thompson. 1991. Accelerated aging and male homosexuality: Australian evidence in a continuing debate. *Journal of Homosexuality* 20: 65–75.

Brekhus, W. 2003. *Peacocks, chameleons, centaurs: Gay suburbia and the grammar of social identity*. Chicago: University of Chicago Press.

Calasanti, T. M. 2004. Feminist gerontology and old men. *Journal of Gerontology* 59B: 305–314.

Calasanti, T. M., and K. F. Slevin. 2001. *Gender, social inequalities, and aging*. Walnut Creek, CA: AltaMira Press.

Calasanti, T. M., and K. F. Slevin. 2006. Introduction: Age matters. In *Age matters: Realigning feminist thinking*, edited by T. M. Calasanti and K. F. Slevin, 1–17. New York: Routledge.

Calasanti, T. M. and N. King. 2005. Firming the floppy penis: Age, class, and gender relations in the lives of old men. *Men and Masculinities* 8: 3–23.

Cantu, L. 2000. Entre hombres/between men: Latino masculinities and homosexualities. In *Gay masculinities*, edited by P. Nardi, 224–246. Thousand Oaks, CA: Sage.

Carpenter, L. M. 2002. Gender and the social construction of virginity loss in the contemporary United States. *Gender & Society* 16: 345–365.

Chase, S. E. 2005. Narrative inquiry: Multiple lenses, approaches, voices. In *Qualitative research*, 3rd ed., edited by N. K. Denzin and Y. Lincoln, 651–679. Thousand Oaks, CA: Sage.

Chen, A. S. 1999. Lives at the center of the periphery, lives at the periphery of the center: Chinese American masculinity and bargaining with hegemony. *Gender & Society* 13: 584–607.

Collins, P. H. 2000. *Black feminist thought: Knowledge, consciousness, and the politics of empowerment*. New York: Routledge.

Connell, R. W. 1995. *Masculinities*. Berkeley: University of California Press.

Connell, R. W. and J. W. Messerschmidt. 2005. Hegemonic masculinity: Rethinking the concept. *Gender & Society* 19: 829–859.

Crenshaw, K. 1991. Mapping the margins: Intersectionality, identity politics, and violence against women of color. *Stanford Law Review* 46: 1241–1299.

Cruikshank, M. 2003. *Learning to be old: Gender, culture, and aging*. Lanham, MD: Rowman and Littlefield.

Dyer, R. 2002. *The culture of queers*. New York: Routledge.

Emslie, C., K. Hunt, and R. O'Brien. 2004. Masculinities in older men: A qualitative study in the west of Scotland. *The Journal of Men's Studies* 12: 207–226.

Faircloth, C. A., ed. 2003. *Aging bodies: Images and everyday experience.* Walnut Creek, CA: AltaMira Press.

Freitas, A., S. Kaiser, D. J. Chandler, D. C. Hall, J. Kim, and T. Hammidi. 1997. Appearance management as border construction: Least favorite clothing, group distancing, and identity not! *Sociological Inquiry* 67: 323–335

Gilleard, C., and P. Higgs. 2000. *Cultures of ageing: Self, citizen and the body.* Harlow, England: Prentice Hall.

Goffman, E. 1963. *Stigma: Notes on the management of spoiled identity.* Englewood Cliffs, NJ: Prentice-Hall.

Han, S. 2000. Asian American gay men's (dis)claim on masculinity. In *Gay masculinities*, edited by P. Nardi, 206–223. Thousand Oaks, CA: Sage.

Heaphy, B. 2007. Sexualities, gender and ageing. *Current Sociology* 55: 193–210.

Hennen, P. 2005. Bear bodies, bear masculinity: Recuperation, resistance, or retreat? *Gender & Society* 19: 25–43.

Hennen, P. 2008. *Faeries, bears, and leathermen: Men in community queering the masculine.* Chicago: University of Chicago Press.

Hostetler, A. J. 2004. Old, gay, and alone? The ecology of well-being among middle-aged and older single gay men. In *Gay and lesbian aging: Research and future directions*, edited by G. Herdt and B. De Vnes. New York: Springer.

Jones, J. and S. Pugh. 2005. Ageing gay men. *Men and Masculinities* 7: 248–260.

Katz, S. 2005. *Cultural aging: Life course, lifestyle, and senior worlds.* Ontario, Canada: Broadview Press.

Kimmel, M. 1996. *Manhood in America: A cultural history.* New York: The Free Press.

Laws, G. 1995. Understanding ageism: Lessons from feminism and postmodernism. *The Gerontologist* 35(1): 112–118.

Lindau, S. T., L. P. Schumm, E. O. Laumann, W. Levmson, C. A. O'Muircheartaigh, and L. J. Waite. 2007. A study of sexuality and health among older adults in the United States. *New England Journal of Medicine* 375: 762–774.

Linneman, T. 2008. How do you solve a problem like Will Truman? The feminization of gay men on Will & Grace. *Men and Masculinities* 10: 583–603.

Loe, M. 2003. *The rise of Viagra: How the little blue pill changed sex in America.* New York: New York University Press.

Loftus, J. 2001. America's liberalization in attitudes toward homosexuality, 1973 to 1998. *American Sociological Review* 66:762–782.

Marshall, B. L. 2006. The new virility: Viagra, male aging and sexual function. *Sexualities* 9: 345–362.

Marshall, B. L., and S. Katz. 2002. Forever functional: Sexual fitness and the ageing male body. *Body & Society* 8: 43–70.

McVittie, C., and J. Willock. 2006. 'You can't fight windmills': How older men do health, ill health, and masculinities. *Qualitative Health Research* 16: 788–801.

Meadows, R. and K. Davidson. 2006. Maintaining manliness in later life: Hegemonic masculinities and emphasized femininities. In *Age matters: Realigning feminist thinking*, edited by T. M. Calasanti and K. F. Slevin, 295–312. New York: Routledge.

Messner, M. A. 1992. *Power at play: Sports and the problem of masculinity.* Boston: Beacon Press.

Nardi, P. 2000. 'Anything for a sis, Mary': An introduction to gay masculinities. In *Gay masculinities*, edited by P. Nardi, 1–11. Thousand Oaks, CA: Sage.

Oberg, P. 2003. Images vs. experiences of the aging body. In *Aging bodies: Images and everyday experience*, edited by C. A. Faircloth, 103–139. Walnut Creek, CA: AltaMira Press.

Prime Timers World Wide. 2008. *Prime Timers World Wide.* http//www.primetimersww.org/about.htm (accessed January 13, 2008).

Quam, J. K., and G. S. Whitford. 1992. Adaptation and age-related expectations of older gay and lesbian adults. *The Gerontologist* 32: 367–374.

Rosenfeld, D. 2003. The homosexual body in lesbian and gay elders' narratives. In *Aging bodies: Images and everyday experience*, edited by C. A. Faircloth, 171–203. Walnut Creek, CA: AltaMira Press.

Slevin, K. F. forthcoming. Disciplining bodies: The aging experiences of old heterosexual and gay men. *Generations.*

Slevin, K. F. 2006. The embodied experiences of old lesbians. In *Age matters: Realigning feminist thinking*, edited by T. M. Calasanti and K. F. Slevin, 247–268. New York: Routledge.

Spector-Mersel, G. 2006. Never-aging stories: Western hegemonic masculinity scripts. *Journal of Gender Studies* 15: 67–82.

Thompson, E. H. 1994. Older men as invisible men in contemporary society. In *Older men's lives*, edited by E. H. Thompson, 1–21. London: Sage.

Thompson, E. H., Jr., and P. M. Whearty. 2004. Older men's social participation: The importance of masculinity ideology. *The Journal of Men's Studies* 13: 5–24.

Turner, B. S. 1996. *The body and society*. 2nd ed. London: Sage.

Wahler, J., and S. G. Gabbay. 1997. Gay male aging: A review of the literature. *Journal of Gay & Lesbian Social Services* 6: 1–20.

IF MEN COULD MENSTRUATE

Gloria Steinem

A white minority of the world has spent centuries conning us into thinking that a white skin makes people superior—even though the only thing it really does is make them more subject to ultraviolet rays and to wrinkles. Male human beings have built whole cultures around the idea that penis-envy is "natural" to women—though having such an unprotected organ might be said to make men vulnerable, and the power to give birth makes womb-envy at least as logical.

In short, the characteristics of the powerful, whatever they may be, are thought to be better than the characteristics of the powerless—and logic has nothing to do with it.

What would happen, for instance, if suddenly, magically, men could menstruate and women could not?

The answer is clear—menstruation would become an enviable, boastworthy, masculine event:

Men would brag about how long and how much.

Boys would mark the onset of menses, that longed-for proof of manhood, with religious rituals and stag parties.

Congress would fund a National Institute of Dysmenorrhea to help stamp out monthly discomforts.

Sanitary supplies would be federally funded and free. (Of course, some men would still pay for the prestige of commercial brands such as John Wayne Tampons, Muhammad Ali's Rope-a-dope Pads, Joe Namath Jock Shields—"For Those Light Bachelor Days," and Robert "Baretta" Blake Maxi-Pads.)

Military men, right-wing politicians, and religious fundamentalists would cite menstruation ("*men*-struation") as proof that only men could serve in the Army ("you have to give blood to take blood"), occupy political office ("can women be aggressive without that steadfast cycle governed by the planet Mars?"), be priests and ministers ("how could a woman give her blood for our sins?"), or rabbis ("without the monthly loss of impurities, women remain unclean").

Male radicals, left-wing politicians, and mystics, however, would insist that women are equal, just different; and that any woman could enter their ranks if only she were willing to self-inflict a major wound every month ("you *must* give blood for the revolution"), recognize the preeminence of menstrual issues, or subordinate her selfness to all men in their Cycle of Enlightenment.

Street guys would brag ("I'm a three-pad man") or answer praise from a buddy ("Man, you lookin' *good*!") by giving fives and saying, "Yeah, man, I'm on the rag!"

TV shows would treat the subject at length. ("Happy Days": Richie and Potsie try to convince Fonzie that he is still "The Fonz," though he has missed two periods in a row.) So would newspapers. (SHARK SCARE THREATENS MENSTRUATING MEN. JUDGE CITES MONTHLY STRESS IN PARDONING RAPIST.) And movies. (Newman and Redford in "Blood Brothers"!)

Men would convince women that intercourse was *more* pleasurable at "that time of the month."

Lesbians would be said to fear blood and therefore life itself—though probably only because they needed a good menstruating man.

Of course, male intellectuals would offer the most moral and logical arguments. How could a woman master any discipline that demanded a sense of time, space, mathematics, or measurement, for instance, without that in-built gift for measuring the cycles of the moon and planets—and thus for measuring anything at all? In the rarefied fields of philosophy and religion, could women compensate for missing the rhythm of the universe? Or for their lack of symbolic death-and-resurrection every month?

Liberal males in every field would try to be kind: the fact that "these people" have no gift for measuring life or connecting to the universe, the liberals would explain, should be punishment enough.

And how would women be trained to react? One can imagine traditional women agreeing to all these arguments with a staunch and smiling masochism ("The ERA would force housewives to wound themselves every month": Phyllis Schlafly. "Your husband's blood is as sacred as that of Jesus—and so sexy, too!": Marabel Morgan.) Reformers and Queen Bees would try to imitate men, and *pretend* to have a monthly cycle. All feminists would explain endlessly that men, too, needed to be liberated from the false idea of Martian aggressiveness, just as women needed to escape the bonds of menses-envy. Radical feminists would add that the oppression of the nonmenstrual was the pattern for all other oppressions. ("Vampires were our first freedom fighters!") Cultural feminists would develop a bloodless imagery in art and literature. Socialist feminists would insist that only under capitalism would men be able to monopolize menstrual blood. . . .

In fact, if men could menstruate, the power justifications could probably go on forever.

If we let them.

MASCULINITY, HEALTH, AND HUMAN RIGHTS: A SOCIOCULTURAL FRAMEWORK

Dr. Shari L. Dworkin

A SOCIOCULTURAL FRAMEWORK

It is clear that women have a right to health. In my own area of research, a very large research literature and public health discourse converge on the main arguments to protect women from HIV, violence, and a lack of sexual and reproductive health. Readers are likely quite familiar with the main claims: Women are culturally, structurally, and interpersonally subordinate to men, which puts them at risk of HIV, violence, and poor reproductive health outcomes. To become more empowered, women need sexual and reproductive rights, human rights, property rights, protection from violence, access to and control over income and assets, improved access to education, safe schools, increased cultural visibility, access to political participation and leadership, household bargaining power, safer sex negotiating power, reproductive health decision-making power, female-initiated methods of HIV/STI protection, and the integration of family planning and HIV/AIDS prevention, treatment, and care activities.[1]

But what do men need to protect their HIV/AIDS risks, their sexual and reproductive health, or their right to health or health care more generally? What do rights have to do with it? When one types "men's right to health" or "men's right

to health care" into Google, it asks "do you mean women's right to health" or "do you mean women's right to health care?" When one types "men's right to health" or "men's right to health care" into PubMed,[2] the number of relevant articles is around 20, many of which are actually about women's health or about involving men to improve reproductive health care outcomes with women. When one types terms about rights to health or health care for women into PubMed, thousands of articles arise. This basic exercise is a signifier of the state of the field, and numerous questions therefore remain: (1) Does gender inequality affect men's health and men's access to health care?; (2) Do men have sexual and reproductive rights?; (3) Are men only privileged and empowered in terms of their right to health relative to women and therefore deserve less attention than women or are there unique aspects of gender relations that disproportionately shape men's negative health outcomes?; (4) If gender inequality negatively influences men's health outcomes or access to health, do all men pay the price equally?; and (5) What right to health or health care will society help men achieve when several of our most prized social institutions (i.e., sports, the military) produce dominant notions of masculinity that not only privilege men and reward men enormously but also disproportionately harm, injure, disable, and kill them?

This paper draws upon a sociocultural framework from masculinity studies and applies it to the case of men's health with the goal of providing the legal field with critical considerations that might shape a stronger future research agenda in the area

Shari Dworkin, "Masculinity, Health, and Human Rights: A Sociocultural Framework" In *Hastings International & Comparative Law Review,* 33(2) Summer, 2010, pp 461–478. Copyright © 2010 Reprinted by permission of the author.

of masculinity, rights, and health. In the sections that follow, I will attempt to lay out a fairly important paradox in the study of men's health: It is well recognized that gender inequality affects women and that men enjoy numerous *cultural and institutional privileges that negatively shape women's health outcome.* These commonly understood drivers of women's poor health have led to crucial and much needed linkages between women's rights and health. However, men do not only enjoy cultural and institutional privileges relative to women and cause harm to women's health. *Men are also deeply negatively affected by gender relations and gender inequality*—and this harms their health and access to health care. Furthermore, men are not homogenous as a group and there are vast *differences and inequalities among men in terms of their health and health care access.* This means that men *do not equally share in the rewards of masculinity and it is marginalized men who in fact disproportionately pay the costs of adhering to narrow definitions of masculinity.* They pay with poor health outcomes and constrained access to health care. They pay this cost not only because of racism and class inequalities but also because of the unique forms that masculinities take among poor and working-class racial/ethnic men.

What I hope to make clear in this article, then, is that even though men enjoy numerous privileges relative to women and enjoy valuations and reward structures that are advantageous to men socially, culturally, and fiscally; *men's and women's health are harmed when men adhere to narrow and constraining definitions of masculinity.* Thus, scholars from numerous disciplines, including legal scholars, need to become keenly aware of the nuances surrounding the role that masculinities play in shaping health. It is vital to consider men's differential social positioning across race, class, and sexuality in societies around the globe. Prior to delving more into the specificities of the sociocultural framework that will be drawn upon in this article, it is first important to assess the state of men's health and access to care: Are men so privileged?

The health of men and men's access to health care in the United States and worldwide is increasingly an area of academic interest and growing concern.[3] An old adage is that "women get sicker, men die quicker. "Indeed, men die nearly seven years younger than women in the U.S., and globally, men's life expectancy is lower than women's in most countries around the world.[4] In addition, in the U.S., the mortality rates of the twelve leading causes of death (coronary artery disease, cerebrovascular accident, cancer, chronic obstructive pulmonary disease, flu, liver disease, pneumonia, diabetes mellitus, HIV, trauma, motor vehicle accident, and homicide) show that men's rates are higher than women's in each and every category.[5] In almost every age category, men die at greater rates than do women; often from preventable causes. In North America, the leading causes of death among males ages 15–19 are car accidents, suicide, and AIDS, and all are at rates higher than for women.[6] Men abuse alcohol and other drugs at least twice as often as women and commit 86% of the violent crimes.[7] Globally, violence, alcohol abuse, accidents, other substance use, homicide, dangerous workplaces, and poor management of stress and anger all contribute to men's higher rates of mortality.[8]

Additionally, the male mortality rate for the ten most common cancers that affect both sexes is double the female mortality rate[9] and men are more likely than women to suffer from severe chronic conditions and fatal diseases.[10] Despite the fact that women are much more often the victims of interpersonal violence at the hands of men than the reverse, it is also crucial to underscore that men kill other men at a significantly higher rate than they do women (the high homicide rate reflects this, in part).[11] Furthermore, men's rate of suicide is much higher than women's in every country in the world.[12] In workplaces in the U.S., men constitute more than ninety percent of those employed in dangerous occupations, and men have a much higher workplace injury rate than do women.[13] Men are also injured in and killed in wars at far greater rates than women; a result of their much greater access to this institution.[14]

Biomedical frameworks that attempt to explain the above trends make claims that men are genetically more susceptible to various illnesses or death. These frameworks stand in contrast to a large body of work that has conceptualized health as being shaped by the social construction of masculinities. A social construction of masculinities perspective considers: (1) the social and structural forces (poverty, migration, prison and criminal justice system, lack of housing) and social institutions (work, military, sports) that organize men into hierarchical cultures and groups that definitively harm men's health; and (2) how normative masculinity itself (e.g., gender norms and roles) can be harmful to men's—and women's—health when enacted.[15] That is, the norms and ideals of masculinity that include toughness, aggressiveness, violence, the perception that health-seeking behaviors are a sign of weakness, and distancing oneself from one's own—and other's—emotions are in and of themselves some of the most formidable barriers to health and health care that exist.[16]

One framework that can be used to critically assess the above trends and pave the way for a future research agenda on rights and health is one that I will apply from Mike Messner, a sociologist and leading masculinities scholar in the U.S. While the framework was not created to examine health disparities or outcomes, it can easily be applied to health and rights issues. In his 1997 work titled Politics of Masculinities, Messner offers a three-part framework in order to explain the experiences of men as a group relative to women as a group and relative to groups of differently positioned men.[17] As applied to health and rights, this framework pushes health researchers to avoid viewing men solely as a group that harms women and to continue examining how sociocultural definitions of masculinities shape health and access to health care.

The first part of the framework highlights that men as a group experience *institutional and cultural privileges* over and above women as a group. Michael Kaufman makes this point clear in his 1994 work when he states that: "Compared to women we are free to walk the streets at night, we have traditionally escaped domestic labor, and on average we have higher wages, better jobs, and more power."[18] This perspective on men's privileges has been applied to many analyses on the harm to women's health. Given that men often have greater access to assets, income, education, and property rights and that women lack these key resources, women are left more vulnerable to a variety of illnesses and their negative effects. In terms of sexual privileges, it is well recognized that, globally, there is a sexual double standard that allows men to have multiple sexual partners, but stigmatizes women for the same behaviors.[19] Culturally, when HIV/AIDS is brought into a home, there is evidence that women are often blamed for the disease, face violence from their male partners, and are disinherited, even though women are most at risk of HIV from their male partners within a marriage who may have extramarital partners.[20] In terms of family planning and condom negotiating power, it is also well recognized that women's decisions are often influenced by their men, who frequently hold greater decision-making power in households and relationships.[21]

Men also have greater access than do women to several key societal institutions that are highly valued such as sports and the military. Honing in on the institution of sport, there is ample historical evidence that sport as an institution was made by men for men at the turn of the nineteenth century to bolster masculinity when work and family roles rapidly changed, with industrialization and a shifting economy destabilizing notions about what it means to be a man.[22] At this time, intense societal fears emerged surrounding the fact that boys would increasingly be socialized by women who were making their way into the public sphere. This led to fears of "social feminization"—that boys would not be made into proper men.[23] Thus, sport formed (as did the Boy Scouts), in part to ensure a separate sphere in which masculinity could be constituted as separate from and superior to women as a group.[24] Women have made great inroads into the institution of sport thanks to societal changes, shifts in media coverage, and Title IX legislation that mandated equal funding under the law for schools that receive federal funding directly.[25] As a result of these advances, women now have greater access to sport's positive health effects.[26] However, women now also face a host of new injuries and health problems within sport that men have long been subject to.[27]

The second part of the framework makes clear that even though men may experience cultural and institutional privileges associated with masculinities, men also face negative and harmful effects from gender inequality. That is, men experience great *costs for adhering to narrow and constraining definitions of masculinity* (referred to as "costs of masculinity") that hurt both men's and women's health. Research indicates that men who endorse a more traditional masculine ideology have an increased risk for negative mental (e.g., depression) and physical (e.g., cardiovascular disease) health outcomes.[28] Men who endorse traditional masculine ideology are also more likely to endorse rape-supportive attitudes and negative attitudes about women, express a likelihood of committing acquaintance or stranger rape, have actually committed sexual aggression against women and engage in higher rates of HIV/AIDS risk behavior.[29] Men who endorse traditional masculinity also show greater substance abuse,[30] more risk-taking and pleasure seeking, less likelihood to stick to one sexual partner,[31] less willingness to see health care providers overall,[32] and are less likely to see a health care provider after clear signs of a heart problem than are men who do not endorse traditional masculinity.[33] There is also a growing body of work that shows that men are less likely than women to seek preventative care.[34] Consequently, men are therefore less likely to be screened for chronic and infectious diseases, less likely to utilize health care services in general, and more likely to wait longer than women do in seeking care when they experience symptoms.[35] They are also less likely to test for HIV than women and when they receive test results, norms of masculinity make it

difficult for men to accept a positive diagnosis and accept care.[36]

Furthermore, simply because men may value and/or enact masculine behavior, it does not mean that they do not experience conflicts associated with this behavior or the beliefs that underlie it. These conflicts are also harmful to men's health. In fact, the impact of traditional masculine ideology on health behavior may be accentuated for men who are experiencing gender-role conflicts (GRC) in particular.[37] In their review, Wester and Vogel indicate that GRC can occur when men: (1) deviate from or violate masculine gender role norms; (2) try, but fail, to meet masculine gender role norms; and/or (3) experience a discrepancy between their real and ideal self-concept of masculine gender role stereotypes.[38] Men who are conflicted about masculinity expectations experience lower levels of well-being, increased problem behaviors, experience anxiety and depression, significantly higher rates of abuse alcohol and other drugs, and do not seek mental or physical health as much as men who are not conflicted about masculine expectations.[39]

Previously, I made mention of men's greater access to the institution of sport and other socially valued institutions than women. Professional athletes in particular often embody the most valued form of masculinity within sport, and are often highly culturally celebrated, well paid, and viewed as heroes. At first glance, they appear to be privileged icons of masculinity and health given the focus on their superhuman performances. They are also focused on a great deal within media reports and research literature, both of which underscore that male athletes have privileged access to multiple sexual partners, have difficulty attaining monogamy and may disproportionately commit violence and sexual assault against women while rarely getting convicted (particularly in violent team sports).[40] And yet, there is a crucial paradox that remains: There are inordinate health risks for these paragons of masculinity and the occupation of sport is extremely hazardous for men's health.[41] As has been noted by several scholars, male athletes in hockey, football, wrestling, boxing, rugby, and other sports naturalize violence against other male athletes, enacting and stretching the rules as much as they can to gain a competitive edge over their opponents.[42] However, instead of casting extremely violent collisions (or in the case of the military, killing others) as an occupational health hazard that men have a right to avoid in the name of health and well-being, or that these realms need to be more highly surveilled or regulated, these actions are framed as "part of the game," "for the team," and "for the nation" within institutional hierarchies where violence is a central feature.

Concerning the sport of football, while it seems obvious that very large, muscular people crashing into each other's bodies and heads with helmets at high speeds and/or with great force would yield health risks, it has only recently been reported that NFL players have nineteen times the rate of Alzheimer's among men aged thirty to forty-nine compared to the general population.[43] The public may be less aware that there is a 100% injury rate in the NFL, and that the shelf life of an NFL players averages five and a half years.[44] Furthermore, NFL players have a life expectancy of approximately fifty-six years.[45] A new study commissioned by the NFL found that ex-pro players over age fifty were five times as likely as the national average to receive a memory-related disease diagnosis and players thirty to forty-nine were nineteen times as likely.[46] Professional athletes, once they retire, will spend much of the money that remains on medical care costs, and many experience permanent and acute damage to their limbs, skulls, and bodies.

In the words of Messner, "Top athletes who are often portrayed as the epitome of good physical conditioning and health are likely to suffer from a very high incidence of permanent injuries, disabilities, alcoholism, drug abuse, obesity, and heart problems. The instrumental rationality which teaches athletes to view their own bodies as machines and weapons with which to annihilate an objectified opponent ultimately comes back upon the athlete as an alien force: the body as weapon ultimately results in violence against one's own body."[47]

In high schools and colleges across the country, while football is viewed as one of the most central

forms of school spirit and can bring in funds at the highest levels, football is undoubtedly the most common source of injury that leads to disability, and fatality.[48] Across other sports, men's rougher style of play also leads to gendered disparities in injuries that are unfavorable to men.[49] Men frequently accept such injuries acritically: They are often unreflective about past disablement, and frequently remain altogether uncritical of the organization of sport.[50]

This section has underscored two main points. First, adherence to narrow and constraining definitions of masculinity harms not just women's but also men's health and creates enormous barriers to men's health and health care. Second, even among the most privileged icons of masculinity who may receive an abundance number of social and financial rewards for enacting masculine success, there are vast health costs that stay quietly under the radar in terms of public health and a right to health. This is because these men are disproportionately "taking it" in the name of masculinity. The costs are great, but the cost of "refusing" such enactments is perhaps perceived to be higher given societal expectations and rewards. It is therefore crucial to not only focus on harms to women that are shaped by masculine enactments, but also those to men.

The third and final part of the framework underscores that not all men equally experience the cultural and institutional privileges of manhood since there are *differences and inequalities among men*. That is, men marginalized due to race and class, and men from sexual minorities do not have easy access to the structural privileges that are associated with dominant forms of masculinity, are disproportionately at risk of numerous health problems, and are subject to barriers to health care.[51] Furthermore, social structural opportunities are stratified by race and gender (referred to as "structures of opportunity") and hence racial-ethnic minority men have disproportionate inclusion into several key male-dominated institutions such as sport and the military, as noted, are particularly harmful to men's health and can cause long-term disability.[52]

I have argued in my previous work[53] that disadvantaged men who are oppressed due to their

race and/or class are frequently kept from traditional definitions of masculine success (e.g., access
to the occupational structure, access to safe housing, avoidance of the prison system). As a result,
marginalized men may be over-reliant on garnering
identity through narrow definitions of masculinity
in order to garner status and respect.[54] Stating this
another way, Courtenay describes this process as
the "signifiers of 'true' masculinity"(e.g., sexual
conquest, physical forms of masculinity, seeing
need as a sign of weakness, violence in the name of
the team or the nation, or in the name of "respect"
from men or women) that are "readily accessible
to men who may otherwise have limited resources
for constructing masculinity."[55] For these men, it is
critical to intervene on their poor health in interventions that offer a safe space to critically reflect on
how norms of masculinities shape their own and
women's health.

In some of my other work,[56] I have delved into
how differences and inequalities among men are
crucial to understanding the HIV/AIDS epidemic.
In the U.S., black men have six times the HIV prevalence of white men and Hispanic men have two
times the rate of white men.[57] Numerous structural
factors shape socially disenfranchised men's risk
to HIV, including residential segregation, unstable
housing and homelessness, unemployment, migra-
tory work, and—in the U.S. in particular—high
rates of incarceration among men of color.[58] Over
ninety percent of prisoners in the United States are
men, and African-American men are seven to eight
times as likely to be incarcerated as white men.[59]
The AIDS rate is up to four times higher in the
prison system than in the general population.[60]

Additionally, large economic shifts stimulated
through de-industrialization in the inner cities have
economically displaced millions of inner city men
of color, dramatically increasing the size of the
urban underclass and, without options for work,
the prison population.[61] The HIV susceptibility of
men who do not live in the U.S. is also affected by
globalization, structural adjustment, and economic
destabilization which has led to large increases in male
migration patterns that can exacerbate HIV/AIDS

risks.[62] And yet, when we think of the links between
human rights, health, and HIV, we often think of
men as perpetrators of HIV/AIDS given men's multiple sexual partnerships or as responsible for wom-
en's health given gender inequality, without creating
urgency among the links between masculinities,
structural inequalities, and men's right to health. It is
high time for a disciplinary shift in thinking.

A RIGHT TO HEALTH: TOWARDS THE STUDY OF GENDER RELATIONS

Public health has recently started to make an otherwise common and important disciplinary shift in
the study of gender relations. This shift is one that
moves away from the common conflation of gender
with *women* and *women's oppression* to the recognition
of *gender relations*, or the ways in which both women
and men are affected by gender inequality. Such an
emphasis is crucial because men and women are differentially positioned in and affected by gender relations and gender inequality.[63] As this article has
made clear, it is also urgent since masculinity as a
set of beliefs and social practices definitively shapes
both men's and women's health outcomes.[64]

Throughout the process of evolution and
change across numerous other disciplines, we have
seen these familiar transitions in terms of the study
of women and men. It would be useful to apply this
historical lens to the study of health and rights to
assess where the field is in terms of studying gender
relations. These transitions:

- Conflate women and gender and leave men out;
- Focus on men as harming women or as being
  irresponsible to women;
- Add men to health programs, but do not make
  these programs gender-specific (e.g. "add men
  and stir," similar to previous criticisms about
  adding women and stirring without making programs gender-specific for women);
- Male inclusion, but only focus on men as
  "being harmed too"—making fully parallel the
  experiences of gender inequality without also
  struggling with the fact that many men enjoy

institutional and cultural privileges over and above women as a group;

- Relationally examine women and men simultaneously, using a frame of gender relations and masculinity, taking into account the different social positioning of women and men while pressing for gender equality and positive health outcomes for both women and men.

On this last point, in the field of violence and HIV/AIDS prevention, prevention interventions with men have increasingly intervened on the norms and practices of masculinities that shape both HIV/AIDS and violence outcomes for women and men.[65] There are certainly many mandates that call for increased male involvement in numerous endeavors related to health, but all too often, the framing has been in terms of the harm that men cause to women.[66] In the rest of the public health field, and particularly in the rights and health field, it will remain critical to press beyond "simplistic explanations of masculinity that focus only on the harms hegemonic masculinities visit upon women, while neglecting the damage done to men by these regressive norms."[67] Peacock, Stemple, Sawires, and Coates analyzed numerous international instruments that have developed mandates to work with men and make the following four suggestions.[68] First, engage men as proponents of gender equality and health. Second, avoid regressive and simplistic stereotyping of men that frames them as a problem for women's health. Third, recognize that men are not monolithic and have unequal access to health care and human rights. Fourth, use policy approaches to take gender transformative work with boys and men to scale.[69] To this I would add that if a human rights approach to health serves to "provide health services and alter the conditions that create, exacerbate, and perpetuate poverty, deprivation, marginalization, and discrimination,"[70] then it is high time to consider how some of our most-valued social institutions not only privilege but also harm men, undermining their right to health. Along these lines, marginalized men who disproportionately pay for the costs of masculinity to men's health are particularly in need of intervention.

I will end with several questions for those interested in men's right to health given the main claims of this paper. What shall those interested in a right to health and health care focus on when it comes to men? The right for men to reject dominant and harmful aspects of masculinity? The right to place a critical lens on masculine institutions where conformity to harmful norms are rewarded and remain all too unchallenged—particularly given that these are frequently a part of successful masculine citizenship? The right for all men, and particularly sexual and racial/ethnic minority men to have access to health care? Other questions include: How will the rights field balance the urgent need to link women's empowerment and health outcomes with the need to also critically examine the ways that masculinity can negatively shape men's and women's health outcomes? How will the field move forward concerning men's right to health care when it is well recognized that programming on women's rights and health has received too much lip service and not enough political will, action, or financial support?[71] These are some questions among many that result from an application of this particular sociocultural framework to men's health. It is my hope that such a framework stimulates much dialogue within and across numerous disciplines in the name of men's health. Men's health depends on it.

AUTHOR'S NOTE

Dr. Shari L. Dworkin, PhD, MS is an Associate Professor of Sociology at the University of California, San Francisco, Department of Social & Behavioral Sciences and is the Director of Doctoral Studies in Sociology. She is Affiliated Faculty at the Center for AIDS Prevention Studies and a Founding Member of the Center of Expertise on Women's Health and Empowerment at the UC Global Health Institute. Dr. Dworkin specializes in the area of gender relations and health; particularly in gender relations and HIV/AIDS prevention for both heterosexually active women and men in Sub-Saharan Africa.

NOTES

1. *See* Ann K. Blanc, *The Effect of Power in Sexual Relationships on Sexual and Reproductive Health: An Examination of the Evidence*, 32(3) STUD. IN FAMILY PLANNING 189, 189–213 (2001); Shari L. Dworkin & Kim Blankenship, *Microfinance and HIV/AIDS Prevention: Assessing its Promise and Limitations*, 13 AIDS & BEHAVIOR 462, 462–469 (2009); Matthew R. Dudgeon & Marcia C. Inhorn, *Men's Influence on Women's Reproductive Health: Medical Anthropological Perspectives*, 59(7) SOC. SCI. & MED. 1379, 1379–1395 (2004); Allen Greig & Dean Peacock, *Men as Partners Programme: Promising Practices Guide*, Jan. 2005, *available at* http://www.genderjustice.org.za/external-resources/external-resources/men-as-partners-programme-promising-practices-guide/download; Geeta Rato Gupta, *Gender, Sexuality and HIV/AIDS: The What, the Why and the How*, INT'L CENTER ON RES. FOR WOMEN, Jul. 12, 2000, http://www.icrw.org/docs/Durban_HIVAIDS_speech700.pdf; Jenny A. Higgins, Susie Hoffman & Shari L. Dworkin, *Rethinking Gender, Heterosexual Men, and Women's Vulnerability to HIV/AIDS*, AM. J. PUB. HEALTH (2010) (EPUB ahead of print); Richard S. Strickland, *To Have and To Hold: Women's Property and Inheritance Rights in the Context of HIV/AIDS in Sub-Saharan Africa*, INT'L CTR. FOR RES. ON WOMEN (Jun. 2004), http://www.icrw.org/docs/2004_paper_haveandhold.pdf; J. Kim & C. Watts, *Gaining a Foothold: Tackling Poverty, Gender Inequality, and HIV in Africa*, 331 BRITISH MED. J. 769 (2005); G.M. Wingood & R.J. DiClemente, *Application of the Theory of Gender and Power to Examine HIV-Related Exposures, Risk Factors, and Effective Interventions for Women*, 27 HEALTH EDUC. BEHAV. 539–565 (2000).

2. PubMed is the most prominent and commonly used database to search for journal articles in the health sciences.

3. *See* Jean J. Bonhomme, *Men's Health: Impact on Women, Children, and Society*, 4(2) J. MEN'S HEALTH & GENDER 124, 124–130 (June 2007); Will H. Courtenay, *Constructions of Masculinity and Their Influence on Men's Well-being: A Theory of Gender and Health*, SOC. SCI. & MED., 50(10) 1385 (2000); Will H. Courtenay, *Behavioral Factors Associated with Disease, Injury, and Death Among Men: Evidence and Implications for Prevention*, J. MEN'S STUDIES 9(1), 81–142 (2000); David C. Dodson, *Men's Health Compared with Women's Health in the 21st Century USA*, J. MEN'S HEALTH & GENDER 4(2), 121–23 (2007); James Harrison, James Chin & Thomas Ficarotto, *Warning: Masculinity May Be Dangerous to Your Health*, in MEN'S LIVES 271–285 (M.S. Kimmel & M.A. Messner eds., 2nd ed. 1989); Debra Kalmuss & Karen Austrian, *Real Men Do ... Real Men Don't: Young Latino and African American Men's Discourses Regarding Sexual Health Care Utilization*, AM. J. MEN'S HEALTH (2009); E. Mankowski & K. Maton, *A Community Psychology of Men and Masculinity: Historical and Conceptual Review*, AM. J. COMM. PSYCHOL. 45, 73 (2010) (E, ahead of print); James R. Mahalik, Shaun M. Burns, & Matthew Syzdek, *Masculinity and Perceived Normative Health Behaviors as a Predictor of Men's Health Behaviors*, SOC. SCI. & MED. 64, 2201–2209 (2007); Siegfried Meryn, *5th Biennial World Congress on Men's Health and Gender: A Special Anniversary*. J. MEN'S HEALTH & GENDER 4(3), 217–219 (Sept. 2007); Donald Sabo & Frederick Gordon, *Rethinking Men's Health and Illness*, in MEN'S HEALTH AND ILLNESS: GENDER, POWER, AND THE BODY 1–21 (Donald Sabo & Frederick Gordon eds., 1995).

4. *See* James Mahalik, Hugh Lagan, & Jay Morrison, *Health Behaviors and Masculinity in Kenyan and U.S. Male College Students*, PSYCHOL. MEN AND MASC. 7(4), 191–202 (2006).

5. *See* Courtenay, *Constructions, supra* note 3; Courtenay, *Behavioral Factors. supra* note 3; Dodson, *supra* note 3; WORLD HEALTH ORGANIZATION [WHO], *The World Health Report: Reducing Risks, Promoting Healthy Life* (2002), *available at* http://www.who.int/whr/2002/en/.

6. WHO, *supra* note 5.

7. Bonhomme, *supra* note 3.

8. International Labor Organization [ILO], *HIV/AIDS Prevention: How Empowering Men and Boys to Promote Gender Equality can Help* (2004), *available at* http://www.ilo.org/global/About_the_ILO/Media_and_publicW_information/Feature_stories/lang-en/WCMS_075584/index.htm; WHO, *supra* note 5.

9. Meryn, *supra* note 3.

10. *See* Courtenay, *Constructions, supra* note 3; Courtenay, *Behavioral Factors, supra* note 3.

11. Medical Research Council/UNISA, *A Profile of Fatal Injuries in South Africa*, 7th Annual Report of the National Injury Mortality Surveillance System (2005), *available at* http://www.sahealthinfo.org/violence/national2005.pdf; Violence Policy Center, *Black Homicide Victimization in the United States: An Analysis of 2007 Homicide Data* (2010), *available at* http://www.vpc.org/studies/blackhomicide10.pdf.

12. WHO, *Primary Health Care: Now More Than Ever* (2008), *available at* http://www.who.int/whr/2008/en/index.html.

13. *See* Courtenay, *Constructions, supra* note 3; Courtenay, *Behavioral Factors, supra* note 3.

14. Hannah Fischer, *United States Military Casualty Statistics: Operation Iraqi Freedom and Operation Enduring Freedom*, CONG. RES. SERVICE, Mar. 25, 2009, *available at* http://fas.org/sgp/crs/natsec/RS22452.pdf.

15. *See* Courtenay, *Constructions, supra* note 3; Courtenay, *Behavioral Factors, supra* note 3; Michael A. Messner, *When Bodies Are Weapons: Masculinity and Violence in Sport*, INT'L REV. FOR THE SOCIO. OF SPORT 25(3), 203–220 (1990).

16. *See* D. Stanley Eitzen & George H. Sage, SOCIOLOGY OF NORTH AMERICAN SPORT (2002); Michael Flood, *Addressing the Sexual Cultures of Heterosexual Men: Key Strategies in Involving Men and Boys in HIV/AIDS Prevention*, U.N. Doc EGM/Men-Boys-GE/2003/EP.6 (Oct. 9, 2003), *available at* http://www.un.org/womenwatch/daw/egm/men-boys2003/EP6-Flood.pdf (last visited Mar. 26, 2010); Greig & Peacock, *supra* note 1; Mankowski & Maton, *supra* note 3.

17. Michael Messner, POLITICS OF MASCULINITIES: MEN IN MOVEMENTS (1997).

18. M. Kaufman, *The Construction of Masculinity and the Triad of Men's Violence*, in GENDER VIOLENCE: INTERDISC. PERSP. 33, 35 (L. Toole & J.R. Schiffman, eds., NYU Press 1994).

19. *See* Susie Hoffman, Anke A. Ehrhardt, Theresa M. Exner & Shari Dworkin, *Beyond the Male Condom: The Evolution of Gender-Specific HIV Interventions for Women*, ANN. REV. SEX RESEARCH 14, 114–136 (2003); Higgins et al., *supra* note 1.

20. *See* Michael Aliber & Cherryl Walker, *The Impact of HIV/AIDS on Land Rights: Perspectives from Kenya*, WORLD DEVELOPMENT, 34(4), 704–727 (2006).; Strickland, *supra* note 1; K. Izumi, *Gender-Based Violence and Property Grabbing in Africa: A Denial of Women's Liberty and Security*, GENDER & DEV. 15(1), 11–23 (2007); S. Newmann et al., *Marriage, Monogamy, and HIV: A Profile of HIV Infected Women in India*, INT'L J. STDs & HIV 11, 250–253 (2000); UNAIDS, *AIDS Epidemic Update*, UNAIDS/09.36E/JC1700E (Nov. 2009), *available at* http://data.unaids.org:80/pub/Report/2009/JC1700_Epi_Update_2009_en.pdf.

21. *See* Blanc, *supra* note 1; Dudgeon & Inhorn, *supra* note 1; Gupta, *supra* note 1; Julie Pulerwitz et al., *Relationship Power, Condom Use and HIV Risk Among Women in the USA*, AIDS CARE 14(6), 789–800 (2002).

22. *See* Todd Crossett, *Masculinity, Sexuality, and the Development of Modern Sport*, in SPORT, MEN, AND THE GENDER ORDER: CRITICAL FEMINIST PERSPECTIVES (Michael A. Messner & Donald F. Sabo eds., Human Kinetics Books 1990); Eitzen & Sage, *supra* note 16; M. Kimmel, *Baseball and the Reconstitution of American Masculinity 1880–1920*, in SPORT, MEN, AND THE GENDER ORDER: CRITICAL FEMINIST PERSP. 55–66 (M. Messner & D. Sabo eds., Human Kinetics 1990); M. Kimmel, MANHOOD IN AMERICA: A CULTURAL HISTORY (1996); Michael A. Messner, *Sports and Male Domination: The Female Athlete as Contested Ideological Terrain*, SOC. SPORTS J. 5, 197–211 (1988); Michael A. Messner, TAKING THE FIELD: WOMEN, MEN, AND SPORTS (2002).

23. *See* Crossett, *supra* note 22; Varda Burstyn, THE RITES OF MEN: MANHOOD, POLITICS, AND THE CULTURE OF SPORT (1999); Michael S. Kimmel, *Men's Responses to Feminism at the Turn of the Century*, GENDER & SOC'Y, 1, 261–283 (Sept., 1987); KIMMEL, MANHOOD, *supra* note 22.

24. *See* Burstyn, *supra* note 23; Kimmel, *Men's Responses, supra* note 23; Kimmel, MANHOOD, *supra* note 22; Michael A. Messner, POWER AT PLAY: SPORTS AND THE PROBLEM OF MASCULINITY (1992); Ann Travers, *The Sport Nexus and Gender Injustice*, STUD. IN SOC. JUST. 2(1), 79–101 (2008).

25. *See* Mary A. Boutilier & Lucinda F. San Giovanni, *Politics, Public Policy and Title X*, in WOMEN, SPORT AND CULTURE (Susan Birrell & Cheryl Cole eds., Human Kinetics Publishers 1994); Leslie Heywood. & Shari L. Dworkin, BUILT TO WIN: THE FEMALE ATHLETE AS CULTURAL ICON (2003).

26. *See* Miller et al., *Health Risks and the Teen Athlete, A Women's Sports Foundation Research Project*, WOMEN'S SPORTS FOUNDATION (2000); Donald Sabo et al., *High School Athletic Participation and Suicide*, INT'L REV. FOR THE SOC. OF SPORT 40(1), 5–23 (2005).

27. *See* Howard L. Nixon, *Explaining Pain and Injury Attitudes and Experiences in Sport in Terms of Gender, Race, and Sports Status Factors*, J. SPORT & SOC. ISSUES 20(1), 33–44 (1996); Richard Pringle, *Competing Discourses: Narratives of a Fragmented Self, Manliness,*

and *Rugby Union*, INT'L REV. Soc. SPORT 36(4), 425–439 (2001); Kevin Young, SPORT, VIOLENCE, AND SOCIETY 2010); Kevin Young & Phillip White, *Sport, Physical Danger, and Injury: The Experiences of Elite Women*, J. SPORT & SOC. ISSUES 19(1), 45–61 (1995).

28. *See* Courtenay, *Constructions, supra* note 3; Courtenay, *Behavioral Factors, supra* note 3; Sabo & Gordon, *supra* note 3; White et al., *Sport Masculinity, and the Injured Body*, in MEN'S HEALTH AND ILLNESS: GENDER, POWER, AND THE BODY 158–182 (Donald Sabo & Frederick Gordon eds., 1995).

29. *See* Gary Barker, DYING TO BE MEN: YOUTH, MASCULINITY, AND SOCIAL EXCLUSION (Routledge 2005); Marcia K. Fitzpatrick et al. *Associations of Gender and Gender-Role Ideology with Behavioral and Attitudinal Features of Intimate Partner Aggression*, 5(2) PSYCHOL. MEN & MASCULINITY 91 (2004); Melanie S. Hill, & Ann R. Fischer, *Does Entitlement Mediate the Link Between Masculinity and Rape-Related Variables?*, J. COUNS. PSYCHOL 48, 39 (2001); M. Jakupcak et al., *The Role of Masculine Ideology and Masculine Gender Role Stress in Men's Perpetuation of Relationship Violence*, PSYCHOL. MEN & MASC. 3, 97–106 (2002); M. Kaufman et al., *Gender Attitudes, Sexual Power, HIV Risk: A Model for Understanding HIV Risk Behavior of South African Men*, AIDS CARE 20(4) 434, 434–441 (2008); Jonathan Schwartz et al., *Gender-Role Conflict and Self-Esteem: Predictors of Partner Abuse in Court Referred Men*, PSYCHOL. OF MEN AND MASCULINITY 6, 109–113 (2005).

30. *See* Mahalik et al., *supra* note 4; D. McCreary et al., *The Male Role, Alcohol Use, and Alcohol Problems: A Structural Modeling Examination in Adult Women and Men*, J. COUNSELING PSYCHOL. 46, 109–124 (Jan. 1999); Joseph H. Pleck. et al., *Masculinity Ideology and Its Correlates*, in GENDER ISSUES IN CONTEMPORARY SOCIETY 85–110 (Stuart Oskamp & Mark Constanzo eds., 1993).

31. *See* Lucia F. O'Sullivan et al. *Men, Multiple Sexual Partners, and Young Adults' Sexual Relationships: Understanding the Role of Gender in the Study of Risk*, J. URBAN HEALTH 83(4), 695–708 (2006); JONNY STEINBERG, SIZWE'S TEST: A YOUNG MAN'S JOURNEY THROUGH AFRICA'S AIDS EPIDEMIC (Simon & Schuster 2008).

32. *See* Kalmuss & Austrian, *supra* note 3; Michael E. Addis & James R. Mahalik, *Men, Masculinity, and the Contexts of Help-Seeking*, AM. PSYCHOLOGIST 58(1), 5–14 (2003).

33. Vicki S. Helgeson, *The Role of Masculinity in a Prognostic Predictor of Heart Attack Severity*, SEX ROLES 22, 755 (1990).

34. *See* Janice Blanchard & Nicole Lurie, *Preventive Care in the United States: Are Blacks Finally Catching Up?*, ETHNICITY & DISEASE 15, 498–504 (2005); Kalmuss & Austrian, *supra* note 3; Mahalik et al., *supra* note 4.

35. *See* David Sandman et al., *Out of Touch: American Men and the Health Care System*, COMMONWEALTH FUND, (2000), *available at* http://www.commonwealthfund.org/~/media/Files/Publications/Fund%20Report/2000/Mar/Out%20of%20Touch%20%20American%20Men%20and%20the%20Health%20Care%20System/sandman_outoftouch_374%20pdf.pdf; STEINBERG, *supra* note 31.

36. *See* Alan Grieg et al., *Gender and AIDS: Time to Act*, JAIDS 22, S35 (2008); Purnima Mane & Peter Aggleton, *Gender and HIV? AIDS: What do Men Have to do With It?*, CURRENT Soc. 49(6), 23–37 (2001); Dean Peacock et al., *Men, HIV/AIDS, and Human Rights*, JAIDS 51(3), S119–125 (2009); Robert Remien et al., *Gender and Care: Access to HIV Testing, Care, and Treatment*, JAIDS 51, S106–110 (2009).

37. Joseph H. Pleck, *The Gender Role Strain Paradigm: An Update*, in A NEW PSYCHOLOGY OF MEN 11–32 (Ronald F. Levant & William S. Pollack eds., 1995).

38. Stephen Wester & David Vogel, *Working With the Masculine Mystique: Male Gender Role Conflict, Counseling Self-Efficacy, and the Training of Male Psychologists*, PROF. PSYCHOL. RES. & PRAC. 33(4), 370–376 (2002).

39. *See* James M. O'Neil, *Summarizing 25 Years of Research on Men's Gender Role Conflict Using the Gender Role Conflict Scale: New Research Paradigms and Clinical Implications*, COUNSELING PSYCHOLOGIST 36(3), 358–445 (2008); Mankowski & Maton, *supra* note 3; Pleck, *supra* note 37; Mark J. Sharpe & Paul P. Heppner, *Gender Role, Gender Role Conflict, and Psychological Well Being in Men*, J. COUNSELING PSYCHOL. 38(3), 323–330 (1991).

40. *See* Jeff Benedict, PUBLIC HEROES, PRIVATE FELONS: ATHLETES AND CRIMES AGAINST WOMEN (Northeastern University Press 1999) (1997); Mary P. Koss & J. Gaines, *The Prediction of Sexual Aggression by Alcohol Use, Athletic Participation, and Fraternity Affiliation*, J. INTERP. VIOLENCE 8(1), 94–108 (1993); Mary P. Koss & Hobart H. Cleveland III, *Athletic Participation, Fraternity Membership, and Date Rape*, VIOLENCE

AGAINST WOMEN 2(2), 33 (1996); Shari L. Dworkin & Faye Linda Wachs, BODY PANIC: GENDER, HEALTH, AND THE SELLING OF FITNESS (NYU Press 2009).

41. *See* Messner *supra* note 15; Messner, *supra* note 24; Messner, *supra* note 22; Kevin Young, et al., *Body Talk: Male Athletes Reflect on Sport, Injury, and Pain*, SOC. OF SPORT J. 11, 175–194 (1994); YOUNG, supra note 27.

42. *See* Timothy J. Curry & Richard H. Strauss, *A Little Pain Never Hurt Anybody: A Photo-Essay on the Normalization of Sport Injuries*, SOC. SPORT J. 11(2), 195–208 (1994); Messner, *supra* note 15; Nixon, *supra* note 27; Pringle, *supra* note 27; Young et al., *supra* note 41; SPORT, VIOLENCE, AND SOCIETY, *supra* note 27.

43. *See* Sean Gregory, *The Problem with Football: How to Make it Safer*, TIME, Jan. 28, 2010, *available at* http://www.time.com/time/nation/article/0,8599,1957046,00.html (last visited Mar. 26, 2010); Alan Schwartz, *Dementia Risk in Players in NFL Study*. N.Y. TIMES. Sept. 29, 2009, at A1, *available at* http://www.nytimes.com/2009/09/30/sports/football/30dementia.html (last visited Apr. 3, 2010).

44. *See* Messner, *supra* note 24; Messner, *supra* note 15.

45. Messner, *supra* note 24.

46. Gregory, *supra* note 43.

47. Messner, *supra* note 15, at 211.

48. YOUNG, *supra* note 27.

49. *See* Eitzen & Sage, *supra* note 16; Nixon, *supra* note 27; Young, *supra* note 27.

50. *See* Messner, *supra* note 24; Pringle, *supra* note 27.

51. *See* Higgins, Hoffman, & Dworkin, *supra* note 1; Robert E. Fullilove, *African Americans, Health Disparities, and HIV/AIDS: Recommendations for Confronting the Epidemic in Black America*, NAT'L MINORITY AIDS COUNCIL, (2006), *available at* http://www.nmac.org/index/cms-filesystem-action?file=grpp/african%20americans,%20health%20disparities%20and%20hiv/aids.pdf (last visited Mar. 26, 2010); Messner *supra* note 24; Messner, *supra* note 17; A.M.W. Young, *Disparities in Health Among Men: Toward a Global Perspective*, J. MEN'S HEALTH & GENDER 4(3), 222–225 (2007).

52. *See* Messner *supra* note 24; Messner, *supra* note 17; Nixon, *supra* note 27; Pringle, *supra* note 27.

53. *See* Shari L. Dworkin et al., *Are HIV/AIDS Prevention Interventions for Heterosexually Active Men in the United States Gender-Specific?*, AM. J. PUBLIC HEALTH 99(6), 981–984 (2009); Higgins, Hoffman & Dworkin, *supra* note 1.

54. *See* Phillippe Bourgois, *In Search of Masculinity: Violence, Respect and Sexuality among Puerto Rican Crack Dealers in East Harlem*, BRIT. J. CRIMINOL. 36, 412–427 (1996); R. Majors & J. Billson, COOL POSE: THE DILEMMAS OF BLACK MANHOOD IN AMERICA (1992); Messner, *supra* note 17.

55. Courtenay, *Constructions, supra* note 3, at 1392.

56. Higgins, Hoffman, & Dworkin, *supra* note 1.

57. *HIV/AIDS Among African Americans: CDC HIV/AIDS Facts*, CENTERS FOR DISEASE CONTROL (2009), http://www.cdc.gov/hiv/topics/aa/resources/factsheets/pdf/aa.pdf.

58. *See* Cynthia Golembeski & Robert Fullilove, *Criminal (in) Justice in the City and its Associated Health Consequences*, AM. J. PUB. HEALTH 95(10), 1701–1706 (2005).

59. *See* Golembeski & Fullilove, *supra* note 58; Jeffrey H. Reiman, THE RICH GET RICHER THE POOR GET PRISON: IDEOLOGY, CLASS, AND CRIMINAL JUSTICE (Allyn & Bacon 1979) (2000); W.J. Wilson, WHEN WORK DISAPPEARS: THE NEW WORLD OF THE URBAN POOR (Vintage Press 1996).

60. *See* Fullilove, *supra* note 51: Golembeski & Fullilove, *supra* note 58; Richard G. Parker et al., *Structural Barriers and Facilitators in HIV Prevention: A Review of International Research*, AIDS 14, S22 (2000).

61. *See* Fullilove, *supra* note 51; W.J. Wilson, THE TRULY DISADVANTAGED: THE INNER CITY, THE UNDERCLASS, AND PUBLIC POLICY (University of Chicago 1990); Wilson, *supra* note 59.

62. *See* Higgins, Hoffman, & Dworkin, *supra* note 1; Parker, et al., *supra* note 60.

63. *See* Dworkin, Fullilove, & Peacock, *supra* note 53; Higgins, Hoffman, & Dworkin, *supra* note 1.

64. *See* Barker, *supra* note 29; Courtenay, *Constructions, supra* note 3; Courtenay, *Behavioral Factors, supra* note 3; Dworkin, Fullilove, & Peacock, *supra* note 53; Robert Morrell, *Of Boys and Men: Masculinity and Gender in Southern African Studies*, J. S. AFRICAN STUD. 24, 605–630 (1998); Robert Morrell, CHANGING MEN

IN SOUTHERN AFRICA (2001); Julie Pulerwitz et al., *Promoting Healthy Relationships and HIV/STI Prevention for Young Men: Positive Findings from an Intervention Study in Brazil*, HORIZONS REPORT (2004), *available at* http://www.popcouncil.org/pdfs/horizons/brgndrnrmsru.pdf; Kim Rivers & Peter Aggleton, *Men and the HIV Epidemic*, UNITED NATIONS DEV. PROGRAM (1999), *available at* http://www.undp.org/hiv/publications/gender/mene.htm; Sabo et al., *supra* note 26.

65. *See* Gary Barker et al., *Engaging Men and Boys in Changing Gender-based Inequity in Health: Evidence from Programme Interventions*, WHO (2007), *available at* http://www.who.int/gender/documents/Engaging_men_boys.pdf; Pulerwitz, Barker, & Sagundo, *supra* note 64; Sonke Gender Justice, *One Man Can Workshop Activities: Talking to Men About Gender, Sexual and Domestic Violence, and HIV/AIDS, available at* http://www.gender-justice.org.za/onemancan/images/publications/workshop/omc_workshopactivities_1sted_eng_lowres.pdf; R. Jewkes et al., *Impact of Stepping Stones on HIV, HSV-2, and Sexual Behavior in Rural South Africa: Cluster Randomized Controlled Trial*, BRITISH MEN'S J. 337, 1–11 (2008).

66. Peacock, Stemple, Sawires, & Coates, *supra* note 36.

67. *Id.* at S119.

68. *See id.*

69. *Id.* at S122–124.

70. Sofia Gruskin, *Rights-Based Approaches to Health: Something for Everyone*, HEALTH & HUM. RTS. 9(2), 5 (2006).

71. Grieg, Peacock, Jewkes & Msimang, *supra* note 36.

GENDER CAPITAL AND MALE BODYBUILDERS

Tristan S. Bridges

I have to keep on being a bodybuilder. I can't use my street credit anywhere else. This is the only place it works. . . . No one else gets us. We're the freaks to lots of people, but here, we're like gods. (Chris, 255 lb, professional bodybuilder, 36, physical trainer, 18 years on the bench)

Bodybuilders are in the business of developing a 'physical' (Shilling, 1993) or 'bodily' capital (Wacquant, 1995a). This is a capital that has greater relative value within specific fields of practice but would be identified as 'masculine' in almost any setting. However, what that masculinity is worth varies by context. As the quote above illustrates, some bodybuilders understand their bodily capital as contextually significant in the distribution of cultural status. Utilizing Bourdieu's notion of cultural capital, this work builds on the conceptualization of hegemonic masculinity by developing a new hybrid concept: gender capital.

Cultural capital is part of a larger theory of the social character of 'taste' that gained widespread popularity following its original conceptualization (Bourdieu and Passeron, 1977). Most broadly, cultural capital refers to the resources (e.g. knowledge, body image, tastes) that individuals employ to gain status in certain contexts. Hegemonic masculinity is another theoretical concept that has received celebratory attention since it was proposed (Carrigan et al., 1985; Connell, 1987). The concept was established to recognize

status asymmetries in inter- and intra-gender relations (Connell, 1998). Thus, it was first conceptualized to discuss the ways that men can be more or less 'manly'. Both concepts have since been re-examined and re-articulated. The purpose of this article is to build on the theoretical strength of both concepts by developing 'gender capital'.

Bodybuilders have also received scholarly attention, particularly among those interested in gender, sport and studies of the body (e.g. Gillett and White, 1992; Klein, 1993; Monaghan, 1999, 2001; Wiegers, 1998). They provide an example of the utility of gender capital. Cultural capital and hegemonic masculinity are strategies for making sense of systems of valuation that vary between and among groups, and by context (Bourdieu, 1984; Connell, 1987, 1995). The development of both concepts enabled studies of not only inter-group variation (e.g. men relative to women), but intra-group relations (e.g. men relative to other men).

In this article, I address two main issues: (1) What is gender capital and how does it build on cultural capital and hegemonic masculinity? (2) How do relations among bodybuilders and between bodybuilders and other men (and women) illustrate the utility of gender capital? Gender capital refers to the value afforded contextually relevant presentations of gendered selves. It is interactionally defined and negotiated. Thus, gender capital – similar to both cultural capital and hegemonic masculinity – is in a state of continuous (though often subtle) transformation. This article illustrates that bodybuilders are often aware of the different contextually contingent and gender-political messages their massive figures send.

From Tristan S. Bridges, "Gender Capital and Male Bodybuilders." *Body & Society*, Vol 15(1): 83–107. Copyright © 2009 Sage Publications, Inc. Reprinted by permission of Sage Publications, Inc.

A METHODOLOGICAL NOTE

> Daren pointed at me and, talking with the three men he was working out with said, 'This man over here think he can study us. . . . I hope he likes hanging out at the gym.' (from author's field notes)

This article emerged from a one-year ethnography of four 'hard-core' bodybuilding gyms[1] in two US East coast cities carried out in 2004–5. One city was a smaller, less urban environment, while the other was a major metropolitan city. I use pseudonyms when referring to the sites I studied, which I am conceptually combining into one gym – 'Mount Olympus' – for heuristic purposes. Separate locations were originally chosen to provide regional variation. However, one of my first findings was the homogeneity of the geographically separate communities. Thus, despite disparate physical locations, these bodybuilders occupy one 'field' with a set of transferable capital, an aesthetic disposition, and tastes all their own.[2] Biographical accounts of bodybuilders (e.g. Fussell, 1992; Schwarzenegger and Hall, 1977; Wacquant, 1995c) also support my findings. Additionally, Crossley (2004, 2005) argues that individuals who use their bodies in similar ways will be similar on a great number of different levels.[3]

My purposive sample is composed of 43 aspiring, amateur and professional male bodybuilders. A large component of this study was participant observation, but I interviewed a number of participants as well. More than half of the interviews came from the larger city (23), as there were more bodybuilders in these gyms. Eleven interviews were performed in the smaller city. The remaining participants (9) were observed but not interviewed. Some men figure more prominently in the research than others: 12 men form the bulk of my observations.

Interviews ranged from 20 minutes to approximately two hours in length, averaging 35 minutes. All interviews were recorded and transcribed. The work of interviewing bodybuilders is often time-intensive as it is necessary to interview them when they are *not* training. However, I found that most welcomed a 'legitimate' reason to procrastinate when performing less exciting lifts. As a result, 'leg day' (a commonly despised muscle group) was the most popular day for interviews.

As a reflexive ethnographer, I trust that my being a young man intrigued by weight-lifting culture aided me in gaining access to this group. While much smaller in stature, my own social history of athletics lent me enough status among the men at least to enable my observations to be less disruptive to their daily routines. Additionally, lifting alongside them allowed me to gain trust and to establish a relationship with them on their own terms (Hammersley and Atkinson, 1995).

Transcripts and field notes were then open coded. Files of field notes and transcripts were scrutinized and re-scrutinized for emergent themes informing and altering subsequent research (Emerson et al., 1995; Glaser and Strauss, 1967). Data that I might not have first considered became intensely important in later interviews and interactions. Interview questions and observational strategies changed as I attempted to gather the most information possible. This is consistent with a grounded theoretical approach to qualitative research (Glaser and Strauss, 1967).

While I make no claims to the theoretical representativeness of this sample, working with these men enabled me to become extremely familiar with the micro-politics and interactional rituals (Goffman, 1989). Certainly interview accounts and ethnographic observations cannot be understood as literal accounts of reality, nor can we precisely identify concepts and their inner workings solely through observation (Hammersley, 1989, 1992). However, these interviews and observations do offer clues for understanding social dynamics, and ethnographic research allows for elaborate understandings and illustrations of social environments and behavior (Hammersley and Atkinson, 1995).

WHY STUDY BODYBUILDERS?

> I don't really know what it is, I guess. We really just see the world in a different way. Whenever I see how much something weighs, I wonder if I can pick it up. When I see guys, I don't see them

like they do or even like other people prob'ly look at 'em. We just see everything different. It's part of who we are. (Derrick, 205 lb, amateur bodybuilder, 28, custodian, 10 years on the bench)

Bodybuilding is a valuable topic for sociological analysis for at least three reasons. First, bodybuilding is similar to other occupations, such as modeling and professional athletics, in which people make a living displaying (Goffman, 1977) and performing (West and Zimmerman, 1987) gender. The bodybuilding community is particularly useful to discuss the 'inscription' of gender (Butler, 1993) – or what Connell (1987) refers to as 'practical transformations' of the body – due to the superficiality and extent of their inscription practices. We live in a 'somatic society', in which social anxiety and political issues are embodied (Turner, 1984, 1992). Part of the difficulty in addressing the fluidity of a concept like hegemonic masculinity is that it is often discussed as having a physical form (e.g. Gillett and White, 1992; Wiegers, 1998). However, Connell (1990) addresses hegemonic masculinity as resisting universal forms, similar to cultural capital. Bodies are subject to situational transformation in both form and meaning (Crossley, 2005; Shilling, 1993).

Second, bodybuilders provide an excellent example of how subcultures monitor cultural (bodily) capital, and what I am calling 'gender capital'. Wacquant (1995a, 1995b) discusses bodily capital to explain the diverse ways through which bodies are evaluated in the boxing world in preparation for fights – how the subculture alters their 'aesthetic dispositions' (Bourdieu, 1984) toward what Wacquant (1995b) terms the 'pugilistic point of view'. Delineating a group's point of view is never a wasted project. Some points of view and presentations of self are more trans-situationally 'durable' than others in that they are similarly evaluated in diverse settings. Bodybuilders are *not* an example of a durable presentation. However, similar to the research of Freud and Goffman, extreme cases are of interest precisely because of the light they shed on the 'normal'.

The third reason to study bodybuilders is to illuminate aspects of wider gender-political agendas inherent in social practice, bodies and identities.

Bodily practices are easily labeled individual issues. However, identities and individual practices are not detached from the wider social arenas in which they occur (Adkins, 2003). In fact, identities and practices are the component parts through which interactional orders are (re)produced (Goffman, 1983; Sassatelli, 1999). Bodies are powerful symbols in social relations (Crossley, 2005; Turner, 2003). Though male bodybuilders' bodies are stigmatized outside the gym setting, their existence is a powerful and political symbol of gender difference (Gillett and White, 1992; Wiegers, 1998). Similarly, women bodybuilders' bodies are powerful symbols of resistance and are stigmatized with different concerns (Aoki, 1996; St Martin and Gavey, 1996). Individual social actors may not be cognizant of the gender-political implications of their actions, bodies and identities. However, this does not mean that gender politics do not exist. It simply means that they often exist in spite of our relative levels of recognition, interest and reflexivity (Adkins, 2003; Connell, 2002a).

> Body-reflexive practices . . . are not internal to the individual. They involve social relations and symbolism; they may well involve large-scale social institutions. Particular versions of masculinity are constituted in their circuits as meaningful bodies and embodied meanings. Through body-reflexive practices, more than individual lives are formed: a social world is formed. (Connell, 1995: 64)

The task for sociologists is not only to discuss the ways that bodybuilders have a relationship with a hegemonic masculine form, but also to discuss the ways that they physically and discursively manage capital field-specifically. Here, I am not interested in cultural, bodily or gender capital per se, but in the ways that the status and meanings of these capitals vary not only between and within groups, but by context as well. For instance, bodybuilders often have high status in the gym. However, their gender capital purchases a different sort of masculinity outside the gym. While it is not new to argue that bodybuilders are peculiar on more than one level (Gillett and White, 1992; Klein, 1986; Wiegers, 1998), this article will explore the ways that their peculiarities are delicately tied to the transformative quality of gender capital.

Cultural Capital and Hegemonic Masculinity

Both cultural capital and hegemonic masculinity rely on a Gramscian conceptualization of hegemony. Hegemony is an important concept to use here, particularly in its distinction from ideology. While ideologies are more static, the notion of hegemony is so powerful precisely because of its fluidity (Gramsci, 2005; Williams, 1977). Adamson defines hegemony as: 'A process of continuous creation which, given its massive scale, is bound to be uneven in the degree of legitimacy it commands and to leave some room for antagonistic cultural expressions to develop' (1980: 174). Hegemony refers to a cultural *process* of domination. It organizes, monitors and restricts the ways in which new ideas or systems of valuation are established, eliminated or naturalized in ways that subtly alter notions of 'common sense' within fields of practice (Gramsci, 2005).

Similarly, reification is a process: converting a concept, idea, etc. to a more static form. Elias discusses this by giving the example of a photograph of a dance presuming to explain the dance (1998: 36–9). In the photograph of the dance, the actors are not *dancing*; they are frozen.[4] Inevitably, theory and scholarship attempting to define processes reify them to a certain extent by putting them down on the page. Something is lost in translation. Hegemonies are similarly difficult to discuss without reifying. Williams (1977: 113) argues that one way of attempting to write about such processes is to speak of what is hegemonic and why, rather than about hegemony per se.

Reifying these concepts does enable certain advantages. For instance, defining precisely what cultural capital is (e.g. knowledge of fine wine, classical music) and what hegemonic masculinity is (e.g. a type 'A' personality, misogynistic, muscular), allows us to empirically search for them in different contexts and discuss their relative prevalence. However, reification also has the effect of making it seem as though some have cultural capital, for example, while others do not. This disguises the fact that what might be of no value in some settings could prove invaluable in others.

Discussing these concepts as processes foregrounds different concerns. It enables a closer understanding of the ways that context actually (re)defines the factors at play in delineating status distinctions which are constantly – if only subtly – transforming (Bourdieu, 1984; Connell, 1995; Goffman, 1959, 1963, 1967). Focusing on process allows for contextual distinction or 'field-specificity' (Bourdieu and Wacquant, 1992; Holt, 1997). A closer examination of the theories of Bourdieu and Connell will illustrate a number of similarities that highlight the value of 'gender capital' more clearly.

Bourdieu's Theory of Taste

> Bodybuilding is really a lifestyle. Guys do this their whole life just to get that feeling, you know . . . that pump. It really changes you once you get into it. Lifting's all I think about, and I don't think I'm all that different from other guys. When I look at some guy, that's the first thing I look to. How big's his chest, arms, you know? (Jeff, 220 lb, amateur bodybuilder, 26, bouncer at a bar/club, 6½ years on the bench)

Bourdieu's theory is defined by three terms (habitus, cultural capital and field) and the relationships between them. He uses these to describe individual tastes and social status distinctions. The central argument of Bourdieu's theory is that individual tastes and aesthetic dispositions (worldviews) are uniquely shaped through interaction with socializing agents (class position, family, social interactions, etc.). These interactions work to reproduce socially situated interactional norms, roles and expectations, along with the status hierarchies and inequality in social life. More generally, *taste* refers to the processes through which individuals appropriate – through choice and desire – routines and practices which have their origins in material constraints (Bourdieu, 1984).

Bourdieu defines the *habitus* as the pre-reflexive, practical mastery of self that arranges social practice in such a way that individuals can continuously adjust to a diversity of social situations without consciously considering each adjustment as it is made (Bourdieu, 1990: 53).[5] Bourdieu argues that social predispositions, proclivities and preferences often thought to constitute the 'self' are actually products of diverse and multi-layered socializing forces stemming from social positioning. Many scholars have commented on the fact that the habitus is a profoundly gendered social entity (Krais, 2006; McNay, 1999). Presentations of self are socially produced and contextually distinct (e.g. Eliasoph, 1998; Goffman, 1959; Mills, 1940). The habitus exists as an embodied form of knowledge and as schemas of evaluation allowing for contextual adaptation. Gender is also practiced at a pre-reflexive level and becomes embodied (McNay, 1999).

Before defining cultural capital we must first clarify what it is that Bourdieu means when he defines 'capital' as:

> [A]n energy which only exists and only produces its effects in the field in which it is produced and reproduced, each of the properties attached to class is given its value and efficacy by the specific laws of each field. (1984: 113)

By defining capital as energy, Bourdieu allows its impact to vary. Capital has much more to do with the perceptual status of – and relations between – resources than it does with the objective resources themselves. *Cultural capital* refers to specific repertoires of knowledge, tastes, dispositions and objects of desire that individuals within particular social spaces perceive and employ for status accumulation. The content of cultural capital only matters as it is evaluated in social practice. It will differ by the individual making use of it, and actors will employ it differently – or employ different situationally relevant cultural resources – in different contexts.

Fields are defined by their boundaries, across which field-specific forms of capital cease to have the identical purchase that they have in the field of interest. The habitus may have more or less mastery in different fields. A *field* is a transforming arrangement of relations in a given social context in which a range of specific types of capital and relations between capital – such as knowledge, status or economic resources – are at stake. The meaning and value of capital varies by field. Certainly there exists a hierarchy of tastes in the dominant culture and a hierarchical relationship among fields,

but fields and the capitals that define them – and are defined by them – are also subject to transformation (Adkins, 2003; Bourdieu, 1984, 1990; Krais, 2006; McNay, 1999).

Connell's Theory of Gender Relations

> Reputation depends on kind of stupid stuff. I mean, like, corporate guys, and suits and stuff, get their reps from money, experts of wine, and ridiculous knowledge of things that don't matter at all. . . . We're really not all that different. I mean, here, like we get reps on how big your chest is, and how striped [defined] your shit [body] is. (Jerome, 240 lb, amateur bodybuilder, 29, security guard, 12 years on the bench)

Connell's theory is concerned with the distinction between gender categories and gender relations: 'The key is to move from a focus on difference to a focus on *relations*. Gender is, above all, a matter of the social relations within which individuals and groups act' (2002a: 9). Difference, dichotomy and categories are included in gender relations, but gender relations are also much more. Gender relations include the processes by which gendered distinctions are made. This is why Garfinkel (1967) refers to gender as an 'ongoing accomplishment', Goffman (1977) discusses gender as a social 'arrangement' and West and Zimmerman (1987) address the 'doing' of gender. Gendered distinctions only make sense within the logic of the fields in which they are made. Connell is also critically concerned with the ways in which power is implicated with gender relations. To discuss power, Connell introduces four concepts: gender regime, gender order, the patriarchal dividend and hegemonic masculinity.

Gender regime is a concept developed to address the issue of field-specificity: why do different contexts have different systems of gender valuation and evaluation? A *gender regime* is a local set of interactional arrangements concerning gender[6] Elements of gender regimes go above and beyond clothing, intellect, styles of speaking, etc. to the very gender of interactional predispositions, proclivities and preferences toward which individuals are inclined. While gender regimes are internally varied and subject to change as well, Connell argues that changes in regimes tend to be resisted (Connell, 1987, 2002a).[7]

Gender regimes are also parts of wider patterns of gender relations that endure over time and space. These wider, more durable patterns are what Connell refers to as the *gender order* (Connell, 1987, 2002a). Separate gender regimes may have different degrees of affinity with the gender order. While Bourdieu might refer to this as 'field-specificity', using Connell's ideas, we might discuss 'regime-specificity'. To connect local regimes with the gender order, Connell develops two relatively fluid concepts: the patriarchal dividend and hegemonic masculinity.

Extending Bourdieu's utilization of economic metaphor, the *patriarchal dividend* refers to the advantages that men (as a group) receive as a result of the maintenance of unequal gender relations (e.g. money, authority, respect, safety). While the patriarchal dividend is distributed universally *to* men, it is not equally distributed *among* them. Thus, individual men may receive more benefits than others, and some may receive no benefits (Connell, 2002a). In doing this, Connell sets up relations of power not only between men and women, but among each as well.

Hegemonic masculinity is the name that Connell gives to the currently accepted form of masculinity that dominates women and other men (Connell, 1995), subordinating not only femininity, but also other masculinities (Connell, 1987). Hegemonic masculinities vary by gender regime, as gender relations are contextually arranged and continually transforming (Connell, 2002a). Counter to this regime-specific conceptualization of hegemonic masculinity, some research has attempted to define it more statically, calling attention to groups of men as upholding the patriarchal order (e.g. Connell, 1990; Gillett and White, 1992; Klein, 1986). However, this denies hegemonic masculinity precisely the transformative capacity that makes it so powerful: it is largely elusive and continually in flux (Connell and Messerschmidt, 2005). Because hegemonic masculinity is negotiated regime-specifically, individuals encounter distinct masculinities occupying the hegemonic position in distinct fields of

interaction and historical moments. '"Hegemonic masculinity" is not a fixed character type, always and everywhere the same. It is, rather, a masculinity that occupies the hegemonic position in a given pattern of gender relations, a position always contestable' (Connell, 1995: 76).

The distinction is subtle but important: *we do not exalt hegemonic masculinities because they are hegemonic; they are hegemonic because we exalt them*. Connell's recent work suggests that perhaps a 'transnational business masculinity' is the current hegemonic masculinity of the global gender order (Connell and Wood, 2005). Gender regimes are hierarchically related to one another, as are fields. Transnational businessmen have more power and influence than bodybuilders in *most* social arenas. But it is still important to acknowledge that many transnational businessmen might experience less masculine status in a bodybuilding gym. 'Hegemony has many different configurations and may be local as distinct from general. . . . Like class relations, gender relations change historically, and the pattern and depth of hegemony changes as well' (Connell, 2002b: 89). In short, hegemonic masculinity is defined regime-specifically. This point might be more productively framed with the help of Pierre Bourdieu.

Gender Capital

All men are tryin' to get to the top of their game. It just depend on what that game is. I always wanted to be big cause that's what me and my guys always used to like, measure each other on . . . you know. I guess big don't have to be the body though. We're all tryin' to be big somehow . . . right? (Andre, 198 lb, pre-professional bodybuilder, 23, part-time mover and restaurant employee, 6½ years on the bench)

Gender capital refers to the knowledge, resources and aspects of identity available – within a given context – that permit access to regime-specific gendered identities. Bodies are not the only source of gender capital, but they are an important source. 'A body is a piece of consequential equipment, and its owner is always putting it on the line. Of course, he can bring other capital goods into many of his moments too, but his body is the only one he can never leave behind'

(Goffman, 1967: 167). Bodies are integral parts of the social construction of gender. As identities are now more deliberately undertaken than ever before (Giddens, 1991), men have increasingly come to see their bodies as 'their responsibility to discipline' (Gill et al., 2005: 55).

Some gender capital maintains similar value across social settings. That is, some forms of gender capital are more trans-situationally 'durable' than others. Bourdieu reasons that this is the result of the capital belonging to larger fields, while Connell argues that certain gender capital is a part of the gender order. However, much gender capital varies significantly by context. Individuals employ different aspects of self in different settings to negotiate differently gendered identities (West and Zimmerman, 1987).[8] Above all, 'gender capital' takes both Bourdieu's bounded fields and Connell's gender regimes as critically important: what is valued in gender identities may vary widely by context and setting. Gender capital attempts to foreground the independent effect of context on the relative value of gendered presentations of self.

Connell argues that although hegemonic masculinity is used in many ways, it should not be abandoned. What makes it hegemonic is that it is culturally exalted, not that it dominates society by means of force (though we sometimes exalt forceful forms). Thus, Connell asserts:

> I do think it possible for hegemony to be a positive force. That was part of Gramsci's original conceptualization of hegemony and class relations, and it is quite conceivable that a certain hegemony could be constructed for masculinities that are less toxic, more cooperative and peaceable, than the current editions. (1998: 476)

While hegemonic masculinity is used differently in different research – even within Connell's writings – this is the conceptualization I find most useful. Hegemonic masculinity is defined by social and symbolic value, making 'capital' a useful metaphor in a discussion of gender relations. Gender capital builds on this use and understanding of hegemonic masculinity.

Gender capital also removes some of the difficulties surrounding the use of hegemonic masculinity. For example, gender capital may differ for men and women in certain respects, and overlap in others. In different settings, confidence may be highly valued whether associated with masculinity or femininity. Factors utilized as gender capital by men have changed much throughout history as well and differ by culture. Long hair was a sign of nobility among men when Benjamin Franklin wore it, and while contemporary rock musicians may retain the ability to utilize long hair as 'masculine' gender capital, few contemporary politicians are capable of doing the same.

Simply put, the value of bodies is dictated largely by the contexts in which they are presented. Building on Featherstone's (1991a, 1991b) analysis of consumer culture, Shilling argues that: '[W]e may be witnessing processes which will make it extremely difficult for any one group to impose as hegemonic, as worthy of respect and deference across society, a single classificatory scheme of "valuable bodies"' (1993: 143). Interactional orders are complete with distinct systems of valuation and, as such, the value of a gendered presentation of self will differ by regime. While the body is certainly invested with great amounts of regime-specific gender capital, gender capital also has to do with aspects of self apart from bodies. Gender capital can exist as practice, knowledge, bodily capital, style, tastes and more: aspects of 'self' and social performance that produce gendered statuses within interactional orders.

Gender capital allows us to discuss the ways in which some things count as masculine or feminine for some, but not for others, in some situations and not in others. Thus, Arnold Schwarzenegger's musculature has assisted him greatly in the production of a masculine self (Messner, 2007). However, Richard Simmons – the 'televangelical' fitness instructor – may not command the same amount of masculine gender capital for fitness and musculature, at least not in the same fields that Schwarzenegger receives social status. Having access to or knowledge about something considered masculine or feminine is not all that matters. Rather, it is the elaborate ways in which social actors interact with gender capital, and the ways that various elements interact with one another, that dictate different exchange values in distinct social contexts. Gender capital is also defined, employed and evaluated within a patriarchal gender order that values a hierarchical relationship between masculinities and femininities, regardless of contextual distinctions. Thus, domination, subordination, marginalization and complicity remain paramount in discussions of gender capital. Bodybuilders help to underline some key dimensions of gender capital. So let us now turn to an examination of gender and identity in the social world I call Mount Olympus.

The Bodybuilders of Mount Olympus

> This is what guys are supposed to do. Sometimes people think it's because we feel like nobody inside, so we get all big and stuff. . . . But that's not it. . . . Everyone is all about making themselves beautiful. Some of these people do it with, like, clothes or whatever, and expensive jewelry. . . . I don't need to buy anything. I spend time on my body. It's the same thing, just looks different. (Kevin, 220 lb, amateur bodybuilder, 27, bouncer at a club, 7½ years on the bench)

If there is a single recurrent theme that dominates many of the representations and discussions of the bodybuilding world – what Appadurai (1988) refers to as a strong trope – it is undoubtedly *insecurity*. The grunts and groans that typify the gym setting are thought not only to be the guttural sounds of strongmen, but also impassioned pleas for attention and recognition. What sociologists have found most interesting about men's bodybuilding is that it transparently illustrates a sense of insecurity in the development of a masculine self (e.g. Connell, 1990; Gillett and White, 1992; Klein, 1986, 1993; Wiegers, 1998) most illustratively portrayed by Klein's (1993) discussion of bodybuilders as 'little big men'. Knowing this, I did not expect to find the confident exteriors I first encountered at Mount Olympus.

As the quote above illustrates, Kevin does not perceive himself as any more insecure than other kinds of men (or people for that matter). His quote expresses the belief that everyone is looking for what they perceive to be an adequately gendered self through the use of regime-specific gender capital. While sports cars work for some men, money and occupational prestige for others, bodybuilding is a similar process of acquiring and utilizing gender capital that purchases temporally and contextually contingent gendered identification and status. The regime-specificity of gender capital is explicitly ignored when bodybuilders are thought of only as insecure, rather than – like most people – insecure in certain contexts. While this article is principally concerned with regime-specificity, I will also briefly address issues to do with power and larger gender-political concerns.

Drew started bodybuilding about six years ago. He now works at a nightclub in the evening checking IDs at the door, breaking up fights and ensuring that patrons do not drive home under the influence. The following excerpts from field notes express the ways in which Drew epitomizes the regime-specificity of gender capital.

> A movie theatre is about two blocks from the gym. New action movies are typically a big topic of conversation [at Mount Olympus], particularly debates concerning the body of the star. Having knowledge of the new action movies is a big deal here. It struck me that, although I enjoy action movies, I am clearly less proud of that fact than these men [bodybuilders]. I walked back from the theatre after a morning workout with Andre, Kevin, and Drew (they all have night jobs and are part-time physical trainers at the gym). . . . Two men walked by us in the opposite direction. As they walked by, they began to laugh and as we looked back at them, they seemed to be laughing at Andre, Kevin and Drew. . . . Drew hung his head, 'Fuck, I hate that.' 'Shake it off man,' Kevin consoled him. *Drew would never have let someone get away with that in the gym.* (from author's field notes, emphasis added)

In the gym, Drew was one of the stronger bodybuilders. Although strength does not necessarily have an impact on the size and definition of the body, stronger bodybuilders regularly tease the less strong. Drew's strength was not understood as an asset on our walk back from the movies. But inside the gym, Drew was different.

> Drew finished a set of incline dumb-bell presses [a chest lift] with 130 lb dumb-bells. He was lifting with Johnny. They spot each other [help each other lift]. Drew set his weights down and asked Johnny what weight he wanted to use as Johnny sat down on the bench. 'Gimme the 100s.' Drew went over and picked up the 100 lb dumb-bells, brought them back over to Johnny and set them down by his feet. [This is typical of lifting buddies so that energy is not expended on carrying the weights over to the bench.] After setting them down, Drew used a lisp to say, 'These weights are so cute. Can I get you drink or something? . . . Bitch. 110s on your third [set]?' (from author's field notes)

This is a very different Drew than the one with whom I walked back from the movies. Drew's gender capital purchased a different sort of identification here. His musculature and strength were not laughed at in the gym; he was given high status for his bodily form. Beyond not being laughed at for his physique, he was able to use it to put others down. Typical of bodybuilders in the gym, Drew is extremely confident and believes that he is among the best in the community I studied. As the judging of bodybuilding competitions is often subject to the subjective whims of judges – something often complained about – confidence is understood as an important resource in this setting. This 'emotional labor' (Hochschild, 1983) might not alter judges' opinions, but it enables bodybuilders to cope with loss and perceived 'negative' evaluations of the gender capital they work so hard to attain. Strength and musculature enable Drew to be confident in the gym, but these resources did not have the same effect outside of the gym. Outside, in a different field, Drew was either less confident in his gender capital, or interactionally aware of the different value his body had in a different setting.

This did not necessitate Drew's conscious awareness of the contextual contingencies of the

social status of his gender capital. Rather, he illustrates through his *interactional* awareness that he understands this feature of social life, likely through repeated socialization and subordination. This could be an analogous process to the ways in which children become interactionally aware of topics that we all know about, but no one discusses, what Zerubavel (2006) refers to as 'open secrets'.

Connell (1987, 1995, 2002a) distinguishes intra-gender status relations by referring to hegemonic masculinity as well as marginalized, subordinated, and complicit masculinities. While there are macro-level gender relations, social actors are also uniquely called upon to evaluate individual contexts as they interact with them in different ways – often only making subtle alterations in the performance of their social selves. Drew occupies a hegemonically masculine status in the gym, but his masculinity appeared more subordinate in the interaction outside of the gym. Hence, the reason for talking about gender *relations* in the first place (Connell, 1987, 1995, 2002a): *gender is relationally (or interactionally) accomplished*. As a result, local regimes have to negotiate nuanced ways of illustrating the 'rules of the game' to newcomers. Humor often plays a distinct role in this socialization process and the reproduction of inequality (Goffman, 1959, 1967).

For example, when Kevin starts to work out with a new bodybuilder, joking is a large part of his socialization. Malik – a young black man who just moved to the city to work out with other competing bodybuilders – works at a storage and loading dock for a large furniture company. Kevin asks him how he likes his 'out-of-gym' employment and if he has to lift too much at work, which could hurt Malik's gym performance. He also asks jokingly if the men Malik works with tease him about being a bodybuilder.

> KEVIN: You work with boys or men?
>
> MALIK: Huh?
>
> KEVIN: Boys or men. . . . What? Okay, that's when . . . okay, a man respect work. Maybe you get big while he get rich, but you both work. A boy . . . man, a boy tell you . . . a boy is when

like, says, like, 'You fag' or like, 'Pretty boy' this. . . . A boy can't handle a man like you, 'cause you work.

MALIK: (laughter) Yeah. Men man, men. Most of these guys [that work with me] are tryin' to get off the street too. I get mine [receive status and respect] for my shit [my dedication to my body]. I'm not tryin' to be a punk [out on the street without a job] (laughter). (field notes taken as soon as possible after the interaction took place)

Kevin is doing two things here. He is asking Malik if he has noticed the contextuality of the gender capital he is accumulating through his work at the gym, and he is instructing him that work environments are available where Malik does not have to be ridiculed for the gender capital in which he has invested time and energy (where he can work with 'men'). While these are not always high-status occupations, it is not atypical for individuals to desire to work and play in environments in which their gender capital is considered valuable.

It is likely the case that a great deal of gender capital has regime-specific status. However, it is particularly clear among bodybuilders because of the stark contrast between gym and non-gym settings, and the extreme type of gender capital they possess. Their bodies often go from the height of exaltation and social status to the subject of ridicule (Fussell, 1992; Monaghan, 1999). Some of the bodybuilders in this study were more capable of dealing with contextual contingencies and status distinctions than others, though it was a constant strain for most. In an interview, Chris, an older bodybuilder conscious of regime-specificity, said: 'I can't use my street credit anywhere else. This is the only place it works. . . . No one else gets us. We're the freaks to lots of people, but here, we're like gods'. While Chris is exaggerating when he states that the gym is the 'only place it works', he carefully points out the regime-specificity of gender capital. Chris has also been around long enough to understand and be comfortable with this.

Bodybuilders have many stories in which their gender capital was a source of ridicule and shame. However, most of the bodybuilders I studied also found social spaces where their gender capital

purchased high status, like Malik. Bouncers and doormen at bars and clubs were also able to utilize bodybuilder gender capital. Not surprisingly, these were extremely popular jobs. Many bodybuilders worked together both in and outside of the gym. When I first found out that some of the men were bouncers I thought that injuries would be a concern, as they can ill-afford to miss workouts and still compete. However, this is something that bodybuilders do not worry about.

Jeff and Bruce worked out together today. It was leg day, so both were struggling to enthusiastically engage with their lifts. To pump each other up, they began talking about the night they were about to have together. While they are both bouncers at clubs, they do not typically work together, but tonight they are because Jeff's manager asked for extra guys due to some men leaving, and Jeff was able to recommend Bruce [who would much rather work at Jeff's club than his current location]. This is Bruce's unofficial 'tryout' for Jeff's club. 'How full will it get tonight?' asked Bruce. Jeff said, 'It's all up [all full]. It's always crazy on Fridays, but we just lost like three guys, so we'll be short tonight.' 'Okay. I can't get hurt though. I only have like two months left [before a competition]', said Bruce. 'Look at you son, nobody can get at you. Big mother fucker. Don't trip . . . and don't say that kind of shit around Dave [the manager].' (from author's field notes)

I later asked Jeff if injuries were a concern despite his discussion with Bruce. He laughed. 'Would you ever hit Bruce?' 'No', I said. 'Nobody else would either', said Jeff. He walked away acting as though I had asked a stupid question.

Bouncing is another field in which male bodybuilder gender capital (and bodily capital) often has purchase, although likely in a different way. In the gym, bodybuilders have high status due to their work ethic, strength and the 'look' of their bodies. As Chris stated after a long day in the gym, 'Props [respect is given] to all those that get in early and get out late.' Bars and clubs afford the gender capital of these men a different status: fear and bodies that stand as symbols of violence. Monaghan (2002) had similar findings among doormen in Britain. '[B]odily capital may be transformed into other forms of capital such as income and masculine validating recognition' (Monaghan, 2002: 337). Jeff explained to me the status of bodybuilders as bouncers. 'Nobody wants a guy like me on 'em. . . . I scare myself. People respect, but they can't, like, they can't really not. You know?'

Jeff and Bruce are extremely large men, both over 200 pounds. They pat patrons down as they enter the club and check IDs, often muttering 'No trouble tonight' to rougher-looking men. In this way, they are also letting people know that they will have to deal with a very large man if they 'start trouble'. They are symbolically in control of the environment long before they would ever have the need to physically control it. Bruce later reiterated this point in an interview.

> I would actually never get in a fight at work. I wouldn't want to risk, like, getting hurt or something. . . . It doesn't matter though. I never had a situation where I mighta' had to. Most times, if there's trouble, I just walk over and say, like, 'Hey, buddy, you need to take it somewhere.' . . . The times that someone looks like he might swing on me or something, I got some other guys with me [for assistance]. One time, this one guy's friends pulled him out the bar 'cause, like, they don't want him to try get mixed up either [fight with me]. So, I don't really worry. (Bruce, 235 lb, amateur bodybuilder, 32, bouncer at a club, 10 years on the bench)

However, later in the same interview, Bruce chuckled, 'Seems nice, yeah? Try getting out of a speeding ticket with this shit (flexing an arm).' He perceived his gender capital as precluding the possibility of receiving only a warning from a police officer for driving too fast.

Interactions with the police were a popular topic of conversation.[9] Bodybuilders were both proud of and frustrated with the ways in which they understood police as 'dealing' with them. Many of the men in my study felt that police seemed to unfairly pick them out of a crowd. Two black bodybuilders at Mount Olympus had the following discussion while taking a lifting break.

> Jerome: 'I fucking hate cops. . . . They always follow me around and shit. I'm not tryin' to do

nothing [illegal]. Kid, they just can't handle these guns' (flexes a bi [bicep] and grins). Others laugh. Derrick agrees with him and talks about being followed at a grocery store like he was going to steal. Lots of laughter. (from author's field notes)

The police represent a different set of gender relations – or gender regime (and perhaps the gender order) – wherein some people are in charge, not because of their individual gender capital, but because of the power of the positions they occupy. This is also interesting because, in the gym, black bodybuilders are treated and interacted with in much the same ways as white bodybuilders. However, outside of this field, it is likely that huge, muscular black men are interpreted in a qualitatively different way from their white counterparts.

The police symbolize a 'masculinity challenge' (Messerschmidt, 2000) among bodybuilders. Messerschmidt (2000) defines masculinity challenges as confrontations between conflicting masculinities. Many bodybuilders understand the police as symbolically representing a masculinity challenge. Though I did not hear of any bodybuilders getting into actual fights or arguments with police, there was another group in the gym that presented similar 'challenges': the powerlifters.

The powerlifters at Mount Olympus occupy a separate gender regime, though many aspects overlap with the bodybuilders. Conflict is ever present, but rarely erupts into arguments or fights. While bodybuilders lift for definition and size, powerlifters lift for strength. Connell notes that: 'It is common for different groups of men, each pursuing a project of hegemonic masculinity, to come into conflict with each other' (1995: 215). Powerlifters provide a sort of ubiquitous masculinity challenge, serving to both reaffirm distinctions between groups and solidarity among them.

Distinctions between bodybuilders and powerlifters also illustrate the ways in which gender regimes are not always represented as geographically separate in terms of *physical* space. 'Different masculinities are [sometimes] produced in the same cultural or institutional setting' (Connell, 1995: 36). Gender regimes represent *social* spaces, or what Goffman (1983) refers to as 'interactional orders'.

An individual can be physically in the middle of a group of individuals who all occupy the same field (or gender regime) while being outside of the field. Think of the experience of 'not getting' a joke that everyone else around you seems to understand. In many cases, context, group-specific knowledge and interactional styles preclude your comprehension of the joke, not that you simply missed the punch line.

Based on the jargon, lifting noises and presence in the 'heavy weight room', both groups might actually appear more similar than they are. I assumed that powerlifters were bodybuilders when I began my study. I thought that they had more recently begun the process of transforming into a bodybuilder and had not yet attained the same level of definition and size as others. The distinctions between the two subcultures are inscribed into their bodies, and while both are groups of very large men, their bodily and gender capital within the gym setting are different from one another. Gender capital distinctions, particularly when both groups interact with one another, become apparent inside the gym setting. What counts as masculine gender capital differs by group:

> Bodybuilders, powerlifters and individuals who want to 'tone up' and 'trim down' might each use dumb-bells and bar-bells, for example, and might even do the same exercises (bench press, squat, etc.). However, the way in which they do those exercises will vary. (Crossley, 2005: 12)

As both groups are very vocal, masculinity challenges are a regular feature of the gym's interactional order.

When I asked one of the more seasoned powerlifters – Javier – why powerlifters and bodybuilders tease each other, his response illuminates a popular way in which powerlifters view bodybuilders.

> Because they are gay. . . . I mean, just look at them. Gay! . . . They are always touching each other and checking each other's bodies and stuff. It's nasty . . . . I think they're just all acting like they don't want to get with guys. . . . That's all they talk about though . . . guys' bodies and different parts and stuff. Nasty! . . . We fuck with those guys [tease them] 'cause they act all gay like that. They

> try to pretend and be all man and all that, but they mostly be shaving their legs and wearing thongs . . . it's just gay. I don't know what else to say. (Javier, powerlifter, 26, 4½ years on the bench)

While I did meet two male bodybuilders who openly identified as homosexual, Javier was not referring to those two. The two homosexual bodybuilders were no different from their heterosexual counterparts in the gym in most respects. Aside from Javier's comments about their sexuality, the rest of his comments are true of bodybuilding subculture. There is a great deal of bodily interaction, they closely examine each others' bodies, they shave their entire bodies (causing razors to be a nearly constant accessory for bodybuilders), and competition requires the use of a very small 'posing suit' that would be referred to as a 'male thong' in almost any other setting. Much of this 'hyper-masculine' behavior is ironically 'feminine' in many other contexts. Bodybuilders' gender capital is highly contingent upon context. This is Javier's point. It was not unusual to hear powerlifters calling bodybuilders 'gay', 'fag', 'fairies', etc. Another powerlifter reiterated this point.

> Bodybuilders are mainly a bunch of fuckin' homos [homosexuals]. Serious though . . . I mean those guys are all over each other (laughing). . . . Nobody takes that shit seriously. They're fags. I don't really think they're all manly or whatever. They're girly to me. (Freddie, powerlifter, 27, construction worker, 6 years on the bench)

Bodybuilders have a different way of talking about powerlifters to illustrate distinctions in gender capital. Bodybuilders value definition and size much more than strength. As a result, lifting as much as possible just to lift as much as possible (the powerlifter philosophy) is seen as 'immature' among bodybuilders. Kevin jokingly explained how bodybuilders view powerlifters:

> Powerlifters are basically a bunch of jocks that never got over leaving high school. They're all like, trying to relive the glory days. . . . I mean, they are just not like us [bodybuilders]. They're like, stupid. They don't lift right and, I'm just

sayin', they are some ugly dudes . . . you know? (Kevin, 220 lb, amateur bodybuilder, 27, bouncer at a club, 7½ years on the bench)

Bodybuilders in my study often attributed the 'dumb jock' stereotype to powerlifters. From the point of view of a bodybuilder like Kevin, it is difficult to understand why someone would disregard technique solely to display power. Although these two groups occasionally work out together, the gender capital distinctions became clear the more I came to learn.

It is common for bodybuilders to criticize the lifting techniques and movements of powerlifters in the gym. The use of 'too much' weight (bodybuilder perspective) does not enable the lifter to maximize the benefit of each lift; rather, it enables the lifter to bear full capacity (powerlifter perspective). Crossley (2005) addresses this by coining reflexive body techniques, which he defines as, 'those body techniques whose primary purpose is to work back upon the body, so as to modify, maintain or thematize it in some way' (2005: 9). As Crossley (2005) seeks to show in his work, groups that maintain similar reflexive body techniques share much more than only bodily forms. Hence, the ways in which exercises are performed can serve to delineate group boundaries.

Bodybuilders also criticize powerlifters for 'football squats', giving full weight to the 'dumb jock' stereotype. Squats are a leg exercise in which the lifter places a barbell behind the neck and across the shoulders, with the legs shoulder width apart. The lifter then proceeds to dip down and press the weight back up into a standing position. A 'football squat' is when the squatter is not able to descend fully as a result of attempting to lift more than he or she is capable of lifting 'correctly' (bodybuilder perspective). While perhaps a useful distinction to newcomers, to tell another lifter that they are performing 'football squats' is an insult taken very seriously at Mount Olympus. As a result, it is typically only used in jest or behind the back of the alleged 'football squatter'.

When instructing Malik how to correctly perform squats, Bruce shows proper form and technique.

He tells Malik, 'You don't want to be doing it like this', as he dips only about half way down. 'That [this lifting technique] makes you look all lumpy [a characteristic 'look' of powerlifters] and like you proving something. . . . Prove it by shredding up [defining] your quads. Lift less, but do it good.' (from author's field notes)

Bruce is illustrating to Malik how to correctly perform a squat, but is also indicating the subtle gender capital distinctions between bodybuilders and men with 'something to prove' – a common bodybuilder assessment of powerlifter subculture. Thus, despite the popular quip about bodybuilders and insecurity – which is not necessarily always incorrect – bodybuilders themselves often situate powerlifters as adhering more closely to the insecurity trope.

Beyond the contextual contingencies of gender capital, issues of power and the gender-political consequences of the mobilization of certain gender capital must remain paramount. This was vital for Connell's (1987) conceptualization of hegemonic masculinity and gender relations, and Bourdieu's (1984) conceptualization of social reproduction and cultural capital. Connell's (1987) book is entitled *Gender and Power* to underline this connection, similar to the ways in which Foucault ties power to knowledge, while Bourdieu's (2001) work on gender – *Masculine Domination* – also explicitly addresses power.

Gender relations are important to understand in both their micro- and macro-level consequences. For example, some scholars have remarked that it is far from ironic that bodybuilding achieved fame in the United States in the 1970s (Gillett and White, 1992; Wiegers, 1998). This occurred at the same time that the US women's movement was making sizeable gains and gender relations were changing at a macro level. Bodybuilders – regardless of individual intentions – forced us to notice gender differences in the face of a cultural shift toward the unification of separate spheres and an increasing prevalence of ideologies of gender similarity. Weight-lifting also became popular at roughly the same time that strong bodies were no longer necessary for economic advantage (Kimmel, 2006).

This could also be part of Faludi's (1991) 'backlash' argument, discussing the subtle cultural messages of the 'comforts' of gender differences at times when feminist change may appear imminent. This was part of Kimmel's (1989) argument when he discussed the ways in which men's gender politics have historically been 'reactions' to changes in women's gender politics rather than innovations. Positions of privilege *react* to changes made among subordinate statuses. This is precisely the power of hegemony. These reactions illustrate the fluidity of cultural capital, hegemonic masculinity and gender capital that make static understandings much less useful, and much less characteristic of the ways in which social life works.

Gender capital means different things to different people in different fields at different times. This transformative capacity is exactly why Connell uses the concept of hegemony. It is important to discuss the ways in which gender-political acts and identities that characterize local gender regimes may have consequences for social relations within the gender order as well. Future research endeavoring to utilize gender capital and discuss regime-specificity should work to address the gender-political consequences of the meanings and mobilizations of gender capital more explicitly.

CONCLUSION

> It's not like I'm the man wherever I go. . . . People gonna treat you different, if like, well, they treat you different. . . . I mean not everybody out there is like, tryin' to make you feel good. You gotta' do that for yourself. So . . . like, me and these guys [the other bodybuilders at Mount Olympus], we hold each other up here [in the gym]. Out there, you hold yourself. That's life. (Malik, 190 lb, aspiring amateur bodybuilder, 25, part-time mover at a furniture warehouse, 4 years on the bench)

Discussions of hegemonic masculinity in the sociology of gender – and perhaps masculinities studies

in particular – have yielded diverse meanings and uses. However, when drawing upon practice theoretical scholarship, as Connell did when formulating this concept (e.g. Bourdieu, Elias, Giddens), an important meaning and intention of hegemonic masculinity is perhaps made more clear. Hegemonic masculinity, like cultural capital, refers to the social value of regime-specific configurations of status, knowledge, body image, performances, etc. While bodybuilders are a population that make this distinction viscerally obvious, I suggest that they are perhaps more similar to the rest of us in their negotiation of multiple fields of gendered interaction than they are different.

Allowing the meaning and content of gender capital to vary regime-specifically opens up new and interesting questions for sociological and feminist research. What types of interactional orders foster hegemonically masculine identifications consistent with the peaceable potential of hegemonic masculinity? How does power operate within gender regimes relative to what is considered 'high-status' gender capital? How does power connect gender regimes to larger fields of interaction (e.g. politics, the economy, the gender order)? When is violence a resource and when is it stigmatized? These types of questions are only available to us if we first acknowledge that what 'count' as dominant forms of masculinity or femininity (what I am referring to as gender capital) are much more fluid or regime-specific than they are sometimes treated.

Finally, introducing gender capital into our vocabulary for describing gender (and perhaps sexuality as well) allows for a few other contributions. First, both men and women possess gender capital, albeit often different types and in different ways. With the recent academic interest in discussions of the 'degendering' of society (e.g. Kimmel, 2007: 339–44; Lorber, 2005) – or what West and Zimmerman (2009) call a society in which gender has been 'redone' – it will be increasingly important to develop a vocabulary that allows us to talk about gender without having to address it as *either* masculine *or* feminine. Connell's conceptualization precludes researchers from addressing gender regimes in which androgynous gender capital is valued, other than identifying them as subordinated from a more macro-social perspective. This is not to argue against the continued use of hegemonic masculinity. In fact, when used as an open concept, I think that this is one of the more powerful conceptual tools sociologists of gender have.

Hegemonic masculinity is a useful term when looking at the ways in which bodybuilders *do* gender. However, it is potentially less useful when attempting to compare the ways in which bodybuilders are doing much the same thing as everyone else, though the value of their presentations of self may be less trans-situationally durable than most. More generally, I suggest that gender capital allows us to compare the gender projects of bodybuilders to those of anyone – not only gender 'extremists'. Future research should pay close attention to the contextual fluidity of gender capital, as well as the gender-political implications that it resists, expresses or attempts to hide.

ACKNOWLEDGEMENTS

Special thanks to the anonymous reviewers at *Body and Society* as well as Rae Lesser Blumberg, Ekaterina Makarova, Tara L. Tober, Portia Bridges, Matthew W. Hughey, Benjamin H. Snyder, Tatiana Omeltchenko, and David Sullivan Morris for helpful comments on earlier portions and drafts of this paper. Finally, I would like to thank the members of Mount Olympus for welcoming me into their community for a period of time and generously assisting my efforts to understand the gender of their lives.

NOTES

1. See Mansfield and McGinn (1993) for a typology of gyms.

2. There are distinctions and variation among bodybuilders (see particularly Monaghan, 1999), but for the purposes of the analysis here, they are grouped together for a few reasons: (1) outside of the gym, they are situated as a single group; (2) they share roughly similar aesthetic dispositions relative to bodily form and function; and (3) they are all engaged in extremely comparable 'body projects' (Featherstone et al., 1991).

3. Certainly there are distinctions between East coast and West coast bodybuilding (e.g. Fussell, 1992; Tyler, 2004; Wayne, 1985), and bodybuilding culture in the US as distinct from abroad (e.g. Aoki, 1996; Monaghan, 1999, 2001; St Martin and Gavey, 1996), but these differences are not critical for the purposes of this study. Additionally, due to online networks facilitated by the largest bodybuilding magazine in the world – *Flex* – it is possible that variation between gyms and cultures is becoming less apparent. The commercialization of bodybuilding has also allowed national gyms to commodify and transport that 'West Coast, Venice Beach feel' to gyms all over the US, and perhaps abroad as well. See Connell and Wood (2005) for a similar argument on the globalization of gender relations.

4. There is also the potential to confuse and falsely separate 'body' and 'self' when thinking of processes as photographs, a potential Crossley (2005) warns against. Photographs are a useful example of this: a dance is not only witnessed, it is also experienced. The experience cannot be divorced from the process if we are to have a complete understanding of the dance.

5. McNay (1999) usefully discusses Bourdieu's notion of habitus with his discussion of '*le sens pratique*' (1990: 52), which roughly translates as 'a feel for the game'. For Bourdieu, this '*sens*' is not natural or sociologically inexplicable, but rather is a field-specific mastery of interactional forms and dynamics, such that a sense of 'intuition' is experienced due to socialization, structural positioning and the predictability of modern life.

6. Connell was not alone in her work to discuss gender as a transforming arrangement of social relations. Many individuals were a part of the critique of structural functionalism and sex role theory (see Connell, 1985 for the clearest critique with which I am familiar). It is worth noting that the term 'gender regime' has been used by another significant figure in gender theory. In *Gender Transformations* (1997), Sylvia Walby uses the term to highlight historical shifts in gender relations. I believe that Connell employs the term in a more nuanced way which seeks to illuminate transformations about and beyond only historical (e.g., cross-cultural, intra-psychic, and contextual).

7. Bodybuilders are, in many ways, a symbolic resistance to feminist changes in society (Gillett and White, 1992). Their rise to popularity took place at roughly the same time as women and men were beginning to play more equal roles in society (Wiegers, 1998). Thus, they provide an interesting example of a group that passionately and prominently displays gender differences.

8. However, when I am discussing individuals 'employing' different aspects of their gender capital, there is a temptation to read this as a cultural rational choice theory (i.e. that actors enter situations and consciously consider which aspects of self to employ to achieve maximum gains). This is an incorrect reading. Rather, it is similar to Bourdieu's notion of the habitus, wherein individual actors make adjustments in their portrayal of self to a great diversity of social interactions and situations without having to actively consider each adjustment as it is made.

9. While I did not have any police who were bodybuilders in my study, I did see some at competitions. The contentious relationship between police and bodybuilders is not one of bodily capital distinction per se. Police may engage in very similar bodily practices, as the gender capital of a bodybuilder might be particularly well suited to their occupation. They may exercise at police facilities or may not. I did not meet anyone who identified themselves as police. The contention (i.e. masculinity challenge) arose surrounding the relationship of the police to bodybuilders as one of civilian and officer.

10. 'Football squats' are squats attributed to American football players. Football players endeavor to 'max out' (lift the most that they can) and in so doing are often criticized for lifting incorrectly as a result of attempting to achieve a higher 'max' on record.

REFERENCES

Adamson, W.L. (1980) *Hegemony and Revolution*. Berkeley, CA: University of California Press.

Adkins, L. (2003) 'Reflexivity: Freedom or Habit of Gender?', *Theory, Culture & Society* 20(6): 21–42.

Aoki, D. (1996) 'Sex and Muscle: The Female Bodybuilder Meets Lacan', *Body & Society* 2(4): 59–74.

Appadurai, A. (1988) 'Putting Hierarchy in its Place', *Cultural Anthropology* 3(1): 36–49.

Bourdieu, P. (1984) *Distinction*. Cambridge, MA: Harvard University Press.

Bourdieu, P. (1990) *The Logic of Practice*. Stanford, CA: Stanford University Press.

Bourdieu, P. (2001) *Masculine Domination*. Stanford, CA: Stanford University Press.

Bourdieu, P. and J. Passeron (1977) *Reproduction in Education, Society and Culture*. London: SAGE.

Bourdieu, P. and L. Wacquant (1992) *An Invitation to Reflexive Sociology*. Chicago, IL: University of Chicago Press.

Butler, J. (1993) *Bodies that Matter: On the Discursive Limits of Sex*. London: Routledge.

Carrigan, T., R.W. Connell and J. Lee (1985) 'Toward a New Sociology of Masculinity', *Theory and Society* 14: 551–602.

Connell, R.W. (1985) 'Theorising Gender', *Sociology* 19(2): 260–72.

Connell, R.W. (1987) *Gender and Power*. Stanford, CA: Stanford University Press.

Connell, R.W. (1990) 'An Iron Man: The Body and Some Contradictions of Hegemonic Masculinity', in M. Messner and D. Sabo (eds) *Sport, Men and the Gender Order*. Champaign, IL: Human Kinetic Books.

Connell, R.W. (1995) *Masculinities*. Berkeley, CA: University of California Press.

Connell, R.W. (1998) 'Reply', *Gender & Society* 12(4): 474–77.

Connell, R.W. (2002a) *Gender*. Cambridge: Polity Press.

Connell, R.W. (2002b) 'On Hegemonic Masculinity and Violence: Response to Jefferson and Hall', *Theoretical Criminology* 6(1): 89–99.

Connell, R.W. and J.W. Messerschmidt (2005) 'Hegemonic Masculinity: Rethinking the Concept', *Gender & Society* 19(6): 829–59.

Connell, R.W. and J. Wood (2005) 'Globalization and Business Masculinities', *Men and Masculinities* 7(4): 347–64.

Crossley, N. (2004) 'The Circuit Trainer's Habitus', *Body & Society* 10(1): 37–69.

Crossley, N. (2005) 'Mapping Reflexive Body Techniques', *Body & Society* 11(1): 1–35.

Elias, N. (1998) *On Civilization, Power, and Knowledge*. Chicago, IL: University of Chicago Press.

Eliasoph, N. (1998) *Avoiding Politics: How Americans Produce Apathy in Everyday Life*. Cambridge: Cambridge University Press.

Emerson, R., R. Fretz and L. Shaw (1995) *Writing Ethnographic Fieldnotes*. Chicago, IL: University of Chicago Press.

Faludi, S. (1991) *Backlash: The Undeclared War against American Women*. New York: Anchor Books.

Featherstone, M. (1991a) 'The Body in Consumer Culture', in M. Featherstone, M. Hepworth and B.S. Turner (eds) *The Body: Social Process and Cultural Theory*. London: SAGE.

Featherstone, M. (1991b) *Consumer Culture and Postmodernism*. London: SAGE.

Featherstone, M., M. Hepworth and B.S. Turner (1991) *The Body: Social Process and Cultural Theory*. London: SAGE.

Fussell, S.W. (1992) *Muscle: Confessions of an Unlikely Bodybuilder*. New York: Harper.

Garfinkel, H. (1967) *Studies in Ethnomethodology*. Cambridge: Polity Press.

Giddens, A. (1991) *Modernity and Self-identity*. Stanford, CA: Stanford University Press.

Gill, R., K. Henwood and C. McLean (2005) 'Body Projects and the Regulation of Normative Masculinity', *Body & Society* 11(1): 37–62.

Gillett, J. and P.G. White (1992) 'Male Bodybuilding and the Reassertion of Hegemonic Masculinity: A Critical Feminist Perspective', *Play and Culture* 5: 358–69.

Glaser, B. and A. Strauss (1967) *The Discovery of Grounded Theory*. Chicago, IL: Aldine Press.

Goffman, E. (1959) *The Presentation of Self in Everyday Life*. New York: Doubleday.

Goffman, E. (1963) *Behavior in Public Places*. New York: Free Press.

Goffman, E. (1967) *Interaction Ritual*. New York: Doubleday.

Goffman, E. (1977) 'The Arrangement between the Sexes', *Theory and Society* 4(3): 301–31.

Goffman, E. (1983) 'The Interaction Order: American Sociological Association, 1982 Presidential Address', *American Sociological Review* 48(1): 1–17.

Goffman, E. (1989) 'On Fieldwork', *Journal of Contemporary Ethnography* 18(2): 123–32.

Gramsci, A. (2005 [1971]) *Selections from Prison Notebooks of Antonio Gramsci*. New York: International Publishers.

Hammersley, M. (1989) 'The Problem of the Concept', *Journal of Contemporary Ethnography* 18(2): 133–59.

Hammersley, M. (1992) *What's Wrong with Ethnography?* London: Routledge.

Hammersley, M. and P. Atkinson (1995) *Ethnography: Principles in Practice*. London: Routledge.

Hochschild, A. (1983) *The Managed Heart*. Berkeley, CA: University of California Press.

Holt, D.B. (1997) 'Distinction in America? Recovering Bourdieu's Theory of Tastes from its Critics', *Poetics* 25: 93–120.

Kimmel, M.S. (1989) 'The Contemporary "Crisis" of Masculinity in Historical Perspective', pp. 121–53 in Harry Brod (ed.) *The Making of Masculinities*. Boston, MA: Allen and Unwin.

Kimmel, M.S. (2006) *Manhood in America*, 2nd edn. New York: Oxford.

Kimmel, M.S. (2007) *Gender and Society*, 3rd edn. New York: Oxford.

Klein, A. (1986) 'Pumping Irony: Crisis and Contradiction in Bodybuilding', *Sport Sociology Journal* 3(2): 112–33.

Klein, A. (1993) *Little Big Men: Bodybuilding Subculture and Gender Construction*. New York: SUNY Press.

Krais, B. (2006) 'Gender, Sociological Theory and Bourdieu's Sociology of Practice', *Theory, Culture & Society* 23(6): 119–34.

Lorber, J. (2005) *Breaking the Bowls*. New York: W.W. Norton.

McNay, L. (1999) 'Gender, Habitus and the Field: Pierre Bourdieu and the Limits of Reflexivity', *Theory, Culture & Society* 16(1): 95–117.

Mansfield, A. and B. McGinn (1993) 'Pumping Irony: The Muscular and the Feminine', in S. Scott and D. Morgan (eds) *Body Matters*. London: Falmer Press.

Messerschmidt, J. (2000) 'Becoming "Real Men": Adolescent Masculinity Challenges and Sexual Violence', *Men and Masculinities* 2(3): 286–307.

Messner, M. (2007) 'The Masculinity of the Governator: Muscle and Compassion in American Politics', *Gender & Society* 21(4): 461–80.

Mills, C. Wright (1940) 'Situated Action and Vocabularies of Motive', *American Sociological Review* 5(6): 904–13.

Monaghan, L.F. (1999) 'Creating "The Perfect Body": A Variable Project', *Body & Society* 5(2–3): 267–90.

Monaghan, L.F. (2001) *Bodybuilding, Drugs and Risk*. London: Routledge.

Monaghan, L.F. (2002) 'Hard Men, Shop Boys, and Others: Embodying Competence in a Masculinist Occupation', *Sociological Review* 50(3): 334–55.

Sassatelli, R. (1999) 'Interaction Order and Beyond: A Field Analysis of Body Culture within Fitness Gyms', *Body & Society* 5(2–3): 227–48.

Schwarzenegger, A. and D.K. Hall (1977) *Arnold: The Education of a Bodybuilder.* New York: Simon and Schuster.

Shilling, C. (1993) *The Body and Social Theory.* London: SAGE.

St Martin, L. and N. Gavey (1996) 'Women's Bodybuilding: Feminist Resistance and/or Femininity's Recuperation?', *Body & Society* 2(4): 45–57.

Turner, B.S. (1984) *The Body and Society.* Oxford: Blackwell.

Turner, B.S. (1992) *Regulating Bodies: Essays in Medical Sociology.* London: Routledge.

Turner, B.S. (2003) 'Social Fluids: Metaphors and Meanings of Society', *Body & Society* 9(1): 1–10.

Tyler, D. (2004) *West Coast Bodybuilding Scene.* Aptos, CA: On Target.

Wacquant, L. (1995a) 'Pugs at Work: Bodily Capital and Bodily Labour among Professional Boxers', *Body & Society* 1(1): 65–93.

Wacquant, L. (1995b) 'The Pugilistic Point of View: How Boxers Think and Feel about their Trade', *Theory and Society* 24: 489–535.

Wacquant, L. (1995c) 'Review Article: Why Men Desire Muscles', *Body & Society* 1(1): 163–79.

Walby, S. (1997) *Gender Transformations.* London: Routledge.

Wayne, R. (1985) *Muscle Wars.* New York: St Martin's Press.

West, C. and D. Zimmerman (1987) 'Doing Gender', *Gender & Society* 1(2): 125–51.

West, C. and D. Zimmerman (2009) 'Accounting for Doing Gender', *Gender & Society* 23(2): 112–122.

Wiegers, Y. (1998) 'Male Bodybuilding: The Social Construction of a Masculine Identity', *Journal of Popular Culture* 32(2): 147–61.

Williams, R. (1977) *Marxism and Literature.* New York: Oxford University Press.

Zerubavel, E. (2006) *The Elephant in the Room: Silence and Denial in Everyday Life.* New York: Oxford.

PART SIX

MEN IN RELATIONSHIPS

Why do many men have problems establishing and maintaining intimate relationships with women? What different forms do male–female relational problems take within different socioeconomic groups? How do men's problems with intimacy and emotional expressivity relate to power inequities between the sexes? Are rape and domestic violence best conceptualized as isolated deviant acts by "sick" individuals, or are they the illogical consequences of male socialization? This complex web of male–female relationships, intimacy, and power is the topic of this part.

And what is the nature of men's relationships with other men? Do men have close friendships with men, or do they simply "bond" around shared activities and interests? How do competition, homophobia, and violence enter into men's relationships with each other? For example, a student recently commented that when he goes to movies with another male friends, they always leave a seat between them, where they put their coats, because they don't want anyone to think they are there "together."

But what are the costs of this emotional and physical distance? And what are the costs of maintaining emotionally impoverished relationships with other men? How is this emotional distance connected to men's intimate relationships with women? Is it related to Billy Crystal's line in *When Harry Met Sally* that women and men can never be friends because "the sex thing always gets in the way"?

Do young guys together constantly brag about heterosexual conquests, real or imagined? Neill Korobov's analysis of young men's conversations with their friends suggests a different sort of gamesmanship and bonding is going on among some male friends: Men become "lovable losers" by telling sexual stories about embarrassing romantic and sexual mishaps and gaffes. Peter Nardi explores the friendship patterns of gay men, finding innovative blendings of friendship and family life, and broadened emotional repertoires. Peggy Giordano and her colleagues describe how adolescent boys are far more romantic than we give them credit for being, although this romanticism often leads to a certain "learned helplessness" when it comes to actually working on a relationship. These sorts of emotional asymmetries between young heterosexual women and men play out later in life, as the final article in this part shows. In the final article, Kathleen Gerson discusses men's resistance to equal sharing with women in relationships and shows how this is a key part of a stalled feminist revolution.

"We've been wandering in the desert for forty years. But he's a man—would he ever ask directions?"

Source: Peter Steiner/The New Yorker Collection/www.cartoonbank.com

'HE'S GOT NO GAME': YOUNG MEN'S STORIES ABOUT FAILED ROMANTIC AND SEXUAL EXPERIENCES

Neill Korobov

INTRODUCTION

During the last decade, there has been an increasing amount of theoretical and analytic attention to masculinity from a discursive orientation (Wetherell and Edley 1999, Gough 2001, Riley 2003, Korobov 2004, 2005, 2006, Korobov and Bamberg 2004). In seizing on rigorous analytic procedures for the close study of talk, discursive work has been instrumental in revealing how oppressive forms of masculinity are not only discursively produced and reproduced, but also how they are routinely denied, inoculated from challenge, and mitigated through irony, humor and parody. It has been in this second vein of analysis, in exposing the plausibly deniable features of masculinity, that discursive work has uniquely illuminated Connell's (1995) argument concerning the flexible, formidably resourceful, and inscrutable composition of what is hegemonic about masculinity. Whereas traditional psychological work often conflates 'hegemonic masculinity' with 'heroic masculinity' (bread-winner, heterosexual, tough, virile), discursive work has revealed that what is sometimes most hegemonic are masculine positions that are knowingly non-heroic or ordinary, i.e. the self-reflexive varieties that casually and playfully parody traditional male stereotypes.

Neill Korobov, "He's Got no Game: Young Men's Stories About Failed Romantic and Sexual Experiences," *Journal of Gender Studies*, 18(2) June, 2009, 99–114. Copyright © 2009. Reprinted by permission of Taylor & Francis.

Nowhere is this more obvious than in the textual and visual construction of masculinities in popular culture magazines, television and films. For instance, consider the interminable barrage of men's lifestyle magazines (*Maxim, Details, FHM, Stuff, Loaded*, etc.) that proffer, in tongue-in-cheek ways, a kind of 'new laddism' – an educated, middle-class, and witty version of masculinity that eschews the wimpishness of the sensitive 'new man' while seeking to re-claim the conservative ethos of beer, women and sport (Benwell 2002). Or consider the television sitcom trend of presenting men as anti-heroes – as hapless, yet affably befuddled and domesticated, who nevertheless remain eminently likable and successful. There are also series such as MTV's *Jackass*, where a group of unassuming white working-class guys turn failure and bodily injury into a 'carnivalesque sadomasochism' that relentlessly mocks heroic masculinity (Brayton 2007). Also popular is the 'white-guy-as-loser' trope that is ubiquitous in beer commercials (Messner and Montez de Oca 2005). This 'lovable loser' finds himself routinely humiliated, usually as a result of pursuing unattainably beautiful women. Yet, he is blissfully self-mocking and ironic about his loser-status, for he is a loser only in contrast to the outdated macho versions of masculinity typical of beer ads in the past. In whatever form, these various media gambits have been successful in serving up an average and ordinary 'everyman' – a youthful and predominately white version of masculinity that is playfully ironic and self-mocking.

When interpreted in the wake of significant post-civil rights advances by women, sexual minorities and ethnic minorities, these new masculine tropes appear as a form of anxious 'white male backlash' (Savran 1996, Robinson 2000), albeit an intentionally mitigated backlash. Commercial forces have commodified these anxious and self-deprecating tendencies, creating a simulacrum of marginalized and victimized masculine positionalities and disseminating them throughout culture (see Benwell 2002, Brayton 2007). Unfortunately, there is a paucity of micro-level research detailing how ordinary young men occasion such positions within mundane social contexts. As these visual and textual depictions of failed masculinity become increasingly woven into the fabric of everyday culture, we are left to wonder if and how young men are adopting them as part of the project of doing homosociality and, if so, how the face of hegemonic masculinity may be slowly changing as a result.

The present study thus takes a keen interest in how young men occasion a variety of self-deprecating masculine tropes in their stories about romantic mishaps and gaffes, often resulting in rejection and embarrassment. These types of stories are the focus of the present study. The aim in studying self-deprecation in the context of romantic experiences is not to voyeuristically indulge in young men's immature behavior; rather, the aim is to use a critical-discursive perspective to examine how young men formulate stories that, at least on the surface, seem contrary to traditional masculine norms, and to finally suggest how a new variety of male homosociality and hegemonic masculinity is emerging as a result.

The 'ordinariness' of hegemonic masculinity

Insight into this new variety of hegemony is not without precedent. In one of the more widely cited discursive studies on masculinity, Wetherell and Edley (1999) found that the most common form of self-positioning with young men did not involve 'heroism' or 'rebelliousness', but rather 'ordinariness'. Most men resisted the macho and 'bad-boy' masculine ideals in favor of positioning themselves as normal and conventional guys. Wetherell and Edley (1999) noticed, however, that their 'ordinariness' was actually a gender-oppressive method of self-presentation. They argue that sometimes one of the most effective ways of endorsing hegemonic masculinity is to demonstrate one's distance from it – that is, to show, with all the weapons of rhetoric, that one has the courage and confidence, as an 'ordinary' man, to resist (and even mock) heroic and macho forms of masculinity.

This lampooning of heroic and macho masculinity and embracing of the 'everyman' is a type of masculine subjectivity slowly being illuminated in a range of subsequent studies (see Gough 2001, Korobov 2005, 2006, Korobov and Thorne 2006, Brayton 2007, Gilmartin 2007). In remarking on the 'generous nonchalance' in heterosexual college-aged men's stories about romantic breakups, Gilmartin (2007) noticed that young men put a considerable amount of effort into making romance a casual, easily-jettisoned topic. In two similar studies, Korobov and Thorne (2006, 2007) found that young men often playfully mitigated the seriousness of their romantic problems so as to appear nonchalant, un-invested, and at times mildly amused by their own and each other's romantic troubles. Gough (2001) found that young men often discursively suppressed their thoughts in particular contexts in order to manage potentially sexist sentiments. The common thread in these studies is not that young men are, as men, simply 'ordinary' sorts of people. Rather, it is that young men are, occupationally speaking, increasingly finding themselves in a culture that mandates the social business of what Harvey Sacks (1984) calls 'doing being ordinary'.

For Sacks (1984), 'ordinariness' is not an aspect of one's personality, but rather is a concerted interactive accomplishment. Sacks (1984, p. 414) notes that 'it is not that somebody *is* ordinary; it is perhaps that that is what one's business is, and

it takes work, as any other business does'. As social business, doing being ordinary becomes an
attributional issue with deviance and normalcy at
stake. It is a way of being 'reciprocally witness-
able' or intelligible to members of a social group
(Sacks 1984). As a member of a social group,
one must not only monitor one's experiences for
features that are story-worthy, but one must also
take care to assure that what gets storied are those
experiences that one is, as an ordinary member,
entitled to have. As a way of creating sociality,
group members are thus obliged to bind up their
experiences by borrowing from the group's common stock of knowledge. The work of being ordinary thus becomes crucially important for telling
stories that break with convention, such as roman-
tic/sexual failures.

The central premise of this study is that formulations of ordinariness are likely to be features in
young men's stories about romantic and/or sexual
mishaps. At stake for these young men is not ordinariness in the sense of their heterosexual *orientation* or their heterosexual *desire*. Those canonical or
'ordinary' heterosexual and masculine elements are
secured by virtue of the fact that the young men's
stories are clearly about pursuits, albeit unsuccessful pursuits, of romantic and sexual experiences
with women. At stake are other aspects of ordinary
masculinity, such as skilful and successful seduction, prowess, glibness, bravura, or what is sometimes euphemistically referred to as 'game', as in the
sports metaphor of 'he's got game' (Brooks 1997,
Levant 1997).

Being normatively masculine is thus only
partially about displaying heterosexual orientation or heterosexual desire; it is also about having 'game', which is to say, being able to display
a set of well-honed romantic skills. Because
these young men's stories celebrate gaffes leading to embarrassment and sometimes rejection,
they break with the canonical masculine norms
of cool seduction or gamesmanship. A new form
of homosociality is thus being created here,
where stories of romantic failure function as a
strategy for coping with the shifting meaning of
'successful' masculinity. The focus of this study
is to understand how positions of failed gamesmanship function in the accomplishment of
these young men's masculine subjectivities, how
a sense of conventionality or ordinariness is reclaimed, and what these processes reveal about
the shifting nature of hegemonic masculinity in
contemporary culture.

BACKGROUND TO THE STUDY

Twelve group discussions were conducted with
three young-adult male friends per group, plus an
adult-male moderator. Each of the 36 participants
was between the ages of 18 and 23 ($M = 19.8$
years, $SD = 0.8$ years), and was living away from
home while enrolled in a public university in
Northern California. Small and casual group discussions were chosen, as opposed to one-on-one
interviews, so as to create a fluid, symmetrical
and collaborative context in which to share stories about potentially delicate topics. Each triad
was required to have known each other for at
least six months and to have been 'good friends'
at the time of the group discussion. The large majority (89%) of the sample self-identified as either
'Caucasian' or 'white'; the remainder declined to
state ethnicity, or indicated either 'Asian' or 'Latino' descent. The entire sample self-identified as
'heterosexual'.

Participants were enlisted informally through
general requests for volunteers in both upper and
lower-level social science university courses. The
study was described as a research project looking at
how young adult same-sex friends talk about their
romantic experiences. Each conversation was audio recorded with permission and fully transcribed
(see Appendix 1 for transcription conventions).
Each group discussion lasted approximately 1.5h
and generated a total of approximately 980 pages of
transcribed dialogue.

The group conversations were relatively unstructured. The moderator casually asked for
small stories about everyday events (see Ochs and
Capps 2001, Bamberg 2004). The discussions were

littered with colorfully co-constructed small stories. It is quite possible that, as a male moderator in his mid-thirties of a similar ethnicity and class as the majority of the participants, the young men felt less inhibited with me than they would with a female or older male researcher. My aim, therefore, was to create a space where the participants felt free to engage in the kinds of conversations that occurred naturally in their everyday contexts. With that in mind, I did not simply remain on the periphery back-channeling the young men with 'mmhs' and 'yeahs', but rather cautiously engaged them, challenged them, and cajoled them when appropriate.

ANALYSIS

The analytic focus is a critical discursive analysis of 'small stories', aligned closely with programs of discursive research that have detailed the subtle and often indirect ways that young men transact compliance and resistance to normative masculinity in everyday conversations (Wetherell and Edley 1999, Gough 2001, Korobov 2004, 2006). The central focus in this form of analysis is how young men indirectly align themselves with the stereotypical aspects of normative masculinity while *at the same time* engaging in talk that is meant to sound sensitive, self-deprecating or vulnerable. This requires an examination of how self-deprecation and self-derogation is *rhetorically* built to simultaneously accommodate and resist an array of social expectations, potential interlocutor challenges and cultural assumptions. It is in this vein that the analyses extend into a discussion of the ideological and gender-political nature of how formulations of self-deprecation and 'failure' become strategically useful for the overall survivability and adaptability of hegemonic masculinity.

Analyses proceeded by first identifying any story that involved talk about romantic or sexual experiences which failed or were embarrassing in some way, i.e. stories about romantic mishaps, gaffes and bad decisions that resulted

in embarrassment, anxiety or rejection. Inductive analyses revealed that these kinds of stories generally touched on one of three general themes. First, many of the failed romantic stories seemed to involve experiences with what some of the participants called '*crazy bitches*'. From what could be gleaned from the conversations, 'crazy bitch' is a colloquially popular, misogynistic phrase used to describe women who are erratic, overly jealous, insecure, vengeful, and sometimes violent. A second common theme was failure in the context of attempted '*hook-ups*'. 'Hook-ups' referred to some form of casual, no-strings-attached sexual experience. And finally, many of the young men told stories of times they made fools out of themselves while being inebriated. The subjects talked about alcohol as providing a kind of '*liquid courage*' that often backfired on them. The analyses that follow examine, in a broad and critical-discursive way, paradigmatic stories for each of the three themes.

Theme 1: '*crazy bitches*'

In this first story, Hal recounts a relatively recent dating experience in which his girlfriend reveals that she might have contracted herpes from another man and that she has continued to have sex with her ex-boyfriend while dating Hal. Rather than disparage this, Hal creates an ironic and bemused incongruity between his ex-girlfriend's outlandish actions/statements and his nonchalant reactions, thus creating a palpable tension the young men find funny.

Story 1

Participants: Hal (H), Gary (G), and Cory (C), Moderator (M)

1. H: maybe a week yeah I'd say about a week into
2. the school year I got a phone call from her and
3. she said 'um I'm sorry but I may have herpes'
4. ((laughter, 2.0))
5. H: yeahha ((laughing)) whic(hah) was a fun
6. phone call to get and then so she told me and
7. what was funny was that on the first date
8. uh one of the things she told me was like

9.   uhh 'hey I just got tested and I'm clean so
10. you don't have to worry' and I said '<that's
11. gre::at> that's wonderful' umm:: and so>
12. but every time we had sex I used a condom
13. <and so but she called me and she's like yeah
14. uh about a week before she met me she said
15. she was at this party and she ended up get-
16. ting drunk and her (.) this is an exact quote
17. '<ended up having sex with some Asian
18. dude in the back of his van>'[…] and so
19. I said '<okay::: um let me call you back in
11. like a day or two once I think about some
12. things>'[…]
13. G: and then two weeks later he gets a text mes-
14.   sage and he looks at it and he just starts (.) I
15.   guess he just started laughing or something I
16.   don't really remember but it said something
17.   along the lines of 'hey what up I'm uh oh
18.   what was it I'm back=
19. H: =I'm back with Bruce again'(.) yeah with
20.   Bruce […] she's crazy she been dating this
21.   guy for about two years and like recently
22.   broke up with him but <did:::n't tell him>
23.   or something cause like when I talked to her
24.   she said 'yeah me and my boyfriend broke
25.   up' and then later that day her boyfriend
26.   called her ex-boyfriend called her and she
27.   picked up n' was like 'oh hey honey what's
28.   up?' and I'm like uh::: so does he know that
29.   he's been broken up with an' I'm like well::
30.   I think he knows and so <I don't think she
31.   ever actually stopped having sex with him>
32.   while we were dating

Although Hal notes that he had sex with this woman, he deviates from the heroic masculine script by positioning himself not as hero but as a victim. He positions her as having a question-able sexual past that put his health in jeopardy; she also cheats on him with her ex-boyfriend. Nevertheless, Hal exploits the self-deprecating aspect of his victim status to both entertain his male friends and, by extension, to position himself as confidently detached and even slightly amused by the 'crazy' behavior of this woman. Hal's casual position of ordinariness is principally brought off through a series of carefully crafted juxtaposi-tions between his girlfriend's reported speech and

his own sarcastic or deadpan reactions to it. For instance, in response to her admission that she is disease-free, Hal slows his speech in an audi-bly long and drawn-out sarcastic way as he says '<that's gre::at> that's wonderful'. His slow and deliberate staging of this evaluation, common in sarcastic rejoinders, instructs the others to hear her admission as odd and to see him as noncha-lant about it. Later, after she casually calls him up to alert him about her sexual encounter with 'some Asian dude in the back of his van' and of the chance they both might now have herpes, he is again affectedly nonchalant as he replies '<okay::: um let me call you back in like a day or two once I think about some things>'. Coupled with Hal's in-structive laughter, there are other instances (lines 4, 23–24) where Hal reports his own speech in an exaggerated, slow and sarcastic way so as to for-ward a surprised but cool and ordinary reaction to 'crazy' admissions from his girlfriend. This ironic tension works to procure laughter, as it illumi-nates the extraordinariness of his girlfriend's non-normative actions in contrast to his own subdued and ordinary reactions.

As seen in the first story, a defensively built form of misogyny often lurks in stories about failed romantic experiences that involve 'crazy' women. This next story is no exception. In it, Gus weaves a very colorful account about a recent run-in with his angry ex-girlfriend, Noel. Prior to this story we learn that Gus recently broke up with Noel, immediately following their first sexual encounter.

Story 2

Participants: Noah (N), Gus (G), Chris (C), Moderator (M)

1. G: so I see Noel at a party last week and um she's
2.   like 'hey Gus' an I was like 'hey' and she's
3.   like 'HEY I got something to tell you' and
4.   I was like 'oh shit' so like she like walks
5.   over to me pretty upset looking and she's
6.   like um just went off (.) she's like 'YOU
7.   THINK YOU CAN HAVE SEX WITH
8.   ME AND JUST NEVER DEAL WITH IT
9.   AGAIN' an blah blah an' she's like <'I outta

10.		make you feel the pain you made me feel'>
11.		((laughter, 1.0))
12.	G:	and so she went like this ((makes clenched
13.		fist)) and she grabbed my balls and was like
14.		<'I hope you're feeling the same pain I was'>
15.		an I was like 'AGGHH SHOOT' an I didn't
16.		know what to do
17.	N:	((smile voice)) and how long was she grab-
18.		bin em?
19.	G:	for a good while like=
11.	M:	=and you just stood there?
12.	G:	well I put my hand over my balls and then
13.		she like she's like 'it's a good thing you cup-
14.		ping em cause I'm squeezing really hard
15.		right now' an I'm like 'ALL:::RIGHT'[. . .]
16.	N:	((laughing)) it was AWESOME
17.	G:	she was freakin out she grabbed my balls and
18.		then like for a good like thirty seconds she
19.		was like ((inhales loudly)) and like staring in
20.		my eyes [...] I didn't know what to say like
21.		I was trying to say ((in falsetto)) 'I'm sorry'
22.		an trying to like explain myself but at the
23.		same time my balls=
24.	M:	= you're talking in falsetto
25.	G:	there was no point in like trying to explain
26.		anything.

Although Gus had sex with Noel, the story is not about bragging about that, but instead is a colorful and self-deprecating admission of how Noel enacted a publicly and personally humiliating form of revenge. Why, we might wonder, would Gus spend an entire story ratcheting up the details of this embarrassing incident? Before focusing on the details of the story, imagine that instead of getting angry, Noel approached Gus with a controlled anger or sadness at having been rejected after having sex with him for the first time. Had that happened, it is unlikely that Gus's story would have worked. In other words, Gus's self-deprecating story, and the victim status that ensues, only works if he can construe her vis-à-vis the irrational 'crazy bitch' trope (see Gilmartin 2007). Moreover, her craziness needs to be illustrated in a remarkably weighty and colorful way so that it serves as a clear foil to his relatively calm response. As Gilmartin (2007) observed in her study of college-aged men's

experiences of romance, guys expected to end relationships and break hearts, and expected women to get really angry with them. Unlike sadness, anger enables a traditionally masculine response (remain stoic, take it, say nothing). Noel's anger confirms Gus's standing in the gender order. Had she not cared, Gus might be less certain of where he stood as a man. And the crazier she seems, the more difficult it becomes to empathize with her pain. By extension, it becomes more difficult to condemn Gus for sexually exploiting her.

The 'crazy bitch' trope is but one essential ingredient in this story. The other essential ingredient, the one that drives the self-deprecation, centers on the spectacle of having one's testicles squeezed by an angry woman in a public setting. Of the image of Gus standing there cupping his testicles in pain, Noah laughingly remarks, 'it was AWESOME' (line 18). It is 'awesome' for these guys both for its physical comedy and for what it represents at a gender-political level. The punishment of the white male body is yet another prop in the project of creating a white-male backlash rhetoric (Savran 1996). The effect is (yet again) a victimized male identity, or more accurately, the simulacrum of a fractured abject hero (see Brayton 2007). Whereas emasculation in-and-of-itself is not 'awesome', the *spectacle* of emasculation, particularly when cloaked in irony, is a useful rhetorical ploy for simultaneously embracing and disavowing the role of victim. What remains is a quiet reassertion of traditional masculinity. In effect, the misogynistic message is: 'these women are crazy, but we can take it and we can laugh about it'.

Theme 2: 'hook-ups'

This simulacrum of victimization can appear in a variety of forms. Aside from being scared by venereal diseases or accosted, many of the young men in this study told stories highlighting their floundering oafishness in sexual 'hook-ups' with women. In the following story, Terry talks about his recent attempt to 'make out' with a young woman. Kyle and Cal have heard the story before, and prompt him (beginning in line 3) to focus on an awkward expression that he apparently used the first time he told them the story.

Story 3

Participants: Kyle (K), Terry (T), Cal (C), Moderator (M)

1.	T:	we're just getting kind of flirty and I try mak-
2.		ing out with her and she totally just like blocks
3.		me n' stuff
4.	K:	but later you were like outside sitting on this
5.		thing and she was sitting on your lap and you
6.		started to:::?
7.	T:	((in deadpan)) playing the vagina ((laughter, 2.0))
8.	M:	((laughing)) wait(hah) <u><playing the vagina></u>?
9.	K:	they weren't even making out he was just
10.		<u><playing</u> the vagina>
11.	T:	((laughing)) I dunno what(hah) I'm doing
12.		down there
13.	M:	((laughing)) you can't say 'playing the va-
14.		gina' what's that? but no wait ((deadpan)) no
15.		seriously keep saying it it's cool
16.	T:	so um we go back in her house and I hop in
17.		her bed an' she's like 'oh no you gotta go' and
18.		I'm just like '<u>what</u>?' I was like 'what the fuck'
19.		like 'why are <u>you</u> telling me to leave like after
11.		all this?'
12.	C:	right (.) you've already touched her vagina
13.	K:	YEAH
14.	T:	YEAH
15.	C:	no <u>played</u> the vagina
16.	T:	((laughing)) ex(h)actly
17.	K:	you played the vagina
18.	C:	((deadpan)) what sport did you play with her
19.		vagina?
20.	T:	pretty much things just didn't happen
21.	C:	no duh

Kyle's interrupted narration in lines 3–4 and the dangling 'and you started to:::' works as a prompt in the first part in a kind of adjacency pair, which Terry completes with staged deadpan in line 5 when he says 'playing the vagina'. Terry apparently used the expression in an earlier telling of this story where Kyle was present (instead of using more common terms, like 'touching' or 'fingering', or even the expression 'playing *with her* vagina'). 'Playing the vagina' is a verbal gaffe that his friends find entertaining. Terry's deadpan in line 5 reveals his

willingness to be complicit with the joke so as to produce the expected group laughter (line 6). What makes the gaffe additionally funny is that they were not, according to Kyle, even 'making out' (line 8) when Terry attempted to touch her vagina. He was only 'trying' to 'make out', as Terry himself attests (line 1). In accounting for this, Terry displays ignorance and laughs as he says 'I dunno what I'm doing down there' (line 9), a concession that admits to a general clumsiness in sexual situations. His laughter, though, mitigates the seriousness of the self-criticism, lacing it with a kind of knowing or hipster irony. In other words, because he knows he's not cool with the ladies, he is in a way, cool. His friend's laughter is also ambiguous. Are they laughing at the courage or the stupidity required to attempt to touch a woman like that while not even really 'making out' to begin with?

When Terry tries to get the story back on track (line 12), thus displaying more of the details of his rejection and of how he feels he was sexually led on by this woman, his friends initially agree (lines 15–17), thereby securing for him a victim status; yet, they quickly derail him yet again and return to enjoying Terry's humorous malapropism. This derailing is a form of displacement (see Edwards 2005), which involves the use of displaced buffer topics, particularly in cases where complaints or troubles are being articulated, that are biased towards a nonserious treatment. It is particularly useful for taking the sting out of sensitive topics, like sexual failure. In lines 1–2 and 12–14, Terry attempts to launch his rejection story, only to have it displaced each time. His friends are arguably helping him out, in a way, to mitigate his romantic failure. Terry displays complicity in both instances (lines 5 and 19), thereby colluding in the fun of laughing at his gaffe. In this particular example, Terry is positioned not simply as a victim of his own fumbling hands, but also of the young woman's (alleged) capriciousness when it comes to sending sexual signals and setting clear boundaries.

In this next story, Kyle talks about a recent attempt to ask a young woman over to his house for a 'hook-up'. What makes the story tellable is not that

Kyle was rejected *per se*, which seemed inevitable, but is the way he went about trying to persuade her to come back to his house and his nonchalant reaction to her rejection.

Story 4

Participants: Kyle (K), Terry (T), Cal (C), Moderator (M)

1. K: like two weeks ago I went over to Ali's house
2.   and there was this girl Jaime that I'd hooked
3.   up with in the past a few times an I was try-
4.   ing to get her to go back to my place but she
5.   wasn't really having it ((laughter, 1.0))
6. M: what were you saying to try to get her to
7.   come back?
8. K: tha:::t's the thing uhmm(hahuh) ((laughs))
9. T: I was there I can vouch [it was like]
10. K: [yea what] I say?
11. T: pretty much that=
12. K: =just 'hey let's go back to my place' ((laugh-
13.   ter, 2.0))
14. T: it's 'are you coming home with me' n'she's
15.   like 'nope I'm going to sleep'[...]
16. M: I think you got dissed ((all laugh, 1.0)) is that
17.   what you think?
18. T: I thought it was pretty funny when we were
19.   going home and he calls her again on the
11.   phone n'he's like 'so are you coming over
12.   soon?' ((laughter, 2.0))
13. K: an she did [°not°
14. T: [not ((laughing)) you tried
15. K: I tried (.) that's all that counts

At stake in this story are Kyle's seduction skills, which Kyle formulates in a *knowingly* glib and unadorned way. Kyle assumes the position of the 'underachieving pick-up artist' who admittedly dispenses with curt pick-up lines ('hey let's go back to my place'; 'are you coming home with me?'; 'so are you coming over soon?') so lacking in creativity or romance that they clearly violate the masculine dictum to display 'game'. What function, we might ask, does his self-deprecating story of failed seduction achieve, other than a laugh or the opportunity to display nonchalance? At the end, Terry and Kyle note that it is the 'trying' that counts. Is this a kind of valorization of a blue-collar work ethic when it comes to romantic seduction? Or is this irony yet

again? After all, Kyle's seduction repertoire is blissfully lazy. His gamesmanship is entirely lacking. He is not *really* trying, though, which seems to be exactly the point. His laziness, and the subsequent rejection that predictably follows, is the formula that makes the story funny to his friends and therefore tellable in the first place.

One way to understand the logic of such failed masculine positions is to interpret them on a broader gender-political level. They reflect what Messner and Montez de Oca (2005) argue is men's increasingly unstable status in contemporary culture when it comes to understanding how to initiate romantic endeavors. Being ironic or self-mocking about such complexities is one way of coping with this tension, or more broadly, with the erosion of the masculine norm to have seduction skills. Kyle's lazy seduction (i.e. 'are you coming home with me?') can thus be viewed as a misogynistic, albeit tongue-in-cheek, backlash against women's increasing autonomy and social power. Rather than risk being genuinely humiliated, either via rejection for actually trying or by appearing genuinely (not playfully) ignorant about the evolving rules of gender relations, men might opt for a kind of 'boys-will-be-boys' defensive ironic posture. The obvious playfulness and staged certitude of quips like 'hey let's go back to my place' inoculates it from charges of blatant sexism. When seen in this light, the 'trying is all that counts' adage is not an endorsement for an actual roll-your-sleeves-up approach to figuring out how to appropriately talk to women, but is a way of rationalizing failure. 'Trying' is futile, in other words, so one might as well have a laugh. It allows men to indirectly define themselves as victims, as the purveyors of a now endangered form of suave masculinity.

Theme 3: 'liquid courage'

Being drunk was another common resource in these young men's self-deprecating stories. There were generally two types of stories involving alcohol and romantic embarrassment. The first type, as illustrated in the next story, usually involved getting drunk and making daring, but foolish, attempts to flirt with attractive women. The second type, as illustrated in Story 6, often involved getting drunk with a woman (usually at a party) and then having something embarrassing happen. In this first story, Ron and Seth co-narrate a recent incident where Ron 'got sloshed', took his pants off, and approached a very attractive and sober female friend and asked her for a date.

Story 5

Participants: Ron (R), Zach (Z), Seth (S), Moderator (M)

1. R: apparently I don't remember this but I lost
2. my pants somehow ((laughter, 2.0)) [...]
3. R: and pounded on one of my housemate's
4. doors and said like 'we should go on a date'
5. and then 'let's set a date' an'she's like =
6. S: = oh that was so funny
7. R: she's 'you won't remember Ron you're
8. sloshed'
9. M: and she's like 'uh:: you're in your underwear
10. Ron'
11. S: this is our other female housemate from this
12. year Ashley
13. Z: she's pretty hot
14. R: yea she's very hot [...] so yea apparently I
15. guess someone had or I guess I had started
16. going to bed and then I went outside and I
17. knocked on Ashley or I <u>pounded</u> I don't
18. know on Ashley's door (.) she was kind of
19. asleep being it four in the morning and uh I
11. just said ((in drunk voice)) 'we should go on
12. a date' you know an it wasn't knowing me
13. it wasn't very sexual at all (.) it was more
14. like cause she's into a lot of guy things she's
15. into Family Guy she's into video games you
16. know so she's pretty cool I have a good time
17. around her you know (.) I can joke around
18. like a guy I don't have to kind of censor
19. myself cause it's a girl and yea so (.) and I
20. just said 'you know what we should go out
21. sometime I like you you're cool you're fun
22. to be around' and <yeah::::> she says <'Ron
23. you're drunk and you won't remember this'>
24. and um of course I didn't the next morning
25. and I get up and Seth's like 'guess what you
26. did last night' and I'm like 'oh god'
27. S: he just wanted me to shut up (.) he just wanted
28. some orange juice and like I just started just

29. started harassing him and asking him if he
30. remembered ANY of the night before and
31. does he remember talking to Ashley and
32. he says 'NO NO NO WAY I didn't do
33. that' ((laughing)) and he(huh) goes 'really
34. I did that?' and he's like 'fu:::ck'

At least three discursive elements intersect to make this kind of story work. First, inebriation stories allow for hazy recollections, where the narrator is able to play 'mind' against 'world' (Edwards 1997). Phrases like 'apparently', 'I don't remember', 'somehow', 'that's a little fuzzy', 'I hear different stories', and 'I guess' are littered throughout Ron's narrative. These rhetorical constructions of ignorance (see Potter 1996, Edwards 1997) make the veracity of the events being narrated a function of the 'world out there', of what his friends have told him, rather than being a product of Ron's actual memory, which is liable to be biased by his own interests. It is, however, counterintuitive it may seem, absolutely crucial that Ron *not* remember. Not remembering insulates Ron from the counter that he was intentionally trying to be cool or courageous, which works against the masculine dictum to be effortless and nonchalant. Not remembering also allows his friends (see Seth's contributions) to own the story, in a way, since they get to remember it, interpret it as cool or funny, pass it along, and most importantly, hold the one who experienced it accountable in terms of masculine norms. In this way, self-deprecating stories are essential for promoting homosociality.

A second way that Ron manages this kind of story is by scripting his actions according to a pervasive and stable dispositional tendency (Edwards 1995). From lines 16–19, Ron suggests that given what is 'known' about him and Ashley, i.e. that they joke around a lot and that she is cool and into guy things, it is likely that his flirtation was meant playfully and not sexually. Where there is a predictable way of acting, then whatever happens (here, Ron taking his pants off and asking Ashley on a date) can be attributed to a kind of scripted repartee between the participants. The effect is that it situates Ron's actions within a pre-established frame of playfulness, thus mitigating the potential for his actions to appear perverse, harassing or desperate. The self-deprecation reveals that he can be himself around her, that he can be playful and boyish, or as he puts it (line 19), 'I don't have to censor myself'. His self-deprecation is thus proof of their chemistry.

Finally, from a gender-political perspective, the entire story treats failure as patriarchal male privilege, and a supposedly endearing one at that, thus reincarnating the 'loser motif' and 'everyman' trope (see Messner and Montez de Oca 1995). It involves male 'buddies' drinking beer together at a house party, a woman who is constructed as a fantasy object or 'hottie', and precarious attempts by one or more 'buddies' to risk humiliation by attempting to broach the space of the 'hottie'. While this happens, the other 'buddies' gleefully enjoy their beer and the voyeurism of watching their friend make his moves (Seth listened through the door, line 19). The attempt at the 'hottie' inevitably fails, and is followed by the kind of rejection that occasions high-fives from the other 'buddies'. They are thus outed as 'losers' but do not seem to care because they have each other, their beer, and now a good story to tell (see Messner and Montez de Oca 1995). When seen this way, stories of failed seduction, though deceptively playful in their telling, cater exclusively to men's insecurities about their unstable status within the contemporary gender order. They invite men to not only take refuge in the victim identity occasioned by this loser status, but to exploit it through irony, and to finally recognize that while 'hotties' may be unavailable, the one thing that men can count on is their shared fraternal bond.

In this second type of inebriation story, Shawn relates a time when he and his girlfriend, Kaly, got drunk at a big fraternity party and went to an upstairs room to have sex.

Story 6

Participants: Shawn (S), Mod (M)

1. S: I brought Kaly with me and uh it was a big
2. party and we were both fairly inebriated
3. and I uh took her by the hand and lead her
4. into my buddy's room [...] and all my other
5. friends are very aware of it and we're takin off
6. each other's clothes and then there's this like
7. pounding on the door 'SHAWN' ((laughing))
8. hahan' I say 'GO AWAY' and they say 'NO::
9. what are you doing come out here' (.) and I
10. guess one of my other drunk buddy's was get-
11. ting a lap dance like outside in the main room
12. (.) so they're like banging down the door and
13. at one point they were really like harassing us
14. like I guess like the door had a crappy lock
15. and there was a way to exploit it um and so
16. they were coming in the room as I was getting
17. a blow job ((laughing)) hahhuh yeah so like
18. Kaly was awesome she like leans against the
19. door to block em so I thought that was pretty
11. cool (.) so we're in this bedroom and we had
12. just finished and we're lying there on the bed
13. and my buddy Paul stumbles in and uh I say
14. 'Paul what are you doing get out of here now'
15. and he just kind of like looks at me with this
16. you know this goofy expression and he kind
17. of like starts stumbling over towards the bed
18. and I say 'Paul what are you doing LEAVE
19. RIGHT NOW' and I'm like yelling at him an
20. uh he goes <'nah::: man it's cool'> ((laugh-
21. ing)) and(ha) so he(huh) sits he like sits down
22. like Indian style just like plops down at the
23. corner of the bed and he goes <'I'm just get-
24. ting my gum'> and like ((laughing)) and he
25. pulls out this pack of like I dunno Orbitz or
26. something ((laughing)) and I'm(ha) like I'm
27. like <u>screaming</u> at him and he uh he says 'Kaly
28. do you want some gum?' and she says 'NO'
29. and she slaps his hand awayn' I said 'Paul get
30. out of here' so I jump off the bed like totally
31. naked I'm like grabbing and I lift him up and
32. I say 'get out' and I throw him out the door
33. and like slammed it shut
34. M: holy crap
35. S: and as I throw Paul out and slam the door
36. I hear my friend Judy scream ((in a high
37. pitched voice)) 'I saw Sean's lil' penis!' hahhe
38. an (ha)so now all my friends=
39. M: = you're like legend there now

This story oscillates between being a traditionally heroic masculine story and an anti-heroic and somewhat humiliating one. With regard to the former, Shawn is having spontaneous sex with his drunk girlfriend at a fraternity party while his buddies are in the other room getting lap dances. Yet, when one looks at how Shawn positions his own character in the telling of the story, his character appears anxious, frustrated and embarrassed. His narration involves people trying to barge in on them and how Paul's nonchalance exposes his own frustration. And finally, Judy sees his penis and yells out to everyone that it was small. There is very little that is cool or suave about the way his character is presented in this narration of sexual activity. It is only in the re-retelling, with the embedded laughter at certain points and with evaluative tags like 'it was awesome' or 'it was funny' that we see he has a different, more nonchalant perspective now.

Like the last story, the self-deprecating aspects of his narrated character allow for 'mind' (i.e. Shawn's intentions and expectations concerning the events at the party) and 'world' (i.e. the actual events at the party) to be played against one another for rhetorical purposes. In allowing his character to appear anxious and embarrassed by the fracas, Shawn-the-narrator is doing interactive work. He is guarding against the view that he intentionally orchestrated the types of events that occur at these parties. As Coates (2003) has shown, although men enjoy telling wild stories, it is a violation of the 'ordinariness' norm to appear to have a hand in making wild things happen for the purpose of having a good story (Sacks 1984). The party needs to have a life of its own. Allowing oneself to appear accidentally, or even reluctantly, embarrassed in the melee of a wild party, is part of the rhetorical project of accounting for potentially anti-normative events. While Shawn can certainly laugh at the events now, as narrator, he must present his character in the story differently. As is true for the other stories analyzed, Shawn's self-deprecation is at the service of creating a discursive identity that is marginalized and victimized by events 'out there'.

CONCLUSION

The analysis of young men's stories about romantic experiences found that, contrary to the expectation that male friends will boast about their romantic endeavors, young men are apt to display self-deprecating positions about romantic and sexual mistakes and gaffes. However, like the 'lovable loser' laddishness that parades itself in the media, these forays into non-heroic masculinity are not straightforward. They are cloaked in a self-reflexivity that makes it difficult to determine whether the young men are complying with or resisting normative masculinity. The analyses lend empirically-grounded weight to discussions about the use of play and irony in masculine gender construction, discussions that, to date, have largely been confined to more macro-level cultural analyses. The micro-level analysis of young men's small stories reveal how formulations of self-deprecation occasion a victim identity that effaced the young men's agency.

If scored on a psychological inventory or scale measuring adherence to traditional masculinity, these young men's stories would not represent paradigmatic complicity; but when analyzed within the sequential arrangement of turns, where double-voicing, irony and innuendo are played up, displays of self-deprecation buy back complicity with traditional masculine norms. While the young men resist looking straightforwardly or obviously macho, they also work to safeguard the traditional masculine values of appearing confident, secure and knowing about what is at stake in displaying their views. As Wetherell and Edley (1999) argue, one of the more subtle ways for young men to reclaim the control associated with hegemonic masculinity is to appear ordinary, flouting the social expectation that their romantic and sexual agenda is simply about mastering seduction and gamesmanship.

This study found that managing ordinariness through candor meant negotiating an ideological dilemma (Billig *et al.* 1988) – the tension between acquiescing to a transparent conformity to stereotypical masculine norms, and working to avoid the perception that one's resistance somehow portrays one as romantically challenged. Displays of failure allowed these young men to deflate the bravado of heroic masculinity while not appearing to be genuine losers. In other words, they seemed discursively skilled at coming off non-seriously, not because success in romantic relationships is unimportant, but as a strategy for coping with the ambiguities of contemporary gender relations. The types of subjectivities evinced in these stories aptly reflect a crisis in masculinity that encourages men to be independent, confident and secure in their masculinity, while simultaneously not taking themselves too seriously, and also being advised to reform or abandon their oppressive habits, to be more open and tolerant, and to practice sensitivity and compassion.

While this may or may not be a tall order, the young men in this study were skilled at indirectly seizing on it in working up the sheen of victimization. While they certainly implicate themselves in the failures narrated, they also work to position women as irrational, capricious or hostile. For instance, the 'crazy bitch' trope is useful for mitigating sexual exploitation. By presenting Noel as crazy, and himself as being able to take it (as well as being entertained by it), Gus works to turn the tables. He tells a humorous story that circumvents the cause of Noel's anger, namely that he used her for sex. While he does nothing to suggest that Noel did not have the right to be angry, his narration construes her as *excessively* angry, thus mitigating his culpability. It is in this vein that I have argued that self-deprecation is often camouflage for sexism.

This has direct repercussions for research concerning the relationship between 'new prejudice' and hegemonic masculinity. 'New prejudice' refers to forms of prejudice that are accomplished in subtle and intricate ways – often, paradoxically, by the speaker espousing egalitarian or liberal values (see Billig *et al.* 1988, Wetherell and Potter 1992). The paradox is that as young men become more socialized to resist 'old fashioned' forms of sexism, while attempting to accommodate women's increased power in heterosexual relationships, the better they may become at normalizing the new sexism found in contemporary, media-driven forms of 'lad-masculinity'. Strategic displays of self-deprecation are one example of a burgeoning discursive practice for trying out 'new' forms of staged sexism. To date, very few discursive researchers (and even fewer psychologists) have examined how these practices are worked-up and managed, or how they become psychologically relevant in the formation of young men's masculinities.

Given the limited sample size and its demographic homogeneity – largely white, heterosexual college-age students – there are limitations regarding the generalizability of this study's findings. Messner and Montez de Oca (2005) have argued that the 'lovable loser' trope popularized in the media caters almost exclusively to young *white* men, rather than men of color. Ethnic minorities may not as easily identify with the playfulness of self-deprecation or the irony of the loser-motif and, as such, may resist them. This remains an open research question, as are questions pertaining to impact of socio-economic status, sexual orientation and age. It is also important to consider whether the context of the adult-moderated group discussions pressed for self-deprecating stories about romantic mishaps. This setting may have been an optimal climate for telling embarrassing romantic stories. Since most of the stories had already been told in previous settings, the threat of teasing, ridicule or rejection is lessened. Future research will have to be more innovative in capturing a variety of conversations in a variety of settings.

To conclude, I return to an issue raised at the beginning: how are we to think about what is currently 'hegemonic' about masculinity? This study has shown that for young heterosexual white males, heroic masculinity may be increasingly supplanted with an 'everyman' form of masculinity that achieves hegemony through knowing self-deprecation, ordinariness and nonchalance. This supplanting is not simply a media phenomenon, but is alive in the quotidian details of men's discursive practices. Being hegemonic in a constantly changing landscape of gender relations means learning to manage a variety of social and cultural expectations within specific contexts while neither over- or under-indulging in traditional masculine norms.

By examining these projects in detail, we can productively begin to identify hegemonic practices as the gradual fine-tuning of a range of discursive techniques that allow men to maintain *multiple* ideological positions within a variety of situations. To do so in ways that become routinely normalized is to effectively and unfortunately guarantee, as Connell (1995) argues, an iterative process of dominance for men. Preventing this kind of iterative recuperation of hegemony will thus require equally creative interventions that alter the discursive resources of men in ways that promote countersexist social practices.

REFERENCES

Bamberg, M., 2004. I know it may sound mean to say this, but we couldn't really care less about her anyway. Form and functions of 'slut-bashing' in male identity constructions in 15-year-olds. *Human development*, 47, 331–353.

Benwell, B., 2002. Is there anything 'new' about these lads? The textual and visual construction of masculinity in men's magazines. *In*: L. Litosseliti and J. Sunderland, eds. *Gender identity and discourse analysis*. Amsterdam/Philadelphia: John Benjamins Publishing.

Billig, M., *et al.*, 1988. *Ideological dilemmas: a social psychology of everyday thinking*. London: Sage.

Brayton, S., 2007. MTV's *Jackass*: transgression, abjection, and the economy of white masculinity. *Journal of gender studies*, 16 (1), 57–72.

Brooks, G.R., 1997. The centerfold syndrome. *In*: R.F. Levant and G.R. Brooks, eds. *Men and sex. New psychological perspectives*. New York: John Wiley & Sons.

Coates, J., 2003. *Men talk: stories in the making of masculinities*. Malden, MA: Blackwell Publishers.

Connell, R.W., 1995. *Masculinities*. Berkeley, CA: University of California Press.

Edwards, D., 1995. Two to tango: script formulations, dispositions, and rhetorical symmetry in relationship troubles talk. *Research on language and social interaction*, 28 (4), 319–350.

Edwards, D., 1997. *Discourse and cognition*. London: Sage.

Edwards, D., 2005. Moaning, whining and laughing: The subjective side of complaints. *Discourse studies*, 7, 5–29.

Gilmartin, S., 2007. Crafting heterosexual masculine identities on campus. *Men and masculinities*, 9, 530–539.

Gough, B., 2001. 'Biting your tongue': negotiating masculinities in contemporary Britain. *Journal of gender studies*, 10(2), 169–185.

Korobov, N., 2004. Inoculating against prejudice: a discursive approach to homophobia and sexism in adolescent male talk. *Psychology of men and masculinity*, 5, 178–189.

Korobov, N., 2005. Ironizing masculinity: how adolescent boys negotiate hetero-normative dilemmas in conversational interaction. *The journal of men's studies*, 13, 225–246.

Korobov, N., 2006. The management of 'nonrelational sexuality': positioning strategies in adolescent male talk about (hetero)sexual attraction. *Men and masculinities*, 8, 493–517.

Korobov, N. and Bamberg, M., 2004. Positioning a 'mature' self in interactive practices: how adolescent males negotiate 'physical attraction' in group talk. *British journal of developmental psychology*, 22, 471–492.

Korobov, N. and Thorne, A., 2006. Intimacy and distancing: young men's conversations about romantic relationships. *Journal of adolescent research*, 21, 27–55.

Korobov, N. and Thorne, A., 2007. How late adolescent friends share stories about relationships: the importance of mitigating the seriousness of romantic problems. *Journal of social and personal relationships*, 24 (6), 971–992.

Levant, R.F., 1997. Nonrelational sexuality in men. *In*: R.F. Levant and G.R. Brooks, eds. *Men and sex. New psychological perspectives*. New York: John Wiley & Sons.

Messner, M. and Montez de Oca, J., 2005. The male consumer as loser: beer and liquor ads in mega sports media events. *Signs: journal of women in culture and society*, 30, 1870–1909.

Ochs, E. and Capps, L., 2001. *Living narrative: creating lives in everyday storytelling*. Cambridge, MA: Harvard University Press.

Potter, J., 1996. *Representing reality: discourse, rhetoric, and social construction*. London: Sage.

Riley, S.C.E., 2003. The management of the traditional male role: a discourse analysis of the constructions and functions of provision. *Journal of gender studies*, 12 (2), 99–113.

Robinson, S., 2000. *Marked men: white masculinity in crisis*. New York: Columbia University Press.

Sacks, H., 1984. On doing 'being ordinary'. *In*: J.M. Atkinson and J. Heritage, eds. *Structures of social action. Studies in conversational analysis*. Cambridge: Cambridge University Press.

Savran, D., 1996. The sadomasochist in the closet: white masculinity and the culture of victimization. *Journal of feminist cultural studies*, 8, 127–152.

Wetherell, M. and Edley, N., 1999. Negotiating hegemonic masculinity: imaginary positions and pscyho-discursive practices. *Feminism and psychology*, 9 (3), 335–356.

Wetherell, M. and Potter, J., 1992. *Mapping the language of racism: discourse and the legitimation of exploitation*. Hemel Hempstead: Harvester Wheatsheaf.

APPENDIX 1 TRANSCRIPTION CONVENTIONS

(.)	Short pause of less than 1 second
(1.5)	Timed pause in seconds
[overlap	Overlapping speech
?	Rising intonation/question
°quieter°	Encloses talk that is quieter than the surrounding talk
LOUD	Talk that is louder than the surrounding talk
Underlined	Emphasis
>faster<	Encloses talk that is faster than the surrounding talk
<slower>	Encloses talk that is slower than the surrounding talk
((comments))	Encloses comments from the transcriber
Rea:::ly	Elongation of the prior sound
=	Immediate latching of successive talk
[...]	Where material from the tape has been omitted for reasons of brevity.

THE POLITICS OF GAY MEN'S FRIENDSHIPS

Peter M. Nardi

Towards the end of Wendy Wasserstein's Pulitzer Prize–winning play, *The Heidi Chronicles*, a gay character, Peter Patrone, explains to Heidi why he has been so upset over all the funerals he has attended recently: "A person has so many close friends. And in our lives, our friends are our families" (Wasserstein 1990: 238). In his collection of stories, *Buddies*, Ethan Mordden (1986: 175) observes: "What unites us, all of us, surely, is brotherhood, a sense that our friendships are historic, designed to hold Stonewall together. . . . It is friendship that sustained us, supported our survival." These statements succinctly summarize an important dimension about gay men's friendships: Not only are friends a form of family for gay men and lesbians, but gay friendships are also a powerful political force.

Mordden's notion of "friends is survival" has a political dimension that becomes all the more salient in contemporary society where the political, legal, religious, economic, and health concerns of gay people are routinely threatened by the social order. In part, gay friendship can be seen as a political statement, since at the core of the concept of friendship is the idea of "being oneself" in a cultural context that may not approve of that self. For many people, the need to belong with others in dissent and out of the mainstream is central to the maintenance of self and identity (Rubin 1985). The friendships formed by a shared marginal identity, thus, take on powerful political dimensions as they organize around

a stigmatized status to confront the dominant culture in solidarity. Jerome (1984: 698) believes that friendships have such economic and political implications, since friendship is best defined as "the cement which binds together people with interests to conserve."

Suttles (1970: 116) argues that:

> The very basic assumption friends must make about one another is that each is going beyond a mere presentation of self in compliance with "social dictates." Inevitably, this makes friendship a somewhat deviant relationship because the surest test of personal disclosure is a violation of the rules of public propriety.

Friendship, according to Suttles (1970), has its own internal order, albeit maintained by the cultural images and situational elements that structure the definitions of friendship. In friendship, people can depart from the routine and display a portion of the self not affected by social control. That is, friendships allow people to go beyond the basic structures of their cultural institutions into an involuntary and uncontrollable exposure of self—to deviate from public propriety (Suttles 1970).

Little (1989) similarly argues that friendship is an escape from the rules and pieties of social life. It's about identity: who one is rather than one's roles and statuses. And the idealism of friendship "lies in its detachment from these [roles and statuses], its creative and spiritual transcendence, its fundamental skepticism as a platform from which to survey the givens of society and culture" (Little 1989: 145). For gay men, these descriptions illustrate the political meaning friendship can have in their lives and their society.

Peter M. Nardi, "The Politics of Gay Men's Friendships." Reprinted by permission of the author.

The political dimension of friendship is summed up best by Little (1989: 154–155):

> [T]he larger formations of social life—kinship, the law, the economy—must be different where there is, in addition to solidarity and dutiful role-performance, a willingness and capacity for friendship's surprising one-to-one relations, and this difference may be enough to transform social and political life. . . . Perhaps, finally, it is true that progress in democracy depends on a new generation that will increasingly locate itself in identity-shaping, social, yet personally liberating, friendships.

The traditional, nuclear family has been the dominant model for political relations and has structured much of the legal and social norms of our culture. People have often been judged by their family ties and history. But as the family becomes transformed into other arrangements, so do the political and social institutions of society. For example, the emerging concept of "domestic partnerships" has affected a variety of organizations, including insurance companies, city governments, private industry, and religious institutions (Task Force on Family Diversity final report 1988).

For many gay people, the "friends as family" model is a political statement, going beyond the practicality of developing a surrogate family in times of needed social support. It is also a way of refocusing the economic and political agenda to include nontraditional family structures composed of both romantic and nonromantic nonkin relationships.

In part, this has happened by framing the discussions in terms of gender roles. The women's movement and the emerging men's movement have highlighted the negative political implications of defining gender roles according to traditional cultural norms or limiting them to biological realities. The gay movement, in turn, has often been one source for redefining traditional gender roles and sexuality. So, for example, when gay men exhibit more disclosing and emotional interactions with other men, it demonstrates the limitations of male gender roles typically enacted among many heterosexual male friends. By calling attention to the impact of

homophobia on heterosexual men's lives, gay men's friendships illustrate the potentiality for expressive intimacy among all men.

Thus, the assumptions that biology and/or socialization have inevitably constrained men from having the kinds of relationships and intimacies women often typically have can be called into question. This questioning of the dominant construction of gender roles is in itself a sociopolitical act with major implications on the legal, religious, and economic order.

White (1983: 16) also sees how gay people's lives can lead to new modes of behavior in the society at large:

> In the case of gays, our childlessness, our minimal responsibilities, the fact that our unions are not consecrated, even our very retreat into gay ghettos for protection and freedom: all of these objective conditions have fostered a style in which we may be exploring, even in spite of our conscious intentions, things as they will someday be for the heterosexual majority. In that world (as in the gay world already), love will be built on esteem rather than passion or convention, sex will be more playful or fantastic or artistic than marital—and friendship will be elevated into the supreme consolation for this continuing tragedy, human existence.

If, as White and others have argued, gay culture in the post-Stonewall, sexual liberation years of the 1970s was characterized by a continuous fluidity between what constituted a friend, a sexual partner, and a lover, then we need to acknowledge the AIDS decade of the 1980s as a source for restructuring of gay culture and the reorganization of sexuality and friendship. If indeed gay people (and men in particular) have focused attention on developing monogamous sexual partnerships, what then becomes the role of sexuality in the initiation and development of casual or close friendships? Clearly, gay culture is not a static phenomenon, unaffected by the larger social order. Certainly, as the moral order in the AIDS years encourages the re-establishment of more traditional relationships, the implications for the ways sexuality and friendships are organized similarly change.

Friends become more important as primary sources of social and emotional support when illness strikes; friendship becomes institutionally organized as "brunch buddies" dating services or "AIDS buddies" assistance groups; and self-help groups emerge centering on how to make and keep new friends without having "compulsive sex." While AIDS may have transformed some of the meanings and role of friendships in gay men's lives from the politicalization of sexuality and friendship during the post-Stonewall 1970s, the newer meanings of gay friendships, in turn, may be having some effect on the culture's definitions of friendships.

Interestingly, the mythical images of friendships were historically more male-dominated: bravery, loyalty, duty, and heroism (see Sapadin 1988). This explained why women were typically assumed incapable of having true friendships. But today, the images of true friendship are often expressed in terms of women's traits: intimacy, trust, caring, and nurturing, thereby excluding the more traditional men from true friendship. However, gay men appear to be at the forefront of establishing the possibility of men overcoming their male socialization stereotypes and restructuring their friendships in terms of the more contemporary (i.e., "female") attributes of emotional intimacy.

To do this at a wider cultural level involves major sociopolitical shifts in how men's roles are structured and organized. Friendships between men in terms of intimacy and emotional support inevitably introduce questions about homosexuality. As Rubin (1985: 103) found in her interviews with men: "The association of friendship with homosexuality is so common among men." For women, there is a much longer history of close connections with other women, so that the separation of the emotional from the erotic is more easily made.

Lehne (1989) has argued that homophobia has limited the discussion of loving male relationships and has led to the denial by men of the real importance of their friendships with other men In addition, "the open expression of emotion and affection by men is limited by homophobia . . . . The expression of more tender motions among men is thought to be characteristic only of homosexuals" (Lehne 1989: 426). So men are raised in a culture with a mixed message:

strive for healthy, emotionally intimate friendships, but if you appear too intimate with another man you might be negatively labelled homosexual.

This certainly wasn't always the case. As a good illustration of the social construction of masculinity, friendship, and sexuality, one need only look to the changing definitions and concepts surrounding same-sex friendship during the nineteenth century (see Smith-Rosenberg 1975; Rotundo 1989). Romantic friendships could be erotic but not sexual, since sex was linked to reproduction. Because reproduction was not possible between two women or two men, the close relationship was not interpreted as being a sexual one:

> Until the 1880s, most romantic friendships were thought to be devoid of sexual content. Thus a woman or man could write of affectionate desire for a loved one of the same gender without causing an eyebrow to be raised (D'Emilio and Freedman 1988: 121).

However, as same-sex relationships became medicalized and stigmatized in the late nineteenth century, "the labels 'congenital inversion' and 'perversion' were applied not only to male sexual acts, but to sexual or romantic unions between women, as well as those between men" (D'Emilio and Freedman, 1988: 122). Thus, the twentieth century is an anomaly in its promotion of female equality, the encouragement of male–female friendships, and its suspicion of intense emotional friendships between men (Richards 1987). Yet, in ancient Greece and the medieval days of chivalry, comradeship, virtue, patriotism, and heroism were all associated with close male friendship. Manly love, as it was often called, was a central part of the definition of manliness (Richards 1987).

It is through the contemporary gay, women's, and men's movements that these twentieth century constructions of gender are being questioned. And at the core is the association of close male friendships with negative images of homosexuality. Thus, how gay men structure their emotional lives and friendships can affect the social and emotional lives of all men and women. This is the political power and potential of gay friendships.

REFERENCES

D'Emilio, John, and Freedman, Estelle. (1988). *Intimate Matters: A History of Sexuality in America*. New York: Harper & Row.

Jerome, Dorothy. (1984). Good company: The sociological implications of friendship. *Sociological Review*, 32(4), 696–718.

Lehne, Gregory K. (1989 [1980]). Homophobia among men: Supporting and defining the male role. In M. Kimmel and M. Messner (Eds.), *Men's Lives* (pp. 416–429). New York: Macmillan.

Little, Graham. (1989). Freud, friendship, and politics. In R. Porter and S. Tomaselli (Eds.), *The Dialectics of Friendship* (pp. 143–158). London: Routledge.

Mordden, Ethan. (1986). *Buddies*. New York: St. Martin's Press.

Richards, Jeffrey. (1987). "Passing the love of women": Manly love and Victorian society. In J. A. Mangan and J. Walvin (Eds.), *Manliness and Morality: Middle-Class Masculinity in Britain and America (1800–1940)* (pp. 92–122). Manchester, England: Manchester University Press.

Rotundo, Anthony. (1989). Romantic friendships: Male intimacy and middle-class youth in the northern United States, 1800–1900. *Journal of Social History*, 23(1), 1–25.

Rubin, Lillian. (1985). *Just Friends: The Role of Friendship in Our Lives*. New York: Harper & Row.

Sapadin, Linda. (1988). Friendship and gender: Perspectives of professional men and women. *Journal of Social and Personal Relationships*, 5(4), 387–403.

Smith-Rosenberg, Carroll. (1975). The female world of love and ritual: Relations between women in nineteenth-century America. *Signs*, 1(1): 1–29.

Suttles, Gerald. (1970). Friendship as a social institution. In G. McCall, M. McCall, N. Denzin, G. Suttles, and S. Kurth (Eds.), *Social Relationships* (pp. 95–135). Chicago: Aldine.

Task Force on Family Diversity. (1988). *Strengthening Families: A Model for Community Action*. Los Angeles, CA: Task Force on Family Diversity.

Wasserstein, Wendy. (1990). *The Heidi Chronicles*. San Diego: Harcourt, Brace, Jovanovich.

White, Edmund. (1983). Paradise found: Gay men have discovered that there is friendship after sex. *Mother Jones*, June, 10–16.

GENDER AND THE MEANINGS OF ADOLESCENT ROMANTIC RELATIONSHIPS: A FOCUS ON BOYS

Peggy C. Giordano   Monica A. Longmore   Wendy D. Manning

Increased interest in heterosexual relationships has long been considered a hallmark of adolescence (Waller 1937; Sullivan 1953). Yet sociological attention to adolescent love and romance is dwarfed by the level of cultural interest, ranging from television and film portrayals to parental concerns about teenage sexuality and pregnancy. Recently, media accounts have declared the end of dating and romance among teens in favor of casual hook-ups that lack feelings of intimacy or commitment (see, e.g., Denizet-Lewis 2004). A large-scale investigation based on a national probability sample of adolescents contradicts this depiction, however: by age 18 over 80 percent of adolescents have some dating experience, and a majority of these liaisons are defined by adolescent respondents as "special romantic relationships" (Carver, Joyner, and Udry 2003). Even relatively young adolescents indicate some romantic relationship experience, and those who do not nevertheless express a strong interest in dating (Giordano, Longmore, and Manning 2001). In spite of the ubiquitous nature of dating relationships during the period, we know little about how adolescents themselves experience the transition from a social life based on same-gender

Peggy C. Giordano, Monica A. Longmore, and Wendy D. Manning, "Gender and the Meanings of Adolescent Romantic Relationships: A Focus on Boys," *American Sociological Review*, 71(2) (April 2006): 260–287. Copyright © 2006 American Sociological Association. Reprinted with permission.

friendships to one that includes romantic involvement (Brown, Feiring, and Furman 1999).

We know much more about the character, meaning, and impact of adolescent peer relations. This research not only underscores that peers and friends are critically important to children and adolescents (see, e.g., Call and Mortimer 2001; Crosnoe 2000; Youniss and Smollar 1985), but it also provides a basis for expecting gender differences in the ways in which adolescents navigate and experience romantic relationships. Maccoby (1990) emphasizes that girls more often forge intimate dyadic friendships and rely on supportive styles of communication, while boys tend to play in larger groups, use a "restrictive" interaction style, and develop a greater emphasis on issues of dominance. In light of these differences, she poses a key developmental question: "What happens, then, when individuals from these two distinctive 'cultures' attempt to interact with one another? People of both sexes are faced with a relatively unfamiliar situation to which they must adapt" (Maccoby 1990: 517).

Maccoby argues that the transition to dating is easier for boys, who tend to transport their dominant interaction style into the new relationship. This is consistent with other research on peer socialization that also adapts a spillover argument. While girls are socialized to center attention on personal relationships (Gilligan 1982) and romance, boys' interactions within male peer groups often lead them to define the heterosexual world as another arena in which they can compete and score

(Eder, Evans, and Parker 1995). Studies from this peer-based research tradition thus provide a theoretical basis for expecting that as adolescents begin to date, boys will do so with greater confidence and less emotional engagement (i.e., the notion that boys want sex, girls want romance), ultimately emerging as the more powerful actors within these relationships.

Research on peer relationships has been critical to an understanding of the adolescent period, and is important in that it foreshadows some of the origins of problematic features of male-female relationships, including intimate violence and gender mistrust. Yet perspectives about dating are too heavily grounded in studies of peer interactions and concerns, rather than in research on romantic encounters themselves. In addition, prior research has focused almost exclusively on issues of sexuality, while the relational and emotional dimensions of early heterosexual experiences have often been ignored. The symbolic interactionist perspective that we develop highlights unique features of adolescent romantic relationships that provide a rich climate for additional socialization. Our view is that meanings may emerge from interaction and communication within the romantic context that significantly alter or supplant those developed through peer interactions. This perspective fosters a different view of the ways in which gender influences the crossing-over process, and suggests fundamental limitations of the focus on spillover effects. Further, depictions of girls' experiences, especially concerning issues of sexuality, have become increasingly nuanced, but in prior work boys have often been cast as especially flat or one-dimensional characters (Forster [1927] 1974). Thus, it is important to explore both girls' and boys' perspectives on romance, but our central objective here is to address consequential gaps in knowledge about boys' relationship experiences.[1] The theoretical perspective and findings presented nevertheless have implications for understanding the character and range of girls' experiences, and provide a basic foundation for additional research focused specifically on girls' perspectives.

BACKGROUND

Prior Research on Adolescent Girls

Most studies of adolescent life emphasize girls' strong relational orientation (e. g., Gilligan 1982; Martin 1996), as well as fundamental gender inequalities that tend to be reproduced as girls learn to center much time and energy on their romantic attachments (Holland and Eisenhart 1990; Pipher 1994). In a study based on social life within a Midwestern middle school, Eder et al. (1995) conclude that emphases within girls' peer groups (e.g., the notion that one must always be in love, the focus on personal appearance, and concerns over reputation) foster these inequalities and serve to distance young women from their sexual feelings (see also Simon, Eder, and Evans 1992). Within their own peer networks, boys emphasize competition on many levels, and ridicule those who express caring and other positive emotions for girls. Consistent with Maccoby's (1990) spillover hypothesis, then, Eder et al. (1995) argue that these peer emphases influence the character of cross-gender relations: "[M]ost male adolescents and many adults continue to associate excitement with a sense of domination and competition . . . [while] most girls fail to develop a sense of the depth of their inner resources and power and thus remain dominated and controlled" (Eder et al. 1995: 148).

Studies that explore girls' early sexual experiences draw similar conclusions about asymmetries of power within romantic relationships. Holland, Ramazanoglu, and Thomson (1996) initially theorize that there is a sense in which female and male adolescents can be considered "in the same boat" due to their relative inexperience. They subsequently discard this notion, however, based on their analysis of girls' and boys' narrative accounts of their first sexual experiences. The authors argue that girls quickly learn that sex is in large part directed to "supporting and satisfying masculine values and needs" (Holland et al. 1996: 159). Thompson's (1995) study of girls' sexual narratives develops a more nuanced portrait, by highlighting significant variations in girls' sexual experiences. Focusing on the highly melodramatic character of many girls' narratives, however, Thompson (1995) concludes that within the contemporary context, the gender gap in orientations toward relationships and sexuality may even have widened. She suggests, for example, that it is no longer as necessary as in earlier eras for boys to engage in preliminary steps of relationship-building to achieve their goal of sexual access, a dynamic that could accentuate rather than diminish traditional differences in perspectives. Interestingly, Risman and Schwartz (2002) have recently developed an alternative hypothesis. Examining aggregate trends that show declining rates of sexual intercourse during the adolescent period, the authors link such changes to "the increasing power of girls in their sexual encounters" (Risman and Schwartz 2002: 21), particularly to negotiate the timing and the context within which sexual behavior occurs. Thus, while interpretations of the nature and effects of these dynamic processes differ, prior research points to power as a key relationship dynamic that warrants more direct, systematic scrutiny.

In summary, the emphases of prior studies have been appropriate, as the dynamics highlighted connect in intimate ways to processes that have been limiting or injurious to young women. Areas of concern range from leveled career aspirations (Holland and Eisenhart 1990) to sexual coercion and partner violence (Eder et al. 1995). Nevertheless, this research is itself limited by the focus on the relatively public face of cross-gender relations, such as joking and teasing that occurs within school lunchrooms or during after-school activities. Here the emphasis remains upon the dynamics of the same-gender peer group, providing only glimpses into the more private world of the romantic dyad. Many studies in this tradition also rely on small non-diverse samples, or concentrate on very young adolescents. The heavy focus on issues of sexuality also provides a restricted view of the broader relationship context within which sexual behaviors unfold; that is, of the more basic emotional and other relational dynamics that characterize these relationships. More fundamentally, this portrait of spillover effects does not sufficiently highlight the communicative strengths and relationship competencies that girls bring to these relationships, nor does this literature confront inherent limits to the idea of carry-over effects. These criticisms apply equally to prior research on boys, where similar themes emerge, even though the research base is even more sketchy and incomplete.

Studies of Boys['] Romantic and Sexual Lives

Boys have certainly not been ignored in prior research on adolescence. Yet within the many studies that concentrate on boys, romantic relationships have not been a frequent subject. Classic investigations of boys' lives often concentrate on group processes within boys' friendship and peer circles, either as ends in themselves (e.g., Fine 1987), or as peers influence specific outcomes such as delinquency (e.g., Cohen 1955; Sullivan 1989; Thrasher 1927) or the reproduction of the class system (e.g., MacLeod 1987; Willis 1977). These studies do, however, sometimes offer characterizations of boys' romantic attachments. For example, MacLeod (1987) in a classic study of boys' delinquency involvement suggests that "women were reduced to the level of commodities and the discussions sometimes consisted of consumers exchanging information" (MacLeod 1987: 280). The relative lack of research on boys' romantic experiences, then, likely stems from scholars' interests in other areas, as well as from their views that male-female relationships are of a limited, or at least a delimited (primarily sexual), interest to adolescent boys themselves. This is consistent with the research reviewed on girls' lives, and again highlights the reach of male peer culture. A consequence, however, is that boys' views about romance are gleaned primarily from analyses of girls' narratives and/or studies based on boys' discourse within the relatively public arena of the male peer group.

A few studies have examined boys' perspectives on romance directly, again often in connection with discussions of sexuality. Wight (1994), for example; observed significant differences in boys' talk about their girlfriends and sex among their peers compared with interviews conducted in more private settings. In the latter context, the working-class Scottish youth whom he studied were much more likely to express insecurities and vulnerabilities regarding the adequacy of their own sexual performances. Nevertheless, Wight (1994: 721) also concludes that only a minority of the boys were engaged emotionally in the relationship aspects of these heterosexual liaisons. He suggests that generally the boys preferred male company and "particularly dislike girls' displays of feminine emotion which make them feel extremely awkward." Despite his more layered view of boys' perspectives, then, Wight's (1994) depiction of boys' attitudes toward romance does not differ greatly from a number of other accounts: "the main excitement of girlfriends is the challenge of chatting them up and getting off with them; once this has been achieved, going out with the girl becomes tedious . . . only a few came close to expressing trust in, or loyalty to, girls in the way they sometimes did for boys" (p. 714). In contrast, Moffatt (1989), relying on older students' written accounts of their sexual lives, found that a significant number (about one third) of the young men's narratives stressed the importance of romance and love in connection with their sexual experiences. It is unclear whether these differences in findings stem from significant age differences across samples, or variations in the methods employed. Thus, it is important to examine specific aspects of the existing portrait of adolescent males' romantic relationship experiences using a larger, more heterogeneous sample of adolescents.

The present study, then, focuses on basic but foundational research questions. Do adolescent boys, as Maccoby (1990) hypothesized, more often than girls express confidence as they cross over to the heterosexual realm? Are adolescent girls more likely to be engaged emotionally, relative to their male counterparts? And, perhaps most central to existing portraits, do boys typically evidence greater power and influence within their early heterosexual liaisons? These questions are interrelated and central to the development of an age-graded, life-course perspective on how gender influences relationship processes.

A Neo-Meadian Perspective on Adolescent Romantic Relationships

In our view, prior work in this area offers an incomplete portrait of the ways in which gender influences the crossing-over process. Further, existing treatments undertheorize the extent to which the romantic relationship itself becomes a potentially important arena of socialization and site for the emergence of meanings. These relationships may occasion new perspectives that coexist with, contradict, and even negate previous peer-based messages. Mead's (1934) symbolic interaction theory and recent extensions in the sociology of emotions tradition (e.g., Collins 2004; Engdahl 2004) provide a useful framework for exploring this general idea.[2]

Two central tenets of symbolic interaction theories are that meanings emerge from the process of social interaction and that the self is continuously shaped by dynamic social processes (Mead 1934). These basic insights foster a highly unfinished, continually emerging view of development, and a caution to the notion that meanings derived from peer interactions are likely to be transported wholesale into the romantic context. As Sandstrom, Martin, and Fine (2002: 10) point out, Mead (1934) and later Blumer (1969) emphasized that "social definitions guide action," but also recognized that this involves much more than a "reflex-like application of these definitions."

> We have to determine which objects or actions we need to give meaning and which we can neglect. Moreover, we must figure out which of the many meanings that can be attributed to a thing are the appropriate ones in this context. . . . [W]hen we find ourselves in some situations, particularly new and ambiguous ones, we discover that no established meanings apply. As a result, we must be flexible enough to learn or devise new meanings. We have this flexibility because we handle the things we encounter through a dynamic and creative process of interpretation. This process allows us to generate new or different meanings and to adjust our actions accordingly.

Scholars such as Corsaro (1985) highlight these dynamics as a way to understand the character of the parents-to-peers transition that reliably occurs during childhood and adolescence (see also Corsaro and Eder 1990). Researchers point out that parental socialization efforts are never fully successful, in that young people inevitably produce novel cultural practices through interaction with their peers. These meanings fit the peer context well, as they are a product of this context. Social forces are thus deeply implicated in the production of meanings; and, as these meanings are shared, they become a further source of social solidarity and self-definition (Fine 1987). This meaning-construction process is never fully stabilized, however, because new "hooks for change" continually present themselves within the environment (Giordano, Cernkovich, and Rudolph 2002). Individuals also possess the unique capacity to develop new plans, including the capacity to carve out new social networks. Yet as Emirbayer and Goodwin (1994) note, these new affiliations will nevertheless in turn have a shaping influence.

These basic insights are integral to many discussions of child and adolescent peer networks, but researchers have not systematically applied the symbolic interactionist or interpretive framework to an understanding of the peers-to-romance transition. It is intuitive to do so for several reasons: First, adolescent romantic relationships definitely qualify as a new situation, one in which interaction and communication hold a central place. Second, the relatively private world of romantic interactions makes it likely that meanings will emerge on site, rather than simply being imported from earlier peer experiences or from the broader culture (see also Simon and Gagnon 1986). The fundamentally reciprocal qualities of dyadic communication enhance these possibilities. Mead ([1909] 1964: 101) theorized that the "probable beginning of human communication was in cooperation, not in imitation, where conduct *differed* [emphasis added] and yet where the act of the one answered to and called out the act of the other." Third, scholars point out that contemporary romantic relationships in Western nations lack the heavily scripted qualities that characterized earlier

eras or courtship practices within more traditional cultural contexts (Giddens 1992). This too leads us to favor a symbolic interactionist perspective on the meaning construction process. In the following discussion, we explore three basic relationship domains—communication, emotion, and influence—that allow us to develop further this symbolic interactionist perspective on adolescent romantic relationships.

Communication. We agree with Maccoby's (1990) key assertion that "both sexes face a relatively unfamiliar situation to which they must adapt" (p. 517), but we offer a different perspective on the ways in which gender-related experiences may influence the crossing-over process. Recall Maccoby's suggestion that the transition is easier for boys, who are seen as frequently transporting their dominant interaction style into the new relationship. A competing hypothesis is that because girls have more experience with intimate dyadic communications by virtue of their own earlier friendship experiences, boys must make what amounts to a bigger developmental leap as they begin to develop this more intimate way of relating to another.

Mead (1913: 378) pointed out that when engaged in familiar, habitual actions, "the self is not self-conscious." In contrast, on those occasions when the individual's previous repertoire proves inadequate to the task at hand (what Mead termed the "problematic situation"), cognitive processes, including feelings of self-consciousness, are fully engaged. While both girls and boys are likely to experience their initial forays into heterosexual territory as instances of Mead's "problematic situation," this may be even more descriptive of boys' experience, by virtue of the especially strong contrast for boys with the form and content of their earlier peer interactions. Thus, our expectation is that boys, at least initially, will experience a greater level of *communication awkwardness* in connection with their romantic liaisons. Following Mead, this also implies that cues within the new situation will be especially important. Mead noted that while the past (here, youths' understandings derived from peer interactions) is never completely discarded, the current perspective will nevertheless be transformed in light of present circumstances and future plans (Mead 1934; see also Joas 1997: 167–98).

Movement into romantic relationships involves more than developing a level of comfort while communicating with the opposite gender. It also requires a full complement of relationship skills, most of them communication based as well. Adolescents must become familiar with the process of making initial overtures, learn how to communicate their needs to partners, manage conflict, and successfully terminate unwanted relationships. Here, too, young women may be more competent and confident in what we will call relationship navigational skills, as they have experienced generally related social dynamics in prior relationships (e.g., friendship troubles and their repair). In addition, norms about dating behavior have become more ambiguous within the contemporary context, but boys are still often expected to make the initial advances. This provides a further reason for them to be more anxious and less certain about how to proceed.

Adolescents' perceived *confidence navigating relationships* requires systematic investigation, however, as prior research has shown that boys frequently score higher on scales measuring general self-esteem and self-efficacy (Gecas and Longmore 2003). Thus focusing only on the self-esteem literature, and the notion that males occupy a position of greater societal privilege, we might expect boys simply to forge ahead with confidence into this new terrain, with little uncertainly about a lack of expertise or preparation. This is also consistent with the idea that girls may lack confidence in their abilities to make their own needs known in relationships, particularly given socialization practices that heighten girls' sensitivities to and concern for the needs of others (Gilligan 1982).

Emotion. Researchers have recently accorded greater significance to the role of emotions in human behavior (e.g., Katz 1999; Massey 2002; Turner 2000). Theorists in the sociology of emotions tradition in particular stress the strongly social basis of emotional processes (e.g., Collins 2004; Thoits 1989). Departing from highly individualistic conceptions of emotions, many sociological treatments focus on the ways in which cultural expectations influence emotion-management as well as emotional expression (e.g., Hochschild 1983). This sociological viewpoint resonates with the peer-based literature reviewed earlier, as it stresses that boys are socialized to avoid or deny softer emotions, and are teased and ridiculed by peers if they reveal signs of weakness or emotionality. In turn, this literature suggests that boys learn to devalue relationships that might engender positive emotions, and to objectify and denigrate the young women who are their partners in romantic interactions. Overall, much previous research provides support for the idea of an emotional closing-off process, as boys are observed making crude comments in the school lunchroom (Eder et al. 1995), describing their romantic relationships as tedious (Wight 1994), or constructing relationships as a game perpetrated on young women for the purpose of sexual conquest (Anderson 1989).

The symbolic interactioinst approach, in contrast, suggests that the new dyadic context opens up additional opportunities for role-taking, defined as "putting oneself in another's position and taking that person's perspective" (Shott 1979: 1323). Such reciprocal interactions may promote new definitions of the situation, as well as the experience of new emotions. Scholars have recently noted that emotions have clarifying and motivational significance (Frijda 2002), in effect providing valence or energy to new lines of action (Collins 2004). Our central argument, then, is that adolescent romantic relationships become a potentially important arena of socialization and reference, one that fosters new definitions and interrelated emotions. Suggesting that girls typically experience heightened emotionality in connection with their romantic endeavors is hardly a novel assertion. In contrast, however, to the emphases within much of the existing adolescence literature, we argue that boys often develop positive emotional feelings toward partners and accord significance and positive meanings to their romantic relationships. The notion that new attitudes and feelings can emerge from these recurrent sequences of interaction is generally consistent with Thorne's (1993: 133) key observation that "incidents of crossing (gender boundaries) may chip away at traditional ideologies and hold out new possibilities."

This educational process and boys' emerging interest, we believe, frequently extends beyond the sexual to include the relationship itself. To the degree that boys engage in a distinctive form of intimate self-disclosure lacking within their peer discourse, and receive both positive identity and social support from a caring female partner, boys in some respects may be seen as more dependent on these relationships than girls, who have a range of other opportunities for intimate talk and social support. Feelings of heightened emotionality or *love* for the partner can be assessed directly, as adolescents are well placed to comment on their own subjective emotional experiences. Here the private interview provides a useful supplement to observational studies of boys' interactions in public settings, as recent work on gender and emotions underscores that the public face of emotions appears more highly gendered than the personal experience of these same emotions (Fischer 2000). It is also important to obtain systematic assessments across a large, heterogeneous sample of adolescents, as most of the research reviewed earlier indicates that some boys develop caring attitudes toward a partner and positive feelings about their romantic relationships. These researchers frequently assert, however, that this adaptation is characteristic of a small subgroup of male adolescents who represent a departure from the more common and traditionally gendered pattern (Anderson 1989; Eder et al. 1995; Wight 1994).

Influence. Social interactions are not only implicated in the production of specific emotional feelings, but as some theorists argue, these emotional processes are capable of transforming the self in more fundamental ways (Engdahl 2004; MacKinnon 1994). The social influence literature emphasizes that the more highly valued the relationship,

the more individuals are willing to accede to influence attempts in order to maintain or enhance their standing with valued others (Blau 1964). Viewed from a neo-Meadian perspective, however, positive interactions with significant others influence self-feelings (emotions) and attitudes that become catalysts in the truest sense. This neo-Meadian viewpoint encompasses but also extends the notion that change is accomplished primarily as a strategic move to preserve the relationship.

If, on the other hand, positive meanings are largely constructed outside the romantic relationship (e.g., as a source of competition and basis for camaraderie with one's male peers), we may expect the romantic partner's influence to be (and to be viewed as) rather minimal (see Collins 2004: 238). This is likely to be the case whether the focus is on change in relationship attitudes/behaviors, influence on other aspects of the adolescent's life, or effects on the young person's emerging identity. Thus the character of communication and levels of emotional engagement in these relationships during adolescence are critical dynamics likely to be implicated in the nature and extent of partner influence. Our expectation, following the arguments developed in the previous sections, is that adolescent girls, owing to their greater familiarity with issues of intimacy and skill in communication, will likely make influence attempts, and boys (highly interested/engaged in this new relationship form) will often be receptive to them. Consequently, we do not expect to find significant gender differences in reports of partner influence, as contrasted with the hypothesis of a highly gendered (i.e., boys have more influence) pattern.

Consistent with prior sociological treatments, it is also useful to distinguish *influence* processes, which may be quite subtle, from *power*, often defined as the ability to overcome some resistance or to exercise one's will over others (Weber 1947). Youniss and Smollar (1985) note that much of the time within same-gender friendship relations, reality is "cooperatively co-constructed." This description reflects that the initial similarity of friends favors the development of a relatively egalitarian style of mutual influence. As a close relationship, romantic relations should also entail many instances of cooperative co-construction—but these relationships to a greater extent than friendships also bridge considerable difference. Thus it is not only likely that differences in perspective and conflict will occur, but also that partners will attempt to control or change the other in some way.

It is conventional to argue that structurally based gender inequalities tend to be reproduced at the couple level. On average the male partner acquires more power and control in the relationship (Komter 1989). While these ideas originally were applied to adult marital relations, as suggested earlier, the notion of gendered inequalities of power is also a recurrent theme within the adolescence literature. These power and influence processes require more systematic study, however, because during adolescence, social forces that are generally understood as fostering gender inequalities are still somewhat at a distance (e.g., child-bearing, gendered access to the labor force and to other bases of power); thus the reproduction process itself may be markedly less than complete. The symbolic interactionist framework also suggests a more situated, constantly negotiated view of power dynamics, in contrast to a straightforward male privilege argument (see, e.g., Sprey 1999). The assumption of boys' greater power and control also connects to the largely untested assumptions that: (a) boys, on average, effect a dominant interaction style in these fledgling relationships (our communication hypothesis), and (b) girls are systematically disadvantaged by their greater commitment and emotional investment in their romantic endeavors (our emotion hypothesis). Asymmetries of various kinds (demographic, relational, status) are common within adolescent romantic relationships (see Carver and Udry 1997; Giordano et al. 2001). Our view, however, is that these imbalances in the contours of the relationship need not—during this phase of life—necessarily and systematically privilege male adolescents. In the current analysis, then, our goal with respect to influence and power is to assess and compare adolescent male and female reports about their romantic partner's *influence attempts, actual influence* (as perceived by the respondent), and perceptions of the *power balance* within the relationship (defined as getting one's way, given some level of disagreement).

DATA AND METHODS

Data

The Toledo Adolescent Relationships Study (TARS) sample was drawn from the year 2000 enrollment records of all youths registered for the 7th, 9th, and 11th grades in Lucas County, Ohio, a largely urban metropolitan environment that includes Toledo (n = 1,316).[3] The sample universe encompassed records elicited from 62 schools across seven school districts. The stratified, random sample was devised by the National Opinion Research Center, and includes over-samples of African American and Hispanic adolescents School attendance was not a requirement for inclusion in the sample, and most interviews were conducted in the respondent's home using preloaded laptops to administer the interview.

From the total sample of 1,316, we focus the present analysis on 957 respondents who reported either currently dating or having recently dated (the previous year).[4] As shown in Table 26.1, 49 percent of the dating sample is male, and the average age is approximately fifteen years. The race/ethnic distribution is: 69 percent white, 24 percent African American, and 7 percent Hispanic. In-depth interviews were also conducted with a subset (n = 100) of the respondents who had participated in the structured interview. These youths were selected based on their race/gender characteristics, and having indicated some dating experience during the structured interview. This subsample is on average older than the sample as a whole, and includes 51 girls and 49 boys. Of these 40 were white, 33 African American, 26 Hispanic, and one was "other" (Filipino).[5]

Measures

Definition of a romantic relationship. We developed a simple definition that precedes the romantic relationships section of the interview schedule: "Now we are interested in your own experiences with

■ TABLE 26.1

Means/Percentages and Standard Deviations for the Total Sample and Separately for Boys and Girls

	Total		Boys		Girls	
	Mean/%	SD	Mean/%	SD	Mean/%	SD
Dependent Variables (range)						
Communication processes						
Awkwardness (4–20)	9.87*	3.3	10.10	3.2	9.64	3.4
Confidence (3–15)	10.40*	2.8	9.92	2.8	11.03	2.7
Heightened emotionality						
Love (4–20)	14.13	3.6	13.91	3.5	14.34	3.6
Influence and power						
Influence attempts (2–10)	3.80*	1.7	4.09	1.7	3.51	1.7
Actual influence (3–15)	6.41*	2.5	6.94	2.5	5.89	2.4
Perceived power balance (4–12)	8.23*	1.8	7.63	1.8	8.80	1.7
Independent Variables						
Gender						
Boys	.49	—	—	—	—	—
Girls	.51	—	—	—	—	—
Race						
White	.69	—	.64	—	.66	—
African American	.24	—	.24	—	.23	—
Hispanic	.07	—	.12	—	.11	—
Age (12–19)	15.49	1.7	15.44	1.7	15.54	1.7
Family structure						
Married biological	.46	—	.46	—	.43	—
Single	.26	—	.25	—	.28	—
Step	.16*	—	.19	—	.14	—
Other	.12*	—	.09	—	.15	—
Mother's monitoring (6–24)	20.55*	2.8	20.17	3.0	20.92	2.4
Peer orientation (1–4)	3.16*	.9	3.25	.9	3.08	.9
Mother's education						
< 12 years	.11	—	.13	—	.12	—
(12 years)	.32	—	.31	—	.31	—
> 12 years	.57	—	.56	—	.57	—
Self-esteem (10–30)	23.80	3.6	23.92	3.4	23.60	3.8
Currently dating						
Yes	.60*	—	.52	—	.67	—
No	.40	—	.48	—	.33	—
Duration of relationship (1–8 months)	4.79*	2.1	4.62*	2.1	4.95	2.1
Sex with romantic partner						
Yes	.28	—	.30	—	.27	—
No	.72	—	.70	—	.73	—
N	957	—	469	—	488	—

Note: Mean/% = mean or percent; N = number; SD = standard deviation.

*$p < .05$ difference between boys and girls (two-tailed tests).

dating and the opposite sex. When we ask about 'dating' we mean when you like a guy, and he likes you back. This does not have to mean going on a formal date."[6] The interview schedule elicits information about a number of different types of relationships, but the items and scales that we later describe and the accompanying analyses focus on the adolescent's relationship with a current or most recent partner.

Relationship Qualities/Dynamics

Communication awkwardness. To measure feelings of communication awkwardness or apprehension we rely on four items: "Sometimes I don't know quite what to say with X," "I would be uncomfortable having intimate conversations with X," "Sometimes I find it hard to talk about my feelings with X," and "Sometimes I feel I need to watch what I say to X" (Powers and Hutchinson 1979) (alpha = .71).

Confidence in navigating romantic relationships. This scale was designed for the TARS study, and it includes three items that tap dating-specific dilemmas and respondents' perceptions of confidence that they would be able to communicate their wishes: "How confident are you that you could . . . refuse a date?" "tell your girlfriend/boyfriend how to treat you?" and "break up with someone you no longer like?" (alpha = .72).

Heightened emotionality. To measure the adolescent's level of emotional engagement we use items drawn from Hatfield and Sprecher's (1986) passionate *love* scale, including "I would rather be with X than anyone else," "I am very attracted to X," "the sight of X turns me on," and "X always seems to be on my mind" (alpha = .85).

Influence. We distinguish between the partner's influence attempts and perceptions of "actual" partner influence. *Influence attempts* are indexed by these items: "X sometimes wants to control what I do" and "X always tries to change me" (alpha = .77). "*Actual*" *influence* reflects the level of agreement that respondents have been influenced by or actually changed things about themselves due to their

relationship with the partner. Items include "X often influences what I do," "I sometimes do things because X is doing them," and "I sometimes do things because I don't want to lose X's respect" (alpha = .71). We note that the influence scales do not require respondents to select who has the most influence in their relationship, but instead to provide an assessment of their perception that partners have made influence attempts and that they have actually made changes or adjustments that they trace to the partner's influence. We then compare girls' and boys' average scores on these indices to gauge perceptions of partner influence.

Power. The measure of power includes a more direct comparative element, as questions focus on the likelihood of getting one's way given some disagreement. This index is modeled on Blood and Wolfe's (1960) *decision power index* revised for use with this younger sample. The scale includes an overall assessment ("If the two of you disagree, who usually gets their way?") and also includes items that reference specific situations: "what you want to do together," "how much time you spend together," and "how far to go sexually." Responses include "X more than me," "X and me about the same," and "me more than X." Higher scores reflect the adolescent's perception of a relatively more favorable power balance, relative to the partner (alpha = .77).

Control variables. Although our primary objective is to examine similarities and differences in the experience of romantic relationships as influenced by the respondent's gender, we also include control variables in our models. This allows us to account for possible differences between the gender subgroups on other basic characteristics and features of adolescents' lives, and to assess whether these variables operate as mediators of any observed gender differences. In addition to the influence of other sociodemographic characteristics, gender differences in reports about relationships might be influenced by girls' generally higher levels of parental monitoring (Longmore, Manning, and Giordano 2001), or males' greater levels of involvement with peers (as suggested in the foregoing literature review). It is particularly important to control for self-esteem, as responses to items about relationship confidence or perceived power may be influenced by the adolescent's generally efficacious or confident self-views. This would be consistent with Maccoby's (1990) argument that boys move ahead with confidence into the heterosexual context. Thus we not only assess whether, on average, boys tend to report greater relationship confidence, but also whether high self-esteem accounts for any observed gender difference. During adolescence, romantic relationships themselves vary significantly—both in terms of duration and level of seriousness (Carver et al. 2003). Thus, our models also include controls for *duration* and whether or not the relationship has become sexually intimate. Teens with romantic relationship experience who were not dating at the time of the interview reported about a "most recent" partner, thus we also add a control for whether the referent is a current or most recent relationship.

In addition to *gender* (female = 1), controls are added for *race/ethnicity* (African American, Hispanic, and white were created), and *age*. We also include dummy variables reflecting variations in *mother's education* as a proxy for socioeconomic status (less than 12, greater than 12, where 12th grade completion is the reference category), a strategy that allows for the observation of nonlinear effects. This measure is derived from a questionnaire completed by parents, rather than from youth reports *Family structure* is represented in the models as a set of dummy variables (single parent, stepparent, other, with married biological as the reference category). *Parental monitoring* is measured by a six-item scale completed by the parent, which includes items such as "When my child is away from home, s/he is supposed to let me know where s/he is," "I call to check if my child is where s/he said," "My child has to be home at a specific time on the weekends" (alpha = .73). A measure of *peer orientation* is included, which asks respondents, "During the past week, how many times did you just hang out with your friends?" *Self-esteem* is measured with a six-item version of Rosenberg's (1979) self-esteem scale

(alpha = .71). Relationship controls include a measure of *duration* of the focal relationship in months, whether *sexual intercourse* has occurred within the relationship (1 = yes), and whether the relationship is *current* (1 = yes) or most recent.

Analytic Strategy

We estimate zero-order models with gender and then add the remaining covariates to the model. This includes the social and demographic factors (e.g., race/ethnicity, age, mother's education), other network and individual characteristics (parental monitoring, peer orientation, self-esteem), and features of the relationship described (duration, whether the relationship includes sex, whether the referent is a current relationship). Given the nature of our dependent variables, we use ordinary least squares (OLS) to estimate our models. Although we do not develop specific hypotheses in this regard, due to the general importance of the adolescent's other social addresses, and the utility of the concept of inter-sectionalities as developed in prior theorizing about gender, we also test for differential effects of gender based on race/ethnicity, mother's education, and age by sequentially estimating each model introducing a series of interaction terms (gender by race, gender by mother's education, and gender by age). This allows us to document whether observed patterns of gender similarity and difference generalize across various race/ethnic, SES, and age categories. We also examine interactions between gender and other features of the focal relationship, including duration and whether intercourse has occurred, in order to determine whether the findings with regard to gender reflect a consistent pattern across relationships that vary in longevity and level of sexual intimacy. We use a Chow test to evaluate whether the influence of the total set of covariates on relationship qualities is sufficiently different for boys and girls to warrant analysis of separate models.

Qualitative Data

The in-depth relationship history narratives that we elicited from a subset of the respondents are useful as they serve to validate the quantitative findings, give depth to our conceptual arguments, and provide a starting point for reconciling our results with themes about gender and relationships that have predominated in prior research. Qualitative methods preserve respondents' own language and narrative emphasis, and thus provide an additional vantage point from which to explore the meaning and importance of these relationships from each respondent's point of view (Morse 1994).

The in-depth interviews were generally scheduled separately from the structured interview, and were conducted by a full-time interviewer with extensive experience eliciting in-depth, unstructured narratives. Areas covered in general parallel the structured protocol, but allow a more detailed consideration of respondents' complete romantic and sexual histories. The interview began by exploring the dating scene at the respondent's high school, and subsequently moved to a more personal discussion of the respondent's own dating career. The prompt stated, "Maybe it would be a good idea if you could just kind of walk me through some of your dating experiences—when did you first start liking someone?" Probes were designed to elicit detail about the overall character and any changes in a focal relationship, and about the nature of different relationships across the adolescent's romantic and sexual career. The resulting relationship narratives were tape-recorded and subsequently transcribed verbatim. We relied on Atlas.ti software to assist with the coding and analysis of the qualitative data. This program was useful in the organization of text segments into conceptual categories and refinement of the categories, while retaining the ability to move quickly to the location of the text within the more complete narrative. We also relied on shorter two-to-three-page summaries for some aspects of our analysis.

Because the current study is based on a combined analytic approach, we do not attempt an overview of the qualitative data, as the systematically collected structured data and related quantitative analyses adequately depict aggregate trends. Here we generally limit our discussion of the qualitative material to narrative segments that (a) illustrate the direction of specific quantitative findings, but that further illuminate them, particularly with reference to the conceptual areas outlined above, and (b) serve to reconcile our results with the perspectives and emphases of prior research. Consistent with our focus in this article, we draw on boys' narratives, recognizing that a comprehensive account of adolescents' heterosexual experiences requires a corollary analysis of girls' perspectives. Other analyses using the TARS data focus specifically on issues of sexuality, both within romantic relationships (Giordano, Manning, and Longmore 2005a) and outside the traditional dating context (Manning, Longmore, and Giordano 2005).

RESULTS

Table 26.1 presents descriptive statistics for all variables included in the analyses. In addition to the focal relationship variables to be discussed presently, results indicate that, consistent with prior research, female respondents score higher on parental monitoring, relative to their male counterparts. Young women also report relationships of significantly longer duration, and they are more likely to reference a current (rather than "most recent") partner. Male respondents score higher on the measure of time spent with peers, but self-esteem scores did not differ significantly by gender. Table 26.2 presents results of analyses of boys' and girls' reports of communication awkwardness, confidence navigating relationships, and feelings of love. Table 26.3 shows results of similar analyses focusing on partner influence attempts and "actual" influence, as well as the perceived power balance within the current/most recent relationship. Results of analyses focused on gender interactions are reported in the text.

Communication

Awkwardness.   The first column in Table 26.2 indicates that, consistent with our hypothesis, boys report significantly higher levels of communication awkwardness in connection to their relationship with a current/most recent partner. Within the context of the more complete relationship-history narratives elicited from a subset of the respondents (recall that

TABLE 26.2

Communication and Emotion within Adolescent Romantic Relationships

Gender	Communication Awkwardness		Confidence Navigating Relationships		"Love"	
	1	2	1	2	1	2
(Male)	—	—	—	—	—	—
Female	−.462*	−.195	1.118***	1.208***	.435	−.020
Race						
(White)	—	—	—	—	—	—
African American	—	.300	—	.167	—	−.553*
Hispanic	—	−.098	—	−.053	—	.104
Age	—	−.094	—	.159**	—	.165*
Family structure						
(Married biological)	—	—	—	—	—	—
Single	—	.002	—	−.129	—	−.465
Step	—	−.061	—	.030	—	−.743*
Other	—	.410	—	−.253	—	−.788*
Parental monitoring	—	−.042	—	.033	—	.042
Peer orientation	—	−.160	—	−.022	—	.017
Mother's education						
< 12 years	—	.060	—	.258	—	−.055
(12 years)	—	—	—	—	—	—
> 12 years	—	−.230	—	.095	—	−.023
Self-esteem	—	−.116	—	.180***	—	.032
Duration of relationship	—	−249***	—	.026	—	.486***
Sex with romantic partner						
(No)	—	—	—	—	—	—
Yes	—	−.635**	—	.442*	—	.185
Currently dating						
(No)	—	—	—	—	—	—
Yes	—	−1.583***	—	−.311	—	1.786*****
F	4.68	11.74	40.89	8.95	3.58	16.42
R^2	.049	.158	.041	.125	.004	.208

Note: Reference category in parentheses. N = 957.
*$p < .05$; **$p < .01$; ***$p < .001$ (two-tailed tests).

■ **TABLE 26.3**
Influence and Power within Adolescent Romantic Relationships

Gender	Influence Attempts		"Actual" Influence		Perceived Power Balance	
	1	2	1	2	1	2
(Male)	—	—	—	—	—	—
Female	−.583***	−.547***	−1.045***	−1.107***	1.173***	1.215***
Race						
(White)	—	—	—	—	—	—
African American	—	.043	—	−.273	—	.375*
Hispanic	—	−.083	—	−.620*	—	.287
Age	—	−.047	—	−.039	—	−.021
Family structure						
(Married biological)	—	—	—	—	—	—
Single	—	.067	—	−.206	—	.126
Step	—	−.149	—	−.293	—	.078
Other	—	.260	—	−.060	—	−.005
Parental monitoring	—	−.015	—	−.023	—	.019
Peer orientation	—	.038	—	−.010	—	.066
Mother's education						
< 12 years	—	.283	—	.349	—	.433*
(12 years)	—	—	—	—	—	—
> 12 years	—	−.093	—	.023	—	.043
Self-esteem	—	−.086***	—	−.112***	—	.024
Duration of relationship	—	.077**	—	.137**	—	−.052
Sex with romantic partner						
(No)	—	—	—	—	—	—
Yes	—	.592***	—	−.092	—	.037
Currently dating						
(No)	—	—	—	—	—	—
Yes	—	−.460***	—	−.084	—	−.023
F	28.0	8.06	44.6	6.38	111.4	9.49
R^2	.029	.114	.045	.092	.105	.132

Note: Reference category in parentheses. N = 957.
*p < .05; **p < .01; ***p < .001 (two-tailed tests).

these youths are, on average, slightly older), these communication difficulties are especially likely to surface in boys' references to the early days of their dating careers or in discussions of how a given relationship had changed over time. Jake, for example, mentioned such communication difficulties in connection to his very first romantic relationship:

> Then I like talked to her on the phone, I don't know it was kind of awkward, like long silences when you're talking and stuff like that, and I don't know, then she like broke up with me a week later . . . [during their conversations] I couldn't like think of anything more to say you know I really didn't know . . . [her]; I really wasn't friends before I asked her out, so it was kind of like talking to somebody I really didn't know. . . . [Jake, 17]

Table 26.2 presents multivariate results, in which other covariates have been taken into account. Gender differences remain significant in a model that controls for race/ethnicity, age, mother's education, family structure, parental monitoring, peer orientation, self-esteem, and whether the relationship had become sexually intimate (results not shown). The gender gap is explained by the other relationship controls (specifically duration and current dating status), as shown in model 2. This indicates that girls' tendency to be involved in relationships of longer duration and their greater likelihood of referencing a current partner influence the observed gender difference in level of communication awkwardness. The addition of the relationship controls also reduces the effect of age—in the reduced model without relationship controls, age is, as expected, inversely related to perceived awkwardness, but the relationship controls reduce this to non-significance. This suggests intuitive connections between age, relationship seriousness, and perceived awkwardness in communication. Having had sex with the romantic partner is also inversely related to perceived communication awkwardness, but this does not influence the findings with regard to gender and age (not shown). Turning to gender interactions, additional analyses indicate a significant gender by race interaction—white

and Hispanic male respondents score significantly higher on communication awkwardness than their female counterparts, but African American male and female respondents do not show this pattern.[7] Interactions of age, mother's education and the various relationship controls (duration, having sex, current dating status) with gender are not significant, however, indicating that, for example, duration has a similar effect on boys' and girls' reports about communication awkwardness.

The findings reported provide general support for the hypothesis outlined, but the relationship between gender and communication awkwardness is relatively modest and not significant in the full model. Aside from the gender differences in duration that we noted, several other factors may have influenced these results, and suggest the need to qualify the hypothesis. First, perceived communication awkwardness is a general feature of early romantic relationships, and undoubtedly characterizes girls' as well as boys' feelings about the crossing-over process. In addition, results point to some variations in the gender pattern by race/ethnicity. Finally, youths completing this section of the interview focused on a specific, and most often, ongoing relationship. While adolescent romantic relationships do contain elements of uncertainty and awkwardness, the narratives also show that the perceived ability to "really communicate" with a particular other often develops as an important basis for both boys' and girls' feelings of positive regard. Although we explore these ideas further in the sections on emotion and influence, quotes such as the following illustrate this countervailing tendency:

> A lot of the other girls I met in high school, I felt like I had to hold back from them, you know you just couldn't talk about everything with them. With Tiffany you could. Like she wants to know what is on your mind. And if there is something bothering me, you don't have to dress it up or you know, you can just be straight with her all the time. [Tim, 17]

Confidence navigating relationships. Table 26.2 also presents the results of analyses examining effects of gender on perceptions of confidence in navigating romantic relationships. This index provides a more general assessment of confidence in navigating various stages of romantic relationships, and is thus not only focused on the current/most recent partner. When we consider this more general scale, male adolescents, consistent with our hypothesis, report significantly lower levels of relationship confidence. Recall that the scale refers to confidence through such items as "to refuse a date," "tell your partner how to treat you," and "break up with someone you no longer like." Gender differences are significant for responses to each of these items examined separately, as well as for the total scale, and gender remains significant in the model that incorporates the control and other relationship variables, as well as self-esteem. As these confidence items were also completed by non-dating youths, we also assessed the perceptions of confidence of youth who had not yet entered the dating world. The gender difference is significant whether we focus on non-daters, daters as shown in Table 26.2, or consider the total sample of over 1,300 male and female respondents. These findings thus reflect a gendered portrait, but one that contrasts with Maccoby's (1990) hypothesis about boys' relatively more confident transition into the heterosexual arena.

With regard to other covariates, race/ethnicity and socioeconomic status are not significant predictors in this model, but age is positively related to perceived confidence. Self-esteem is also positively related to these assessments of relationship confidence, and focusing on the other relationship controls, having had sex with the romantic partner is related to greater overall feelings of confidence. None of the gender interactions assessed is significant. This indicates a consistent pattern of gender differences across the various race/ethnic groups, and the lack of a significant interaction of gender and mother's education suggests that this gendered confidence gap is found across various levels of socioeconomic status. Further, while age is positively related to perceived confidence, the age by gender interaction is not statistically significant—the observed gender disparity is evident in reports of older as well as younger respondents. Similarly, while

teens who had sex with their boy/girlfriend report greater feelings of confidence navigating their relationships, a gender and sexual intercourse interaction term is not significant, reflecting a consistent pattern of gender differences in "confidence navigating relationships," whether or not the respondents reported that the relationship had become sexually intimate. Duration by gender and self-esteem by gender interactions are also not significant.

As suggested previously, the relationship-history narratives give respondents the opportunity to elaborate on ways in which they have experienced different stages of a number of different relationships (e.g., as they discuss the initial phase of starting a relationship or how they experience a particular breakup). These more wide-ranging discussions align well with the gender differences described earlier. Boys frequently reflect on their lack of confidence when talking about the beginning stages of a relationship, or a desired relationship that never materialized:

> I don't know why I'm so scared to let girls know I like them . . . like I said I was always nervous at asking them out but that one experience where I crashed and burned that just killed my confidence completely and I have been scared ever since to ask girls out and stuff . . . [Michael, 17]

This excerpt is useful as it clearly depicts feelings of concern and even inadequacy, feelings that Michael connects to one unfortunate early experience. Michael makes reference earlier within his narrative to what appears to be a generally positive self-image (*I know that I'm like a good-looking guy and everything, but I just get so nervous*), even as he offers a candid description of these relationship insecurities. While Michael's discussion includes the notion that such feelings may abate with time and additional experience (e.g., *I don't know how I'm going to be later but hopefully I'll just loosen up*), this awareness does not serve to lessen current feelings of discomfort. Undoubtedly, some of these feelings connect to boys' more often being cast in the role of initiators, but the feelings that some boys describe nevertheless provide a sharp contrast to depictions of boys' confident, privileged positions within these dating situations. Young men who do not appear to possess characteristics viewed as desirable within the context of what Waller (1937) termed "the rating and dating complex" were even more likely to include references to a lack of confidence. James, a slightly built sixteen year old, originally from Latin America, stressed that "girls still think of me as a little shy guy and short . . . with an accent . . . young . . . well it's hard for me because I'm not too experienced." These quantitative and qualitative data thus add to Wight's (1994) observation that adolescent boys frequently experience feelings of anxiety about the adequacy of their sexual performances, as here we document considerable insecurity extending to the broader relationship realm.

The quantitative findings and open-ended narratives also suggest that these feelings of insecurity are not limited to the early stages of the relationship-navigation process. For example, within the context of the structured interview, boys express less confidence about "telling your partner how to treat you," an interview question that was specifically developed with girls in mind. Further, the narratives provide evidence that corresponds with the item that asks about confidence to "break up with someone you no longer like." For example, Bobby indicated that he had experienced considerable trepidation about how to go about breaking up with his girlfriend Sara:

> It really took me like a while I guess to [breakup] because I didn't want to like hurt her so I kinda like waited too long to do it, which was stupid by me. I just kept on like, I couldn't do it. I felt really bad. . . . I just put myself in her shoes and I felt like awful like you know. . . . Just like she saw a girl with my sweatshirt on and she just felt like what the heck's going on and everything just probably went down for her I couldn't. . . . do it, I just kept waiting too long to do it. . . . I didn't want to like hurt her really bad which I knew it would that's why I just kept on waiting so. [Bobby, 16]

Bobby felt sufficiently uncomfortable about the prospect of breaking up that he continued to let

things slide rather than speaking directly with Sara about his desire to end the relationship (for example, he repeats some version of "I just couldn't do it" eight times within the longer narrative). From an outsider's perspective, Bobby had rather callously started up a relationship with a new partner, without properly ending things with his current girlfriend. Bobby's own narrative, however, reveals feelings of insecurity and discomfort, concern for Sara's reaction, and intimate connections between these two sets of feelings. This suggests at least the rudiments of a role-taking experience, and the possibility that Bobby has learned important lessons that could be carried forward into the next relationship. When asked about what he had taken from this relationship, Bobby replied, "If I'm feeling a certain way I should just tell them and not just sit there and wait and wait and not tell her." This is consistent with our argument that for adolescent males schooled in the peer dynamics described at the outset, the romantic context itself represents an especially important arena of socialization. Bobby's own narrative does not suggest a complete aversion to such lessons, but at least a general receptivity to learning from them.

Emotion

An examination of reports of feelings of love across the total sample does not reveal a significant gender difference in these feelings of heightened emotionality in connection with the current or most recent relationship. Recall that the scale contains items such as "I would rather be with X than anyone else," "X always seems to be on my mind," and "the sight of X turns me on." The multivariate model shown in Table 26.2 mirrors the bivariate findings: boys and girls report similar levels of feelings of love in connection with the focal relationship. Race/ethnicity (African American or Hispanic, relative to white youth) is not related to reports of heightened emotionality at the bivariate level, but being African American emerges as a significant predictor in the multivariate analysis.[8] The multivariate results also reveal a developmental trend—age is positively related to reports of feelings of love for the partner. Youths living with both parents relative to those residing in single or stepparent families also scored higher on the love scale, but mother's education is not related to reports of love. Longer-duration relationships are also characterized by higher scores on this scale, and, perhaps not surprisingly, when the current partner is the referent, scores are also significantly higher. Sexual intercourse within the relationship is not, however, related to variations in adolescents' reports of feelings of love. Race/ethnicity and gender interactions are not significant, indicating that the pattern of responses by gender is similar across race/ethnic groups. Analyses indicate no significant gender interaction by mother's education. Duration has a similar effect for boys and girls, and the gender by intercourse interaction is not statistically significant. This indicates that having sex does not exert a differential impact on reports of feelings of love provided by male and female respondents.

It could be argued that the items within the love scale capture feelings of sexual attraction as much or more than a strong emotional connection to the partner, or positive feelings about the relationship. The narratives are thus an important adjunct to the quantitative findings, as they allow us further to explore questions of meaning from respondents' own subjectively experienced and uniquely articulated points of view. Many quotes from the narratives are congruent with the quantitative results, and inconsistent with Wight's (1994) conclusion that boys have little interest in the relationship aspects of these liaisons. One index that adolescent relationships can be said to "matter" to many adolescent boys is the sheer length of the relationship-history narratives that they often produced.[9] Here we refer to total length, as well as to lengthy sections discussing particular girlfriends. Will's 74-page narrative contains a very long section about his history with his current girlfriend Jenny, including a detailed story of how they met and a discussion of the various phases within their relationship's development. Will commented directly on the relationship's importance:

I: How important is your relationship to Jenny in your life?

R: About as important as you get. You know, well, you think of it as this way, you give up your whole life, you know, know, to save Jenny's life, right? That's how I feel. I'd give up my whole life, to save any of my friends' life too. But it's a different way. Like, if I could save Jon's life, and give up my own, I would, because that is something you should, have in a friend, but I wouldn't want to live without Jenny, does that make some sense? [Will, 17]

It is important to note that such expressions of positive regard and heightened emotionality are not contained only within the narratives of white middle-class youth, since prior research on African American youth in particular often includes the notion that romance is constructed largely as a kind of disingenuous game or con (e.g., Anderson 1989). Ron and Steve, two African American respondents who participated in the in-depth interview, express intense emotional feelings about their girlfriends:

Yeah, I ain't never, I ain't never like, felt that way about somebody. . . . I tell her that [he loves her] everyday too! Everyday, I see her. [Ron, 17]

I: So, you remember all the dates and stuff?
R: Yeah, I'm like a little girl in a relationship. . . . [at first] just seemed like every time I was around her I couldn't talk, I was getting butterflies in my stomach, I just was like, discombobulated or something. [Steve, 17]

When asked to be more specific about features of the relationship that make it special or important, many adolescent boys reference themes that have long been emphasized in the literature on intimacy and social support (e.g., Duck 1997; Prager 2000), including opportunities for self-disclosure (see e.g., Tim's quote on page 274), and the importance of having a partner who is always there for them:

Because she was always there for me. Like with everything. Like when my parents separated, she was there for me to comfort me then. And she helped me pull up my grades up to good grades and she was just always there for me. She always comforted me when I needed a hug. [Nick, 17]

We do not believe that such statements were produced primarily to please the interviewer, since the detailed answers frequently reference concrete instances where emotional support was provided. The narrative histories also frequently include descriptions of the endings of relationships. Breakups often involve disillusionment and other negative feelings, but such discussions also telegraph feelings of loss, providing a further indication of boys' own constructions of the meanings of these relationships:

> I: I mean a year and three months is a long...
> R: I'm not doing that good but my friends and my mother, they're helping me.
> I: In what ways aren't you doing so well?
> R: Ah emotionally I, I can't sleep I really can't eat that much.
> I: I'm sorry.
> R: That's okay.
> I: How long and this just happened?
> R: About a week.
> I: Oh wow. So this is very fresh ...
> I: Do you believe them [friends and mom] that you'll get over it?
> R: Yes. Some, someday I'll get over this but hopefully soon. [Eric, 17]
> R: She just broke it down to me like, "Yeah, we're at different schools, we're young, we need to see other people."
> I: So, why were you upset that you broke up?
> R: I don't know 'Cause I loved her so much. [Derrick, 17]

> She kept insisting I wasn't going to work out and I kept insisting I wanted to try it and one night, and like I said I couldn't sleep, and I wrote her a letter, front and back, crying the whole time and then I handed the letter to her the next morning.... It was really emotional, like how she hurt me and how it wasn't right. [Cody, 17]

These narratives often specifically mention the emotional realm (e.g., "It was really emotional"; "I'm not doing that good"; "my feelings was hurt"), or referenced behavioral indicators of psychological distress (e.g., "can't sleep," "really can't eat"). It is, however, also important to highlight that while Derrick's narrative communicated that the breakup

did have a significant effect on him, he did not possess the social knowledge that other boys may also experience similar emotions (as he attempted to explain his bad mood to his mother, "I'm on my weekly [sic] cycle.").

Influence

Table 26.3 presents results of analyses examining reports of influence attempts, actual influence, and the perceived power balance within the current or most recent romantic relationship, as constructed by these adolescent respondents. Although most of the arguments developed in the existing literature focus specifically on issues of power, it is useful to consider the power results alongside the broader and perhaps ultimately more useful dynamic of interpersonal influence. Power assumes competing interests and only one victor, while influence focuses on whether the individual has taken the partner into account and actually made some adjustments. This need not involve a strong contrary view that needs to be overcome by the assertion of a power privilege. In line with this, recall that the questions about influence do not require the respondent to make a choice about who has the most influence in the relationship, but only to indicate whether and to what degree respondents believe that they have been influenced by their partner. The power items, in contrast, require a specific comparison of the respondent's own, relative to the partner's ability to get his or her way in a disagreement.

Attempted and actual influence. Results regarding influence attempts indicate a consistent pattern of gender differences: in both the zero-order and multivariate models, male respondents score higher on partner influence attempts. In the multivariate model, lower self-esteem youth report higher levels of partner influence attempts, and all of the relationship controls are significant: youths involved in more serious relationships (as measured by duration and sexual intimacy) report higher levels of partner influence attempts. Youths also describe former partners as making more attempts to influence, relative to reports about current partners. These relationship covariates have similar effects for boys and girls (results not shown).

More surprising than this pattern, however, is the finding that boys also report higher levels of "actual" influence from the romantic partner. The second set of models in Table 26.3 show a significant gender gap in reports of "actual" partner influence. In addition to a significant effect of gender, Hispanic youth scored lower on partner influence relative to their white counterparts. Lower self-esteem is associated with greater partner influence, and youths involved in longer-duration relationships also scored higher on "actual" influence. Sexual intercourse was not related to perceptions of partner influence. The interactions of gender with other sociodemographic variables as well as other relationship measures were not significant in this model. Thus, these results indicate that the gender gap is consistent across youths who vary in developmental stage, race/ethnicity, mother's education, and seriousness of the relationship.

The scales measuring partner influence (attempts and actual) are rather general (e.g., "X influences what I do"), and thus do not provide a full picture of (a) specific mechanisms of influence, (b) the areas or domains in which boys believe they have been influenced, or (c) the nature of their reactions to various influence attempts. Although a comprehensive examination of these issues is beyond the scope of this analysis, the narrative data do provide a more in-depth portrait of these processes.[10] The specific domains referenced within the narrative accounts are of particular interest, because they indicate influence on many potentially important relationship dynamics and behavioral outcomes—ranging from boys' behavior within the romantic context to academic performance and delinquency involvement. Given boys' initial lack of familiarity and confidence with intimate ways of relating, it is perhaps not surprising to find that some boys indicate that girlfriends had influenced their ability to relate in a more intimate fashion:

> Yeah, well it was a while . . . like about three months. Her mom was having problems . . . and so like she just kept talking to me a lot you know what I'm saying, and I listened and I tried to help and I had problems and you know we just, that was somebody we could open up to each other, so it was like I could talk to her and she could talk to me. [Todd, 17]

Todd described a gradual process that began with Caroline's willingness to open up to him about some of her own family problems. Eventually Todd found that he could not only be helpful to her, but that he also increasingly began to talk with Caroline about some of his own problems. Although he does not state this directly, Caroline may have influenced not only his willingness to engage in intimate self-disclosure, but the way in which he chose to handle problems that the two had discussed in this more intimate fashion.

In addition to modifications in their relationship-based selves, a number of the narratives reference specific changes that the youths indicate they had made in other important areas of their lives, shifts in perspective and behavior that respondents specifically connect to the influence of their romantic partners. Consider the following narrative excerpts:

> [Julie] makes me want to do better in school and stuff. I want to do well because of her because she is really smart and she's got a real good grade point average. Mine isn't as high as hers so I try to be up there and I don't want to look stupid. I don't think she would want me to be dumb. [Rob, 18]

> For like um the past two years, you know that I've been with her it has been, you know, about school. We both are carrying 3.8 averages and stuff. You know we're both kind of you know, kind of pushing each other along like, "you should really go do this." So academically, we help each other like a lot. [Dan, 17]

> I don't know it's weird but certain things make me want to go out and do better. I don't know why . . . You know Melanie, Melanie makes me want to do a hell of a lot better you know . . . [Chad, 18]

As the first quote makes clear, Julie is not simply one more friend who has been added to Rob's total mix of definitions favorable to academic achievement, and this hints at potentially distinctive influence mechanisms across types of reference others (notably peers versus romantic partners). Reciprocal role-taking experiences that elicit positive emotions provide an enriched social terrain for further development, as cognitive, emotional, and behavioral changes reciprocally influence self-views, including views of self in relation to these valued others. Here the positive emotions elicited within the romantic context can be seen as providing energy and valence to compatible or even new lines of action (e.g., Collins 2004). The last quote from Chad nicely evokes this notion of an energizing component.

Theorists have often noted that similar others (e.g., close same-gender friends) are very important as a source of reference. This is a sound assertion, based on basic principles of identification. Nevertheless, relationships based in elements of difference are also potentially important, as contrasts offer more in the way of a developmental challenge (see, e.g., Cooley [1902] 1970:380), and at times a blueprint for how to make specific changes and adjustments (Giordano 1995; Giordano et al. 2002). For example, Todd learns about self-disclosure through his partner's own tendency to self-disclose, as well as her encouragement of his own efforts to do so. Yet describing romantic relationships only in terms of contrasts provides an incomplete portrait of these relationships. If difference were the only dynamic involved, individuals might not be inclined to enter into the type of sustained interaction that results in a social influence process. In short, some level of identification or social coordination necessarily precedes role-taking and in effect makes it possible (see, e.g., Engdahl 2004; Miller 1973).[12] This neo-Meadian view, along with other sociology of emotions theorizing, tends to position emotions at the center of change processes, as individuals draw inspiration from their points of connection and a new direction via the element of contrast.[13]

Perceived power balance. The findings and discussion focus on influence processes that may be subtle and incremental. In the examples relating to

school performance, Rob wants Julie to think well of him, and Dan and his romantic partner are even more in tune, both having a strong commitment to keeping up their high grade point averages. Yet not all influence attempts lead individuals in a direction they wish to go. As stated at the outset, many of the significant differences that male and female adolescents bring to romantic relationships are not entirely overcome by a developing mutuality of perspectives that we described in the previous section. When interests clearly diverge, considerations of power become especially important.

Table 26.3 presents results of analyses focused on the perceived power balance in the current or most recent relationship (who has the most say in a disagreement—overall and in relation to specific domains). In the zero-order model, the gender coefficient is statistically significant; boys' scores are lower, indicating on average a relatively less favorable (to self) view of the power balance within their relationship. It is important to point out that the modal response to each question is egalitarian (having equal say); thus these findings reflect a significant gender difference where respondents have diverged from this more common response across the four items that make up this scale. We note also, however, that gender differences are significant for each of the items making up the scale (regarding overall say in relation to decisions about what the couple does and how much time they spend together, as well as about how far to go sexually) and for the total scale score.

Turning to the multivariate results, additional statistical analyses reveal that the best fitting model is a separate model for boys and girls (results not shown).[14] Most of the covariates are similar in their effects on reports of power (youths whose mothers have less than a high school degree saw themselves as having a relatively more favorable power position, and African American youth are also likely to describe a relatively more favorable level of power in their relationships). Some gendered effects of covariates, however, are masked when a combined model is estimated. We find that relationship duration does not influence girls' reports, but longer duration of the relationship is related to *less* perceived power in the case of male respondents. In contrast, while sexual intercourse experience was again not related to girls' reports about power, boys who reported that the relationship had become sexually intimate reported a *more* favorable (to self) power balance, compared with the reports of male adolescents whose relationships had not become sexually intimate. It is important to highlight that within models focused only on the subsample of sexually active male and female youths, the overall gender difference remains significant, with boys reporting a less favorable power balance relative to similarly situated girls. Nevertheless, these intriguing interaction results warrant additional scrutiny and exploration, as we did not have a theoretical basis for expecting these patterns. In addition, it is of interest that the two findings operate in an apparently distinct fashion—the association between duration and lower perceived power on the part of boys is somewhat unexpected from a traditional inequality point of view, while the findings regarding intercourse are more consistent with the idea that sexual involvement is a more pivotal event or marker for male adolescents (Holland et al. 1996).

The quantitative findings provide indications that, in contrast to the direction of much theorizing within the adolescence literature, when male and female respondents departed from an egalitarian description of the power dynamics within their relationships, males were more likely to describe a tilt favoring the partner's greater decision-making power. A number of narratives also highlight distinct interests on the part of partners, and a perceived power balance that corresponds with the statistical results:

> I guess she was more mature than I was and I guess I wasn't on her level you know because she wanted to do it [have sex] more than I did . . . she said that I wasn't mature enough and you know all that stuff . . . I was too young, I was scared, I didn't know what I was doing I wasn't ready for it I think I felt like I was too young . . . she was my girlfriend and that's what she wanted. [David, 18]

> She's like okay we're going out now, and I tried making plans with my friends, but Amy's like

"No we're going out here and we're doing this." I just wasn't going to live with that anymore . . . there was something about her she always wanted to change me. She wanted me to do this and wear this and do that. I was like okay. Whatever I'd do it but I don't see it [as] right. [Josh, 17]

David's longer narrative confirms that this adolescent did have sex with his girlfriend, even though he felt that he was not "ready for it." Josh also admitted that he often went along with his former girlfriend's preferences, even though his narrative clearly telegraphed that he experienced this power balance in a negative way ("I don't see it as right," "I just wasn't going to live with that anymore"). The latter quote, then, provides support for the direction of the quantitative results, while reflecting the continuing impact of traditional gender scripts.

Variations

Further support for characterizations emphasized in the peer-based literature can be found when we confront the variability in boys' orientations and relationship styles evident within the narrative histories. This heterogeneity is necessarily somewhat obscured by our focus here on aggregate trends. A symbolic interactionist framework can accommodate explorations of subtypes and variations, as theorists have emphasized that while interactions influence identities, as identities begin to solidify, they become a kind of cognitive filter for decision-making (Matsueda and Heimer 1997). Over time, these differentiated identities increasingly structure social interaction in line with these self-conceptions. For example, Donny, a 17 year old, had apparently developed a strong identity as a player within his high school. Donny's first sexual experience occurred at an early age, and this respondent estimated about 35 sexual partners. Donny was also unable to recall the names of all of the young women with whom he had become sexually intimate ("I don't know I would have to go through some letters"). While he considered some of these young women girlfriends, he nevertheless often cheated on them, and indicated that he had control within his relationships. Consistent with this portrait, Donny admitted physically abusing at least one young woman he had dated and reacted aversively to the idea of expressing his feelings ("I really don't like talking about my feelings . . . I don't know I just don't like talking about it").

Donny's narrative thus departs significantly from the aggregate portrait that emerges from the quantitative analysis; yet these types of cases and corresponding identities are important, as they are vivid representations of traditional masculinity that virtually demand attention. Thorne (1993) noted the heavy societal and even research focus on what she termed the "Big Man" social type. It has been important to highlight that the aggregate findings and many narratives do not accord with Donny's perspective; indeed a number of boys specifically position away from this social type in discussions of their own self-views. Yet the number of references to players and other traditional gender attitudes itself affirms the continuing impact of such gender scripts:

> I rather focus on one girl than a whole bunch because I don't think that I'm like some player or something and I really don't like those people that go out and have a bunch of girlfriends and stuff and they think that they're some big pimp or whatever. [Michael, 16]

Additional research on masculine styles such as the player are needed, because (a) a host of negative social dynamics are directly and indirectly associated with this orientation, and (b) adolescents apparently believe that this is a more prevalent and highly valued social role than appears to be the case. Such shared misunderstandings are consequential, and are undoubtedly heavily influenced by the character of peer interactions that have been so effectively captured in prior research. For example, Eric explained why he does not engage in intimate self-disclosure with his male friends: "most of them don't, they don't probably think the way I think or have the feelings that I, feelings that I have for girls." We also saw evidence of this in earlier quotes (e.g., Steve's admission that he is "like the little girl in the relationship," or Derrick's reference to negative emotions after his girlfriend broke up with him,

"I'm on my weekly cycle."). Undoubtedly differences between discussions within peer settings and the more private experience of these relationships serves to perpetuate boys' beliefs about the uniqueness of their feelings and emotional reactions.

CONCLUSIONS

In this article, we developed a symbolic interactionist perspective on adolescent romantic relationships that draws on Mead's basic insights, as well as recent treatments of the role of emotions in social interaction and self-development processes. Relying on structured interview data collected from a large stratified random sample of adolescents, we found support for hypotheses that differ significantly from traditional accounts of the role of gender as an influence on the relationship dynamics within these romantic liaisons. Results suggest a portrait of adolescent boys as relatively less confident and yet more emotionally engaged in romantic relationships than previous characterizations would lead us to expect. The findings regarding power and influence are also unexpected from a straightforward gender inequality point of view. Although we did not specifically predict systematic gender differences in reports of power and partner influence, these results do follow logically from our conceptual discussion and fit well with the findings concerning communication and emotion.

As boys make the transition from peers to romance, they lack experience with intimate ways of relating (as evidenced by lower perceived confidence in navigating relationships and at the bi-variate level, among white and Hispanic respondents, by greater perceived communication awkwardness), even as they are beginning to develop a high interest and at times strong emotional attachment to certain romantic partners (as evidenced by the absence of strong gender differences on reports of feelings of love for the current/most recent partner). In line with our symbolic interactionist framework, we argued that these relationships set up conditions favorable to new definitions, to the emergence of new emotions, and, at least within these relationship contexts, to glimpses of a different and more connected view of self. The argument that boys move in a straight line toward autonomy, or the declaration that "heterosexuality is masculinity" (Holland et al. 1996) are global assertions that do not take into account the adjustments that boys as well as girls continually make as they begin to forge this new type of intimate social relationship.

Although additional research is needed on these and other relationship processes, we do not believe that the results derive from unique peculiarities of our measurement approach. First, the findings across various indices are themselves quite consistent. For example, differences on the power and influence scales are all significant and vary in the same direction. In addition, findings fit well with observations based on a range of methods employed during preliminary phases of the TARS study (see, e.g., Giordano et al. 2001), and are further validated by the content of in-depth relationship-history narratives that we also collected and drew upon in the present analysis. We also estimated a series of interactions that in most instances support the idea that documented similarities (feelings of love) and differences (boys' lower confidence levels, perceptions of greater partner power and influence) generalize across respondents who vary significantly in race/ethnic backgrounds, socioeconomic status levels, and age. We also estimated models that contained gender by sexual intercourse and duration interactions, and the lack of significance of these interactions in most models suggests that the observed gender patterns are not strongly influenced by length of the relationship or whether it had become sexually intimate. Exceptions were associations between sexual intercourse experience and duration of the relationship and boys' reports of power, findings that warrant additional research scrutiny. Finally, controls for variations in family and peer dynamics, other basic features of the relationship, and self-esteem, although sometimes significant, did not strongly influence or attenuate these results.

The symbolic interactionist theoretical perspective described at the outset provides a generally useful framework for interpreting our results.

As we have suggested throughout this analysis, it is important to avoid an adult vantage point when focusing on early heterosexual relationships. It is quite possible that as boys gain in social maturity and confidence, and links to traditional sources of inequality become more salient, dynamic features within these romantic relationships will more often and more directly correspond to traditional gender scripts. In line with this idea, prior research has shown that certain transition events such as the move from cohabitation to marriage more often depend on male rather than female preferences (see, e.g., Brown 2000). Another possibility is that the nature of reports of relationship qualities and dynamics we documented in this study reflect cohort changes associated with broader societal level transformations. This interpretation would be consistent with Risman and Schwartz's (2002) recent discussion of apparent temporal shifts in adolescent sexual behavior patterns.

More research is also needed on the heterogeneity within this and other sample groups, as briefly described earlier. Our observations of variation are similar to those described by Moffatt (1989), who found that some university men emphasized love and romance in their personal narratives, while those whom he labeled the "Neanderthals" and "Neoconservatives" held more traditionally gendered views that appeared to influence their relationship styles and sexual behaviors significantly. Since few studies had directly assessed relationship processes during adolescence (and the results provide a strong contrast with key assertions about them contained within the existing literature), our findings should provide a useful background for exploring such variations in more detail in subsequent analyses.

It would also be useful to examine factors linked to within-individual shifts and variations in the ascendance or movement away from more traditionally gendered patterns and relationship styles (Thorne 1993). This suggests a more situated (again resonant with the symbolic interactionist framework) rather than a fixed or overarching gender inequalities approach to relationship processes. Aside from connections to major life-course transitions, for example, researchers could explore how certain relationship experiences connect to such shifts in perspective. Even within a focal relationship or time period, situations that link to boys' enactment of traditional/nontraditional repertoires need to be further highlighted. As an example, some of the same boys who expressed caring sentiments about their girlfriends undoubtedly make denigrating comments about girls when in the company of their circle of friends. Some boys also described tensions between their wish to spend time with friends and also to be responsive to their girlfriends. The fear of being seen as controlled by their girlfriends and subsequently ridiculed by friends reflects well that boys care very much what their friends think of them (a primary emphasis of prior research), but also what their girlfriends think of them (a conclusion of the present study). In line with this notion, we found that male respondents scored higher on a scale measuring perceived influence from friends as well as on the index of influence from romantic partners (results available on request). The idea of crosscurrents of social influence should in the long run prove more useful than the theme of autonomy so often highlighted as the central dynamic associated with boys' development.

The current analysis focused primarily on boys' perspectives on romance, as this was a particularly noticeable gap in the existing adolescence literature. Nevertheless, a comprehensive understanding of these social relationships obviously awaits more systematic investigations of girls' experiences. Where research has delved into the role of romantic involvement on girls' development, the focus of sociological investigations has, as suggested in the literature review, remained almost exclusively on sexuality or alternatively, negative outcomes—for example, establishing links to depression (Joyner and Udry 2000) and to relationship violence (Hagan and Foster 2001; Halpern et al. 2001), or pointing out how dating derails young women's academic pursuits (Holland and Eisenhart 1990). The conceptual framework and data presented here provide a starting point for a more multifaceted approach to girls' relationship experiences. Future research

linking dating and particular outcomes needs not only to assess whether adolescents have entered the dating world, but also to capture variations in partners' attitude and behavioral profiles, as well as the qualitative features of these romantic relationships. It is important to note that girls' narratives provide support for the direction of the results reported here, while also highlighting significant variations. Some young women described what they viewed as egalitarian relationships or a favorable power balance (e.g., "he wears what I want him to wear"), but others stressed that boyfriends had engaged in a range of controlling, intrusive behaviors. The aggregate findings are an important backdrop for further exploring the impact of these variations, as the subset of girls who describe themselves as having low power may experience this power balance in an especially detrimental way (for reasons highlighted in prior work, and because such girls may compare their own situations to those of other teens whose relationships are characterized by less traditionally gendered dynamics). A full exploration from girls' points of view also requires moving beyond the immediate confines of the dating context to consider some of the indirect ways in which involvement in the heterosexual world influences girls' well-being, including concerns about weight and appearance (Pipher 1994), and connections to relationships with parents (e.g., Joyner and Udry [2000] found that some of the gender difference in the dating-depression link was associated with increases in girls' conflicts with their parents).

Finally, the symbolic interactionist perspective highlights the importance of adolescents' own constructions of the nature and meanings of their relationships. This framework recognizes that many important relationship features are inherently subjective (e.g., adolescents are better positioned than others to comment upon their own confidence levels or feelings of love). It is, however, important to supplement the perceptual accounts described here with findings based on other methodological strategies. For example, teens may report a relatively egalitarian power balance, or even greater power on the part of the female partner, but laboratory-based studies or other methods may well uncover more traditionally gendered communication and relationship dynamics that are not well appreciated by adolescents themselves. Yet we hope that researchers will continue to explore the subjectively experienced aspects of adolescent romantic relationships, as these provide an important supplement to peer-focused ethnographies and the behavioral emphasis of large-scale surveys such as the National Longitudinal Study of Adolescent Health (Add Health).

NOTES

1. This analysis is also limited to a consideration of heterosexual relationships, as we are particularly interested in the process of "crossing over" from a social life based primarily on same-gender friendships to involvement with heterosexual partners. In addition, the number of respondents who self-identify as homosexual or bisexual at wave one is too small to support a separate analysis. Nevertheless, our conceptual framework and associated measurement emphasis could potentially be useful in connection with future investigations that explore the broader relationship contexts within which gay, lesbian, and bisexual youths' romantic and sexual experiences unfold.

2. The focus on emotions as an important dynamic within social interactions represents a shift from Mead's original cognitive emphasis, but it can be considered neo-Meadian since his more general ideas (e.g., the concept of role-taking and focus on self-processes) are applicable to understanding the emotional as well as cognitive realms of experience (see Engdahl 2004; MacKinnon 1994).

3. All of the schools eventually complied with our requests for these data, as this information is legally available under Ohio's Freedom of Information Act.

4. Furman and Hand (2004) found similarities in dating involvement in TARS and in their own study. Both studies document higher rates of dating involvement by age than are evident within the National Longitudinal Study of Adolescent Health (Add Health). We note that our reports of (for example) sexual intercourse by age parallel those in Add Health, but a higher percentage of respondents at each age report current romantic involvement: 32 percent of 7th, 41 percent of 9th graders, and 59 percent of 11th grade TARS respondents, compared with 17 percent, 32 percent, and 44 percent of Add Health respondents.

5. This respondent was excluded from the quantitative analysis, but included in our study of the relationship history narratives.

6. This introduction and definition were selected after extensive pre-testing and reflects contemporary trends in dating that are less focused than in earlier eras on formal activities. In addition, the latter type of definition is strongly class-linked, and would tend to exclude lower socioeconomic-status (SES) youth. Our definition also differs from that used in Add Health, where respondents are asked whether they currently have a "special romantic relationship." We wished to avoid selecting on a relationship that the respondent specifically defines as special, since understanding the patterning of relationship qualities is a primary objective of the study.

7. Further examination of the means for all groups indicates that African American male respondents perceive significantly less communication awkwardness than African American girls. In general, this fits with Staples's (1981) hypothesis about the greater social and communication ease of African American youths, but we document a significant gender difference in this regard. These distinct patterns highlight the importance of examining the nature of relationship dynamics among diverse groups of teens, since the bulk of prior research on adolescent relationships focuses on samples of white adolescents or largely white samples of college students (see also Carver et al. 2003).

8. We note that no racial/ethnic differences are observed in multivariate models that include demographic, family, and peer controls. African American youth report relationships of longer duration, and relationships are more likely to include sexual intercourse; when these variables are introduced, the African American coefficient becomes significant. These findings suggest that African American youth may accord differential meanings and emotional significance to different types of relationships. The role of race/ethnicity warrants more systematic investigation than we give it in the current analysis (see Giordano, Manning, and Longmore 2005b for an analysis of race/ethnicity effects on romantic relationships using Add Health data).

9. 2005b (1996) makes a similar point in her discussion of the length of girls' romance narratives, but she concludes from her own study that boys "rarely express the feelings of romantic love that girls do" (Martin 1996: 68). Our results are not in accord with this conclusion.

10. For a more detailed discussion of specific mechanisms of influence and reactions to influence attempts, see Trella (2005).

11. These narratives provide a strong contrast with Frost's (2001) description of boys' singular concern with what peers think of them, citing Kimmel (1994:128–29): "this kind of policing of identity construction, reflects a profound need to be accepted and approved by men: 'There is no strong concern for women's approval as they are in too low a place on the social ladder.'"

12. Our own interpretation of this dynamic differs slightly from Engdahl (2004) and Miller's (1973) emphases, as we posit a level of recognition of these points of connection on the part of the actors involved.

13. Research is needed on specific domains (e.g., achievement, delinquency, sexuality), where complex portraits of partner influence and gender effects will undoubtedly emerge. TARS data document effects of romantic partners' grades on respondents' grades, net of peer and parent influences, but we find a stronger effect for boys (Phelps et al. 2006). Using Add Health data, we found an effect of partners' minor deviance on respondents' deviance for male and female respondents, but a stronger effect for girls. Effects of the romantic partner's involvement in serious delinquency were comparable for boys and girls (Haynie et al. 2005).

14. Based on statistical tests, we do not find support for separate gender models for any of the other relationship qualities (communication awkwardness, confidence navigating relationships, love, and influence attempts or "actual" influence).

REFERENCES

Anderson, Elijah. 1989. "Sex Codes and Family Life among Poor Inner-City Youths." *Annals of the American Academy of Political Social Science* 501:59–79.

Blau, Peter M. 1964. *Exchange and Power in Social Life.* New York: Wiley.

Blood, Robert O. and Donald M. Wolfe. 1960. *Husbands and Wives: The Dynamics of Married Living.* Glencoe, IL: Free Press.

Blumer, Herbert. 1969. *Symbolic Interactionism: Perspective and Method.* Berkeley, CA: University of California Press.

Brown, B. Bradford, Candice Feiring, and Wyndol Furman. 1999. "Missing the Love Boat: Why Researchers Have Shied away from Adolescent Romance." pp. 1–18 in *The Development of Romantic Relationships in Adolescence*, edited by W. Furman, B. B. Brown, and C. Feiring. New York: Cambridge University Press.

Brown, Susan L. 2000. "Union Transitions among Cohabitors: The Significance of Relationship Assessments and Expectations." *Journal of Marriage and the Family* 62:833–46.

Call, Kathleen T. and Jeylan T. Mortimer. 2001. *Arenas of Comfort in Adolescence: A Study of Adjustment in Context.* Mahwah, NJ: Lawrence Erlbaum Associates.

Carver, Karen P. and J. Richard Udry. 1997. *Reciprocity in the Identification of Adolescent Romantic Partners.* Presented at the annual meeting of the Population Association of America, March 28, Washington, DC.

Carver, Karen P., Kara Joyner, and J. Richard Udry. 2003. "National Estimates of Adolescent Romantic Relationships." pp. 23–56 in *Adolescent Romantic Relations and Sexual Behavior*, edited by P. Florsheim. Mahwah, NJ: Lawrence Erlbaum Associates.

Cohen, Albert K. 1955. *Delinquent Boys: The Culture of the Gang.* New York: Free Press.

Collins, Randall. 2004. *Interaction Ritual Chains.* Princeton, NJ: Princeton University Press.

Cooley, Charles H. [1902] 1970. *Human Nature and the Social Order.* New York: Scribner.

Corsaro, William A. 1985. *Friendship and Peer Culture in the Early Years.* Norwood, NJ: Ablex.

Corsaro, William A. and Donna Eder. 1990. "Children's Peer Cultures." *Annual Review of Sociology* 16:197–220.

Crosnoe, Robert. 2000. "Friendships in Childhood and Adolescence: The Life Course and New Directions." *Social Psychology Quarterly* 63:377–91.

Denizet-Lewis, Benoit. 2004. "Whatever Happened to Teen Romance? (And What Is a Friend with Benefits Anyway?): Friends, Friends with Benefits and the Benefits of the Local Mall." *New York Times*, May 30, p. 30.

Duck, Steve, ed. 1997. *Handbook of Personal Relationships: Theory, Research, and Interventions.* New York: Wiley.

Eder, Donna, Catherine Evans, and Stephen Parker. 1995. *School Talk: Gender and Adolescent Culture.* New Brunswick, NJ: Rutgers University Press.

Emirbayer, Mustafa and Jeff Goodwin. 1994. "Network Analysis, Culture, and the Problem of Agency." *American Journal of Sociology* 99:1411–54.

Engdahl, Emma. 2004. "A Theory of the Emotional Self from the Standpoint of a Neo-Meadian." Ph.D. dissertation, Department of Sociology, Örebro University, Örebro, Sweden.

Fine, Gary A. 1987. *With the Boys: Little League Baseball and Preadolescent Culture*. Chicago, IL: University of Chicago Press.

Fischer, Agneta H. 2000. *Gender and Emotion Social Psychological Perspectives* Cambridge, England Cambridge University Press

Forster, Edward M. [1927] 1974. *Aspects of the Novel, and Related Writings*. New York: Holmes and Meier.

Frijda, Nico H. 2002. "Emotions as Motivational States." Pp. 11–32 in *European Review of Philosophy Emotion and Action*, vol 5, edited by E. Pacherie. Stanford, CA: CSLI Publications.

Frost, Liz. 2001. *Young Women and the Body: A Feminist Sociology*. New York: Palgrave Macmillan.

Furman, Wyndol and Laura S. Hand. 2004. "The Slippery Nature of Romantic Relationships: Issues in Definition and Differentiation." Presented at the Pennsylvania State Family Symposium, October, Philadelphia, PA.

Gecas, Viktor and Monica A. Longmore. 2003. "Self-Esteem." Pp. 1419–24 in *International Encyclopedia of Marriage and Family Relationships*, 2d ed., edited by J. J. Ponzetti, Jr. New York: Macmillan Reference.

Giddens, Anthony. 1992. *The Transformation of Intimacy: Sexuality, Love, and Eroticism in Modern Societies*. Stanford, CA: Stanford University Press.

Gilligan, Carol. 1982. *In a Different Voice: Psychological Theory and Women's Development*. Cambridge, MA: Harvard University Press.

Giordano, Peggy C. 1995. "The Wider Circle of Friends in Adolescence." *American Journal of Sociology* 101:661–97.

Giordano, Peggy C., Monica A. Longmore, and Wendy D. Manning. 2001. "A Conceptual Portrait of Adolescent Romantic Relationships." Pp. 111–39 in *Sociological Studies of Children and Youth*, edited by D. A. Kinney. London, England: Elsevier Science.

Giordano, Peggy C., Stephen A. Cernkovich, and Jennifer L. Rudolph. 2002. "Gender, Crime, and Desistance Toward a Theory of Cognitive Transformation." *American Journal of Sociology* 107:990–1064.

Giordano, Peggy C., Wendy D. Manning, and Monica A. Longmore. 2005a. "The Qualities of Adolescent Relationships and Sexual Behavior." Presented at the annual meeting of the Population Association of America, April 1, Philadelphia, PA.

——. 2005b. "The Romantic Relationships of African American and White Adolescents." *The Sociological Quarterly* 46:545–68.

Hagan, John and Holly Foster. 2001. "Youth Violence and the End of Adolescence." *American Sociological Review* 66:874–99.

Halpern, Carolyn T., Selene G. Oslak, Mary L. Young, Sandra L. Martin, and Lawrence L. Kupper. 2001. "Partner Violence among Adolescents in Opposite-Sex Romantic Relationships: Findings from the National Longitudinal Study of Adolescent Health." *American Journal of Public Health* 91:1679–85.

Hatfield, Elaine and Susan Sprecher. 1986. "Measuring Passionate Love in Intimate Relations." *Journal of Adolescence* 9:383–410.

Haynie, Dana L., Peggy C. Giordano, Wendy D. Manning, and Monica A. Longmore. 2005. "Adolescent Romantic Relationships and Delinquency Involvement." *Criminology* 43:177–210.

Hochschild, Arlie R. 1983. *The Managed Heart: Commercialization of Human Feeling*. Berkley, CA: University of California Press.

Holland, Dorothy C. and Margaret A. Eisenhart. 1990. *Educated in Romance: Women, Achievement, and College Culture*. Chicago, IL: University of Chicago Press.

Holland, Janet, Caroline Ramazanoglu, and Rachel Thomson. 1996. "In the Same Boat? The Gendered (In)experience of First Heterosex." Pp. 143–60 in *Theorizing Heterosexuality: Telling it Straight*, edited by D. Richardson. Philadelphia, PA: Open University Press.

Joas, Hans. 1997. *G H Mead: A Contemporary Reexamination of His Thought*. Cambridge, MA: MIT Press.

Joyner, Kara and J. Richard Udry. 2000. "You Don't Bring Me Anything but Down: Adolescent Romance and Depression." *Journal of Health and Social Behavior* 41:369–91.

Katz, Jack. 1999. *How Emotions Work*. Chicago, IL: University of Chicago Press.

Kimmel, Michael S. 1994. "Masculinity as Homophobia Fear, Shame, and Silence in the Construction of Gender Identity." Pp. 119–41 in *Theorizing Masculinities*, edited by H. Brod and M. Kaufman. London, England: Sage.

Komter, Aafke. 1989. "Hidden Power in a Marriage." *Gender and Society* 3:187–216.

Longmore, Monica A., Wendy D. Manning, and Peggy C. Giordano. 2001. "Preadolescent Parenting Strategies and Teens' Dating and Sexual Initiation." *Journal of Marriage and the Family* 63:322–35.

Maccoby Eleanor. 1990. "Gender and Relationships: A Developmental Account." *American Psychologist* 45:513–20.

MacKinnon, Neil J. 1994. *Symbolic Interactionism as Affect Control*. Albany, NY: State University of New York Press.

MacLeod, Jay. 1987. *Ain't No Makin' It Leveled Aspirations in a Low-Income Neighborhood*. Boulder, CO: Westview Press.

Manning, Wendy D., Monica A. Longmore, and Peggy C. Giordano. 2005. "Adolescents' Involvement in Non-Romantic Sexual Activity." *Social Science Research* 34:384–407.

Martin, Karin A. 1996. *Puberty, Sexuality, and the Self Boys and Girls at Adolescence*. New York: Routledge.

Massey, David S. 2002. "A Brief History of Human Society: The Origin and Role of Emotion in Social Life." *American Sociological Review* 67:1–29.

Matsueda, Ross L. and Karen Heimer. 1997. "A Symbolic Interactionist Theory of Role-Transitions, Role-Commitments, and Delinquency." Pp. 163–213 in *Developmental Theories of Crime and Delinquency*, edited by T. P. Thornberry. New Brunswick, NJ: Transaction.

Mead, George H. [1909] 1964. "Social Psychology as Counterpart to Physiological Psychology." Pp. 94–104 in *Selected Writings George Herbert Mead*, edited by A. J. Reck. Chicago, IL: University of Chicago Press.

———. 1913. "The Social Self." *Journal of Philosophy, Psychology, and Scientific Methods* 10:374–80.

———. 1934. *Mind, Self, and Society from the Standpoint of a Social Behaviorist*. Chicago, IL: University of Chicago Press.

Miller, David L. 1973. *George Herbert Mead Self, Language, and the World*. Austin, TX: University of Texas Press.

Moffatt, Michael. 1989. *Coming of Age in New Jersey: College and American Culture*. New Brunswick, NJ: Rutgers University Press.

Morse, Janice M. 1994. "Designing Funded Qualitative Research." Pp. 220–35 in *Handbook of Qualitative Research*, edited by N. Denzin and Y. Lincoln. Thousand Oaks, CA: Sage.

Phelps, Kenyatta D., Peggy C. Giordano, Wendy D. Manning, and Monica A. Longmore. 2006. "The Influence of Dating Partners on Adolescents' Academic Achievement." Presented at the annual meeting of the North Central Sociological Association, March 23–25, Indianapolis, IN.

Pipher, Mary. 1994. *Reviving Ophelia: Saving the Lives of Adolescent Girls*. New York: Ballentine.

Powers, William G. and Kevin Hutchinson. 1979. "The Measurement of Communication Apprehension in the Marriage Relationship." *Journal of Marriage and the Family* 41:89–95.

Prager, Karen J. 2000. "Intimacy in Personal Relations." Pp. 229–42 in *Close Relationships: A Sourcebook*, edited by C. Hendrick and S. S. Hendrick. Thousand Oaks, CA: Sage.

Risman, Barbara and Pepper Schwartz. 2002. "After the Sexual Revolution: Gender Politics in Teen Dating." *Contexts* 1:16–24.

Rosenberg, Morris. 1979. *Conceiving the Self*. New York: Basic Books.

Sandstrom, Kent L., Daniel D. Martin, and Gary A. Fine. 2002. *Symbols, Selves, and Social Reality: A Symbolic Interactionist Approach to Social Psychology and Sociology*. Los Angeles, CA: Roxbury.

Shott, Susan. 1979. "Emotion and Social Life: A Symbolic Interactionist Analysis." *American Journal of Sociology* 84:1317–34.

Simon, Robin W., Donna Eder, and Cathy Evans. 1992. "The Development of Feeling Norms Underlying Romantic Love among Adolescent Females." *Social Psychology Quarterly* 55:29–46.

Simon, William and John H. Gagnon. 1986. "Sexual Scripts: Permanence and Change." *Archives of Sexual Behavior* 15:97–120.

Sprey, Jetse. 1999. "Family Dynamics: An Essay on Conflict and Power." Pp. 667–85 in *Handbook of Marriage and the Family*, 2d ed., edited by M. R. Sussman, S. K. Steinmetz, and G. W. Peterson. New York: Plenum.

Staples, Robert. 1981. *The World of Black Singles: Changing Patterns of Male-Female Relationships*. Westport, CT: Greenwood.

Sullivan, Harry S. 1953. *The Interpersonal Theory of Psychiatry*. New York: Norton.

Sullivan, Mercer L. 1989. *"Getting Paid" Youth Crime and Work in the Inner City*. Ithaca, NY: Cornell University Press.

Thompson, Sharon. 1995. *Going All The Way Teenage Girls' Tales of Sex, Romance, and Pregnancy*. New York: Hill and Wang.

Thoits, Peggy A. 1989. "The Sociology of Emotions." *Annual Review of Sociology* 15:317–42.

Thorne, Barrie. 1993. *Gender Play Girls and Boys in School.* New Brunswick, NJ: Rutgers University Press.

Thrasher, Frederic M. 1927. *The Gang: A Study of 1,313 Gangs.* Chicago, IL: University of Chicago Press.

Trella, Deanna L. 2005. "Control and Power Dynamics in Adolescent Romantic Relationships." Masters thesis, Department of Sociology, Bowling Green State University, Bowling Green, OH.

Turner, Jonathan H. 2000. *On the Origin of Human Emotion: A Sociological Inquiry into the Evolution of Human Affect.* Stanford, CA: Stanford University Press.

Waller, Walter. 1937. "The Rating and Dating Complex." *American Sociological Review* 2:727–34.

Weber, Max. 1947. *The Theory of Social and Economic Organization.* Translated by A. M. Henderson and T. Parsons. Edited by T. Parsons. Glencoe, IL: Free Press.

Wight, Daniel. 1994. "Boys' Thoughts and Talk about Sex in a Working-Class Locality of Glasgow." *Sociological Review* 42:703–38.

Willis, Paul E. 1977. *Learning to Labor.* Aldershot, England: Gower.

Youniss, James and Jacqueline Smollar. 1985. *Adolescent Relations with Mothers, Fathers and Friends.* Chicago, IL: University Of Chicago Press.

MEN'S RESISTANCE TO EQUAL SHARING

Kathleen Gerson

WHILE GENDER INEQUITIES MAY explain why young women prepare for "second best" options, men are not immune from similar concerns. The increased fragility of marriage, growing time demands and insecurities at work, and women's rising standards for a relationship all confront men with new dilemmas of their own. Though men's responses may differ, they also face options likely to fall short of their ideals.

Young men share women's doubts about their chances of striking a good balance between earning and caring, but they experience this conflict in a different way. If women worry about the economic, social, and psychological risks of depending too much on someone else, men are more apprehensive about their financial ability to support others. And if women worry about having to assume the lion's share of family caretaking whether or not they marry or have a paid job, men face rising pressures to do more at home and earn more at work if they do marry.

Perceiving different obstacles, men form different fallback strategies. Uneasy about the price equality might exact, seven out of ten men look to modified traditionalism, in which they retain the position of a family's main breadwinner while also granting their partner the right, and need, to work. If equality proves impossible or just too costly, these men seek to preserve some distinct gender divisions that most women resist.[1]

The minority of men who do not fall back on modified traditionalism share women's skepticism about traditional marriage. In contrast to women who

are preparing to do it all on their own, however, these men are more likely to emphasize freedom *from* family obligations. Anxious about achieving a cultural ideal equating "being a man" with supporting a family, they stress self-reliance as a route to autonomy more than to connectedness. These men are drawn to the freedom side of the tension between commitment and freedom. This tension has pervaded American culture since its inception as a frontier society, but it takes a special form in a world where men face declining economic opportunities and expanding options to reject marriage.[2] This mix of new constraints and opportunities has increased the lure of autonomy, especially for men who doubt they can live up to the cultural injunction to be a breadwinner or the rising pressure to take on more responsibility at home.

Faced with different options and fears, men are adopting fallback strategies that clash with women's. Yet men's outlooks, no less than women's, reflect the need to pursue second-best scenarios because more desirable options seem out of reach. Most men, like most women, prefer a more egalitarian, flexible balance between breadwinning and caretaking. Their aspirations are converging, even if their strategies do not.

It's Hard to Do It All

Today's young men face an uncertain economic landscape and rising expectations for equality in relationships. Each may be a cause for concern, but together, these forces create conflicting pressures. They press men to give more time and energy to both work and family, leaving most to wonder if they can succeed—or even survive—in their jobs or at home. Indeed, a recent study of the American workforce found that 45 percent of employed men report experiencing either "some" or "a lot" of work-life conflict (compared to 34 percent in 1977), and among men in dual-earner couples, that number rises to almost 60 percent.[3] Like these men, Adam worried about whether he could pursue a medical career and also live up to his father's example as an involved parent as well as a successful dentist and good provider:

> I would like to think I'm gonna earn enough money to live a nice life, [but] I'm afraid of not doing as well as my father—either career-wise or family-wise.

Although Mitch's dad was a psychologist who spent plenty of time at home, his own job in banking left him doubtful about the chances of finding work that would allow a similar balance and still ensure a steady income:

> [My dad] certainly set a good example, a paradigm model if you want to call it. In the ideal world, I'd love to work until 4:00, 4:30, then spend time with my family. I want my children to have a real father as opposed to someone who just kisses them good night. I'd like to have a fairly equal balance, kind of like my dad, but it would be tough to attain because a lot of careers are downsizing, and they want you to work weekends and around the clock.

Men also face new pressures for involvement at home. Although acknowledging the loss, in Sam's words, of a "get out of housework free" card, most focus more on the obstacles to building an equal relationship. Chris hoped to re-create his father's flexible approach, but feared striking such a balance in his own life would be arduous and costly:

> I thought you could have just a relationship, and I've learned that you've got to be able to draw that line. It's a difficult thing. And that would be my fear—where am I cutting into my job too much, where am I cutting into the relationship too much, and how do I divide it, and can it actually be done at all?

Lawrence knew even the most rewarding domestic activities would place limits on his independence:

> A large part of me wants to have the picket fence, big house, big family, and coach the Little League team and be the head of PTA. And then there's the other side that wants a lot more freedom.

These cross-pressures have raised the stakes on men, leaving them skeptical about whether they can live up to their own ideals or the expectations of others. Reflecting on his hard-working Chinese parents' struggle to keep the family afloat, even though they relied on two incomes, Justin blamed the economy:

> You don't want to be in a situation where in order to put food on the table, you can't meet the child's needs in another way. I have a high standard. I don't want to be a sloppy father. So it's a conundrum. I don't think it's as simple as it was in the past.

Joel pointed to his own "high standards," and especially his hope to avoid the pitfalls of his parents' unhappy traditional marriage, but he agreed his goal of equal parenting was on a collision course with successful breadwinning:

> I feel sometimes that my standards are too high, and I want it all, and it's just not reasonable or feasible in this world. I don't feel I'm as strong a person as that situation would require—someone who is on top of everything and sort of a superman. It doesn't really seem like I'd be able to keep up that pace.

Young men face trade-offs that mirror those facing women. Like women, they believe the ideal work-family balance will have to give way to a fallback scenario, but men are inclined to fall back on emphasizing their breadwinning rights and duties. Josh felt strongly that, despite his professed support for equality, he could not surrender his duty to be the primary earner:

> I'll work as hard as I could to support them. I just think it's a responsibility. It conflicts with what I said about women, but that's just something I feel—that a man's first responsibility is to take care of his family. I know it's kind of contradictory.

Matthew agreed:

> I want family life to be the most important thing. If I could have the ideal world, I'd like to have a

partner who's making as much as I am—someone who's ambitious and likes to achieve. [But] if it can't be equal, I would be the breadwinner and be there for helping with homework at night.

Yet not all men agree with this view. Some seek more independence than a traditional marriage allows. They neither want to submit to the strictures of conventional jobs nor hope to find a domestically oriented partner. Divorced and on his own in his late twenties, Nick vowed to avoid his father's nine-to-five routine:

I don't want to end up being your every day, run-of-the-mill Joe Commuter, like those uptight people who worry about this bill and that. I don't want to be stuck in one place for twenty-five years. I want to do it my way.

Men's fallback positions reverse rather than mimic women's. Though women disproportionately favor self-reliance, men favor more traditional patterns. They are prone to stress their own economic responsibilities and prerogatives, even if a marriage contains two earners.[4] Figures 27.1 and 27.2 show that a majority of men from all types of

backgrounds prefer breadwinning as a fallback, although African-Americans, Latinos, and those from single-parent homes and working-class or poor families are more evenly divided. For these groups, who continue to face more constricted job opportunities, lower rates of educational attainment, and higher incarceration rates, a larger proportion stress freedom from breadwinning, even in the context of an intimate relationship (including slightly more than a third of African-American and Latino men, and close to half of men from single-parent homes).[5]

Because men face different options than women, their versions of both traditionalism and self-reliance also differ. For men, traditionalism means taking on the privileges and responsibilities of primary breadwinning, while self-reliance means *not* being responsible for the care and feeding of a family. Yet even though young men's fallback positions differ from women's, they are "second best" strategies nonetheless.

Falling Back on Breadwinning

Like women who look to domesticity, men who fall back on breadwinning place marriage and family at the center of their plans. For men, this means being a good provider. Parental examples, lessons on the job,

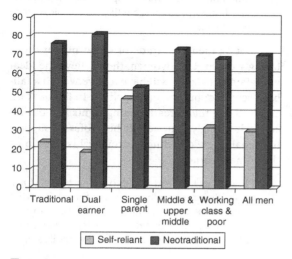

■ FIGURE 27.1
Men's fallback positions, by family background and class.

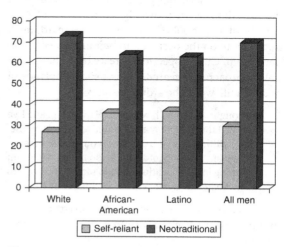

■ FIGURE 27.2
Men's fallback positions, by ethnic background.

and experiences in relationships have convinced them that, when push comes to shove, they need to take responsibility for their family's financial welfare. Some view breadwinning as a privilege, while others see it as an obligation, but they all agree that no matter what the gender revolution prescribes, it is still paramount for men to earn a living and support their families, which also implies taking a backseat as a caregiver.

FATHERS' AMBIGUOUS MODELS

Since over three-quarters of men from both traditional and dual-earner homes, as well as over half of those from single-parent homes, plan to fall back on breadwinning, fathers' choices do not predict sons' strategies. Most harbor mixed reactions to their fathers' choices, but nevertheless see breadwinning as the most reasonable alternative.

Men who grew up in two-parent homes had ambivalent reactions to their parents' arrangements, whether their mothers stayed home or had paid jobs. Jonathan did not share his father's attraction to "the traditional thing":

> I don't want or feel it's right to have a traditional one like my parents, where I was the only one working. Having such a simple, standard, pretty traditional upbringing, I wish it had been more challenging.

Justin had no desire to become an overworked and disengaged parent like his father:

> I don't want to have the type of relationship my father had with me. You get home at 7:00, 7:30. You're wiped out, and [the kids] are ready for bed. That's the greatest fear.

Neither wished to repeat his father's pattern, yet both expected to become primary breadwinners. In the end, they agreed it would be wrong to forfeit the "good provider" mantle or rely on a wife's income, as Jonathan explained:

> I like an even relationship, but if it got to the situation where my wife didn't want to work, I need to be able to support [her].

And Justin added:

> I saw how hard [my mom] worked, and I didn't feel that was right, so this is the way I'm changing

from what my dad did. I realize it's not perfect, and maybe it's paternalistic, but because of the way I grew up, I feel I need to be in a situation where I can take care of her, provide for her.

Sons were even more conflicted when their fathers abandoned the family. Close to half shared women's skepticism about marriage, but the other half agreed with Hank, whose father's departure strengthened his resolve to become a responsible family man:

> I'm not afraid to be in a relationship or get married. It's number one. I think I learned that from my father, from his saying "I'm gonna go get cigarettes," and not seeing him till three years later. So I'll be faithful.

Over two-thirds of men reared in a traditional or dual-earner home fell back on breadwinning, yet their enthusiasm is muted. Even men with successful breadwinning fathers were mindful of the dangers. Paul worried about repeating his father's pattern of overwork as a lawyer for an oil company:

> I didn't want to go into the corporate world because I saw what it did to my father. He worked all the time. So I realized early on that I didn't want to do that. Unfortunately, I think I'm developing a lot more of these ambitious feelings that I saw in my father growing up and I disliked. I think it's closely tied to the economic comforts that provides.

Although overwork did not concern Manny, he realized he might be unable to support a family on the modest earnings his construction worker father relied on:

> Life is scary today, because I know she's my responsibility and the mother of my child.

THE PULL OF THE WORKPLACE

In a world that questions whether a man who does not carry his own economic weight is "marriageable," having children, a family, and even love seems to hinge on the ability to bring home a "big enough" paycheck.[6] As Jonathan put it:

> Success is getting to the point where you can say, "I've got this great marriage, great kids, this is what I do with my life." But a lot of it's financial—to be able to provide for my family, like I got provided for.

Men from all class backgrounds measured success in market terms. Although those who plan to fall back on autonomy are skeptical about the chances of earning a "good living," most men counted on jobs to ease the way to primary breadwinning. Work opportunities, often invisible or taken for granted, pulled these men into the workplace and away from home. Their routes differ by class and ethnic background, but everyone who turned toward breadwinning focused on their economic prospects.

Invisible Opportunities

Middle-class men largely assumed from an early age that they would enter a demanding occupational niche, while those from more modest economic backgrounds generally took more winding, ambiguous paths. Growing up in an affluent suburb, Adam's professional aspirations emerged early and never wavered:

> I always wanted to be a professional. I would never settle for second-best. Even today, it makes me crazy if I don't do as well as I could have—financially, in a career. That's something that won't go away, and it's my own pressure.

In contrast, Ray, an African-American from a working-class home, became an enthusiastic worker only after he joined the lower ranks of the prison system and rose unexpectedly into management:

> I would do just enough to pass school, but I found out I love work. I became a manager, and I'm so gung ho. So I'm not gonna abuse my job.

Few men attributed their improving prospects to having a gender advantage, but there continues to be an "invisible inequality" in women's and men's occupational opportunities that still allows some men, especially if they are non-Hispanic whites, to "coast" in school and still succeed at work.[7] On average, men continue to earn more than women and to outpace them in professional careers, despite the fact that women are more likely to go to college, earn a college degree, and report studying more and relaxing less.[8] Yet over the long run, most men can still expect to outearn their female peers, and among people with a four-year college degree,

the gap between men's and women's pay has actually widened slightly since the mid-1990s.[9] But even those men who drifted through school did not notice these advantages when they found their careers taking off. Jim never liked studying, barely graduated from high school, and dropped out of college after one semester. Yet after "kind of falling into" a job in the court system, he rose up the civil service ladder. Beginning at the "bottom of the barrel" as a guard, he rose to a "supervisory level" by his late twenties and expected to keep moving up:

> What I'm doing, it's pretty much the ideal. I came in as an officer, and now I'm a supervisor. My pay has gone up pretty much within a couple of years. I don't have a college degree, [but] there are a lot of people with college degrees who don't use them. As far as getting ahead, I make more money than my sister, who's an accountant. So I feel very positive about my career. I see myself on the path, and I want to get ahead as far as possible.

Whether anticipated or unexpected, promising careers offer reassurance about the chances of succeeding at breadwinning. But this reassurance comes with a cost, since the demands required to build a career also undermine the chances of striking a balance between work and home.

No Time for "Equal Time"

As financial rewards accrue at work, the heavy time investments required to sustain them make it harder to balance work with the rest of life. The paradigm of a committed worker as someone who works full-time—and overtime—for decades, with no time-outs or even cutting back, creates what Joan Williams calls a "maternal wall" for women, but it leaves men with a shrinking window for sharing at home.[10] Jim believed the need to work "full-time, all the time" meant that, faced with a choice, he would have to spend more time at work:

> Even though I didn't go to school a lot, you can get by in school without being there every day. But now it's different. How are you gonna get ahead if you're not at work? So if somebody's gonna be the breadwinner, it's going to be me. I always feel the need to work.

New economic uncertainties have raised the stakes even higher, making workweeks that extend well beyond forty hours typical in the most demanding professions.[11] In a "winner take all" economy with less room at the top, high- and lesser-earning men alike feel uneasy about taking time away from work.[12] Despite Justin's early financial accomplishments, he felt compelled to work harder and longer just to stay even:

> This society, there's no security. So for a twenty-eight-year-old, I'm successful, but I look around and there are plenty of young people who are successful, too. I'm not the smartest, the brightest, the best, or whatever. So if I'm ahead, then I make a new goal. Once you stop doing it, you start to slide. So everything's relative.

Inexorably escalating job demands, along with intensifying competition for occupational rewards, leave primary breadwinning men with little hope of striking an equal work-family balance. Peter became pessimistic about the possibilities for either balance or equality:

> The biggest challenge is the balance between work and home. I want as even a split as it could be, but with my hours, I don't think it would be very even . . . because work will be very difficult.

Chris became increasingly wary of a two-career marriage:

> Two careers, it's gonna be very difficult. I see it with the director of our lab. They're both professionals—she's an executive, and I see how he comes in so tired because his wife had to go do her presentation. So I've seen how tricky it gets. It really can run you haggard.

Most greet the prospect of putting so much time into a job with ambivalence and wistfulness. Justin longed to leave his fast-paced corporate career to become a teacher, but felt unable to resist the pressure to "make very good money" for his family:

> If it weren't for money, I would like to be a teacher and live a quiet life. But it's not possible, I'm beginning to realize, because of the financial needs. The more likely scenario [is] I would have to

continue in this line of work. I don't feel there's a choice, really.

MOVING TOWARD MARRIAGE

In contrast to self-reliant women, who are skeptical of marriage, breadwinning men are drawn to its benefits. Like women, they are postponing marriage, but most (though certainly not all, as we shall see) view marriage as a goal they want and expect to reach. Some breadwinning men never questioned the attraction of marriage, while others overcame doubts as they grew older. Many were surprised to see their skepticism melt. Ray changed his outlook after a brief but intense period of "wildness":

> I always wanted to have kids, but I didn't want to get married. Then I started quieting down. At twenty-one, I already had money, had traveled, done the wild things. I was tired.

Daniel vowed to be a responsible husband and father after watching his "wilder" brother make mistakes:[13]

> Scott's the divorced one, but he's much different than I am. When he got married, he still wanted to be a drinker and a partyer. That was his problem. I've already gotten rid of those things, so I don't see that being my problem.

Supportive partners also help skeptical men develop a more sanguine view of lasting commitment. Carlos felt fortunate, if surprised, when his girlfriend gave him hope for creating the happy marriage that eluded his parents:

> I was always like, "I'm not ever gonna get married." With her, I can see myself getting married, having kids. She's a real close friend. It's better than my parents, 'cause even when it comes to a point where we're about to disagree, we talk instead of argue.

William went even further. Though he enjoyed the advantages of middle-class affluence, he once feared his life had no direction or purpose. But creating a "real" relationship with his fiancée gave William a newfound faith in himself. At twenty-eight, he marveled at how their relationship had helped him find his way and had given him optimism about the future:

> The course of my life, the past eleven years have not gone the way I think my life ought to have gone. I dropped out of college, diddled around doing this and that. So I'm lucky to be where I am now, just finishing my bachelor's degree. Lindsey is very assertive and has taught me a lot . . . I'm learning to believe in myself in a real way. I was really unhappy for a long time, but now I'm really happy. Dealing in a more real way with another person in a relationship, a lot of what I went through is getting self-confidence and learning to believe in myself. I look forward to my future, and I'm sure it's going to be great. You've got to understand, it comes after years of dread. You know, I'm never gonna have a midlife crisis.

Eduardo grew up in a working-class Latino home, where neither parent had gone to college, but he had a similar story to tell:

> I met Mary six years ago. [It made] a big difference. If it wasn't for her, I wouldn't be here right now. I'd be lost, dreaming somewhere. She's come through with me. She's made me feel really good about myself. She's really important to me and really wants to stay with me.

Supportive partners not only fuel optimism about work and marriage; they also help men anchor their identity in breadwinning by providing moral and practical support. As Manny put it, "I know she's the one 'cause I love the way she takes care of me." For men who fall back on breadwinning, marriage is as a package of commitments that promises intimacy, love, emotional sustenance, and social status. In fact, contemporary men are generally less skeptical about marriage and parenthood than women, who are more supportive of childlessness and hold more cautious views about marriage.[14] Men's more optimistic outlook is well founded, since married men enjoy a range of personal and social benefits, including better health and higher earnings. Not only do married men do better than single men at work, but fathers are more likely than childless men to be hired and offered higher salaries.[15] Ken sensed this advantage when his previous boss, who had remained single well into his thirties, offered an unappealing contrast

to his current boss, whose "perfect family" seemed integral to his workplace success:

> My former employer, I don't want to be like that. He's about thirty-six and never been married. My current employer is more of a role model. He's got two daughters, a pretty wife, up there in the company, very advanced. He's a great guy, too.

Marriage is clearly associated with benefits for men, but it is difficult to disentangle cause and effect. Does marriage confer advantages, or are healthier, more successful men more likely to marry? In either case, marriage and parenthood help men in myriad ways. At work, they enjoy a wage bonus, and in private life, they are less vulnerable to disease and have larger social networks.[16] Most young men sense this link and hope to create it for themselves.

FROM PARENTING TO MOTHERING

Where do children fit into time-demanding jobs? This question poses the biggest challenge to the ideal of equal sharing. Most agree with Paul, who "always envisioned two earners, but that would obviously be a problem when children start coming into the picture." To resolve this conundrum, breadwinning men distinguish between "equal but different" forms of caring. They profess support for the ideal of *equal parenting*, but they fall back on the practical advantages of *devoted mothering*.

Only a Parent Will Do

With few exceptions, neotraditional men do not believe mothers are inherently more qualified than fathers to care for children; but they do believe *parents* are inherently more qualified than other caregivers. While Eric assumed mothers and fathers should be equally responsible for children's care, he did not feel caretaking should be delegated:

> I would primarily like it to be a family member—either one of us. I would like for the child to have one or both parents there at the beginning.

Phil echoed this point:

> If children come into the picture, that's when I've got the old, traditional values—not that women should

be home, but somebody—one of the parents—should always be there to take care of the kids. Where my part would come, I would deal with it then, but one of us would always be at home.

In principle, a reluctance to rely on babysitters and day care centers does not leave the bulk of parenting to women. Yet few men can envisage finding two flexible full-time jobs or living on two part-time incomes. Phil continued:

> I would like to work certain days and she would work certain days. This way, one of the parents is always there, and it's not always the same. I would like to work my schedule around my kids, but that's not going to happen.

Although the reluctance to delegate coexists with egalitarian principles, its practical implication makes equality close to impossible. Without the option to divide child care equally, neotraditional men look to their partners to pick up an added share of the load.

Market Work and the Gender of Caretaking

Most men feel justified in leaving mothers as the default caretaker because they assume their own market advantages mean their work needs to come first.[17] Although women's yearly earnings, as a percent of men's, have risen from 64 percent in 1955 to 78 percent in 2008, husbands continue to outearn wives in most marriages. Some embrace this circumstance, while others regret it, but they all see it as unavoidable. Justin felt his wife's lower earnings as a freelance writer deprived them both of the option to be equal caretakers:

> She doesn't want to have babysitters, and I agree. If she was in a job that pulls down the same type of money, then either of us could quit. But we don't, so the problem is I have to work, unless she can get another job.

Jim, on the other hand, believed his higher earnings and better job prospects justified an arrangement his wife, a math teacher, did not prefer:

> This may sound sexist, but she'll just have to take time off. As far as a macho thing, if she made a much better salary, it would be different. [But]

she's pretty much going to stay at that level, and I'm going to move up as far as I can.

Whether or not they prefer the outcome, an earnings advantage and more promising career prospects lends an air of inevitability to men's reliance on women's caretaking. Yet almost every young man rejected the idea of staying at home, even if it *were* possible.[18] Josh felt it would be irresponsible for him to rely on a woman's paycheck, even if she could earn more:

> I would never stay home. I have a friend who's like that, and I strongly disapprove. The father just stays home. I think it's wrong, 'cause his wife's out there working seven days a week, and he's doing nothing except stay home.

Hank agreed:

> I can't sit home and have a woman pay the bills. Sharing the child care—I would do it once I'm home, but the kids have to have somebody to come home to. So if she makes more than me, then I'll have to get two jobs.

By equating responsible manhood with earning a "good enough" living, breadwinning men relieve their partner of an economic weight that even self-reliant women are reluctant to assume. Coupled with the resistance to delegating child care, however, this view leads inexorably, if unconsciously, to the assumption that a mother will take the main responsibility for the care work. The ideal of intensive parenting becomes the need for *maternal* responsibility. Engaged to be married, Manny moved seamlessly from believing "only a parent will do" to assuming his fiancée would be the one to do it:

> Especially at an early age, you don't leave your child with anyone. So she would have to take care of the baby, 'cause I wouldn't like anybody with my child and I'll be working.

Breadwinning in an Age of Women's Work

Though men face powerful incentives to fall back on breadwinning, they cannot ignore the attendant conflicts. Placing paid work first and counting on someone else to do more of the domestic work complicates the search for balance and flexibility, especially when most families need two incomes and most women want to work.[19] This tension prompts neotraditional men to develop mental strategies to resolve the clash. They refashion the core ideals of work-family balance, equal sharing, and the importance of women's work to fit better their need to see themselves as breadwinners first.

BALANCE IS A STATE OF MIND

Breadwinning men have not relinquished the ideal of work-family balance, but they hope to redefine it. In contrast to self-reliant women, who expect to combine work and parenting as best they can, and neotraditional women, who expect to fit paid work around their family tasks, neotraditional men stress how their earnings *substitute* for time and other forms of care. Patrick believed being a good father means giving priority to financial contributions:

> Ideally, my children would be more important than my job. But I need to work to support my family.

Matthew also reluctantly focused on making money before spending time:

> What premium are you going to put on having time or money? Certainly, to give your children any sort of chance takes material things.

To fit "balance" into this framework, some make a mental distinction between time and personal priorities. For Thomas, what matters most is how he *feels*, not what he actually *does*:

> Time-wise, I spend a lot of time on work, so if you slice up the day into a pie, I'll spend more time at work than doing anything else. But in terms of rank in significance, it's fifty-fifty.

Others take a longer view, defining "balance" as a sequence of changing priorities. These men hope putting in long hours early in their careers will pave the way for more family involvement later on. Ken hoped to put work first and then family:

> After I've exhausted my corporate life and saved enough money, it would be very nice to contribute to raising my child. Maybe then [my wife] can

work full-time, and I'll go to school and raise the child.

Matthew proposed a similar scenario:

> I'd like to have it such that work dominates my life until my children turn five, six, and then have work taper off such that by the time my kids are in high school, I'll have a job with complete flexibility.

By stressing the long-run nature of the work-family balance, breadwinning men can focus on work in the short run. But these plans presume someone else will pick up the slack in the early stages of child rearing, when the demands of both careers and children are especially intense. For Hank, this meant his wife's presence could stand in for his own:

> I'd never want to work so much that the kids grow up and say, "My father never spent time with me, and that's why I'm a screwup." But if there's someone who represents you at home and doing the same thing I would, hopefully that makes up for it.

Neotraditionalism preserves some semblance of the idea of work-family balance by adopting cognitive strategies that place men's work first. Defining balance as a state of mind helps men resolve inner conflicts between the ideal of involved fatherhood and the reality of time-demanding jobs. Yet this strategy leaves the underlying structure of work unchallenged, leaving genuine balance beyond everyone's grasp.

THE PLACE OF WOMEN'S WORK

Most neotraditional men assume that wives and mothers should be able to pursue careers and see their earnings as important and desirable.[20] Those who fall back on breadwinning do not expect their partners to reject paid work. Although Lucius hoped to be the primary earner, he did not expect or want to be the only one:

> I'm gonna make enough money so that I'll be able to hold it down. But I'd rather that we both work. It helps.

Brian agreed:

> It's more on a man to bring home money, but it's not bad if you have the woman bringing home

money, too. Otherwise, in twenty years, you've been shelling out money for her.

These men walk a thin line in blending their support for working partners with the image of themselves as good providers. They believe everyone should have a work ethic, but they grant more value to their own paycheck. A partner, they reason, can—and *should*—work, but not in the same way or to the same degree.

Her Job Comes Second

Neotraditional men find value in women's work as a source of income, a protection from boredom, a marker of maturity, and an avenue of personal and social esteem. They neither wish nor plan for their partner to stay home over the long run. Yet even though they frown on full-time homemaking, they nevertheless place women's jobs in a different category than their own. Like notions of women as a "reserve labor force," they view a woman's paid work as something that can ebb and flow depending on family needs.[21] Allen expected to find a career-oriented partner, but hoped she would take time out when children arrived:

> Someone I knew would just stay home—that wouldn't be my first choice. I'd like to marry somebody who has a career. But I'd like it if she stayed home for a few years.

Matthew planned for his partner to "shift down":

> I'd like to have a partner who's making as much as I am—has a high-powered job where we can put the money aside quickly. So by the time we have a kid, she can shift down. Now she works with the kids and spends her time working for the Humane Society or whatever.

Seeing a partner's career as "extra"—and less essential—helps men discount the costs women (and all these men are heterosexual) bear by putting work on the back burner, even temporarily. Peter argued that pulling back to care for children would not exact a heavy price on his wife's career as long as it did not become a permanent arrangement:

> She should work and just adjust her schedule after they're born. After the children reach a certain age, I would feel, if I were her, that if I didn't go on and pursue my own objectives, I would always feel that I missed out on doing something.

And even though Jim recognized the highly professional nature of his wife's accomplishments, he distinguished between her relatively flat career ladder as a teacher and his own plans to move up the civil service ladder:

> She's a professional woman and does very well at her job, so she would go on forever. But to take a year or two off—it's fine, 'cause as a math teacher, it's not gonna be a problem. If she had a job that was more demanding, it would be a bigger problem.

Placing women's work second allows men to affirm a two-earner arrangement without undermining their own identities as breadwinners. It also justifies holding her responsible for domestic work whether or not she holds a job. Although Sam granted his partner the option to work, he did not give himself an offsetting responsibility to share at home:

> If she wanted to work, I would assume it's her responsibility to drop the kids off at grandma's house or something. She's in charge of the kids. If she's gonna work, fine, but you still have responsibilities.

Given most women's determination to preserve their autonomy through paid work, it may be wishful thinking for these men to presume they can find a partner willing to put work aside. As a short-run strategy, it nevertheless allows them to focus on their own economic prospects and identities as family providers. These efforts make room for women's work, but they also represent a pattern that is well short of equal sharing.

DEFINING EQUALITY AS "CHOICE"

How do neotraditional men reconcile the ideal of equality with the identity of a good provider? Alex defined equality as a malleable concept, whose meaning can shift with changing circumstances:

> I would like it to be egalitarian, but I don't have a set definition for what an egalitarian relationship would be like. If she thought, "At this point in my life, I don't want to work, it's more important to stay home," then that would be fine for one person to do more work in some respects.

Because these men believe they should, in Peter's words, "be responsible for the money," they distinguish between a woman's "choice" to work and their own obligation to do so. Dwayne explained that equality means offering a partner the choice *not* to work:

> If we're struggling and you're gonna lay around, then I can't see that. But if things is going as they're supposed to and I'm making good money, if you choose not to work, that's on you.

Daniel sounded a similar theme:

> It's probably much easier for us to earn the money we're gonna need if both of us are working, but if somehow my job makes enough money, my wife doesn't *have* to work. As long as there's enough money for the family, then it doesn't matter.

Using the language of choice as a frame for women's work narrows men's work options but expands their leverage at home. The responsibility of being the economic mainstay makes it easier to select which forms of domestic work they prefer. It is thus telling that, over the last several decades, men's involvement in child care has risen more substantially than their participation in housework.[22] Lawrence, like most, distinguished between child care and housework:

> I can really imagine myself raising kids. It's the housework-type stuff I can't imagine.

Mitch proposed a similar division:

> I'd like sharing equally—certainly child raising and also financially. I'd like my mate to be able to balance and maybe switch them, but I do not want to do cooking.

Many also hope to resolve the potential conflicts by delegating the least appealing tasks to a third party. Delegating tasks once performed routinely by wives and mothers is part of a long-term trend of outsourcing household tasks, a process that has been under way since the workplace and children's schooling moved out of the private household.[23] Wayne viewed paid help as a reasonable extension of this process and the best solution to contemporary pressures:

> We both gotta work, so I hope we get help. 'Cause I don't want my wife to be working and doing housework chores. And I don't want to be doing it. I did enough of that already.

While self-reliant women define equality as their right to seek independence, breadwinning men typically use the language of choice to distinguish between a partner's option to work and their own obligation to do so. This frame allows men to reconcile the abstract ideal of equal sharing with the real difficulties of putting it into practice, but it also re-creates gender boundaries by preserving personal discretion about how—and how much—to participate at home.[24]

PLUS ÇA CHANGE, PLUS C'EST LA MÊME CHOSE?

Breadwinning men stress the importance of paternal involvement, but they redefine work-family balance as a state of mind. They are prepared to find a work-committed partner, but they expect her to place work in the background if and when needed. They value equality, but frame working as optional for women and their own domestic participation as a matter of choice. These strategies reaffirm men's moral responsibility to support a family while also helping them reconcile the ideals of involved fatherhood and equal sharing with their identity as a good provider. But they also imply that women should be ready and willing to do it all, as Lucius explained:

> I want a woman who knows how to do everything if she has to. She can be independent and domestic at the same time. Independent means a career-minded woman, and domestic means she knows how to take care of home stuff.

Isaiah put it this way:

> Let's say I don't get to that point where I can do it alone, then depending on the situation, I would know that person [can] go either way,

whatever they decide. That's why they have to be independent.

By softening the gender boundaries of previous eras without erasing them, these men have developed a neotraditional vision that grants some gender flexibility without surrendering gender distinctions. If most women do not find this "equal, but different" perspective reassuring, most men view it as an unavoidable consequence of circumstances beyond their control. As Lucius acknowledged, "I wouldn't like it if the shoe was on the other foot, but there's a lot of things in life that's unfair."

The same forces pushing and pulling women toward self-reliance prevent a commensurate shift among men toward domesticity. Men, no less than women, understand that market work must come first—not just for survival, but also for self-respect.[25] Because paid work bestows social status as well as economic rewards, few men can sidestep the pressure to measure their own worth in terms of market value. Those who try to resist must cope with pervasive social cues reminding them of its importance. Since care work remains devalued and largely invisible, market logic leaves men with little incentive or opportunity to shift the balance.[26] Despite a professed desire for change, neotraditional men see little alternative to placing the demands of work and the validation it provides before the ideal of equal sharing.[27]

Autonomy through Men's Eyes

Not all men stress primary breadwinning as their fallback strategy. About three in ten of the men I interviewed are wary of marriage as an institution, feel reluctant to assume economic responsibility for another adult, and find a general, if vague, vision of personal freedom more appealing. Thomas contrasted his ideal of a fulfilling relationship with a path that looked achievable:

> My ideal is [to] go through life [with] no philandering, committed to the relationship, going for a decent relationship—no yelling on the sidewalk every day on my way to work. But if not, then I see myself sitting on the beach in the Caribbean, with a swizzle stick in my glass.

While these men do not all plan a life of travel and leisure, they all agree adulthood does not require supporting another adult. As Gabriel put it, "I refuse to support somebody. If I have a kid, yes, but I refuse to support a wife." They stress independence *from* and autonomy *within* relationships.

Like self-reliant women, autonomous men resist the breadwinner-homemaker ethic, even in a neotraditional form. Yet they differ from their female counterparts in crucial ways. Self-reliance offers women protection against the dangers of ceding one's personal identity and economic security to another; autonomy provides men with insulation from the perils of too much financial responsibility. Skepticism about finding secure work and growing doubts about traditional marriage set them on this path.

ECONOMIC UNCERTAINTY AND THE LURE OF SINGLEHOOD

In contrast to the "invisible opportunities" pulling neotraditional men toward time-demanding jobs, about a third of the men expressed substantial pessimism about their career prospects. Most were reared in working-class and minority neighborhoods, including many whose homes teetered on the edge of poverty, but about two-fifths are white men who could look back on a financially secure childhood. Yet economic uncertainties and the demoralizing effects of regimented jobs prompted all of these men to take a different approach to work and family life. If equality proves impossible, they prefer autonomy to the more rigid requirements of breadwinning.

Losing Faith in the American Dream

Although breadwinning continues to form the core of "hegemonic masculinity," the shrinking pool of traditional jobs undermines autonomous men's desire to seek and ability to find steady, secure work. While this view is most prevalent among men with modest economic and educational resources, people from all backgrounds concur.[28] At twenty-nine, Nick believed downsizing and "deskilling" would leave him unable to find the kind of economic security his working-class father enjoyed:

> I'm worried about the future because I am still unemployed. There are a lot of people who are a lot less skilled than I am, [who have] a lot less determination and a lot less communication skills, getting positions because [employers] don't feel like paying the top dollar.

Antonio reached a similar conclusion about his chances of reproducing the middle-class standard he enjoyed as a child:

> In the future, I see a lot of chaos. I wake up with nightmares about the money being gone. We're now middle-class, but that's not gonna exist years from now. You're either gonna be at the top or at the bottom.

If breadwinning men respond to rising competition by vowing to work longer hours, autonomous men are tempted to withdraw from the contest. Demoralized by his low-paying jobs, Jermaine, a high school dropout, decided paid work hardly seemed worth the effort:

> I'm tired of working. I've been working off and on since I was thirteen, fourteen, and I don't have money in the bank. Maybe there's something out there I would like to see through to the end, but nothing comes to mind. Who wants to work twenty-five, thirty years in the same place, and then when it's time to collect a pension, you're too old to enjoy it?

Also in his mid-twenties but with a college degree, Jeff reached a similar conclusion about his more lucrative, but suffocating, career in finance:

> I had plans to be a financial analyst for six, seven years. Now I don't give a shit about any of that. I'd just like to cruise around and say, "screw it all." Most people, they'll stay put somewhere, but I'd like to maybe go down to Australia [where] I think culturally they're more into anarchy.

Demoralized by poorly paid or overly demanding jobs, autonomous men soured on the goal of building a traditional (male) career and chose riskier paths. Antonio planned to seek his fortune outside the structure of a bureaucratic organization:

> Jobs in corporations—I was getting paid, but so what? So I was going late, wasn't enthused to be at the job. I felt like I was selling my soul to this company, like this is gonna be my life now.

Richard sought freedom from the relentless monotony of mainstream work:

> I don't want to be stuck here doing the same thing nine-to-five every day for the rest of my life. I just don't know if I want to work. I sound like a dreamer, and I am, but I want lots of time. One summer, I went to Mexico and just painted. I want to be able to do that. I need time to explore and do what I need to do.

Putting Family on the Back Burner

Men's doubts about finding or wanting a steady job foster equally strong doubts about marrying. Comparing his own uncertainty with the opportunities enjoyed by his parents, Angel found family commitments taking a mental backseat:

> I really don't know what's gonna happen, if I'm gonna have kids. Before I bring any life to this planet, I want to be well off, situated where I don't have to worry—like my parents.

And Antonio planned to put off becoming a husband or father indefinitely:

> I'm not rushin' into marriage. I'm very cynical. Things are gonna get real hard. I wouldn't bring kids into this. If I'm not stable, my kid ain't gonna be stable. I'm more focused on dealing with my own instability, the economic revolution that's going on.

Men stressing autonomy do not view their reluctance to marry as a lack of proper "family values," but rather as a morally responsible response to economic uncertainties. Michael argued it would be irresponsible to marry before achieving financial stability:

> I have the correct values—strong family, religious, moral values. I'm gonna do the right thing. But you need [to] make a paycheck so you can afford to do the right thing. Work is not promised to you, and that's what you really have to focus on.

And like a growing number of women, Jermaine viewed independence as a necessary step on the path to self-development:

> I don't want to live with anybody right now. I haven't done anything for *me* yet! If I'm gonna have a place, I want it to be *my* place. I really don't want to be in a relationship . . . until my feet are firmly cemented in the ground.

Poor work prospects, pessimism about the future, and a desire to avoid stifling jobs prompt men to fall back on autonomy. Some are reacting to the growing time demands and false promises in white-collar careers, while others focus on the dwindling rewards and shrinking opportunities in blue-collar occupations. These different routes lead in a similar direction: men's version of "opting out."

Although the overwhelming majority of Americans eventually marry, marriage rates have declined among most income and ethnic groups. The decline is steeper for the less educated and for members of racial minorities, where men's school and work opportunities are especially squeezed.[29] Indeed, the largest gender disparities in educational achievement are among racial and ethnic minorities, where girls have graduated from high school and college at higher rates than boys.[30] Since half as many African-American men as women now graduate from college, and African-American men have suffered a 12 percent decline in their median income over the last three decades (while African-American women have experienced a 75 percent increase), it is not surprising they have the lowest marriage rate of any racial group.[31] Yet regardless of race or ethnicity, as long as a breadwinning ethic pervades our notions of what makes a man "marriageable," low-earning men with dim job prospects face a declining incentive to marry and better-educated women have similarly low motivation to choose them as a partner.

TYING A LOOSE KNOT

Autonomous men do not reject the possibility of finding a lasting relationship, but they see marriage as only one among a range of alternatives. For David, marriage remained an option, but not a requirement:

> I don't see marriage as an absolute priority. I'm glad that I don't think of it that way. I don't feel pressured.

Jeff also planned to resist the pressure:

> I couldn't really set a goal saying I need to be married, because you do that to yourself and all of a sudden you're marrying somebody you're not gonna be happy with.

Accordingly, these men rejected the institution of marriage as the only route to mature manhood.[32] Like self-reliant women, they view marriage an option to be taken only under the most propitious circumstances.

Low on the List

Autonomous men place marriage low on their list of priorities, and, like self-reliant women, set a very high standard for choosing it. Turning the tables on those who argue that singlehood devalues marriage, autonomous men believe they valued it more.[33] Watching his parents stay together throughout his childhood only to divorce after he left home convinced Noah it would be better to remain single than to seek marital ideals he could not achieve:

> I would never jump into marriage. I would tell her everything about what my parents were about so she knew what kind of baggage I was carrying. It's the most important decision I might make. We have to spend enough time to see each other at our worst.

Although Joel's parents stayed together, he agreed:

> I'll definitely look at my situation and see if I'm in danger of making the same mistakes. It's such a huge commitment, it seems that people don't actually sit down and think of how it's really going to be.

Taking pride in resisting the pressure to marry, these men distinguish between marriage as a legal matter and commitment as a state of mind. Married and divorced by twenty-nine, Nick had good reason to decide that "a piece of paper does not mean you're married." Still in his early twenties and never married, Richard also believed that only a very high standard for marrying would help him avoid divorce:

> I haven't found anyone I'd like to marry, and I don't know if she's out there. I'm going to make sure she is 100 percent what I want—because I don't want to go through any divorce. People nowadays take marriage for granted—we'll get married just because we're supposed to. It's a very loose thing. You get married, divorced, no problem. There's no sacred bond anymore. So that's the way it's affected me. I wouldn't get married just for someone I think is really cool.

To avoid making the "wrong" choice, autonomous men set conditions for any relationship to meet. Noah insisted on a prearranged plan to resolve conflicts and "build" a worthy partnership:

> I would make a prenuptial agreement to seek counseling if we ever felt that we would fall apart, and that would be something we'd have to promise to prepare for.

Michael believed any marriage would need a prior blueprint similar to those he drew up as an engineer:

> If you look at it statistically, it doesn't make sense. Over fifty percent of marriages end in divorce. So you have to nurture the kind of marriage you want. You have to draw it out before you can go into it. I want to blueprint how I want marriage to be.

Although most men, and women, do ultimately marry, autonomous men plan to postpone as long as possible. Not concerned about a ticking biological clock, they have the luxury of time. At twenty-five, Jeff vowed to postpone a decision for as long as possible and took no firm position on what that decision might ultimately be:

> I may have thought I would be with somebody at this point, but it's been like, "Stay single as long as possible." And it was always everybody saying, "Don't get married." So I don't feel the pressure.

Blaming his parents' troubles on their rush to marry, Gabriel concurred:

> I'm now thinking it could easily be forty. I want to go into something like that being sure it's what I want to do. There's no reason to rush. [My

parents] got married in their early twenties, and I don't want to make the mistake of marrying too young.

In setting a high standard and placing marriage low on their list of priorities, autonomous men seek to avoid the neotraditional bargain outlined by their breadwinning peers. Married or not, they favor relationships where both partners retain a considerable measure of independence.

Seeking a Self-Sufficient Partner

Autonomous men use a metric of equal freedom, rather than equal sharing, to define the ideal of equality. In return for preserving their independence, they grant a large measure of it to others. Luis took pride in giving his ex-girlfriend the same leeway that he reserved for himself:

> We were living together, but I always told her, I tell her still, "If it wasn't working out for you, you just had to say so." If you get along well, it works out. If it doesn't, I always felt like I never owned her. So if she wanted to move on, I enjoyed the good times. I'm not a grudge-holding person.

Mark believed his long-term, live-apart relationship succeeded precisely because each could retreat to their own separate space:

> The space we have in the relationship—that's a big factor in why we stayed together all these years. I can have my own space, do my own thing, but then I have her there. I'd feel alienated if I was to settle down—the control factor.

Since independence requires a financial base, autonomous men also reject the neotraditional view that employment should be optional or secondary for women. Only a work-committed person would make a suitable mate. With no desire or intention to support a wife, Daniel appreciated knowing the women he dated would never want to depend on him for their livelihood:

> If she doesn't work, and she's a deadbeat—I don't think I'd date a girl like that, not for more than two days. Cheryl won't take money from me. I don't see her ever going, "I don't want to work anymore." She hates her job, but she does it because she's earning her own money.

And Mark concurred:

In terms of having a wife who doesn't work, that's a lot of pressure on me to carry the whole weight of the family. I'd rather have a working partner. My girlfriend could never *not* work. That's the farthest thing from her mind.

Work offers a crucial source of psychological as well as financial independence for the women in their lives. These men found it difficult to fully respect a partner who lacks an identity beyond hearth and home. Gabriel could not imagine having a partner who did not have a base outside the home:

I just want, need someone who can stand on their own. I wouldn't mind having someone make more—not for the sake of leeching off her, but so that she was independent. I have to respect her, so she has to be a doer. I need someone to think for themselves.

Richard agreed:

Life is too short, and it shouldn't revolve around a household. There are so many things I need see, do, experience, and I'd feel trapped being in a house. I wouldn't want it for me, so I wouldn't want anyone else to like it.

Men who fell back on autonomy do not reject partnerships, but they seek ones that do not impinge too greatly on their own freedom. This means finding someone with an independent income and identity, who can and will be financially and emotionally self-sustaining.

Paternal Ambivalence

Since it is not possible for children to support or care for themselves, autonomous men are ambivalent about fatherhood. Most plan to postpone parenthood indefinitely, but some are fathers who do not live with their offspring.[34] All of these men reject the view that "being responsible" requires bearing children or living with the children they had borne. At twenty-seven, Luis felt resisting parenthood went hand in hand with resisting breadwinning, since being "child-free" relieved him of having to bring home a big paycheck:

In ten, twenty years, maybe. 'Cause I like doing my own thing. If something else came along that I

wanted to do, all I have to do is make sure someone takes care of the cat. If I had a family, I would have to have a job that's making nice money. If I had kids, I'd have to provide for them.

Single fathers did not have the luxury of postponing parenthood, but they did resist obligations to the mothers of their children. Michael distinguished the importance of having a tie with his daughter from his willingness to support her mother. Though involved in his child's life, he refused his girlfriend's requests to marry or even live together until—and unless—she became secure in her own career:

I'm very close to Chandra, and I love her mother, but Kim has to get her act together before I consider marrying. Commitment is fine and dandy, but you can't fall into a trap. She's got some bad habits, and one of them is being lazy. Before we move in, I want her to be established in her career, motivated in herself, and not live through me. When she does that, I don't have a problem.

Whether they postponed fatherhood, plan to remain childless, or live apart from their children, these men do not view their choice as irresponsible. After watching his parents and siblings struggle in unhappy marriages, Nick decided that no one—least of all his son—would benefit from his staying in a forced and flawed union:

I wanted to stay together, because that's the way my parents did it, but then I realized that I don't believe anybody should stay together because of a child. I've seen that happen with my brother's son. They stayed together just because of him, and now he's seven and in therapy. A lot could have been avoided by not getting married.

Steve, at twenty-six and openly gay, viewed childlessness as the best option as long as he felt unprepared to make the needed sacrifices:

I don't rule anything out, but even thinking of the future, I'm not planning it. The kid's got to be the priority. When I get to that point, maybe. For now, it's me doing what I want to do for myself.

By remaining childless, becoming a father-at-a-distance, or rejecting a necessary link between paternity and marriage, autonomous men seek to redefine the terms and conditions of fatherhood. This outlook upholds the ideal of personal independence and provides an escape from the pressures of primary breadwinning, but it allows little room for equal parenting.

GENDER AND THE MEANING OF AUTONOMY

Autonomous men, like self-reliant women, view independence as a survival strategy, not an ideal. Yet women view self-reliance as a way to avoid dependence on a man while still being able to care for children and forge ties to others. Autonomous men are more inclined to avoid such ties unless and until they can achieve a level of financial stability that seems not only elusive but hard to define.[35] Concerns that neither economic security nor a lasting relationship will come their way make this starker version of singlehood and independence more acceptable. It nevertheless reflects the continuing strictures on visions of masculinity, which stress men's breadwinning despite the decline in their economic entitlement.[36] Such a strategy reduces an unbearable weight, but it also leaves autonomous men with tenuous social connections, a situation few greeted with enthusiasm.[37] Noah admitted:

> I don't see myself as having a family because I just don't see that progression. If I think about it, that's going to be too much to handle . . . because I'm commitmentless and alone.

Dilemmas and Uncertainties in Men's Lives

In a mirror image of women's outlooks, most men fall back on modified traditionalism, while some favor personal autonomy over breadwinning obligations. Because equal sharing threatens to exact a toll on men's occupational and economic achievement, most men prefer to reassert their place as a primary breadwinner, while leaving room for their partner to make additional contributions. By defining equality as women's "choice" to add work onto mothering, neotraditionalism allows men to acknowledge women's desire for a life beyond the home and also to rely on the financial cushion of a second income.

This strategy accepts the end of an era of stay-at-home mothers, but not the disappearance of distinct gender boundaries. Breadwinning men instead define separate spheres of responsibility for fathers and mothers, even if two-earner families are here to stay.

A sizeable minority of men, however, prefer another alternative. Poor work prospects and skepticism about marriage have left them wary of breadwinning and searching for a relationship with a self-sustaining partner who does not depend on their financial support. These men seek independence in lieu of equal sharing, but they give autonomy a different twist than self-reliant women by stressing "freedom from" breadwinning rather than "freedom to" support themselves.

Despite the differences between neotraditional and autonomous men, both outlooks are adaptive responses, not inherent attributes, and they can shift as circumstances change. Autonomous men realize they might welcome marriage and commitment in the long run, especially if their financial prospects improve, while breadwinning men concede the future might not bring the opportunities they anticipate. Brian planned to be a breadwinner, but recognizing "anything could happen," he admitted, "I could be making a lot of money, or I could be out of a job and totally stuck." In contrast, Gabriel harbored strong doubts about marriage, but conceded his skepticism could dissolve if circumstances changed his mind:

> If you asked me five years ago, I'd say there was absolutely no way of ever getting married. Because I didn't know anybody who was happy and married. But even in the last year—meeting and getting involved with Val and just seeing that marriage doesn't have to be like that—came a level of maturity that I've never had.

Whether they fall back on breadwinning or autonomy, young men face an uncertain future that may—and probably will—change at unexpected times and in unexpected ways. Their life paths, like those of women, ultimately depend on the opportunities and obstacles they encounter along the way.

NOTES

1. For an early statement on why men resist e quality, even when it may be in their longer-term interest to support it, see William Goode (1982). In contrast, Robert Jackson (1998) argues that over the long run, most men ultimately support gender equality as part of a larger package of egalitarian movements that are integral to modern social organization.

2. In a brilliant analysis of the tensions of manhood in American culture, Fiedler (1966) charts how great American novels, from *Moby Dick* to *Huckleberry Finn*, involve a male protagonist who forsakes domestic life and heterosexual commitment to find his identity as a man alone. For powerful statements about the dual strains of individualism and commitment in modern American culture, see Swidler (1980) and Bellah et al. (1985).

3. Galinsky et al. (2009).

4. This outlook preserves the essential elements of twentieth-century "hegemonic Masculinity" (to use a term coined by R.W. Connell, 1987, 1995), including the assumption of heterosexuality. It is thus not surprising that none of the "neotraditional" men identified as gay.

5. Among the many studies documenting continuing racial disadvantage, see Pager (2007), Manza and Uggen (2006), Massey (2007), and Western (2006).

6. The term "marriageable men," as used by William Julius Wilson (1987), refers to men who earn enough to be a suitable mate. In Wilson's analysis, a dwindling pool of jobs has drastically constricted the pool of acceptable husbands in poor communities. More generally, however, few have questioned the assumption that income should be the primary yardstick for measuring a man's suitability as a husband. As we have seen, women increasingly expect their partner to be a sharing caretaker, but they also want him to be a responsible earner.

7. Annette Lareau uses the concept of "invisible inequality" to distinguish between middle-class and working-class childhoods. Christine Williams (1989, 1995) documents how a "glass escalator" helps men rise in female-dominated fields even though women continue to hit glass ceilings in male-dominated ones. For incisive analyses of continuing discrimination against women at the workplace, see Correll et al. (2007), Correll (2004), Ridgeway and Correll (2004), and Valian (1998).

8. Women now make up 58 percent of those enrolled in two- and four-year colleges and are also the majority in graduate schools and professional schools, although many of these women concentrate in historically female fields that remain underpaid compared to male-dominated ones (Jacobs, 2003). The 2005 National Survey of Student Engagement, which studied 90,000 students at 530 institutions, found that college men are significantly more likely than women to say they skipped classes, did not complete their homework, and did not turn it in on time (Lewin, 2006).

9. Cotter, Hermsen, and Vanneman (2004).

10. Joan Williams (2000).

11. Epstein et al. (1999) show that forty-hour workweeks are now considered part time in most law firms. Louise Roth's study of Wall Street financial firms (2006) found them more likely to support equal opportunity policies, which give women an equal right to work interminable hours, than to support family-friendly policies, which undermine the principle that work should supersede family needs.

12. See, for example, Frank and Cook (1996). The economic crisis has intensified this concern.

13. The varied outcomes among siblings who grew up in the same household point to the indeterminate nature of family experiences as well as to the diverse influences a father's model can have on sons. Dalton Conley (2004) shows how within family differences in adults income attainment are greater than between family differences. Although he focuses on how parents apportion unequal investments among siblings, I would add that siblings also develop different reactions to similar circumstances and are likely to encounter different opportunities and obstacles in the wider world.

14. Koropeckyj-Cox and Pendell (2007).

15. Glauber (2008), Correll et al. (2007), and Correll (2004).

16. The "case for marriage" (as Linda Waite and Maggie Gallagher put it) appears compelling for men, but much less so for women, who are more likely to pay a price, literally and figuratively, for being a wife and mother. In Correll's experimental research, she also finds that mothers are significantly less likely to be hired and are offered lower salaries than equally qualified childless women. Mothers are rated as less competent, less committed, and less suitable for promotion and training, and they are also held to higher performance standards, while fathers are not rated lower than other men and benefited on some measures. Budig and England (2001) add that mothers suffer a substantial per-child wage penalty not explained by other factors, such as amount of schooling or work experience. In sum, men enjoy a marriage and fatherhood advantage, while women experience a marriage and motherhood penalty.

17. Institute for Women's Policy Research, 2008 and Drago, Black, and Wooden (2005) report that approximately 20 percent of couples contain a wife whose earnings exceed her husband's by more than 10 percent, but only about a quarter of these couples remain in this state in the following year. Winslow-Bowe (2006) reports that "although a significant minority of women outearn their husbands in one year, considerably fewer do so for five consecutive years." In sum, although the gender wage gap has declined, a husband's earnings continue to outstrip a wife's in most marriages, especially in the longer run. (Also see Charles and Grusky, 2004; Cotter, Hermsen, and Vanneman, 2004; and Blau, Brinton, and Grusky, 2006.)

18. The percentage of couples relying on a wife as the primary provider (defined as earning 60 percent or more of total couple earnings) remains low, although it increased from 4 percent in 1970 to 12 percent in 2001 (Raley, Mattingly, and Bianchi, 2006).

19. Even though "gender" is an ambiguous category in same-sex partnerships, they face similar work and child-rearing constraints. Same-sex couples tend to create more egalitarian arrangements, but they also tend to devise ways to divide responsibility for caretaking, as Carrington (1999) shows. In her study of African-American lesbian couples, Mignon Moore (2008) finds that biological motherhood shapes parenting strategies and that these couples are more concerned with economic independence than with having an equal distribution of domestic work.

20. Women's earnings are the major reason that contemporary households have maintained a standard of living on a par with the households of several decades ago. Warren and Tyagi (2003) focus on the drawbacks of this trend, while Barnett and Rivers (1996) delineate the advantages of two-income families. Bradbury and Katz (2004) report that in recent decades, families that have moved ahead or maintained their position have had wives with high and rising employment rates, work hours, and pay. In fact, the annual earnings of wives in upwardly mobile families have increased relative to the earnings of their husbands.

21. See, for example, Hartmann (1976). Potuchek (1997) analyzes how dual-earner couples still tend to designate one partner, usually but not always the husband, as the main bread winner and how this designation is crucial to shaping the domestic dynamics of contemporary couples.

22. For studies that distinguish among fathers who are helpers, equal partners, and primary caretakers, see Risman (1986, 1998) and my own study of men's parenting and work commitments (1993). Recent decades have seen a notable rise in men's participation in domestic work, but stay-at-home fathers remain a very small group (Smith, 2009).

23. The history of modern family life has been one of continual "outsourcing." This process of "structural differentiation" (a term used by Parsons and Bales, 1955) first involved moving such tasks as raising food, weaving cloth, sewing clothes, and educating the young out of the home. The growing reliance on day care, takeout, and prepared food is a postindustrial extension of this process. If "commodification" has dangers, especially in reinforcing class inequality, it is also a logical and practical response to women's entry into the world of paid work in the absence of a comparable increase in men's domestic involvement. Rather than lamenting the inevitable rise in families' reliance on other caretakers, the larger challenge is to make this shift more equal and fair by increasing the economic and social value of both paid and unpaid care work. See, for example, Hondagneu-Sotelo (2001), Folbre (2001), and Zimmerman, Litt, and Bose (2006).

24. Linda Hirshman (2006) argues that "choice feminism" leaves women short of equality because it does not effectively address the *domestic* glass ceiling.

25. For an overview of how the rise of the market transformed cultural definitions of manhood, see Kimmel (1996). Lamont (2000) richly details the place of work in the lives of contemporary working-class men. See also Sennett and Cobb (1972) and Bourdieu (1984) on the importance of class as a cultural marker, a habitus, as well as an economic status.

26. For compelling analyses of how providing essential, but unpaid or poorly paid, care exacts costs from society as well as from individual care workers and providers, see Folbre (2008) and Crittenden (2001).

27. For an original analysis of how social and cultural arrangements shape market worth, see Zelizer (1994, 2005).

28. Mooney (2008) discusses how economic transformations have undermined young middle-class Americans' ability to achieve their parents' standard of living.

29. See Porter and O'Donnell (2006). Uchitelle (2006) and Greenhouse (2008) document the decline of economic options and the rise of economically squeezed workers, especially at the bottom of the income ladder.

30. Lewin (2008).

31. Jones (2006), *USA Today* (2007).

32. Despite the rise of alternatives to marriage, extended bachelorhood continues to have an aura of immaturity. Many neoconservative analysts argue that marriage exerts a "civilizing" influence on men. In this view, unmarried men are prone to behave badly, while marriage—and by implication, the influence of women—reins in their sexual and violent impulses. See, for example, Nock (1998) and James Q. Wilson (2002). The evidence on the high rates of marital infidelity among both husbands and wives undermines this argument.

33. Popenoe (1988, 1996) argues that declining marriage rates indicate a decline of the family.

34. Given the rising rates of children born to single mothers, it is difficult to ascertain the full contours of unmarried paternity. Not only are some men unwilling to acknowledge it, but others may not be aware that they have fathered children (England and Edin, 2007).

35. Haney (2002) provides an insightful analysis of the culturally variable meanings of "dependency" for women. See also Fraser (1989) and Orloff (2008).

36. Kimmel (2008) and Risman and Seale (2010) analyze the cultural strictures that continue to constrain definitions of masculinity even as women's cultural options expand.

37. Ehrenreich (1983) argues that women's fight for equality also allowed men to flee commitment by making it acceptable for them to remain unmarried. Yet research shows that, in the long run, men who are unconnected to families are more likely to suffer adverse consequences, particularly because they are less likely than women to draw on a wider network of family and friends. McPherson, Smith-Lovin, and Brashears (2006) find that men are especially likely to lack close social ties other than a marital partner. For the classic study of "his and her" marriages, see Bernard (1982).

REFERENCES

Barnett, Rosalind C. and Caryl Rivers 1996. *She works/he works: How two-income families are happier, healthier, and better-off.* San Francisco: Harper San Francisco.

Bellah, Robert N. et al. 1985. *Habits of the heart: Individualism and commitment in American life.* Berkeley and Los Angeles: University of California Press.

Bernard, Jessie 1982. *The future of marriage.* New Haven, CT: Yale University Press.

Blau, Judith, Mary Brinton and David Grusky 2006. *The declining significance of gender?* New York: Russell Sage Foundation.

Bourdieu, Pierre 1984. *Distinction: A social critique of the judgment of taste.* Cambridge, MA: Harvard University Press.

Bradbury, Katherine and Jane Katz 2004. "Wives' work and family income mobility." Boston, MA: Federal Reserve Bank of Boston, Public Policy Discussion Report No. 04–3, July.

Budig, Michelle and Paula England 2001. "The wage penalty for motherhood." *American Sociological Review 66*: 204–225.

Carrington, Christopher 1999. *No place like home: Relationships and family life among lesbians and gay men.* Chicago: University of Chicago Press.

Charles, Maria and David Grusky 2004. *Occupational ghettos: The worldwide segregation of women and men.* Stanford, CA: Stanford University Press.

Conley, Dalton 2004. *The pecking order: Which siblings succeed and why.* New York: Pantheon Books.

Connell, R. W. 1987. *Gender & Power.* Stanford, CA: Stanford University Press.

Connell, R. W. 1995. *Masculinities.* Berkeley: University of California Press.

Correll, Shelley J. 2004. "Constraints into preferences: Gender, status, and emerging career aspirations." *American Sociological Review 69*: 93–133.

Cotter, David A., Joan M. Hermsen, and Reeve Vanneman 2004. "Gender inequality at work." In *The American people: Census 2000*, 1–32. New York and Washington, DC: Russell Sage Foundation and Population Reference Bureau.

Crittendon, Ann 2001. *The price of motherhood: Why the most important job in the world is still the least valued.* New York: Metropolitan Books.

Drago, Robert, David Black and Mark Wooden. 2005. "Female breadwinner families: Their existence, persistence, and sources." *Journal of Sociology 41*: 343–362.

Ehrenreich, Barbara 1983. *The hearts of men: American dreams and the flight from commitment.* New York: Anchor Books.

England, Paula and Kathryn Edin, editors 2007. *Unmarried couples with children.* New York: Russell Sage Foundation.

Epstein, Cynthia F., Carroll Seron, Bonnie Oglensky, and Robert Saute 1999. *The part-time paradox: Time norms, professional lives, family and gender.* New York: Routledge.

Feidler, Leslie A. 1966. *Love and death in the American novel.* New York: Stein and Day.

Folbre, Nancy 2008. *Valuing Children: Rethinking the economics of the family.* Cambridge, MA: Harvard University Press.

Folbre, Nancy 2001. *The invisible heart: Economics and family values.* New York: New Press.

Frank, Robert and Phillip J. Cook. 1996. *The winner-take-all society: Why the few at the top get so much more than the rest of us.* New York: Penguin Books.

Fraser, Nancy, ed. 1989. *Unruly practices: Power, discourse, and gender in contemporary social theory.* Minneapolis: University of Minnesota Press.

Gallinsky, Ellen, KerstenAumann, and James T. Bond 2009. "Times are changing: Gender and generation at work and at home." New York: Families and Work Institute.

Gerson, Kathleen 1993. *No man's land: Men's changing commitments to family and work.* New York: Basic Books.

Glauber, Rebecca 2008. "Gender and race in families at work: The fatherhood wage premium." *Gender & Society 22*: 8–30.

Goode, William 1963. *World revolution and family patterns.* New York: Free Press.

Greenhouse, Steven 2008. *The big squeeze: Tough times for the American worker.* New York: Alfred A. Knopf.

Haney, Lynne 2002. *Inventing the needy: Gender and the politics of welfare in Hungary.* Berkeley: University of California Press.

Hartmann, Heidi 1976. "Capitalism, patriarchy, and job segregation by sex." *Signs 1*: 137–169.

Hirshman, Linda 2006. *Get to work: A manifesto for women of the world.* New York: Viking.

Hondagneu-Sotelo, Pierrette 2001. *Domestica: Immigrant women workers cleaning and caring in the shadows of affluence.* Berkeley and Los Angeles: University of California Press.

Institute for Women's Policy Research 2008. "The gender wage ratio: Women's and men's earnings." Washington, DC: IWPR Fact Sheet No. C350 (February).

Jackson, Robert Max 1998. *Destined for equality.* Cambridge, MA: Harvard University Press.

Jacobs, Jerry 2003. "Detours on the road to equality: Women, work and higher education." *Contexts 2*: 32–41.

Jones, Joy 2006. "Marriage is for white people." *Washington Post*, March 26.

Kimmel, Michael 1996. *Manhood in America: A cultural history.* New York: The Free Press.

Kimmel, Michael 2008. *Guyland: The perilous world where boys become men.* New York: HarperCollins.

Koropeckyj-Cox, Tanya and Gretchen Pendell 2007. "The gender gap in attitudes about childlessness in the United States." *Journal of Marriage and Family 9*: 899–915.

Lamont, Michele 2000. *The dignity of working men: Morality and the boundaries of race, class and immigration.* Cambridge, MA: Harvard University Press.

Lewin, Tamar 2006. "At colleges, women are leaving men in the dust." *New York Times*, July 9.

Lewin, Tamar 2008. "Girls' gains have not cost boys, report says." *New York Times*, May 20.

Manza, Jeff and Christopher Uggen 2006. *Locked out: Felon disenfranchisement and American democracy*. New York: Oxford University Press.

McPherson, Miller, Lynne Smith-Lovin, and Matthew E. Brashears 2006. "Social isolation in America, 1985–2004." *American Sociological Review 71*: 353–375.

Mooney Nan 2008. *(Not) keeping up with our parents: The decline of the professional middle class*. Boston, MA: Beacon Press.

Moore, Mignon 2008. "Gendered power relations among women: A study of household decision making in black, lesbian stepfamilies."*American Sociological Review 73*: 335–356.

Nock, Steven 1998. *Marriage in men's lives*. New York: Oxford University Press.

Orloff, Ann 2008. "Farewell to maternalism?: Welfare reform, ending entitlements for poor single mothers, expanding the claims of poor employed parents." Unpublished manuscript.

Pager, Devah 2007. *Marked: Race, crime, and finding work in an era of mass incarceration*. Chicago: University of Chicago Press.

Parsons, Talcott and Robert F. Bales 1955. *Family, socialization, and interaction process*. Glencoe, IL: Free Press.

Popenoe, David 1988. *Disturbing the nest: Family change and decline in modern societies*. New York: Aldine de Gruyter.

Popenoe, David 1996. *Life without father: Compelling new evidence that fatherhood and marriage are indispensible for the good of children and society*. New York: Martin Kessler.

Porter, Eduardo and Michelle O'Donnell 2006. "Facing middle age with no degree, and no wife." *New York Times*, August 6.

Potuchek, Jean L. 1997. *Who supports the family? Gender and breadwinning in dual-earner marriages*. Stanford, CA: Stanford University Press.

Raley, Sara B., Marybeth J. Mattingly and Suzanne M. Bianchi 2006. "How dual are dual income couples? Documenting change from 1970–2001." *Journal of Marriage and Family 68*: 11.

Ridgeway, Cecilia and Shelley J. Correll 2004. "Motherhood as a status characteristic." *Journal of Social Issues 60*: 683–700.

Risman, Barbara J. 1986. "Can men 'mother'? Life as a single father." *Family Relations 35*: 95–102.

Risman, Barbara J. 1998. *Gender vertigo: American families in transition*. New Haven, CT: Yale University Press.

Risman, Barbara and Elizabeth Seale 2010. "Betwixt and between: Gender contradictions among middle schoolers." In *Families as they really are*, edited by Barbara J. Risman. New York: W. W. Norton.

Roth, Louise 2006. *Selling women short: Gender and money on wall street*. Princeton, NJ: Princeton University Press.

Sennett, Richard and Jonathan Cobb 1972. *The hidden injuries of class*. New York: Alfred A. Knopf.

Smith, Jeremy A. 2009. *The daddy shift: How stay-at-home dads, breadwinning moms, and shared parenting are transforming the American family*. Boston: Beacon Press.

Swidler, Ann 1980. "Love and adulthood in American culture," In *Themes of love and work in adulthood*. Edited by Erik Erikson and Neil J. Smelser, 120–147. Cambridge, MA: Harvard University Press.

Uchitelle, Louis 2006. *The disposable American: Layoffs and their consequences*. New York: Alfred A. Knopf.

USA Today 2007. "Downward mobility trend threatens black middle class." November 19.

Valian, Virginia 1998. *Why so slow? The advancement of women*. Cambridge, MA: MIT Press.

Warren, Elizabeth and Amelia W. Tyagi 2003. *The two-income trap: Why middle class mothers and fathers are going broke*. New York: Basic Books.

Western, Bruce 2006. *Punishment and inequality in America*. New York: Russell Sage Foundation.

Williams, Christine 1989. *Gender differences at work: Men and women in nontraditional occupations*. Berkeley: University of California Press.

Williams, Christine 1995. *Still a man's world: Men who do women's work*. Berkeley: University of California Press.

Williams, Joan C. 2000. *Unbending gender: Why family and work conflict and what to do about it*. New York: Oxford University Press.

Wilson, James Q. 2002. *The marriage problem: How our culture has weakened families*. New York: Harper Collins.

Wilson, William Julius 1987. *The truly disadvantaged*. Chicago: University of Chicago Press.

Winslow-Bowe, Sarah 2006. "The persistence of wives' income advantage." *Journal of Marriage and Family 68 (4)*: 824–842.

Zelizer, Viviana 1994. *The social meaning of money*. New York: Basic Books.

Zelizer, Viviana 2005. *The purchase of intimacy*. Princeton, NJ: Princeton University Press.

Zimmerman, Mary K, Jacqueline S. Litt, and Christine Bose 2006. *Global dimensions of gender and carework*. Stanford, CA: Stanford University Press.

PART SEVEN

MALE SEXUALITIES

How do many men learn to desire women? What are men thinking about when they are sexual with women? Are gay men more sexually promiscuous than straight men? Are gay men more obsessed with demonstrating their masculinity than straight men, or are they likely to be more "effeminate"? Recent research indicates that there are no simple answers to these questions. It is increasingly clear, however, that men's sexuality, whether homosexual, bisexual, or heterosexual, is perceived as an experience of their gender.

Since there is no anticipatory socialization for homosexuality and bisexuality, future straight and gay men receive the same socialization as boys. As a result, sexuality as a gender enactment is often a similar internal experience for all men. Early socialization teaches us—through masturbation, locker-room conversations, sex-ed classes and conversations with parents, and the tidbits that boys will pick up from various media—that sex is private, pleasurable, guilt provoking, exciting, and phallocentric, and that orgasm is the goal toward which sexual experience is oriented.

The articles in this part explore how male sexualities express the issues of masculinity. Michael Messner describes how he "became" 100 percent straight, and M. Rochlin's questionnaire humorously challenges us to question the normative elements of heterosexuality. Robert Jensen reopens the debate about whether men's consumption of pornography fuels misogyny and inspires rape and violence. Chong-suk Han suggests that racial and ethnic stereotypes remain fully operative in the world of gay male sexuality. Finally, Julia O'Connell Davidson and Jacqueline Sanchez Taylor examine the recent phenomenon of sex tourism and raise important questions about masculinity on the one hand and global sex trafficking, globalization, and consumer culture on the other.

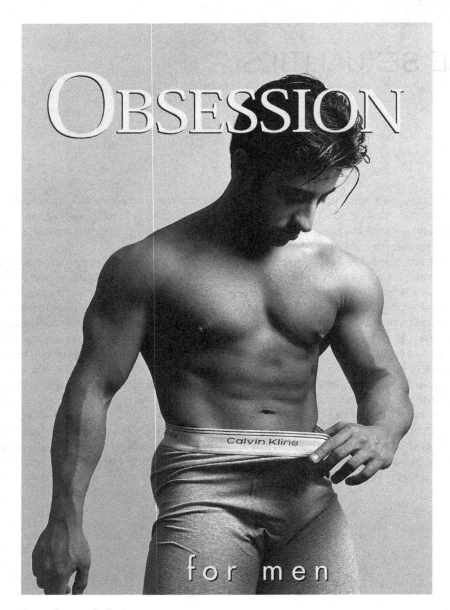

Source: Courtesy of adbusters.org

BECOMING 100 PERCENT STRAIGHT

Michael A. Messner

In 1995, as part of my job as the President of the North American Society for the Sociology of Sport, I needed to prepare an hour-long presidential address for the annual meeting of some 200 people. This presented a challenge to me: how might I say something to my colleagues that was interesting, at least somewhat original, and, above all, not boring. Students may think that their professors are especially dull in the classroom, but, believe me, we are usually much worse at professional meetings. For some reason, many of us who are able to speak to our classroom students in a relaxed manner, using relatively jargon-free language, seem to become robots, dryly reading our papers—packed with impressively unclear jargon—to our yawning colleagues.

Since I desperately wanted to avoid putting 200 sport studies scholars to sleep, I decided to deliver a talk which I entitled "Studying up on sex." The title, which certainly did get my colleagues' attention, was intended as a play on words, a double entendre. "Studying up" has one generally recognizable colloquial meaning, but in sociology it has another. It refers to studying "up" in the power structure. Sociologists have perhaps most often studied "down"—studying the poor, the blue- or pink-collar workers, the "nuts, sluts and perverts," the incarcerated. The idea of "studying up" rarely occurs to sociologists unless and until we live in a time when those who are "down" have organized movements that

challenge the institutional privileges of elites. For example, in the wake of labor movements, some sociologists like C. Wright Mills studied up on corporate elites. Recently, in the wake of racial and ethnic civil rights movements, some scholars like Ruth Frankenberg have begun to study the social meanings of "whiteness." Much of my research, inspired by feminism, has involved a studying up on the social construction of masculinity in sport. Studying up, in these cases, has raised some fascinating new and important questions about the workings of power in society.

However, I realized that when it comes to understanding the social and interpersonal dynamics of sexual orientation in sport we have barely begun to scratch the surface of a very complex issue. Although sport studies have benefited from the work of scholars such as Helen Lenskyj (1986, 1997), Brian Pronger (1990), and others who have delineated the experiences of lesbians and gay men in sports, there has been very little extension of their insights into a consideration of the social construction of heterosexuality in sport. In sport, just as in the larger society, we seem obsessed with asking "how do people become gay?" Imbedded in this question is the assumption that people who identify as heterosexual, or "straight," require no explanation, since they are simply acting out the "natural" or "normal" sexual orientation. We seem to be saying that the "sexual deviants" require explanation, while the experience of heterosexuals, because we are considered normal, seems to require no critical examination or discussion. But I knew that a closer look at the development of sexual orientation or sexual identity reveals an extremely complex process. I decided to challenge myself and my colleagues by arguing that although we have begun to "study up" on corporate elites in sport, on whiteness, on masculinity, it is now time to extend that by studying up on heterosexuality.

But in the absence of systematic research on this topic, where could I start? How could I explore, raise questions about, and begin to illuminate the social construction of heterosexuality for my colleagues? Fortunately, for the previous two years I had been working with a group of five men (three of whom identified as heterosexual, two as gay) mutually to explore our own biographies in terms of the earlier bodily experiences that helped to shape our gender and sexual identities. We modeled our project after that of a German group of feminist women, led by Frigga Haug, who created a research method which they call "memory work." In short, the women would mutually choose a body part, such as "hair," and each would then write a short story based on a particularly salient childhood memory that related to their hair (for example, being forced by parents to cut one's hair, deciding to straighten one's curly hair in order to look more like other girls, etc.). Then the group would read all of the stories and discuss them one by one in the hope of gaining a more general understanding of, and raising new questions about, the social construction of "femininity." What resulted from this project was a fascinating book called *Female Sexualization* (Haug 1987), which my men's group used as the inspiration for our project.

As a research method, memory work is anything but conventional. Many sociologists would argue that this is not really a "research method" at all. The information that emerges from the project cannot be used very confidently as a generalizable "truth," and in this sort of project the researcher is simultaneously part of what is being studied. How, my more scientifically oriented colleagues might ask, is the researcher to maintain his or her objectivity? My answer is that in this kind of project objectivity is not the point. In fact, the strength of this sort of research is the depth of understanding that might be gained through a systematic group analysis of one's experience, one's subjective orientation to social processes. A clear understanding of the subjective aspect of social life—one's bodily feelings, emotions, and reactions to others—is an invaluable window that allows us to see and ask new sociological questions about group interaction and social structure. In short, group memory work can provide an important, productive, and fascinating insight on social reality, though not a complete (or completely reliable) picture.

As I pondered the lack of existing research on the social construction of heterosexuality in sport, I decided to draw on one of my own stories from my memory work in the men's group. Some of my most salient memories of embodiment are sports memories. I grew up as the son of a high school coach, and I eventually played point guard on my dad's team. In what follows, I juxtapose my story with that of a gay former Olympic athlete, Tom Waddell, whom I had interviewed several years earlier for a book on the lives of male athletes (Messner and Sabo 1994).

Many years ago I read some psychological studies that argued that even for self-identified heterosexuals it is a natural part of their development to have gone through "bisexual" or even "homosexual" stages of life. When I read this, it seemed theoretically reasonable, but did not ring true in my experience. I have always been, I told myself, 100 percent heterosexual! The group process of analyzing my own autobiographical stories challenged the concept I had developed of myself, and also shed light on the way in which the institutional context of sport provided a context for the development of my definition of myself as "100 percent straight." Here is one of the stories:

> When I was in the 9th grade, I played on a "D" basketball team, set up especially for the smallest of high school boys. Indeed, though I was pudgy with baby fat, I was a short 5'2", still prepubescent with no facial hair and a high voice that I artificially tried to lower. The first day of practice, I was immediately attracted to a boy I'll call Timmy, because he looked like the boy who played in the *Lassie* TV show. Timmy was

short, with a high voice, like me. And like me, he had no facial hair yet. Unlike me, he was very skinny. I liked Timmy right away, and soon we were together a lot. I noticed things about him that I didn't notice about other boys: he said some words a certain way, and it gave me pleasure to try to talk like him. I remember liking the way the light hit his boyish, nearly hairless body. I thought about him when we weren't together. He was in the school band, and at the football games, I'd squint to see where he was in the mass of uniforms. In short, though I wasn't conscious of it at the time, I was infatuated with Timmy—I had a crush on him. Later that basketball season, I decided—for no reason that I could really articulate then—that I hated Timmy. I aggressively rejected him, began to make fun of him around other boys. He was, we all agreed, a geek. He was a faggot. Three years later, Timmy and I were both on the varsity basketball team, but had hardly spoken a word to each other since we were freshman. Both of us now had lower voices, had grown to around six feet tall, and we both shaved, at least a bit. But Timmy was a skinny, somewhat stigmatized reserve on the team, while I was the team captain and starting point guard. But I wasn't so happy or secure about this. I'd always dreamed of dominating games, of being the hero. Halfway through my senior season, however, it became clear that I was not a star, and I figured I knew why. I was not aggressive enough.

I had always liked the beauty of the fast break, the perfectly executed pick and roll play between two players, and especially the long twenty-foot shot that touched nothing but the bottom of the net. But I hated and feared the sometimes brutal contact under the basket. In fact, I stayed away from the rough fights for rebounds and was mostly a perimeter player, relying on my long shots or my passes to more aggressive teammates under the basket. But now it became apparent to me that time was running out in my quest for greatness: I needed to change my game, and fast I decided one day before practice that I was gonna get aggressive. While practicing one of our standard plays, I passed the ball to a teammate, and then ran to the spot at which I was to set a pick on a defender. I knew that one could sometimes get away with

setting a face-up screen on a player, and then as he makes contact with you, roll your back to him and plant your elbow hard in his stomach. The beauty of this move is that your own body "roll" makes the elbow look like an accident. So I decided to try this move. I approached the defensive player, Timmy, rolled, and planted my elbow deeply into his solar plexus. Air exploded audibly from Timmy's mouth, and he crumbled to the floor momentarily.

Play went on as though nothing has happened, but I felt bad about it. Rather than making me feel better, it made me feel guilty and weak. I had to admit to myself why I'd chosen Timmy as the target against whom to test out my new aggression. He was the skinniest and weakest player on the team.

At the time, I hardly thought about these incidents, other than to try to brush them off as incidents that made me feel extremely uncomfortable. Years later, I can now interrogate this as a sexual story, and as a gender story unfolding within the context of the heterosexualized and masculinized institution of sport. Examining my story in light of research conducted by Alfred Kinsey a half-century ago, I can recognize in myself what Kinsey saw as a very common fluidity and changeability of sexual desire over the life course. Put simply, Kinsey found that large numbers of adult, "heterosexual" men had previously, as adolescents and young adults, experienced sexual desire for males. A surprisingly large number of these men had experienced sexual contact to the point of orgasm with other males during adolescence or early adulthood. Similarly, my story invited me to consider what is commonly called the "Freudian theory of bisexuality." Sigmund Freud shocked the post-Victorian world by suggesting that all people go through a stage, early in life, when they are attracted to people of the same sex.[1] Adult experiences, Freud argued, eventually led most people to shift their sexual desire to what he called an appropriate "love object"—a person of the opposite sex. I also considered my experience in light of what lesbian feminist author Adrienne Rich called the institution of compulsory heterosexuality. Perhaps the extremely high levels of homophobia that are often endemic in boys' and men's organized sports led me to deny and repress my own homoerotic desire through a direct and overt rejection of Timmy, through homophobic banter with male peers, and the resultant stigmatization of the feminized Timmy. Eventually I considered my experience in the light of what radical theorist Herbert Marcuse called the sublimation of homoerotic desire into an aggressive, violent act as serving to construct a clear line of demarcation between self and other. Sublimation, according to Marcuse, involved the driving underground, into the unconscious, of sexual desires that might appear dangerous due to their socially stigmatized status. But sublimation involves more than simple repression into the unconscious. It involves a transformation of sexual desire into something else—often into aggressive and violent acting out toward others. These acts clarify the boundaries between oneself and others and therefore lessen any anxieties that might be attached to the repressed homoerotic desire.

Importantly, in our analysis of my story, the memory group went beyond simply discussing the events in psychological terms. The story did perhaps suggest some deep psychological processes at work, but it also revealed the importance of social context—in this case, the context of the athletic team. In short, my rejection of Timmy and the joining with teammates to stigmatize him in ninth grade stands as an example of what sociologist R. W Connell calls a moment of engagement with hegemonic masculinity, where I actively took up the male group's task of constructing heterosexual/masculine identities in the context of sport. The elbow in Timmy's gut three years later can be seen as a punctuation mark that occurred precisely because of my fears that I might be failing in this goal.

It is helpful, I think, to compare my story with gay and lesbian "coming out" stories in sport. Though we have a few lesbian and bisexual coming out stories among women athletes, there are very few from gay males. Tom Waddell, who as a closeted gay man finished sixth in the decathlon in the 1968 Olympics, later came out and started the Gay Games, an athletic and cultural festival that draws tens of thousands of people every four years. When I interviewed Tom Waddell over a decade ago about his sexual identity and athletic career, he made it quite clear that for many years sports was his closet:

> When I was a kid, I was tall for my age, and was very thin and very strong. And I was usually faster than most other people. But I discovered rather early that I liked gymnastics and I liked dance. I was very interested in being a ballet dancer [but] something became obvious to me right away— that male ballet dancers were effeminate, that they were what most people would call faggots. And I thought I just couldn't handle that I was totally closeted and very concerned about being male. This was the fifties, a terrible time to live, and everything was stacked against me. Anyway, I realized that I had to do something to protect my image of myself as a male—because at that time homosexuals were thought of primarily as men who wanted to be women. And so I threw myself into athletics—I played football, gymnastics, track and field . . . I was a jock—that's how I was viewed, and I was comfortable with that

Tom Waddell was fully conscious of entering sports and constructing a masculine/heterosexual athletic identity precisely because he feared being revealed as gay. It was clear to him, in the context of the 1950s, that being known as gay would undercut his claims to the status of manhood. Thus, though he described the athletic closet as "hot and stifling," he remained there until several years after his athletic retirement. He even knowingly played along with locker room discussions about sex and women as part of his "cover."

> I wanted to be viewed as male, otherwise I would be a dancer today. I wanted the male, macho image of an athlete. So I was protected by a very hard shell. I was clearly aware of what I was doing . . . I often felt compelled to go along with a lot of locker room garbage because I wanted that image—and I know a lot of others who did too.

Like my story, Waddell's points to the importance of the athletic institution as a context in which peers mutually construct and reconstruct narrow definitions of masculinity. Heterosexuality is considered to be a rock-solid foundation of this concept of masculinity. But unlike my story, Waddell's may invoke a dramaturgical analysis.[2] He seemed to be consciously "acting" to control and regulate others' perceptions of him by constructing a public "front stage" persona that differed radically from what he believed to be his "true" inner self. My story, in contrast, suggests a deeper, less consciously strategic repression of my homoerotic attraction. Most likely, I was aware on some level of the dangers of such feelings, and was escaping the risks, disgrace, and rejection that would likely result from being different. For Waddell, the decision to construct his identity largely within sport was to step into a fiercely heterosexual/masculine closet that would hide what he saw as his "true" identity. In contrast, I was not so much stepping into a "closet" that would hide my identity; rather, I was stepping out into an entire world of heterosexual privilege. My story also suggests how a threat to the promised privileges of hegemonic masculinity—my failure as an athlete—might trigger a momentary sexual panic that can lay bare the constructedness, indeed, the instability of the heterosexual/masculine identity.

In either case, Waddell's or mine, we can see how, as young male athletes, heterosexual masculinity was not something we "were," but something we were doing. It is significant, I think, that although each of us was "doing heterosexuality," neither of us was actually "having sex" with women (though one of us desperately wanted to). This underscores a point made by some recent theorists that heterosexuality should not be thought of simply as sexual acts between women and men. Rather, heterosexuality is a constructed identity, a performance, and an institution that is not necessarily linked to sexual acts. Though for one of us it was more conscious than for the other, we were both "doing heterosexuality" as an ongoing practice through which we sought to do two things:

- avoid stigma, embarrassment, ostracism, or perhaps worse if we were even suspected of being gay;

- link ourselves into systems of power, status, and privilege that appear to be the birthright of "real men" (i.e., males who are able to compete successfully with other males in sport, work, and sexual relations with women).

In other words, each of us actively scripted our own sexual and gender performances, but these scripts were constructed within the constraints of a socially organized (institutionalized) system of power and pleasure.

QUESTIONS FOR FUTURE RESEARCH

As I prepared to tell this sexual story publicly to my colleagues at the sport studies conference, I felt extremely nervous. Part of the nervousness was due to the fact that I knew some of them would object to my claim that telling personal stories can be a source of sociological insights. But a larger part of the reason for my nervousness was due to the fact that I was revealing something very personal about my sexuality in such a public way. Most of us are not accustomed to doing this, especially in the context of a professional conference. But I had learned long ago, especially from feminist women scholars, and from gay and lesbian scholars, that biography is linked to history. Part of "normal" academic discourse has been to hide "the personal" (including the fact that the researchers are themselves people with values, feelings, and yes, biases) behind a carefully constructed facade of "objectivity." Rather than trying to hide or be ashamed of one's subjective experience of the world, I was challenging myself to draw on my experience of the world as a resource. Not that I should trust my experience as the final word on "reality." White, heterosexual males like me have made the mistake for centuries of calling their own experience "objectivity," and then punishing anyone who does not share their worldview by casting them as "deviant." Instead, I hope to use my experience as an example of how those of us who are in dominant sexual/racial/gender/class categories can get a new perspective on the "constructedness" of our identities by juxtaposing our subjective experiences against the recently emerging worldviews of gay men and lesbians, women, and people of color.

Finally, I want to stress that in juxtaposition neither my own nor Tom Waddell's story sheds much light on the question of why some individuals "become gay" while others "become" heterosexual or bisexual. Instead, I should like to suggest that this is a dead-end question, and that there are far more important and interesting questions to be asked:

- How has heterosexuality, as an institution and as an enforced group practice, constrained and limited all of us—gay, straight, and bi?
- How has the institution of sport been an especially salient institution for the social construction of heterosexual masculinity?
- Why is it that when men play sports they are almost always automatically granted masculine status, and thus assumed to be heterosexual, while when women play sports, questions are raised about their "femininity" and sexual orientation?

These kinds of questions aim us toward an analysis of the working of power within institutions—including the ways that these workings of power shape and constrain our identities and relationships—and point us toward imagining alternative social arrangements that are less constraining for everyone.

NOTES

1. The fluidity and changeability of sexual desire over the life course is now more obvious in evidence from prison and military populations, and single-sex boarding schools. The theory of bisexuality is evident, for example, in childhood crushes on same-sex primary schoolteachers.

2. Dramaturgical analysis, associated with Erving Goffman, uses the theater and performance to develop an analogy with everyday life.

REFERENCES

Haug, Frigga (1987) *Female Sexualization: A Collective Work of Memory*, London: Verso.

Lenskyj, Helen (1986) *Out of Bounds Women, Sport and Sexuality*, Toronto: Women's Press.

———. (1997) "No fear" Lesbians in sport and physical education," *Women in Sport and Physical Activity Journal* 6(2): 7–22.

Messner, Michael A. (1992) *Power at Play Sports and the Problem of Masculinity*, Boston: Beacon Press.

———. (1994) "Gay athletes and the Gay Games: An Interview with Tom Waddell," in M. A. Messner and D. F. Sabo (eds), *Sex, Violence and Power in Sports: Rethinking Masculinity*, Freedom, CA: The Crossing Press, pp. 113–119.

Pronger, Brian (1990) *The Arena of Masculinity Sports, Homosexuality, and the Meaning of Sex*, New York: St Martin's Press.

THE HETEROSEXUAL QUESTIONNAIRE

M. Rochlin

1. What do you think caused your heterosexuality?
2. When and how did you decide you were a heterosexual?
3. Is it possible that your heterosexuality is just a phase you may grow out of?
4. Is it possible that your heterosexuality stems from a neurotic fear of others of the same sex?
5. If you have never slept with a person of the same sex, is it possible that all you need is a good gay lover?
6. Do your parents know that you are straight? Do your friends and/or roommate(s) know? How did they react?
7. Why do you insist on flaunting your heterosexuality? Can't you just be who you are and keep it quiet?
8. Why do heterosexuals place so much emphasis on sex?
9. Why do heterosexuals feel compelled to seduce others into their lifestyle?
10. A disproportionate majority of child molesters are heterosexual. Do you consider it safe to expose children to heterosexual teachers?
11. Just what do men and women *do* in bed together? How can they truly know how to please each other, being so anatomically different?
12. With all the societal support marriage receives, the divorce rate is spiraling. Why are there so few stable relationships among heterosexuals?
13. Statistics show that lesbians have the lowest incidence of sexually transmitted diseases. Is it really safe for a woman to maintain a heterosexual lifestyle and run the risk of disease and pregnancy?
14. How can you become a whole person if you limit yourself to compulsive, exclusive heterosexuality?
15. Considering the menace of overpopulation, how could the human race survive if everyone were heterosexual?
16. Could you trust a heterosexual therapist to be objective? Don't you feel s/he might be inclined to influence you in the direction of her/his own leanings?
17. There seem to be very few happy heterosexuals. Techniques have been developed that might enable you to change if you really want to. Have you considered trying aversion therapy?
18. Would you want your child to be heterosexual, knowing the problems that s/he would face?

A PORNOGRAPHIC WORLD [WHAT IS NORMAL?]

Robert Jensen

MY STORY

I am a normal guy in a world in which no guy is really normal. I was raised in a conventional household (two parents, three siblings, one dog) in a part of the United States not known for radical thinking or countercultural lifestyles (Fargo, North Dakota). There I was exposed to the standard US ideology of male dominance, white supremacy, the inherent superiority of capitalism, and America's role as the moral exemplar of the world. I was raised to be a nice white guy who took his place in the world, worked hard, and didn't complain too much.

At the same time, there are aspects of my biography that are not so normal, such as experiences of abuse early in my life. But it turns out, when you start talking to guys, such things happened to lots of us. My sexual profile also might, at first glance, seem outside the norm; I have had sexual relationships with men and women, though most of my life has been lived as a heterosexual. But it turns out that such sexual ambiguity isn't so unusual for lots of men either.

As a child growing up, until my late teens, I typically was the shortest boy in my class and painfully thin. As a small, "faggy" kid, I knew I was an easy target. So, I spent a lot of energy trying not to appear to be homosexual. And it turns out that a lot of the men of my generation whom I have talked to over the years—no matter how macho they appeared on the surface—worried at some point about being tagged as gay when they were young.

Even with my lack of physical ability, I managed to be minimally competent in sports and played on baseball and basketball teams through junior high. Emotionally, I was what's typically called a "sensitive child," but I managed to fake my way through the routine interactions with other boys without getting beaten up. Other boys were not so lucky. I remember one in particular in junior high who endured endless cruelty for being a gangly, socially awkward kid. When other boys teased and attacked him, I stepped aside. I didn't actively participate in that abuse, but I never defended the boy; my fear of being similarly targeted kept me silent. As I write this, 35 years later, I can recall how deeply I empathized with his suffering, and how terrified I was of those boys turning on me.

I have never felt like a "real man," but it turns out that almost no man I know feels much confidence in that realm; even those who fit the specifications more closely rarely feel like they are fulfilling their masculine obligations. So, I wasn't normal, and at the same time I was well within the norm. Most important, I was raised to be normal. I was socialized to be a man, even if I lacked some of the physical or emotional attributes to fill the role very well. And part of that socialization involved the use of pornography.

PORNOGRAPHY USE

I was born in 1958, in the post-*Playboy* world. My first recollection of viewing sexual material is from early grade school, when one of the boys in my school got his hands on a biker magazine that had pictures of women with exposed breasts. I have no recollection of the specific images but do retain a clear memory of gathering in the backyard of a neighborhood boy's house to look at the magazine, which we had hidden under a leaf pile. It was at about the same time I began "playing doctor," exploring bodies with other boys and girls in the neighborhood. So, as I was consciously becoming aware of sexuality, my first recognizable cultural lesson on the subject came in a male-bonding ritual around men's use of an objectified woman, who existed only to provide sexual excitement for us.

[A footnote: This memory is so powerful that every time I see a poster called "Celebrate the Whole Boy" I am reminded of it. The picture on the poster is of five grade-school boys after football practice in the park as they listen to one of the boys playing the violin. In the picture it is fall, with leaves on the ground. Three of the boys are kneeling around the violin case, with the other two standing. The obvious irony is that a poster with a healthy message—that the culture's narrow conception of masculinity limits boys' development and that we should think of all the ways to nurture them—reminds me of the patriarchal training it is critiquing.]

That grade-school experience is the first recollection I have of what Sheila Jeffreys calls "the idea of prostitution," the notion that men can buy women's sexuality in various forms. Rather than seeing men's control and use of women for sex as natural and stemming from a biological imperative, Jeffreys argues that such behavior is socially constructed. "The idea of prostitution has to exist in a man's head first if he is to consider using a woman that way," she writes. "A necessary component of this idea is that it will be sexually exciting to so use a woman."[1]

So, let's mark my introduction into the idea of prostitution at age seven, gathered around the leaf pile, one of a group of boys experiencing our emerging sexuality in an act of male dominance, the ideological assertion of dominance made into a material reality in a picture. That magazine would decay by winter but, in those few months of fall, it taught us something about what it meant to be a man.

The story goes downhill from there.

In the 1960s and 70s, as I went through public school, the main medium for pornography was the

magazine, and in my circle of friends there was a reasonably steady supply of them, tucked away under beds, shoved in the back of closets, and carefully hidden under piles of leaves. Some were pilfered from relatives—we all knew where dads and big brothers hid their stash. Others were retrieved from dumpsters; we knew when stores that sold pornography threw away out-of-date stock. Sometimes we looked at them in groups, sometimes alone.

At the end of junior high school and my first year of high school, I was hanging out with a group of guys who had learned the art of sneaking into movie theaters without paying. One of our targets was the Broadway Theater in Fargo, my hometown's only "dirty movie theater," where I saw parts of several hardcore pornographic films as a teenager. At the time I had no sexual experience beyond a few sessions of sexual experimentation with other kids (boys and girls) in grade school, and I really didn't understand much of what was happening on the screen, though I was transfixed by the intensity of my sexual reaction. At a conventional movie theater we sneaked in to see *Last Tango in Paris*, to which I had the same reaction and of which I understood even less.

[Another footnote: In one of those episodes at the Broadway, three of us approached the rear door in the alley with the intention of sneaking in. At the last minute, one of the other boys backed out, claiming to be nervous. But he encouraged us to go ahead, which we did. Once in the theater, we were extremely nervous, desperately afraid of being caught. A few minutes into the film, my companion thought he heard an usher coming toward us and decided to bolt for the exit, with me a few steps behind. He hit the exit door at full speed and met some resistance, but pushed it open and tumbled into the alley, falling over garbage cans. The friend who had stayed behind had dragged the cans in front of the door, assuming that when we tried to exit, we would find it blocked and get scared. Although we were angry at him in the moment, it never occurred to me that such a prank was quite a strange thing to do to a friend. Such cruelty was simply part of growing up male.]

In college, after becoming legally able to enter adult bookstores and theaters, I made occasional visits. Because there was only one such bookstore in Fargo and we risked being seen by friends or relatives while entering or leaving (not to mention while inside), most of those forays took place during trips to Minneapolis, again sometimes with friends and sometimes alone. While in college I also saw a few X-rated movies with friends (both all-male and mixed-gender groups), who treated the outings as campy fun, and I went to a couple of those movies on my own.

[One last footnote: One of my friends from college with whom I made a couple of those trips was a man with whom I had a sexual experience after we had graduated. He was among the most militantly heterosexual men I have ever known and, to the best of my knowledge, did not have a secret gay life. That experience is a reminder that the way most men present themselves to the world in sexual terms does not reflect the complexity of our lives, and we rarely have places to talk openly about that experience. It's one of the most obvious ways in which heterosexism/homophobia limits all men.]

In my 20s, as a working professional, I had a complex relationship to pornography. I typically did not purchase pornography to use at home, although through the years I occasionally bought magazines such as *Playboy* and *Penthouse*. I never showed pornography to women with whom I was involved, with the exception of one trip to an adult theater with a woman in college. I have never made home-made pornography or recorded sexual activity.

Throughout my 20s I would sometimes visit the stores or theaters, though I was increasingly uncomfortable using the material, I had no political critique at that point, nor did I have moral qualms about it, I was then, and remain today, a secular person and had no theological conflicts about the subject. My hesitations were emotional—it just felt wrong. I fell into what I later learned was a common pattern: I would feel intense sexual excitement, masturbate, and immediately feel a sense of shame. That experience would typically lead to a decision to stop using pornography, which would last for some weeks or months. But eventually I would find myself back in a bookstore or theater.

PORNOGRAPHIC FALLOUT

That pattern continued until I was about 30 years old, when I started graduate school and began studying the feminist critique of pornography. Since then, I have used pornography only in the course of four research projects on the content of video and internet pornography.

When people ask me the last time I used pornography—not as a researcher but as a consumer—my answer is "yesterday." By that, I don't mean that I watched a pornographic film yesterday, but that for those of us with a history of "normal" pornography use as children and young adults, quitting pornography doesn't necessarily mean we are pornography-free. My sexual imagination was in part shaped by the use of pornography. I still have in my head vivid recollections of specific scenes in pornographic films I saw 25 years ago. To the degree possible, I try to eliminate those images when I am engaging in sexual activity today (whether alone or with my partner), and I think I'm pretty successful at it. The longer I'm away from pornography, the easier it gets. But the key term is "to the degree possible."

Even with the advances in neuroscience, we really don't know all that much about human memory, consciousness, and behavior. What is pretty clear is that what goes on in our heads and bodies is far more complex than we can ever fully understand. It would not be surprising if the images and ideas that we encounter during the act of achieving orgasm—especially early in our development—would have a powerful influence on us, one that might last in various ways throughout our lives.

What goes on in my body sexually is the result of not just what I think and feel in the moment, but a lifetime of training and experience. I wish I could neatly segregate and eliminate not only the effects of my past pornography use but the effects of all the ugly sexist training I have received in my life about sexuality. I wish I could wall myself off from the sexist messages and images that are all around me today. I wish I could find a way to create a space untouched by those forces in which I could live.

But if I am to be honest, I have to admit something that is painful to face: I still struggle against those forces. I have to work to bracket out of my mind—to the degree possible—those images. I have to work to remember that I can deepen my own experience of intimacy and sexuality only when I let go of those years of training in how to dominate.

It's hard to be honest about these things, because so much of what lives within us is rooted in that domination/subordination dynamic. But it's a good rule of thumb that the things that are difficult are the most important to confront. That's easy to say but hard to practice.

THE CULTURE'S STORY

When I was born in 1958, the cultural conversation on pornography took place largely within a framework of moral assertions. The obscenity law that regulated sexual material was typically defended as necessary because such uses of sex were immoral, while defenders of pornography argued that individuals should be free to use such material because there was no harm to others and the state should not make moral decisions for people. The anti-pornography view was articulated mostly by conservative and religious people; liberals and secular people dominated the defense of pornography.

Beginning in the late 1970s, feminist anti-violence activists began to focus on the connections between men's violence against women and mass media, especially pornography. The framework for that critique was political; feminists were not arguing that any particular expression of sexuality was immoral. Instead, they focused on the political—on differences in power and men's subordination of women, and the concrete harms that followed.

By the mid-1990s, the feminist critique of pornography mostly had been pushed out of the public discussion and a new economic framework emerged. Journalists began writing routinely about pornography as an ordinary business that raised no particular moral or political concerns. These stories sometimes mentioned opposition to the industry, but simply as one aspect of doing business that pornographers had to cope with. Neither the conservative/religious objections to pornography[2] nor the feminist critique[3] has disappeared, but the shift in the framework—the predominant way in which the culture engages pornography—is revealing. Opposition to pornography in the United States, rooted either in conservative religious faith or feminist politics, must articulate that position in a society that largely takes pornography as an uncontroversial part of contemporary culture. This is the normalization or mainstreaming of pornography.

I had been observing that normalization trend for two decades when I went for the first time, in January 2005, to the Adult Entertainment Expo [AEE] sponsored by *Adult Video News* [AVN], the preeminent trade magazine of the pornography industry. Although I had been studying the industry for years, I had always avoided going to the AVN convention, which is held in Las Vegas. When I went in 2005 as part of the crew for a documentary on the industry, I finally understood why I had always instinctively stayed away.

LAS VEGAS

My job at the AEE was to move around on the convention floor with the film's director, Miguel Picker, and talk to the pornography producers, performers, and fans about why they make, distribute, and consume sexually explicit media. As we roamed the huge Sands Expo and Convention Center, which accommodated about 300 booths and thousands of people a day, rock music pulsated from multiple directions. There were photos of naked women everywhere, video screens running porn loops scattered throughout the hall, display tables of dildos and sex dolls. And around every corner were performers in various states of undress, signing posters and posing for pictures. Flashes popped constantly as fans photographed their favorite stars.

At the end of the first day of shooting, Miguel and I were tired. We had spent the day surrounded by images of women being presented and penetrated for the sexual pleasure of men. I had listened to young men tell me that pornography had taught them a lot about what women really want sexually. I had listened to a pornography producer tell me that he thinks anal sex is popular in pornography because men like to think about fucking their wives and girlfriends in the ass to pay them back for being bitchy. And I interviewed the producer who takes great pride that his Gag Factor series was the first to feature exclusively aggressive "throat fucking."

We walked silently from the convention center to the hotel, until I finally said, "I need a drink."

I don't want to feign naïveté. I wasn't particularly shocked by anything I saw that day. There was no one thing I learned on the convention floor that surprised me, nothing anyone said that was really that new to me. I had been working on the issue for more than 15 years at that point; it would have been hard for me to find anything at AEE shocking.

We stopped at the nearest hotel bar (which didn't take long, given how many bars there are in a Las Vegas hotel). I sat down with a glass of wine, and Miguel and I started to talk, searching for some way to articulate what we had just experienced, what we felt. I struggled to hold back tears, and then finally stopped struggling.

I hadn't had some sort of epiphany about the meaning of pornography. It's just that in that moment, the reality of the industry—of the products the industry creates and the way in which they are used—all came crashing down on me. My defenses were inadequate to combat a simple fact: The pornographers had won. The feminist arguments about justice and the harms of pornography had lost. The pornographers not only are thriving, but are more mainstream and normalized than ever. They can fill up a Las Vegas convention center, with the dominant culture paying no more notice than it would to the annual boat show.

My tears at that moment were for myself, because I realized in a more visceral way than ever that the pornographers had won and are helping to construct a world that is not only dangerous for women and children, but also one in which I have fewer and fewer places to turn as a man. Fewer places to walk and talk and breathe that haven't been colonized and pornographized. As I sat there, all I could say to Miguel was, "I don't want to live in this world."

I think Miguel didn't quite know what to make of my reaction. He was nice to me, but he must have thought I was going a bit over the top. I don't blame him; I was a bit over the top. After all, we were there to make a documentary film about the industry, not live out a melodrama about my angst in a Las Vegas hotel bar. The next day Miguel and I hit the convention floor again. At the end of that day, as we walked away, I made the same request. We sat at the same bar. I had another glass of wine and cried again. I think Miguel was glad it was the last day. So was I.

Two days after we left Las Vegas, Miguel called me from New York. This time he was the one crying. He told me that he had just come to his editing studio and had put on some music that he finds particularly beautiful, and then the floodgates opened. "I understand what you meant in the bar," he said, speaking through his own tears.

I tell this story not to highlight the sensitivity of two new-age men. Miguel actually is a sensitive person, though not very new age. I'm not new age, and I don't feel particularly sensitive these days. I often feel harsh and angry. Instead, I tell the story to remind myself that I am alive, that I haven't given up, that I still feel.

I tell the story to remind myself that I'm not alone in that struggle. In a world that trains men to struggle with each other for dominance and keep their emotional distance from each other, Miguel and I could connect. He's a musician and artist from Chile; I'm a journalist and professor from North Dakota. On the surface, we don't have much in common, except our humanity.

I have to remind myself of those things because in the short term, things are grim. The feminist critique that could help this culture transcend its current crisis—on every level, from the intimate to the global—has been attacked and marginalized, and the feminists with the courage to take the critique to the public have been demonized and insulted.

That's the short term. In the long term, I believe human society will move out of patriarchy and into some other organizing principle that will emerge through struggle. The problem is, as the economist John Maynard Keynes put it, in the long run we're all dead.

Hope in the long run is rational only when we are willing to face difficult analyses and action in the short term.

NOTES

1. Sheila Jeffreys, *The Idea of Prostitution* (North Melbourne, Australia Spinifex, 1997), 3.

2. See Morality in Media, http://www.moralityinmedia.org/.

3. See National Feminist Antipornography Movement, http://feministantipornographymovement.org/.

THEY DON'T WANT TO CRUISE YOUR TYPE: GAY MEN OF COLOR AND THE RACIAL POLITICS OF EXCLUSION

Chong-suk Han

INTRODUCTION

Thirty minutes after the posted starting time, men, and a handful of women, continue to wander into the second floor auditorium of a long neglected performance hall in the center of the city's gayborhood. Like many things gay, the scheduled forum on race, sponsored by one of the largest gay-identified organization in the city, begins on gay time. As the audible levels of conversations begin to wane, organizers urge the audience of some 200 men, and a handful of women, to take their seats so we can all begin. Within minutes, a representative of the host agency lays out the ground rules of discussion—most noticeably that we will not, given the limited time, try to define racism while quickly offering that, 'everyone is capable of racism', a definition that many men of color in the audience would, if given the chance, vehemently dispute. Perhaps it wouldn't have been such an issue if members of the community who were invited to help plan the forum hadn't spent weeks arguing for the need to discuss racism in the gay community, rather than focus solely on race. Or perhaps it wouldn't have been such a slight if they were asked to provide an alternative definition of racism, particularly who is able, within the larger social structure, to practise

it rather than being left with only one definition of it. In fact, the title 'Race Forum' was specifically chosen, against the suggestions offered by members of the community, so that the focus could be on 'race' rather than the trickier topic of 'racism'.

'It's like they didn't hear a thing', a member of the 'community' told me immediately after the announcement. 'Why did we go to the meetings? It's like we weren't even there. We might as well be invisible.' Though flabbergasted, he also told me that, 'It's no surprise'. It seems that for this member of the community, speaking up and being ignored has come to be a common occurrence. After all, being a gay man of color is to experience the unnerving feeling of being invited to a potluck while being told not to bring anything since nobody would be interested in what you bring, and then not being offered any food since you didn't bring anything anyway.

Looking around the audience, two things become immediately clear. First, the auditorium is noticeably empty given the tendency of other forums hosted by this agency to fill to capacity and then some. More importantly, the faces are overwhelmingly darker than those at other forums sponsored by this organization. One could conclude, if one were so inclined, that this forum on race was not as popular with many of the gay men who normally attend while bringing out other men who wouldn't normally attend events that would have a broader gay appeal. However, the composition of the audience reflects a larger picture of the broader gay community where issues of race and racism are often ignored.

Looking around any gayborhood, something becomes blatantly clear. Within the queer spaces that have sprung up in once neglected and forgotten neighborhoods, inside the slick new storefronts and trendy restaurants, and on magazine covers—as well as between the covers for that matter—that are no longer covered in plain brown paper and kept behind the counter, gay America has given a whole new meaning to the term 'whitewash'.

We, as a collective, have rehabilitated homes in neglected neighborhoods. We've planted flowers, we've painted the walls, fixed old roofs, and generally have increased the 'value' of areas that were once in urban decline. Whitewash.

We've revived old storefronts, bringing a multitude of retail shops (and the accompanying tax base) to streets once reserved for activities outside the law—not that everything we do within our own houses, or behind the storefronts for that matter, are well within the comfortable boundaries of a legally sanctioned activity. Whitewash.

We've fought hard to counter the stereotypes so famous in mainstream culture of the nellie queens or the lecherous sex stalker and replace them with images that reflect the 'true' gay experience. Rather than accept the images thrown upon us by the mainstream press, we've given gay American a face we can all be proud of. Whitewash.

Whiteness in the gay community is everywhere, from what we see, what we experience, and more importantly, what we desire. The power of whiteness, of course, derives from appearing to be nothing in particular (Lipsitz, 1998). That is, whiteness is powerful precisely because it is everywhere but nowhere in particular. When we see whiteness, we process it as if it doesn't exist or that its existence is simply natural. We don't see it precisely because we see it constantly. It blends into the background and then becomes erased from scrutiny. And this whiteness is imposed from both outside and inside of the gay community. According to Allan Bérubé, the gay community is overwhelmingly portrayed in the heterosexual mind as being 'white and well-to-do' (2001, p. 234). Media images now popular in television and film such as *Will and Grace, My Best*

Friend's Wedding, In and Out, Queer as Folks, Queer Eye for the Straight Guy, etc. promote a monolithic image of the gay community as being overwhelmingly upper-middle class—if not simply rich—and white. For example, in the movie, *Boat Trip*, about the comic misadventures of two straight men booked on a gay cruise by a gay travel agent hell-bent on preserving the honor of his lover, all the gay men, with one exception, are white. The juxtaposition of Cuba Gooding Jr. as the protagonist who stumbles his way through a boat filled with hundreds of gay men, also works to mark racial boundaries. Gay men are white and the straight man is not. Clearly, in this movie, 'men of color' and 'gay' are mutually exclusive categories. While mass media will often use stereotypes to sell minority characters to majority audiences, the gay media are no less to blame for the promotion of the 'gay equals white' misconception. Even the most perfunctory glance through gay publications exposes the paucity of non-white gay images. It's almost as if no gay men of color exist outside of fantasy cruises to Jamaica, Puerto Rico, or the 'Orient'. And even then, they exist only to fulfill the sexual fantasies of gay white men. 'Exotic' vacations to far away places are marketed to rich white men and poor colored bodies are only another consumable product easily purchased with western dollars. As such, gay men of color, whether found within western borders or conveniently waiting for white arrival in the far off corners of the globe, are nothing more than commodities for consumption.

It's not just the media, both straight and gay, that robs gay men of color of equal representation, the gay 'community' is no less to blame. Gay organizations themselves promote and reinforce the whiteness of gay life. The gay movement that once embodied the ideals of liberation, freedom, and social justice quickly turned to the causes of promoting gay pride through visibility and lobbying efforts that forced established institutions—particularly media institutions—to re-examine mainstream heterosexist bias against gay men and women. Doing so, however, led to the unfortunate consequence of ignoring non-gay issues such as 'homelessness, unemployment, welfare, universal health care, union organizing, affirmative action, and abortion rights' (Bérubé, 2001, p. 235). Promoting gay issues meant promoting acceptance rather than liberation. To do so, gay activists adapted various whitening practices to sell gay America to the heartland of America by:

> *mirroring* the whiteness of men who run powerful institutions as a strategy for winning credibility, acceptance, and integration; *excluding* people of color from gay institutions; *selling* gay as white to raise money, make a profit, and gain economic power; and daily wearing the *pale protective coloring* that camouflages the unquestioned assumptions and unearned privileges of gay whiteness. (Bérubé, 2001, p. 246)

Unfortunately, this mirroring of the mainstream community to promote gay causes has meant ignoring the 'non-gay issues' that impact the lives of gay men and women of color as members of racial minority groups such as affirmative action, unemployment, educational access, etc. It has even ignored immigration debates, as is evident in a recent Advocate.com editorial which suggested that focusing on immigrant rights would take away from gay rights. What such arguments ignore is that many in the gay community are members of immigrant groups. As such, to be gay in America today is to be white. More specifically, it means to be white and well-to-do. This is obvious in the ways that gay organizations and businesses mark and market themselves to the larger community, both gay and straight. Gay publications tout the affluence of the gay community when fighting for advertising dollars. Non-profit organizations (NPO) and gay-identified businesses that serve a multi-racial clientele are marked as being raced and, in turn, mark themselves as such. For example, organizations such as Brother to Brother, Gay Asian Pacific Support Network, Hombres Latinos, etc. mark the racial borders of patronage. Gay businesses, too, mark these borders. Bars populated by non-white clients exist merely to support white male fantasies about gay men of color are marked with appropriately

fetishized names such as the Voodoo Lounge in Seattle, Papicock in New York, and Red Dragon in Los Angeles. The Blatino Bronx Factory not only marks the club as raced but also quite blatantly specifies which races they are marking. Yet gay-identified organizations with mostly, and sometimes exclusively, white clientele—both businesses and NPOs—are never marked in this way. In fact, they vehemently oppose such characterizations, arguing instead that they serve all gay people. It is never the 'Gay White Support/Social Organization', but rather, 'Gay Support/Social Organization'. In doing so, the implication is that they speak for all gay people, a claim they make while ignoring certain voices. Their concerns, those of largely gay white men, become the *de facto* concerns for gay men of color. As such, whiteness takes center stage and it becomes synonymous with gay where gay comes to mean white and white comes to mean gay.

Despite all of this, it would be a mistake to assume that whiteness is not actively maintained. Rather, the illusion of normalcy requires active maintenance of racial borders. 'White' doesn't become normal because it is so, it becomes normal because we make it so. More often than not, whiteness is maintained through active exclusion of those who are non-white. In this paper, I examine the forms of racism that are found in gay communities and show how race is implicated in the construction of gay identities. Particularly, I focus on subtle forms and blatant forms of racism that negate the existence of gay men of color and how racism affects the way we see gay men. In this way, I hope to add another dimension to Bérubé's theory about how 'gay' remains white. In addition, I examine the homophobia found in racial and ethnic communities to examine the further marginalization of gay men of color.

Of course, in discussing gay men of color, it is important to point out that this group includes people with vastly different backgrounds along every imaginable social delineation. Care should be taken when referencing the experiences of this group. At the same time, this essay is not about gay men of color as it is about racism in the larger gay community, as well as homophobia found elsewhere, and how that racism and homophobia, both subtle and overt, manifests itself. I'm not so much interested here in the values, beliefs, and cultures of gay men of color as I am with the discriminatory practices of gay white men and the institutions that they control. I'm certain that the racist discourse that justifies such behavior is uniquely modified to fit different racial/ethnic groups that are targeted. My interest is to point out that despite different constructions of race and ethnicity, the end results of exclusion and objectification are similar for racialized groups. As such, this paper should not be read as an exploration into the lives of gay men of color but to the practices of gay white men that work to marginalize the previous group.

INVISIBLE . . . YOU MAKE ME FEEL INVISIBLE: SUBTLE FORMS OF RACISM

Not surprisingly, allusions to invisibility are common in the writings and media productions created by gay men of color. For example, in *Tongues untied*, black film maker Marlon Riggs had this to say about San Francisco:

> I pretended not to notice the absence of black images in this new gay life, in bookstores, poster shops, film festivals, even my own fantasies. Something in Oz was amiss, but I tried not to notice. I was intent on my search for my reflection, love, affirmation, in eyes of blue, gray, green. Searching, I discovered something I didn't expect, something decades of determined assimilation cannot blind me to. In this great, gay Mecca, I was an invisible man. I had no shadow, no substance, no place, no history, no reflection. (Riggs, 1989)

Likewise, Joseph Beam (1986) in his work, *In the Life* wrote:

> Visibility is survival . . . It is possible to read thoroughly two or three consecutive issues of the Advocate, the national biweekly gay newsmagazine, and never encounter, in the words or images, Black gay men . . . We ain't family. Very

clearly, gay male means: White, middle-class, youthful, nautilized, and probably butch, there is no room for Black gay men within the confines of this gay pentagon. (quoted in Manalansan, 1996, p. 402)

Standing at the door of various gay bars, I've been asked, on several occasions, by doormen if I was aware that it was a gay bar. In one particular instance, one doorman added after I answered in the affirmative, 'You must really want a drink'. In these instances, unlike other instances of blatant racism that I discuss below, it just didn't occur to the doormen that being gay *and* Asian was within the realm of the possible. Following their logic, if gay men are white, non-white men must not be gay. As such, the non-white man entering this 'gay' establishment must obviously be in great need of libation rather than sexual encounter. In addition to lived experiences, this sense of invisibility is found in writings by gay Asian men as well. Song Cho writes:

> The pain of being a gay Asian, however, is not just the pain of direct discrimination but the pain of being negated again and again by a culture that doesn't acknowledge my presence . . . Not only did I have to deal with the question of sexual invisibility as a gay man, there was also the issue of racial invisibility. (Cho, 1998, p. 2)

Another writer describes his experiences at gay bathhouses in this way:

> When I go to the baths, I usually go home empty handed without even one guy having hit or making a pass at me. . . . When I first started going to the baths, I could not understand why no one was interested in me. I would hang out for hours and hours and no one would give me a second look. What was more disheartening was the fact that I saw some weird combinations at the baths. Drop dead gorgeous white men would not even give me a second look, yet be with someone who (in my mind) was below average in the looks department . . . When I came out, it never occurred to me that I would become invisible and undesirable and truly worthless in the eyes of so many gay men . . .

Gay Asians are invisible to the gay white community. (Anonymous, n.d.)

At the same time that they are invisible, gay Asian men are also seen as being exotic, submissive fantasies for white men. However, being seen as exotic and submissive is yet another form of subtle racism where gay Asian men are not seen as individuals but as a consumable product for white male fantasy (Ayres, 1999).

Gay Native American men also felt this 'disconnection' from the gay community, even when they are active in gay politics. Jaline Quinto quotes one gay Native American activist as stating:

I was doing a lot of things in the community, but feeling still that disconnection from the larger mainstream gay community because I was Native . . . There was this ideal of what constituted beauty, part of it had to do with if you don't have blonde hair and blue eyes, you don't meet the standard. (Quinto, 2003, p. 14)

Gay Latino men don't fare much better in the larger gay community. As Munoz (1999) points out, the mainstream gay community either ignores or exoticizes Latino bodies. That is to say, Latino men, like other men of color, also fall into two categories within the gay community. Either they are invisible or exist only as props for white male consumption. Miguel Flores is quoted by Joel P. Engardio as stating:

I hate being a fetish. They don't see you as a person. Just an object, Latin meat . . . When I found out about this city, it seemed like a dream. But when I got here [San Francisco], I realized even in the gay capital of the U.S., I'm still Mexican . . . I didn't come all this way to go through the same shit. (Engardio, 1999, p. 7)

Perhaps no example of racial fetishization of gay men of color is more blatant than the use of the 'Indian' character in the 1970s disco group, Village People. Singing songs embedded with gay metaphors, the Village People rose to cult status among both gay and straight listeners and were, perhaps, the most popular music group during the gay-active

1970s. A brain child of music producer, Jacques Morali, each 'character' in the band represented a gay fetish. While the 'Indian' was a character unto his own, representing the idea that a man of color can be a fetish just by being a man of color, the other characters were given an occupational or behavioral role often fetishized within the gay community such as cowboy, biker, construction worker, soldier, and cop. The implication, of course, is that while men of color are fetishized for what they are, white men are fetishized for what they do. Thus, white men can choose when they want to be objectified, but men are color are simply objects.

As discussed above, existing only as props for white male consumption represents another subtle form of racism. As Tony Ayres notes:

First, there is overt belligerence: the drunk queens who shout in my face, 'Go back to your own country'; the tag line at the end of gay personal classifieds—'No Fates, Femmes, or Asians'; the guys who hissed at me in the back room, 'I'm not into Asians'. Still, these incidents are rare and easily dealt with. The second response is the exact opposite of this racist antagonism. It is an attraction to me because of my Asianness, my otherness . . . This has nothing to do with my individual qualities as a person. It is the fact that I conveniently fit into someone else's fantasy. They expect me to be so flattered by the attention of a white man that I will automatically bend over and grab my ankles. (1999, p. 89)

Whereas Asian men become the object of white male fantasy due to their perceived feminine qualities, Black men suffer the opposite stereotype. Rather than subservient geishas who will submissively tend to all of the white male fantasies of domination, black men are the overly sexual predators racially capable of fulfilling white male sexual lust. If Asian men are the vassals for white men's domination fantasies, black men are the tools required for white male submissive fantasies. As Frantz Fanon explains, the black 'man' no longer exists in the white sexual imagination. Instead, 'one is no longer aware of the negro, but only of a penis. The Negro is eclipsed. He is turned into a penis. He is a penis' (1970, p. 120). Rather than existing as individuals, black men exist as sexual tools, ready to fulfill, or violate, white male sexual fetishes. This fetishization of the black man's penis is perhaps most evident in nude photographs of black men, taken by white men, and meant for white (straight, gay, male and female) consumption. Perhaps nowhere is this more evident than in the photography of Robert Mapplethorpe, particularly the collection of photographs published in *Black Book*. As Mercer (1991) points out, images, such as those presented by Mapplethorpe, help to objectify and fetishize black men as being nothing more than giant penises. Ironically, whereas the objectification of Asian men is largely based on the desire to dominate, the objectification of black men is based on the fear of domination (Fung, 1991; Marriott, 2000).

THEY DON'T WANT TO CRUISE YOUR TYPE: BLATANT FORMS OF RACISM

Sometimes racism in the gay community takes on more explicit forms. Like racism everywhere, these forms tend to operate with the goal of excluding, in this case, men of color from gay institutions. Perhaps the most notorious has been the events surrounding Badlands, a popular bar in the Castro district in San Francisco. In the summer of 2004, Badlands became the site of weekly picketing after a group of racially diverse Bay Area residents filed a complaint with the San Francisco Human Rights Commission, the San Francisco Entertainment Commission, the California Department of Fair Employment and Housing, and the state Alcoholic Beverage Control Department claming racial discrimination at the bar. Among the complaints were that not only was the owner practising job discrimination at the bar but also that non-white customers were being either turned away at the door or were being expunged from the bar. According to complainants, people of color were routinely denied employment and promotional opportunities and entrance into the establishment. Most obvious incidents were the fact that black men were required to provide two forms of I.D. at the door while white men were required to only show one. Michael Kinsley, a former bouncer at the club, stated:

> One of my tasks while working at the Badlands was to stand guard and judge whether or not to allow entrance into the bar. Introductory bouncer etiquette, courtesy of Les (the owner), was a short course in discriminating between 'Badlands' and 'non-Badlands' customers. During this introduction there were continual references to the characteristics of the undesirable customers—if they looked like 'street people' or if they were not 'dressed' like 'Badlands customers'. As a new initiate into the field of adult door monitor there were, in the first few weeks, instances where Les would politely walk a person to the door and escort them from the premises. These instances were all accompanied by an admonishing, 'This person was not a Badlands customer', or 'He had a backpack. We don't let in people with backpacks. They are often street people or have no money'. All of these individuals had one common feature and it was painfully obvious to me—everyone escorted out was black. (And Castro for All, 2004)

Max Killen, another former Badlands doorman, was also quoted as stating:

> He (Les Natali, the owner) sat me down and he told me, 'There are certain types of people that we don't want in here. And those people can go across the street'. He didn't say the Pendulum (another Castro street bar with a large black clientele), but . . . it was really obvious that he was talking about the bar. He wasn't talking about hanging out in the parking lot or at the other places there. It was the Pendulum. (And Castro for All, 2004)

It is interesting to note that the racist policies are cloaked in discourses of class. By doing so, it allows gay businesses to escape the stigma of racism while ultimately maintaining racial borders. Ironically, the mirroring of the gay community with the white mainstream, as discussed earlier, contributes to such actions. Such mirroring actions allow gay business owners to mask issues of race and class under the justification of running a 'successful' business.

An isolated incident might have been easily forgotten, but the events at Badlands struck a cord with
the city's non-white gay and lesbian residents. For
them, it was just another incident in a long history
of racial discrimination in the city's gayborhood. As
Don Romesburg (2004) notes,

> The most recent troubles surrounding the Badlands
> [were] just the latest incarnation of a long-standing
> struggle in the Castro's LGBT community regard-
> ing racial discrimination and exclusion.

In fact, the policy of requiring multiple forms of
I.D. from non-white patrons had a long history in
the Castro, starting with the Mine Shaft, a Castro
bar that required three forms of I.D. for men of
color during the mid-1970s. Rodrigo Reyes, in an
interview with Richard Marquez in 1991, recalls
this about the early 1980s:

> There were also some racist discriminatory prac-
> tices on the part of the bars in that sometimes they
> would ask for an inordinate amount of IDs from
> people of color . . . They would ask for two, three
> picture IDs. So it wasn't a very happy time for
> Latino gays . . . We were still a marginal group.
> The dominant group was still white gay men.
> (quoted in Ramirez, 2003, p. 232)

Also during the early 1980s, an informal study
conducted by the Association of Lesbian and Gay
Asians (ALGA) found that multiple carding was a
fairly widespread practice among gay bars throughout San Francisco, not just in the Castro district.
Recalling the ensuing boycott following the release
of the study, Dinoa Duazo notes:

> The most insidious aspect of the whole situation
> was how proprietors felt completely justified to
> practice such casual discrimination. Unfortu-
> nately, just because a community has faced op-
> pression, there's no guarantee that its members
> won't practice it themselves. (1999, p. 5)

In fact, during an on-air debate on KPFA, a local
radio station, one bar owner told Randy Kikukawa,
one of the organizers of the boycott, that 'Your people
don't drink. We have to make money', and 'It's a
cruise bar, we would lose money because they don't
want to cruise your type' (Duazo, 1999, p. 5). Also,
the practice of multiple carding was not unique to
San Francisco. In Washington DC, two bars, Lost
& Found and Grand Central, were targeted by community activists for blatantly requiring two forms of
I.D. from non-white patrons while allowing white
patrons easy access. In 1984, the 'Boston Bar Study'
conducted by Men of All Colors Together Boston
(MACTB) cited numerous examples of widespread
discrimination at gay bars in Boston against black
men. Similar types of discrimination have also been
cited in Los Angeles and New York (Wat, 2002).
Even more troubling is that this type of behavior
seems to be international as well—anywhere that
gay white men come into contact with gay men of
color (Ridge, Hee & Minichiello, 1999). One can
only imagine how many others never make it into
the new stories. Rather than isolated events attributable to racist owners of single bars, the attempt
to patrol the borders of whiteness in gay-owned
business establishments seems to be a systematic
practice to ensure only certain types of people are
allowed into 'gay' bars.

I JUST WANT AN 'ALL AMERICAN' BOY

The primacy of white images in the gay community often leads to detrimental results for gay men
of color, particularly manifested as internalized
racism. In 'No blacks allowed', Keith Boykin argues that 'in a culture that devalues black males and
elevates white males', black men deal with issues
of self-hatred that white men do not. 'After all', he
notes, 'white men have no reason to hate themselves
in a society that reinforces their privilege'. Boykin
argues that this racial self-hatred makes gay black
men see other gay black men as unsuitable sexual
partners. Obviously, such racial self-hatred rarely
manifests itself as such. Instead, gay black men who
don't want to date other black men simply rely on
stereotypes to justify their behavior rather than confront their own self-hatred. For example, Boykin
notes that most of these men justify excluding other
black men as potential partners by relying on old

stereotypes of the uneducated, less intelligent black male. Ironically, the same black men who rely on these stereotypes to exclude members of their own race rarely enforce them on gay white men, as evidenced by Boykin's example of the gay black man who has no problem with dating blue-collar white men but excludes black men on the assumption that they are, 'uneducated and less successful than he is'. What's worse is that not only do gay black men fail to see each other as sexual partners, white men also ignore them. In such an environment, black men compete with each other for the allusive white male partner (Boykin, 2002, p. 1).

This desire for white male companionship is not limited just to black men, and neither is racial self-hatred. Rather, it seems to be pandemic among many gay men of color. For example, Tony Ayres explains that:

> The sexually marginalized Asian man who has grown up in the West or is western in his thinking is often invisible in his own fantasies. [Their] sexual daydreams are populated by handsome Caucasian men with lean, hard Caucasian bodies. (1999, p. 91)

Likewise, Kent Chuang writes about how he tried desperately to avoid anything related to his Chinese heritage and his attempts to transform his 'shamefully slim Oriental frame . . . into a more desirable western body' (1999, p. 33). Asian men, too, rely on stereotypes to justify their exclusive attraction to white men. For example, a gay Asian man is cited as stating:

> For me, I prefer dating white men because I want something different from myself. I think that dating another Asian would be like dating my sister. I mean, we would have so much in common, what would there be for us to learn about? Where would the excitement come from? (Han, 2005)

Here, gay Asian men rely on the old stereotype of an 'Asian mass' to justify their own prejudices towards other Asian men. All Asians are presented as homogenous masses with each person being interchangeable with another. Ironically, white men who exclusively

date white men rarely rely on such tactics. There is no need to argue, from a white male position, that dating other white men would be like 'dating their brothers'. Also, the man's characterization of other Asian men as 'sister' also points to the stereotypical ways that Asian men are seen in the larger gay community. Stereotyped as overly feminine, gay Asian men become unappealing to gay men who desire men who are masculine or 'straight acting'.

Partner preference among Latino men also seems to follow the hierarchy of the 'white is best' mentality. Ramirez notes that the competition for a white 'trophy' boyfriend among gay Latino men has often hindered community formation. Rather than seeing each other as allies, gay Latino men may see each other as competitors for the attention of the few white men who prefer Latino men to other white men. For example, one Latino man was quoted as saying:

> One of the things that I saw that really bothered me and I told them, I said, 'What the problem here is everybody is after the white trophy. That's the problem here. And unless two people are comadres [godmothers], you don't want to have nothing to do with each other. But that's the problem. After the white trophy, nobody has time. And it's like, you tear each other down . . . viciousness, because you're after the white trophy. And to have a white lover is ooohhh! Don't you see?' (Ramirez, 2003, p. 229)

After complaining to other Latino men about the pedestalization of white men among gay Latino men, this particular gay Latino man was labeled a 'radical lesbian'. The implication here is that any Latino man who chooses to be with another Latino man, rather than a white man that has come to dominate gay male sexual fantasies, must be a 'lesbian', a woman who prefers other women. The limited definition of desirable masculinity within the gay community leads to white males as being 'men' while men of color are placed lower on the hierarchy much in the same way that the mainstream creates a hierarchy of men and women. As such, men of color are seen lower on the gendered hierarchy within the gay community where white masculinity is valued over all other forms of masculinity. Should they prefer other men of color, they are easily conflated with 'lesbians', two people lower on the gender hierarchy who prefer the sexual companionship of each other over that of the gender dominant group.

While information about racial preference for Native American men is scarce, Brown (1997) reported that only one of their five gay Native American male informants reported ever having a sexual relationship with another Native American male.

Rather than less, race seems to matter more to gay men than to straight men when it comes to mate selection. Examining personal ads, Phua and Kaufman (2003) found that gay men were significantly more likely to prefer one race and suggest that they may be more likely to exclude certain races as well. According to their data, gay men of color were much more likely to explicitly exclude members of their own race and much more likely to request another race (overwhelmingly white) than even gay white men.

THERE'S NO NAME FOR THIS

It would be too easy to throw racism at the doorstep of gay white men and blame them for all of the problems encountered by gay men of color. But racial and ethnic communities must also take some of the blame for whatever psychological assaults gay men of color have endured. If we are invisible in the dominant gay community, perhaps we are doubly so in our racial/ethnic communities.

In the film, *There is no name for this*, produced by Ming-Yuen S. Ma and Cianna Pamintuan Stewart, Chwee Lye Chng, a gay Asian man explains:

> There are words in Malay, in Chinese, or what have you that describes, you know, that is used in the culture. But it's more akin to the word, a transvestite. We just don't know, there is no vocabulary for that and I think that's why it was so difficult to, to perhaps, come out because if I thought I'm gay, I almost have to accept the very distorted definition in the culture of, I'm going to be a cross dresser, I'm going to stand in the street corner and service me. (Ma & Stewart, 1997)

As can be noted from the above quote, the prominence of negative gay stereotypes in Asian cultures makes it difficult for them to discuss their sexual orientation with their families. In addition, the absence of vocabulary also makes it difficult to discuss sexual matters. Anna Jiang in describing the difficulty of discussing her sister's sexuality with her parents stated:

> I have some relatives who only speak Chinese. When I tried to explain Cecilia's character to them, I don't know how to do it. I don't know how to explain the term 'gay' and 'lesbian' to them. (Ma & Stewart, 1997)

Likewise, Doug Au explained:

> It's not just coming out, it's not just saying that I'm queer or that I'm gay but really being able to sit down with someone and explain to them in a way they could understand. (Ma & Stewart, 1997)

Gay and lesbian Asians are not alone in feeling invisible within their ethnic communities. One gay Latino man was quoted by Edgar Colon as stating:

> My family acts as if my sexual orientation does not exist. Moreover, I have no ongoing contact with my family. In this way, we can make sure that I remain invisible. (2001, p. 86)

In Latino cultures, much as in some Asian cultures, 'there is no positive or self-validating word for one who identifies himself as homosexual' (Manalansan, 1996, p. 399). Rather, to self-identify as 'gay' means taking on the maligned and feminine label of *maricon*, implying that one takes the passive role in sexual intercourse. Embedded within the *machisimo* framework of Latin male sexuality, the passive partner during gay intercourse is doubly stigmatized as not only being one who engages in sexual acts with other men but also as taking the feminine, passive role during execution.

Likewise, many Native American gay men have also been forced to leave reservations and families after disclosing that they are gay. As Karina Walters notes:

> In some cases, [first nations gay, lesbian, bisexual, transgendered, two-spirits] leave reservations at very young ages and with little education, eventually trading sex to survive in cities. Prejudice in [first nations] communities manifests itself in the denial of the existence of [first nations gay, lesbian, bisexual, transgendered, two-spirits], avoidance in discussing the subject, and cultural beliefs that nonhetero-sexual behavior is sinful, immoral, and against traditions. (Walters *et al.*, 2002, p. 317)

In black communities, much has been debated recently regarding the 'down low' phenomenon when men, who may be either bisexual or closeted homosexuals, have openly heterosexual lives but engage in covert sexual acts with other men (King, 2004). While it should be noted that black men are not the only men to engage in homosexual activity while leading heterosexual lives, the common belief is that they are more likely than white men to engage in such behavior. True, there are ample examples of homophobia in the black community. At the same time, there is evidence to indicate that it is a mistake to attribute homophobia as simply a black phenomenon, or a phenomenon specific to any racial/ethnic community. Rather, as Manalansan (1996) explains, homophobia in the black community may have much to do with class, self-identification of gay men and women, and other situational factors associated with being a minority group in a racialized society than with blacks being inherently more homophobic than whites.

BORROW THE WORDS BUT IGNORE THE MEANING

The irony, of course, is that even as the 'gay' community uses the language of the civil rights movement to further the cause of equality for gays and lesbians, many within the community continue to ignore the lessons that should be apparent within the language that they have adopted. For example,

the National Gay and Lesbian Task Force describes itself in this way:

> Founded in 1973, the National Gay and Lesbian Task Force Foundation (the Task Force) was the first national lesbian, gay, bisexual and transgender (LGBT) civil rights and advocacy organization and remains the movement's leading voice for freedom, justice and equality. We work to build the grassroots political strength of our community by training state and local activists and leaders, working to strengthen the infrastructure of state and local allies, and organizing broad-based campaigns to build public support for complete equality for LGBT people.

The use of the terms civil rights, movement, justice, equality, grassroots, activist, etc., clearly harkens back to the language of the civil rights movement. The language of the civil rights movement has resonated with numerous 'gay' organizations and as such, they have presented the movement as being one of equality and justice rather than sexual preference. While the Task Force has done an admirable job in promoting issues of race within the gay community, and several men and women of color hold leadership positions on their board of directors, the majority of other gay organizations have not followed suit, particularly at the local level.

Predictably, the use of civil rights language has been met with contesting viewpoints about its validity when applied to gay rights. On the one hand, it has been met positively with Julian Bond, board chairman of the NAACP stating:

> Are gay rights civil rights? Of course they are. 'Civil rights' are positive legal prerogatives—the right to equal treatment before the law. These are rights shared by all—there is no one in the United States who does not—or should not—share in these rights . . . We ought to be flattered that our movement has provided so much inspiration for others, that it has been so widely imitated, and that our tactics, methods, heroines and heroes, even our songs, have been appropriated by or served as models for others . . . Many gays and lesbians worked side by side with me in the '60s Civil Rights Movement. Am I to tell them 'thanks'

for risking life and limb helping me win my rights—but they are excluded because of a condition of their birth? They cannot share now in the victories they helped to win? (Bond, 2004, p. 142)

Others have been less generous with their support, such as the Reverend Fred L. Shuttlesworth, the interim president of the Southern Christian Leadership Conference:

> I was among the original five who started the Southern Christian Leadership Conference (SCLC), and our primary focus back then was to put an end to racial segregation under the Jim Crow system. As SCLC's first secretary, I never took down anything in our minutes that addressed the issue of gay rights. The issue of gay rights was not our focus, and should not be confused with the Civil Rights Movement. (Shuttlesworth, 2004, p. 142)

The problem here is that whether one supports the analogy with the civil rights movement or not, both perspectives seem to negate the possibility that people can be both gay and a racial minority, a point made clear by Mary F. Morten, the former liaison to the gay community under Chicago mayor Richard Daley, when she states:

> A major problem is that gay and lesbian life is associated with privilege because it is depicted far too often from a white perspective. We have few positive images of African American gays and lesbians, and we rarely see African American gays and lesbians on TV. So for many people being gay is associated with being white . . . We have always had visibly gay and lesbian folks in our community, whether we talked about it or not . . . We need to be much more open about the reality that you live next door to some gays and lesbians, that we're in your family, that we're literally everywhere in our community. (Morten, 2004, p. 144)

Clearly, for Morten, acknowledging that racial communities include gay members and, by extension, acknowledging that gay communities include members of racial minority groups, is a top priority.

DISCUSSION

Given the prevalence of negative racial attitudes in the larger gay community and the homophobia in racial communities, gay men of color have had to build identities along the margins of both race and sexuality. More often than not, this has been a difficult road. Looking for a space to call his own, Eric Reyes asks, while referring to Michiyo Cornell's early writing that America is a 'great lie':

> I ask which America should I call a lie. Is it the Eurocentric and heterosexual male-dominated America, the white gay male-centered Queer America, the marginalized People of Color (POC) America, or our often-romanticized Asian America? As a Queer API, I ask where is this truth situated that betrays our belief that we have a space here in this place called America? Locating this space from which we draw our strength and our meaning is the part of coming out that never ends. (Reyes, 1996, p. 85)

The difficulty for gay men of color in coming out as gay has to do with both the homophobia found in racial communities and the racism found in gay communities. True, men of color are dependent on ethnic communities. Michiyo Cornell explains, 'because of Asian American dependence on our families and Asian American communities for support, it is very difficult for us to be out of the closet' (1996, p. 83). At the same time, this 'dependence' may have more to do with lacking alternatives rather than self-inflicted internal homophobia. As Richard Fung points out:

> As is the case for many other people of color and especially immigrants, our families and our ethnic communities are a rare source of affirmation in a racist society. In coming out, we risk (or feel that we risk) losing this support. (Fung, 1991, p. 149)

Other gay men of color have also pointed out the need to maintain ties to their racial and ethnic communities in order to maintain a sense of self-esteem. In fact, the two-spirit movement among gay Native Americans has played a powerful part in bolstering self-esteem among gay Native American men and women. Rather than attempting to 'fit' into white definitions of 'gay' or 'lesbians', Native Americans have reclaimed a long cultural practice of valuing a third gender that is not rigidly linked to the European definitions of 'man' and 'woman' (Brown, 1997; Quinto, 2003; Walters, 1999). In fact, Walters demonstrates that enculturation into Native communities is critical for mental health among gay Native Americans (Walters, 1999).

In this paper, I examined both the racism found in the gay community and the homophobia found in racial and ethnic communities and argue that both racism and homophobia affect men of color negatively in ways that may be multiplicative rather than additive. That is, gay men of color don't simply experience racism because they are racial minorities and homophobia because they are sexual minorities. Instead, they experience a unique type of racism and homophobia because they are gay and of color. Certainly, gay Asian men experience these forces differently from gay black men. In addition, the mirroring of the mainstream by the gay community can also be seen to occur in communities of color, where they favor heterosexuality above homosexuality in an attempt to mirror the dominant society. Within this framework, gay men and women of color are relegated to the bottom of the hierarchy in both communities. While I have limited my discussion to gay men, it is likely that examining the lives of bisexual men of color, bisexual women of color, and lesbian women of color, would lead to a fuller understanding of multiple sites of oppression. Future research and theoretical work will need to tease out the specific experiences of multiply marginalized groups in order to truly understand how race, sexuality, class, etc. may be intersected in the lives of subaltern groups rather than focus on single categories of oppression and expect these to be additive rather than multiplicative. Only then can we truly understand the methods of domination and oppression that mark groups and the implications that such categorization may have.

REFERENCES

And Castro for All. (2004). Is badlands bad? Retrieved 10 August 2005 from www.isbadlandsbad.com

Anonymous. (n.d.). *Racism or preference (at the baths?).* Retrieved 10 February 2005 from *Bathhouse Diaries,* www.bathhouseblues.com/racism.html

Ayres, T. (1999). China doll: The experience of being a gay Chinese Australian. In P. A. Jackson & G. Sullivan (Eds.), *Multicultural queer: Australian narratives.* New York: The Haworth Press.

Beam, J. (1986). Introduction. In J. Beam (Ed.), *In the life: A Black gay anthology.* Boston: Alyson.

Bérubé, A. (2001). How gay stays white and what kind of white it stays. In B. Brander Rasmussen, E. Klinenberg, I. J. Nexica & M. Wray (Eds.), *The making and unmaking of whiteness.* Durham, NC: Duke University Press.

Bond, J. (2004). Is gay rights a civil rights issue? Yes. *Ebony, 59*(9), 142–46.

Boykin, K. (2002). No blacks allowed. Retrieved 25 September 2005 from *Temenos,* www.temenos.net/articles/12-23-04.shtml

Brown, L. (1997). Women and men, not-men and not-women, lesbians and gays: American Indian gender style alternatives. *Journal of Gay and Lesbian Social Services, 6*(2), 5–20.

Cho, S. (1998). *Rice: Explorations into gay Asian culture and politics.* Toronto: Queer Press.

Chuang, K. (1999). Using chopsticks to eat steak. *Journal of Homosexuality, 36*(3/4), 29–41.

Colon, E. (2001). An ethnographic study of six Latino gay and bisexual men. *Journal of Gay and Lesbian Social Services, 12*(3/4), 77–92.

Cornell, M. (1996). Living in Asian America: An Asian American lesbian's address before the Washington Monument (1979). In R. Leong (Ed.), *Asian American sexualities: Dimensions of the gay and lesbian experience.* New York: Routledge.

Duazo, D. (1999). Looking back in homage. *Lavender Godzilla,* April, 1–5.

Engardio, J. P. (1999). You can't be gay, you're Latino: A gay Latino identity struggles to emerge, somewhere between the macho Mission and Caucasian Castro. *SF Weekly,* 7.

Fanon, F. (1970). *Black skin, white masks.* London: Paladin.

Fung, R. (1991). Looking for my penis: The eroticized Asian in gay video porn. In Bad Object-Choice

(Ed.), *How do I look: Queer film and video*. Seattle: Bay Books.

Han, C.-S. (2005). Gay Asian men and negotiating race and sexual behavior. Unpublished manuscript.

King, J. L. (2004). *On the down low: A journey into the lives of 'straight' black men who sleep with men*. New York: Broadway Books.

Lipsitz, G. (1998). *Possessive investment in whiteness*. Philadelphia: Temple University Press.

Ma, M.-Y. S., & Stewart, C. P. (1997). *There is no name for this*. API Wellness Center.

Manalansan, M. R. (1996). Double minorities: Latino, black and Asian men who have sex with men. In R. Savin Williams & K. Cohen (Eds.), *The lives of lesbians, gays, and bisexuals: Developmental, clinical and cultural issues*. Forth Worth: Harcourt, Brace and Co.

Marriott, D. (2000). *On black men*. New York: Columbia University Press.

Mercer, K. (1991). Skinhead sex thing: Racial difference and the homoerotic imaginary. In Bad Object-Choice (Ed.), *How do I look: Queer film and video*. Seattle: Bay Books.

Morten, M. (2004). Is gay rights a civil rights issue? Maybe. *Ebony, 59*(9), 142–46.

Munoz, J. E. (1999). *Disidentifications: Queers of color and the performance of politics*. Minneapolis: University of Minnesota Press.

National Gay and Lesbian Task Force Foundation. (1973). Retrieved from www.thetaskforce.org/aboutus/whatwedo.cfm

Phua, V., & Kaufman, G. (2003). The crossroads of race and sexuality: Date selection among men in internet 'personal' ads. *Journal of Family Issues, 24*(8), 981–94.

Quinto, J. (2003). Northwest two-spirit society. *Colors Northwest, 3*(3), 12–15.

Ramirez, H. N. R. (2003). 'That's my place!': Negotiating racial, sexual, and gender politics in San Francisco's Gay Latino Alliance, 1975–1983. *Journal of the History of Sexuality, 12*(2), 224–58.

Reyes, E. (1996). Strategies for queer Asian and Pacific Islander spaces. In R Leong (Ed.), *Asian American sexualities: Dimensions of the gay and lesbian experience*. New York: Routledge.

Ridge, D., Hee, A., & Minichiello, V. (1999). 'Asian' men on the scene: Challenges to 'gay communities'. *Journal of Homosexuality, 36*(3/4), 43–68.

Riggs, M. (1989). *Tongues untied*. MTR Production.

Romesburg, D. (2004). Racism and reaction in the Castro: A brief, incomplete history. Retrieved 20 October 2005 from www.isbadlandsbad.com/archives/000039.html

Shuttlesworth, F. (2004). Is gay rights a civil rights issue? No. *Ebony, 59*(9), 142–46.

Walters, K. (1999). Negotiating conflicts in allegiances among lesbians and gays of color: Reconciling divided selves and communities. In G. P. Mallon (Ed.), *Foundations of social work practice*. New York: Harrington Park Press.

Walters, K., Longress, J., Han, C.-S., & Icard, L. (2002). Cultural competence with gay and lesbian persons of color. In D. Lum (Ed.), *Culturally competent practice: A framework for understanding diverse groups and justice issues*. Pacific Grove, CA: Thomson Brooks/Cole.

Wat, E. C. (2002). *The making of a gay Asian community: An oral history of pre-AIDS Los Angeles*. Lanham, MD: Rowman and Littlefield.

FANTASY ISLANDS: EXPLORING THE DEMAND FOR SEX TOURISM

Julia O'Connell Davidson　　　　Jacqueline Sanchez Taylor

In a useful review of prostitution cross-culturally and historically, Laurie Shrage observes that "one thing that stands out but stands unexplained is that a large percentage of sex customers seek (or sought) sex workers whose racial, national, or class identities are (or were) different from their own" (Shrage 1994: 142). She goes on to suggest that the demand for African, Asian, and Latin American prostitutes by white Western men may "be explained in part by culturally produced racial fantasies regarding the sexuality of these women" and that these fantasies may be related to "socially formed perceptions regarding the sexual and moral purity of white women" (ibid: 48–50). Kempadoo also draws attention to the "over-representation of women of different nationalities and ethnicities, and the hierarchies of race and color within the [international sex] trade" and observes, "That sex industries today depend upon the eroticization of the ethnic and cultural Others suggest we are witnessing a contemporary form of exoticism which sustains post-colonial and post-cold war relations of power and dominance" (Kempadoo 1995: 75–76).

This chapter represents an attempt to build on such insights. Drawing on our research with both male and female Western heterosexual sex tourists in the Caribbean,[1] it argues that their sexual taste for "Others" reflects not so much a wish to engage in any specific sexual practice as a desire for an extraordinarily high degree of control over the management of self and others as sexual, racialized, and engendered beings. This desire, and the Western sex tourist's power to satiate it, can only be explained through reference to power relations and popular discourses that are simultaneously gendered, racialized, and economic.

WHITE WESTERN MEN'S SEX TOURISM

Empirical research on sex tourism to Southeast Asia has fairly consistently produced a portrait of Western male heterosexual sex tourists as men whose desire for the Other is the flip side of dissatisfaction with white Western women, including white Western prostitute women. Lee, for example, explores the demand for sex tourism as a quest for racially fantasized male power, arguing that this is at least in part a backlash against the women's movement in the West: "With an increasingly active global feminist movement, male-controlled sexuality (or female passivity) appears to be an increasingly scarce resource. The travel advertisements are quite explicit about what is for sale: docility and submission" (Lee 1991: 90; see also Jeffreys 1997). Western sex tourists' fantasies of "docile" and "willing" Asian women are accompanied, as Kruhse-Mount Burton (1995: 196) notes, by "a desexualization of white women . . . who are deemed to be spoiled, grasping and, above all, unwilling or inferior sexual partners." These characteristics are also attributed to white prostitute women. The sex tourists interviewed by Seabrook (1997: 3) compared Thai prostitutes "very favorably with the more mechanistic and functional behavior of most Western sex workers." Kruhse-Mount Burton states that where many impose their own boundaries on the degree of physical intimacy implied by the prostitution contract (for example refusing to kiss clients on the mouth or to engage in unprotected penetrative and/or oral sex) and are also in a position to turn down clients' requests to spend the night or a few days with them is likewise experienced as a threat to, or denial of, traditional male identity.

Though we recognize that sex tourism provides Western men with opportunities "to reaffirm, if only temporarily, the idealized version of masculine identity and mode of being," and that in this sense sex tourism provides men with opportunities to manage and control both themselves and others as engendered beings, we want to argue that there is more to the demand for sex tourism than this (ibid: 202). In the remainder of this chapter we therefore interrogate sex tourists' attitudes toward prostitute use, sexuality, gender, and "race" more closely, and further complicate matters by considering white Western women's and black Western men and women's sex tourism to the Caribbean.

WESTERN SEXUALITY AND PROSTITUTE USE

Hartsock observes that there is "a surprising degree of consensus that hostility and domination, as opposed to intimacy and physical pleasure" are central to the social and historical construction of sexuality in the West (Hartsock 1985: 157). Writers in the psychoanalytic tradition suggest that the kind of hostility that is threaded through Western sexual expression reflects an infantile rage and wish for revenge against the separateness of those upon whom we depend. It is, as Stoller puts it, "a state in which one wishes to harm an object," and the harm wished upon objects of sexual desire expresses a craving to strip them of their autonomy, control, and separateness—that is, to dehumanize them, since

a dehumanized sexual object does not have the power to reject, humiliate, or control (Stoller 1986: 4).

The "love object" can be divested of autonomy and objectified in any number of ways, but clearly the prostitute woman, who is in most cultures imagined and socially constructed as an "unnatural" sexual and social Other (a status which is often enshrined in law), provides a conveniently ready dehumanized sexual object for the client. The commercial nature of the prostitute–client exchange further promises to strip all mutuality and dependency from sexual relations. Because all obligations are discharged through the simple act of payment, there can be no real intimacy and so no terrifying specter of rejection or engulfment by another human being. In theory, then, prostitute use offers a very neat vehicle for the expression of sexual hostility and the attainment of control over self and others as sexual beings. Yet for many prostitute users, there is a fly in the ointment:

> Prostitute women may be socially constructed as Others *and fantasized* as nothing more than objectified sexuality, but in reality, of course, they are human beings. It is only if the prostitute is imagined as stripped of everything bar her sexuality that she can be *completely* controlled by the client's money/powers. But if she were dehumanized to this extent, she would cease to exist as a person. . . . Most clients appear to pursue a contradiction, namely to control as an object that which cannot be objectified. (O'Connell Davidson 1998: 161)

This contradiction is at the root of the complaints clients sometimes voice about Western prostitutes (Graaf et al. 1992; Plumridge and Chetwynd 1997). It is not always enough to buy access to touch and sexually use objectified body parts. Many clients want the prostitute to be a "lover" who makes no claims, a "whore" who has sex for pleasure not money, in short, a person (subject) who can be treated as an object. This reflects, perhaps, deeper inconsistencies in the discourses which surround prostitution and sexuality. The prostitute woman is viewed as acting in a way wholly inconsistent with her gender identity. Her perceived sexual agency degenders her (a woman who takes an impersonal, active, and instrumental approach to sex is not a "real" woman) and dishonors her (she trades in something which is constitutive of her personhood and cannot honorably be sold). The prostitute-using man, by contrast, behaves "in a fashion consistent with the attributes associated with his gender (he is active and sexually predatory, impersonal, and instrumental), and his sexual transgression is thus a minor infraction, since it does not compromise his gender identity" (O'Connell Davidson 1998: 127). A paradox thus emerges:

> The more that men's prostitute use is justified and socially sanctioned through reference to the fiction of biologically determined gender roles and sexuality, the greater the contradiction implicit in prostitution. In order to satisfy their "natural" urges, men must make use of "unnatural" women. (ibid: 128)

All of this helps to explain the fact that, even though their sexual interests may be powerfully shaped by a cultural emphasis on hostility and domination, prostitute use holds absolutely no appeal for many Western men.[2] Fantasies of unbridled sexual access to willingly objectified women are not necessarily fantasies of access to prostitute women. Meanwhile, those who do use prostitutes in the West imagine and manage their own prostitute use in a variety of different ways (see O'Connell Davidson 1998). At one extreme are men who are actually quite satisfied with brief and anonymous sexual use of women and teenagers who they imagine as utterly debased and objectified "dirty whores." (For them, the idea of using a prostitute is erotic in and of itself.) At the other extreme are those who regularly visit the same prostitute woman and construct a fiction of romance or friendship around their use of her, a fiction which helps them to imagine themselves as seen, chosen, and desired, even as they pay for sex as a commodity. Between these two poles are men who indulge in a range of (often very inventive) practices and fantasies designed to create

the illusion of balance between sexual hostility and sexual mutuality that they personally find sexually exciting. How does this relate to the demand for sex tourism?

Let us begin by noting that not all Western male sex tourists subjectively perceive their own sexual practices abroad as a form of prostitute use. This reflects the fact that even within any one country affected by sex tourism, prostitution is not a homogeneous phenomenon in terms of its social organization. In some countries sex tourism has involved the maintenance and development of existing large-scale, highly commoditized sex industries serving foreign military personnel (Truong 1990; Sturdevant and Stoltzfus 1992; Hall 1994). But it has also emerged in locations where no such sex industry existed, for instance, in Gambia, Cuba, and Brazil (Morris-Jarra 1996; Perio and Thierry 1996; Sanchez Taylor 1997). Moreover, even in countries like Thailand and the Philippines, where tourist-related prostitution has been grafted onto an existing, formally organized brothel sector serving military demand, tourist development has *also* been associated with the emergence of an informal prostitution sector (in which prostitutes solicit in hotels, discos, bars, beaches, parks, or streets, often entering into fairly protracted and diffuse transactions with clients).

This in itself gives prostitution in sex tourist resorts a rather different character to that of prostitution in red-light districts in affluent, Western countries. The sense of difference is enhanced by the fact that, in many places, informally arranged prostitution spills over into apparently noncommercial encounters within which tourists who do not self-identify as prostitute users can draw local/migrant persons who do not self-identify as prostitutes into profoundly unequal and exploitative sexual relationships. It also means that sex tourism presents a diverse array of opportunities for sexual gratification, not all of which involve straightforward cash for sex exchanges in brothels or go-go clubs or on the streets, and so provides the sex tourist with a veritable "pic 'n' mix" of ways in which to manage himself as a sexual and engendered being. He can indulge in overt forms of sexual hostility (such as selecting a numbered brothel prostitute from those on display in a bar or brothel for "short time" or buying a cheap, speedy sexual service from one of many street prostitutes), or he can indulge in fantasies of mutuality, picking up a woman/teenager in an ordinary tourist disco, wining and dining and generally simulating romance with her for a day or two and completely denying the commercial basis of the sexual interaction. Or, and many sex tourists do exactly this, he can combine both approaches.

Now it could be argued that, given the fact that Western men are socialized into a view of male sexuality as a powerful, biologically based need for sexual "outlets," the existence of multiple, cheap, and varied sexual opportunities is, in itself, enough to attract large numbers of men to a given holiday resort. However, it is important to recognize the numerous other forms of highly sexualized tourism that could satisfy a wish to indulge in various sexual fantasies and also a desire for control over the self as a sexual and engendered being. Sex tourists could, for example, choose to take part in organized holidays designed to facilitate sexual and romantic encounters between tourists (such as Club 18–30 and other singles holidays), or they could choose to take all-inclusive holidays to resorts such as Hedonism or destinations renowned for promiscuous tourist–tourist sex, such as Ibiza or Cap d'Azur. These latter offer just as many opportunities for anonymous and impersonal sex in a party atmosphere as well as for intense but ultimately brief and noncommitted sexual romances. What they do not offer is the control that comes from paying for sex or the opportunity to indulge in racialized sexual fantasies, which helps to explain why sex tourists reject them in favor of sexual experience in what they term "Third World" countries. This brings us to questions about the relationship between the construction of "Otherness" and sex tourism.

"OTHERNESS" AND WESTERN MEN'S SEX TOURISM

For obvious reasons, sex tourists spend their time in resorts and *barrios* where tourist-related prostitution is widespread. Thus they constantly encounter what appear to them as hedonistic scenes—local "girls" and young men dancing "sensuously," draping themselves over and being fondled by Western tourists, drinking and joking with each other, and so on. Instead of seeing the relationship between these scenes and their own presence in the resort, sex tourists tend to interpret all this as empirical vindication of Western assumptions of "non-Western peoples living in idyllic pleasure, splendid innocence or Paradiselike conditions—as purely sensual, natural, simple and uncorrupted beings" (Kempadoo 1995: 76). Western sex tourists (and this is true of black as well as white informants) say that sex is more "natural" in Third World countries, that prostitution is not really prostitution but a "way of life," that "They" are "at it" all of the time.

This explains how men who are not and would not dream of becoming prostitute users back home can happily practice sex tourism (the "girls" are not really like prostitutes and so they themselves are not really like clients, the prostitution contract is not like the Western prostitution contract and so does not really count as prostitution). It also explains the paranoid obsession with being cheated exhibited by some sex tourists, who comment on their belief that women in certain sex tourist resorts or particular brothels or bars are "getting too commercial" and advise each other how to avoid being "duped" and "exploited" by a "real professional," where to find "brand new girls," and so on (see Bishop and Robinson 1998; O'Connell Davidson 1998).

It also points to the complex interrelations between discourses of gender, "race," and sexuality. To begin with, the supposed naturalness of prostitution in the Third World actually reassures the Western male sex tourist of his racial or cultural superiority. Thus we find that sex tourists continue a traditional Western discourse of travel which rests on the imagined opposition between the "civilized" West and the "barbarous" Other (Grewal 1996: 136; Kempadoo 1994: 76, see also Brace and O'Connell Davidson 1996). In "civilized" countries only "bad" women become prostitutes (they refuse the constraints civilization places upon "good" women in favor of earning "easy money"), but in the Third World (a corrupt and lawless place where people exist in a state of nature), "nice girls" may be driven to prostitution in order to survive ("they have to do it because they've all got kids" or "they're doing it for their families"). In the West, "nice girls" are protected and supported by their menfolk, but in the Third World, "uncivilized" Other men allow (or even demand that) their womenfolk enter prostitution. In interviews, Western male sex tourists contrast their own generosity, humanity, and chivalry against the "failings" of local men, who are imagined as feckless, faithless, wife-beaters, and pimps. Even as prostitute users, Other men are fantasized as inferior moral beings who cheat and mistreat the "girls."

In this we see that sex tourism is not only about sustaining a male identity. For white men it is also about sustaining a *white* identity. Thus, sex tourism can also be understood as a collective behavior oriented toward the restoration of a generalized belief about what it is to be white: to be truly white is to be served, revered, and envied by Others. For the black American male sex tourists we have interviewed, sex tourism appears to affirm a sense of Westernness and so of inclusion in a privileged world. Take, for example, the following three statements from a 45-year-old black American sex tourist. He is a New York bus driver and ex-vice cop, a paid-up member of an American-owned sex tourist club, Travel & the Single Male, and he has used prostitutes in Thailand, Brazil, Costa Rica, and the Dominican Republic:

> There's two sides to the countries that I go to. There's the tourist side and then there's the real people, and I make a habit of going to the real people, I see how the real people live, and when I see something like that . . . I tend to look at the little bit I've got at home and I appreciate it . . . .
>
> I've always been proud to be an American . . . . I always tip in US dollars when I arrive. I always keep dollars and pesos, because people tend to think differently about pesos and dollars . . . .
>
> They always say at hotels they don't want you to bring the girls in; believe me, that's crap, because you know what I do? Reach in my pocket and I go anywhere I want.

Meanwhile, sexualized racisms help the sex tourist to attain a sense of control over himself and Others as engendered and racialized sexual beings. Here it is important to recognize the subtle (or not so subtle) variations of racism employed by white Western men. The sex tourists we have interviewed in the Caribbean are not a homogeneous group in terms of their "race" politics, and this reflects differences of national identity, age, socioeconomic background, and racialized identity. One clearly identifiable subgroup is comprised of white North American men aged forty and above, who, though perhaps not actually affiliated with the Klan, espouse a white supremacist worldview and consider black people their biological, social, and cultural inferiors. They use the word "nigger" and consider any challenge to their "right" to use this term as "political correctness." As one sex tourist complained, in the States "You can't use the N word, nigger. Always when I was raised up, the only thing was the F word, you can't use the F word. Now you can't say cunt, you can't say nigger."

For men like this, black women are imagined as the embodiment of all that is low and debased, they are "inherently degraded, and thus the appropriate partners for degrading sex" (Shrage 1994: 158). As unambiguous whores by virtue of their racialized identity, they may be briefly and anonymously used, but they are not sought out for longer term or quasi-romantic commercial sexual relationships. Thus, the sex tourist quoted above told us that when he and his cronies (all regular sex tourists to the Dominican Republic) see another American sex tourist "hanging round" with a local girl or woman who has the phenotypical characteristics they associate with African-ness, they call out to him, "How many bananas did it take to get her down out of the tree?" and generally deride him for transgressing a racialized sexual boundary which should not, in their view, be openly crossed.

The Dominican females that men like this want sexual access to are light skinned and straight haired (this is also true in Cuba and in the Latin American countries where we have undertaken fieldwork). They are not classified as "niggers" by these white racists, but instead as "LBFMs" or "Little Brown Fucking Machines," a catch-all category encompassing any female Other not deemed to be either white or "African." The militaristic and imperialist associations of this term (coined by American GIs stationed in Southeast Asia) simultaneously make it all the more offensive and hostile and all the more appealing to this type of sex tourists, many of whom have served in the armed forces (a disturbing number of whom have also been or currently are police officers in the United States) and the rest of whom are "wanna-be vets"—men who never made it to Vietnam to live out their racialized-sexualized fantasies of masculine glory.

Shrage and Kruhse-Mount Burton's comments on the relationship between fantasies of hypersexual Others and myths about white women's sexual purity are also relevant to understanding this kind of sex tourist's worldview. An extract from an article posted on an Internet site written by and for sex tourists entitled "Why No White Women?" is revealing:

> **Q:** Is it because white women demand more (in terms of performance) from their men during Sex? and white men cannot deliver?
>
> **A:** In my case, it's just that my dick is not long enough to reach up on the pedestal they like to stand on.

If whiteness is imagined as dominance, and woman is imagined as subordination, then "white woman" becomes something of a contradiction. As Young notes, "For white men, white women are both self and other: they have a floating status. They can reinforce a sense of self through common racial identity or threaten and disturb that sense through their sexual Otherness" (Young 1996: 52). White supremacists have to place white women on a pedestal (iconize them as racially, morally, and sexually pure), since whiteness and civilization are synonymous and "civilization" is constructed as the rejection of base animalism. But keeping them on their pedestal requires men to constantly deny what they imagine to be their own needs and nature and thus white women become the object of profound resentment.

Not all Western male sex tourists to the Caribbean buy into this kind of overt, denigrating racism. In fact, many of them are far more strongly influenced by what might be termed "exoticizing" racisms. Younger white Europeans and North Americans, for example, have been exposed to such racisms through the Western film, music, and fashion industries, which retain the old-school racist emphasis on blackness as physicality but repackage and commoditize this "animalism" so that black men and women become the ultimate icons of sporting prowess, "untamed" rebelliousness, "raw" musical talent, sexual power, and so on (see hooks 1992, 1994; Young 1996). As a consequence, many young (and some not so young) white Westerners view blackness as a marker of something both "cool" and "hot."

In their own countries, however, their encounters with real live black people are not only few and far between, but also generally something of a disappointment to them. As one British sex tourist to Cuba told us, black people in Britain are "very standoffish . . . . They stick to their own, and it's a shame, because it makes divisions." What a delight it is for men like this to holiday in the Caribbean, then, where poverty combined with the exigencies of tourist development ensure that they are constantly faced by smiling, welcoming black folk. The small black boy who wants to shine their shoes; the old black woman who cleans their hotel room; the cool, young, dreadlocked black man on the beach who is working as a promoter for some restaurant or bar; the fit, young black woman soliciting in the tourist disco—all want to "befriend" the white tourist. Finally, interviews with black American male sex tourists suggest that they too sexualize and exoticize the women they sexually exploit in the Third World ("Latin women are hot," "Latin girls love sex").

Both the sexualized racism that underpins the category LBFM and the exoticizing sexualized racism espoused by other sex tourists help to construct the Other prostitute as the embodiment of a contradiction, that is, as a "whore" who does it for pleasure as much as for money, an object with a subjectivity completely attuned to their own, in short, the embodiment of a masturbatory fantasy. Time and again Western sex tourists have assured us that the local girls really are "hot for it," that Third World prostitutes enjoy their work and that their highest ambition is to be the object of a Western man's desire. Their belief that Third World prostitutes are genuinely economically desperate rather than making a free choice to prostitute for "easy money" is clearly inconsistent with their belief that Third World prostitutes are actually acting on the basis of mutual sexual desire, but it is a contradiction that appears to resolve (at least temporarily) an anxiety they have about the relationship between sex, gender, sexuality, and "race."

The vast majority of the sex tourists we have interviewed believe that gender attributes, including sexual behavior, are determined by biological sex. They say that it is natural for women to be passive and sexually receptive as well as to be homemakers, child rearers, dependent upon and subservient toward men, which is why white Western women (prostitute and nonprostitute alike) often appear to them as unsexed. Thus the sex tourist quoted at the beginning of this chapter could only explain women's presence on traditional male terrain by imagining them as sexually "unnatural" ("Most of these girls are dykes anyways"). White women's relative economic, social, and political power as well as their very whiteness makes it hard for Western male sex tourists to eroticize them as nothing more than sexual beings. Racism/ethnocentrism can collapse such tensions. If black or Latin women are naturally physical, wild, hot, and sexually powerful, there need be no anxiety about enjoying them as pure sex. Equally, racism settles the anxieties some men have about the almost "manly" sexual power and agency attributed to white prostitutes. A Little Brown Fucking Machine is not unsexed by prostituting, she is "just doing what comes naturally." Since the Other woman is a "natural" prostitute, her prostitution does not make her any the less a "natural woman." All these points are also relevant to understanding the phenomenon of female sex tourism.

"OTHERNESS" AND FEMALE SEX TOURISM

Western women's sexual behavior abroad (both historically and contemporaneously) is often viewed in a rather different light compared to that of their male counterparts, and it is without doubt true that Western women who travel to Third World destinations in search of sex differ from many of the Western male sex tourists discussed above in terms of their attitudes toward prostitution and sexuality. Few of them are prostitute users back home, and few of them would choose to visit brothels while abroad or to pay street prostitutes for a quick "hand job" or any other sexual service (although it should be noted that some women do behave in these ways). But one of the authors' (Sanchez Taylor) ongoing interview and survey research with female sex tourists in Jamaica and the Dominican Republic suggests that there are also similarities between the sexual behavior of Western women and men in sex tourist resorts.

The Caribbean has long been a destination that offers tourist women opportunities for sexual experience, and large numbers of women from the United States, Canada, Britain, and Germany as well as smaller numbers of women from other European countries and from Japan (i.e., the same countries that send male sex tourists) engage in sexual relationships with local men while on holiday there (Chevannes 1993; Karch and Dann 1981; Pruitt and LaFont 1995). Preliminary analysis of data from Sanchez Taylor's survey of a sample of 104 single Western female tourists in Negril, Sosúa, and Boca Chica shows that almost 40 percent had entered into some form of sexual relationship with a local man.[3] The survey data further suggest that these were not chance encounters but rather that the sexually active female tourists visit the islands in order to pursue one or more sexual relationships. Only 9 percent of sexually active women were on their first trip; the rest had made numerous trips to the islands, and over 20 percent of female sex tourists reported having had two or more different local sexual partners in the course of a two- to three-week stay. Furthermore female sex tourists, as much as male sex tourists, view their sexual experiences as integral to their holiday— "When in Jamaica you have to experience everything that's on offer," one black American woman explained, while a white woman working as a tour representative for a U.S. package operator said: "I tell my single women: come down here to love them, fuck them, and leave them, and you'll have a great time here. Don't look to get married. Don't call them."

Like male sex tourists, these women differ in terms of their age, nationality, social class, and racialized identity, including among their ranks young "spice girl" teenagers and students as well as grandmothers in their sixties, working-class as well as middle-class professionals, or self-employed women. They also differ in terms of the type of sexual encounters they pursue and the way in which they interpret these encounters. Some are eager to find a man as soon as they get off the plane and enter into multiple, brief, and instrumental relationships; others want to be romanced and sweet-talked by one or perhaps two men during their holiday. Around 40 percent described their relationships with local men as "purely physical" and 40 percent described them as "holiday romances." Twenty percent said that they had found "true love." Almost all the sexually active women surveyed stated that they had "helped their partner(s) out financially" by buying them meals, drinks, gifts, or by giving cash, and yet none of them perceived these relationships as commercial sexual transactions. Asked whether they had ever been approached by a gigolo/prostitute during their stay in Jamaica, 90 percent of them replied in the negative. The data collected in the Dominican Republic revealed similar patterns of denial.

The informal nature of the sexual transactions in these resorts blurs the boundaries of what constitutes prostitution for Western women just as it does for Western men, allowing them to believe that the meals, cash, and gifts they provide for their sexual partners do not represent a form of payment for services rendered but rather an expression of their own munificence. It is only when women repeatedly enter into a series of extremely brief sexual encounters that they begin to acknowledge that, as one put it, "It's all about money." Even this does not lead them to view themselves as prostitute users, however, and again it is notions of difference and Otherness that play a key role in protecting the sex tourist from the knowledge that they are paying for the sexual attentions they receive. As Others, local men are viewed as beings possessed of a powerful and indiscriminate sexuality that they cannot control, and this explains their eagerness for sex with tourist women, regardless of their age, size, or physical appearance. Again, the Other is not *selling* sex, just "doing what comes naturally."

As yet, the number of black female sex tourists in Sanchez Taylor's survey and interview sample is too small to base any generalizations upon,[4] but so far their attitudes are remarkably consistent with those voiced by the central character in Terry Macmillan's 1996 novel *How Stella Got Her Groove Back*, in which a black American woman finds "love and romance" with a Jamaican boy almost half her age and with certainly less than half her economic means.[5] Stella views her own behavior in a quite different light from that of white male sex tourists—she disparages an older white male tourist as "a dirty old man who probably has to pay for all the pussy he gets" (Macmillan 1996: 83). It is also interesting to note the ways in which Macmillan "Otherizes" local men: the Jamaican boy smells "primitive"; he is "exotic and goes with the island"; he is "Mr. Expresso in shorts" (ibid: 142, 154). Like white female sex tourists interviewed in the course of research, Macmillan further explains the young Jamaican man's disinterest in Jamaican women and so his sexual interest in an older American woman by Otherizing local women through the use of derogatory stereotypes. Thus, Jamaican women are assumed to be rapacious, materialistic, and sexually instrumental— they only want a man who owns a big car and house and money—and so Jamaican men long for women who do not demand these things (i.e., American women who already possess them).

Like their male counterparts, Western female sex tourists employ fantasies of Otherness not just to legitimate obtaining sexual access to the kind of young, fit, handsome bodies that would otherwise be denied to them and to obtain affirmation of their own sexual desirability (because the fact is that some female sex tourists are themselves young and fit looking and would be easily able to secure sexual access to equally appealing male bodies at home), but also to obtain a sense of power and control over themselves and others as engendered, sexual beings and to affirm their own privilege as Westerners. Thus they continually stress their belief that people in the Caribbean "are different from Westerners." Sexual life is one of the primary arenas in which this supposed difference is manifest. More than half of the female sex tourists surveyed in Jamaica stated that Jamaicans are more relaxed about teen-age sex, casual sex, and prostitution than Westerners. In response to open-ended questions, they observed that "Jamaican men are more up front about sex," that "Jamaicans are uninhibited about sex," that "Jamaicans are naturally promiscuous," and that "sex is more natural to Jamaicans." In interviews, female sex tourists also reproduced the notion of an opposition between the "civilized" West and the "primitive" Third World. One Scots grandmother in her early forties described the Dominican Republic as follows: "It's just like Britain before its industrial phase, it's just behind Britain, just exactly the same. Kids used to get beat up to go up chimneys, here they get beaten up to go polish shoes. There's no difference."

Western female sex tourists' racisms, like those of male sex tourists, are also many-layered and nuanced by differences in terms of nationality, age, and racialized identity. There are older white American female sex tourists whose beliefs about "race" and attitudes toward interracial sex are based upon an ideology that is overtly white supremacist. The black male represents for them the essence of an animalistic sexuality that both fascinates and repels. While in their own country they would not want to openly enter a sexual relationship with a black man, in a holiday resort like Negril they can transgress the racialized and gendered codes that normally govern their sexual behavior, while maintaining their honor and reputation back home. As one Jamaican gigolo commented:

> While they are here they feel free. Free to do what they never do at home. No one looking at them. Get a Black guy who are unavailable at home. No one judge them. Get the man to make they feel good then they go home clean and pure.

This observation, and all the sexual hostility it implies, is born out by the following extract from an interview with a 45-year-old white American woman from Chicago, a regular sex tourist to Negril:

> [Jamaican men] are all liars and cheats . . . . [American women come up Negril because] they get what they don't get back home. A girl who no one looks twice at back home, she gets hit on all the time here, all these guys are paying her attention, telling her she's beautiful, and they really want her . . . . They're obsessed with their dicks. That's all they think of, just pussy and money and nothing else . . . . In Chicago, this could never happen. It's like a secret, like a fantasy and then you go home.

When asked whether she would ever take a black boyfriend home and introduce him to her friends and family, she was emphatic that she would not—"No, no, never. It's not like that. This is something else, you know, it's time out. Like a fantasy." This is more than simply a fantasy about having multiple anonymous sexual encounters without getting caught and disgraced. It is also a highly racialized fantasy about power and vengeance. Women like the sex tourist quoted above are looking for black men with good bodies, firm and muscle-clad sex machines that they can control, and this element of control should not be overlooked. It is also important to female sex tourists who reject white supremacist ideologies, and there are many of these, including white liberals and young white women who value Blackness as a "cool" commodity in the same way that many young white men do, and black American and black British female sex tourists.

These latter groups do not wish to indulge in the overtly hostile racialized sexual fantasy described by the woman quoted above, but they do want to live out other fantasies, whether they be "educating and helping the noble savage," or being the focus of "cool" black men's adoring gaze, or being the central character of a Terry Macmillan novel.[6] No matter what specific fantasy they pursue, female sex tourists use their economic power to initiate and terminate sexual relations with local men at whim, and within those relationships, they use their economic and racialized power to control these men in ways in which they could never command a Western man. These are unaccustomed powers, and even the female sex tourists who buy into exoticizing rather than hostile and denigrating racisms appear to enjoy them as such.

For white women, these powers are very clearly linked to their own whiteness as well as to their status and economic power as tourist women. Thus they contrast their own experience against that of local women (remarking on the fact that they are respected and protected and not treated like local women) *and* against their experience back home (commenting on how safe they feel in the Caribbean walking alone at night and entering bars and discos by themselves, observing that local men are far more attentive and chivalrous than Western men). Take, for example, the comments of "Judy," a white American expatriate in the Dominican Republic, a woman in her late fifties and rather overweight:

> When you go to a disco, [white] men eye up a woman for her body, whatever. Dominicans don't care because they love women, they love women. It's not that they're indifferent or anything. They are very romantic, they will never be rude with you, while a white man will say something rude to you, while Dominican men are not like that at all. A white man will say to me, like, "slut" to me and I have been with a lot of Dominican men and they would never say anything like that to you. They are more respectful. Light cigarettes, open doors, they are more gentlemen. Where white men don't do that. So if you have been a neglected woman in civilization, when you come down here, of course, when you come down here they are going to wipe you off your feet.

The Dominican Republic presents women like Judy with a stage upon which to simultaneously affirm their femininity through their ability to command men and exact revenge on white men by engaging sexually with the competition, i.e., the black male. For the first time she is in a position to call the shots. Where back home white female sex tourists' racialized privilege is often obscured by their lack of gender power and economic disadvantage in relation to white men, in sex tourist resorts it is recognized as a source of personal power and power over others. Meanwhile, their beliefs about gender and sexuality prevent them from seeing themselves as sexually exploitative. Popular discourses about gender present women as naturally sexually passive and receptive, and men as naturally indiscriminate and sexually voracious. According to this essentialist model of gender and sexuality, women can never sexually exploit men in the same way that men exploit women because penetrative heterosexual intercourse requires the woman to submit to the male—she is "used" by him. No matter how great the asymmetry between female tourist and local male in terms of their age or economic, social, and racialized power, it is still assumed that the male derives benefits from sex above and beyond the purely pecuniary and so is not being exploited in the same way that a prostitute woman is exploited by a male client. This is especially the case when the man so used is socially constructed as a racialized, ethnic, or cultural Other and assumed to have an uncontrollable desire to have sex with as many women as he possibly can.

CONCLUSION

The demand for sex tourism is inextricably linked to discourses that naturalize and celebrate inequalities structured along lines of class, gender, and race/Otherness; in other words, discourses that reflect and help to reproduce a profoundly hierarchical model of human sociality. Although sex tourists are a heterogeneous group in terms of their background characteristics and specific sexual interests, they share a common willingness to embrace this hierarchical model and a common pleasure in the fact that their Third World tourism allows them either to affirm their dominant position within a hierarchy of gendered, racialized, and economic power or to adjust their own position upward in that hierarchy. In the Third World, neocolonial relations of power equip Western sex tourists with an extremely high level of control over themselves and others as sexual beings and, as a result, with the power to realize the fantasy of their choosing. They can experience sexual intimacy without risking rejection; they can evade the social meanings that attach to their own age and body type; they can transgress social rules governing sexual life without consequence for their own social standing; they can reduce other human beings to nothing more than the living embodiments of masturbatory fantasies.

In short, sex tourists can experience in real life a world very similar to that offered in fantasy to pornography users: "Sexuality and sexual activity are portrayed in pornography as profoundly distanced from the activities of daily life. The action in pornography takes place in what Griffin has termed 'pornotopia,' a world outside real time and space" (Hartsock 1985: 175). To sex tourists, the resorts they visit are fantasy islands, variously peopled by Little Brown Fucking Machines, "cool" black women who love to party, "primitive smelling" black studs who only think of "pussy and money," respectful Latin gentlemen who love women. All the sex tourist has to do to attain access to this fantasy world is to reach into his or her pocket, for it is there that the sex tourist, like other individuals in capitalist societies, carries "his social power as also his connection with society" (Marx 1973: 94). That the Western sex tourist's pocket can contain sufficient power to transform others into Others, mere players on a pornographic stage, is a testament to the enormity of the imbalance of economic, social, and political power between rich and poor nations. That so many Westerners *wish* to use their power in this way is a measure of the bleakness of the prevailing model of human nature and the human sociality that their societies offer them.

NOTES

1. In 1995 we were commissioned by ECPAT (End Child Prostitution in Asian Tourism) to undertake research on the identity, attitudes, and motivations of clients of child prostitutes. This involved ethnographic fieldwork in tourist areas in South Africa, India, Costa Rica, Venezuela, Cuba, and the Dominican Republic. We are currently working on an Economic and Social Research Council-funded project (Award no. R 000 23 7625), which builds on this research through a focus on prostitution and the informal tourist economy in Jamaica and the Dominican Republic. Taking these projects together, we have interviewed some 250 sex tourists and sexpatriates and over 150 people involved in tourist-related prostitution (women, children, and men working as prostitutes, pimps, procurers, brothel keepers, etc.).

2. The fact that not all men are prostitute users is something that is often forgotten in radical feminist analyses of prostitution which, as Hart has noted, encourage us to view "either all men as prostitutes' clients or prostitutes' clients as somehow standing for/being symbolic of men in general" (Hart 1994: 53).

3. Because the survey aims to support exploration and theory development in a previously underresearched field, purposive (nonprobability) sampling methods were employed (Arber 1993: 72). Sanchez Taylor obtained a sample by approaching all single female tourists in selected locations (a particular stretch of beach, or a given bar or restaurant) and asking them to complete questionnaires.

4. Four out of eighteen single black British and American female tourists surveyed had entered into sexual relationships with local men. Sanchez Taylor also interviewed four more black female sex tourists.

5. In Negril, gigolos often refer to black American female sex tourists as "Stellas," after this fictional character.

6. Macmillan hints at the transgressive elements of a black Western female sex tourist's excitement—Stella's desire for the "primitive"-smelling younger man makes her feel "kind of slutty," but she likes the feeling.

REFERENCES

Arber, Sarah. "Designing Samples." *Researching Social Life*, ed. Nigel Gilbert, 68–92. London: Sage, 1993.

Bishop, Ryan and Lillian S. Robinson. *Night Market: Sexual Cultures and the Thai Economic Miracle*. New York: Routledge, 1998.

Brace, Laura and Julia O'Connell Davidson. "Desperate Debtors and Counterfeit Love: The Hobbesian World of the Sex Tourist." *Contemporary Politics* 2.3 (1996): 55–78.

Chevannes, Barry. "Sexual Behaviour of Jamaicans: A Literature Review." *Social and Economic Studies* 42.1 (1993).

Graaf, Ron de, Ine Vanwesenbeck, Gertjan van Zessen, Straver Visser, and Jan Visser. "Prostitution and the Spread of HIV." *Safe Sex in Prostitution in The Netherlands*, 2–24, Amsterdam: Mr A. de Graaf Institute, 1992.

Grewal, Inderpal. *Home and Harem: Nation, Gender, Empire and the Cultures of Travel*. London: Leicester University Press, 1996.

Hall, C. Michael. "Gender and Economic Interests in Tourism Prostitution: The Nature, Development and Implications of Sex Tourism in South-East Asia." *Tourism: A Gender Perspective*, ed. Vivien Kinnaird and D Hall. London: Routledge, 1994.

Hart, Angie. "Missing Masculinity? Prostitutes' Clients in Alicante, Spain." *Dislocating Masculinity: Comparative Ethnographies*, ed. Andrea Cornwall and Nancy Lindisfarne, 48–65. London: Routledge, 1994.

Hartsock, Nancy. *Money, Sex, and Power*. Boston: Northeastern University Press, 1985.

hooks, bell. *Black Looks: Race and Representation*. London: Turnaround, Boston: South End Press, 1992.

———. *Outlaw Culture: Resisting Representations*. London: Routledge, 1994.

Jeffreys, Sheila. *The Idea of Prostitution*. Melbourne: Spinifex, 1997.

Karch, Cecilia A. and G. H. S. Dann. "Close Encounters of the Third Kind." *Human Relations* 34 (1981): 249–68.

Kempadoo, Kamala. "Prostitution, Marginality, and Empowerment: Caribbean Women in the Sex Trade." *Beyond Law* 5.14 (1994): 69–84.

———. "Regulating Prostitution in the Dutch Caribbean." Paper presented at the 20th annual conference of the Caribbean Studies Association, Caraçao, Netherlands Antrilles, May 1995.

Kruhse-Mount Burton, Suzy. "Sex Tourism and Traditional Australian Male Identity." *International Tourism Identity and Change*, ed. Marie-Françoise Lanfant, John Allcock, and Edward Bruner, 192–204. London: Sage, 1995.

Lee, Wendy. "Prostitution and Tourism in South-East Asia." *Working Women: International Perspectives on Labour and Gender Ideology*, ed. N. Redclift and M. Thea Sinclair, 79–103. London: Routledge, 1991.

Macmillan, Terry. *How Stella Got Her Groove Back*. New York: Penguin, 1996.

Marx, Karl. *Grundisse*. Harmondsworth, England: Penguin, 1973.

Morris-Jarra, Monica. "No Such Thing as a Cheap Holiday." *Tourism in Focus* 26 (Autumn 1996): 6–7.

O'Connell Davidson, Julia. *Prostitution, Power and Freedom*. Cambridge: Polity Press, 1998.

Perio, Gaelle and Dominique Thierry. *Tourisme Sexuel au Bresil et en Colombie*. Rapport D'Enquete, TOURGOING, 1996.

Plumridge, Elizabeth and Jane Chetwynd. "Discourses of Emotionality in Commercial Sex." *Feminism & Psychology* 7.2 (1997): 165–81.

Pruitt, Deborah and Suzanne LaFont. "For Love and Money: Romance Tourism in Jamaica." *Annals of Tourism Research* 22.2 (1995): 422–40.

Sanchez Taylor, Jacqueline. "Marking the Margins: Research in the Informal Economy in Cuba and the Dominican Republic." Discussion Paper No. 597/1, Department of Sociology, University of Leicester, 1997.

Seabrook, Jeremy. *Travels in the Skin Trade: Tourism and the Sex Industry*. London: Pluto Press, 1997.

Shrage, Laurie, *Moral Dilemmas of Feminism*. London: Routledge, 1994.

Stoller, Robert, *Perversion: The Erotic Form of Hatred*. London: Karnac, 1986.

Sturdevant, Saundra and Brenda Stoltzfus. *Let the Good Times Roll: Prostitution and the U.S. Military in Asia*. New York: The New Press, 1992.

Truong, Than Dam. *Sex, Money and Morality: The Political Economy of Prostitution and Tourism in South East Asia*. London: Zed Books, 1990.

Young, Lola. *Fear of the Dark: "Race," Gender and Sexuality in the Cinema*. London: Routledge, 1996.

PART EIGHT

MEN IN FAMILIES

Are men still taking seriously their responsibilities as family breadwinners? Are today's men sharing more of the family housework and child care than those in previous generations? The answers to these questions are complex, and often depend on which men we are talking about and what we mean when we say "family."

Many male workers long ago won a "family wage" and, with it, made an unwritten pact to share that wage with a wife and children. But today, as Barbara Ehrenreich argues in her influential book *The Hearts of Men*, increasing numbers of men are revolting against this traditional responsibility to share their wages, thus contributing to the rapidly growing impoverishment of women and children. Ehrenreich may be correct, at least with respect to the specific category of men who were labeled "yuppies" in the 1980s. But if we are looking at the growing impoverishment of women and children among poor, working-class, and minority families, the causes have more to do with dramatic shifts in the structure of the economy—including skyrocketing unemployment among young black males—than they do with male irresponsibility. Increasing numbers of men have no wage to share with a family.

But how about the new dual-career family? Is this a model of egalitarianism, or do women still do what sociologist Arlie Hochschild called "the second shift"—the housework and child care obligations that come after their workplace shift is done? In this part, Scott Coltrane examines the shifting roles of American fathers, as they engage in new realities and a new household division of labor. Has the dual-career family also become a dual-carer family?

Family life for men varies by race, class, ethnicity, and sexuality. The article by Anne Shelton and Daphne John explores some of these differences for different ethnic groups. Judith Stacey and Dana Berkowitz each explore different aspects of family life for gay men, both in the distribution of housework and child care, and the assumption of different roles in their respective works.

FATHERING: PARADOXES, CONTRADICTIONS, AND DILEMMAS

Scott Coltrane

The beginning of the 21st century offers a paradox for American fathers: Media images, political rhetoric, and psychological studies affirm the importance of fathers to children at the same time that men are becoming less likely to live with their offspring. Although the average married father spends more time interacting with his children than in past decades, marriage rates have fallen, and half of all marriages are predicted to end in divorce. Additionally, the proportion of births to unmarried mothers has increased dramatically for all race and ethnic groups, and single-mother households have become commonplace. These contradictory tendencies—more father-child interaction in two-parent families but fewer two-parent families in the population—have encouraged new research on fathers and spawned debates about how essential fathers are to families and normal child development (Blankenhorn, 1995; Silverstein & Auerbach, 1999).

Scholars attribute the current paradox in fathering to various economic and social trends. Whereas most men in the 20th century were sole breadwinners, contemporary fathers' wages can rarely support a middle-class standard of living for an entire family. The weakening of the good-provider model, coupled with trends in fertility, marriage, divorce, and custody, has resulted in the average man spending fewer years living with children (Eggebeen,

2002). Simultaneously, however, men rank marriage and children among their most precious goals, single-father households have increased, and fathers in two-parent households are spending more time with co-resident children than at any time since data on fathers were collected (Pleck & Masciadrelli, 2003). Although married fathers report that they value their families over their jobs, they spend significantly more time in paid work and less time in family work than married mothers, with most men continuing to serve as helpers to their wives, especially for housework and child maintenance activities (Coltrane, 2000). Personal, political, religious, and popular discourses about fathers reveal similar ambivalence about men's family involvements, with ideals ranging from stern patriarchs to nurturing daddies, and public portrayals frequently at odds with the actual behavior of average American fathers (LaRossa, 1997). We can understand these contradictions by recognizing that fatherhood has gained symbolic importance just as men's family participation has become more voluntary, tenuous, and conflicted (Griswold, 1993; Kimmel, 1996).

In this chapter, I summarize how fathering practices have varied across cultures and through history; highlight how different social, economic, and political contexts have produced different types of father involvement; review how social scientists have measured father involvement; and examine findings about causes and consequences of father involvement. I end with a short analysis of debates over family policy and offer tentative predictions about the future of fathering in America.

CROSS-CULTURAL VARIATION

Fatherhood defines a biological and social relationship between a male parent and his offspring. *To father* means to impregnate a woman and beget a child, thus describing a kinship connection that facilitates the intergenerational transfer of wealth and authority (at least in patrilineal descent systems such as ours). Fatherhood also reflects ideals about the rights, duties, and activities of men in families and in society and generalizes to other social and symbolic relationships, as when Christians refer to "God the Father," Catholics call priests "Father," and Americans label George Washington "the Father" of the country. Fatherhood thus reflects a normative set of social practices and expectations that are institutionalized within religion, politics, law, and culture. Social theories have employed the concept of *social fatherhood* to explain how the institution of fatherhood links a particular child to a particular man (whether father or uncle) in order to secure a place for that child in the social structure (Coltrane & Collins, 2001).

Fathering (in contrast to *fatherhood*) refers more directly to what men do with and for children. Although folk beliefs suggest that fathering entails behaviors fixed by reproductive biology, humans must learn how to parent. In every culture and historical period, men's parenting has been shaped by social and economic forces. Although women have been the primary caretakers of young children in all cultures, fathers' participation in child rearing has varied from virtually no direct involvement to active participation in all aspects of children's routine care. Except for breastfeeding and the earliest care of infants, there are no cross-cultural universals in the tasks that mothers and fathers perform (Johnson, 1988). In some societies, the social worlds of fathers and mothers were so separate that they rarely had contact and seldom performed the same tasks; in other societies, men participated in tasks like infant care and women participated in tasks like hunting (Coltrane, 1988; Sanday, 1981).

Drawing on worldwide cross-cultural comparisons, scholars have identified two general patterns of fathers' family involvement, one intimate and the other aloof. In the intimate pattern, men eat and sleep with their wives and children, talk with them during evening meals, attend births, and participate actively in infant care. In the aloof pattern, men often eat and sleep apart from women, spend their leisure time in the company of other men, stay away during births, and seldom help with child care (Whiting & Whiting, 1975). Societies with involved fathers are more likely than societies with aloof fathers to be peaceful, to afford women a role in community decision making, to have intimate husband–wife relationships, to feature more gender equality in the society, and to include nurturing deities of both sexes in their religions. Aloof-father societies are more likely to have religious systems with stern male gods, social institutions that exclude women from community decision making, marriage systems in which husbands demand deference from wives, and public rituals that focus on men's competitive displays of masculinity (Coltrane, 1988, 1996; Sanday, 1981).

Research on fathering among indigenous peoples such as the African Aka suggests why involved fathering and gender egalitarianism are associated (Hewlett, 1991). Anthropologists such as Hewlett have drawn on Chodorow's (1974) work to suggest that when fathers are active in infant care, boys develop an intimate knowledge of masculinity, which makes them less likely to devalue the feminine, whereas when fathers are rarely around, boys lack a clear sense of masculinity and construct their identities in opposition to things feminine by devaluing and criticizing women (Hewlett, 2000). In reviews of data on father involvement over the past 120,000 years, Hewlett concluded that fathers contribute to their children in many ways, with the relative importance of different contributions varying dramatically, that different ecologies and modes of production have a substantial impact on the contributions of fathers to their children, and that fathers' roles today are relatively unique in human history (Hewlett, 1991, 2000).

HISTORICAL VARIATION

Historical studies have focused on practices in Europe and North America, chronicling and emphasizing men's public lives: work, political exploits, literary accomplishments, scientific discoveries, and heroic battles. This emphasis shows how various economic, political, and legal practices have structured privileges and obligations within and beyond families. For example, the historical concept of family in the West is derived from the Latin *famulus*, meaning servant, and the Roman *familia*, meaning the man's domestic property. Linking institutional arrangements with linguistic forms tells us something important about men's relationships to families. Recent historical studies have focused more directly on men's ideal and actual behaviors in families, thereby documenting complexity and diversity in past fathering practices (e.g., Griswold, 1993; Kimmel, 1996; LaRossa, 1997; Mintz, 1998; Pleck & Pleck, 1997).

Before these studies, many scholars erroneously assumed that changes in fatherhood were linear and progressive (Coltrane & Parke, 1998). For example, early family history emphasized that peasant families were extended and governed by stern patriarchs, whereas market societies produced nuclear families, companionate marriages, and involved fathers. In fact, historical patterns of fathering have responded to a complex array of social and economic forces, varying considerably across regions, time periods, and ethnic or cultural groups. Although it is useful to identify how men's work and production have shaped their public and private statuses, actual family relations have been diverse, and fatherhood ideals have followed different trajectories in different regions of the same country (Griswold, 1993; Mintz, 1998; Pleck & Pleck, 1997).

The economy of the 17th and 18th centuries in Europe and America was based on agriculture and productive family households. For families that owned farms or small artisan shops, their place of work was also their home. Slaves, indentured servants, and others were expected to work on family estates in return for food, a place to live, and sometimes other rewards. In this pattern of household or family-based production, men, women, and children worked together. Regional variations could be large, and fathers and mothers often did different types of work, but many tasks required for subsistence and family survival were interchangeable, and both mothers and fathers took responsibility for child care and training (Coltrane & Galt, 2000).

Because most men's work as farmers, artisans, and tradesmen occurred in the family household, fathers were a visible presence in their children's lives. Child rearing was a more collective enterprise than it is today, with family behaviors and attitudes ruled primarily by duty and obligation. Men introduced sons to farming or craft work within the household economy, oversaw the work of others, and were responsible for maintaining harmonious household relations. The preindustrial home was a system of control as well as a center of production, and both functions reinforced the father's authority (Griswold, 1993). Though mothers provided most direct care for infants and young children, men tended to be active in the training and tutoring of children. Because they were moral teachers and family heads, fathers were thought to have greater responsibility for and influence on children than mothers and were also generally held responsible for how the children acted outside the home (Pleck & Pleck, 1997).

Because the sentimental individualism of the modern era had not yet blossomed, emotional involvement with children in the Western world during the 17th and early 18th centuries was more limited than today. Prevailing images of children also were different from modern ideas about their innocence and purity. Religious teachings stressed the corrupt nature and evil dispositions of children, and fathers were admonished to demand strict obedience and use swift physical punishment to cleanse children of their sinful ways. Puritan fathers justified their extensive involvement in children's lives because women were seen as unfit to be disciplinarians, moral guides, or intellectual teachers. Griswold (1997) pointed out, however, that stern unaffectionate fathering, though not confined to Puritans, was not representative of all of the population. In fact, most American fathers attempted to shape and guide their children's characters, not break them or beat the devil out of them. As more privileged 18th-century fathers gained enough affluence to have some leisure time, many were affectionate with their children and delighted in playing with them (Griswold, 1997).

As market economies replaced home-based production in the 19th and 20th centuries, the middle-class father's position as household head and master and moral instructor of his children was slowly transformed. Men increasingly sought employment outside the home, and their direct contact with family members declined. As the wage labor economy developed, men's occupational achievement outside the household took on stronger moral overtones. Men came to be seen as fulfilling their family and civic duty, not by teaching and interacting with their children as before, but by supporting the family financially. The middle-class home, previously the site of production, consumption, and virtually everything else in life, became a nurturing, child-centered haven set apart from the impersonal world of work, politics, and other public pursuits. The separate-spheres ideal became a defining feature of the late 19th and early 20th centuries (Bernard, 1981; Coltrane & Galt, 2000; Kimmel, 1996).

The ideal that paid work was only for men and that only women were suited to care for family members remained an unattainable myth rather than an everyday reality for most families. Many working-class fathers were not able to earn the family wage assumed by the separate-spheres ideal, and a majority of African American, Latino, Asian American, and other immigrant men could not fulfill the good-provider role that the cultural ideal implied. Women in these families either had to work for wages, participate in production at home, or find other ways to make ends meet. Although the emerging romantic ideal held that women should be sensitive and pure keepers of the home on a full-time basis, the reality was that women in less advantaged households had

no choice but to simultaneously be workers and mothers. In fact, many working-class and ethnic minority women had to leave their homes and children to take care of other people's children and houses (Dill, 1988). Even during the heyday of separate spheres in the early 20th century, minority women, young single women, widows, and married women whose husbands could not support them worked for wages.

As noted above, attempts to understand the history of fatherhood have often painted a simple before-and-after picture: *Before* the Industrial Revolution, families were rural and extended, and patriarchal fathers were stern moralists, *after* the Industrial Revolution, families were urban and nuclear, and wage-earning fathers became companionate husbands, distant breadwinners, and occasional playmates to their children. This before-and-after picture captures something important about general shifts in work and family life, but its simple assumption of unidirectional linear change and its binary conceptualization contrasting men's patriarchal roles in the past with egalitarian roles in the present is misleading (Coontz, 1992). Stage models of family history have ignored the substantial regional and race/ethnic differences that encouraged different family patterns (Pleck & Pleck, 1997). For example, as most of the United States was undergoing industrialization, large pockets remained relatively untouched by it. The experience of white planters in the antebellum South was both like and unlike that of men in the commercial and industrial North (Griswold, 1993). Another major drawback of early historical studies is the tendency to overgeneralize for the entire society on the basis of the experience of the white middle class. Even during the heyday of separate spheres at the turn of the 20th century, minority and immigrant men were unlikely to be able to support a family. Race and class differences also intersect with regional differences: Not only did southern fathering practices differ from northern ones, but slave fathers and freedmen in the South had much different experiences than either group of white men (Griswold, 1993; McDaniel, 1994).

THE EMERGENCE OF MODERN FATHERING

Throughout the 20th century, calls for greater paternal involvement coexisted with the physical presence, but relative emotional and functional absence, of fathers (LaRossa, 1997). Nevertheless, some fathers have always reported high levels of involvement with their children. By the 1930s, even though mothers bore most of the responsibility for care of homes and families, three out of four American fathers said they regularly read magazine articles about child care, and nearly as many men as women were members of the PTA (Kimmel, 1996). Increases in women's labor force participation during the 1940s briefly challenged the ideal of separate family and work roles, but in the postwar era, high rates of marriage and low rates of employment reinforced the ideology of separate spheres for men and women. The ideal father at mid-century was seen as a good provider who "set a good table, provided a decent home, paid the mortgage, bought the shoes, and kept his children warmly clothed" (Bernard, 1981, pp. 3–4). As they had during the earlier Victorian era, middle-class women were expected to be consumed and fulfilled by wifely and motherly duties. With Ozzie and Harriet–style families as the 1950s model, women married earlier and had more children than any group of American women before them. Rapid expansion of the U.S. economy fueled a phenomenal growth of suburbs, and the consumer culture from that era idolized domestic life on radio and television. Isolated in suburban houses, many mothers now had almost sole responsibility for raising children, aided by occasional reference to expert guides from pediatricians and child psychologists (Hays, 1996). Fathers of the 1950s were also told to get involved with child care—but not *too* involved (Kimmel, 1996). The separate spheres of white middle-class men and women were thus maintained, though experts deemed them permeable enough for men to participate regularly as a helper to the mother (Coltrane & Galt, 2000; Hays, 1996).

During the mid-20th century, separate-spheres ideology and the popularity of Freud's ideas about mother–infant bonding led to widespread acceptance of concepts like *maternal deprivation*, and few researchers asked who besides mothers took care of children, although some researchers began to focus on *father absence* during the baby boom era (roughly 1946–64). Empirical studies and social theories valued the symbolic significance of fathers' breadwinning, discipline, and masculine role modeling, even though few studies controlled for social class or measured what fathers actually did with children. Studies including fathers found that they were more likely than mothers to engage in rough and tumble play and to give more attention to sons than daughters (Parke, 1996; Pleck, 1997). In general, research showed that child care was an ongoing and taken-for-granted task for mothers but a novel and fun distraction for fathers (Thompson & Walker, 1989).

Compared to the wholesome but distant good-provider fathers pictured on television programs like *Ozzie and Harriet* and *Father Knows Best* in the 1950s, a new father ideal gained prominence in the 1980s (Griswold, 1993). According to Furstenberg (1988), "[T]elevision, magazines, and movies herald the coming of the modern father—the nurturant, caring, and emotionally attuned parent. . . . Today's father is at least as adept at changing diapers as changing tires" (p. 193). No longer limited to being protectors and providers, fathers were pictured on television and in magazines as intimately involved in family life. Fatherhood proponents focused on the potential of the new ideals and practices (Biller, 1976), but researchers in the 1980s reported that many fathers resisted assuming responsibility for daily housework or child care (Thompson & Walker, 1989). Some researchers claimed that popular images far exceeded men's actual behaviors (LaRossa, 1988), and others suggested that men, on the whole, were less committed to families than they had been in the past (Ehrenreich, 1984). In the 1990s, researchers also began to examine how the modern ideal of the new father carried hidden messages about class and race, with some suggesting that the image of the sensitive and involved father was a new class/ethnic icon because it set middle-class fathers apart from working-class and ethnic minority fathers, who presented a more masculine image (Messner, 1993). Others suggested that the sensitive or androgynous parenting styles of new fathers might lead to gender identity confusion in sons (Blankenhorn, 1995).

MEASURING FATHER INVOLVEMENT

Before the 1980s, the rare researchers who included fathers focused on simple distinctions between father-present and father-absent families, finding that children from families with co-resident fathers generally fared better, on average, than those without co-resident fathers. Although the structural aspects of fatherhood (marriage, paternity, co-residence) sometimes correlate with various child and family outcomes, most researchers now agree that what fathers do with and for children is more important than co-residence or legal relationship to the mother and recommend that dichotomous measures (e.g., father presence/absence) be replaced by more nuanced ones.

The most influential refinement in fathering measurement was offered by Lamb, Pleck, Charnov, and Levine (1987), who suggested three components: (a) interaction, the father's direct contact with his child through caregiving and shared activities; (b) availability (or accessibility), a related concept concerning the father's potential availability for interaction, by virtue of being accessible to the child (whether or not direct interaction is occurring); and (c) responsibility, the role the father takes in ascertaining that the child is taken care of and in arranging for resources to be available for the child. Within each of these categories, two further distinctions should be made. First, it is critical to distinguish the amount from the quality of involvement. Both are important to child development and parental well-being (Parke, 1996). Second, absolute as well as relative (in relation to partner) indices of involvement are independent and may affect children and adults in different ways (Pleck, 1997).

A recent tabulation of father involvement assessment in 15 large social science family data sets showed that all but one measured father "presence/absence," with most also measuring some aspects of fathers' "availability," "teaching," "monitoring," or "affection." About half measured the fathers' "communication" or "emotional support," only a few measured "thought processes" (e.g., worrying, dreaming) or "planning" (e.g., birthdays, vacations, friend visits), and none measured "sharing interests" (e.g., providing for instruction, reading together) or "child maintenance" (e.g., cleaning or cooking for the child) (Federal Interagency Forum, 1998, pp. 144; Palkovitz, 1997, pp. 209–210). Structural availability is thus the most common fathering indicator, with various routine parent–child interactions and support activities sometimes assessed, and with fathers' planning and responsibility rarely measured. In addition, many studies collect fathering data from just one reporter, even though self-reports of fathers' involvement tend to be higher than mothers' reports of fathers' involvement, especially for nonresident fathers (Coley & Morris, 2002; Smock & Manning, 1997).

LEVELS AND PREDICTORS OF FATHERS' INVOLVEMENT

Research on fathering in two-parent households shows a noticeable and statistically significant increase in men's parenting involvement, both in absolute terms and in relation to mothers. Simultaneously, however, average levels of fathers' interaction with, availability to, and responsibility for children lag well behind those of mothers (Marsiglio, Amato, Day, & Lamb, 2000; Parke, 1996; Pleck & Masciadrelli, 2003). Measurement strategies vary, with time-use diaries generally producing the most accurate estimates of fathers' interaction and availability. On average, in the 1960s to early-1980s, fathers interacted with their children about a third as much as mothers and were available about half as much as mothers (Lamb et al., 1987). During the mid-1980s to early-1990s, the average co-resident father interacted about two fifths as much as mothers and was available to his children almost two thirds as much (Pleck, 1997). In the late 1990s, he was available to his children about three fourths as much as mothers, interacting on weekdays about two thirds as often, but over four fifths as much on weekends (Pleck & Masciadrelli, 2003; Yueng, Sandberg, Davis-Kean, & Hofferth, 2001). In an estimated 20% of two-parent families, men are now about as involved as mothers interacting with and being available to their children. At the same time, in most families, fathers share much less of the responsibility for the planning, scheduling, emotional management, housework, and other maintenance activities associated with raising children (Deutsch, 1999; Hochschild, 1989).

Researchers have begun to isolate the effects of income, race/ethnicity, education, family structure, marriage, employment, work schedules, and other factors on father involvement, though results are often incomplete or contradictory. For example, the relation between socioeconomic status and father involvement is complex. Income is often found to be positively correlated with father involvement among various ethnic groups (Fagan, 1998; Parke, 1996). Relative income contributions by wives are also associated with higher proportionate levels of father involvement in housework and child care (Coltrane, 2000; Yueng et al., 2001), though some studies still find that financially dependent husbands do less domestic work than others (Brines, 1994). Wealthier men do little routine family work, but the amount their wives do varies dramatically, with higher-earning wives more likely to purchase domestic services (e.g., child care, house cleaning, laundry) (Cohen, 1998; Oropesa, 1993).

Although most contemporary studies of fathering have been based on white, middle-class, two-parent families, we are beginning to get a more complete picture about similarities and differences across family types. When financial stability is hard to achieve, fathers only minimally involved with their children may nevertheless see themselves as "good fathers" because they work hard to provide financially. Because of inequities in the labor market, men of color are disproportionately likely to face difficulties being adequate providers (Bowman & Sanders, 1998; Hamer & Marchioro, 2002). Comparisons between white, African American, and Latino fathers suggest

similar levels of involvement with infants and similar styles of engagement with young children (e.g., proportionately more play and less caretaking than mothers, Coltrane, Parke, & Adams, 2001; Toth & Xu, 1999). Contrary to cultural stereotypes, some research also shows that Latino fathers are more likely than their European American counterparts to spend time in shared activities with children, to perform housework and personal care, and to engage in monitoring and supervising children's activities (Coltrane et al., 2001; Toth & Xu, 1999; Yueng et al., 2001). Results for African American fathers in two-parent households are mixed, with most reporting levels of father–child interaction comparable to other race/ethnic groups, and several studies finding that black men do more housework than white men, net of other predictors (Ahmeduzzaman & Roopnarine, 1992; Broman, 1991; Hossain & Roopnarine, 1993; John & Shelton, 1997), and that nonresident black fathers contribute more to children than nonresident white fathers (Wilson, Tolson, Hinton, & Kiernan, 1990). Studies of African American and Latino fathers reveal a wide range of behaviors across families, depending on employment, income, education, gender and religious ideology, family structure, marital status, age of children, immigration status, neighborhood context, cultural traditions, and presence of extended or fictive kin, and a similar pattern of association between social contextual variables and levels and styles of paternal participation (Auerbach, Silverstein, & Zizi, 1997; Cabrera, Tamis-LeMonda, Bradley, Hofferth, & Lamb, 2000; Hossain & Roopnarine, 1993; Hunter & Davis, 1994; Padgett, 1997; Pleck & Steuve, 2001; Silverstein, 2002).

Fathers tend to spend more time with young children than they do with older children and adolescents, probably because younger children require more attention and care, even though many men feel more comfortable interacting with older children. Most research finds that a father's availability (as determined by work hours) is a strong predictor of his involvement in child care. When mothers of preschool children are employed, a father's time availability predicts whether he will serve as a primary caregiver (Brayfield, 1995; Casper & O'Connell, 1998). Fathers and mothers with non-overlapping work shifts are the most likely to share child care (Presser, 1995). When mothers of school-aged children are employed more hours, their husbands tend to do a greater portion of the child care and housework, and fathers tend to be more involved to the extent that they view their wives' career prospects more positively (Pleck, 1997). For instance, Brewster (2000) found that fathers in the late 1980s and 1990s were likely to use non-working discretionary hours for child care, whereas in the late 1970s and early 1980s they tended to use those hours for other activities.

As demonstrated in comprehensive reviews (Pleck, 1997; Pleck & Masciadrelli, 2003), father involvement is multiply determined, with no single factor responsible for the different types of involvement. In addition, studies often report contradictory effects of factors like income, education, age, family size, and birth timing. One of the most consistent findings is that men are more involved with sons than with daughters (Harris, Furstenberg, & Marmer, 1998; Harris & Morgan, 1991; Marsiglio, 1991; McBride, Schoppe, & Rane, 2002), especially with older children (Pleck, 1997). However, some recent studies have found no differences in father involvement by sex of child (Fagan, 1998; Hofferth, 2003), leading Pleck and Masciadrelli (2003) to suggest that fathers' preference for sons may be weakening. Some researchers also find that if fathers get involved during pregnancy or early infancy they tend to sustain that involvement later in children's lives (Coltrane, 1996; Parke, 1996).

Lamb, Pleck, and colleagues suggested that for fathers to become actively involved, they required four facilitating factors: (a) motivation, (b) skills and self-confidence, (c) social approval, and (d) institutional support (Lamb et al., 1987, see also Pleck, 1997). Many studies find that fathers are more involved and show more warmth if they believe in gender equality (Cabrera et al., 2000; Hofferth, 1998), though others find no significant association (Marsiglio, 1991; Pleck, 1997). Others find that fathers get more involved when they have a strong

fatherhood identity or actively embrace the father role (Beitel & Parke, 1998; Hawkins, Christiansen, Sargent, & Hill, 1993; Pasley, Ihinger-Tallman, & Buehler, 1993; Rane & McBride, 2000; Snarey, 1993). In general, fathers feel more competent as parents when they are more involved with their children, though it is difficult to say whether this competence is a precursor or a result of active fathering (Beitel & Parke, 1998; McHale & Huston, 1984). Evidence suggesting that competence leads to involvement comes from interventions designed to develop fathers' parenting skills (e.g., Cowan & Cowan, 2000; McBride, 1990). In terms of social support, fathers tend to be more involved when the children's mothers facilitate it, when the mothers had positive relationships with their own fathers when they were children (Allen & Hawkins, 1999; Cowan & Cowan, 2000; McBride & Mills, 1993; Parke, 1996), and when kin and other community members support father involvement (Pleck, 1997). Finally, institutional supports can include factors such as fewer work hours and more flexible work schedules (Pleck, 1993).

Another approach to identifying predictors of father involvement is based on a process model of parenting (Belsky, 1984; McBride et al., 2002). This framework suggests that fathering is shaped by three categories of influence: (a) characteristics of the father (e.g., personality, attitudes toward child rearing), (b) characteristics of the child (e.g., temperament, age, gender), and (c) contextual sources of stress and support (e.g., marital relationships, social support networks, occupational experiences). Many of these facilitating influences overlap with factors in the Lamb and Pleck model, but this approach also includes consideration of things like child temperament and parental stress. Emergent findings suggest that child temperament or other characteristics may have a larger influence on father–child involvement than mother–child involvement, probably because fathering is seen as more discretionary than mothering (Cabrera et al., 2000; McBride et al., 2002).

The nature of the marital relationship is also associated with paternal involvement, though causality is sometimes difficult to assess. Some find that greater marital satisfaction leads to greater father involvement (Parke, 1996), and others suggest that higher levels of men's relative contributions to child care lead to women's greater marital satisfaction (Brennan, Barnett, & Gareis, 2001; Ozer, Barnett, Brennan, & Sperling, 1998). In addition, satisfaction with men's levels of family involvement appears to be strongly related to mothers' and fathers' gender ideals and expectations. We cannot simply assume that more father involvement is better for all families. As the emerging gatekeeping literature (e.g., Allen & Hawkins, 1999; Beitel & Parke, 1998) attests, too much involvement by fathers can be interpreted as interference rather than helpfulness. In general, if family members want a father to be more involved, his participation has positive effects on family functioning. If family members feel that fathers should not change diapers or do laundry, then such practices can cause stress (Coltrane, 1996).

THE POTENTIAL INFLUENCE OF FATHERS

As scholars pay more attention to fathers, they are beginning to understand what influence their involvement might have on child development. Most researchers find that father–child relationships are influential for children's future life chances (Federal Interagency Forum, 1998; Parke, 1996; Pleck & Masciadrelli, 2003). The focus of this research tends to be on the positive aspects of fathers' involvement, though it should be noted that because men are more likely than women to abuse children or to use inappropriate parenting techniques, increased male involvement can lead to increased risk and negative outcomes for children, particularly if the father figure does not have a long-term relationship with the mother (Finkelhor, Hotaling, Lewis, & Smith, 1990; Margolin, 1992; National Research Council, 1993; Radhakrishna, Bou-Saada, Hunter, Catellier, & Kotch, 2001).

Many researchers continue to focus on fathers' economic contributions to children and report that fathers' resources improve children's life chances. Longitudinal research shows that children from one-parent households (usually mother headed) are at greater risk for negative adult outcomes (e.g., lower educational and occupational achievement, earlier childbirth, school dropout, health problems, behavioral difficulties) than those from two-parent families (Marsiglio et al., 2000; McLanahan & Sandefur, 1994). Although comparisons between children of divorced parents and those from first-marriage families show more problems in the former group, differences between the two are generally small across various outcome measures and do not necessarily isolate the influence of divorce or of father involvement (Crockett, Eggebeen, & Hawkins, 1993; Furstenberg & Harris, 1993; Seltzer, 1994). For children with nonresident fathers, the amount of fathers' earnings (especially the amount that is actually transferred to children) is a significant predictor of children's well-being, including school grades and behavior problems (Amato & Gilbreth, 1999; McLanahan, Seltzer, Hanson, & Thomson, 1994; Marsiglio et al., 2000). Because the great majority of children from single-parent homes turn out to be happy, healthy, and productive adults, debates continue about how such large-group comparisons should be made and how we should interpret their results in terms of fathers' economic or social contributions (Amato, 2000; Coltrane & Adams, 2003).

Earlier reviews suggested that the level of father involvement has a smaller direct effect on infant attachment than the quality or style of father interaction, though time spent parenting is also related to competence (Lamb et al., 1987; Marsiglio et al., 2000). Preschool children with fathers who perform 40% or more of the within-family child care show more cognitive competence, more internal locus of control, more empathy, and less gender stereotyping than preschool children with less involved fathers (Lamb et al., 1987; Pleck, 1997). Adolescents with involved fathers are more likely to have positive developmental outcomes such as self-control, self-esteem, life skills, and social competence, provided that the father is not authoritarian or overly controlling (Mosley & Thomson, 1994; Pleck &

Masciadrelli, 2003). Studies examining differences between the presence of biological fathers versus other father figures suggest that it is the quality of the father–child relationship rather than biological relationship that enhances the cognitive and emotional development of children (Dubowitz et al., 2001; Hofferth & Anderson, 2003; Silverstein & Auerbach, 1999). Reports of greater father involvement when children were growing up have also been associated with positive aspects of adult children's educational attainment, relationship quality, and career success (Amato & Booth, 1997; Harris et al., 1998; Nock, 1998; Snarey, 1993). Because of methodological inadequacies in previous studies such as not controlling for maternal involvement, most scholars recommend more carefully controlled studies using random samples and multirater longitudinal designs, as well as advocating caution in interpreting associations between fathering and positive child outcomes (Amato & Rivera, 1999; Parke, 1996; Pleck & Masciadrelli, 2003). It will take some time to isolate the specific influence of fathers as against the influence of mothers and other social-contextual factors such as income, education, schools, neighborhoods, communities, kin networks, and cultural ideals.

We do know that when fathers share child care and housework with their wives, employed mothers escape total responsibility for family work, evaluate the division of labor as more fair, are less depressed, and enjoy higher levels of marital satisfaction (Brennan et al., 2001; Coltrane, 2000; Deutsch, 1999). When men care for young children on a regular basis, they emphasize verbal interaction, notice and use more subtle cues, and treat sons and daughters similarly, rather than focusing on play, giving orders, and sex-typing children (Coltrane, 1996; 1998; Parke, 1996). These styles of father involvement have been found to encourage less gender stereotyping among young adults and to encourage independence in daughters and emotional sensitivity in sons. Most researchers agree that these are worthy goals that could contribute to reducing sexism, promoting gender equity, and curbing violence against women (but see Blankenhorn, 1995).

DEMOGRAPHIC CONTEXTS FOR FATHER INVOLVEMENT

As Furstenberg (1988) first noted, conflicting images of fathers are common in popular culture, with nurturing, involved "good dads" contrasted with "bad dads" who do not marry the mother of their children or who move out and fail to pay child support. Recent research suggests that both types of fathers are on the rise and that the demographic contexts for fatherhood have changed significantly over the past few decades. In many industrialized countries, at the same time that some fathers are taking a more active role in their children's lives, growing numbers of men rarely see their children and do not support them financially. In the United States, for example, single-parent households are increasing, with only about half of U.S. children eligible for child support from nonresident parents via court order, and only about half of those receive the full amount (Scoon-Rogers, 1999). Both trends in fatherhood—toward more direct involvement and toward less contact and financial support—are responses to the same underlying social developments, including women's rising labor force participation and the increasingly optional nature of marriage.

Marriage rates have fallen in the past few decades, with people waiting longer to get married and increasingly living together without marrying. Women are having fewer children than they did just a few decades ago, waiting longer to have them, and not necessarily marrying before they give birth (Eggebeen, 2002; Seltzer, 2000). One of three births in the United States is to an unmarried woman, a rate that is three times higher than it was in the 1960s, with rates for African American women highest, followed by Latinas, and then non-Hispanic whites (National Center for Health Statistics, 2000). It is often assumed that nonmarital births produce fatherless children, but recent studies show that most of the increase in nonmarital childbearing from the 1980s to the 1990s is accounted for by the increase in the number of cohabiting women getting pregnant and carrying the baby to term without getting married. Historically, if an unmarried woman became pregnant, she would marry to legitimate the birth. Today, only a minority of women do so.

In addition, an increasingly large number of American fathers live apart from their children because of separation or divorce. Because most divorcing men do not seek (or are not awarded) child custody following divorce, the number of divorced men who are uninvolved fathers has risen (Eggebeen, 2002; Furstenberg & Cherlin, 1991), although recent research shows that the actual involvement of fathers with children after divorce varies enormously, sometimes without regard to official postdivorce court orders (Braver, 1998; Hetherington & Stanley-Hagan, 1999; McLanahan & Sandefur, 1994; Seltzer, 1998). The number of men with joint physical (residential) custody has grown, though joint legal (decision-making) custody is still a more common postdivorce parenting arrangement (Maccoby & Mnookin, 1992; Seltzer, 1998). And although single-father households have increased in recent years, single-mother households continue to outpace them five to one. Demographers suggest that because of all these trends, younger cohorts will be less likely to experience sustained involved fathering than the generations that immediately preceded them (Eggebeen, 2002).

Marriage and the traditional assumption of fatherhood have become more fragile, in part because an increasing number of men face financial difficulties. Although men continue to earn about 30% higher wages than women, their real wages (adjusted for inflation) have declined since the early 1970s, whereas women's have increased (Bernstein & Mishel, 1997). As the U.S. economy has shifted from heavy reliance on domestic manufacturing to global interdependence within an information and service economy, working-class men's prospects of earning a family wage have declined. At the same time, women's labor force participation has risen steadily, with future growth in the economy predicted in the areas where women are traditionally concentrated (e.g., service, information, health care, part-time work). The historical significance of this shift cannot be overestimated. For most of the 19th

and 20th centuries, American women's life chances were determined by their marriage decisions. Unable to own property, vote, or be legally independent in most states, daughters were dependent on fathers and wives were dependent on their husbands for economic survival. Such dependencies shaped family relations and produced fatherhood ideals and practices predicated on male family headship. As women and mothers have gained independence by entering the labor force in record numbers, it is not surprising that older ideals about marriage to a man legitimating childbearing have been challenged.

GENDER AND THE POLITICS OF FATHERHOOD

In the 1990s, popular books and articles revived a research and policy focus that had been popular in the 1960s: father absence. For example, Popenoe (1996) suggested that drug and alcohol abuse, juvenile delinquency, teenage pregnancy, violent crime, and child poverty were the result of fatherlessness and that American society was in decline because it had abandoned traditional marriage and child-rearing patterns. Such claims about father absence often rely on evolutionary psychology and sociobiology and define fathers as categorically different from mothers (Blankenhorn, 1995; Popenoe, 1996). Even some proponents of nurturing fathers warn men against trying to act too much like mothers (Pruett, 1993). Following this reasoning, some argue for gender-differentiated parenting measurement strategies: "[T]he roles of father and mother are different and complementary rather than interchangeable and thus the standards for evaluating the role performance of fathers and mothers should be different" (Day & Mackey, 1989, p. 402). Some label the use of measures developed on mothers to study fathers and the practice of comparing fathers' and mothers' parenting as the *deficit model* (Doherty, 1991) or the *role inadequacy perspective* (Hawkins & Dollahite, 1997).

Because parenting is a learned behavior for both men and women, most social scientists focus on the societal conditions that create gender differences in parenting or find proximate social causes of paternal investment that outweigh assumed biological causes (e.g., Hofferth & Anderson, 2003). Nevertheless, questioning taken-for-granted cultural ideals about families can cause controversy. When Silverstein and Auerbach (1999) challenged assertions about essential differences between fathers and mothers in an *American Psychologist* article entitled "Deconstructing the Essential Father," they received widespread public and academic criticism. Their scholarly article (based on a review of research findings) was ridiculed as "silliness" and "junk science" by Wade Horn (1999; formerly of the National Fatherhood Initiative and now Assistant Secretary in the U.S. Department of Health and Human Services), and the U.S. House of Representatives debated whether to pass a resolution condemning the article (Silverstein, 2002). Clearly, debates about fathers, marriage, and family values carry symbolic meanings that transcend scientific findings. The contentious political and scholarly debates about fathers that emerged in the 1990s appear to be framed by an older political dichotomy. Conservatives tend to focus on biological parenting differences and stress the importance of male headship and breadwinning, respect for authority, and moral leadership (Blankenhorn, 1995; Popenoe, 1996), whereas liberals tend to focus on similarities between mothers and fathers and stress the importance of employment, social services, and possibilities for more equal marital relations (Coontz, 1992; Silverstein & Auerbach, 1999; Stacey, 1996).

A full analysis of contemporary family values debates is beyond the scope of this chapter, but elsewhere I analyze marriage and fatherhood movements using data and theories about political opportunities, resource mobilization, and the moral framing of social issues (Coltrane, 2001; Coltrane & Adams, 2003, see also Gavanas, 2002). In general, cultural tensions in the larger society are mirrored in policy proposals and academic debates about the appropriate roles of fathers and the importance of marriage. One cannot adjudicate among various scholarly approaches to fathering without acknowledging gendered interests and understanding the political economy of expert knowledge production.

Recent policies and programs promoting marriage and fatherhood using faith-based organizations are designed to advance a particular vision of fatherhood. Whether they will benefit the majority of American mothers and children is a question that cannot be resolved without more sophisticated research with controls for mothers' parenting and various other economic and social-contextual issues (Marsiglio et al., 2000; Marsiglio & Pleck, in press).

PROSPECTS FOR THE FUTURE

The forces that are driving changes in fathers' involvement in families are likely to continue. In two-parent households (both married and cohabiting), men share more family work if their female partners are employed more hours, earn more money, and have more education. All three of these trends in women's attainment are likely to continue for the foreseeable future. Similarly, fathers share more family work when they are employed fewer hours and their wives earn a greater portion of the family income. Labor market and economic trends for these variables are also expected to continue for several decades. Couples also share more when they believe that family work should be shared and that men and women should have equal rights. According to national opinion polls, although the country has become slightly more conservative about marriage and divorce than it was in the 1970s and 1980s, the belief in gender equality continues to gain acceptance among both men and women. In addition, American women are waiting longer, on average, to marry and give birth, and they are having fewer children—additional factors sometimes associated with more sharing of housework and child care. Thus, I predict that increasing economic parity and more equal gender relations will allow women to buy out of some domestic obligations and/or recruit their partners to do more. Middle- and upper-class wives and mothers will rely on working-class and immigrant women to provide domestic services (nannies, housekeepers, child care workers, fast food employees, etc.), thereby reducing their own hours of family labor but simultaneously perpetuating race, class, and gender hierarchies in the labor market and in the society. Some fathers in dual-earner households will increase their contributions to family work, whereas others will perform a greater proportion of housework and child care by virtue of their wives' doing less. Other men will remain marginal to family life because they do not stay connected to the mothers of their children, do not hold jobs allowing them to support their children, or do not seek custody or make regular child support payments. These two ideal types—of involved and marginalized fathers—are likely to continue to coexist in the popular culture and in actual practice.

The context in which American couples negotiate fathering has definitely changed. The future is likely to bring more demands on fathers to be active parents if they want to stay involved with the mothers of their children. For fathers to assume more responsibility for active parenting, it may be necessary to change cultural assumptions that men are entitled to domestic services and that women are inherently predisposed to provide them. Further changes in fathering are likely to be driven by women's increasing independence and earning power. Ironically, women's enhanced economic position also makes them able to form families and raise children without the fathers being present. In the future, men will be even less able to rely on their superior earning power and the institution of fatherhood to maintain their connection to families and children. Increasingly, they will need to adopt different fathering styles to meet specific family circumstances and to commit to doing things men have not been accustomed to doing. Some men will be able to maintain their economic and emotional commitments to their children, whereas others will not. Some men will participate in all aspects of child rearing, whereas others will hardly see their children. Unless living wages and adequate social supports are developed for all fathers (as well as for mothers and children), we can expect that the paradoxes, contradictions, and dilemmas associated with fathering described in this chapter will continue for the foreseeable future.

AUTHOR'S NOTE

This chapter incorporates some material from a November 21, 2002, National Council on Family Relations (NCFR) Annual Conference Special Session "Future Prospects for Increasing Father Involvement in Child Rearing and Household Activities," reprinted as "The Paradox of Fatherhood: Predicting the Future of Men's Family Involvement" in *Vision 2003* (Minneapolis, MN: NCFR/Allen Press). I thank Marilyn Coleman, Lawrence Ganong, Joseph Pleck, Carl Auerbach, and two anonymous reviewers for valuable feedback on an earlier draft of this chapter.

REFERENCES

Ahmeduzzaman, M., & Roopnarine, J. L. (1992). Sociodemographic factors, functioning style, social support, and fathers' involvement with preschoolers in African American intact families. *Journal of Marriage and the Family, 54*, 699–707.

Allen, S. M., & Hawkins, A. J. (1999). Maternal gatekeeping. *Journal of Marriage and the Family, 61*, 199–212.

Amato, P. (2000). Diversity within single-parent families. In D. H. Demo, K. R. Allen, & M. A. Fine (Eds.), *Handbook of family diversity* (pp. 149–172). New York: Oxford University Press.

Amato, P., & Booth, A. (1997). *A generation at risk: Growing up in an era of family upheaval.* Cambridge, MA: Harvard University Press.

Amato, P., & Gilbreth, J. (1999). Nonresident fathers and children's well-being: A meta-analysis. *Journal of Marriage and the Family, 61*, 557–573.

Amato, P., & Rivera, F. (1999). Paternal involvement and children's behavior problems. *Journal of Marriage and the Family, 61*, 375–384.

Auerbach, C., Silverstein, L., & Zizi, M. (1997). The evolving structure of fatherhood. *Journal of African American Men, 2*, 59–85.

Beitel, A. H., & Parke, R. D. (1998). Paternal involvement in infancy: The role of maternal and paternal attitudes. *Journal of Family Psychology, 12*, 268–288.

Belsky, J. (1984). The determinants of parenting. *Child Development, 55*, 83–96.

Bernard, J. (1981). The good provider role: Its rise and fall. *American Psychologist, 36*, 1–12.

Bernstein, J., & Mishel, L. (1997). Has wage inequality stopped growing? *Monthly Labor Review, 120*, 3–17.

Biller, H. B. (1976). The father and personality development. In M. E. Lamb (Ed.), *The role of the father in child development*. New York: John Wiley.

Blankenhorn, D. (1995). *Fatherless America*. New York: Basic Books.

Bowman, P. J., & Sanders, R. (1998). Unmarried African American fathers. *Journal of Comparative Family Studies, 29*, 39–56.

Braver, S. L. (1998). *Divorced dads*. New York: Jeremy Tarcher/Putnam.

Brayfield, A. (1995). Juggling jobs and kids. *Journal of Marriage and the Family, 57*, 321–332.

Brennan, R. T., Barnett, R. C., & Gareis, K. C. (2001). When she earns more than he does: A longitudinal study of dual-earner couples. *Journal of Marriage and Family, 63*, 168–182.

Brewster, K. L. (2000, March). *Contextualizing change in fathers' participation in child care*. Paper presented at "Work and Family" Conference, San Francisco.

Brines, J. (1994). Economic dependency, gender, and the division of labor at home. *American Journal of Sociology, 100*, 652–688.

Broman, L. L. (1991). Gender, work, family roles, and psychological well-being of blacks. *Journal of Marriage and the Family, 53*, 509–520.

Cabrera, N., Tamis-LeMonda, C., Bradley, R., Hofferth, S., & Lamb, M. (2000). Fatherhood in the 21st century. *Child Development, 71*, 127–136.

Casper, L. M., & O'Connell, M. (1998). Work, income, the economy, and married fathers as child-care providers. *Demography, 35*, 243–250.

Chodorow, N. (1974). Family structure and feminine personality. In M. Z. Rosaldo & L. Lamphere (Eds.), *Woman, culture and society* (pp. 43–66). Palo Alto, CA: Stanford University Press.

Cohen, P. N. (1998). Replacing housework in the service economy: Gender, class, and race-ethnicity in service spending. *Gender and Society, 12*, 219–231.

Coley, R. L., & Morris, J. E. (2002). Comparing father and mother reports of father involvement among low-income minority families. *Journal of Marriage and the Family, 64*, 982–997.

Coltrane, S. (1988). Father-child relationships and the status of women. *American Journal of Sociology, 93*, 1060–1095.

Coltrane, S. (1996). *Family man*. New York: Oxford University Press.

Coltrane, S. (1998). *Gender and families*. Newbury Park, CA: Pine Forge/Alta Mira.

Coltrane, S. (2000). Research on household labor. *Journal of Marriage and the Family, 62*, 1209–1233.

Coltrane, S. (2001). Marketing the marriage "solution." *Sociological Perspectives, 44*, 387–422.

Coltrane, S., & Adams, M. (2003). The social construction of the divorce "problem": Morality, child victims, and the politics of gender. *Family Relations, 52*, 21–30.

Coltrane, S., & Collins, R. (2001). *Sociology of marriage and the family* (5th ed.). Belmont, CA: Wadsworth/ Thomson Learning.

Coltrane, S., & Galt, J. (2000). The history of men's caring. In M. H. Meyer (Ed.), *Care work: Gender, labor, and welfare states* (pp. 15–36). New York: Routledge.

Coltrane, S., & Parke, R. D. (1998). *Reinventing fatherhood: Toward an historical understanding of continuity and change in men's family lives* (WP 98-12A). Philadelphia: National Center on Fathers and Families.

Coltrane, S., Parke, R. D., & Adams, M. (2001, April). *Shared parenting in Mexican-American and European-American families*. Paper presented at the biennial meeting of the Society for Research in Child Development, Minneapolis, MN.

Coontz, S. (1992). *The way we never were*. New York: Basic Books.

Cowan, C. P., & Cowan, P. A. (2000). *When partners become parents*. Mahwah, NJ: Lawrence Erlbaum.

Crockett, L. J., Eggebeen, D. J., & Hawkins, A. J. (1993). Fathers' presence and young children's behavioral and cognitive adjustment. *Journal of Family Issues, 14*, 355–377.

Day, R. D., & Mackey, W. C. (1989). An alternate standard for evaluating American fathers. *Journal of Family Issues, 10*, 401–408.

Deutsch, F. (1999). *Halving it all*. Cambridge, MA: Harvard University Press.

Dill, B. T. (1988). Our mother's grief: Racial ethnic women and the maintenance of families. *Journal of Family History, 13*, 415–431.

Doherty, W. J. (1991). Beyond reactivity and the deficit model of manhood. *Journal of Marital and Family Therapy, 17*, 29–32.

Dubowitz, H., Black, M. M., Cox, C. E., Kerr, M. A., Litrownik, A. J., Radhakrishna, A., English, D. J., Schneider, M. W., & Runyan, D K. (2001). Father involvement and children's functioning at age 6 years: A multisite study. *Child Maltreatment, 6*, 300–309.

Eggebeen, D. (2002). The changing course of fatherhood. *Journal of Family Issues, 23*, 486–506.

Ehrenreich, B. (1984). *The hearts of men.* Garden City, NY: Anchor Press/Doubleday.

Fagan, J. A. (1998). Correlates of low-income African American and Puerto Rican fathers' involvement with their children. *Journal of Black Psychology, 3*, 351–367.

Federal Interagency Forum on Child and Family Statistics. (1998). Report of the Working Group on Conceptualizing Male Parenting (Marsiglio, Day, Evans, Lamb, Braver, & Peters). In *Nurturing fatherhood* (pp. 101–174). Washington, DC: Government Printing Office.

Finkelhor, D., Hotaling, G., Lewis, I., & Smith, C. (1990). Sexual abuse in a national survey of adult men and women. *Child Abuse and Neglect, 14*, 19–28.

Furstenberg, F. F. (1988) Good dads—bad dads. In A. Cherlin (Ed.), *The changing American family and public policy* (pp. 193–218). Washington, DC: Urban Institute Press.

Furstenberg, F. F., & Cherlin, A. (1991). *Divided families.* Cambridge, MA: Harvard University Press.

Furstenberg, F. F., & Harris, K. (1993). When and why fathers matter. In R. Lerman & T. Ooms (Eds.), *Young unwed fathers* (pp. 150–176). Philadelphia: Temple University Press.

Gavanas, A. (2002). The fatherhood responsibility movement. In B. Hobson (Ed.), *Making men into fathers* (pp. 213–242). New York: Cambridge University Press.

Griswold, R. L. (1993). *Fatherhood in America: A history.* New York: Basic Books.

Griswold, R. L. (1997). Generative fathering: A historical perspective. In A. J. Hawkins & D. Dollahite (Eds.), *Generative fathering* (pp. 71–86). Thousand Oaks, CA: Sage.

Hamer, J., & Marchioro, K. (2002). Becoming custodial dads: Exploring parenting among low-income and working-class African American fathers. *Journal of Marriage and the Family, 64*, 116–129.

Harris, K. H., Furstenberg, F. F., & Marmer, J. K. (1998). Paternal involvement with adolescents in intact families. *Demography, 35*, 201–216.

Harris, K. H., & Morgan, S. P. (1991). Fathers, sons and daughters: Differential paternal involvement in parenting. *Journal of Marriage and the Family, 53*, 531–544.

Hawkins, A. J., Christiansen, S. L., Sargent, K. P., & Hill, E. J. (1993). Rethinking fathers' involvement in child care. *Journal of Family Issues, 14*, 531–549.

Hawkins, A. J., & Dollahite, D. C. (1997). Beyond the role-inadequacy perspective of fathering. In A. J. Hawkins & D. C. Dollahite (Eds.), *Generative fathering: Beyond deficit perspectives* (pp. 3–16). Thousand Oaks, CA: Sage.

Hays, S. (1996). *The cultural contradictions of motherhood.* New Haven, CT: Yale University Press.

Hetherington, E. M., & Stanley-Hagan, M. M. (1999). Stepfamilies. In M. E. Lamb (Ed.), *Parenting and child development in "nontraditional" families* (pp. 137–159). Mahwah, NJ: Lawrence Erlbaum.

Hewlett, B. S. (1991). *The nature and context of Aka pygmy paternal infant care.* Ann Arbor: University of Michigan Press.

Hewlett, B. S. (2000). Culture, history, and sex: Anthropological contributions to conceptualizing father involvement. *Marriage and Family Review, 29*, 59–73.

Hochschild, A. R. (1989). *The second shift.* New York: Viking.

Hofferth, S. L. (1998). *Healthy environments, healthy children: Children in families.* Ann Arbor: Institute for Social Research, University of Michigan.

Hofferth, S. L. (2003). Race/ethnic differences in father involvement in two-parent families: Culture, context, or economy? *Journal of Family Issues, 24*, 185–216.

Hofferth, S. L., & Anderson, K. G. (2003). Are all dads equal? Biology versus marriage as a basis for paternal investment. *Journal of Marriage and the Family, 65*, 213–232.

Horn, W. (1999). Lunacy 101: Questioning the need for fathers. Retrieved April 29, 2003, from the Smart Marriages Web site: http://listarchives.his.com/smartmarriages/smartmarriages.9907/msg00011.html.

Hossain, Z., & Roopnarine, J. L. (1993). Division of household labor and child care in dual-earner African-American families with infants. *Sex Roles, 29*, 571–583.

Hunter, A. G., & Davis, J. E. (1994). Hidden voices of black men: The meaning, structure, and complexity of manhood. *Journal of Black Studies, 25*, 20–40.

John, D., & Shelton, B. A. (1997). The production of gender among black and white women and men: The case of household labor. *Sex Roles, 36*, 171–193.

Johnson, M. (1988). *Strong mothers, weak wives.* Berkeley: University of California Press.

Kimmel, M. (1996). *Manhood in America: A cultural history.* New York: Free Press.

Lamb, M. E., Pleck, J., Charnov, E., & Levine, J. (1987). A biosocial perspective on parental behavior and involvement. In J. B. Lancaster, J. Altman, & A. Rossi (Eds.), *Parenting across the lifespan* (pp. 11–42). New York: Academic Press.

LaRossa, R. (1988). Fatherhood and social change. *Family Relations, 37,* 451–457.

LaRossa, R. (1997). *The modernization of fatherhood: A social and political history.* Chicago: University of Chicago Press.

Maccoby, E., & Mnookin, R. (1992). *Dividing the child.* Cambridge, MA: Harvard University Press.

Margolin, L. (1992). Child abuse by mother's boyfriends. *Child Abuse and Neglect, 16,* 541–551.

Marsiglio, W. (1991). Paternal engagement activities with minor children. *Journal of Marriage and the Family, 53,* 973–986.

Marsiglio, W., Amato, P., Day, R. D., & Lamb, M. E. (2000). Scholarship on fatherhood in the 1990s and beyond. *Journal of Marriage and the Family, 62,* 1173–1191.

Marsiglio, W., & Pleck, J. H. (in press). Fatherhood and masculinities. In R W Connell, J Hearn, & M. Kimmel (Eds.), *The handbook of studies on men and masculinities.* Thousand Oaks, CA: Sage.

McBride, B. A. (1990). The effects of a parent education/play group program on father involvement on child rearing. *Family Relations, 39,* 250–256.

McBride, B. A., & Mills, G. (1993). A comparison of mother and father involvement with their preschool age children. *Early Childhood Research Quarterly, 8,* 457–477.

McBride, B. A., Schoppe, S., & Rane, T. (2002). Child characteristics, parenting stress, and parental involvement: Fathers versus mothers. *Journal of Marriage and the Family, 64,* 998–1011.

McDaniel, A. (1994). Historical racial differences in living arrangements of children. *Journal of Family History, 19,* 57–77.

McHale, S. M., & Huston, T. L. (1984). Men and women as parents: Sex role orientations, employment, and parental roles with infants. *Child Development, 55,* 1349–1361.

McLanahan, S., & Sandefur, G. (1994). *Growing up with a single parent: What hurts, what helps.* Cambridge, MA: Harvard University Press.

McLanahan, S., Seltzer, J., Hanson, T., & Thomson, E. (1994). Child support enforcement and child well-being. In I. Garfinkel, S. S. McLanahan, & P. K. Robins (Eds.), *Child support and child well-being* (pp. 285–316). Washington, DC: Urban Institute.

Messner, M. (1993) "Changing men" and feminist politics in the U.S. *Theory and Society, 22,* 723–737.

Mintz, S. (1998). From patriarchy to androgyny and other myths. In A. Booth & A. C. Crouter (Eds.), *Men in families* (pp. 3–30). Mahweh, NJ: Lawrence Erlbaum.

Mosley, J., & Thomson, E. (1994). Fathering behavior and child outcomes. In W. Marsiglio (Ed.), *Fatherhood* (pp. 148–165). Thousand Oaks, CA: Sage.

National Center for Health Statistics. (2000, January). Nonmarital birth rates, 1940–1999. Retrieved on April 29, 2003, from the Centers for Disease Control and Prevention Web site: www.cdc.gov/nchs/data/nvsr/nvsr48.

National Research Council. (1993). *Understanding child abuse and neglect.* Washington, DC: National Academy Press.

Nock, S. (1998). *Marriage in men's lives.* New York: Oxford University Press.

Oropesa, R. S. (1993). Using the service economy to relieve the double burden: Female labor force participation and service purchases. *Journal of Family Issues, 14,* 438–473.

Ozer, E. M., Barnett, R. C., Brennan, R. T., & Sperling, J. (1998). Does childcare involvement increase or decrease distress among dual-earner couples? *Women's Health: Research on Gender, Behavior, and Policy, 4,* 285–311.

Padgett, D. L. (1997). The contribution of support networks to household labor in African American families. *Journal of Family Issues, 18,* 227–250.

Palkovitz, R. (1997). Reconstructing "involvement." In A. Hawkins & D. Dollahite (Eds.), *Generative fathering* (pp. 200–216). Thousand Oaks, CA: Sage.

Parke, R. D. (1996). *Fatherhood.* Cambridge, MA: Harvard University Press.

Pasley, K., Ihinger-Tallman, M., & Buehler, C. (1993). Developing a middle-range theory of father involvement postdivorce. *Journal of Family Issues, 14,* 550–576.

Pleck, E. H., & Pleck, J. H. (1997). Fatherhood ideals in the United States: Historical dimensions. In M. E. Lamb (Ed.), *The role of the father in child development* (3rd ed., pp. 33–48). New York: John Wiley.

Pleck, J. H. (1993). Are "family-supportive" employer policies relevant to men? In J. C. Hood (Ed.), *Men, work, and family* (pp. 217–237). Newbury Park, CA: Sage.

Pleck, J. H. (1997). Paternal involvement: Levels, sources, and consequences. In M. E. Lamb (Ed.), *The role of the father in child development* (3rd ed., pp. 66–103). New York: John Wiley.

Pleck, J. H., & Masciadrelli, B. P. (2003). Paternal involvement: Levels, sources, and consequences. In M. E. Lamb (Ed.), *The role of the father in child development* (4th ed). New York: John Wiley.

Pleck, J. H., & Steuve, J. L. (2001). Time and paternal involvement. In K. Daly (Ed.), *Minding the time in family experience* (pp. 205–226). Oxford, UK: Elsevier.

Popenoe, D. (1996). *Life without father: Compelling new evidence that fatherhood and marriage are indispensable for the good of children and society.* New York: Free Press.

Presser, H. B. (1995). Job, family and gender. *Demography, 32*, 577–598.

Pruett, K. D. (1993). The paternal presence. *Families in Society, 74*, 46–50.

Radhakrishna, A., Bou-Saada, I. E., Hunter, W. M., Catellier, D. J., & Kotch, J. B. (2001). Are father surrogates a risk factor for child maltreatment? *Child Maltreatment, 6*, 281–289.

Rane, T. R., & McBride, B. A. (2000). Identity theory as a guide to understanding father's involvement with their children. *Journal of Family Issues, 21*, 347–366.

Sanday, P. R. (1981). *Female power and male dominance.* New York: Cambridge University Press.

Scoon-Rogers, L. (1999). Child support for custodial mothers and fathers. *Current Population Reports*, P60–196. Washington, DC: US Bureau of the Census.

Seltzer, J. A. (1994). Consequences of marital dissolution for children. *Annual Review of Sociology, 20*, 235–266.

Seltzer, J. A. (1998). Father by law: Effects of joint legal custody on nonresident fathers' involvement with children. *Demography, 35*, 135–146.

Seltzer, J. A. (2000). Families formed outside of marriage. *Journal of Marriage and the Family, 62*, 1247–1268.

Silverstein, L. B. (2002). Fathers and families. In J. McHale & W. Grolnick (Eds.), *Retrospect and prospect in the psychological study of fathers* (pp. 35–64). Mahwah, NJ: Lawrence Erlbaum.

Silverstein, L. B., & Auerbach, C. F. (1999). Deconstructing the essential father. *American Psychologist, 54*, 397–407.

Smock, P., & Manning, W. (1997). Nonresident parents' characteristics and child support. *Journal of Marriage and the Family, 59*, 798–808.

Snarey, J. (1993). *How fathers care for the next generation.* Cambridge, MA: Harvard University Press.

Stacey, J. (1996). *In the name of the family.* Boston: Beacon.

Thompson, L., & Walker, A. J. (1989). Gender in families: Women and men in marriage, work, and parenthood. *Journal of Marriage and the Family, 51*, 845–871.

Toth, J. F., & Xu, X. (1999). Ethnic and cultural diversity in fathers' involvement: A racial/ethnic comparison of African American, Hispanic, and white fathers. *Youth and Society, 31*, 76–99.

Whiting, J., & Whiting, B. (1975). Aloofness and intimacy of husbands and wives. *Ethos, 3*, 183–207.

Wilson, M. N., Tolson, T. F. J., Hinton, I. D., & Kiernan, M. (1990). Flexibility and sharing of childcare duties in black families. *Sex Roles, 22*, 409–425.

Yueng, W. J., Sandberg, J. F., Davis-Kean, P. E., & Hofferth, S. L. (2001). Children's time with fathers in intact families. *Journal of Marriage and Family 63*, 136–154.

CRUISING TO FAMILYLAND: GAY HYPERGAMY AND RAINBOW KINSHIP

Judith Stacey

> *Promiscuity was rampant because in an all-male-subculture there was no one to say 'no'*
> *—no moderating role like that a woman plays in the heterosexual milieu. (Shilts, 1987)*
>
> *Because men are naturally promiscuous, two men will stick together as naturally as the two*
> *north poles of a magnet. (Davis and Phillips, 1999)*
>
> *There is room for both monogamous gay couples and sex pigs in the same big tent of gay*
> *community. (Rofes, 1998: 221)*

Does masculine sexuality threaten bourgeois family and social order? Scholars, critics and activists who hold incommensurate ideological and theoretical views about gender, family and sexuality, nonetheless seem to share the belief that it does. To religious and social conservatives, gay male sexual culture signifies masculine libido incarnate, the dangerous antithesis of family and community. "In the Christian right imagination," as Arlene Stein points out, "homosexuals represent undisciplined male sexuality, freed of the 'civilizing' influence of women" (Stein, 2001: 107). "Untrammeled homosexuality can take over and destroy a social system," warns Paul Cameron, a leading anti-gay ideologue in the US. Indeed, Cameron unwittingly hints that sexual jealousy, marital frustration and not-so-latent homoerotic desire propel his hostility to homosexuality when he concedes that:

> Marital sex tends toward the boring end. Generally, it doesn't deliver the kind of sheer sexual

Judith Stacey, "Cruising to Familyland: Gay Hypergamy and Rainbow Kinship." *Current Sociology*, March 2004, 52(2): 181–197. Reprinted by permission of SAGE Publications, Inc.

pleasure that homosexual sex does. The evidence is that men do a better job on men, and women on women, if all you are looking for is orgasm. (Quoted in Dreyfuss, 1999)

Quite a few mainstream gay male leaders, like the late journalist and AIDS victim Randy Shilts, agree that gay male sexual culture, which legitimates pursuit of recreational sex with an unlimited number of partners as an end in itself, represents the dangerous excesses of *masculine* sexuality. In *And the Band Played On*, Shilts charged unfettered masculine sexuality with escalating the epidemic spread of AIDS. In his view, gay baths, bars and cruising grounds serve masculine, rather than specifically homoerotic male desires: "Some heterosexual males confided that they were enthralled with the idea of the immediate, available, even anonymous sex a bathhouse offered, if they could only find women who would agree. Gay men, of course, agreed quite frequently" (Shilts, 1987: 89). Similarly, pessimistic assessments of undomesticated masculinity that undergird the views of reactionary antifeminists, like George Gilder (1986), echo in the discourse of mainstream gay men. For example, "the conservative case for gay marriage" that neo-conservative gay journalist Andrew Sullivan puts forth maintains that:

> . . . the discipline of domesticity, of shared duties and lives, of the inevitable give-and-take of cohabitation and love with anyone, even of the same sex, tends to benefit men more than the option of constant, free-wheeling, etiolating bachelorhood. (Sullivan, 1997: 151)

Right-wing opponents of same-sex marriage endorse the diagnosis that masculine eros is anti-social, but reject the remedy Sullivan proposes as insufficient and naive. Thus, the scornful second extract at the start of this article by Britain's moralistic *Daily Mail* columnist Melanie Phillips concludes: "It is not marriage which domesticates men—it is women" (Davis and Phillips, 1999: 17).

Writing from an antithetical ideological perspective, the late gay sociologist Martin Levine likewise interpreted gay male cruising culture as an arena of hypermasculinity, where men operate free of the restraints that negotiating with women imposes on heterosexual men:

> . . . without the "constraining" effects of feminine erotic standards, gay men were able to focus more overtly and obviously on the sexual activities in finding sexual partners. . . . Cruising, in this sense, is a most masculine of pastimes. Gay men were simply more honest—and certainly more obvious—about it. (Levine, 1998: 79–80)

Likewise, queer theorists, such as Michael Warner (1999), who also hold political and sexual values quite hostile to those of Andrew Sullivan as well as to the right-wing authors quoted above, nonetheless share Sullivan's view (or, in Warner's case, fear) that the contemporary gay rush to the altar and the nursery will erode the liberatory, transgressive character of queer sexual culture. Gays who have succumbed to what comedian Kate Clinton terms "mad vow disease," Warner charges, fail to recognize that "marriage has become the central legitimating institution by which the state penetrates the sexuality of its subjects; it is the 'zone of privacy' outside which sex is unprotected" (Warner, 1999: 128). Critics on all sides take gay male sexual culture to be a potent source of oppositional values and cultural resistance.

In short, sexual radicals and conservatives converge in viewing gay male sexual norms and practices as a realm of unadulterated masculine desire that is subversive to bourgeois domesticity and committed family ties. "If you isolate sexuality as something solely for one's own personal amusement," Paul Cameron warns, "and all you want is the most satisfying orgasm you can get—and that is what homosexuality seems to be—then homosexuality seems too powerful to resist" (quoted in Dreyfuss, 1999).

Yet, *is* orgasm, or even carnal pleasure, all that gay men are looking for when they cruise? And, more to the point, is that all they find? In this article, I draw from ethnographic research I conducted on gay male intimacy and kinship in Los Angeles to challenge these widely shared assumptions. Gay male cruising culture, I suggest, yields social and familial consequences far more complex and contradictory than most critics (or even a few fans) seem to imagine. The gay cruising arena of unencumbered, recreational sex certainly does disrupt conventional family norms and practices. At the same time, however, it also generates bonds of kinship and domesticity. Gay male sexual cruising serves, I suggest, as an underappreciated cultural resource for the creative construction of those "families of choice" (Weston, 1991; Weeks et al., 2001) and "invincible communities" (Nardi, 1999) that scholars have identified as the distinctive character of non-heterosexual family and kinship formations. In particular, the unfettered pursuit of masculine sexuality facilitates opportunities for individual social mobility and for forging rainbow kinship ties that have not yet attracted much attention from scholars or activists.

GAY "EL LAY"

Los Angeles is home to the second largest, and likely the most socially diverse, yet comparatively understudied population of gay men on the planet.

Arguably no city better symbolizes sexual excess, consumer culture and the antithesis of family values, and perhaps no population more so than the gay male denizens who crowd the bars, beats and boutiques of West Hollywood. To many observers, numerous gay men among them, "Weho" culture particularly signifies gay male decadence in situ, the epitome of the sexual culture that both Andrew Sullivan and Paul Cameron denounce. Cursory contact with gay culture in Los Angeles readily reinforces stereotypes about gay men's narcissistic preoccupation with erotic allure. Advertisements for corporeal beautification and modification flood the pages, airwaves and websites of the local gay male press: familiar and exotic cosmetic surgery and body sculpture procedures, including penile, buttock and pec implants; liposuction; laser resurfacing; hair removal or extensions; cosmetic dentistry; personal trainers and gym rat regimens; tattooing and tattoo removal; body piercing; hair coloring, growing and styling; tinted contact lenses; manicures, pedicures and body waxing; as well as color, style and fashion consultants and the commodified universe of couture, cosmetics and personal grooming implements that they service.

Nonetheless, conducting local field research on gay men's intimate affiliations from 1999 to 2003, I encountered tinker toys as often as tinsel. Los Angeles might well be the cosmetic surgery capital of "planet out," but much less predictably, the celluloid metropolis is also at the vanguard of gay fatherhood. Organized groups of "Gay Fathers" and of "Gay Parents" formed in the city as early as the mid-1970s and contributed to the genesis of Family Pride, Incorporated, currently among the leading national grassroots organizations of its kind anywhere (Miller, 2001: 226–9). Los Angeles also gave birth to Growing Generations, the world's first and only gay-owned, assisted reproduction agency founded to serve an international gay clientele.[1] Several of its first clients were among nine families who in 1998 organized the PopLuckClub (PLC), a pioneering local support group for gay fathers and their children.[2]

The thriving PLC sponsors monthly gatherings, organizes special events and provides information, referrals, support and community to a membership that now includes nearly 200 families of varying shapes, sizes, colors and forms. A PLC subgroup of at-home dads and their children meet weekly for a play-date and lunch in a West Hollywood playground; single gay dads and "prospective SGDs" seeking "to meet others who understand how parenting affects our lives" hold monthly mixers that feature "friendly folks, scintillating snacks, and brilliant banter—about the best brand of diapers!" (PLC listserv, 2003), and additional PLC focus groups, for prospective gay dads or adoptive dads, for example, as well as satellite chapters in neighboring counties continually emerge.

Between June 1999 and June 2003, I conducted field research in the greater Los Angeles area that included lengthy multisession, family life history interviews with 50 self-identified gay men born between 1958 and 1973 and with members of their designated kin, as well as within their community groups, religious institutions and organizations, like the PLC. My primary subjects came of age and came out after the Stonewall era of gay liberation and after the AIDS crisis was widely recognized. Popular discourses about safe sex, the gayby boom, gay marriage, domestic partnerships and "families we choose" informed their sense of familial prospects. This is the first cohort of gay men young enough to be able to contemplate parenthood outside heterosexuality and mature enough to be in a position to choose or reject it. The men and their families include diverse racial, ethnic, geographic, religious and social class backgrounds.[3] They also practice varied relational and residential options. My research sample included 16 gay men who were single at the time of my study; 31 who were coupled, some in open relationships, others monogamous, most of whom cohabited, but several who did not; and a committed, sexually exclusive, trio. It included men who reside or parent alone, with friends, lovers, former lovers, biological, legal and adopted kin, and children of every "conceivable" origin.[4] More than a few of these men cruised their way to several genres of gay hypergamy and to unconventional forms of rainbow kinship.

CRUISING TO KINSHIP: CASE STUDIES

In anthropological terminology, hypergamy designates a marriage system in which women, but not men, may "marry up" the social status ladder. In the classic situation, lower rank kin groups trade on the youth, beauty and fertility of their daughters in efforts to marry them (and thereby the fortunes of their natal families) to older, wealthier, often less attractive men from higher ranking families. Modern western residues of this preindustrial patriarchal pattern persist, of course, as the fact that there is a dictionary entry for "trophy wife" (but none for "trophy husband") underscores: "An attractive, young wife married to a usually older, affluent man" (*The American Heritage® Dictionary of the English Language*, 2000). The more pejorative and even more sexist definition for "gold-digger" ("a woman who seeks money and expensive gifts from men") reveals that heterosexual women still can barter youth, beauty and erotic appeal (and sometimes even fertility) for intimate affiliations with older men with greater economic, cultural and social resources (*The American Heritage® Dictionary of the English Language*, 2000).

TWO RAINBOW FAMILIES

And so can some gay men. Cruising culture, combined with the greater fluidity of gay male gender conventions, allows gay men to engage more frequently than is common in intimate encounters that cross conventional social borders. While the majority of these may be fleeting and anonymous, the sheer volume of gay erotic exchanges outside the customary bounds of public scrutiny and social segregation provides opportunities to form more enduring socially heterogeneous attachments. Brief sketches of two cases from my field research illustrate how gay men can cruise their way to creative, multicultural permutations of hypergamous kinship.

Ozzie and Harry—A Gay Pygmalion Fable[5]

Ozzie, Harry and their two young children, a picture-perfect, affluent, adoring nuclear family who own an elegant, spacious Spanish home, represent an utterly improbable, gay fairy-tale romance of love, marriage and the baby-carriage. A transracial, transnational, cross-class, interfaith couple who have been together eight years, Ozzie and Harry claim to have fallen in love at first sight on a Roman street in 1995. Harry, then 31 years old and a prosperous, white, Jewish, New England ivy-league educated, successful literary agent, was vacationing in Europe when he spotted and cruised 24-year-old Ozzie on a crowded street. Talented but undereducated, a Catholic Afro-Brazilian raised in an impoverished single-mother family, Ozzie had migrated to Italy several years earlier as a guest worker.

Although the lovers met by cruising, they both claim to have fallen in love instantly. Ozzie says he told Harry that he loved him that very first night: "I just knew. I just told him what I felt." They report sharing all of their "hopes and dreams" from the moment they met, and preeminent among these was the desire to have children: "When we first met we talked about everything," Harry recalled:

> . . . and all of our dreams, and one of them was to have a family and what it meant to be gay, you know, if we were together, and what we would be giving up potentially, what the sacrifices might be; and so that was one of the things that was going to be a potential sacrifice was not being able to have children.

"Me too," Ozzie interjected. "I always knew I wanted to have children." "But we talked about how we didn't think it was possible to have them together," Harry continued. "We both talked about how it was a dream that we both had, and that it was kind of something that we thought we might have to forsake together."

The new lovers plunged headlong into a deeply romantic, intense, committed, monogamous love affair that seems only to have deepened after nearly a decade of bourgeois domesticity. After a year of transatlantic (and translinguistic) courtship, Harry sponsored his beloved's immigration to the US, financed Ozzie's education in computer technology and vocal music, and assisted his rapid acquisition of fluency in English and bourgeois cultural habitus, all domains in which Ozzie proved gifted. After the couple celebrated their union with an interfaith commitment ceremony in 1998, they had dinner with a gay couple who had recently become fathers through surrogacy. "It was all kind of Kismet," Harry recalled. "They told us about their two sons, and we kind of admitted that it was something we fantasized about." Inspired by this example, Ozzie and Harry contacted Growing Generations and decided immediately to engage a "traditional" surrogate[6] in order to realize the dream of fatherhood that they had feared they would have to sacrifice on the altar of gay love. The agency successfully matched them with a white woman who has since borne them two babies—first a white daughter conceived with Harry's sperm, and three years later, a biracial, genetic half-sister, conceived with Ozzie's.

No gay union in my study encapsulates a more dramatic example of successful hypergamy, or one that transcends a wider array of social structural inequalities and cultural differences than the bond between Ozzie and Harry. Formally, the younger, buff and beautiful Ozzie occupies a disadvantaged position across a staggering number of social divisions and cultural resources—including income, wealth, education, occupation, race, nation, language, citizenship, not to mention access to the ongoing support of his natal world of kin, long-term friendship, community and culture. Moreover, because the co-parents share a strong prejudice against hired childcare, Ozzie has become a full-time, at-home parent and economically dependent on Harry, to boot. "We don't use babysitters at all," Harry boasted, as he burped their first infant daughter during my initial visit. "We don't want any nannies, babysitters, nothing," he emphasized, espousing a childrearing credo few contemporary mothers in the West could contemplate affording, even if they were to desire it:

Nothing, NOTHING. We don't believe in it. No baby nurse, nothing. Just us; and one of us always will be with her. If you wait this long to do this. We're mature adults. I mean I'm 38. I have no dreams left, other than being a good dad and a good mate for my Ozzie.

"The same with me," Ozzie volunteered, draping both arms around his spouse with adoration. Initially, Harry had stayed home several months blissfully caring for their first newborn while Ozzie was employed. However, because Harry commands far greater earning power, he decided that it was in his family's interest that he resume the breadwinner role. He has supported Ozzie as full-time, at-home parent ever since.

Nonetheless, despite forms of structural inequity glaring enough to make Betty Friedan's (1963) critique of the feminine mystique seem tepid, this is no transvestite version of the male-dominant, female-dependent, breadwinner–homemaker patriarchal bargain of the 1950s' modern family. Defying all sociological odds, Ozzie seems to enjoy substantive and emotional parity with Harry both as partner and parent. In deference to Ozzie's jealous, possessive wishes, Harry relinquished friendships with his former lovers. Harry regards his breadwinner role to be a sacrificial burden rather than a creative outlet or source of status and power: "I hate work," Harry maintains "It's a necessary evil." He conducts as much of his professional work from home as he can in order to participate as fully as possible in the hands-on burdens and blessings of early parenting—diapering, feeding, dressing, toilet-training, bathing, along with playing, reading, cuddling, educating, cajoling, consoling, disciplining and chauffeuring. Indeed, not only does Harry dread the unavoidable business trips that periodically separate him from his children and spouse, he seems genuinely to envy Ozzie's uninterrupted quotidian contact with the children. "I don't need to make my mark," Harry claims. "There's nothing else I need to accomplish. So that's the most important job [being a parent and mate] I have which is why it's a real conflict." What's more, Harry has voluntarily relinquished the weighty patriarchal power of the purse by taking legal measures to fully share all property, as well as child custody of both daughters, with Ozzie. Few heterosexual marriages—whether hypergamous or homogamous—share resources, responsibilities, or romance so fully or harmoniously as these two seem to do.

Mother Randolph and His Foundling Boys

Dino, an 18-year-old, fresh "wetback," Salvadoran immigrant, was waiting at a bus stop in 1984 when a 45-year-old Anglo entertainment lawyer with a taste for young Latino men cruised by and picked him up. Discovering that his gregarious, sexy, young trick was homeless and unemployed, the lawyer brought Dino home to live and keep house for him for several weeks. There the eager youth began to acquire the mores and mentors, along with the mistakes, from which he has since built his life as an undocumented immigrant among chosen kin in gay L.A.

Among the mentors, Randolph eventually proved to be the most significant. Now in his mid-sixties, Randolph is a cultivated, but bawdy, financially secure and generous, former interior designer recently disabled by post-polio syndrome. Much earlier, Randolph had met his life partner of 17 years while cruising in a "stand-up sex club." Ten years into the committed, but sexually open, relationship that ensued, Randolph's lover shocked him by choosing to undergo male-to-female sex reassignment surgery. Randolph was traumatized, and the couple's relationship foundered. After a year-long separation and his lover's successful transition from male to female, however, Randolph recognized that his love for the person transcended his strong homoerotic sexual preference, and so the couple reunited. Paradoxically, this gender and sexual upheaval compelled Randolph to perform a semblance of the life of heterosexual masculinity that he had renounced as inauthentic, at considerable risk, but to his great relief, a full decade before the Stonewall rebellion.

Several years after her surgical transformation, however, Randolph's lover was diagnosed with AIDS, a cruel legacy of her prior life as a sexually active gay man. By then too, Randolph's post-polio syndrome symptoms had begun to emerge, and he lacked the physical ability to take care of his lover, or of himself. Blessed with ample financial, social and spiritual resources, Randolph gradually assembled a rainbow household staff of five gay men, who have come to regard him and each other as family.

Chance encounters through sexual cruising generated many of these relationships, as it had the union between Randolph and his lover. A former employee of Randolph's met Dino at a gay bar in 1993 and introduced him to his benefactor. By then Dino had been diagnosed as HIV-positive and was drinking heavily. Randolph has a long history and penchant for rescuing gay "lost boys," and so he hired Dino to serve as his household's primary live-in cook and manager. Now sober, grateful and devoted, Dino remains asymptomatic thanks to the health care that Randolph purchases for him. Dino resides at Randolph's Mondays through Fridays and spends weekends with his lover of five years, a 50-something, Anglo dental hygienist who cruised him at a Gay Pride parade. Dino's lover pays him weekly overnight conjugal visits in Randolph's household and also participates in the holiday feasts that Dino prepares for Randolph's expansive, extended, hired and chosen family.

Randolph employs three additional men who work staggered shifts as physical attendant, practical nurse and chauffeur, and a fourth as part-time gardener and general handyman. The day nurses are Mikey, a 23-year-old, white former street hustler and drug abuser, and Ricardo, the newest of Mikey's three roommates in another multicultural and intergenerational gay male household. The devoutly Catholic Ricardo, who is also 20-something, is a recent illegal Mexican immigrant still struggling with religious guilt over his homosexual desires. Randolph's night nurse, Bernard, is a married, closeted, bisexual African-American man in his fifties with whom Randolph used to enjoy casual sex. Finally, Randolph employs his friend Lawrence as his gardener, a white gay man now in his late forties and also HIV-positive, with whom Randolph has been close ever since they hooked up in a San Diego tea room more than three decades ago.

Randolph refers to Dino and his day nurses parentally as his "boys." "Well, I'm their father and their mother," he explains. Since Randolph's lover died in 1999, "these boys are certainly the most important family that I have these days. They mean more to me, and *for* me than anyone else." From his wheelchair-throne, "Mother Randolph," as he parodically identifies himself, presides with love, wit, wisdom and, it must be acknowledged, financial control, as well as responsibility, over a multicultural, mutually dependent, elastically extended, chosen family somewhat reminiscent of the black drag houses immortalized in the documentary *Paris Is Burning* (1990, directed by Jennie Livingston). Few of these intimate attachments remain erotic. However, a serendipitous series of hypergamous sexual encounters initiated most of the creative kin ties in this expansive rainbow "family of man."

THE GAY FAMILY CRUISE

Most advocates and opponents of gay, recreational sexual cruising culture, whether straight or gay, believe it threatens mainstream "family values." To be sure, gay male cruising directly challenges norms of heteronormativity, monogamy and premarital chastity. Indeed, unless the pure pursuit of sexual pleasure is culturally sanctioned, in the face of "marital boredom," as Paul Cameron warns, "it seems too powerful to resist" and is often threatening to secure and stable intimate attachments. In fact, for reasons like these, a sizable constituency of gay men find sexual transgression to be as disturbing and threatening as does mainstream heterosexual culture. Although Ozzie and Harry met by cruising, they, along with many men "in the family," practice sexual exclusivity and strongly disapprove of polyamory and recreational sex. These more sexually conservative family values appear to be particularly prevalent among gay men who are fathers, among the religiously observant, and the generation of gay men who came of age in the period immediately following discovery of the AIDS virus.

However, as my field research illustrates, the gay male arena of sexual sport also spawns less obvious, more productive effects on intimacy and kinship. Sexual cruising, as we have seen, initiates lasting familial ties more than is commonly recognized. Anonymous erotic encounters occasionally yield fairly conventional forms of love and "marriage." "Sexual encounters are often pursued as a route to more long-term, committed, emotional relationships," as Weeks et al. (2001: 144) observe. "Particularly for some men who are not in a couple relationship, casual sexual relationships can offer the potential for meeting the 'right' person." Or, as a gay friend of mine puts it more humorously, "Sex can be a great icebreaker." Randolph, as we have seen, cruised his deceased mate, Dino met his current lover, and even the implausibly idyllic, romantic, monogamous union and nuclear family formed by Harry and Ozzie commenced on a sexual cruise. Many other interviewees also reported histories of long-term relationships initiated through anonymous sexual encounters.[7]

Within what Giddens (1992) has termed the modern western "transformation of intimacy," the search for everlasting "confluent love" occupies a status akin to a religious quest. Just as Puritans who subscribed to the Protestant ethic took material success to signify their spiritual salvation, so do many believers in the "pure relationship" seek its earthly signs in the appearance of instantaneous erotic "chemistry." Syndicated gay sex advice columnist-provocateur Dan Savage endorses this comparatively mainstream family cruise route with uncharacteristic sentimentality:

> Desire brought my boyfriend and me together. And it's simple desire that brings most couples, gay or straight, together. Responsibly acted on, this desire is a good thing in and of itself, and it can often lead to other good things. Like strong, healthy families. (Savage, 2003)

Momentary sexual adventures also yield more innovative genres of "healthy" family life. Anonymous gay sexual encounters do not ordinarily lead to conjugal coupling, but not infrequently they commence enduring friendships that evolve into kin-like ties, whether or not sexual interest continues. Through such side-effects of casual sex, Randolph met his close friend and gardener; Dino acquired, at first temporary, and later his long-term lodging, employment and familial support; and Mikey repeatedly found refuge from Hollywood's mean streets. Thus, even when a gay man ostensibly *is* "only looking for the most satisfying orgasm" he can get, sexual cruising allows him to find a whole lot more. "Some people like the sport of chasing somebody and seeing if they can get them," Mother Randolph acknowledged. "For some people the game is worth more than the candle. My interest is specifically in the candle." When I asked Randolph, however, whether an orgasm constituted the candle, he quickly identified more enduring embers:

> Yes, and also the love-making, if it was that sort of situation. If I had a guy home in bed, I was big on foreplay and all of that. In fact, often I didn't want my partner to go home after fucking. I often liked them to stay over. And a lot of my sexual partners became eventual friends. Mr. Baldwin [the gardener] over there at the sink being one of them.

A venerable gay history of cruising to kinship and community long antedated the contemporary popularity of gay family discourse. Even in the first two decades of the 20th century, as George Chauncey's (1994) prize-winning historical study, *Gay New York*, copiously documents, gay men frequented bars and bathhouses seeking not only quick sexual encounters, but also because they "formed more elaborate social relationships with the men they met there, and came to depend on them in a variety of ways." Chauncey draws on the extensive diaries of Charles Tomlinson Griffes, a successful early 20th-century composer who:

> . . . was drawn into the gay world by the baths not just because he had sex there, but because he met men there who helped him find apartments and otherwise make his way through the city, who appreciated his music, who gave him new insights into his character, and who became his good friends. (Chauncey, 1994: 224)

Thus, socially heterogeneous intimate affiliations (whether long-term or more ephemeral) are among the underappreciated byproducts of gay cruising grounds. Thanks in part to this arena of sexual sport, interracial intimacy occurs far more frequently in the gay world, and particularly among gay men, than in heterosexual society. US census data indicate this contrast, even though, because they only tabulate co-residential couples who elected to self-identify as same-sex partners, they vastly understate the degree of both gay and interracial intimacy in the US. In 1990, the first time the US census form allowed co-residing, same-sex partners to declare their couple status, 14.6 percent of those who did so were interracial pairs, compared with only 5.1 percent of married heterosexual couples. In the 2000 Census, 15.3 percent of declared same-sex male couples and 12.6 percent of lesbians compared with 7.4 percent of married and 15 percent of unmarried heterosexual pairs bridged racial differences.[8] The percentage of interracial pairs in my nonrepresentative sample was substantially higher, a product, most likely, of my decision to stratify in order to encompass broad racial and social diversity. Of 31 men in my sample who identified themselves as coupled at the time of the interviews, 14 were paired with someone of a different race.[9]

One of the provocative byproducts of sexual cruising culture is the greater access to social mobility that it offers gay men from subordinate social classes, races and cultural milieux than their straight siblings and peers enjoy.[10] In the unvarnished prose of William J. Mann (1997), an established gay writer in the US, "the dick dock in Provincetown is a great equalizer. I've watched my share of condo owners suck off their share of houseboys." While it is likely that only a small percentage of those "houseboys" garner more than a quickly lit "candle" from these encounters, these nonetheless represent a social mobility opportunity very few of their non-gay peers enjoy. Marveling over his personal meteoric rise from working-class origins in a small factory town, Mann reflects:

> "*How the hell did you ever wind up here, kid?*" I've asked myself time and again . . . how did I

end up sharing a house in the tony west end of Provincetown every summer for the entire summer, year after year? It's simple: I'm gay. Had I not been gay—had I been my brother, for example—I would never have discovered the access that led me to a different place. (Mann, 1997: 221)

Both Mann and his brother attended the same state university near their hometown. "But only *I* ventured into a world my parents had never known. Had I not been a gay kid," Mann recognizes, "I would never have been invited into that world." A visiting gay lecturer, for example, took the youthful Mann to dinner and later introduced him to prominent writers, and to a gay world: "I met people, I read books, I listened to speeches" (Mann, 1997: 221).

Ozzie, Dino, Mikey and Ricardo are among 10 of the 50 gay men in my study who have traversed even greater social, geographic, economic and cultural distances, all beneficiaries of what I am choosing to call gay hypergamy. But for its gender composition, the Cinderella fairy-tale character of Ozzie's marriage to Harry, represents hypergamy in nearly the classic anthropological sense of marrying up through an exchange of beauty and youth for cultural status and material resources. In no way do I mean to imply that Ozzie or Harry intentionally deployed strategic, let alone manipulative, bartering tactics in this exchange. By the same token, I do not believe that most contemporary, hypergamous, heterosexual marriages involve the cynical exploitation or motives connoted by terms like "gold-digger" or "trophy wife." Rather, I aim to highlight some unrecognized gender and social effects of the asymmetrical exchanges of sex appeal for status that represent the contemporary cultural residue of patriarchal hypergamy.

Expanding the concept somewhat, gay hypergamy can be used to designate even relatively brief and informal intimate affiliations between exotic, erotic youth and older men with greater material resources and cultural capital. Cruising on the "dick dock" in Provincetown, in the baths of old New York, at a bus stop in Los Angeles, and at beats, cottages, tea rooms and ports of call around the world (see, for example, Altman, 2001; Dowsett, 1996) allows for more democratic social mixing and matching and greater opportunities for upward mobility than heterosexual society generally offers. Whether or not the "candle" ignites a satisfying orgasm, it can melt social barriers—as icebreakers are meant to do—and thereby expand the bonds of kinship, as in the rainbow family ties between Mother Randolph and his adopted, and hired, "boys." In this respect, the world of sexual sport resembles athletic sport, which also provides some ghetto male youth opportunities for social mobility and cross-racial bonds, but because sexual sport is simultaneously more intimate and unregulated, it is also far more socially transgressive.[11]

It turns out that gay male "promiscuity" is not as inherently antithetical to healthy, committed, or even to comparatively conventional, family values, as its critics and some of its champions imagine. However, gay men who breach sexual norms often find themselves challenging social divides as well, cruising their way into hypergamous intimate attachments and a social rainbow of kinship bonds. The culture of unbridled masculine sexuality represents no utopian arena of egalitarian, liberated "sexual citizenship." Hypergamous, erotic exchanges among gay men that cross racial, generational and social class boundaries can yield the same sort of exploitative, abusive, humiliating and destructive effects on the more vulnerable party that women too often suffer in asymmetrical heterosexual exchanges. Gender does effect a crucial difference, however, in the social geometry of heterosexual and gay hypergamy. The exclusively masculine arena of gay hypergamy allows for greater reciprocity of sexual and cultural exchanges over the life-cycle than women can typically attain. The heterosexual double standard of beauty and aging inflicts severe erotic and romantic constraints on even very prosperous, high status, aging "gold-diggers" or "trophy" widows. Although aging gay men also suffer notable declines in their erotic options, they operate on a gender-free playing field. Unlike heterosexual women, formerly subordinate beneficiaries of gay hypergamy, like Ozzie and Dino, can come to enact the opposite side of the exchange over the life course. Gay men who cruise to higher status can anticipate ultimately enjoying the power to exchange whatever cultural and material capital they attained through gay hypergamy for intimacy with less socially privileged, younger, attractive men.

Gay men aboard the family cruise ship are reconfiguring eros, domesticity, parenthood and kinship in ways that simultaneously reinforce and challenge conventional gender and family practices and values.[12] Although by no means a utopian arena of race and class harmony, gay cruising does facilitate more democratic forms of intimate social (as well as sexual) intercourse across more social boundaries (including race, age, class, religion, nation, education, ideology and even sexual orientation) than occur almost anywhere else. Enduring bonds of chosen family and kinship are among the significant consequences of these transgressive assignations. Whether or not Melanie Phillips is correct in her view that men are "naturally promiscuous," she is clearly wrong that masculine erotic impulses preclude two men from forming enduring attachments. Whether for "monogamous gay couples" like Ozzie and Harry, or for unapologetic "sex pigs" like Mother Randolph and his foundlings, it turns out that sexual cruising can be a creative mode of family travel.

NOTES

1. See www.growinggenerations.com

2. See www.popluckclub.org

3. My primary sample of 50 men included 10 Latinos, seven blacks, four Asians and 29 of white Anglo or Jewish origins. Nine men were also immigrants, both documented and undocumented, five of these from Latin America, two from the Caribbean and two from Europe. Religious upbringings and affiliations ranged from fundamentalist, Catholic, Jewish and Protestant, to Buddhist and atheist. Social class locations in the US are, of course, vastly more difficult to conceptualize or assign. The men's natal family backgrounds ranged from destitute to almost aristocratic, with the majority, unsurprisingly, from self-identified "middle-class" origins. Current income and occupational statuses encompassed the unemployed and indebted as well as extremely wealthy and successful members of the local professional, creative, managerial and community elite.

4. In order to study the broad array of paternal strategies and configurations, I intentionally oversampled gay fathers. Thus, 26 of the 50 men have some sort of paternal relationship to children, whether biological, social and/or legal, and whether or not their children reside with them.

5. I employ pseudonyms and have altered identifying details to protect privacy of informants.

6. In the terminology of assisted reproduction clinics in the US, a "traditional" surrogate is also the biological mother of a child conceived via alternative insemination with sperm, generally supplied by a contracting father. A "gestational" surrogate, in contrast, does not contribute genetic material to the child she bears under contract, but is hired to gestate an ovum supplied by an egg donor, fertilized in vitro and transplanted to her uterus.

7. Because I cannot reliably tally the aggregate number of couple relationships which all 50 interviewees have collectively experienced over their lifespans, I cannot provide meaningful data on the proportion of these that were initiated through sexual cruising. However, 10 of the 31 men who were in committed couple relationships when interviewed reported that they had met their mates in this way.

8. An analysis of these census data by the Williams Project at the UCLA School of Law examined 23 cities where most same-sex couples are concentrated. Project director William Rubenstein reports that 7 percent of married couples and 14.1 percent of unmarried heterosexual couples are interracial compared with 18.4 percent of same-sex couples in these urban areas. The project defines "interracial" as the mix of two racial groups and/or a Hispanic partner and non-Hispanic partner. For more information, contact William Rubenstein, The Williams Project, UCLA School of Law.

9. Of these 14 interracial intimacies, eight were black/white couples, four were Latino/white and two were an Asian/white couple. Additional men in the sample reported prior cross-racial unions.

10. Studies have found substantial differences in occupational ladders and career paths between heterosexual and non-heterosexual individuals. Nimmons (2002: 51) cites the as yet unpublished study by Dr. John Blandford at the University of Chicago, who analyzed a large sample

from standard US census figures to find that gay men in same-sex partnered households were "greatly over-represented" compared with heterosexual counterparts in "Professional and Specialty" occupations, particularly in teaching, nursing and the arts. Gay men, however, were scarcely represented at all in traditionally masculine working-class jobs, such as heavy equipment operators, miners, explosive workers, brick layers, etc. Rothblum and Factor's (2001) study of lesbians and their straight sisters found that sisters who grew up in the same age cohort, of the same race/ethnicity and with parents of the same education, occupation and income displayed quite dissimilar outcomes on demographic variables. Lesbians were significantly more educated, more likely to live in urban areas and more geographically mobile than their heterosexual sisters.

11. See, for example, Messner (1992: 90): "several white and black men told me that through sport they had their first real contact with people from different racial groups, and for a few of them, good friendships began . . . competitive activities such as sport mediate men's relationships with each other in ways that allow them to develop a powerful bond while at the same time preventing the development of intimacy."

12. These contradictory practices have historical antecedents. Chauncey (1994: 290) describes the "idiom of kinship" popular in the early 20th century among gay men who used camp culture "to undermine the 'natural' categories of the family and to reconstitute themselves as members of fictive kinship systems." Men involved in relationships that enacted a gendered division of labor often defined themselves as "husbands" and "wives," thereby inverting and undermining the meaning of "natural" categories, while repeated use simultaneously confirmed their significance.

BIBLIOGRAPHY

Adam, Barry (2003) "The 'Defense of Marriage Act' and American Exceptionalism," *Journal of the History of Sexuality* 12(2): 259–76.

Altman, Dennis (2001) *Global Sex*. Chicago, IL: University of Chicago Press.

Asher, Jon ben (2003) "Pope Declares Gay Families In authentic," *Integrity-L Digest* 28 January (#2003–29) from PlanetOut News Front, at: www.365Gay.com

Barbeau v. British Columbia (Attorney General) (2003) BCCA 251, Court of Appeal for British Columbia.

Bawer, Bruce (1993) *A Place at the Table: The Gay Individual in American Society*. New York: Simon and Schuster.

Browning, Frank (1994) *The Culture of Desire: Paradox and Perversity in Gay Lives Today*. New York: Vintage Books.

Budgeon, Shelley and Roseneil, Sasha (2002) "Cultures of Intimacy and Care Beyond 'The Family': Friendship and Sexual/Love Relationships in the Twenty-First Century," paper presented at the International Sociological Association, Brisbane, July.

Butler, Judith (1990) *Gender Trouble: Feminism and the Subversion of Identity*. New York: Routledge.

Chauncey, George (1994) *Gay New York Gender: Urban Culture, and the Making of the Gay Male World 1890–1940*. New York: Basic Books

Davis, Evan and Phillips, Melanie (1999) "Debate: Gay Marriage," *Prospect Magazine* 40 (April): 16–20.

Dowsett, Gary W. (1996) *Practicing Desire: Homosexual Sex in the Era of AIDS*. Stanford, CA: Stanford University Press.

Dreyfuss, Robert (1999) "The Holy War on Gays," *Village Voice* 18 (March): 38–41.

Fagan, Craig (2002) "Buenos Aires Legalizes Same-Sex Unions," at: www.salon.com/mwt/wire/2002/12/13/brazil_marriage/index.html

Friedan, Betty (1963) *The Feminine Mystique*. New York: Norton.

Giddens, Anthony (1992) *The Transformation of Intimacy: Sexuality, Love and Eroticism in Modern Societies*. Cambridge: Polity Press.

Gilder, George (1986) *Men and Marriage*. Gretna: Pelican.

Heath, Melanie and Stacey, Judith (2002) "Transatlantic Family Travail," *American Journal of Sociology* 108(3): 658–68.

Integrity Press Release (2003) "Integrity Uganda Begins Same-Sex Blessings," 12 April; at: www.integrity-usa.org/UgandaJournal/index.htm

Levine, Martin (1998) *Gay Macho: The Life and Death of the Homosexual Clone*. New York: New York University Press.

Lewin, Ellen (1998) *Recognizing Ourselves: Ceremonies of Lesbian and Gay Commitment*. New York: Columbia University Press.

Mann, William J. (1997) "A Boy's Own Class," in Susan Raffo (ed.) *Queerly Classed*, pp. 217–26. Boston, MA: South End Press.

Messner, Michael A. (1992) *Power at Play: Sports and the Problem of Masculinity*. Boston, MA: Beacon Press.

Miller, John C. (2001) "'My Daddy Loves Your Daddy': A Gay Father Encounters a Social Movement," in Mary Bernstein and Renate Reimann (eds) *Queer Families, Queer Politics: Challenging Culture and the State*, pp. 221–30. New York: Columbia University Press.

Nardi, Peter (1999) *Gay Men's Friendships: Invincible Communities*. Chicago, IL: University of Chicago Press.

Nimmons, David (2002) *The Soul Beneath the Skin: The Unseen Hearts and Habits of Gay Men*. New York: St. Martin's Press.

"Oppose the Federal Marriage Amendment" (2003) at: www.petitiononline.com/0712t001/petition.html (accessed 30 May 2003).

PLC listserv (2003) "The Lusty Month of May Mixer," 5 May.

Rauch, Jonathan (1994) "A Pro-Gay Pro-Family Policy," *Wall Street Journal* 29 November: A22.

Rofes, Eric (1998) *Dry Bones Breathe: Gay Men Creating Post-AIDS Identities and Cultures*. New York: Harrington Park Press.

Rothblum, Esther D. and Factor, Rhonda (2001) "Lesbians and Their Sisters as a Control Group: Demographic and Mental Health Factors," *Psychological Science* 12: 63–9.

Savage, Dan (2003) "G.O.P. Hypocrisy," *New York Times* 25 April: A31.

Shilts, Randy (1987) *And the Band Played On*. New York: St Martin's Press.

Stein, Arlene (2001) *The Stranger Next Door: The Story of a Small Community's Battle over Sex, Faith, and Civil Rights*. Boston, MA: Beacon Press.

Stuever, Hank (2001) "Is Gay Mainstream?" *Washington Post* 27 April: C1.

Sullivan, Andrew (1997) "The Conservative Case," in Andrew Sullivan (ed.) *Same-Sex Marriage Pro and Con*, pp. 146–54. New York: Vintage Books.

The American Heritage® Dictionary of the English Language (2000) 4th edn. Boston, MA: Houghton Mifflin.

United States Congress (1996) *The Defense of Marriage Act: Committee on the Judiciary, United States Senate*. Washington, DC: US Government Printing Office.

Warner, Michael (1999) *The Trouble with Normal: Sex, Politics, and the Ethics of Queer Life*. New York: Free Press.

Weeks, Jeffrey, Heaphy Brian and Donovan, Catherine (2001) S*ame Sex Intimacies: Families of Choice and Other Life Experiments*. London: Routledge.

Weston, Kath (1991) *Families We Choose: Lesbians, Gays, Kinship*. New York: Columbia University Press.

Wetzstein, Cheryl (2003) "Bill to Define Marriage Tried Again in House as 2 States Mull Cases," *Washington Times*, at: www.washingtontimes.com/national/20030525-155459-1812r.htm

ETHNICITY, RACE, AND DIFFERENCE: A COMPARISON OF WHITE, BLACK, AND HISPANIC MEN'S HOUSEHOLD LABOR TIME

Anne Shelton   Daphne John

Most of the recent research on household labor concerns the impact of women's labor force participation on the allocation of tasks or responsibilities. Researchers routinely recognize that women's household labor time is associated with their employment status, as well as with a variety of other sociodemographic characteristics, including age and education. A great deal has been written about the ways in which time commitments and sex role attitudes affect the division of household labor (Coverman 1985; Huber and Spitze 1983; Perrucci, Potter, and Rhoads 1978; Pleck 1985; Ross 1987). Men are by definition included in the analyses that focus on the division of household labor, but these studies typically ignore the relationship between men's work and family roles.

Some researchers have examined the relationship between men's work and family roles (Coverman 1985; Pleck 1977, 1985), but the relative scarcity of these studies means that although some questions about men's household roles have been examined, a number of issues remain unexamined. In particular, there has been little research on the impact of men's paid labor time on their household labor time and there has been only limited research on racial and ethnic variations in men's household labor time.

In this analysis we begin to examine some of the neglected issues in the study of men's household labor time by focusing on how married men's paid labor time affects their family roles as defined by their household labor time and specific household tasks. Although there is less variation in men's paid labor time than in women's, there is some variation, and just as paid labor time affects women's household labor time, it may also affect men's. Moreover, the amount of time men have available to them may affect the specific household tasks they perform, with men with more time performing more nondiscretionary tasks than men who have less time available to them.

Recently, increased awareness of the need to examine links between gender and race have led many to argue that race and gender cannot, in fact, be discussed separately (Collins 1990; Reid and Comas-Diaz 1990; Zinn 1991). Moreover, "gender studies" should not be limited only to women. Therefore, we assess the impact of selected sociodemographic characteristics on men's household labor time with a special emphasis on race and ethnicity.

LITERATURE REVIEW

The changes in women's labor force participation have resulted in a large number of dual-earner couples. Kimmel (1987) notes that this shift has created not only new role demands for women, but also new

Anne Shelton and Daphne John, "Ethnicity, Race, and Difference: A Comparison of White, Black, and Hispanic Men's Household Labor Time." *Men Work and Family*, pp. 131–150. Copyright © 1993. Reprinted by permission of SAGE Publications, Inc.

demands for men. Just as women have expanded their roles in the paid labor force, men also have expanded their roles in the family. The transition in men's and women's roles may, however, vary by race and ethnicity because of the historically different patterns of black, white, and Hispanic women's labor force participation (Beckett and Smith 1981; McAdoo 1990).

Although researchers routinely examine the impact of women's paid labor time on the household division of labor, the impact of men's paid labor time on the household division of labor is generally ignored. The lack of attention to the impact of men's paid work time on their household labor time may reflect the fact that there is less variability in men's paid labor time than in women's. Those studies that have examined the impact of men's paid work time on their household labor time have yielded conflicting results (Barnett and Baruch 1987; Coverman and Sheley 1986; Pleck 1985; Thompson and Walker 1989). Some find that men's time spent in paid labor is negatively associated with their household labor time (Rexroat and Shehan 1987; Atkinson and Huston 1984), whereas others find no association (Kingston and Nock 1985). Because this research rarely focuses on racial/ethnic variation, we have little information about the ways that paid labor and household labor demands may be related differently for white, black, and Hispanic men.

Research on black and Hispanic households indicates that the images of the egalitarian black household and the gender-stratified Hispanic household may be inaccurate depictions of reality derived from superficial examinations. In the case of black households, egalitarianism is commonly attributed to black women's high rates of labor force participation (McAdoo 1990). If, however, black women's labor force participation reflects economic pressures rather than egalitarian sex role attitudes (Broman 1988, 1991), women's employment may be unrelated to the division of labor.

Research on the division of labor in black households does not consistently indicate how black and white households differ. Some research on the division of household labor finds that black families have a more egalitarian division of labor than white families (Beckett 1976; Beckett and Smith 1981; Broman 1988, 1991). Other studies by J. A. Ericksen, Yancey, and E. P. Ericksen (1979) and Farkas (1976) also suggest that black men do more household labor than their white counterparts (see also Miller and Garrison 1982). However, Broman (1991, 1988) argues that although some egalitarian patterns do exist in black households, there is no gender equity. For example, in married couple households the proportions of men who state they do most of the household chores is much smaller than the proportion of women responding that they do all the household chores. Although unemployed men respond that they do more of the household chores more frequently than employed men, they do not make this claim nearly as often as women, regardless of women's employment status. Broman (1988) also notes that women are likely to report being primarily responsible for traditionally female tasks.

Other researchers argue that the image of the egalitarian black family is inaccurate (Cronkite 1977; Staples 1978; Wilson, Tolson, Hinton, and Kiernan 1990). For example, Wilson et al. (1990) point out that black women are likely to be responsible for child care and household labor. Cronkite (1977) says that black men prefer more internal differentiation in the household than do white men. That is, she argues that they prefer a more traditional division of household labor, with women responsible for housework and child care. Others claim that black families are similar to white families in egalitarianism and that the differences that do exist often are based on social class rather than on race per se (McAdoo 1990; Staples 1978). Staples (1978) also claims that class differences are consistent across race. McAdoo (1990) argues, in much the same vein, that black and white fathers are similarly nurturant to their children and that black and white middle- and upper-income fathers have similar parenting styles. In contrast to the view that black men are less traditional than white men, Ransford and Miller (1983) find that middle-class black men have more traditional sex role attitudes than white middle-class men.

The literature regarding the division of household labor within Hispanic households is more limited, and much of what is available deals only with Chicanos, excluding other Hispanics. The research on Hispanic households yields conflicting results. Golding (1990) finds that Mexican American men do less household labor than Anglo men, whereas Mexican American women do more household labor than Anglo women. Differences between Hispanic and Anglo men's housework and child care time, like the differences between black and white men, may be due to other differences between them (Golding 1990; McAdoo 1990; Staples 1978). Golding (1990) finds that education is correlated with ethnicity and household labor time such that after removing the effects of education, the impact of ethnicity on the division of labor in the household is not significant. Thus, although she finds a more traditional division of labor within Mexican American households than in Anglo households', this division of labor reflects educational differences rather than solely ethnicity effects. Similarly, Ybarra (1982) finds that although acculturation does not significantly affect who performs the household labor, wives' employment does. She finds that the division of labor in dual-worker households is more equal than in male provider households.

In other research, Mirandé (1979) discusses the patterns of shared responsibility for domestic work in Mexican American households. Although men's participation in household labor may give the appearance of egalitarianism, it does not necessarily indicate equality. For example, men may participate but spend less time than women. Vega and colleagues (1986) argue that Mexican American families are similar to Anglo families but that in terms of their adaptability to change in family roles they appear to be more flexible than Anglo families. Thus the male provider role may be less firmly entrenched in Mexican American than in Anglo households, resulting in a less rigid division of household labor. Similarly, Zinn (1980) asserts

that Mexican American women's changing work roles may change their role identification.

There also is research indicating that decision making is not shared in Hispanic households (Williams 1990). Williams (1990) finds that Mexican American men continue to have more authority than wives, but that the patterns of decision making are not as traditional as in the past.

Some research suggests that the differences among white, black, and Hispanic men's family roles may reflect differences in the way that they internalize the provider role. Wilkie (1991) argues that black men's ability to fulfill the provider role may be associated with their rates of marriage (see also Tucker and Taylor 1989). Similarly, Stack (1974) found that when black men are unable to provide financially for their family, they also are less likely to participate in the household (e.g., housework and child care) (Cazenave 1979; Wilkie 1991). Although the findings of Wilkie (1991) and Tucker and Taylor (1989) do not directly indicate a relationship between the provider role and men's participation in the household, we can speculate that this association may exist. Thus, to the extent that there are differences among black, white, and Hispanic men's internalization of the provider role, we might also expect to find that the relationship between work and family roles varies by race/ethnicity.

We focus on the definition of egalitarianism based on the division of labor within the household. Hood (1983) notes that there are a number of ways in which an egalitarian marriage is defined. For our purposes, egalitarianism is defined in terms of household labor time. Some studies discuss decision making and role sharing, which are logically associated with the division of household labor, but which are not unproblematically related to it (Blumstein and Schwartz 1983).

A problem with much of the research on men's household labor time is the failure to incorporate wives' characteristics into the analyses. Just as men's paid labor time may act as a constraint on their household labor time, wives' paid labor time may create a demand for them to spend more time on household labor. The use of couples as the units of analysis in this chapter helps us understand the inter-action between spouses' characteristics.

We further examine white, black, and His-panic men's household labor time to determine the nature of the association between men's paid labor time and household labor time. In addition, we examine racial/ethnic differences in men's house-hold labor time and assess the extent to which any observed differences may reflect differences in paid labor time, education, or other sociodemographic characteristics. We also incorporate wives' paid la-bor time and attitudes about family roles into our analysis to determine the ways in which husbands' and wives' characteristics interact to affect men's household labor time.

DATA AND METHODS

The data for this study are from the 1987 National Survey of Families and Households (NSFH) (Sweet, Bumpass, and Call 1988), a national probability sample of 9,643 persons with an oversampling of 3,374 minority respondents, single parents, cohabit-ing persons, recently married persons, and respon-dents with stepchildren. One adult per household was selected randomly to be the primary respondent and his or her spouse/partner (if applicable) was also given a questionnaire designed for secondary respondents. Portions of the main interview with the primary respondent were self-administered, as was the entire spouse/partner questionnaire. In this analysis, we include only married respondents with a completed spouse questionnaire.

In the analyses to follow we begin by describing black, white, and Hispanic men's and women's house-hold labor time. In addition to comparing household labor time across racial/ethnic groups, we also com-pare this time by work status.

In the second stage of the analysis, we examine the relationship between ethnicity and men's house-hold labor time after controlling for a variety of other factors, including age, education, sex role attitudes, and both husbands' and wives' paid work. We use multiple regression analysis to determine if there are race/ethnic differences in household labor time or

in the impact of paid labor time on household labor time that are independent of sociodemographic dif-ferences between white, black, and Hispanic men.[1]

In addition to determining whether or not a race/ethnicity effect on household labor time ex-ists once other characteristics have been taken into account, we look at the relationship between husbands' and wives' paid labor and household la-bor time. We expect to find that men who spend more time in paid work will spend less time on household labor once other characteristics have been held constant. Moreover, to the extent that wives' market work time may act as a demand on men, we expect to find that the more time wives spend in paid labor the more time husbands will spend on household labor, once other variables have been held constant.

Our analyses include separate estimates of white, black, and Hispanic men's and women's household labor time. Hispanics include Mexican Americans as well as other Hispanic respondents. Paid labor time is measured in hours usually spent per week at work for both respondents and spouses. Education and age are measured in years.

Respondents' and spouses' sex role attitudes are measured by their responses to two attitude items. Each item was scored from 1 to 5. Respon-dents were asked if they agreed with the following statements:

1. If a husband and a wife both work full-time, they should share household tasks equally.
2. Preschool children are likely to suffer if their mother is employed.

Responses to the two items were summed and divided by two so that the range of the summated measure is 1 to 5. A high score indicates more lib-eral sex role attitudes and a low score indicates more traditional sex role attitudes.

Presence of children was included as an inde-pendent variable in some of the analyses. A score of 0 indicates that the respondent has no children under the age of 18 in the household, whereas a score of 1 indicates that there are children under the age of 18 in the household.

FINDINGS

Findings in Table 35.1 reveal that black and Hispanic men spend significantly more time on household labor than do white men. Women's household labor time also varies by race/ethnicity, but in a different pattern. Hispanic women spend significantly more time on household labor than white women. They also spend more time on household labor than black women, but a t-test of the difference is not significant. Nevertheless, the gap is of substantive interest because the lack of statistical significance is largely a function of inflated standard deviations due to the small number of black and Hispanic respondents. As the results in Table 35.1 indicate, the divergent patterns of variation in household labor time by race and gender combine in such a way that men's proportionate share of household labor also varies by ethnicity.

Black men spend an average of 25 hours per week on household labor compared to 19.6 hours for white men and 23.2 hours for Hispanic men. The absolute size of the gap between black and Hispanic men's household labor time is small, with both groups of men spending significantly more time on household labor than white men. Nevertheless, black men spend more time on household labor than Hispanic men, although the gap is not statistically significant. This pattern both partially confirms and contradicts earlier research. Black men's relatively high household labor

time is consistent with the view that black households may have a more equal division of labor than other households. The data in Table 35.1 do not, however, allow us to determine the source of black men's household labor time investments. It is possible, for example, that on average, black men spend less time in paid labor and therefore more time on household labor. The pattern also could reflect a number of other possible differences in the sociodemographic characteristics of black and white men that we examine in a later section.

Hispanic men's relatively high time investment in household labor is consistent with previous research finding that Hispanic men participate at least as much as Anglo men in household labor, and contradicts those who argue that Hispanic men participate in household labor less than Anglo men. Of course, much of the research on Hispanic men's family roles examines decision making or the distribution of power, rather than household labor time. Most of the research on household labor assumes that it is onerous duty and that only someone without the power to avoid it (or without any decision-making authority) will do it (Ferree 1987). Thus, researchers whose focus is on decision making often assume that egalitarian patterns of decision making are associated with an egalitarian division of household labor.

Women's household labor time also varies by race/ethnicity, with Hispanic women spending

■ **TABLE 35.1**
Household Labor Time by Gender and Race/Ethnicity

	White	Black	Hispanic	t-Test Blk/Wht	t-Test Hsp/Wht	t-Test Blk/Hsp
Men	19.6 (19.3)	25.0 (28.7)	23.2 (19.2)	2.3**	2.2*	.6
Women	37.3 (21.6)	38.0 (26.3)	41.8 (24.5)	.3	1.9*	1.2
Men's % of Household Labor Time	34%	40%	36%			

Notes: *p ≤ .05; **p ≤ .01. Standard deviation in parentheses.

significantly more time on household labor than either black or white women. Hispanic women spend an average of 41.8 hours per week on household labor compared to 37.3 hours for white women and 38 hours per week for black women. Thus, Hispanic men and women spend significantly more time on household labor than white men and women, whereas black women's household labor time is not significantly different from white women's household labor time. Women's and men's different investments in household labor time affect men's proportionate share of household labor time. The data on black men and women indicate that black men do 40 percent of the household labor (done by men and women only) whereas Hispanic and Anglo men do 36 percent and 34 percent of the household labor, respectively. Thus, Table 35.1 confirms earlier research reporting that black households have a more equal division of household labor than white households and also confirms research indicating that Anglo and Hispanic households may have few differences in division of labor. In addition, the findings for Hispanic households suggest that there may be even more changes in the traditional patterns of Hispanic households than Williams's (1990) research on decision-making indicates.

We begin to examine the source of some of the gap in Table 35.2, where we present white, black, and Hispanic men's household labor time by employment status using multiple classification analysis. We do this in order to determine if black men's relatively high levels of household labor time reflect their lower paid labor time.

With respect to employment status, there are some interesting patterns. For both white and Hispanic men, those who are employed spend less time on household labor than those who are not employed, although the pattern is statistically significant only for white men. For blacks, however, the pattern is quite different. Black men who are not employed spend less time on household labor than black men who are employed, although the difference is not statistically significant. These findings indicate that the relationship between paid labor time and household labor time varies by race/ethnicity and that differences in black, white, and Hispanic men's household labor time are not simply a function of differences in their employment status.

The relationship between black men's employment status and their household labor time may indicate that black men who are not employed are different from nonemployed white and Hispanic men. To the extent that black men are not employed involuntarily, the results in Table 35.2 may reflect the age structure of those who are not employed. It also may indicate the presence of a distinct group of black men characterized by both low time investments in paid labor and low investments in household labor. The argument that the apparent egalitarianism of the black family may be a function of black men's reduced hours in paid labor is not supported by these findings. If anything, these findings indicate that, among blacks, the division of household labor is likely to be more equal in households where the man is employed than in households where he is not. Although this is in some sense counterintuitive, it may indicate that the "breadwinner" role is internalized in such a way that even black men who are not employed may opt out of the family per se, rather than compensating

■ **TABLE 35.2**

Men's Household Labor Time by Race/Ethnicity and Employment Status

	White	Black	Hispanic
Employment Status			
Not employed	23.5	19.5	23.0
Employed PT			
(1–39 hrs.)	19.1	26.6	22.7
Employed FT	18.2	27.0	22.3
Eta	.12***	.13	.03
N	2798	183	164

Notes: We use 39 hours as our break between part-time and full-time in order to ensure an adequate *n* for the part-time category. Eta is a measure of association.
***p ≤ .001.

for their reduced paid work with more household labor (Komarovsky 1940; Stack 1974). Among the men in this sample, the expression of their "opting out" may be to avoid household labor. (See Cazenave 1984; Hood 1986, for more discussion of the importance of subjective perceptions of work and family roles.)

Up to this point we have examined men's household labor time without taking into consideration a variety of sociodemographic characteristics, sex role attitudes, or wives' work status. Thus, some of the observed race/ethnic differences may reflect other differences among white, black, and Hispanic households. In Table 35.3 we examine the impact of race/ethnicity on men's household labor time by estimating the direct effect of race/ethnicity on household labor time as well as by estimating the ways that paid labor time may affect white, black, and Hispanic men's household labor time differently, after taking other factors into account. Thus, in Table 35.3 we can determine if the previously observed association between race/ethnicity and household labor time or the race/ethnic differences in the impact of paid labor time on household labor time are artifacts of other differences among white, black, and Hispanic men.

The results in Table 35.3 show that after controlling for respondents' education, age, children, men's sex role attitudes, wives' sex role attitudes and paid labor time, race/ethnicity is not significantly associated with men's household labor time. Thus, the differences among white, black, and Hispanic men's household labor time that we observed earlier appear to reflect other differences among them. For example, they may reflect differences in social class or education as McAdoo (1990) and Golding (1990) have argued. They may also, however, reflect differences in the presence of children or in wives' paid labor time.

Although we find no direct effects of race/ethnicity on men's household labor time in our multivariate analysis, the differential effect of paid labor time on men's household labor time remains.[2] For white and Hispanic men, each additional hour spent in paid labor is associated with their spending

■ TABLE 35.3

Regression of Men's Household Labor Time on Paid Labor Time, Race/Ethnicity, Presence of Children, Education, Age, Sex Role Attitudes, Wives' Paid Labor Time, and Wives' Sex Role Attitudes

	beta	standard error
Paid labor	−.10***	.02
Black	−3.4	2.4
Hispanic	−.67	3.2
Black/paid	.27***	.07
Hispanic/paid	.08	.08
Children	3.7***	.81
Education	−.15	.12
Age	.02	.03
Men's sex role attitudes	1.5***	.52
Wives' paid labor time	.07***	.02
Wives' sex role attitudes	.76	.51
Constant	13.4	3.4
R^2	.033	
N	2782	

Note: ***p ≤ .001.

slightly more than six fewer minutes per day on household labor. For black men, however, each additional hour in paid labor is associated with them spending more time on household labor, even after controlling for sociodemographic and household characteristics. Thus, the pattern we observed in the bivariate analyses is repeated in the multivariate analyses. The more time black men spend in paid labor the more time they spend on household labor, whereas the association between paid labor time and household labor time is negative for Anglo and Hispanic men.

There are a variety of possible explanations for the different association between paid labor time and household labor time for black men than for white or Hispanic men. Black men may define the breadwinner role more narrowly than white or Hispanic men, such that when they are not employed and unable to contribute to their family's financial well-being they may retreat from the family in other ways (Stack 1974). The race/ethnic variation in the association between men's paid labor time and household labor time may reflect differences in housing patterns. If households with nonemployed black men are more likely to live in apartments, and those with employed black men are more likely to live in single-family houses, the pattern we see may reflect the amount of household labor that must be done. The different association for white and Hispanic men may be the result of different housing patterns. That is, households with non-employed white or Hispanic men may not be as concentrated in apartments as is the case with black households. Thus there may be variation in the amount of household labor that must be done associated with men's employment status.

The pattern of the effects of some of the control variables is also interesting. For example, men with children spend more time on household labor than men without children, and men with more egalitarian sex role attitudes spend more time on household labor than men with more traditional attitudes. Wives' sex role attitudes are not associated with men's household labor time, but the more time wives spend in paid labor, the more time husbands spend on household labor. Interestingly, after controlling for other variables, men's age is not significantly associated with their household labor time.

In Table 35.4 we further examine the relationship between men's employment status and their household labor time by examining white, black, and Hispanic men's time spent on specific household tasks, after controlling for sociodemographic and household characteristics. Among those men employed full-time, black men spend more time than white and Hispanic men cleaning house, shopping, and repairing automobiles. Cleaning house and shopping are typically "female-typed" tasks

■ **TABLE 35.4**

Men's Time Spent on Specific Household Tasks by Employment Status and Race/Ethnicity

	Not Employed	Employed Part-Time	Employed Full-Time
Preparing Meals			
White	3.3	2.9	2.3
Black	4.2	4.9	3.3
Hispanic	5.8	3.2	2.2
Beta	.09+	.09	.02
Washing Dishes			
White	2.7	2.2	1.9
Black	1.6	4.5	2.7
Hispanic	4.0	4.1	2.1
Beta	.06*	.22**	.05
Cleaning House			
White	2.3	1.8	1.7
Black	2.3	3.2	3.0
Hispanic	4.3	3.9	2.2
Beta	.08+	.20**	.11***
Outdoor Tasks			
White	7.5	5.0	5.6
Black	5.8	4.8	5.4
Hispanic	5.2	3.7	3.9
Beta	.06	.06	.06*
Shopping			
White	2.9	2.4	2.3
Black	2.7	2.6	4.0
Hispanic	2.5	3.5	3.1
Beta	.02	.08	.14***
Laundry			
White	.7	.8	1.2
Black	.9	1.5	.6
Hispanic	1.3	.4	.6
Beta	.06	.11	.08***
Paying Bills			
White	1.6	1.4	1.5
Black	2.5	2.2	2.4
Hispanic	2.1	4.1	2.5
Beta	.07	.26***	.09***
Auto Maintenance			
White	1.4	1.6	2.0
Black	1.4	2.5	3.4
Hispanic	2.1	3.2	2.9
Beta	.04	.21***	.08***
Driving			
White	1.2	1.3	1.5
Black	1.1	1.7	2.7
Hispanic	1.9	1.4	1.5
Beta	.04	.04	.08

Notes: Controlling for respondents' sex role attitudes, education, age, spouses' paid work time, spouses' sex role attitudes, and number of children. Beta is a partial measure of association. +$p \leq .10$; *$p \leq .05$; **$p \leq .01$; ***$p \leq .001$.

indicating that employed black men's household labor time represents less gender stratification rather than simply more time spent on tasks typically done by men. Nevertheless, there are some "female-typed" tasks on which white men spend more time. White men employed full-time spend more time on laundry than black or Hispanic men. Not all of the differences in housework time result from variation in time spent on "female-typed" tasks. White and black men employed full-time spend more time than Hispanic men on outdoor tasks, and black and Hispanic men employed full-time spend more time paying bills than white men.

Among those who are employed part-time or not at all, Hispanic men are most likely to spend more time on specific household tasks than either white or black men, although in a number of cases black and Hispanic men's household task time is similar. Hispanic men employed part-time spend the most time cleaning house, but black men also spend more time cleaning house than white men. Similarly, black men spend significantly more time washing dishes than other men, although Hispanic men spend almost as much time as black men. Among those who are not employed, Hispanic men spend more time than black or white men preparing meals, washing dishes, and cleaning house; thus more time among "female-typed" tasks than other men.

The patterns observed in Table 35.4 indicate that there is more variation by race/ethnicity among men who are employed full-time than among those who are employed part-time or not at all. Although we should use care when comparing across employment statuses in Table 35.4 (because there may be sociodemographic differences among the groups), we can see that black men's greater household labor time, with respect to white and Hispanic men, appears to be among those who are employed full-time, whereas there are fewer and less definite patterns among those employed fewer hours or not at all.

With respect to specific household tasks, Table 35.4 shows that black men who are employed full-time spend more time on a variety of household tasks, rather than on only a few or male-typed tasks. The pattern of greater involvement in traditionally female tasks among black men employed full-time indicates that among black households there are more egalitarian patterns of family work when the husband is employed than when he is not.

CONCLUSION

Our findings point to several important patterns. Just as women's paid labor time is associated with their household labor time, we find that men's paid labor time is associated with their household labor time. Thus, although there is less variation in men's paid labor time than in women's, there is enough that it warrants some research attention. Interestingly, the pattern of association between paid labor time and household labor time varies by race/ethnicity. Employed black men do more household labor than those who are not employed, whereas employed white and Hispanic men do less household labor than those who are not employed. These different patterns illustrate the dangers of analyses that fail to examine not only the direct effect of race/ethnicity on household labor time but also the way that race/ethnicity may affect the relationship among other variables. The relationship between men's work and family roles is not such that we can talk about a relationship: the relationship varies by race/ethnicity. This difference in the relationship between work and family suggests that we need to conduct more research on the nature of work and family trade-offs and how they vary by race and ethnicity.

Our analyses also indicate some differences in the family roles (as measured by household labor time) of white, black, and Hispanic men. Our findings from bivariate analyses show that Hispanic and black men spend more time on household labor than white men. Even with Hispanic women's relatively high levels of household labor time, Hispanic men's proportionate share of household labor time is higher than white men's. Black men's relatively high proportionate share of household labor time confirms earlier research indicating that black households may be more egalitarian than white households. Unlike some speculation, however, we find that this pattern is not the result of differences in black men's paid labor time, but that employed black men are the ones who are spending more time on household labor. This somewhat surprising finding indicates the need to examine the relationship between black men's work and family roles in more detail. Given previous findings about black men's attachment to family and work roles (Cazenave 1979), black men's attachments to the provider role as well as their perceptions of family obligations may be the most fruitful place to begin future studies. In addition, the different patterns observed indicate the complex nature of the work–family linkage for men more generally. Further analyses might also focus on the characteristics of nonemployed black men as compared to nonemployed white and Hispanic men to determine what may account for the different patterns of work and family role trade-offs.

Finally, we find that higher household labor time among black men employed full-time reflects their greater time investments in traditionally female tasks, rather than differences in time investments in "male-typed" tasks. In addition, the pattern of Hispanic men's time spent on specific household tasks indicates that they often spend more time on "female-typed" tasks than Anglo men. Thus, even though Anglo and Hispanic men's total household labor time is not significantly different once sociodemographic characteristics have been taken into account, Hispanic men may spend more time on typically "female-typed" tasks like meal preparation, washing dishes, and cleaning house than do Anglo men (see also Mirandé 1985; Zinn 1980). In addition, our findings indicate that there may be more changes in the Hispanic household than some who have found changing patterns suggest (Mirandé 1985; Williams 1990).

In future research we must give more attention to racial/ethnic variation in men's family patterns as well as to the different trade-offs that men may make between work and family. We simply cannot assume that the trade-offs are the same for men as for women, just as we have often argued that we cannot assume that women's labor force experiences can be modeled in the same way that we model men's. At the same time, our findings argue for the systematic inclusion of ethnicity and race in studies of the work–family trade-off for both men and women. We need to examine differences among black, white, and Hispanic men's perceptions of their family responsibilities if we are to understand how they balance work and family responsibilities.

NOTES

We appreciate the very helpful comments of Jane Hood, Norma Williams, Maxine Baca Zinn, and Marta Tienda.

1. The lack of statistical significance is a result of the relatively small number of black and Hispanic respondents in the survey.

2. To determine the differential effects of paid labor time for white, black, and Hispanic respondents we included interaction terms for race/ethnicity and paid labor time in our analysis. The nonsignificant effect for the interaction term between Hispanic and paid labor time indicates that the impact of paid labor time on Hispanic men's household labor time is not significantly different from the impact of paid labor time on white men's household labor time. The significant interaction term for black men indicates that there is a significant difference in the impact of paid labor time on black and white men's household labor time. By adding the coefficient for paid labor time to the coefficient for the black/paid labor time interaction term, we can see that even after controlling for sociodemographic and household characteristics, paid labor time is positively associated with black men's household labor time. Thus, the more time black men spend in paid labor the more time they spend in household labor, whereas the association between paid labor time and household labor time is negative for Anglo and Hispanic men.

REFERENCES

Atkinson, J., and Huston, T. L. 1984. "Sex Role Orientation and Division of Labor Early in Marriage." *Journal of Personality and Social Psychology* 46, no. 2: 330–345.

Barnett, R. C, and Baruch, G. K. 1987. "Determinants of Fathers' Participation in Family Work." *Journal of Marriage and the Family* 49: 29–40.

Beckett, J. O. 1976. "Working Wives: A Racial Comparison." *Social Work,* November, 463–471.

Beckett, J. Q., and Smith, A. D. 1981. "Work and Family Roles: Egalitarian Marriage in Black and White Families." *Social Service Review* 55, no. 2: 314–326.

Blumstein, P., and Schwartz, P. 1983. *American Couples.* New York: Pocket Books.

Broman, C. 1988. "Household Work and Family Life Satisfaction of Blacks." *Journal of Marriage and the Family* 50: 743–748.

———. 1991. "Gender, Work-Family Roles, and Psychological Well-Being of Blacks." *Journal of Marriage and the Family* 53: 509–520.

Cazenave, N. 1979. "Middle-Income Black Fathers: An Analysis of the Provider Role." *Family Coordinator* 28: 583–593.

———. 1984. "Race, Socioeconomic Status, and Age: The Social Context of Masculinity." *Sex Roles* 11, no. 7–8: 639–656.

Collins, P. H. 1990. *Black Feminist Thought: Knowledge, Consciousness and the Politics of Empowerment.* Cambridge, Mass.: Unwin Hyman.

Coverman, S. 1985. "Explaining Husbands' Participation in Domestic Labor." *Sociological Quarterly* 26, no. 1: 81–98.

Coverman, S., and Sheley, J. F. 1986. "Change in Men's Housework and Child-Care Time, 1965–1975." *Journal of Marriage and the Family* 48: 413–422.

Cronkite, R. C. 1977. "The Determinants of Spouses' Normative Preferences for Family Roles." *Journal of Marriage and the Family* 39: 575–585.

Ericksen, J. A., Yancey, W. L., and Ericksen, E. P. 1979. "The Division of Family Roles." *Journal of Marriage and the Family* 41: 301–313.

Farkas, G. 1976. "Education, Wage Rates, and the Division of Labor Between Husband and Wife." *Journal of Marriage and the Family* 38: 473–483.

Ferree, M. M. 1987. "Family and Job for Working-Class Women: Gender and Class Systems Seen from Below." In N. Gerstel and H. E. Gross, eds, *Families and Work,* 289–301. Philadelphia: Temple University Press.

Golding, J. M. 1990. "Division of Household Labor, Strain and Depressive Symptoms Among Mexican Americans and Non-Hispanic Whites." *Psychology of Women Quarterly* 14: 103–117.

Hood, J. C. 1983 *Becoming a Two-Job Family.* New York: Praeger.

———. 1986. "The Provider Role: Its Meaning and Measurement." *Journal of Marriage and the Family* 48: 349–359.

Huber, J., and G. Spitze. 1983. *Sex Stratification: Children, Housework and Jobs.* New York: Academic Press.

Kimmel, M. S. 1987. "Rethinking 'Masculinity': New Directions in Research." In M. S. Kimmel, ed., *Changing Men: New Directions of Research on Men and Masculinity,* 9–24. Newbury Park, Calif.: Sage.

Kingston, P. W., and Nock, S. L. 1985. "Consequences of the Family Work Day." *Journal of Marriage and the Family* 47, no. 3: 619–630.

Komarovsky, M. 1940. *The Unemployed Man and His Family.* New York: Dryden.

McAdoo, H. P. 1990. "A Portrait of African American Families in the United States." In S. E. Rix, ed., *The American Woman 1990–1991: A Status Report,* 71–93. New York: Norton.

Miller, J., and Garrison, H. H. 1982. "Sex Roles: The Division of Labor at Home and in the Workplace." *Annual Review of Sociology* 8: 237–262.

Mirandé, A. 1979. "A Reinterpretation of Male Dominance in the Chicano Family." *Family Coordinator* 28, no. 4: 473–480.

———. 1985. *The Chicano Experience: An Alternative Perspective.* Notre Dame, Ind.: University of Notre Dame Press.

Perrucci, C. C., Potter, H. R., and Rhoads, D. L. 1978. "Determinants of Male Family-Role Performance." *Psychology of Women Quarterly* 3, no. 1: 53–66.

Pleck, J. H. 1977. "The Work-Family Role System." *Social Problems* 24: 417–427.

———. 1985. *Working Wives / Working Husbands.* Beverly Hills: Sage.

Ransford, E., and Miller, J. 1983. "Race, Sex, and Feminist Outlooks." *American Sociological Review* 48: 46–59.

Reid, P. T., and Comas-Diaz, L. 1990. "Gender and Ethnicity: Perspectives on Dual Status." *Sex Roles* 22, no. 7–8: 397–408.

Rexroat, C., and Shehan, C. 1987. "The Family Life Cycle and Spouses' Time in Housework." *Journal of Marriage and the Family* 49, no. 4: 737–750.

Ross, C. E. 1987. "The Division of Labor at Home." *Social Forces* 65, no. 3: 816–834.

Stack, C. B. 1974. *All Our Kin.* New York: Harper Colophon.

Staples, R. 1978. "Masculinity and Race: The Dual Dilemma of Black Men." *Journal of Social Issues* 34, no. 1: 169–183.

Sweet, J., Bumpass, L., and Call, V. 1988. *The Design and Content of the National Survey of Families and Households*. Working Paper NSFH-1. Madison: University of Wisconsin-Madison, Center for Demography and Ecology.

Thompson, L., and Walker, A. J. 1989. "Gender in Families: Women and Men in Marriage, Work and Parenthood." *Journal of Marriage and the Family* 51: 845–871.

Tucker, M. B., and Taylor, R. J. 1989 "Demographic Correlates of Relationship Status Among Black Americans." *Journal of Marriage and the Family* 51: 655–665.

Vega, W. A., Patterson, T., Sallis, J., Nader, P., Atkins, C., and Abramson, I. 1986. "Cohesion and Adaptability in Mexican American and Anglo Families." *Journal of Marriage and the Family* 48: 857–867.

Wilkie, J. R. 1991. "The Decline in Men's Labor Force Participation and Income and the Changing Structure of Family Economic Support." *Journal of Marriage and the Family* 53, no. 1: 111–122.

Williams, N. 1990. *The Mexican American Family: Tradition and Change*. Dix Hills, N.Y.: General Hall.

Wilson, M. N., Tolson, T. F. J., Hinton, I. D., and Kiernan, M. 1990. "Flexibility and Sharing of Childcare Duties in Black Families." *Sex Roles* 22, no. 7–8: 409–425.

Ybarra, L. 1982. "When Wives Work: The Impact on the Chicano Family." *Journal of Marriage and the Family* 44: 169–178.

Zinn, M. B. 1980. "Gender and Ethnic Identity Among Chicanos." *Frontiers* 2: 8–24.

———. 1991. "Family Feminism, and Race in America." In J. Lorber and S. A. Farrell, eds., *The Social Construction of Gender,* 110–134. Newbury Park, Calif.: Sage.

CAN A GAY MAN BE A HOUSEWIFE?
Gay Fathers Doing Gender, Family, and Parenting

Dana Berkowitz

Heteronormative assumptions about appropriate parents, gender norms, and child socialization continue to underpin the hegemonic view of family. Lesbian and gay families challenge these gender and heteronormative assumptions and expose the widening gap between the complex reality of contemporary families and the simplistic ideology that pervades modern family thought, scholarship, rhetoric, and policies. This paper advances theoretical understanding on how gay men discursively construct their procreative consciousness and fathering experiences. I maintain that attention to such discourse opens doors to new understandings of how societal surveillance fueled by heterosexism, homophobia, and constricting gender norms shapes gay men's fathering thoughts and experiences.

I draw upon my current research that explores the narratives of 22 gay fathers and 19 childless gay men. I detail how many of the men I spoke with relied upon dominant narratives of gender, kinship, biogenetics, and responsibility in the context of the interview setting. Participants described how they negotiate gender, sexuality, and real or imagined families within explicit gendered and heterosexist social boundaries; ultimately reifying certain discourses that I expected them to subvert or at least transgress. I argue that because these men and their families

Dana Berkowitz, "Can a Gay Man Be a Housewife? Gay Fathers Doing Gender, Family and Parenting." Edited from a version first presented at the American Sociological Association Annual Meeting, August 2007. Reprinted by permission of the author.

are under extreme surveillance and public scrutiny, they are forced to draw upon the very discourses that many family scholars expect them to reject.

BACKGROUND

I expand upon the procreative identity framework—a conceptual lens that was initially developed to explain how heterosexual men experience the procreative arena (Marsiglio & Hutchinson, 2002). The procreative identity framework is a useful conceptual lens to explore gay men's experiences in the reproductive realm because procreative consciousness is viewed as the cognitive and emotional awareness and expression of self as a person capable of creating and caring for life. Moreover, the framework treats this self-expression as a process-oriented phenomenon tied to situational contingencies, global sentiments, and romantic relationships. Although gay men's experiences are distinct in some ways, the basic conceptual lens is relevant to gay men because it accentuates how men's procreative consciousness is activated and evolves. Furthermore, the model's emphasis on both individual-based and relationship-based modes for expressing procreative consciousness draws attention to how gay men, on their own and in conjunction with partners, learn to frame their view about becoming fathers.

While it is sensible to extend the procreative identity framework to the experiences of gay men, extending a model originally conceptualized for heterosexual men is complicated. I hesitate to take knowledge developed by and for heterosexual men and risk incorrectly extending this knowledge to the experience of gay men. Although gay men's desire for parenthood may be similar in some situations to heterosexuals' feelings, gay men's access to fatherhood and fathering experiences are constructed within a heterosexually defined realm embedded with ideological proscriptions. To address this consideration, I draw upon the theoretical contributions of feminist sociologist Dorothy Smith. Smith maintains that women's consciousness has been created by men occupying positions of power (1987, 1990). I borrow from and expand on this framework positing that gay men's procreative consciousness has been constructed within a world that has traditionally assumed heterosexuality and continues to privilege heterosexual parenting. Smith maintains that consciousness is not merely something going on in people's heads, rather it is produced by people and it is a social product (Smith, 1990). Thus, in order to more completely understand gay men's procreative consciousness and their possible fantasies of fathering, there is a necessity to link this consciousness with the institutions that create, maintain, challenge, and eventually change how gay men have historically imagined fatherhood and families. Smith's framework helps to anchor gay men's personal thoughts and experiences about fatherhood within the political, historical, economic, and social process that shapes them. Smith's theoretical paradigm highlights how certain institutions and ruling relations, such as adoption and fertility agencies, and the institutionalization of both fatherhood and the gay subculture shape the processes by which gay men contemplate and experience fatherhood. For example, even though gay men's desire for parenthood and experiences of fathering may be similar in some situations to heterosexuals' feelings, gay men's access to adoption and assisted reproductive technologies is mediated by a bureaucratic apparatus that affects the conditions under which they can father (Lewin, 2006). This is especially important for this study because the majority of data were collected in Florida and New York. The former is currently one of the only states with explicit statutes prohibiting adoption by gay men and lesbians and

in the latter state all use of surrogate mothers is illegal (Horowitz & Maruyama, 1995; Mallon, 2004; Weltman, 2005).

I also draw upon the concept of doing fathering to show how men engage in fathering actions, behaviors, and processes. This concept emerges from West and Zimmerman's construct of doing gender (1987). The metaphor of doing gender was one of the first to reconceptualize gender as not so much a set of traits residing with individuals, but as something people do in their social interactions. "A person's gender is not simply an aspect of what one is, but more fundamentally, it is something that one does, recurrently, in interaction with others" (West and Zimmerman, 1987: 126). By using this conceptual lens to frame my analysis, fathering and more broadly family are viewed as situated accomplishments of my participants, and when fathering and family are viewed as such, the focus of analysis moves from matters internal to the individual to interactional and eventually institutional arenas. Thus, one is not only a father but one does fathering, just as one does gender. The concept of accountability is of primary significance here because given that much of society still defines family as a heterosexual two-parent nuclear structure, the families in my study came to be held accountable for every action each member performed. Accountability is relevant to both those actions that conform and deviate from prevailing normative conceptions about family. I stress that while individuals are the ones who do fathering and family, the process of rendering something accountable is both interactional and institutional.

The concept of accountability becomes critical as I move into a theoretical discussion of how heterosexual domination influences how gay men discursively do fathering and family. Accountability is of primary importance in the specific context of gay and lesbian headed families. Gay fathers are consistently viewed with suspicion because of myths surrounding issues of pedophilia, a desire to "replicate their lifestyle" and a perceived lack of ability to properly socialize children and inscribe them with stereotypical gendered norms.

Gay men's thoughts about fatherhood and fathering experiences are complex and dynamic. Thus, each of these theoretical lenses is necessary to expand the procreative identity framework and disentangle the convoluted web of gay men's fathering talk.

METHOD

As a qualitative method, in-depth interviewing accentuates the subjective quality of different life experiences, the contextual nature of knowledge, the production of social meanings, and the interactive character of human action. I use this interviewing technique to study the process by which gay men express their procreative consciousness, father identities, and fathering experiences.

Recruitment

Analysis draws on audiotaped, in-depth interviews conducted with a sample of 19 childless gay men and 22 gay fathers who have created families through nonheterosexual means. The participants were recruited through a variety of methods in diverse locales from 2004–2006. In South and North Central Florida, I used both snowball sampling and posted fliers in areas frequented by members of the gay community such as gay community centers, shopping malls, eating and drinking establishments, hair salons, and gay activist organizations. The fliers for the recruitment of childless gay men were a broad call for participants who might be interested in discussing their thoughts about fatherhood, without screening them for whether they intended to have children. The fliers for gay fathers specified that we were searching for men who had become fathers through any means other than heterosexual intercourse.

Participants

The group of childless gay men differed substantially from those who chose to become fathers through nonheterosexual means. These differences should not be regarded as a substantive finding of my research, but an artifact of my recruitment strategies. The childless gay participants were more racially,

ethnically, and economically diverse than the fathers. Three of the childless men were African American, 1 was Chinese-American, 2 were Latino, and 13 were White. Three participants had not completed college, 5 were enrolled in college with the intentions of graduating, 7 had graduated from a four-year university, and 4 had an advanced graduate degree. Two participants were Jewish, 1 was Presbyterian, 3 were Christian, 4 were Catholic, 1 was Buddhist and Catholic and 8 reported to have no religious affiliation. Six participants were students and the remaining participants were employed in either the service sector or the professional sector. Annual income for these men ranged from under $15,000 to over $75,000 annually. Ages of the childless men ranged from 19–53 and the mean age was 31.

Consistent with other research on gay fathers (Johnson & Connor, 2002; Mallon, 2004), the gay fathers participating in this research were White and predominantly upper middle class. All but 2 of these men earned over $75,000 annually, the remaining 2 earned between $30,000–$60,000, and the majority of participants were employed in the professional sector. Similarly, all participants except 2 had completed college and 8 had an advanced graduate degree. Fathers' ages ranged from 33–55 with a mean age of 43.5. Nine participants were Jewish, 5 were Catholic, 4 were Christian, 2 were Unitarian, and 3 claimed to have no religious affiliation. Participants created their families in diverse ways, including various forms of adoption, traditional and gestational surrogacy arrangements, and co-parenting with a lesbian woman or women.

Interviews

Semi-structured interviews were conducted that lasted from 45–120 minutes. They took place in a variety of settings (e.g., participants' households or work offices, coffee shops, eating and drinking establishments, the researcher's office, and over the telephone). Although it was my intention to conduct all interviews individually, 6 men who were coupled and had young children opted to be interviewed together. The qualitative interviews were preceded by a brief sociodemographic background survey. Interviews were open-ended and designed to generate rich, detailed information. Participants were encouraged to discuss their thoughts, feelings, experiences, and personal narratives regarding their images and decisions about fatherhood. Interviews were designed to explore the men's emerging identity as a prospective or real father, including how their father identity emerged out of interactions with other children, friends, family members, birth mothers, agency coordinators, and romantic partners.

Analysis

The initial textual material was analyzed with grounded theory methodology for qualitative data analysis (Glaser & Strauss, 1967; Strauss & Corbin, 1998). As ideas, terms, moods, and so on surfaced in multiple interviews, they were coded and given tentative labels during the open phase of coding. Open coding is a process of comparing concepts found in the text for classification as examples of some phenomenon. As similarities in experience, patterns, and emergent themes appeared, categories of phenomena were labeled and entered into a code list. This process of open coding enabled me to create an analytic process for identifying key categories and their properties (Strauss & Corbin, 1998).

My final stage of selective coding allowed me to compare themes identified in this study to existing literature exploring fathering talk among both gay and heterosexual men. The themes derived from this work unveil the dynamic and complex process of how gay men discursively construct their procreative and father identities in a socially constructed world that privileges heterosexuality.

FINDINGS

The remainder of this paper addresses how the men I spoke with drew upon dominant gender and familial discourses. First, I explore how men's descriptions of their procreative consciousness was framed within an essentialized context. Next, I move to a discussion of how men described their ideal fathering experiences and detail aspects related to the

privileging of biological ties and the dominant two-parent nuclear family. Finally, I examine how participants narrated their thoughts about engendering their children and their experiences of gender accountability. In each and every phase of procreative and fathering talk, men drew upon a discourse associated with the hegemonic family and/or normative gender stereotypes.

An Essentialized Procreative Consciousness

Regardless of one's sexuality, parenthood has become a reflective process in contemporary Western society. "Paths to parenthood no longer appear natural, obligatory, or uniform, but are necessarily reflexive, uncertain, self-fashioning, plural, and politically embattled" (Stacey, 2006, p. 28). Children have moved from an economic asset to an economic responsibility and even a liability. Thus, "an emotional rather than economic calculus governs the pursuit of parenthood" (Stacey, 2006, p. 28). Openly identified gay men who seek fatherhood face these dimensions of postmodern parenting in an exaggerated way. Furthermore, it has been documented that the thought processes that gay men undergo to become fathers are quite different from those experienced by their heterosexual counterparts (Barret & Robinson, 2000; Bigner & Jacobsen, 1989; Mallon, 2004). Many of the men I spoke with were well aware of emerging legal and reproductive opportunities that made their once outlandish daydreams of becoming a father now a viable reality. Yet, they also were well aware of how structural and institutional constraints shaped their experiences in the procreative realm.

More interestingly however was how some men explained their fathering desires within the constraints of dominant gender discourse. Nick, a soft-spoken 26-year-old who moved from the Midwest to Miami Beach a year earlier eloquently discussed his burning desire to father as equivalent to a woman's natural drive to mother:

> Because I was always gay and I did have some maternal instinct. Maybe at the time that women first, whenever, somewhere in adolescence, was when

I first started thinking I want to have a child . . . the older I got the more I considered it the same way as finding Mr. Right . . . this very important thing that would complete me. The only thing that could [complete me].

Nick cited identifying as gay as being tantamount to having a maternal urge. Further, he recognized that as a human being, the only thing that would fully complete him was creating a family of his own. Ross, a childless single man, echoed Nick's sentiments regarding a desire to father. He asserted that fatherhood is "the greatest thing that somebody can do. I think it enriches your life . . . you can give back to someone your good experiences, so they can become a good person."

That men discussed their procreative fantasies in terms of having a "maternal instinct," "the greatest thing that somebody can do" and "needing something to complete me" clearly speaks to our contemporary pronatalist milieu. It also touches on the notion of generativity, or the nurturing quality in individuals whereby they seek to "create and guide younger generations" (Marsiglio, 1995, p. 84). While some refer to gay men choosing fatherhood as postmodern pioneers (Stacey, 2006), the yearning to procreate, father, nurture, and have someone depend on you is a particularly modern characteristic. What is unique about this desire is only that it is being articulated by gay men, a population who because of gender and heterosexist norms are not expected to have these yearnings. Clearly, because gay men are raised within a socially constructed society that stresses pronatalism and generativity, their procreative desires and discourses are not so different from their heterosexual counterparts.

However, when we listen to how gay men negotiate these modern desires for fatherhood with their gay identity, essential ideologies associated with gender and sexuality surface. For example, while Luke wanted children in his future, he maintained that:

Gay men were not meant to be that way, if it was meant to be that way then two people would have stood beside each other and had a baby. Obviously there is a reason that our bodies are built to procreate and for a woman to go through that process.

Luke described his procreative urges within the constraints of a heteronormative discourse. If we take Luke's statement and juxtapose it against those of Nick and Ross, it illuminates how gay men's reliance on dominant familial, heterosexual, and gender discourse underscores the need for a more inclusive way of talking about parenting. Furthermore, because we live in a society that conflates and confuses gender and sexuality, gay men's procreative fantasies are narrated within the constraining framework of Western conceptions of gender and sexuality. Yet while many of the men describe their procreative desires within a gendered and heteronormative context, there were a few exceptions. Not surprisingly, one of these exceptions surfaced in my conversation with Segal, a fellow sociologist who is a leading scholar on gender and sexuality. He mentioned that my study should critically examine how heterosexism "hinders and hurts gay men." This reliance upon dominant gender and familial discourse is a theme that surfaced more than I would have ever imagined and confirms Segal's statement of how heterosexism constrains gay men's narrative abilities.

Essentializing Biology

The formation of a father identity for some of the men is mediated by the anticipated or actual presence of biological ties. Childless participants diverged in whether they desired a child who was biologically related to them. Some men explained that they preferred a child who would have blood ties to them, whereas others talked about wanting to adopt their future child. Zach, a childless 33-year-old Chinese-American restaurant manager, confessed that the only way he would have a child was if that child was biologically related to him. He elaborated:

I would love more than anything to have a child. My own as well. . . . If I am going to have a child, I want it to be a part of me . . . I want it to have some of my characteristics . . . I want to have a little piece of me . . . I think that if anything, that is really what drives all of it. I do want to have someone, a little piece of me out there doing a little something to contribute to the world.

Zach was one of the few childless men who was so explicit in his desire for a biological child. A handful of other childless men claimed that although a biological tie was preferred, adoption would be a second option. Taylor, also childless, explained, "adoption would just be the second option, like a fall back . . . I'd rather conceive a child with someone I know and trust . . . I guess I would rather have my own . . . but if that's not an option, adoption wouldn't change anything." Although Taylor and a few other men ideally preferred a biological relation between themselves and their child, as gay men and as prospective fathers, they realized their options were quite limited. Many other men, both childless and fathers, questioned their ability to feel the same level of affection for a child not biologically related to them as compared to a genetically related child. These statements illuminate how the men I spoke with still greatly valued biogenetic ties. Although I found a great deal of creative negotiation within these families, it is significant to recognize that such negotiations were regulated with the conventional privileging of biological relatedness at the forefront of these men's consciousness.

The Essential Family

The majority of childless men I spoke with perceived their futures as residing in an intimate partnership raising children. Noah articulated that, "I know that that's going to be the only way for me to have a kid, but I would like to, I would like to provide that child with more of a structured family than just a single parent." Walter echoed Noah's sentiments when he explained, "I'm not religious, but I think God made it so that two people have to create a child because it usually takes two people to parent a child." In an ideal family, most of these men saw themselves raising children in a (post)modern nuclear family: two men, two children, a pet, a suburban style house and a white picket fence. While gay men are marginalized from traditional family arrangements, my participants' narratives underscore that their ideal visions of family and fatherhood are forged within a dominant understanding of normative images of family. Moreover, men's visions of an ideal family were fashioned with the dominant mother as nurturer, father as provider familial ideology.

Noah fantasized his ideal parenting experience:

I definitely see myself being like the quintessential little housewife, if a gay man can be a housewife. Like, I very much and like take on the maternal role in the family, and in a relationship, I'm very much like the little wife. And I'm always cooking and cleaning for them, and like taking care of them, and so I think it's, when I think of myself having kids, I very much think of myself being like the soccer mom . . . I think about . . . where we would live and our family and I'd have my Volvo Sedan, my Sedan, my Volvo SUV with my SLK hardtop convertible, for when I want to have like mommy time, and be the soccer mom.

Noah's ideal fathering—or rather, mothering—visions take place within a 1950s glorified and somewhat postmodern conception of a Leave It to Beaver–esque family. The reliance by so many men on a dominant gender and family discourse points to a very uninclusive way of speaking about family. That Noah envisioned his parenting roles as a caretaker and nurturer and automatically equates these roles with taking on the role of a soccer mom speaks to the insidiousness of socially constructed gender norms within the family.

Gender Essentialism

A final theme that surfaced was how men spoke about negotiating the real or imagined gender of children. Many of the gay men's narratives underscored uncertainty with regards to how they envisioned coping with public bathroom issues, menstruation, bra-shopping, and the first dates of their future or present daughters. A vast majority of gay fathers painted a mental picture of a menstruating, bra-shopping, sexually active teenager and I heard constant concern from these men wondering if two dads could adequately deal with the "harsh" realities of a thirteen-year-old girl's pubescent phase. Rick and Art, fathers of a three-year-old boy spoke about how they fantasized about the challenges of having a little girl because, "We knew boy issues; we knew what to expect . . . we also thought girls were more difficult in terms of later on, with puberty and all that." Both Rick and Art questioned if two dads could adequately deal with the realities of a 13-year-old girl's pubescent phase.

When envisioning raising a girl child, many men discussed the importance of securing a suitable role model for her, particularly during her pubescent phase. Noah explained:

> I like to think that like my mother or my partner's mother or my female friends would be there and that they would . . . like help her out and like if she's having like maybe, if I had a daughter and she's 12 years old, and she's got her period, and like I'd like to have help with that, but I understand where she would feel uncomfortable coming to me, so, I see that you know the presence of like other women or a mother or someone who'd be involved is beneficial.

When men envisioned taking up the tasks of raising a girl, preparation and planning become critical. Such planning always includes guaranteeing a suitable role model for their girl children to assist with milestones like menstruation.

If I were to follow a folk logic, it makes sense that two men would have anxiety about raising a girl child because in their minds, their own experiences would not easily parallel hers. However, some participants wondered how their gender and sexuality would interact to negatively affect their boy children's future socialization. Marc, the proud single father of a four-year-old girl explained, "If I have a boy, will I be as good as a role model? You know, dads take their sons to ball games and things like that, which I am just not into . . . if I had a boy, it might be somewhat difficult to do that 'macho' role model." Because Marc was never the stereotypical masculine athlete, he questioned whether he could participate with his imagined son in "normal"

male-bonding activities. In most cases, it is taken for granted that someone can appropriately raise a child of the same gender, but in some cases, like Marc's own, gender atypical behavior is cited as a reason for not being a suitable role model for children of the same gender. Hence, the men's perceptions of their future children's gender socialization helped forge the men's child and fathering visions as well as their procreative and father identities. However, such considerations were clearly framed within rigid gender stereotypes.

Sanctions against gay men for doing gender incorrectly are rampant in heterosexist U.S. society. These sanctions are exacerbated in the case of gay parents, in that they have a unique type of surveillance surrounding both their own normative gendered behavior as well as their children's gendered actions and attitudes. Because the heterosexual nuclear family has become institutionalized as an "ideological code" (Smith, 1990), gay fathers are held accountable for the gendered outcomes of their children. Thus, the panoptic gaze of the heterosexual eye serves as a surveillance mechanism that commands these fathers to engage in self-monitoring their children's gendered actions, to become per Foucault (1977) "docile bodies" inscribed with normative gender standards.

This becomes more lucid when we explore how men spoke about how they actually did fathering. Lawrence is a gay father with two teenage sons who never doubted his own ability to instill his teenage boys with "proper" masculine ideals. Nevertheless, he recalled a scenario when an outsider who happened to be in close proximity to him and his son scrutinized his fathering skills:

> I remember once Issac [older son] was crying, he was like 3-years-old, and he hurt himself and he was crying, and there was this painter in the house, and the painter kept saying, "be a man, be a man." And my instinct is to hug him and wait until he stopped crying, and let him sit there and calm down, you know. But this man's thing was "be a man" which is I think what many people would say. . . . So, I just took him away, and I didn't say any more.

Gender scholars have argued that normative definitions such as No Sissy Stuff, The Big Wheel, The Sturdy Oak, and Give 'em Hell give men a blueprint for how to live their lives (Brannon, as cited in Connell, 1995 and Kimmel, 1994). As an adult gay man reared with these gendered blueprints, Lawrence was acutely aware of the rigid definitions of masculinity in contemporary society. As such, he was keenly attentive to the pressures of raising a man in a socially constructed world that defines masculinity in such strict terms. In contemporary society, raising a boy to be a "proper" and "suitable" man is simultaneous with preparing him to fit into the historically and socially constructed version of hegemonic masculinity that is culturally dominant (Connell, 1995, 2000).

Lawrence also elaborated on another time when an outsider commented on his son's masculine development. Many years prior to the interview, Lawrence was with his two young sons at a local playground. He clearly remembered another father approaching his younger son, who had recently been wounded and was wailing at the pain. The man exclaimed, "Oh stop crying, you're acting like a girl" to the young boy. Although Lawrence was tempted to retort "What is wrong with being a girl?" he quickly stopped himself from succumbing to his immediate response and simply picked up his boy and walked away. Lawrence explained that he was uncomfortable with having another adult man fill his son's head with stereotypical masculine ideals. At the same time, Lawrence clearly did not want to get in a verbal argument in a public playground about the unfairness of the expectation that boys should not display emotion. Furthermore, Lawrence was in a paradoxical dilemma: he should not want his son to have to act in accordance with hegemonic ideals of masculinity, yet he understood that in order to survive as a man in contemporary society, one needs to adapt to certain normative gender standards.

DISCUSSION

This paper details how gay men discursively construct their procreative and father identities within the constrictions of a gendered and heteronormative discourse. My analysis underscores the needs to move beyond the social and structural constraints in attaining fatherhood to distinguish what type of father identities and families are produced in these distinct settings. Expanding the pro-creative identity framework developed for heterosexual men with Smith's feminist sociology, West and Zimmerman's (1987) concept of accountability and a Foucaultian power/knowledge (1977) framework brings us closer to grasping the insidious effects of heterosexual surveillance on gay and lesbian parents.

Whereas the closet as a strategy of accommodating to heterosexual domination is becoming less salient, this does not necessarily denote that heterosexual domination is a remnant of the past. The discourses of my participants demonstrate that whether it is the 1970s, 80s, 90s or today, gay men are still growing up in a world organized by heterosexuality. Although many individuals today can choose to live beyond the closet, they must still reside in a world where most institutions maintain heterosexual domination. My conversations with these men show how heterosexual dominance is deeply rooted in the institutions and culture of American society and must be understood as not simply a product of laws or individual prejudice, but institutionalized pervasive dominance (Seidman, 2004).

The insights I generate about gay men and their fathering talk should be viewed in context and their limitations noted. Meanwhile, because the process of becoming a gay father through nonheterosexual means is often financially costly, and because of my recruitment strategies, the fathers who participated in my study were primarily white and in the professional class. Regrettably, I am unable to speak to how minority men and gay men of more limited financial means discursively construct their procreative and father identities. That is an area for further research.

LITERATURE CITED

Barret, R. L., & Robinson, B. E. (2000). *Gay Fathers*. San Francisco: Jossey-Bass.

Bigner, J. J., & Jacobsen, R. B. (1989). The value of children to gay and heterosexual fathers. *Journal of Homosexuality*, 18:12, 163–172.

Connell, R. W. (1995). *Masculinities.* Berkeley: University of California Press.

Foucault, M. (1977). *Power/Knowledge: Selected interviews and other writings, 1972–1977.* New York: Pantheon.

Glaser, B. G., & Strauss, A. L. (1967). *The discovery of grounded theory: Strategies for qualitative research.* Hawthorne, NY: Aldine de Gruyter.

Horowitz, R. M., & Maruyama, H. (1995). *Legal issues in gay and lesbian adoption: Proceedings from the Fourth Annual Pierce-Warwick Adoption Symposium.* Washington, DC: Child Welfare League of America.

Johnson, S. M., & Connor, E. M. (2002). *The gay baby boom: The psychology of gay parenthood.* New York: New York University Press.

Kimmel, M. (1994). Masculinity as homophobia: Fear, shame, and silence in the construction of gender identity. In Harry Brod and Michael Kaufman (Eds.), *Theorizing masculinities* (pp. 119–141). Thousand Oaks, CA: Sage.

Lewin, E. (2006). Family values: Gay men and adoption in America. In K. Wegar (Ed.) Adoptive families in a diverse society (pp. 129–145). New Brunswick, NJ: Rutgers University Press.

Mallon, G. P. (2004). *Gay men choosing parenthood.* New York: Columbia University Press.

Marsiglio, W. (1995). *Procreative man.* New York: New York University Press.

Marsiglio, W., & Hutchinson, S. (2002). *Sex, men, and babies: Stories of awareness and responsibility.* New York: New York University Press.

Seidman, S. (2004). *Beyond the closet: The transformation of gay and lesbian life.* New York: Routledge.

Smith, D. (1987). *The everyday world as problematic: A feminist sociology.* Toronto: University of Toronto Press.

Smith, D. (1990). *Conceptual practices of power: Toward a feminist sociology of knowledge.* Boston: Northeastern University Press.

Stacey, J. (2006). Gay parenthood and the decline of paternity as we knew it. *Sexualities, 9,* 27–55.

Strauss, A., & Corbin, J. (1998). *Basics of qualitative research: Techniques and procedures for developing grounded theory* (2nd ed.). Newbury Park, CA: Sage.

Weltman, J. J. (2004, August 26). Surrogacy in New York. *Resolve of New York.* Retrieved September 1, 2005, from http://www.surrogacy.com/Articles/news_view.asp?ID=128.

West, C., and Zimmerman, D. (1987). Doing gender. *Gender & Society, 1,* 2: 125–151.

MASCULINITIES IN RELIGION

GOD IS A MAN! was the full-page headline of the *New York Post*, a local tabloid newspaper, on June 17, 1991. Apparently, during a Father's Day sermon, John Cardinal O'Connor, then the Archbishop of New York City, had excoriated radical feminists who had suggested the possibility of a more androgynous, all-embracing deity.

Well, is he—or she? All the monotheistic religions tend to think so: in Islam, Christianity and Judaism, God is always depicted and understood as masculine. (not necessarily so in other religious traditions)

And what does it mean? All over the globe the twin trends are dramatic secularization—as scientific criteria dominate more and more of our understanding of life itself—and dramatic religious resurgence (except in Europe), as people return to the faiths of their forbears to explain the most basic questions of existence.

More than just the gender of God, masculinity is deeply implicated in all aspects of religion—from the gender of canonical texts to the gender of the people who are authorized to speak.

In this part, we present several different approaches to thinking about the relationship between masculinity and religion. Theologian Leonard Swidler turns conventional gender stereotypes on their heads by asserting that Jesus was a feminist. Michael S. Kimmel uses his own experiences to explore the associations between Judaism, masculinity, and feminism, while Yasemin Besen and Gilbert Zicklin develop an empirical study of the relationship between masculinity, religion, and attitudes toward gay men. Finally, the article by Sally Gallagher and Sabrina Wood looks inside a recent religious movement designed to bring manly men back to God.

YOUNG MEN, RELIGION AND ATTITUDES TOWARDS HOMOSEXUALITY

Yasemin Besen   Gilbert Zicklin

Attitudes towards gays and lesbians are an important topic for social scientists, politicians and policy makers. Many recent studies have documented the increasing acceptance of gays and lesbians in the United States (Loftus, 2001; Werum and Winders, 2001).

While many organizations have become more accepting and supportive of gay rights, religions and religious institutions have in general been unsupportive. Young people have therefore come of age caught between increasing support for and acceptance of gays from secular authorities and a strong counter-mobilization from the religious right. Young men in particular constitute an interesting research area, as they show less acceptance and tolerance towards gays than their female counterparts, despite the fact that young people on the whole are more tolerant than the rest of the population. Young men, therefore, seem to be situated at the intersection of two forces: one making them more tolerant, the other less. This paper focuses on young men and explores the effects of age, gender and particularly religiosity on their attitudes towards gay men and lesbians. We investigate the complex relationship of religiosity, masculinity and gay rights and unravel the effects of these seemingly contrasting influences.

Yasemin Besen_Cassino and Gilbert Zicklin, "Young Men, Religion and Attitudes Towards Homosexuality," *Journal of Men, Masculinities and Spirituality*, 1(3) November, 2007.

PRIOR RESEARCH

Prior research consistently shows that attitudes towards gay men and women have generally tended to be negative (Louderback and Whitley Jr., 1997). This anti-gay prejudice has been distinct and well documented in research done with convenience samples from college students (Herek, 1984, 1986; Kite, 1994) as well as large scale, representative surveys (Herek, 1991; Herek and Capitanio, 1996; Herek and Glunt, 1993). Overall, attitudes towards gay men and lesbians seem to be improving consistently over time as Americans become increasingly liberal in their opinions about civil liberties (Brooks, 2000). They have gained social acceptance from some parts of the U.S. population, but face opposition from others (Loftus, 2001; Werum and Winders 2001).

Attitudes towards gay men and lesbians have been explained by numerous factors. Individuals holding negative attitudes towards gay men and women tend to be more authoritarian, less educated, more traditional in sex roles and show negative attitudes towards minority groups (Herek, 1984 and 1991).

MEN

One of the most central factors in attitudes towards homosexuality is the sex of the respondent. Many studies show that men on average have more negative attitudes towards gays and lesbians than women (Glenn and Weaver, 1979; Lottes and Kuriloff, 1992; Herek and Glunt, 1993; Kirkpatrick, 1993;

Louderback and Whitley, 1997; Marsiglio, 1993; Kerns and Fine, 1994; Kite and Whitley, 1996; LaMar and Kite, 1998; Aberson, Swan and Emerson, 1999; Cotten-Huston and Waite, 2000; Wills and Crawford, 2000; Brown and Amoroso, 1975; Kite and Whitley, 1996; Glassner and Owen, 1976; Gurwitz and Marcus, 1978; Hansen, 1982; Kite, 1984; Laner and Laner, 1979; Millham et al., 1976; Minnigerode, 1976; Steffensmeier and Steffensmeier, 1974; Storms, 1978; Weiss and Dein, 1979). However, even though this sex difference is well documented, few attempts have been made to explain it (Herek, 1988).

Further inquiries also show that attitudes towards gay men and women differ based on the sex of the target in interaction with the respondent's sex (Kite and Whitley, 1996). Mary Kite and Bernard Whitley (1996) show that men are more negative towards gay men than women are while there are no differences between men and women in their attitudes towards lesbian women.

Kite and Whitley (1996) explain this difference based on gender belief systems. Gender belief systems define appropriate behaviors for men and women: people use these gender stereotypes to define what is feminine and masculine, and form opinions about others depending on how well they conform to them. They suggest that attitudes towards homosexuals are shaped by these existing gender belief systems. Because society has more strict expectations of masculinity than femininity (Herek, 1986; Hort, Fagot and Leinbach, 1990), men who display feminine traits receive more negative reaction than women who display masculine traits. We would therefore expect that gay men who violate male gender stereotypes to receive more negative reaction than gay women who violate female gender stereotypes. Furthermore, the more one is invested in the gender belief system, the more one is likely to have a negative view of gays and lesbians because they deviate from the gender norm, possibly forcing one to question the system itself. An additional explanation could be found in men's traditional definitions of masculinity. To the extent that gay men differ from heterosexual men's definitions of traditional, normative masculinities,

heterosexual men's masculine identities might be threatened (Epstein, 1995, 1998; Herek and Capitanio, 1999), leading to more negative feelings towards gay men.

Support for this view of masculinity threat leading to more negative views of gay men can be found in the differential views of men and women towards both gay men and women. In addition to the main effect of sex on attitudes towards homosexuality, where men have more negative attitudes on average towards gays than women do, there is also an indirect effect of sex on attitudes towards homosexuality. While women show no difference in their attitudes towards gay men and women, men have more negative attitudes towards gay men that towards gay women. While gay men seem to threaten heterosexual male's gender belief systems, lesbianism is seen as erotic and therefore unthreatening (Reiss, 1986; Louderback and Whitley, 1997).

RELIGION

Religion is an important factor in the understanding of discrimination against gay men and lesbians (McFarland, 1989). First, religious orientation is identified as a factor leading to discrimination, not just against gay men and lesbians, but racial discrimination as well (Allport and Ross, 1967; Batson, 1971). In the now-classic Allport and Ross model (1967), religious orientation is classified as *extrinsic*, where the individual uses religion to gain "security, comfort, status or social support" (p. 441) or intrinsic, where the individual uses religion only for personal and individual reasons. Similarly, C. D. Batson's (1971) three factor model classifies religious orientation as *Religion as Means*, where religion is a means to reach an end, *Religion as End*, where religion is as an end in itself and finally *Religion as Quest*, where religion is a way to reach truth. Extensive research shows extrinsic religion is positively related, intrinsic religion unrelated and quest religion negatively related with discrimination (McFarland, 1989). Most of this research focuses on racial discrimination, however. Some prior studies point to the effects of religious orientation on gender discrimination and discrimination towards gays and lesbians; unfortunately, there is little research focusing exclusively on attitudes towards gays and lesbians. Extant research points to higher discrimination against women and gays and lesbians in intrinsic religion (McClain, 1979; McFarland, 1989), suggesting that the relationship between religious categories and attitudes towards gays is similar to that of religious categories and attitudes towards blacks.

Recent studies that focus exclusively on gay and lesbian discrimination show that some religions are more conservative and less accepting of gays and lesbians than others. Jews, those with no religious affiliation, and inactive Christians have higher rates of gay and lesbian support than Catholics, who are, in turn, more tolerant than Protestants, who show the lowest levels of tolerance towards gays and lesbians (Irwin and Thompson, 1977; Glenn and Weaver, 1979; Henley and Pincus 1978; Lottes and Kuriloff, 1992; Wills and Crawford, 2000).

RELIGIOSITY

In addition to the overall effect of religious orientation, fundamentalism and being a born-again Christian are specifically identified as factors associated with negative attitudes towards gays and lesbians (Herek, 1987). Within the large category of Protestants, fundamentalism – a belief in the literal truth of the Bible – is a particular factor related to attitudes towards gays and lesbians. Herek's (1987) findings show that fundamentalism increased prejudice towards gays and lesbians. Other studies confirm the effects of fundamentalism on negative attitudes towards gays and lesbians (Wagenaar and Barton, 1977; Herek and Glunt, 1993; Kirkpatrick, 1993; Marsiglio, 1993; Cutton, Hudson and Waite, 2000). Unfortunately, since fundamentalism is not included as a control in other studies (i.e. McClain, 1979), it is hard to predict the direct and indirect effects of religion and fundamentalism.

Finally, in addition to religion and fundamentalism, religiosity or attending services is identified as a distinct factor associated with negative attitudes towards gay men and lesbians. Many studies have found that the more individuals attend services, outside of weddings and funerals, the less tolerant they are of gays and lesbians (Beatty and Walker, 1984; Cochran and Beeghley, 1991; Herek and Glunt, 1993). Randy Fisher et al. (1994), however, point out that for individuals who belong to more progressive and accepting religions, attendance at services has no effect on attitudes towards homosexuality. It remains unclear if the effects are due to the reinforcement of an anti-gay message at less progressive churches, or due to a selection effect, with less tolerant individuals attending church more often.

POLITICAL IDEOLOGY

Religiosity is also closely related to political ideology as both deal with the idea of morality. According to Paul Brewer (2003), public opinion on gays and lesbians is partially explained as an issue of equality (McClosky and Zaller, 1984; Wilcox and Wolpert, 1996 and 2000), partially linked to political party affiliation and political ideology (Haeberle, 1999; Lewis and Rogers, 1999; Wilcox and Norrander, 2002) and partially as a moral issue (Lewis and Rogers, 1999). Therefore, the political affiliation and views of individuals are an important factor in understanding their views on gay issues.

CONTACT

Furthermore, knowing someone who is gay tends to lead to more positive attitudes towards gays and lesbians (Gentry, 1987; Herek, 1988; Schneider and Lewis, 1984). Further and more recent studies confirm these findings (Ellis and Vasseur, 1993; Herek and Capitanio, 1996; LaMar and Kite, 1998; Cotten-Huston and Waite, 2000; Wills and Crawford, 2000). However, this interpretation has been criticized methodologically because just as having openly gay relatives and friends could make one more likely to have positive attitudes, the direction of causality could be in the other direction, so that it could be argued that people who support gay rights tend to associate with people who are openly gay.

Further research also points to other correlates such as income, education, geographic region and race and ethnicity (Herek, 1984; Schneider and Lewis, 1984), which are important control factors.

ATTITUDES AND POLICY AREAS

In the literature, partly due to data restrictions, attitudes towards gay men and lesbians are generally measured as a unified category, mostly through a feeling thermometer as to how positive or negative one feels towards gay men and lesbians on a scale from 0–100. However, attitude towards gay men and lesbians is not a single unified category. While feeling thermometers are useful, it is important to see the inner differences within the overall attitude. Unpacking policy views in this way will give us crucial insight into the differences in opinion regarding different issues. Different factors may be associated with different concrete aspects of gay related issues: for instance, having gays in the military may be more of a threat to heterosexual men's masculinity than allowing gays to adopt children. Therefore, we shall look at concrete, policy related issues such as gay marriage, gay adoption and gays in the military.

Furthermore, each of these issues is separate and divides survey respondents in distinct ways. Rather than grouping them all together, it is important to model approvals and factors explaining opinion in each category separately. This will allow for a more nuanced understanding of attitudes towards gays and lesbians.

By exploring attitudes towards these issues, this paper focuses on the complex and interrelated relationship between gender, age and religion. The intersection of these areas creates a unique place for young men. While men are traditionally less supportive of gay rights, young people are more supportive. Young men, therefore, are at the center of two opposing social forces. How does belonging to two categories of contrasting views predominate young men's attitudes towards gays and lesbians? Furthermore, religion and religiosity are central factors in explaining support for gay rights: we will pay special attention to the attitudes of young religious men and unravel the intertwined relationship of gender, age and religiosity in explaining attitudes towards gay men and lesbians.

METHODS

Our data come from the Pew Center, which conducts regular national surveys that measure social and political attitudes, values and public attentiveness. Our data come from the recent March 2006 survey on attitudes towards homosexuality. This dataset provides extensive information on factors predicting attitudes towards gays and lesbians, ranging from demographic factors to attitudinal factors, providing the opportunity to estimate a comprehensive model in understanding opinions. It offers a very large, nationally representative sample (n = 1405).

Our aim is to understand attitudes towards gay men and lesbians. As noted before, however, though these attitudes are multi-faceted, most datasets on the topic do not typically include many different variables. The dataset allows us to see differential opinions based on the issue, measured by three dependent variables: approval of gay marriage, approval of gay adoption and approval of openly gay people serving in the military. These three variables were recoded as dichotomous variables, coded 1 if the respondent approved and 0 otherwise.

Three separate models were estimated, predicting the above dependent variables. Since the dependent variables are dichotomous, logistic regression models were estimated. The independent variables included in the models were uniform to enable comparison. The first set of independent variables included in the model is demographic variables. Sex of the respondent was recoded as a dummy variable where 1 = male and 0 = female. Age of the respondent was asked in years as a continuous variable. However, in addition to age as a continuous variable, a dummy variable for being 18–24-year-olds was included (labeled "youth" in the tables presenting the regression results). While the continuous age variable captures the gradual effect of age, the dummy variable should capture any threshold effect. Income, measured in dollars was included, as was race, recoded into a dummy variable as white = 1 and non-white = 0; Hispanic was coded as 1 if Hispanic and 0 otherwise. Finally, marital status and parenthood are important demographic factors, which could potentially affect attitudes towards gay men and lesbians, especially given their established relationship with authoritarianism (Altemeyer, 1996). Therefore, both these variables were recoded to test for the effects of being married, coded 1 if married and 0 otherwise and being a parent, coded 1 if parent and 0 otherwise. Finally, political affiliation was included as two separate dummy variables: Republican (coded 1 if Republican and 0 otherwise) and Democrat (coded 1 if Democrat and 0 otherwise), leaving political independents as the excluded category.

In addition to demographic factors which affect attitudes towards homosexuality, we have included a series of factors on religion, religiosity and being a born-again Christian. First, we have coded the religious affiliations of the respondents as dummy variables. In addition to the effects of religious affiliation, religiosity was measured through attending services aside from weddings and funerals, measured in number of times the respondent attends religious services on a weekly basis.

Finally, being a born-again Christian was included as a separate category, where the respondents who identified themselves as born-again Christians were coded as 1 and 0 otherwise. While being born-again is not exactly the same as fundamentalism, it is a closely related concept, and should be indicative of many of the same attitude structures.

We have also included attitudinal variables in predicting attitudes towards gay men and lesbians, such as attitudes towards abortion, coded as 1 if approve and 0 otherwise. This inclusion is not intended to imply that views on abortion lead to views on policies relating to homosexuals, but rather to control for general attitudes towards culture war issues (Lindaman and Haider-Markel, 2002). Controlling for these attitudes in such a way allows us to isolate the effects of the other variables specifically on gay rights issues, rather than on the broader category of cultural policy questions. Furthermore, we have included a measure of media exposure, predicting attitudes towards homosexuality such that respondents, who have access to media and are exposed to homosexuality would have more positive views, through access to the Internet coded 1 for access and 0 otherwise.

In addition to the direct effects of these variables, in explaining attitudes towards gay marriage, gay adoption and gays in the military, we have included a series of interaction effects to capture the interactive effects of these variables through gender. We hypothesize that being a male, particularly a young male, would affect how some of the above variables would affect attitudes towards homosexuality. For this purpose, we have included interaction effects of male by white, parent, married, born-again, Republican, Democrat, Internet Access, Abortion Attitudes, Religiosity and Age.

To explain attitudes towards gay men and lesbians, three logistic regression models were estimated, predicting attitudes towards gay marriage, gay adoption and gays in the military, all using the same independent variables to allow for easy comparison. To isolate the effects of being male and young instead of dividing the dataset and losing sample size, dummy variables were employed instead as well as interactions to capture both direct and indirect effects.

INITIAL RESULTS

First, we looked at the descriptive statistics on attitudes towards gay marriage, gay adoption and gays in the military. While these three aspects all constitute attitudes towards gay men and lesbians in our society, each issue differs in terms of approval rates. Table 37.1 shows attitudes towards each issue in percentages in the overall population and amongst 18–24-year-old men.

■ **TABLE 37.1**

Attitudes towards gay marriage, adoption and military for young men and the overall population (in percentages)

		Overall Population	Men 18–24
Gay Marriage	Strongly Favor	9.5	17.4
	Favor	29.6	26.1
	Oppose	28.2	17.4
	Strongly Oppose	32.7	39.1
Gay Adoption	Strongly Favor	13.3	19.6
	Favor	33.5	32.1
	Oppose	25.7	21.4
	Strongly Oppose	27.5	26.8
Gay Military	Strongly Favor	20.7	32.3
	Favor	43.7	35.5
	Oppose	20.1	16.1
	Strongly Oppose	15.4	16.1

Source: Pew Center, 2006.

Among these three, allowing gays to serve openly in the military has the highest approval rate, at 64.4 percent of the overall population, with 20.7 percent strongly favoring. This is followed by gay adoption, with 46.8 percent (13.3 percent strongly favoring) of the overall population supporting policies that would allow gays to adopt children. This is followed closely by gay marriage, with 39.1 percent of the overall population supporting gay marriage, though only about 10 percent strongly support it.

When we look specifically at young men between the ages 18 and 24 – the same group represented by the dummy variable in the logistic regression models – we see that young men have higher levels of support on all three issues. However, their ranking of support follows the same pattern as the overall population, even though their approval in every category is higher. The highest approval rate is for gays in the military, where 67.8 percent of young men support openly gay people serving in the military, almost half of those

strongly supporting it. This is followed by gay adoption, where 51.7 percent of young men support gay adoption (19.6 percent of them strongly) and finally 43.5 percent of young men support gay marriage, while an almost equal number, 39.1 percent, strongly oppose it.

Compared to the overall population, young men between the ages 18 and 24 show higher support for three issues, but they follow general society's rankings of these issues. As Figure 37.1 shows, young men also seem to cluster around more extreme categories: strongly agree, strongly disagree, rather than in the middle categories.

On all three issues, young men are more likely to "strongly support" gay-friendly policies. Also, the proportion of young men strongly opposing gay adoption and gays in the military are much lower than those in the overall population. The exception is in gay marriage, where the proportion strongly opposing is rather higher at 39.1 percent, opposed to 32.7 in the overall population.

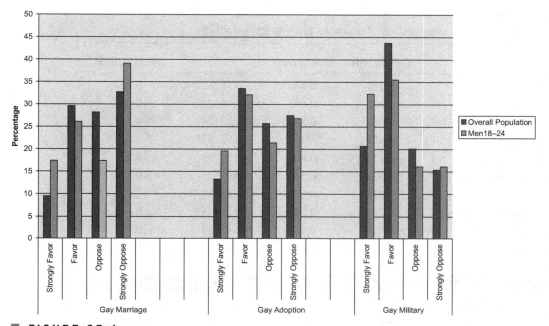

■ **FIGURE 37.1**
Comparative Attitudes for Young Men and Overall Population.

LOGISTIC REGRESSION RESULTS

While these descriptive statistics show us initial differences between young men and the overall population, a more accurate picture requires that we isolate the effects of sex and age. The first logistic regression model explains attitudes towards gay marriage.

Interestingly, there is no independent effect of sex on attitudes towards gay marriage, meaning that, on the whole, men are not less likely than women to approve of gay marriage. Also, there is no threshold effect of age, meaning that the effect of age on approval is relatively linear, and that 18 to 24 year-olds are not different as a group than members of other age groups. The linear effect of age can be seen in the age variable, which shows that the older people are, the less likely they are to approve of gay marriage. So, while age is a marginally significant predictor, young men do not show differential approval rates.

Overall, approval of gay marriage is predicted by a combination of demographic, attitudinal and religious variables. Higher income, being a Democrat, being Roman Catholic and favoring abortion increases the likelihood of approving of gay marriage. Being religious, identifying oneself as a born-again Christian, being a Republican and being a parent decreases the likelihood of approving gay marriage.

While men and women show no differences in their attitudes towards gay marriage, the one marginally significant interaction effect is between being male and being a parent. While being a parent makes one less likely to approve of gay marriage, this is not the case for men who are parents: they are more likely to approve of gay marriage.

So, overall, when we look specifically at gay marriage and model its approval, we see that young people are more supportive, yet being a male has no significant direct effect.

■**TABLE 37.2**
Logistic regression estimates predicting attitudes towards gay marriage

	Coefficient	Std. Error	t	Significance
Male × White	−0.295	0.771	−0.38262	0.702
Male × Parent	1.002	0.602	1.664452	0.096
Male × Born Again	0.663	0.576	1.151042	0.249
Male × Republican	0.622	0.64	0.971875	0.331
Male × Democrat	−0.471	0.607	−0.77595	0.438
Male × Internet Use	0.395	0.584	0.67637	0.498
Male × Married	−0.019	0.561	−0.03387	0.973
Male × Abortion Views	0.273	0.543	0.502762	0.615
Male × Religiosity	−0.078	0.18	−0.43333	0.667
Male × Age	0.032	0.02	1.6	0.104
Male	−2.582	1.564	−1.6509	0.099
Democrat	0.865	0.424	2.040094	0.042
Age × Church Attendance	−0.006	0.006	−1	0.314
Youth	−0.228	0.704	−0.32386	0.746
Abortion	−1.705	0.379	−4.49868	0
Internet	−0.294	0.418	−0.70335	0.482
Roman Catholic	0.742	0.306	2.424837	0.015
Born Again	−0.918	0.413	−2.22276	0.026
Republican	−0.979	0.472	−2.07415	0.038
Parent	−1.022	0.425	−2.40471	0.016
Marital Status	−0.197	0.369	−0.53388	0.594
Hispanic	−0.33	0.565	−0.58407	0.559
Race	0.454	0.555	0.818018	0.414
Income	0.115	0.056	2.053571	0.04
Religiosity	0.739	0.335	2.20597	0.028
Age	−0.041	0.022	−1.86364	0.063
Constant	0.726	1.574	0.461245	0.645

Note: Shaded coefficients significant at $\alpha = 0.05$.

Our second model looks at approval of gay adoption. While age was a significant factor in explaining gay marriage – younger people were more likely to approve – age does not seem to be a factor in approval for gay adoption, either as a continuous or threshold effect. Sex also has no direct effect: men and women on average do not seem significantly different in their attitudes towards gay adoption. Therefore, solely being a young male does not seem to lead to differences in approval of gay adoption.

The direct significant effects seem comparable to attitudes towards gay marriage. The significant predictors of approval of gay marriage are religiosity, where the more often the respondent attends services, the less likely he or she is to approve of gay marriage, being married, where being married makes the respondent less likely to approve of gay adoption, being a Republican, which makes one less likely to approve of gay adoption, being a born-again Christian, which makes one less likely to approve of gay marriage, being Roman Catholic, which makes one more likely to approve and approving of abortion, which makes one more likely to approve of gay adoption. This final result indicates that as with approval of gay marriage, being more liberal on other culture war issues makes it more likely that the respondent will be more liberal with regard to gay adoption. A new significant predictor is Internet access, which makes people more likely to approve of gay adoption. This might be because the Internet provides more exposure and provides more information, leading to more positive attitudes towards gay adoption. However, it could also be interpreted as a self-selection bias, where younger and more liberal people, in ways not captured by other variables, tend to have Internet access.

While being male has no direct effects on approval of gay adoption, there are many significant and interesting interaction effects. Overall, the less frequently a respondent attends religious services, the more likely he or she is to approve of gay adoption. However, men who attend services are less likely than women who attend religious services to approve of gay adoption.

Also, among married people – even though being married makes one less likely to approve of gay adoption – married men, compared to married women, are more likely to approve. Finally, white men are less likely than white women to approve of gay adoption.

Our final model deals with attitudes towards gays in the military. Here, we see a completely different picture. While being male had no significant effects on the gay marriage and gay adoption, it is a significant predictor of approval of gays in the military, where men are more likely to approve of allowing gays to serve openly in the military. Age, however has no significant effect: there is no difference between older and younger people in their attitudes towards gays in the military.

Religiosity is a significant predictor of approval of gays in the military. Interestingly, we also detect a significant interaction effect of religiosity and being male. Being a religious man, compared to a religious woman, makes one less likely to approve of gays in the military. Similarly, male parents are less approving of gays in the military than their female counterparts.

DISCUSSION

This analysis yields a complex mapping of relationship between young men's attitudes towards different gay rights issues and their religiosity. In all three issues, we see religiosity and being born-again as leading to disapproval. Parallel with the argument made by Glock and Stark (1966), our results show that more religious and fundamentalist people display a more "closed-minded, ethnocentric mindset, which is shown here as a general tendency to discriminate" (McFarland, 1989, p. 333).

However, men do not have less support for all three issues. When we separate the issues, for gay marriage, gender has no effect: therefore men and women are not different in their attitudes on at least one of the issues. This might also be because of the lack of a linear relationship: it is possible that some men approve and some disapprove, resulting in a curvilinear relationship between gender and support for gay marriage, which requires further research. Age, however, is not as important as we predicted.

■ **TABLE 37.3**

Logistic regression estimates predicting attitudes towards gay adoption

	Coefficient	Std. Error	t	Significance
Male × White	−0.938	0.472	−1.98729	0.047
Male × Parent	0.119	0.384	0.309896	0.757
Male × Born Again	0.21	0.36	0.583333	0.561
Male × Republican	0.403	0.401	1.004988	0.315
Male × Democrat	0.001	0.397	0.002519	0.997
Male × Internet Use	0.215	0.384	0.559896	0.576
Male × Married	0.729	0.359	2.030641	0.042
Male × Abortion Views	−0.19	0.338	−0.56213	0.574
Male × Religiosity	−0.245	0.119	−2.05882	0.039
Male × Age	−0.012	0.012	−1	0.312
Male	0.513	0.985	0.520812	0.603
Democrat	0.264	0.265	0.996226	0.319
Age × Church Attendance	−0.003	0.003	−1	0.411
Youth	0.06	0.411	0.145985	0.884
Abortion	−1.169	0.221	−5.28959	0
Internet	0.788	0.257	3.066148	0.002
Roman Catholic	0.775	0.19	4.078947	0
Born Again	−0.876	0.235	−3.72766	0
Republican	−0.768	0.285	−2.69474	0.007
Parent	−0.391	0.274	−1.42701	0.154
Marital	−0.466	0.232	−2.00862	0.045
Hispanic	0.098	0.34	0.288235	0.772
Race	0.48	0.332	1.445783	0.149
Income	0.036	0.034	1.058824	0.288
Religiosity	0.473	0.192	2.463542	0.014
Age	0	0.012	0	0.969
Constant	−0.863	0.908	−0.95044	0.342

Note: Shaded coefficients significant at $\alpha = 0.05$.

TABLE 37.4

Logistic regression estimates predicting attitudes towards gays in the military

	Coefficient	Std. Error	t	Significance
Male × White	−0.527	0.713	−0.73913	0.459
Male × Parent	−1.175	0.565	−2.07965	0.037
Male × Born Again	0.269	0.496	0.542339	0.587
Male × Republican	−0.77	0.55	−1.4	0.161
Male × Democrat	−0.876	0.58	−1.51034	0.131
Male × Internet Use	−0.687	0.529	−1.29868	0.194
Male × Married	0.313	0.503	0.622266	0.534
Male × Abortion Views	−0.258	0.476	−0.54202	0.588
Male × Religiosity	−0.45	0.182	−2.47253	0.013
Male × Age	−0.022	0.018	−1.22222	0.209
Male	2.932	1.477	1.985105	0.047
Democrat	0.661	0.413	1.600484	0.109
Age × Church Attendance	−0.003	0.005	−0.6	0.572
Youth	0.115	0.653	0.17611	0.86
Abortion	−0.351	0.327	−1.07339	0.282
Internet	1.05	0.376	2.792553	0.005
Roman Catholic	0.362	0.269	1.345725	0.178
Born Again	−0.663	0.341	−1.94428	0.052
Republican	−0.003	0.406	−0.00739	0.994
Parent	0.402	0.431	0.932715	0.35
Marital	−0.103	0.346	−0.29769	0.766
Hispanic	0.602	0.538	1.118959	0.263
Race	0.057	0.526	0.108365	0.914
Income	−0.037	0.046	−0.80435	0.429
Religiosity	0.596	0.293	2.03413	0.042
Age	0.004	0.016	0.25	0.787
Constant	−0.925	1.283	−0.72097	0.471

Note: Shaded coefficients significant at $\alpha = 0.05$.

While it has a marginally positive effect on approval of gay marriage, it does not affect men differently than women.

When it comes to gay adoption, there is no direct effect of being a man, but there are interaction effects, where religious men are less supportive than religious women and white men are less supportive than white females of gay adoption. However, married men are more supportive than married women. Therefore, in attitudes towards gay adoption, gender is a complex issue. In both issues, however, age does not seem to be important: younger and older men do not seem significantly different.

Gays in the military is a very different issue than the previous ones, for men. This is the only issue in which being a man leads to more support of gay rights. While men who are religious are less supportive of gays in the military than religious females, the direct effects of gender are in the opposite direction. Such a finding shows that for men, attitudes towards homosexuality are not a unified category, but one that is separated by issues.

CONCLUSION AND FUTURE DIRECTION LIMITATIONS

This paper has looked at the attitudes towards homosexuality in the United States and shows they do not consist of one issue, but rather have inner differences based on the issue, which result in different attitudes. Traditional studies have agreed upon the effects of gender, age and religiosity on attitudes towards homosexuality. But rather than simply looking at "attitudes towards homosexuality" as a large, reified category, this paper looks at three main issues: attitudes towards gay marriage, adoption, and gays in the military. Furthermore, rather than making assumptions about young men, this paper looks at young men's attitudes in-depth and provides a more nuanced understanding. Attitudes towards gay marriage and adoption are not different for men, though men are more likely to support allowing gays to serve openly in the military.

What is also interesting is to see the interaction effects of men and religiosity: where religious

men, rather than religious women, are less likely to support gay adoption and allowing gays in the military. Overall, rather than looking at simplistic relationships between men and attitudes towards homosexuality, we have tried to demonstrate the complexity of the relationship, and the next step would be to unravel why men see these issues so differently through in-depth interviews.

REFERENCES

Aberson, C. L., Swan, D. C., & Emerson, E. P. (1999). Covert discrimination against gay men by U.S. college students. *The Journal of Social Psychology, 39*, 323–334.

Allport, G. W., & Ross, J. M. (1967). Personal religious orientation and discrimination. *Journal of Personality and Social Psychology, 5*, 432–443.

Altemeyer, R. A. (1996). *The authoritarian spectre.* Cambridge, MA: Harvard University Press.

Batson, C. D. (1971). *Creativity and religious development: Toward a structural functional psychology of religion.* Doctoral Dissertation. Princeton University.

Beatty, K. M., & Walter, O. (1984). Religious preference and practice: Reevaluating their impact on political tolerance. *Public Opinion Quarterly, 48*, 318–329.

Brewer, P. (2003). The shifting foundations of public opinion about gay rights. *Journal of Politics, 65*, 1208–1220.

Brooks, C. (2000). Civil rights liberalism and the suppression of a republican political realignment in the United States, 1972 to 1996. *American Sociological Review, 65*, 483–505.

Brown, M., & Amoroso, D. (1975). Attitudes towards homosexuality among West Indian male and female college students. *Journal of Social Psychology, 977*, 163–168.

Cochran. J. K., & Beeghley, L. (1991). The influence of religion on attitudes toward nonmarital sexuality: A preliminary assessment of reference group theory. *Journal of Scientific Study of Religion, 30*, 45–62.

Cotten-Huston, A. L., & Waite, B. M. (2000). Antihomosexual attitudes in college students: Predictors and classroom interventions. *Journal of Homosexuality, 38*, 117–133.

Ellis, A. L., & Vasseur, R. B. (1993). Prior interpersonal contact with and attitudes towards gays and lesbians in an interviewing context. *Journal of Homosexuality*, 25, 31–45.

Epstein, D. (1995). Keeping them in their place: Hetero/sexist harassment, gender and the enforcement of heterosexuality. In J. Holland & L. Adkins (Eds.), *Sex, sensibility and the gendered body* (pp. 202–221). London: Macmillan.

———. (1998). Real boys don't work: Underachievement, masculinity and the harassment of sissies. In *Failing boys? Issues in gender and achievement* (pp. 96–108). London: Open University Press.

Finlay, B., & Walther, C. S. (2003). The relation of religious affiliation, service attendance, and other factors to homophobic attitudes among university students. *Review of Religious Research*, 44, 370–393.

Fisher, R. D., Derison, D., Polley, C. F., Cadman, J., & Johnston, D. (1994). Religiousness, religious orientation, and attitudes towards gays and lesbians. *Journal of Applied Social Psychology*, 24, 614–630.

Gentry, C. S. (1987). Social distance regarding male and female homosexuals. *Journal of Social Psychology*, 127, 199–208.

Glassner, B., & Owen, C. (1976). Variations in attitude toward homosexuality. *Cornell Journal of Social Relations*, 11, 161–176.

Glenn, N. D., & Weaver, C. N. (1979). Attitudes toward premarital, extramarital and homosexual relations in the U.S. in the 1970s. *Journal of Sex Research*, 15, 108–118.

Glock, C. Y., & Stark, R. (1966). *Christian beliefs and anti-Semitism*. New York: Harper and Row.

Gurwitz, S. B., & Marcus, M. (1978). Effects of anticipated interaction, sex and homosexual stereotypes in first impressions. *Journal of Applied Social Psychology*, 8, 47–56.

Haeberle, S. H. (1999). Gay and lesbian rights: Margining trends in public opinion and voting behavior. In E. D. B. Riggle & B. L. Tadlock (Eds.), *Gays and lesbians in the democratic process* (pp. 146–169). New York: Columbia University Press.

Hansen, G. L. (1982). Measuring prejudice against homosexuality (homosexism) among college students: A new measure. *Journal of Social Psychology*, 117, 233–236.

Henley, N. M., & Pincus, F. (1978). Interrelationship of sexist, racist and anti-homosexual attitudes. *Psychological Report*, 42, 83–90.

Herek, G. M. (1984). Beyond "homophobia": A social-psychological perspective on attitudes towards lesbians and gay men. *Journal of Homosexuality*, 10, 1–21.

———. (1986). On heterosexual masculinity: Some physical consequences of social construction of gender and sexuality. *American Behavioral Scientist*, 29, 563–577.

———. (1988). Heterosexuals' attitudes towards lesbians and gay men: Correlates and gender differences. *Journal of Sex Research*, 5, 451–477.

———. (1991). Stigma, prejudice and violence against lesbians and gay men. In J. Gonsiorek and J. Weinrich (Eds.), *Homosexuality: Research implications for public policy* (pp. 60–80). Newbury Park, CA: Sage.

Herek, G. M., & Capitanio, J. P. (1996). Some of my best friends: Inter-group contact, concealable stigma, and heterosexuals' attitudes towards gay men and lesbians. *Personality and Social Psychology Bulletin*, 22, 412–424.

———. (1999). Sex differences in how heterosexuals think about lesbians and gay men: Evidence from survey context effects. *Journal of Sex Research*, 36(4), 348–360.

Herek, G. M., & Glunt, E. K. (1993). Interpersonal contact and heterosexuals' attitudes towards gay men: Results from a national survey. *Journal of Sex Research*, 30, 239–244.

Hort, B. E., Fagot, B. I., & Leinbach, M. D. (1990). Are people's notions of maleness more stereotypically framed than their notions of femaleness? *Sex Roles*, 23, 197–212.

Irwin, P., & Thompson, N. L. (1977). Acceptance of the rights of homosexuals: A social profile. *Journal of Homosexuality*, 3, 107–121.

Kerns, J. G., & Fine, M. A. (1994). The relation between gender and negative attitudes toward gay men and lesbians: Do gender role attitudes mediate this relation? *Sex Roles*, 31, 297–307.

Kirkpatrick, L. A. (1993). Fundamentalism, Christian orthodoxy, and intrinsic religious orientation as predictors of discriminatory attitudes. *Journal of Scientific Study of Religion*, 32, 256–268.

Kite, M. E. (1984). Sex differences in attitudes toward homosexuals: A meta-analytic review. *Journal of Homosexuality*, 10, 69–81.

———. (1994). When perceptions meet reality: Individual differences in reaction to lesbians and gay men. In B. Greene and G. M. Herek (Eds.), *Lesbian and gay psychology: Theory, research and clinical applications* (pp. 25–53). Thousand Oaks, CA: Sage.

Kite, M. E., & Whitley, Jr., B. E. (1996). Sex differences in attitudes towards homosexual persons, behaviors and civil rights: A meta analysis. *Personality and Social Psychology Bulletin*, 22, 336–352.

LaMar, L., & Kite, M. (1998). Sex differences in attitudes toward gay men and lesbians: A multidimensional perspective. *Journal of Sex Research*, 35, 189–196.

Laner, M. R., & Laner, R. H. (1979). Personal style or sexual preference: Why gay men are disliked. *International Review of Modern Sociology*, 9, 215–228.

Lewis, G. B., & Rogers, M. A. (1999). Does the public support equal employment rights for gays and lesbians? In E. D. B. Riggle and B. L. Tadlock (Eds.), *Gays and lesbians in the democratic process* (pp. 118–145). New York: Columbia University Press.

Lindaman, K., & Haider-Markel, D. P. (2002). Issue evolution, political parties and the culture wars. *Political Research Quarterly*, 55, 91–110.

Loftus, J. (2001). America's liberalization in attitudes toward homosexuality, 1973 to 1998. *American Journal of Sociology*, 66, 762–782.

Lottes, I. L., & Kuriloff, P. J. (1992). The effects of gender, race, religion, and political orientation on the sex role attitudes of college freshmen. *Adolescence*, 27, 675–688.

Louderback, L. A. & Whitley, B. E. Jr. (1997). Perceived erotic value of homosexuality and sex role attitudes as mediators of sex differences in heterosexual college students' attitudes toward lesbians and gay men. *Journal of Sex Research*, 34, 175–182.

Marsiglio, W. (1993). Attitudes towards homosexual activity and gays as friends: A national survey of heterosexual 15- to 19-year-old males. *Journal of Sex Research*, 30, 12–17.

McClain, E. W. (1979). Religious orientation as the key to psycho-dynamic differences between feminists and non-feminists. *Journal for the Scientific Study of Religion*, 18, 40–45.

McClosky, H., & Zaller, J. (1984). *The American ethos: Public attitudes towards democracy and capitalism*. Cambridge, MA: Harvard University Press.

McFarland, S. G. (1989). Religious orientations and the targets of discrimination. *Journal for the Scientific Study of Religion*, 28, 324–336.

Millham, J., San Miguel, C. L., & Kellog, K. (1976). A factor analytic conceptualization of attitudes towards male and female homosexuals. *Journal of Homosexuality*, 2, 3–10.

Minnigerode, F. (1976). Attitudes towards homosexuality: Feminist attitudes and sexual conservatism. *Sex Roles*, 2, 347–357.

Smith. A. (1998). General assembly backgrounder: Sexuality and ordination. *Presbyterian News Science, No. 98184.*

Schneider, W., & Lewis, I. A. (1984). The straight story on homosexuality and gay rights. *Public Opinion*, 7, 16–20, 59–60.

Steffensmeier, D., & Steffensmeier, R. (1974). Sex differences in reactions to homosexuals: Research continuities and further developments. *Journal of Sex Research*, 10, 52–67.

Storms, M. D. (1978). Attitudes toward homosexuality and femininity in men. *Journal of Homosexuality*, 3, 257–263.

Wagenaar, T. C., & Barton, P. E. (1977). Orthodoxy and attitude of clergymen towards homosexuality and abortion. *Review of Religious Research*, 18, 114–125.

Weiss, C. B., & Dein, R. N. (1979). Ego development and sex attitudes in heterosexual and homosexual men and women. *Archives of Sexual Behavior*, 8, 341–356.

Werum, R., & Winders, B. (2001). Who's "in" and who's "out": State fragmentation and the struggle over gay rights, 1974–1999. *Social Problems*, 48, 386–410.

Wilcox, C., & Norrander, B. (2002). Of moods and morals: The dynamic of opinion on abortion and gay rights. In B. Norrander and C. Wilcox (Eds.), *Understanding public opinion* (pp. 121–148). Washington: Congressional Quarterly Press.

Wilcox, C., & Wolpert, R. (1996). President Clinton, public opinion and gays in the military. In C. Rimmerman (Ed.), *Gay rights and military wrongs: Political perspectives on lesbians and gays in the military* (pp. 127–145). New York: Garland Publishing.

Wilcox, C., & Wolpert, R. (2000). Gay rights in the public sphere: Public opinion on gay and lesbian equality. In C. Rimmerman & K. D. Wald (Eds.), *Politics of gay rights* (pp. 409–432). Chicago: University of Chicago Press.

Wills, G., & Crawford, R. (2000). Attitudes toward homosexuality in Shreveport-Bossier City Louisiana. *Journal of Homosexuality*, 38, 97–116.

JESUS WAS A FEMINIST

Leonard Swidler

Definition of Terms: By Jesus is meant the historical person who lived in Palestine two thousand years ago, whom Christians traditionally acknowledge as Lord and Savior, and whom they should "imitate" as much as possible. By a feminist is meant a person who is in favor of, and who promotes, the equality of women with men, a person who advocates and practices treating women primarily as human persons (as men are so treated) and willingly contravenes social customs in so acting.

To prove the thesis it must be demonstrated that, so far as we can tell, Jesus neither said or did anything which would indicate that he advocated treating women as intrinsically inferior to men, but that on the contrary he said and did things which indicated he thought of women as the equals of men, and that in the process he willingly violated pertinent social mores.

The negative portion of the argument can be documented quite simply by reading through four Gospels. Nowhere does Jesus treat women as "inferior beings." In fact, Jesus clearly felt especially sent to the typical classes of "inferior beings," such as the poor, the lame, the sinner—and women— to call them all to the freedom and equality of the Kingdom of God. But there are two factors which raise this negative result exponentially in its significance: the status of women in Palestine at the time of Jesus, and the nature of the Gospels. Both need to be recalled here in some detail, particularly the former.

THE STATUS OF WOMEN IN PALESTINE

The status of women in Palestine during the time of Jesus was very decidedly that of inferiors. Despite the fact that there were several heroines recorded in the Scriptures, according to most rabbinic customs of Jesus' time—and long after—women were not allowed to study the Scriptures (Torah). One first-century rabbi, Eliezer, put the point sharply: "Rather should the words of the Torah be burned than entrusted to a woman . . . Whoever teaches his daughter the Torah is like one who teaches her lasciviousness."

In the vitally religious area of prayer, women were so little thought of as not to be given obligations of the same seriousness as men. For example, women, along with children and slaves, were not obliged to recite the Shema, the morning prayer, nor prayers at meals. In fact, the Talmud states: "Let a curse come upon the man who must needs have his wife or children say grace for him. . . ." Moreover, in the daily prayers of Jews there was a threefold thanksgiving: "Praised be God that he has not created me a gentile; praised be God that he has not created me a woman; praised be God that he has not created me an ignorant man." (It was obviously a version of this rabbinic prayer that Paul controverted in his letter to the Galatians: "There is neither Jew nor Greek, there is neither slave or free, there is neither male nor female; for you are all one in Christ Jesus.")

Women were also grossly restricted in public prayer. It was (is) not even possible for them to be counted toward the number necessary for a quorum to form a congregation to worship communally— they were again classified with children and slaves, who similarly did not qualify (there is an interesting parallel to the current canon 93 of the *Codex Juris Canonici* which groups married women, minors, and the insane). In the great temple at Jerusalem, they were limited to one outer portion, the women's court, which was five steps below the court for the men. In the synagogues, the women were also separated from the men; and, of course, they were not allowed to read aloud or take any leading function. (The same is still true in most synagogues today— cannon 1262 of the CJC also states that "in church the women should be separated from the men.")

Besides the disabilities women suffered in the areas of prayer and worship, there were many others in the private and public forums of society. As a Scripture scholar, Peter Ketter, noted, "A rabbi regarded it as beneath his dignity, as indeed positively disreputable, to speak to a woman in public." The *Proverbs of the Fathers* contain the injunction: "Speak not much with a woman." Since a man's own wife is meant here, how much more does not this apply to the wife of another? The wise men say: "Who speaks much with a woman draws down misfortune on himself, neglects the words of the law, and finally earns hell. . . ." If it were merely the too free intercourse of the sexes which was being warned against, this would signify nothing derogatory to woman. But since the rabbi may not speak even to his wife, daughter or sister in the street, then only male arrogance can be the motive. Intercourse with uneducated company is warned against in exactly the same terms. One is not so much as to greet a woman. In addition, save in the rarest instances, women were not allowed to bear witness in a court of law. Some Jewish thinkers, as for example, Philo, a contemporary of Jesus, thought women ought not leave their households except to go to the synagogues (and that only at a time when most of the other people would be at home); girls ought even not cross the threshold that separated the male and female apartments of the household.

In general, the attitude toward women was epitomized in the institutions and customs surrounding marriage. For the most part, the function of women was thought rather exclusively in terms of childbearing and rearing; women were almost always under the tutelage of a man, either the father or husband, or if a widow, the dead husband's brother. Polygamy—in the sense of having several wives, but not in the sense of having several husbands—was legal among Jews at the time of Jesus. Although probably not heavily practiced, he merely had to give her a writ of divorce. Women in Palestine, on the other hand, were not allowed to divorce their husbands.

Rabbinic sayings about women also provide an insight into the attitude toward women: "It is well for those whose children are male, but ill for those whose children are female. . . . At the birth of a boy all are joyful, but at the birth of a girl all are sad. . . . When a boy comes into the world, peace comes into the world; when a girl comes, nothing comes. . . . Even the most virtuous of women is a witch. . . . Our teachers have said: 'Four qualities are evident in women: They are greedy at their food, eager to gossip, lazy and jealous.'"

The condition of women in Palestinian Judaism was bleak.

THE NATURE OF THE GOSPELS

The Gospels, of course, are not the straight factual reports of eyewitnesses of the events in the life of Jesus of Nazareth as one might find in the columns of the *New York Times* or in the pages of a critical biography. Rather, they are four different faith statements reflecting at least four primitive Christian communities who believed that Jesus was the Messiah, the Lord and Savior of the world. They were composed from a variety of sources, written and oral, over a period of time and in response to certain needs felt in the commonalities and individuals at the time; consequently they are many-layered. Since the Gospel writers-editors were not twentieth-century critical historians, they were not particularly intent on recording *ipissima verba Christi*, nor were they concerned to winnow out all of their own cultural biases and assumptions; indeed, it is doubtful they were particularly conscious of them.

This modern critical understanding of the Gospels, of course, does not impugn the historical character of the Gospels; it merely describes the type of historical documents they are so their historical significance can more accurately be evaluated. Its religious value lies in the fact that modern Christians are thereby helped to know much more precisely what Jesus meant by certain statements and actions as they are reported by the first Christian communities in the Gospels. With this new knowledge of the nature of the Gospels it is easier to make the vital distinction between the religious truth that is to be handed on and the time-conditioned categories and customs involved in expressing it.

When the fact that no negative attitudes by Jesus toward women are portrayed in the Gospels is set side by side with the recently discerned "communal faith-statement" understanding of the nature of the Gospels, the importance of the former is vastly enhanced. For whatever Jesus said or did comes to us only through the lens of the first Christians. If there were no very special religious significance in a particular concept or custom, we would expect that current concept or custom to be reflected by Jesus. The fact that the overwhelmingly negative attitude toward women in Palestine did not come through the primitive Christian communal lens by itself underscores the clearly great religious importance Jesus attached to his positive attitude—his feminist attitude—toward women: feminism, that is, personalism extended to women, is a constitutive part of the Gospel, the Good News, of Jesus.

WOMEN DISCIPLES OF JESUS

One of the first things noticed in the gospels about Jesus' attitude toward women is that he taught them the Gospel, the meaning of the Scriptures, and religious truths in general. When it is recalled that in Judaism it was considered improper, and even "obscene," to teach women the Scriptures, this action of Jesus was an extraordinary deliberate decision to break with a custom invidious to women. Moreover, women became disciples of Jesus, not only in the sense of learning from Him, but also in the sense of following Him in His travels and ministering to Him. A number of women, married and unmarried,

were regular followers of Jesus. In Luke 8:1ff., several are mentioned by name in the same sentence with the Twelve: "He made his way through towns and villages preaching and proclaiming the Good News of the Kingdom of God. With him went the Twelve, as well as certain women . . . who provided for them out of their resources." (Cf: Mk. 15:40f. The Greek word translated here as "provided for" and in Mark as "ministered to" is *diekonoun*, the same basic word as "deacon"; indeed apparently the tasks of the deacons in early Christianity were much the same as these women undertook.) The significance of this phenomenon of women following Jesus about, learning from and ministering to Him, can be properly appreciated when it is recalled that not only were women not to read or study the Scriptures, but in the more observant settings they were not even to leave their household, whether as a daughter, a sole wife, or a member of a harem.

The intimate connection of women with resurrection from the dead is not limited in the Gospels to that of Jesus. There are accounts of three other resurrections in the Gospels—all closely involving a woman. The most obvious connection of a woman with a resurrection account is that of the raising of a woman, Jairus' daughter (Mt. 9:18ff.; Mk. 5:22ff.; Lk. 8:41ff.). A second resurrection Jesus performed was that of the only son of the widow of Nain: "And when the Lord saw her, he had compassion on her and he said to her, 'Do not weep.'" (Cf. Lk. 7:13ff.). The third resurrection Jesus performed was Lazarus' at the request of his sisters Martha and Mary (Cf. Jn. 11:43-44). From the first, it was Martha and Mary who sent for Jesus because of Lazarus' illness. But when Jesus finally came, Lazarus was four days dead. Martha met Jesus and pleaded for his resurrection: "Lord, if you had been here, my brother would not have died. And even now I know that whatever you ask from God, God will give you." Later, Mary came to Jesus and said much the same. "When Jesus saw her weeping, and the Jews who came with her also weeping, he was deeply moved in spirit and troubled"; and he said, "Where have you laid him?" They said to him, "Lord, come and see." Jesus wept. Then followed the raising from the dead. Thus, Jesus raised one woman from the dead and raised two other persons largely because of women.

There are two further details that should be noted in these three resurrection stories. The first is that only in the case of Jairus' daughter did Jesus touch the corpse—which made him ritually unclean. In the cases of the two men, Jesus did not touch them but merely said, "Young man, I say to you, arise," or "Lazarus, come out." One must at least wonder why Jesus chose to violate the laws of ritual purity in order to help a woman, but not a man. The second detail is in Jesus' conversation with Martha after she pleaded for the resurrection of Lazarus. Jesus declared himself to be the resurrection, ("I am the resurrection and the life.") the only time he did so that is recorded in the Gospels. Jesus, here again, revealed the central event, the central message in the Gospel—the resurrection, His resurrection, His being the resurrection—to a woman.

WOMEN AS SEX OBJECTS

There are, of course, numerous occasions recorded in the Gospels where women are treated by various men as second-class citizens. There are also situations where women were treated by others, not at all as persons but as sex objects, and it was expected that Jesus would do the same. The expectations were disappointed. One such occasion occurred when Jesus was invited to dinner at the house of a skeptical Pharisee (Lk. 7:36ff.) and a woman of ill repute entered and washed Jesus' feet with her tears, wiped them with her hair and anointed them. The Pharisee saw her solely as an evil sexual creature: "The Pharisee . . . said to himself, 'If this man were a prophet, he would know who this woman is who is touching him and what a bad name she has.'" But Jesus deliberately rejected this approach to the woman as a sex object. He rebuked the Pharisee and spoke solely of the woman's human, spiritual actions; he spoke of her love, her non-love, that is, her sins, of her being forgiven, and her faith. Jesus then addressed her (It was not "proper" to speak to women in public, especially "improper" women) as

a human person: "Your sins are forgiven. . . . Your faith has saved you; go in peace."

A similar situation occurred when the scribes and Pharisees used a woman reduced entirely to a sex object to set a legal trap for Jesus. It is difficult to imagine a more callous use of a human person than the "adulterous" woman was put to by the enemies of Jesus. First, she was surprised in the intimate act of sexual intercourse (quote possibly a trap was set up ahead of time by the suspicious husband), and then dragged before the scribes and Pharisees, and then by them before an even larger crowd that Jesus was instructing: "making her stand in full view of everybody." They told Jesus that she had been caught in the very act of committing adultery and that Moses had commanded that such women be stoned to death (Deut. 22:22ff.). "What have you to say?" The trap was partly that if Jesus said "Yes" to stoning, He would be violating the Roman law, which restricted capital punishment; and if He said "No," He would appear to contravene Mosaic law. It could also partly have been to place Jesus' reputation for kindness toward, and championing the cause of, women in opposition to the law and the condemnation of sin. Jesus, of course, eluded their snares by refusing to become entangled in legalisms and abstractions. Rather, he dealt with both the accusers and the accused directly as spiritual, ethical, human persons. He spoke directly to the accusers in the context of their own personal ethical conduct: "If there is one of you who has not sinned, let him be the first to throw a stone at her." To the accused woman he likewise spoke directly with compassion, but without approving her conduct: "Woman, where are they? Has no one condemned you?" She said, "No one, Lord." And Jesus said, "Neither do I condemn you; go, and do not sin again."

(One detail of this encounter provides the basis for a short excursus related to the status of women. The Pharisees stated that the woman had been caught in the act of adultery and, according to the law of Moses, was, therefore, to be stoned to death. Since the type of execution mentioned was stoning, the woman must have been a "virgin betrothed," as referred to in Deut. 22:23f. There provision is made for the stoning of both the man and the woman although in the Gospel story only the woman is brought forward. However, the reason given for why the man ought to be stoned was not because he had violated the woman, or God's law, but "because he had violated the wife of his neighbor." It was the injury of the man by misusing his property—his wife—that was the great evil.)

JESUS' REJECTION OF THE BLOOD TABOO

All three of the synoptic Gospels insert into the middle of the account of raising Jairus' daughter from the dead the story of the curing of the woman who had an issue of blood for twelve years (Mt. 9:20ff; Mk. 5:25ff.; Lk. 8:43ff.). Especially touching about this story is that the affected woman was so reluctant to project herself into public attention that, "she said to herself, 'If I only touch his garment, I shall be made well'." Her shyness was not because she came from the poor, lower classes; for Mark pointed out that over the twelve years she had been to many physicians—with no success—on whom she had spent all her money. It was probably because for the twelve years, as a woman with a flow of blood, she was constantly ritually unclean (Lev. 15:19ff.), which not only made her incapable of participating in any cultic action and made her in some sense "displeasing to God" but also rendered anyone and anything she touched (or anyone who touched what she had touched!) similarly unclean. (Here is the basis for the Catholic Church not allowing women in the sanctuary during Mass—she might be menstruating and hence unclean.) The sense of degradation and contagion that her "womanly weakness" worked upon her over the twelve years doubtless was oppressive in the extreme. This would have been especially so when a religious teacher, a rabbi, was involved. But not only does Jesus' power heal her, in one of His many acts of compassion on the downtrodden and afflicted, including women, but Jesus also makes a great to-do about the event, calling extraordinary attention to the publicity-shy woman: "And Jesus, perceiving in himself that power had gone forth from him, immediately

turned about in the crowd, and said 'Who touched my garments?' And the disciples said to him, 'You see the crowd pressing around you, and yet you say, 'Who touched me?' And he looked around to see who had done it. But the woman, knowing what had been done to her, came in fear and trembling and fell down before Him and told Him the whole truth. And He said to her, 'Daughter, your faith has made you well; go in peace, and be healed of your disease'." It seems clear that Jesus wanted to call attention to the fact that He did not shrink from the ritual uncleanness incurred by being touched by the "unclean" woman (on several occasions Jesus rejected the notion of ritual uncleanness), and by immediate implication rejected the "uncleanness" of a woman who had a flow of blood, menstruous or continual. Jesus apparently placed a great importance on the dramatic making of this point, both to the afflicted woman herself and the crowd, than He did on avoiding the temporary psychological discomfort of the embarrassed woman, which in light of Jesus' extraordinary concern to alleviate the pain of the afflicted, meant He placed a great weight on the teaching of this lesson about the dignity of women.

JESUS AND THE SAMARITAN WOMAN

On another occasion, Jesus again deliberately violated the then common code concerning men's relationship to women. It is recorded in the story of the Samaritan woman at the well of Jacob (John 4:5ff). Jesus was waiting at the well outside the village while His disciples were getting food. A Samaritan woman approached the well to draw water. Normally, a Jew would not address a Samaritan as the woman pointed out: "Jews, in fact, do not associate with Samaritans." But also normally a man would not speak to a woman in public (doubly so in the case of a rabbi). However, Jesus startled the woman by initiating a conversation. The woman was aware that on both counts, her being a Samaritan and being a woman, Jesus' action was out of the ordinary; for she replied: "How is it that you, a Jew, ask a drink of me, a woman of Samaria?" As hated as the Samaritans were by the Jews, it is nevertheless clear that Jesus' speaking with a woman was considered a much more flagrant breach of conduct than His speaking with a Samaritan. John related: "His disciples returned and were surprised to find him speaking to a woman, though none of them asked, 'What do you want from her?' or 'Why were you talking to her?'" However, Jesus, bridging of the gap of inequality between men and women, continued further; for in the conversation with the woman He revealed himself in a straightforward fashion as the Messiah for the first time: "The woman said to him, 'I know that Messiah is coming' . . . Jesus said to her, 'I who speak to you am he.'"

Just as when Jesus revealed Himself to Martha as "the resurrection," and to Mary as the "risen one" and bade her to bear witness to the apostles, Jesus here also revealed Himself in one of his key roles, as Messiah, to a woman who immediately bore witness of the fact to her fellow villagers. (It is interesting to note that apparently the testimony of women carried greater weight among the Samaritans than among the Jews, for the villagers came out to see Jesus: "Many Samaritans of that town believed in him on the strength of the woman's testimony. . . ." It would seem that the John the Gospel writer deliberately highlighted this contrast in the way he wrote about this event, and also that he clearly wished to reinforce Jesus' stress on the equal dignity of women.)

One other point should be noted in connection with this story. As the crowd of Samaritans was walking out to see Jesus, Jesus was speaking to His disciples about the fields being ready for the harvest and how He was sending them to reap what others had sown. He was clearly speaking of the souls of men and most probably was referring directly to the approaching Samaritans. Such exegesis is standard. It is also rather standard to refer to others in general, and only Jesus in particular, as having been the sowers whose harvest the apostles were about to reap (e.g., in the Jerusalem Bible). But it would seem that the evangelist also meant specifically to include the Samaritan woman among those sowers; for immediately after he recorded Jesus' statement to the disciples about their reaping what others had sown, he added the above mentioned verse: "Many

Samaritans of that town had believed in him on the strength of the woman's testimony. . . ."

MARRIAGE AND THE DIGNITY OF WOMEN

One of the most important stands of Jesus in relation to the dignity of women was His position on marriage. His unpopular attitude toward marriage (cf. Mt. 19:10: "The disciples said to Him, 'If such is that case of a man with his wife, it is not expedient to marry.'") presupposed a feminist view of women; they had rights and responsibilities equal to men. It is quite possible in Jewish law for men to have more than one wife (this was probably not frequently the case in Jesus' time, but there are recorded instances, e.g., Herod, Josephus) though the reverse was not possible. Divorce, of course, also was a simple matter, to be initiated only by the man. In both situations, women were basically chattels to be collected or dismissed as the man was able and wished to. The double moral standard was flagrantly apparent. Jesus rejected both by insisting on monogamy and the elimination of divorce. Both the man and the woman were to have the same rights and responsibilities in their relationship toward each other (cf. Mk. 10:2ff; Mt. 19:3ff.). This stance of Jesus was one of the few that was rather thoroughly assimilated by the Christian Church (in fact, often in an over-rigid way concerning divorce, but how to understand the ethical prescriptions of Jesus is another article), doubtless in part because it was reinforced by various sociological conditions and other historical accidents, such as the then current strength in the Greek world of the Stoic philosophy. However, the notion of equal rights and responsibilities was not extended very far within the Christian marriage. The general role of women was *Kürche, Künder, Kuche* [church, children, kitchen]— and only a supplicant's role in the first.

THE INTELLECTUAL LIFE FOR WOMEN

However, Jesus clearly did not think of woman's role in such restricted terms; she was not to be limited to being only a housekeeper. Jesus quite directly rejected the stereotype that the proper place of all women is "in the home," during a visit to the house of Martha and Mary (Lk. 10:38ff.). Martha took the typical woman's role: "Martha was distracted with much serving." Mary however, took the supposedly "male" role: she "sat at the Lord's feet and listened to his teaching." Martha apparently thought Mary was out of place in choosing the role of the "intellectual," for she complained to Jesus. But Jesus' response was a refusal to force all women into the stereotype; he treated Mary first of all as a person (whose highest faculty is the intellect, the spirit) who was allowed to set her own priorities, and in this instance has "chosen the better part." And Jesus applauded her: "It is not to be taken from her." Again, when one recalls the Palestinian restriction on women studying the Scriptures or studying with rabbis, that is, engaging in the intellectual life or acquiring any "religious authority," it is difficult to imagine how Jesus could possibly have been clearer in his insistence that women were called to the intellectual, the spiritual life just as were men.

There is at least one other instance recorded in the Gospels when Jesus uttered much the same message (Lk. 11:27f.). One day as Jesus was preaching, a woman from the crowd apparently was very deeply impressed and, perhaps imagining how happy she would be to have a son, raised her voice to pay Jesus a compliment. She did so by referring to His mother, and did so in a way that was probably not untypical at that time and place. But her linage of a woman was sexually reductive in the extreme (one that largely persists to the present): female genitals and breasts. "Blessed is the womb that bore you, and the breasts that you sucked!" Although this was obviously meant as a compliment and although it was even uttered by a woman, Jesus clearly felt it necessary to reject this "baby-machine" image of women and insist again on the personhood, the intellectual and moral faculties, being primary for all: "But he said, 'Blessed rather are those who hear the word of God and keep it!'" Looking at this text, it is difficult to see how the primary point could be anything substantially other than this. Luke and the traditional

and Christian communities he depended on must also have been quite clear about the sexual significance of this event. Otherwise, why would he (and they) have kept and included such a small event from the years of Jesus' public life? It was not retained because Jesus said blessed are those who hear and keep God's word, but because that was stressed by Jesus as being primary in comparison to a woman's sexuality. Luke, however, seems to have had a discernment here and elsewhere concerning what Jesus was about in the question of women's status that has not been shared by subsequent Christians (nor apparently by many of his fellow Christians); for, in the explanation of this passage, Christians for two thousand years did not see its plain meaning—doubtless because of unconscious presuppositions about the status Christians gave it. For, in the explanation of this passage, Christians for two thousand years did not see its plain meaning—doubtless because of unconscious presuppositions about the status.

GOD AS A WOMAN

In many ways, Jesus strove to communicate the equal dignity of women. In one sense, that effort was capped by his parable of the woman who found the lost coin (Lk. 15:8ff.), for here Jesus projected God in the image of woman! Luke recorded that the despised tax collectors and sinners were gathering around Jesus; and, consequently, the Pharisees and scribes complained. Jesus, therefore, related three parables in a row, all of which depicted God being deeply concerned for that which was lost. The first story was of the shepherd who left the ninety-nine sheep to see the one lost—the shepherd is God. The third parable is on the prodigal son—the father is God. The second story is of the woman who sought the lost coin—the woman is God! Jesus did not shrink from the notion of God as feminine. In fact, it would appear that Jesus included this womanly image of God quite deliberately at this point for the scribes and Pharisees were among those who most of all denigrated women—just as they did "tax-collectors and sinners."

There have been some instances in Christian history when the Holy Spirit has been associated with a feminine character, for example, in the Syrian Didascalia where, in speaking of various offices in the Church, it states: "The Deaconess however should be honored by you as the linage of the Holy Spirit." It would make an interesting investigation to see if these images of God presented here by Luke were ever used in a Trinitarian manner—thereby giving the Holy Spirit a feminine linage. A negative result to the investigation would be as significant as a positive one, for this passage would seem to be particularly apt for Trinitarian interpretation: the prodigal son's father is God the Father (this interpretation has in fact been quite Common in Christian history). Since Jesus elsewhere identified himself as the Good Shepherd, the shepherd seeking the lost sheep is Jesus, the Son (this standard interpretation is reflected in, among other things, the often-seen picture of Jesus carrying the lost sheep on his shoulders). The woman who sought the lost coin should "logically" be the Holy Spirit. If such an interpretation has existed, it surely has not been common. Should such lack of "logic" be attributed to the general cultural denigration of women of the abhorrence of pagan goddesses although Christian abhorrence of pagan gods did not result in a Christian rejection of a male linage of God?

CONCLUSION

From this evidence it should be clear that Jesus vigorously promoted the dignity and equality of women in the midst of a very male-dominated society: Jesus was a feminist, and a very radical one. Can his followers attempt to be anything less—*De Imitatione Christi?*

GODLY MANHOOD GOING WILD?: TRANSFORMATIONS IN CONSERVATIVE PROTESTANT MASCULINITY

reference
The Warrior
Narrative

The journey of
John The Baptist

Sally K. Gallagher   Sabrina L. Wood

This article assesses shifting ideals of masculinity among conservative Protestants focused on the current best seller, *Wild at heart*, by John Eldredge (2001). First, we compare Eldredge's notion of manhood as essentially "heroic, slightly dangerous, alive and free" with the ideals of responsible manhood central to much Promise Keepers literature. Second, we explore the salience of this shift for men's relationships with each other, their wives and female friends. Analysis of interview data with a sample of married men and women in two churches and one para-church campus ministry highlight the active and selective reading of religious texts across gender and age. Overall, Eldredge's "slightly dangerous" masculinity represents a re-articulation of the nineteenth century myth of the "self-made man" and is both a reaction against the rationalized nature of paid employment, as well as the responsible and "feminized" expectations of Promise Keepers' ideal of servant leadership and involved fatherhood.

This article presents an analysis of shifting ideals of masculinity among conservative Protestants after the "demise" of the Promise Keepers. For over a decade, Promise Keepers ethos of responsible manhood dominated conservative Protestant rhetoric on manhood, fatherhood, and marriage.

Sharon Mazer, "The Power Team: Muscular Christianity and the Spectacle of Conversation." *TDR/The Drama Review*, 38:4 (T144-Winter, 1994) 162–188. © 1994 by New York University and the Massachusetts Institute of Technology. Reprinted with permission.

The "seven promises" of a Promise Keeper set the standard for evangelical men in terms of vibrant, expressive faith in Jesus Christ; commitment to the local church and its leadership; moral and sexual purity; unity across race and ethnicity; building strong marriages through "love, protection and biblical values"; and being held accountable for all of these through investing in relationships with a small group of like minded men (McCartney 1994). Yet from a high over a million attendees at twenty-two stadium conferences in 1996, the organization has struggled financially, reduced its focus on large conferences (450,000 attending in 1998 and less than half that number in 2003), and faded from the national visibility it held in the mid-1990s.

The question this article addresses, then, has to do with shifting interpretations of gender ideals within conservative Protestantism—most specifically, the vision of responsible manhood after the reorganization of the Promise Keepers. During the 1970s and 1980s evangelical gender debates focused on the implications of individualism and women's employment for notions of godly womanhood (Clark 1980; Cooper 1974; Elliot 1976; Getz 1977; Hurley 1981; Piper and Grudem 1991), and the case evangelical feminists had begun to make for mutual submission in marriage and women's ordination (Bilezikian 1985; Bristow 1988; Gallagher 2004a; Gundry 1980; Mickelsen 1986; Mollenkott 1977; Scanzoni and Hardesty 1974; Van Leeuwen 1990). By the late 1980s the focus had shifted away from increasingly refined theological debates to a wide range of practical advice intended to help evangelical couples balance and maintain a symbolic commitment to husbands' headship with the pragmatic egalitarianism that characterized the majority of evangelical households (Bartkowski 2001; Gallagher 2003, 2004b). Nearly all of this advice literature was addressed to women. That changed, however, in the early 1990s when men, masculinity and fatherhood appeared on the scene as the new focus of evangelical efforts to reinforce and strengthen "family values." Promise Keepers embodied this latter development (Bartkowski 2004; Mathisen 2001). As Promise Keepers developed into the dominant evangelical men's movement of the late twentieth century, evangelical publishers began to expand their marriage and parenting listings to include a growing number of books on how men also might more responsibly balance paid work and family, communicate better, be more involved at home, and more accountable to each other (McCartney 1997; Smalley & Trent 1992; Weber 1993, 1997).

In 2001, however, a book appeared that countered much of this emerging subcultural consensus about responsible manhood with the notion that masculinity is in essence "wild, dangerous, unfettered and free" (Eldredge 2001:12). The book was *Wild at Heart: Discovering the Secret of a Man's Soul*, by self-employed therapist, outdoorsman, former Focus on the Family employee, and father of three (boys), John Eldredge. It was an immediate success. The year after its publication, it sold over 200,000 copies and was the fourth best selling Christian book in the nation (Christian Booksellers Association 2004).

In the analysis that follows, we explore the symbolic and practical salience of the message of *Wild at heart* for evangelical notions of godly masculinity. We begin by systematically contrasting Eldredge's notion of godly manhood as essentially "heroic, slightly dangerous, alive and free" with the ideals of responsible manhood central to much of the Promise Keepers literature of the 1990s. Second, based on interviews with a cross section of conservative Protestant men and women, we explore the personal and practical salience of this shift in norms of masculinity for identity and men's relationships with each other, their

wives and female friends. Data for this section of the analysis come from three sets of interviews with a sample of married men and women in two churches and with young adult men and women involved in a para-church evangelical campus ministry. Based on these interviews, we assess the degree to which Eldredge's "slightly dangerous" masculinity represents a re-articulation of the nineteenth century myth of the "self-made man" (Kimmel 1996; Rotundo 1994), and is both a reaction against the rationalized nature of paid employment (Schwalbe 1996), as well as the responsible and "feminized" expectations of Promise Keepers' ideal of servant leadership and involved fatherhood. As we will argue, ordinary evangelicals employ a flexible hermeneutic in interpreting popular texts, in the same way that they employ a range of hermeneutical approaches in interpreting biblical texts on family and gender (Bartkowski 1996, 2004; Gallagher 2003).

CONTRASTING IDEALS FOR GODLY MANHOOD

Although early research on Promise Keepers described the movement as an anti-feminist backlash intended to restore men to their rightful place as benign patriarchs within the family (Hackstaff 1999; Hardisty 1999; Messner 1997; Messner & Anderson 1998), a growing body of literature has begun to explore the polyvocal and multi-dimensional ideals of masculinity articulated by movement leaders and participants (Bartkowski 2001, 2004; Lockhart 2000). Although less institutionally robust than in the 1990s, Promise Keepers rhetoric continues to frame men's expressiveness and nurturing as an extension of masculine leadership and authority within the household.

Bartkowski's (2001, 2004) analyses of this literature demonstrates the breadth of gender perspectives within the organization. In addition to the Rational Patriarch model advocated in evangelical men's literature in the 1970s and 1980s (e.g. Christenson 1970; Cole 1982; Elliot 1981; Farrar 1990), Bartkowski identifies strands of PK literature in the 1990s—the expressive egalitarian; the tender warrior; and "multicultural man." Writing by Gary Oliver, *Real men have feelings, too* (1993), and Gary Smalley and John Trent's, *The hidden value of a man* (1992) typifies the first of these styles—the "expressive egalitarian." In these works, evangelical men are urged to communicate better with their wives, cultivate emotional vulnerability, and connect themselves to both their children and other men.

A second iteration of godly manhood Bartkowski identifies within PK literature is the "multicultural man" that draws on PK concerns with "racial reconciliation." PK authors recognize that historical and economic factors have played a role in creating and sustaining inequality, yet present the problem of racism as fundamentally one of personal sin. As a result, they argue that racial reconciliation is only possible through forgiveness and connection between individuals (Cooper 1995; Porter 1996; Washington and Kehrein 1997). (See Bartkowski (2004) and Allen (2000) for a more thorough analysis of this theme).

The third iteration of masculinity within PK literature is typified by the popular writings of Stu Weber (1993, 1997, 1998), in which he presents the case that authentic masculinity is characterized by four pillars: king, warrior, mentor and friend. At the center of godly masculinity is the responsibility to provide, protect, teach and love (1993:40–43). Like gender conservative evangelicals of an earlier generation Weber argues that these characteristics have been hard-wired into humanity by God, in dimorphic gender differences that mirror eternal spiritual realities and the very character of God. For Weber, "the core of masculinity is initiation—the provision of direction, security, stability and connection (1993:45)." It is also responsibility, particularly when marriage and fatherhood are involved.

> Husband. The noun form of husband means "manager." A husband is a "steward." A caretaker. The man responsible. In its verb form the term means "to direct, to manage." Those are strong terms that imply effective leadership. In a word, husbanding is responsibility. To be a husband is to be responsible (1993:88).

This image of responsible manhood expresses itself not only in protecting and directing family life, but also in loving "sacrificial" leadership, without domination.

> Manly love. Men must develop a thorough, biblical, manly love. Now what is that? In a word—*headship*. It is leadership with an emphasis upon responsibility, duty, and sacrifice. Not rank or domination (97).

While clearly not advocating the egalitarian possibilities hinted at in the literature by "expressive egalitarians," Weber's pastoral concern for the struggles of dual career couples lends itself to a pragmatic masculinity that supports a modicum of flexibility in "roles" at home, as well as committed relationships with other men, while preserving notions of men's ultimate authority.

Alternatives to Responsible Manhood: Wildness & Following Your Heart

Every few years, a book appears that becomes "mandatory reading" within evangelical subculture. Unlike perennial favorites such as Dobson's works on parenting, these books create and are accompanied by a flash flood of marketing, videos, study guides, special editions, gift bindings, and seminars. Recent examples include *The prayer of Jabez* (Wilkenson 1999), *The purpose driven life* (Warren 2002), and the fictional *Left behind* series (LaHaye and Jenkins 1996). John Eldredge's *Wild at heart* is such a book. Since its publication in 2001 it has ranked in the top four best selling Christian books overall by the Evangelical Christian Publishers Association.[1] It was a finalist for the ECPA Book of the Year award in 2003, and winner of the ECPA Gold Medallion in Inspirational Books in 2003.

---

[1]In August 2004, *Wild at heart* was ranked #3 in overall best sellers by the Christian Booksellers Association (2004), just behind Rick Warren's *Purpose driven life* (2002) and newest book *You have what it takes: What every father needs to hear* (2004). It has been ranked #1 in the "Christian Living" category multiple times since publication.

Given this enormous popularity, what is it about *Wild at heart* that has so captured the evangelical imagination? What model of godly manhood does Eldredge present, and how does it compare to the responsible and connected masculinity of much PK literature?

Contrasting WAH & *PK Ideals for Men*. Compared to most PK literature, *Wild at heart* offers less connected masculinity, one directed by the passions of the heart rather than duty, responsibility or accountability.[2] In fact, Eldredge offers his book as a counter point, if not antithesis, to Promise Keepers' ideas of connected and responsible masculinity.

> Do we really need another book for men? No. . . . We need permission. To be what we are—men made in God's image. Permission to live from the heart and not from the list of "should" and "ought to" that has left so many of us tired and bored. . . . So I offer this book, not as the seven steps to being a better Christian, but as a safari of the heart to recover a life of freedom, passion and adventure (xi–xii).

While never directly criticizing the Promise Keepers movement or its leaders, Eldredge's emphasis is clearly on the personal struggle of men to free themselves from feelings of inadequacy and move "westward into the wilderness" in their relationship with God, rather than their need to be responsible providers and leaders at church and at home. In one brief paragraph he supports the notion that men need each other, yet goes on to argue . . .

> Thanks to the men's movement the church understands now that a man needs other men, but what we've offered is another two-dimensional solution:

[2]The themes of desire, passion, and following one's heart appear in no fewer than eight books and workbooks by John Eldredge over the past seven years. Three of these— *The Sacred Romance* (Curtis and Eldredge 1997); *Journey of desire* (Eldredge 2000); and *Wild at heart* (Eldredge 2001)—were followed by the publication of an associated workbook, and were reissued as a set of "classics" in 2001. Since then, the *Wild at heart* phenomena has spawned numerous seminars, boot camps for men, and a video-book-tape-field guide boxed set for small group use (2003b). The theme of following one's heart continues in Eldredge's recent work (2002, 2003a).

"Accountability" groups or partners. Ugh. That sounds so old covenant: "you're really a fool and you're just waiting to rush into sin, so we'd better post a guard by you to keep you in line." We don't need accountability groups; we need fellow warriors, someone to fight alongside, someone to watch our back (175).

Like Weber, the book draws heavily on warrior metaphors. But whereas Weber argues that a godly man is a "tender warrior" who draws his strength from a community of men who are emotionally intimate and committed to "holding each other accountable," Eldredge downplays accountability in favor of men supporting each other in taking individual risks. He exaggerates Weber's "tender warrior" motif—bypassing initiation in favor of aggression as "part of the masculine *design* . . . (10)," arguing that "a man is a dangerous thing . . ." (82), whose "strength is wild and fierce (149)," who above all takes risks (202–03). For Eldredge, this iteration of masculinity is like God who also takes risks (in creation), and Jesus who was "fierce and wild and romantic to the core" (203).

Eldredge's vision of godly manhood is defined as much by what it is not as for what it is. The soul of a man is made for adventure (205). It is most emphatically not domestic. It thrives when it is embattled (141). For Eldredge, every man longs for "a great mission to his life that involves and yet transcends even home and family (141)". Finding that mission involves paying careful attention to one's own desires.

Following this adventure leads a man outside the household, into the wilderness. Men should "pay attention to our desire . . . to head into the wilderness" (207), because "the core of a man's heart is undomesticated *and that is good*" (4). Eldredge explains men's "wildness" by appealing to a detail in the Genesis creation account in which man is created *outside* the garden and brought in; while the woman is created inside. From this, he infers the basis of men's and women's essentially different natures—one uncultivated and "wild," the other domesticated. (One might as plausibly argue that the text demonstrates how Adam was incomplete until he was brought into the garden—that essential manhood is one that isn't finished until it is applied to the cultivation and nurture of growing things—but this is not the point Eldredge draws from the text.) Here, in the very beginning, lie the roots of male wildness, male aggression, and male desire for wilderness in which to roam free. Repeatedly posing Mr. Rogers and Braveheart as competing alternatives for manhood, Eldredge comes down firmly on the position that above all, godly men are not "nice."

> The whole crisis in masculinity today has come because we no longer have a warrior culture, a place for men to learn to fight like men. We don't need a meeting of Really Nice Guys; we need a gathering of Really Dangerous Men (175).

Eldredge pushes the metaphor further, writing specifically against anything associated with gentleness, meekness, humility or tenderness. The godly man "takes risks (202–03), "has a vision" (142), is "cunning" and "knows how to fight" both spiritual enemies (143), and for the heart of a woman (15). This latter theme, "the beauty to fight for" runs throughout the book. Every man "wants to be the hero to the beauty . . . he needs someone to fight *for* (15)." What prevents this heroism is the wounds men receive from fathers who undermine the very qualities that lie at the center of authentic masculinity. Describing his own struggle to develop emotional intimacy with his wife, Eldredge writes, "Will you fight for her? That's the question Jesus asked me many years ago (192)."

Finally, Eldredge's message is tempered by occasional qualifications—godly manhood is "wild" but not irresponsible; it is "free" but not a solo enterprise; it is "slightly dangerous" but "the warrior is in this for good"(193). Echoing a theme that is central to PK accountability groups, Eldredge writes:

> Don't even think about going into battle alone. Don't even try to take the masculine journey without at least one man by your side. Yes, there are times a man must face the battle alone, in the wee hours of the morn, and fight with all he's got. But don't make that a lifestyle of isolation (174).

Yet against scattered statements encouraging community and cooperation stand illustration upon illustration of the solo hero battling unimaginable odds and stories of intensive counseling of individuals he has helped. These examples weigh clearly against the notion of men needing other groups of men—a theme that is central to much PK literature—or men being responsible, even submitting themselves, to the authority of a pastor or other spiritual leader. Rather than drawing their strength from an institution or community, Eldredge's godly man is more likely to struggle within and against the stultifying effects of established institutions.

Eldredge also hedges against the criticism that advocating male wildness promotes selfishness or irresponsibility.

> I'm not suggesting that the Christian life is chaotic or that a real man is flagrantly irresponsible. . . . What I am saying is that our false self demands a formula before he'll engage; he wants guarantee of success, and mister, you aren't going to get one. There comes a time in a man's life when he's got to break away from all that and head off into the unknown with God (213).

The "false self that Eldredge alludes to here, is the self who is afraid to risk—the wounded self of the mythopoetic men's movement in which men are encouraged to find their true masculine hearts through retreat, workshops, and recognition of their inner warrior and wildman (Kimmel 1996; Messner 1997; Schwalbe 1996). Sounding much like an evangelical version of Robert Bly, Eldredge argues that godly manhood takes risks and heads off "into the unknown with God." Authentic men are willing to take professional risks, as evidenced by Eldredge's account of leaving the security of Focus on the Family Ministries and became a freelance author and therapist. Nowhere does he provide any discussion of the risks of male wildness for women who live with truly dangerous men whose pursuit of their passions harms both wives and children (for a discussion of domestic violence in evangelical families see Nason-Clark and Kroeger 2004). Instead, wildness is understood as means to more authentic career choices and richer family life as men resist stagnation and are encouraged to engage in the dangerous business of living "free" in a rationalized world. Against the seven promises of a Promise Keeper, Eldredge writes:

> This is not a book about the seven things a man ought to do to be a nicer guy. It is a book about the recovery and release of a man's heart, his passions, his true nature, which he has been given by God . . . . If you are going to know who you truly are as a man, if you are going to find a life worth living, if you are going to love a woman deeply and not pass on your confusion to your children, you simply must get your heart back. You must head up into the high country of the soul, into wild and uncharted regions and track down that elusive prey (18).

Authority & Evidence in Wild at Heart

Although evangelicals and other conservative Protestants are often characterized as biblical literalists, much evangelical advice literature appeals as frequently to personal experience and popular culture as to the Bible. *Wild at heart* typifies this approach. Coding and counting these themes through the book shows nearly identical proportions of the text devoted to these three types of evidence—personal/autobiographical anecdotes, popular culture and the Bible. In emphasizing the "self evident" and "obvious" nature of his case and in drawing on personal experience as much as the Bible, *Wild at heart* is a quintessentially evangelical text (Noll 1994). The heros in "Braveheart," "Saving Private Ryan" and "The legends of the fall" figure as dominantly as Moses, David and Jesus in his analysis. Perhaps most important is his use of material from Robert Bly's *Iron man*, whose work is highlighted nearly a dozen times in the book, and is clearly a key source for Eldredge's imaginative vision. Here in particular, *Wild at heart* stands opposite that of PK author Stu Weber who mentions Bly, but writes scathingly about the mythopoetic men's movement, calling it self-indulgent and shallow, and contrasting its vision of self-involved masculinity to his challenge to evangelical men to prioritize wives and children above self and career (Weber 1993).

INTERPRETING WILD AT HEART

Given the emphasis on responsible providing and involved fatherhood that is central to so much PK advice literature for men, and given the anti-promise keepers themes implicit within Eldredge's *Wild at heart*, what can we say about shifting ideals of masculinity among evangelical Protestants? How do ordinary readers interpret and apply the styles of masculinity advocated by this literature? To what extent are the readings of *Wild at heart* gendered—that is, do men and women read it in different ways? And how do age and marital status affect the personal meanings ordinary evangelicals draw from the book?

Research Methods

To answer these questions, we talked with a cross section of self-identified evangelical men and women, asking them what they thought about the book and how they saw themselves applying it in their own lives. More specifically, we interviewed a sample of married husbands and wives in two local congregations (a Presbyterian (PCUSA) and an Assemblies of God). We also talked with young adult men and women involved in an evangelical campus ministry.

The two sets of church-going men that we interviewed had studied the book together. At one church it was used as teaching material for a large Sunday school class of sixty to eighty men; in the other as the basis for discussion in an early morning men's Bible study of twelve to fifteen men. The men in the para-church fellowship did not read the book as part of a formal study group, rather the book was recommended and discussed informally among friends.

Because the early morning church bible study group had been meeting for years, and because the men and women in the para-church ministry frequently met for informal discussion we did group interviews with these three sets of respondents (interviewing men and women separately was a methodological decision that turned out to be strategically important in given the divergent responses that appeared across gender and age). Coordinating group

■ **TABLE 39.1**
Sample Characteristics

	Presbyterian	Pentecostal	Para-Church Organization	Total #
men n =	n = 9	n = 6	n = 5	20
$\bar{x}$ age	58	52	23.2	
Women	n = 8	n = 6	n = 5	19
$\bar{x}$ age	46	50	21.8	
% married	94	100	0	
% professional	80	80	—	
% Euro-American	100	100	80	
TOTAL #	17	12	10	39

meetings with the men who studied the book for Sunday school but were no longer meeting, and coordinating meetings with the wives of both groups of church-going men proved to be quite difficult. After multiple failed attempts, we interviewed the sample of men from the second church and the wives from both churches individually over the telephone.[3]

[3]In considering the effects of mixing interview techniques, it is possible that some of those interviewed in the group settings may have been be hesitant to speak as freely as they might in a personal interview. It is also possible for a few dominant individuals to limit the amount of input from less outspoken participants in a group. Two points give us some confidence that these potential problems did not significantly undermine the quality of our data. First, the men and women we interviewed together had a history of meeting to talk about faith, relationships, American culture, etc., so that a significant degree of trust within the group was already established. Second, we encouraged all individuals to speak in an effort to prevent one or two leaders from dominating the group interviews. We began by offering each person opportunity to respond to opening questions about how they heard about the book and what they thought, liked and didn't like about it. We also made note to return to less outspoken members, asking their ideas about the particular aspect of the book under discussion. Moreover, it is possible that the men in the large Sunday school class and the wives of the church-going men (e.g. those respondents who were not part of any long term study or discussion group) were more open over the telephone than they might have been had we interviewed them in groups. However, we have no way to systematically assess the degree to which that was the case.

Among the married women in the local churches, only one had read the entire book. The remainder knew their husbands were reading it and a handful had discussed it with their husbands. None had been motivated to take time to read it themselves. Within the campus fellowship, the men who read the book were so passionate about its message that some of their female friends decided to read it themselves. As we describe below their reaction was passionate too, but of a different sort. The book spurred numerous heated debates about gender within the fellowship and led to a rethinking of both relationships and approaches to ministry on campus. In all, twenty men and nineteen women participated in these discussions (see Table 39.1 for sample description[4]). All interviews were recorded with permission and fully transcribed for analysis.

[4]Nearly all of the men and women connected to the local churches were married. None of the young adults associated with the university para-church ministry were married (one woman was engaged and another couple were seriously dating). Most of the men and women in the church samples were in their late forties and early fifties; with two older couples in their late seventies. The overall age of the church sample was fifty-five years old. The young adults associated with the para-church college group ranged from nineteen to twenty-seven years old, with a mean age of about twenty-two. As in other samples of self-identified evangelical Protestants, our sample was middle- and upper middle class, white, and fairly well educated (see Smith 1998).

Multiple Meanings, Gender & Age

Two primary domains distinguished the meanings appropriated from reading *Wild at heart*—gender and age. Interpretations differed between younger and older men; and for women and men regardless of age.

Para-Church University Men

The men associated with the para-church ministry were unanimously positive in their overall reactions to the book. Ideas about men's "instinctive need" for adventure and women's need to be viewed as a "beauty to be rescued" echoed what most of them hoped or already thought were true about gender difference. As one young man explained

> [The book] made more sense than anything I ever read before, and it feels beneficial. I can be who I am . . . and that should be beneficial to the women I'm around. . . . Men need to have a battle to fight, a beauty to rescue, adventure . . . What a women needs is for me to be alive and free and full of life. To be active and not passive. Any woman wants that, over me just checking out and not being there.

Eldredge's imagery of men being made for risk and adventure was particularly salient. One young man said "I realized internally in my soul there were parts of me that were dying because everyone was communicating to me to be safe." Others argued that "men need to be 'slightly dangerous'" and to "stand up and not be afraid to show how much you care." For those in dating relationships and those hoping for relationships, images of masculine leadership and initiative rang true. They resonated with metaphors encouraging men to risk moving relationships forward to new levels of intimacy and commitment. As one of the men explained

> The point I came to was if I am dating her and I want to marry her, what is to honoring her? I am not just having fun, I am going to show that I am serious by going there and pursuing the "beauty." That's helped. Now she sees that I care and that I am serious.

This encouragement to "make a move" worked across levels of dating relationships—so that young men who were approaching decisions about marriage, as well as those just contemplating asking a woman out on a date heard a similar message—theirs was the responsibility to take the initiative and risk the danger of rejection and failure in their relationships with women. The rationale for this was the underlying belief that "women want to marry a man who has life and excitement—a purpose—not just someone who is a 'yes' man." The notion that "what women want is a man who sees life as an adventure" was the kind of motivation some men needed to "take the risk" of a more personal relationship. When women protested this notion, arguing (as those in the fellowship had) that they would prefer to be partners in a joint adventure rather than join in one that is really "his" one of the men dismissed the objection as false consciousness and self-delusion.

> *All* the women I know, women who are strong women, who two years ago would never have expressed a desire to be beautiful or pursued, now they realize that's what they want. . . . There's a realization that it's actually true. All the women I know who are more mature will say . . . deep down, they want to be "the beauty" and be pursued. That's a fundamental difference between male desires and female desires. I think its what they really want, but they don't realize its what they want. They say they want someone who is safe originally, but down the road . . .

So compelling was the image of the beauty to be rescued that the same men who acknowledged "there's a range among women . . ." and argued that taking risk and adventure "aren't gender specific at all—he calls both men and women out," were nevertheless supportive of the notion that deep down, even if they don't realize it, what women really want is to beautiful and pursued.

Minimally critical of the book's gender messages, the men in the fellowship were much more concerned about the narrowness of Eldredge's vision across race and class. The theme of racial reconciliation (a major emphasis within Promise Keepers) had been a focus of the fellowship during the past year, and echoed in their comments on the "whiteness" of *Wild at heart*. They described how most of the book applied only to men who, like themselves and like Eldredge, were educated, white and relatively privileged. One who had grown up in a large urban area summarized this discussion by saying:

> I felt that he was writing to white men who live in the suburbs. Like where he tells the kid to punch the bully back. If you did that at my high school a kid might come at you with a baseball bat.

Most of Eldredge's metaphors for wild, adventurous, and even free masculinity seemed applicable only to the lives of privileged men. Adventuring in the West, counseling sessions with a family therapist, white water rafting and kayaking all seemed useful and exciting, but were hard to imagine as ordinary experience for men across race and class. None of them, however, interpreted the inapplicability of much of the book to most men as a challenge to its basic premise—that men, by design, are slightly dangerous, alive and free.

Para-Church University Women

The women involved in the campus fellowship had quite a different reaction and set of perspectives on the book. If it made the young men cheer, it made the women cry. Literally. It made them cry; it made them angry. In short, they hated it.

Why this extraordinary difference? Like the men in the fellowship, the women also read *Wild at heart* as confirmation of gender stereotypes. Yet while this was good news for the men, it was acutely bad news for the women—especially the notion that "everyone has to look like this."

> If everything in this book is "essential manhood" then I don't know what I am. . . . I don't have that much different an experience with my father [than he does with his]. I like to walk around outside, I like to get muddy, I like to get dirty, whatever. . . . in my world that doesn't make someone essentially a man or a woman.

The fellowship women found it initially problematic that Eldredge would presume to make such absolutist claims about a woman's essential nature and deepest needs. While not denying that being beautiful or desirable is important, they felt Eldredge exaggerated these characteristics. Women want to be beautiful as persons and partners, not passive beauties waiting to be rescued.

> When he talks about women's deepest desire as wanting to be considered beautiful or sought after, I think that is two desires I have . . . but I think that my deepest desire is to have partnership and have someone to come along side and consider me an equal.

The women also voiced concern that Eldredge's model of femininity was simply an inversion of idealized masculinity, "as though for masculinity to increase, femininity must decrease, like a woman isn't whole." Although he does acknowledge variety among women and men (38), the overall message of the book was that masculinity is inherently strong, adventurous, risk taking and brave. Femininity, by association, seemed emptied of the possibility of those virtues.

> I get really mad when I hear femininity being described as the opposite of masculinity. It isn't. He builds this whole argument about what masculinity is, and femininity is the opposite. That's just not true.

The characteristics Eldredge argues are the essence of masculinity were some of the same characteristics women said they both saw and wanted to cultivate in themselves. They described "following Jesus" as a terrific adventure. It puzzled and disturbed them that in areas as diverse as evangelism and rock climbing, they would be passionate about things Eldredge argues are distinctly masculine. "What does this mean, I'm a man? I'm a bad woman? How am I supposed to respond to being told you're basically deluded about what you think it means to be a godly woman?" For them strength, courage, adventure seemed human, not gendered. And in both their lives and in the lives of their relatives and friends they saw enormous variation in character.

The women reject essentialism

He kept reiterating that there was this *masculine* journey and that . . . masculine aggression is a holy thing. I never considered just masculinity as aggressive. There might be something to that, but I felt he was defining masculinity from his own experience. I could write the same from my own experience.

Not only did these women believe that love for adventure and risk taking are distributed to various degrees across women and men, they saw these as narrow caricatures of the real men with whom they were friends. In some cases, they thought "dangerous" and "free" might describe some of the men that they knew. But they also knew women who were like that and some men who were not.

I am wondering and have been praying about a lot this: it feels like to talk about "godly gender" is almost a paradox or wrong, cause there is so much cultural influence that's hard to filter (out). God allows so much variation along gender lines than we would like to give him. I value the book because it wants to give these masculine men a place to be dangerous that most churches don't allow, but I question whether it will allow for women to be this way, too . . . or for other men to say, "this doesn't fit me".

The young women were especially critical of the narrowness of Eldredge's vision of godly manhood. They were offended by his repetitive pitting of "Mr. Rogers" against "Braveheart" styles of masculinity. Not only did they think that manliness could be expressed in a wider range of activities than rafting, climbing and other outdoor adventures, they worried that these characteristics might not always be qualities God wanted to develop in a man's life. "What about compassion," "what about mercy" they wondered. "How is this supposed to help a man nurture children or care for the poor?" For them, "kindness" or "niceness" or even "meekness" were neither antithetical to their own ideals for godly manhood, nor were they synonymous with a man being a pathetic, weak or domesticated "nice guy."

Finally, the para-church women were highly critical of the degree to which Eldredge's image of godly manhood could be applied across race and class. Similar to the men, the women thought *Wild at heart* was written for a white middle-class audience. So thick is the book with examples of rafting, rock climbing, and bronco busting, that they could not imagine how it could be useful to men who were not white, privileged, outdoorsmen who could afford to cultivate such an adventurous lifestyle. As one woman explained

I think that's really dangerous because not all men are like him at all. From my personal experience, my brother grew up in Hong Kong. He was never in the outdoors, he doesn't desire that at all. He came here when he was twelve, and he hated the idea of "be a man," be macho . . . have guns and play with frogs.

Even if economic resources were not a constraint on adventurous living, they could think of men they considered "Godly guys" who had no desire to go rafting or rock climbing. It seemed implausible that this image of aggressive manhood could apply to an entire world of men in multiple countries, cultures, and ethnicities.

Middle-Age Church-going Men

Compared to those in the para-church fellowship, several interesting contrasts emerged in the interviews conducted with the mostly middle-age sample of church-going women and men. First, men from both churches were somewhat more temperate in their response to *Wild at heart*. For some, the moderation of their enthusiasm reflected years of living with "real women." Other than the idea that all women want to be pursued—a notion interpreted as both leading to emotional as well as sexual intimacy—most of the married men were quick to identify Eldredge's gender ideals as unrealistically narrow. The romanticized notion of "a beauty to fight for" was appealing, but they laughed out loud at the thought that their wives, whom they'd seen living "outside the tower," were maidens locked away in distress.

I think there are lots of models to be a man, so he generalizes what it would look like. Men in general, and women too, have a need to face challenge. It's not an exclusive thing. It might be played out more in men but I know lots of women who face challenges.

For some of the men, a little "wildness" seemed an attractive thing in women as well as men. The generalization seemed much too narrow, given the real and ideal of women they know.

I think he really generalizes about what women want. Otherwise, why do we have stories from history of women who never marry, who contributed greatly in lives of adventure? Florence Nightingale: she spent her life waiting to be rescued [they laugh at the sarcasm]. . . . There's a painting in my office of a woman wrangler and *she* isn't waiting for anyone to rescue her. She's the un-stereotype of a woman. I really like it, it just points out what we men have thought about the stereotype role of woman. He generalizes way too much.

About a third of the men saw the book as sending different messages on both gender and accountability than they'd picked up in reading PK literature and attending PK events.

I saw that crack on accountability groups. I've been to two or three PK events and think PK is a little more even handed and don't go after quite the same generalizations towards women. I see them as saying more "stick to the promises you have made to women, you promised to love them and provide for them, now get your tail to work and do it." I don't think PK is advocating at all for the Stone Age sort of stuff. I'm not sure Eldredge does either, but I think his views on women are a little outdated.

Although Eldredge is critical of the concept of PK style "accountability groups," reading the book together provided a context in which men could share areas of their lives they might never had otherwise. "It has been beneficial to get to know these guys. In how many churches do men see each other's faces Sunday after Sunday and don't know anything about each other. Maybe that is what fellowship is about." Reading the book as a group deepened their understanding of each other,

provided opportunity to hear each other's life stories, and a context for sharing fears and struggles with family and career.

It touched on a lot of subjects that men just don't want to talk about. It gets to the point and uses lots of illustrations so it was easy for all the guys to connect to what he was saying. It gave us a chance to talk about fear and relationships with wives and kids. Some guys just don't want to talk about this stuff cause their image is of being so cool or whatever. It's just hard for people to discuss some of this. But we had some really good discussions.

In sharing their personal struggles, a second area of contrast between older and younger men was their discussion of "the father wound." The younger men saw this as an area in which they should seek healing, while many of the older men had a difficult time identifying what the nature of this wound might be. For the few who felt they *had* been wounded, the damage appeared to be something they had already resolved. As one of the men in the AOG congregation explained:

I was supposed to be teaching a Sunday school class on that section and both I and the other fellow couldn't figure out what to do with it because we just couldn't relate. Neither one of us felt like that described our relationships with our dads. And most of the guys we know who have had trouble have worked it out long ago.

Part of the difference between older and younger men's approach to the "father wound" is a difference in what older and younger men expect from their fathers. When older men talked about their fathers they expressed gratitude for their hard work and spoke fondly of the bonding trips they had taken together. As one man in his 80s expressed

[Eldredge] put a big emphasis about wounding from the father and I tried and I just can't dig up anything. I think in terms of my father, he was very busy and we didn't spend a lot of time together, but I always felt supported and respected, and he gave me a lot of good advice in times when I needed it.

These varying generational expectations may have had some affect on how older and younger men approached the question of personal healing. One set of men who had read the book together talked about this portion of the book as a valuable opportunity to share about their fathers and childhoods with a group of other men. While appreciating the opportunity to share a part of their lives they might never had otherwise, the framework of a need to heal "the father wound" was not particularly salient.

On the other hand, the middle aged and older men *did* use this theme as an opportunity to rethink their relationship with their own children. Here it meant a chance to reconsider the degree to which they might be overly demanding or set unrealistic expectations for their children. It provided modest motivation for how they might approach asking their adult sons to forgive them for past mistakes, saying "One of the things this has prompted me to do is go back and talk to my kids . . . did I wound you? Was I too harsh? Did I neglect you?" Men with younger children were quick to point out how the book had provided them ammunition for countering their wives' concerns about doing risky and dangerous things with their children, to "go easy" on their sons, "connect more" and "mentor" their daughters.

Yet overall, the most important aspect of the book for the men in the church samples was the encouragement they received for taking risks in their jobs. Two thirds of the married men in our sample were white collar, highly paid professional men—most working in large bureaucratic corporations or in family businesses of their own. Their reading did nothing to discourage their sense of responsibility at home by taking off for the weekend into the wilderness. But did encourage them to rethink complacency at work and the dulling effects of years in a career.

> I think he's right that our society is trying keep people "safe." I think that's dangerous. The state tries to protect people from anything that could possibly conceivably hurt them. We are so afraid of risk that we risk losing the ability to act at all.

For one man in particular, the book was a real turning point in his career, providing the impetus to leave his high paying position in management and take several months to rethink what he really wanted to do with the second half of his life. More often, it reshaped how men described thinking about the balance of time and energy they were spending at work and at home.

> I'd read his other book, *Journey of desire*, and felt compelled to read this one when it came out. It spoke to where I've been the past two years, on a journey from being so independent and focused on me to being much more involved with my family and other men. My wife loves it: I've had a heart change. I'm definitely more available.

Along with being more involved at home and taking risks by scaling back careers, these older men made the case that perseverance, self-control and personal sacrifice—themes they thought were clear in the Promise Keepers literature they had read—were important aspects of godly manhood that *Wild at heart* neglected.

> I think he's right, but in my own estimate, these things in a man's heart are good but should be controlled. He doesn't say an awful lot about the matter of control, and there are all kinds of battles to be fought that aren't physical or even necessarily emotional. But they require real stamina in modern life, not just heroism.

Finally, one area of agreement between older and younger cohorts was the class and race biases of the book. It was hard for them to envision the book appealing to men in less privileged positions. One of them wondered aloud at how much money Eldredge had made from sales of the book and the degree to which "his brothers and sisters around the world were sharing in that."

Wives of Church-going Men

The final sample of people with whom we talked were the wives of the middle aged and older men. The most remarkable thing about these interviews was their length—the women did not read the book, and so had very little to say about either it or how they saw it affecting their husband's lives. A couple of the wives had read parts of it. Only one had read the whole. When asked why, they said they "just never thought of it," "had other things to do," or "it seemed like a guys book, so I wasn't that interested." And so they didn't bother.

Still, even within these interviews, two points of contrast with the younger women's interviews emerged. First, several of the women did talk briefly (one at length) about how the book seemed good for their husbands' sense of being able to take risks at work. As we mentioned above, this translated into one wife encouraging her husband to leave his career. In most cases, however, women felt the book had helped their husbands in a general way to be willing to voice disagreement with supervisors or provide critical, but difficult, personnel reviews.

The most dramatic contrast that emerges out of the wives' interviews was their very different response to Eldredge's images of godly manhood and womanhood. For women in the Assemblies of God church, the emphasis on gender difference sounded both familiar and "right." "Men and women are different," they said. "Our society doesn't want to admit it, but they are. It was nice to hear someone say so." The married women with whom we talked were neither offended nor threatened by Eldredge's gender essentialism. Among those for whom the image of women as beauties desiring to be pursued did not ring true, they simply dismissed the entire line of argument as exaggerated and not particularly relevant.

> I think he may be right about some things, like how guys need to get out there and take risks. But I'm not like the women he describes. There's a lot more to both of us than that. What's important is that we both be willing to go out there and do whatever God wants us to do. Whether that's with our kids or jobs or whatever. Sometimes that gender stuff helps, sometimes it doesn't.

For married women who had already shared a number of years living with particular men, whether they agreed with Eldredge's gender essentialism or not, the overall impression of the book was that if it helped their husbands get in touch with other men, pay more attention to how they interacted with their kids, and gave them the push they needed to take hard stands at work, it was good. The rest of the story was not all that important.

Denominational Distinctives

While the most significant contrasts we identified were across age and gender, different ways of interpreting and appropriating the messages of *Wild at heart* were evident across religious tradition as well. Styles of discourse, metaphor and points of emphasis all subtly differed among men whose church culture, theology, style of worship and heroes of the faith were connected to broader Reformed or Pentecostal streams of Christianity. Men in the Assembly of God church were much more likely to use military and adventurer language in describing the role of men in family life, saying things like "the book really lays out who we are as men . . . what God designed us to be. . . . we're designed as men to be leaders and warriors." The warrior motif was applied to men being designed to fight both spiritual and relational battles, and appeared most prominently in AOG discussions of "putting on the armor of God," "going into battle," "being the spiritual leader," "the need for a man to lay down his life for his wife and kids" or more generally having "a beauty to rescue" because "God designed us to be that person." Clearly, the specific responsibilities of husbands and wives may have changed, but these men saw their primary responsibilities as extensions of the protector and provider husbands of the 1950s.

> Then men worked came home and worked and came home and did their jobs. Their role was to be the provider. It still is, but men are called to be bigger than that, to *be* Braveheart and Gladiator fighting for our families and the church. Somebody has to step up.

This model of strong masculine involved leadership appeared as a much-needed challenge to the "light weight" and "feminized" models of masculinity AOG men saw as coming to dominate American culture. In contrast, men affiliated with the Presbyterian church were less likely to spiritualize their struggles at home or work using metaphors of adventure, warfare or combat, but rather described these as areas in which God expected them to act responsibly vis a vis both family and employers.

The concerns these middle age church-going men also had with the book differed somewhat across denomination. For men connected with the Pentecostal church, two issues arose. First, the notion that *Wild at heart* might somehow encourage men to disregard their pastor's authority or the accountability of other men and opt to "fly solo." As one of the men, involved in leadership in the church expressed:

Some things you have to take with a grain of salt, like his slamming the church-going man. What sells is controversy and some people picked it up because of that. Here's a guy who [sounds like he] attends church six or eight times a year and thinks he has all the answers. But he doesn't talk about who he's accountable to . . . I have guys throughout the United States where I never make a major move without consulting them and I didn't see any of that [in the book]. He doesn't talk about great times of fellowship with his men's leader, or major players in his life.

The men in the Presbyterian church also expressed concern that the book might encourage "solo Christianity," but the connection they thought was lacking was less a relationship of subordination to church leaders and more in a set of mutually supportive (and now somewhat more intimate) male friends.

The guys by-and-large don't think its that great. Its not deep. But it does have some good ideas. I think they have appreciated the conversations and that we have beared [sic] our souls a little better. In a sense it validates his thesis that men need other men. So pastorally its been very worth while, cause I think the guys have talked more.

Clearly, these two approaches to authority within the church reflect the different denominational cultures of the Assembly of God and Presbyterianism in the United States. Moreover, in attitudes and policies regarding gender, specifically women in church leadership, men also differed. The men in the Presbyterian church were much more skeptical about the narrowness of the gender stereotypes and limited application across race and class than were men in the AOG church. In fact, none of the AOG men thought that Eldredge's gender stereotypes were particularly problematic. Although the image of women as needing to be pursued and rescued did not resonate as deeply as it did with the younger men, the men in the AOG study group were unanimous in their agreement that men and women are "just different"—an idea that confirmed their belief that husbands should be providers, protectors and spiritual leaders at home.

As a husband and a father it showed me that my role is to provide opportunity to let my wife dance on the stage of life. Before it was all about me . . . my job, my influence, my money . . . how much I was earning. Now I see there has to be less of my self, dying to myself and my goals, my job. And now much more about my family.

Across denomination, reading the book increased men's awareness of the how much they were connected to family. Yet the degree to which gender differences were used to explain that connection was more prominent among the AOG men than the men at the Presbyterian church.

Finally, these middle aged church-going men differed in their thoughts about how the book was most useful or effective. Men in the Assembly, like the younger men in the para-church campus ministry, saw the book as a useful tool in evangelism as well as personal growth.

I was very confident in my masculinity already . . . but you get a lot of guys who are into different things and there's no place for that in the church. Like you can separate your secular and sacred life. That's not right. If you can't use whatever you're into ministry wise, then maybe you ought to think again . . . maybe it shouldn't be in your life. So this weekend we're doing a "coast ride" for guys with bikes. Last time, we had 40 guys in leather with their Harleys, etc.

Not your typical white shirt Baptist thing. We want all kinds of guys to know that the church is for them!

Or as another man put it:

You know, the culture has evolved and if we don't evolve too, the gospel won't be heard. He puts the gospel in a way that men today can hear. It is very solid. The gospel has to be presented in the terms of the culture otherwise it won't have an impact. Just talking, like in traditional churches, from the scripture in a sermon—well, that's harder for men in our culture to hear. So Eldredge tells the gospel in a way that men today can hear. His word is something that God is using to raise up men and call them out.

In contrast, none of the men in the Presbyterian church described *Wild at heart* as a useful evangelism strategy. For them, its usefulness was found in help balancing commitments and enriching relationships with family and at work.

Although our sample is quite small, these differences across Pentecostal and non-Pentecostal men are consistent with findings from other research in which men and women in charismatic or Pentecostal churches tend to hold more essentialist notions of godly manhood and womanhood (Gallagher 1999, 2003). Moreover they mirror specific denominational and theological distinctives: cultural relevance versus the "just talking from the scripture"; responsibility to church leadership versus responsibility to a group of men peers; spiritual warfare versus relational sensitivity; resisting domestication versus being involved fathers. In these ways, even this small sample points to the significance of embeddedness in a particular Christian theological story, in shaping how men interpret the particular stories they encounter in popular Christian advice literature.

SUMMARY & DISCUSSION

While this analysis is based on a small set of case studies across local church and para-church fellowships, the findings speak to a number of broader theoretical and methodological issues within the sociology of religion.

First, it is clear that the social location of the reader has enormous influence over the messages heard and applied from family advice literature. By itself, this is hardly news. Each of us has a set of lenses with which we read that are colored by gender, age, ethnicity, class, cohort and history. These shape how particular themes are interpreted as meaningful, foci narrowed and ideas emphasized and adopted in the process of selecting, reading and remembering religious texts. When it comes to interpreting the bible, evangelicals are intensely concerned that they employ a hermeneutic that preserves ideas of biblical authority and inspiration, while also being sensitive to cultural-historic specifics that inform its application to everyday life. Questions of hermeneutics are given less attention when it comes to other religious texts, yet they are nonetheless active in shaping their interpretation. As our analysis demonstrates, readers are remarkably active and selective consumers of the messages presented in books such as *Wild at heart*. Just as they employ a range of hermeneutical approaches in interpreting the scriptures, so too do they employ a range of perspectives in interpreting popular evangelical texts.

Among the multiple sets of lenses that shape the appropriation of ideas, two emerged as particularly salient in affecting ordinary readers' interpretations of *Wild at heart*—gender and age. Both older and younger men understood the message of the book as a challenge to take risks in relationships. However, the younger men were more likely to emphasize and celebrate Eldredge's messages of gender difference as a relational strategy, while the older and middle-aged men focused on the need to take risks in their careers and in cultivating more nurturing relationships with their children. For men in the middle of their lives the book was less a confirmation of gender stereotypes than a challenge to resist complacency. Perhaps most importantly, it provided a coherently evangelical language with which to resist (or at least consider resisting) the stultifying effects of rationalization (Schwalbe 1996).

Gender was also, not surprisingly, enormously important in readings of *Wild at heart*. For younger women the ideal of femininity as passive antithesis and response to the agency of a man felt like an attack on their personhood. They dreamed of having their own adventures, not simply finding someone whose adventure they could join. At a time in their lives when committed relationships are being formed, the narrowness of Eldredge's gender vision appeared as more of a death trap than a doorway to life. In contrast, the gender essentialism of *Wild at heart* hardly raised an eyebrow among middle-aged married women. They recognized the story, but ignored the plot line. Maybe he's right, maybe he's not—it made little difference. The real men with whom they shared their real lives appeared to be helped, and that was good enough.

From these interpretive strands, what more broadly can we learn about evangelical ideals for godly manhood? First, we are reminded that the range of masculinities and femininities among ordinary believers is much broader than those presented in most conservative Protestant family advice literature. More importantly, our analysis demonstrates that even narrow and gender essentialist messages can be read by ordinary believers as broader, more qualified, and more nuanced than the texts suggest. This selective appropriation of gender ideals highlights the need for researchers to attend to multiple meanings as well as messengers, if we are to more adequately describe and explain the workings of religion in everyday life.

Exploring the selective reading of these texts also helps explain the process through which evangelicals can be simultaneously symbolic traditionalists and pragmatic egalitarians (Gallagher 2003; Gallagher and Smith 1999) and "tack" between two seemingly contradictory sets of ideals (Bartkowski 2004). The most common expression of this process can be seen in cases where practice overrides literalist interpretation. The experience of married couples did not prevent them from hearing and even (in some cases) celebrating messages about essential gender difference. Their life experience, however, was a powerful filter that shaped how those messages were actually appropriated and applied. Among evangelicals for whom gender ideology does important subcultural religious

boundary work, we are likely to see a shift toward ever greater spiritualization of the "rules" for men and women, and emphasis on partnership and effective communication in marriage rather than a "chain of command" and "God given roles." In these ways, the experience of ordinary evangelicals may be reshaping the production of evangelical culture as much as evangelical cultural producers shape the subculture itself.

Second, the selective reading and multi-vocal character of evangelical gender texts underscores the centrality of ideals of gender that are both essentialized *and* flexible to the subcultural strength of American evangelicalism (see Gallagher 2003; Smith 1998). The various interpretations and selective appropriation of ideas from books like *Wild at heart* reflect the very core of what makes evangelical subculture tick. Both methodologically and thematically it captures the essence of evangelical identity. Methodologically, it appeals to two domains of religious authority that are most salient to evangelicals—personal experience and the bible (Gallagher 2003). Eldredge, as do other evangelical authors, presents his argument as resting on evidence that is both self evident and obvious. In doing so, he stands well within a tradition of anti-intellectualism and "Scottish Common Sense Realism" that historian Mark Noll argues have long been characteristic of American Evangelicalism (Noll 1994). Thematically also borrows heavily (we might say shamelessly) from the ideas of popular culture. It re-articulates ideas of muscular Christianity (Kimmel 1996; Putney 2003; Rotundo 1994) that framed conservative Protestant gender debates nearly a century ago, and romanticizes the ideal of the independent "self-made" man from the same era. It repackages themes from the mythopoetic men's movement of the 1980s, translating these into the language and style that dominates evangelical self-help literature. The prominence of Robert Bly as an authority on masculine identity and the "father wound" highlights the degree to which *Wild at heart* borrows from this literature—problematizing the inner struggles of rationalized and emotionally isolated hegemonic manhood. Here, it stands somewhat in contradiction to much Promise Keepers literature, particularly the writing of Stu Weber, which emphasizes responsibility and stability and is critical of the perceived self-indulgence and self-centeredness of the men's movement (Weber 1993).

Overall, then, Eldredge's *Wild at heart* is a quintessentially evangelical text. It places non-negotiable, dimorphous gender identity at the center of the story. It appeals to the most salient sources of religious authority, the bible and personal experience, as the basis for believing these are true. And it links these truths to well known myths, movies and media, as though there were a kind of gender essentialist "common grace" through which the characteristics of masculinity and femininity can be clearly known. Thus, connecting religious gender identity to popular culture, Eldredge's *Wild at heart* speaks to the heart of evangelical identity and its mandate to be both orthodox and culturally relevant—to be both in but not of "the world."

For men, that struggle involves not so much the fight against irresponsibility or selfishness, but a fight against the fear of failure and the willingness to abandon one's deepest desires for personal security and safety. For Stu Weber's "tender warrior" the latter might be interpreted as the personal sacrifices of a responsible man; for Eldredge it is acquiescing to rationalization and the death of the soul. For evangelical men across generation and tradition, popular texts such as these offer an easily assessable narrative that provides a plot-line for framing significant decisions, encouragement for greater connectedness at home, and a vision for how manhood and faith should express themselves in the world.

REFERENCES

Allen, L. D. 2000. Promise keepers and racism. *Sociology of Religion* 16:55–72.

Bartkowski, J. P. 1996. Beyond biblical literalism and inerrancy. *Sociology of Religion* 57:259–72.

———. 2001. *Remaking the godly marriage*. New Brunswick, N.J.: Rutgers University Press.

———. 2004. *The Promise Keepers*. New Brunswick, N.J.: Rutgers University Press.

Bilezikian, G. 1985. *Beyond sex roles*, second edition. Grand Rapids, Mich.: Baker Book House.

Bristow, J. T. 1988. *What Paul really said about women*. San Francisco: Harper San Francisco.

Christian Booksellers Association. 2004. Online report: http://www.ecpa.org/ECPA/best-sell.html.

Christenson, L. 1970. *The Christian family*. Minneapolis: Bethany.

Clark, S. B. 1980. *Man and woman in Christ*. Ann Arbor, Mich.: Servant Publications.

Cole, E. L. 1982. *Maximized manhood*. New Kensington, Penn.: Whitaker House.

Cooper, D. 1974. *You can be the wife of a happy husband*. Wheaton, I.L.: Victor Books.

Cooper, R. 1995. *We stand together*. Chicago: Moody Press.

Curtis, B. and J. Eldredge. 1997. *The sacred romance*. Nashville: Thomas Nelson.

Eldredge, J. 2000. *Journey of desire*. Nashville: Thomas Nelson.

———. 2001. *Wild at heart*. Nashville: Thomas Nelson.

———. 2002. *Dare to desire*. Nashville: Thomas Nelson.

———. 2003a. *Waking the Dead*. Nashville: Thomas Nelson.

Eldredge, J. 2003b. *Wild at heart multi-media facilitator's kit*. Nashville: Thomas Media Group.

———. 2004. *What every man needs to hear*. Nashville, TN: Thomas Nelson.

Elliot, E. 1976. *Let me be a woman*. Wheaton, IL.: Tyndale.

———. 1981. *Mark of a Man*. Wheaton, IL. Tyndale.

Farrar, S. 1990. *Point man*. Portland, OR: Multnomah.

Gallagher, S. K. 2003. *Evangelical identity and gendered family life*. New Brunswick, NJ.: Rutgers University Press.

———. 2004a. The marginalization of evangelical feminism. *Sociology of Religion* 65:215–37.

———. 2004b. Where are the anti-feminist evangelicals? *Gender & Society* 18:451–72.

Gallagher, S. K. &. C. Smith. 1999. Symbolic traditionalism and pragmatic egalitarianism. *Gender & Society* 13:211–233.

Getz, G. 1977. *The measure of a woman*. Ventura, CA: Regal Books.

Gundry, P. 1980. *Heirs together*. Grand Rapids, MI: Zondervan.

Hackstaff, K. 1999. *Marriage in a culture of divorce*. Philadelphia, PA: Temple University Press.

Hardisty, J. 1999. *Mobilizing resentment*. Boston: Beacon Press.

Hurley, J. B. 1981. *Man and woman in biblical perspective.* Grand Rapids, MI: Zondervan.

Kimmel, M. 1996. *Manhood in America.* New York, NY: The Free Press.

LaHaye, T. and J. B. Jenkins. 1996. *Left behind.* Wheaton, IL: Tyndale House Publishers.

Lockhart, W. H. 2000. "We are one life," but not of one gender ideology. *Sociology of Religion* 61:73–92.

Mathisen, J. A. 2001. The strange decade of the Promise Keepers. *Books & Culture* 7:36.

McCartney, B. 1997. *Sold out.* Waco, TX: Word.

———. 1994. *Seven promises of a Promise Keeper.* Colorado Springs, CO: Focus on the Family.

Messner, M. 1997. *The politics of masculinities.* Thousand Oaks, CA: Sage.

Messner, M. A. and C. Anderson. 1998. Miles to go before they sleep. Paper presented at the Annual Meeting of the Pacific Sociological Association, August, San Francisco.

Mickelsen, A. 1986. *Women, authority and the bible.* Downers Grove, IL: InterVarsity Press.

Mollenkott, V. R. 1977. *Women, men and the bible.* Nashville, TN.: Abingdon Press.

Nason-Clark, N. and C. C. Kroeger. 2004. *Refuge from abuse.* Downers Grove, IL: InterVarsity Press.

Noll, M. A. 1994. *The scandal of the evangelical mind.* Grand Rapids, MI: Eerdmans.

Oliver, G. 1993. *Real men have feelings too.* Chicago, IL: Moody Press.

Piper, J. and W. Grudem. 1991. *Recovering biblical manhood and womanhood.* Wheaton, IL: Crossway.

Porter, P. with W. T. Whalin. 1996. *Let the walls fall down.* Orlando, FL: Creation House.

Putney, C. 2003. *Muscular Christianity.* Cambridge, MA: Harvard University Press.

Rotundo, E. A. 1994. *American manhood.* New York, NY: Basic Books.

Scanzoni, L. D. and N. A. Hardesty. 1974. *All we're meant to be.* Waco, TX: Word.

Schwalbe, M. 1996. *Unlocking the iron cage.* New York, NY: Oxford University Press.

Smalley, G. and J. Trent. 1992. *The hidden value of a man.* Wheaton, IL: Tyndale House.

Smith, C. 1998. *American evangelicals.* Chicago, IL: University of Chicago Press.

Van Leeuwen, M. S. 1990. *Gender and grace.* Downers Grove, IL: InterVarsity Press.

Warren, R. 2002. *The purpose driven life.* Grand Rapids, MI: Zondervan.

Washington, R. and G. Kehrein. 1997. *Break down the walls.* Chicago, IL: Moody Press.

Weber, S. 1993. *Tender warrior.* Sisters, OR: Multnomah Books.

———. 1997. *The four pillars of a man's heart.* Sisters, OR: Multnomah Books.

———. 1998. *All the king's men.* Sisters, OR: Multnomah.

Wilkenson, B. 1999. *The prayer of Jabez.* Sisters, OR: Multnomah Books.

JUDAISM, MASCULINITY AND FEMINISM

Michael Kimmel

In the late 1960s, I organized and participated in several large demonstrations against the war in Vietnam. Early on—it must have been 1967 or so—over 10,000 of us were marching down Fifth Avenue in New York urging the withdrawal of all U.S. troops. As we approached one corner, I noticed a small but vocal group of counter-demonstrators, waving American flags and shouting patriotic slogans, "Go back to Russia!" one yelled. Never being particularly shy, I tried to engage him. "It's my duty as an American to oppose policies I disagree with. This is patriotism!" I answered. "Drop dead, you commie Jew fag!" was his reply.

Although I tried not to show it, I was shaken by his accusation, perplexed and disturbed by the glib association of communism, Judaism, and homosexuality. "Only one out of three," I can say to myself now, "is not especially perceptive." But yet something disturbing remains about that linking of political, religious, and sexual orientations. What links them, I think, is a popular perception that each is not quite a man, that each is less than a man. And while recent developments may belie this simplistic formulation, there is, I believe, a kernel of truth to the epithet, a small piece I want to claim, not as vicious smear, but proudly. I believe that my Judaism did directly contribute to my activism against that terrible war, just as it currently provides the foundation for my participation in the struggle against sexism.

What I want to explore here are some of the ways in which my Jewishness has contributed to

becoming an anti-sexist man, working to make this world a safe environment for women (and men) to fully express their humanness. Let me be clear that I speak from a cultural heritage of Eastern European Jewry, transmuted by three generations of life in the United States. I speak of the culture of Judaism's effect on me as an American Jew, not from either doctrinal considerations—we all know the theological contradictions of a biblical reverence for women, and prayers that thank God for not being born one—nor from an analysis of the politics of nation states. My perspective says nothing of Middle-Eastern machismo; I speak of Jewish culture in the diaspora, not of Israeli politics.

The historical experience of Jews has three elements that I believe have contributed to this participation in feminist politics. First, historically, the Jew is an *outsider*. Wherever the Jew has gone, he or she has been outside the seat of power, excluded from privilege. The Jew is the symbolic "other," not unlike the symbolic "otherness" of women, gays, racial and ethnic minorities, the elderly and the physically challenged. To be marginalized allows one to see the center more clearly than those who are in it, and presents grounds for alliances among marginal groups.

This essay was originally prepared as a lecture on "Changing Roles for the American Man" at the 92nd Street Y in November, 1983. I am grateful to Bob Brannon and Harry Brod for comments and criticisms of an earlier draft.

But the American Jew, the former immigrant, is "other" in another way, one common to many ethnic immigrants to the United States. Jewish culture is, after all, seen as an ethnic culture, which allows it to be more oppressive and emotionally rich than the bland norm. Like other ethnic subgroups, Jews have been characterized as emotional, nurturing, caring. Jewish men hug and kiss, cry and laugh. A little too much. A little too loudly. Like ethnics.

Historically, the Jewish man has been seen as less than masculine, often as a direct outgrowth of this emotional "respond-ability." The historical consequences of centuries of laws against Jews, of anti-Semitic oppression, are a cultural identity and even a self-perception as "less than men," who are too weak, too fragile, too frightened to care for our own. The cruel irony of ethnic oppression is that our rich heritage is stolen from us, and then we are blamed for having no rich heritage. In this, again, the Jew shares this self-perception with other oppressed groups who, rendered virtually helpless by an infantilizing oppression, are further victimized by the accusation that they are, in fact, infants and require the beneficence of the oppressor. One example of this cultural self-hatred can be found in the comments of Freud's colleague and friend Weininger (a Jew) who argued that "the Jew is saturated with femininity. The most feminine Aryan is more masculine than the most manly Jew. The Jew lacks the good breeding that is based upon respect for one's own individuality as well as the individuality of others."

But, again, Jews are also "less than men" for a specific reason as well. The traditional emphasis on literacy in Jewish culture contributes in a very special way. In my family, at least, to be learned, literate, a rabbi, was the highest aspiration one could possibly have. In a culture characterized by love of learning, literacy may be a mark of dignity. But currently in the United States literacy is a cultural liability. Americans contrast egghead intellectuals, divorced from the real world, with men of action—instinctual, passionate, fierce, and masculine. Senator Albert Beveridge of Indiana counseled in his 1906 volume *Young Man and the World* (a turn of the century version of *Real Men Don't Eat Quiche*) to "avoid books, in fact, avoid all artificial learning, for the forefathers put America on the right path by learning from completely natural experience." Family, church and synagogue, and schoolroom were cast as the enervating domains of women, sapping masculine vigor.

Now don't get me wrong. The Jewish emphasis on literacy, on mind over body, does not exempt Jewish men from sexist behavior. Far from it. While many Jewish men avoid the Scylla of a boisterous and physically harassing misogyny, we can often dash ourselves against the Charybdis of a male intellectual intimidation of others. "Men with the properly sanctioned educational credentials in our society," writes Harry Brod, "are trained to impose our opinions on others, whether asked for or not, with an air of supreme self-confidence and aggressive self-assurance." It's as if the world were only waiting for our word. In fact, Brod notes, "many of us have developed mannerisms that function to intimidate those customarily denied access to higher educational institutions, especially women." And yet, despite this, the Jewish emphasis on literacy has branded us, in the eyes of the world, less than "real" men.

Finally, the historical experience of Jews centers around, hinges upon our sense of morality, our ethical imperatives. The preservation of a moral code, the commandment to live ethically, is the primary responsibility of each Jew, male or female. Here, let me relate another personal story. Like many other Jews, I grew up with the words "Never Again" ringing in my ears, branded indelibly in my consciousness. For me they implied a certain moral responsibility to bear witness, to remember—to place my body, visibly, on the side of justice. This moral responsibility inspired my participation in the anti-war movement, and my active resistance of the draft *as a Jew*. I remember family dinners in front of the CBS Evening News, watching Walter Cronkite recite the daily tragedy of the war in Vietnam. "Never Again," I said to myself, crying myself to sleep after watching napalm fall on Vietnamese villagers. Isn't this the brutal terror we have sworn ourselves to preventing when we utter those two words? When I allowed myself to feel the pain of those people, there was no longer a choice; there was, instead, a moral imperative to speak out, to attempt to end that war as quickly as possible.

In the past few years, I've become aware of another war. I met and spoke with women who had been raped, raped by their lovers, husbands, and fathers, women who had been beaten by those husbands and lovers. Some were even Jewish women. All those same words—Never Again—flashed across my mind like a neon meteor lighting up the darkened consciousness. Hearing that pain and that anger prompted the same moral imperative. We Jews say "Never Again" to the systematic horror of the Holocaust, to the cruel war against the Vietnamese, to Central American death squads. And we must say it against this war waged against women in our society, against rape and battery.

So in a sense, I see my Judaism as reminding me every day of that moral responsibility, the *special* ethical imperative that my life, as a Jew, gives to me. Our history indicates how we have been excluded from power, but also, as men, we have been privileged by another power. Our Judaism impels us to stand against any power that is illegitimately constituted because we know only too well the consequences of that power. Our ethical vision demands equality and justice, and its achievement is our historical mission.

NOTE

1. Harry Brod, "Justice and a Male Feminist" in *The Jewish Newspaper* (Los Angeles) June 6, 1985, p. 6.

PART TEN

MASCULINITIES IN THE MEDIA AND POPULAR CULTURE

Men are daily bombarded with images of masculinity—in magazines, television, movies, music, even the Internet. We see what men are supposed to look like, act like, be like. And social scientists are only now beginning to understand the enormous influence that the media have in shaping our ideas about what it means to be a man.

For one thing, it is clear that the media can create artificial standards against which boys as well as girls measure themselves. Just as idealized human female models can only approximate the exaggeratedly large breasts and exaggeratedly small waistline of Barbie, virtually no men can approach the physiques of the cartoon version of Tarzan or even G.I. Joe. The original G.I. Joe had the equivalent of 12.2-inch biceps when he was introduced in 1964. Ten years later, his biceps measured the equivalent of 15.2 inches. By 1994, he had 16.4-inch biceps, and today his biceps measure a simulated 26.8 inches—nearly 7 inches larger than Mark McGwire's 20-inch muscles. "Many modern figures display the physiques of advanced bodybuilders and some display levels of muscularity far exceeding the outer limits of actual human attainment," notes Dr. Harrison Pope, a Harvard psychiatrist.

No wonder boys and men so often feel like we fail the test of physical manhood. Media provide unrealistic images against which we measure ourselves, as the article by Ken Gillam and Shannon Wooden suggest. Michael Messner and Jeffrey Montez de Oca look at the portrayal of masculinity in beer ads—where we don't fare particularly well either. Media may offer images of idealized masculinity alongside a notion of idealized femininity—or, in the case of rap music, Ronald Weitzer and Charis Kubrin argue, a femininity that is hypersexualized only in relation to masculinity. And entire genres of media are offered to us as gendered, as Kathy Sandford and Leanna Madill suggest in their examination of video games as a "boy thing."

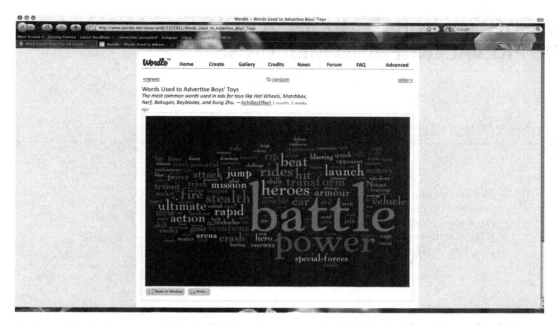

Source: Jonathan Feinberg.

Source: Jonathan Feinberg.

MISOGYNY IN RAP MUSIC: A CONTENT ANALYSIS OF PREVALENCE AND MEANINGS

Ronald Weitzer   Charis E. Kubrin

That's the way the game goes, gotta keep it strictly pimpin',
Gotta have my hustle tight, makin' change off these women.
You know it's hard out here for a pimp,
When he tryin' to get this money for the rent.
"It's Hard Out Here For a Pimp"

Three 6 Mafia

The 2005 Academy Award for best original song in a feature film went to Three 6 Mafia's controversial "It's Hard Out Here For a Pimp" from the film *Hustle and Flow*. The song was performed at the Oscars, and immediately provoked a storm of criticism for glorifying the exploitation of women. This is only the most recent chapter in the mounting criticism directed at rap music's presentation of women. A few years earlier, rapper Eminem won a Grammy for his 2001 album, *The Marshall Mathers LP*—an album whose lyrics contained extreme hostility and violence toward women. Women's groups promptly condemned the award. More recently, the African American women's magazine *Essence* launched a campaign in 2005 against sexism in rap music. The magazine lamented the depiction of black women in rap and solicited feedback from readers on ways to challenge it.

Much of the criticism of rap music is impressionistic and based on a handful of anecdotes, rather than a systematic analysis. Exactly how prevalent are misogynistic themes in this music and what specific messages are conveyed to the listeners? The current study addresses this question through a content analysis of over 400 rap songs. We document five themes related to the portrayal of women in rap music and link them to the larger cultural and music industry norms and the local, neighborhood conditions that inspired this music.

IMAGES OF WOMEN IN POPULAR MUSIC

Gender stereotypes are abundant in popular music, where women are often presented as inferior to men or are trivialized and marginalized (Tuchman 1978). Women are not portrayed monolithically, however (Butruille and Taylor 1987; Lay 2000; van Zoonen 1994), and lyrical depictions appear to have changed somewhat over time. It has been argued that the overall trend is one of "greater diversity, more complexity, and dramatically mixed messages about the individual female persona and women's roles in society" (Lee 1999:355). Despite this variegation, it remains uncommon for women to be presented as independent, intelligent, enterprising, or superior to men (Lee 1999). Derogatory images are far more common.

A body of research documents depictions of men and women in different genres. A content analysis of rock music videos found that a majority (57 percent) presented women in a "condescending" manner (e.g., unintelligent, sex object, victim) and a fifth placed them in a traditional sex role (e.g., subservient, nurturing, domestic roles), while 8 percent displayed male violence against women (Vincent, Davis, and Boruszkowski 1987). Only 14 percent presented women as fully equal to men. A more recent study of rock videos found that traditional sex role stereotypes continue to predominate: 57 percent of videos in which women were present depicted them in a "conventional" manner (passive, dependent on men, accenting physical appearance), while a third presented them as strong and independent (Alexander 1999).

Country music also casts women in subordinate roles. A study of 203 country music videos featuring male performers found that two-thirds devalued women (portraying them in a condescending manner or in traditional roles), while only 9 percent presented women as fully equal to men (Andsager and Roe 1999). Of the 80 videos by female artists, by contrast, half fit the fully equal category. Interestingly, country songs and videos do not feature violence against women or portray them as strippers and prostitutes, apparently because of strong industry norms against such images (Andsager and Roe 1999:81). In fact, one study found that country music advertisers pressure radio stations to screen out misogynistic songs in order to attract desired female listeners (Ryan and Peterson 1982).

Although rap music has been a topic of heated public debate for years, systematic content analyses are rare. One analysis of rap and heavy metal songs from 1985–1990 found that rap was more sexually explicit and graphic whereas heavy metal's allusions to sexual acts or to male domination were fairly subtle (Binder 1993), which is consistent with other studies of heavy metal songs and videos that have found that "blatant abuse of women is uncommon"

in this genre (Walser 1993:117). Binder's comparative analysis was limited to only 20 songs which she deemed "controversial," and the time period examined preceded rap's ascendancy in the music field. In a unique study of Chicano rap songs from 1999–2002, McFarland (2003) identified two main themes: a critique of racial inequality and injustice and an endorsement of male supremacy over women. Of the 263 songs that mentioned women, 37 percent depicted them "simply as objects of male desire and pleasure," while 4 percent justified violence against them. McFarland's sampling frame was based on songs he identified as popular in focus groups and on the Brown Pride website, rather than a more objective measure of popularity. Armstrong (2001) conducted a content analysis of 490 rap songs during 1987–1993. Lyrics featuring violence against women were found in 22 percent of the songs, and the violence perpetrated against women included assault, rape, and murder. Although his study makes a valuable contribution to the literature in its systematic focus on violence against women, it does not discuss other (nonviolent) depictions of women, provides little indication of coding procedures, and presents the lyrics in a brief and sketchy manner, decontextualized from larger song segments. Other content analyses of rap music (Kubrin 2005a, 2005b; Martinez 1997) do not examine the depiction of women or gender relations more broadly. The present paper addresses this issue.

SOCIAL SOURCES OF RAP LYRICS

Most of the studies reviewed above did not attempt to *explain why* lyrics portray women as they do—an admittedly difficult task. Yet artists do not work in a vacuum. We suggest that rappers whose songs portray women negatively are influenced by three major social forces: larger gender relations, the music industry, and local neighborhood conditions. The most diffuse influence is the larger gender order, which includes the cultural valorization of a certain type of masculinity. *Hegemonic masculinity* has been defined as attitudes and practices that perpetuate heterosexual male domination over women. It involves "the currently most honored way of being a man, it requires all other men to position themselves in relation to it, and it ideologically legitimates the global subordination of women to men" (Connell and Messerschmidt 2005:832). For this type of masculinity, to be a "man" requires the acceptance of attitudes that objectify women, practices that subordinate them, and derogation of men who adopt an egalitarian orientation, equally affirmative of men and women and all sexual orientations (Connell 1987; Connell and Messerschmidt 2005; Donaldson 1993). Hegemonic masculinity exists alongside and in competition with what Connell calls "subordinated masculinities," and to remain normative, it requires ongoing reproduction via the mass media, the patriarchal family, and other socializing institutions. Media representations of men, for example, often glorify men's use of physical force, a daring demeanor, virility, and emotional distance (see Hanke 1998). Popular music is a case in point: As indicated by the studies reviewed above, only a minority of songs, across music genres, espouse egalitarian gender relations or alternative masculinities, whereas the majority can be viewed as texts on hegemonic masculinity. We argue that rap, like the other music genres, is part of this broader culture of gender relations, even as some of the music challenges the dominant culture (Lay 2000).[1]

Some argue that popular music over the past three decades is also part of a larger cultural resistance to feminism, an attempt to block progress toward gender equality and resuscitate male domination. As Lay (2000:239) argues, "Popular music can be read as a vehicle for heterosexual male concerns [over the advancement of women and gays] and, more importantly, for the recuperation of hegemonic masculinity." Stated differently, this music can be seen as part of a larger ideological process of persuading the population that heterosexual male supremacy is natural and normal. Rap is part of this backlash. Collins (2000:82, 144) considers rap to be one of the contemporary "controlling images" used to subordinate black women, and Oliver (2006:927) argues that rap's sexist lyrics "provide justifications for engaging in acts of violence against black women" (see also

hooks 1994; Rhym 1997). But it may also be seen as an effort to control *all* women, since rap is consumed by youth from all racial and ethnic groups. Such images have real-world effects insofar as they contribute to gendered socialization and perpetuate gender inequality (Barongan and Hall 1995; Johnson et al. 1995; Martino et al. 2006; Wester et al. 1997).

Rap artists are also influenced by pressures from elites in the music industry. To maximize sales, record industry moguls encourage provocative, edgy lyrics. Producers not only encourage artists to become "hardcore" but they also reject or marginalize artists who go against the grain. As a result of such practices, a directly proportional relationship has developed between rap music's explicitness and the sale of its records.

In response to corporate pressures, many rappers abandon political and social messages and focus instead on material wealth and sexual exploits (Powell 2000). In his documentary, "Hip-Hop: Beyond Beats and Rhymes," Byron Hurt (2007) asks one aspiring rapper why rap artists focus on violence and misogyny. The rapper freestyles a verse about whether he could have been a doctor, a father, or police officer. He then says, "That's nice, but nobody wanna hear that right now. They don't accept that shit." When Hurt asks, "Who is 'they'," the rapper answers, "The industry. They usually don't give us deals when we speak righteously." Indeed, Kitwana (1994:23) finds that artists in search of securing record deals are often told their message is not hard enough, they are too clean cut, that "hardcore" is what is selling now, and that they should no longer engage in social commentary (see also Krims 2000:71). The consequence? According to Smith (1997:346), "Many of today's rappers make the ghetto visible in order to sell and to be sold."

The pressure for artists to rap about hardcore themes is perhaps most evident in gangsta rap.[2] A statement by Carmen Ashhurst-Watson, former President of Def Jam Records, is revealing:

The time when we switched to gangsta music was the same time that the majors [record companies] bought up all the [independent] labels. And I don't think that's a coincidence. At the time that we were able to get a bigger place in the record stores, and a bigger presence because of this major marketing capacity, the music became less and less conscious. (Ashhurst-Watson, quoted in Hurt 2007)

Her account is confirmed by recent research which documents that as rap increasingly became produced by major record labels, its content became more hardcore to encourage sales. In a longitudinal analysis of rap music production and lyrical content, Lena (2006:488) finds that "starting in 1988 the largest record corporations charted substantially more 'hardcore' rap songs than did independent labels. In the eight years between 1988 and 1995, majors charted up to five and a half times as many hardcore rap singles as all their independent competitors combined." She concludes that "major record labels produced the majority of puerile rap" during this later time period. This was in stark contrast to earlier periods of production where rap lyrics emphasized features of the local environment and hostility to corporate music production and values.

The bias fostered by record companies is recapitulated in the kind of rap music that gets the greatest airplay on radio stations. Hip-hop historian Kevin Powell points out that "in every city you go to in America . . . [rap stations are] playing the same 10–12 songs over and over again. So what it does is perpetuate the mindset that the only way you can be a man—a black man, a Latino man—is if you hard. To denigrate women. To denigrate homosexuals. To denigrate each other. To kill each other" (Kevin Powell, quoted in Hurt 2007). This privileging of hegemonic masculinity and negative depiction of women is driven by an interest in selling records (Rhym 1997). As long as this type of music continues to sell, "record labels will continue to put ethics and morality aside to release [violent or sexist rap]" (McAdams and Russell 1991:R-22).

Consumers play a key role in this process. Misogynistic representations of women and the more general marketing of "hood narratives" (Watkins 2001:389) occur, in part, in response to a perceived consumer demand for stereotypical representations

of the ghetto, and specifically of young black men and women. Listeners of rap, many of whom are white youth, can vicariously experience the ghetto, a place symbolizing danger and deviance (Quinn 2005:85). As one white listener of rap music claims,

> I've never been to a ghetto. I grew up in upper middle-class, basically white suburbia. . . . And to listen to [rap music] is a way of us to see . . . a completely different culture. It's something that most of us have never had the opportunity to experience. . . . And the stuff in the music, it appeals to our sense of learning about other cultures and wanting to know more about something that we'll never probably experience. (quoted in Hurt 2007)

Such cross-cultural learning may be quite biased. As Quinn (2005:91) argues, "with its provocative pop-cultural portrayals of the ghetto, there can be little doubt that gangsta rap helps to reinforce racial stereotypes held by many whites." Indeed, when Hurt asked the white listener quoted above whether the music reinforces stereotypes, she answered affirmatively. While explicit lyrics and misogynistic representations of women have made rap music highly marketable, they have also "reinvigorated popular beliefs about black deviance and social pathology" (Watkins 2001:389). In short, the production and lyrical content of rap music are inextricably linked; as such, music industry interests can be viewed as one important source of rap music lyrics.

Rap music also has local roots, which help shape the content of the lyrics. More so than other genres, rap is a "localized form of cultural expression" (Bennett 1999a:77; 1999b). Hip-hop and rap initially developed out of the lived experiences of youth in disadvantaged, black neighborhoods and was "incubated in the black community's house parties, public parks, housing projects, and local jams" (Powell 1991:245; Rose 1994a). And although the music industry's influence has become increasingly apparent, even today rap continues to be marketed as a cultural reflection of life on "the streets" of America's inner-cities. In fact, the music industry sends agents into these neighborhoods for the express purpose of gathering "street intelligence" on what is popular; they do this by visiting record stores, clubs, and parties (Negus 1999:502).

The degree to which a particular music genre, and particularly male artists within that genre, endorse male supremacy in their lyrics may be related to broader, societal opportunities for affirming hegemonic masculinity—opportunities that vary to some extent by racial and class background. Poor, marginalized black males have historically faced obstacles to asserting their masculinity, and they continue to be denied access to conventional institutional avenues through which masculinity may be established. According to Skeggs (1993), music historically served as a medium that provided black men with an alternative resource for asserting their masculinity.

This opportunity structure can be linked specifically to the conditions in disadvantaged neighborhoods. It has been argued that the content of rap music reflects, at least to some extent, gender relations among youth in many inner-city communities. Several ethnographic studies provide evidence of discord between men and women in disadvantaged, minority neighborhoods. The harsh conditions of the ghetto and barrio provide residents with few conventional sources of self-esteem (Bourgois 1995; Horowitz 1983; Liebow 1967), which can lead to unconventional means to win respect. Violence is one means of eliciting respect from others or punishing those who withhold it (Kubrin and Weitzer 2003), but men are also admired for economically and sexually exploiting women. Four decades ago, Liebow's (1967:140–144) ethnographic study of a low-income, black neighborhood described how important it was for men to be seen as "exploiters of women," even if they did not always treat women in this way. Recent research indicates that exploitation and degradation of young women is still a feature of some inner-city communities today and continues to shape gender relations (Miller and White 2003). Anderson's (1999) study of an African American community identified several dimensions of a distinctive neighborhood culture, what he calls the

"code of the street." For many young men in such neighborhoods, the street code places a high value on sexual conquest, promiscuity, and the manipulation of women:

> Because of the implications sex has for their local social status and esteem, the young men are ready to be regaled with graphic tales of one another's sexual exploits . . . Status goes to the winner, and sex is prized as a testament not of love but of control over another human being. The goal of the sexual conquests is to make a fool of the young woman . . . [The male] incurs sanctions [from his peers] for allowing a girl to "rule" him or gains positive reinforcement for keeping her in line. . . . In many cases the more the young man seems to exploit the young woman, the higher is his regard within the peer group. (Anderson 1999:150, 153, 154)

A similar male street culture is documented in an ethnographic study of a Puerto Rican barrio in New York City (Bourgois 1995, 1996). Rooted in conditions of socioeconomic disadvantage which strip men of traditional sources of dignity, this street culture is characterized by a high level of male promiscuity, the "celebration of the gigolo image," the value of "being an economic parasite" on one's girlfriends, and justifications for violence against women (Bourgois 1995:276–295).

We do not argue that either neighborhood or industry forces, as just described, are necessarily direct causes of the lyrical content or images, but instead that these forces are an essential part of the *context* within which the messages contained in rap are best understood. Our study thus can be situated within the recent literature on gender relations, which recognizes the importance of multiple contexts in which gender roles and identities are reproduced (Connell and Messerschmidt 2005).

RESEARCH METHODS

The current study focuses on a time period that has not been examined in previous research on this topic. All rap albums from 1992 through 2000 that attained platinum status (selling at least one million copies) were identified (N = 130). Sampling only platinum albums ensured that the music had reached a substantial segment of the population. To identify the sample, we obtained a list of all albums that went platinum between 1992 and 2000 from the Recording Industry Association of America (RIAA). The RIAA, which compiles, analyzes, and reports on the quantity and value of recorded music shipped into market channels, is considered the premier source for comprehensive market data on music trends in the U.S. We went through the list and used the Web site ARTISTdirect (http://www.artistdirect.com) to identify "rap" albums. ARTISTdirect is a comprehensive online network of resources that provides, among other things, detailed information about artists/groups. We typed in the name of each artist/group and the Web site classified the precise music genre.

Our analysis begins in 1992 because gangsta rap began to flourish around this time (Kelley 1996:147; Keyes 2002:104; Kitwana 2002:xiv; Krims 2000:83; Smith 1997:346; Watkins 2001:389).[3] Our interest in this starting point is related to the fact that misogyny and related themes (i.e., violence) are popularly thought to be more prevalent in gangsta rap than in rap generally. Yet these themes are not exclusive to gangsta rap, which is why we selected all rap albums rather than just gangsta albums. As noted by Krims (2000:87), rap albums typically mix genres and so songs that contain misogynistic lyrics would have been left out of the analysis had we only sampled gangsta rap albums.

The analysis ends in 2000 because that year marked a turning point in the industry's increasing commercialization and greater detachment from its neighborhood sources (Kitwana 1994:23; Krims 2000:71; Watkins 2001:382). This time frame thus captures a period when rap music more closely reflected grassroots values and local conditions on the street and was somewhat less commercialized than today, although the interests of record labels were important during this time period as well.

The 130 albums contained a total of 1,922 songs. Using SPSS, a simple random sample of 403 songs was drawn and then analyzed.[4] Each song

was listened to twice in its entirety by the authors, while simultaneously reading the lyrics. The lyrics were obtained from *The Original Hip-Hop/Rap Lyrics Archive* (www.ohhla.com/all.html). Each line was coded to identify major misogynistic themes. *Misogyny* refers to lyrics that encourage, condone, or glorify the objectification, exploitation, or victimization of women. In cases of uncertainty regarding the meaning of a particular word or phrase, we consulted *The Rap Dictionary* (www.rapdict.org), a comprehensive online dictionary of rap terms. During the coding, careful attention was paid to the context in which the lyrics were stated. This is especially important in rap, given that it is rooted in the Black oral tradition of signifying and other communicative practices (Smitherman 1997:4). Signifying is a way of speaking that involves ritual insult (commonly referred to as "playing the dozens") and double entendre (Lee 2005:83; see also Keyes 2002). With signifying, words have alternative meanings beyond their conventional practices and should not necessarily be taken literally. In our coding, we were careful to interpret the lyrics within their larger contexts. Finally, an independent researcher coded a random subset (16 percent of the sample songs) in order to assess inter-coder reliability. With respect to misogyny, agreement occurred in 73.4 percent the songs, indicating fairly strong consensus.

FINDINGS

Misogyny was present in 22 percent of the 403 songs (N = 90 songs, by 31 rappers).[5] This means that misogyny is much less pervasive in rap music than some critics believe, but is clearly a significant theme. Female rappers accounted for only 5 of the 90 misogynistic songs, as well as an additional 8 songs (out of the remaining 313) that did not have misogynistic lyrics. The scarcity of female artists shows just how male-dominated rap was during this time period, especially at the platinum level (George 1998; Troka 2002: 82). We include a separate analysis of the 8 non-misogynistic songs by female artists for purposes of comparison to the messages contained in our main sample.

Misogynistic Themes

Theme	Frequency in Songs (%)*
Naming and Shaming	49
Sexual Objectification	67
Can't Trust 'Em	47
Legitimating Violence	18
Prostitutes and Pimps	20

*Frequency in songs identified as misogynistic, not within the larger sample of rap songs (where 22 percent of the songs were categorized as misogynistic).

Although misogynistic messages appear less frequently in rap than is commonly believed, significance is not simply a matter of frequency. Also important is the nature and intensity of the messages. Our content analysis identified five misogynistic themes that appear with some frequency: (1) derogatory naming and shaming of women, (2) sexual objectification of women, (3) distrust of women, (4) legitimation of violence against women, and (5) celebration of prostitution and pimping. Our presentation of findings identifies the frequency of each theme, substantive messages and subthemes in the lyrics, and the ways in which the lyrics reflect societal gender relations, record industry pressures, and neighborhood conditions in disadvantaged communities.

Naming and Shaming

A number of rap songs can be described as a full-fledged "status degradation ceremony" directed at women—a "ritual destruction of the person denounced" (Garfinkle 1956: 421). In these songs, it is typically women in general, rather than a specific person, who are shamed with derogatory names. This theme was present in half (49 percent) of the misogynistic songs.

Our analysis identified instances of naming-and-shaming but, as discussed earlier, we did not automatically assume that all conventionally "negative" labels were necessarily disparaging.

For instance, in rap culture the terms "bitch" and "ho" are not necessarily intended to be derogatory, depending on the lyrical context (Keyes 2002; Kitwana 1994:25). Ice Cube talks about a "wholesome ho," and Too $hort refers to his "finest bitches" and a "top-notch bitch." While recognizing that some listeners consider such terms offensive in all usage, we coded conservatively by including in our naming-and-shaming category only lyrics that were unambiguously derogatory. For example, Eminem's song *Kill You* talks about "vile, venomous, volatile bitches." Other rappers condemn the slut, tramp, whore, hoochie, "lying-ass bitch," "shitty hoe," "prima donna bitch," and so forth. A favorite rap term is "chickenhead," which reduces a woman to a bobbing head giving oral sex. Status degradation was the sole theme of some songs, present in every verse. Sweeping attacks are sometimes generalized, while other lyrics reveal particular rationales for degradation, such as women's failure to cooperate with men:

> We couldn't get no play from the ladies
> With seven niggas in a Nav [Navigator] is you crazy? . . .
> So we all said "fuck you bitch" and kept rolling.
> (Snoop Dogg, *DP Gangsta*)

Even rappers' female relatives are not immune from such attacks. Eminem says that "all bitches is hoes, even my stinkin' ass mom" (*Under the Influence*). Eminem's unbridled hostility toward all women, including relatives, is somewhat extreme but not unique in this music genre.[6]

The flipside of this naming process is found in lyrics that praise men who treat women poorly. In these lyrics, it is a badge of honor for men to verbally and physically abuse women, and men win respect from other men when they act like "players," "pimps," and exploiters of women—financially, sexually, and emotionally. This theme is reflected throughout the data, closely mirroring the neighborhood street code described by Anderson and others. The variety of disparaging labels for women is not paralleled for men, either in rap or in the larger culture. Insofar as rappers derogate other men, they tend to use feminized terms, such as bitch or pussy—a staple of hegemonic masculinity.

It is important to point out that these lyrics essentialize women by portraying them as inherently "Other" and different from men by nature. Many of the labels refer to women's anatomy or sexuality, and the lyrics endorse the age-old notion that "biology is destiny."

Some rappers report that verbal abuse of women is encouraged and rewarded by the music industry:

> Rappers like me always disrespectin' ladies,
>
> Wonder why it's like that, well so do I.
>
> But I just turn my back and then I go get high,
>
> 'Cause I get paid real good to talk bad about a bitch.
>
> And you bought it, so don't be mad I got rich.
> (Too $hort, *Thangs Change*)

In an interview, Brother Marquis from 2 Live Crew, echoed these sentiments: "I'm degrading [women] to try to get me some money. . . . And besides, you let me do that. You got pimps out here who are making you sell your body. Just let me talk about you for a little while . . . and make me a little money" (quoted in Collins 2000:143–144). By this logic, because women are already exploited by pimps, there is no harm in subjecting them to lyrical shaming. The larger point is that rap industry norms, more so than in other types of music, encourage artists to disparage women (Kitwana 1994:23; Krims 2000:71; Smith 1997:346).

Sexual Objectification   *Exploitation*

Sexual objectification of women was evident in 67 percent of our misogynistic songs. Sexual objectification refers to the idea that women are good only for sex. These lyrics mirror the street code's exhortation that men avoid commitment, marriage, and caring for children; instead, women are to be sexually used and then quickly discarded (Anderson 1999; Bourgois 1995; Liebow 1967; Miller and White 2003). N.W.A. captures this theme with a song titled "Findum, Fuckum, and Flee." Puff

Daddy offers another example: "Call me Sean if you suck, call me gone when I nut. That's the end of us, get your friend to fuck" (Sean "Puffy" Combs, on Notorious B.I.G., *Notorious B.I.G.*). Consider also the following songs:

> Bitches ain't shit but hoes and tricks
>
> Lick on these nuts and suck the dick
>
> Get's the fuck out after you're done
>
> And I hops in my ride to make a quick run.
> (Dr. Dre, *Bitches Ain't Shit*)

> I'm only out to fuck a bitch, fuck tryin' to charm her.
>
> I treat a fine ass bitch like dirt
>
> No money in her purse, a fuck is all it's worth.
>
> 'Cause Short Dawg'll never cater to you hoes
>
> And if you ain't fuckin,' I say "later" to you hoes.
> (Too Short, *Coming up $hort*)

High value is placed on having scores of sexual partners and even sharing them, another way in which women are de-individualized:

> I meet a bitch, fuck a bitch
>
> Next thing you know you fuckin' the bitch.
> (Notorious B.I.G., *Friend of Mine*)

Anderson (1999) discusses the extreme peer pressure on young men in disadvantaged neighborhoods to have casual sex with women as a way of affirming their masculinity. This norm is a hallowed one in song lyrics:

> I had niggas making bets like, did he fuck her yet?
>
> Ask her did he touch her bra, when I say nah they say ahh
>
> So tomorrow I use that pressure to undress her
>
> But the more I caress her, more I feel like a molester.
> (Mase, *I Need to Be*)

By the end of this stanza, peer pressure has resulted in sexual aggression.

Some rappers make it clear that they intend to put women "in their place" by demeaning strong and independent women: Redman boasts, "I turn an independent woman back into a hoochie" (*Keep On '99*) and Notorious B.I.G. raps, "I like 'em . . . educated, so I can bust off on they glasses" (*Big Booty Hoes*). Some of the lyrics in this thematic category, therefore, may be seen as resistance to women's growing autonomy, education, and independence—messages that cross-cut the other themes in this music as well. As indicated earlier, this backlash against women's liberation and reassertion of traditional masculinity can be found in other popular music genres as well.

Sexual objectification of women has a flip side in the sexual empowerment of men. Male sexual bravado and hypersexuality were present in 58 percent of the misogynistic songs. A common practice is bragging about how easy it is for "players" to get women to have sex: "Witness me holla at a hoochie, see how quick the game takes" (2Pac, *All 'Bout U*).

Men win respect from other men for a high number of sexual conquests without commitment. Although present throughout the culture, it appears to be especially prized in disadvantaged neighborhoods where men often lack other sources of dignity and self-esteem. In fact, there is a striking correspondence between the street code in inner-city communities and this music theme. Just as young men earn respect from their peers if they are viewed as having casual sex with many women (Anderson 1999; Bourgois 1995, 1996; Liebow 1967; Miller and White 2003), rappers likewise frequently brag about their sexual exploits, and are rewarded for doing so. A good example is rapper 50 Cent, who in the last several years has been frequently nominated for Grammy Awards for songs with precisely these themes (e.g., *Candy Shop* and *Magic Stick*). Both in rap songs and among neighborhood peers, bragging earns respect. Low sexual achievers and those who seek a long-term relationship with a woman are ridiculed and subordinated because they are less active practitioners of this (extremely utilitarian) version of hegemonic masculinity: "their games [are] seen as inferior, and their identities devalued" (Anderson 1999:151).

If having multiple sex partners earns respect, men also face an ongoing threat of sexual competition

from other men. In other words, "Women provide heterosexual men with sexual validation, and men compete with each other for this" (Donaldson 1993:645). Men are thus instructed to use their sexual talents or material goods to steal other men's women:

> Say dog, what kinda nigga be on top of the world?
> Million dollar status got me on top of ya girl.
> (Hot Boys, *Fired Up*)

Men are also rewarded for demonstrating that they are sexually superior to other men:

> Get freaky, and do it wild
> On the floor, doggy style.
> While your bitch be crying "please don't stop". . . .
> I fuck her like I know you won't.
> If that's your bitch, homeboy you'd better keep her
> 'Cause she won't stay off my beeper.
> You can't fuck her and I appreciate it
> Even though I know you hate it.
> (Too Short, *Step Daddy*)

Finally, sexual objectification is expressed in gangbanging. In these songs, several men have sex with one woman, whether consensually or not, and the woman is highly depersonalized. Some involve gangbangs with underage girls, while others describe sex with heavily intoxicated women:

> All on the grass [marijuana], every bitch passed [out]
> A first not last, when we all hit the ass.
> Doin' tricks jacked up like a six
> One pussy, and thirteen dicks.
> (Westside Connection, *The Gangsta, the Killa, and the Dope Deala*)

> Kisha got did right yeah
> Fucked the whole Cash Money clique all in one night yeah.
> (Lil' Wayne, *Kisha*)

There is evidence that such gangbanging takes place in some disadvantaged minority neighborhoods.

One study of black youth in north St. Louis, for example, reported that 40 percent of the young men interviewed admitted they had engaged in such behavior, which helped them gain status among their peers (Miller and White 2003:1219).

The sexual objectification of women and the hypersexuality of black men portrayed in these lyrics can be linked to larger stereotypes about black sexuality—stereotypes that date back to colonialism and slavery and that are still quite salient for consumers of rap music today (Skeggs 1993). Rappers exploit these stereotypes in their music.

Can't Trust 'Em

Suspicion of women is a significant theme in rap songs—a tension that is mirrored to some extent in the communities in which rap originated (Anderson 1999). Almost half (47 percent) of the misogynistic songs displayed deep distrust of women. There is both a diffuse sense of distrust (e.g., Dr. Dre's verse, "How could you trust a ho?", *Bitches Ain't Shit*) and several specific reasons to be suspicious of women, who are seen as prone to entrap, betray, exploit, or destroy men. First, it is claimed that teenage girls lie about their age:

> See nowadays man you got to know these bitches age
>
> 'Cause they ass be real fast when they be goin' through that phase.
>
> You fuck a girl that's young, and you gonna end up in the cage
> (Mase, *I Need to Be*)

Second, women stand accused of making false rape accusations in order to get a financial settlement:

> Don't take the pussy, if she fightin'
>
> 'Cause you saw what happened to Tupac and Mike Tyson.
>
> 'Specially if you large [famous], some hoes is trife [petty]
>
> Get you on a rape charge, have you servin' your life.
> (Nas, *Dr. Knockboot*)

Third, men are warned to be wary of the *femme fatale*—especially women who seek to set them up for robbery, assault, or murder. Ice Cube's song, *Don't Trust 'Em*, talks about a woman who lured a man to her home where there were four men who beat the man, stole his money, and killed him. The song ends, "I told you the bitch was a trap. Don't trust 'em." This scenario seems to be fairly common, judging from our data:

> You know they [women] might be the one to set me up
>
> Wanna get they little brother to wet [kill] me up. . . .
>
> Bitches be schemin', I kid ya not
>
> That's why I keep my windows locked and my Glock cocked.
> (Notorious B.I.G., *Friend of Mine*)

The *femme fatale* is iconic in popular culture, as illustrated in many films (e.g., *Double Indemnity*, *Fatal Attraction*, *Basic Instinct*), all of which feature a villainous woman who uses her beauty and sexuality to exploit or victimize innocent men. These women are presented as thoroughly evil and condemned for departing from their traditional gender role. Interestingly, there is no equivalent label for men who act this way toward women. What is especially remarkable about rap's use of this icon is its claim that *all* young women are potential *femmes fatales*; the music sends a strong signal to men to be wary of women generally.

A fourth refrain is that women frequently lie to men in order to get pregnant. The value many young poor women place on having babies, as one of the few sources of dignity in their lives, is quite strong (Anderson 1999:162–166; Edin and Kefalas 2005). For many young men in these neighborhoods, a woman's pregnancy is viewed quite differently, something to be feared and denied: "To own up to a pregnancy is to go against the peer-group street ethic of hit and run" (Anderson 1999:156). Rappers express an identical concern. 2Pac asks, "Why plant seeds in a dirty bitch, waitin' to trick me? Not the life for me" (*Hell 4 a Hustler*). Paying child support is just one of the fears. Snoop Dog raps:

> I ain't lettin' nothin' leak cause if things leak, then I'm a get caught
>
> And I can't get caught cause you know how they do it about that child support.
>
> Shit, bitches is cold on a nigga who ain't got his game tight
>
> Getting 18.5 percent [child support payments] half your life.
> (Snoop Dogg, *Freestyle Conversation*)

Too $hort describes an even worse scenario after getting a woman pregnant:

> No more player, no Shorty the Pimp
>
> I get paid, divert a check and get 40 percent.
>
> All the homies talkin' bad, hair down, walkin' sad
>
> Got the broad livin' with me, baby sayin' "Dad!". . .
>
> I could try to mack again but the bitches won't want me
>
> 'Cause I'm all washed up, broke, fat, and funky.
>
> I lost everything that I worked to be
>
> Never thought I'd be a trick, payin' hoes to serve me.
> (Too $hort, *Coming Up Short*)

Young men who fall prey to such women are ridiculed by their peers (Anderson 1999). It is not only the material costs of fathering a child that is feared in these songs, but also fatherhood in general. This may be regarded as an extreme form of traditional masculinity, where the father is largely absent from his children's lives. As Donaldson (1993:650) states, "In hegemonic masculinity, fathers do not have the capacity or the skill or the need to care for children . . . Nurturant and care-giving behavior is simply not manly." Our rap songs convey this message in no uncertain terms.

Even more common than the other subthemes in this category is our final one: The woman as gold digger only interested in men for their money:

> Watch the honeys check your style
>
> Worthless, when they worship what you purchase.
>
> They only see ice [diamonds], not me, under the surface
>
> What's the purpose?
> (The Lox, *I Wanna Thank You*)

> You must be used to all the finer things
>
> Infatuated by what money brings.
>
> It seems to me you hoes will never change
> (Scarface, *Fuck Faces*)

It is significant that the 2006 Grammy Award for Best Rap Solo Performance went to Kanye West's song, "Gold Digger," which complains about a woman who seduces a man to get his money. Such recognition can be interpreted as one way in which the music industry helps to perpetuate stereotyped images of women.

Several female rappers in our sample reinforce the idea of women as gold diggers interested solely in exploiting men (cf. Pough 2004). Missy Misdemeanor Elliott sings, "If you want me, where's my dough? Give me money, buy me clothes" (*All 'N My Grill*), and in another song:

> Hot boys
>
> Baby you got what I want.
>
> See 'cause y'all be drivin' Lexus jeeps
>
> And the Benz jeeps, and the Lincoln jeeps.
>
> Nothin' cheaper, got them Platinum Visa's
> (Missy Misdemeanor Elliott, *Hot Boys*)

As does Lil' Kim:

> I fuck with dudes with Member's Only jackets
>
> That sleep on brass beds, with money for a mattress.
>
> Everything I get is custom made
>
> Niggas wanna get laid; I gotta get paid.
> (Lil' Kim, *Custom Made*)

Men's fear of being exploited by women has a long history and is by no means unique to rap music. Yet, the gold digger fear is especially acute among men who are *nouveau riche* such as the newly successful rapper. They have achieved rapid upward mobility and celebrity status, and thus have precarious new wealth that can be lost. It may be less salient among poor men who have few assets to lose.

Legitimating Violence

Norms regarding appropriate conduct are ineffectual if not backed up with sanctions for those who disregard the norms. Violent punishment is one such sanction. Compared to the previous themes, condoning violence against women was less frequent but does appear in almost one-fifth (18 percent) of the misogynistic songs. Violence is portrayed in these songs, first of all, as the most appropriate response to women who act disrespectfully toward men, just as it is for men who disrespect other men (Anderson 1999; Kubrin 2005a; Kubrin and Weitzer 2003). Juvenile asks, "If she think you're jokin', is she goin' get a quick chokin'?" (*March Nigga Step*), and Dr. Dre tells us that "snobby-ass bitches get slapped out of spite" (*Ackrite*). Violence is seen as fitting for other "offenses" as well. Mase raps, "If she make my nuts itch [from an STD], I kill that slut bitch" (*I Need to Be*); N.W.A. has a song titled *To Kill a Hooker*; and Eminem tells listeners to "rape sluts" (*Who Knew*), prostitutes, and other women:

> Slut, you think I won't choke no whore
>
> 'Til the vocal cords don't work in her throat no more?!
>
> Shut up slut, you're causin' too much chaos
>
> Just bend over and take it like a slut, okay Ma? (Eminem, *Kill You*)

Several rappers threaten women with assault or rape if they refuse sex:

> Slap you with my paw, all across your jaw
>
> Break fool [act violent] on these bitches while I'm breakin' the law
>
> You come up in my room, look bitch you takin' it off.
> (Snoop Dogg, on Notorious B.I.G., *Dangerous MC's*)

These sorts of justifications for the use of violence are mirrored, to some extent, in disadvantaged communities, as borne out in some ethnographic research. For instance, Miller and White (2003:1237) found that both girls and boys in the inner city believed that male violence was appropriate when the girl seemed to have "forgotten her place." Examples of such misconduct include girls who "run their mouth," "act a fool," dress inappropriately, or drink too much. As in rap music, violence in these communities is portrayed as situationally appropriate. By contrast, girls' violence was defined by boys as "rooted in their greater emotionality," which is another example of how gender differences are naturalized (Miller and White 2003:1242).

A related subtheme is the positive value placed on sex that is aggressive and injurious to women. Rappers take pride in women being "drilled," "wrecked," and otherwise roughed up during intercourse. Men demonstrate their dominance over women by such representations of rough sex. This subtheme was also evident in rap during the preceding time period, as documented in Armstrong's (2001) study of songs produced in 1987–1993.

In the songs in this category, rappers (1) pride themselves on sex acts that appear to harm women, (2) justify other acts of violence, (3) warn women who challenge male domination that they will be assaulted, and (4) seem to invite male violence against women. There is a dual message here, one for women and one for men: Violence is portrayed as the most appropriate response to women who violate gendered etiquette or who don't "know their place" and men are encouraged to abide by this principle. The main purpose of such songs, therefore, appears to be the *normalization of violence against women as a means of social control*. The music both espouses a set of gendered norms and advocates sanctions for those who violate these norms.

Women as Prostitutes, Men as Pimps

Pimp chic is a recent cultural innovation. It draws on pimp imagery and the language of pimping and prostitution, but has broader meaning. As Quinn (2000:116) observed, "The divergent articulations of the pimp as trope and type point to the versatility of this misogynist, street-heroic figure." To "pimp" something can mean to promote it or to accessorize it. MTV, for example, has a show called "Pimp My Ride," where old cars are spruced up with expensive gadgets to create the ultimate pimpmobile. The term pimp is often synonymous with "player," a man who excels at attracting women or glamorized hustlers who conspicuously display their riches. Here, "the pimp image is more central than his occupation" (Quinn 2000:124). The celebration of both pimp imagery and real pimps is pervasive in rap culture. Ice-T, Snoop Dogg, Jay-Z, and others claim to have been real-life pimps; at least one rapper (K-Luv the Pimp) has been arrested for pimping and pandering; a 2003 film called *Lil' Pimp* starred a 9 year old boy as the film's hero; and a year after Nelly released his 2002 song and video, "Pimp Juice," he launched a new energy drink of the same name.

Although the mainstreaming of pimp chic is a fascinating cultural trend, we do not include it in this thematic category. Instead, we use the conventional, narrow definitions—namely, men who employ prostitutes. In coding, we were careful to distinguish references to prostitution and pimping, in the strict sense, from pimp chic. Women as prostitutes/men as pimps was a theme in 20 percent of the misogynistic songs.

Prostitutes are the quintessential figures of sexual objectification and exploitation, even if many of them see themselves as exploiting customers instead (Weitzer 2005). In rap, both prostitution and pimping are defined as legitimate economic pursuits and celebrated—themes which are almost non-existent in other music genres (Quinn 2000). The notion that women are only good for sex is epitomized in male discourse regarding prostitutes, and some rappers go to great lengths to present such women in one-dimensional, impersonal terms:

Let's me and you lay in these hoes

And show 'em what they pussy made fo' . . .

Let's leave without payin' these hoes

And show 'em what they pussy made fo'.
(Scarface, *Use Them Ho's*)

Here women are reduced to their sex organs, and not even worth paying for their services.

Some artists describe the hardships faced by pimps, such as Ice-T's "Somebody's Gotta Do It, Pimpin' Ain't Easy!" and Three 6 Mafia's academy award winning song, "It's Hard Out Here for a Pimp." Others revel in the multiple benefits of pimping:

Around the world, getting money,

I'm pimpin' hoes on Sunday.

I'm the kind of nigga you'll work all night fo' . . .

Wanna see how much pussy these hoes can sell.

It's like hypnosis, I pimps your mother, I pimps yo sis'

Hoes be nothin' but slaves for me, ready to go to their graves for me.
(Too Short, *Pimp Me*)

Pimping and prostitution are glorified:

Nuthin' like pimpin' . . .

I'll make the White House a hoe house, and all the pimps

To just set up shops like they do in Vegas

Legalize pimpin' for all the playas.

Puttin' fine ass bitches in the streets and the hood

Every year a nigga trade for a new Fleetwood [Cadillac].
(Too Short, *Ain't Nothing Like Pimpin'*)

And rappers ask listeners to give pimps the respect they deserve:

This ho, that ho make me rich . . .

I'm back in the game, getting' my dough

And fuck any motherfucker that say it ain't so.
(Snoop Dogg, *Buck 'Em*)

Quinn (2000:117, 135) argues that simply by drawing attention to pimps' exploitative practices and misogyny, these lyrics contain a "dissident" subtext that partially undermines such conduct even as it reinforces and condones it. This interpretation, of dual and perhaps contradictory messages, is a function of

Quinn's broad definition of pimping to include both "players" and traditional pimps. In our sample of lyrics we found celebration, not critique, to be the norm with respect to the pimp-prostitute relationship.

Street prostitution is typically located in both disadvantaged and marginal/transitional neighborhoods. Residents of these areas face obstacles in finding work, and prostitution and pimping may be seen as preferable to dead-end, low-paying jobs. Insofar as rap music emerged out of conditions in these neighborhoods, we might expect the sex trade to be one theme, and indeed it is in one-fifth of our misogynistic songs. At the same time, neighborhood conditions do not exist in a vacuum but interact with external factors. Ice-T invokes legendary pimp Iceberg Slim's book, *Pimp: The Story of My Life*, as the inspiration for his lyrics: "Ghetto hustlers in my neighborhood would talk this nasty dialect rich with imagery of sex and humor. My buddies and I wanted to know where they picked it up, and they told us, 'You better get into some of the Iceberg stuff!'" (quoted in Quinn 2000:123). Several rappers also claim to have been influenced by the romanticization of the iconic pimps featured in the blaxploitation films of the 1970s (Quinn 2000). Snoop Dogg, for instance, states, "When I started seeing those movies in the '70s, like *The Mack* and *Superfly*, that helped me to more or less pick who I wanted to be in life, how I wanted to live my life, how I wanted to represent me" (quoted in Moody 2003). Those films not only painted pimps as role models for young black men but also purported to describe life in the ghetto—well illustrated in the 1999 documentary, *American Pimp*. Coming full circle, several famous pimps have appeared in rap videos. Rap's glorification of pimping is thus linked to both neighborhood conditions and a larger, preexisting pimp culture (in films and books), which itself originated on the streets.

THE VOICES OF FEMALE RAPPERS

According to one analyst, "Rap provides a medium to mobilize feminist strategies of resistance, to give voice to the experience and concerns shared by young black women, or to explore and articulate

various aspects of desire and pleasure" (Forman 1994:54). Did the lyrics of female rappers, during this time period, contain elements of an oppositional subculture directed at misogynistic male rap? Did they call hegemonic masculinity into question and reject the negative images and messages regarding women? Or were they silent or compliant with respect to male constructions of proper gender relations?

To determine whether female rappers objected to the negative portrayal of women in rap, we analyzed lyrics by female rappers that were not included in our original sample (because they did not contain misogynistic themes). Recall that only 13 of our 403 songs were by women; 8 of these 13 did not contain misogynistic lyrics. Analysis of these 8 songs reveals very little resistance to sexism during the time period under study. Only one song by Eve (*Love is Blind*) directly challenges male mistreatment of women. In this song, Eve alternates between cursing a man who abused her girlfriend and questioning her girlfriend's decision to stay with this "snake motherfucker." In one stanza, she asks her friend:

> What kind of love from a nigga would black your eye?
>
> What kind of love from a nigga every night make you cry?
>
> What kind of love from a nigga make you wish he would die?
>
> And you stayed, what made you fall for him?
>
> That nigga had the power to make you crawl for him. . . .
>
> Smacked you down cause he said you was too tall for him, huh?
> (Eve, *Love Is Blind*)

This song stands alone in its rejection of violence towards women. This is not to suggest that female rappers accepted misogynistic lyrics; instead, the fact that they offered such little resistance likely reflects industry norms at the time. During the 1990s, women were grossly underrepresented in rap generally, and gangsta rap in particular, and were channeled instead into hip-hop and R&B. For women to gain acceptance in this male-dominated industry, they had to conform to existing industry norms and required male sponsors, who often appeared on one of their songs or in their videos (Emerson 2002; Nelson 1998:184). For this reason, the most common theme in our sample of songs by female artists involves the entry-level claim to being a bona fide, skilled rapper. Like many male artists at the time (Kubrin 2005a), women demanded respect for their talents as rappers and would boast about this. In nearly all cases, bragging about one's skills on the microphone was the entire point of the song.

Apart from Eve's oppositional song, there was one remaining theme associated with gender relations—competition and fighting over men. In these songs, female rappers disparaged other women who they accused of trying to steal their men:

> Get your own stacks [money]
> Why you think these niggas pussy hungry?
> Cause you actin' triflin'
> Layin' up, takin' his money.
> (Eve, *Let's Talk About*)

In other scenarios, female rappers claimed ownership of their man even if he had sex with other women, usually because the former was the man's wife or longtime girlfriend:

> Shit, I got the ring bitch and his last name. . . .
> Any bitch could luck up and have a kid
> Any chick could fuck a nigga for spite
> But the nigga got to love you if he make you his wife
> Ughh, ya'll chicks is lonely, I'm ownin' that dick
> And on top of all this bullshit, I'm still his chick.
> (Foxy Brown, *It's Hard Being Wifee*)

Although our sample of female rappers is too small for definitive conclusions, most did not challenge the degradation of women by male artists at the time. Some female artists adopt the persona and status afforded them by men: Lil' Kim calls herself "Queen Bitch," Mia X is a "Boss Bitch" (Pough

2004), and others pride themselves on being gold diggers. But it is also important to remember that most songs by women neither accepted nor opposed such degradation. This pattern appears to have changed subsequent to the time period covered by our study. Currently female rappers more actively confront male domination and seek to empower women, although songs by female artists today still contain a contradictory mix of themes that both challenge and perpetuate misogynistic themes (Emerson 2002; Jennings 2004; Pough 2004:85–87; Troka 2002:83).

CONCLUSION

According to one review of popular music over the past century, the portrayal of women has increasingly shown "greater diversity, more complexity, and dramatically mixed messages about the individual female persona and women's roles in society" (Cooper 1999:355). Much rap music, at least rap produced by male artists, runs counter to this larger trend. Indeed, a segment of rap music naturalizes certain alleged characteristics of men and women and, in accordance with these imputed differences, seeks to restrict, rather than broaden, women's proper roles and resuscitate male domination. The messages are thus both essentialist and normative—portraying men and women as inherently different and unequal and espousing a set of conduct norms for each gender's proper behavior toward the other and sanctions for those who violate these norms.

Some analysts describe rap music as part of a larger reaction against the feminist movement, seeking to perpetuate women's inequality and re-empower men. As bell hooks (1994:6) argues, "Gangsta rap is part of the anti-feminist backlash that is the rage right now." The music contains a variety of "controlling images" directed at women (Collins 2000), and goes to great lengths to define strict gender roles, with women subordinate to men in several ways. In this sense rap speaks to larger gender relations by making universalistic claims and instructing all men on appropriate conduct toward women. But rap artists are not solely responsible for the content of their work. The entertainment industry plays an essential role, cultivating sexist lyrics and rewarding artists who produce them with huge sums of money, Grammy and Oscar awards, and spin-off products like Pimp Juice. In addition to this top-down dynamic, we have also pointed to a bottom-up process in which, as Negus (1999:490) argues, neighborhood "culture produces industry" as much as "industry produces culture." In other words, rap's messages have been incubated and resonate in communities where men have few opportunities for socioeconomic success and dignity and where respect is instead often earned by mistreating young women (Anderson 1999; Bourgois 1996; Liebow 1967) as well as other men (Kubrin and Weitzer 2003). As Connell and Messerschmidt (2005) point out, hegemonic masculinity is reinforced reciprocally at multiple levels—societal, community, and interactional.

It is important to emphasize that, like other music genres, rap is more varied in its content than is often recognized. For instance, this music has served as a consciousness-raising, politically progressive, liberating form of popular culture (Martinez 1997). Therefore, we want to emphasize that misogyny does not characterize rap music as a whole. This is an important finding in itself. A majority of songs in our sample do *not* degrade women, which we consider a major finding in itself. And there are rappers who actively challenge rap's misogynistic messages and endorse a more egalitarian form of masculinity. At the same time, a sizeable segment (more than one-fifth) of this genre does contain such messages, and our analysis indicates that these messages are rather extreme. While women are presented as subordinate to men in a majority of rock and country songs as noted earlier, rap stands out for the *intensity* and *graphic* nature of its lyrical objectification, exploitation, and victimization of women. Other genres, in the aggregate, make more subtle allusions to gender inequality or present more muted criticisms of women (Andsager and Roe 1999; Binder 1993; Cooper 1999; Rhym 1997; Ryan and Peterson 1982; Walser 1993). Furthermore, it is important to consider what themes are largely *absent* in rap lyrics.

Rare are lyrics that describe women as independent, educated, professional, caring, and trustworthy. While the majority of songs in the original sample did not contain misogynistic lyrics, even these songs failed to present women in a favorable light. In other words, absence of misogyny does not equate with a positive representation of women.

Given its sources, we argue that changing the content of this music—specifically with respect to the portrayal of women—requires in part changing the conditions under which it is created, conditions that lie at the intersection of three important forces: socioeconomic disadvantage and associated gender relations in local communities, the material interests of the record industry, and the larger cultural objectification of women and associated norms of hegemonic masculinity.

AUTHORS' NOTE

For their helpful comments on this paper, we are grateful to Ivy Ken, Michael Kimmel, Theresa Martinez, and the anonymous reviewers, and for research assistance we thank Ami Lynch.

NOTES

1. It is important to recognize that rap is not monolithic. There are various themes in rap music, ranging from Afro-Centric community building to support for liberation struggles, to celebration of partying to problems of racism and drug dealing. See Kitwana (1994:32) and Krims (2000:55) for evidence of rap music's varied content.

2. Gangsta rap is a subgenre of rap music. It describes life in the ghetto, and has been controversial in part because it provides an insiders' view of crime, violence, and social conflict in the inner city (Kitwana 1994: 19; Krims 2000:70). More so than other rap genres, gangsta rap is noted for its violent and misogynistic lyrics, which depart from the rich political and social commentary that characterizes some other rap music (Kelley 1996:147).

3. We recognize that a few artists, such as NWA, produced gangsta rap songs before this time period. However, gangsta rap gained ascendancy in the early 1990s.

4. Originally a random sample of one-third of the 1,922 songs was selected to be analyzed (N = 632). The findings are based on a final sample size of 403 because, during the course of coding, after song 350 we no longer encountered new themes. Nevertheless, we coded an additional 53 songs to ensure that we had reached saturation, which is standard practice in qualitative analysis (Glaser and Strauss 1967:111).

5. At first glance, it might appear that negative portrayals of women were less frequent in rap than in the other music genres reviewed earlier, based on the percentage differences. However, each study operationalized such depictions in somewhat different ways, so study findings cannot be directly compared. Similarly, our finding on rap music cannot be compared to Armstrong's (2001) study of earlier rap songs because he focused on expressions of violence against women whereas our measure of misogyny is more inclusive.

6. Eminem has marketed himself as a poor or working-class white youth, which gives him some "street credibility" among black rappers and record producers, and it has been argued that his misogynistic lyrics are intended to gain credibility as a rapper (Stephens 2005).

REFERENCES

Alexander, Susan. 1999. The gender role paradox in youth culture: An analysis of women in music videos. *Michigan Sociological Review* 13:46–64.

Anderson, Elijah. 1999. *Code of the street: Decency, violence, and the moral life of the inner city*. New York: W.W. Norton.

Andsager, Julie, and Kimberly Roe. 1999. Country music video in country's year of the woman. *Journal of Communication* 49:69–82.

Armstrong, Gerald. 2001. Gangsta misogyny: A content analysis of the portrayals of violence against women in rap music, 1987–1993. *Journal of Criminal Justice and Popular Culture* 8:96–126.

Barongan, Christy, and Gordon Hall. 1995. The influence of misogynous rap music on sexual aggression against women. *Psychology of Women Quarterly* 19:195–207.

Bennett, Andy 1999a. Rappin' on the Tyne: White hip-hop culture in northeast England. *Sociological Review* 47:1–24.

——. 1999b. Hip hop am Main: The localization of rap music and hip hop culture. *Media, Culture & Society* 21:77–91.

Binder, Amy. 1993. Media depictions of harm in heavy metal and rap music. *American Sociological Review* 58:753–767.

Bourgois, Philippe. 1995. *In search of respect: Selling crack in El Barrio*. New York: Cambridge University Press.

——. 1996. In search of masculinity: Violence, respect, and sexuality among Puerto Rican crack dealers in East Harlem. *British Journal of Criminology* 36:412–427.

Butruille, Susan, and Anita Taylor. 1987. Women in American popular song. In *Communication, gender, and sex roles in diverse interactional contexts*, eds. L. Stewart and S. Ting-Toomey, 179–188. Norwood, NJ: Ablex.

Collins, Patricia Hill. 2000. *Black feminist thought*. 2nd Edn. New York: Routledge.

Connell, R.W. 1987. *Gender and power*. Cambridge: Polity.

Connell, R.W., and James Messerschmidt. 2005. Hegemonic masculinity: Rethinking the concept. *Gender & Society* 19:829–859.

Donaldson, Mike. 1993. What is hegemonic masculinity? *Theory and Society* 22:643–657.

Edin, Kathryn, and Maria Kefalas. 2005. *Promises I can keep: Why poor women put motherhood before marriage*. Berkeley: University of California Press.

Emerson, Rana. 2002. "Where my girls at?" Negotiating black womanhood in music videos. *Gender and Society* 16:115–135.

Forman, Murray. 1994. "Moving closer to an independent funk": Black feminist theory, standpoint, and women in rap. *Women's Studies* 23:35–55.

——. 2002. *The 'hood comes first: Race, space, and place in rap and hip hop*. Middletown, CT: Wesleyan University Press.

Garfinkle, Harold. 1956. Conditions of successful degradation ceremonies. *American Journal of Sociology* 61:420–424.

George, Nelson. 1998. *Hip hop America*. New York: Penguin Books.

Glaser, Barney, and Anselm Strauss. 1967. *The discovery of grounded theory*. Chicago: Aldine.

Hanke, Robert. 1998. Theorizing masculinity within the media. *Communication Theory* 8:183–203.

Henderson, Errol A. 1996. Black nationalism and rap music. *Journal of Black Studies* 26:308–339.

hooks, bell. 1994. Misogyny, gangsta rap, and the piano. *Z Magazine*, February.

Horowitz, Ruth. 1983. *Honor and the American dream: Culture and identity in a Chicano community*. New Brunswick, NJ: Rutgers University Press.

Hurt, Byron. 2007. *Hip hop: Beyond beats and rhymes*. Independent Lens series, PBS. First broadcast February 20th.

Jennings, Tom. 2004. Dancehall dreams. *Variant 2* (Summer):9–13.

Johnson, James, Mike Adams, Leslie Ashburn, and William Reed. 1995. Differential gender effects of exposure to rap music on African American adolescents' acceptance of teen dating violence. *Sex Roles* 33:597–605.

Kelley, Robin. 1996. Kickin' reality, kickin' ballistics: Gangsta rap and postindustrial Los Angeles. In *Droppin' science: critical essays on rap music and hip hop culture*, ed. W. Perkins, 117–158. Philadelphia: Temple University Press.

Keyes, Cheryl L. 2002. *Rap music and street consciousness*. Chicago: University of Chicago Press.

Kitwana, Bakari. 1994. *The rap on gangsta rap*. Chicago: Third World Press.

———. 2002. *The hip hop generation: Young blacks and the crisis of African American culture*. New York: Basic Books.

Krims, Adam. 2000. *Rap music and the poetics of identity*. Cambridge: Cambridge University Press.

Kubrin, Charis E. 2005a. Gangstas, thugs, and hustlas: Identity and the code of the street in rap music. *Social Problems* 52:360–378.

———. 2005b. I see death around the corner: Nihilism in rap music. *Sociological Perspectives* 48:433–459.

Kubrin, Charis E. and Ronald Weitzer. 2003. Retaliatory homicide: Concentrated disadvantage and neighborhood culture. *Social Problems* 50:157–180.

Lay, Frank. 2000. "Sometimes we wonder who the real men are": Masculinity and contemporary popular music. In *Subverting masculinity: Hegemonic and alternative versions of masculinity in contemporary culture*, ed. R. West and F. Lay, 227–246. Amsterdam: Rodopi.

Lee, Carol D. 2005. Intervention research based on current views of cognition and learning. In *Black education: A transformative research and action agenda for the new century*, ed. J. King, 73–114. Washington, D.C.: American Educational Research Association.

Lee, Cooper B. 1999. From Lady Day to Lady Di: Images of women in contemporary recordings, 1938–1998. *International Journal of Instructional Media* 26:353–358.

Lena, Jennifer C. 2006. Social context and musical content of rap music, 1979–1995. *Social Forces* 85:479–495.

Liebow, Elliot. 1967. *Tally's corner*. Boston: Little, Brown.

McAdams, Janine, and Deborah Russell. 1991. Rap breaking through to adult market. *Hollywood Reporter* Sept. 19:4.

McFarland, Pancho. 2003. Challenging the contradictions of Chicanismo in Chicano rap music and male culture. *Race, Gender, and Class* 10: 92–107.

Martino, Steven, Rebecca Collins, Marc Elliott, Amy Strachman, David Kanouse, and Sandra Berry. 2006. Exposure to degrading versus nondegrading music lyrics and sexual behavior among youth. *Pediatrics* 118:430–441.

Martinez, Theresa A. 1997. Popular culture as oppositional culture: Rap as resistance. *Sociological Perspectives* 40:265–286.

Miller, Jody, and Norman White. 2003. Gender and adolescent relationship violence. *Criminology* 41:1207–1247.

Moody, Nekesa Mumbi. 2003. Pimps: The new gangstas of rap. *Associated Press*, July 21.

Negus, Keith. 1999. The music business and rap: Between the street and the executive suite. *Cultural Studies* 13:488–508.

Oliver, William. 2006. The streets: An alternative black male socialization institution. *Journal of Black Studies* 36:918–937.

Pough, Gwendolyn. 2004. *Check it while I wreck it: Black womanhood, hip-hop culture, and the public sphere*. Boston: Northeastern University Press.

Powell, Catherine T. 1991. Rap music: An education with a beat from the street. *Journal of Negro Education* 60:245–259.

Powell, Kevin. 2000. My culture at the crossroads: A rap devotee watches corporate control and apolitical times encroach on the music he has loved all his life. *Newsweek*, October 9:66.

Quinn, Eithne. 2000. "Who's the mack?" The performativity and politics of the pimp figure in gangsta rap. *Journal of American Studies* 34:115–136.

———. 2005. *Nuthin' but a "G" thang: The culture and commerce of gangsta rap*. New York: Columbia University Press.

Rhym, Darren. 1997. "Here's for the bitches": An analysis of gangsta rap and misogyny." *Womanist Theory and Research* 2:1–14.

Rose, Tricia. 1994a. *Black noise: Rap music and black culture in contemporary America.* Hanover, NH: Wesleyan University Press.

——. 1994b. Contracting rap: An interview with Carmen Ashhurst-Watson. In *Microphone fiends: Youth music and youth culture,* ed. A. Ross and T. Rose, 122–44. New York: Routledge.

Ryan, John W. and R. A. Peterson. 1982. The product image: The fate of creativity in country music songwriting. *Sage Annual Reviews of Communication Research* 10:11–32.

Skeggs, Beverley. 1993. Two minute brother: Contestation through gender, race, and sexuality. *Innovation: The European Journal of Social Sciences* 6:299–323.

Stephens, Vincent. 2005. Pop goes the rapper: A close reading of Eminem's genderphobia. *Popular Music* 24:21–36.

Smith, Christopher H. 1997. Method in the madness: Exploring the boundaries of identity in hip hop performativity. *Social Identities* 3:345–374.

Smitherman, Geneva. 1997. "The chain remain the same": Communicative practices in the hip hop nation. *Journal of Black Studies* 28:3–25.

Troka, Donna. 2002. "You heard my gun cock": Female agency and aggression in contemporary rap music. *African American Research Perspectives* 8:82–89.

Tuchman, Gaye. 1978. The symbolic annihilation of women by the mass media. In *Hearth and home: Images of women in the mass media,* eds. G. Tuchman, A. Daniels, and J. Benet, 3–38. New York: Oxford University Press.

van Zoonen, Liesbet. 1994. *Feminist media studies.* Thousand Oaks: Sage.

Vincent, Richard, Dennis Davis, and Lilly Boruszkowski. 1987. Sexism on MTV: The portrayal of women in rock videos. *Journalism Quarterly* 64:750–755.

Walser, Robert. 1993. *Running with the Devil: Power, gender, and madness in heavy metal music.* Hanover, NH: Wesleyan University Press.

Watkins, S. Craig. 2001. A nation of millions: Hip hop culture and the legacy of black nationalism. *The Communication Review* 4:373–398.

Weitzer, Ronald. 2005. New directions in research on prostitution. *Crime, Law, and Social Change* 43:211–235.

Wester, Stephen, Cynthia Crown, Gerald Quatman, and Martin Heesacker. 1997. The influence of sexually violent rap music on attitudes of men with little prior exposure. *Psychology of Women Quarterly* 21:497–508.

RESISTANCE THROUGH VIDEO GAME PLAY: IT'S A BOY THING

Kathy Sanford   Leanna Madill

Youth, in particular boys, are finding many literacy activities, largely outside the realm of the school institution, that engage them and sustain long-term interest, e.g., video games (including computer and console systems). These games provide an interesting, engaging, dynamic, social space for many types of boys, both those who succeed at school literacy and those who struggle; they do not have to fit into any particular affinity group, they can engage without interference or sanction from adults, whenever they choose or when they have opportunities, and in ways that provide social capital for making connections with peers in real-time and virtual spaces. The lack of boys' success in formal schooling activities, so frequently reported in public press, can, we argue, be framed as resistance, both unconscious and conscious, against meaningless, mindless, boring schooling or workplace activities and assignments; instead, they engage in activities that provide them with active involvement and interest. Videogame play also serves as a form of resistance to stereotypical views of boys as a category who, by virtue of the fact that they are boys, has been categorized as unsuccessful learners – videogames are spaces where players can be successful in their endeavours.

VIDEO GAME CULTURE, GENDER, AND NEW AND CRITICAL LITERACIES

Video Game Culture

According to the Kaiser Family Foundation study *Kids, Media, and the New Millennium*, boys and girls differ in the amount of time engaged with media. Girls aged 8–18 spent less time per day than boys with the combination of media surveyed. Boys spent more time with TV, video games, and computers than did girls who spent more time with music media and print materials (as cited in Newkirk, 2002, p. 42). Rowan, Knobel, Bigum, and Lankshear (2002) report similar findings, claiming that "girls use the internet more than do the boys surveyed, but the girls use it more for educational purposes" (p. 131). The Canadian Teachers' Federation (2003), in *Kids' Take on Media: Summary of Findings*, report that almost 60 per cent of boys in grades 3–6 play video or computer games almost every day, 38 per cent for boys in grade 10. For girls, 33 per cent of grade-3 girls play interactive games every day, but only 6 per cent of grade 10 girls (p. iv).

Boys and male youth are far more involved in videogames than are girls. By engaging in these activities that resist traditional literacy learning, video game players are keeping up with the changing technological world faster and more productively than schools are. Gee (2000) describes this changing world: "If our modern, global, high-tech, and science-driven world does anything, it certainly gives rise to new semiotic domains and transforms old ones at an even faster rate" (p. 19).

"Attempts to assess the effects of video games on young people have been extensive," report Alloway and Gilbert (1998), "and have come from a variety of research domains and methodologies" (p. 95). Although some studies (Alloway & Gilbert, 1998; Alvermann, 2002; Rowan, Knobel, Bigum, & Lankshear, 2002) have focused on connections between gender and videogame play, many have focused on these issues separately, addressing videogame play and learning (Gee, 2003), identity development through videogame play (Filiciak, 2003), the nature of computer games (Myers, 2003), the value of videogames (Newman, 2004), and gendered marketing strategies for videogames (Ray, 2004).

Although videogame culture is strongly male-focused and masculinist, developing aggressive themes and situations (Alloway & Gilbert, 1998), often children and youth are represented as a homogeneous group, ignoring issues of difference connected to gender (Kline, 2004) and differing impacts on diverse populations.

Gender and Masculinity

Gender as a social construct impacts learning both in and out of school, dictating what is and can be learned and what is out of bounds. Gender, and therefore masculinity, is not fixed in advance of social interaction, but is constructed in interaction, and masculinity must be understood as an aspect of large-scale social structures and processes (Connell, 1995, p. 39). From a poststructural perspective, there are multiple ways of being a male and creating/negotiating male subjectivity. These multiple and diverse positions open up the possibility of constituting subjectivity as multiple and contradictory (Davies, 1992): every individual male accesses, performs, and transforms multiple versions of masculinity in various contexts and at various times. There are multiple ways that masculinity is performed; however hegemonic versions of masculinity are most highly valued, that is, performances of masculinity that embody "the currently accepted answer to the

problem of the legitimacy of patriarchy, which guarantees (or is taken to guarantee) the dominant position of men and the subordination of women" (Connell, 1995, p. 77).

Family activities and values transfer into schooling practices where notions of masculinity (often linked to images of such things as strength, cleverness, winning, power, and status) are further developed and reinforced, creating powerful sites for gendered messages to be reinforced by teachers and young people themselves (Browne, 1995; Sanford, 2002). Hegemonic masculinity not only naturalizes masculine behaviours, but also male discipline areas, such as science, mathematics, mechanics, and technology – those areas seen to require rational, unemotional engagement.

Males and females develop attitudes towards science and machines differently, and at a very young age. As Ray (2004) notes, the concept of the computer as a male object is reinforced in children very early in their lives. Males, given machine-type toys, including computers, are encouraged to experiment with them; they are more likely to receive training (formal and informal) in using computers. One young participant in our study commented, "You've got to know how to make what go where and stuff. I learned some of that from a game manual, mostly just clicking around . . . that's how I learn that kind of thing, just trial and error." Males, like this participant, are socialized to engage with computers and video games.

New and Critical Literacies

In this article, we have discussed not only how males use videogames to create resistances, but also our concerns related to videogame play when viewed simply as another form of "text." We have raised questions about operational, cultural, and critical dimensions of learning. Based on a sociocultural perspective in examining new or alternative literacies comprehensively, we draw on Green's (1997) three-dimensional model that considers operational, cultural, and critical dimensions of literacy and learning. Operational literacy "includes but also goes beyond competence with the tools, procedures, and techniques involved in being able to handle the written language system proficiently. It includes being able to read and write/key in a range of contexts in an appropriate and adequate manner" (Lankshear & Knobel, 2003, p. 11). Cultural literacy "involves competence with the meaning system of a social practice; knowing how to make and grasp meanings appropriately within the practice . . . this means knowing what it is about given contexts of practice that makes for appropriateness or inappropriateness of particular ways of reading and writing" (Lankshear & Knobel, 2003, p. 11). Critical literacy addresses "awareness that all social practices, and thus all literacies, are socially constructed and 'selective': they include some representations and classifications – values, purposes, rules, standards, and perspectives – and exclude others" (Lankshear & Knobel, 2003, p. 11). We believe that as educators embrace videogames as a powerful learning tool (Gee, 2003), they must also find ways to raise critical questions relating to these texts and to disrupt unexamined hegemonic masculine attitudes related to power, status, and exclusivity.

METHODOLOGY

In this article, we examine video games as a domain that many boys and men choose to resist traditional school-based literacy, and examine how they use games to resist controlling societal forces and so-called feminized spaces such as home, daycare, and school. Given the considerable and growing involvement of boys with this alternative form of learning about literacy, technology, and the world, it is critical for both males and females that researchers and educators examine the implication of this male immersion into these new semiotic and technological domains.

In this study, we elucidate the complexity of the interplay between gender and videogame play, to better understand the nature of the learning done by male youth, and to consider the impact of this learning on them and on others in society. We observed the youths (predominantly male) in this

study as they engaged in the literacy practice of videogame play as a discursive tool. These observations provided a context in which we examined the performance of gender subjectivities through a range of alternative literacy practices (Gee, 1992; Street, 1984).

Participants and Data Collection

The informants for this study included two groups of participants/players. The first group, six young adolescent males attending a middle school in a small Canadian community, volunteered to participate in this study. Throughout the year, we observed them at school, both in classrooms and in less regulated spaces such as the hallways, out-of-doors, and in computer labs. We interviewed each participant twice throughout the year, where the discussion focused on his use of and interest in computers generally and game playing particularly. We transcribed the interviews, and used the first interview to shape the discussion of the second interview.

Our second group of participants, five young adult males, referred to us by acquaintances and selected for their interest in videogame play, were observed and videotaped in their home environments, playing videogames both independently and with a friend. We interviewed them in-depth two to three times over three months, where they discussed the nature of their videogame playing and reflected on the influences of videogame play on their lives. As with the first group, we transcribed the interviews, using the first interview to shape the focus of subsequent interviews. Both groups of participants, from the same geographical region, were predominantly from white, middle-class backgrounds. Our gender as two white females might have initially imposed barriers; however, the participants became very willing to share their ideas and expertise about videogames and helped us understand their specific references and to share their insider knowledge.

The interviews were analyzed and coded using NVivo text analysis software program. The data were coded into categories, mapped, searched, synthesized, and analyzed. We also conducted manual coding of themes to supplement the computer analysis which we shared with boys. To recognize themes of significance, we used critical discourse analysis to identify oppositions, recurrent key terms, and subjects spoken about by the participants and connected to the videogames identified by the participants.

FINDINGS

A significant theme that we identified through the analysis was the participants' perception of resistance as they engaged in videogame play: resistance to institutional authority, hegemonic masculinity, and femininity. These themes often overlapped or were sometimes even contradictory as the participants talked about how and why they played. Some of the forms of resistance were consciously selected (resistance to societal rules and resistance to school) while others were not consciously selected, but seemed to us to be pushing back on some of the restrictions and taboos they faced in school and current Western society (versions of restrictive masculinity and at the same time all types of femininity).

Through discussions with the participants, we learned what games they played, the types of games available, and their operational critique of the games (Lankshear & Knobel, 2003). We observed and videotaped the young adult players as they engaged in a variety of games (e.g., NBA Live 2005; Grand Theft Auto: Vice City; Counter Strike). Surprisingly to us, the games discussed by the adolescents and the young adults were very similar. They identified a range of game types: role play games – RPG (Final Fantasy, Halo), First Person Shooter – FPS (Max Payne, Medal of Honour, James Bond), Strategy/Simulation (Sims), Real Time Strategy – RTS (Counterstrike), Multi-genre role play/First Person Shooter (Grand Theft Auto), sports games (NBA 2005; Triple Play 2001, NHL Hockey 2002), and Movie games (Harry Potter, Star Wars, Punisher, Man Hunt) as being games they chose to spend hours playing, with their friends or on their own. Boys and male youth are engaging in the same types of videogames as adults, even though the

games are intended for mature adult players (Canadian Teachers' Federation study, 2003).

Sites of Resistance

We examined the role(s) that videogames play for males in challenging existing societal norms and expectations as they sought to define their masculine subjectivities in appropriate ways. Popular culture and media have historically been used as sites of resistance, whether through music, banners, graffiti, or alternative newspapers (Guzzetti & Gamboa, 2004) and this use of popular media continues today to resist constricting forms of education that stereotype, limit learning opportunities for segments of the population, and prevent meaningful learning for a rapidly increasingly global, technological, and digital world. Videogame players demonstrate many examples of resistance through challenges to rules and structures imposed by existing societal regulation and through challenges to restrictive identity formations and stereotypes.

Three significant areas of potential conflict and resistance include: institutional authority, hegemonic masculinity, and femininity. There are many ways in which students, particularly boys, overtly resist the hegemony of adult authority, and videogame play offers them a safe place to contest these power structures.

Resistance to Institutional Authority. Whether purposefully or unconsciously, youth engage in practices that serve to resist imposition of structures and rules currently prevailing in society. These rules are challenged in both private and social spaces. Even when speaking to us as researchers, the participants seemed more willing to share their expertise once it was clear that we were not negatively judging their videogame play. Players shared their frustrations and (either overtly or subtly) opposed authority within their cultural groups, ignoring and reshaping the rules. As they gained skills and confidence in playing games, they felt more able to resist traditional authority, relying on their fellow gamers for support and understanding – of the risks, the meaning, and the value. "I like lots of videogames" said one younger participant, "though there are some games that I had to defend that adults would think are stupid." They received immediate feedback not only from the game but also from their peers as they developed greater skill and confidence in playing the game.

The world of school, followed by the world of work, offers many routinized, dull tasks that do not offer the qualities reported by males as required for meaningful engagement, that is, personal interest, action, fun, purpose, or opportunities for success (Blair & Sanford, 2004; Smith & Wilhelm, 2002). Instead, they faced a world of ordinariness, lacking excitement or purpose. "I get bored quite a bit," one adolescent participant told us, "at school and at home. Then I usually go up and play on the computer." All the adult male participants explained that they used games to "zone out," to stop thinking or engaging with real people in their lives who have demands and remind them of their responsibilities. Videogames enabled players to create fantasy worlds for themselves where they were heroic, active, and respected.

Videogames also offer opportunities for players to learn information in alternate multi-modal ways through playing videogames, unlike traditional school learning that is most often linear and book based. Engaging in *Medal of Honor: Pacific Assault* allows youth to gain information about a significant historic event, but goes far beyond transmission of facts because adrenaline allows the players to feel the experience through sound and vibration, newer aspects of videogame play. Simulation games (Sim City, Speed Racing, Air Strike) enable players to learn about valued workplace and life skills, such as driving a car, flying a plane, or building a city. The immersion experiences that are promised, engaging players in the action, enabling them to feel the exhilaration and the fear, create a far more powerful and memorable learning experience than the reading of a textbook. One young adolescent participant reported, "I've learned tons about history, tons and tons, from *Civilization 3*. You just learn lots of stuff, and you don't really think about it." Not a far stretch, then for students to begin to challenge the

material (both content and format) being presented in school, and to resist the linear, uni-dimensional approach to learning that is so often used in school.

Videogames provide many opportunities for players to explore alternatives to the reality of adult society and its patriarchal, imposed rules. These rules, or laws, create restrictive structures that adolescents yearn to resist. As one young adult commented, ". . . it's cool, you can just explore . . . you can fly with a jet pack, break into an airport, grab some pizza . . . you're not limited to what you can do." Through videogame play, they can try out resistant and dangerous choices and experience the consequences, all within the safety of game play. The opportunity to adopt an alternative persona and to experience characters' perceptions and actions, which are often inappropriate or illegal actions in the real world, and usually have no consequences, was a powerful enticement. One young adult participant commented,

> "You take street racing that's illegal and you take new cars and you soup them up and you make them look all flashy and crazy . . . and you race them on the street, swerving in and around other cars and things like that – it's slightly rebellious or whatever, but I'd like to see what that's like."

The players assume authority as the game character and thereby gives their individual consent for the actions and attitudes that they role play (Leonard, 2004). Playing games that transgress societal, family, and school rules and norms enables a freedom to experiment with and challenge existing restrictions that, while providing safety, are also limiting and dull. Trying on resistant thoughts and actions is highly appealing to our participants.

The technology of videogames allows players to cheat by downloading codes or finding glitches in the game. One participant explained that players use cheats[1] because "at the moment they're so angry or frustrated with the game that they just want to go ahead, or they wonder, Wow! It would be so great if I had that." By using cheats, and engaging in a community that understands the purpose of cheats and the importance of them, players can band together to resist traditional and mainstream rules as a community, using their social connections to succeed at their game play.

Many videogame story lines encourage players to resist society's expectations. From stealing cars to killing enemies or random people, the game allows players to play out scenarios that they would never actually do: "It's kinda fun to do because it's not something that you would do everyday, obviously." Videogames allow players to forego the rules of the real world and engage in a new fantasy frontier where they can be mavericks, able to ignore rules that others have to abide. When players state that the reason they play video games is to escape, they suggest that they are not having to think critically about what they play: "I definitely play it to get into the role and forget about other things" and "I just go and play it and space out" are answers from our adult participants as to why they play video games. This attitude allows them the right to ignore stereotypes, prejudices, or other usually conflicting messages that they would otherwise not be allowed to (or even want to) participate with. "It's like a feeling of power, but it's sadistic," one adult participant explained, "You really enjoy it, like killing someone, blasting them in the head . . . maybe it's cause you can't do it, it's such a forbidden thing, but like they make it so real and powerful, like in a game you can have the ability to smoke people continuously." Another participant commented, "I don't know why I enjoy it, I imagine myself living in Vice City [Grant Theft Auto] just doing missions and you can kill people and steal cars and just do bad stuff. You do all these things that you don't necessarily want to do, but it gives you so much power. . .". To succeed the participants engaged in the rules of the game, even if the rules did not match socially constructed values or rules.

Resistance to Hegemonic Masculinity. Western society has responded to expanded and alternative gender positions with a rigid homophobic stance regarding masculinity. Young males today are faced with a fierce policing of traditional masculinity, and the rules of masculinity are enforced in many overt and subtle ways. Being a male who does not exhibit characteristics of physical strength, individuality, and machismo can find the world dangerous and lonely space (Connell, 1995; Frank, Kehler, & Davison, 2003; Kehler, 2004; Martino & Pallotta-Chiarolli, 2001). Videogames provide players with spaces in which to experiment with identity: to safely resist traditional masculinities currently prevailing in society, or conversely, to demonstrate their heterosexual masculinity and resist connections to the feminine, and to challenge societal expectations of appropriateness regarding attitude, appearance, or behaviour. By adopting roles through which they can experiment with their identity formation, they can expand their sense of self and understand their world from new perspectives. One adult participant negotiated his identity as he described a game, "In *Halo*, I really like that it is shoot 'em up, not that I am a killer, but you know . . . I just like that it is go and shoot, shoot, and kill, kill, kill."

In another interview, an adult male participant was asked what characteristics of male video game characters he admired. He responded: "I'd like to have the big body, a six-pack not an 8 pack! . . . I'd like to be built; I don't want to be a drug dealer, king of the city." When he was asked, "What about saving the girl?" he answered, "That would be neat. . . . I've often had dreams about that, meeting a girl by doing something courageous, you know." Another adult participant commented on his desire to be a hockey player. "I didn't ever play hockey; I don't know the rules. But in the game I'm always trying to start a body check or start a fight . . . I like all the silly things like how the glass breaks when you do a body check."

Videogames provide a way to resist traditional hegemonic masculinities in a safe space, to play out alternative personas, such as personas of men of colour or of females. In reality, not all males are strong and macho (and may not want to be), but they may wish to try on the persona of a rugged heroic figure who rescues the weak from dangerous situations. By using online forums and Internet gameplay, subjectivities can be disguised and trans/reformed in myriad ways. One participant talked about a friend

[whom] he described as a "very fairy tale type of person, similar to the *Everquest* type of thing. He's kind of creative, and likes imaginary types of stuff." This friend was able to engage in the videogame as a character who did not display traditional masculinity traits, yet in the context of the game it was safe for him to do so. However, his alternative masculine persona might not have been as safe to perform in reality.

As suggested earlier in this article, the media and the public have categorized boys as regularly experiencing failure in school, of under-performing, and of being less literate than girls. Videogames provide spaces where boys can dominate and create an alternative sense of success. They are finding many activities that engage them and sustain long-term interest; videogames provide an interesting, engaging, dynamic social space for many types of boys who do not have to fit into any particular category. Videogames also allow for the creation of additional social spaces where boys from various social groups (athletes, trades, academics, rebels) can belong, resisting imposed societal roles and positions. By creating fantasy personas for themselves, heroic powerful figures able to rescue innocent girls and garner the respect of their peers, they resist the traditionally stereotypical ways they are viewed in society. Additionally they develop skills that are valued in the workplace, giving them future social capital through which to be successful.

By connecting to communities, face-to-face or on-line communities, and engaging in extensive rounds of play, players gain skills in manual dexterity, ability to read multiple screens or texts simultaneously, and make quick, accurate decisions based on information provided. These operational literacies referred to earlier in this article (Lankshear & Knobel, 2003) teach the mostly male players how to use many functions of computers, to make repairs and adjustments to programs and glitches, to make accurate predictions, and to apply their knowledge to new situations – most importantly, they gain a confidence in their ability to use computers effectively, not just videogames, but many aspects of computers. This confidence enables them to resist

traditional school literacies, choosing instead modes of literacy that support the particular type of masculine persona they have selected for themselves, and make a commitment to that self-selected identity. As Gee (2003) comments, "Such a commitment requires that they are willing to see themselves in terms of a new identity, that is, to see themselves as the *kind of person* who can learn, use, and value the new semiotic domain" (p. 59, italics in original). And if they are successful, then they will be valued by and accepted in that affinity group.

Rejecting Femininity. One way that male game players use videogames as a form of resistance is to create a clearly non-female identity, that is, muscular, big, and dangerous-looking. Although it is interesting to try on different personas, even those of females, it is personally dangerous to associate oneself with the feminine. One young adult male participant explained how sometimes a friend of his might choose to be the princess in a Mario Bros, game and they would all tease him. "We started calling him princess." This adult participant is a football player in real life and he attempted to masculinize his interest in videogames; he comments,

> "I don't think many girls are too interested in playing a game of *Dead or Alive* and seeing another girl's scantily clad body bounce around like it is, that kind of stuff appeals to guys. It's on more of a primal level, just kinda like one-on-one combat. It really turns guys on for some reason."

He differentiates males from females in this sexual way, and includes himself in this masculine description; he is not sure why males are drawn to these primal interests but is not inclined to question his theory or his participation in this world.

A similar example of resistance within the role playing games is the type of avatars (game characters) that players select to become in the videogames. The selected character is often the strong, independent rebel, such as in *Max Payne*, all the *Grand Theft Auto* games, *Man Hunt*, and *Counter Strike*; one adult gamer described these characters as "not really dependent on anyone else, very like 'I am going to do this my way'." The players' desire to shape their identity as rugged, independent, and strong precludes them from making choices of characters who seem weak, dependent, and feminine. This same participant talked about Max Payne as a character he admired. "He's kind of a dark and lonely character, very dark and devious, and he talks with kind of a low deep voice and he's very masculine and he usually gets with one woman in the storyline."

Although choice of creating videogame characters helps the players to experiment with diverse subjectivities, again the hegemonic masculinity model looms large in most of the games the participants report playing regularly. As they negotiate their sense of self through various videogame characters, we worry that they are reinforcing the binary that relegates females to subordinate positions and does not allow any space or opportunity for a critical reading of the gender positions offered in the games.

DISCUSSION

There is no question in our minds that videogames encourage resistance to school values, parental authority, and societal expectations, and partly because of the perception of resistance are hence a major attraction for youth. Videogames are fun, and this is partly because they are perceived as dangerous, entering forbidden territory. There is no doubt that videogame players are developing an understanding of learning principles through playing games, as suggested by Gee (2003), in relation to text design, intertextuality, semiotics, transfer of knowledge, or probing and identifying multiple approaches. However, we are not convinced that, as Gee claims, there is significant learning about cultural models. We did not find evidence that learners were thinking consciously and reflectively about cultural models of the world, or that they were consciously reflecting on the values that make up their real or videogame worlds. The resistance that we have observed in one area of the players' lives did not necessarily lead to resistance of imposed stereotypical and potentially harmful beliefs and attitudes.

Resistance to hegemonic hypermasculinity in game play does not necessarily lead the players to challenge gender stereotypes, or present themselves to the world in alternative representations of masculinity. And although resistance to anything feminine enables male players to develop their own subjectivity, it does not cause them to be more aware of their privileged positions of power or to respect difference in any significant way. We are concerned that the resistances made possible by videogame play serves only to reify the traditional stereotypes and cement them firmly in place.

There is, perhaps, a place to encourage resistance on a more conscious and responsive level through videogame play. Is it possible that spaces for critical questioning can be identified and taken up in relation to the images, actions, attitudes, and values being presented at hyperdrive speeds throughout the duration of a videogame? As we began to see in our interviews with young adult males, there is a place for them to critically examine their motivation and attitudes as they engage in games. Critical questions, such as those posed by Rowan and colleagues (2002), can help to shape resistances that change the world, rather than merely playing with the world as it exists.

- Who and what are included? What groups of people are included or excluded? How do you know?
- What do those who are included get to do? What roles are taken by men/boys, women/girls? What evidence do you have?
- Which people and roles are valued and how is this communicated?
- Who has control? Who has access to power? Who exercises power? Who acts independently? Who initiates action?
- What are various people rewarded for and with?
- In what ways does the inclusion or exclusion reflect to your own life?
- What are the consequences of this relationship?
- What alternatives are there? (pp. 117–118)

These types of questions enable engagement with and purpose for resistance, encouraging videogame players to look beyond the superficial qualities of action, speed, and excitement to a consideration of more fundamental levels of meaning and value that includes issues of power, control, and difference.

CONCLUSION

Popular media has historically been used as sites of resistance, through underground newspapers, graffiti, and music. And it is being used today to resist constricting forms of education that stereotype, limit learning opportunities, and prevent meaningful learning for a rapidly and increasingly global, technological, and digital world. The speed at which literacies are being challenged and reshaped defies institutional support and knowledge from maintaining the pace. Children create connections when they learn: "Our experiences in the world build patterns in our mind, and then the mind shapes our experience of the world (and the actions we take in it), which, in turn, reshapes our mind" (Gee, 2003, p. 92). Gee acknowledges that the harmful side of patterned thinking can lead to prejudices or stereotypes. If videogames are a main area from which players gain knowledge about a certain type of person, setting, or event then knowledge is heavily influenced by the limitations, biases, and values found in the videogames. It is these potentially harmful effects that cause us to draw on Lankshear and Knobel's (2003) framework that includes a critical dimension of literacy and learning, and to recognize the need for further research into the effects of videogame playing in the longterm, both for boys and for girls.

Through an examination of the opportunities for resistance to traditional authority and identity formation through videogame play, we can see the multiple types of literacy learning that are possible. Players are developing a wide range of useful operational knowledge that can be used as social capital in the workplace. As discussed previously, they are gaining a confidence in using new technologies, a belief that they can use and create programs effectively; they are becoming accomplished at making speedy decisions and reactions, developing a new

level of manual dexterity, and are able to read/process multiple pieces of information (text or screen) simultaneously.

However, as Gee (2003) points out, it is the potentially harmful effects of such opportunities for subversive and localized resistance as videogame play afford that also need to be interrogated. Educators and researchers need to be aware of the cultural and critical literacies that may or may not be addressed through the extensive videogame play that is currently in vogue with many boys and young men. Resistance to the videogame representations of gender, race, and sexual orientation are generally uni-dimensional and highly stereotypical; these can serve to reinforce societal prejudices that maintain hegemonic patriarchal power structures and understandings if the various types of resistance available to game players are not recognized and encouraged. More thought needs to be given to considerations of appropriateness related to specific contexts, indeed appropriateness of values and respect for diverse perspectives needs to be encouraged and supported.

In our observations of videogame play, we believe that the speed of decision making and action taking in videogames mitigates any reflective element of the game beyond how to win – during game play there is often little opportunity to consider alternative, more complex issues and decisions. There is opportunity to learn and experience historical events in multiple modes, but space and encouragement to reflect upon which of these perspectives holds more evidence of ethical and moral truth is also important.

Clearly evident in discussion with these videogame players is an element of critical literacy in relation to technical and technological qualities of videogames, in relation to the realism of visual components of the games, and in relation to comparisons with other modes of interaction. The participants are highly articulate about aspects of the game that function well, glitches in the games, and visual elements of the game. However, we are concerned about a lack of demonstrated critical thought in relation to alternate worldviews and perspectives on socio-cultural issues. As Lankshear and Knobel (2003) suggest,

> to participate effectively and productively in any literate practice, people must be socialized into it. But if individuals are socialized into a social practice without realizing that it is socially constructed and selective, and that it can be acted on and transformed, they cannot play an active role in changing it. (p. 11)

If players are not critically engaged in the literacies of videogames, they will not be able to understand the transformative and active production aspects of meaning making; rather they will be limited to existing in and engaging with literacies as they are created by others. There will be little room for players to consider the origins of the games, who creates the characters and the commercial aspects of the games, and the values that are subtly (or overtly) being perpetuated and encouraged.

Both educators and researchers need to consider whether the resistance to authority and to identity shaping enables future citizens to engage critically in the world, or whether their resistance is limited to small acts of adolescent defiance. Is the nature of their resistance limited itself to the individual or self-selected affinity group, or does their engagement in oppositional interactions engage the broader world? Do videogames desensitize players from moral and ethical responsibility for the world? Do videogames support concern for environmental and ecological realities that continue to consume the human and natural world or do they provide escapes from these global issues?

Further, how are schools developing the increased sophistication in operational literacies, but also creating opportunities for students to engage with cultural and critical literacies that are so necessary for the twenty-first century? How are schools understanding and addressing the knowledge capital that will be needed by our future generations for being successful in an increasingly technological and changing world? These are some of the concerns that need to be taken up by educators and researchers as they attempt to gain deeper and broader understandings of the nature of videogame learning and the nature of resistance.

NOTE

1. Cheat is a code a player can enter into the game to make play easier.

REFERENCES

Alloway, N., & Gilbert, P. (1998). Video game culture: Playing with masculinity, violence and pleasure. In S. Howard (Ed.), *Wired Up: Young people and the electronic media* (pp. 95–114). London, UK: UCL Press.

Alvermann, D. (Ed.). (2002). *Adolescents and literacies in a digital world*. New York: Peter Lang.

Blair, H. & Sanford, K. (2004). Morphing literacy: Boys reshaping their school-based literacy practices. *Language Arts*, 81(6), 452–460.

Browne, R. (1995). Schools and the construction of masculinity. In R. Browne & R. Fletcher (Eds.), *Boys in schools: Addressing the real issues* (pp. 224–233). Sydney, AU: Finch Publishing.

Canadian Teachers' Federation. (2003). *Kids' take on media: Summary of finding*. Retrieved April 6, 2006, from www.ctf-fce.ca/en/projects/MERP/summaryfindings.pdf

Connell, R. W. (1995). *Masculinities*. Berkeley and Los Angeles, CA: University of California Press.

Davies, B. (1992). Women's subjectivity and feminist stories. In C. Ellis & M. Flaherty (Eds.), *Investigating subjectivity: Research on lived experience* (pp. 53–76). London, UK: Sage Publications.

Filiciak, M. (2003). Hyperidentities: Postmodern identity patterns in massively multiplayer online role-playing games. In M. Wolf & B. Perron (Eds.), *The videogame theory reader* (pp. 87–102). New York: Routledge.

Frank, B., Kehler, ML., & Davison, K. (2003). A tangle of trouble: Boys, masculinity and schooling, future directions. *Educational Review*, 55(2), 119–133.

Gee, J. P. (1992). *The social mind: Language, ideology and social practice*. New York: Bergin & Harvey.

Gee, J. P. (2000). Teenagers in new times: A new literacy perspective. *Journal of Adolescent & Adult Literacy*, 43, 412–420.

Gee, J. P. (2003). *What video games have to teach us about learning and literacy*. New York: Palgrave MacMillan.

Green, B. (1997, May). Literacies and school learning in new times. Keynote address at the Literacies in Practice: Progress and Possibilities Conference, South Australian Department of Education and Children's Services and the Catholic Education office, Adelaide, Australia.

Guzzetti, B. J., & Gamboa, M. (2004). Zining: The unsanctioned literacy practice of adolescents. In C. Fairbanks, J. Worthy, B. Maloch, J. Hoffman & D. L. Schallert (Eds.), *53rd yearbook of the National Reading Conference* (pp. 208–217). Oak Creek, WI: National Reading Conference.

Kehler, M. (2004). "The Boys" interrupted: Images constructed, realities translated. *Education and Society*, 22(2), 83–99.

Kline, S. (2004, January). Technologies of the imaginary: Evaluating the promise of toys, television and video games for learning. Paper presented at the Sixth Australian and New Zealand Conference on the First Years, Tasmania.

Lankshear, C., & Knobel, M. (2003). *New literacies: Changing knowledge and classroom learning*. Buckingham, UK: Open University Press.

Leonard, D. (2004). Unsettling the military entertainment complex: Video games and a pedagogy of peace.

Studies in Media & Information Literacy Education, 4(4). Retrieved September 25, 2005, from http://www.utpjournals.com/jour.ihtml?lp=simile/issue16/leonardl.html

Martino, W., & Pallotta-Chiarolli, M. (Eds.). (2001). *Boys' stuff: Boys talking about what matters*. Sydney, AU: Allen & Unwin.

Myers, D. (2003). *The nature of computer games: Play as semiosis*. New York: Peter Lang.

Newkirk, T. (2002). Foreword. In M. Smith & J. Wilhelm (Eds.), *Reading don't fix no Chevys: Literacy in the lives of young men* (pp. ix–xi). Portsmouth, NH: Heinemann.

Newman, J. (2004). *Videogames*. London, UK: Routledge.

Ray, S. G. (2004). *Gender inclusive game design: Expanding the market*. Hingham, MA: Charles River Media, Inc.

Rowan, L., Knobel, M., Bigum, C., Lankshear, C. (2002). *Boys, literacies and schooling*. Buckingham, UK: Open University Press.

Sanford, K. (2006). Gendered literacy experiences: The effects of expectation and opportunity for boys' and girls' learning. *Journal of Adult and Adolescent Literacy*, 49(4), 302–314.

Smith, M., & Wilhelm, J. (2002). *Reading don't fix no Chevys: Literacy in the lives of young men*. Portsmouth, NH: Heinemann.

Street, B. (1984). *Literacy in theory and practice*. New York: Cambridge University Press.

POST-PRINCESS MODELS OF GENDER: THE NEW MAN IN DISNEY/PIXAR

ex plain homosocial

Ken Gillam   Shannon R. Wooden

Lisping over the Steve McQueen allusion in Pixar's *Cars* (2006), our two-year-old son, Oscar, inadvertently directed us to the definition(s) of masculinity that might be embedded in a children's animated film about NASCAR. The film overtly praises the "good woman" proverbially behind every successful man: the champion car, voiced by Richard Petty, tells his wife, "I wouldn't be nothin' without you, honey." But gender in this twenty-first-century bildungsroman is rather more complex, and Oscar's mispronunciation held the first clue. To him, a member of the film's target audience, the character closing in on the title long held by "The King" is not "Lightning McQueen" but "Lightning the queen"; his chief rival, the always-a-bridesmaid runner-up "Chick" Hicks.

Does this nominal feminizing of male also-rans (and the simultaneous gendering of success) constitute a meaningful pattern? Piqued, we began examining the construction of masculinity in major feature films released by Disney's Pixar studios over the past thirteen years. Indeed, as we argue here, Pixar consistently promotes a new model of masculinity, one that matures into acceptance of its more traditionally "feminine" aspects.

Ken Gillam, and Shannon R. Wooden, "Post-Princess Models of Gender: The New Man in Disney/Pixar," *Journal of Popular Film and Television*, 36(1): 2–8, January 4, 2008. Copyright © 2008. Taylor & Francis Group. Reprinted by permission. http://www.informaworld.com

Cultural critics have long been interested in Disney's cinematic products, but the gender critics examining the texts most enthusiastically gobbled up by the under-six set have so far generally focused on their retrograde representations of women. As Elizabeth Bell argues, the animated Disney features through *Beauty and the Beast* feature a "teenaged heroine at the idealized height of puberty's graceful promenade [. . . , f]emale wickedness [. . .] rendered as middle-aged beauty at its peak of sexuality and authority [. . . , and] [f]eminine sacrifice and nurturing [. . .] drawn in pear-shaped, old women past menopause" (108). Some have noted the models of masculinity in the classic animated films, primarily the contrast between the ubermacho Gaston and the sensitive, misunderstood Beast in *Beauty and the Beast*,[1] but the male protagonist of the animated classics, at least through *The Little Mermaid*, remains largely uninterrogated.[2] For most of the early films, this critical omission seems generally appropriate, the various versions of Prince Charming being often too two-dimensional to do more than inadvertently shape the definition of the protagonists' femininity. But if the feminist thought that has shaped our cultural texts for three decades now has been somewhat disappointing in its ability to actually rewrite the princess trope (the spunkiest of the "princesses," Ariel, Belle, Jasmine, and, arguably, even Mulan, remain thin, beautiful, kind, obedient or punished for disobedience, and headed for the altar), it has been surprisingly effective in rewriting the type of masculine power promoted by Disney's products.[3]

Disney's new face, Pixar studios, has released nine films—*Toy Story* (1995) and *Toy Story 2* (1999);

A Bug's Life (1998); *Finding Nemo* (2003); *Monsters, Inc.* (2001); *The Incredibles* (2004); *Cars* (2006); *Ratatouille* (2007); and now *WALL•E* (2008)—all of which feature interesting male figures in leading positions. Unlike many of the princesses, who remain relatively static even through their own adventures, these male leads are actual protagonists; their characters develop and change over the course of the film, rendering the plot. Ultimately these various developing characters particularly Buzz and Woody from *Toy Story*, Mr. Incredible from *The Incredibles*, and Lightning McQueen from *Cars*—experience a common narrative trajectory, culminating in a common "New Man" model[4]: they all strive for an alpha-male identity; they face emasculating failures; they find themselves, in large part, through what Eve Sedgwick refers to as "homosocial desire" and a triangulation of this desire with a feminized object (and/or a set of "feminine" values); and, finally, they achieve (and teach) a kinder, gentler understanding of what it means to be a man.

EMASCULATION OF THE ALPHA MALE

A working definition of *alpha male* may be unnecessary; although more traditionally associated with the animal kingdom than the Magic Kingdom, it familiarly evokes ideas of dominance, leadership, and power in human social organizations as well. The phrase "alpha male" may stand for all things stereotypically patriarchal: unquestioned authority, physical power and social dominance, competitiveness for positions of status and leadership, lack of visible or shared emotion, social isolation. An alpha male, like Vann in *Cars*, does not ask for directions; like Doc Hudson in the same film, he does not talk about his feelings. The alpha male's stresses, like Buzz Lightyear's, come from his need to save the galaxy; his strength comes from faith in his ability to do so. These models have worked in Disney for decades. The worst storm at sea is no match for *The Little Mermaid*'s uncomplicated Prince Eric—indeed, any charming prince need only ride in on his steed to save his respective princess. But the postfeminist world is a different place for men, and

the post-princess Pixar is a different place for male protagonists.

Newsweek recently described the alpha male's new cinematic and television rival, the "beta male": "The testosterone-pumped, muscle-bound Hollywood hero is rapidly deflating. [. . .] Taking his place is a new kind of leading man, the kind who's just as happy following as leading, or never getting off the sofa" (Yabroff 64). Indeed, as Susan Jeffords points out, at least since *Beauty and the Beast*, Disney has resisted (even ridiculed) the machismo once de rigueur for leading men (170). Disney cinema, one of the most effective teaching tools America offers its children, is not yet converting its model male protagonist all the way into a slacker, but the New Man model is quite clearly emerging.

> Pixar consistently promotes a new model of masculinity, one that matures into acceptance of its more traditionally "feminine" aspects.

Cars, *Toy Story*, and *The Incredibles* present their protagonists as unambiguously alpha in the opening moments of the films. Although Lightning McQueen may be an as-yet incompletely realized alpha when *Cars* begins, not having yet achieved the "King" status of his most successful rival, his ambition and fierce competitiveness still clearly valorize the alpha-male model: "Speed. I am speed . . . I eat losers for breakfast," he chants as a prerace mantra. He heroically comes from behind to tie the championship race, distinguishing himself by his physical power and ability, characteristics that catapult him toward the exclusively male culture of sports superstars. The fantasies of his life he indulges after winning the coveted Piston Cup even include flocks of female cars forming a worshipful harem around him. But the film soon diminishes the appeal of this alpha model. Within a few moments of the race's conclusion, we see some of Lightning's less positive macho traits; his inability to name any friends, for example, reveals both his isolation and attempts at emotional stoicism. Lightning McQueen is hardly an unemotional character, as can be seen when he prematurely jumps onto the stage to accept what he assumes to be his victory. For this happy emotional outburst, however, he is immediately disciplined by a snide comment from Chick. From this point until much later in the film, the only emotions he displays are those of frustration and anger.

Toy Story's Buzz Lightyear and Sheriff Woody similarly base their worth on a masculine model of competition and power, desiring not only to be the "favorite toy" of their owner, Andy, but to possess the admiration of and authority over the other toys in the playroom. Woody is a natural leader, and his position represents both paternalistic care and patriarchal dominance. In an opening scene, he calls and conducts a "staff meeting" that highlights his unambiguously dominant position in the toy community. Encouraging the toys to pair up so that no one will be lost in the family's impending move, he commands: "A moving buddy. If you don't have one, GET ONE." Buzz's alpha identity comes from a more exalted source than social governance—namely, his belief that he is the one "space ranger" with the power and knowledge needed to save the galaxy; it seems merely natural, then, that the other toys would look up to him, admire his strength, and follow his orders. But as with Lightning McQueen, these depictions of masculine power are soon undercut. Buzz's mere presence exposes Woody's strength as fragile, artificial, even arbitrary, and his "friends," apparently having been drawn to his authority rather than his character, are fair-weather at best. Buzz's authority rings hollow from the very beginning, and his refusal to believe in his own "toy-ness" is at best silly and at worst dangerous. Like Lightning, Buzz's and Woody's most commonly expressed emotions are anger and frustration, not sadness (Woody's, at having been "replaced") or fear (Buzz's, at having "crash-landed on a strange planet") or even wistful fondness (Woody's, at the loss of Slink's, Bo Peep's, and Rex's loyalty). Once again, the alpha-male position is depicted as fraudulent, precarious, lonely, and devoid of emotional depth.

An old-school superhero, Mr. Incredible opens *The Incredibles* by displaying the tremendous physical strength that enables him to stop speeding trains, crash through buildings, and keep the city safe from

criminals. But he too suffers from the emotional isolation of the alpha male. Stopping on the way to his own wedding to interrupt a crime in progress, he is very nearly late to the service, showing up only to say the "I dos." Like his car and toy counterparts, he communicates primarily through verbal assertions of power—angrily dismissing Buddy, his meddlesome aspiring sidekick; bantering with Elastigirl over who gets the pickpocket—and limits to anger and frustration the emotions apparently available to men.

Fraught as it may seem, the alpha position is even more fleeting: in none of these Pixar films does the male protagonist's dominance last long. After Lightning ties, rather than wins, the race and ignores the King's friendly advice to find and trust a good team with which to work, he browbeats his faithful semi, Mack, and ends up lost in "hill-billy hell," a small town off the beaten path of the interstate. His uncontrolled physical might destroys the road, and the resultant legal responsibility—community service—keeps him far from his Piston Cup goals. When Buzz appears as a gift for Andy's birthday, he easily unseats Woody both as Andy's favorite and as the toy community's leader. When Buzz becomes broken, failing to save himself from the clutches of the evil neighbor, Sid, he too must learn a hard lesson about his limited power, his diminished status, and his own relative insignificance in the universe. Mr. Incredible is perhaps most obviously disempowered: despite his superheroic feats, Mr. Incredible has been unable to keep the city safe from his own clumsy brute force. After a series of lawsuits against "the Supers," who accidentally leave various types of small-time mayhem in their wake, they are all driven underground, into a sort of witness protection program. To add insult to injury, Mr. Incredible's diminutive boss fires him from his job handling insurance claims, and his wife, the former Elastigirl, assumes the "pants" of the family.

Most of these events occur within the first few minutes of the characters' respective films. Only Buzz's downfall happens in the second half. The alpha-male model is thus not only present and challenged in the films but also is, in fact, the very structure on which the plots unfold. Each of these films is about being a man, and they begin with an outdated, two-dimensional alpha prototype to expose its failings and to ridicule its logical extensions: the devastation and humiliation of being defeated in competition, the wrath generated by power unchecked, the paralyzing alienation and fear inherent in being lonely at the top. As these characters begin the film in (or seeking) the tenuous alpha position among fellow characters, each of them is also stripped of this identity—dramatically emasculated—so that he may learn, reform, and emerge again with a different, and arguably more feminine, self-concept.

"Emasculated" is not too strong a term for what happens to these male protagonists; the decline of the alpha-male model is gender coded in all the films. For his community service punishment, Lightning is chained to the giant, snorting, tar-spitting "Bessie" and ordered to repair the damage he has wrought. His own "horsepower" (as Sally cheerfully points out) is used against him when literally put in the service of a nominally feminized figure valued for the more "feminine" orientation of service to the community. If being under the thumb of this humongous "woman" is not emasculating enough, Mater, who sees such subordination to Bessie as a potentially pleasurable thing, names the price, saying, "I'd give my left two lug nuts for something like that!"

Mr. Incredible's downfall is most clearly marked as gendered by his responses to it. As his wife's domestic power and enthusiasm grow increasingly unbearable, and his children's behavior more and more out of his control, he surreptitiously turns to the mysterious, gorgeous "Mirage," who gives him what he needs to feel like a man: superhero work. Overtly depicting her as the "other woman," the film requires Elastigirl to intercept a suggestive-sounding phone call, and to trap her husband in a lie, to be able to work toward healing his decimated masculinity.

In *Toy Story*, the emasculation of the alpha male is the most overt, and arguably the most comic. From the beginning, power is constructed in terms conspicuously gender coded, at least for adult viewers: as they watch the incoming birthday presents,

the toys agonize at their sheer size, the longest and most phallic-shaped one striking true fear (and admiration?) into the hearts of the spectators. When Buzz threatens Woody, one toy explains to another that he has "laser envy." Buzz's moment of truth, after seeing himself on Sid's father's television, is the most clearly gendered of all. Realizing for the first time that Woody is right, he is a "toy," he defiantly attempts to fly anyway, landing sprawled on the floor with a broken arm. Sid's little sister promptly finds him, dresses him in a pink apron and hat, and installs him as "Mrs. Nesbit" at her tea party. When Woody tries to wrest him from his despair, Buzz wails, "Don't you get it? I AM MRS. NESBIT. But does the hat look good? Oh, tell me the hat looks good!" Woody's "rock bottom" moment finds him trapped under an overturned milk crate, forcing him to ask Buzz for help and to admit that he "doesn't stand a chance" against Buzz in the contest for Andy's affection, which constitutes "everything that is important to me." He is not figured into a woman, like Buzz is, or subordinated to a woman, like Lightning is, or forced to seek a woman's affirmation of his macho self, like Mr. Incredible is, but he does have to acknowledge his own feminine values, from his need for communal support to his deep, abiding (and, later, maternal) love of a boy. This "feminine" stamp is characteristic of the New Man model toward which these characters narratively journey.

Homosociality, Intimacy, and Emotion

Regarding the "love of a boy," the "mistress" tempting Mr. Incredible away from his wife and family is not Mirage at all but Buddy, the boy he jilted in the opening scenes of the film (whose last name, Pine, further conveys the unrequited nature of their relationship). Privileging his alpha-male emotional isolation, but adored by his wannabe sidekick, Mr. Incredible vehemently protects his desire to "work alone." After spending the next years nursing his rejection and refining his arsenal, Buddy eventually retaliates against Mr. Incredible for rebuffing his advances. Such a model of homosocial tutelage as Buddy proposes at the beginning of the film certainly evokes an ancient (and homosexual) model of masculine identity; Mr. Incredible's rejection quickly and decisively replaces it with a heteronormative one, further supported by Elastigirl's marrying and Mirage's attracting the macho superhero.[5] But it is equally true that the recovery of Mr. Incredible's masculine identity happens primarily through his (albeit antagonistic) relationship with Buddy, suggesting that Eve Sedgwick's notion of a homosocial continuum is more appropriate to an analysis of the film's gender attitudes than speculations about its reactionary heteronormativity, even homophobia.

Same-sex (male) bonds—to temporarily avoid the more loaded term *desire*—are obviously important to each of these films. In fact, in all three, male/male relationships emerge that move the fallen alphas forward in their journeys toward a new masculinity. In each case, the male lead's first and/or primary intimacy—his most immediate transformative relationship—is with one or more male characters. Even before discovering Buddy as his nemesis, Mr. Incredible secretly pairs up with his old pal Frozone, and the two step out on their wives to continue superheroing on the sly; Buddy and Frozone are each, in their ways, more influential on Mr. Incredible's sense of self than his wife or children are. Although Lightning falls in love with Sally and her future vision of Radiator Springs, his almost accidentally having befriended the hapless, warm Mater catalyzes more foundational lessons about the responsibilities of friendship—demanding honesty, sensitivity, and care—than the smell-the-roses lesson Sally represents. He also ends up being mentored and taught a comparable lesson about caring for others by Doc Hudson, who even more explicitly encourages him to resist the alpha path of the Piston Cup world by relating his experiences of being used and then rejected. Woody and Buzz, as rivals-cum-allies, discover the necessary truths about their masculine strength only as they discover how much they need one another. Sedgwick further describes the ways in which the homosocial bond is negotiated through a triangulation of desire; that is, the intimacy emerging "between men" is constructed through an overt and shared desire for a

feminized object. Unlike homosocial relationships between women—that is, "the continuum between 'women loving women' and 'women promoting the interests of women'"—male homosocial identity is necessarily homophobic in patriarchal systems, which are structurally homophobic (3). This means the same-sex relationship demands social opportunities for a man to insist on, or prove, his heterosexuality. Citing Rene Girard's *Deceit, Desire, and the Novel*, Sedgwick argues that "in any erotic rivalry, the bond that links the two rivals is as intense and potent as the bond that links either of the rivals to the beloved" (21); women are ultimately symbolically exchangeable "for the primary purpose of cementing the bonds of men with men" (26).

This triangulation of male desire can be seen in *Cars* and *Toy Story* particularly, where the homosocial relationship rather obviously shares a desire for a feminized third. Buzz and Woody compete first, momentarily, for the affection of Bo Peep, who is surprisingly sexualized for a children's movie (purring to Woody an offer to "get someone else to watch the sheep tonight," then rapidly choosing Buzz as her "moving buddy" after his "flying" display). More importantly, they battle for the affection of Andy—a male child alternately depicted as maternal (it is his responsibility to get his baby sister out of her crib) and in need of male protection (Woody exhorts Buzz to "take care of Andy for me!").[6] *Cars* also features a sexualized romantic heroine; less coquettish than Bo Peep, Sally still fumbles over an invitation to spend the night "not with me, but . . ." in the motel she owns. One of Lightning and Mater's moments of "bonding" happens when Mater confronts Lightning, stating his affection for Sally and sharing a parallel story of heterosexual desire. The more principal objects of desire in *Cars*, however, are the (arguably) feminized "Piston Cup" and the Dinoco sponsorship. The sponsor itself is established in romantic terms: with Lightning stuck in Radiator Springs, his agent says Dinoco has had to "woo" Chick instead. Tia and Mia, Lightning's "biggest fans," who transfer their affection to Chick during his absence, offer viewers an even less subtly gendered goal, and Chick uses this to taunt

Lightning. It is in the pursuit of these objects, and in competition with Chick and the King, that Lightning first defines himself as a man; the Piston Cup also becomes the object around which he and Doc discover their relationship to one another.

The New Man

With the strength afforded by these homosocial intimacies, the male characters triumph over their respective plots, demonstrating the desirable modifications that Pixar makes to the alpha-male model. To emerge victorious (and in one piece) over the tyrannical neighbor boy, Sid, Buzz, and Woody have to cooperate not only with each other but also with the cannibalized toys lurking in the dark places of Sid's bedroom. Incidentally learning a valuable lesson about discrimination based on physical difference (the toys are not monsters at all, despite their frightening appearance), they begin to show sympathy, rather than violence born of their fear, to the victims of Sid's experimentation. They learn how to humble themselves to ask for help from the community. Until Woody's grand plan to escape Sid unfolds, Sid could be an object lesson in the unredeemed alpha-male type: cruelly almighty over the toy community, he wins at arcade games, bullies his sister, and, with strategically placed fireworks, exerts militaristic might over any toys he can find. Woody's newfound ability to give and receive care empowers him to teach Sid a lesson of caring and sharing that might be microcosmic to the movie as a whole. Sid, of course, screams (like a girl) when confronted with the evidence of his past cruelties, and when viewers last see him, his younger sister is chasing him up the stairs with her doll.

Even with the unceremonious exit of Sid, the adventure is not quite over for Buzz and Woody. Unable to catch up to the moving van as Sid's dog chases him, Woody achieves the pinnacle of the New Man narrative: armed with a new masculine identity, one that expresses feelings and acknowledges community as a site of power, Woody is able to sacrifice the competition with Buzz for his object of desire. Letting go of the van strap, sacrificing

himself (he thinks) to Sid's dog, he plainly expresses a caretaking, nurturing love, and a surrender to the good of the beloved: "Take care of Andy for me," he pleads. Buzz's own moment of truth comes from seizing his power as a toy: holding Woody, he glides into the family's car and back into Andy's care, correcting Woody by proudly repeating his earlier, critical words back to him: "This isn't flying; it's falling with style." Buzz has found the value of being a "toy," the self-fulfillment that comes from being owned and loved. "Being a toy is a lot better than being a space ranger," Woody explains. "You're *his toy*" (emphasis in original).

Mr. Incredible likewise must embrace his own dependence, both physical and emotional. Trapped on the island of Chronos, at the mercy of Syndrome (Buddy's new super-persona), Mr. Incredible needs women—his wife's superpowers and Mirage's guilty intervention—to escape. To overpower the monster Syndrome has unleashed on the city, and to achieve the pinnacle of the New Man model, he must also admit to his emotional dependence on his wife and children. Initially confining them to the safety of a bus, he confesses to Elastigirl that his need to fight the monster alone is not a typically alpha ("I work alone") sort of need but a loving one: "I can't lose you again," he tells her. The robot/monster is defeated, along with any vestiges of the alpha model, as the combined forces of the Incredible family locate a new model of postfeminist strength in the family as a whole. This communal strength is not simply physical but marked by cooperation, selflessness, and intelligence. The children learn that their best contributions protect the others; Mr. Incredible figures out the robot/monster's vulnerability and cleverly uses this against it.

> The postfeminist world is a different place for men, and the post-princess Pixar is a different place for male protagonists.

In a parallel motif to Mr. Incredible's inability to control his strength, Buddy/Syndrome finally cannot control his robot/monster; in the defeat, he becomes the newly emasculated alpha male.

But like his robot, he learns quickly. His last attempt to injure Mr. Incredible, kidnapping his baby Jack-Jack, strikes at Mr. Incredible's new source of strength and value, his family. The strength of the cooperative family unit is even more clearly displayed in this final rescue: for the shared, parental goal of saving Jack-Jack, Mr. Incredible uses his physical strength and, with her consent, the shape-shifting body of his super-wife. He throws Elastigirl into the air, where she catches their baby and, flattening her body into a parachute, sails gently back to her husband and older children.

Through Lightning McQueen's many relationships with men, as well as his burgeoning romance with Sally, he also learns how to care about others, to focus on the well-being of the community, and to privilege nurture and kindness. It is Doc, not Sally, who explicitly challenges the race car with his selfishness ("When was the last time you cared about something except yourself, hot rod?"). His reformed behavior begins with his generous contributions to the Radiator Springs community. Not only does he provide much-needed cash for the local economy, but he also listens to, praises, and values the residents for their unique offerings to Radiator Springs. He is the chosen auditor for Lizzy's reminiscing about her late husband, contrasting the comic relief typically offered by the senile and deaf Model T with poignancy, if not quite sadness. Repairing the town's neon, he creates a romantic dreamscape from the past, a setting for both courting Sally ("cruising") and, more importantly, winning her respect with his ability to share in her value system. For this role, he is even physically transformed: he hires the body shop proprietor, Ramone, to paint over his sponsors' stickers and his large race number, as if to remove himself almost completely from the Piston Cup world, even as he anticipates being released from his community service and thus being able to return to racing.

Perhaps even more than Buzz, Woody, and Mr. Incredible do, the New Man McQueen shuns the remaining trappings of the alpha role, actually refusing the Piston Cup. If the first three protagonists are ultimately qualified heroes—that is, they still retain their authority and accomplish their

various tasks, but with new values and perspectives acquired along the way—Lightning completely and publicly refuses his former object of desire. Early in the final race, he seems to somewhat devalue racing; his daydreams of Sally distract him, tempting him to give up rather than to compete. The plot, however, needs him to dominate the race so his decision at the end will be entirely his own. His friends show up and encourage him to succeed. This is where the other films end: the values of caring, sharing, nurturing, and community being clearly present, the hero is at last able to achieve, improved by having embraced those values. But Lightning, seeing the wrecked King and remembering the words of Doc Hudson, screeches to a stop inches before the finish line. Reversing, he approaches the King, pushes him back on the track, and acknowledges the relative insignificance of the Piston Cup in comparison to his new and improved self. He then declines the Dinoco corporate offer in favor of remaining faithful to his loyal Rust-eze sponsors. Chick Hicks, the only unredeemed alpha male at the end, celebrates his ill-gotten victory and is publicly rejected at the end by both his fans, "the twins," and, in a sense, by the Piston Cup itself, which slides onto the stage and hits him rudely in the side.

CONCLUSION

The trend of the New Man seems neither insidious nor nefarious, nor is it out of step with the larger cultural movement. It is good, we believe, for our son to be aware of the many sides of human existence, regardless of traditional gender stereotypes. However, maintaining a critical consciousness of the many lessons taught by the cultural monolith of Disney remains imperative. These lessons—their pedagogical aims or results—become most immediately obvious to us as parents when we watch our son ingest and express them, when he misunderstands and makes his own sense of them, and when we can see ways in which his perception of reality is shaped by them, before our eyes. Without assuming that the values of the films are inherently evil or representative of an evil "conspiracy to undermine American youth" (Giroux 4), we are still compelled to critically examine the texts on which our son bases many of his attitudes, behaviors, and preferences.

Moreover, the impact of Disney, as Henry Giroux has effectively argued, is tremendously more widespread than our household. Citing Michael Eisner's 1995 "Planetized Entertainment," Giroux claims that 200 million people a year watch Disney videos or films, and in a week, 395 million watch a Disney TV show, 3.8 million subscribe to the Disney Channel, and 810,000 make a purchase at a Disney store (19). As Benjamin Barber argued in 1995, "[T]he true tutors of our children are not schoolteachers or university professors but filmmakers, advertising executives and pop culture purveyors" (qtd. in Giroux 63). Thus we perform our "pedagogical intervention[s]" of examining Disney's power to "shap[e] national identity, gender roles, and childhood values" (Giroux 10). It remains a necessary and ongoing task, not just for concerned parents, but for all conscientious cultural critics.

NOTES

1. See Susan Jeffords, "The Curse of Masculinity: Disney's *Beauty and the Beast*," for an excellent analysis of that plot's developing the cruel Beast into a man who can love and be loved in return: "Will he be able to overcome his beastly temper and terrorizing attitude in order to learn to love?" (168). But even in this film, she argues, the Beast's development is dependent on "other people, especially women," whose job it is to tutor him into the new model of masculinity, the "New Man" (169, 170).

2. Two articles demand that we qualify this claim. Indirectly, they support the point of this essay by demonstrating a midcentury Disney model of what we call "alpha" masculinity. David Payne's "Bambi" parallels that film's coming-of-age plot, ostensibly representing a "natural" world, with the military mindset of the 1940s against which the film was drawn. Similarly, Claudia Card, in "Pinocchio," claims that the Disneyfied version of the nineteenth-century Carlo Collodi tale replaces the original's model of bravery and honesty with "a macho exercise in heroism [. . . and] avoid[ing] humiliation" (66–67).

3. Outside the animated classics, critics have noted a trend toward a postfeminist masculinity—one characterized by emotional wellness, sensitivity to family, and a conscious rejection of the most alpha male values—in Disney-produced films of the 1980s and 1990s. Jeffords gives a sensible account of the changing male lead in films ranging from *Kindergarten Cop* to *Terminator 2*.

4. In Disney criticism, the phrase "New Man" seems to belong to Susan Jeffords's 1995 essay on *Beauty and the Beast*, but it is slowly coming into vogue for describing other postfeminist trends in masculine identity. In popular culture, see Richard Collier's "The New Man: Fact or Fad?" online in *Achilles Heel: The Radical Men's Magazine* 14 (Winter 1992/1993). http://www.achillesheel.freeuk.com/article14_9.html. For a literary-historical account, see *Writing Men: Literary Masculinities from Frankenstein to the New Man* by Berthold Schoene-Harwood (Columbia UP, 2000).

5. Critics have described the superhero within some framework of queer theory since the 1950s, when Dr. Fredric Wertham's *Seduction of the Innocent* claimed that Batman and Robin were gay (Ameron Ltd, 1954). See Rob Lendrum's "Queering Super-Manhood: Superhero Masculinity, Camp, and Public Relations as a Textual Framework" (*International Journal of Comic Art* 7.1 [2005]: 287–303) and Valerie Palmer-Mehtan and Kellie Hay's "A Superhero for Gays? Gay Masculinity and Green Lantern" (*Journal of American Culture* 28.4 [2005]: 390–404), among myriad nonscholarly pop-cultural sources.

6. Interestingly, Andy and *Toy Story* in general are apparently without (human) male role models. The only father present in the film at all is Sid's, sleeping in front of the television in the middle of the day. Andy's is absent at a dinner out, during a move, and on the following Christmas morning. Andy himself, at play, imagines splintering a nuclear family: when he makes Sheriff Woody catch One-Eyed Black Bart in a criminal act, he says, "Say goodbye to the wife and tater tots . . . you're going to jail."

WORKS CITED

Bell, Elizabeth. "Somatexts at the Disney Shop: Constructing the Pentimentos of Women's Animated Bodies." Bell, *From Mouse to Mermaid* 107–24.

Bell, Elizabeth, Lynda Haas, and Laura Sells, eds. *From Mouse to Mermaid: the Politics of Film, Gender, and Culture.* Bloomington: Indiana UP, 1995.

Card, Claudia. "Pinocchio." Bell, *From Mouse to Mermaid* 62–71.

Cars. Dir. John Lasseter. Walt Disney Pictures/Pixar Animation Studios, 2006.

Collier, Richard. "The New Man: Fact or Fad?" *Achilles Heel: The Radical Men's Magazine* 14 (1992–93). <http://www.achillesheel.freeuk.com/article14_9.html>.

Eisner, Michael. "Planetized Entertainment." *New Perspectives Quarterly* 12.4 (1995): 8.

Giroux, Henry. *The Mouse that Roared: Disney and the End of Innocence*. Oxford, Eng.: Rowman, 1999.

The Incredibles. Dir. Brad Bird. Walt Disney Pictures/Pixar Animation Studios, 2004.

Jeffords, Susan. "The Curse of Masculinity: Disney's *Beauty and the Beast*." Bell, *From Mouse to Mermaid* 161–72.

Lendrum, Rob. "Queering Super-Manhood: Superhero Masculinity, Camp, and Public Relations as a Textual Framework." *International Journal of Comic Art* 7.1 (2005): 287–303.

Palmer-Mehtan, Valerie, and Kellie Hay. "A Superhero for Gays? Gay Masculinity and Green Lantern." *Journal of American Culture* 28.4 (2005): 390–404.

Payne, David. "Bambi." Bell, *From Mouse to Mermaid* 137–47.

Schoene-Harwood, Berthold. *Writing Men: Literary Masculinities from Frankenstein to the New Man*. Columbia: Columbia UP, 2000.

Sedgwick, Eve Kosofsky. *Between Men: English Literature and Male Homosocial Desire*. New York: Columbia UP, 1985.

Toy Story. Dir. John Lasseter. Walt Disney Pictures/Pixar Animation Studios, 1995.

Wertham, Fredric. *Seduction of the Innocent*. New York: Reinhart, 1954.

Yabroff, Jennie. "Betas Rule." *Newsweek* 4 June 2007: 64–65.

THE MALE CONSUMER AS LOSER: BEER AND LIQUOR ADS IN MEGA SPORTS MEDIA EVENTS

Michael A. Messner   Jeffrey Montez de Oca

The historical development of modern men's sport has been closely intertwined with the consumption of alcohol and with the financial promotion and sponsorship provided by beer and liquor producers and distributors, as well as pubs and bars (Collins and Vamplew 2002). The beer and liquor industry plays a key economic role in commercialized college and professional sports (Zimbalist 1999; Sperber 2000). Liquor industry advertisements heavily influence the images of masculinity promoted in sports broadcasts and magazines (Wenner 1991). Alcohol consumption is also often a key aspect of the more dangerous and violent dynamics at the heart of male sport cultures (Curry 2000; Sabo, Gray, and Moore 2000). By itself, alcohol does not "cause" men's violence against women or against other men; however, it is commonly one of a cluster of factors that facilitate violence (Koss and Gaines 1993; Leichliter et al. 1998). In short, beer and liquor are central players in "a high holy trinity of alcohol, sports, and hegemonic masculinity" (Wenner 1998).

GENDER, MEN'S SPORTS, AND ALCOHOL ADS

Although marketing beer and liquor to men is not new, the imagery that advertisers employ to pitch their product is not static either. Our analysis of past

Super Bowls and *Sports Illustrated* beer and liquor ads suggests shifting patterns in the gender themes encoded in the ads.

Ads from the late 1950s through the late 1960s commonly depicted young or middle-aged white heterosexual couples happily sharing a cold beer in their suburban backyards, in their homes, or in an outdoor space like a park.

In these ads, the beer is commonly displayed in a clear glass, its clean, fresh appearance perhaps intended to counter the reputation of beer as a working-class male drink. Beer in these ads symbolically unites the prosperous and happy postwar middle-class couple. By the mid-1970s, women as wives and partners largely disappeared from beer ads. Instead of showing heterosexual couples drinking in their homes or backyards, these ads began primarily to depict images of men drinking with other men in public spaces. Three studies of beer commercials of the 1970s and 1980s found that most ads pitched beer to men as a pleasurable reward for a hard day's work. These ads told men that "For all you do, this Bud's for you." Women were rarely depicted in these ads, except as occasional background props in male-dominated bars (Postman et al. 1987; Wenner 1991; Strate 1992).

The 1950s and 1960s beer ads that depicted happy married suburban couples were part of a moment in gender relations tied to postwar culture and Fordist relations of production. White, middle-class, heterosexual masculinity was defined as synonymous with the male breadwinner, in symmetrical relation to a conception of femininity grounded in the image of the suburban housewife. In the 1970s and early 1980s, the focus on men's laboring bodies, tethered to their public leisure with other men, expressed an almost atavistic view of hegemonic masculinity at a time when women were moving into public life in huge numbers and blue-collar men's jobs were being eliminated by the tens of thousands.

Both the postwar and the postindustrial ads provide a gendered pedagogy for living a masculine lifestyle in a shifting context characterized by uncertainty. In contrast to the depiction of happy white families comfortably living lives of suburban bliss, the postwar era was characterized by anxieties over the possibility of a postwar depression, nuclear annihilation, suburban social dislocation, and disorder from racial and class movements for social justice (Lipsitz 1981; May 1988; Spigel 1992). Similarly, the 1970s and 1980s beer ads came in the wake of the defeat of the United States in the Vietnam War, the 1972 gas crisis, and the turbulence in gender relations brought on by the women's and gay/lesbian liberation movements.

The 2002 and 2003 ads that we examine here primarily construct a white male "loser" whose life is apparently separate from paid labor. He hangs out with his male buddies, is self-mocking and ironic about his loser status, and is always at the ready to engage in voyeurism with sexy fantasy women but holds committed relationships and emotional honesty with real women in disdain. To the extent that these themes find resonance with young men of today, it is likely because they speak to basic insecurities that are grounded in a combination of historic shifts: deindustrialization, the declining real value of wages and the male breadwinner role, significant cultural shifts brought about by more than three decades of struggle by feminists and sexual minorities, and challenges to white male supremacy by people of color and by immigrants. This cluster of social changes has destabilized hegemonic masculinity and defines the context of gender relations in which today's young men have grown toward adulthood.

TWO MEGA SPORTS MEDIA EVENTS

This article examines the gender and sexual imagery encoded in two mega sports media events: the 2002 and 2003 Super Bowls and the 2002 and 2003 *Sports Illustrated* swimsuit issues.

Mega sports media events are mediated cultural rituals (Dayan and Katz 1988) that differ from everyday sports media events in several key ways: sports media actively build audience anticipation and excitement throughout the year for these single events; the Super Bowl and the swimsuit issue are each preceded by major pre-event promotion and hype—from the television network that will broadcast the Super Bowl to *Sports Illustrated* and myriad other print and electronic media; the Super Bowl and the swimsuit issue are used as marketing tools for selling the more general products of National Football League (NFL) games and *Sports Illustrated* magazine subscriptions; the Super Bowl and the swimsuit issue each generate significant spin-off products (e.g., videos, books, "making of" TV shows, calendars, frequently visited Web pages); the Super Bowl and the swimsuit issue generate significantly larger audiences than does a weekly NFL game or a weekly edition of *Sports Illustrated*; and advertisements are usually created specifically for these mega sports media events and cost more to run than do ads in a weekly NFL game or a weekly edition of *Sports Illustrated*.

SUPER BOWL ADS

Since its relatively modest start in 1967, the NFL Super Bowl has mushroomed into one of the most expensive and most watched annual media events in the United States, with a growing world audience (Martin and Reeves 2001), the vast majority of whom are boys and men. Increasingly over the past decade, Super Bowl commercials have been specially created for the event Newspapers, magazines, television news shows, and Web sites now routinely run pre–Super Bowl stories that focus specifically on the ads, and several media outlets run post–Super Bowl polls to determine which ads were the most and least favorite. Postgame lists of "winners" and "losers" focus as much on the corporate sponsors and their ads as on the two teams that— incidentally?—played a football game between the commercials.

Fifty-five commercials ran during the 2003 Super Bowl (not counting pregame and postgame shows), at an average cost of $2.1 million for each thirty-second ad. Fifteen of these commercials were beer or malt liquor ads. Twelve of these ads were run by Anheuser-Busch, whose ownership of this Super Bowl was underlined at least twenty times throughout the broadcast, when, after commercial breaks, the camera lingered on the stadium scoreboard, atop which was a huge Budweiser sign. This represented a slight increase in beer advertising since the 2002 Super Bowl, which featured thirteen beer or malt liquor commercials (eleven of them by Anheuser-Busch), at an average cost of $1.9 million per thirty-second ad. In addition to the approximately $31.5 million that the beer companies paid for the 2003 Super Bowl ad slots, they paid millions more creating and testing those commercials with focus groups. There were 137.7 million viewers watching all or part of the 2003 Super Bowl on ABC, and by far the largest demographic group watching was men, aged twenty-five to fifty-five.

SPORTS ILLUSTRATED SWIMSUIT ISSUE ADS

Sports Illustrated began in 1964 to publish an annual February issue that featured five or six pages of women modeling swimsuits, embedded in an otherwise normal sixty-four-page magazine (Davis 1997). This modest format continued until the late 1970s, when the portion of the magazine featuring swimsuit models began gradually to grow. In the 1980s, the swimsuit issue morphed into a special issue in which normal sports coverage gradually disappeared. During this decade, the issue's average length had grown to 173 pages, 20 percent of which were focused on swimsuit models. By the 1990s the swimsuit issue averaged 207 pages in length, 31 percent of which featured swimsuit

models. The magazine has continued to grow in recent years. The 2003 issue was 218 pages in length, 59 percent of which featured swimsuit models. The dramatic growth in the size of the swimsuit issue in the 1990s, as well as the dropping of pretence that the swimsuit issue had anything to do with normal "sports journalism," were facilitated by advertising that began cleverly to echo and spoof the often highly sexualized swimsuit imagery in the magazine. By 2000, it was more the rule than the exception when an ad in some way utilized the swimsuit theme. The gender and sexual themes of the swimsuit issue became increasingly seamless, as ads and *Sports Illustrated* text symbiotically echoed and played off of each other. The 2002 swimsuit issue included seven pages of beer ads and seven pages of liquor ads, which cost approximately $230,000 per full page to run. The 2003 swimsuit issue ran the equivalent of sixteen pages of beer ads and thirteen pages of liquor ads. The ad space for the 2003 swimsuit issue sold for $266,000 per full-page color ad.

The millions of dollars that beer and liquor companies spent to develop and buy space for these ads were aimed at the central group that reads the magazine: young and middle-aged males. *Sports Illustrated* estimates the audience size of its weekly magazine at 21.3 million readers, roughly 76 percent of whom are males. Nearly half of the male audience is in the coveted eighteen- to thirty-four-year-old demographic group, and three quarters of the male. *Sports Illustrated* audience is between the ages of eighteen and forty-nine. A much larger number of single-copy sales gives the swimsuit issue a much larger audience, conservatively estimated at more than 30 million readers.[1]

The Super Bowl and the *Sports Illustrated* swimsuit issue are arguably the biggest single electronic and print sports [media] events annually in the United States. Due to their centrality, size, and target audiences, we suggest that mega sports media events such as the Super Bowl and the swimsuit issue offer a magnified view of the dominant gender and sexual imagery emanating from the center of the sports-media-commercial complex.

LOSERS AND BUDDIES, HOTTIES AND BITCHES

In the 2002 and 2003 beer and liquor ads that we examined, men's work worlds seem mostly to have disappeared. These ads are less about drinking and leisure as a reward for hard work and more about leisure as a lifestyle in and of itself. Men do not work in these ads; they recreate. And women are definitely back in the picture, but not as wives who are partners in building the good domestic life. It is these relations among men as well as relations between men and women that form the four dominant gender themes in the ads we examined. We will introduce these four themes by describing a 2003 Super Bowl commercial for Bud Lite beer.

Two young, somewhat nerdy-looking white guys are at a yoga class, sitting in the back of a room full of sexy young women. The two men have attached prosthetic legs to their bodies so that they can fake the yoga moves. With their bottles of Bud Lite close by, these voyeurs watch in delight as the female yoga teacher instructs the class to "relax and release that negative energy . . . inhale, arch, *thrust* your pelvis to the sky and exhale, *release* into the stretch." As the instructor uses her hands to push down on a woman's upright spread-eagled legs and says "focus, focus, focus," the camera (serving as prosthesis for male spectators at home) cuts back and forth between close-ups of the women's breasts and bottoms, while the two guys gleefully enjoy their beer and their sexual voyeurism. In the final scene the two guys are standing outside the front door of the yoga class, beer bottles in hand, and someone throws their fake legs out the door at them. As they duck to avoid being hit by the legs, one of them comments, "*She's* not very relaxed."

We begin with this ad because it contains, in various degrees, the four dominant gender themes that we found in the mega sports media events ads:

1. Losers: Men are often portrayed as chumps, losers. Masculinity—especially for the lone man—is precarious. Individual men are always on the cusp of being publicly humiliated, either by their own stupidity, by other men, or, worse, by a beautiful woman.
2. Buddies: The precariousness of individual men's masculine status is offset by the safety of the male group. The solidity and primacy—and emotional safety—of male friendships are the emotional center of many of these ads.
3. Hotties: When women appear in these ads, it is usually as highly sexualized fantasy objects. These beautiful women serve as potential prizes for men's victories and proper consumption choices. They sometimes serve to validate men's masculinity, but their validating power also holds the potential to humiliate male losers.
4. Bitches: Wives, girlfriends, or other women to whom men are emotionally committed are mostly absent from these ads. However, when they do appear, it is primarily as emotional or sexual blackmailers who threaten to undermine individual men's freedom to enjoy the erotic pleasure at the center of the male group.

To a great extent, these four gender themes are intertwined in the Super Bowl "Yoga Voyeurs" ad. First, the two guys are clearly not good-looking, high-status, muscular icons of masculinity. More likely they are intended to represent the "everyman" with whom many boys and men can identify. Their masquerade as sensitive men allows them to transgress the female space of the yoga class, but they cannot pull the masquerade off and are eventually "outed" as losers and rejected by the sexy women. But even if they realize that they are losers, they do not have to care because they are so happy and secure in their bond with each other. Their friendship bond is cemented in frat-boy-style hijinks that allow them to share close-up voyeurism of sexy women who, we can safely assume, are way out of these men's league. In the end, the women reject the guys as pathetic losers. But the guys do not seem too upset. They have each other and, of course, they have their beers.

Rarely did a single ad in our study contain all four of these themes. But taken together, the ads show enough consistency that we can think of these themes as intertwined threads that together make up the ideological fabric at the center of mega sports media events. Next, we will illustrate how these themes are played out in the 2002 and 2003 ads, before discussing some of the strains and tensions in the ads.

REAL FRIENDS, SCARY WOMEN

Five twenty-something white guys are sitting around a kitchen table playing poker. They are laughing, seemingly having the time of their lives, drinking Jim Beam whiskey. The caption for this ad reflects the lighthearted, youthful mood of the group: "Good Bourbon, ice cubes, and whichever glasses are clean." This ad, which appeared in the 2002 *Sports Illustrated* swimsuit issue, is one in a series of Jim Beam ads that have run for the past few years in *Sports Illustrated* and in other magazines aimed at young men.[2] Running under the umbrella slogan of "Real Friends, Real Bourbon," these Jim Beam ads hail a white, college-age (or young college-educated) crowd of men with the appeal of playful male bonding through alcohol consumption in bars or pool halls. The main theme is the safety and primacy of the male group, but the accompanying written text sometimes suggests the presence of women. In one ad, four young white guys partying up a storm together and posing with arms intertwined are accompanied by the caption, "Unlike your girlfriend, they never ask where this relationship is going." These ads imply that women demand levels of emotional commitment and expression undesirable to men, while life with the boys (and the booze) is exciting, emotionally comfortable, and safe. The comfort that these ads suggest is that bonding and intimacy have clear (though mostly unspoken) boundaries that limit emotional expression in the male group. When drinking with the guys, a man can feel close to his friends, perhaps even drape an arm over a friend's shoulder, embrace him, or tell him that he loves him. But the context of alcohol consumption provides an escape hatch that contains and rationalizes the eruption of physical intimacy.

Although emotional closeness with and commitment to real women apparently are to be avoided, these ads also do suggest a role for women. The one ad in the Jim Beam series that includes an image of a woman depicts only a body part (*Sports Illustrated* ran this one in its 2000 swimsuit issue in 3-D). Four guys drinking together in a bar are foregrounded by a set of high-heeled legs that appear to be an exotic dancer's. The guys drink, laugh, and seem thoroughly amused with each other. "Our lives would make a great sitcom," the caption reads, and continues, "of course, it would have to run on cable." That the guys largely ignore the dancer affirms the strength and primacy of their bond with one another—they do not need her or any other women, the ad seems to say. On the other hand—and just as in the "Yoga Voyeurs" commercial—the female dancer's sexualizing of the chronotopic space affirms that the bond between the men is safely within the bounds of heterosexuality.

Although these ads advocate keeping one's emotional distance from women, a commitment to heterosexuality always carries the potential for developing actual relationships with women. The few ads that depict real women portray them consistently as signs of danger to individual men and to the male group. The ads imply that what men really want is sex (or at least titillation), a cold beer, and some laughs with the guys. Girlfriends and wives are undesirable because they push men to talk about feelings and demonstrate commitment to a relationship. In "Good Listener," a 2003 Super Bowl ad for Budweiser, a young white guy is sitting in a sports bar with his girlfriend while she complains about her best friend's "totally self-centered and insensitive boyfriend." As he appears to listen to this obviously boring "girl talk," the camera pulls to a tight close-up on her face. She is reasonably attractive, but the viewer is not supposed to mistake her for one of the model-perfect fantasy women in other beer ads. The close-up reveals that her teeth are a bit crooked, her hair a bit stringy, and her face contorts as she says of her girlfriend that "she has these *emotional* needs he can't meet." Repelled, the guy spaces out and begins to peer over her shoulder at the television. The camera takes the guy's point of view and focuses on the football game while the speaking woman is in the fuzzy margins of his view. The girlfriend's monologue gets transposed by a football announcer describing an exciting run. She stops talking, and just in time his gaze shifts back to her eyes. She lovingly says, "You're such a great listener." With an "aw-shucks" smile, he says "thanks," and the "Budweiser TRUE" logo appears on the screen. These ads suggest that a sincere face and a bottle of beer allow a guy to escape the emotional needs of his partner while retaining regular access to sex. But the apparent dangers of love, long-term commitment, and marriage remain. The most overtly misogynist ad in the 2003 Super Bowl broadcast was "Sarah's Mom." While talking on the phone to a friend, a young, somewhat nerdy-looking white guy prepares to meet his girlfriend's mother for the first time. His friend offers him this stern advice: "Well, get a good look at her. 'Cause in twenty years, that's what Sarah's gonna look like." The nerd expresses surprised concern, just as there is a knock on the door. Viewed through the door's peephole, the face of Sarah's mother appears as young and beautiful as Sarah's, but it turns out that Sarah's mother has grotesquely large hips, thighs, and buttocks. The commercial ends with the screen filled mostly with the hugeness of the mother's bottom, her leather pants audibly stretching as she bends to pet the dog, and Sarah shoveling chips and dip into her mouth, as she says of her mother, "Isn't she incredible?" The guy replies, with obvious skepticism, "yeah."

The message to boys and men is disturbing. If you are nerdy enough to be thinking about getting married, then you should listen to your male friends' warnings about what to watch out for and what is important. If you have got to have a wife, make sure that she is, and always will be, conventionally thin and beautiful.

In beer ads, the male group defines men's need for women as sexual, not emotional, and in so doing it constructs women as either whores or bitches and then suggests ways for men to negotiate the tension between these two narrow and stereotypical categories of women. This, we think, is a key point of tension that beer and liquor companies are attempting to exploit to their advantage. They do so by creating a curious shift away from the familiar "madonna-whore" dichotomy of which Western feminists have been so critical, where wives/mothers/girlfriends are put on a pedestal and the women one has sex with are put in the gutter. The alcohol industry would apparently prefer that young men not think of women as madonnas. After all, wives and girlfriends to whom men are committed, whom they respect and love, often do place limits on men's time spent out with the boys, as well as limits on men's consumption of alcohol. The industry seems to know this: as long as men remain distrustful of women, seeing them either as bitches who are trying to ensnare them and take away their freedom or as whores with whom they can party and have sex with no emotional commitment attached, then men remain more open to the marketing strategies of the industry.

WINNERS AND LOSERS

In the 2002 and 2003 Super Bowls, Budweiser's "How Ya Doin'?" ads featured the trope of a country bumpkin, or hick, in the big city to highlight the rejection of men who transgress the symbolic boundaries of the male peer group. These ads also illustrate the communication and emotional processes that police these boundaries. Men may ask each other "how's it goin'," but they do not want to hear how it's *really* goin'. It is these unspoken limits that make the group bond feel like an emotionally safe place: male buddies at the bar will not ask each other how the relationship is going or push each other to get in touch with their feminine sides. But men who transgress these boundaries, who do not understand the unwritten emotional rules of the male group, are suspect, are branded as losers, and are banished from the inner circle of the group.

REVENGE OF THE REGULAR GUYS

If losers are used in some of these ads to clarify the bounds of masculine normality, this is not to say that hypermasculine men are set up as the norm. To the contrary, overly masculine men, muscle men, and men with big cars who flash their money around are often portrayed as the real losers, against whom regular guys can sometimes turn the tables and win the beautiful women. In the ads we examined, however, this "regular guy wins beautiful fantasy woman" outcome was very rare. Instead, when the regular guy does manage to get the beautiful fantasy woman's attention, it is usually not in the way that he imagined or dreamed. A loser may want to win the attention of—and have sex with—beautiful women. But ultimately, these women are unavailable to a loser; worse, they will publicly humiliate him if he tries to win their attention. But losers can always manage to have another beer.

If white-guy losers risk punishment or humiliation from beautiful women in these ads, the level of punishment faced by black men can be even more severe. Although nearly all of the television commercials and print ads that we examined depict white people, a very small number do focus centrally on African Americans.[3] In "Pick-Up Lines," a Bud Lite ad that ran during the 2002 Super Bowl, two black males are sitting at a bar next to an attractive black female. Paul, the man in the middle, is obviously a loser; he's wearing a garish shirt, and his hair looks like an Afro gone terribly wrong. He sounds a bit whiny as he confides in his male friend, "I'm just not good with the ladies like you, Cedric." Cedric, playing Cyrano de Bergerac, whispers opening pickup lines to him. The loser turns to the woman and passes on the lines. But just then, the bartender brings another bottle of beer to Cedric, who asks the bartender, "So, how much?" Paul, thinking that this is his next pickup line, says to the woman, "So, how much?" Her smile turns to an angry frown, and she delivers a vicious kick to Paul's face, knocking him to the floor. After we see the Budweiser logo and hear the voice-over telling us that Bud Lite's great taste "will never let you down," we see a stunned

Paul rising to his knees and trying to pull himself up to his bar stool, but the woman knocks him down again with a powerful backhand fist to the face.

This Bud Lite "Pick-Up Lines" ad—one of the very few ads that depict relations between black men and black women—was the only ad in which we saw a man being physically beaten by a woman. Here, the African American woman as object turns to subject, inflicting direct physical punishment on the African American man. The existence of these very few "black ads" brings into relief something that might otherwise remain hidden: most of these ads construct a youthful white masculinity that is playfully self-mocking, always a bit tenuous, but ultimately lovable. The screwups that white-guy losers make are forgivable, and we nearly always see these men, in the end, with at least a cold beer in hand. By contrast, the intersection of race, gender, and class creates cultural and institutional contexts of suspicion and punishment for African American boys and men (Ferguson 2000). In the beer ads this translates into the message that a black man's transgressions are apparently deserving of a kick to the face.

EROTIC INTERTEXTUALITY

One of the dominant strategies in beer and liquor ads is to create an (often humorous) erotic tension among members of a "threesome": the male reader/viewer, a woman depicted as a sexy fantasy object, and a bottle of cold beer. This tension is accomplished through intertextual referencing between the advertising text and the sport text. For instance, on returning to live coverage of the Super Bowl from a commercial break, the camera regularly lingered on the stadium scoreboard, above which was a huge Budweiser sign.

One such occasion during the 2003 Super Bowl was particularly striking. Coors had just run its only commercial (an episode from its successful "Twins" series) during this mega sports media event that seemed otherwise practically owned by Anheuser-Busch. Immediately on return from the commercial break to live action, the handheld field-level camera focused one by one on dancing cheerleaders (once coming so close that it appears that the camera bumped into one of the women's breasts), all the while keeping the Budweiser sign in focus in the background. It was almost as though the producers of the Super Bowl were intent on not allowing the Coors "twins" to upstage Anheuser-Busch's ownership of the event.

Omnipresent advertising images in recent years have continued to obliterate the already blurry distinction between advertising texts and other media texts (Goldman and Papson 1996). This is surely true in the world of sport: players' uniforms, stadium walls, the corner of one's television screen, and even moments within telecasts are regularly branded with the Nike swoosh or some other corporate sign. When ads appropriate or make explicit reference to other media (e.g., other ads, celebrities, movies, television shows, or popular music), they engage in what Robert Goldman and Stephen Papson call "cultural cannibalism" (1998, 10). Audiences are then invited to make the connections between the advertised product and the cultural meanings implied by the cannibalized sign; in so doing, the audience becomes "the final author, whose participation is essential" (O'Donohoe 1997, 259). As with all textual analyses that do not include an audience study, we must be cautious in inferring how differently situated audiences might variously take up, and draw meanings from, these ads. However, we suspect that experiences of "authorship" in the process of decoding and drawing intertextual connections are a major part of the pleasure of viewing mass media texts.

The 2002 and 2003 *Sports Illustrated* swimsuit issues offer vivid examples of texts that invite the reader to draw intertextual connections between erotically charged ads and other non-ad texts. Whereas in the past the *Sports Illustrated* swimsuit issue ran ads that were clearly distinct from the swimsuit text, it has recently become more common for the visual themes in the ads and the swimsuit text to be playfully intertwined, symbiotically referencing each other. A 2003 Heineken ad shows a close-up of two twenty-four-ounce "keg cans" of Heineken beer, side by side. The text above the two cans reads, "They're big. And yeah, they're real." As if the reference to swimsuit models' breast size (and questions about whether some of the models have breast implants) were perhaps too subtle, *Sports Illustrated* juxtaposed the ad with a photo of a swimsuit model, wearing a suit that liberally exposed her breasts.

For the advertisers and for *Sports Illustrated*, the payoff for this kind of intertextual coordination is probably large: for the reader, the text of the swimsuit issue becomes increasingly seamless, as ads and swimsuit text melt into each other, playfully, humorously, and erotically referencing each other. As with the Super Bowl ads, the *Sports Illustrated* swimsuit issue ads become something that viewers learn not to ignore or skip over; instead, the ads become another part of the pleasure of consuming and imagining.

In 2003, Miller Brewing Company and *Sports Illustrated* further developed the symbiotic marketing strategy that they had introduced in 2002. The 2003 swimsuit issue featured a huge Miller Lite ad that included the equivalent of fourteen full pages of ad text. Twelve of these pages were a large, pull-out poster, one side of which was a single photo of "Sophia," a young model wearing a bikini with the Miller Lite logo on the right breast cup. On the opposite side of the poster were four one-page photos and one two-page photo of Sophia posing in various bikinis, with Miller Lite bottles and/or logos visible in each picture. As it did in the 2002 ad, Miller invites viewers to enter a contest to win a trip to the next *Sports Illustrated* swimsuit issue photo shoot. The site of the photo shoot fuses the text-based space of the magazine with the real space of the working models in exotic, erotic landscapes of desire that highlight the sexuality of late capitalist colonialism (Davis 1997). The accompanying text invites the reader to "visit http://www.cnnsi.com" to "check out a 360 degree view of the *Sports Illustrated* swimsuit photo shoot." And the text accompanying most of the photos of Sophia and bottles of Miller Lite teasingly encourages the reader to exercise his consumer power: "So if you had to make a choice, which one would it be?"

This expansive ad evidences a multilevel symbiosis between *Sports Illustrated* and Miller Brewing Company. The playful tease to "choose your favorite" (model, swimsuit, and/or beer) invites the reader to enter another medium—the *Sports Illustrated* swimsuit Web site, which includes access to a *Sports Illustrated* swimsuit photo shoot video sponsored by Miller. The result is a multifaceted media text that stands out as something other than mere advertisement and other than business-as-usual *Sports Illustrated* text. It has an erotic and commercial charge to it that simultaneously teases the reader as a sexual voyeur and hails him as an empowered consumer who can freely choose his own beer and whichever sexy woman he decides is his "favorite."

"LIFE IS HARSH": MALE LOSERS AND ALCOHOLIC ACCOMMODATION

In recent years, the tendency in the *Sports Illustrated* swimsuit issue to position male readers as empowered individuals who can "win" or freely choose the sexy fantasy object of their dreams has begun to shift in other directions. To put it simply, many male readers of the swimsuit issue may find the text erotically charged, but most know that these are two-dimensional images of sexy women who in real life are unavailable to them. In recent years, some swimsuit issue ads have delivered this message directly. In 1997, a two-page ad for Tequila Sauza depicted six women in short red skirts, posing flirtatiously, some of them lifting their blouses provocatively to reveal bare midriffs, or opening their blouses to reveal parts of their breasts. In small letters, across the six women's waists, stretching all the way across the two pages, the text reads, "We can say with 99.9% accuracy that there is no possible way whatsoever in this lifetime that you will ever get a date with one of these women." Then, to the side of the ad is written "LIFE IS HARSH. Your tequila shouldn't be." A similar message appears in other ads. For instance, in the 1999 swimsuit issue, a full-page photo of a Heineken bottle included the written text "The only heiny in this magazine you could actually get your hands on."

These ads play directly to the male reader as loser and invite him to accommodate to his loser status, to recognize that these sexy fantasy women, though "real," are unavailable to him, and to settle for what he can have: a good bottle of Tequila Sauza or a cold (rather than a hot) "Heiny." The Bud Lite Super Bowl commercials strike a similar chord. Many Bud Lite ads either titillate the viewer with sexy fantasy women, point to the ways that relationships with real women are to be avoided, or do both simultaneously. The break that appears near the end of each Bud Lite ad contrasts sharply with the often negative depiction of men's relations with real women in the ad's story line. The viewer sees a close-up of a bottle of Bud Lite. The bottle's cap explodes off, and beer ejaculates out, as a male voice-over proclaims what a man truly can rely on in life: "For the great taste that won't fill you up, and never lets you down . . . make it a Bud Lite."

REVENGE OF THE LOSERS

The accommodation theme in these ads may succeed, momentarily, in encouraging a man to shift his feelings of being a sexual loser toward manly feelings of empowerment through the consumption of brand-name beers and liquor. If the women in the ads are responsible for heightening tensions that result in some men's sense of themselves as losers, one possible outcome beyond simply drinking a large amount of alcohol (or one that accompanies the consumption of alcohol) is to express anger toward women and even to take revenge against them. This is precisely a direction that some of the recent ads have taken.

A full-page ad in the 2002 swimsuit issue showed a large photo of a bottle of Maker's Mark Whiskey. The bottle's reflection on the shiny table on which it sits is distorted in a way that suggests an hourglass-shaped female torso. The text next to the bottle reads, "'Your bourbon has a great body and fine character. I WISH the same could be said for my girlfriend.' D. T., Birmingham, AL." This one-page ad is juxtaposed with a full-page photo of a *Sports Illustrated* model, provocatively using her thumb to begin to pull down the right side of her bikini bottom.

Together, the ad text and *Sports Illustrated* text angrily express the bitch-whore dichotomy that we discussed above. D. T.'s girlfriend is not pictured, but the description of her clearly indicates that not only does she lack a beautiful body; worse, she's a bitch. While D. T.'s girlfriend symbolizes the real woman whom each guy tolerates, and to whom he avoids committing, the juxtaposed *Sports Illustrated* model is the beautiful and sexy fantasy woman. She is unavailable to the male reader in real life; her presence as fantasy image highlights that the reader, like D. T., is stuck, apparently, with his bitchy girlfriend. But at least he can enjoy a moment of pseudo-empowerment by consuming a Maker's Mark whiskey and by insulting his girlfriend's body and character. Together, the Maker's Mark ad and the juxtaposed *Sports Illustrated* model provide a context for the reader to feel hostility toward the real women in his life.

This kind of symbolic male revenge toward women is expressed in a different way in a four-page Captain Morgan rum ad that appeared in the 2003 *Sports Illustrated* swimsuit issue. On the first page, we see only the hands of the cartoon character "Captain Morgan" holding a fire hose spraying water into the air over what appears to be a tropical beach. When one turns the page, a three-page foldout ad reveals that "the Captain" is spraying what appears to be a *Sports Illustrated* swimsuit issue photo shoot. Six young women in tiny bikinis are laughing, perhaps screaming, and running for cover (five of them are huddled under an umbrella with a grinning male character who looks suspiciously like Captain Morgan). The spray from the fire hose causes the women's bathing suits to melt right off their bodies. The readers do not know if the swimsuits are painted on or are made of meltable candy or if perhaps Captain Morgan's ejaculate is just that powerfully corrosive. One way or the other, the image suggests that Captain Morgan is doing a service to the millions of boys and men who read this magazine. Written across a fleeing woman's thigh, below

her melting bikini bottom, the text reads "Can you say birthday suit issue?"

Two men—apparently photographers—stand to the right of the photo, arms raised to the heavens (with their clothing fully intact). The men in the picture seem ecstatic with religious fervor. The male reader is perhaps invited to identify with these regular guys: like them, he is always good enough to look at these beautiful women in their swimsuits but never good enough to get them to take it off for him. But here, "the Captain" was clever enough to strip the women naked so that he and all of his male buddies could enjoy a vengeful moment of voyeurism. The relational gender and sexual dynamics of this ad—presented here without overt anger and with cartoonish humor—allegorize the common dynamics of group sexual assaults (Beneke 1982). These sexy women have teased men enough, the ad suggests. First they arouse men, and then they inevitably make them feel like losers. They deserve to be stripped naked against their will. As in many male rape fantasies, the ad suggests that women ultimately find that they like it. And all of this action is facilitated by a bottle of rum, the Captain's magical essence.

TENSION, STABILIZATION, AND MASCULINE CONSUMPTION

We argued in our introduction that contemporary social changes have destabilized hegemonic masculinity. Examining beer and liquor ads in mega sports media events gives us a window into the ways that commercial forces have seized on these destabilizing tendencies, constructing fantasy narratives that aim to appeal to a very large group—eighteen- to thirty-four-year-old men. They do so by appealing to a broad zeitgeist among young (especially white, heterosexual) men that is grounded in widespread tensions in the contemporary gender order.[4] The sexual and gender themes of the beer and liquor ads that we examine in this article do not stand alone; rather they reflect, and in turn contribute to, broader trends in popular culture and marketing to young white males. Television shows like *The Man Show*, new soft-core porn magazines like *Maxim* and *FHM*, and radio talk shows like the syndicated *Tom Leykus Show* share similar themes and are targeted to similar audiences of young males. Indeed, radio talk show hosts like Leykus didactically instruct young men to avoid "girlie" things, to eschew emotional commitment, and to think of women primarily as sexual partners (Messner 2002, 107–8). These magazines and television and radio shows construct young male lifestyles saturated with sexy images of nearly naked, surgically enhanced women; unabashed and unapologetic sexual voyeurism shared by groups of laughing men; and explicit talk of sexual exploits with "hotties" or "juggies." A range of consumer products that includes—often centrally, as in *The Man Show*—consumption of beer as part of the young male lifestyle stitches together this erotic bonding among men. Meanwhile, real women are either absent from these media or they are disparaged as gold diggers (yes, this term has been resuscitated) who use sex to get men to spend money on them and trick them into marriage. The domesticated man is viewed as a wimpy victim who has subordinated his own pleasures (and surrendered his paychecks) to a woman. Within this framework, a young man should have sex with as many women as he can while avoiding (or at least delaying) emotional commitments to any one woman. Freedom from emotional commitment grants 100 percent control over disposable income for monadic consumption and care of self. And that is ultimately what these shows are about: constructing a young male consumer characterized by personal and emotional freedom who can attain a hip lifestyle by purchasing an ever-expanding range of automobile-related products, snack foods, clothes, toiletries, and, of course, beer and liquor.

At first glance, these new media aimed at young men seem to resuscitate a 1950s "*Playboy* philosophy" of men's consumption, sexuality, and gender relations (Ehrenreich 1983). Indeed, these new media strongly reiterate the dichotomous bitch-whore view of women that was such a linchpin of Hugh Hefner's "philosophy." But today's tropes of masculinity do not simply reiterate the past: rather, they give a postfeminist twist to the *Playboy* philosophy. A half-century ago, Hefner's pitch to men to recapture the indoors by creating (purchasing) one's own erotic "bachelor pad" in which to have sex with women (and then send them home) read as a straightforwardly masculine project. By contrast, today's sexual and gender pitch to young men is delivered with an ironic, self-mocking wink that operates, we think, on two levels. First, it appears to acknowledge that most young men are neither the heroes of the indoors (as Hefner would have it) nor of the outdoors (as the 1970s and 1980s beer ads suggested). Instead, the ads seem to recognize that young white men's unstable status leaves them always on the verge of being revealed as losers. The ads plant seeds of insecurity on this fertile landscape, with the goal of creating a white guy who is a consistent and enthusiastic consumer of alcoholic beverages. The irony works on a second level as well: the throwback sexual and gender imagery—especially the bitch-whore dichotomization of women—is clearly a defensively misogynistic backlash against feminism and women's increasing autonomy and social power. The wink and self-mocking irony allow men to have it both ways: they can engage in humorous misogynist banter and claim simultaneously that it is all in play. They do not take themselves seriously, so anyone who takes their misogyny as anything but boys having good fun just has no sense of humor. The humorous irony works, then, to deflect charges of sexism away from white males, allowing them to define themselves as victims, as members of an endangered species. We suspect, too, that this is a key part of the process that constructs the whiteness in current reconstructions of hegemonic masculinity. As we have suggested, humorous "boys-will-be-boys" misogyny is unlikely to be taken ironically and lightly when delivered by men of color.

Caught between the excesses of a hypermasculinity that is often discredited and caricatured in popular culture and the increasing empowerment of women, people of color, and homosexuals, while simultaneously being undercut by the postindustrial economy, the "Average Joe" is positioned as the ironic, vulnerable but lovable hero of beer and liquor ads. It is striking that the loser is not, or is rarely, your "José Mediano," especially if we understand the construction as a way to unite diverse eighteen- to thirty-four-year-old men. This is to say that the loser motif constructs the universal subject as implicitly white, and as a reaction against challenges to hegemonic masculinity it represents an ongoing possessive investment in whiteness (Lipsitz 1998).

Our analysis suggests that the fact that male viewers today are being hailed as losers and are being asked to identify with—even revel in—their loser status has its limits. The beer and liquor industry dangles images of sexy women in front of men's noses. Indeed, the ads imply that men will go out of their way to put themselves in position to be voyeurs, be it with a TV remote control, at a yoga class, in a bar, or on the *Sports Illustrated*/Miller Beer swimsuit photo shoot Web site. But ultimately, men know (and are increasingly being told in the advertisements themselves) that these sexy women are not available to them. Worse, if men get too close to these women, these women will most likely humiliate them. By contrast, real women—women who are not model-beautiful fantasy objects—are likely to attempt to ensnare men into a commitment, push them to have or express feelings that make them uncomfortable, and limit their freedom to have fun watching sports or playing cards or pool with their friends. So, in the end, men have only the safe haven of their male friends and the bottle.

This individual sense of victimization may feed young men's insecurities while giving them convenient scapegoats on which to project anger at their victim status. The cultural construction of white males as losers, then, is tethered to men's anger at and desire for revenge against women. Indeed, we have observed that revenge-against-women themes are evident in some of the most recent beer and liquor ads. And it is here that our analysis comes full circle. For, as we suggested in the introduction, the cultural imagery in ads aimed at young men does not simply come from images "out there." Instead, this imagery is linked to the ways that real people live their lives. It is the task of future research—including audience research—to investigate and flesh out the specific links between young men's consumption of commercial images, their consumption of beer and liquor, their attitudes toward and relationships with women, and their tendencies to drink and engage in violence against women.

NOTES

1. In addition to *Sports Illustrated*'s 3,137,523 average weekly subscribers, the company's rate card claims 1,467,228 single-copy sales of the swimsuit issue. According to the same multiplier of 6.55 readers per magazine that *Sports Illustrated* uses for estimating the total size of its weekly audience, the swimsuit issue audience is over 30 million. More than likely, the multiplier for the swimsuit issue is higher than that of the weekly magazine, so the swimsuit issue audience is probably much larger than 30 million.

2. Most of the Jim Beam "Real Friends" ads discussed here did not appear in the two *Sports Illustrated* swimsuit issues on which we focus. However, it enhances our understanding of the gender themes in the Jim Beam ads to examine the thematic consistencies in the broader series of Jim Beam "Real Friends" ads.

3. Of the twenty-six beer and malt liquor ads in the two Super Bowls, twenty-four depicted people. Among the twenty-four ads that depicted people, eighteen depicted white people only, three depicted groups that appear to be of mixed race, and three focused on African American main characters. Thirteen of the twenty-four beer and liquor ads in the two *Sports Illustrated* swimsuit issues depicted people: twelve depicted white people only, and one depicted what appears to be the silhouette of an African American couple. No apparent Latino/as or Asian Americans appeared in any of the magazine or television ads.

4. These same beer companies target different ads to other groups of men. Suzanne Danuta Walters (2001) analyzes Budweiser ads, e.g., that are aimed overtly at gay men.

REFERENCES

Beneke, Timothy. 1982. *Men on Rape*. New York: St. Martin's.

Collins, Tony, and Wray Vamplew. 2002. *Mud, Sweat, and Beers: A Cultural History of Sport and Alcohol*. New York: Berg.

Curry, Timothy. 2000. "Booze and Bar Fights: A Journey to the Dark side of College Athletics." In *Masculinities, Gender Relations, and Sport*, ed. Jim McKay, Donald F. Sabo, and Michael A. Messner, 162–75. Thousand Oaks, CA: Sage.

Davis, Laurel L. 1997. *The Swimsuit Issue and Sport: Hegemonic Masculinity in* Sports Illustrated. Albany, NY: SUNY Press.

Dayan, Daniel, and Elihu Katz. 1988. "Articulating Consensus: The Ritual and Rhetoric of Media Events." In *Durkheimian Sociology: Cultural Studies*, ed. Jeffrey C. Alexander, 161–86. Cambridge: Cambridge University Press.

Ehrenreich, Barbara. 1983. *The Hearts of Men: American Dreams and the Flight from Commitment*. New York: Anchor Doubleday.

Ferguson, Ann Arnett. 2000. *Bad Boys: Public Schools in the Making of Black Masculinity*. Ann Arbor: University of Michigan Press.

Goldman, Robert, and Stephen Papson. 1996. *Sign Wars: The Cluttered Landscape of Advertising*. New York: Guilford.

———. 1998. *Nike Culture: The Sign of the Swoosh*. Thousand Oaks, CA: Sage.

Koss, Mary, and John A. Gaines. 1993. "The Prediction of Sexual Aggression by Alcohol Use, Athletic Participation, and Fraternity Affiliation." *Journal of Interpersonal Violence* 8(1):94–108.

Leichliter, Jami S., Philip W. Meilman, Cheryl A. Presley, and Jeffrey R. Cashin. 1998. "Alcohol Use and Related Consequences among Students with Varying Levels of Involvement in College Athletics." *Journal of American College Health* 46(6):257–62.

Lipsitz, George. 1981. *Class and Culture in Cold War America: "A Rainbow at Midnight."* New York: Praeger.

———. 1998. *The Possessive Investment in Whiteness: How White People Profit from Identity Politics*. Philadelphia: Temple University Press.

Martin, Christopher R., and Jimmie L. Reeves. 2001. "The Whole World Isn't Watching (but We Thought They Were): The Super Bowl and U.S. Solipsism." *Culture, Sport, and Society* 4(2):213–54.

May, Elaine Tyler. 1988. *Homeward Bound: American Families in the Cold War Era*. New York: Basic Books.

Messner, Michael A. 2002. *Taking the Field: Women, Men, and Sports*. Minneapolis: University of Minnesota Press.

O'Donohoe, Stephanie. 1997. "Leaky Boundaries Intertextuality and Young Adult Experiences of Advertising." In *Buy This Book Studies in Advertising and Consumption*, ed. Mica Nava, Andrew Blake, Ian McRury, and Barry Richards, 257–75. London: Routledge.

Postman, Neil, Christine Nystrom, Lance Strate, and Charlie Weingartner. 1987. *Myths, Men, and Beer: An Analysis of Beer Commercials on Broadcast Television, 1987*. Washington, DC: AAA Foundation for Traffic Safety.

Sabo, Don, Phil Gray, and Linda Moore. 2000. "Domestic Violence and Televised Athletic Events: 'It's a man thing'." In *Masculinities, Gender Relations, and Sport*, ed. Jim McKay, Don Sabo, and Michael A. Messner, 127–46. Thousand Oaks, CA: Sage.

Sperber, Murray. 2000. *Beer and Circus: How Big-Time College Sports Is Crippling Undergraduate Education*. New York: Henry Holt.

Spigel, Lynn. 1992. *Make Room for TV: Television and the Family Ideal in Postwar America*. Chicago: University of Chicago Press.

Strate, Lance. 1992. "Beer Commercials: A Manual on Masculinity." In *Men, Masculinity, and the Media*, ed. Steve Craig, 78–92. Newbury Park, CA: Sage.

Walters, Suzanna Danuta. 2001. *All the Rage: The Story of Gay Visibility in America*. Chicago: University of Chicago Press.

Wenner, Lawrence A. 1991. "One Part Alcohol, One Part Sport, One Part Dirt, Stir Gently: Beer Commercials and Television Sports." In *Television Criticism Approaches and Applications*, ed. Leah R. Vende Berg and Lawrence A. Wenner, 388–407. New York: Longman.

———. 1998. "In Search of the Sports Bar: Masculinity Alcohol, Sports, and the Mediation of Public Space." In *Sport and Postmodern Times*, ed. Genevieve Rail, 303–32. Albany, NY: SUNY Press.

Zimbalist, Andrew. 1999. *Unpaid Professionals: Commercialism and Conflict in Big-Time College Sports*. Princeton, NJ: Princeton University Press.

PART ELEVEN

VIOLENCE AND MASCULINITIES

Nightly, we watch news reports of suicide bombings in the Middle East, terrorist attacks on the United States, racist hate crimes, gay-bashing murders, or Colombian drug lords and their legions of gun-toting thugs. Do these reports ever mention that virtually every single one of these terrorists, suicide bombers, or racist gang members is male?

This fact is so obvious that it barely needs to be mentioned. Virtually all the violence in the world today is committed by men. Imagine, for a moment, if all that violence were perpetrated entirely by women. Would that not be *the* story?

Take a look at the numbers: Men constitute 99 percent of all persons arrested for rape, 88 percent of those arrested for murder, 92 percent of those arrested for robbery, 87 percent for aggravated assault, 85 percent of other assaults, 83 percent of all family violence, and 82 percent of disorderly conduct. Nearly 90 percent of all murder victims are killed by men.

From early childhood to old age, violence is the most obdurate, intractable behavioral gender difference. The National Academy of Sciences puts the case starkly: "The most consistent pattern with respect to gender is the extent to which male criminal participation in serious crimes at any age greatly exceeds that of females, regardless of source of data, crime type, level of involvement, or measure of participation." "Men are always and everywhere more likely than women to commit criminal acts," write criminologists Michael Gottfredson and Travis Hirschi.[1]

What can we, as a culture, do to understand, let alone prevent the casual equation of masculinity and violence? The articles in this part approach that equation in a variety of arenas. Michael Kaufman's alliterative description of men's violence offers a clever entry into a world that many of us would like to pretend is really about a few "bad" guys and most of us nonviolent "good" guys. Nick Pappas, Partick McKenry, and Beth Catlett look at violence in sports, especially in ice hockey. (Ice hockey is interesting because the rules of the game are so gendered: for men, aggression and fighting are prescribed, but female ice hockey strictly prohibits such behavior.) Tim Beneke describes how ordinary men might justify the use of violence and sexual aggression.

Violence isn't only interpersonal; it is also institutional. Cynthia Enloe's chilling examination of the scandal at Abu Ghraib prison shows how both individual and institutional ideals of masculinity lead to specifically gendered forms of humiliation and torture. Finally, Edward Heisler and Michael Firmin show systematically how college guys are beginning to organize around issues of violence on their campuses.

NOTE

1. National Academy of Sciences, cited in Michael Gottfredson and Travis Hirschi. *A General Theory of Crime* (Stanford: Stanford University Press, 1990), p. 145. See also Steven Barkan, "Why Do Men Commit Almost All Homicides and Assault?" in *Criminology: A Sociological Understanding* (Englewood: Prentice Hall, 1997); Lee Bowker, ed., *Masculinities and Violence* (Thousand Oaks, CA: Sage Publications, 1998).

THE SEVEN P'S OF MEN'S VIOLENCE

Michael Kaufman

For a moment my eyes turned away from the workshop participants and out through the windows of the small conference room and towards the Himalayas, north of Kathmandu. I was there, leading a workshop, largely the outgrowth of remarkable work of UNICEF and UNIFEM which, a year earlier, had brought together women *and* men from throughout South Asia to discuss the problem of violence against women and girls and, most importantly, to work together to find solutions.[1]

As I turned back to the women and men in the group, it felt more familiar than different: women taking enormous chances – in some cases risking their lives – to fight the tide of violence against women and girls. Men who were just beginning to find their anti-patriarchal voices and to discover ways to work alongside women. And what pleasantly surprised me was the positive response to a series of ideas I presented about men's violence: until then, I wasn't entirely sure if they were mainly about the realities in North and South America and Europe – that is largely-Europeanized cultures – or whether they had a larger resonance.

Here, then, is the kernel of this analysis:

PATRIARCHAL POWER: THE FIRST "P"

Individual acts of violence by men occurs within what I have described as "the triad of men's violence." Men's violence against women does not occur in isolation but is linked to men's violence against other men and to the internalization of violence, that is, a man's violence against himself.[2]

Indeed male-dominated societies are not only based on a hierarchy of men over women but some men over other men. Violence or the threat of violence among men is a mechanism used from childhood to establish that pecking order. One result of this is that men "internalize" violence – or perhaps, the demands of patriarchal society encourage biological instincts that otherwise might be more relatively dormant or benign. The result is not only that boys and men learn to selectively use violence, but also, as we shall later see, redirect a range of emotions into rage, which sometimes takes the form of self-directed violence, as seen, for example in substance abuse or self-destructive behaviour.

This triad of men's violence – each form of violence helping create the others – occurs within a nurturing environment of violence: the organization and demands of patriarchal or male dominant societies.

What gives violence its hold as a way of doing business, what has naturalized it as the *de facto* standard of human relations, is the way it has been articulated into our ideologies and social structures. Simply put, human groups create self-perpetuating forms of social organization and ideologies that explain, give meaning to, justify, and replenish these created realities.

Violence is also built into these ideologies and structures for the simpler reason that it has brought enormous benefits to particular groups: first and foremost, violence (or at least the threat of violence), has helped confer on men (as a group) a rich set of privileges and forms of power. If indeed the original forms of social hierarchy and power are those based on sex, then this long ago formed a template for all the structured forms of power and privilege enjoyed by others as a result of social class or skin color, age, religion, sexual orientation, or physical abilities. In such a context, violence or its threat become a means to ensure the continued reaping of privileges and exercise of power. It is both a result and a means to an end.

THE SENSE OF ENTITLEMENT TO PRIVILEGE: THE SECOND "P"

The individual experience of a man who commits violence may not revolve around his desire to maintain power. His conscious experience is not the key here. Rather, as feminist analysis has repeatedly pointed out, such violence is often the logical outcome of his sense of entitlement to certain privileges. If a man beats his wife for not having dinner on the table right on time, it is not only to make sure that it doesn't happen again, but is an indication of his sense of entitlement to be waited on. Or, say a man sexually assaults a woman on a date, it is about his sense of entitlement to his physical pleasure even if that pleasure is entirely one sided. In other words, as many women have pointed out, it is not only inequalities of power that lead to violence, but a conscious or often unconscious sense of entitlement to privilege.

THE THIRD "P": PERMISSION

Whatever the complex social and psychological causes of men's violence, it wouldn't continue if there weren't explicit or tacit permission in social customs, legal codes, law enforcement, and certain religious teachings. In many countries, laws against wife assault or sexual assault are lax or non-existent;

in many others laws are barely enforced; in still others they are absurd, such as those countries where a charge of rape can only be prosecuted if there are several male witnesses and where the testimony of the woman isn't taken into account.

Meanwhile, acts of men's violence and violent aggression (in this case, usually against other men) are celebrated in sport and cinema, in literature and warfare. Not only is violence permitted, it is glamorized and rewarded. The very historic roots of patriarchal societies is the use of violence as a key means of solving disputes and differences, whether among individuals, groups of men, or, later, between nations. I am often reminded of this permission when I hear of a man or women who fails to call the police when they hear a woman neighbour or child being beaten. It is deemed a "private" affair. Can you imagine someone seeing a store being robbed and declining to call the police because it is a private affair between the robber and the store owner?

THE FOURTH "P": THE PARADOX OF MEN'S POWER

It is my contention, however, that such things do not in themselves explain the widespread nature of men's violence, nor the connections between men's violence against women and the many forms of violence among men. Here we need to draw on the paradoxes of men's power or what I have called "men's contradictory experiences of power."[3]

The very ways that men have constructed our social and individual power is, paradoxically, the source of enormous fear, isolation, and pain for men ourselves. If power is constructed as a capacity to dominate and control, if the capacity to act in "powerful" ways requires the construction of a personal suit of armor and a fearful distance from others, if the very world of power and privilege removes us from the world of child-rearing and nurturance, then we are creating men whose own experience of power is fraught with crippling problems.

This is particularly so because the internalized expectations of masculinity are themselves impossible to satisfy or attain. This may well be a problem inherent in patriarchy, but it seems particularly true in an era and in cultures where rigid gender boundaries have been overthrown. Whether it is physical or financial accomplishment, or the suppression of a range of human emotions and needs, the imperatives of manhood (as opposed to the simple certainties of biological maleness), seem to require constant vigilance and work, especially for younger men.

The personal insecurities conferred by a failure to make the masculine grade, or simply, the threat of failure, is enough to propel many men, particularly when they are young, into a vortex of fear, isolation, anger, self-punishment, self-hatred, and aggression. Within such an emotional state, violence becomes a *compensatory mechanism*. It is a way of re-establishing the masculine equilibrium, of asserting to oneself and to others ones masculine credentials. This expression of violence usually includes a choice of a target who is physically weaker or more vulnerable. This may be a child, or a woman, or, as it may be social groups, such as gay men, or a religious or social minority, or immigrants, who seem to pose an easy target for the insecurity and rage of individual men, especially since such groups often haven't received adequate protection under the law. (This compensatory mechanism is clearly indicated, for example, in that most 'gay-bashing' is committed by groups of young men in a period of their life when they experience the greatest insecurity about making the masculine grade.)

What allows violence as an individual compensatory mechanism has been the widespread acceptance of violence as a means of solving differences and asserting power and control. What makes it possible are the power and privileges men have enjoyed, things encoded in beliefs, practices, social structures, and the law.

Men's violence, in its myriad of forms, is therefore the result both of men's power, the sense of entitlement to the privilege, the permission for certain forms of violence, and the fear (or reality) of not having power.

But there is even more.

THE FIFTH "P": THE PSYCHIC ARMOUR OF MANHOOD

Men's violence is also the result of a character structure that is typically based on emotional distance from others. As I and many others have suggested, the psychic structures of manhood are created in early childrearing environments that are often typified by the absence of fathers and adult men – or, at least, by men's emotional distance. In this case, masculinity gets codified by absence and constructed at the level of fantasy. But even in patriarchal cultures where fathers are more present, masculinity is codified as a rejection of the mother and femininity, that is, a rejection of the qualities associated with caregiving and nurturance. As various feminist psychoanalysts have noted, this creates rigid ego barriers, or, in metaphorical terms, a strong suit of armor.

The result of this complex and particular process of psychological development is a dampened ability for empathy (to experience what others are feeling) and an inability to experience other people's needs and feelings as necessarily relating to one's own. Acts of violence against another person are, therefore, possible. How often do we hear a man say he "didn't really hurt" the woman he hit? Yes, he is making excuses, but part of the problem is that he truly may not experience the pain he is causing. How often do we hear a man say, "she wanted to have sex"? Again, he may be making an excuse, but it may well be a reflection of his diminished ability to read and understand the feelings of another.

MASCULINITY AS A PSYCHIC PRESSURE COOKER: THE SIXTH "P"

Many of our dominant forms of masculinity hinge on the internalization of a range of emotions and their redirection into anger. It is not simply that men's language of emotions is often muted or that our emotional antennae and capacity for empathy are somewhat stunted. It is also that a range of natural emotions have been ruled off limits and invalid. While this has a cultural specificity, it is rather typical for boys to learn from an early age to repress feelings of fear and pain.

On the sports field we teach boys to ignore pain. At home we tell boys not to cry and act like men. Some cultures celebrate a stoic manhood. (And, I should stress, boys learn such things for survival: hence it is important we don't blame the individual boy or man for the origins of his current behaviours, even if, at the same time, we hold him responsible for his actions.)

Of course, as humans, we still experience events that cause an emotional response. But the usual mechanisms of emotional response, from actually experiencing an emotion to letting go of the feelings, are short-circuited to varying degrees among many men. But, again for many men, the one emotion that has some validation is anger. The result is that a range of emotions get channeled into anger. While such channeling is not unique to men (nor is it the case for all men), for some men, violent responses to fear, hurt, insecurity, pain, rejection, or belittlement are not uncommon.

This is particularly true where the feeling produced is one of not having power. Such a feeling only heightens masculine insecurities: if manhood [is] about power and control, not being powerful means you are not a man. Again, violence becomes a means to prove otherwise to yourself and others.

THE SEVENTH "P": PAST EXPERIENCES

This all combines with more blatant experiences for some men. Far too many men around the world grew up in households where their mother was beaten by their father. They grew up seeing violent behaviour towards women as the norm, as just the way life is lived. For some men this results in a revulsion towards violence, while in others it produces a learned response. In many cases it is both: men who use violence against women often feel deep self-loathing for themselves and their behaviour.

But the phrase "learned response" is almost too simplistic. Studies have shown that boys and girls who grow up witnessing violence are far more likely to be violent themselves. Such violence may be a way of getting attention; it may be a coping mechanism, a way of externalizing impossible-to-cope-with feelings. Such patterns of behaviour continue beyond

childhood: most men who end up in programs for men who use violence either witnessed abuse against their mother or experienced abuse themselves.

The past experiences of many men also includes the violence they themselves have experienced. In many cultures, while boys may be half as likely to experience sexual abuse than girls, they are twice as likely to experience physical abuse. Again, this produces no one fixed outcome, and, again, such outcomes are not unique to boys. But in some cases these personal experiences instill deep patterns of confusion and frustration, where boys have learned that it is possible to hurt someone you love, where only outbursts of rage can get rid of deeply-imbedded feelings of pain.

And finally, there is the whole reign of petty violence among boys which, as a boy, doesn't seem petty at all. Boys in many cultures grow up with experiences of fighting, bullying, and brutalization. Sheer survival requires, for some, accepting and internalizing violence as a norm of behaviour.

ENDING THE VIOLENCE

This analysis, even presented in such a condensed form, suggests that challenging men's violence requires an articulated response that includes:

- Challenging and dismantling the structures of men's power and privilege, and ending the cultural and social permission for acts of violence. If this is where the violence starts, we can't end it without support by women and men for feminism and the social, political, legal, and cultural reforms and transformations that it suggests.
- The redefinition of masculinity or, really, the dismantling of the psychic and social structures of gender that bring with them such peril. The paradox of patriarchy is the pain, rage, frustration, isolation, and fear among that half of the species for whom relative power and privilege is given. We ignore all this to our peril. In order to successfully reach men, this work must be premised on compassion, love, and respect, combined with a clear challenge to negative masculine norms and their destructive outcomes.

Pro-feminist men doing this work must speak to other men as our brothers, not as aliens who are not as enlightened or worthy as we are.

- Organizing and involving men to work in cooperation with women in reshaping the gender organization of society, in particular, our institutions and relations through which we raise children. This requires much more emphasis on the importance of men as nurturers and caregivers, fully involved in the raising of children in positive ways free of violence.

- Working with men who commit violence in a way that simultaneously challenges their patriarchal assumptions and privileges *and* reaches out to them with respect and compassion. We needn't be sympathetic to what they have done to be empathetic with them and feel horrified by the factors that have led a little boy to grow up to be a man who sometimes does terrible things. Through such respect, these men can actually find the space to challenge themselves and each other. Otherwise the attempt to reach them will only feed into their own insecurities as men for whom violence has been their traditional compensation.

- Explicit educational activities, such as the White Ribbon Campaign, that involve men and boys in challenging themselves and other men to end all forms of violence.[4] This is a positive challenge for men to speak out with our love and compassion for women, boys, girls, and other men.

Toronto, Canada
October 1999

NOTES

1. This workshop was organized by Save the Children (UK). Travel funding was provided by Development Services International of Canada. Discussion of the 1998 Kathmandu workshop is found in Ruth Finney Hayward's book *Breaking the Earthenware Jar* (forthcoming 2000). Ruth was the woman who instigated the Kathmandu meetings.

2. Michael Kaufman, "The Construction of Masculinity and the Triad of Men's Violence," in M. Kaufman, ed. *Beyond Patriarchy: Essays by Men on Pleasure, Power and Change*, Toronto: Oxford University Press, 1985. Reprinted in English in Laura L. O'Toole and Jessica R. Schiffman, *Gender Violence* (New York: NY University Press, 1997) and excerpted in Michael S. Kimmel and Michael A. Messner, *Men's Lives* (New York: Macmillan, 1997); in German in BauSteineMänner, *Kritische Männerforschung* (Berlin: Arument Verlag, 1996); and in Spanish in *Hombres: Poder, Placer, y Cambio* (Santo Domingo: CIPAF, 1989.)

3. Michael Kaufman, *Cracking the Armour: Power, Pain and the Lives of Men* (Toronto: Viking Canada, 1993 and Penguin, 1994) and "Men, Feminism, and Men's Contradictory Experiences of Power," in Harry Brod and Michael Kaufman, eds., *Theorizing Masculinities*, (Thousand Oaks, CA: Sage Publications, 1994), translated into Spanish as "Los hombres, el feminismo y las experiencias contradictorias del poder entre los hombres," in Luz G. Arango el. al. eds., *Genero e identidad. Ensayos sobre lo feminino y lo masculino,* (Bogota: Tercer Mundo, 1995) and in a revised form, as "Las experiences contradictorias del poder entre los hombres," in Teresa Valdes y Jose Olavarria, eds., *Masculinidad/es. Poder y crisis*, Ediciones de las Jujeres No. 23. (Santiago: Isis International and FLACSO-Chile, June 1997).

4. White Ribbon Campaign, 365 Bloor St. East, Suite 203, Toronto, Canada M4W 3L4 1-416-920-6684 FAX: 1-416-920-1678 info@whiteribbon.ca www.whiteribbon.com

My thanks to those with whom I discussed a number of the ideas in this text: Jean Bernard, Ruth Finney Hayward, Dale Hurst, Michael Kimmel, my colleagues in the White Ribbon Campaign, and a woman at Woman's World '99 in Tromso, Norway who didn't give her name but who, during a discussion period of an earlier version of this paper, suggested it was important to explicitly highlight "permission" as one of the "p's". An earlier version of this paper was published in a special issue of the magazine of the International Association for Studies of Men, v.6, n.2 (June 1999) www.ifi.uio.no/~eivindr/iasom).

ATHLETE AGGRESSION ON THE RINK AND OFF THE ICE: ATHLETE VIOLENCE AND AGGRESSION IN HOCKEY AND INTERPERSONAL RELATIONSHIPS

Nick T. Pappas   Patrick C. McKenry   Beth Skilken Catlett

Athletes recently have appeared on television and in news headlines because of their involvement in instances of aggression and violence. Although much of the documented violence takes place in the context of sports competition, not all athlete aggression is restricted to sports opponents. Indeed, the past decade has witnessed documentation of athlete aggression directed toward other males outside the sports arena, as well as aggression directed toward women in both intimate and nonintimate situations. What remains unclear, however, is whether athletic participation—in particular, the violent strategies learned in sport—contributes to the likelihood that athletes will be violent in interpersonal relationships (Coakley 1989; Crosset 1999).

Public concern about the links between sports participation and interpersonal violence has spawned work over the past decade that documents athlete violence, especially in the area of sexual aggression. Specifically, several studies have indicated that college athletes are overrepresented among those who are involved in aggressive and violent sexual behavior on college campuses. In a study of male undergraduates at a large southeastern

university, Boeringer (1996) found that 60 percent of athletes reported at least one instance of using verbal coercion to obtain sexual favors, 28 percent reported using alcohol and drugs to obtain sexual favors, and 15 percent reported using physical force. Moreover, Boeringer found that athletes reported higher percentages than nonathletes in all such categories of aggressive behavior. In a similar vein, Frintner and Rubinson (1993) found that although the population of male athletes at a large midwestern university was less than 2 percent of the male student population, 21 percent of the reported sexual assaults, 18 percent of the attempted sexual assaults, and 14 percent of the cases of sexual abuse were committed by members of sports teams or sports clubs on campus. Berkowitz (1992) similarly reported that in one review of alleged gang rapes by college students since 1980, twenty-two out of twenty-four documented cases were perpetuated by either members of fraternities or intercollegiate athletic teams. And Crosset, Benedict, and McDonald (1995) reviewed police records at twenty colleges and universities as well as the records of offices of judicial affairs and found that male athletes were overrepresented in reports of sexual assault; while athletes accounted for 3 percent of the male student population, they perpetrated 35 percent of the physical battering reports on the college campuses.

Young (1993) argues that the links between sport and interpersonal violence parallel the problems of violence elsewhere in society. In fact, this notion is consistent with research that indicates that violence in one social domain is highly correlated with violence in other domains (Fagan and Browne 1994; National Research Council 1996). Yet it should be noted that while much is known regarding athlete-athlete violence as a part of the sport, there is little empirical validation of athlete violence outside the sports arena (Benedict and Klein 1997; Coakley 1989; Young 2000). Moreover, while initial explorations have theorized a link between athletic participation and interpersonal violence, many studies have found only a weak association between sports violence and outside the sport violence (e.g., Koss and Gaines 1993) and some have found no association at all (Carson, Halteman, and Stacy 1997; Schwartz and Nogrady 1996).

The mixed results of early empirical research highlight the need to clarify the connections between athletic participation and violence. Indeed, researchers such as Boeringer (1996) and Crosset (1999, 2000) note the pressing need to explore the dynamics surrounding athlete violence beyond the sports context, including inquiries into how team members, coaches, and fans promote and defend violent behavior, variations in the experiences of athletes in different sports contexts, and the role of intervening variables that may be more predictive of male violence than athletic participation per se (Crosset 1999; Crowell and Burgess 1996). One intervening variable, alcohol consumption, is worth particular note. As Crosset (1999) argues, missing from current discussions of athletes and violence is any discussion of drinking. This omission is conspicuous in light of the strong association between drinking and sport. Furthermore, alcohol has been strongly implicated in much of the research on violence against women; although alcohol consumption is not necessarily considered a cause of such violence, many scholars theorize that it has a complex role in men's violence.

The need for such exploration is perhaps nowhere more pertinent than in the sport of hockey. In recent years, several incidents in professional hockey have resulted in an intensified concern regarding aggression and violence associated with the sport. For instance, Toronto Maple Leafs' Nick Kyupreos

sustained a severe concussion that led to his early retirement from hockey. In another incident, Vancouver's Donald Brahshear was struck on the head by Boston's Marty McSorley; he missed 20 games because of the injury. Furthermore, several publicized incidents of athlete violence outside the sports context have caused substantial concern, in particular, about the links between male athletic participation and violence against women. One case, for example, involves AHL Wilkes-Barre rookie, Billy Tibbetts, who lost four seasons of hockey due to a jail sentence for raping a 15-year-old girl at a party.

Thus, the purpose of this study is to explore, through in-depth interviews with five former college/professional hockey players, the nature of aggression and violence in their sport and its relationship to violent interpersonal behaviors both inside and outside the sport. Violence is defined as male-to-male physical sport-related violence, male-to-male physical out-of-sport interpersonal violence; and male-to-female physical, sexual, and emotional aggression and abuse.

SOCIALIZATION FOR VIOLENCE

While an instinctive drive and a drive stimulated by frustration may partially explain sports aggression, Terry and Jackson (1985) contend that a powerful socialization process is the primary determinant of sport and sport-related violence. Hargreaves (1986) notes that sports offers an ideal means for males to develop and exhibit traditional masculine qualities including power, strength, and violence while rejecting traditionally ascribed feminine values. Terry and Jackson see sports aggression as behavior learned in a culture that reinforces and models violence. In sport, reinforcement for acts of violence emanate from a variety of sources, which may be grouped under three categories: (1) the immediate reference group of the athlete, especially coaches, teammates, and family; (2) the structure of the sport and the implementation of rules by governing bodies and referees; and (3) the attitude of the fans, media, courts of law, and society in general.

REFERENCE GROUPS

Cultural ideals of sport and of masculinity combine to create a context within which violence in athletics is not only tolerated but encouraged (Messner 1995). Coaches and parents contribute to the legitimacy of sports violence as they argue that sport aggression prepares boys for success as a man in an adult world (Fine 1987). Messner and Sabo (1990) contend that male tolerance of risk and injury in sports is not a socially passive process but rather is one through which violence, injury, and disablement become reframed as masculinizing by society at all levels. Demonstration of these behaviors is thus linked to gender legitimacy.

In a review of biographies of athletes who come to understand the rewards of aggression and violence, Crosset (1999) suggests that these individuals learn from coaches and peers to be violent. Studies of hockey players, in particular, provide prototypic examples of such socializing influences. For instance, Smith (1979b) found that displays of toughness, courage, and willingness to fight are important means of establishing a positive identity among both peers and coaches in hockey. Moreover, Weinstein, Smith, and Wiesenthal (1995) found that players' aggression, demonstrated especially through fistfighting, often produced greater teammate and coach perceptions of player competence than playing or skating skills. In general, players who backed away from fights were often labeled as "chicken" and were viewed as exhibiting signs of personal failure and weak character. These authors suggest that players will often participate in hockey fights and violence to avoid demeaning labels, which are not easily removed.

Key concepts from West and Zimmerman's (1987) classic work on "doing gender" provide an apt interpretive framework for understanding the impact of hockey culture on athletes' displays of violence and aggression. Under this view, violent behavior can be seen as a way of constructing oneself as masculine and demonstrating one's place in the masculinity hierarchy (Connell 1995). Violence and aggression may be displayed as a way to meet the gender expectations of the peer group as well as the hegemonic notions of masculinity more broadly (Coakley 1989, Levinson 1989).

Furthermore, Crosset (1999) argues that training for sport in the context of an already patriarchal society may also be training men to be violent toward women. For example, coaches employ images of antifemininity and castration to chastise players. The descriptive works of Curry (1991, 1998, 2000) found team dynamics that openly express support for violence against women and demonstrate how resistance to these norms is discouraged. Indeed, teammates in many contact sports clearly reinforce and model sexist behaviors, focusing on sex, aggression, and negative attitudes toward women (Curry 1991).

STRUCTURE OF THE SPORT AND IMPLEMENTATION OF THE RULES

Many athletes are presented with a conflict inherent to competitive sports—that is, they are presented with the apparent dilemma of having to win at all costs and yet, at the same time, to adhere to moral and ethical sport behavior. Young (1993) reflected this conflict when he compared professional sports to a hazardous and violent workplace with its own unique form of industrial disease. Male athletes are expected to be tough and to live up to cultural expectations of manliness, which often encourage the use of violence and performance-enhancing drugs such as steroids. Indeed, Messner (1990) contends that violent behaviors are occupational imperatives in contact sports with practical consequences if not performed. Athletes constantly are encouraged to ignore their own pain and at the same time are encouraged to inflict pain on others or they risk being belittled by their coaches and peers.

Smith (1979a) specifically describes the hockey subculture in terms of an occupational culture based on a theme of violence. By age 15, boys are identified by coaches for their ability to mete out and withstand illegal physical coercion—attributes desired by professional hockey teams. The structure of the system compels conformity to prevailing professional standards that include the necessity of employing violence. Weinstein, Smith, and Weisenthal (1995) found even among youth and preprofessional junior hockey teams that there was a strong imperative toward violence. These authors state that fighting and intimidation are essential elements in the tradition and culture of hockey.

From an early age, hockey players undergo a specialized socialization process in the production of a tough fighting unit; players are taught that competence is linked to aggressive play, including penalties (Vaz 1979, 1980; Weinstein, Smith, and Wiesenthal 1995). Toughness and willingness to fight are attributes that impress coaches and management (Smith 1983). Players understand the possibility of violence on the ice, and they know that fighting is advocated as a proactive means for not being easily intimidated and guarding against further aggression. Players also are required to create trouble for opponents and to employ tactics that create anxiety in adversaries (Faulkner 1974; Weinstein, Smith, and Wiesenthal 1995).

ATTITUDES OF THE COMMUNITY AND SOCIETY IN GENERAL

In general, there appears to be widespread support, both institutional and community, for violence associated with sport, both within and outside the sports context. Institutional support for alleged perpetrators of violence outside the sport often blames the victims and fails to hold athletes responsible for their actions. The inability of institutions to hold athletes accountable also extends to the court system (Crosset 1999). In spite of higher rates of violence within sport communities, conviction rates present a striking difference that favors the accused athlete (Benedict and Klein 1997). Benedict and Klein examined arrest and conviction rates for collegiate and professional athletes accused of felony sexual assaults against women and compared these with national crime data to determine differential patterns of treatment in the criminal justice system. In sum, these authors found that of 217 athletes who were initially reported

to police for a felonious sex crime, only 24 percent were successfully prosecuted. The comparison national sample was 54 percent of arrests leading to conviction. In addition, Benedict (1997) found in their 150 case studies of reported violence that athletes were convicted in only 28 cases, mainly through plea-bargaining agreements. Only 10 cases went to trial, and 6 of these resulted in guilty verdicts.

Curry (2000), among others, has focused on the sports bar as a safe haven in the community arena for aggression outside the sport. Curry found that aggression and assault are encouraged by bars' privileging of male athletes—allowing them to drink for free, taking their sides during fights, and giving them an arena in which to operate. Curry describes the striving for status among peers in the bars through drinking, fighting, and public display of sexual activity. Indeed, Curry (1998) contends that these bars were permissive to the point of allowing the male athletes to take advantage of situations where they could prey on the physical inequalities of others.

Fans also play an important role in the reinforcement of violence, in particular within hockey culture. For example, in a national opinion poll, 39 percent of Canadians reported that they like to see fighting at hockey games (Macleans-Goldfarb 1970, cited in Smith 1979a). In a similar vein, Smith (1979b) found that 61 percent of the players he surveyed perceived spectators at these games as approving of fighting.

Based on this overview of the literature and the socialization into a culture of violence theoretical perspective, the following research questions were developed and addressed: (1) In what ways does participation in hockey promote a culture of aggression and violence? and (2) To what extent does hockey aggression and violence affect off-ice behavior, and what factors seem influential?

METHOD

Participants in this study were five former hockey players whose ages ranged between twenty-five and thirty years old with a mean age of twenty-six years. Four of the five athletes consisted of former players that the researcher formerly coached at the collegiate level. Each of the athletes had competed at either the collegiate level, the professional minor league level, or both. Four of the athletes played collegiate hockey, two of the athletes played professionally in the minor leagues, and one player played both college and professional hockey. Three of the five players were Canadian and played Canadian junior hockey before playing collegiate or professional hockey. It is important to note that the style of Canadian junior hockey is fundamentally different from collegiate hockey in that it allows and encourages fighting to a much greater extent than American collegiate hockey. The two American players had competed at either the high school and/or prep school level before playing collegiate hockey.

The first author has a history of extensive involvement in the culture of ice hockey, with a keen understanding of the perspectives of the players, as well as the phenomenon of violence inside and outside the sports arena. This experience has occurred through participation in American and Canadian junior hockey, over five years of professional playing experience in both the minor leagues and in Europe, and coaching at numerous levels, including three years at the men's collegiate level. It is through being deeply involved in the culture of ice hockey as both a player and a coach over the span of twenty years that the first author has a unique, insider knowledge of ice hockey and its associated violence.

In fact, the first author's unique position as a participant observer within the culture of hockey allowed him ready access for recruitment of players to participate in this study. Four of the five informants were players that the first author coached in college, and the fifth was a referral from one of the four former players. Each of these athletes has at least ten years of professional competition and is thought to be fully immersed into the culture of ice hockey. In addition, the researcher has a long personal and professional relationship with the four players he coached.

The primary source of data for this study was in-depth interviews. The interviews can be considered as semistructured because they were guided by a set of predetermined questions with a number of branching questions that were used to facilitate more detail and more focused attention to the study's domains of interest. Probing questions were also used in a spontaneous manner to prompt elaboration and specificity. The questions were derived from previous inquiries into sport violence as well as previous focused discussions with participants in ice hockey regarding the use of violence. Five major questions were asked during the interviews: (1) Describe your overall experience as a player in organized hockey; (2) How do you think contact sports such as hockey promote violence/aggression within the sport itself? (3) Describe any situations of violence/aggression perpetrated by athletes that you have either seen, heard of, or participated in that occurred outside of sports competition; (4) What are some of the ways that you think participation in hockey encourages off-ice aggression? and (5) What are some ways to prevent athlete violence and aggression off-ice? The participants determined the settings for the interviews, which, in four of the five cases were their homes; this helped to ensure privacy and confidentiality.

It is important to note that these participants were asked to (1) discuss their own personal involvement in hockey, both on and off the ice and (2) to comment on their observations of others in the sport and their overall view of violence and aggression associated with the culture of hockey. Because the principal investigator had a strong personal connection to and history with the respondents, and because he wanted to ensure honest and open exploration of sensitive topics such as violence, sexual aggression, and alcohol and drug use, he did not insist that participants specify whether their narrative responses pertained to their own personal experiences or experiences observed of other athletes. Thus, these participants are best considered key informants who inform this in-depth exploration of the culture of violence and aggression among hockey players.

The data analysis began with a verbatim transcription of the audio-recorded interviews. Once this was completed, a qualitative content analysis was conducted by two independent coders. Specifically, coders first identified and subsequently organized themes that emerged from the transcribed text. The interview responses were examined for salient topics covered, patterns, regularities, and differences within and across the cases. Then, initially coded categories were generated from the topics and patterns, and these coding schemes were developed, continuously modified, and redefined through the data collection process and afterwards. Finally, the topics and patterns were placed into conceptually focused analytical themes related to the study's theoretical foundation (Berg 1998; Bogdan and Biklen 1992).

RESULTS

All of the participants' narratives contained detailed accounts of both their own and other athletes' involvement in violence and aggression within the context of sports competition, as well as outside of the competitive arena. These narratives described varied experiences with and observations of aggression perpetrated against teammates, opponents, bystanders, and women. Moreover, each of the participants provided their own subjective insights about the interconnections between hockey and aggression/violence. In this analysis, we first discuss, in an introductory fashion, the participants' accounts of the extent of violence in ice hockey. Next, we review the ways in which hockey socialization and athletes' notions of masculinity combine to create a culture of aggression and violence. We then turn to an examination of two central factors—consumption of alcohol and the objectification of women—that contribute to exporting violence outside the athletic arena.

FREQUENCY OF VIOLENCE

All of the research participants were easily able to identify a number of situations in which they had either participated in violence or they had observed such violence among their friends and teammates. Moreover, these narratives illustrate the way in which such violence and aggression is considered routine in this population. For example, one athlete described his social life in this way:

> It seemed like every time we would go out . . . at someone's house or a bar . . . at least once a weekend, there would probably be a fight . . . if you took a random sample of 20 guys that didn't play sports and went out on a Friday or Saturday, I don't think you would find the frequency in them getting into fights compared to the 20 guys that I hung out with that I played hockey with.

The narrative accounts of two other participants reflected parallel sentiments with respect to the conventions of aggression and violence in this community:

> More things I've seen has been guys hitting other guys—in a bar—get a couple of drinks in some of these guys, and they want to fight everyone as if they're invincible—the worst I've seen is that guys will get a bunch of teeth knocked out or their face beat in—black eyes and brown eyes and all of that . . .

> I mean, I had quite a lot of brawls in the summer—one time, a guy had sold drugs to my younger sister and I confronted the guy, and he brought back a bunch of his friends, and I went after the whole gang of them and . . . I beat them up quite badly . . . they beat me over the head with a fishing bat and they cut me open, but I'd also cut a bunch of them open pretty bad too—and I went to the hospital and they had come after me at the hospital. I was out of town very shortly after that, so that was good.

These players' perspectives align well with extant research that asserts that conformity to a violent sport ethic is common and that this conformity can lead male athletes to see aggression as a natural part of their sport and a natural part of who they are as athletes and men (Young 1993). The question that remains, however, is, Are people who choose to play heavy contact sports more likely than others to see aggression as an appropriate way to deal with life stressors? An answer to this question is embedded within the research participants' reflections on the potential causes of aggressive behavior among hockey players. In particular, several respondents speculated that men with aggressive tendencies may be attracted to the sport of hockey:

> It's the old what-came-first-the-chicken-or-the-egg syndrome—were these guys violent before they played hockey or did they become violent because they played hockey . . . I think that guys I played with . . . had some antisocial behavior and had it before they ever got into hockey, and then you mix the two and you can get yourself into a lot of trouble. . . . I played junior C in Canada, and guys were getting out of jail on weekends to play hockey—you know, get in trouble with the law and all sorts of crazy stuff before they were really ever really involved with the game, and I think the game for them was almost a chance to vent their anger or whatever it was they were dealing with in a way that wouldn't get them thrown [back] into jail . . .
>
> I played against guys that do a lot of fighting in hockey that were just plain whacked—you know, that would sit there across from you before the game, hyperventilating and stuff, some of them I knew that were actually crazy—but . . . with one guy in particular, I knew that he had a chemical imbalance and he just happens to also be a really good hockey player that snaps . . .
>
> I think, from my experiences, with some of these guys who are getting into trouble on the ice have a lot more going on off the ice than you think. The rink becomes the hunting grounds for a lot of these guys, and I don't know all their stories in and out, but troubled guys getting in trouble on the ice as well whether it's family, school, or what. . . . I think it's a place for violence to come out—because it's allowed.

These narratives are somewhat inconsistent with a sports socialization perspective. That is, these informants' speculations that men with pre-existing aggressive tendencies actualize such proclivities within the acceptable context of hockey play is somewhat contrary to an explanation that emphasizes the socialization of the athlete in which violence learning takes place within sport culture. However, the multifaceted interpretations offered by the informants in this study are compatible with

Coakley's (1989) assertion that the origins of this phenomenon are heterogeneous, and that there is no single cause of violence in sport.

HOCKEY SOCIALIZATION AND THE CULTURE OF MASCULINITY

The socialization of hockey differs from socialization for other contact sports because fighting plays a central role in hockey competition. Indeed, according to Gruneau and Whitson (1993), high rates of violence in hockey are to be expected because physical contact affords opportunities for hockey sticks to be defined and used as weapons, and norms within the community celebrate toughness and a willingness to fight, seek retribution, and intimidate opponents. According to the participants in this study, this context promotes a unique set of dynamics that is unlike most other contact sports. Players enhance their value to their team by demonstrating toughness through display of fighting skills; indeed, the ability to fight effectively becomes a coveted trait, operating even as a means to indirectly win games through intimidation of the opposition and targeting of key opposing players. Fighting is seen to be far more important than skating skills to player success (Weinstein, Smith, and Wiesenthal 1995). These concepts can be seen in the following observations of three study participants:

> Hockey definitely promotes violence. . . . I mean, they have a penalty for fighting . . . and just the reasoning behind that is that they say hey, we don't want fighting in the game, but if they didn't want fighting in the game, they wouldn't have a penalty for it—they would just basically kick the person out of the sport . . . and just the nature of the sport . . . how you win a game—you're physically dominant over another person—being bigger, stronger, faster than the person . . . it's just inherent in the nature of the sport . . . that promotes violence . . .
>
> Hockey players or others in a contact sport could be prone to instigate a fight . . . hockey players instigating fights is part of the game . . . instigating a fight can work to your advantage . . . you can get them [opposition] off their game . . . you know . . .

red card

make them push themselves, push their manhood . . . I'm not sure if it [hockey] makes you more prone to violence, but it almost does . . .

Actually, it [fighting] was the thing that was paying my meal ticket so to speak, you know—and you get good at it and you have to do it—or you weren't going to play or they would find somebody else that would do it. I mean, if I was going to make it to the NHL, I was going to have to fight my way there, and it wasn't going to be through some other role on the team, and you have your role on the team.

The narrative data in this study also reflect the pressure that hockey players feel from coaches who are perceived to promote aggression in their players. These athletes' accounts are replete with references to coaches' win-at-all-cost mentality, as well as descriptions of the ethically questionable methods that a number of their former coaches used against their players to motivate them toward aggressive behavior. For example, one player described the way in which a coach used aggression himself as a sort of modeling strategy:

There's pressure from all around. The coaches will use name calling or in some situations use physical—not to hurt, but wrestle you around a bit—if they don't think you are doing your job and being aggressive and taking guys out of the play, that kind of thing. I've been in situations where coaches have used their hand or their stick in certain ways to get you fired up—hand in the back of the head, stick in the balls, you know.

Other coaches may not have engaged in aggressive behavior themselves, but players certainly believed that their coaches had a role in encouraging aggression, perhaps by active promotion or simply tacit acceptance of violent and aggressive behavior. The following narratives serve as prototypic examples:

Your teammates may expect you to watch their back . . . but, generally, it's the coach that will tell you to start with the violence . . . to agitate— sometimes those are elements that the team is

lacking . . . it really is . . . coaches like guys . . . who take a hit . . . most coaches I've played with have not had a problem with sending someone out . . . a heavy person [enforcer] out . . . if they believe that a rival would possibly injure one of his good players . . . it makes sense . . . you've got to keep your scorers to win the game . . .

I've been involved in situations before where people are asked to go and fight [by the coach]. Someone is being dirty on the ice—takes a cheap shot at a smaller guy and basically they [coach] will . . . say, hey, I want you to go fight that guy just because they don't want them to take liberties and try to intimidate . . . so that's a definite influence, and, of course, you are rewarded by the coaches . . .

I smacked a guy in the dressing room one time and the coach asked me why I did it at the next practice. I said he shot his mouth off in front of the whole team and I told him to shut it or I was going to smack him—if I back down in front of the whole team and let him shoot his mouth off, how do you expect these guys to rely on me the next game out there—he [coach] said that's fine.

These quotes are consistent with Crosset's (1999) findings that athletes fully understand that their knowledge of the rewards for being mean are linked to coaching behaviors.

Fan pressures and influences also promote aggression and violence because the reinforcement through cheering and positive comments is extremely appealing to the athletes. Although winning was usually viewed as being most important, the use of aggression and violence could at times be considered an extremely significant secondary aspect in terms of what hockey fans wanted to see. The pressure players felt as a result of spectator comments is described through the following accounts:

The first thing that comes into my head is the cheering every time somebody gets hit into the boards and a fight breaks out everyone stands up and cheers—that kind of thing, and when they see blood. A lot of fans came to see that and they got bored if there wasn't some kind of violence going on. In my personal conversations with them and how they react to the game, it was enough for me to see that they wanted to see that violence thing, and it does promote it—I mean, when the crowd is behind you and cheer when you knock people into the boards—I'm not going to lie, it gets you fired up and wants to make you do more banging of guys into the boards, and lots of times, if it takes that to get the team fired up, then that's what you're going to do. It always helps to get the fans behind you—they definitely have a role in promoting violence in the sport.

Like even at universities or . . . back in the days of juniors . . . basically, if you go out in a fight and beat someone up . . . after the game . . . you'd get recognition for that—fans would come up to you and say, that's a great fight you were in, you really beat the crap out of that guy . . . and, basically, you're getting rewarded for . . . fighting with someone, and people remember that . . . if you're constantly getting rewarded for something you do . . . you're going to do that again and again.

Such findings are consistent with Smith's (1979b) findings that 61 percent of the players perceived spectators at hockey games approved of fighting.

The reinforcement of violent behaviors can be usefully framed with the observations offered by Vaz (1980). He found that violence is virtually non-existent among young boys just starting to play hockey. But as they are influenced by older players and professionals within the hockey community, rough play is encouraged and "under certain conditions, failure to fight is variously sanctioned by coaches and players" (145). This hockey subculture plays itself out against a larger backdrop of conventions of masculinity in contemporary society. For instance, several players discussed the ways in which hockey players are likely to equate manliness with a willingness to engage in violent behavior. Three narratives, in particular, illustrate this inclination:

I think of people that you know and hang out with . . . expect you to be strong, kind of macho, and stick up or you know stick up for yourself . . . someone would never walk up to you and say, hey that was a great move you made walking away from fighting that guy, I mean I probably never heard that in my life but I definitely heard a person

being put down because he backed away from a physical confrontation both on the ice and off the ice . . . you were generally perceived as weak if you didn't go fight . . . it would lower their opinion of you whereas if you went out and fought . . . you were generally seen . . . in higher standards . . . you're a team guy, you're a guy that would stick up for the other players . . . you were tough . . . you're a lot of things that people respected back then . . . I think it's more trying to prove yourself . . . trying to prove your physical dominance . . . to yourself, your coach, your teammates, the fans that you know . . . hey, I might have lost the last fight, but hey, I'm strong enough to win this fight against this guy . . . and trying to make yourself look better in front of . . . especially your teammates . . . your teammates tend to remember a lot of things that I think most of the fans that come will forget . . .

If someone were to try to fight you on the ice and you backed away . . . it would be more perceived as he's weak, he's backed away from a physical confrontation and generally most people don't want to be seen like that . . . so I think there was a lot of pressure to stick up for yourself and I think the same goes over into your social behavior often . . . you're kind of expected to stick up for yourself and people think you should and kind of have the perception that if you are not, you're not as manly.

As this last narrative reflects, embedded within many of these players' narratives is the implicit recognition that the tendency to draw parallels between manliness and violence extends beyond the competitive arena into broader social relations (cf. Coakley 1989). For example, one player described the similarities between problem solving in hockey competition and problem solving in social relationships in this way:

You might have something like guys having problems in school and with their girlfriend or . . . away from home and pressure from not being around his family . . . maybe at an older level, like in juniors, maybe leaving home for the first time, a combination of all those things contributing to maybe a little bit more of a downer attitude—not feeling good about themself—and maybe having to beat someone up to feel better about themself— you get a lot of that with athletes.

As this thematic analysis indicates, hockey socialization and players' ideals of masculinity combine to create a culture of aggression and violence within the sport. Specifically, the socializing influences on which the research participants focused their attention included hockey competition per se, teammates, coaches, and fans. Cultural imagery surrounding masculinity—in particular, ideals of physical dominance, strength, and toughness—joins with these primary hockey influences to create a culture within which violence and aggression are not only tolerated but even encouraged. Moreover, the narrative data in this study demonstrate that the conventions of aggression and violence that typify sports competition apply as well in the nonsports environment. In fact, one player's narrative powerfully illustrates his belief that this link is indeed inevitable:

> They make demands on athletes to be tough because they want to see it, it [aggression] automatically carries over when you see some guy who's huge and charged with beating his wife. It's like, what—so they think this is some sort of surprise, because if you're paying a guy three million dollars a year to knock somebody's block off, do you expect them to turn it off? No way, and you're praising him to be this animal, you know, you want him to be a destructive force on the field but then you want him to be some sort of pussy cat off the field?

In addition to discussing this inherent connection between violence within and outside of sports competition, the athletes discussed two factors that promoted the exportation of violence outside the athletic context: (1) consumption of alcohol and (2) objectification of women.

ALCOHOL CONSUMPTION

Previous research—for example, Gallmeier (1988)—has found that alcohol use is nearly universal among professional hockey players. Its use is apparently related to the extreme pressures of the game, as well as to the desire to suppress or deaden feelings. Likewise, all of the participants in this study discussed the common role of alcohol in the lives of hockey players. Moreover, these athletes associated violence with consumption of alcohol and other substances. For some, alcohol consumption was mentioned merely as a contextual feature in their descriptions of violent episodes. Some of the participants, however, perceived alcohol as a causal agent, explaining that it facilitated the transition of violence from the competitive venue into everyday social interaction. One player explained it in this way:

> It is the major factor of talk and off-ice violence—alcohol and testosterone and after-sport smack talking—you know, I was doing this and I did that and I played great, and when they start drinking, they think that they can do anything . . . it's the major factor in off-ice violence. Alcohol is the thing that leads to fights—in my experience in college, there wasn't one sober, off-ice violence [incident] that I ever witnessed or heard of or anything—never.

Other players may not have identified alcohol as "the major factor" but they certainly described, with great clarity, the role alcohol and drugs often play in creating a context within which athletes can act out their machismo. Two narratives illustrate this phenomenon:

> Alcohol after a game adds a strange element—I think it makes a person more conducive to violence off the ice—definitely—just because beer and muscles . . . you feel a little bit more invincible once you have a six-pack in you . . . that much more macho . . . alcohol is good for socializing, helps you relax, but it can also get people on edge . . . especially more high-strung people . . .

> I think it just adds fuel to the fire—if you've already got a kid who's aggressive by nature and you throw a catalyst in there [alcohol], it just makes everything worse—especially with hockey as there's a lot of drinking that goes on with it—you mix that with guys who are maybe lonely or depressed and you got trouble off the ice—if things are going on on the ice that they may not be happy with and then you're drinking and doing drugs, it makes everything worse—so it's just adding fuel to the fire.

In essence, all these players describe some way that alcohol and drugs act to promote aggression and violence. Indeed, these findings are consistent with previous work in this area. For instance, although alcohol has not been identified as the cause of abuse, it has been associated with violence and is thought to play a complex role in its occurrence; it may impair reasoning and communication, be part of premeditated strategy (Crowell and Burgess 1996), and/or be used to excuse violent behavior (Benedict 1997). Furthermore, the complex relationship between alcohol, violence, and constructions of masculinity that is implicated in the narrative data in this study is mirrored by Messerschmidt (1993), who theorizes that alcohol cannot be separated from demonstrating masculinity as it is often used to decrease communication and increase men's capacity to be violent.

Although the athletes in this study talked about the connection between alcohol and violence rather generally, there is research to indicate that excessive alcohol use within male peer groups contributes to sexual violence against women (Koss and Dinero 1988). In addition, Koss and Gaines (1993) linked alcohol consumption, athletic participation, and violence against women; they found that while athletic participation per se was associated with sexual aggression, alcohol consumption was even more highly correlated with sexual aggression. Thus, this analysis now turns to an examination of the role of hockey players' sexual relationships with women.

OBJECTIFICATION OF WOMEN

Commentaries, theoretical analyses, and empirical studies have begun to focus on whether participation in certain sports is related to misogyny, high rates of physical and sexual assault, and the occurrence of rape and gang rape (Coakley 1998). For instance, Sanday (1990) argues that when men become emotionally bound together in all-male groups that emphasize physical dominance, they often express their sense of togetherness by demeaning women. The narrative data in this study provide support for these assertions. For example, two participants talk extensively about the way in which their peers objectify women:

> I think that date rape is prevalent among the jock culture. There are things that are not violent but they just seem kind of wrong that guys do in terms of how they relate to women—off ice. They treat women like objects—sexual objects. They talk about them as if they aren't there, as if they [the athletes] were in the locker room talking . . . and don't care what they say at all because they think they're still going to have sex or whatever. Things like that machismo group mentality, that locker room mentality, comes out in off-ice behavior . . . treating women really bad . . . like one-nighters or short-term girlfriends or someone they didn't care very much, just as objects or sex partners.

> Locker room talk [is] definitely machismo without doubt, and that carries over when the team is all out you're talking to a girl and all the team's around and they say, what are you going to do to her—and all that stuff. That kind of talk breeds, does breed that kind of certain behavior in the group when men have the group thing going with a not-caring attitude towards women—that kind of carries over when a guy's with a girl—he doesn't care what happens to the girl as long as he is getting what he wants—or getting what the group wants—like, sometimes, I've heard where two guys will have sex with one woman, group sex, or, if she's drunk or passed out or whatever—sometimes, the girl's into it—and that's a rarity—and then you hear about that stuff in the locker room—I mean, it happens, and sometimes they're willing and sometimes they're not—I'm not sure . . . if they're kind a coaxed, you know, 'cause there are more than one male in the room—stuff like that.

From the first author's knowledge of athlete behavior, these players are describing situations that are very common to the male sport culture, and they reflect only a small extent of the actual sexual behaviors that occur. It has been this researcher's experience that objectification of women occurs as a natural outgrowth and continuation of traditional male socialization that begins in early childhood. Such socialization encourages boys and men to see women as inferior and as sexual objects who are supposed to meet the needs of men. The culture of hockey reinforces this objectification because of the focus on traditional male behaviors conducive to sports success and the large amount of time men spend exclusively with other males. These conversations occur frequently as part of the bonding experience.

Moreover, according to the athlete informants in this study, such demeaning attitudes and talk often carry over into actual violent behaviors. One player's account provides an apt illustration:

> A guy back in juniors I played with when he was 16—a tough kid off the farm—cucumber farm—he got his girlfriend pregnant—knocked her up—she was about 15—and while I never saw it—he was actually taken away right out of the rink one night because she went to the cops and told them he had been beating her when she was even pregnant with the kid—so that was probably one of the worst stories I had heard because there was a baby involved.

Two other players also commented on their knowledge of violence against women. Although these athletes do not concede to engaging in violence against women themselves, they discuss it as if it is a somewhat routine occurrence within male hockey cultures:

> Yeah, I remember certain things that had happened. . . . My friends would get abusive with their girlfriends and stuff like that. I definitely know people that have gotten like that—not necessarily hit, but they'd be abusive and kind of push them and things like that, and we'd always stop them.

> I'd heard stories of guys roughing up a girl a bit. Most of it was guys talking about other guys they knew that were in situations like that.

SUMMARY AND CONCLUSIONS

The findings of this study indicate that interpersonal aggression is common in the lives of these hockey players, both on and off the ice. For these hockey professionals, aggressive behaviors were seen as manifestations of existent tendencies as well as products of sport socialization. Future studies should examine personality characteristics and psychological symptoms of particularly aggressive athletes to determine the role of individual factors as opposed to the culture of sport in producing violent behaviors. Increasingly, studies of interpersonal violence are employing biopsychosocial perspectives, noting the relevance of all three domains in predicting violence (e.g., McKenry, Julian, and Gavazzi 1995).

The participants in this study readily explored the ways in which hockey socialization created a context within which violence and aggression are not only tolerated but also encouraged. Much was said about the culture of hockey itself as an instigating mechanism of male violence. Clearly, hockey was viewed as a violent sport and a sports culture that encouraged violent behaviors on the ice, the players, management, and indeed the fans expected and desired it. It was not mindless violence but functional despite some prohibition. Consistent with Weinstein, Smith, and Wiesenthal's (1995) survey of youth and preprofessional junior hockey players, violent behaviors were seen as only mildly penalized and generally viewed as essential for team and individual player success. For example, referees do not intervene in professional hockey fights as long as only two players are involved, and teammates and coaches judge players' competence more on their willingness to engage in violence (especially fist fighting) than playing and skating skills. Messner (1995) notes that men are raised to view the world as competitive and hierarchal, taught to get the job done regardless of the consequences to others—what Balkan (1966) termed "unmitigated agency." Thus, when tasks become more important than people, violence is sometimes a problem-solving mechanism, for example, intentionally hurting an opposing player. Aggression and violence were important components to competitive success, and they were not limited to the ice rink; a united front perpetuating violent behaviors carried over to social situations. In addition, coaches often were negligent, if not somewhat encouraging, of players remaining tough and aggressive off the ice.

A culture of masculinity can be seen to characterize the teams the players described. The athletes tended to share a set of ideological beliefs related to traditional forms of masculine expression, for example, preoccupation with achievement and maintaining status through fighting or risk taking, acquiring an identity of toughness (Weisfeld et al. 1987). Research has found that hockey players with the strongest levels of endorsement of traditional masculine ideologies are more likely to fight than are other players (Weinstein, Smith, and Wiesenthal 1995). Kilmartin (2000) contends that violent behaviors by athletes are motivated by one athlete's perception that another is trying to hurt him. This too was represented in the players' comments regarding the need to be on guard, the necessity to protect oneself from the violence inherent in the game, and the dominance perspective wherein the athlete is constantly battling against teammates and opposition who are motivated toward domination. The culture of masculinity was also seen in the pack mentality that emerged among the players and carried over to off-ice activities. The strong bonds that emerged reinforced aggressive behaviors but also resulted in strong bonds of allegiance and loyalty.

In his examination of sport and violence, Young (2000) asserts that while knowledge of player violence within sport is substantial, little is actually known about other forms of sport-related violence. This in-depth exploration of hockey culture begins to fill this knowledge gap; its unique contribution is a more nuanced understanding of athletes' expressions of aggression and violence outside the sports context. As noted previously, the players in this study viewed aggression in broader social relationships as a logical extension of on-ice violent behavior. This relationship between participation in violence in sport and in other social contexts is consistent with the well-established relationship between and among various types of violent displays consistently found in the literature (Fagan and Browne 1994; Levinson 1989). Moreover, when asked specifically to provide explanations for off-ice violence based on their experiences, many mentioned the role of alcohol specifically, but also

in combination with other factors. The players typically drew a causal relationship between alcohol use and violent behaviors. Alcohol was used to a great extent to self-medicate as a means of handling the stresses associated with the game. Gustafson (1986) contends that alcohol is a societally sanctioned aggressive solution for men to use when frustrated. Also, hockey seems to be a culture that is defined, in part, by the use of alcohol in leisure. Others have noted that drinking is a cultural symbol of masculinity (Lemle and Mishkind 1989). The complex role that alcohol plays in aggression should be explored in greater depth, especially as it interacts with social situations, psychological factors, and other drugs.

The informants in this study also identified athletes' tendency to objectify women as a factor that contributes to the exportation of violence off the ice. Interestingly, the men defined sexual abuse of women broadly to include verbal aggression and general disrespectful behaviors, that is, treatment of women as sexual objects. Some connected sexual aggression or violence to what they termed a locker-room-talk mentality wherein certain male sexual bravado in the peer culture was carried off the ice to their relationships with women. The respondents tended to differentiate between general physical violence and sexual aggression or violence, seeing the latter as less serious and more understandable than general physical violence. In general, the athletes seemed to speak of a culture that had a lesser regard for women.

In general, the findings of this study have illuminated men's subjective experiences as participants in the sport of hockey. As such, they have brought personal insights to bear on our understanding of aggression and violence in sports. Because this was a small-scale intensive study, the voices of a variety of other participants who could have provided more insights into couple violence were excluded, for example, actual male aggressors of women and women victims. The researchers rely on the perspectives of respondents who had a particularly close relationship with the first author; perhaps a larger number of informants who were not acquainted with the researcher would have yielded additional information.

Many questions remain to be addressed. Because violent behaviors first emerge in high school and continue into college play, these would be useful arenas for generating a fuller understanding of the development of violent behaviors in this sport. Other sports have also been associated with violence outside the sport itself, for example, football and basketball; a question emerges as to whether the development of violence is similar for other sports. In addition, as more women enter contact sports, it would be interesting to see if they create a similar sport culture and become more aggressive both in and outside the sport. Factors that have been implicated in domestic violence research in general, for example, masculine identity, family-of-origin issues, male peer group influences, and stress need to be explored in future work on this topic.

REFERENCES

Balkan, D. 1966. *The duality of human existence*. Chicago: Rand McNally.

Benedict, J. R. 1997. *Public heroes, private felons*. Boston: Northeastern University Press.

Benedict, J., and A. Klein. 1997. Arrest and conviction rates for athletes accused of sexual assault. *Sociology of Sport Journal* 14:86–94.

Berg, B. L. 1998. *Qualitative research methods in the social sciences*. Needham Heights, MA: Allyn & Bacon.

Berkowitz, A. 1992. College men as perpetrators of acquaintance rape and sexual assault: A review of recent literature. *Journal of American College Health* 40:157–65.

Boeringer, S. 1996. Influences of fraternity membership, athletics, and male living arrangements on sexual aggression. *Violence Against Women* 2:135–47.

Bogdan, R. C., and S. K. Biklen. 1992. *Qualitative research for education: An introduction to theory and methods*. 2nd ed. Boston: Allyn & Bacon.

Carson, S. K., W. A. Halteman, and G. Stacy. 1997. Athletes and rape: is there a connection? *Perceptual and Motor Skills* 85:1379–83.

Coakley, J. J. 1989. *Sport in society issues and controversies*. Boston: Irwin McGraw-Hill.

Connell, R. W. 1995. *Masculinities*. Los Angeles: University of California Press.

Crosset, T. W. 1999. Male athletes' violence against women: A critical assessment of the athletic affiliation, violence against women debate. *Quest* 51:244–57.

———. 2000. Athletic affiliation and violence against women: toward a structural prevention project. In *Masculinities, gender relations, and sport*, edited by J. McKay, M. A. Messner, and D. Sabo, 147–61. Thousand Oaks, CA: Sage.

Crosset, T. W., J. R. Benedict, and M. M. McDonald. 1995. Male student-athletes reported for sexual assault: A survey of campus. *Journal of Sport and Social Issues* 19:126–40.

Crowell, N., and A. Burgess, eds. 1996. *Understanding violence against women*. Washington, DC: National Academy Press.

Curry, T. J. 1991. Fraternal bonding in the locker room: A profeminist analysis of talk about competition and women. *Sociology of Sport Journal* 8:119–35.

———. 1998. Beyond the locker room: Campus bars and college athletes. *Sociology of Sport Journal* 15:205–15.

———. 2000. Booze and bar fights: A journey to the dark side of college athletics. In *Masculinities, gender relations, and sport*, edited by J. McKay, M. A. Messner, and D. Sabo, 162–75. Thousand Oaks, CA: Sage.

Fagan, J., and A. Browne. 1994. Violence between spouses and intimates: Physical aggression between women and men in intimate relationships. In *Understanding and preventing violence: social influences*, edited by A. J. Reiss, Jr., and J. A. Roth, 115–292. Washington, DC: National Academy Press.

Faulkner, R. 1974. Making violence by doing work, selves, situations and the world of professional hockey. *Sociology of Work and Occupations* 1:288–312.

Fine, G. A. 1987. *With the boys: Little league baseball and preadolescent culture*. Chicago: University of Chicago Press.

Frintner, M. P., and L. Rubinson. 1993. Acquaintance rape: The influence of alcohol, fraternity, and sports team membership. *Journal of Sex Education and Therapy* 19:272–84.

Gallmeier, C. P. 1988. Juicing, burning, and tooting: Observing drug use among professional hockey players. *Arena Review* 12:1–12.

Gruneau, R., and D. Whitson. 1993. *Hockey night in Canada: Sport, identities, and cultural politics*. Toronto, Canada: Garamond.

Gustafson, R. 1986. Threat as a determinant of alcohol-related aggression. *Psychological Reports* 58:287–97.

Hargreaves, J. 1986. Where's the virtue? Where's the grace? A discussion of the social production of gender relations in and through sport. *Theory, Culture, and Society* 3:109–21.

Kilmartin, C. T. 2000. *The masculine self.* Boston: McGraw-Hill.

Koss, M. P., and T. E. Dinero. 1988. Predictors of sexual aggression among a national sample of male college students. *Annals of the New York Academy of Sciences* 528:133–46.

Koss, M. P., and J. A. Gaines. 1993. The prediction of sexual aggression by alcohol use, athletic participation, and fraternity affiliation. *Journal of Interpersonal Violence* 8:94–108.

Lemle, R., and M. E. Mishkind. 1989. Alcohol and masculinity. *Journal of Substance Abuse Treatment* 6:213–22.

Levinson, D. 1989. *Family violence in cross-cultural perspective.* Newbury Park, CA: Sage.

McKenry, P. C., T. W. Julien, and N. Gavazzi. 1995. Toward a biopsychosocial model of domestic violence. *Journal of Marriage and the Family* 57:307–20.

Messerschmidt, J. W. 1993. *Masculinities and crime: Critique and reconceptualization of theory.* Lanham, MD: Rowman & Littlefield.

Messner, M. 1990. When bodies are weapons: Masculine violence in sport. *International Review for the Sociology of Sport* 25:203–21.

———. 1995. Boyhood, organized sports, and the construction of masculinity. In *Men's lives*, edited by M. A. Kimmel and M. S. Messner, 102–14. Boston: Allyn & Bacon.

Messner, M., and D. Sabo. 1990. *Sports, men, and the gender order: Critical feminist perspectives.* Champaign, IL: Human Kinetics.

Miller, M. B., and A. M. Haberman. 1994. *Qualitative data analyses: A new sourcebook of methods.* Newbury Park, CA: Sage.

National Research Council. 1996. *Understanding violence against women.* Washington, DC: National Academy Press.

Sanday, P. 1990. *Fraternity gang rapes: Sex, brotherhood, and privilege on campus.* New York: New York University Press.

Schwartz, M., and C. Nogrady. 1996. Frat membership, rape myths, and sexual aggression on a college campus. *Violence Against Women* 2:158–62.

Smith, M. D. 1979a. Hockey violence: A new test of the violent subculture hypothesis. *Social Problems* 27:235–47.

———. 1979b. Towards an explanation of hockey violence: A reference other approach. *Canadian Journal of Sociology* 4:105–24.

———. 1983. *Violence and sport.* Toronto, Canada: Butterworths.

Terry, P. C., and J. J. Jackson. 1985. The determinants and control of violence in sport. *Quest* 37:27–37.

Vaz, E. W. 1979. Institutionalized rule violation and control in organized minor league hockey. *Canadian Journal of Sports Sciences* 4:83–90.

———. 1980. The culture of young hockey players: Some initial observations. In *Jock: Sports and male identity*, edited by D. F. Sabo and R. Runfola, 142–57. Englewood Cliffs, NJ: Prentice Hall.

Weinstein, M. D., D. S. Smith, and D. L. Wiesenthal. 1995. Masculinity and hockey violence. *Sex Roles* 33:831–47.

Weisfeld, G. E., D. M. Muczenski, C. C. Weisfeld, and D. R. Omark. 1987. Stability of boys' social success among peers over an eleven-year period. In *Interpersonal relations: family, peers, and friends*, edited by J. A. Meacham, 58–80. Basel, UK: Karger.

West, C., and D. H. Zimmerman. 1987. Doing gender. *Gender & Society* 1:125–51.

Young, K. 1993. Violence, risk, and liability in male sports culture. *Sociology of Sport Journal* 10:373–96.

———. 2000. Sport and violence. In *Handbook of sports studies*, edited by J. Coakley and E. Dunning, 23–59. London: Sage.

MEN ON RAPE

Tim Beneke

Rape may be America's fastest growing violent crime; no one can be certain because it is not clear whether more rapes are being committed or reported. It *is* clear that violence against women is widespread and fundamentally alters the meaning of life for women; that sexual violence is encouraged in a variety of ways in American culture; and that women are often blamed for rape.

Consider some statistics:

- In a random sample of 930 women, sociologist Diana Russell found that 44 percent had survived either rape or attempted rape. Rape was defined as sexual intercourse physically forced upon the woman, or coerced by threat of bodily harm, or forced upon the woman when she was helpless (asleep, for example). The survey included rape and attempted rape in marriage in its calculations. (Personal communication)
- In a September 1980 survey conducted by *Cosmopolitan* magazine to which over 106,000 women anonymously responded, 24 percent had been raped at least once. Of these, 51 percent had been raped by friends, 37 percent by strangers, 18 percent by relatives, and 3 percent by husbands. 10 percent of the women in the survey had been victims of incest. 75 percent of the women had been "bullied into making love." Writer Linda Wolfe, who reported on the survey, wrote in reference to such bullying: "Though such harassment stops short of rape, readers reported that it was nearly as distressing."
- An estimated 2–3 percent of all men who rape outside of marriage go to prison for their crimes.[1]
- The F.B.I. estimates that if current trends continue, one woman in four will be sexually assaulted in her lifetime.[2]
- An estimated 1.8 million women are battered by their spouses each year.[3] In extensive interviews with 430 battered women, clinical psychologist Lenore Walker, author of *The Battered Woman,* found that 59.9 percent had also been raped (defined as above) by their spouses. Given the difficulties many women had in admitting they had been raped, Walker estimates the figure may well be as high as 80 or 85 percent (personal communication). If 59.9 percent of the 1.8 million women battered each year are also raped, then a million women may be raped in marriage each year. And a significant number are raped in marriage without being battered.
- Between one in two and one in ten of all rapes are reported to the police.[4]
- Between 300,000 and 500,000 women are raped each year outside of marriage.[5]

What is often missed when people contemplate statistics on rape is the effect of the *threat* of sexual violence on women. I have asked women repeatedly, "How would your life be different if rape were suddenly to end?" (Men may learn a lot by asking this question of women to whom they are close.) The threat of rape is an assault upon the meaning of the world;

it alters the feel of the human condition. Surely any attempt to comprehend the lives of women that fails to take issues of violence against women into account is misguided.

Through talking to women, I learned: *The threat of rape alters the meaning and feel of the night.* Observe how your body feels, how the night feels, when you're in fear. The constriction in your chest, the vigilance in your eyes, the rubber in your legs. What do the stars look like? How does the moon present itself? What is the difference between walking late at night in the dangerous part of a city and walking late at night in the country, or safe suburbs? When I try to imagine what the threat of rape must do to the night, I think of the stalked, adrenalated feeling I get walking late at night in parts of certain American cities. Only, I remind myself, it is a fear different from any I have known, a fear of being raped.

It is night half the time. If the threat of rape alters the meaning of the night, it must alter the meaning and pace of the day, one's relation to the passing and organization of time itself. For some women, the threat of rape at night turns their cars into armored tanks, their solitude into isolation. And what must the space inside a car or an apartment feel like if the space outside is menacing?

I was running late one night with a close woman friend through a path in the woods on the outskirts of a small university town. We had run several miles and were feeling a warm, energized serenity.

"How would you feel if you were alone?" I asked.

"Terrified!" she said instantly.

"Terrified that there might be a man out there?" I asked, pointing to the surrounding moonlit forest, which had suddenly been transformed into a source of terror.

"Yes."

Another woman said, "I know what I can't do and I've completely internalized what I can't do. I've built a viable life that basically involves never leaving my apartment at night unless I'm directly going some place to meet somebody. It's

unconsciously built into what it occurs to women to do." When one is raised without freedom, one may not recognize its absence.

The threat of rape alters the meaning and feel of nature. Everyone has felt the psychic nurturance of nature. Many women are being deprived of that nurturance, especially in wooded areas near cities. They are deprived either because they cannot experience nature in solitude because of threat, or because, when they do choose solitude in nature, they must cope with a certain subtle but nettlesome fear.

Women need more money because of rape and the threat of rape makes it harder for women to earn money. It's simple: if you don't feel safe walking at night, or riding public transportation, you need a car. And it is less practicable to live in cheaper, less secure, and thus more dangerous neighborhoods if the ordinary threat of violence that men experience, being mugged, say, is compounded by the threat of rape. By limiting mobility at night, the threat of rape limits where and when one is able to work, thus making it more difficult to earn money. An obvious bind: women need more money because of rape, and have fewer job opportunities because of it.

The threat of rape makes women more dependent on men (or other women). One woman said: "If there were no rape I wouldn't have to play games with men for their protection." The threat of rape falsifies, mystifies, and confuses relations between men and women. If there were no rape, women would simply not need men as much, wouldn't need them to go places with at night, to feel safe in their homes, for protection in nature.

The threat of rape makes solitude less possible for women. Solitude, drawing strength from being alone, is difficult if being alone means being afraid. To be afraid is to be in need, to experience a lack; the threat of rape creates a lack. Solitude requires relaxation; if you're afraid, you can't relax.

The threat of rape inhibits a woman's expressiveness. "If there were no rape," said one woman, "I could dress the way I wanted and walk the way I wanted and not feel self-conscious about the responses of men. I could be friendly to people. I wouldn't have to wish I was ugly. I wouldn't have to make myself small when I got on the bus. I wouldn't have to respond to verbal abuse from men by remaining silent. I could respond in kind."

If a woman's basic expressiveness is inhibited, her sexuality, creativity, and delight in life must surely be diminished.

The threat of rape inhibits the freedom of the eye. I know a married couple who live in Manhattan. They are both artists, both acutely sensitive and responsive to the visual world. When they walk separately in the city, he has more freedom to look than she does. She must control her eye movements lest they inadvertently meet the glare of some importunate man. What, who, and how she sees are restricted by the threat of rape.

The following exercise is recommended for men.

> Walk down a city street. Pay a lot of attention to your clothing; make sure your pants are zipped, shirt tucked in, buttons done. Look straight ahead. Every time a man walks past you, avert your eyes and make your face expressionless. Most women learn to go through this act each time we leave our houses. It's a way to avoid at least some of the encounters we've all had with strange men who decided we looked available.[6]

To relate aesthetically to the visual world involves a certain playfulness, spirit of spontaneous exploration. The tense vigilance that accompanies fear inhibits that spontaneity. The world is no longer yours to look at when you're afraid.

I am aware that all culture is, in part, restriction, that there are places in America where hardly anyone is safe (though men are safer than women virtually everywhere), that there are many ways to enjoy life, that some women may not be so restricted, that there exist havens, whether psychic, geographical, economic, or class. But they are *havens,* and as such, defined by threat.

Above all, I trust my experience: no woman could have lived the life I've lived the last few years. If suddenly I were restricted by the threat of rape, I would feel a deep, inexorable depression. And it's not just rape; it's harassment, battery, Peeping Toms, anonymous phone calls, exhibitionism, intrusive stares, fondlings—all contributing to an atmosphere of intimidation in women's lives. And I have only scratched the surface; it would take many carefully crafted short stories to begin to express what I have only hinted at in the last few pages. I have not even touched upon what it might mean for a woman to be sexually assaulted. Only women can speak to that. Nor have I suggested how the threat of rape affects marriage.

Rape and the threat of rape pervade the lives of women, as reflected in some popular images of our culture.

"SHE ASKED FOR IT"—BLAMING THE VICTIM[7]

Many things may be happening when a man blames a woman for rape.

First, in all cases where a woman is said to have asked for it, her appearance and behavior are taken as a form of speech. "Actions speak louder than words" is a widely held belief; the woman's actions—her appearance may be taken as action—are given greater emphasis than her words; an interpretation alien to the woman's intentions is given to her actions. A logical extension of "she asked for it" is the idea that she wanted what happened to happen; if she wanted it to happen, she *deserved* for it to happen. Therefore, the man is not to be blamed. "She asked for it" can mean either that she was consenting to have sex and was not really raped, or that she was in fact raped but somehow she really deserved it. "If you ask for it, you deserve it," is a widely held notion. If I ask you to beat me up and you beat me up, I still don't deserve to be beaten up. So even if the notion that women asked to be raped had some basis in reality, which it doesn't, on its own terms it makes no sense.

Second, a mentality exists that says: a woman who assumes freedoms normally restricted to a man (like going out alone at night) and is raped is doing the same thing as a woman who goes out in the rain without an umbrella and catches a cold. Both are considered responsible for what happens to them. That men will rape is taken to be a legitimized given, part of nature, like rain or snow. The view reflects a massive abdication of responsibility for rape on the part of men. It is so much easier to think of rape as natural than to acknowledge one's part in it. So long as rape is regarded as natural, women will be blamed for rape.

A third point. The view that it is natural for men to rape is closely connected to the view of women as commodities. If a woman's body is regarded as a valued commodity by men, then of course, if you leave a valued commodity where it can be taken, it's just human nature for men to take it. If you left your stereo out on the sidewalk, you'd be asking for it to get stolen. Someone will just take it. (And how often men speak of rape as "going out and *taking* it.") If a woman walks the streets at night, she's leaving a valued commodity, her body, where it can be taken. So long as women are regarded as commodities, they will be blamed for rape.

Which brings us to a fourth point. "She asked for it" is inseparable from a more general "psychology of the dupe." If I use bad judgment and fail to read the small print in a contract and later get taken advantage of, "screwed" (or "fucked over"), then I deserve what I get; bad judgment makes me liable. Analogously, if a woman trusts a man and goes to his apartment, or accepts a ride hitchhiking, or goes out on a date and is raped, she's a dupe and deserves what she gets. "He didn't *really* rape her" goes the mentality—"he merely took advantage of her." And in America it's okay for people to take advantage of each other, even expected and praised. In fact, you're considered dumb and foolish if you don't take advantage of other people's bad judgment. And so, again, by treating them as dupes, rape will be blamed on women.

Fifth, if a woman who is raped is judged attractive by men, and particularly if she dresses to look attractive, then the mentality exists that she attacked him with her weapon so, of course, he counter-attacked with his. The preview to a popular movies states: "She was the victim of her own *provocative beauty.*" Provocation: "There is a line which, if crossed, will *set me off* and I will lose control and no longer be responsible for my behavior. If you punch me in the nose then, of course, I will not be responsible for what happens: you will have provoked a fight. If you dress, talk, move, or act a certain way, you will have provoked me to rape. If your appearance *stuns* me, *strikes* me, *ravishes* me, *knocks me out,* etc., then I will not be held responsible for what happens; you will have asked for it." The notion that sexual feeling makes one helpless is part of a cultural abdication of responsibility for sexuality. So long as a woman's appearance is viewed as a weapon and sexual feeling is believed to make one helpless, women will be blamed for rape.

Sixth, I have suggested that men sometimes become obsessed with images of women, that images become a substitute for sexual feeling, that sexual feeling becomes externalized and out of control and is given an undifferentiated identity in the appearance of women's bodies. It is a process of projection in which one blurs one's own desire with her imagined, projected desire. If a woman's attractiveness is taken to signify one's own lust and a woman's lust, then when an "attractive" woman is raped, some men may think she wanted sex. Since they perceive their own lust in part projected onto the woman, they disbelieve women who've been raped. So long as men project their own sexual desires onto women, they will blame women for rape.

And seventh, what are we to make of the contention that women in dating situations say "no" initially to sexual overtures from men as a kind of pose, only to give in later, thus revealing their true intentions? And that men are thus confused and incredulous when women are raped because in their sexual experience women can't be believed? I doubt that this has much to do with men's perceptions of rape. I don't know to what extent women actually "say no and mean yes"; certainly it is a common theme in male folklore. I have spoken to a couple of women who went through periods when they wanted to be sexual but were afraid to be, and often rebuffed initial sexual advances only to give in later. One point is clear: the ambivalence women may feel about having sex is closely tied to the inability of men to fully accept them as sexual beings. Women have been traditionally punished for being openly and freely sexual; men are praised for it. And if many men think of sex as achievement of possession of a valued commodity, or aggressive degradation, then women have every reason to feel and act ambivalent.

These themes are illustrated in an interview I conducted with a 23-year-old man who grew up in Pittsburgh and works as a file clerk in the financial district of San Francisco. Here's what he said:

"Where I work it's probably no different from any other major city in the U.S. The women dress up in high heels, and they wear a lot of makeup, and they just look really *hot* and really sexy, and how can somebody who has a healthy sex drive not feel lust for them when you see them? I feel lust for them, but I don't think I could find it in me to overpower someone and rape them. But I definitely get the feeling that I'd like to rape a girl. I don't know if the actual act of rape would be satisfying, but *the feeling* is satisfying.

"These women look so good, and they kiss ass of the men in the three-piece suits who are *big* in the corporation, and most of them relate to me like 'Who are *you*? Who are *you* to even *look* at?' They're snobby and they condescend to me, and I resent it. It would take me a lot longer to get to first base than it would somebody with a three-piece suit who had money. And to me a lot of the men they go out with are superficial assholes who have no real feelings or substance, and are just trying to get ahead and make a lot of money. Another thing that makes me resent these women is thinking, 'How could she want to hang out with somebody like that? What does that make her?'

"I'm a file clerk, which makes me feel like a nebbish, a nerd, like I'm not making it, I'm a failure. But I don't really believe I'm a failure because

I know it's just a phase, and I'm just doing it for the money, just to make it through this phase. I catch myself feeling like a failure, but I realize that's ridiculous."

What exactly do you go through when you see these sexy, unavailable women? "Let's say I see a woman and she looks really pretty and really clean and sexy, and she's giving off very feminine, sexy vibes. I think, 'Wow, I would love to make love to her,' but I know she's not really interested. It's a tease. A lot of times a woman knows that she's looking really good and she'll use that and flaunt it, and it makes me feel like she's laughing at me and I feel *degraded.*

"I also feel dehumanized, because when I'm being teased I just turn off, I cease to be human. Because if I go with my human emotions. I'm going to want to put my arms around her and kiss her, and to do that would be unacceptable. I don't like the feeling that I'm supposed to stand there and take it, and not be able to hug her or kiss her; so I just turn off my emotions. It's a feeling of humiliation, because the woman has forced me to turn off my feelings and react in a way that I really don't want to.

"If I were actually desperate enough to rape somebody, it would be from wanting the person, but it would be a very spiteful thing, just being able to say, 'I have power over you and I can do anything I want with you,' because really I feel that *they* have power over *me* just by their presence. Just the fact that they can come up to me and just melt me and make me feel like a dummy makes me want revenge. They have power over me so I want power over them. . . .

"Society says that you have to have a lot of sex with a lot of different women to be a real man. Well, what happens if you don't? Then what are you? Are you half a man? Are you still a boy? It's ridiculous. You see a whiskey ad with a guy and two women on his arm. The implication is that real men don't have any trouble getting women."

How does it make you feel toward women to see all these sexy women in media and advertising using their looks to try to get you to buy something? "It makes me hate them. As a man you're taught that men are more powerful than women, and that men always have the upper hand, and that it's a man's society; but then you see all these women and it makes you think, 'Jesus Christ, if we have all the power how come all the beautiful women are telling us what to buy?' And to be honest, it just makes me hate beautiful women because they're using their power over me. I realize they're being used themselves, and they're doing it for money. In *Playboy* you see all these beautiful women who look so sexy and they'll be giving you all these looks like they want to have sex so bad; but then in reality you know that except for a few nymphomaniacs, they're doing it for the money; so I hate them for being used and for using their bodies in that way.

"In this society, if you ever sit down and realize how manipulated you really are it makes you pissed off—it makes you want to take control. And you've been manipulated by women, and they're a very easy target because they're out walking along the streets, so you can just grab one and say, 'Listen, you're going to do what I want you to do,' and it's an act of revenge against the way you've been manipulated.

"I know a girl who was walking down the street by her house, when this guy jumped her and beat her up and raped her, and she was black and blue and had to go to the hospital. That's beyond me. I can't understand how somebody could do that. If I were going to rape a girl, I wouldn't hurt her. I might *restrain* her, but I wouldn't *hurt* her. . . .

"The whole dating game between men and women also makes me feel degraded. I hate being put in the position of having to initiate a relationship. I've been taught that if you're not aggressive with a woman, then you've blown it. She's not going to jump on *you,* so *you've* got to jump

on *her.* I've heard all kinds of stories where the woman says, 'No! No! No!' and they end up making great love. I get confused as hell if a woman pushes me away. Does it mean she's trying to be a nice girl and wants to put up a good appearance, or does it mean she doesn't want anything to do with you? You don't know. Probably a lot of men think that women don't feel like real women unless a man tries to force himself on her, unless she brings out the 'real man,' so to speak, and probably too much of it goes on. It goes on in my head that you're complimenting a woman by actually staring at her or by trying to get into her pants. Lately, I'm realizing that when I stare at women lustfully, they often feel more threatened than flattered."

NOTES

1. Such estimates recur in the rape literature. See *Sexual Assault* by Nancy Gager and Cathleen Schurr, Grosset & Dunlap, 1976, or *The Price of Coercive Sexuality* by Clark and Lewis, The Women's Press, 1977.

2. *Uniform Crime Reports*, 1980.

3. See *Behind Closed Doors* by Murray J. Strauss and Richard Gelles, Doubleday, 1979.

4. See Gager and Schurr (above) or virtually any book on the subject.

5. Again, see Gager and Schurr, or Carol V. Horos, *Rape,* Banbury Books, 1981.

6. From "Willamette Bridge" in *Body Politics* by Nancy Henley, Prentice-Hall, 1977, p. 144.

7. I would like to thank George Lakoff for this insight.

WIELDING MASCULINITY INSIDE ABU GHRAIB: MAKING FEMINIST SENSE OF AN AMERICAN MILITARY SCANDAL

power of the situation

Cynthia Enloe

In April, 2004, a year after the US government launched its massive military invasion of Iraq, a series of shocking photographs of American soldiers abusing Iraqi prisoners began appearing on television news programs and the front pages of newspapers around the world. American male and female soldiers serving as prison guards in a prison called Abu Ghraib were shown deliberately humiliating and torturing scores of Iraqi men held in detention and under interrogation. The American soldiers were smiling broadly. They appeared to be taking enormous pleasure in humiliating their Iraqi charges.

Most people who saw these photographs—people in Seattle and Seoul, Miami and Madrid, Bangkok and Boston—can still describe the scenes. An American male soldier standing self-satisfied with his arms crossed and wearing surgical blue rubber gloves, while in front of him, an American woman soldier, smiling at the camera, is leaning on top of a pile of naked Iraqi men forced to contort themselves into a human pyramid. An American woman soldier, again smiling, holding a male Iraqi prisoner on a leash. An American woman soldier pointing to a naked Iraqi man's genitals, apparently treating them as a joke. American male soldiers intimidating naked Iraqi male prisoners with snarling guard dogs.

From Cynthia Enloe, "Wielding Masculinity Inside Abu Ghraib: Making Feminist Sense of an American Military Scandal," *Asian Journal of Women's Studies* 10(3): 89–102. © 2004. Used by permission of the author.

An Iraqi male prisoner standing alone on a box, his head hooded, electrical wires attached to different parts of his body. An Iraqi male prisoner forced to wear women's underwear. Not pictured, but substantiated, were Iraqi men forced to masturbate and to simulate oral sex with each other, as well as an Iraqi woman prisoner coerced by several American male soldiers into kissing them (Hersh, 2004a).

What does a feminist curiosity reveal about the causes and the implications of the American abuses of Iraqi prisoners at Abu Ghraib? Few of the US government's official investigators or the mainstream news commentators used feminist insights to make sense of what went on in the prison. The result, I think, is that we have not really gotten to the bottom of the Abu Ghraib story. One place to start employing a feminist set of tools is to explain why one American woman military guard in particular captured the attention of so many media editors and ordinary viewers and readers: the twenty-one-year-old enlisted army reservist Lynndie England.

What proved shocking to the millions of viewers of the prison clandestine photos were several things. First, the Abu Ghraib scenes suggested there existed a gaping chasm between, on the one hand, the US Bush administration's claim that its military invasion and overthrow of the brutal Saddam Hussein refime would bring a civilizing sort of "freedom" to the Iraqi people and, on the other hand, the seemingly barbaric treatment that American soldiers were willfully meting out to Iraqis held in captivity without trial. Second, it was shocking to witness such blatant abuse of imprisoned detainees by soldiers representing a government that had signed both the international Geneva Conventions against mistreatment of wartime combatants and the UN Convention Against Torture, as well as having passed its own anti-torture laws.

Yet there was a third source of shock that prompted scores of early media commentaries and intense conversations among ordinary viewers: seeing women engage in torture. Of the seven American soldiers, all low-ranking Army Reserve military police guards, whom the Pentagon charged and initially court-martialed, three were women. Somehow, the American male soldier, the man in the blue surgical gloves (his name was Charles Graner), was not shocking to most viewers and so did not inspire much private consternation and/or a stream of op-ed columns. Women, by conventional contrast, were expected to appear in wartime as mothers and wives of soldiers, occasionally as military nurses and truck mechanics, or most often as the victims of the wartime violence. Women were not—according to the conventional presumption—supposed to be the wielders of violence, certainly not the perpetrators of torture. When those deeply gendered presumptions were turned upside down, many people felt a sense of shock. "This is awful; how could this have happened?"

Private First Class Lynndie England, the young woman military guard photographed holding the man on a leash, thus became the source of intense public curiosity. The news photographers could not restrain themselves two months later, in early August, 2004, from showing England in her army camouflaged maternity uniform when she appeared at Fort Bragg for her pre-trial hearing. She had become pregnant as a result of her sexual liaison with another enlisted reservist while on duty in Abu Ghraib. Her sexual partner was Charles Graner. Yet Charles Graner's name was scarcely mentioned. He apparently was doing what men are expected to do in wartime: have sex and wield violence. The public's curiosity and its lack of curiosity thus matched its pattern of shock. All three were conventionally gendered. Using a feminist investigatory approach,

one should find this lack of public and media curiosity about Charles Graner just as revealing as the public's and media's absorbing fascination with Lynndie England.

Responding to the torrent of Abu Ghraib stories coming out of Iraq during the spring and summer of 2004, President George W. Bush and his Secretary of Defense, Donald Rumsfeld, tried to reassure the public that the graphically abusive behavior inside the prison was not representative of America, nor did it reflect the Bush administration's own foreign policies. Rather, the Abu Ghraib abuses were the work of "rogue" soldiers, a "few bad apples." The "bad apple" explanation always goes like this: the institution is working fine, its values are appropriate, its internal dynamics are of a sort that sustain positive values and respectful, productive behavior. Thus, according to the "bad apple" explanation, nothing needs to be reassessed or reformed in the way the organization works; all that needs to happen to stop the abuse is to prosecute and remove those few individuals who refused to play by the established rules. Sometimes this may be true. Some listeners to the Bush administration's "bad apple" explanation, however, weren't reassured. They wondered if the Abu Ghraib abuses were not produced by just a few bad apples found in a solid, reliable barrel, but, instead, were produced by an essentially "bad barrel." They also wondered whether this "barrel" embraced not only the Abu Ghraib prison, but the larger US military, intelligence and civilian command structures (Hersh, 2004b; Hersh, 2004c; Human Rights Watch, 2004).

What makes a "barrel" go bad? That is, what turns an organization, an institution, or a whole system into one that at least ignores, perhaps even fosters abusive behavior by the individuals operating inside it? This question is relevant for every workplace, every political system, every international alliance. Here too, feminists have been working hard over the past three decades to develop a curiosity and a set of analytical tools with which we can all answer this important question. So many of us today live much of our lives within complex organizations, large and small—work places, local and national governments, health care systems, criminal justice systems, international organizations. Feminist researchers have revealed that virtually all organizations are gendered: that is, all organizations are shaped by the ideas about, and daily practices of, masculinities and femininities (Bunster-Burotto, 1985; Ehrenreich, 2004; Enloe, 2000; Whitworth, 2004). Ignoring the workings of gender, feminist investigators have found, makes it impossible for us to explain accurately what makes any organization "tick." That failure makes it impossible for us to hold an organization accountable. Yet most of the hundred-page long official reports into the Abu Ghraib abuse scandal were written by people who ignored these feminist lessons. They acted as if the dynamics of masculinity and femininity among low-level police and high-level policy-makers made no difference. That assumption is very risky.

A series of US Senate hearings, along with a string of Defense Department investigations tried to explain what went wrong in Abu Ghraib and why. The most authoritative of the Defense Department reports were the "Taguba Report," the "Fay/Jones Report" (both named after generals who headed these investigations) and the "Schlesinger Report" (named after a civilian former Secretary of Defense who chaired this investigatory team) (Human Rights Watch, 2004; Jehl, 2004; Lewis and Schmitt, 2004; Schmitt, 2004; Taguba, 2004). In addition, the CIA was conducting its own investigation, since its officials were deeply involved in interrogating—and often hiding in secret prisons—captured Afghans and Iraqis. Moreover, there were several human rights groups and journalists publishing their own findings during 2004. Together, they offered a host of valuable clues as to why this institutional "barrel" had gone bad. First was the discovery that lawyers inside the Defense and Justice Departments, as well as the White House, acting on instructions from their civilian superiors, produced interpretations of the Geneva Conventions and US law that deliberately shrank the definitions of "torture" down so far that American military and CIA personnel could order and conduct interrogations of Iraqis and Afghans in detention using techniques that otherwise would have been deemed violations of US and international law.

Second, investigators found that an American general, Geoffrey Miller, commander of the US prison at Guantanamo Bay, Cuba, was sent by Secretary Rumsfeld to Iraq in September, 2003, where he recommended that American commanders overseeing military prison operations in Iraq start employing the aggressive interrogation practices that were being used on Afghan and Arab male prisoners at Guantanamo. Somewhat surprisingly, General Miller later was named by the Pentagon to head the Abu Ghraib prison in the wake of the scandal. Third, investigators discovered that the intense, persistent pressure imposed on the military intelligence personnel by the Defense Department to generate information about who was launching insurgent assaults on the US occupying forces encouraged those military intelligence officers to put their own pressures on the military police guarding prisoners to "soften up" the men in their cell blocks, thus undercutting the military police men's and women's own chain of command (which led up to a female army general, Janis Karpinski, who claimed that her authority over her military police personnel had been undermined by intrusive military intelligence officers). This policy change, investigators concluded, dangerously blurred the valuable line between military policing and military interrogating. A fourth finding was that non-military personnel, including CIA operatives and outside contractors hired by the CIA and the Pentagon, were involved in the Abu Ghraib military interrogations in ways that may have fostered an assumption that the legal limitations on employing excessive force could be treated cavalierly: We're under threat, this is urgent, who can be bothered with the Geneva Conventions or legal niceties?

Did it matter where the women were inside the prison and up and down the larger American military and intelligence hierarchies—as low level police reservists, as a captain in the military intelligence unit, as a general advising the chief US commander in Iraq? Investigators apparently didn't ask. Did it matter what exactly Charles Graner's and the other male military policemen's daily relationships were to their female colleagues, who were in a numerical minority in the military police unit, in the military interrogation unit and in the CIA unit all stationed together at Abu Ghraib? The official investigators seemed not to think that asking this question would yield any insights. Was it significant that so many of the abuses perpetrated on the Iraqi prisoners were deliberately sexualized? Was hooding a male prisoner the same (in motivation and in result) as forcing him to simulate oral sex? No one seemed to judge these questions to be pertinent. Was it at all relevant that Charles Graner, the older and apparently most influential of the low-ranking guards charged, had been accused of physical intimidation by his former wife? No questions asked, no answers forthcoming. Among all the lawyers in the Defense and Justice Departments and in the White House who were ordered to draft guidelines to permit the US government's officials to sidestep the Geneva Conventions outlawing torture, were there any subtle pressures imposed on them to appear "manly" in a time of war? This question too seems to have been left on the investigative teams' shelves to gather dust.

Since the mid-1970s, feminists have been crafting skills to explain when and why organizations become arenas for sexist abuse. One of the great contributions of the work done by the "Second Wave" of the international women's movement has been to throw light on what breeds sex discrimination and sexual harassment inside organizations otherwise as dissimilar as a factory, a stock brokerage, a legislature, a university, a student movement, and a military (Bowers, 2004; Kwon, 1999; Ogasawara, 1998; Stockford, 2004; Whitworth, 2004). All of the Abu Ghraib reports' authors talked about a "climate," an "environment," or a "culture," having been created inside Abu Ghraib that fostered abusive acts. The conditions inside Abu Ghraib were portrayed as a climate of "confusion," of "chaos." It was feminists who gave us this innovative concept of organizational climate.

When trying to figure out why in some organizations women employees were subjected to sexist jokes, unwanted advances, and retribution for not going along with the jokes or not accepting those

advances, feminist lawyers, advocates and scholars began to look beyond the formal policies and the written work rules. They explored something more amorphous but just as, maybe even more, potent: that set of unofficial presumptions that shapes workplace interactions between men and men, and men and women. They followed the breadcrumbs to the casual, informal interactions between people up and down the organization's ladder. They investigated who drinks with whom after work, who sends sexist jokes to whom over office email, who pins up which sorts of pictures of women in their lockers or next to the coffee machine. And they looked into what those people in authority did not do. They discovered that inaction is a form of action: "turning a blind eye" is itself a form of action. Inaction sends out signals to everyone in the organization about what is condoned. Feminists labeled these webs of presumptions, informal interactions, and deliberate inaction an organization's "climate." As feminists argued successfully in court, it is not sufficient for a stock brokerage or a college to include anti-sexual harassment guidelines in their official handbooks; employers have to take explicit steps to create a workplace climate in which women would be treated with fairness and respect.

By 2004, this feminist explanatory concept—organizational "climate"—had become so accepted by so many analysts that their debt to feminists had been forgotten. Generals Taguba, Jones and Fay, as well as former Defense Secretary Schlesinger, may never have taken a Women's Studies course, but when they were assigned the job of investigating Abu Ghraib they were drawing on the ideas and investigatory skills crafted for them by feminists.

However, more worrisome than their failure to acknowledge their intellectual and political debts was those journalists' and government investigators' ignoring the feminist lessons that went hand in hand with the concept of "climate." The first lesson: to make sense of any organization, we always must dig deep into the group's dominant presumptions about femininity and masculinity. The second lesson: we need to take seriously the experiences of women as they try to adapt to, or sometimes resist those dominant gendered presumptions—not because all women are angels, but because paying close attention to women's ideas and actions will shed light on why men with power act the way they do.

It is not as if the potency of ideas about masculinity and femininity had been totally absent from the US military's thinking. Between 1991 and 2004, there had been a string of military scandals that had compelled even those American senior officials who preferred to look the other way to face sexism straight on. The first stemmed from the September, 1991, gathering of American navy aircraft carrier pilots at a Hilton hotel in Las Vegas. Male pilots (all officers), fresh from their victory in the first Gulf War, lined a hotel corridor and physically assaulted every woman who stepped off the elevator. They made the "mistake" of assaulting a woman navy helicopter pilot who was serving as an aide to an admiral. Within months members of Congress and the media were telling the public about "Tailhook"— why it happened, who tried to cover it up (Office of the Inspector General, 2003). Close on the heels of the Navy's "Tailhook" scandal came the Army's Aberdeen training base sexual harassment scandal, followed by other revelations of military gay bashing, sexual harassment and rapes by American male military personnel of their American female colleagues (Enloe, 1993, 2000).

Then in September, 1995, the rape of a local school girl by two American male marines and a sailor in Okinawa sparked public demonstrations, new Okinawan women's organizing and more US Congressional investigations. At the start of the twenty-first century American media began to notice the patterns of international trafficking in Eastern European and Filipina women around American bases in South Korea, prompting official embarrassment in Washington (an embarrassment which had not been demonstrated earlier when American base commanders turned a classic "blind eye" toward a prostitution industry financed by their own male soldiers because it employed "just" local South Korean women). And in 2003, three new American military sexism scandals caught Washington policy-makers' attention: four

American male soldiers returning from combat missions in Afghanistan murdered their female partners at Fort Bragg, North Carolina; a pattern of sexual harassment and rape by male cadets of female cadets—and superiors' refusal to treat these acts seriously—as revealed at the US Air Force Academy; and testimonies by at least sixty American women soldiers returning from tours of duty in Kuwait and Iraq described how they had been sexually assaulted by their male colleagues there—with, once again, senior officers choosing inaction, advising the American women soldiers to "get over it" (Jargon, 2003; Lutz and Elliston, 2004; The Miles Foundation, 2004; Moffeit and Herder, 2004).

So it should have come as no surprise to American senior uniformed and civilian policy makers seeking to make sense of the abuses perpetrated in Abu Ghraib that a culture of sexism had come to permeate many sectors of US military life. If they had thought about what they had all learned in the last thirteen years—from Tailhook, Aberdeen, Fort Bragg, Okinawa, South Korea and the US Air Force Academy—they should have put the workings of masculinity and femininity at the top of their investigatory agendas. They should have made feminist curiosity one of their own principal tools. Perhaps Tillie Fowler did suggest to her colleagues that they think about these military sexual scandals when they began to delve into Abu Ghraib. A former Republican Congresswoman from Florida, Tillie Fowler, had been a principal investigator on the team that looked into the rapes (and their cover-ups) at the US Air Force Academy. Because of her leadership in that role, Fowler was appointed to the commission headed by James Schlesinger investigating Abu Ghraib. Did she raise this comparison between the Air Force Academy case and Abu Ghraib? Did her male colleagues take her suggestion seriously?

Perhaps eventually the investigators did not make use of the feminist lessons and tools because they imagined that the lessons of Tailhook, the Air Force Academy and Okinawa were relevant only when all the perpetrators of sexualized abuse are men and all the victims are women. The presence of Lynndie England and the other women in

Abu Ghraib's military police unit, they might have assumed, made the feminist tools sharpened in these earlier gendered military scandals inappropriate for their explorations. But the lesson of Tailhook, Okinawa and the most recent military scandals was not that the politics of masculinity and femininity matter only when men are the perpetrators and women are the victims. Instead, the deeper lesson of all these other military scandals is that we must always ask: Has this organization (or this system of interlocking organizations) become masculinized in ways that privilege certain forms of masculinity, feminize its opposition and trivialize most forms of femininity?

With this core gender question in mind, we might uncover significant dynamics operating in Abu Ghraib and in the American military and civilian organizations that were supposed to be supervising the prison's personnel. First, American military police and their military and CIA intelligence colleagues might have been guided by their own masculinized fears of humiliation when they forced Iraqi men to go naked for days, to wear women's underwear and to masturbate in front of each other and American women guards. That is, belief in an allegedly "exotic," frail Iraqi masculinity, fraught with fears of nakedness and homosexuality, might not have been the chief motivator for the American police and intelligence personnel; it may have been their own home-grown American sense of masculinity's fragility—how easily manliness can be feminized—that prompted them to craft these prison humiliations. In this distorted masculinized scenario, the presence of women serving as military police might have proved especially useful. Choreographing the women guards' feminized roles so that they could act as ridiculing feminized spectators of male prisoners might have been imagined to intensify the masculinized demoralization. Dominant men trying to utilize at least some women to act in ways that undermine the masculinized self-esteem of rival men is not new.

What about the American women soldiers themselves? In the US military of 2004 women comprised 15 percent of active duty personnel, 17 percent of all Reserves and National Guard (and a surprising 24 percent of the Army Reserves alone).

From the very time these particular young women joined this military police unit, they, like their fellow male recruits, probably sought to fit into the group. If the reserve military police unit's evolving culture—perhaps fostered by their superiors for the sake of "morale" and "unit cohesion"—was one that privileged a certain form of masculinized humor, racism and bravado, each woman would have had to decide how to deal with that. At least some of the women reservist recruits might have decided to join in, play the roles assigned to them in order to gain the hoped-for reward of male acceptance. The facts that the Abu Ghraib prison was grossly understaffed during the fall [of] 2003 (too few guards for spiraling numbers of Iraqi detainees), that it was isolated from other military operations, and that its residents endured daily and nightly mortar attacks, would only serve to intensify the pressures on each soldier to gain acceptance from those unit members who seemed to represent the group's dominant masculinized culture. And Lynndie England's entering into a sexual liaison with Charles Graner? We need to treat this as more than merely a "lack of discipline." We need to ask what were the cause and effect dynamics between their sexual behaviors and the abuses of prisoners and staging of the photographs. Feminists have taught us never to brush off sexual relations as if they have nothing to do with organizational and political practices.

Then there is the masculinization of the military interrogators' organizational cultures, the masculinization of the CIA's field operatives and the workings of ideas about "manliness" shaping the entire US political system. Many men and women—as lawyers, as generals, as Cabinet officers, as elected officials—knew full well that aggressive interrogation techniques violated both the spirit and the language of the Geneva Conventions, the UN Convention Against Torture and the US federal law against torture. Yet during the months of waging wars in Afghanistan and Iraq most of these men and women kept silent. Feminists have taught us always to be curious about silence. Thus we need to ask: Did any of the American men involved in interrogations keep silent because they were afraid of being labeled "soft," or "weak," thereby jeopardizing their status as "manly" men. We need also to discover if any of the women who knew better kept silent because they were afraid that they would be labeled "feminine," thus risking being deemed by their colleagues untrustworthy, political outsiders.

We are not going to get to the bottom of the tortures perpetrated by Americans at Abu Ghraib unless we make use of a feminist curiosity and unless we revisit the feminist lessons derived from the scandals of Tailhook, Fort Bragg, Annapolis, Okinawa and the Air Force Academy. Those tools and lessons might shed a harsh light on an entire American military institutional culture and maybe even the climate of contemporary American political life. That institutional culture and that political climate together have profound implications not only for Americans. They are being held up as models to emulate in Korea, Japan, the Philippines, Afghanistan and Iraq. That, in turn, means that the insights offered by feminist analysts from those societies who have such intimate experiences with this US institutional culture and this political climate are likely to teach Americans a lot about themselves.

REFERENCES

Bowers, Simon (2004), "Merrill Lynch Accused of 'Institutional Sexism,'" *The Guardian,* (London), June 12.

Bunster-Burotto, Ximena (1985), "Surviving beyond Fear: Women and Torture in Latin America," *Women and Change in Latin America,* eds. June Nash and Helen Safa, South Hadley, MA: Bergin and Garvey Publishers: 297–325.

Enloe, Cynthia (1993), *The Morning After: Sexual Politics at the End of the Cold War,* Berkeley: University of California Press.

—— (2000), *Maneuvers: The International Politics of Militarizing Women's Lives,* Berkeley and London: University of California Press.

Ehrenreich, Barbara (2004), "All Together Now," Op. Ed., *New York Times,* July 15.

Hersh, Seymour (2004a), "Annals of National Security: Torture at Abu Ghraib," *The New Yorker,* May 10: 42–47.

—— (2004b), "Annals of National Security: Chain of Command," *The New Yorker,* May 17: 38–43.

—— (2004c), "Annals of National Security: The Gray Zone," *The New Yorker,* May 24: 38–44.

Human Rights Watch (2004), *The Road to Abu Ghraib,* New York: Author.

Jargon, Julie (2003), "The War Within," Westword, January.

Jehl, Douglas (2004), "Some Abu Ghraib Abuses are Traced to Afghanistan," *The New York Times,* August 26.

Kwon, Insook (1999), "Militarization in My Heart," unpublished PhD Dissertation, Women's Studies Program, Clark University, Worcester, MA, USA.

Lewis, Neil A. and Eric Schmitt (2004), "Lawyers Decided Bans on Torture Didn't Bind Bush," *New York Times,* June 8.

Lutz, Catherine and Jori Elliston (2004), "Domestic Terror," *Interventions: Activists and Academics Respond to Violence,* eds. Elizabeth Castelli and Janet Jackson, New York: Palgrave.

The Miles Foundation (2004), "Brownback/Fitz Amendment to S. 2400," email correspondence, June 14, from Milesfdn@aol.com.

Moffeit, Miles and Amy Herder (2004), "Betrayal in the Ranks," *The Denver Post,* May, Available on the Web at: http://www.denverpost.com.

Office of the Inspector General (2003), *The Tailhook Report, US Department of Defense,* New York: St Martin's Press.

Ogasawara, Yuko (1998), *Office Ladies and Salaried Men: Power, Gender and Work in Japanese Companies,* Berkeley and London: University of California Press.

Schmitt, Eric (2004), "Abuse Panel Says Rules on Inmates Need Overhaul," *The New York Times,* August 25.

Stockford, Marjorie A. (2004), *The Bellwomen: The Story of the Landmark AT&T Sex Discrimination Case,* New Brunswick, NJ: Rutgers University Press.

Taguba, Antonio (2004), "Investigation of the 800th Military Police Brigade," Washington, D.C.: US Department of Defense, April.

Whitworth, Sandra (2004), *Men, Militarism and UN Peacekeeping: A Gendered Analysis,* Boulder, CO Lynne Rienner Publishers.

MALE COMMITMENT TO GENDER EQUITY AND ANTIVIOLENCE: A NATIONAL COLLEGE STUDY

Edward Heisler   Michael W. Firmin

Violence against women is a significant problem on college campuses across the United States. The Centers for Disease Control and Prevention (2007) reported that 20 to 25% of college women experienced attempted or completed rape during their college careers. According to the National Center for Victims of Crime (2007), young women ages 16 to 24 experienced the highest rates of relationship violence in 2000. Despite the predominant amount of male-perpetrated violence experienced by their female classmates, campus men have largely remained on the sidelines in terms of formal attempts to curb this problem.

Sexism and men's violence against women sabotage campus goals of supporting the fulfillment of each student's potential. Having recognized this and many other costs of gender inequality and violence against women, many campus leaders have increased efforts to create safe, equitable, and respectful campus communities, free from sexual and domestic violence. As a result, interest in men's gender equality and antiviolence groups is growing. Small groups of college men are allying with women to end the repressive campus environments

created by ongoing threats of men's violence, harassment, intrusion, and sexism. This movement toward men's involvement represents an exciting shift in social norms, because more men are identifying gender equality and antiviolence work as vocations or part of their larger purpose in life.

Nonetheless, despite an apparent rise in campus support for ending gender inequality and men's violence against women, student activists for gender equity and antiviolence often feel unsupported in their campus community. This illustrates a struggle that feminist women have articulated for years: Working for gender equality is an uphill battle, and campuses have yet to achieve that goal. This circumstance poses a number of questions related to engaging men: What causes men to care about sexism and men's violence against women as a social issue? Why would men commit to gender equality work despite a lack of support from the greater community? What can campuses do to create a supportive environment for gender equality and antiviolence groups?

These are key questions that guided an exploratory project at the 1st National Conference for Campus-Based Men's Gender Equality & Antiviolence Groups at St. John's University in Collegeville, Minnesota. The conference was a groundbreaking gathering of representatives from campus-based men's groups across the country, providing an excellent opportunity to gather data. Fourteen male students were interviewed in an attempt to further understand how and why men are committing themselves to promoting gender equality and ending violence against women. Their responses have implications for the way campus leaders approach the engagement of men and the way campuses think about encouraging gender equality and antiviolence efforts. Their statements can also inform the way one supports men as they identify vocations related to gender equality and antiviolence work.

METHOD

Participants

The present research study used a purposeful sample (Arminio & Hulgren, 2002), consisting of 14 participants from 10 colleges and universities across the United States. Participants ranged from age 18 to 23, with an average age of 20.5 years. Each participant was involved in campus-related activities associated with gender equality and antiviolence work for at least one semester. Participants included majors from women's studies to mechanical engineering. Eight participants identified themselves as Caucasian/white, three participants identified themselves as Black/African-American, two participants identified themselves as Latino/Mexican, and one participant identified himself as biracial. Twelve participants indicated they were straight/heterosexual (two students identified their sexual orientation as male), one participant indicated he was gay, and one did not disclose. Project participants were recruited through a posting on the conference Web page. Potential participants completed a personal statement before the conference as well as a semi-structured, personal interview while at the national conference. Interview questions focused on understanding the nature of each participant's commitment, perspective, and experience related to gender equality and ending violence against women. Questions included: How did you first get involved in work connected to gender equality and violence against women? What are the greatest challenges and rewards related to your involvement? How has your involvement impacted your life?

Procedure

The study followed the protocol for a phenomenological, qualitative research investigation. This is a research protocol that explores and reports the perceptions of participants, from their own perspectives, giving voice to how the individuals view their worlds and personal constructs (Bailey, 2007). Interviews were digitally recorded for later analysis. The interviews were semi-structured (Seidman, 2006), allowing the participants to relate their own perspectives, stories, accounts, and sentiments—explaining their phenomenological perspectives freely and without coaching. Coding procedures for analyzing the data utilized an inductive methodology. That is, preestablished axial categories were not imposed on the data. This was due to the exploratory nature of the investigation. Consequently, open coding (Maxwell, 2005) strategies were more apt for studying the phenomenon of interest.

The interviews were assessed by repeated review and appraising the data for frequent words, phrases, constructs, and ideas. Concept mapping organizational review (Gay, Mills, & Airasian, 2009) helped to provide an organizational framework for the data analysis. At times, original codes were combined in order to keep the number manageable, and some codes were later discarded if they failed to reflect the sentiments of most participants. Constant comparison among the transcript data produced a set of codes that eventually led to the themes reported in the present research article (Bereska, 2003). Themes were only reported if they represented the consensus of most participants interviewed in the study. Initials used in the printed version of the article are fabricated in order to preserve the confidentiality of the research participants.

Internal validity for the study was enhanced primarily via two mechanisms. One was to generate a data trail (Daytner, 2006). This is a qualitative research technique of systematically supporting each reported theme in a study with citations and direct quotes from the respective participants. It helps to ensure that the themes reported in a study are adequately grounded in the collected research data. Additionally, the data trail was submitted to an expert qualitative researcher who was independent of the data collection and analysis. This qualitative research methodology helps to provide an objective appraisal of the process and reported findings, helping to ensure that the study possesses adequate rigor (Merriam, 2002). The independent expert supported the conclusions drawn, helped to sharpen the accuracy of the present research findings, and provided valuable assistance in assuring the overall quality of research design and execution.

RESULTS

Of the 14 participants, all but 2 strongly asserted that they would remain involved in gender equality and antiviolence work for the rest of their lives. For most participants, striving for gender equality and a world free from men's violence against women had become part of their identity and life purpose. Most men described a connection and self-identification with gender equality work similar to the following participant's account:

> I respect and love women due to seeing my mother and grandmother. I acquired the knowledge of what women go through in the world today. With that said, I just want to help in every way possible. Women are fighting for equality everyday. So as long as they're fighting, I'm going to be right beside them, fighting with them. . . . I feel as though if I wasn't doing this kind of work I wouldn't be being me, you know? (JA)

Participants specifically explained that involvement in gender equality and antiviolence groups anchored their deep personal commitment to the mission of such programs. As such, these men expressed a perceived calling to which they felt more than a passing attachment. It was not said to be a fad or hobby. Rather, it was perceived to be a long-term commitment or moral obligation. For example, another participant explained:

> I feel like since I know so much now I can never go back. I'm always going to be progressive from now on. So no matter where I go, if I'm in college or I'm working, whenever I feel like this issue comes

up I feel like I can address it because I know how to. I've learned values and I've learned different skills that can help me address this issue. (HM)

Overall, the path leading to each student's commitment, though filled with unique details, suggested at least four common themes: knowledge and empathy, social/peer support and exploration of masculinity, guidance and encouragement, and self-improvement and altruism.

Knowledge and Empathy

It was common for participants to describe a presentation on sexism and violence against women that initially caught their attention, challenged their thinking, and called them to action. However, participants reported that learning in this area extended beyond conference-based or other intellectual learning. It is interesting to note that a small majority of participants had taken classes related to gender equality and violence against women, but academic study was not the central focus of participants' commitment. It was, however, common for participants to allude to a sharp and continuous learning curve, whether it began with a campus group, class, or volunteer experience. Participants seemed to be gaining knowledge, even though the medium for their learning was not strictly a classroom setting.

Additionally, participants shared that knowledge was only the beginning of the commitment they experienced. For most participants, empathy for the harm caused by male dominance and violence against women was at the heart of their commitment. Presentation activities intended to personalize men's violence against women for the audience frequently formed the foundation of their passion. Ongoing discussions in groups and classrooms, along with friends, family members, classmates, and campus faculty/staff, built on this foundation. One participant stated: "It has opened my eyes to some of the things unseen, such as hegemonic masculinity and the terror that women are put through, especially by their male counterparts" (RA). Engagement of the mind headed the path toward empathy in the heart.

For all but one of the men, empathy was amplified by detailed knowledge of a woman they knew who had suffered male-perpetrated violence and gender inequality. For example, some participants grew up in households with domestic violence, and this strongly impacted the empathy they experienced: "My mother keeps me motivated[;] thinking back to the violence she experienced will always be in my mind. I will always remain involved in the fight for this issue" (BE). Many participants also had close relationships with a female relative or friend who experienced male violence. Often, this exposure served as a catalyst in the lives of participants. That is, the issue became real and personal: "One of my best friends was raped my freshman year. So I think that's what really propelled me [to become involved]" (NP). The subject went from the theoretical to the tangible and practical for the research participants. As such, close experiences with violence against women seemed to force participants to struggle with what had happened and relate to the harm that resulted. One participant explained:

> I had a sister who, four years ago, her boyfriend at the time turned violent against her. . . . My sister felt like she, like she did something wrong. She felt, you know, "Why, why did I stay with this guy?" . . . And just thinking inside it's like, "You know this is none of your fault at all." (BT)

In multiple cases, participants indicated they were not aware of abuse that was impacting someone close to them until they were involved in gender equality or antiviolence groups for some time. They were not necessarily naïve, but insulated until they participated in prevention programs that illuminated the dynamics and effects of abuse. One participant aptly explained: "As a student in Sociology and Gender Studies, I knew it was around and carried passion for those who experience it. . . . However, it directly hit my heart when I found out my mom was being abused" (ST). He continued to elaborate on how his awareness had expanded:

> It's hard for me because I feel like I victimized my mom a lot. She's very outspoken. If she doesn't like it, she'll say it. And it got labeled as "she's

crazy" from my dad, my brother, and I. That's the toughest part is that I can be a part of that structure. (LK)

Men's violence against women often carries with it significant shame and secrecy. Furthermore, children experience male dominance, and unhealthy beliefs develop, such as *women are irrational* and *women are objects*, which support inequality and violence against women. This phenomenon can make it very difficult for men entering college to have an intimate understanding of the amount and impact of women's experiences with inequality and violence. Participants in this project suggested that, as their awareness of the inequality and victimization that women experience increased, they were more likely to take responsibility for making things better.

Participants further suggested that personal connections with women highlight the difference between seeing sexism and men's violence against women as a subject versus an experience. In order to do well in a class or on a paper related to a presentation, students are required to study gender inequality and violence against women as a subject. They gain knowledge and understanding, which they apply to various life situations. Participants suggested that these learning experiences piqued their interest. Once the heart was engaged, however, participants perceived sexism and men's violence against women as an experience that impacted their lives as well as the lives of women around them. As a result, knowledge and understanding led to empathy and deeper evaluation of the world. Whether in a classroom, a presentation, or a men's group, higher levels of thinking and commitment seemed to occur when men stopped seeing sexism and men's violence against women as a subject and connected the issue with real women that existed in their lives.

Though most of the men in this project had a very intimate connection to men's violence against women, coming from an abusive background or having a close relationship with a woman who was sexually assaulted or battered was not required to connect the issue with the everyday reality of women.

Participants often referenced victimization and perpetration statistics for men's violence against women. As one student wrote in his personal statement:

> My experience in [a campus men's group] has both opened my eyes to staggering and devastating statistics with regard to sexual assault and rape on college campuses—nearly one in four women is a victim of sexual assault at some point in her college career—and filled me with an enthusiasm and determination I had never felt before. (PC)

Empathy for victimized women was said to have been enhanced through the personal connections participants made once they became aware of the immense scope of the issue. In this way, exposure to the real-life situation of women made cogent impressions on the males in the sample.

Participants also highlighted the fact that violence against women is predominately committed by men: "We have to face the reality that men are perpetrating ninety-five percent of the time, and women are primarily survivors of this issue" (AR). Each participant was asked what he thought caused violence against women. Participants almost uniformly identified socially constructed masculinity: "It's definitely masculinity I think . . . socialization . . . we promote rape culture. We promote violence" (TL). The sense of connectedness to the root cause of violence against women seemed to be a powerful influence. A participant expressed a sense of responsibility, as a man, to address it:

> I found that, as a man, it was my responsibility to take a stand and say that misogynist, male-dominant attitudes are not healthy attitudes for men or women. Also, because I am a son, grandson, nephew, cousin, and friend to many women, these issues are around me and I cannot sit by while they continue. (CG)

It appears that a deep personal engagement for the issues, through both participants' minds and hearts, and a strong sense of responsibility as men, combined to create the beginnings of a commitment to gender equality and antiviolence work rooted deeply in participants' identity.

Social/Peer Support and Exploration of Masculinity

The influence of a strong leader, friend, or close relative played a significant role in facilitating all but one participant's initial commitment to gender equality and antiviolence work. Influence came from a variety of sources. As one participant recalled, "A few [teammates] told me to get involved; it seemed like a good cause. My advisor at the time recommended me to the program as well" (OR). Participants' experiences suggested that one of the most effective methods for recruiting student involvement was for students, faculty, or staff to personally invite men into the group. One participant recalled:

> After watching Don McPherson speak for the second time[,] I talked to [two student leaders] to receive more information about [a campus men's group]. They were the ones who strongly encouraged me to keep the conversation going and to get more involved. Without them I wouldn't be filling out this form today. (IJ)

Some participants suggested that male students who appeared similar and had similar interests made the difference in becoming involved. When invited to participate by a male student with whom they were able to identify, participants reportedly felt much more comfortable about becoming involved.

The concept of a *man box*, often described as the restrictive hegemonic socialization of men based on domination and control, appeared frequently in interviews. Participants suggested social support from a group of men was valuable for thinking about their role as men and living outside the man box. As one participant wrote, "It's very rewarding. I have learned a lot of things about gender equality. More importantly, I am stepping outside the 'hegemonic male box,' and that alone is an amazing feeling" (MG). Participants clearly sought the social connections and support provided by a men's group, not only to step outside the man box but also to do something meaningful. One participant explained:

> It's seeing a problem, knowing that there's something wrong and you want to do something about

it, and you finally have an outlet to do it. You finally see other people who have been feeling the same way you have been feeling. (TC)

Social and peer support was of critical importance to participants for reasons including personal growth and influencing the greater campus. Each participant reportedly found support in some way from the men and women in their lives.

Guidance and Encouragement

Individual mentoring from adult leaders was said to have had a major impact on participants' commitment to gender equality and antiviolence work. Participants were cogently influenced by their mentors. One participant suggested that his mentors were " . . . like moms [to him]. They showed great passion for me to get involved. They saw that I had the resources to help football players to think critically about gender" (HT). Many participants described an intense appreciation for the way faculty/staff mentors and student leaders encouraged them, created an environment for them to grow, provided enough structure to make groups purposeful, and actually guided them through the process of becoming leaders and identifying this issue with their purpose in life.

Outside of their group, participants did not have the same support. Because women face sexism and the threat of physical and sexual violence every day, it is important to note that the lack of support participants described for their commitment to gender equality centered on discomfort. None of the participants mentioned fearing for their personal safety or feeling completely isolated on a campus. Actually, some participants received a great deal of praise, largely from individual women in their lives. Regardless, participants experienced discomfort from frequent resistance to gender equality on campus. For example, one participant recalled: "I have been shut down by men and women about critically analyzing gender. One man told me not to bring this feminist bullshit to the locker room" (OR). Participants' experiences with negative responses to their commitment helped highlight the importance

of guidance and encouragement through strong leadership. Participants described being ostracized and ridiculed as well as feeling like they were going against the tide—many men in their lives were saying and doing things that directly contradicted participants' beliefs. Participants particularly noted a threat of isolation.

Sometimes I will invent a fake job when people ask me what I do. I don't want to tell them I'm a rape crisis counselor. At a party they'll just walk away from me because they think I'm the downer . . . or they'll constantly be trying to throw these rape myths at me. Sometimes it's just eas[i]er to be a guy, "I work at a desk job, it's really boring." (LJ)

The threat of discomfort and lack of support made it more challenging for participants to live up to their own expectations of themselves. Participants talked about difficulties in turning beliefs into practice. It can be much easier not to fight the tide. As one participant explained:

It's hard to speak out sometimes. Like within the group it's easy because you all agree with the general idea anyway. But when you're out there, you know, you might get criticized for speaking out and that can be kind of hard. (DF)

This statement highlights the challenging connection between male privilege and commitment to gender equality. Participants tended to identify with male privilege as a concept, namely unearned benefits men get for being men. They described male privilege through examples, such as being able to walk alone at night, getting more credibility as a public speaker, and receiving higher salaries than women. Most participants did not connect male privilege to the challenges and values surrounding their daily commitment to end sexism and men's violence against women. Men grow up learning to expect male privilege. Aside from having power over women, these privileges can include the expectation of comfort both inside and outside oneself. When facing resistance, then, many participants seemed to struggle with having to give something up, such as the comfortable relationship with some of the men in their lives, to challenge gender inequality as the status quo. Participants sometimes seemed frustrated that they could not live up to their own personal expectations without some discomfort. These findings suggest adult leaders and mentors should help men identify and work through their own discomfort, using the lens of male privilege, as individuals and in a group. The findings also support a call to create accountable connections with feminist women on campus. Formalizing a commitment to feminist organizations and their mission statements would keep male privilege more visible in men's gender equality groups and help men's groups remain centered on their goals of ending sexism and men's violence against women.

Participants recognized, to varying degrees, that the resistance they experienced from many men and some women might be related to socialized complacency for structural sexism. Academic institutions, like other major institutions, often reflect normalized gender inequality. This can create environments that implicitly support resistance to gender equality work—and participants in the study reported resistance was high on their respective campuses. Many men are threatened by men working to end sexism and men's violence against women, especially when gender equality groups are challenging perspectives and institutionalized male privilege. Men committed to gender equality shook the status quo on their respective campuses—and received resistance due to the resulting discomfort. Facing an uphill battle, participants rallied around the support they found from their group on campus and focused on strengthening their ability to live in a way that reflects gender equality. Group leaders' guidance and encouragement also were major sources of inspiration.

Self-improvement and Altruism

Participants spoke of focusing heavily on self-improvement—becoming better men. They highlighted how their involvement in gender equality and antiviolence groups helped shape them. For example: "I've grown as a person. What matters to me and what I care about, it's changed because of this group. I respect myself. I respect others so much more"

(LG). Participants illustrated how their involvement had improved their present-day lives. They talked about improved relationships with their mothers and other family members, more fulfilling relationships with their romantic partners, better relationships with other men, a feeling of purpose in life, and more fulfilling experiences at their colleges or universities.

> And to really make it personal, it's a group that makes me stay at college, at the school I'm at right now. . . . And it's like, I feel motivated when I go to the meetings. I feel like, "Oh, I got to catch up on my studying because I've been slacking a bit. I've got to step my game up." (SL)

For many participants, campus gender equality and antiviolence groups helped create a more supportive, respectful, enjoyable campus environment, where they felt more equipped to achieve their fullest potential.

Participants expressed a strong sense that their exposure and commitment to gender equality and antiviolence work would positively shape and impact their lives in the future. This sentiment was seemingly deep-seated and proactive. For example, one participant articulated, "Our favorite statement is 'The man who views the world the same way at age 50 as he did at age 30 has wasted 20 years of his life'" (LH). Continued growth and development were commonly referenced throughout the interviews. Participants similarly discussed having a sense of purpose and better relationships: "I think being involved with this will help me in the future become a better husband, a better father, a better partner" (MB). They further explained a number of expectations and goals they had set for themselves. Statements, such as "I want to be present for, you know, everything that my kid does" (KA), were common. Ultimately, a clear sense of purpose and identity connected to gender equality seemed to be at the center of the numerous self-improvement benefits participants described. Gender equality and antiviolence groups helped participants form the internal beliefs and values that would shape the rest of their lives.

A sense of altruism was a universal component of each participant's commitment to gender equality and ending men's violence against women. Some participants described growing up with an understanding of the harm caused by male domination and men's violence against women. Others shared a more recent path to their understanding of the terrible impact of women's oppression. In all cases, participants shared a desire to make the world a better place. One participant illustrated this when sharing his personal creed, "If you make an observation, you have an obligation" (PO). He further explained, "In other words, I got tired of seeing males treat women like animals and abuse them" (PO). Another participant said, "That's always my goal is to help someone. I don't care if it's one person, I've helped someone" (EW). Many participants spoke about the duty they felt to make the world a better place for women. They wanted to be a catalyst to change the world, and the change was both internal and external for participants: "I'm making a difference and stepping outside the confined box of what it is to be a man and realizing that these are problems in our society that we need to tackle" (JG).

DISCUSSION

Campus-based gender equality and antiviolence groups were found to help men identify a greater purpose in life and possibly a vocation related to gender equality, contributing toward the creation of a world free from men's violence against women. In this context, the present research study provided insight into the motivation and experiences of men committed to such work and illuminated some opportunities and challenges facing men as they form deep, lifelong commitments to gender equality. Findings imply the following recommendations to those wishing to engage men on campus. These recommendations require fighting a strong current of normalized male dominance.

- The heart is central to facilitating commitment. Engage the mind to raise awareness, and connect campus men's lives to the pain, frustration, and sadness felt by women due to male domination and violence. Empathy is the most salient reason men make commitment, despite an evident lack of support from the greater community.

- Student leaders and adult mentors should personally encourage men to attend men's groups and become involved.
- Create a welcoming, challenging, and open space for men to socialize with like-minded men as a way to learn more about themselves and issues related to sexism and men's violence against women.
- Leaders and mentors should build personal relationships with group participants and guide them as they form strong personal commitments to the issue. Committed men should be challenged to find ways to shape their daily environments so they reflect gender equality. They will need help identifying and working through their resulting personal discomfort by using the lens of male privilege.
- Support participants as they recognize and embrace the deep personal impact their involvement could have on their lives.
- Help group participants cultivate an altruistic sense of identity and purpose for the rest of their lives.

The findings from the present study suggest that college men committing to gender equality and antiviolence work feel a lack of support from their campus environment. Insight from this project can help inform a conversation on how campuses can meaningfully support gender equality and antiviolence efforts. In many contexts, this will involve redoubling efforts to create an environment that serves as a model. Some helpful questions to consider for such a campaign might include the following: (a) What would our campus look like if it reflected the philosophies of gender equality and antiviolence groups? (b) What would the dorms be like? (c) What would be different about the athletic department and student union? (d) What sort of education and organizational policy and practices could begin creating those environments? (e) How could we support women's and men's efforts to organize around gender equality and ending men's violence against women? Support could take many forms, including staff and administrative participation in the groups, highlighting active groups during tours for prospective students and at first-year orientation, featuring the groups in literature about the campus, using institutional language that highlights equality, attracting media attention to the efforts of the groups, and funding. Students need resources, mentors, and approval from the campus community in order for these groups to thrive.

Aside from organizing campuses around gender equality, this project raises questions about what committed men can do to help create an equal world free from men's violence against women. Despite declaring a strong, long-term commitment, many participants had not thought very deeply about what they could do after college in order to create such a world. Project participants seemed to hold to the few examples of concrete activities they knew they could do. Some men talked about going to graduate school in a field related to gender. Others hoped to educate in some way about gender inequality and men's violence against women. Still others spoke about mentoring younger men. Overall, participants focused on personal changes they could make and a larger outlook for the world that they would like to see actualized.

Each participant's sense of purpose and altruism creates a significant opportunity for potential widespread action, but the lack of a deeply deliberated post-college plan of action threatens to limit his impact to a personal sphere. To maximize the impact of campus men committed to gender equality and ending men's violence against women, campus leaders should help men realize their potential as leaders and allies to women. Adult leaders must create on-campus opportunities to work toward transforming the campus climate through organizational practices and policies that will prevent sexism and men's violence against women. These opportunities should meet a parallel goal of preparing men to work outside campus to end sexism and violence against women. As campus men approach graduation and begin identifying work to end sexism and violence against women as a vocation, they must think beyond the few concrete examples of how men can be involved after college. Campus men should work to identify how they might have the greatest impact and strive to create those

opportunities for themselves in the culture. Feminist women did the very same thing as they created the sexual assault and battered women's movements. Committed men can contribute to these movements by creating opportunities for themselves that are in line with feminist women's organizations and their mission statements.

Two more recommendations address this gap between commitment and action: (a) Embark on an in-depth study of feminism as part of the group's weekly process and (b) create structured partnerships between committed men and feminist women's groups on campus. Have conversations and create written statements with feminist groups about accountability. Commitment to the goals and mission statements of feminist organizations is critical to men's ability to partner with women as safe and effective allies in ending sexism and men's violence against women.

Guiding men to partner as allies with women also will help them learn and identify more clearly how they can use their talents and skills for the broader movement. Too few examples existed of men's groups creating strong and sustained allied connections with women's groups among the participants in this study, and conversation about accountability to feminist groups or organizations and their mission was rare. Understanding of and identification with feminism was also varied with this group of participants. A stronger focus on feminism, the dynamics of men's involvement, and close, structured, and accountable connections between committed men and feminist women might better prepare men for an ongoing commitment as they end their academic careers.

Participants in this project represented a wealth of positive and exciting efforts on campuses across the nation. In the face of a reality where men are commonly resistant or unengaged, participants were committed to changing themselves and working toward gender equality and a world free from men's violence against women. These men represent a shifting of momentum, a changing social norm.

Campuses and the greater movement to end men's violence against women can guide and encourage this momentum. Imagine a campus where male and female students are working together with faculty, staff, and administration to ensure their campus is an environment supporting gender equality. Efforts to change social norms by engaging campus men as effective, accountable allies with women represent great potential to actualize this vision.

FUTURE RESEARCH

The present research study was an exploratory study of a salient need in contemporary higher education. Namely, men's involvement in violence prevention programs across American university campuses is a growing movement but also one where further empirical data are needed in order to better understand and serve the needs of campus programming. Future research studies should include survey data from regional and national samples. Such research should draw substantially from the findings of the present study. Good survey questions should be based partly in previous research findings and sufficiently grounded from empirically based conclusions (De Rada, 2005). The present study significantly contributes to this end.

Additionally, while the sample size of the present study was adequate for its intended, exploratory purpose, future studies should expand sample sizes in order to help bolster the present study's external validity. Ultimately, external validity in qualitative projects is achieved through replication (Firmin, 2006). Repeating the present study, therefore, at a variety of regional and national conferences will help show the interconnections among various participants and manifest clear patterns among reported data points.

Most of the participants were Caucasian, because this reflected the predominant race of the conference participants from which the sample was drawn. Further studies should expand this subject pool to include additional participants from racial minority populations. A study that focuses specifically on minority men would be of particular interest, comparing the results with the present findings. If samples could be adequately drawn, then a series

of studies drawn from independent minority groups (e.g., African-American, Asian-American, Hispanic) would be useful in order to compare how different minority individuals might view their respective participations with violence prevention for women.

REFERENCES

Arminio, J.L., & Hulgren, F.H. (2002). Breaking out from the shadow: The question of criteria in qualitative research. *Journal of College Student Development, 43,* 447–460.

Bailey, C.A. (2007). *A guide to qualitative field research* (2nd ed.). Thousand Oaks, CA: Sage.

Bereska, T.M. (2003). How will I know a code when I see it? *Qualitative Research Journal, 3,* 60–74.

Centers for Disease Control and Prevention & National Center for Injury Prevention and Control. (2007). *Understanding sexual violence.* Retrieved from http://www.cdc.gov/ncipc/pub-res/images/SV%20Factsheet.pdf

Daytner, K. (2006, June). *Validity in qualitative research: Application of safeguards.* Paper presented at the 18th Annual Ethnographic & Qualitative Research Conference, Cedarville, OH.

De Rada, V.D. (2005). The effect of follow-up mailings on the response rate and response quality in mail surveys. *Quality and Quantity, 39,* 1–18.

Firmin, M. (2006). External validity in qualitative research. In M. Firmin & P. Brewer (Eds.). *Ethnographic & qualitative research in education* (Vol. 2, pp. 17–29). New Castle, UK: Cambridge Scholars Press.

Gay, L.R., Mills, G.E., & Airasian, P. (2009). *Educational research* (9th ed.). Upper Saddle River, NJ: Pearson.

Maxwell, J.A. (2005). *Qualitative research design* (2nd ed.). Thousand Oaks, CA: Sage.

Merriam, S.B. (2002). Assessing and evaluating qualitative research. In S. Merriam (Ed.), *Qualitative research in practice* (pp. 18–33). San Francisco: Jossey-Bass.

National Center for Victims of Crime. (2007). *Teen dating violence fact sheet.* Retrieved from http://www.cdc.gov/ncipc/pub-res/images/SV%20Factsheet.pdf

Seidman, I. (2006). *Interviewing as qualitative research* (3rd ed.). New York: Teachers College Press.

PART TWELVE

MEN, MOVEMENTS, AND THE FUTURE

Q: Why did you decide to record again?

A: Because this housewife would like to have a career for a bit! On October 9, I'll be 40, and Sean will be 5 and I can afford to say, "Daddy does something else as well." He's not accustomed to it—in five years I hardly picked up a guitar. Last Christmas our neighbors showed him "Yellow Submarine" and he came running in, saying, "Daddy, you were singing . . . Were you a Beatle?" I said, "Well—yes, right."

—John Lennon, interview for *Newsweek*, 1980

Are men changing? If so, in what directions? Can men change even more? In what ways should men be different? We posed many of these questions at the beginning of our exploration of men's lives, and we return to them here, in the last part of the book, to examine the directions men have taken to enlarge their roles, to expand the meaning of masculinity, to change the rules.

The articles in this part address the possibility and the direction of change for men: how shall we, as a society, understand masculinity in the modern world? Raewyn Connell provides a global overview of institutional masculinities. The Statement of the United Nations Commission on the Status of Women outlines the importance of involving men in the global struggles for gender equality.

On the more personal side of the ledger, Erin Casey and Tyler Smith offer a sociological perspective on the moral and political efforts by men to support gender equality in moral and political terms, and Jackson Katz examines the ways in which individual men are stepping up for equality and, in the process, redefining masculinity.

CHANGE AMONG THE GATEKEEPERS: MEN, MASCULINITIES, AND GENDER EQUALITY IN THE GLOBAL ARENA

Raewyn Connell

Equality between women and men has been a doctrine well recognized in international law since the adoption of the 1948 *Universal Declaration of Human Rights* (United Nations 1958), and as a principle it enjoys popular support in many countries. The idea of gender equal rights has provided the formal basis for the international discussion of the position of women since the 1975–85 UN Decade for Women, which has been a key element in the story of global feminism (Bulbeck 1988). The idea that men might have a specific role in relation to this principle has emerged only recently.

The issue of gender equality was placed on the policy agenda by women. The reason is obvious: it is women who are disadvantaged by the main patterns of gender inequality and who therefore have the claim for redress. Men are, however, necessarily involved in gender-equality reform. Gender inequalities are embedded in a multidimensional structure of relationships between women and men, which, as the modern sociology of gender shows, operates at every level of human experience, from economic arrangements, culture, and the state to interpersonal relationships and individual emotions (Holter 1997; Walby 1997; Connell 2002). Moving toward a gender-equal society involves profound institutional change as well as change in everyday life and personal conduct. To move far in this direction requires widespread social support, including significant support from men and boys.

Further, the very gender inequalities in economic assets, political power, and cultural authority, as well as the means of coercion, that gender reforms intend to change, currently mean that men (often specific groups of men) control most of the resources required to implement women's claims for justice. Men and boys are thus in significant ways gatekeepers for gender equality. Whether they are willing to open the gates for major reforms is an important strategic question.

In this article, I will trace the emergence of a worldwide discussion of men and gender-equality reform and will try to assess the prospects of reform strategies involving men. To make such an assessment, it is necessary to set recent policy discussions in the wider context of the cultural problematization of men and boys, the politics of "men's movements," the divided interests of men and boys in gender relations, and the growing research evidence about the changing and conflict-ridden social construction of masculinities.

In an article of this scope, it is not possible to address particular national agendas in detail. I will refer to a number of texts where these stories can be found. Because my primary concern is with the global character of the debate, I will give particular attention to policy discussions in UN forums. These discussions culminated in the 2004 meeting of the UN Commission on the Status of Women, which produced the first world-level policy document on the role of men and boys in relation to gender equality (UN Commission on the Status of Women 2004).

MEN AND MASCULINITIES IN THE WORLD GENDER ORDER

In the last fifteen years, in the "developed" countries of the global metropole, there has been a great deal of popular concern with issues about men and boys. Readers in the United States may recall a volume by the poet Robert Bly, *Iron John: A Book about Men* (1990), which became a huge best seller in the early 1990s, setting off a wave of imitations. This book became popular because it offered, in prophetic language, simple solutions to problems that were increasingly troubling the culture. A therapeutic movement was then developing in the United States, mainly though not exclusively among middle-class men, addressing problems in relationships, sexuality, and identity (Kupers 1993; Schwalbe 1996).

More specific issues about men and boys have also attracted public attention in the developed countries. Men's responses to feminism, and to gender-equality measures taken by government, have long been the subject of debate in Germany and Scandinavia (Metz-Göckel and Müller 1985; Holter 2003). In anglophone countries there has been much discussion of "the new fatherhood" and of supposed changes in men's involvement in families (McMahon 1999). There has been public agonizing about boys' "failure" in school, and in Australia there are many proposals for special programs for boys (Kenway 1997; Lingard 2003). Men's violence toward women has been the subject of practical interventions and extensive debate (Hearn 1998). There has also been increasing debate about men's health and illness from a gender perspective (Hurrelmann and Kolip 2002).

Accompanying these debates has been a remarkable growth of research about men's gender identities and practices, masculinities and the social processes by which they are constructed, cultural and media images of men, and related matters. Academic journals have been founded for specialized research on men and masculinities, there have been many research conferences, and there is a rapidly growing international literature. We now have a far more sophisticated and detailed scientific understanding of issues about men, masculinities, and gender than ever before (Connell 2003a).

This set of concerns, though first articulated in the developed countries, can now be found worldwide (Connell 2000; Pease and Pringle 2001). Debates on violence, patriarchy, and ways of changing men's conduct have occurred in countries as diverse as Germany, Canada, and South Africa (Hagemann-White 1992; Kaufman 1993; Morrell 2001a). Issues about masculine sexuality and fatherhood have been debated and researched in Brazil, Mexico, and many other countries (Arilha, Unbehaum Ridenti, and Medrado 1998; Lerner 1998). A men's center with a reform agenda has been established in Japan, where conferences have been held and media debates about traditional patterns of masculinity and family life continue (Menzu Senta 1997; Roberson and Suzuki 2003). A "traveling seminar" discussing issues about men, masculinities, and gender equality has recently been touring in India (Roy 2003). Debates about boys' education, men's identities, and gender change are active from New Zealand to Denmark (Law, Campbell, and Dolan 1999; Reinicke 2002). Debates about men's sexuality, and changing sexual identities, are also international (Altman 2001).

The research effort is also worldwide. Documentation of the diverse social constructions of masculinity has been undertaken in countries as far apart as Peru (Fuller 2001), Japan (Taga 2001), and Turkey (Sinclair-Webb 2000). The first large-scale comparative study of men and gender relations has recently been completed in ten European countries (Hearn et al. 2002). The first global synthesis, in the form of a world handbook of research on men and masculinities, has now appeared (Kimmel, Hearn, and Connell 2005).

The rapid internationalization of these debates reflects the fact—increasingly recognized in feminist thought (Bulbeck 1998; Marchand and

Runyan 2000)—that gender relations themselves have an international dimension. Each of the substructures of gender relations can be shown to have a global dimension, growing out of the history of imperialism and seen in the contemporary process of globalization (Connell 2002). Change in gender relations occurs on a world scale, though not always in the same direction or at the same pace.

The complexity of the patterns follows from the fact that gender change occurs in several different modes. Most dramatic is the direct colonization of the gender order of regions beyond the metropole. There has also been a more gradual recomposition of gender orders, both those of the colonizing society and the colonized, in the process of colonial interaction. The hybrid gender identities and sexualities now much discussed in the context of postcolonial societies are neither unusual nor new. They are a feature of the whole history of imperialism and are visible in many contemporary studies (e.g., Valdés and Olavarría 1998).

Imperialism and globalization change the conditions of existence for gender orders. For instance, the linking of previously separate production systems changes the flow of goods and services in the gendered division of labor, as seen in the impact of industrially produced foods and textiles on household economies. Colonialism itself often confronted local patriarchies with colonizing patriarchies, producing a turbulent and sometimes very violent aftermath, as in southern Africa (Morrell 1998). Pressure from contemporary Western commercial culture has destabilized gender arrangements, and models of masculinity, in Japan (Ito 1992), the Arab world (Ghoussoub 2000), and elsewhere.

Finally, the emergence of new arenas of social relationship on a world scale creates new patterns of gender relations. Transnational corporations, international communications systems, global mass media, and international state structures (from the United Nations to the European Union) are such arenas. These institutions have their own gender regimes and may form the basis for new configurations of masculinity, as has recently been argued for transnational business (Connell 2000) and the international relations system (Hooper 2001). Local gender orders now interact not only with the gender orders of other local societies but also with the gender order of the global arena.

The dynamics of the world gender order affect men as profoundly as they do women, though this fact has been less discussed. The best contemporary research on men and masculinity, such as Matthew C. Gutmann's (2002) ethnographic work in Mexico, shows in fine detail how the lives of particular groups of men are shaped by globally acting economic and political dynamics.

Different groups of men are positioned very differently in such processes. There is no single formula that accounts for men and globalization. There is, indeed, a growing polarization among men on a world scale. Studies of the "super-rich" (Haseler 2000) show a privileged minority reaching astonishing heights of wealth and power while much larger numbers face poverty, cultural dislocation, disruption of family relationships, and forced renegotiation of the meanings of masculinity.

Masculinities, as socially constructed configurations of gender practice, are also created through a historical process with a global dimension. The old-style ethnographic research that located gender patterns purely in a local context is inadequate to the reality. Historical research, such as Robert Morrell's (2001b) study of the masculinities of the colonizers in South Africa and T. Dunbar Moodie's (1994) study of the colonized, shows how a gendered culture is created and transformed in relation to the international economy and the political system of empire. There is every reason to think this principle holds for contemporary masculinities.

SHIFTING GROUND: MEN AND BOYS IN GENDER-EQUALITY DEBATES

Because of the way they came onto the agenda of public debate, gender issues have been widely regarded as women's business and of little concern to men and boys. In almost all policy discussions, to adopt a gender perspective substantially means to address women's concerns.

In both national and international policy documents concerned with gender equality, women are the subjects of the policy discourse. The agencies or meetings that formulate, implement, or monitor gender policies usually have names referring to women, such as Department for Women, Women's Equity Bureau, Prefectural Women's Centre, or Commission on the Status of Women. Such bodies have a clear mandate to act for women. They do not have an equally clear mandate to act with respect to men. The major policy documents concerned with gender equality, such as the UN *Convention on the Elimination of All Forms of Discrimination against Women* (United Nations [1979] 1989), often do not name men as a group and rarely discuss men in concrete terms.

However, men are present as background throughout these documents. In every statement about women's disadvantages, there is an implied comparison with men as the advantaged group. In the discussions of violence against women, men are implied, and sometimes named, as the perpetrators. In discussions of gender and HIV/AIDS, men are commonly construed as being "the problem," the agents of infection. In discussions of women's exclusion from power and decision making, men are implicitly present as the power holders.

When men are present only as a background category in a policy discourse about women, it is difficult to raise issues about men's and boys' interests, problems, or differences. This could be done only by falling into a backlash posture and affirming "men's rights" or by moving outside a gender framework altogether.

The structure of gender-equality policy, therefore, created an opportunity for antifeminist politics. Opponents of feminism have now found issues about boys and men to be fertile ground. This is most clearly seen in the United States, where authors such as Warren Farrell (1993) and Christina Hoff Sommers (2000), purporting to speak on behalf of men and boys, bitterly accuse feminism of injustice. Men and boys, they argue, are the truly disadvantaged group and need supportive programs in education and health, in situations of family breakup, and so forth. These ideas have not stimulated a social movement, with the exception of a small-scale (though active and sometimes violent) "father's rights" movement in relation to divorce. The arguments have, however, strongly appealed to the neoconservative mass media, which have given them international circulation. They now form part of the broad neoconservative repertoire of opposition to "political correctness" and to social justice measures.

Some policy makers have attempted to straddle this divide by restructuring gender-equality policy in the form of parallel policies for women and men. For instance, some recent health policy initiatives in Australia have added a "men's health" document to a "women's health" document (Schofield 2004). Similarly, in some school systems a "boys' education" strategy has been added to a "girls' education" strategy (Lingard 2003).

This approach acknowledges the wider scope of gender issues. But it also risks weakening the equality rationale of the original policy. It forgets the relational character of gender and therefore tends to redefine women and men, or girls and boys, simply as different market segments for some service. Ironically, the result may be to promote more gender segregation, not less. This has certainly happened in education, where some privileged boys' schools have jumped on the "gender equality" bandwagon and now market themselves as experts in catering to the special needs of boys.

On the other hand, bringing men's problems into an existing framework of policies for women may weaken the authority that women have so far gathered in that policy area. In the field of gender and development, for instance, some specialists argue that "bringing men in"—given the larger context in which men still control most of the wealth and institutional authority—may undermine, not help, the drive for gender equality (White 2000).

The role of men and boys in relation to gender equality emerged as an issue in international discussions during the 1990s. This development crystallized at the Fourth World Conference on Women, held in Beijing in 1995. Paragraph 25 of the *Beijing*

Declaration committed participating governments to "encourage men to participate fully in all actions towards equality" (United Nations 2001). The detailed "Platform for Action" that accompanied the declaration prominently restated the principle of shared power and responsibility between men and women and argued that women's concerns could be addressed only "in partnership with men" toward gender equality (2001, pars. 1, 3). The "Platform for Action" went on to specify areas where action involving men and boys was needed and was possible: in education, socialization of children, child care and housework, sexual health, gender-based violence, and the balancing of work and family responsibilities (2001, pars. 40, 72, 83b, 107c, 108e, 120, 179).

Participating member states followed a similar approach in the twenty-third special session of the UN General Assembly in the year 2000, which was intended to review the situation five years after the Beijing conference. The "Political Declaration" of this session made an even stronger statement on men's responsibility: "[Member states of the United Nations] emphasise that men must involve themselves and take joint responsibility with women for the promotion of gender equality" (United Nations 2001, par. 6). It still remained the case, in this and the accompanying "Outcome Document," that men were present on the margins of a policy discourse concerned with women.

The role of men and boys has also been addressed in other recent international meetings. These include the 1995 World Summit on Social Development, its review session in 2000, and the special session of the General Assembly on HIV/AIDS in 2001. In 1997 the UN Educational, Scientific, and Cultural Organization (UNESCO) convened an expert group meeting about "Male Roles and Masculinities in the Perspective of a Culture of Peace," which met in Oslo and produced studies on the links among personal violence, war, and the construction of masculinities (Breines, Connell, and Eide 2000).

International meetings outside the UN system have addressed similar issues. In 1997 the Nordic Council of Ministers adopted the *Nordic Action Plan*

for Men and Gender Equality. In the same year the Council of Europe conducted a seminar on equality as a common issue for men and women and made the role of men in promoting equality a theme at a ministerial conference. In 1998 the Latin American Federation of Social Science (FLACSO) began a series of conferences about masculinities, boys, and men across Latin America and the Caribbean. The first conference in this series had the specific theme of gender equity (Valdés and Olavarría 1998). The European Commission has recently funded a research network on men and masculinities.

DIVIDED INTERESTS: SUPPORT AND RESISTANCE

There is something surprising about the worldwide problematizing of men and masculinities, because in many ways the position of men has not greatly changed. For instance, men remain a very large majority of corporate executives, top professionals, and holders of public office. Worldwide, men hold nine out of ten cabinet-level posts in national governments, nearly as many of the parliamentary seats, and most top positions in international agencies. Men, collectively, receive approximately twice the income that women receive and also receive the benefits of a great deal of unpaid household labor, not to mention emotional support, from women (Gierycz 1999; Godenzi 2000; Inter-Parliamentary Union 2003).

The UN Development Program (2003) now regularly incorporates a selection of such statistics into its annual report on world human development, combining them into a "gender-related development index" and a "gender empowerment measure." This produces a dramatic outcome, a league table of countries ranked in terms of gender equality, which shows most countries in the world to be far from gender-equal. It is clear that, globally, men have a lot to lose from pursuing gender equality because men, collectively, continue to receive a patriarchal dividend.

But this way of picturing inequality may conceal as much as it reveals. There are multiple dimensions in gender relations, and the patterns of inequality in these dimensions may be qualitatively different. If we look separately at each of the sub-structures of gender, we find a pattern of advantages for men but also a linked pattern of disadvantages or toxicity (Connell 2003c).

For instance, in relation to the gender division of labor, men collectively receive the bulk of income in the money economy and occupy most of the managerial positions. But men also provide the workforce for the most dangerous occupations, suffer most industrial injuries, pay most of the taxation, and are under heavier social pressure to remain employed. In the domain of power men collectively control the institutions of coercion and the means of violence (e.g., weapons). But men are also the main targets of military violence and criminal assault, and many more men than women are imprisoned or executed. Men's authority receives more social recognition (e.g., in religion), but men and boys are underrepresented in important learning experiences (e.g., in humanistic studies) and important dimensions of human relations (e.g., with young children).

One could draw up a balance sheet of the costs and benefits to men from the current gender order. But this balance sheet would not be like a corporate accounting exercise where there is a bottom line, subtracting costs from income. The disadvantages listed above are, broadly speaking, the conditions of the advantages. For instance, men cannot hold state power without some men becoming the agents of violence. Men cannot be the beneficiaries of women's domestic labor and "emotion work" without many of them losing intimate connections, for instance, with young children.

Equally important, the men who receive most of the benefits and the men who pay most of the costs are not the same individuals. As the old saying puts it, generals die in bed. On a global scale, the men who benefit from corporate wealth, physical security, and expensive health care are a very different group from the men who provide the workforce of developing countries. Class, race, national, regional, and generational differences cross-cut the category "men," spreading the gains and costs of

gender relations very unevenly among men. There are many situations where groups of men may see their interest as more closely aligned with the women in their communities than with other men. It is not surprising that men respond very diversely to gender-equality politics.

There is, in fact, a considerable history of support for gender equality among men. There is certainly a tradition of advocacy by male intellectuals. In Europe, well before modern gender-equality documents were written, the British philosopher John Stuart Mill published "The Subjection of Women" (1912), which established the presumption of equal rights; and the Norwegian dramatist Henrik Ibsen, in plays like *A Doll's House* ([1923] 1995), made gender oppression an important cultural theme. In the following generation, the pioneering Austrian psychoanalyst Alfred Adler established a powerful psychological argument for gender equality (Connell 1995). A similar tradition of men's advocacy exists in the United States (Kimmel and Mosmiller 1992).

Many of the historic gains by women's advocates have been won in alliance with men who held organizational or political authority at the time. For instance, the introduction of equal employment opportunity measures in New South Wales, Australia, occurred with the strong support of the premier and the head of a reform inquiry into the public sector, both men (Eisenstein 1991). Sometimes men's support for gender equality takes the form of campaigning and organizing among men. The most prominent example is the U.S. National Organization of Men against Sexism (NOMAS), which has existed for more than twenty years (Cohen 1991). Men's groups concerned with reforming masculinity, publications advocating change, and campaigns among men against violence toward women are found widely, for instance, in the United Kingdom, Mexico, and South Africa (Seidler 1991; Zingoni 1998; Peacock 2003).

Men have also been active in creating educational programs for boys and young men intended to support gender reform. Similar strategies have been developed for adult men, sometimes in a religious and sometimes in a health or therapeutic context. There is a strong tradition of such work in Germany, with programs that combine the search for self-knowledge with the learning of antisexist behavior (Brandes and Bullinger 1996). Work of the same kind has developed in Brazil, the United States, and other countries (Denborough 1996; Lyra and Medrado 2001).

These initiatives are widespread, but they are also mostly small-scale. What of the wider state of opinion? European survey research has shown no consensus among men either for or against gender equality. Sometimes a third/third/third pattern appears, with about one-third of men supporting change toward equality, about one-third opposing it, and one-third undecided or intermediate (Holter 1997, 131–34). Nevertheless, examinations of the survey evidence from the United States, Germany, and Japan have shown a long-term trend of growing support for change, that is, a movement away from traditional gender roles, especially among members of the younger generation (Thornton 1989; Zulehner and Volz 1998; Mohwald 2002).

There is, however, also significant evidence of men's and boys' resistance to change in gender relations. The survey research reveals substantial levels of doubt and opposition, especially among older men. Research on workplaces and on corporate management has documented many cases where men maintain an organizational culture that is heavily masculinized and unwelcoming to women. In some cases there is active opposition to gender-equality measures or quiet undermining of them (Cockburn 1991; Collinson and Hearn 1996). Research on schools has also found cases where boys assert control of informal social life and direct hostility against girls and against boys perceived as being different. The status quo can be defended even in the details of classroom life, for instance, when a particular group of boys used misogynist language to resist study of a poem that questioned Australian gender stereotypes (Kenworthy 1994; Holland et al. 1998).

Some men accept change in principle but in practice still act in ways that sustain men's dominance of the public sphere and assign domestic labor and child care to women. In strongly gender segregated societies, it may be difficult for men to recognize alternatives or to understand women's experiences (Kandiyoti 1994; Fuller 2001; Meuser 2003). Another type of opposition to reform, more common among men in business and government, rejects gender-equality measures because it rejects all government action in support of equality, in favor of the unfettered action of the market.

The reasons for men's resistance include the patriarchal dividend discussed above and threats to identity that occur with change. If social definitions of masculinity include being the breadwinner and being "strong," then men may be offended by women's professional progress because it makes men seem less worthy of respect. Resistance may also reflect ideological defense of male supremacy. Research on domestic violence suggests that male batterers often hold very conservative views of women's role in the family (Ptacek 1988). In many parts of the world, there exist ideologies that justify men's supremacy on grounds of religion, biology, cultural tradition, or organizational mission (e.g., in the military). It is a mistake to regard these ideas as simply outmoded. They may be actively modernized and renewed.

GROUNDS FOR OPTIMISM: CAPACITIES FOR EQUALITY AND REASONS FOR CHANGE

The public debates about men and boys have often been inconclusive. But they have gone a long way, together with the research, to shatter one widespread belief that has hindered gender reform. This obstacle is the belief that men *cannot* change their ways, that "boys will be boys," that rape, war, sexism, domestic violence, aggression, and self-centeredness are natural to men.

We now have many documented examples of the diversity of masculinities and of men's and boys' capacity for equality. For instance, life-history research in Chile has shown that there is no unitary Chilean masculinity, despite the cultural homogeneity of the country. While a hegemonic model is widely diffused across social strata, there are many men who depart from it, and there is significant discontent with traditional roles (Valdés and Olavarría 1998). Though groups of boys in schools often have a dominant or hegemonic pattern of masculinity, there are usually also other patterns present, some of which involve more equal and respectful relations with girls.

Research in Britain, for instance, shows how boys encounter and explore alternative models of masculinity as they grow up (Mac an Ghaill 1994; O'Donnell and Sharpe 2000).

Psychological and educational research shows personal flexibility in the face of gender stereotypes. Men and boys can vary, or strategically use, conventional definitions of masculinity. It is even possible to teach boys (and girls) how to do this in school, as experiments in Australian classrooms have shown (Davies 1993; Wetherell and Edley 1999).

Changes have occurred in men's practices within certain families, where there has been a conscious shift toward more equal sharing of housework and child care. The sociologist Barbara J. Risman (1998), who has documented such cases in one region of the United States, calls them "fair families." It is clear from her research that the change has required a challenge to traditional models of masculinity. In the Shanghai region of China, there is an established local tradition of relative gender equality, and men are demonstrably willing to be involved in domestic work. Research by Da Wei Wei (Da 2004) shows this tradition persisting among Shanghai men even after migration to another country.

Perhaps the most extensive social action involving men in gender change has occurred in Scandinavia. This includes provisions for paternity leave that have had high rates of take-up, among the most dramatic of all demonstrations of men's willingness to change gender practices. Øystein Holter sums up the research and practical experience: "The Nordic 'experiment' has shown that a *majority* of men can change their practice when circumstances are favorable. . . . When reforms or support policies are well-designed and targeted towards an on-going

cultural process of change, men's active support for gender-equal status increases" (1997, 126). Many groups of men, it is clear, have a capacity for equality and for gender change. But what reasons for change are men likely to see?

Early statements often assumed that men had the same interest as women in escaping from restrictive sex roles (e.g., Palme 1972). Later experience has not confirmed this view. Yet men and boys often do have substantial reasons to support change, which can readily be listed.

First, men are not isolated individuals. Men and boys live in social relationships, many with women and girls: wives, partners, mothers, aunts, daughters, nieces, friends, classmates, workmates, professional colleagues, neighbors, and so on. The quality of every man's life depends to a large extent on the quality of those relationships. We may therefore speak of men's relational interests in gender equality.

For instance, very large numbers of men are fathers, and about half of their children are girls. Some men are sole parents and are then deeply involved in caregiving—an important demonstration of men's capacity for care (Risman 1986). Even in intact partnerships with women, many men have close relationships with their children, and psychological research shows the importance of these relationships (Kindler 2002). In several parts of the world, young men are exploring more engaged patterns of fatherhood (Olavarría 2001). To make sure that daughters grow up in a world that offers young women security, freedom, and opportunities to fulfil their talents is a powerful reason for many men to support gender equality.

Second, men may wish to avoid the toxic effects that the gender order has for them. James Harrison long ago issued a "Warning: The Male Sex Role May Be Dangerous to Your Health" (1978). Since then health research has documented specific problems for men and boys. Among them are premature death from accident, homicide, and suicide; occupational injury; higher levels of drug abuse, especially of alcohol and tobacco; and in some countries at least, a relative unwillingness by men to seek medical help when it is needed. Attempts to assert a tough and dominant masculinity sustain some of these patterns (Sabo and Gordon 1995; Hurrelmann and Kolip 2002).

Social and economic pressures on men to compete in the workplace, to increase their hours of paid work, and sometimes to take second jobs are among the most powerful constraints on gender reform. Desire for a better balance between work and life is widespread among employed men. On the other hand, where unemployment is high the lack of a paid job can be a damaging pressure on men who have grown up with the expectation of being breadwinners. This is, for instance, an important gender issue in postapartheid South Africa. Opening alternative economic paths and moving toward what German discussions have called "multioptional masculinities" may do much to improve men's well-being *(Widersprüche* 1998; Morrell 2001a).

Third, men may support gender change because they see its relevance to the well-being of the community they live in. In situations of mass poverty and underemployment, for instance in cities in developing countries, flexibility in the gender division of labor may be crucial to a household that requires women's earnings as well as men's. Reducing the rigidity of masculinities may also yield benefits in security. Civil and international violence is strongly associated with dominating patterns of masculinity and with marked gender inequality in the state. Movement away from these patterns makes it easier for men to adopt historically "feminine" styles of nonviolent negotiation and conflict resolution (Zalewski and Parpart 1998; Breines, Connell, and Eide 2000; Cockburn 2003). This may also reduce the toxic effects of policing and incarceration (Sabo, Kupers, and London 2001).

Finally, men may support gender reform because gender equality follows from their political or ethical principles. These may be religious, socialist, or broad democratic beliefs. Mill argued a case based on classical liberal principles a century and a half ago, and the idea of equal human rights still has purchase among large groups of men.

GROUNDS FOR PESSIMISM: THE SHAPE OF MASCULINITY POLITICS

The diversity among men and masculinities is reflected in a diversity of men's movements in the developed countries. A study of the United States found multiple movements, with different agendas for the remaking of masculinity. They operated on the varying terrains of gender equality, men's rights, and ethnic or religious identities (Messner 1997). There is no unified political position for men and no authoritative representation of men's interests.

Men's movements specifically concerned with gender equality exist in a number of countries. A well-known example is the White Ribbon Campaign, dedicated to mobilizing public opinion and educating men and boys for the prevention of men's violence against women. Originating in Canada, in response to the massacre of women in Montreal in 1989, the White Ribbon Campaign achieved very high visibility in that country, with support from political and community leaders and considerable outreach in schools and mass media. More recently, it has spread to other countries. Groups concerned with violence prevention have appeared in other countries, such as Men against Sexual Assault in Australia and Men Overcoming Violence (MOVE) in the United States. These have not achieved the visibility of the White Ribbon Campaign but have built up a valuable body of knowledge about the successes and difficulties of organizing among men (Lichterman 1989; Pease 1997; Kaufman 1999).

The most extensive experience of any group of men organizing around issues of gender and sexual politics is that of homosexual men, in antidiscrimination campaigns, the gay liberation movement, and community responses to the HIV/AIDS pandemic. Gay men have pioneered in areas such as community care for the sick, community education for responsible sexual practices, representation in the public sector, and overcoming social exclusion, which are important for all groups of men concerned with gender equality (Kippax et al. 1993; Altman 1994).

Explicit backlash movements also exist but have not generally had a great deal of influence. Men mobilizing as men to oppose women tend to be seen as cranks or fanatics. They constantly exaggerate women's power. And by defining men's interests in opposition to women's, they get into cultural difficulties, since they have to violate a main tenet of modern patriarchal ideology—the idea that "opposites attract" and that men's and women's needs, interests, and choices are complementary.

Much more important for the defense of gender inequality are movements in which men's interests are a side effect—nationalist, ethnic, religious, and economic movements. Of these, the most influential on a world scale is contemporary neoliberalism—the political and cultural promotion of free-market principles and individualism and the rejection of state control.

Neoliberalism is in principle gender neutral. The "individual" has no gender, and the market delivers an advantage to the smartest entrepreneur, not to men or women as such. But neoliberalism does not pursue social justice in relation to gender. In Eastern Europe, the restoration of capitalism and the arrival of neoliberal politics have been followed by a sharp deterioration in the position of women. In rich Western countries, neoliberalism from the 1980s on has attacked the welfare state, on which far more women than men depend; supported deregulation of labor markets, resulting in increased casualization of women workers; shrunk public sector employment, the sector of the economy where women predominate; lowered rates of personal taxation, the main basis of tax transfers to women; and squeezed public education, the key pathway to labor market advancement for women. However, the same period saw an expansion of the human-rights agenda, which is, on the whole, an asset for gender equality.

The contemporary version of neoliberalism, known as neoconservatism in the United States, also has some gender complexities. George W. Bush was the first U.S. president to place a woman in the very heart of the state security apparatus, as national security adviser to the president. And some of the regime's actions, such as the attack on the Taliban regime in Afghanistan, were defended as a means of emancipating women.

Yet neoconservatism and state power in the United States and its satellites such as Australia remain overwhelmingly the province of men—indeed, men of a particular character: power oriented and ruthless, restrained by little more than calculations of likely opposition. There has been a sharp remasculinization of political rhetoric and a turn to the use of force as a primary instrument in policy. The human-rights discourse is muted and sometimes completely abandoned (as in the U.S. prison camp for Muslim captives at Guantanamo Bay and the Australian prison camps for refugees in the central desert and Pacific islands).

Neoliberalism can function as a form of masculinity politics largely because of the powerful role of the state in the gender order. The state constitutes gender relations in multiple ways, and all of its gender policies affect men. Many mainstream policies (e.g., in economic and security affairs) are substantially about men without acknowledging this fact (Nagel 1998; O'Connor, Orloff, and Shaver 1999; Connell 2003b).

This points to a realm of institutional politics where men's and women's interests are very much at stake, without the publicity created by social movements. Public-sector agencies (Jensen 1998; Mackay and Bilton 2000; Schofield, forthcoming), private-sector corporations (Marchand and Runyan 2000; Hearn and Parkin 2001), and unions (Corman et al. 1993; Franzway 2001) are all sites of masculinized power and struggles for gender equality. In each of these sites, some men can be found with a commitment to gender equality, but in each case that is an embattled position. For gender-equality outcomes, it is important to have support from men in the top organizational levels, but this is not often reliably forthcoming.

One reason for the difficulty in expanding men's opposition to sexism is the role of highly conservative men as cultural authorities and managers. Major religious organizations, in Christianity, Islam, and Buddhism, are controlled by men who sometimes completely exclude women, and these organizations have often been used to oppose the emancipation of women. Transnational media organizations such as Rupert Murdoch's conglomerate are equally active in promoting conservative gender ideology.

A specific address to men is found in the growing institutional, media, and business complex of commercial sports. With its overwhelming focus on male athletes; its celebration of force, domination, and competitive success; its valorization of male commentators and executives; and its marginalization and frequent ridicule of women, the sports/business complex has become an increasingly important site for representing and defining gender. This is not traditional patriarchy. It is something new, welding exemplary bodies to entrepreneurial culture. Michael Messner (2002), one of the leading analysts of contemporary sports, formulates the effect well by saying that commercial sports define the renewed centrality of men and of a particular version of masculinity.

On a world scale, explicit backlash movements are of limited importance, but very large numbers of men are nevertheless engaged in preserving gender inequality. Patriarchy is defended diffusely. There is support for change from equally large numbers of men, but it is an uphill battle to articulate that support. That is the political context with which new gender-equality initiatives have to deal.

WAYS FORWARD: TOWARD A GLOBAL FRAMEWORK

Inviting men to end men's privileges, and to remake masculinities to sustain gender equality, strikes many people as a strange or Utopian project. Yet this project is already under way. Many men around the world are engaged in gender reforms, for the good reasons discussed above.

The diversity of masculinities complicates the process but is also an important asset. As this diversity becomes better known, men and boys can more easily see a range of possibilities for their own lives, and both men and women are less likely to think of gender inequality as unchangeable. It also becomes possible to identify specific groups of men who might engage in alliances for change.

The international policy documents discussed above rely on the concept of an alliance between men and women for achieving equality. Since the growth of an autonomous women's movement, the main impetus for reform has been located in women's groups. Some groups within the women's movement, especially those concerned with men's violence, are reluctant to work with men or are deeply skeptical of men's willingness to change. Other feminists argue that alliances between women and men are possible, even crucial. In some social movements, for instance, environmentalism, there is a strong ideology of gender equality and a favorable environment for men to support gender change (Connell 1995; Segal 1997).

In local and central government, practical alliances between women and men have been important in achieving equal-opportunity measures and other gender-equality reforms. Even in the field of men's violence against women, there has been cooperation between women's groups and men's groups, for instance, in prevention work. This cooperation can be an inspiration to grass-roots workers and a powerful demonstration of women and men's common interest in a peaceful and equal society (Pease 1997; Schofield, forthcoming). The concept of alliance is itself important, in preserving autonomy for women's groups, in preempting a tendency for any one group to speak for others, and in defining a political role for men that has some dignity and might attract widespread support.

Given the spectrum of masculinity politics, we cannot expect worldwide consensus for gender equality. What is possible is that support for gender equality might become hegemonic among men. In that case it would be groups supporting equality that provide the agenda for public discussion about men's lives and patterns of masculinity.

There is already a broad cultural shift toward a historical consciousness about gender, an awareness that gender customs came into existence at specific moments in time and can always be transformed by social action (Connell 1995). What is needed now is a widespread sense of agency among men, a sense that this transformation is something they can actually share in as a practical proposition. This is precisely what was presupposed in the "joint responsibility" of men invoked by the General Assembly declaration of the year 2000.[1]

From this point of view, the recent meeting of the UN Commission on the Status of Women (CSW) is profoundly interesting. The CSW is one of the oldest of UN agencies, dating from the 1940s. Effectively a standing committee of the General Assembly, it meets annually, and its current practice is to consider two main themes at each meeting. For the 2004 meeting, one of the defined themes was "the role of men and boys in achieving gender equality." The section of the UN secretariat that supports the CSW, the Division for the Advancement of Women, undertook background work. The division held, in June–July 2003, a worldwide online seminar on the role of men and boys, and in October 2003 it convened an international expert group meeting in Brasilia on the topic.

At the CSW meetings, several processes occur and (it is to be hoped) interact. There is a presentation of the division's background work, and delegations of the forty-five current member countries, UN agencies, and many of the nongovernmental organizations (NGOs) attending make initial statements. There is a busy schedule of side events, mainly organized by NGOs but some conducted by delegations or UN agencies, ranging from strategy debates to practical workshops. And there is a diplomatic process in which the official delegations negotiate over a draft document in the light of discussions in the CSW and their governments' stances on gender issues.

This is a politicized process, inevitably, and it can break down. In 2003 the CSW discussion on the issue of violence against women reached deadlock. In 2004 it was clear that some participating NGOs were not happy with the focus on men and boys, some holding to a discourse representing men exclusively as perpetrators of violence. Over the two weeks of negotiations, however, the delegations did reach consensus on a statement of "Agreed Conclusions."

Balancing a reaffirmation of commitment to women's equality with a recognition of men's and boys' potential for action, this document makes specific recommendations across a spectrum of policy fields, including education, parenthood, media, the labor market, sexuality, violence, and conflict prevention. These proposals have no force in international law—the document is essentially a set of recommendations to governments and other organizations. Nevertheless, it is the first international agreement of its kind, treating men systematically as agents in gender-equality processes, and it creates a standard for future gender-equality discussions. Most important, the CSWs "Agreed Conclusions" change the logic of the representation of men in gender policy. So far as the international discourse of gender-equality policy is concerned, this document begins the substantive presentation of gender equality as a positive project for men.

Here the UN process connects with the social and cultural possibilities that have emerged from the last three decades of gender politics among men. Gender equality is an undertaking for men that can be creative and joyful. It is a project that realizes high principles of social justice, produces better lives for the women whom men care about, and will produce better lives for the majority of men in the long run. This can and should be a project that generates energy, that finds expression in everyday life and the arts as well as in formal policies, and that can illuminate all aspects of men's lives.

NOTE

1. Twenty-third special session, UN General Assembly, "Political Declaration," par. 6.

REFERENCES

Altman, Dennis. 1994. *Power and Community: Organizational and Cultural Responses to AIDS*. London: Taylor & Francis.

———. 2001. *Global Sex*. Chicago: University of Chicago Press.

Arilha, Margareth, Sandra G. Unbehaum Ridenti, and Benedito Medrado, eds. 1998. *Homens e Masculinidades: Outras Palavras*. Sao Paulo: ECOS/Editora 34.

Bly, Robert. 1990. *Iron John: A Book about Men*. Reading, MA: Addison-Wesley.

Brandes, Holger, and Hermann Bullinger, eds. 1996. *Handbuch Männerarbeit*. Weinheim, Germany: Psychologie Verlags Union.

Breines, Ingeborg, Robert Connell, and Ingrid Eide, eds. 2000. *Male Roles, Masculinities and Violence: A Culture of Peace Perspective*. Paris: UNESCO.

Bulbeck, Chilla. 1988. *One World Women's Movement*. London: Pluto.

———. 1998. *Re-orienting Western Feminisms: Women's Diversity in a Postcolonial World*. Cambridge: Cambridge University Press.

Cockburn, Cynthia. 1991. *In the Way of Women: Men's Resistance to Sex Equality in Organizations*. Ithaca, NY: ILR Press.

———. 2003. *The Line: Women, Partition and the Gender Order in Cyprus*. London: Zed.

Cohen, Jon. 1991. "NOMAS: Challenging Male Supremacy." *Changing Men* (Winter/Spring): 45–46.

Collinson, David L., and Jeff Hearn, eds. 1996. *Men as Managers, Managers as Men: Critical Perspectives on Men, Masculinities and Managements*. London: Sage.

Connell, R. W. 1995. *Masculinities*. Berkeley: University of California Press.

———. 2000. *The Men and the Boys*. Sydney: Allen & Unwin Australia.

———. 2002. *Gender*. Cambridge: Polity.

———. 2003a. "Masculinities, Change and Conflict in Global Society: Thinking about the Future of Men's Studies." *Journal of Men's Studies* 11(3):249–66.

———. 2003b. "Men, Gender and the State." In *Among Men: Moulding Masculinities*, ed. Søren Ervø and Thomas Johansson, 15–28. Aldershot: Ashgate.

———. 2003c. "Scrambling in the Ruins of Patriarchy: Neo-liberalism and Men's Divided Interests in Gender Change." In *Gender—From Costs to Benefits*, ed. Ursula Pasero, 58–69. Wiesbaden: Westdeutscher.

Corman, June, Meg Luxton, D. W. Livingstone, and Wally Seccombe. 1993. *Recasting Steel Labour: The Stelco Story*. Halifax: Fernwood.

Da Wei Wei. 2004. "A Regional Tradition of Gender Equity: Shanghai Men in Sydney." *Journal of Men's Studies* 12(2):133–49.

Davies, Bronwyn. 1993. *Shards of Glass: Children Reading and Writing beyond Gender Identities*. Sydney: Allen & Unwin Australia.

Denborough, David. 1996. "Step by Step: Developing Respectful and Effective Ways of Working with Young Men to Reduce Violence." In *Men's Ways of Being*, ed. Chris McLean, Maggie Carey, and Cheryl White, 91–115. Boulder, CO: Westview.

Eisenstein, Hester. 1991. *Gender Shock: Practising Feminism on Two Continents*. Sydney: Allen & Unwin Australia.

Farrell, Warren. 1993. *The Myth of Male Power: Why Men Are the Disposable Sex*. New York: Simon & Schuster.

Franzway, Suzanne. 2001. *Sexual Politics and Greedy Institutions*. Sydney: Pluto.

Fuller, Norma. 2001. "The Social Constitution of Gender Identity among Peruvian Men." *Men and Masculinities* 3(3):316–31.

Ghoussoub, Mai. 2000. "Chewing Gum, Insatiable Women and Foreign Enemies: Male Fears and the Arab Media." In *Imagined Masculinities: Male Identity and Culture in the Middle East*, ed. Mai Ghoussoub and Emma Sinclair-Webb, 227–35. London: Saqi.

Gierycz, Dorota. 1999. "Women in Decision-Making: Can We Change the Status Quo?" In *Towards a Women's Agenda for a Culture of Peace*, ed. Ingeborg Breines, Dorota Gierycz, and Betty A. Reardon, 19–30. Paris: UNESCO.

Godenzi, Alberto. 2000. "Determinants of Culture: Men and Economic Power." In *Breines, Connell, and Eide 2000*, 35–51. Paris: UNESCO.

Gutmann, Matthew C. 2002. *The Romance of Democracy: Compliant Defiance in Contemporary Mexico*. Berkeley: University of California Press.

Hagemann-White, Carol. 1992. *Strategien gegen Gewalt im Geschlechterverhältnis: Bestandsanalyse und Perspektiven*. Pfaffenweiler, Ger.: Centaurus.

Harrison, James. 1978. "Warning: The Male Sex Role May Be Dangerous to Your Health." *Journal of Social Issues* 34(1):65–86.

Haseler, Stephen. 2000. *The Super-Rich: The Unjust New World of Global Capitalism*. London: Macmillan.

Hearn, Jeff. 1998. *The Violences of Men: How Men Talk about and How Agencies Respond to Men's Violence to Women*. Thousand Oaks, CA: Sage.

Hearn, Jeff, and Wendy Parkin. 2001. *Gender, Sexuality, and Violence in Organizations: The Unspoken Forces of Organization Violations*. Thousand Oaks, CA: Sage.

Hearn, Jeff, Keith Pringle, Ursula Müller, Elzbeieta Oleksy, Emmi Lattu, Janna Chernova, Harry Ferguson, et al. 2002. "Critical Studies on Men in Ten European Countries: (1) The State of Academic Research." *Men and Masculinities* 4(4):380–408.

Holland, Janet, Caroline Ramazanoğlu, Sue Sharpe, and Rachel Thomson. 1998. *The Male in the Head: Young People, Heterosexuality and Power*. London: Tufnell.

Holter, Øystein Gullvåg. 1997. *Gender, Patriarchy and Capitalism: A Social Forms Analysis*. Oslo: Work Research Institute.

———. 2003. *Can Men Do It? Men and Gender Equality— The Nordic Experience*. Copenhagen: Nordic Council of Ministers.

Hooper, Charlotte. 2001. *Manly States: Masculinities, International Relations, and Gender Politics*. New York: Columbia University Press.

Hurrelmann, Klaus, and Petra Kolip, eds. 2002. *Geschlecht, Gesundheit und Krankheit: Männer und Frauen im Vergleich*. Bern: Hans Huber.

Ibsen, Henrik. (1923) 1995. *A Doll's House*. Cambridge: Cambridge University Press.

Inter-Parliamentary Union. 2003. "Women in National Parliaments: Situation at 30 December 2003." Available online at http://www.ipu.org/wmn-e/world.htm.

Ito, Kimio. 1992. "Cultural Change and Gender Identity Trends in the 1970s and 1980s." *International Journal of Japanese Sociology* 1(1):79–98.

Jensen, Hanne Naxø. 1998. "Gender as the Dynamo: When Public Organizations Have to Change." In *Is There a Nordic Feminism? Nordic Feminist Thought on Culture and Society*, ed. Drude von der Fehr, Bente Rosenberg, and Anna G. Jóasdóttir, 160–75. London: UCL Press.

Kandiyoti, Deniz. 1994. "The Paradoxes of Masculinity: Some Thoughts on Segregated Societies." In *Dislocating Masculinity: Comparative Ethnographies*, ed. Andrea Cornwall and Nancy Lindisfarne, 197–213. London: Routledge.

Kaufman, Michael. 1993. *Cracking the Armour: Power, Pain and the Lives of Men*. Toronto: Viking.

———, ed. 1999. "Men and Violence." Special issue, *International Association for Studies of Men Newsletter* 6, no. 2.

Kenway, Jane, ed. 1997. *Will Boys Be Boys? Boys' Education in the Context of Gender Reform*. Canberra: Australian Curriculum Studies Association.

Kenworthy, Colin. 1994. "'We want to resist your resistant readings': Masculinity and Discourse in the English Classroom." *Interpretations* 27(2):74–95.

Kimmel, Michael S., Jeff Hearn, and R. W. Connell, eds. 2005. *Handbook of Studies on Men and Masculinities*. Thousand Oaks, CA: Sage.

Kimmel, Michael S., and Thomas E. Mosmiller. 1992. *Against the Tide: Profeminist Men in the United States, 1776–1990: A Documentary History*. Boston: Beacon.

Kindler, Heinz. 2002. *Väter und Kinder*. Weinheim, Germany: Juventa.

Kippax, Susan, R. W. Connell, G. W. Dowsett, and June Crawford. 1993. *Sustaining Safe Sex: Gay Communities Respond to AIDS*. London: Falmer.

Kupers, Terry. 1993. *Revisioning Men's Lives: Gender, Intimacy, and Power*. New York: Guilford.

Law, Robin, Hugh Campbell, and John Dolan, eds. 1999. *Masculinities in Aotearoa/New Zealand*. Palmerston North, NZ: Dunmore.

Lerner, Susana, ed. 1998. *Varones, sexualidad y reproducción: Diversas perspectivas teórico-metodológicas y hallazgos de investigación*. El Colegio de México, México.

Lichterman, Paul. 1989. "Making a Politics of Masculinity." *Comparative Social Research* 11:185–208.

Lingard, Bob. 2003. "Where to in Gender Policy in Education after Recuperative Masculinity Politics?" *International Journal of Inclusive Education* 7(1):33–56.

Lyra, Jorge, and Benedito Medrado. 2001. "Constructing an Adolescent Father in Brazil." Paper presented at the Third International Fatherhood Conference, Atlanta, May 28–30.

Mac an Ghaill, Mairtin. 1994. *The Making of Men: Masculinities, Sexualities and Schooling*. Buckingham: Open University Press.

Mackay, Fiona, and Kate Bilton. 2000. *Learning from Experience: Lessons in Mainstreaming Equal Opportunities*. Edinburgh: Governance of Scotland Forum.

Marchand, Marianne H., and Anne Sisson Runyan, eds. 2000. *Gender and Global Restructuring: Sightings, Sites and Resistances*. London: Routledge.

McMahon, Anthony. 1999. *Taking Care of Men: Sexual Politics in the Public Mind*. Cambridge: Cambridge University Press.

Menzu Senta (Men's Center Japan). 1997. *Otokotachi no watashisagashi* (How are men seeking their new selves?). Kyoto: Kamogawa.

Messner, Michael A. 1997. *The Politics of Masculinities: Men in Movements*. Thousand Oaks, CA: Sage.

———. 2002. *Taking the Field: Women, Men and Sports*. Minneapolis: University of Minnesota Press.

Metz-Göckel, Sigrid, and Ursula Müller. 1985. *Der Mann: Die Brigitte-Studie*. Hamburg: Beltz.

Meuser, Michael. 2003. "Modernized Masculinities? Continuities, Challenges, and Changes in Men's Lives." In *Among Men: Moulding Masculinities*, vol. 1, ed.

Søren Ervø and Thomas Johansson, 127–48. Aldershot: Ashgate.

Mill, John Stuart. 1912. "The Subjection of Women." In his *On Liberty; Representative Government; The Subjugation of Women: Three Essays*, 427–548. London: Oxford University Press.

Mohwald, Ulrich. 2002. *Changing Attitudes towards Gender Equality in Japan and Germany*. Munich: Iudicium.

Moodie, T. Dunbar. 1994. *Going for Gold: Men, Mines and Migration*. Johannesburg: Witwatersrand University Press.

Morrell, Robert. 1998. "Of Boys and Men: Masculinity and Gender in Southern African Studies." *Journal of Southern African Studies* 24(4):605–30.

———, ed. 2001a. *Changing Men in Southern Africa*. Pietermaritzburg, S.A.: University of Natal Press.

———. 2001b. *From Boys to Gentlemen: Settler Masculinity in Colonial Natal, 1880–1920*. Pretoria: University of South Africa Press.

Nagel, Joane. 1998. "Masculinity and Nationalism: Gender and Sexuality in the Making of Nations." *Ethnic and Racial Studies* 21(2):242–69.

Nordic Council of Ministers. 1997. *Nordic Action Plan for Men and Gender Equality, 1997–2000*. Copenhagen: Nordic Council of Ministers.

O'Connor, Julia S., Ann Shola Orloff, and Sheila Shaver. 1999. *States, Markets, Families: Gender, Liberalism and Social Policy in Australia, Canada, Great Britain, and the United States*. Cambridge: Cambridge University Press.

O'Donnell, Mike, and Sue Sharpe. 2000. *Uncertain Masculinities: Youth, Ethnicity and Class in Contemporary Britain*. London: Routledge.

Olavarría, José. 2001. *Y todos querian ser (buenos) padres: Varones de Santiago de Chile en conflicto*. Santiago: FLACSO-Chile.

Palme, Olof. 1972. "The Emancipation of Man." *Journal of Social Issues* 28(2):237–46.

Peacock, Dean. 2003. "Building on a Legacy of Social Justice Activism: Enlisting Men as Gender Justice Activists in South Africa." *Men and Masculinities* 5(3):325–28.

Pease, Bob. 1997. *Men and Sexual Politics: Towards a Pro-feminist Practice*. Adelaide: Dulwich Centre.

Pease, Bob, and Keith Pringle, eds. 2001. *A Man's World? Changing Men's Practices in a Globalized World*. London: Zed.

Ptacek, James. 1988. "Why Do Men Batter Their Wives?" In *Feminist Perspectives on Wife Abuse*, ed. Kersti Yllö and Michele Bograd, 133–57. Newbury Park, CA: Sage.

Reinicke, Kenneth. 2002. *Den Hele Mand:Manderollen i forandring*. Aarhus, Denmark: Schønberg.

Risman, Barbara J. 1986. "Can Men 'Mother'? Life as a Single Father." *Family Relations* 35(1):95–102.

———. 1998. *Gender Vertigo: American Families in Transition*. New Haven, CT: Yale University Press.

Roberson, James E., and Nobue Suzuki, eds. 2003. *Men and Masculinities in Contemporary Japan: Dislocating the Salaryman Doxa*. London: Routledge.

Roy, Rahul. 2003. "Exploring Masculinities—A Travelling Seminar." Unpublished manuscript.

Sabo, Donald, and David Frederick Gordon, eds. 1995. *Men's Health and Illness: Gender, Power, and the Body*. Thousand Oaks, CA: Sage.

Sabo, Donald, Terry A. Kupers, and Willie London, eds. 2001. *Prison Masculinities*. Philadelphia: Temple University Press.

Schofield, Toni. 2004. *Boutique Health? Gender and Equity in Health Policy*. Sydney: Australian Health Policy Institute.

———. Forthcoming. "Gender Regimes in Public Policy Making." Unpublished manuscript, Faculty of Health Sciences, University of Sydney.

Schwalbe, Michael. 1996. *Unlocking the Iron Cage: The Men's Movement, Gender Politics, and American Culture*. New York: Oxford University Press.

Segal, Lynne. 1997. *Slow Motion: Changing Masculinities, Changing Men*. 2nd ed. London: Virago.

Seidler, Victor J., ed. 1991. *The Achilles Heel Reader: Men, Sexual Politics and Socialism*. London: Routledge.

Sinclair-Webb, Emma. 2000. "'Our bülent is now a commando': Military Service and Manhood in Turkey." In *Imagined Masculinities: Male Identity and Culture in the Modern Middle East*, ed. Mai Ghoussoub and Emma Sinclair-Webb, 65–92. London: Saqi.

Sommers, Christina Hoff. 2000. *The War against Boys: How Misguided Feminism Is Harming Our Young Men*. New York: Simon & Schuster.

Taga, Futoshi. 2001. *Dansei no Jendâ Keisei: "Otoko-Rashisa" no Yuragi no Naka de* (The gender formation of men: Uncertain masculinity). Tokyo: Tôyôkan Shuppan-sha.

Thornton, Arland. 1989. "Changing Attitudes toward Family Issues in the United States." *Journal of Marriage and the Family* 51(4):873–93.

United Nations. 1958. *Universal Declaration of Human Rights*. New York: Department of Public Information, United Nations.

———. (1979) 1989. *Convention on the Elimination of All Forms of Discrimination against Women*. New York: Department of Public Information, United Nations.

———. 2001. *Beijing Declaration and Platform for Action, with the Beijing +5 Political Declaration and Outcome Document*. New York: Department of Public Information, United Nations.

United Nations Commission on the Status of Women. 2004. *The Role of Men and Boys in Achieving Gender Equality: Agreed Conclusions*. Available online at http://www.un.org/womenwatch/daw/csw/csw48/ac-men-auv.pdf

United Nations Development Program (UNDP). 2003. *Human Development Report 2003*. New York: UNDP and Oxford University Press.

Valdés, Teresa, and José Olavarría. 1998. "Ser hombre en Santiago de Chile: A pesar de todo, un mismo modelo." In their *Masculinidades y equidad de género en América Latina*, 12–36. Santiago: FLACSO/UNFPA.

Walby, Sylvia. 1997. *Gender Transformations*. London: Routledge.

Wetherell, Margaret, and Nigel Edley. 1999. "Negotiating Hegemonic Masculinity: Imaginary Positions and Psycho-Discursive Practices." *Feminism and Psychology* 9(3):335–56.

White, Sara C. 2000. "Did the Earth Move? The Hazards of Bringing Men and Masculinities into Gender and Development." *IDS Bulletin* 31(2):33–41.

Widersprüche. 1998. "Multioptionale Männlichkeiten?" Special issue, no. 67.

Zalewski, Marysia, and Jane Parpart, eds. 1998. *The "Man" Question in International Relations*. Boulder, CO: Westview.

Zingoni, Eduardo Liendro. 1998. "Masculinidades y violencia desde un programa de acción en México." In *Masculinidades y equidad de género en América Latina*, ed. Teresa Valdés and José Olavarría, 130–36. Santiago: FLACSO/ UNFPA.

Zulehner, Paul M., and Rainer Volz. 1998. *Männer im Aufbruch: Wie Deutschlands Männer sich Selbst und wie Frauen Sie Sehen*. Ostfildern, Ger.: Schwabenverlag.

THE ROLE OF MEN AND BOYS IN ACHIEVING GENDER EQUALITY

Agreed Conclusions March 12, 2004, as Adopted

United Nations Commission on the Status of Women Forty-Eighth Session, March 1–12, 2004

1. The Commission on the Status of Women recalls and reiterates that the Beijing Declaration and Platform for Action[1] encouraged men to participate fully in all actions towards gender equality and urged the establishment of the principle of shared power and responsibility between women and men at home, in the community, in the workplace and in the wider national and international communities. The Commission also recalls and reiterates the outcome document adopted at the twenty-third special session of the General Assembly entitled "Gender equality, development and peace in the twenty-first century"[2] which emphasized that men must take joint responsibility with women for the promotion of gender equality.

2. The Commission recognizes that men and boys, while some themselves face discriminatory barriers and practices, can and do make contributions to gender equality in their many capacities, including as individuals, members of families, social groups and communities, and in all spheres of society.

3. The Commission recognizes that gender inequalities still exist and are reflected in imbalances of power between women and men in all spheres of society. The Commission further recognizes that everyone benefits from gender equality and that the negative impacts of gender inequality are borne by society as a whole and emphasizes, therefore, that men and boys, through taking responsibility themselves and working jointly in partnership with women and girls, are essential to achieving the goals of gender equality, development and peace. The Commission recognizes the capacity of men and boys in bringing about change in attitudes, relationships and access to resources and decision making which are critical for the promotion of gender equality and the full enjoyment of all human rights by women.

4. The Commission acknowledges and encourages men and boys to continue to take positive initiatives to eliminate gender stereotypes and promote gender equality, including combating violence against women, through networks, peer programmes, information campaigns, and training programmes. The Commission acknowledges the critical role of gender-sensitive education and training in achieving gender equality.

5. The Commission also recognizes that the participation of men and boys in achieving gender equality must be consistent with the empowerment of women and girls and acknowledges that efforts must be made to address the undervaluation of many types of work, abilities and

roles associated with women. In this regard, it is important that resources for gender equality initiatives for men and boys do not compromise equal opportunities and resources for women and girls.

6. The Commission urges Governments and, as appropriate, the relevant funds and programmes, organizations and specialized agencies of the United Nations system, the international financial institutions, civil society, including the private sector and nongovernmental organizations, and other stakeholders, to take the following actions:

   a) Encourage and support the capacity of men and boys in fostering gender equality, including acting in partnership with women and girls as agents for change and in providing positive leadership, in particular where men are still key decision makers responsible for policies, programmes and legislation, as well as holders of economic and organizational power and public resources;

   b) Promote understanding of the importance of fathers, mothers, legal guardians and other caregivers, to the well being of children and the promotion of gender equality and of the need to develop policies, programmes and school curricula that encourage and maximize their positive involvement in achieving gender equality and positive results for children, families and communities;

   c) Create and improve training and education programmes to enhance awareness and knowledge among men and women on their roles as parents, legal guardians and caregivers and the importance of sharing family responsibilities, and include fathers as well as mothers in programmes that teach infant child care development;

   d) Develop and include in education programmes for parents, legal guardians and other caregivers information on ways and means to increase the capacity of men to raise children in a manner oriented towards gender equality;

   e) Encourage men and boys to work with women and girls in the design of policies and programmes for men and boys aimed at gender equality and foster the involvement of men and boys in gender mainstreaming efforts in order to ensure improved design of all policies and programmes;

   f) Encourage the design and implementation of programmes at all levels to accelerate a socio-cultural change towards gender equality, especially through the upbringing and educational process, in terms of changing harmful traditional perceptions and attitudes of male and female roles in order to achieve the full and equal participation of women and men in the society;

   g) Develop and implement programmes for pre-schools, schools, community centers, youth organizations, sport clubs and centres, and other groups dealing with children and youth, including training for teachers, social workers and other professionals who deal with children to foster positive attitudes and behaviours on gender equality;

   h) Promote critical reviews of school curricula, textbooks and other information education and communication materials at all levels in order to recommend ways to strengthen the promotion of gender equality that involves the engagement of boys as well as girls;

   i) Develop and implement strategies to educate boys and girls and men and women about tolerance, mutual respect for all individuals and the promotion of all human rights;

   j) Develop and utilize a variety of methods in public information campaigns on the role of men and boys in promoting gender equality, including through approaches specifically targeting boys and young men;

   k) Engage media, advertising and other related professionals, through the development of training and other programmes, on the importance of promoting gender equality, non-stereotypical portrayal of women and girls and men and boys and on the harms caused by portraying women and girls in a demeaning or exploitative manner, as well as on the enhanced participation of women and girls in the media;

l) Take effective measures, to the extent consistent with freedom of expression, to combat the growing sexualization and use of pornography in media content, in terms of the rapid development of ICT, encourage men in the media to refrain from presenting women as inferior beings and exploiting them as sexual objects and commodities, combat ICT- and media-based violence against women including criminal misuse of ICT for sexual harassment, sexual exploitation and trafficking in women and girls, and support the development and use of ICT as a resource for the empowerment of women and girls, including those affected by violence, abuse and other forms of sexual exploitation;

m) Adopt and implement legislation and/or policies to close the gap between women's and men's pay and promote reconciliation of occupational and family responsibilities, including through reduction of occupational segregation, introduction or expansion of parental leave, flexible working arrangements, such as voluntary part-time work, tele-working, and other home-based work;

n) Encourage men, through training and education, to fully participate in the care and support of others, including older persons, persons with disabilities and sick persons, in particular children and other dependants;

o) Encourage active involvement of men and boys through education projects and peer-based programmes in eliminating gender stereotypes as well as gender inequality in particular in relation to sexually transmitted infections, including HIV/AIDS, as well as their full participation in prevention, advocacy, care, treatment, support and impact evaluation programmes;

p) Ensure men's access to and utilization of reproductive and sexual health services and programmes, including HIV/AIDS-related programmes and services, and encourage men to participate with women in programmes designed to prevent and treat all forms of HIV/AIDS transmission and other sexually transmitted infections;

q) Design and implement programmes to encourage and enable men to adopt safe and responsible sexual and reproductive behaviour, and to use effectively methods to prevent unwanted pregnancies and sexually transmitted infections, including HIV/AIDS;

r) Encourage and support men and boys to take an active part in the prevention and elimination of all forms of violence, and especially gender-based violence, including in the context of HIV/AIDS, and increase awareness of men's and boys' responsibility in ending the cycle of violence, inter alia, through the promotion of attitudinal and behavioural change, integrated education and training which prioritize the safety of women and children, prosecution and rehabilitation of perpetrators, and support for survivors, and recognizing that men and boys also experience violence;

s) Encourage an increased understanding among men how violence, including trafficking for the purposes of commercialized sexual exploitation, forced marriages and forced labour, harms women, men and children and undermines gender equality, and consider measures aimed at eliminating the demand for trafficked women and children;

t) Encourage and support both women and men in leadership positions, including political leaders, traditional leaders, business leaders, community and religious leaders, musicians, artists and athletes to provide positive role models on gender equality;

u) Encourage men in leadership positions to ensure equal access for women to education, property rights and inheritance rights and to promote equal access to information technology and business and economic opportunities, including in international trade, in order to provide women with the tools that enable them to take part fully and equally in economic and political decision-making processes at all levels;

v) Identify and fully utilize all contexts in which a large number of men can be reached, particularly in male-dominated institutions, industries and associations, to sensitize men on their roles and responsibilities in the promotion of gender equality and the full enjoyment of all human rights by women, including in relation to HIV/AIDS and violence against women;

w) Develop and use statistics to support and/or carry out research, inter alia, on the cultural, social and economic conditions, which influence the attitudes and behaviours of men and boys towards women and girls, their awareness of gender inequalities and their involvement in promoting gender equality;

x) Carry out research on men's and boys' views of gender equality and their perceptions of their roles through which further programmes and policies can be developed and identify and widely disseminate good practices. Assess the impact of efforts undertaken to engage men and boys in achieving gender equality;

y) Promote and encourage the representation of men in institutional mechanisms for the advancement of women;

z) Encourage men and boys to support women's equal participation in conflict prevention, management and conflict resolution and in post-conflict peace-building;

7. The Commission urges all entities within the UN system to take into account the recommendations contained in these agreed conclusions and to disseminate these agreed conclusions widely.

NOTES

1. Report of the Fourth World Conference on Women, Beijing 4–15 September 1995 (United Nations publications, Sales No. E. 96. IV.13).

2. A/RES/S-23/3, annex.

"HOW CAN I NOT?": MEN'S PATHWAYS TO INVOLVEMENT IN ANTI-VIOLENCE AGAINST WOMEN WORK

Erin Casey   Tyler Smith

Engaging boys and men as antiviolence allies is an increasingly core element of efforts to end violence against women. In the past decades, men have become more of a presence in long-established domestic and sexual violence organizations and have created myriad men's organizing groups aimed at educating, engaging, and mobilizing other men to take an active stand against sexual and intimate partner violence. Based in the reality that the majority of perpetrators of violence are male (Tjaden & Thoennes, 1998), that risk for violence is connected to traditional notions of appropriate "masculinity," (Heise, 1998; Murnen. Wright, & Kaluzny, 2002), and that men are more likely to be influenced by other men (Earle, 1996; Flood, 2005), there is increasingly widespread agreement that the project of ending domestic and sexual violence requires male participation (Flood, 2005; DeKeseredy, Schwartz, & Alvi, 2000). Existing programs engage males in a continuum of involvement, ranging from raising men's awareness about violence against women to encouraging their active involvement in taking a stand against the abuse of women (being an "ally"). Examples include The Men's Program, a prevention intervention for men that has been shown to reduce rape-related attitudes and behaviors among some college students (Foubert, Newberry, &

Tatum, 2007); Mentors in Violence Prevention (Katz, 1995); and Men Can Stop Rape's Men of Strength Clubs (Hawkins, 2005), ally-building programs considered "promising" prevention strategies (Barker, Ricardo, & Nascimento, 2007).

Still, knowledge building regarding men's antiviolence work is in its early stages. In particular, little data exist on the routes through which men initiate involvement in antiviolence efforts or come to define themselves as antiviolence "allies." In addition, although theorizing has developed regarding ally building in other social justice endeavors such as antiracism work, theoretical frameworks relative to men's antiviolence engagement are relatively new. Enhancing this knowledge and theory base holds promise for expanding outreach efforts to diverse men and for understanding how best to engage them. The purpose of this article, therefore, is to summarize research and theory regarding the process of initially engaging men, to present findings from a study of male allies about their involvement in antiviolence work and to evaluate the degree of congruence between these men's experiences and existing theoretical perspectives on ally development.

MODELS OF SOCIAL JUSTICE ALLY BUILDING

Engaging men as partners in efforts to end violence against women can be seen as parallel to "ally" development in other social justice arenas. Allies are typically defined as "members of dominant social groups (e.g., men, Whites, heterosexuals) who are working to end the system of oppression that gives them greater privilege and power based on their social-group membership" (Broido, 2000, p. 3). Significant model-building work describing the processes of ally building has occurred, particularly in relation to the development of antiracism allies. These models are likely instructive for enhancing theorizing and practice relevant for engaging men, particularly as many male allies may see their role as working to dismantle multiple forms of oppression (Funk, 2008) and because violence itself is inextricably linked with mechanisms of oppression (Sokoloff & Dupont, 2005).

Models of social justice ally formation are typically developmental in nature, noting the factors over time that collectively shape an individual's awareness of and commitment to rectifying social inequities. Across these models, critical elements of ally development include learning experiences regarding issues of racism and social inequity coupled with ongoing opportunities to process, discuss, and reflect on those experiences (Broido, 2000; Reason, Miller, & Scales, 2005) and opportunities to experience being a "minority" or to examine the parts of one's personal identity that are marginalized by "dominant" groups (Bishop, 2002; Reason et al., 2005). Specific invitations to participate in social justice work and modeling by respected peers or mentors is also important (Reason et al., 2005; Tatum, 1994). Finally, many models of social justice ally development highlight the central importance of developing self-awareness of personal sources of unearned social privilege in relation to other groups (Bishop, 2002; Reason et al., 2005; Tatum, 1994). Drawing on social identity theory, such as Helms' (1990) theory regarding White racial identity development, these models suggest that ally behavior is predicated on a "status" of identity development characterized by the acknowledgment of racism and other forms of social inequities, coupled with an awareness of how one's own privilege may be complicit in the marginalization of others. Taken together, these models highlight the multilayered nature of ally-promoting dynamics, which include intrapersonal factors (such as the ability to critically self-reflect), interpersonal factors (opportunities to engage with others across racial or gender "difference"), and environmental factors (concrete opportunities for involvement). These factors are likely highly applicable to male antiviolence ally development.

THEORETICAL PERSPECTIVES ON ENGAGING MEN AS ALLIES

Although empirical models specific to male antiviolence ally formation have not been developed, researchers have proposed applying existing theoretical frameworks, such as cognitive behavioral theory and the Transtheoretical Model (TTM), to violence prevention and ally building efforts. For example, Crooks and colleagues (Crooks, Goodall, Hughes, Jaffe, & Baker, 2007) suggest that the cognitive behavioral principles of surfacing and reshaping an individual's core beliefs about an issue, identifying specific behaviors that build toward a desired behavior, and building opportunities to practice new behaviors could address common barriers to men's antiviolence involvement, such as ambivalence about the seriousness or relevance of the topic of violence against women and uncertainty about or lack of skill related to specific actions they can take.

Similarly, scholars argue that principles from the TTM are instructive in tailoring violence prevention and ally-building efforts (Banyard, Eckstein, & Moynihan, 2010; Berkowitz, 2002). A stages of change model, the TTM suggests that individuals occupy different statuses in terms of their readiness to engage in behavior change over time and that intervention strategies should be matched to an individual's current change stage (Prochaska, Redding, & Evers, 2002). Applying the model to a bystander-focused sexual assault prevention program, Banyard et al. (2010) found that participants' preintervention stage of awareness regarding sexual assault (ranging from denial of the problem to active involvement in prevention activities) was associated with the magnitude of the program's impact on the participants, with respondents in the "precontemplation" stage evidencing less change following the program. Although applied to a mixed-gender audience in this case, these findings suggest that the TTM can offer a helpful framework for thinking about differentially tailoring engagement efforts for men with different levels of awareness or concern for the issue of violence against women. This concept is echoed in previous conceptualizations of men's degree of engagement, such as Funk's (2006) "continuum of male attitudes toward sexism and sexist violence" (p. 78) that ranges from "overtly hostile" to "activist" in describing men's possible orientations to the issue of violence against women.

To date, however, the implementation of either cognitive behavioral or TTM principles in engaging male allies has not been expressly tested, nor do these models necessarily address the combination of internal or environmental precipitating factors that might motivate men to seek or avoid an opportunity to learn about the issue of violence against women in the first place.

FACTORS ASSOCIATED WITH MEN'S ANTIVIOLENCE INVOLVEMENT

From the handful of studies that have explicitly examined factors associated with men's involvement in antiviolence or gender equity efforts, three themes are apparent. First, exposure to or personal experiences with issues of sexual or domestic violence appear to be a critical element (Coulter, 2003; Funk, 2008). Second, receiving support or encouragement from peers, role models, and specifically, female mentors is associated with initiation into antiviolence efforts (Coulter, 2003). This theme of peer support is echoed in findings that men's willingness to intervene in sexist peer behavior or a situation that may lead to violence against a woman is related to men's perceptions of their male peers' willingness to do the same (Fabiano, Perkins, Berkowitz, Linkenbach, & Stark, 2003; Stein, 2007). Finally, longer term dedication to antiviolence work is associated with employing a social justice analysis of violence that includes issues of racism and homophobia and that links violence against women to sexism (DeKeseredy et al., 2000; Funk, 2008).

Although these findings suggest that peers, mentors, and an awareness of violence or other social justice issues constitute a few of the possible important building blocks that support men's entrée into antiviolence involvement, little is known about the particular ways that these factors influence men. Other possible pathways in the probably complex process involved in deciding to join an antiviolence effort are also not yet elucidated. Furthermore, unlike more general models of social justice ally development, the degree to which social identity development and an awareness of male privilege are central to initial antiviolence ally formation is unknown. Although some approaches to engaging men in antiviolence work incorporate a focus on critically examining notions of masculinity, such as Men Can Stop Rape's focus on "re-storying" dominant narratives of manhood (www.mencanstoprape.org), the extent to which male antiviolence involvement is predicated on a critical awareness of male privilege remains unclear. As a whole, the specific factors influencing men's pathways to involvement have been identified by practitioners and current male allies as topics ripe for future research and investigation (e.g., Funk, 2008).

SUMMARY AND PURPOSE OF THE STUDY

In summary, although models of ally development have emerged from more general social justice arenas, the accuracy of these models in describing men's experiences of initiating antiviolence involvement is unknown. Furthermore, little data are available regarding the specific internal, interpersonal, and environmental factors that mutually facilitate men's antiviolence participation. Elucidating these gaps holds promise for more effectively reaching out to men and fostering their positive involvement in ending violence. To this end, this study examines qualitative data from interviews with 27 men who recently initiated membership or involvement in an anti-sexual or domestic violence effort. Specifically, this study aims to (a) describe the pathways through which these men became involved in antiviolence efforts, (b) build a conceptual model of participants' initiation into antiviolence work, and (c) evaluate the degree of overlap between extant theorizing about social justice ally development and the participants' descriptions of their own experiences.

METHOD

Participant Recruitment

In accordance with procedures approved by the human subjects review committee, potential respondents were recruited in four ways. First, notices about the study were disseminated via several topic-relevant national email listserves, including the Prevention Institute's sexual violence prevention listserve and the Men Against Violence listserve on Yahoo. Permission to forward these notices to other relevant interest groups was included. Second, the first author attended relevant local community or agency meetings to announce and disseminate information about the study. Third, leaders of local men's antiviolence organizing groups were contacted and provided with information about the study. Finally, men who contacted the researcher regarding participation were invited to refer other potentially eligible men. Respondents contacted the researcher directly and were screened for eligibility. Participation eligibility criteria included initiating involvement in an antiviolence against women organization, event, or group within the past 2 years at the time of contacting the study and being a man 18 years or older. Consistent with the goals of the study, recent initiation into antiviolence work was included as an eligibility criterion to assess *current* factors and strategies associated with men's involvement; some data on factors associated with long-term antiviolence activism already exist (e.g., Funk, 2008). Eligible participants were then scheduled for a phone or in-person interview, depending on location.

SAMPLE

A total of 43 men were screened for participation in the study. Fourteen described long-term antiviolence involvement and were therefore ineligible for participation. An additional two men did not return consent forms and therefore could not be

interviewed. The final sample consisted of 27 men, aged 20 to 72. All but one identified as White; one man identified as Latino. This article, therefore, largely reflects the experiences of White men in coming to view the issue of violence as relevant to and actionable in their own lives. Of the 16 men whose length of participation or lack of consent form excluded them from the study, 5 identified as African American, 1 as Latino, and 10 as White. Participants from locations across the United States were recruited and represented all regions of the country. Length of involvement in antiviolence work at the time of the interview ranged from 1 to approximately 30 months.

Participants' involvement in antiviolence work generally fell into two categories: employment/volunteer work or involvement in a college campus-based organization. Of the 27 men, 10 (37%) were postcollege-aged men who worked or volunteered with a domestic and/or sexual violence-related program or government agency. These men's roles ranged from doing direct advocacy with survivors of violence to volunteering in a prevention education program for youth. Of these, 5 reported that part of their organizational role was to engage other men or boys around the issue of violence. Sixteen (59%) of the participants (aged 20–42) joined a campus-based antiviolence group or effort at the college or university in which they were enrolled. Typical activities in which these participants were engaged included facilitating educational presentations for other college students, organizing campus-wide antiviolence awareness events, or designing activities or events aimed at garnering additional male participation. Finally, one participant described his participation as being a part of a men's discussion group that had partnered in fundraising efforts with a local domestic violence agency.

Data Collection

Nine participants were interviewed in person and the remaining 18 were interviewed by phone. Interviews varied from 45 to approximately 90 min in length and were semistructured, with standardized general questions designed to elicit involvement narratives, followed by tailored follow-up questions to explore relevant issues in greater depth. Question topics included the nature of men's involvement; the factors precipitating their initiation into antiviolence work; their perceptions of effective and ineffective strategies for engaging other men; the impact of antiviolence involvement on their beliefs, attitudes, and behaviors; and their perceptions of the factors that sustain men's antiviolence efforts. For example, men were asked to describe what prompted them to become involved in their organization or event, followed by in-depth prompts to expand on any personal and/or environmental influences. All interviews were digitally recorded and transcribed.

Data Analysis

Data analysis was conducted using Grounded Theory techniques and principles (Strauss & Corbin, 1998). An inductive analysis strategy useful for building conceptual frameworks from data, Grounded Theory, emphasizes the development of conceptual categories derived through constant comparison of the dimensions of analytic concepts emerging from participants' data. Analysis was conducted by two researchers using the qualitative analytic software program ATLAS.ti. Coding was initially done separately by each researcher on several transcripts and then compared and negotiated until agreement was reached on categories in the data for the purposes of analyzing remaining transcripts. Coding proceeded in two phases. First, all transcripts were coded for general domains, with like domains pertaining to men's pathways to involvement grouped together. Second, close inductive coding on relevant domains was done using extensive memoing to uncover concepts within the data and relationships between those concepts. Particular attention was paid to the dimensions and qualities of the factors reported by participants as salient to their initiation into antiviolence involvement. Once saturation of concepts was reached, all transcripts were reread and compared for both confirming and disconfirming cases. When agreement between researchers was reached regarding concepts and their theoretical relationships, trustworthiness

was enhanced through the use of six member checks (Lincoln & Guba, 1985) and through third-party checks by two independent readers who evaluated the face validity of concepts and the data used to support them.

RESULTS

Participants' descriptions of the specific factors related to their antiviolence involvement fell into three arenas. These arenas and the proposed relationships between them are summarized in Figure 52.1. First, all men but one had some sort of "sensitizing" or priming experience that raised their level of consciousness regarding issues of violence or gender inequity and seemed to lay the groundwork for being open to involvement when an opportunity arose. Second, all men had at least one tangible opportunity or entrée into an antiviolence group, volunteer opportunity, or job. Third, the meaning that participants had come to attach to the initial sensitizing and/or to the opportunity experience seemed to be a critical component of men's decision to devote time to antiviolence work. In other words, the impact of a sensitizing or opportunity experience or the particular ways men made sense of it, constituted the motivating factor that allowed men to take or seek an opportunity to get involved. Pathways of men's movement through these arenas are reflected in Figure 52.1 and described more fully below.

Sensitizing Experiences

Most men identified more than one previous experience that rendered the issue of violence against women more salient or visible. The sensitizing experience may have made the issue of violence more important or "real" and was the first influential involvement factor for 25 (92%) of the participants. One participant did not describe any sensitizing experiences, and a second participant encountered a sensitizing experience after his first involvement opportunity. The most common sensitizing experience was hearing a *disclosure of domestic or sexual violence* from a close female friend, family member, or girlfriend or witnessing violence in childhood.

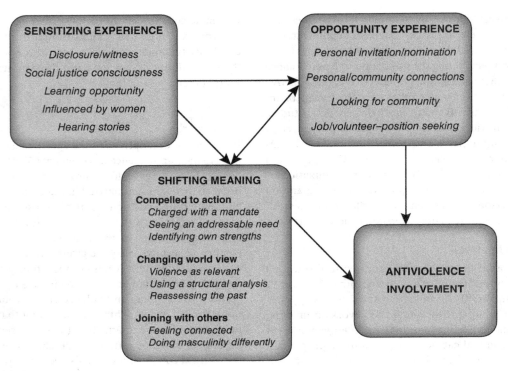

■ FIGURE 52.1
Conceptual model of men's pathways to antiviolence involvement

Fifteen respondents (56%) reported exposure to violence or a disclosure of violence, and many of these participants described reevaluating the meaning of that exposure over time or as other sensitizing or opportunity incidents arose. Next, 8 respondents (30%) described a preexisting *social justice consciousness* or egalitarian value system as a factor in sensitizing them to issues of men's use of violence. This often stemmed from a respondent's own experiences of marginalization or from previous exposure to connected issues of racism, classism, and sexism. Another 8 respondents (30%) reported that they were exposed to a specific *learning opportunity* related to violence against women. For most of these men, this learning was a college-based prevention presentation on dating violence or sexual assault. Others were exposed to content through courses or lectures. Five participants (18%) reported that *close*

relationships with influential women (mostly mothers) made them more aware of threats to women's safety or fostered a feminist consciousness. Finally, 4 participants (15%) reported that they had been moved or troubled by a story or *stories of violence survivors* who were not personal acquaintances of the men. These stories emerged in a variety of contexts, including church, a work-related setting, and Take Back the Night marches.

Opportunity Experiences

Similar to their sensitizing experiences, many men encountered more than one tangible entrée into antiviolence involvement. Nine respondents (33%) were formally invited or nominated to become a part of an antiviolence group or event by an acquaintance, professor, or supervisor. Seven (26%) of the participants were members of a friendship group or community in which others who were involved in antiviolence work encouraged the respondent to come to a meeting or communicated that participation was important, inspiring, or fun. Ten men (37%) reported that they were looking for a group, a "way to make a difference" or a community of similarly minded friends and that this active search precipitated involvement. Most of these men also knew someone involved in the group or effort that they ultimately joined. Finally, 5 participants (18%) initiated antiviolence work as the result of a job or volunteer position search. For 2 men, a formal involvement opportunity was the first influential factor precipitating their participation in some kind of antiviolence effort.

Shift in Meanings

As men discussed the nature and qualities of the experiences that led to their antiviolence involvement, they described specific meanings they had derived from these experiences. For 17 of the men, a meaning evolved over time from a sensitizing event, which then became a precipitate or motivating factor in seeking or accepting an opportunity to become active. For the remaining 10 participants, the meanings emerged following a tangible involvement opportunity, which often generated new reflection on earlier sensitizing experiences or exposure to additional sensitizing events. This new meaning making in turn precipitated accepting an offer to join an antiviolence effort or prompted the respondent to seek one. In both cases, the meaning that men attached to their sensitizing and opportunity experiences appeared to be a critical motivating factor in involvement. Three primary meanings surfaced, each with subthemes, and most men identified with more than one meaning. These are described more fully below.

Compelled to Action

This group of three subthemes was generally related to a sense of feeling obligated to take action or seeing a tangible opportunity for making a difference. Collectively, men who derived these meanings from their sensitizing or opportunity experiences felt that they no longer had a choice to do nothing, newly

perceived doing nothing as contributing to the problem, or had a clear sense of how their own strengths could make a contribution to addressing violence.

Charged with a mandate. The first of these subthemes, "charged with a mandate," was reported by 9 participants (33%). These men reported a sense that their new knowledge or awareness of violence rendered them responsible for taking action. Several men felt that having this knowledge eliminated the option of being uninvolved or of not speaking up as long as women's safety was jeopardized. For example, the following respondent reflected on how his growing understanding of sexual violence led him to equate inaction with acquiescence and deepened his commitment to taking an active antiviolence stance:

> Instead of seeing isolated incidences of people that I knew who had been assaulted, [I] started looking at that as a systemic issue. And I think once I started doing that, it was like, okay, how can I not? . . . And I think I started putting that together . . . that it's a generalizable experience. Even people who haven't been assaulted experience some of this fear. I just knew what side of that I wanted to be on, and I knew that . . . not being active about it was being silent about it, and, therefore, in a sense condoning it. (MAV27)

Other men reported an increased awareness that simply not using violence in their own lives and being "decent" was not sufficient to reduce violence or to maintain the safety of women they care about. Describing the meaning he derived from a campus-wide presentation, one participant stated,

> The thing that Jackson Katz was talking about is that, you could say, we're all good men here because we don't hit our girlfriends or wives, but he was saying, "Well, that's not good enough. You've got to be better men." And so that kind of inspired me. (MAV9)

Perceiving an addressable need. The second subtheme under the meaning "compelled to action," was "perceiving an addressable need," reported by 6 respondents (22%). The meaning is characterized by men's perception that violence against women is a problem that can be addressed or made tangibly better, perhaps more so than other social issues, as reflected in this respondent's statement, "I can't stop global warming tomorrow, and I can't stop poverty tomorrow, but tomorrow someone might not get hit" (MAV4). Other men got involved because they identified or were exposed to a specific need or to a contribution they could make. The following participant described the appeal of a full-time role in an antiviolence agency:

> I feel like I'm making a difference on a day-to-day basis by changing and/or having people listen to the story of the women. . . . Or the other day I got funded for a grant that I wrote. . . . And to get that notice in the mail saying we want to support what you're doing, you know those things are just huge for me. And I just feel like I'm making a difference every day. (MAV6)

Identifying own strengths. Finally, 5 respondents (18%) noted that the sensitizing or opportunity experience had the effect of highlighting or identifying a particular skill or quality in them that was needed. As a result, these participants felt that they had something specific to contribute, or felt trusted, honored, or recognized by encouragement to participate or by a disclosure from a survivor. Describing his reaction to a friend's disclosure of abuse one participant noted,

> I don't know if I knew the full power or the level of trust that's involved in telling someone else this, but I remember feeling really glad or good that she could trust me enough to say that . . . and that made me want to do that more. (MAV20)

On receiving a nomination to join an antiviolence education group, another participant learned about how his own skills could be tangibly useful, which motivated him to pursue the involvement opportunity:

> I went through the interview process, you know I found out that the work they do was very presentation based, and I consider myself a very strong public speaker who's talking to a lot of male populations, or all male populations . . . and I thought

that I could be a good, forceful speaker and really have a helpful role in trying to communicate with these populations. (MAV7)

Changing Worldview

As a result of processing their sensitizing or opportunity events, several respondents reported experiencing a deep shift in their thinking about their own experiences or behavior or in their level of comprehension of the ongoing vulnerability of women. This shift often served to connect the issue of violence much more closely to their own reality or priorities, or foster a previously absent emotional connection to the issue. Three subthemes also emerged in relation to the "changing worldview" meaning.

Violence as relevant. First, 11 respondents (41%) reported a heightened awareness of the relevance of violence to their own lives, and particularly to lives of women they care about. Participants described feeling frightened, disturbed, or suddenly conscious of the multiple ways that violence against women manifests in their own communities. For many participants, disclosures of or learning opportunities about violence had the impact of splintering assumptions that violence is not a significant issue in circles close to them. For example, one participant described the magnitude of the impact of learning that his mother is a survivor of violence:

> To be completely honest, I really didn't think sexual assault was a very pertinent issue for me as a man until about my sophomore year. And, frankly, like probably until my sophomore year of college . . . I probably would have argued about the whole one in four statistic and other things like that. Like I never thought sexual assault was a big problem on our University. And during a break I went home and found out through an argument that my mom and sister were having that my mom was actually a victim and survivor of sexual assault. And it really kind of turned my whole . . . my world over. (MAV12)

For many men, processing a sensitizing experience created a sudden awareness of ongoing vulnerability of people they love and generated an emotional connection to the issue of violence that was previously absent. This emotional connection in turn seemed to lay the groundwork for antiviolence involvement for these participants.

Employing a structural analysis was the second subtheme related to a changing worldview. Eight respondents (30%) reported that as they gained greater exposure to the issue of violence against women, they began to see it as connected with other social justice issues to which they were already committed. Linking sexual and domestic violence to social issues about which they had a preexisting concern, such as racism or homophobia, rendered the issue of violence against women more pressing or relevant. In making these connections, men felt that they could address larger issues of oppression by becoming involved in antiviolence efforts. For example, the following respondent employed an analysis in which he connected violence to two issues he cared deeply about, oppression and environmentalism, both of which he viewed as related to systems of domination and alienation:

> And so when I work on the issue of sexualized violence, I'm conscious that I'm working specifically on the issue of sexualized violence, but I'm also conscious in that in working on that issue of sexualized violence, I'm also working on the general issue of violence itself and even more generally on that relationship between self and other, and if I can contribute toward undoing sexualized violence, then I see that as a contribution towards environmentalism, too. (MAV24)

For other respondents, employing a structural analysis was related to linking violence against women to other forms of oppression that they had experienced or witnessed in their own lives. Again, making this connection with personal experiences of marginalization rendered violence a more focal, "actionable" concern for these men:

> I saw a lot of my friends growing up experience hate crimes and experience physical violence. . . . And so I guess I just . . . I was thinking about how I wanted to be as an ally to women in general. So I think that the way that I got involved in doing

anti-violence work was through a lot of the anti-oppression work that I was doing when I was a youth. . . . I mean I started doing a lot of activism and stuff when I was 14, and you know I've been doing it pretty consistently since then. And so I think that my strong relationship to doing anti-oppression work really helped segue me into doing anti-violence work. (MAV 15)

In addition to the 8 respondents who identified a preexisting social justice consciousness or concern for social equality as a precipitating factor in their involvement, an additional 8 men spoke about how their antiviolence work has subsequently helped them form an analysis of violence that links it to social inequity in general, and patriarchal norms or "traditional" forms of masculinity in particular. These men explicitly made connections between violence against women and issues of sexism, male privilege, and race or sexuality-based oppression. In contrast, 8 men made no overt linkage between violence against women and broader issues of gender inequity or male privilege. Finally, 3 men could be characterized as beginning the process of examining how gender inequities are related to violence.

Reassessing the past. Finally, 4 respondents (15%) spoke about how their sensitization or opportunity experiences led them to reevaluate past experiences or behavior. For these men, new learning about or new exposure to violence sparked additional reflection on past experiences, and perhaps viewing those experiences in a new way. The following 2 men spoke specifically about how their exposure to survivors of violence triggered a reassessment of past aggressive behavior that ultimately motivated antiviolence involvement.

> I guess I felt I sort of owed it to myself, if not society, and the universe to balance out who I used to be . . . so when this thing happened in high school, you know the accused . . . we literally kicked him out of our lives. And while I don't necessarily regret it. I do realize that is was ultimately probably not productive. And he probably went on to be a rapist or an abuser. He's probably more likely to turn out that way because of what we did. And so in a way

it's like . . . sort of coming into my adulthood with this stuff, you know, I'm wanting to balance out the stupid, vigilante, adolescent emotions around this issue with adult proaction. (MAV3)

My part in DV work is part of my redemption, a part of reconciliation with my violent past. Not guilt or shame, but redemption. (MAV31)

Reevaluating past responses to disclosure was also part of reassessment for two respondents. For these men, new learning about violence against women prompted uneasiness about the way they had handled past situations and motivated a desire to gain the knowledge and skills to provide support to survivors.

In my senior year, the girl I was dating was actually sexually assaulted [by someone else], and there was a lot of gray in the sense that I didn't really recognize fully what had happened at the time. . . . I was really affected by that, and I felt very powerless. You know, I wasn't able to help her. I certainly blame myself a little bit for not realizing what had happened when it initially did. (MAV2)

Joining With Others

The third major meaning to emerge from men's sensitizing or opportunity experiences was a realization that antiviolence work was an opportunity to enact their own ideals with like-minded others or was a way of joining a compelling group that offered connection and support. Two subthemes are related to joining with others.

Feeling connected. The first subtheme was described by 4 respondents (15%). Primarily through opportunity experiences, these men began to see antiviolence work as a way to build or enhance connection with others, particularly with other men. For these men, involvement was part of building community and a sense of mutual support. This is reflected in the following participant's description of his internal processing following his first exposure to a Take Back the Night event:

Knowing that there was a community of people who cared and in caring, the community substantially contributed to the healing of individuals who

were . . . being so vulnerable, and knowing that there was a community to work with and that we could support each other in this process because something as pernicious and insidious as sexual violence does not just affect individuals; it affects whole communities, and it's all of our burden to bear. And so knowing there was a community willing to stand in the face of that truth and stand together and then say no and then do the work to try and change some things . . . meant so much to me and made it worthwhile and continues to do so. (MAV13)

Doing masculinity differently. Another 5 participants described the appeal of realizing that they could work with other men in a way that was different from "traditional" approaches to masculinity or male friendship. These men expressed relief or excitement at the prospect of having close friendships with men in which they could express vulnerability, work collaboratively, and find broader ways of "being masculine" than masculine stereotypes might suggest. One participant noted,

It was something about just sitting in a circle with a couple of guys and talking about, you know, how men dance compared to women, like how it's not okay to put your hands above your head when you dance or something [laughs]. Just things like that, that you would *never* talk about just walking through campus or anything . . . and I thought that was really unique and really just honest, and it kind of lifts the weight off of your chest. Because I think a lot of the times, men walk around with this shield up, this . . . or we talk about the male stereotype *box* that we're always living in. Even if we don't want to, we're still put into that box, and that was the first time in my life where I didn't have that box around me. And I liked it. It was fun. (MAV30)

DISCUSSION

Men's descriptions of the influences that precipitated their involvement in antiviolence work suggest that factors at multiple levels over the course of time coalesce into taking an active stand against violence.

Specifically, initial sensitizing exposures to the issue of violence or to survivors, coupled with internal meanings that men attach to these experiences, and tangible involvement opportunities were critical to these men's pathways to engagement. Across these three arenas, four general commonalities characterizing men's antiviolence involvement surfaced. First, all participants described their initiation into active antiviolence participation as a *process* that unfolded over time and had multiple influences. Men's decision to take a stand against violence against women, attend an event or meeting, or join an antiviolence group was never constituted of or influenced by a single event or factor, but was rather precipitated by a combination of experiences and internal reflection that sparked or deepened men's interest in involvement. Second, respondents described specific ways in which the issue of violence against women had become personalized or emotion laden for them in some way. Their antiviolence involvement was predicated, in part, on discovering ways that violence was personally relevant to their own lives or those close to them or on making an empathic connection with the emotional consequences of violence. Third, the vast majority of participants became involved through or because of existing personal connections and social networks. Finally, many respondents made connections between their involvement and a sense of community: these participants felt that their initiation into antiviolence efforts was supported by their own community or was part of an effort to find or build a sense of community for themselves. Collectively, these findings hold implications both for enhancing model development regarding antiviolence ally development and for the practice of engaging men in violence prevention endeavors. These are discussed in turn below.

Implications for Models of Ally Development

Men's descriptions of their experiences leading to antiviolence involvement evidence both areas of overlap and disconnect with the models of social justice ally development presented in the introduction to this article. Similar to the social justice ally

models, antiviolence ally formation was a process that occurred over time, with factors at multiple levels (intrapersonal, interpersonal, and community) convening to influence involvement. Specifically, similar to models developed by Broido (2000) and Reason et al. (2005), men's pathways to involvement relied on initial exposure opportunities, engagement in reflection and meaning making over time, personal connections to the issue of violence against women, and tangible, clear invitations or opportunities to join an ally effort within their personal communities. These factors are likely important to retain and adapt in refining models of male antiviolence engagement. Future research could seek to more fully elucidate the mechanisms or intervention approaches that best foster the kinds of precipitating experiences, reflection, and meaning making described by both ally-development models and by men in this study.

A point of departure between models of social justice ally development and the experiences of men in this study is the degree to which male antiviolence allies engaged with their own social identities and male privilege as a precursor to involvement. Although approximately one third of the respondents described linking violence against women to structural justice issues as a meaning that fostered their involvement, this sometimes but not always took the form of interrogating their own social identities, ideas about "masculinity," or the role of male privilege in perpetuating woman abuse. About one third of men in the study made no explicit connection between violence against women and larger social inequities, such as sexism, even after a period of involvement. Although these men may have framed violence as problematic or people they love as in need of protection, there was an absence of exploration about the roles of gender and power in the perpetuation of woman abuse. Furthermore, only about 15% of the men in the study (those endorsing the "reassessing the past" meaning) explicitly described exploring the ways that their own past or current behavior might have reflected sexism as a step in their process of involvement. Unlike models of ally development more generally, therefore, the degree to which an awareness of gender-based social privilege is (or should be) a necessary prerequisite to antiviolence involvement remains a somewhat open question.

Several possible interpretations of the variance in men's engagement with issues of sexism exist. On a pragmatic level, interview probes may not have been specific enough to prompt all men to reflect on the ways that they engaged with the notion of male privilege as part of their involvement process. It may also be that the nature of many violence-related sensitizing or opportunity experiences (such as hearing a specific survivor's story, or receiving an invitation to attend an antiviolence event) do not contain explicit linkages between abuse and sexism, whereas sensitizing exposure experiences regarding racism or heterosexism likely contain, by their very nature, clear connections to notions of oppression and unearned social privilege.

It may also be that the relatively recent nature of participants' initiation into antiviolence work means that some are at the beginning stages of the process of employing a social justice analysis. The ongoing development of a critical awareness of gender inequity may be fostered by entrance into antiviolence work itself, as it was for about a third of men in this study. Practitioners have noted that initial awareness building and engagement efforts need to meet men "where they are" and that starting with conversations about male privilege may raise defensiveness and deter preliminary participation from some men who have important contributions to make (e.g., Funk, 2006). At the same time, a lack of awareness of male privilege may create risk for recreating patterns of sexism within antiviolence work as more men become involved. Several practitioners have noted the need for men's antiviolence groups to continually consult with and be accountable to women and women's antiviolence networks to ensure that men's prevention efforts honor the considerable history of women's contributions to ending violence and do not replicate structures of inequity (Berkowitz, 2002; Funk, 2006). Although there is likely a middle ground of tailored engagement efforts for men that also gradually work

toward a critical understanding of male privilege, the long-term effectiveness of ally efforts depend on tackling gender-based and other social inequities, as these ultimately buttress enduring violence. Further research is needed that examines the impact of involvement in antiviolence work over time on men's analysis of the roots of violence and how men's degree of engagement with issues of sexism and male privilege relates to their impact and effectiveness as "allies."

Principles from the Transtheoretical Model (TTM) may provide helpful strategies for moving men through the process from a lack of awareness about abuse, to engagement, to a more critical evaluation of sexism and its links to violence against women. Combining social justice ally models with processes identified by the TTM to support behavioral change may enhance both the accuracy and the interventive relevance of these models. For example. Prochaska et al. (2002) identify consciousness raising (increasing an understanding of the causes, impacts, and dynamics of a specific behavior) and environmental reevaluation (examining the impact of inaction or an unhealthy behavior on others) as typical processes associated with moving from denial of a problem to "contemplation," or a readiness to engage in new behaviors. Coupling these specific processes with initial factors in social justice ally development (such as sensitizing or exposure experiences) may increase the model's explanatory power and guide intervention development related to engaging men around deeper issues of sexism and violence.

Implications for Practice

As noted above, for most of the men in this study, the decision to become part of an antiviolence effort was influenced by multiple factors and occurred over time. Engaging men is a multifaceted process that likely demands repeated and diverse opportunities for exposure to the issue of violence against women as well as built-in mechanisms for men to discuss, reflect on, and make sense of the ways that violence is relevant to their worlds. Previously discussed applications of multiple, diverse strategies for men at different "stages" in their relationship to the issue of violence are needed, both to provide initial "sensitizing" experiences and the opportunities to create meaning from them. For example, large-scale community or educational events might be supported with a network of follow-up conversations, both formally and informally through peer groups, to allow for the kind of processing that could foster men's development as allies.

At the same time, although the men in this study were influenced by many different factors over time, a strong commonality among participants was the importance of personal connections and community in making linkages with concrete antiviolence opportunities. All but 5 participants located an opportunity for involvement through a friend or community member and 9 joined an antiviolence effort as the result of a formal personal invitation. This highlights the primacy of social networks as recruiting and engagement vehicles. Although many study participants were exposed to the topic of violence against women through educational presentations, community events, or college courses, these "learning opportunities" did not directly precipitate involvement on their own. Rather, encouragement and engagement from trusted peers or mentors constituted the tangible involvement opportunity that brought most of the men into antiviolence efforts. This echoes Broido (2000) and Reason et al. (2005) who found that the social justice allies in their studies did not actively seek action opportunities but initiated their social justice activities only after explicit invitations to do so. The project of engaging men and encouraging them to view themselves as allies is therefore perhaps best done individually through existing social networks and by admired peers and necessitates specific, personalized invitations to become a part of the work. Popular Opinion Leader (POL) approaches, which have previously been applied to HIV (Fernandez et al., 2003) and smoking prevention (Campbell et al., 2008), capitalize on the power of natural leaders in existing social networks and may be a relevant approach here. At the same time, engagement through social networks can build on "sensitizing experiences" that many

men have likely already had and can foster the kind of meaning making from those experiences that supports antiviolence engagement.

Finally, this "meaning making" is likely central to men's process in coming to see themselves as antiviolence allies. Efforts to provide sensitizing experiences (such as learning opportunities or occasions to hear survivor stories) or to engage men through personal contact in their social networks may be bolstered by explicitly cultivating the kinds of meanings that men in this study came to attach to the issue of violence. These might include unambiguously issuing a charge of responsibility to addressing the issue, identifying specific needs and the ways that individual men's strengths and talents may contribute to ameliorating those needs, fostering connections with supportive groups or community, relaying the unacceptability and dangers of inaction, making explicit linkages between violence and other social issues men may care about, and highlighting the experiences of violence survivors in a way that helps men to interrogate their own underestimation of the degree to which sexual and domestic violence affect their communities and the people they love. Relaying information about the prevalence and impact of violence against women in general terms is likely insufficient to support men in seeing the issue as personally relevant; rather, helping men to form these deeper connections appears critical. Such efforts are reflected in existing men's engagement programs, such as A Call To Men (www.acalltomen. org), a national training organization dedicated to "galvanizing" men's antiviolence participation, and Men Can Stop Rape (www.mencanstoprape. org), which encourages young men to reframe and then act on "strength" in service of ending men's violence against women. Explicitly fostering several of these "meaning shifts" is likely an important element of any male antiviolence building effort.

Limitations

Study limitations should be noted. Perhaps most important, the sample of men in this study almost exclusively identified as White. Findings presented here, therefore, largely reflect White men's antiviolence ally development and the meanings and factors significant to their journey. A glaring gap in both the findings presented here and research about male antiviolence allies more generally is the experiences of men of color around antiviolence mobilization. Future research should examine both the unique factors that might influence the involvement of men of color as well as how racism affects men's relationships to ally movements and to taking a stand around issues of violence. A second limitation is the small, volunteer nature of the sample. Men in this sample self-selected to participate and therefore may represent a subgroup of male antiviolence allies who have particular interests or experiences relative to their work, which may not be more broadly generalizable. Future research with larger, more diverse samples is needed to evaluate the replicability of these findings. Finally, because this study focused only on men who have successfully been engaged in antiviolence work, it is not possible to contrast their stories with those of men who have had sensitizing or opportunity experiences but have not chosen to become involved or with those of men who have disengaged. Additional scholarship focusing on the discriminating factors separating male antiviolence allies from noninvolved men may shed additional light on how to design engagement strategies to maximize effective male participation.

CONCLUSION

Given that engaging and partnering with men is increasingly recognized as an important component of the formidable challenge of ending violence against women, it is critical to build on our understanding of the processes through which men incorporate antiviolence work into their own lives. This study suggests that, similar to existing models of social justice ally development, exposure to issues of violence, opportunities to critically reflect and make meaning from those exposures, and tangible invitations for involvement are some of the general interrelated factors that motivate men's antiviolence involvement over time. As the practice of engaging men and the models developed to describe it are

refined over time, additional work is needed regarding the particular strategies that best foster the kinds of opportunities and meaning making associated with men's commitment to antiviolence efforts. This may be assisted by adapting elements of theoretical frameworks, such as the Transtheoretical Model, with models of ally formation to maximize the efficacy of efforts to broaden the range of men dedicated to ending violence in women's lives.

AUTHORS' NOTE

The authors would like to thank the 27 men who volunteered their time to participate in this study, along with the many individuals who provided consultation throughout the process of the research, including Jonathan Grove, Taryn Lindhorst, Kevin Miller, Joshua O'Donnell, and Gayle Stringer.

REFERENCES

Banyard, V. L., Eckstein, R. P., & Moynihan, M. M. (2010). Sexual violence prevention: The role of stages of change. *Journal of Interpersonal Violence, 25,* 111–135.

Barker, G., Ricardo, C., & Nascimento, M. (2007). *Engaging men and boys in changing gender-based inequity in health: Evidence from programme interventions.* Retrieved July 29, 2009, from www.who.int/gender/documents/Engaging_men_boys.pdf

Berkowitz, A. (2002). Fostering men's responsibility for preventing sexual assault. In P. A. Schewe (Ed.). *Preventing violence in relationships: Interventions across the life span* (pp. 163–196). Washington, DC: American Psychological Association.

Bishop, A. (2002). *Becoming an ally: Breaking the cycle of oppression in people* (2nd ed.). Halifax, Nova Scotia, Canada: Fernwood.

Broido, E. M. (2000). The development of social justice allies during college: A phenomenological investigation. *Journal of College Student Development, 41,* 3–18.

Campbell, R., Starkeya, F., Holliday, J., Audrey, S., Bloorc, M., Parry-Langdon et al. (2008). An informal school-based peer-led intervention for smoking prevention in adolescence (ASSIST): A cluster randomised trial, *Lancet, 371,* 1595–1602.

Coulter, R. P. (2003). Boys doing good: Young men and gender equity. *Educational Review. 55*, 135–145.

Crooks, C. V., Goodall, G. R., Hughes, R., Jaffe, P. G., & Baker, L. L. (2007). Engaging men and boys in preventing violence against women: Applying a cognitive-behavioral model. *Violence Against Women, 13*, 217–239.

DeKeseredy, W. S., Schwartz, M. D., & Alvi, S. (2000). The role of profeminist men in dealing with woman abuse on the Canadian college campus. *Violence Against Women, 6*, 918–935.

Earle, J. P. (1996). Acquaintance rape workshops: Their effectiveness in changing the attitudes of first-year college men. *NASPA Journal, 34*, 2–18.

Fabiano, P. M., Perkins, H. W., Berkowitz, A. D., Linkenbach, J., & Stark, C. (2003). Engaging men as social justice allies in ending violence against women: Evidence for a social norms approach. *Journal of American College Health, 52*, 105–112.

Fernandez, M. I., Bowen, G. S., Gay, C. L., Mattson, T. R., Bital, E., & Kelly, J. A. (2003). HIV, sex and social change: Applying ESID principles to HIV prevention research. *American Journal of Community Psychology, 32*, 333–344.

Flood, M. (2005). Changing men: Best practice in sexual violence education. *Women Against Violence, 18*, 26–36.

Foubert, J. D., Newberry, J. T., & Tatum, J. L. (2007). Behavior differences seven months later: Effects of a rape prevention program on first-year men who join fraternities. *NASPA Journal, 44*, 728–749.

Funk, R. (2006). *Reaching men: Strategies for preventing sexist attitudes, behaviors, and violence.* Indianapolis, IN: JIST.

Funk, R. (2008). Men's work: Men's voices and actions against sexism and violence. *Journal of Intervention and Prevention in the Community, 36*, 155–171.

Hawkins, S. R. (2005). *Evaluation findings: Men Can Stop Rape, Men of Strength Clubs 2004–2005.* Retrieved August 8, 2007, from www.mencanstoprape.org

Heise, L. L. (1998). Violence against women: An integrated, ecological framework. *Violence Against Women, 4*, 262–290.

Helms, J. E. (1990). Toward a model of White racial identity development. In J. E. Helms (Ed.), *Black and White racial identity: Theory, research and practice* (pp. 67–80). Westport, CT: Greenwood.

Katz, J. (1995). Reconstructing masculinity in the locker room: The Mentors in Violence Prevention Project. *Harvard Educational Review, 65*, 163–174.

Lincoln, Y. S., & Guba, E. G. (1985). *Naturalistic inquiry.* Newbury Park, CA: Sage.

Murnen, S. K., Wright, C., & Kaluzny, G. (2002). If "boys will be boys," then girls will be victims? A meta-analytic review of the research that relates masculine ideology to sexual aggression. *Sex Roles, 46*, 359–375.

Prochaska, J. O., Redding, C. A., & Evers, K. E. (2002). The Transtheoretical Model and stages of change. In K. Glanz, B. K. Rimer, & F. M. Lewis (Eds.), *Health behavior and health education: Theory, research and practice* (3rd ed., pp. 99–120). San Francisco, CA: Jossey-Bass.

Reason, R. D., Miller, E. A. R., & Scales, T. C. (2005). Toward a model of racial justice ally development. *Journal of College Student Behavior, 46*, 530–546.

Sokoloff, N. J., & Dupont, I. (2005). Domestic violence at the intersections of race, class and gender. *Violence Against Women, 11*, 38–64.

Stein, J. L. (2007) Peer educators and close friends as predictors of male college students' willingness to prevent rape. *Journal of College Student Development, 48*, 75–89.

Strauss, A., & Corbin, J. (1998). *Basics of qualitative research: Techniques and procedures for developing Grounded Theory.* Thousand Oaks, CA: Sage.

Tatum, B. (1994). Teaching White students about racism: The search for White allies and the restoration of hope. *Teachers College Record, 95*, 462–476.

Tjaden, P., & Thoennes, N. (1998). *Prevalence, incidence and consequences of violence against women: Findings from the National Violence Against Women Survey.* Washington, DC: National Institute of Justice and Centers for Disease Control.

MORE THAN A FEW GOOD MEN

Jackson Katz

"As long as we take the view that these are problems for women alone to solve, we cannot expect to reverse the high incidence of rape and child abuse . . . and domestic violence. We do know that many men do not abuse women and children; and that they strive always to live with respect and dignity. But until today the collective voice of these men has never been heard, because the issue has not been regarded as one for the whole nation. From today those who inflict violence on others will know they are being isolated and cannot count on other men to protect them. From now on all men will hear the call to assume their responsibility for solving this problem."—President Nelson Mandela, 1997, National Men's March, Pretoria, South Africa

Since the very beginning of the women-led movements against domestic and sexual violence in the 1970s, there have been men who personally, professionally, and politically supported the work of those women. In addition, over the past several decades there have been repeated attempts by men to create organizations and targeted initiatives to address men's roles in ending men's violence against women. Some of the early efforts were undertaken by groups of concerned men who responded to the challenge from women's organizations to educate, politicize, and organize other men. Some of these men chose to volunteer in supportive roles with local rape crisis centers or battered women's programs. Others contributed to the development of the fledgling batterer intervention movement in

the late 1970s and 1980s. Some of the better known programs for batterers were Emerge in Cambridge, Massachusetts; RAVEN (Rape and Violence End Now) in St. Louis, Missouri; and Men Stopping Violence in Atlanta, Georgia. Still other men created political and activist educational organizations, like the National Organization for Men Against Sexism (NOMAS), which has held "Men and Masculinity" conferences annually since 1975; the Oakland Men's Project in the San Francisco Bay Area; Men Stopping Rape in Madison, Wisconsin; DC Men Against Rape; and Real Men, an anti-sexist men's organization I co-founded in Boston in 1988.

The rapidly growing field of "men's work" also produced community centers that combine batterer-intervention and counseling services for men with educational outreach and social activism. One of the groundbreaking programs in this field is the Men's Resource Center of Western Massachusetts, founded in Amherst in 1982. In the 1990s anti-sexist men's initiatives in the U.S. and around the world increased dramatically. One of the most visible has been the White Ribbon Campaign, an activist educational campaign founded by a group of men in Canada in 1991. They started the WRC in response to a horrific incident on December 6, 1989, at the University of Montreal, where an armed twenty-five-year-old man walked into a classroom, separated the women from the men and proceeded to shoot the women. Before he finished his rampage, he had murdered fourteen women in cold blood—and shaken up an entire country. The significance of the white ribbon—which has been adopted on hundreds of college campuses and communities in the U.S. as well as a number of other countries—is that men wear it to make a visible and public pledge "never to commit, condone, nor remain silent about violence against women."

Despite these notable efforts over the past thirty years, the movement of men committed to ending men's violence against women has only recently picked up significant momentum. There are more men doing this work in the United States and around the world than ever before. Halfway through the first decade of the twenty-first century there is reason for optimism, especially about the emergence of a new generation of anti-sexist men. But there are nowhere near enough men yet involved to make a serious dent in this enormous problem. Several key challenges lie ahead:

- How to increase dramatically the number of men who make these issues a priority in their personal and professional lives
- How to expand the existing infrastructure of men's anti-rape and domestic violence prevention groups, and other campus and community-based initiatives
- How to institutionalize gender violence prevention education at every level of the educational system
- How to build multiracial and multiethnic coalitions that unite men across differences around their shared concerns about sexist violence and the sexual exploitation of children
- How to insure that federal, state, and local funding for efforts to reduce gender violence are maintained and expanded in the coming years
- And finally, how to make it socially acceptable—even cool—for men to become vocal and public allies of women in the struggle against all forms of men's violence against women and children

A "BIG TENT" APPROACH

As I have made clear in this book, there is much that we can do to prevent men's violence against women—if we find the collective will in male culture to make it a priority. I am convinced that

millions of men in our society are deeply concerned about the abuse, harassment, and violence we see—and fear—in the lives of our daughters, mothers, sisters, and lovers. In fact, a recent poll conducted for Lifetime Television found that 57 percent of men aged sixteen to twenty-four believe gender violence is an "extremely serious" problem. A 2000 poll conducted by the Family Violence Prevention Fund found that one-quarter of men would do more about the issue if they were asked. And some compelling social norms research on college campuses suggests that one of the most significant factors in a man's decision to intervene in an incident is his perception of how other men would act in a similar situation. Clearly, a lot of men are uncomfortable with other men's abusive behaviors, but they have not figured out what to do about it—or have not yet mustered the courage to act on their own. So there is great potential to increase dramatically the number of men who commit personal time, money, and institutional clout to the effort to reduce men's violence against women. But in order to achieve this we need to think outside the box about how to reach into the mainstream of male culture and social power.

One promising approach employs elements of what might be called "big tent" movement building. The big tent concept comes from politics, where it has been used most famously to describe efforts to unite various constituencies and single-issue special-interest groups under the Republican Party label. A number of questions arise when this concept is applied to gender violence prevention: How do we attract individuals and organizations not known for their advocacy of the issues of men's violence? What are some of the necessary compromises required in order to broaden the coalition of participating individuals and groups? What are some of the costs and benefits of engaging new partners, who might not have the depth of experience or the ideological affinities of the majority of women and men currently in the movement?

Growing pains always accompany growth. A bigger movement will inevitably create new conflicts. One way to think about the question of

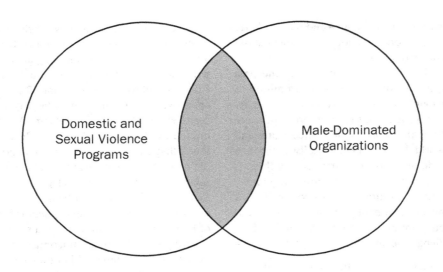

broadening the base of the movement is to consider the concept embodied in the geometric model of the Venn diagram. The Venn diagram captures the idea that coalition building involves identifying shared objectives between groups with different interests, not creating a perfect union between fully compatible partners. The diagram consists of two overlapping circles. In this case we might say that one circle represents the needs and interests of the battered women's and rape crisis movements. The other circle represents any men's organization that has not historically been part of these movements. Clearly, there are large areas where the circles do not overlap. But the big tent approach does not dwell on the areas of disconnection. It focuses on the center area, where there are points of agreement and shared objectives. If individuals and groups of men and women can agree that reducing men's violence against women is an urgent objective, then perhaps they can agree for the moment to table their other differences.

CHALLENGES

There are obvious downsides to incautiously expanding the big tent. Take, for example, the costs and benefits of working with men in the sports culture. Many women in domestic and sexual violence advocacy have long seen the benefit to partnering with athletic teams or utilizing high-profile male athletes in public service campaigns. But some of these same women worry about the potential risks inherent in such collaboration. They fear that a male athlete who speaks out publicly against men's violence could undermine the integrity of the movement if his private behavior does not match his public rhetoric. Happily, in recent years this fear has begun to dissipate as more male athletes speak out, in part because with increased men's participation there is less pressure on any one man to be the "perfect" poster child for anti-violence efforts. We can also never lose sight of the fact that professional sports teams are not social justice organizations. They are businesses that sometimes have huge investments in players. Say a team takes a public stand against men's violence, and then at some point one of its star players is arrested for domestic violence or sexual assault. Is the team likely to respond based on what they think is best for the community, or for their own bottom line?

The participation of faith-based organizations in the big tent presents significant opportunities, but comes with its own unique set of challenges. As the Rev. Dr. Marie Fortune, a pioneer in the movements against domestic and sexual violence and founder of the FaithTrust Institute in Seattle, Washington, points out, "Millions of men participate in faith-based communities whose leaders, often male, typically enjoy significant moral authority and shape in important ways the values and behaviors of men in their congregations." There are male clergy in every denomination who are strong allies of women in the domestic and sexual violence prevention movements. But many clergy and religious leaders have received no training on the issue of men's violence against women. To this day many male clergy are reluctant to take strong public stands on issues of sexual and domestic violence. What further complicates matters is that many religious traditions have "reflected and reinforced," in the words of Rev. Fortune, "patriarchal values that have been at the core of violence against women." But perhaps even more troubling are the clergy sex abuse scandals that have become routine in recent years. It is plain to see that even men with impeccable religious credentials can be private hypocrites.

The participation of faith-based organizations in gender violence prevention also raises the question of how much ideological incompatibility is tolerable in the quest for big tent inclusiveness. Can feminist religious and secular leaders work in coalition with religious leaders who have resisted the advancement of women in the family and the pulpit? Can progressive religious and secular leaders who support full sexual equality work side by side with religious leaders who oppose gay civil rights?

Similar questions arise about an organization like the Boy Scouts. Scouting plays an important role in the lives of millions of boys and adolescent males. Many local Boy Scout chapters have participated in events of domestic violence and sexual assault awareness month. But if the Scouts went a step further and made participation in gender violence prevention a major nationwide organizational goal, they could have a tremendous impact, especially since the Scouts have a presence in many communities where there is currently little male participation in domestic and sexual violence programs. But many progressive organizations refuse to work with the Boy Scouts because their official policy discriminates against openly gay scouts and scoutmasters. Does their anti-gay stance make the Boy Scouts an unacceptable coalition partner in the struggle against teen-relationship abuse and sexual assault?

Until now most men in the movement to end men's violence against women have been pro-feminist and politically liberal or progressive. But this does not preclude them from framing one aspect of the gender-violence issue in language about crime and punishment that resonates with conservatives. In fact, many politically conservative men have played an important role in this fight—particularly men in law enforcement, the military, and government. After all, domestic and sexual violence are more than social problems; they are crimes. Nonetheless, millions of abusive men continue to receive suspended sentences, probation, and other light penalties, which signals that their crimes are not taken seriously. In order to be effective, decisive action is required by police, prosecutors, and judges. The goal of punishment is to send the message to would-be perps that the price for transgression is steep. Conservative as well as progressive men who take the idea of personal responsibility seriously should support policies that hold law-breakers accountable, and advocacy that strengthens the community's desire to do so. But a criminal justice approach is also fraught with potential problems. For one thing, there are not enough jail cells to house all the men who could be prosecuted for domestic and sexual violence. As I have discussed, class bias and racism are factors in any discussion about the criminal justice system. Efforts to attract conservative men's support by emphasizing a law enforcement approach might exact too high a cost—and jeopardize the increased participation of people of color who are concerned about both gender violence *and* the over-representation of men in color in the "prison industrial complex." In addition, since most gender violence—including the vast majority of rape—is currently not reported, it is questionable how effective a criminal justice approach can be.

MEN AND WOMEN

The special challenge of gender violence prevention politics is that women's trust of men is not a given. Some women are understandably wary of men's motivations and skeptical about their commitment to gender justice. As increasing numbers of men get involved, they worry that men might try to "take over" the movement, or take it in a direction that suits men's needs rather than women's. Women are always eager to see whether men "walk their talk." For example, an administrator in a domestic-violence agency recently told me about a talented young man who had applied for a youth outreach position. He seemed to know the issues really well, she explained, and he grasped some of the subtle racial and ethnic issues involved in this work. He also had an engaging personal style. But he had not yet mastered the "micro-politics" of how to interact with women in positions of leadership. He often cut off women co-presenters, or talked over them in an effort to prove his knowledge. Was it worth the risk of hiring him?

For their part, some men are well-meaning but oblivious to the sensitivities required for effective inter-gender collaboration on an issue where women have historically been the leaders. For example, I have heard stories too many times about earnest young men on college campuses who were inspired to start anti-rape groups, but neglected first to check in with women who were already engaged in rape prevention work, like the director of the campus women's center. These sorts of political missteps can cause unnecessary tension and discord at the earliest stages and can undermine successful coalition-building.

Even so, there are numerous examples across the country of men and women working together to create and sustain sexual and domestic violence prevention initiatives. In fact, many successful college men's anti-violence programs have actually been started by women. Among the more well-known are Men Against Violence at Louisiana State University, begun by Dr. Luoluo Hong, and the Fraternity Anti-Violence Education Project at West Chester University in Pennsylvania, led by Dr. Deborah Mahlstedt.

WHAT CAN MEN DO?

At a small state college in the Northeast, a controversy erupted in early 2005 when the editors of the student newspaper distributed a sex survey across campus that included a question about which professor on campus they would most like to "get it on with." The person chosen was the coordinator of the women's studies program, who responded with a lengthy letter to the editor in which she wrote that it was "offensive and hurtful" to be disrespected by students in this way, and as a professional it undermined her ability to do her job. In her letter she posed a number of questions for an alternative survey, including one to men which asked, "What are you willing to do to help reduce rape and sexual assault among college students?" In response, a male columnist for the student newspaper wrote dismissively: "I will not rape anyone. Is there anything more I should add to this?" The student's response might have been glib and a bit obnoxious, but he spoke for a lot of men. Many of them have never even considered the wide range of choices men have to reduce rape and sexual assault, and every other type of gender violence. What follows is a brief discussion about how men can be effective anti-sexist agents, both as individuals and in their various public and private leadership roles within institutions.

HAVE THE COURAGE TO LOOK INWARD

One of the most important steps any man can take if he wants to be an ally to women in the struggle against gender violence is to be honest with himself. A key requirement for men to become effective anti-sexist agents is their willingness to examine their own attitudes and behaviors about women, sex, and manhood. This is similar to the sort of introspection required of anti-racist whites. It is not an easy process, especially when men start to see that they have inadvertently perpetuated sexism and violence through their personal actions, or their participation in sexist practices in male culture. Because defensiveness is the enemy of introspection, it is vital that men develop ways to transcend their initial defensive reactions about men's mistreatment of women and move toward a place where they are grounded enough to do something about it.

SUPPORT SURVIVORS

In a social climate where women who report sexual and domestic violence are often disbelieved and called "accusers," it is crucial that men personally and publicly support survivors—girls and boys, women and men. This can mean the offer of a supportive ear in a conversation, or a shoulder for a friend to cry on. It can also mean challenging others—men and women—who seek to discredit victims' accounts of their victimization. For example, when a girl or woman reports a sexual assault and her alleged attacker is a popular guy with a network of supporters, people often rally around him—even when they have nothing more than his word to go on that she is lying. Sadly, some of them try to smear her character and reputation. It is not fair to assume the man's guilt; he is entitled to a presumption of innocence until proven guilty. But alleged victims are entitled to a presumption as well—the presumption that they are telling the truth about what was done to them. They also have the right to be treated with respect, and to expect the people around them to defend their integrity if it is ever questioned.

SEEK HELP

Men who are emotionally, physically, or sexually abusive to women and girls need to seek help now. But first they have to acknowledge to themselves that they have a problem. I once gave a speech about men's violence against women at a big state university in the West. After the event was over, a blond-haired college student in jeans and a T-shirt approached me in the main lobby of the student center. His voice quivered as he said, "I just realized that I have done bad things to women." He did not elaborate, nor did I ask him to. But I could tell he had a troubled conscience by the look in his

eyes, and because he waited nearly half an hour to talk to me. The question of what to do about men who have been abusive will take on ever greater urgency as more men become involved in the movement against gender violence. Many men who were formerly abusive to women have become effective professionals in batterer intervention programs. They share their personal stories and serve as models for how men can grow and change. This is crucial because millions of men have committed mild or severe acts of cruelty toward women and children, and whether they were charged with and convicted of a crime or not, we have to figure out ways to integrate most of them back into our families and communities. Of course, sometimes this is easier said than done. For example, in recent years families in communities across the U.S. have faced the challenge of living in neighborhoods alongside convicted child molesters. This raises another set of questions: When do the rights of children and their parents to be free from the threat of sexual abuse and violence out-weigh the rights of men (or women) who have served their sentences and are seeking to rebuild their lives? If a man has committed acts of sexual or domestic violence, should those acts define him for the rest of his life?

REFUSE TO CONDONE SEXIST AND ABUSIVE BEHAVIOR BY FRIENDS, PEERS, AND COWORKERS

As I have argued in this book, if we want to dramatically increase the number of men who make men's violence against women a priority, it is not useful to engage them as perpetrators or potential perpetrators. Instead, it makes sense to enlist them as empowered bystanders who can do something to confront abusive peers, or who can help to create a climate in male peer culture that discourages some men's sexist attitudes and behaviors. This is often easier said than done, because it can be quite awkward for men to confront each other about how they talk about and treat women. Consider an experience I had when I was in my early thirties at a wedding of an old friend of mine. A few minutes after I was introduced to the best man at a cocktail reception the day before the wedding, he confidently told me and a group of other guys a tasteless joke about battered women. I was not sure how to react. If I said something, I feared that it could create a chill between us, and this was the first day of a long weekend. But if I did not say something, I feared my silence might imply approval of the joke. I felt similar to how I would have felt if a white friend had told a racist joke. There was an added concern: How could I—or anyone else— know the full context of his joke-telling? The guy may have been personally harmless, but at the very least his gender politics were suspect, and at the worst he also may have been a closeted batterer who was subtly seeking public approval for his private behavior. I managed to mutter a feeble objection, something like, "Surely you have other topics to joke about." But I never told the guy how I really felt.

Sometimes men who take a strong stand against gender violence can face serious interpersonal consequences for their efforts. Mike LaRiviere, a police officer who is deeply committed to domestic and sexual violence prevention, trains police across the country in domestic violence policies and procedures. He recounts an incident many years ago when he was relatively new to his small-city New England police force. He and his more senior partner answered a domestic violence call, and when they arrived at the apartment it was obvious that the man had assaulted the woman. Mike thought it was clear they should make an arrest, both for the victim's safety and to hold the man accountable for what he had done. But the senior partner had another idea.

He just wanted to tell the guy to cool down. Mike and he had a hushed but heated conversation in another room about what to do. They finally arrested the man, but for the next five or six months, Mike's partner barely spoke with him. The atmosphere in the squad car was tense and chilly, which in police work can be dangerous as well as unpleasant, because you can never be certain that someone who seethes with resentment will always have your back.

In spite of how difficult it can be for men to challenge each other about sexism, it does happen. In fact, it might happen more often than many people realize. In any case, it is important for men to hear each other's stories about this type of intervention, so they can see that other men feel as they do and so they can get potentially useful ideas. I heard one such story about a bachelor party road trip that Al Emerick, a leader of Men Against Violence Against Women in Jacksonville, Florida, took a couple of years ago with some friends. They were a group of well-off white guys in their thirties who had been playing poker together for nine years. There were four married men in the car along with the groom, and the discussion came up about strip clubs. The best man was ready to drop a pile of one-dollar bills on some "fine ladies' asses." Al said he would not be joining them, and the guys immediately got on him. "Whattya gay?" "What's the big deal, the wife's not here." "Cut loose." Because the guys had known Al for quite some time, they knew he was no prude, nor were his objections based on his religious beliefs. But they did know he had been working with a men's group that was affiliated with the local domestic violence shelter. He told them he did not want to take part because he had a problem with the objectification of women—even when it is voluntary. As he tells it, this group of friends spent two hours in an "intense but wonderful" conversation about sexism, domestic violence, male privilege, power, and control. In the course of the conversation Al fielded a range of predictable challenges like: "I'm not an abuser because I look at chicks." He countered with questions like, "What about men in the audience who might be abusers or rapists? By us being there and supporting the action, aren't we reinforcing their behaviors?" In the end, they never went to the strip clubs. Since that event, they have had further conversations about these issues, and according to Al, one of the guys has even offered to help produce a public service announcement for the anti-sexist men's group.

MAKE CONNECTIONS BETWEEN MEN'S VIOLENCE AGAINST WOMEN AND OTHER ISSUES

Gender violence contributes to a wide range of social problems that include youth violence, homelessness, divorce, alcoholism, and the transmission of HIV/AIDS. Men who care about these problems need to educate themselves about the relationship between gender violence and these issues, and then integrate this understanding in their work and daily life.

Perhaps nowhere are the effects of gender violence more pronounced than with HIV/AIDS, the global pandemic that has already killed twenty million people and infected forty-five million. Across the world, there is an inextricable linkage between men's violence against women and transmission of the virus. Forms of gender violence that are fueling transmission include sexual coercion and rape, men's refusal to wear condoms, and married or monogamous men's solicitation of prostitutes followed by unprotected sex with their wives or partners. Gender violence also takes the form of civil and customary laws that perpetuate male privilege and prerogative and deny women's human rights. This might include civil and customary laws that do not recognize marital rape or the dangers of early marriage, as well as systematic prohibitions against females inheriting wealth and property—a reality that ultimately forces millions of widows and daughters to lives of abject poverty and economic dependence on men. But according to M.I.T. research fellow and United Nations consultant Miriam Zoll, while heterosexual transmission may be the primary route of HIV/AIDS infection today, few HIV-prevention programs actually address the underlying gender, power, and sexual dynamics between men and women that contribute to infection, including violence. In a 2004 report entitled "Closing the HIV/AIDS Prevention Gender Gap?" Zoll surveyed men's and women's attitudes about gender and sexuality on several continents. She found that men and women's cultural definitions and perceptions of masculinity and femininity often reinforced men's power over women in ways that

make sexually transmitted infections more likely. In the report, Zoll featured the work of men and women who are implementing promising gender-based prevention strategies. For example, Dean Peacock is a white South African who lived for many years in the U.S., where he worked in San Francisco as a facilitator in a batterer intervention program. Peacock returned to South Africa a couple of years ago to lead HIV prevention work with men in a program called Men As Partners, sponsored by Engender Health and Planned Parenthood of South Africa. As Zoll reports, from his unique vantage point Peacock observed with groups of men in prevention trainings in South Africa many of the same ideas about masculinity that he encountered with batterers in the U.S.: "A real man doesn't negotiate with a woman." "A real man doesn't use condoms." "A real man doesn't worry about his health status." "A real man doesn't get tested." "A real man has sex with multiple partners." Even so, Peacock says that men in South Africa with whom he has worked are very open to gender equitable work. "The paradox of the HIV/AIDS epidemic is that it has opened the door to gender equality. We say to these men, 'If you work with us, your life will become richer.' We appeal to them as moral agents. We ask them, 'What is your responsibility to take this to the community, to challenge other men's behaviors, to confront men who are violent, to confront other men who are placing their partners at risk?'"

CONTRIBUTE FINANCIAL RESOURCES

Men with significant financial resources need to think creatively about what they can do to help support the growing number of domestic and sexual-assault prevention initiatives that target boys and men. This is the cutting edge of prevention work, and the field is new enough that a small number of wealthy men could make an enormous impact. Ted Waitt, founder of the Gateway Computer Company, has been one of the early leaders in this area. Philanthropic individuals and organizations can and should continue to fund services for women and girls who are victims and survivors of men's violence, especially when state and federal funds are being cut; funds that target work with men and boys should never compete with funds for direct services for women and girls. But they should not have to, because the pool of available resources should increase as more influential men get involved and bring new ideas and energy to the task of preventing men's violence against women.

BE CREATIVE AND ENTREPRENEURIAL

A number of enterprising men have used their imagination and creativity to raise other men's awareness of sexism, and to challenge the sexist attitudes and behaviors of men around them. Any list of these individuals is necessarily subjective and abbreviated, but I would nonetheless like to spotlight a handful of exemplary anti-sexist activist men. Chris Kilmartin, a professor of psychology at Mary Washington University, performs a one-man show around the country where he uses his skills as a stand-up comedian to satirize traditional masculinity. His first solo theatre performance was called *Crimes against Nature*, and his most recent show is entitled *Guy Fi: The Fictions That Rule Men's Lives*. Through these dramatic presentations and scholarship, Kilmartin has helped to expand the focus of sexual assault prevention to include discussions about the pressures on young men to conform to gender norms that limit their humanity as well as set them up to hurt women.

Another man who has made a unique contribution to this work is Hank Shaw, who in 2000 produced a glossy brochure about men and gender violence that is called, "It's Time for Guys to Put an End to This." Shaw, whose day job is in marketing and corporate communications, wanted to reach average guys with a piece written in "guy language" for men who would likely never read a book about gender violence. The brochure, tens of thousands of which have been distributed across the U.S., Canada, and elsewhere, is cleverly written and beautifully illustrated, and contains such features as the "Mancipation Proclamation": "Henceforth

guys are no longer under any gender-oriented, testosterone-derived, penis-related or penis-associated obligation to hurt, harass, or otherwise mess up (or mess with) the lives of female employees, coworkers, students, family members, friends, neighbors, or other female personages who may or may not be personally known to the party of the first part. When all people of the male persuasion get this message, it will spare everyone a whole lot of grief. Plus it will save the country about a gazillion dollars per year."

Another man who has become influential in the gender violence prevention field is Don McPherson, the former professional football player and star quarterback for Syracuse University in the late 1980s. One of the first highly successful black quarterbacks, McPherson runs the Sports Leadership Institute at Adelphi University in New York, and travels widely and gives speeches about violence toward women and what it means to be a man to a variety of high school, college, and professional audiences. What makes McPherson an effective gender violence prevention educator is that while he has the credentials as "The Man" due to his success in sports, he openly admits that he was never comfortable in the role that so many men fantasize about: "I had to carry myself in a different way," he told Oprah Winfrey, "sometimes not showing emotion, not showing weakness or any kind of vulnerability. It meant being in control all of the time. Most people expected me to be shallow . . . I struggled with who I really was on the inside versus my need to be a part of the guys who were cool." In his popular lecture, entitled, "You Throw Like a Girl," McPherson makes the connection between what the culture expects of "real men," and men's widespread mistreatment of women.

New technologies are changing the nature of social activism, and this is as true for anti-sexist men's work as it is for any social movement. In particular, the Internet and the Web have become indispensable tools in anti-sexist men's organizing. The ability to instantaneously transmit information and facilitate connection between people across the country and the world continues to amaze some of us who have vivid memories from the 1980s and

1990s of standing on street corners handing out leaflets. One man who has made a significant contribution to harnessing the power of the Internet is Marc Dubin, founder and executive director of CAVNET, Communities Against Violence Network, at www. cavnet.org. CAVNET is a diverse network of professionals and advocates who work on issues related to violence against women and children, human rights, genocide, and crime victims with disabilities. People in the network regularly share a wealth of information and resources—including points of contact for anti-sexist men's organizations nationally and internationally. Dubin, who works tirelessly—and virtually without pay—to maintain and expand CAVNET's database and connect people to each other, is a former federal prosecutor with extensive experience prosecuting domestic violence, sexual assault, rape, child abuse, and hate crimes. He formerly served as special counsel to the Violence Against Women Office at the United States Department of Justice and is an expert in the federal civil rights of people with disabilities.

START ANTI-SEXIST MEN'S GROUPS

The power of individuals to catalyze change increases exponentially when they work together to create new institutions and organizations. A growing number of organizations have made significant contributions in recent years to gender violence prevention efforts with men and boys. Some of these groups have paid staff and operate along the lines of traditional non-profit educational organizations; others are more grass roots and volunteer-oriented. It is not possible to provide anything close to a comprehensive list of these various initiatives, but consider a handful of examples from around the country: The Washington, D.C.-based group Men Can Stop Rape regularly conducts anti-rape trainings with high school, college, and community organizations. Their "strength campaign" posters and other materials have been widely circulated. The Institute on Domestic Violence in the African American Community, headed by Dr. Oliver Williams, regularly brings together scholars and activists to discuss issues

of particular interest to men (and women) of color, such as the potential role of the hip-hop generation in preventing men's violence against women. The anti-rape men's group One in Four has chapters on dozens of college campuses. In 1999, a group of men in the famous fishing town of Gloucester, Massachusetts—carpenters and clergy, bartenders and bankers—started Gloucester Men Against Domestic Abuse. They march annually in the town's popular Fourth of July parade and sponsor a billboard that says "Strong Men Don't Bully," a public testimonial of sorts that features the names of five hundred Gloucester men. The Men's Leadership Forum in San Diego, California, is a high-profile annual conference held on Valentine's Day. Since 2001, MLF has brought together a diverse group of men and boys (and women) from across the city to learn how men in business, labor unions, the sports culture, education, the faith community, and the human services can contribute to ending men's violence against women. Some men are politicized about sexism out of concern for their daughters, or as a result of things that have happened to them. One of the most effective organizations that addresses these concerns is Dads and Daughters, a Duluth, Minnesota-based advocacy group led by Joe Kelly. Part of the mission of DADS is to mobilize concerned fathers to challenge companies whose marketing is sexist and exploitative—especially when it involves the sexualization of young girls or adolescents, or treats men's violence against women as a joke.

In addition to some of these now well-established organizations, anti-sexist men on college campuses and in local communities have worked—often in collaboration with women's centers or domestic and sexual violence programs—to educate men and boys about the role men can play in confronting and interrupting other men's abusive behaviors. One venue for this collaboration has been the proliferating number of V-Day events held on college campuses. While V-Day is woman-centered, male students have played all sorts of supportive roles, such as organizing outreach efforts to men and coproducing and promoting performances of the Eve Ensler play *The Vagina Monologues*.

Some anti-sexist men's efforts have been ad hoc and customized to fit the needs and experiences of various communities. For example, in 2003 a group of Asian American men in Seattle organized to support the local chapter of the National Asian Pacific American Women's Forum in their opposition to a restaurant that was promoting "naked sushi" nights, where patrons took sushi off the bodies of semi-nude models wrapped in cellophane. And in the summer of 2004, a group of men (and women) in the "punk, indie, alternative" music scene organized a Different Kind of Dude Fest in Washington, D.C. Along the lines of the Riot Girrls and Girlfest, Hawaii, they sought to use art as an organizing tool. Their goal was to call attention to the ways in which progressive political punk culture, while promising liberation from other forms of social conformity and oppression, nonetheless helped to perpetuate sexism and patriarchal domination. The organizers of the music festival also explicitly affirmed the need for men to be allies of feminists in the fight for gender justice and social equality.

CHAMPION INSTITUTIONAL REFORM

Men who hold positions of power in government, non-profit organizations, business, and labor unions can do much to prevent men's violence against women if they take two critical steps: 1.) Recognize domestic and sexual violence prevention as a leadership issue for men, and 2.) Start to think creatively about how they can push their institutions to address it. The problem is that many men in positions of institutional authority do not yet see gender violence prevention in this way. That is why I strongly suggest that public or private institutions who want to begin serious primary prevention initiatives first arrange trainings for men in positions of senior leadership—and the more senior, the better. If done well, gender violence prevention training for men can be transformative. Men often come out of such trainings with an entirely new sensibility about their professional and personal responsibilities to women and children, as well as to other men. This is important because in the long term, dramatic reductions

in the incidence of men's violence against women in the U.S. and around the world will only come about when people with power—which often means *men* in power—make gender violence issues a priority. Among other things, this means that male leaders must set and maintain a tone—in educational institutions, corporations, the military—where sexist and abusive behavior is considered unacceptable and unwelcome, not only because women don't like it but because other men will not stand for it. This sounds good, but people often ask me how to get powerful men to take these issues seriously. For example, how do you convince male legislators, educational administrators, business leaders, or military commanders to attend gender violence prevention training? There are a variety of strategies, but the bottom line is that they do not necessarily have to be motivated—at least initially—by altruism or concerns about social justice. They need instead to be persuaded that prevention is a widely shared institutional goal, and that it is their responsibility to be as knowledgeable and proactive about these issues as possible.

THINK AND ACT LOCALLY AND GLOBALLY

The focus of this book has been mostly on the U.S., but obviously men's violence against women is an issue everywhere in the world. Since 9/11, many Americans have learned what many people around the world have long known—in the modern era, what happens in foreign cultures thousands of miles away can affect people right here at home, sometimes in ways that are impossible to predict. That is the irrevocable reality of the global environment in which we now live. As I have maintained throughout, gender violence is best seen not as aberrational behavior perpetrated by a few bad men but as an expression of much more deeply seated structures of male dominance and gender inequality. This is much easier to see when you are looking at someone else's culture. For example, in radical fundamentalist Islamic countries, women have few rights, and in many instances men's violence against them is legal and even expected—especially when they defy male authority. In other words, men's violence against women functions in some cultures to maintain a highly authoritarian, even fascistic male power structure. In that sense, gender violence is clearly a political crime with potentially far-reaching consequences. As a result, the way that men in distant lands treat women—individually and as a group—cannot be dismissed as a private family or cultural matter. It has too much bearing on political developments that could affect all of us—like the possibility of nuclear war, or the constant threat of terrorist attacks.

At the same time, it is tempting for some Americans to hear and read about the way men mistreat women in foreign cultures and attribute that mistreatment to cultural deficiencies and even barbarism. But it is important to remember that by world standards, the incidence of men's violence against women here in the U.S. is embarrassingly high. No doubt many American men would be offended to hear people in other countries speculating about the shortcomings of American men—and the inferiority of the culture that produced them.

Fortunately, the growing movement of men who are speaking out about men's violence against women is international in scope. There are anti-sexist men's initiatives in scores of countries across the world. In addition, one of the most promising developments in the history of international human rights law is the growing international movement to identify men's violence against women as a human rights issue. A pivotal moment in that movement came in 2001, when the United Nations war crimes tribunal named rape and sexual slavery as war crimes. And today, a number of international organizations—most prominently Amnesty International—have begun to focus on gender violence and link the physical and sexual exploitation of women to a host of other social and political problems. One of the major challenges for American anti-sexist men in the coming years will be to make connections between men's violence against women in the U.S. with violence around the world, and to support efforts everywhere to reduce men's violence

and advance gender equality—not only because it is the right thing to do, but also because it is arguably in our national interest.

WHAT'S IN IT FOR MEN?

Men who occupy positions of influence in boys' lives—fathers, grandfathers, older brothers, teachers, coaches, religious leaders—need to teach them that men of integrity value women and do not tolerate other men's sexism or abusive behavior. Obviously they have to lead by example. But that is not enough. In a cultural climate where the objectification of women and girls has accelerated, and boys are exposed to ever more graphic displays of brutality toward women disguised as "entertainment," men need to preemptively provide clear guidelines for boys' behavior. This does not always have to be defined in negative terms, e.g., "Don't hit women." It can be framed as a positive challenge to young men, especially if they aspire to something more special than being "one of the guys" at all costs.

In fact, when I give talks about men's violence against women to groups of parents, I am often asked by parents of sons if there is something positive we can offer young men as a substitute for what we are taking away from them. "We constantly say to our kids, 'Don't do this, don't do that, I wish you wouldn't listen to this music.' We tell them they shouldn't treat girls a certain way, they shouldn't act tough. We spend a lot of time telling our sons what they shouldn't be. It's so negative. Why shouldn't they just tune us out? What's in it for them?"

My answer is really quite simple, and it is as true for the fathers as it is for the sons. When we ask men to reject sexism and the abuse of women, we are not taking something away from them. In fact, we are giving them something very valuable—a vision of manhood that does not depend on putting down others in order to lift itself up. When a man stands up for social justice, non-violence, and basic human rights—for women as much as for men—he is acting in the best traditions of our civilization. That makes him not only a better man, but a better human being.

CONTRIBUTORS

TIM BENEKE is a freelance writer and editor living in the San Francisco Bay Area. He is the author of *Men on Rape* and *Proving Manhood*.

DANA BERKOWITZ is an assistant professor in the Department of Sociology and the Program in Women's and Gender Studies at Louisiana State University. Her research and teaching interests focus on the social construction of gender, sexualities, and families. She has published extensively on gay men's procreative, fathering, and family identities.

YASEMIN BESEN is an associate professor of sociology at Montclair State University. She received her Ph.D. in sociology from SUNY Stony Brook in 2005. Her work focuses on gender, work, and youth.

GREG BORTNICHAK will soon graduate from college and put his barista days behind him. He plays guitar and cello in his band, "The Sparta Philharmonic." His article originally appeared in *Men Speak Out: Views on Gender, Sex, and Power*, ed. Shira Tarrant (Routledge, 2008).

TRISTAN BRIDGES is a Ph.D. candidate in sociology at the University of Virginia. His dissertation—*Liquid Masculinities: Transformations in Gender and Politics among Men*—compares the ways that three very different groups of men interact with feminist ideologies and practices and mobilize of setting-specific masculine identities and discourses of inequality and privilege.

ROCCO L. (CHIP) CAPRARO, senior associate dean and assistant professor of history, is the founding coordinator of the men's studies program and founding director of the rape prevention education program for men at Hobart and William Smith Colleges, Geneva, New York. He received his B.A. from Colgate University and his Ph.D. from Washington University, and is a consultant and public speaker in the areas of gender and diversity, with an emphasis on masculinity, and is currently writing a brief history of rock and roll from a men's studies perspective.

ERIN CASEY is an associate professor of social work at the University of Washington, Tacoma. She received her M.S.W. and Ph.D. in social welfare at the University of Washington, Seattle and has over 10 years of practice experience in the fields of domestic and sexual violence. Her research interests include the etiology of sexual and intimate partner violence perpetration, examining ecological approaches to violence prevention, and exploring intersections between violence, masculinities, and sexual risk.

BETH SKILKEN CATLETT is an assistant professor of women's studies at DePaul University. She received her doctorate from the Ohio State University, where her studies focused on feminist approaches to studying families. She has been particularly interested in applying a feminist paradigm to understanding male aggression.

SCOTT COLTRANE is dean of the College of Arts and Sciences, Oregon University. His research focuses on families, gender, and social inequality.

RAEWYN CONNELL is a professor at the University of Sydney, a fellow of the Academy of Social Sciences in Australia, and one of Australia's leading social scientists. Her most recent books are *Southern Theory* (2007), about social thought beyond the global metropole; *Gender: In World Perspective* (2009); and *Confronting Equality* (2011), about social science and politics. Her other books include *Masculinities, Schools & Social Justice, Ruling Class Ruling Culture, Gender & Power*, and *Making the Difference*. Her work is widely cited internationally, and has been translated into fifteen languages. She has taught at universities in Australia, Canada, and the USA, in departments of sociology, political science, and education. A long-term participant in the labor movement and peace movement, Raewyn has tried to make social science relevant to social justice.

ANGELA COWAN is a postgraduate student in the Department of Sociology at the University of Newcastle. Her thesis topic is an investigation of the discursive world of young children. She is a trained primary school teacher and has worked as an observer on a number of psychiatric research projects.

JULIA O'CONNELL DAVIDSON is a professor of sociology at the University of Nottingham in the United Kingdom with a focus on gender, race, class and global inequalities, and contract, employment relations, selfhood, and human rights. She has conducted studies of entrepreneurial prostitution, sex tourism, and children's involvement in the global sex trade.

SHARI L. DWORKIN is an associate professor and vice chair in the Department of Social and Behavioral Sciences at the University of California at San Francisco. She is an affiliated faculty at the Center for AIDS Prevention Studies and in UCSF Global Health Sciences.

CYNTHIA ENLOE is a research professor at Clark University. Among her recent books are *Maneuvers: The International Politics of Militarizing Women's Lives*; *Curious Feminist: Searching for Women in a New Age of Empire*; and *Globalization and Militarism: Feminists Make the Link*.

YEN LE ESPIRITU is a professor of ethnic studies at the University of California, San Diego. She is the author of *Asian American Panethnicity: Bridging Institutions and Identities*, *Filipino American Lives*, and *Asian American Women and Men: Labor, Laws, and Love*. She is also serving as the president of the Association of Asian American Studies.

ANN FERGUSON is an assistant professor of women's studies and African American studies at Smith College. She received her Ph.D. in sociology from the University of California at Berkeley.

MICHAEL FIRMIN is a professor of psychology at Cedarville University in Cedarville, OH. He is editor of the *Journal of Ethnographic & Qualitative Research* and directs a national qualitative research conference, now in its 23rd annual year. He is a licensed psychologist and has been a university professor since 1988.

EDWARD FLORES is an assistant professor of sociology at Loyola University in Chicago.

SALLY K. GALLAGHER is a professor of sociology in the School of Public Policy at Oregon State University. She is author of *Evangelical Identity and Gendered Family Life* (Rutgers 2003) and numerous articles on religion, gender, and family. She is currently writing in the area of gender, identity, and congregational culture and has a forthcoming book on gender, resources, and religion in Damascus, Syria.

KATHLEEN GERSON is a professor of sociology and collegiate professor of arts and science at New York University, where her research focuses on gender, work, and family change in contemporary societies. Her most recent book, *The Unfinished Revolution: Growing Up in a New Era of Gender, Work, and Family*, provides a first-hand account of the experiences, outlooks, and strategies of the generation who grew up amid the gender revolution of the last several decades.

KEN GILLAM, the director of composition at Missouri State University, studies popular culture from text-messaging to a variety of instructional technologies, especially for composition, focusing on our society's trending toward disembodied rhetorical identities. He also closely examines the films that socialize his young sons and is currently collaborating (with Shannon Wooden) on a book that examines boy culture as constructed by Pixar.

PEGGY C. GIORDANO is a distinguished research professor of sociology at Bowling Green State University. Her research centers on basic social network processes, including friendships and dating relationships, and the ways in which these influence a variety of developmental outcomes, especially adolescent sexual behavior and delinquency involvement.

CHONG-SUK HAN is an assistant professor of sociology (teaching/instructional) at Temple University. His research focuses on the intersection of race, gender, and sexuality, particularly among gay Asian American men. His publications have appeared in a number of journals including *Sexuality and Culture*, *Social Identities*, *AIDS Education and Prevention*, and *Contemporary Justice Review*, among others. In 2006, he was the recipient of the Martin Levine Dissertation Award from the Sexualities Section of the American Sociological Association.

FRANK HARRIS III is an associate professor of postsecondary education at San Diego State University. His research focuses on the social construction of masculinities in college and university contexts. He is co-editor of *College Men and Masculinities: Theory, Research, and Implications for Practice*.

ROBERT JENSEN is a journalism professor at the University of Texas at Austin and a board member of the Third Coast Activist Resource Center. His latest book, *All My Bones Shake*, was published in 2009 by Soft Skull Press. He also is the author of *Getting Off: Pornography and the End of Masculinity* (South End Press, 2007); *The Heart of Whiteness: Confronting Race, Racism and White Privilege* (City Lights, 2005); *Citizens of the Empire: The Struggle to Claim Our Humanity* (City Lights, 2004); and *Writing Dissent: Taking Radical Ideas from the Margins to the Mainstream* (Peter Lang, 2002). Jensen can be reached at rjensen@uts.cc.utexas.edu and his articles can be found online at http://uts.cc.utexas.edu/~rjensen/index.html.

DAPHNE JOHN is associate professor and chair of the department of sociology at Oberlin College. Her teaching and research focuses on issues related to work and family, and gender stratification.

ELLEN JORDAN is a senior lecturer in the Department of Sociology at the University of Newcastle. She was for many years a teacher in primary schools. Her major research interests are women's work in nineteenth-century Britain and gender construction in early childhood.

EMILY W. KANE is the Whitehouse professor of sociology, and a member of the Program in Women and Gender Studies, at Bates College in Lewiston, Maine. Much of her research focuses on beliefs about gender inequality, including quantitative analysis of such beliefs in the United States and cross-nationally, and on gender and parenting. She is currently working on a book based on the qualitative interview data included in her article within this collection. She is also interested in community engagement, teaching courses and working on research that addresses the intersections of social inequality, public sociology, and community-based research.

JACKSON KATZ is co-founder of the mixed-gender, racially diverse mentors in Violence Prevention (MVP) program, the leading gender violence prevention initiative in college and professional athletics. He is the creator and co-creator of educational videos including "Tough Guise" (2000), "Wrestling with Manhood" (2002), and "Spin the Bottle" (2004). His book *The Macho Paradox: Why Some Men Hurt Women and How All Men Can Help* was published by Sourcebooks in 2006. He lectures widely in the United States and internationally about masculinities, media, and violence.

MICHAEL KAUFMAN, Ph.D., is an educator and writer focused on engaging men and boys to promote gender equality and end violence against women. He has worked in forty-five countries, including extensively with the United Nations. He is the co-founder of the White Ribbon Campaign, the largest effort in the world of men working to end violence against women, and is the author or editor of seven books, including an award-winning novel. His articles and books have been translated into 14 languages.

MICHAEL S. KIMMEL is a distinguished professor of sociology at SUNY at Stony Brook. His books include *Changing*

Men (1987), *Men Confront Pornography* (1990), *Men in the United States* (1992), *Manhood in America* (1996), *The Politics of Manhood* (1996), *The Gendered Society* (2000), and *Guyland* (2008). He is the editor of *Men and Masculinities*, a scholarly journal, and national spokesperson for the National Organization for Men Against Sexism (NOMAS).

PAUL KIVEL is a trainer, activist, writer, and violence prevention educator. He is the author of several books including *Men's Work*, *Uprooting Racism*, and *Boys Will Be Men*. He is also co-author of several widely used curricula including Making the Peace, Young Men's Work, and Young Women's Lives. His newest book is *You Call This a Democracy? Who Benefits, Who Pays, and Who Really Decides*. He can be reached at pkivel@mindspring.com, or at www.paulkivel.com.

NEILL KOROBOV is an assistant professor in the Department of Psychology at the University of West Georgia, USA. His research focuses primarily on the ways young men narrate their romantic and sexual experiences, with a particular interest in the how they use self-deprecation and irony as methods to handle incipient sexism.

CHARIS E. KUBRIN is an associate professor in the Department of Criminology, Law and Society at the University of California, Irvine. She is co-editor of *Crime and Society: Crime*, 3rd ed. (Sage Publications 2007) and co-author of *Researching Theories of Crime and Deviance* (Oxford University Press 2008) and *Privileged Places: Race, Residence, and the Structure of Opportunity* (Lynne Rienner 2006). In 2005, Charis received the American Society of Criminology's Ruth Shonle Cavan Young Scholar Award and the Morris Rosenberg Award for Recent Achievement from the District of Columbia Sociological Society.

MONICA A. LONGMORE is a professor of sociology at Bowling Green State University. Her interests include social psychological processes, including the nature and consequences of dimensions of the self-concept, especially the impact of self-conceptions on adolescent dating and sexual behavior.

LEANNA MADILL is an instructor at the University of Victoria in the Department of Curriculum and Instruction. She researches gender, assessment, alternative literacies, as well as video game learning. Her dissertation examined the experiences of parents with adolescent children who play video games.

WENDY D. MANNING is a professor of sociology at Bowling Green State University and the director of the

Center for Family and Demographic Research. Her research focuses on relationships that exist outside the boundaries of marriage, including cohabitation, adolescent dating, and nonresident parenting.

MARTHA MCCAUGHEY is a professor of women's studies and sociology at Appalachian State University. Her work examines the body, gender, science, technology, and popular culture. She is most recently the author of *The Caveman Mystique: Pop-Darwinism and the Debates Over Sex, Violence, and Science* (Routledge, 2008).

PATRICK MCKENRY is a professor of human development and family science at the Ohio State University. He received his doctorate in child and family studies from the University of Tennessee. His research has focused on family conflict, including domestic violence. He has published over 100 journal articles and book chapters.

MICHAEL A. MESSNER is a professor of sociology and gender studies at the University of Southern California. He is author of several books, including most recently *It's All For the Kids: Gender, Families and Youth Sports* (2009), and *King of the Wild Suburb: A Memoir of Fathers, Sons and Guns* (2011).

JEFFREY MONTEZ DE OCA is a doctoral candidate in sociology at the University of Southern California. He teaches classical and contemporary theory as well as media analysis. His dissertation examines postwar physical education and American football's relation to cold war masculinities.

PETER M. NARDI is a professor of sociology at Pitzer College. He has published articles on AIDS, anti-gay crimes and violence, magic and magicians, and alcoholism and families. His books include *Men's Friendships* (1993) and *Growing up before Stonewall* (1994), with David Sanders and Judd Marmor. He has served as co-president of the Los Angeles chapter of the Gay and Lesbian Alliance against Defamation.

NICK T. PAPPAS is a graduate in human development and family science from the Ohio State University. He is a former professional hockey player and coach and former adjunct professor at Indiana University of Pennsylvania. He is the founder of Personal & Athletic Solutions, working as a motivational speaker and personal life coach.

C. J. PASCOE is an assistant professor of sociology at Colorado College. She is the author of the book, *Dude, You're a Fag: Masculinity and Sexuality in High School*.

BETH A. QUINN is an associate professor in the Department of Sociology at Montana State University-Bozeman. She received her Ph.D. in criminology, law, and society from the University of California, Irvine. Drawing primarily on feminist and masculinity theories and neo-institutional organizational theory, her research focuses on legal complaint-making and discrimination law. Her research has been published in journals such as *Law and Social Inquiry* and *Gender & Society*. She is currently exploring how human resources understand and deal with sexual harassment law.

HERNAN RAMIREZ is an assistant professor of sociology at Florida State University. His research focuses on Mexican immigrant entrepreneurship, immigrant social mobility, gender and work.

M. ROCHLIN is the creator of "The Heterosexual Questionnaire."

DON SABO, Ph.D., is a professor of Health Policy at D'Youville College in Buffalo, New York. He has co-authored *Humanism in Sociology, Jock: Sports & Male Identity*, and *Sport, Men and the Gender Order: Critical Feminist Perspectives*. His most recent books include *Sex, Violence and Power in Sports: Rethinking Masculinity*, and *Men's Health & Illness: Gender, Power & the Body*. He has conducted many national surveys on gender issues in sport, is a trustee of the Women's Sports Foundation, and co-authored the 1997 Presidents' Council on Physical Fitness and Sports report "Physical Activity & Sport in the Lives of Girls."

KATHY SANDFORD is an associate professor in the Faculty of Education at the University of Victoria. Her recent research projects include *Literacy Learning through Videogames: Adolescent Boys' Perspectives* and *Teacher Education beyond the Classroom: Supporting Learning in Community Places and Spaces*. Her research interests include issues of gender and engagement with videogames, the nature of games and play, and youth participation in the new digital economy.

KRISTEN SCHILT is an assistant professor of sociology at the University of Chicago. Her research examines gender inequality in the workplace through the lens of transgender workplace experiences.

ANNE SHELTON is a professor in the Department of Sociology and Anthropology at the University of Texas at Arlington. She is author of *Women, Men and Time: Gender Differences in Paid Work, Housework and Leisure*, Westport, CT: Greenwood, 1992.

KATHLEEN F. SLEVIN is a chancellor professor of sociology at The College of William and Mary. Her research interests include aging, gender, and work. With Toni Calasanti she is the co-editor of *Age Matters: Realigning Feminist Thinking* (Routledge, 2006) and a Gender Lens Series book: *Gender, Social Inequalities, and Aging* (AltaMira Press, 2001).

TYLER SMITH is a member of the Social Work and Care Coordination Team at the University of Washington – Medical Center and Disease Intervention Specialist for Public Health – Seattle & King County. In addition to medical systems and infectious disease research, his other areas of interest include health care administration and relevant application of social work theory, intimate partner violence in same-gender relationships and examining the experiences of LGBTQ youth within the child welfare system.

JUDITH STACEY is a professor of sociology and professor of gender and sexuality at New York University. She is author of many articles and books on gender, sexualities, and families, including *In the Name of the Family: Rethinking Family Values in a Postmodern Age* (Boston: Beacon Press, 1996).

GLORIA STEINEM is a founding editor of *Ms.*, and the author of *Outrageous Acts and Everyday Rebellions* and *Revolution from Within*.

JACQUELINE SANCHEZ TAYLOR is a researcher on adult sex tourism and child sexual exploitation in Latin America, India, South Africa, and the Caribbean. Her Ph.D. focuses on sexual economic exchanges between female tourists and local men in Jamaica and the Dominican Republic. She is currently a sociology lecturer at the University of Leeds.

LEONARD SWIDLER is a professor of Catholic thought and interreligious dialogue at Temple University, Philadelphia, PA where he has taught since 1966. He is the co-founder (in 1964, with Arlene Swidler) and editor of the *Journal of Ecumenical Studies* (quarterly). He is also the founder/president of the Dialogue Institute – Interreligious, Intercultural, International (born 1978), and the founder/president of the Association for the Rights of Catholics in the Church (1980–).

RONALD WEITZER is a professor of sociology at George Washington University. He has written extensively on both police-minority relations (in the U.S. and some other countries) and sex work, including two recent books *Sex For Sale* (2nd ed., Routledge, 2010) and *Legalizing Prostitution* (NYU Press, 2011).

CHRISTINE L. WILLIAMS is a professor of sociology at the University of Texas at Austin. She is author of *Gender Differences at Work* (1989), *Still a Man's World* (1997), and editor of *Doing "Women's Work": Men in Nontraditional Occupations* (1993).

ADIA HARVEY WINGFIELD is an assistant professor of sociology at Georgia State University and has written several books and articles that examine the ways intersections of race, gender, and class impact workers in different occupations and professions. She is the author of *Doing Business with Beauty: Black Women, Hair Salons, and the Racial Enclave Economy, Yes We Can? White Racial Framing and the 2008 Presidential Campaign*, and *Changing Times for Black Professionals*.

SABRINA WOOD is a graduate of Oregon State University with interests in gender, social inequality, and education. She is currently working in school administration and beginning a new project in school wide evaluations.

SHANNON WOODEN, an associate professor of English at Missouri State University, teaches British literature, critical theory, and creative writing, and studies ethical approaches to the literatures of illness, disability, race, and gender. She has published on women writers and feminist pedagogy, but raising two young sons has inspired interest in a wider spectrum of gender identity. She is collaborating (with Ken Gillam) on a book that examines Pixar's contributions to a post-feminist boy culture.

JEWEL WOODS is a gender analyst specializing in men's issues and executive director of the Renaissance Male Project. He is also the co-author of *Don't Blame It on Rio: The Real Deal Behind Why Men Go to Brazil for Sex.*

GIL ZICKLIN received his Ph.D. from University of California, Davis. He is the author of *Countercultural Communes: A Sociological Perspective* and currently teaches in the Sociology Department and directs the GLBTQ Studies Program at Montclair State University.